BFI FILM AND TELEVISION
HANDBOOK
2000

bfi British Film Institute

Information Services
Statistics Manager: Peter Todd
Statistics Research: Erinna Mettler, Phil Wickham
Statistics Tabulation: Ian O'Sullivan

Additional Research/Editorial Assistance:
John Atkinson, Tom Brownlie, Sean Delaney, Allen
Eyles, David Fisher, Alan Gregory, Michael Henry,
Anastasia Kerameos, Laura Pearson,
Mandy Rosencrown, David Sharp, Linda Wood
Database consultant: Lavinia Orton
Marketing: John Atkinson, Rebecca Watts,
Sarah Prosser
Cover design: Ketchup

Advertisement Managers: The Great Partnership
4th Floor, 17 Shaftesbury Avenue,
Piccadilly, London W1V 7RL
Tel: 020 7439 3334
Fax: 020 7439 2935

With many thanks to those who assisted with
photographs: BBC, BSkyB, *bfi*, Buena Vista, Carlton,
Columbia TriStar, Entertainment Film Distributors,
FilmFour Distributors, Granada, Miramax, Pathé
Distribution, PolyGram Filmed Entertainment,
Twentieth Century Fox, Universal Pictures
International, United International Pictures,
The Walt Disney Company, Warner Bros

The views expressed in this book are those of the
author, and do not necessarily reflect *bfi* policy in any
given area.

© British Film Institute 1999
21 Stephen Street
London WIP 2LN

Printed in Great Britain by Bath Press, Bath

A catalogue record for this book is available from the
British Library.

ISBN 0 85170 764 5

Front Cover images:
The majority of images for the front cover were provided by the *bfi*'s
Regional Publicity Unit and represent the diverse range of films
promoted via its bfi supported regional film theatres throughout 1999.
Other images come from *bfi* Publishing's Film Classics and Modern
Film Classics series. The remainder are from the Museum of the
Moving Image which was temporarily closed on 31st August 1999.

Contents

Twentieth Century Fox

Fox Searchlight Pictures

Fox Animation Studios

Fox 2000

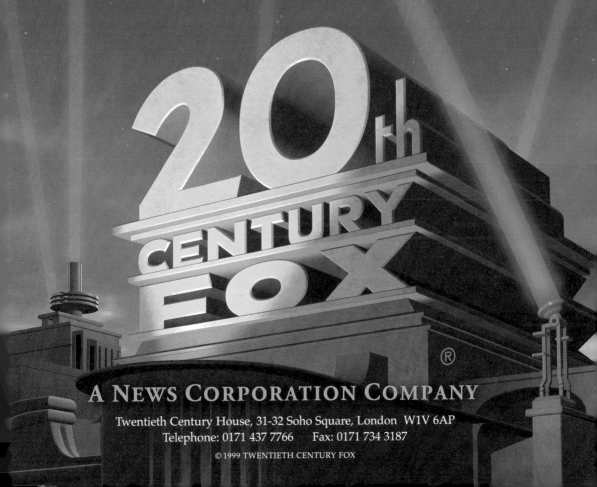

A NEWS CORPORATION COMPANY

Twentieth Century House, 31-32 Soho Square, London W1V 6AP
Telephone: 0171 437 7766   Fax: 0171 734 3187

ACKNOWLEDGMENTS

My sincere thanks go out to all the individuals who have supported the *bfi* Film and Television Handbook throughout the year by keeping me updated with movements and changes within the industry.

Within the *bfi* I would like to salute all those who joined with me to compile the 2000 edition. Those named below made outstanding contributions to this years book.

Top of the list is Tom Cabot who cheerfully fulfiled many roles throughout the year – sounding block, palette and production controller.

To my part-time assistants Sean Delaney and Laura Pearson I offer warm and heartfelt gratitude.

John Atkinson had the unenviable job of editing my commentary, which he did with commendable fortitude, while Mandy Rosencrown sacrificed her time and eyes for some much needed last minute adjustments to the book.

My usual thanks go to my fellow travellers on the information highway. Peter Todd and his team in the Information Service of the *bfi* responded to this year's challenges in an unflustered, meticulous way. Phil Wickham, Erinna Mettler and Ian O'Sullivan, in particular, demonstrated the finer side to number-crunching in the statistical section.

Other colleagues in the *bfi* National Library also made useful contributions to the Handbook, not least David Sharp, who not only fully supported my toils and endeavours, but also provided the Careers and Training sections. Anastasia Keraemos diligently compiled the Books section.

I'd also like to express my thanks to Tony Worron for taking the calls and offering serene, relaxation therapy.

Special thanks go to my special colleagues in *bfi* Publishing for never obfuscating my progress. And of course, to all at Ketchup – for love not money.

Elsewhere in the *bfi,* Alan Gregory and RPU provided endless stills and a healthy 'can do' attitude, while Lavinia Orton did essential work on the database.

Other useful back-up and encouragement came from the likes of Mark Batey, Chris Chandler, Eugene Finn, Matt Kerr, Sarah Prosser, Markku Salmi, Martin Sheffield,

Rebbeca Watts and last, but by no means least, to Linda Wood for her painstaking work on the index.

Credit is also due to Peter Duncan and the Great Partnership for a very productive year.

Screen Finance, Screen International, and *Screen Digest* all continued to cooperate fully with access to their statistics – without their support the statistical section of this book would not have been possible.

Thanks also go to the following organisations and individuals: The BBC, The British Film Commission (BFC), British Screen Finance, British Videogram Association (BVA), Central Statistical Office (CSO), Cinema Advertising Association (CAA), Entertainment Data Inc. (EDI), The Department for Culture, Media and Sport (DCMS), Independent Television Commission (ITC), Roger Bennett at ELPSA, Tom Brownlie, Lavinia Carey, Peter Cowie, Allen Eyles, David Fisher, Patrick Frater, Allan Hardy, Michael Henry, Neil McCartney, Barrie McDonald and Steve Perrin.

Eddie Dyja, Handbook Editor, October 1999

Telephone number changes

From 22 April 2000 changes in the UK's telephone numbering system come into effect. Code and number will change for Cardiff, Coventry, London, Northern Ireland, Portsmouth or Southampton.

Cardiff (029)
changes from (01222) to (029)
add 20 to the front of the existing six-digit local number to create the new eight-digit local number: **(01222) becomes (029) 20xx xxxx**

Coventry (024)
changes from (01203) to (024)
add 76 to the front of the existing six-digit local number to create the new eight-digit local number: **(01203) becomes (024) 76xx xxxx**

London (020)
changes from (0171) or (0181) to (020)
create the new eight-digit local number by adding 7 or 8 to the front of the existing local number, depending on whether you are in an existing 0171 or 0181 area: **0171 becomes (020) 7xxx xxxx**
      0181 becomes (020) 8xxx xxxx

Portsmouth (023)
changes from (01705) to (023)
add 92 to the front of the existing six-digit local number to create the new eight-digit local number: **(01705) becomes (023) 92xx xxxx**

Southampton (023)
changes from (01703) to (023)
add 80 to the front of the existing six-digit local number to create the new eight-digit local number: **(01703) becomes (023) 80xx xxxx**

Northern Ireland (028)
(028) will be the code for the whole of Northern Ireland
local five and six digit numbers will become eight digit local numbers. (Two examples):
Belfast (six-digit) (01232) xxxxxx becomes (028) 90xx xxxx
Ballygawley (five-digit) (016625) xxxxx becomes (028) 855x xxxx
For further information (and a list of all the Northern Ireland code changes) phone 0808 22 4 2000. Website: www.numberchange.org

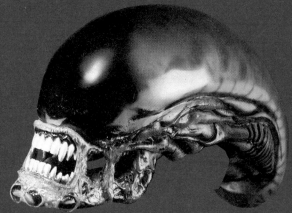

FOREWORD

by The Rt. Hon. Chris Smith MP,
Secretary of State for Culture, Media and Sport

The moving image is playing an increasingly vital role in our daily lives. Films, television and video programming engage most of us at different times, supplying information, entertainment and learning. For most of the 20th century, the British Film Institute has provided a range of distinctive and distinguished public services, promoting greater understanding of the history and future potential of moving image media.

From 2000, the *bfi* will, for the first time, agree its activities with the Film Council, the new government-backed strategic organisation overseeing both the UK film industry and film culture and education. Audiences UK-wide will quite properly remain the *bfi's* focus, and I welcome the Institute's plans to raise its profile amongst a broader cross-section of the public.

The impressive array of information contained in the following pages offers something of value to a very diverse population. From awards to websites, from libraries to funding schemes, from CD-ROMs to production companies, the *bfi Handbook* is a well-established, authoritative guide to the moving image, presenting key information in an easily accessible form. In my own office, previous editions have served as a regular reference source, and I am delighted to commend this latest edition to you.

INTRODUCTION

by John Woodward
Director of the British Film Institute

I sit down to write this introduction in a week where the British Film Institute has re-released Ken Loach's *Kes*, launched the children's 'Puffin on Screen' tour and contributed further to the Hitchcock centenary with a book from *bfi* Publishing and an annotated bibliography of his life from the *bfi* National Library. The London Film Festival brochure has just landed on my desk, and I read in *Sight and Sound* that the *bfi*'s first title on DVD will be Kurosawa's *Seven Samurai*. I mention all these events because they are tangible evidence that the re-constituted *bfi* is not only up and running, but also in good health.

Last year was a period of massive change at the *bfi* and the focus was on review, restructure and redefinition of our ideas – the three R's if you like. Driving this process was a real need to clarify what the Institute stands for, and what we should be offering audiences in the next millennium. This was not just an exercise in navel-gazing; this is an instruction, a challenge even, from the Department for Culture, Media and Sport (DCMS), for the *bfi* to justify its existence and its public funding.

It seemed obvious to me that education should be the key criterion determining our activities. I am relieved that the Government also took this view. The DCMS's Film Policy Review, published in March 1998, recommended that the *bfi* should give priority to widening understanding of film among the general public and develop a strategy to increase and broaden the audience for film – a broad brush-stroke, but clear enough to create a new focus for the Institute.

Whilst our own review was progressing, the Government was establishing the framework for the new Film Council – which included bringing together the British Film Commission and the Lottery department of the Arts Council of England. *bfi* Production will also be subsumed into the new Council – which will be up and running by April 2000. For the *bfi* this means that in future we shall agree our overall programme of activities

with the Film Council rather than the DCMS, and the Film Council in turn will fund the *bfi*.

1999 has also offered other challenges for us. The go-ahead was given to start work on the South Bank, which meant that our dream of having a *bfi* under one roof to include a much needed expanded Library and office space, as well as a new NFT and Museum, started to move towards reality. On 31 August 1999 the Museum of the Moving Image was closed down temporarily. The closure was a tough decision to take, but the next few years will give us time and opportunity to plan for a new Museum – one that will be in tune with the needs of a 21st century audience.

Indeed, the fact that further major surgery on the Institute has been avoided means that we can now build firm foundations in order to reach out to existing and new audiences with renewed confidence and vigour.

bfi FACTS & FIGURES – April 1998 – April 1999

bfi holdings

*bfi*Collections now contain over 275,000 film titles and 200,000 television programmes.

The newly audited *bfi* Stills Library contains seven million images, posters and designs from films and television programmes.

In 1998, more than 2,000 fiction films, 1,450 documentary titles and 20,000 television programmes were acquired and added to the *bfi*'s Collections.

The *bfi* National Library collections include 41,000 books in 15 languages, 145,000 periodicals from over 45 countries and over 2 million newspaper cuttings dating from the 1930s.

Over 23,000 references were added to the *bfi*'s SIFT (Summary of Information on Film and Television) database.

bfi audiences

The *bfi* National Film Theatre on London's South Bank screened 2,000 different feature films, shorts, TV programmes and videos, attracting a total of more than 176,000 admissions. The adjacent riverside Film Café, in its first full year of operation, served 650,000 customers.

The *bfi* provided services and facilities to 28 independent local cinemas throughout the UK.

The 12th London Lesbian and Gay Film Festival attracted audiences of 6,000 during its four-month tour to cinemas UK-wide.

In 1998, the 42nd London Film Festival attracted 102,000 attendances over its 15 days, and a two-week pilot tour to 8 regional cities attracted 4,575 admissions.

Over 150 film and media teachers attended the *bfi*'s media studies conference in June 1998. The Museum of the Moving Image Education Unit organised 97 events, reaching over 5,000 people.

bfi Publishing published 28 new books; more than 86,000 copies were sold. *bfi* Video Publishing released some 30 new titles.

Almost 500 researchers visited the *bfi* Conservation Centre's Cataloguing Unit and an additional 5,000 enquiries were received.

The monthly circulation of *Sight and Sound* magazine exceeded 26,000 copies.

Approximately 500 films from *bfi* Collections played each month in a variety of venues UK-wide.

Approximately 150 telephone calls were made every day to the enquiry service of the *bfi* National Library.

Two new feature films were completed by *bfi* Production during the year.

Films For The Cinematographer

VISION 500T film 7279/5279
Tungsten-500 EI   Daylight-320* EI
With improved grain and sharpness, this high speed tungsten balanced stock offers rich colours and excellent detail in low and very low light conditions.

VISION 800T film 7289/5289
Tungsten-800 EI   Daylight-500* EI
The world's fastest tungsten-balanced stock. Offers the sharpness and grain structure you would expect only in slower products. Allows for increased creative flexibility in low light, fast action, anamorphic, super 35mm, and other filming conditions, where systems speed is vitally important.

VISION 320T film 7277/5277
Tungsten-320 EI   Daylight-200* EI
This unique tungsten balanced stock offers a less saturated look with slightly lower contrast whilst providing superb shadow detail and clean white highlights.

VISION 250D film 7246/5246
Daylight-250 EI   Tungsten-64** EI
A high speed daylight balanced film stock providing the highest image quality for its speed. It delivers a rich reproduction of blacks in natural and mixed lighting conditions.

EXR 100T film 7248/5248
Tungsten-100 EI   Daylight-64* EI
A medium speed tungsten balanced stock with wide exposure latitude. Very good grain and saturation producing excellent highlights and shadow detail.

VISION 200T film 7274/5274
Tungsten-200 EI   Daylight-125* EI
A higher speed tungsten balanced stock with fine grain and outstanding sharpness, offering a wide exposure latitude and excellent colour reproduction. A very good all round stock that works very well in almost any lighting condition.

EXR 50D film 7245/5245
Daylight-50 EI   Tungsten-12** EI
A daylight balanced stock, extremely sharp and virtually grain free. This film offers a wide exposure latitude with rich, natural colours. An excellent choice for bright exteriors.

*With **Kodak** Wratten 85 filter. **With **Kodak** Wratten 80A filter.
The Kodak device, Kodak, Eastman, Vision, EXR, T-grain and Wratten, are all trade marks.

Professional Motion Imaging

Contact Numbers

To order film stock dial the Order Services Department direct:

Hemel Hempstead (01442) 845945

or phone through the Kodak National Switchboard using your local area Kodak number shown.

Your order will be handled by: Ann Johnson or Julie Jackson

The direct fax line is (01442) 844458

Head Office: Kodak House, PO Box 66, Station Road, Hemel Hempstead, (01442) 261122

Area	Number
Belfast	01232 328549
Birmingham	0121 7177766
Bristol	01179 298121
Glasgow	0141 248 4071
Liverpool	0151 546 2101
London	0171 405 6137
	0181 427 4380
Manchester	0161 998 7055
Nottingham	01623 756333
Ask for Ext 45945	

ROUTLEDGE

Media Studies

An Introduction to Film Studies 2nd Edition

Edited by Jill Nelmes, Pontypridd College and Glamorgan Centre for Art and Technology

"The second edition builds on the success of the first, ... incorporating more cross-referencing, useful 'think points' and new material such as spectatorship. It is now an even more valuable resource."
- Jim Hillier, ex-Chief Examiner, A-Level Film Studies

June 1999: 544pp:186 b&w photos
Hb: 0-415-17309-4: £55.00
Pb: 0-415-17310-8: £16.99

Adaptations

From Text to Screen, Screen to Text
Edited by Deborah Cartmell and Imelda Whelehan, both at De Montfort University

Adaptations considers the theoretical and practical issues surrounding the translation of a text into a film.

June 1999:272pp:8 b&w photos
Hb: 0-415-16737-X: £40.00
Pb: 0-415-16738-8: £13.99

Film as Social Practice 3rd Edition

Graeme Turner, University of Queensland

A new edition of a classic student textbook, which explores feature films as entertainment, as narrative and as cultural event.

September 1999:240pp:20 b&w photos
Hb: 0-415-21594-3: £40.00
Pb: 0-415-21595-1: £11.99

French Film - 2nd Edition

Texts and Contexts
Edited by Susan Hayward, University of Exeter and Ginette Vincendeau, University of Warwick

Investigates the nature and history of French film through analyses of key films, including *A bout de souffle*, *Cyrano de Bergerac* and *La Haine*.
"This is film criticism at its most professional."
- Choice

January 2000: 304pp
Hb: 0-415-16117-7: £45.00 Pb: 0-415-16118-5: £13.99

Screen Acting

Edited by Alan Lovell, Staffordshire University and Peter Kramer, University of East Anglia

Reveals the centrality of the actor's performance to a film's success and offers new directions for the study of performance on film.

November 1999:208pp
Hb: 0-415-18293-X: £45.00 Pb: 0-415-18294-8: £13.99

TV Living

Television, Culture and Everyday Life
David Gauntlett, University of Leeds and Annette Hill, University of Westminster

Presents the eagerly-awaited findings of the BFI Audience Tracking Study analysing the lives and viewing habits of 500 participants over five years.

April 1999: 234x156: 328pp
Hb: 0-415-18485-1: £45.00 Pb: 0-415-18486-X: £14.99

Uses of Television

Introduction to Television Studies
John Hartley, University of Wales, Cardiff

An immensely innovative, thought-provoking, iconoclastic and ambitious book ... it both expands and clarifies the academic field. **-Mica Nava, University of East London**

January 1999: 256pp: 20 b&w pictures
Hb: 0-415-08508-X: £45.00 Pb: 0-415-08509-8: £13.99

For more information on Routledge Media titles or a free catalogue contact Media Marketing at: Routledge, 11 New Fetter Lane, London EC4P 4EE

Phone 0171 842 2032 or **Fax** 0171 842 2303 **e-mail:** info.media@routledge.co.uk

For details of all Routledge titles, access our internet site at: **www.routledge.com**

Order hotline 08700 768 853

ROUTLEDGE
Taylor & Francis Group

UK FILM, TELEVISION AND VIDEO: OVERVIEW

by Eddie Dyja

Welcome to the 21st Century and the digital age. The white-hot heat of interactive, multi-media technology is here now, and most probably in your living room, if not today, then soon. However, as we leave the 20th Century, a common paradox may be applied to the current state of film, television and video in Britain – much has changed, yet, there is little change.

Film

Since the publication in March 1998 of *A Bigger Picture*, the report of the Film Review Group set up by the Department for Culture, Media and Sport (DCMS), there has been a flurry of activity to begin implementing the report's recommendations aimed at improving the British film industry's performance over the next decade.

In December 1998 the DCMS announced the formation of a new body, The Film Council, to pursue an integrated strategy for film culture and the film industry. The laudable objective of the Film Council to develop a sustainable domestic film industry comes at a time when, despite one or two outstanding exceptions, the majority of British films continue to perform dismally at the UK box office. Despite the wealth of talent in actors, directors and technicians there is still an air of vulnerability about the British film industry as a whole.

News that the next two *Star Wars* prequels will be moving from Leavesden Studios for Australia, and that American companies are being attracted to Canada to make films more cheaply, should set alarm bells ringing. Exactly how 'sustainable' would the British film industry be if American companies pulled out of Britain altogether?

The demise of British-based distributors PolyGram Filmed Entertainment (which became Universal Pictures International [UPI] part of US major Universal Studios)

High hopes for Mike Leigh's Topsy-Turvy

and First Independent left a hole in the UK's fragile distribution sector. As a result British films are in danger of being left in limbo. This was confirmed by the fact that "64 of the 103 UK producer-linked films which went into production in 1997 have yet to receive a UK theatrical release – more than 62 per cent of the total." (*Screen Finance, 13 May 1999*).

The fate of many of these low-budget films is in the hands of new British distributors such as Redbus Film Distribution, Downtown and Guerilla Films. To make matters worse, financial resources to widen the cinema release of most British films beyond a fortnight are currently unavailable. As a result the self-fulfilling prophecy that British films perform poorly at the box office is proved true time after time.

It is against this backdrop that the Film Council will open for business in April 2000. Hopefully, it will learn the lessons from recent history and not get bogged down in bureaucracy, or spend money unwisely, and, will instead,

Jane Horrocks about to become Little Voice

work towards providing a robust infrastructure that supports film producers, distributors and exhibitors in the UK.

As well as responsibility for providing grant-in-aid to the British Film Institute, the Film Council will take over the distribution of National Lottery funds for film from the Arts Council. It is worth repeating Terry Ilott's comments about the distribution of Lottery money from his commentary in the 1996 Handbook.

"Monies should be invested in training, education, specialised exhibition, distribution and, probably, development as much as they are invested in production itself...The Lottery distributor, the Arts Council, is surely not competent to allocate monies to commercial film projects."

The track record of returns for Lottery-funded films has been poor. In May 1999 Charles Denton, the Arts Council's Lottery Film Panel chairman stated that no Lottery financed film had made a profit. Since then *An Ideal Husband* (produced by Pathé) appears set to be the first to claim that prize. Prior to that, *The Woodlanders, True Blue* and *Shooting Fish* have been the most successful Lottery-funded films.

Yet, Lottery funding has also gone into critically acclaimed and award-winning films such as *Love is the Devil, Hilary and Jackie* and *Beautiful People* and provided experience to first-time filmmakers from which they could either return to make better films – or never make another film again.

Whether the Film Council will be as generous with Lottery money remains to be seen. However, if we only invested in films designed to perform well at the box office our output would exist entirely of literary adaptations, costume dramas and romantic comedies. Luckily, and some would say foolishly, there are still risk takers in the British film industry.

In August the DCMS opened the perennial film-can of worms by adding a new definition of what qualifies as a 'British film'. The Government cited *Little Voice* as an example of a film which could not be defined as British under the old Films Act 1985 (since, while being filmed in the UK, with a UK cast, too much of its soundtrack had been recorded outside the UK). Under the Government's new rules the main qualification for classification as a 'British film' will be that 70 per cent of a film's budget should be spent in the UK – still allowing effectively for a third of the film's budget on location abroad. The system also requires filmmakers to spend 70 per cent of their labour costs (for personnel involved in the film) on European and Commonwealth citizens, but it also allows for the occasional 'star' import to take part in a film (like Julia Roberts in *Notting Hill*).

Audiences in the meantime will perceive *Shakespeare in Love* and *Little Voice* as British, and films like *Fargo* as American. It was interesting to note that *The Third Man* was voted top British film of all time in the *bfi's* 100 poll. Just how culturally British is *The Third Man*? Here is a film set in Vienna, with American lead actors and cinematography by Australian-born Robert Krasker (not to mention Anton Karas' defining zither music). The debate on what is and what isn't a British film can be applied to many other films, particularly American-financed films. Perhaps the bottom line should be – where does the majority of the profit of the film go?

The redefinition exercise came on the back of the March 1999 budget when Chancellor Gordon Brown announced an extension to the Government's tax scheme for new films made in Britain until 1 July 2002. The scheme, designed to encourage filmmaking in Britain, allows the production costs of British films with budgets of £15m or less to be written off when the film is completed.

Further evidence of the partnership between the Government and the film industry was the announcement in May 1999 of a Skills Investment Fund (SIF). The training programme designed to assist cinematic skills such as camera and sound work, editing and set design was to be funded by voluntary contributions from film production budgets.

It is easy to forget that ten years ago the British film industry was in a dire state. Only 30 films were produced in the UK in 1989. The only constant funders of film in Britain were British Screen and Channel 4 and the Government stubbornly kept its distance. Perhaps we should be amazed that from this standing start British films managed to make such an impact in the latter part of the 1990s.

The perceived renaissance of British films can be charted by the following list of box office hits: *Four Weddings and a Funeral* (1994), *GoldenEye* (1995), *Trainspotting* (1996), *The Full Monty* (1997), *Bean* (1997), *Sliding Doors* (1998), *Lock, Stock and Two Smoking Barrels* (1999), *Shakespeare in Love* (1999) and *Notting Hill* (1999).

To this can be added an impressive secondary list of highly acclaimed British films: *Shallow Grave* (1994), *The Madness of King George* (1994), *Land and Freedom* (1995), *Brassed Off* (1996), *Secrets and Lies* (1996), *Nil By Mouth* (1997), *Mrs Brown* (1997), *Elizabeth* (1998), *Hilary and Jackie* (1998), *Little Voice* (1998) and *This Year's Love* (1999).

However, it is worth putting these successes into perspective. None of the films in the secondary list would make it onto the top 20 films of the UK box office in 1998, which is dominated by Hollywood. It is this statistic that the Government and the Film Council will be trying to change over the next ten years.

Television

Dumbing down, faked documentaries, bogus guests on chat shows, endless repeats, criticism of news presentation, *News at Ten* sacrificed for its primetime slot, endless attacks on the BBC – the television industry has had a bad press over the past year. Yet, even if you agree with the notion that the current state of television is in decline, one thing is certain: you will be offered more viewing opportunities than ever before.

Digital television is here to stay. The switch over from analogue broadcasting is now likely to happen sooner (within the next seven to ten years) rather than later.

Digital television brings greater picture clarity and better quality sound. In terms of innovation, television sport, and mainly football, has benefited the most. Already interactive television has been used in the coverage of football matches. Football fans are offered the chance to select their camera angles, play back action in slow motion and pull down vital statistics during a match. It remains to be seen whether programmes other than sport will encourage the same level of interaction. Where interaction will come to the fore will be in on-screen transactions – whether this be shopping, or merely pre-selecting an evening's worth of programmes to watch.

If you feel that there is still nothing worth watching you might want to watch the race to gain subscribers to digital television instead. The UK has become the first country in the world where three methods of delivering digital television are in competition with each other. Digital satellite transmissions began on 1 October 1998, courtesy of British Sky Broadcasting (BSkyB), soon followed by digital terrestrial television (DTT) via land-based transmitters from ONdigital. Thirdly, dragging its heels behind the other two, digital cable arrived in the summer of 1999.

By July 1999 BSkyB announced that it had signed up more than one million subscribers. This figure was boosted by its policy of giving away free receiving equipment to subscribers. ONdigital also saw subscribers signing up after a similar marketing campaign.

There is a sense of *déjà vu* in BSkyB and ONdigital's attempts to entice customers to subscribe – remember Sky and BSB; the dish or the squarial? After ten years of broadcasting satellite and cable penetration in UK homes has yet to hit the 50 per cent mark. The multi-channel environment did not bring with it a cornucopia of original, homegrown, groundbreaking programmes – just more repeats. The majority of people in the UK still tune in to ITV and BBC1 for the bulk of their viewing.

The race for Digital TV subscribers is on

In June 1999 Greg Dyke was appointed John Birt's successor as Director-General of the BBC. It came during a time when the Corporation lost out on the rights to screen live FA Cup matches, England's football and rugby matches, Test cricket, and Formula One. Criticism was also piled on the BBC for spending money on management consultants rather than on quality programmes.

The report on the future funding of the BBC, chaired by Gavin Davies, Chief International Economist at Goldman Sachs International, was published in August 1999 and amongst its recommendations was a temporary digital supplement of £23.88 per year to be paid on top of the existing licence fee. This proposal was met with protest not least from other terrestrial broadcasters. The Government called for a period of consultation before coming to a decision at the end of 1999.

The public service ethos demands quality rather than ratings. It is surely asking too much in such a competitive environment. Whether the BBC can reinvent itself by becoming a commercial operator and still carry the flag as a public service provider is debatable.

A survey entitled *Television Industry Tracking Study* by the *bfi*, of production personnel working in the television industry, found that 70 per cent felt the quality of television output had declined since 1994. Cost cutting was seen as the biggest cause of this decline by those surveyed. But is quality television really in such a decline as commentators suggest?

There is a tendency to look back fondly at a golden age of television and cite outstanding programmes – *Cracker, the Singing Detective, GBH, Brideshead Revisited, Monty Python, Dad's Army, The Forsyte Saga, The Prisoner, The Avengers* – but you can bet there was always something forgettable on during the same period of time.

Perhaps the establishment of digital television will empower the viewer after all. The technology is certainly in place for viewers to create a tailor-made television environment in the home. So, in theory, viewers can tune in to hours of carefully selected quality programmes every night.

If TV audiences are accused of being conservative in their tastes, then programme planners must take some responsibility for years of unimaginative scheduling. Take a look at the programme planning on both ITV and BBC for August in the early Saturday evening slot over the last 40 years in the panel opposite – it reveals a shocking lack of variety.

40 Years of Early Evening Saturday TV Entertainment in August

22 August – 1959
7.30pm *Top Town Parade* (BBC1)
6.00pm *Holiday Town Parade* (ITV)

30 August – 1969
7.30pm *Music, Music, Music* (BBC1)
6.15pm *The Frankie Howerd Show* (ITV)

25 August – 1979
8.20pm *Seaside Special from the Isle of Man* (BBC1)
7.15pm *Cannon and Ball* (ITV)

26 August – 1989
7.05pm *Michael Barrymore's Saturday Night Out* (BBC1)
7.45pm *Beadle's Box of Tricks* (ITV)

21 August – 1999
6.55pm *The Other Half* (BBC)
6.05pm *Would I Lie To You?* (ITV)

Dad's Army was transmitted on 29th August 1999 (BBC2), 28th August 1979 (BBC1) and 29th August 1969 (BBC1). Three decades of the same programme (but not the same episode).

Television at its best enables friends, families and colleagues to engage in a collective viewing experience with conversations about their favourite programme – whether it be last night's soap or something more weighty like *The Sopranos*. Good quality programmes warrant a repeat showing, in the same way that people watch their favourite film. However, quality programmes still need to be made – otherwise there will be nothing left to repeat on all those digital channels.

Video

To DVD or not to DVD? Rather like the impact of CDs on vinyl in record shops, Digital Versatile Discs have entered video store shelves around the country and will, we are told, eventually replace VHS video cassettes. There are expected to be around 1,000 film titles to choose from by the end of 1999. DVDs are being aimed at the casual movie goer and the film buff alike. Rather like digital television, the main selling points of DVD are superior image, sound quality and, in some cases, an interactive element.

One advert for a DVD player suggests that DVD is like going to the cinema – in fact it's better because you don't get people coming in late and walking in front of the screen. The prospect of home systems to reproduce the sounds of your local multiplex fills the potential buyer with awe (and the potential buyer's neighbours with dread). With pull-down menus giving filmographic details of the film and its stars, the cinema trailer and the ability to select favourite scenes from the film, the DVD viewer gets a little more than the VHS viewer.

It will be interesting to see how quickly DVD establishes itself. Its main advantage is that it is the technology of the present and is set to replace the technology of the past. Perhaps the one thing preventing it really taking off is that you can't record from DVD – yet. Recordable DVD for the home is likely to appear in a couple of years' time.

But it is hard to imagine film and TV fans giving up their VHS collections spanning a period of 20-odd years – interactive additions or not. It is also absurd to feel that VHS quality is so inferior to DVD that your old collection is now unwatchable. Indeed, VHS films have come down in price – there are now some collectable films for around the £3.99 mark or less. Nevertheless, it is probable that within five years' time VHS and VTRs will become rather like vinyl and turntables are today.

The DVD player is set to replace the Video machine

DVD looks set to replace the VHS video format

2001

Essentially, as statistics in this Handbook show, the majority of people in Britain are conservative in their tastes and feel comfortable with the familiar. Acceptance of change usually comes with a caveat, illustrated by the following joke.

Q: How many film buffs does it take to change a light bulb?

A: One to insert a bigger, brighter, more powerful bulb and the rest to reflect that they don't make light bulbs like they used to do.

Two years ago relatively few people in the UK had an internet site or access to one. Now it is taken for granted. E-tailing concepts and selling online are no longer new – delivery of programming to the home and for connection to interactive services for shopping, banking and a range of e-commerce possibilities mean that we can conduct the majority of our business and social transactions from the comfort of our armchair. Technology is moving fast and fully integrated home entertainment systems featuring phone, fax, internet, DVD and personal computers are merely online orders waiting to be delivered. It comes as no surprise to learn that computer software giant Microsoft has bought into two of the major UK cable operators, NTL and Telewest. Expect to see further interactive developments in the future with the internet connection merging with the delivery of television channels or even showing the premieres of films. In both cases information surrounding the programme can be downloaded to some related background data files or linked to a host of relevant websites.

Digital cameras and digital films like *A Bug's Life* and *Star Wars* are rewriting film history. With digital camcorders everyone has the opportunity to be a filmmaker. With interactive digital TV everyone has the opportunity to become a programme planner or a TV editor.

But of course we don't have to buy completely into this multimedia utopia. During the IMAX film *Destiny in Space* a short clip from *2001: A Space Odyssey* appears. Here is a film about the future made in the 1960s being shown in a huge format in the present. It is a bizarre moment in timelessness. 21st century technology may well enable us to view things differently – with greater definition, volume and clarity – but purveyors of new technology should be reminded of what happens in Kubrick's film, when the computer running the space ship begins taking over the astronauts' lives.

They turn HAL off.

They don't make them like they used to do – A Matter of Life and Death due to be revived in 2000

2001: A Space Odyssey goes back to the future

Star Wars: The Phantom Menace (left) and digital icon Lara Croft (right)

A Bug's Life – byte sized digital animation

Kate Winslett in Holy Smoke made in 1999

① Number and Value of UK Films*
1981–1998

Year	Titles produced	Current prices (£m)	Production cost (£m) (1999 prices)
1981	24	61.2	134.8
1982	40	141.1	286.3
1983	51	251.1	487.4
1984	53	270.4	495.4
1985	54	269.4	469.4
1986	41	165.8	279.4
1987	55	195.3	315.3
1988	48	175.2	272.2
1989	30	104.7	149.7
1990	60	217.4	280.2
1991	59	243.2	294.1
1992	47	184.9	215.1
1993	67	224.1	260.7
1994	84	455.2	518.3
1995	78	402.4	454.7
1996	128	741.4	809.3
1997	116	562.8	599.9
1998	88	509.3	525.0

Source: Screen Finance/x25 Partnership/BFI

*UK films are defined here as films produced in the UK or with a UK financial involvement. They include majority and minority co-productions

All smiles as Notting Hill reaps box office rewards

Film Production

UK film production continued its gradual drop with a total of 88 films produced in 1998 after 1996/97's heady 100 plus years (Table 1). However, taking the decade as a whole, the upward trend in film production is still evident. It is best illustrated by totalling the number of films produced in the first five years of the decade – 317 compared with the four years from 1995, when the total reached 410.

The £509.3 million spent on these films, compared to the £562.8 million spent in 1997, represents a fall of around 9 percent and suggests a gradual levelling out rather than a cause for concern. The average budget for all these productions is £5.72 million, which perhaps might serve as a useful indicator as we divide UK films into their respective categories.

Nearly half the films produced in 1998 fall into Category A – films that are stand-alone UK productions (Table 2). The average budget of £2.49 million for these 43 films marks an increase over past years.

Notting Hill (£15 million) and *Topsy Turvy* (£13.50 million) contributed to just over 25 per cent of the total budget. These budgets compare favourably with American financed or part-financed films in the UK (Tables 5 and 6) whose average is around the £12 million mark. With the benefit of hindsight it is possible to say the budget on *Notting Hill* has reaped rewards at box offices around the world.

None of the other wholly UK product cracked the £5.72 million figure. Indeed, only 14 films managed budgets of over £2.26 million, leaving 19 with budgets of under £2 million.

Despite the critical acclaim that some of these low-budget UK films receive, they rarely perform well at the box office against the big budget muscle of American productions. And, sadly, some of the films included in the Table 1 figure won't receive a theatrical release at all.

There were fewer major UK co-productions in 1998 than in the previous couple of years (Table 3). However, the average budget of £5.46 million for these films was greater than 1997 (3.23 million) and 1996 (5 million). This trend is also reflected in the number of minority UK co-productions in 1998 (Table 4). There were significantly fewer minority co-productions – 8 compared to 17 in 1997 – but these were offset with larger average budgets of £4.47 million compared to £3.11 million in 1997.

UK Film Production 1998 – Category A

Feature Films where the cultural and financial impetus is from the UK and where the majority of personnel are British.

Title	Production companies	Production cost (£m)
Anxiety	Mortal Films	1.00
Ashes to Ashes	Red Moon Films	1.00
Being Considered	Serendipity Films	1.00
Beautiful People	Tall Stories Prods/ Film Four/BFI/ MIDA/ British Screen/ACE	1.11
The Clandestine Marriage	Portman Productions	5.00
The Darkest Light	Footprint Films/Pathe/ Becker Pictures/BBC	2.00
The Debt Collector	Dragon Pictures/Film Four/Glasgow Film Fund	3.00
East is East	Assassin Films/Film Four/BBC	2.40
Elephant Juice	HAL Films	5.00
Everybody Loves Sunshine	The Mission Prods/Isle of Man Film Commission	2.20
Fanny and Elvis	Film Consortium/Scala Prods/ITV	3.20
Following	Syncopy Films	0.10
Freak Out	Beyond Therapy Entertainment	0.10
Gregory's Two Girls	Young Lake Prods/Film Four/Scottish Arts Council	3.50
Human Traffic	Fruit Salad Films/BBC Wales	2.20
An Ideal Husband	Scorpio Prods/Wilde Films	1.00
Janice Beard 45 wpm	Film Consortium/Dakota Films/Film Four	2.50
The Killing Zone	Seventh Twelfth Collective	0.01
The Last Yellow	Scala Prods/Jolyon Symonds Film/BBC/ACE	2.00
Lighthouse	Winchester Ent./Tungsten Pictures/British Screen/ACE	1.50
Mad Cows	Flashlight Films/Entertainment	2.20
Make Believe	Make Believe Prods	0.25
Milk	Gummfluh Films/BSkyB	2.00
Notting Hill	Notting Hill Pictures/Bookshop Prods/PolyGram	15.00
Out of Depth	Out of Depth plc	0.52
Rancid Aluminium	Fiction Factory/Entertainment	4.72
Ratcatcher	Pathé/BBC	2.00
A Room for Romeo Brass	Company Pictures/BBC/ACE	3.20
Saintly	Cool Beans Prods	2.00
Simon Magus	Silesia Films/Jonescompany/Film Four/ACE	3.00
Small Time Obsession	Solo Films/Seventh Twelfth Collective	0.45
Summer Rain	Enterprise Films	1.00
This Year's Love	Kismet Film Company/Entertainment/Scottish Arts Council	2.75
Three Days	Austin Hill	0.10
Topsy–Turvy	Pathé/Thin Man Films/Greenlight Fund	13.50
Trouble on Earth	Rollercoaster Films	1.00
Tube Tales	Horsepower Productions/BSkyB	4.20
24 Hours in London	One World Films	1.30
Two Bad Mice	April Films	0.10
The Wedding Tackle	Viking Films	1.00
The War Zone	Film Four/Sarah Radclyffe Prods/Portobello Pictures	2.00
Weak at Denise	Peninsula Films	1.00
Wonderland	Revolution Films/Kismet Film Company/BBC/PolyGram	4.00

TOTAL NUMBER OF FILMS   43

TOTAL COST   £107.11m

AVERAGE COST   £2.49 m

Source: Screen Finance/X25 Partnership/BFI

UK Film Production 1998 – Category B

Majority UK Co-Productions. Films in which, although there are foreign partners, there is a UK cultural content and a significant amount of British finance and personnel.

Title	Production companies/participating countries	Production cost (£m)
Accelerator	Imagine Films/Gazboro/Irish Film Board/Irish Section 48 Tax Incentive (**Eire**)	2.60
Best	Smoke and Mirrors/ Pembridge Prods/BSkyB/Isle of Man Film Commission (**Eire**)	5.00
Eight and a Half Women	Woodline/Movie Masters/Delux/Continent/TF1/Dutch Film Fund/Eurimages (**Neths/France/Germany /Luxembourg**)	8.24
Felicia's Journey	Marquis Films/Alliance/Artisan (**Canada/US**)	4.00
Grey Owl	Grey Owl Ajawaan Prods/Richard Attenborough Prods/Largo Entertainment (**Canada/US**)	15.00
Hold Back the Night	Parallax Pictures/C4/ACE/Wave Films/Alta Films (**France/Spain/Denmark**)	1.76
I Could Read the Sky	Hot Property/Spider Pictures/Liquid Films/BFI/C4/ACE/Irish Film Board (**Eire**)	0.48
The Last September	Scala/Ima Films/Zaglos/BSkyB/RTE/British Screen/Irish Film Board (**Eire/France**)	4.00
The Lost Son	Film Consortium/Scala/Ima Films/FilmFour/Canal Plus/TF1(**France**)	7.00
Mad about Mambo	First City/ Plurabelle/ACNI/Irish Film Board(**Eire**)	5.00
The Trench	Blue PM/Skyline/Galatee/Entertainment/Portman/ACE/British Screen/ European Coproduction Fund (**France**)	2.20
To Walk with Lions	Studio Eight/Kingsborough Greenlight/Cavco(**Canada**)	10.30

TOTAL NUMBER OF FILMS   12

TOTAL COST   £65.58 m

AVERAGE COST   £5.46 m

Screen Finance/X25 Partnership/BFI

UK Film Production 1998 – Category C

Minority UK Co-productions. Foreign (non US) films in which there is a small UK involvement in finance or personnel.

Title	Production companies/participating countries	Production cost (£m)
Conquest	Shaftesbury Films/Greenpoint (**Canada**)	1.50
Esther Khan	Zephyr/Why Not Films/Canal Plus/Films Alain Sarde/ACE/British Screen (**France**)	7.00
The German Undertaker	Claussen and Woebke/Media II/German Lander Funding	2.30
Lalla	Frankfurter Film/ZDF(**Germany**)	1.05
Ordinary Decent Criminal	Little Bird/TATfilm/Icon/Greenlight Fund/Irish Film Board/Irish Section 35 Tax Incentive (**Eire/Germany/US**)	7.34
Straight Shooter	Perathon/Senator/German Lander Funding(**Germany**)	3.90
Tea with Mussolini	Film and General/Medusa/Cineritmo (**Italy**)	8.50
The Wrong Blonde	Pathe/Renn Prods/UGC(**France**)	4.20

TOTAL NUMBER OF FILMS   8

TOTAL COST   £35.79m

AVERAGE COST   £4.47m

Source: Screen Finance/X25 Partnership/BFI

UK Film Production – Category D

American financed or part–financed films made in the UK. Most titles have a British cultural content.

Title	Production company(ies)	Production cost (£m)
Alien Love Triangle (Part 1)	Figment Films/Miramax/Dimension Films	3.00
The Big Tease	Crawford Prods/Warner Bros	1.00
Chicken Run	Pathé/Aardman Animations/Dreamworks SKG	27.40
The Closer You Get	Redwave/Fox Searchlight	4.72
Dreaming of Joseph Lees	Midsummer Films/Fox Searchlight	2.00
Entrapment	Fountainbridge/Fox	51.60
Greenwich Mean Time	Anvil Films/Icon Entertainment	5.00
An Ideal Husband	Pathé/Fragile Films/Miramax/Icon Entertainment	6.50
Mansfield Park	Miramax Hal/BBC/ACE	6.64
The Match	Rafford Films/Propaganda/PolyGram	4.20
The Mummy	Universal Pictures	30.35
Onegin	Onegin Prods/Entertainment/Rysher Entertainment	8.40
Shakespeare in Love	Miramax/Universal/Bedford Falls	15.00
Sleepy Hollow	Scott Rudin Films/Paramount	42.00
Soldier	Impact/Jerry Weintraub Prods/Warner Bros/Morgan Creek	30.00
Still Crazy	Marmot Tandy/Columbia TriStar/Greenlight Fund	7.00
Swing	Last Time Prods/Entertainment/Kushner Locke Co.	4.00
Three Businessmen	Exterminating Angel/VPRO (Neths)	0.73
Virtual Sexuality	Noel Gay Co/Canal Plus/Sony	3.70
With or Without You	Revolution Films/Miramax/Film Four	2.40
The Winslow Boy	Sony Pictures Classics	6.00

TOTAL NUMBER OF FILMS   **21**

TOTAL COST   **£261.24m**

AVERAGE COST   **£12.44m**

Source: Screen Finance/X25 Partnership/BFI

UK Film Production – Category E

US Films with some British financial involvement

Title	Production company(ies)	Production cost (£m)
Arlington Road	Samuelson Prods/Lakeshore Entertainment/PolyGram	16.83
Texas Funeral	TF Prods/J and M	4.20
Mickey Blue Eyes	Simian Films/Castle Rock	22.00
The Weekend	Granada Films/Yellow Room Productions	5.00

TOTAL NUMBER OF FILMS   **4**

TOTAL COST   **£48.03m**

AVERAGE COST   **£12.00m**

Source: Screen Finance/X25 Partnership/BFI

Ten years ago commentators in the Handbook had high hopes for European co-productions and many saw them as the only chance of providing a vibrant UK and European film industry. While European co-productions certainly bolstered film production in the early '90s, both in terms of output and budget, the films have failed to ignite at the box office. These films tend to be labelled arthouse and therefore assumed to have only a minority appeal to conservative UK audiences.

What commentators failed to anticipate was that the most financially successful partnerships of the '90s would come via the Americans, who not only were responsible for investing in co-productions but also cinema circuits in the UK.

This is clearly reflected in Table 5 and Table 6. The average budgets of both are easily double the total average budget of UK films of £5.72 million. The films in Table 5 that catch the eye are *Entrapment* (£51.6 million) and *Sleepy Hollow* (£42 million) – compare the combined total budgets of these two films with the 43 wholly UK productions and the impact and input of American financed films is obvious. The remaining films in Table 5 have far smaller budgets – even so just over half exceed the £5.72 million benchmark.

⑦ EU Film Production 1998		
Country	**No of films (inc Co-Prods)**	**Investment ($m)**
Austria	12	16.9
Belgium	7	17.8
Denmark	18	39.0
Finland	8	18.1
France	183	963.4
Germany	119	342.5
Greece	20	7.4
Ireland	25	128.5
Italy	92	361.6
Luxembourg	3	2.1
Netherlands	18	54.5
Portugal	10	4.5
Spain	65	206.4
Sweden	20	43.9
UK	88	317.3
TOTAL	**688**	**2,523.9**

Source: Screen Digest

American money has financed some of the UK's recent big successes – *Shakespeare in Love, Sliding Doors* and *The Full Monty,* and filled studios with big budget productions: *Star Wars: The Phantom Menace, Saving Private Ryan* and *Mission Impossible.* Of course not everything has turned to gold: *The Avengers* being a good example.

However, we should not take this partnership for granted. For while the number of US/UK co-productions has increased from 14 (1997) to 21 (1998) the actual average budget fell by £6.07 million from £18.51 million (1997) to £12.44 million (1998). Previous Handbook commentators have noted that the level of American activity rises and falls according to a host of factors, including the exchange rate. Nevertheless, the UK still remains an attractive option for those willing to invest in technical expertise and artistic integrity.

Shakespeare in Love conquers all

Types of Release for UK films 1997

Proportions of films with a UK involvement which achieved;

a) Wide release. Opening or playing on 30 or more screens around the country within a year of production prior to 1 January 1999

b) Limited release, mainly in art house cinemas or a short West End run, prior to 1 January 1999.

c) Released or planned to be released during 1999

d) Unreleased with no plans to do so during 1999

Year	(a)%	(b)%	(c)%	(d)%
1997	15.5	19.0	22.4	43.1

Source: Screen Finance/X25 Partnership/ACNielsen EDI/BFI

Types of Release for UK films 1984–1997

Proportions of films with a UK involvement which achieved;

a) Wide release. Opening or playing on 30 or more screens around the country within a year of production

b) Limited release, mainly in art house cinemas or a short West End run

c) Unreleased a year after production

Year	(a)%	(b)%	(c)%
1984	50.00	44.00	6.00
1985	52.80	35.90	11.30
1986	55.80	41.90	2.30
1987	36.00	60.00	4.00
1988	29.50	61.20	9.30
1989	33.30	38.90	27.80
1990	29.40	47.10	23.50
1991	32.20	37.30	30.50
1992	38.30	29.80	31.90
1993	25.40	22.40	52.20
1994	31.00	22.60	46.40
1995	23.10	34.60	42.30
1996	19.00	14.00	67.00
1997	15.50	19.00	68.50

Source: Screen Finance/X25 Partnership/ACNielsen EDI/BFI

In terms of European Film Production (Table 7) the UK is fourth behind France, Germany and Italy, both in number of films produced and size of investment. These three European countries have consolidated their position at the head of the European film production chart. France produced 183 films in 1998. Even taking into account co-productions it is an extremely high output. The sum of $963.4 million invested in French production works out at about a third of the whole investment total.

The evidence currently shows that across Europe audiences still see American films ahead of homegrown product. It will be interesting to see whether the ambitions of the top four European film-producing nations will bear fruit as regards respective box office figures, or whether the films being made will make their way straight to digital television or video.

It is only when we look at the depressing statistics down in Table 8 that the chances of UK films actually reaching UK audiences is put into perspective. Fewer UK films are receiving a wide release (defined as playing on 30 or more screens around the country within a year of production). Only 15.5 per cent of UK films managed a full release. At the same time around 68.5 per cent of films remain unreleased a year after production.

This year the Handbook has broken down these statistics further to show that as many as 43.1 per cent of films produced in 1997 remain unreleased with no plans to do so during 1999.

If ever there was an issue to address on Day One of the Film Council it is the failure of the UK film industry to provide financial back-up in terms of distribution and marketing of UK product. It may be desirable to promote the interests of British films but how realistic are the chances of the objectives being met if money is not invested in promoting films?

Looking at the statistics dating from around the mid-'90s (the period which coincidentally saw a so-called resurgence in interest in British films) reveals a marked decline in the release of UK films. This also coincides with a period when the distribution network for UK films has become fragmented and all the major players are from America. At this moment in time it would be hard to put a convincing argument to the major distributors that British films will out-perform American films at the box office. Even taking into account the success of films like *Notting Hill*, *The Full Monty* and *Lock, Stock and Two Smoking Barrels* there are too many micro-budget risks around to warrant a sudden change of heart.

What Happened to 1997 UK Films?

Distribution of 1997 UK productions and foreign films made in the UK up to 30 September 1999

Released theatrically in 1997/8
(* signifies previous titles)

The Avengers
Babymother
The Big Lebowski
Dad Savage
Dancing at Lughnasa
Divorcing Jack
Elizabeth
The General
Girls' Night
The Governess
Guru in Seven
Hilary and Jackie (*Jackie)
If Only
I Want You
Keep the Aspidistra Flying
The Land Girls
Les Miserables
The Life of Stuff
Little Voice
Lock, Stock and Two Smoking Barrels
Lost in Space
Love is the Devil
Martha – Meet Frank, Daniel and Laurence
Middleton's Changeling
My Name is Joe
On Connait La Chanson
Palookaville
The Parent Trap
The Real Howard Spitz
Resurrection Man
Saving Private Ryan
Sliding Doors
A Soldier's Daughter Never Cries
Spice World
Titanic Town
Tomorrow Never Dies
24 7 TwentyFourSeven
Up N' Under
Velvet Goldmine
The Wisdom of Crocodiles

Films in bold signifies those films
which opened or played on 30 or more
screens around the country within a
year of production prior to 1
January 1999

Released theatrically in 1999
All the Little Animals
Among Giants
Bedrooms and Hallways
Captain Jack
The Croupier
Crushproof (*Hooligans)
Don't Go Breaking My Heart (*Us
Begins with You)
The Final Cut
Get Real
Heart
Hideous Kinky
The HiLo Country
Los Angeles Without a Map
The Misadventures of Margaret
Orphans
Parting Shots
Plunkett and MacLeane
A Price Above Rubies
Prometheus
The Red Violin
Rogue Trader
Star Wars: The Phantom Menace
The Theory of Flight
Vigo: Passion for Life
Waking Ned
Woundings

**Distribution deal but no release
date**
Death and The Loss of Sexual innocence
A Kind of Hush
My Life So Far
The Tichborne Claimant
Urban Ghost Story

Straight to TV
The Commissioner
Speak Like a Child
St. Ives
Tom's Midnight Garden
What Rats Won't Do

Straight to video
Mistress of the Craft
Sunset Heights
Underground

No UK release
The Dance

Unfinished
Buskers
Dirty British Boys
Hard Edge

No distribution deal
Alien Blood
Appetite
Arzoo
Basil
Beach Boys
Comic Act
Crossmaheart
Dangerous Obsession
Day Release
The Devil's Snow
Fast Food
Himalaya – A Chief's Childhood
Jilting Joe
Jinnah
The Jolly Boys Last Stand
Laid Up
Last Seduction 2
Lucia
The Nutcracker Prince
Owd Bob
Red Mercury
The Sea Change
The Secret Laughter of Women
Shadow Run
Such a Long Journey
Sugar Sugar
Table 5
Talisman
Time Enough
Treasure Island
Understanding Jane
Vent de Colere
The Wolves of Kromer

As of September 1999
**Source: Screen Finance/X25
Partnership/ACNielsen EDI/BFI**

10 Number of UK Feature Films Produced 1912–1998

Year	Number	Year	Number
1912	2	1960	122
1913	18	1961	117
1914	15	1962	114
1915	73	1963	113
1916	107	1964	95
1917	66	1965	93
1918	76	1966	82
1919	122	1967	83
		1968	88
1920	155	1969	92
1921	137		
1922	110	1970	97
1923	68	1971	96
1924	49	1972	104
1925	33	1973	99
1926	33	1974	88
1927	48	1975	81
1928	80	1976	80
1929	81	1977	50
		1978	54
1930	75	1979	61
1931	93		
1932	110	1980	31
1933	115	1981	24
1934	145	1982	40
1935	165	1983	51
1936	192	1984	53
1937	176	1985	54
1938	134	1986	41
1939	84	1987	55
		1988	48
1940	50	1989	30
1941	46		
1942	39	1990	60
1943	47	1991	59
1944	35	1992	47
1945	39	1993	67
1946	41	1994	84
1947	58	1995	78
1948	74	1996	128
1949	101	1997	116
		1998	88
1950	125		
1951	114	**Source: Screen**	
1952	117	**Digest/Screen**	
1953	138	**Finance/BFI**	
1954	150		
1955	110		
1956	108		
1957	138		
1958	121		
1959	122		

It is also worth saying that quantity does not equal quality and there are always going to be 'turkeys' around that should never have been made in the first place. However, even to get a micro-budget film made implies a certain amount of faith on the part of the producer.

The fate of films produced in 1997 (Table 9) shows the extent of the waiting list. Yet, to counter the pessimism it is worth looking down at the column of films that did get theatrical releases and note the variety of UK product and sufficient quality around.

The fact, identified in last year's Handbook, that it is easier to produce a film in the UK should be counter-balanced with the fact that it is harder to get a UK film released theatrically. This coincides with a period where there are over 750 cinema sites in the UK and over 2,500 screens. So, don't expect too many of the 88 films produced in the UK in 1998 to make it to a screen near you.

The Woodlanders – an adaptation from Hardy's novel

Waking Ned – funded without Lottery money

National Lottery

Total funding from the National Lottery, via the four UK Arts Councils, for film production projects in 1998 dropped for the second successive year to around £19.5 million compared with £23.7 million in 1997.

Two out of the three Lottery franchises registered their intentions with the Film Consortium spreading an initial £3.5 million over 12 projects (seven for development) compared with Pathé Pictures' allocation of £2.3 million for three features. In the meantime some eyebrows were being raised at the the the DNA Films camp who were not appearing to be in a hurry to launch their slate of films.

The Film Consortium's feature *Fanny and Elvis* was awarded £30,500 for development on top of the £1 million for production which gave it the highest amount of Lottery funding of the three franchises. The highest award of all films in 1998 went to *Daniel Deronda*, an adaptation of the novel by George Eliot, which received £2 million from a total budget of £9,500,000.

The Arts Council of England distributed the lion's share of total Lottery grants taking about 85 per cent of the total awards. The Arts Councils of Scotland, Wales and Northern Ireland allocated awards to 14 features/shorts. Of those *Gregory's Two Girls'* award of £1m represented the highest investment.

One lesson already learned from the Lottery is that throwing money in the direction of filmmakers on the basis that they filled in a good application form does not guarantee box office success. The bottom line – that Lottery funding would be allocated to films which looked likely to repay the amounts invested – seems retrospectively to be a good idea in theory but a naive notion in practice. A look at the current difficulties of distributing UK products shows that expectations of returns were based more on hope than on design. Furthermore, the cocktail of bureaucracy, altruism, creativity and commercialism has left a largely unsatisfying taste in the mouth. In addition, the problem for the Arts Council has been what to do with the productions that failed to recoup the money invested.

The implication in the announcement that the Film Council would take on responsibility for distribution of Lottery grants for film production is that the Government is looking for a better return on the money invested. It is clear that the Film Council will have to reassess the criterion for Lottery funding if its desire is

to stimulate a thriving film production base. It also needs to be clear whether commercial success is the sole objective of Lottery funded films. At the same time it must decide what to do with about the performance of non-commercial films before it can even begin to address the idea of the Alpha Fund – ironically, a fund to encourage the development of innovative films which are deemed to be non-commercial.

Hideous Kinky produced by The Film Consortium

An Ideal Husband produced by Pathé Pictures

Funding of Film Productions by National Lottery Awards 1998

Title	Amount of Award(£)	Total Budget(£)
THE FILM CONSORTIUM *		
1 The Boggart	30,000 (Development)	
2 Calcio	1,000,000	4,000,000
3 Fanny and Elvis	1,000,000 + 30,500 (Development)	3,200,000
4 Hideous Kinky	225,000	
5 Hold Back the Night	560,000	1,760,000
6 Janice Beard 45 wpm	833,000	2,500,00
7 The Navigators	9,928 (Development)	
8 1934	36,965 (Development)	
9 Out of It	10,000 (Development)	
10 The Streets Above Us	13,000 (Development)	
11 Vera	20,000 (Development)	
12 Wounded Knee	8,000 (Development)	
TOTAL	**3,776,393**	
DNA FILMS*		
(No titles in 1998)		
PATHÉ PICTURES*		
1 The Darkest Light	708,000	2,000,000
2 An Ideal Husband	1,000,000	6,500,000
3 Ratcatcher	615,000	2,000,000
TOTAL	**2,323,000**	
ARTS COUNCIL OF ENGLAND – Features		
1 Another Life	935,000	2,500,000
2 Beautiful People	553,823	1,100,000
3 Daniel Deronda	2,000,000	9,500,000
4 Esther Khan	700,000	7,000,000
5 I Could Read the Sky	234,327	468,655
6 The Last Yellow	550,000	2,060,000
7 The Lighthouse	412,474	1,500,000
8 Mansfield Park	1,000,000	6,460,000
9 A Room for Romeo Brass	850,000	3,200,000
10 Simon Magus	946,250	3,000,000
11 Solomon and Gaenor	250,000	1,600,000
12 Somme	700,000	2,197,640
13 William	997,000	3,150,000
14 Warriors at Heart	10,000 (Development)	
TOTAL	**10,138,879**	
ARTS COUNCIL OF ENGLAND – Short Films		
1 Banana Rollercoaster	14,603	36,652
2 The English Goodbye	19,624	50,919
3 Hester	20,500	38,000
4 Home Road Movies	47,500	90,000
5 The Night Frontier	18,635	37,270
6 Little Dark Poet	46,321	96,643
7 Pig Iron	45,000	90,000
8 Pitch Black	45,000	80,000
9 The Promise	34,351	72,617
10 Wildlife	31,010	62,010
TOTAL	**322,549**	

*Lottery Franchise Consortia

Title	Amount of Award(£)	Total Budget(£)
SCOTTISH ARTS COUNCIL – Features		
1 Gregory's Two Girls	1,000,000	3,500,000
2 This Year's Love	750,000	2,750,000
SCOTTISH ARTS COUNCIL – Shorts		
1 Duck	15,000	60,000
2 First It's Dark	15,000	64,000
3 Two Wrongs	15,000	60,000
TOTAL	**1,795,000**	
ARTS COUNCIL OF WALES – Features		
1 One of the Hollywood Ten	250,000	3,000,000
2 Solomon and Gaenor	250,000	1,600,000
ARTS COUNCIL OF WALES – Shorts		
1 Aml Bai	38,765	50,000
TOTAL	**538,765**	
ARTS COUNCIL OF NORTHERN IRELAND – Features		
1 Country	75,000	1,000,000
2 Days Like This	200,000	5,300,000
3 The Follower	75,000	1,200,000
4 Mad About Mambo	50,000	4,003,952
ARTS COUNCIL OF NORTHERN IRELAND – TV Series		
1 Eureka Street	160,000	3,260,382
ARTS COUNCIL OF NORTHERN IRELAND – Short		
1 The Shoemaker	28,072	39,000
TOTAL	**588,072**	
TOTAL AWARD	**19,482,658**	

Source: Screen Finance/X25/ACNI

Gregory's Two Girls (left) and This Year's Love (right) two films funded by the Scottish Arts Council

12 Cinema Admissions 1933–1998 (millions)

Year	Admissions	Year	Admissions
1933	903.00		
1934	950.00	1970	193.00
1935	912.33	1971	176.00
1936	917.00	1972	156.60
1937	946.00	1973	134.20
1938	987.00	1974	138.50
1939	990.00	1975	116.30
		1976	103.90
1940	1,027.00	1977	103.50
1941	1,309.00	1978	126.10
1942	1,494.00	1979	111.90
1943	1,541.00		
1944	1,575.00	1980	101.00
1945	1,585.00	1981	86.00
1946	1,635.00	1982	64.00
1947	1,462.00	1983	65.70
1948	1,514.00	1984	54.00
1949	1,430.00	1985	72.00
		1986	75.50
1950	1,395.80	1987	78.50
1951	1,365.00	1988	84.00
1952	1,312.10	1989	94.50
1953	1,284.50		
1954	1,275.80	1990	97.37
1955	1,181.80	1991	100.29
1956	1,100.80	1992	103.64
1957	915.20	1993	114.36
1958	754.70	1994	123.53
1959	581.00	1995	114.56
		1996	123.80
1960	500.80	1997	139.30
1961	449.10	1998	135.50
1962	395.00		
1963	357.20		
1964	342.80		
1965	326.60		
1966	288.80		
1967	264.80		
1968	237.30		
1969	214.90		

Source: Screen Digest/Screen Finance/BFI

13 UK Box Office 1998

Admissions	135.5 million
Total Cinema Sites	759
Total Cinema Screens	2,564
Total Multiplex Sites	167
Total Multiplex Screens	1,488
Box Office Gross	£514.73 m
Average Ticket Price	£3.83

Source: Screen Finance/X25 Partnership/CAA/ACNielsen/EDI/Media Salles

Cinema

Cinema admissions fell slightly in 1998 (Table 12), with a total of 135.5 million, compared with 139.9 million in 1997. Yet, this was still the second highest total since 1974. Furthermore, UK cinemas took a total of £514.73 million (Table 13) which was actually £8.46 million greater than 1997. Not surprisingly, this was due to an increase in ticket prices – which average out at £3.83.

The growth in multiplexes continued with 25 sites adding 266 screens to their impressive totals. Multiplex screens now account for 58 per cent of total screens in the UK. New multiplex sites are being developed and so there is little sign that building work will stop.

Cinema attendances and the increase in the number of sites have gone hand-in-hand since the lowest point in 1984, when attendances sank to 54 million. Since then a whole cinemagoing generation has grown used to a multi-screen, family-friendly environment.

If you like going to the cinema then this is a good era to live in. There are now 759 sites in the UK (Table 13) – if you didn't go to the cinema in 1998 it wasn't due to a lack of screens. Even within this expansive environment the competition for customers remains fierce.

Previous Handbook commentators have speculated that the growth in sites and screens might eventually have led to the possibility of mini-circuits catering for specific niches. This hasn't really happened. The overwhelming product remains that of American mainstream movies aimed at 15–24 year-olds.

In fact, the demographic breakdown of cinemagoing rarely alters (Table 15). Numbers attending once a month or more may increase slightly (as they did in 1998) –

Sliding Doors – top UK film at the UK box office in 1998

(14) UK Sites and Screens 1984-1998

Year	Total Sites	Total Screens
1984	660	1,271
1985	663	1,251
1986	660	1,249
1987	648	1,215
1988	699	1,416
1989	719	1,559
1990	737	1,685
1991	724	1,789
1992	735	1,845
1993	723	1,890
1994	734	1,969
1995	743	2,019
1996	742	2,166
1997	747	2,383
1998	759	2,564

Source: Screen Finance/X25 Partnership

Hilary and Jackie featured women in lead roles

however, this increase is across the board. The age and social class boundaries remain more or less the same.

The best served audiences are the 15–24 year-olds. In terms of size this is the smallest number of people (6.9 million) but represents the most regular cinemagoers. The second largest demographic group are 25–34 year-olds followed reasonably closely by 7–14 year-old age groups.

These three age groups add up to 24.33 million people. However, the largest demographic group, the 35-plus audience (30.15 million) is the group that goes least to the cinema. It represents 11 per cent of those who go to the cinema fortnightly or more. Year after year this potentially lucrative audience is left at home. Perhaps the 35-plus audience who go to the cinema more than once a year may only ever go to the cinema with the 7–14 year-old audience, and that is during school holidays.

It is interesting to note the breakdown of figures representing men and women, which we have introduced this year. The statistics show small differences in the attendance trends of the sexes but what they don't show is that women are returning to the cinema. Well-defined male lead characters and marginalised women have meant that generations of women have had to view films from a predominantly male perspective. While this situation hasn't exactly changed (see Table 30), there have been a few more films made recently with women in lead roles – *Career Girls, Elizabeth, Girls' Night, Hilary and Jackie, Land Girls, Little Voice, Sliding Doors, Stella Does Tricks, Wings of the Dove* and *The Winter Guest.*

While studying the list of box office statistics it is worth returning to the demographic chart to see which films fit which categories.

(15) Frequency of Cinemagoing 1998

Age Group	7–14	15–24	25–34	35 +	ABC1	C2DE	Male	Female
No.of People (m)	8.30	6.96	9.07	30.15	26.39	28.09	26.79	27.69
Once a month or more	31(%)	53 (%)	33 (%)	11 (%)	27 (%)	20 (%)	24 (%)	22 (%)
Less than once a month	48 (%)	37 (%)	44 (%)	33 (%)	41 (%)	34 (%)	37 (%)	39 (%)
Once a year or Less	13 (%)	7(%)	18 (%)	30 (%)	20 (%)	25 (%)	21 (%)	23 (%)
Total who ever go to the cinema	92 (%)	97(%)	95 (%)	74 (%)	99 (%)	79 (%)	82 (%)	84 (%)

Source: Screen Finance/X25 Partnership/CAVIAR

UK Box Office for UK Feature Films 1998

UK Films

Title	Distributor	Country of Origin	Box Office Gross (£m)
1 Lock, Stock and Two Smoking Barrels (18)	PolyGram	UK	11,520,069
2 Elizabeth (15)	PolyGram	UK	4,497,977
3 Up'n'Under (12)	Entertainment	UK	3,206,994
4 Martha – Meet Frank, Daniel and Laurence (15)	Film Four	UK	1,365,704
5 24 7 (15)	Pathé Releasing	UK	235,126
6 Stiff Upper Lips (15)	Metrodome	UK	203,003
7 The Woodlanders (PG)	Pathé Releasing	UK	177,442
8 Kurt & Courtney (18)	Downtown	UK	161,796
9 My Son The Fanatic (15)	Feature Film Co.	UK	123,976
10 Resurrection Man (18)	PolyGram	UK	120,932
11 Bring Me The Head Of Mavis Davis (15)	Feature Film Co.	UK	63,956
12 Babymother (15)	Film Four	UK	62,928
13 Chubby Goes Down Under (18)	PolyGram	UK	58,695
14 Stella Does Tricks (18)	BFI	UK	41,127
15 The Big Swap (18)	Film Four	UK	31,145
16 A Soldier's Daughter Never Cries (15)	Roseland	UK	28,342
17 Mojo (15)	Portobello	UK	26,560
18 The Girl With Brains In Her Feet (15)	Alliance	UK	21,115
19 The Wisdom Of Crocodiles (18)	Entertainment	UK	19,856
20 Guru In Seven (18)	Ratpack	UK	19,792
21 I Want You (18)	PolyGram	UK	16,816
22 Dad Savage (18)	PolyGram	UK	15,131
23 Different For Girls (15)	Blue Dolphin	UK	11,868
24 Razor Blade Smile (18)	Palm Pictures	UK	8,260
25 Monk Dawson (18)	Winstone	UK	7,211
26 Like It Is (18)	Dangerous to Know	UK	5,971
27 Sixth Happiness (not submitted)	NFT	UK	2,818
28 Designated Mourner (not submitted)	NFT	UK	1,371
29 Life Of Stuff (not submitted)	NFT	UK	1,214

29 Titles   **22,057,195**

US/UK Co-productions

Title	Distributor	Country of Origin	Box Office Gross (£m)
1 Sliding Doors (15)	UIP	US/UK	12,434,715
2 Lost In Space (PG)	Entertainment	US/UK	10,664,453
3 The Wings Of The Dove (15)	BVI	US/UK	2,142,932
4 The Big Lebowski (18)	PolyGram	US/UK	1,893,347
5 Still Crazy (15)	Columbia TriStar	US/UK	896,325
6 Girl's Night (15)	Granada	US/UK	717,673
7 Velvet Goldmine (18)	Film Four	US/UK	454,263
8 The Winter Guest (15)	Film Four	US/UK	250,689
9 Cousin Bette (15)	20th C Fox	US/UK	107,575
10 Best Men (15)	Film Four	US/UK	45,576
11 The Secret Agent (12)	20th C Fox	US/UK	13,617
12 Déjà Vu (15)	UIP	US/UK	5,412
13 Body Count (18)	PolyGram	US/UK	4,071

13 Titles   **29,630,648**

Other UK Co-productions

	Film	Distributor	Country of Origin	Box Office Gross (£m)
1	Paws (PG)	PolyGram	AU/UK	2,175,278
2	The General (15)	Warner Bros.	IE/UK	1,694,028
3	The Land Girls (12)	Film Four	UK/FR	1,463,805
4	The Boxer (15)	UIP	US/UK/IE	1,343,129
5	Hard Rain (15)	PolyGram	US/UK/JP/DL/DK	1,077,387
6	Dancing At Lughnasa (PG)	Film Four	UK/US/IE	801,009
7	My Name Is Joe (15)	Film Four	UK/DL/FR/IT/ES	785,594
8	Divorcing Jack (15)	Mosaic	UK/FR	469,961
9	Love And Death On Long Island (15)	Pathé	UK/CA	394,372
10	Love Is The Devil (18)	Artificial Eye	UK/FR/JP	277,366
11	Mrs Dalloway (PG)	Artificial Eye	UK/US/NL	236,793
12	The Governess (15)	Alliance	UK/FR	122,518
13	If Only (15)	Pathé	UK/ES/FR/CA/LU	91,679
14	Dance Of The Wind (U)	Artificial Eye	DL/IN/UK/FR	58,283
15	Metroland (18)	Metrodome	UK/ES/FR	49,497
16	Amy Foster (12)	Columbia Tristar	UK/US/FR	48,711
17	On Connait La Chanson (PG)	Pathé	FR/UK/CZ/IT	47,772
18	Downtime (15)	Film Four	UK/FR	28,135
19	Bent (18)	Film Four	UK/US/JP	27,962
20	Something To Believe In (PG)	Warner Bros.	UK/DL	27,904
21	The James Gang (15)	Polygram	UK/CA	25,400
22	This Is The Sea (15)	Alliance Releasing	UK/US/IE	14,747
23	The Boys (18)	Film Four	UK/AU	12,038
24	Real Howard Spitz (PG)	The MOB	UK/CA	11,947
25	Victory (15)	Feature Film Co.	UK/DL/FR	10,416
26	The Disappearance Of Finbar (15)	Rattray	UK/IE/SE/FR	3,100
27	Guy (18)	PolyGram	UK/DL	1,932
28	Wednesday 19 7 1961 (-)	J. Balfour	UK/DL/FI/RU	1,148
29	Bride Of War (-)	Sgrin	UK/PL	712
30	Dandy Dust (-)	Millivres	UK/AT	482

30 Titles — **11,303,105**

TOTAL 72 TITLES — **62,990,948**

Source: **AC Nielsen EDI/Screen Finance/X25 Partnership/BFI**
Box office totals are for UK and Republic of Ireland

In terms of UK (or co-UK) product there was no repeat of the phenomenal success of *The Full Monty* (which incidentally, was still being screened in some cinemas in the UK up to the end of March 1998). *Sliding Doors* was the top Box Office UK film of 1998 (Table 16 & 18). It was another of those films that gave all appearances of being typically British, but was made with American money. Gwyneth Paltrow continued to play British characters and on the strength of her roles in *Emma*, *Sliding Doors* and *Shakespeare in Love* it is easy to see why some people naturally assume that she is British.

However, there still was a surprise package in the success of *Lock, Stock and Two Smoking Barrels* (Tables 16 & 18), Guy Ritchie's energetic debut. Rather like *The Full Monty*, its strength lay in the ensemble cast which included an ex-footballer (Vinnie Jones) and pop star (Sting). Another reason for its success was that it tapped into the highly marketable concept of Laddism – all that lager and those geezers.

In the third category (other UK co-productions) the top film was the family-orientated fantasy *Paws* (Table 16) which was co-produced with Australia.

It is only when we look at the bigger picture by comparing how UK films performed against their US counterparts (Table 17 with Table 18) that the box office peformance of UK films is put into perspective.

Only three UK films register in the list of top twenty films at the UK box office – *Sliding Doors*, *Lock Stock and Two Smoking Barrels* and *Lost in Space*. The latter film is one of those films that looks American but was made in Britain (as was *Saving Private Ryan*).

Top 20 Films at the UK Box Office 1998

Film	Distributor	Country of Origin	Box Office Gross (£m)
1 Titanic (12)	20th C Fox	US	68,971,532
2 Doctor Dolittle (PG)	20th C Fox	US	19,854,598
3 Saving Private Ryan (15)	UIP	US	17,875,260
4 Armageddon (12)	BVI	US	16,506,605
5 Godzilla (PG)	Columbia TriStar	US	15,974,736
6 There's Something About Mary (15)	20th C Fox	US	15,665,386
7 Sliding Doors (15)	UIP	US/UK	12,434,715
8 Lock, Stock and Two Smoking Barrels (18)	PolyGram	UK	11,520,069
9 Flubber (U)	BVI	US	10,891,774
10 Lost In Space (PG)	Entertainment	US/UK	10,664,453
11 Deep Impact (12)	UIP	US	10,199,634
12 The Truman Show (PG)	UIP	US	9,929,680
13 Antz (PG)	UIP	US	9,672,036
14 As Good As It Gets (15)	Columbia TriStar	US	9,613,181
15 The Wedding Singer (12)	Entertainment	US	9,256,114
16 Mulan (U)	BVI	US	8,902,296
17 The X Files (15)	20th C Fox	US	8,426,489
18 Scream 2 (18)	BVI	US	8,280,725
19 Mouse Hunt (PG)	UIP	US	8,218,817
20 Good Will Hunting (15)	UIP	US	7,806,051

Source: Screen Finance/X25 Partnership/EDI
Box office totals are for UK and Republic of Ireland

 Top 20 UK Films at the UK Box Office 1998

Film	Distributor	Country of Origin	Box Office Gross (£m)
1 Sliding Doors (15)	UIP	US/UK	12,434,715
2 Lock, Stock and Two Smoking Barrels (18)	PolyGram	UK	11,520,069
3 Lost In Space (PG)	Entertainment	US/UK	10,664,453
4 Elizabeth (15)	PolyGram	UK	4,497,977
5 Up 'n' Under (12)	Entertainment	UK	3,206,994
6 Paws (PG)	PolyGram	AU/UK	2,175,278
7 The Wings Of The Dove (15)	BVI	US/UK	2,142,932
8 The Big Lebowski (18)	PolyGram	US/UK	1,893,347
9 The General (15)	Warner Bros.	IE/UK	1,694,028
10 Land Girls (12)	Film Four	UK/FR	1,463,805
11 Martha – Meet Frank, Daniel and Laurence (15)	Film Four	UK	1,365,704
12 The Boxer (15)	UIP	US/UK/IE	1,343,129
13 Hard Rain (15)	PolyGram	US/UK/JP/DL/DK	1,077,387
14 Still Crazy (15)	Columbia TriStar	UK/US	896,325
15 Dancing At Lughnasa (PG)	Film Four	UK/US/IE	801,009
16 My Name Is Joe (15)	Film Four	UK/DL/FR/IT/ES	785,594
17 Girls Night (15)	Granada	UK/US	717,673
18 Divorcing Jack (15)	Mosaic	UK/FR	469,961
19 Velvet Goldmine (18)	Film Four	UK/US	454,263
20 Love And Death On Long Island (15)	Pathé	UK/CA	394,372

Source: Screen Finance/X25 Partnership/EDI
Box office totals are for UK and Republic of Ireland

19 **Breakdown of UK Box Office by Country of Origin 1998**

Territories	No Of Titles	Box Office	%
US	159	431,736,833	83.87
US/UK	14	29,678,307	5.76
UK	30	22,057,195	4.28
Other UK co-productions	31	11,349,748	2.20
EU (including co-productions with non-EU countries)	50	11,300,639	2.19
Co-productions (rest of world)	9	4,692,856	0.91
Rest of world (foreign)	26	3,234,381	0.62
Rest of world (English)	10	683,366	0.13
Total	**329**	**514,733,325**	

nb. does not include films released in 1997

Source: ACNielsen EDI/Screen Finance/X25 Partnership/BFI
Box office totals are for UK and Republic of Ireland

The most disappointing aspect of the statistics is the performance of critically well-received films like Oscar-nominated *Elizabeth* and Shane Meadows' *24 7* in the UK. The former film does not make it onto the list of top 20 films at the UK box office. The film at number 20, *Good Will Hunting* (Table 17) took over £7.5 million at the box office. Comparing that total with the £4.5 million for *Elizabeth* would put *Good Will Hunting* ahead of all but three UK films in 1998 (Table 18). However, according to Table 20, *Elizabeth* performed considerably better in the US, coming top; it brought in receipts of $30,034,124 which put it ahead of *Sliding Doors* ($11,841,544) and *Lock, Stock and Two Smoking Barrels* ($3,753,929).

The fate of *24 7* does not have a similarly bright side. That film, with receipts of £235,126, does not make it onto the top 20 UK films at the UK box office (Table 16). So much for critical recommendations. What really carries the big punch is marketing and the more hype the better. It is no good our bleating about the poor performance of UK films unless we are prepared to quit sparring and 'put our money where our mouth is'. In the meantime UK films will continue to get pulled from cinemas before they realise their full potential.

It is noticeable when comparing the box office tables to see that over half of the top films in 1998 carried a (PG), (12) or (U) certificate. In other words – family films. Compare this with the 2 out of 29 wholly-UK titles

20 **Top 10 US Box Office Revenue of UK Films Released Domestically 1998**

	Title	Distributor US	Country	Box Office ($m)
1	Elizabeth * (15)	Gramercy	UK	30,034,124
2	The Wings of a Dove (15)	Miramax	US/UK	13,692,948
3	Sliding Doors (15)	Miramax	US/UK	11,841,544
4	The Governess (15)	Sony Classics	UK/FR	3,919,509
5	Lock, Stock and Two Smoking Barrels (15)	Gramercy	UK	3,753,929
6	Love and Death on Long Island (15)	Lions Gate	UK/CA .	2,581,012
7	A Soldier's Daughter Never Cries (15)	October	UK	1,782,005
8	Velvet Goldmine (18)	Miramax	US/UK	1,053,788
9	The Winter Guest (15)	New Line	US/UK	870,290
10	Firelight	Buena Vista	US/UK	785,482
				70,314,631

*Still on Release Jan 99

Source: AC Nielsen EDI/Screen Finance/X25 Partnership/BFI

21   **Foreign Language Films Released in the UK 1998**

	Title	Distributor	Country	Box Office (£)
1	Kuch Kuch Hota Hai	Yash Raj	IN	1,498,006
2	Live Flesh	Pathé	ES/FR	632,925
3	Hana-Bi	Alliance Releasing	JP	218,215
4	Shall We Dance	Film Four	JP	216,442
5	Lucie Aubrac	Pathé	FR	174,895
6	Un Air De Famille	Metro	FR	123,660
7	The Dream Life Of Angels	Gala	FR	99,493
8	Rien Ne Va Plus	Artificial Eye	FR/CZ	88,356
9	Doh Sajake Rakhna	Eros	IN	82,999
10	Mehndi	UFDL	IN	81,318
11	Jhooth Bole Kauwa Kaate	UFDL	IN	75,913
12	Bandhan	Eros	IN	73,299
13	Happy Together	Artificial Eye	HK	71,515
14	Junk Mail	Metro	NO/DK	69,244
15	Mr Nice Guy	Entertainment	HK	65,291
16	La Grande Illusion (Re)	BFI	FR	62,481
17	Love Etc.	Pathé	FR	60,726
18	The Prisoner Of The Mountains	Metro	RU/KZ	60,126
19	Dance Of The Wind	Artificial Eye	DL/UK/FR/NL/IN	58,283
20	The Thief	Artificial Eye	RU/FR	58,116
21	The Taste Of Cherry	Artificial Eye	IR	56,782
22	Das Boot (re)	Feature Film Co.	DL	52,535
23	Wajwood	UFDL	IN	48,708
24	Ponette	Metro	FR	48,037
25	On Connait La Chanson	Pathé	FR/UK/CZ/IT	47,772
26	Kudrat	Eros	IN	47,531
27	Western	Artificial Eye	FR	46,117
28	Les Voleurs	Metro	FR	40,500
29	The Eel	Artificial Eye	JP	40,273
30	Funny Games	Metro	AT	33,727
31	The Bandit	Rio	TR/BG/FR	33,172
32	Haman	ICA	TR/IT/ES	29,622
33	La Vie De Jesus	ICA	FR	28,222
34	Prem Aggan	UFDL	IN	28,162
35	Ugetsu Monogatari (re)	BFI	JP	26,054
36	Clubbed To Death	Artificial Eye	FR/PT/NL	23,003
37	Pardesi Babu	UFDL	IN	22,258
38	Mother And Son	Blue Light	RU/DL	21,940
39	The Apple	Artificial Eye	IR/FR	20,012
40	Battleship Potemkin (re)	Contemporary	RU	18,779
41	Pretty Village Pretty Flame	Pathé	SER	16,032
42	Majorettes In Space	BFI	FR	16,955
43	Marquise	Downtown	FR/IT/CZ/ES	15,829
44	The Knowledge Of Healing	Artificial Eye	CZ	15,608
45	Angel Sharks	Bluelight	FR	13,773
46	China Gate	Eros	IN	11,428
47	The River	BFI	TW	11,115
48	Tales Of The Taira Clan (re)	BFI	JP	10,071
49	Journey to the Centre of The World	Artificial Eye	FR/PT	8,128
50	Character	Gala	NL	8,113
51	Pepe Le Moko (re)	BFI	FR	8,639
52	Secret Défense	Artificial Eye	FR/CZ/IT	7,447
53	Caresses	Dangerous	ES	6,515
54	The Hands	Kino	RU	6,474
55	Rothschild's Violin	Winstone	FR/HU/CZ	6,464
56	Fists In Pocket (re)	BFI	IT	6,067
57	Kuhle Wampe (re)	BFI	DL	4,267
58	April Story	Rockwell	JP	3,901
59	Moment Of Innocence	ICA	IR/FR/CZ	3,642
60	Salut Cousin	Arrow	FR/BE/DZ/LU	1,828
61	Wednesday 19-7-1961	J. Balfour	RU/DL/UK/FI	1,148

61 Titles   **4,767,953**

Source:ACNielsen EDI/Screen Finance/BFI
Box office totals are for UK and Republic of Ireland

Top 20 Admissions of Films Distributed in Europe 1998

Based on analysis of 72% of admissions in European Union in 1998

	Title	Country	Admissions
1	Titanic	US	84,683,816
2	Armageddon	US	20,533,583
3	Saving Private Ryan	US	18,224,863
4	There's Something About Mary	US	13,975,358
5	Godzilla	US	13,811,086
6	Mulan	US	13,662,316
7	Dr Dolittle	US	13,380,870
8	As Good as It Gets	US	12,571,907
9	Deep Impact	US	10,765,008
10	Lethal Weapon 4	US	10,492,315
11	The Horse Whisperer	US	10,330,813
12	The Truman Show	US	10,204,528
13	The Man in the Iron Mask	US	9,409,775
14	Le dîner de cons	FR	8,996,894
15	Les couloirs du temps	FR	8,795,987
16	Flubber	US	8,726,410
17	The X Files	US	8,576,071
18	Anastasia	US	7,985,720
19	Six Days, Seven Nights	US	7,561,313
20	The Jackal	US	7,235,744

Source: European Audiovisual Observatory

 **Top 20 of Admissions to European Films
Distributed in the European Union 1998**

Data taken from data generated by 11 European countries. The data represents approximately 72% of admissions to cinemas in the European Union

	Title	Country	Admissions
1	Le dîner des cons	FR	8,996,894
2	Les couloirs du temps	FR	8,795,987
3	Taxi	FR	6,693,334
4	La Vita è Bella	IT	6,549,903
5	The Full Monty	UK	5,342,127
6	Sliding Doors	UK/US	5,312,966
7	Tomorrow Never Dies	UK/US	5,295,275
8	Spice World The Movie	UK	3,470,577
9	Lock, Stock and Two Smoking Barrels	UK/US	3,016,910
10	Torrente, el Brazo Tonto de la Ley	SPA	2,835,220
11	Tre Uomini e una Gamba	IT	2,762,798
12	Comedian Harmonists	GER	2,313,152
13	Lola Rennt	GER	2,136,556
14	Elizabeth	UK	2,110,604
15	Cosi e la Vita	IT	2,000,124
16	Gallo Cedrone	IT	1,616,042
17	La Vie Rêvée des Anges	FR	1,545,820
18	Merkwürdige Verhalten Geschlechtsreifer Grosstädter zur Paarungszeit	GER	1,325,242
19	Abre los Ojos	SPA	1,295,713
20	Pippi Longstocking	CAN/SWE/GER	1,158,127

Source: European Audiovisual Observatory

(Table 16). In the meantime, compare the relative success of (18) certificate films at the UK box office – 2 out of 20 (Table 17) with the amount of wholly UK-produced films – 13 out of 29. If we really want to compete at the box office with UK product we need to learn the best way of targeting UK audiences. In order to do this it seems obvious that we need a distributor to offer the US majors some competition and demonstrate that UK product will do well in UK cinemas.

Titanic topped the UK box office list and cruised past *The Full Monty* as the most successive box office film in UK history, taking £68,971,532. Significantly, the film, with an Anglo–American theme and splattering of British actors, was not a UK/US co-production. Quite simply, we do not have the money to produce films on this scale. Yet, there are no signs to suggest that UK cinema audiences have lost their appetite for big-budget blockbusters.

One argument in favour of UK films is that their box office to budget ratios tend to give favourable returns. According to *Variety, Lock, Stock and Two Smoking Barrels* was the fourth most profitable film in 1998 – behind *Life is Beautiful, There's Something About Mary* and *Pi. Sliding Doors* and *Spice World* also perfomed profitably.

It is no surprise therefore to see the scale of US domination of the UK sector (Table 19). US product represents a massive 84 per cent of the market. Indeed, that market share increased by 15 per cent from 1997.

Lock, Stock and Two Smoking Barrels – profitable

24 Breakdown of UK Box Office by Distributor 1998

	Distributor	Titles	Box office
1	20th C Fox	17	129,562,323
2	UIP	36	119,378,163
3	Buena Vista	27	98,013,512
4	Warner	25	46,967,601
5	Columbia	15	32,750,941
	Total US Majors	**120**	**426,672,540**
1	Entertainment	22	45,404,914
2	PolyGram	22	25,421,233
3	Film Four	12	5,328,848
4	Pathé	16	3,196,645
5	First Independent	7	1,516,921
6	Artificial Eye	18	1,345,749
7	Alliance	11	1,044,382
8	Metrodome	8	910,578
9	Eros	6	820,277
10	Feature Film Co.	11	644,646
11	Metro	10	544,271
12	Mosaic	1	469,961
13	BFI	16	433,603
14	Downtown	3	343,843
15	UFDL	3	152,783
16	Gala	2	107,606
17	ICA	4	63,509
18	Blue Light	2	35,713
19	Rio	1	33,172
20	Blue Dolphin	4	32,265
21	Roseland	1	28,342
22	Portobello	1	26,560
23	Ratpack	1	19,792
24	NFT	7	19,769
25	Contemporary	1	18,779
26	Winstone	3	14,909
27	City	1	12,791
28	Dangerous To Know	2	12,486
29	The MOB	1	11,947
30	Jones	1	9,206
31	Manga	2	8,393
32	KINO KINO	1	6,474
33	United Media	1	5,988
34	Rockwell	1	3,901
35	Barbican	1	3,259
36	Rattray	1	3,100
37	Arrow	1	1,828
38	J.Balfour	1	1,148
39	Sgrin	1	712
40	Millivres	1	482
	Total (Independents)	**209**	**88,060,785**
	Total	**329**	**514,733,325**

Source: ACNielsen EDI/BFI/Screen Finance/X25 Partnership
Box office totals are for UK and Republic of Ireland

UK Cinema Circuits 1984-1998
s (sites) scr (screens)

Year	ABC		Virgin		Cine UK		Odeon		Showcase		UCI		Warner Village		Small Chains		Independents	
	s	scr	s	scr	s	scr	s	scr	s	scr	s	scr	s	scr	s	scr	s	scr
1984	-	-	-	318	-	-	-	205	-	-	-	-	-	-	-	-	-	-
1985	-	-	158	403	-	-	76	194	-	-	3	17	1	5	-	-	-	-
1986	-	-	173	443	-	-	74	190	-	-	3	17	1	5	-	-	-	-
1987	-	-	154	408	-	-	75	203	-	-	5	33	1	5	-	-	-	-
1988	-	-	140	379	-	-	73	214	7	85	12	99	1	5	-	-	-	-
1989	-	-	142	388	-	-	75	241	7	85	18	156	3	26	-	-	-	-
1990	-	-	142	411	-	-	75	266	7	85	21	189	5	48	-	-	-	-
1991	-	-	136	435	-	-	75	296	8	97	23	208	6	57	-	-	-	-
1992	-	-	131	422	-	-	75	313	9	109	25	219	7	64	-	-	-	-
1993	-	-	125	408	-	-	75	322	10	127	25	219	9	84	-	-	-	-
1994	-	-	119	402	-	-	76	327	11	141	26	232	10	93	-	-	437	631
1995	-	-	116	406	-	-	71	320	11	143	26	232	12	110	-	-	469	716
1996	92	244	24	162	2	24	73	362	14	181	26	232	16	143	58	139	437	679
1997	80	225	29	213	5	66	73	362	15	197	26	263	17	152	68	166	434	739
1998	81	234	34	290	10	116	79	415	15	199	29	287	22	200	73	100	416	633

Source: Screen Finance/X25 Partnership

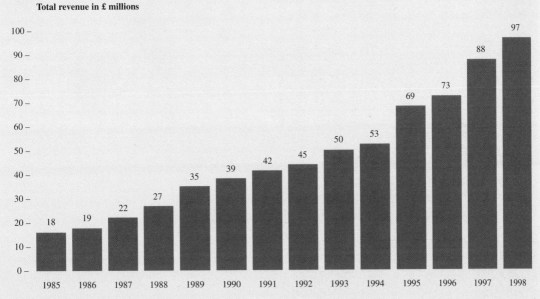

UK Cinema Advertising Revenue 1985-1998

Total revenue in £ millions

1985	1986	1987	1988	1989	1990	1991	1992	1993	1994	1995	1996	1997	1998
18	19	22	27	35	39	42	45	50	53	69	73	88	97

Source: CAA

If UK films have a tough time on their home territory, then foreign language films, and in particular European foreign language films, have a torrid time (Table 21). However, in 1998 the most interesting development has been the emergence of films from India. The influence of Bollywood has been overlooked in previous Handbooks. Yet the success of *Kuch Kuch Hota Hai* (which wasn't even reviewed by *Empire* or *Sight and Sound*) shows that there is a small but significant market for films from India – they represent about a third of the foreign language films in the list of top twenty foreign language films. *Kuch Kuch Hota Hai* opened on 16 October on 20 screens and was the first Indian film to be screened at the Empire Cinema in London's West End (*Screen Finance 21 January 1999*). In some cases Hindi films have made it to multiplexes in areas with large Asian communities. It is likely that the clout of Bollywood will continue to make interesting inroads into the UK market.

The notion that UK audiences do not like foreign films with subtitles might well be challenged in next year's statistics, with the performance of the multi-award winner from Italy *La Vita e Bella/Life is Beautiful*. In the meantime the multiplex generation can plead ignorance of anything that isn't in the English language.

US films dominate European Union cinema circuits (Table 22) with only two French films – *Le diner de cons* and *Les couloirs du temps* – making any impact on the top 20 admissions. *Titanic* again proved to be universally popular.

UK films performed reasonably well in Europe (Table 23). While the top films were represented by three French films and Italy's *La Vita è Bella/Life is Beautiful*, a pack of five UK (or UK/US) films led by *The Full Monty* gave the UK a prominent presence in the European top 10.

The success of *Titanic* enabled 20th Century Fox, who in the previous year basked in the glory of *The Full Monty*, to retain their slot at the head of the distributor table (Table 24) with 25 per cent of the market share. This they did with fewer titles than UIP, Buena Vista and Warner. Indeed, only 3 other titles made it into the top 20 (Table 17): *Doctor Dolittle, There's Something About Mary* and *The X Files*.

UIP's second position came as a result of 36 titles which included *Saving Private Ryan* and *Sliding Doors*. They

Titanic – a triumph out of a disaster

swopped places with Buena Vista. Warner and Columbia continued to lose ground.

Entertainment was the top independent distributor and took overall fifth spot ahead of Columbia. Only Entertainment and PolyGram came close to matching the dominance of the US majors. PolyGram's share of the market dropped from £55,753,927 in 1997 to £25,421,233. In 1999 PolyGram, who had distributed the two aforementioned UK successes *Lock, Stock and Two Smoking Barrels* and *Elizabeth*, was taken over by Universal Pictures International (UPI).

The list of independents shows how fragmented the market has become, with 45 per cent made up of companies who released a single film. A distribution franchise system for small distributors to combine their resources and benefit from Lottery funding was mooted at one stage by the Arts Council, but was shunted into the sidings by the short lived Government proposal of an All Industry Fund to support the development, distribution and marketing of British films. The trend of one-off distributors looks likely to continue.

In addition, beyond Entertainment and PolyGram the box office receipts dip dramatically, with FilmFour, who, while improving their performance, over 1997 by claiming third placed spot, only claimed around 1 per cent of the UK market.

In the exhibition sector, 1998 was a record-breaking year for UK multiplex openings. Twenty-five new multiplexes (266 screens) opened; all cinema chains, with the exception of Showcase, have expanded, to a greater or lesser extent (Table 25). All indicators show that these expansion programmes have yet to end, with operators planning to open 29 multiplexes by the end of the millennium. This growth was also reflected in the continuing steady rise in advertising revenue which looks set to break the £100 million mark in 1999 (Table 26).

However, it is worth observing that the independent cinemas have lost 18 sites and 106 screens. Sooner or later the multiplexes will reach saturation point. It is a sobering thought that the cinema circuits rely heavily on blockbusters to enable them to expand. There is a mad scurry by exhibitors and distributors alike based on how well a film opened, which increasingly seems to determine its fate. Should the public tire of this kind of film, or should the latest crop of big budget films flop and the lure of home entertainment become increasingly attractive, then the building boom is likely to come to an abrupt end.

La Vita è Bella – a foreign language success

Elizabeth – performed better in the US than the UK

Video

Those of you who are old enough will remember how video first came onto the commercial scene in the mid-1970s. Video revolutionised access to films. No longer were people dependent solely on what was shown at their local cinema or whatever films BBC or ITV chose to screen. People could enjoy a wide choice of films in the comfort of their homes. Even when cable and satellite were launched, with their promised plethora of movie channels, people did not abandon the video. Most films still get into video shops more quickly than they get onto cable and satellite, and the film you rent or buy isn't tied down to a cable, satellite or TV schedule.

Twenty-two years later and the VHS video is about to be ushered into semi-retirement by DVD, the new kid on the block. It will be interesting to chart the DVD's growth in both the retail and rental sectors over the next couple of years, as people decide whether to cross over completely or go for both formats depending on the availability of films. Fears that DVD films might prove too expensive have been unfounded. DVD films retail at around £15 while rental prices show little price difference to VHS. However, the clamour to buy a DVD player, subscribe to digital television, and plug in to the internet, even in our consumer-driven society, may prove too much, too soon for the public. Either way the desire to consume films in whatever format is set to continue into the next millennium.

Robin Duval joined the British Board of Film Classification in January in 1999 as its new director replacing James Ferman and sparking various debate

27 BBFC Censorship of Videos 1998

Certificate	Number of Films passed after cuts
U	6
PG	27
12	5
15	18
18	246
R18	23
Rejected	4

Source: BBFC

The Exorcist – passed for video release by the BBFC

28 The UK Video Market 1986-1998

Year	Retail Transactions (millions)	Value (£m)		Rental Transactions (millions)	Value (£m)
1986	6	55		233	284
1987	12	110		251	326
1988	20	184		271	371
1989	38	345		289	416
1990	40	374		277	418
1991	45	440		253	407
1992	48	506		222	389
1993	60	643		184	350
1994	66	698		167	339
1995	73	789		167	351
1996	79	803		175	382
1997	87	858		161	369
1998	100	940		186	437

Source: BVA

29 Top Twenty Rental Videos in the UK 1998

	Film	Distributor	Country
1	Men in Black (PG)	Columbia Tristar	US
2	Face/Off (18)	Buena Vista	US
3	Air Force One (15)	Buena Vista	US
4	Starship Troopers (15)	Buena Vista	US
5	The Fifth Element (PG)	Fox Pathé	FR
6	The Full Monty (15)	Fox Pathé	US/UK
7	The Lost World (PG)	CIC	US
8	The Devil's Advocate (18)	Warner	US
9	Austin Powers (15)	Fox Pathé	US
10	The Jackal (18)	CIC	US
11	My Best Friend's Wedding (15)	Columbia TriStar	US
12	Conspiracy Theory (15)	Warner	US
13	L.A. Confidential (18)	Warner	US
14	Tomorrow Never Dies (12)	MGM	US/UK
15	As Good as it Gets (15)	Columbia Tristar	US
16	Scream (18)	Buena Vista	US
17	Volcano (12)	Fox Pathé	US
18	Alien Resurrection (15)	Fox Pathé	US
19	Event Horizon (18)	CIC	US/UK
20	The Peacemaker (15)	CIC	US

Source: Rental Monitor/BVA

about censorship and the organisation that issues certificates (Table 27). The release of *The Exorcist* helped to keep the role of the BBFC in the spotlight and there was also speculation after the death of Stanley Kubrick about the possible re-release of *A Clockwork Orange* in the UK. It will be interesting to see how the BBFC develops in an era where accountability to the public is in vogue.

30 Distributors Share of UK Rental Transactions (%)1998

	Distributor	% share
1	Buena Vista	20.6
2	Fox Pathe	16.3
3	CIC	15.5
4	Warner/MGM	15.0
5	Columbia Tristar	12.2
6	EV	10.6
7	PolyGram	6.6
8	First Independent	1.0
9	Film Four	0.9
10	High Fliers	0.5

Source:Rental Monitor/BVA

Here come the Men in Black – top rental video

Meanwhile, retail transactions for video rose by almost 10 per cent to £940 million in 1998 and hit the 1 billion transactions mark (Table 28). Needless to say, that represents a sizeable number of videos which people have collected gradually over the last twenty years. Rental activity continued to grow, with the value of transactions rising to £437 million in 1998, compared with £369 million in the previous year.

The top 20 rental chart (Table 29) has the sweaty essence of testosterone all over it. The majority of the titles in this chart can be found on shelves in video stores under 'Action'. Unlike previous years there were few surprises in the top rental titles. Most performed well in the cinemas, especially *Men in Black,* which tops the chart and was the second most popular film in the UK in 1997 (behind *The Full Monty*).

By comparison the retail sector is traditionally family-orientated and only four rental titles – *The Full Monty, Men in Black, The Lost World and Tomorrow Never Dies* make it onto the top 20 retail chart. There are two observations to make from the evidence of this and previous retail charts.

The first is in regard to the dearth of UK films aimed at children – which contrasts with the abundance of popular children's TV programmes and animated shorts such as *Teletubbies, Postman Pat, Thomas the Tank Engine* and *Wallace and Gromit.* The market isn't exactly short of this kind of family entertainment.

Top 20 Retail Videos in the UK 1998

	Title	Distributor	Country
1	Titanic (12)	20th Century Fox	US
2	The Full Monty (15)	20th Century Fox	US/UK
3	The Lady and the Tramp (U)	Buena Vista	US
4	Men in Black (PG)	Columbia Tristar	US
5	Hercules (U)	Buena Vista	US
6	Flubber (U)	Buena Vista	US
7	Cats	PolyGram	US
8	Peter Pan (U)	Buena Vista	US
9	Anastasia (U)	20th Century Fox	US
10	The Lost World (PG)	CIC	US
11	The Little Mermaid (U)	Buena Vista	US
12	Spice World (PG)	PolyGram	UK
13	Romeo + Juliet (12)	20th Century Fox	US/CA
14	Billy Connolly-Erect for 30 Years	VVL	UK
15	Rudolph the Red Nosed Reindeer	Carlton	UK
16	Feet of Flames	VVL	UK
17	Mousehunt (PG)	CIC	US
18	Beauty & Beast Enchanted Xmas (U)	Buena Vista	US
19	Tomorrow Never Dies (12)	MGM	US/UK
20	George of the Jungle (U)	Buena Vista	US

Source: BVA/CIN

Video Retail Company Market Share by Volume 1998 (%)

	Distributor	% share
1	20th Century Fox	15.0
2	PolyGram Group	14.5
3	Buena Vista	14.2
4	Warner/MGM	13.7
5	CIC	8.8
6	Columbia Tristar	7.1
7	VCI	7.0
8	BBC	5.3
9	Carlton	2.1
10	EV	1.9

Source: BVA/CIN

The UK Video Games Market 1998 Computer Software Sales

Value:	£890 million
Units:	23.4 million

Source: Chartrack/© ELPSA 1999

The Full Monty outstripped most in the retail chart

The second is in regard to a generation of children who in years to come may be able to quote word for word from any number of films featuring Disney characters, dinosaurs, or whales being set free. It will be interesting to see how these children figure in any future debates on cine-literacy.

For Twentieth Century Fox the twentieth century leaving party featuring the two box office giants *Titanic* and *the Full Monty* doesn't look like flagging with *Star Wars: The Phantom Menace* still to come. They ended top of the retail chart (Table 32). Buena Vista, who normally expect to dominate the retail sector, were nudged into third place by PolyGram. However, Buena Vista did do well in the rental sector, taking 20.6 per cent of the market (Table 32).

By this time next year we will get a clearer idea of the impact of DVDs on the video rental and retail market and whether there is justification in changing the title of this section to Video/DVD.

Television

Against all the odds and expectations, the daily audience viewing figure rose by a full two minutes in 1998 (Table 34). The increase may be unspectacular but it is an indicator that the long heralded decline in TV viewing has yet to arrive. In fact, never before have the British public had so many TV channels to choose from. If nothing else a curiosity value ought to be taken into account as more people tune in to digital TV.

Judging by the statistics in this section the British TV audience remains predictably conservative in its choices of popular shows. Whereas Hollywood dominates the big screen, the East End of London and Manchester still dominate the small screen.

It is surprising that in the ten years since the launch of Sky, ITV and BBC have retained such a strong share of the market (Table 35). However, ITV, BBC1, BBC2 and

34   **Trends in Television Viewing 1998**

Average Daily Hours Viewing	3.61
Number of TV Households	23.9 million

Source: BARB/Taris

35   **Average TV Audience Share (%) of TV Channels**

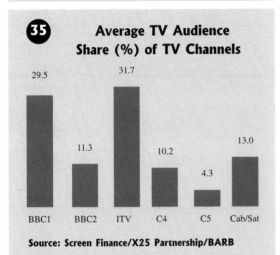

BBC1	BBC2	ITV	C4	C5	Cab/Sat
29.5	11.3	31.7	10.2	4.3	13.0

Source: Screen Finance/X25 Partnership/BARB

36   **Cable and Satellite Penetration 1998**

	cable	satellite
No. of subscribers	2.7m	4.1m
Penetration %	12*	17

There is a 23.7 % TV take up in Cabled areas.
50% of TV households have been passed by broadband cable.

Source: ITC

Televised football – the TV ratings battlefield

37   **ITV Companies Programme Supply to the Network**

Company	Hours (New Programmes)
Anglia	244
Border	2
Carlton	105
Central	173
Channel	-
Grampian	2
Granada	690
HTV	34
LWT	296
Meridian	42
STV	113
Tyne Tees	57
UTV	1
West Country	8
Yorkshire	203

Source: ITC

38 Top 20 Programmes for all Terrestrial Channels 1998

Only top rated episodes of each series are included

	Title	Channel	TX date	Audience(m)
1	England v Argentina (World Cup)	ITV	30/06/98	23.8
2	England v Romania (World Cup)	ITV	22/06/98	19.5
3	England v Columbia (World Cup)	BBC1	26/06/98	19.1
4	Coronation Street	ITV	16/11/98	18.6
5	Eastenders	BBC1	29/12/98	16.9
6	Heartbeat	ITV	22/02/98	16.5
7	Celebrity Stars in Their Eyes	ITV	02/12/98	16.3
8	Casualty	BBC1	28/02/98	15.7
9	Brazil v France (World Cup Final)	BBC1	12/07/98	15.6
10	Men Behaving Badly	BBC1	28/12/98	15.2
11	Forrest Gump	BBC1	01/01/98	15.1
12	France v Croatia (World Cup Semi-final)	BBC1	08/07/98	14.6
13	Brazil v Holland (World Cup Semi-final)	ITV	07/07/98	14.1
14	You've Been Framed	ITV	13/09/98	13.9
15	Goodnight Mr.Tom	ITV	25/10/98	13.8
16	Birds of a Feather	BBC1	19/01/98	13.3
17	Emmerdale	ITV	10/02/98	13.3
18	National Lottery Live	BBC1	28/02/98	13.2
19	The Cruise	BBC1	13/01/98	12.9
20	London's Burning	ITV	11/01/98	12.8

Source: BARB

Channel 4 all lost ground to Channel 5 and cable and satellite. Channel 5's rise of 2 per cent from 1997 is the most surprising statistic of all. However, the gamble of showing England's away football matches and other European games has certainly attracted audiences. They also attracted advertisers with a healthy revenue of £142 million generated in 1998 (Table 40) – settling in to take a 4.8 per cent share of the total market.

Coronation Street – the nation's favourite soap

Ten years ago commentators were speculating that film channels would win viewers over to cable and satellite. No one really predicted that live football would be the lure. Nevertheless, two significant film-related developments have happened since last year. The first was the launch of FilmFour, a channel with a far wider range of films on offer than other cable and satellite film channels. The second was the exclusive premieres on BSkyB's Moviemax channel of films that didn't get theatrical releases in the UK. The first of these was Pierce Brosnan's *The Nephew*. In both cases the exclusiveness of the choice of films has been the key in attracting new viewers.

While it is true that cable and satellite continue to eat into the overall market share, the rate of growth has been slow. Satellite penetration actually dropped from 18 per cent to 17 per cent in 1998, while the total number of cable subscribers rose from 10 per cent to 12 per cent. This is worth noting when anticipating the rush of subscribers to digital TV. Perhaps most significant of all is the breakdown of advertising revenue (Table 40). Channel 4 still attracts more advertisers than cable and satellite despite its lower market share. It seems probable that advertisers will continue placing their faith in terrestrial TV in the near future at least.

39   Top Original Drama Productions 1998

Including soap operas, series, serials and UKTV Movies.
Ratings are for highest rated episode of each production

	Title	Producer/Sponsor	Tx Date	Audience (m)
1	Coronation Street	Granada	16/11/98	18.6
2	Eastenders	BBC	29/12/98	16.9
3	Heartbeat	Yorkshire	22/02/98	16.5
4	Casualty	BBC	28/02/98	15.7
5	Goodnight Mister Tom	Carlton	25/10/98	13.8
6	Emmerdale	Yorkshire	10/02/98	13.3
7	London's Burning	LWT	11/01/98	12.8
8	Inspector Morse: The Wench is Dead	Central	11/11/98	12.4
9	The Bill	Pearson/Carlton	30/01/98	12.3
10	Coming Home	Portman/LWT	13/04/98	11.9
11	Where the Heart Is	United/Anglia	07/06/98	11.8
12	March in Windy City	Yorkshire	25/03/98	11.6
14	Taggart	Scottish TV	01/03/98	11.4
15	Midsomer Murders	Bentley Prods/Yorkshire	22/03/98	11.4
16	Real Women	BBC	26/02/98	11.1
17	Jonathan Creek	BBC	28/02/98	10.9
18	Ballykissangel	World Prods/BBC	08/03/98	10.9
19	Inspector Wexford Mysteries: Road Rage	Blue Heaven/Meridian	08/11/98	10.5
20	Peak Practice	Central	23/03/98	10.5

Source: BARB/Taris/BFI

Whether advertising will eventually make its way onto the BBC, albeit through sponsorship, is the hot potato debate of the moment. The licence fee (Table 43) has come in for intense media scrutiny, particularly in the wake of recommendations in the Davies report that a transitional digital levy be added on to the existing fee. Some people have questioned whether those with so many channels other than the BBC to choose from should pay the licence fee at all.

Football appears to be the battlefield in the TV rating wars. In 1998 the World Cup was staged in France, which accounts for the six football matches in the top 20 programmes on terrestrial television (Table 38). The top three programmes charted the England team's key matches in the tournament, culminating in the all-too-familiar heroic exit from the competition after a penalty shoot-out match with Argentina which gained the top audience of 23.8 million. ITV had the luck of the draw in televising that particular match. However, the key battle in the ratings war came when 15.9 million people preferred tuning in to the BBC's coverage of the World Cup Final rather than ITV's coverage. ITV was to have the last laugh by securing rights to Champions' League matches in 1999 - and acquiring the pulling power of presenter Desmond Lynam from the BBC in a much publicised move.

Carlton's Goodnight Mister Tom – a suprise success

(40) Television Advertising 1998

	£m
Net TV Advertising Revenue	2,948
ITV	1,834
C4	562
C5	142
Cable and Satellite	365*
In addition total sponsorship income	45

*Figures only available up to September 1998 for Cable/Satellite

Source : ITC

Brassed Off – top film premiered on Channel 4

Getting away from football, the top 20 programmes had a pretty familiar look about them. *Coronation Street* overtook regular favourites *Eastenders* and *Heartbeat* as the top original drama (Table 39).

However, in amongst all these programmes came a genuine surprise package. This was Carlton's TV film

Goodnight Mister Tom This gentle, family-orientated, wartime drama tells of an unlikely friendship that develops when an anxious boy is billeted to the home of an outwardly stern widower (played by John Thaw). The audience of 13.8 million for the programme transmitted in October was greater than all films shown on terrestrial television with the exception of *Forrest Gump* (Tables 41

(41) UK TV Films Premiered 1998

Title	Tx date	BARB Rating (m)
BBC1		
Our Boy	15-Feb	6.40
My Summer with Des	25-May	7.00
The Gift	5-Jul	5.60
Speedy Death	31-Aug	8.10
Big Cat	6-Sep	6.60
Mrs Brown	27-Dec	11.50
BBC2		
Small Faces*	1-Jan	1.30
Getting Hurt	8-Mar	2.40
Stand and Deliver	15-Mar	1.30
Guiltrip*	22-Mar	0.90
Anorak of Fire	5-Apr	2.10
The Tribe	21-Jun	3.30
Swann	19-Jul	1.10*
An Awfully Big Adventure	26-Jul	2.00
Two Deaths	26-Jul	0.90
Peggy Su!	16-Aug	1.00
The Designated Mourner	23-Aug	0.30
Touch and Go	15-Sep	5.10
Ted and Ralph	27-Dec	3.10
A Rather English Marriage	30-Dec	4.00

Source: BFI/BARB

Title	Tx date	BARB Rating (m)
ITV		
Wuthering Heights	5-Apr	7.70
The Stalker's Apprentice	25-May	6.90
Neville's Island	4-Jun	7.30
Inspector Pitt:		
The Cater Street Hangman	23-Sep	7.80
Kiszko: Life After Life	4-Oct	7.30
Goodnight Mr.Tom	25-Oct	13.80
Inspector Morse:		
The Wench is Dead	11-Nov	12.40
C4		
Jack and Sarah*	8-Feb	4.40
The Neon Bible*	14-Mar	0.40
Frankie Starlight*	21-Mar	0.40
Institute Benjamenta*	28-Mar	0.20
Secrets and Lies*	13-Apr	2.90
Smalltime*	16-Apr	0.40
Brassed Off*	24-May	4.90
Fever Pitch*	29-Nov	2.50
Jump the Gun*	1-Dec	0.30
Remember Me?	25-Dec	1.00
Alive and Kicking	30-Dec	0.10

* denotes previous cinema release

42   Top 20 Feature Films Shown on Terrestrial TV 1998

Title	Country	Year	Channel	Audience (m)
1 Forrest Gump	US	1994	BBC1	15.10
2 Die Hard with a Vengeance	US	1995	ITV	11.60
3 Mrs Brown	UK/US	1997	BBC1	11.50
4 Indiana Jones and the Last Crusade	US	1989	BBC1	10.90
5 Beverly Hills Cop 3	US	1994	BBC1	10.80
6 Jurassic Park	US	1993	BBC1	9.90
7 Speed	US	1994	BBC1	9.80
8 Babe	Aus	1995	BBC1	9.30
9 Waterworld	US	1995	BBC1	9.00
10 The Three Musketeers	US	1993	ITV	8.90
11 Stargate	US	1994	BBC1	8.70
12 Kindergarten Cop	US	1990	BBC1	8.70
13 Se7en	US	1995	BBC1	8.70
14 The Bodyguard	US	1992	ITV	8.70
15 Licence to Kill	US	1989	ITV	8.70
16 Home Alone	US	1990	ITV	8.60
17 Philadelphia	US	1993	ITV	8.50
18 Lethal Weapon 3	US	1992	ITV	8.50
19 Robin Hood Prince of Thieves	US	1991	BBC1	8.40
20 Maverick	US	1994	ITV	8.30

Source: BARB/BFI

& 42). Indeed, *Goodnight Mister Tom* attracted 2.3 million more viewers than the Oscar-nominated *Mrs Brown* which was premiered on 27 December (Table 41).

Nevertheless, *Mrs Brown* was not only the BBC's top film, it was also the only British film to make it onto the list of top 20 feature films shown on terrestrial television. *Brassed Off* was Channel 4's most watched film, attracting an audience of 4.90 million.

ITV's decision to scrap *News at Ten* in order to free up prime time for new dramas and films (and the advertising revenue that went with these programmes) attracted a fair amount of criticism.

The comforting thought for terrestrial channel executives lies in the public's current faith in the familiar and this is likely to be the case for as long as the analogue signal holds out. However, once digital TV takes off, the picture may start to change. After all, the cable and satellite channels have had a ten-year start in refining their multi-channel environments and dipping their big toes into the pay-per-view markets. The future of the terrestrial channels may be determined by what happens following coverage of the next football World Cup finals in 2002.

Mrs Brown was screened in December 1998

43   UK General Statistics 1998

Population	59.1 million
Number of Households	24.3 million
Inflation	3.10%
Gross Domestic Product (Current Prices)	£837,618 million
Total TV Licences in force	22.3 million
Licence Fee Income	£2,009.7 million

Source: CSO/BBC

Further Reading

BRITISH BOARD OF
FILM CLASSIFICATION
Annual Report 1998.
London: BBFC, 1999.

BRITISH BROADCASTING
CORPORATION
Annual Report 1998/99.
London: BBC, 1999.

BROADCASTING STANDARDS
COMMISSION
Annual report 1998/99.
London: Broadcasting Standards Council,
1999.

BUSINESS RATIO PLUS: THE FILM &
TV INDUSTRY (14th ed.)
Hampton, Middlesex: ICC Business
Publications, 1999.

BVA YEARBOOK 1999
London: British Video Association, 1999.

CABLE AND SATELLITE YEARBOOK
1999
FT Media & Telecoms 1999.

CHANNEL FOUR TELEVISION
Annual Report 1998.
London: Channel Four, 1999.

CULTURAL TRENDS
Issue 30 1998 Media.
London: Policy Studies Institute, 1999.

CAVIAR REPORT
No.12 (3 vol set).
CAVIAR Consortium, 1995.

CENTRAL STATISTICAL OFFICE
Overseas Transactions of the Film and TV
industry.
London: CSO, 1997.

CINEMAGOINGEUROPE
Volume 1: UK & Ireland.
Leicester: Dodona Research, 1999.

EDI DATABASE REPORTS
London: AC Nielsen EDI, 1998-1999.

EDI RELEASE SCHEDULE UK.
London: AC Nielsen EDI, 1998-1999.

EUROPEAN CINEMA YEARBOOK 1998
Milan: Media Salles, 1999.

FILM AND TELEVISION INDUSTRY:
ICC FINANCIAL SURVEY (26th ed.)
Hampton, Middlesex: ICC Business
Publications, 1998.

FILM EDUCATION WORKING GROUP
Making movies matter: report of the Film
Education Working Group.
London: BFI, 1999.

FILM POLICY REVIEW GROUP
A bigger picture: the report of the Film
Policy
Review Group.
London: Department of Culture, Media
and Sport, 1998.

GAUNTLETT, David & HILL, Annette
TV Living: television, culture and
everyday life.
London: Routledge (in association with the
BFI), 1999.

GB CINEMA EXHIBITORS (Quarterly)
London: Central Statistical Office, 1998.

GRAHAM, Andrew (et. al.)
Public purposes in broadcasting: funding
the BBC.
Luton: University of Luton Press, 1999.

HAMILTON-DEELEY, Gavin (et al.)
The cost of making dreams: accounting for
the British film industry.
London: Deloitte & Touche, 1999.

HART-WILDEN, Paul
A practical guide to film financing.
London: FT Media & Telecoms, 1997.

THE FILM INDUSTRY: MARKET
REPORT
(Key Note Market Report).
Hampton, Middlesex: Key Note, 1998.

INDEPENDENT TELEVISION
COMMISSION
Annual Report 1998.
London: ITC, 1999.

INDEPENDENT TELEVISION
COMMISSION
Television: the public's view 1998.
London: ITC, 1999.

MEDIA GUIDE 1999
London: 4th Estate, 1999.

THE MEDIA MAP OF EASTERN
EUROPE 1999
THE MEDIA MAP OF WESTERN
EUROPE 1999
Exeter: CIT Publications, 1999.

OVERSEAS TRANSACTIONS OF THE
FILM & TV INDUSTRY 1997
London: Central Statistical Office, 1998.

RADIO AND TELEVISION SYSTEMS
IN EUROPE
(4 vol set).
Strasbourg: European Audiovisual
Observatory, 1998.

STATISTICAL YEARBOOK: CINEMA,
TELEVISION, VIDEO AND NEW
MEDIA IN EUROPE
Strasbourg: European Audiovisual
Observatory, 1999.

TARIS UK TELEVISION BOOK 1999
(Formerly AGB Television Yearbook).
London, Taylor Nelson Sofres, 1999.

TOP UK MEDIA OWNERS
London: Zenith Media, 1998.

VIDEO AND AUDIOVISUAL
INDUSTRY: ICC FINANCIAL
SURVEY. (23rd ed.)
Hampton, Middlesex: ICC Business
Publications, 1998.

THE WORLD FILM & TELEVISION
MARKET
(IDATE Report).
Montpellier: Institute de l'audiovisuel et
des télécommunications en Europe
(IDATE), 1999.

BEST
OF BRITISH

Film Images presents the *COI Footage File* – a unique visual record of Britain's culture, heritage, way of life and aspirations covering the last 60 years.

The collection begins with John Grierson's documentary masterpiece "Drifters". It moves on to include a wealth of material shot by the Crown Film Unit in the 40s and 50s and now encompasses an outstanding and constantly updated selection of Government commissioned material covering every decade.

Footage File is a kaleidoscope of imagery – social, historical, geographical, scientific and political. Whether you're looking for a single shot or a whole programme, landscapes or laser surgery, churches or Churchill, forestry or forensic science, our experienced staff will make sure that you get the very best of British every time.

fourth floor, 184-192 drummond street, london nw1 3hp. tel: (020) 7 383 2288

The FOUNDATION FOR ART & CREATIVE TECHNOLOGY presents:

MITES

MITES continues to be England's national exhibition technology
resource. Its expanded and upgraded range of services includes:

- a full DVD-Video mastering service for artists offering the opportunity to
  encode video and audio from tape to author complex DVD interactive
  structures and to produce one-off DVD-R disk masters.
- subsidised exhibition equipment hire
- technical management and installation
- specialist training - course formats & tailormade packages
- complimentary specialist advice and on-line support

For costs and details
contact Simon Bradshaw
at MITES:
Tel: 0151 707 2881
Fax: 0151 707 2150
e-Mail: mites@fact.co.uk
MITES web pages:
http://mites.org.uk

VIDEO POSITIVE 2000: THE OTHER SIDE OF ZERO

- 4 March - 30 April 2000 at venues across Liverpool.

THE FACT CENTRE

- a national centre for moving image cultural practice opening in Liverpool
  autumn 2001.

For further information,
please contact
Alison Edbury,
Development &
Communications Manager,
FACT, Bluecoat
Chambers, School Lane,
Liverpool L13BX
Tel: 0151 709 2663
Fax: 0151 707 2150
email: fact@fact.co.uk
http://www.fact.co.uk

THE MEDIA LAW PARTNERSHIP

Films are our speciality

Please call Adam Sutcliffe or Jonathan Rowell for a quotation for your legal work

187 WARDOUR STREET

LONDON

WIV 3FA

Tel. +44 (0) 20 7437 1552

Fax. +44 (0) 20 7437 1558

email mail@medialaw.uk.com

ARCHIVES AND FILM LIBRARIES

International Organisations

FIAF (International Federation of Film Archives)
1 Rue Defacqz
B-1000 Brussels
Belgium
Tel: (32) 2 538 3065
Fax: (32) 2 534 4774
email: info@fiafnet.org
Website: www.cinema.ucla.edu/FIAF/
Christian Dimitziu
Founded in 1938, FIAF is a collaborative association of the world's leading film archives whose purpose is to ensure the proper preservation and showing of motion pictures. More than 100 archives in over 60 countries collect, restore, and exhibit films and cinema documentation spanning the entire history of film. It also publishes handbooks on film archiving practice which can be obtained from the above address

FIAT/IFTA (International Federation of Television Archives)
Tevearkivet
Sveriges Television AB RH-N2G
S-105 10 Stockholm
Sweden
Tel: (+468) 784 5740
Fax: (+468) 660 4000
email: lasse.nilsson@svt.se
Lasse Nilsson (General Secretary)
FIAT membership is mainly made up of the archive services of broadcasting organisations. However, it also encompasses national archives and other television-related bodies. It meets annually and publishes its proceedings and other recommendations concerning television archiving

European Archives

Below are selected some European Film Archives of countries in the European Union. For more specialised information consult *Film and Television Collections in Europe – The MAP-TV Guide* published by Blueprint

AUSTRIA

Österreichishes Filmarchiv (Austrian Film Library)
Rauhensteingasse 5
1010 Wien
Tel: 43 1 512 99 36
Fax: 43 1 513 53 30
Dr Josef Schuchnig

BELGIUM

Cinémathèque Royale/Koninklijk Filmarchief (Royal Film Archives)
Palais des Beaux Arts 23
Rue Ravenstein 1000
Bruxelles
Gabrielle Claes
The Film Museum grants 5 annual awards, each amounting to 250,000 BF, to assist the distribution of quality films in Belgium. These grants, funded with the help of the Ministry of the French Community of Belgium and of the Region of Brussels Capital, are presented to films which are unreleased in Belgium and have not yet been picked up by a distributor for the Belgian market. In addition, one film from among these 5 award winners is singled out by the jury for the Age d'Or Prize, a further 250,000 BF

DENMARK

Det Danske Filmmuseum
Store Søndervoldstraede 4
1419 København
Tel: 45 31 57 65 00
Fax: 45 31 54 12 12
Ib Monty, Director

FINLAND

Suomen Elokuva-Arkisto (Finnish Film Archive)
PO Box 177
00151 Helsinki
Tel: 358 0 171 417
Fax: 358 0 171 544
Matti Lukkarila

FRANCE

Les Archives du Film du Centre National de la Cinématographie – CNC
7 bis rue Alexandre-Turpault,
78390 Bois-D'Arcy
Tel: 33 1 30 14 80 00
Fax: 33 1 34 60 52 25
Eric Le Roy

GERMANY

Deutsche Rundfunkarchiv, Standort Berlin, Fernseharchiv (German Broadcasting Service, Berlin, Television Archive)
Rudower Chaussee
12489 Berlin
Tel: 49 30 63 81 60 55
Fax: 49 30 6 77 40 07
Sigrid Ritter, Head Archivist

GREECE

Teniothiki Tis Elladas (Greek Film Archives)
1 Kanari Street
Athens 1067
Tel: 30 1 3612046
Fax: 30 1 3628468
Theodoros Adamopoulos, Director

IRELAND

Irish Film Archive
Film Institute of Ireland
6 Eustace Street
Dublin 2
Republic of Ireland
Tel: 353 1 679 5744
Fax: 353 1 677 8755
Lar Joye, Head of Archive
Sunniva O'Flynn, Archive Curator
Liam Wylie, Keeper of Film & Magnetic Collections
Emma Keogh, Librarian/Paper Archivist

ITALY

Cineteca Nazionale (National Film Archive)
Centro Sperimentale di Cinematografia
Via Tuscolana
1524, 00173 Roma
Tel: 39 6 722941
Fax: 39 6 7223131
Angelo Libertini, General Director

LUXEMBOURG

Cinémathèque Municipale de Luxembourg/Ville de Luxembourg (Luxembourg National Film Archive/City of Luxembourg)
10 rue Eugene Ruppert
2453 Luxembourg
Tel: 352 47 96 26 44
Fax: 352 40 75 19
Claude Bertemes

THE NETHERLANDS

Nederlands Filmmuseum, Stichting (Nederlands Film Museum)
Vondelpark 3
1071 AA Amsterdam
Tel: 31 20 5891400
Fax: 31 20 6833401
Peter Westervoorde, Head of Cataloguing Department

PORTUGAL

Cinemateca Portuguesa – Museu do Cinema (Portuguese Film Archive – Museum of Cinema)
Rua Barata Salgueiro, No 39
1200 Lisboa
Tel: 351 1 546279
Fax: 351 1 3523180
José Manuel Costa, Head of Film Archive

SPAIN

Filmoteca Española (Spanish National Film Theatre)
Carretera de la Dehesa de la Villa s/n
28040, Madrid
Tel: 34 1 549 00 11
Fax: 34 1 549 73 48

SWEDEN

Svenska Filminstitutet (Swedish Film Institute)
PO Box 27 126
102 52 Stockholm
Tel: 46 8 665 11 00
Fax: 46 8 661 18 20
Rolf Lindfors, Head of Archive

National Archives

National Film and Television Archive
21 Stephen Street
London W1P 2LN
Tel: 020 7255 1444
Fax: 020 7580 7503
Website: http://www.bfi.org.uk
Anne Fleming
The NFTVA preserves and makes permanently available a national collection of moving images which have value as examples of the art and history of cinema and television, or as a documentary record of the twentieth century. The collection now holds over 300,000 titles dating from 1895 to the present. The Archive also preserves and makes accessible the BFI's collection of stills, posters and designs

Scottish Film and Television Archive
1 Bowmont Gardens
Glasgow G2 9LR
Tel: 0141 337 7400
Fax: 0141 337 7413
email: info@scottishscreen.com
Website: www.scottishscreen.com
Janet McBain: Curator
Anne Docherty: Enquiries
Almost exclusively non-fiction film, the collection dates from 1896 to the present day and concerns aspects of Scottish social, cultural and industrial history. Available to broadcasters, programme makers, educational users and researchers. Access charges and conditions available on request

Wales Film and Television Archive
Unit 1, Aberystwyth Science Park
Cefn Llan
Aberystwyth
Dyfed SY23 3AH
Tel: 01970 626007
Fax: 01970 626008
Director: Iola Baines
The Archive locates, preserves and catalogues film and video material relating to Wales. The collection is made accessible where possible for research and viewing. The Archive is part of Sgrín, Media Agency for Wales
Chief Executive: J Berwyn Rowlands

Regional Collections

East Anglian Film Archive
University of East Anglia
Norwich NR4 7TJ
Tel: 01603 592664
Fax: 01603 458553
email: eafa@uea.ac.uk
Website: www.uea.ac.uk/eafa/
David Cleveland, Director
Jane Alvey, Deputy Director
Preserving non-fiction films and videos, both amateur and professionally made, showing life and work in Bedfordshire, Cambridgeshire, Essex, Hertfordshire, Norfolk and Suffolk

North West Film Archive
Manchester Metropolitan University
Minshull House
47-49 Chorlton Street
Manchester M1 3EU
Tel: 0161 247 3097
Fax: 0161 247 3098
email: n.w.filmarchive@mmu.ac.uk
Website: www.nwfa.mmu.ac.uk
Maryann Gomes: Director
Enquiries: Liza Warren/Anoush Simon
Preserves moving images showing life in the North West and operates as a public regional archive. Urban and industrial themes are particularly well illustrated

Northern Region Film and Television Archive
Blanford House
Blanford Square
Newcastle upon Tyne NE1 4JA
Tel: 0191 232 6789
Fax: 0191 230 2614
Chris Galloway, Project Director
A northern regional collection incorporating the former Northeast Television Film Archives which featured television newsfilms from BBC Northeast and documentary film from Tyne Tees Televison and the former Northern Film and Television Archive with its emphasis on industry, especially coal mining, and its community

South East Film & Video Archive
University of Brighton
Grand Parade
Brighton BN2 2JY
Tel: 01273 643213
Fax: 01273 643214
Established in 1992 the function of

this regional film and video archive is to locate, collect, preserve and promote films and video tapes made in the four counties of Surrey, Kent, East Sussex and West Sussex

The South West England Film and Television Archive
New Cooperage
Royal William Yard
Stonehouse
Plymouth
Devon PL1 3RP
Tel: 01752 202650
Fax: 01752 205025
Website: http:www.geocities.com/Athens/Atlantis/1802/fta.htm
The official film archive for the South West of England. Holds south western film material and includes three television collections covering news coverage between 1961 to 1992 – Westward Television, Television South West and BBC South West

Wessex Film and Sound Archive
Hampshire Record Office
Sussex Street
Winchester SO23 8TH
Tel: 01962 847742
Fax: 01962 878681
email: sadedm@hants.gov.uk.
David Lee
Preserves and makes publicly accessible for research, films, video and sound recordings of local interest to central southern England

Yorkshire Film Archive
College of Ripon and York St John
College Road
Ripon HG4 2QX
Tel: 01765 602691
Fax: 01765 600516
email: s.howard@ucrysj.ac.uk
Sue Howard
The Yorkshire Film Archive exists to locate, preserve and show film about the Yorkshire region. Material dates from 1897 and includes newsreels, documentaries, advertising and amateur films

Newsreel, Production and Stock Shot Libraries

Adventure & Wildlife Stock Shot Library
Church House,
18 Park Mount, Leeds
Yorkshire LS5 3HE
Tel: 0113 230 7150
Fax: 0113 274 5387
Chris Lister
A wide range of adventure sports and wildlife footage, most shot on 16mm or Super 16mm and available on Beta SP or film

Archive Film Agency
21 Lidgett Park Avenue
Roundhay
Leeds LS8 1EU
Tel: 0113 2662454
Fax: 0113 2662454
Agnèse Geoghegan
Film from 1898 to present day, including a current worldwide stock shot library. Specialists in early fiction, newsreel, documentary, Music Hall, Midlands, Yorkshire, British 1930s stills. Cassette services

Associated Press Television News (APTN)
The Interchange
Oval Road
Camden Lock
London NW1 7DZ
Tel: 020 7410 5353
Fax: 020 7413 8327
email: info@aptnlibrary.com
Website: www.aptnlibrary.com
David Simmons
Newsfilm and video from 1896 – and adding every day up to 100 new items from around the world. Hard news, stock footage, features, personalities, annual compilations, background packages etc. Story details and shotlists are stored on full-text easy-to-search database. Database also available on CD-Rom and online (see website address above)

BBC Information & Archives – Television Archive
Reynard Mills Industrial Estate
Windmill Road
Brentford TW8 9NF
Tel: 020 8576 9211/9212
Fax: 020 8569 9374
Margaret Kirby

The largest collection of broadcast programmes in the world reflecting the whole range of BBC output

BFI Archival Footage Sales Unit
21 Stephen Street
London W1P 2LN
Tel: 020 7957 8934
Fax: 020 7580 5830
email: footage.films@bfi.org.uk
Website: www.bfi.org.uk
Jan Faull or Simon Brown
Material from the largest collection of film footage in Britain – the National Film and Television Archive. Television, films, documentaries, newsreels and animation are all covered with over 350,000 titles to choose from, including material dating back to 1895. First stop for serious research on subjects that have shaped the 20th century. Research facilities available

Boulton-Hawker Films
Hadleigh, Ipswich
Suffolk IP7 5BG
Tel: 01473 822235
Fax: 01473 824519
Peter Boulton
Educational films produced over 50 years. Subjects include: health, biology, botany, geography, history, archaeology, and the arts

The British Defence Film Library
SSVC, Chalfont Grove
Narcot Lane
Chalfont St. Peter
Gerrards Cross
Bucks SL9 8TN
Tel: 01494 878278/878252
Fax: 01494 878007
email: robertd@ssvc.com
Robert Dungate: BDFL Librarian
SSVC has many years experience in providing both entertainment and support for the military. The British Defence Library (BDFL) is an independent department within SSVC which holds and distributes audio visual training materials for use by the armed forces which have been specifically commissioned by the Ministry of Defence. The Library also supplies this footage to the film and television industry offering a unique collection of British military material

British Movietonews
North Orbital Road
Denham
Middx UB9 5HQ
Tel: 01895 833071
Fax: 01895 834893

Barbara Heavens
One of the world's major film archives featuring high quality cinema newsreels from the turn of the century, with an emphasis on 1929–1979. The library now represents on an exclusive basis the TV-AM News Library with over 1,100 hours of British and World news covering the period 1983–1991. This material is available on re-mastered digital tape

British Pathé Plc
60 Charlotte Street
London W1P 2AX
Tel: 020 7323 0407
Fax: 020 7436 3232
email: pathe@enterprise.net
Website: www.britishpathe.com/ search.html
Larry McKinna: Chief Librarian
50 million feet of newsreel and social documentary from 1896 to 1970. Rapid research and sourcing through computerised catalogue
Pinewood Studios
Pinewood Road
Iver, Bucks SL0 0NH
Tel: 01753 630 361
Fax: 01753 655365
Ron Saunders

Canal + Image UK Ltd
Pinewood Studios
Pinewood Road, Iver
Bucks SL0 0NH
Tel: 01753 631111
Fax: 01753 655813
John Herron
Feature films, TV series, stock shot and stills, b/w and colour, 35mm, 1925 to present day

Central Office of Information Footage File
4th Floor
184-192 Drummond Street
London NW1 3HP
Tel: 020 7383 2292
Fax: 020 7383 2333
Website: www.film-images.com
Tony Dykes
40,000 Crown Copyright titles from the Government's News and Information archives spanning over 75 years of British social and business history. Most of the collection has been thoroughly shot listed and is available on VHS viewing cassettes

Chain Production
2 Clanricarde Gardens
London W2 4NA
Tel: 020 7219 4277
Fax: 020 7229 0861
Specialist in European films and world cinema, cult classics, handling European Film Libraries with all rights to over 1,000 films – also clip rights and clip search

Channel Four Clip Library
124 Horseferry Road
London SW1P 2TX
Tel: 020 7306 8490/8155
Fax: 020 7306 8362
email: caustin@channel4.co.uk
Claire Austin/Eva Kelly
An ever-growing portfolio of programmes and a diverse collection of library material

Clips & Footage
PO Box 28417
London N19 3AF
Tel: 020 7281 4918
Fax: 020 7263 1164
email: clipsetc@easynet.co.uk
Supplies historical and modern colour footage to broadcast, corporate and commercial producers. Special collections include B movies, feature film trailers, destinations, timelapse and lifestyle

Contemporary Films
24 Southwood Lawn Road
Highgate
London N6 5SF
Tel: 020 8340 5715
Fax: 020 8348 1238
Documentaries on China, USSR, Cuba, Nazi Germany, South Africa. The library also covers areas like the McCarthy witch hunts in the '50s, the civil rights movements of the '60s, hippie culture, feminism

Editions Audiovisuel Beulah
66 Rochester Way
Crowborough TN6 2DU
Tel: 01892 652413
Fax: 01892 652413
email: iainlogan@enterprise.net
Website: www.homepages.enterprise. net/ beulah/
Beulah publishes the following videos – Vintage Music, Inland Waterways, Royal Navy, Military Transport, Yesterday's Britain. It also incorporates Film Archive Management (FAME)

Educational and Television Films (ETV)
247a Upper Street
London N1 1RU
Tel: 020 7226 2298
Fax: 020 7226 8016
Documentaries on Eastern Europe, USSR, China, Vietnam, Cuba and British Labour movement, b/w and colour, 16mm and 35mm, 1896 to present day

Environmental Investigation Agency
69-85 Old Street
London EC1V 9HX
Tel: 020 7490 7040
Fax: 020 7490 0436
email: eiauk@gn.apc.org
Extensive and exclusive library of video and stills showing the exploitation of wildlife and the environment worldwide. Subjects include dolphin and whale slaughter, the bird trade, bear farms, animal products illegally on sale in shops and to undercover investigators, and other aspects of endangered species trade. All film sales help to fund future investigations and campaigns

Film Images
4th Floor
184-192 Drummond Street
London NW1 3HP
Tel: 020 7383 2288
Fax: 020 7383 2333
Website: www.film-images.com
Angela Saward
Thousands of hours of classic and contemporary film images from hundreds of different sources around the world. All fully catalogued and immediately available for viewing on VHS or U-Matic. Suppliers include Central Office of Information and Overseas Film and Television

Film Research & Production Services Ltd
Suite 211-213, Mitre Street
177-183 Regent House
London W1R 8LA
Tel: 020 7734 1525
Fax: 020 7734 8017
Amanda Dunne, James Webb
Film research and copyright clearance facilities, also third party clearance. Film holding of space footage

GB Associates
80 Montalt Road
Woodford Green
Essex IG8 9SS
Tel: 020 8505 1850
Fax: 020 8504 6340
email: filmview@aol.com
Malcolm Billingsley
An extensive collection, mainly on 35mm, of fact and fiction film from the turn of the century. The collection is particularly strong in vintage trailers, the early sound era, early colour systems and adverts

Fred Goodland Film, Video & Record Collections
81 Farmilo Road
Leyton

London E17 8JN
Tel: 020 8539 4412
Fax: 020 8539 4412
Fred Goodland MBKS
Diverse actuality and entertainment material on film and disc (1890s-1990s). Specialist collections include early sound films and a wide range of musical material. 100s of original 78 rpm discs in excellent condition represent the authentic sounds of the 20th century, VHS tapes with B.I.T.C. available to film researchers

Granada Media Clip Sales – London Weekend TV Images
London Television Centre
Upper Ground
London SE1 9LT
Tel: 020 7261 3690/3771
Fax: 020 7261 3456
email: clips.london@granadamedia.com
Julie Lewis
Clips and stockshots available from London Weekend Television's vast programme library, dating from 1968. Drama, entertainment, music, arts and international current affairs. Plus London's news, housing, transport, politics, history, wildlife etc

Ronald Grant Archive
The Cinema Museum
The Master's House
The Old Lambeth Workhouse
2 Dugard Way
(off Renfrew Road,Kennington)
London SE11 4TH
Tel: 020 7840 2200
Fax: 020 7840 2299
email: martin@cinemamuseum.org.uk
Martin Humphries
15 million feet of fact and fiction film, mainly 35mm, from 1896 onwards. Also 1 million film stills, posters, programmes, scripts and information. The museum is a FIAF subscriber

Huntley Film Archives
78 Mildmay Park
Newington Green
London N1 4PR
Tel: 020 7923 0990
Fax: 020 7241 4929
email: huntleyarchives.com
Website: www.huntleyarchives.com
Amanda Huntley, John Huntley
Archive film library for broadcast, corporate and educational purposes, specialising in documentary footage 1900-1980. Phone to make an appointment or write for brochure detailing holdings. Now also 50,000 stills from films and film history

Index Stock Shots
12 Charlotte Mews
London W1P 1LN
Tel: 020 7631 0134
Fax: 020 7436 8737
email: index@msn.com
Philip Hinds
Unique stock footage on 35mm film and tape. Including extremes of nature and world climate, time-lapse and aerial photography, cities, landmarks, aviation, wildlife

ITN Archive
200 Gray's Inn Road
London WC1X 8XZ
Tel: 020 7430 4480
Fax: 020 7430 4453
Website: www.itnarchive.com/
John Flewin
Worldwide TV news coverage on film and video tape, from 1955 to the present day. Complete library archive on site including multi-format transfer suite. Also an online stills from video service, available via ISDN. A newspaper cuttings reference library with cuttings back to 1955 is available

London Film Archive
c/o 78 Mildmay Park
Newington Green
London N1 4PR
Tel: 020 7923 4074
Fax: 020 7241 4929
Dedicated to the acquisition and preservation of film relating to the Greater London region. The collection consists of material from 1895 to the present day and represents professional and amateur features and documentary films

The Lux Centre
2-4 Hoxton Square
London N1 6NU
Tel: 020 7284 4588
Fax: 020 7267 6078
email: lea@easynet.co.uk
Website: www.lux.org.uk
Britain's national centre for video and new media art, housing the most extensive collection of video art in the country. Artists' work dating from the 1970s to the present

Medi Scene
32-38 Osnaburgh Street
London NW1 3ND
Tel: 020 7387 3606
Fax: 020 7387 9693
Aurora Salvador-Bennett
Wide range of accurately catalogued medical and scientific shots available on film and video. Part of the Medi Cine Group

Moving Image Communications
The Basement
2-4 Dean Street
London W1V 5RN
Tel: 020 7437 5688
Fax: 020 7437 5649
email: moving-image@compuserve.com
Website: www.moving_image.co.uk
Patrick Smith: Library Manager
Over 11,000 hours of contemporary and archive images including: WPA Film Library; RSPB Film Library; Britain – British Tourist Authority, Landscapes and Seascapes, Tida Films, Business and Industry; World Destinations – Lonely Planet, Endangered World, Travelogue Classics; News & Current Affairs – London News Network, TVAM 1983 to 1992, Universal Newsreels, Cuban Archive; Natural History – Channel 4, The Key Animal Collection; Space and Technology – Space Exploration (NASA), Medical Technology; Special Collections – The Freud Home Movies, Silent Films

Nova Film and Video Library
11a Winholme
Armthorpe
Doncaster DN3 3AF
Tel: 01302 833422
Fax: 01302 833422
email: Library@novaonline.co.uk
Website: www.novaonline.co.uk
An extensive collection of unique archive material. The library holds a huge selection of amateur cine film documenting the changing social life of Britain, dating back to 1944 and has a dedicated collection of transport footage, from 1949 to the present day. The library also holds a selection of specially shot footage and interviews. A catalogue and showreel is available

The Olympic Television Archive Bureau
4th Floor Axis Centre
Burlington Lane
Chiswick
London W4 2TH
Tel: 020 8233 5353
Fax: 020 8233 5354
David Williams
The International Olympic Committee owns a unique collection of film and television material covering the entire history of the Olympic Games from 1896 to 1994. Now it can be accessed via the Olympic Television Archive Bureau, which is administered by Trans World International

Oxford Scientific Films
Lower Road
Long Hanborough
Oxford OX8 8LL
Tel: 01993 881881
Fax: 01993 882808 or 01993 883969
Jane Mulleneux, Rachel Roberts,
Sandra Berry
Stock footage on 16mm, 35mm film
and video. Wide range of wildlife,
special fx, timelapse, slow motion,
scenics, agriculture, traffic, macro,
micro etc. Catalogue and showreel
available. Extensive stills library

Pearson Television International Ltd
1 Stephen Street
London W1P 1PJ
Tel: 020 7691 6732/6733
Fax: 020 7691 6080
Len Whitcher
Over 15,000 hours of a wide range of
TV programmes including all
Thames, Grundy, Alomo, ACI and all
American programming

Post Office Film and Video Library
PO Box 145, Sittingbourne
Kent ME10 1NH
Tel: 01795 426465
Fax: 01795 474871
email: poful@edist.co.uk
Barry Wiles, Linda Gates
Holds a representative selection of
documentary programmes made
under the GPO Film Unit, including
the classic Night Mail. Catalogue
available which also lists recent
releases. New series of programmes
on Millennium stamps now available

Reuters Television Library
(Managed and Distributed by ITN
Archive)
200 Grays Inn Road
London WC1X 8XE
Tel: 020 7430 4480
Fax: 020 7430 4453
email: archive.sales@itn.co.uk
Website: www.itnarchive.com
Caroline Hurley
Full shot listed online. Newsreel, TV
news, special collections. Colour and
b/w, 16mm, 35mm, 1896 to present
day and all material pre-1951 and
post-July 1981 on 1" video

RSPB Film and Video Unit
The Lodge
Sandy
Bedfordshire SG19 2LN
Tel: 01767 680551
Fax: 01767 692365
Colin Skevington: Head of Film &
Video
Producer: Mark Percival

Wildlife documentary filmmakers
and corporate production. Over 500
hours of archive footage, mostly
European birds and other animal and
plant life including habitats and
scenics

Sky News Library Sales
British Sky Broadcasting Ltd
Grant Way
Isleworth
Middlesex TW7 5QD
Tel: 020 7705 2872/3132
Fax: 020 7705 3201
Sue Stewardson, Ben White
Extensive round the clock news and
current affairs coverage since 1989.
Entire library held on Beta SP on
site. Library operates 24 hours a day

TCB Releasing
Stone House, Rudge
Frome
Somerset BA11 2QQ
Tel: 01373 830769
Fax: 01373 831028
Angus Trowbridge
Sales of jazz and blues music
programmes to broadcast television
and the home-video media

TWI Archive
Trans World International
Axis Centre
Burlington Lane
Chiswick
London W4 2TH
Tel: 020 8233 5500/5300
Fax: 020 8233 5301
Rita Costantinou
Includes golf, tennis, World Cup
rugby, America's Cup, Test cricket,
skating, snooker, gymnastics,
yachting, motorsport, adventure
sport, many minor and ethnic sports
plus expanding catalogue of
worldwide stockshots

Undercurrents Archive
16b Cherwell Street
Oxford OX4 1BG
Tel: 01865 203 663
Fax: 01865 243 562
email: underc@gn.apc.org
Website: www.undercurrents.org
Roddy Mansfield
Undercurrents video archive features
grassroots dissent of the '90s and
contains over 1500 hours of footage
of radical protest

World Backgrounds Film Production Library
Imperial Studios
Maxwell Road
Borehamwood, Herts
Tel. 020 8207 4747
Fax: 020 8207 4276
Ralph Rogers

Locations around the world. Fully
computerised. All 35mm including
3,000 back projection process plates.
Numerous video masters held.
Suppliers to TV commercials,
features, pop promos, TV series,
corporate videos etc

Photographic Libraries

BBC Photograph Library
B116 Television Centre
Wood Lane
London W12 7RJ
Tel: 020 8225 7193
Fax: 020 8746 0353
The BBC's unique archive of radio
and television programme stills,
equipment, premises, news and
personalities dating from 1922. B/w
and colour. Visits by appointment

BFI Stills, Posters and Designs
21 Stephen Street
London W1P 2LN
Tel: 020 7255 1444
Fax: 020 7323 9260
A visual resource of around seven
million images, illustrating every
aspect of the development of world
cinema and television. The collection
also holds approximately 15,000 film
posters and 2,000 production and
costume designs. Other material
includes animation models,
storyboards, sketches and plans

The Bridgeman Art Library
17-19 Garway Road
London W2 4PH
Tel: 020 7727 4065
Fax: 020 7792 8509
email: info@bridgeman.co.uk
Website: www.bridgeman.co.uk
From cave paintings to contemporary
design, The Bridgeman Art Library
provides a one stop-source for the
world's art. Representing over 750
collections and contemporary artists
worldwide, the library offers large
format colour transparencies, a picture
research service, CD-ROM catalogues,
image and copyright databases

Corbis Images
12 Regents Wharf
All Saints Street
London N1 9RL
Tel: 0800 731 9995
Fax: 020 7278 1408
email: info@corbisimages.com
Website: www.corbisimages.com
Photographic stills agency/library

Hulton Getty Picture Collection
Unique House
21-31 Woodfield Road
London W9 28A
Tel: 020 7266 2660
Fax: 020 7266 2414

email: ask@getty-images.com
Website: www.hultongetty.com
One of the world's largest stills
archives with over 15 million
photographs, prints and engravings
covering the entire history of
photojournalism

The Image Bank
17 Conway Street
London W1 6EE
Tel: 020 7312 0300
Fax: 020 7391 9123

Image Diggers Picture and Tape Library
618b Finchley Road
London NW11 7RR
Tel: 020 8455 4564
Fax: 020 8455 4564
35mm slides, stills, postcards, sheet
music, magazine and book material
for hire. Cinema, theatre and
literature clippings archive.
Audio/visual tape resources in
performing arts and other areas, plus
theme research

image.net
18 Vine Hill
London EC1
Tel: 0541 522 333
Fax: 020 7729 5098
Simon Townsley

Imperial War Museum
Photograph Archive
All Saints Annexe
Austral Street
London SE11 4SL
Tel: 020 7416 5333/8
Fax: 020 7416 5355
email: photos@iwm.org.uk
A collection of some 6 million images
illustrating all aspects of 20th century
warfare. Film stills can also be made
from material held by the IWM's Film
& Video Archive, by prior
arrangement

Institute of Contemporary History & Wiener Library
4 Devonshire Street
London W1N 2BH
Tel: 020 7636 7247
Fax: 020 7436 6428
email: lib@wl.u-net.com
Rosemarie Nief: Head Librarian
Ben Barkow: Photo Archive,
Christine Patel: Video Collection
The Wiener Library is a private
research library and institute
specialising in contemporary
European and Jewish history,
especially the rise and fall of the
Third Reich, Nazism and Fascist
movements, Anit-Semitism, racism,
the Middle East and post war
Germany. It holds Britain's largest

collection of documents, testimonies,
books and videos on the Holocaust.
The photographic archive contains
stills, postcards, posters and portraits,
illustrated books, plus approx. 2,000
videos and recordings

Kobal Collection
4th Floor
184 Drummond Street
London NW1 3HP
Tel: 020 7383 0011
Fax: 020 7383 0044
David Kent
One of the world's leading film photo
archives in private ownership. Film
stills and portraits, lobby cards and
posters, from the earliest days of the
cinema to modern times

Mckenzie Heritage Picture Archive
90 Ardgowan Road
London SE6 1UU
Tel: 020 8697 0147
Fax: 020 8697 0147
email: MkHeritage@aol.com
Mckenzie Heritage picture archive
specialises in pictures of black
communities from Britain and abroad

The Moviestore Collection Ltd
3 Jonathan Street
London SE11 5NH
Tel: 020 7820 3820
Fax: 020 7820 8420

Pearson Television Stills Library
Teddington Studios
Broom Road
Teddington TW11 9NT
Tel: 020 8781 2789
Fax: 020 8614 2250
Website: www.pearsontv.com/
pages/stillslibrary.htm
Colleen Kay
Stills from Thames TV, Alomo,
Grundy

Retrograph Nostalgia Archive Ltd
164 Kensington Park Road
London W11 2ER
Tel: 020 7727 9378
Fax: 020 7229 3395
email: MBreese999@aol.com
Jilliana Ranicar-Breese
Hiring out transparencies or colour
laser prints from original labels,
packaging, advertising, posters,
prints. Commercial and fine art
material from 1860-1960. Supply to
publishers, film and television
companies, record and CD companies
and gift manufacturers. Visual
research service and photography
service. Most subjects available but
travel, food and drink a speciality

Museums

Bill Douglas Centre for the History of Cinema and Popular Culture The
University of Exeter
Queen's Building
Queen's Drive
Exeter EX4 4QH
Tel: 01392 264263
Fax: 01392 264361
Website: www.ex.ac.uk/bill.douglas/
The Centre's collection was assembled over many years by film-maker Bill Douglas and his friend Peter Jewell. It comprises a huge range of books, periodicals, programmes, posters, sheet music, cards, toys and games related to the cinema, in addition to 19th century pre-cinema artefacts such as zoetropes, magic lanterns, panoramas, peepshows and other optical toys and devices

The Cinema Museum
(See Ronald Grant Archive)
The Cinema Museum
The Master's House
The Old Lambeth Workhouse
2 Dugard Way
(off Renfrew Road,Kennington)
London SE11 4TH
Tel: 020 7840 2200
Fax: 020 7840 2299
email: martin@cinemamuseum.org.uk

Imperial War Museum Film and Video Archive
Lambeth Road
London SE1 6HZ
Tel: 020 7416 5000
Fax: 020 7416 5379
The national museum of twentieth century conflict, illustrating and recording all aspects of modern war. The Archive reflects these terms of reference with an extensive collection of film and video material, which is widely used by historians and by film and television companies

Laurel and Hardy Museum
4C Upper Brook Street
Ulverston
Cumbria LA12 7BQ
Tel: 01229 582292
Website: www.wwwebguides.com/britain/cumbria/furness/laure.html
The museum is in Ulverston, Cumbria, Stan Laurel's birthplace. Open all year, seven days a week for talks about Laurel and Hardy. It contains photos, letters, and memorabilia

National Museum of Photography Film & Television
Pictureville
Bradford BD1 1NQ
Tel: 01274 202030
Fax: 01274 723155
Website: www.nmsi.ac.uk/nmpft
The world's only museum devoted to still and moving pictures, their technology and history. Features Britain's first giant IMAX film system; the world's only public Cinerama; interactive galleries and 'TV Heaven', reference library of programmes and commercials

AWARDS

This section features some of the principal festival prizes and awards from January 1998 to June 1999. Compiled by Laura Pearson

Awards 1998

BAFTA FILM AWARDS
Awarded in London 19th April 1998

The Alexander Korda Award for Outstanding British Film of the Year
NIL BY MOUTH (UK)
Dir Gary Oldman
Audience Award
The FULL MONTY (US/UK)
Dir Peter Cattaneo
Best Actor
Robert Carlyle for The FULL MONTY (US/UK)
Dir Peter Cattaneo
Best Actress
Judi Dench for MRS BROWN (UK/US/Ireland)
Dir John Madden
Best Adapted Screenplay
Baz Luhrmann, Craig Pearce for
WILLIAM SHAKESPEARE'S ROMEO +JULIET (US/UK)
Dir Baz Luhrmann
Best Cinematography
Eduardo Serra for WINGS OF THE DOVE (US/UK)
Dir Iain Softley
Best Costume Design
Deirdre Clancy for MRS BROWN (UK/US/Ireland)
Dir John Madden
Best Director
Baz Luhrmann for WILLIAM SHAKESPEARE'S
ROMEO + JULIET (US/UK)
Best Film
The FULL MONTY (US/UK)
Dir Peter Cattaneo
Best Editing
Peter Honess for L.A. CONFIDENTIAL (US)
Dir Curtis Hanson
Best Foreign Language Film
L'APPARTEMENT (France/Spain/Italy)
Dir Gilles Mimouni
Best Make-Up/Hair
Sallie Jaye, Jan Archibald for
WINGS OF THE DOVE (US/UK)
Dir Iain Softley
Anthony Asquith Award for Achievement in Film Music
for WILLIAM SHAKESPEARE'S ROMEO + JULIET (US/UK)
Dir Baz Luhrmann
Best Original Screenplay
Gary Oldman for NIL BY MOUTH (UK)
Dir Gary Oldman
Best Production Design
Catherine Martin for
WILLIAM SHAKESPEARE'S ROMEO + JULIET (US/UK)
Dir Baz Luhrmann

Best Supporting Actor
Tom Wilkinson for The FULL MONTY (US/UK)
Dir Peter Cattaneo
Best Supporting Actress
Sigourney Weaver for The ICE STORM (US)
Dir Ang Lee
Best Short Film
The DEADNESS OF DAD (UK)
Dir Philippa Cousins
Best Short Animated Film
STAGE FRIGHT (UK)
Dir Steve Box
Best Special Visual Effects
Le CINQUIÈME ÉLÉMENT (France)
Dir Luc Besson
Best Sound
L.A. CONFIDENTIAL (US)
Dir Curtis Hanson
The Academy Fellowship
Sean Connery
Outstanding British Contribution to Cinema
Michael Robert

BAFTA TELEVISION AWARDS
Awarded in London 18th May 1998

Best Single Drama
NO CHILD OF MINE (Stonehenge Films and United
Film & TV Productions for ITV)
Best Drama Series
JONATHAN CREEK (BBC entertainment for BBC1)
Best Drama Serial
HOLDING ON (BBC drama for BBC2)
Best Factual Series
The NAZIS – A WARNING FROM HISTORY (BBC
documentary & history for BBC2)
Best Light Entertainment (programme or series)
The FAST SHOW (BBC entertainment for BBC2)
Best Comedy (programme or series)
I'M ALAN PARTRIDGE (Talkback Productions for BBC2)
Best Actress
Daniela Nardini for THIS LIFE
(World Productions for BBC2)
Best Actor
Simon Russell Beale for A DANCE TO THE MUSIC OF
TIME (Table Top for C4)
Best Light Entertainment Performance
Paul Whitehouse for The FAST SHOW
(BBC entertainment for BBC2)
Best Comedy Performance
Steve Coogan for I'M ALAN PARTRIDGE
(Talkback Productions for BBC2)
Huw Wheldon Award for Best Arts Programme or Series
GILBERT AND GEORGE – THE SOUTH BANK
SHOW (LWT for ITV)
Sports/Events Coverage in Real Time
RUGBY UNION (Sky Sports)
News and Current Affairs Journalism
VALENTINA'S STORY – PANORAMA (BBC1)

The Flaherty Documentary Award
The GRAVE – TRUE STORIES (Soul Purpose for C4)
Original Television Music
TOM JONES (BBC drama for BBC1)
Best Make-Up/Hair
TOM JONES (BBC drama for BBC1)
Best Photography (Factual)
POLAR BEAR WILDLIFE SPECIAL
(BBC Natural History for BBC1)
Best Photography and Lighting (Fiction/Entertainment)
The WOMAN IN WHITE (BBC/Carlton for BBC1)
Best Costume Design
TOM JONES (BBC drama for BBC1)
Best Graphic Design
ELECTION '97 (BBC Resources for BBC1)
Best Sound (Factual)
AIRPORT (BBC documentaries and history for BBC1)
Best Sound (Fiction/Entertainment)
The LAKES (BBC drama for BBC1)
Best Editing (Factual)
The NAZIS – A WARNING FROM HISTORY (BBC
documentaries and history for BBC2)
Best Editing (Fiction/Entertainment)
The LAKES (BBC drama for BBC1)
Best Design
The WOMAN IN WHITE (BBC/Carlton for BBC1)
The Academy Fellowship
Bill Cotton
**The Alan Clarke Award for Outstanding Creative
Contribution to Television**
Ted Childs
**The Richard Dimbleby Award for Outstanding
Personal Contribution to Factual Television**
David Dimbleby
The Dennis Potter Award
Kay Mellor
Best International Programme or Series
FRIENDS
The Special Award
Roger Cook
**The Lew Grade Award for the Most Popular Television
Programme**
A TOUCH OF FROST (Yorkshire TV for ITV)

48th BERLIN INTERNATIONAL FILM FESTIVAL
Held in Berlin 11th-22nd February 1998

Golden Berlin Bear (Grand Prix)
CENTRAL DO BRASIL (Brazil/France/Spain/Japan)
Dir Walter Salles
Silver Berlin Bear – Special Jury Prize
WAG THE DOG (US)
Dir Barry Levinson
**Silver Berlin Bear – Lifetime Contribution to Arts of
Cinematography**
Alain Resnais for ON CONNAÎT LA CHANSON
(France/Switzerland/UK)
Dir Alain Resnais
Silver Berlin Bear – Best Director
Neil Jordan for The BUTCHER BOY (Ireland/US)
Silver Berlin Bear – Best Actress
Fernanda Montenegro for CENTRAL DO BRASIL
(Brazil/France/Spain/Japan)
Dir Walter Salles
Silver Berlin Bear – Best Actor
Samuel L. Jackson for JACKIE BROWN (US)
Dir Quentin Tarantino

Silver Berlin Bear – Best Single Achievement
Matt Damon as scriptwriter and actor for GOOD WILL
HUNTING (US)
Dir Gus Van Sant
The Blue Angel
Jeroen Krabbé for LEFT LUGGAGE
(Netherlands/Belgium/US)
Dir Jeroen Krabbé
Alfred Bauer Prize
YUE KUAI LE, YUE DUO LUO (Hong Kong)
Dir Stanley Kam-Pang Kwan
**A Special Mention for the Promising Performances –
Actress**
Isabella Rossellini for LEFT LUGGAGE (Netherlands/
Belgium/US)
Dir Jeroen Krabbé
**A Special Mention for the Promising Performances –
Actor**
Eamonn Owens for The BUTCHER BOY (Ireland/US)
Dir Neil Jordan
Special Mention
Slawomir Idziak for I WANT YOU (UK)
Dir Michael Winterbottom
Prizes for Short Films
Golden Berlin Bear
I MOVE SO I AM (Netherlands)
Dir Gerrit van Dijk
Silver Berlin Bear
CINEMA ALCAZAR (Nicaragua)
Dir Florence Jaugey

bfi FELLOWSHIPS
Awarded at the NFT at the end of the London Film
Festival, November 1998
Jeremy Thomas, Bernardo Bertolucci

BROADCASTING PRESS GUILD TELEVISION AND RADIO AWARDS 1997
Awarded in London 2nd April 1998

Best Single Drama
BREAKING THE CODE (The Drama House for BBC1)
Best Drama Series/Serial
HOLDING ON (BBC2)
Best Documentary Series
The NAZIS – A WARNING FROM HISTORY (BBC2)
Best Single Documentary
CUTTING EDGE: THE DINNER PARTY (Granada
Television for Channel 4)
Best Entertainment
I'M ALAN PARTRIDGE (Talkback Productions for BBC2)
Best Actor
Simon Russell Beale for A DANCE TO THE MUSIC OF
TIME (Channel 4)
Best Actress
Helen Baxendale for COLD FEET (Granada Television
for Channel 4) and AN UNSUITABLE JOB FOR A
WOMAN (Ecosse Films/HTV/WGHB (Boston) for ITV)
Best Performer (Non-Acting)
Jeremy Paxman for UNIVERSITY CHALLENGE
(Granada Television for BBC2), NEWSNIGHT (BBC2),
ELECTION NIGHT 1997 (BBC1)
Writer's Award
David Renwick for ONE FOOT IN THE GRAVE (BBC1)
Radio Programme of the Year
I'M SORRY I HAVEN'T A CLUE (Radio 4)
Radio Broadcaster of the Year
Susan Sharpe for MIDWEEK CHOICE (Radio 3)

Harvey Lee Award for Outstanding Contribution to Broadcasting
Michael Wearing (Head of Drama Serials, BBC TV)

51st CANNES FESTIVAL
Held in Cannes 13th-24th May 1998

Palme d'Or
MIA EONIOTITA KE MIA MERA (An Eternity and a Day) (Greece/France)
Dir Theo Angelopoulos
Grand Jury Prize
La VITA È BELLA (Italy)
Dir Roberto Benigni
Best Actress
Élodie Bouchez and Natacha Regnier for La VIE RÊVÉE DES ANGES (France)
Dir Erick Zonca
Best Actor
Peter Mullan for MY NAME IS JOE (UK/Germany)
Dir Ken Loach
Best Director
John Boorman for The GENERAL (Ireland/UK)
Best Screenplay
Hal Hartley for HENRY FOOL (US)
Dir Hal Hartley
Jury Technical Prize
Vittorio Storaro for TANGO (Spain/Argentina/France)
Dir Carlos Saura
Special Jury Prize
La CLASSE DE NEIGE (France)
Dir Claude Miller, and FESTEN (Denmark)
Dir Thomas Vinterberg
Best Artistic Contribution Prize
VELVET GOLDMINE (UK/US)
Dir Todd Haynes
Camera d'Or
SLAM (US)
Dir Marc Levin
Best Short Film
L'INTERVIEW (France)
Dir Xavier Giannoli
Short Film Second Prize
GASMAN (UK)
Dir Lynne Ramsay, and HORSESHOE (UK)
Dir David Lodge

23rd CÉSARS
Awarded in Paris 28th February 1998

Best Film
ON CONNAÎT LA CHANSON (France/Switzerland/UK)
Dir Alain Resnais
Best Director
Luc Besson for Le CINQUIÈME ÉLÉMENT (France)
Best Actress
Ariane Ascaride for MARIUS ET JEANNETTE (France)
Dir Robert Guédiguian
Best Actor
André Dussolier for ON CONNAÎT LA CHANSON (France/Switzerland/UK)
Dir Alain Resnais
Best First Film
DIDIER (France)
Dir Alain Chabat
Best Screenplay
Agnès Jaoui et Jean-Pierre Bacri for ON CONNAÎT LA CHANSON (France/Switzerland/UK)

Dir Alain Resnais
Best Supporting Actress
Agnès Jaoui for ON CONNAÎT LA CHANSON (France/Switzerland/UK)
Dir Alain Resnais
Best Supporting Actor
Jean-Pierre Bacri for ON CONNAÎT LA CHANSON (France/Switzerland/UK) Dir Alain Resnais
Best Promising Young Actress
Emma de Caunes for Un FRÉRE (France)
Dir Sylvie Verheyde
Best Promising Young Actor
Stanislas Merhar for NETTOYAGE À SEC (France/Spain)
Dir Anne Fontaine
Best Foreign Film
BRASSED OFF (UK/S)
Dir Mark Herman
Best Photography
Thierry Arbogast for Le CINQUIÈME ÉLÉMENT (France)
Dir Luc Besson
Best Sound
Pierre Lenoir et Jean-Pierre Laforce for ON CONNAÎT LA CHANSON (France/Switzerland/UK)
Dir Alain Resnais
Best Decor
Dan Weil for Le CINQUIÈME ÉLÉMENT (France)
Dir Luc Besson
Best Costumes
Christian Gasc for Le BOSSU (France/Italy/Germany)
Dir Philippe De Broca
Best Editing
Hervé de Luze for ON CONNAÎT LA CHANSON (France/Switzerland/UK)
Dir Alain Resnais
Best Music
Bernardo Sandoval for WESTERN (France)
Dir Manuel Poirer
Best Short Film
Des MAJORETTES DANS L'ESPACE (France)
Dir David Fournier
Best Honor Awards:
Michael Douglas, Clint Eastwood, Jean-Luc Godard

52nd EDINBURGH INTERNATIONAL FILM FESTIVAL
Held 16th-30th August 1998, Edinburgh
88 Lothian Road
Edinburgh EH3 9BZ
Tel: (44) 131 228 4051
Web site: www.edfilmfest.org.uk/

Standard Life Gala Award
GET REAL (UK/South Africa)
Dir Simon Shore
Pathé Best British Performance Award
Daniel Craig and Derek Jacobi for LOVE IS THE DEVIL STUDY FOR A PORTRAIT OF FRANCIS BACON (UK/France/Japan)
Dir John Maybury
Documentary Award
SHIVREI TMNUNOT JERUSHALÏM (Israel)
Dir Ron Havilio
Best New British Feature
LOVE IS THE DEVIL STUDY FOR A PORTRAIT OF FRANCIS BACON (UK/France/Japan)
Dir John Maybury

New Director's Award
Todd Haynes for VELVET GOLDMINE (UK/US)
Best British Short
I JUST WANT TO KISS YOU (UK)
Dir Jamie Thraves and WEE THREE (UKScotland) Dir
Matt Hulse
Best British Animation
HUMDRUM (UK)
Dir Peter Peake

EMMY AWARDS – 26th INTERNATIONAL EMMY AWARDS
Awarded in New York 23rd November 1998
Web site: www.intlemmyawards.com/

Best Drama
The TATTOOED WIDOW (Sweden)
Best Documentary
EXILE IN SARAJEVO (Australia) (Exile
Productions/Australian Film Commission/SBS
Independent)
Best Arts Documentary
The WAR SYMPHONIES SHOSTAKOVICH AGAINST
STALIN (Netherlands)
Best Performing Arts
The JUDAS TREE (UK) (NVC)
Best Popular Arts
The VICAR OF DIBLEY (BBC1)
LOVE AND MARRIAGE (UK) (Tiger Aspect for BBC1)
Best Children and Young People Category
BLABBERMOUTH AND STICKY BEAK (UK) (Double
Exposure for Channel 4 Schools)

EMMY AWARDS – NATIONAL ACADEMY FOR TELEVISION ARTS AND SCIENCES
50th PRIMETIME AWARDS CREATIVE ARTS
WINNERS – Awarded in Pasadena on 29th August 1998
Web site:www.emmys.org/

Outstanding Cinematography for a Series
Constantine Makris for LAW & ORDER (Wolf
Films/Universal TV)
**Outstanding Music Composition for a Series
(Dramatic Underscore)**
Christophe Beck composer for BUFFY THE
VAMPIRE SLAYER: BECOMING, PART 1 (Warner Bros.)
**Outstanding Music Composition for a Miniseries or a
Movie (Dramatic Underscore)**
Bruce Broughton composer for
GLORY & HONOR (Turner Broadcasting System)
Outstanding Music Direction
Bill Conti music director for The 70TH ANNUAL
ACADEMY AWARDS (Academy
of Motion Picture Arts and Sciences)
Outstanding Music and Lyrics
Alf Clausen (composer) and Ken Keeler (lyrics)
"You're Checkin' In"
The SIMPSONS (Fox Network)
Outstanding Guest Actress in a Comedy Series
Emma Thompson for ELLEN (Black/Marlens
Productions/TouchstoneTelevision)
Outstanding Guest Actor in a Comedy Series
Mel Brooks for MAD ABOUT YOU (Infront
Productions/Nuance Productions/Tri-Star TV)
Outstanding Guest Actress in a Drama Series
Cloris Leachman for PROMISED LAND (CBS Productions)

Outstanding Guest Actor in a Drama Series
John Larroquette for The PRACTICE (David E. Kelley
Productions)
Outstanding Non-Fiction Series
The AMERICAN EXPERIENCE
(WNET/KCET/WGBH(Boston))
Outstanding Special Visual Effects for a Series
Pedro Pires, computer graphic design for
YO-YO MA INSPIRED BY BACH
(Rhombus Media/Sony Classical for BBC2)
**Outstanding Special Visual Effects for a Miniseries or
a Movie**
Tim Webber, Stefan Lange, Matthew Cope, Richard
Conway, Tim Greenwood, George Roper, Murray Butler,
Angus Wilson, Pedro Sabrosa, William Bartlett,
Avtar Bains for MERLIN
PART 1 (Hallmark Entertainment)
Outstanding Animated Programme
The SIMPSONS (Fox Network)
Outstanding Art Direction for a Series
Graeme Murray, Greg Loewen and Shirley Inget for THE
X-FILES:
THE POST-MODERN PROMETHEUS (Ten Thirteen
Productions/Twentieth Century Fox Film Corporation)
Outstanding Art Direction for a Miniseries or a Movie
Roger Hall, John King, Mike Boone and Karen Brookes
for MERLIN
PART 1 (Hallmark Entertainment)
**Outstanding Cinematography for a Miniseries or a
Movie**
Eric Van Haren Noman for WHAT THE DEAF
MAN HEARD (Hallmark of Fame)
Outstanding Children's Programme
MUPPETS TONIGHT (Jim Henson Organisation)

TELECAST WINNERS – Awarded in Los Angeles
13 September 1998
Outstanding Comedy Series
FRASIER (Grub Street/Paramount Pictures)
Outstanding Directing for a Comedy Series
Todd Holland for The LARRY SANDERS SHOW
(Brillstein Grey/HBO)
Outstanding Lead Actor in a Comedy Series
Kelsey Grammer for FRASIER
(Grub Street/Paramount Pictures)
Outstanding Lead Actress in a Comedy Series
Helen Hunt for MAD ABOUT YOU
(Infront Productions/Nuance Productions/Tri-Star Television)
Outstanding Supporting Actress in a Comedy Series
Lisa Kudrow for FRIENDS (Bright,Kaufmann,Crane
Productions/Warner Bros. Television)
Outstanding Supporting Actor in a Comedy Series
David Hyde Pierce for FRASIER
(Grub Street/Paramount Pictures)
Outstanding Writing for a Comedy Series
Peter Tolan and Garry Shandling for
The LARRY SANDERS SHOW (Brillstein Grey/HBO)
Outstanding Directing for a Variety or Music Programme
Louis J. Horvitz for The 70TH ANNUAL ACADEMY
AWARDS (Academy of Motion Pictures Arts and Sciences)
Outstanding Writing for a Variety or Music Programme
Eddie Feldmann, Dennis Miller, David Feldman, Leah
Krinsky, Jim Hanna, David Weiss, Jose Arroyo for
DENNIS MILLER LIVE (Tribune Entertainment Co.)
**Outstanding Performance in a Variety or Music
Programme**
Billy Crystal for The 70TH ANNUAL ACADEMY
AWARDS (Academy of Motion Pictures Arts and Sciences)

Outstanding Drama Series
The PRACTICE (David E. Kelley Productions)
Outstanding Directing for a Drama Series
Mark Tinker for BROOKLYN SOUTH (Steven Bochco
Productions)
and Paris Barclay for NYPD BLUE
LOST ISRAEL -PART 2 (Steven Bochco Productions)
Outstanding Lead Actor in a Drama Series
Andre Braugher for HOMICIDE
LIFE ON THE STREET (Baltimore
Pictures/Fatima Productions/Sterling Entertainment/NBC)
Outstanding Lead Actress in a Drama Series
Christine Lahti for CHICAGO HOPE
(David E. Kelley Productions)
Outstanding Supporting Actress in a Drama Series
Camryn Manheim for The PRACTICE
(David E. Kelley Productions)
Oustanding Supporting Actor in a Drama Series
Gordon Clapp for NYPD BLUE
(Steven Bochco Productions)
Outstanding Writing for a Drama Series
Nicholas Wootton, David Milch, Bill Clark for NYPD
BLUE LOST ISRAEL – PART 2
(Steven Bochco Productions)
Outstanding Miniseries
FROM THE EARTH TO THE MOON
(HBO/Imagine Entertainment)
Outstanding Directing for a Miniseries or a Movie
John Frankenheimer for GEORGE WALLACE
(Turner Network Television)
Outstanding Lead Actor in a Miniseries or a Movie
Gary Sinise for GEORGE WALLACE
(Turner Network Television)
Outstanding Lead Actress in a Miniseries or a Movie
Ellen Barkin for BEFORE WOMEN HAD WINGS
(OPRAH WINFREY PRESENTS) (Harpo Pictures)
**Outstanding Supporting Actor in a Miniseries or a
Movie**
George C. Scott for 12 ANGRY MEN
(MGM Worldwide Television)
**Outstanding Supporting Actress in a Miniseries or
Movie**
Mare Winningham for GEORGE WALLACE
(Turner Network Television)
Outstanding Writing for a Miniseries or a Movie
Kario Salem for DON KING ONLY IN AMERICA
(HBO Pictures)
Outstanding Variety, Music or Comedy Special
The 1997 TONY AWARDS (CBS)
Outstanding Variety, Music or Comedy Series
The LATE SHOW WITH DAVID LETTERMAN (CBS)
Outstanding Made for Television Movie
DON KING ONLY IN AMERICA (HBO Pictures)

11th EUROPEAN FILM AWARDS
4th December 1998, London
European Film Academy
Kurfürstendamm 225
D-10719 Berlin
Tel: (49) 30 887 167 0
Web site:www.europeanfilmacademy.org/

Best Documentary Award
CLAUDIO PAZIENZA (for various works)
Five Continents Award
The TRUMAN SHOW (US)
Dir Peter Weir
Best European Cinematographer
Adrian Biddle for The BUTCHER BOY (Ireland/US)
Dir Neil Jordan
European Actress of the Year
Élodie Bouchez for La VIE RÊVÉE DES ANGES
(France)
Dir Erick Zonca and
Natacha Regnier for La VIE RÊVÉE DES ANGES
(France)
Dir Erick Zonca
European Actor of the Year
Roberto Benigni for La VITA È BELLA (Italy)
Dir Roberto Benigni
European Film of the Year
La VITA È BELLA (Italy)
Dir Roberto Benigni
Best European Script/Screenwriter
Peter Howitt for SLIDING DOORS (US/UK)
Dir Peter Howitt
European Discovery of the Year
Erick Zonca for La VIE RÊVÉE DES ANGES (France)
Dir Erick Zonca and Thomas Vinterberg for FESTEN
(Denmark)
Dir Thomas Vinterberg
European Achievement in World Cinema
Stellan Skarsgård for AMISTAD (US)
Dir Steven Spielberg and for
GOOD WILL HUNTING (US)
Dir Gus Van Sant
Best European Short Film
Un JOUR (France)
Dir Marie Paccou
FIPRESCI Critics Prize
BURE BARUTA
(France/Greece/Turkey/Serbia/Macedonia)
Dir Goran Paskaljevic
Audience Award for Best European Actress
Kate Winslet for TITANIC (US)
Dir James Cameron
Audience Award for Best European Actor
Antonio Banderas for The MASK OF ZORRO (US)
Dir Martin Campbell
Audience Award for Best European Director
Roland Emmerich for GODZILLA (US)

EVENING STANDARD FILM AWARDS 1998
Awarded in London 1st February 1998

Best Actress
Katrin Cartlidge for CAREER GIRLS (UK)
Dir Mike Leigh
Best Actor
Robert Carlyle for The FULL MONTY (US/UK)
Dir Peter Cattaneo

Best Film
The FULL MONTY (US/UK)
Dir Peter Cattaneo
Best Screenplay
Jeremy Brock for MRS BROWN (UK/US/Ireland)
Dir John Madden
Best Technical Achievement
Maria Djurkovic for WILDE (UK/US/Japan/Germany)
Dir Brian Gilbert
Most Promising Newcomer
Jude Law for WILDE (UK/US/Japan/Germany)
Dir Brian Gilbert
Peter Sellers Award for Comedy
MRS BROWN (UK/US/Ireland)
Dir John Madden
Special Jury Award
Kenneth Branagh for HAMLET (US/UK)
Special Award
Roy Boulting

55th GOLDEN GLOBE AWARDS
Awarded in Los Angeles 19th January 1998

FILM – Drama
TITANIC (US)
Dir James Cameron
Actress (Drama)
Judi Dench for MRS BROWN (UK/US/Ireland)
Dir John Madden
Actor (Drama)
Peter Fonda for ULEE'S GOLD (US)
Dir Victor Nunez
Musical or Comedy
AS GOOD AS IT GETS (US)
Dir James L. Brooks
Actress (Musical or Comedy)
Helen Hunt for AS GOOD AS IT GETS (US)
Dir James L. Brooks
Actor (Musical or Comedy)
Jack Nicholson for AS GOOD AS IT GETS (US)
Dir James L. Brooks
Foreign Language Film
MA VIE EN ROSE (France/Belgium/UK/Switzerland)
Dir Alain Berliner
Supporting Actress (Drama, Musical or Comedy)
Kim Basinger for L.A. CONFIDENTIAL (US)
Dir Curtis Hanson
Supporting Actor (Drama, Musical or Comedy)
Burt Reynolds for BOOGIE NIGHTS (US)
Dir Paul Thomas Anderson
Best Director
James Cameron for TITANIC (US)
Best Screenplay
Matt Damon and Ben Affleck for
GOOD WILL HUNTING (US)
Dir Gus Van Sant
Original Score
James Horner for TITANIC (US)
Dir James Cameron
Original Song
James Horner and Will Jennings for
"My Heart Will Go On"
TITANIC (US)
Dir James Cameron

TELEVISION- Drama Series
The X-FILES

Actress (Drama Series)
Christine Lahti for CHICAGO HOPE
Actor (Drama Series)
Anthony Edwards for ER
Musical or Comedy Series
ALLY McBEAL
Actress (Musical or Comedy Series)
Calista Flockhart for ALLY McBEAL
Actor (Musical or Comedy Series)
Michael J. Fox for SPIN CITY
Miniseries or Television Movie
GEORGE WALLACE
Actress in Miniseries or Television Movie
Alfre Woodard for MISS EVERS' BOYS
Actor in Miniseries or Television Movie
Ving Rhames for DON KING
ONLY IN AMERICA
Supporting Actress in Miniseries or Television Movie
Angelina Jolie for GEORGE WALLACE
Supporting Actor in Miniseries or Television Movie
George C. Scott for 12 ANGRY MEN
Cecil B. DeMille Award
Shirley MacLaine

38th GOLDEN ROSE OF MONTREUX
Held 23rd-28th April 1998, Montreux

Golden Rose
YO-YO MA INSPIRED BY BACH: SIX GESTURES
(UK/Canada) (Rhombus)
Silver Rose (Music)
The CANADIAN BRASS
A CHRISTMAS EXPERIMENT (UK/Canada) (CDN)
Silver Rose (Sitcom)
OPERATION GOOD GUYS
FRISK 'EM (UK) (BBC2)
Silver Rose/Special Prize of the City of Montreux
HARRY ENFIELD & CHUMS (UK) (Tiger Aspect)
Silver Rose (Variety)
CRONICAS MARCIANAS (Spain) (Gestmusic Zepp)
Silver Rose (Special)
QUEEN – "BÉJART BALLET FOR LIFE"
(UK) (Queen Productions)
Bronze Rose (Music)
GAEL FORCE (Ireland) (Tyrone/RTE)
Bronze Rose (Sitcom)
FATHER TED – ARE YOU RIGHT THERE? (UK)
(Channel 4)
Bronze Rose (Comedy)
The CHAMBER QUINTET (Israel) (Matar Arts +)
Bronze Rose (Special)
FAME AND FORTUNE: OZZY OSBOURNE (UK)
(Channel 5)
Bronze Rose (Variety)
DAVID BLAINE STREET MAGIC (US)
(David Blaine Productions)
Press Prize
DAVID BLAINE STREET MAGIC (US)
(David Blaine Productions)
Special Prize
Il SEGRETO DI PULCINELLA (Switzerland) (RTSI)
Ex-Aqueo
OPERATION GOOD GUYS: FRISK 'EM (UK) (BBC2)
UNDA Award
YO-YO MA INSPIRED BY BACH: SIX GESTURES
(UK/Canada) (Rhombus)

The GRIERSON AWARD for 1997
The SYSTEM – THE NATURE OF THE BEAST
(Peter Dale/BBC2)

33rd KARLOVY VARY INTERNATIONAL FILM FESTIVAL
Held 3rd July-11th July 1998, Karlovy Vary
Panska 1
110 00 Prague 1
Czech Republic
Tel: (420) 224 23 54 13
Web site: www.iffkv.cz/

Crystal Globe
Le COEUR AU POING (Canada)
Dir Charles Binamé
Special Prize
DENJ POLNOLUNIYA (Russia)
Dir Karen Shakhnazarov
Best Director
Charles Binamé for Le COEUR AU POING (Canada)
Best Actress
Julia Stiles for WICKED (US)
Dir Michael Steinberg
Best Actor
Olaf Lubaszenko for JE TREBA ZABÍT SEKALA (Czech Republic/Poland/France/Slovakia) Dir Vladimír Michálek
Special Prize
The GOVERNESS (UK)
Dir Sandra Goldbacher
Best Documentary
MOMENT OF IMPACT (US)
Dir Julia Loktev and SLADKÉ STOLETÍ (Czech Republic) Dir Helena Trestíková
Special Mention
KISANGANI DIARY (France/Austria)
Dir Hubert Sauper and GOLOSA (Russia)
Dir Andrej Osipov
Special Prize for Oustanding Contribution to World Cinema
Michael Douglas, Frantisek Vlácil, Saul Zaentz
Life Achievement Prize
Lauren Bacall, Rod Steiger
FIPRESCI Prize
TIC TAC (Sweden)
Dir Daniel Alfredson
Special Mention
DENJ POLNOLUNIYA (Russia)
Dir Karen Shakhnazarov
Ecumenical Jury Prize
COMEDIAN HARMONISTS (Germany/Austria)
Dir Joseph Vilsmaier
Jury Special Mention
JE TREBA ZABÍT SEKALA (Czech Republic/Poland/France/Slovakia)
Dir Vladimír Michálek
FICC Jury Don Quijot Prize
TIC TAC (Sweden)
Dir Daniel Alfredson
Jury Special Mention
The SUGAR FACTORY (Australia)
Dir Robert Carter and KILLER (Kazakhstan/France)
Dir Darezhan Omirbaev
Audience Prize Kodak Vision
The GOVERNESS (UK)
Dir Sandra Goldbacher

51st LOCARNO INTERNATIONAL FILM FESTIVAL
Held 5th-15th August 1998, Locarno
Via Bluini 3
6600 Locarno 1
Switzerland
Tel: (41) 91 751 0232
Web site: www.pardo.ch/

Special Prize
Rossy de Palma in HORS JEU (France)
Dir Karim Dridi and Adam Bousdoukos, Aleksandar Jovanovic and Mehmet Kurtulus in KURZ UND SCHMERZLOS (Germany)
Dir Fatih Akin
Youth Jury UBS Award
TULENNIELIJÄ (Finland/Sweden)
Dir Pirjo Honkasalo
FIPRESCI Award
El ARBOL DE LAS CEREZAS (Spain)
Dir Marc Recha
FIPRESCI Award (Special Mention)
SIB (Iran/France)
Dir Samira Makhmalbaf
Golden Leopard
ZHAO XIANSHENG (China/Hong Kong)
Dir Lu Yue
Silver Leopard (New Cinema)
RAGHS-E-KHAK (Iran)
Dir Abolfazl Jalili
Silver Leopard (Young Cinema)
BESHKEMPIR (France/Kyrgyzstan)
Dir Aktan Abdykalykov
Youth Jury Award (Euro<26)
23 NICHTS IST SO WIE ES SCHEINT (Germany)
Dir Hans-Christian Schmid
Youth Jury Award (Environment is Quality of Life)
RAGHS-E-KHAK (Iran)
Dir Abolfazl Jalili
Don Quixote Award
BESHKEMPIR (France/Kyrgyzstan)
Dir Aktan Abdykalykov
Don Quixote Award (Special Mention Young Cinema)
TULENNIELIJÄ (Finland/Sweden)
Dir Pirjo Honkasalo
Don Quixote Award (Special Mention New Cinema)
23 NICHTS IST SO WIE ES SCHEINT (Germany)
Dir Hans-Christian Schmid
Prize of the Ecumenical Jury
TITANIC TOWN (UK/Germany/France/Ireland)
Dir Roger Michell
Prize of the Ecumenical Jury (Special Mention)
BESHKEMPIR (France/Kyrgyzstan)
Dir Aktan Abdykalykov and
IKINAI (Japan)
Dir Hiroshi Shimizu
C.I.C.A.E. Award
RAGHS-E-KHAK (Iran)
Dir Abolfazl Jalili
C.I.C.A.E. Award (Special Mention)
SOMBRE (France)
Dir Philippe Grandrieux
Leopard of Honour
Joe Dante
Swissair/Crossair Special Prize
VREMYA TANTSORA (Russia)
Dir Vadim Abdrashitov

LONDON CRITICS' CIRCLE FILM AWARD
Awarded in London 5th March 1998

Best British Actress
Judi Dench for MRS BROWN (UK/US/Ireland)
Dir John Madden
Best British Actor
Robert Carlyle for The FULL MONTY (UK/US)
Dir Peter Cattaneo, FACE (UK) Dir
Antonia Bird, CARLA'S SONG (UK/Germany/Spain)
Dir Ken Loach
Best British Film
The FULL MONTY (UK/US)
Dir Peter Cattaneo
Best British Producer
Uberto Pasolini for The FULL MONTY (UK/US)
Dir Peter Cattaneo
Best British Screenwriter
Simon Beaufoy for The FULL MONTY (UK/US)
Dir Peter Cattaneo
Best English-Language Film
L.A. CONFIDENTIAL (US)
Dir Curtis Hanson
Best Newcomer of the Year
Peter Cattaneo for The FULL MONTY (UK/US)
Dir Peter Cattaneo
Lifetime Achievement Awards:
Paul Scofield, Woody Allen, Michael Caine, Martin
Scorsese

38th MONTE CARLO TELEVISION FESTIVAL
Awarded in Monte Carlo 20th-26th February 1998

FILMS FOR TV
Gold Nymph (Best Film)
L'ORANGE DE NOEL (King Movies) (France)
Silver Nymph (Best Director)
Jean-Louis Lorenzi for L'ORANGE DE NOEL (King
Movies) (France)
Silver Nymph (Best Script)
Stuart Urban for DEADLY VOYAGE (BBC2)
Silver Nymph (Best Actress)
Meredith Baxter for AFTER JIMMY (Worldvision
Enterprises) (US)
Silver Nymph (Best Actor)
Omar Epps for DEADLY VOYAGE (BBC2)
Special Mention
CORRERE CONTRO (SACIS Spa) (Italy)
MINI-SERIES
Gold Nymph (Best Mini-Series)
CLEAN SHEET (Danmarks Radio/TV) (Denmark)
Silver Nymph (Best Director)
Daniel Afredson for CLEAN SHEET (Danmarks
Radio/TV) (Denmark)
Silver Nymph (Best Script)
John Brown for CLEAN SHEET (Danmarks Radio/TV)
(Denmark)
Silver Nymph (Best Actress)
Alex Kingston for MOLL FLANDERS (Granada
Television) (UK)
Silver Nymph (Best Actor)
Ole Ernst for CLEAN SHEET (Danmarks Radio/TV)
(Denmark)
Special Mention
Edward Klosinski, director of photography for GRAND
AVENUE (HBO Enterprises) (US)

NEWS PROGRAMMES
Gold Nymph
LIZENZ ZUM QUALEN (ZDF) (Germany)
Silver Nymph
The SELLING OF INNOCENTS (Associated Producers
Inc.) (Canada)
Silver Nymph
ENVOYE SPECIAL
ENQUETE SUR UN MASSACRE (France 2/Point du
Jour) (France)
Silver Nymph
Le POINT
LES NOUVEAUX GOULAGS (Société Radio Canada)
(Canada)

70th OSCARS – ACADEMY OF MOTION PICTURES ARTS AND SCIENCES
Awarded in Los Angeles 23rd March 1998
for 1997 films

Best Film
TITANIC (US)
Dir James Cameron
Best Foreign Language Film
KARAKTER (Netherlands/Belgium)
Dir Mike van Diem
Best Director
James Cameron for TITANIC (US)
Best Actress
Helen Hunt for AS GOOD AS IT GETS (US)
Dir James L. Brooks
Best Actor
Jack Nicholson for AS GOOD AS IT GETS (US)
Dir James L. Brooks
Best Supporting Actress
Kim Basinger for L.A. CONFIDENTIAL (US)
Dir Curtis Hanson
Best Supporting Actor
Robin Williams for GOOD WILL HUNTING (US)
Dir Gus Van Sant
Best Original Screenplay
Matt Damon and Ben Affleck for GOOD WILL
HUNTING (US)
Dir Gus Van Sant
Best Screenplay Adaptation
Brian Helgeland and Curtis Hanson for L.A.
CONFIDENTIAL (US)
Dir Curtis Hanson
Best Cinematography
Russell Carpenter for TITANIC (US)
Dir James Cameron
Best Editing
Conrad Buff, James Cameron and Richard A. Harris for
TITANIC (US)
Dir James Cameron
Best Original Dramatic Score
James Horner for TITANIC (US)
Dir James Cameron
Best Original Musical or Comedy Score
Anne Dudley for The FULL MONTY (UK/US)
Dir Peter Cattaneo
Best Original Song
James Horner and Will Jennings for "My Heart Will Go On"
TITANIC (US)
Dir James Cameron
Best Art Direction/Set Decor
Peter Lamont and Michael Ford for TITANIC (US)

Dir James Cameron
Best Costume Design
Deborah L. Scott for TITANIC (US)
Dir James Cameron
Best Make-Up
Rick Baker and David LeRoy Anderson for MEN IN
BLACK (US)
Dir Barry Sonnenfeld
Best Sound
Gary Rydstrom, Tom Johnson, Gary Summers and Mark
Ulano for TITANIC (US)
Dir James Cameron
Best Sound Effects Editing
Tom Bellfort and Christopher Boyes for TITANIC (US)
Dir James Cameron
Best Short Film (Animated)
GERI'S GAME
Dir Jan Pinkava
Best Short Film (Live Action)
VISAS AND VIRTUE (US)
Dir Chris Tashima
Best Documentary Feature
The LONG WAY (US)
Dir Mark Jonathan Harris
Best Documentary Short
A STORY OF HEALING (US)
Dir Donna Dewey
Best Visual Effects
Robert Legato, Mark Lasoff, Thomas L. Fisher and
Michael Kanfer for TITANIC (US) Dir James Cameron
Life Achievement Award
Stanley Donen

ROYAL TELEVISION SOCIETY AWARDS
Awarded in London 17th March 1998

Best Actress
Sinead Cusack for HAVE YOUR CAKE AND EAT IT
(BBC1)
Best Actor
Simon Russell-Beale for A DANCE TO THE MUSIC OF
TIME (Table Top Productions for Channel 4)
Best Single Drama
GRANTON STAR CAUSE (Channel 4)
Best Drama Series
THIS LIFE (BBC2)
Best Television Performance
Chris Morris for BRASS EYE (Channel 4)
Best Children's Entertainment Programme
TELETUBBIES (BBC2)
Best Entertainment Programme
HARRY ENFIELD & CHUMS (BBC1)
Gold Medal
Trevor McDonald
The Cyril Bennett Judges Award
Michael Wearing
Best Presenter
Jeremy Clarkson for TOP GEAR (BBC2)
Best Sitcom
The VICAR OF DIBLEY (BBC1)

55th VENICE FILM FESTIVAL
Held in Venice 3rd-13th September 1998
Biennale Di Venezia
Ca Giustinian
30124 San Marco
Italy
Tel: (39) 041 521 87 11
Website: 194.185.28.38/

Golden Lion
COSÌ RIDEVANO (Italy)
Dir Gianni Amelio
Little Golden Lion
BLACK CAT WHITE CAT
(Germany/France/Yugoslavia/Austria/Greece)
Dir Emir Kusturica
Silver Lion (Best Director)
Emir Kusturica for BLACK CAT WHITE CAT
(Germany/France/Yugoslavia/Austria/Greece)
Volpi Cup for Best Actress
Catherine Deneuve for PLACE VENDÔME
(France/Belgium/UK)
Dir Nicole Garcia
Volpi Cup for Best Actor
Sean Penn for HURLYBURLY (US)
Dir Anthony Drazan
OCIC Award
LÔALBERO DELLE PERE (Italy)
Dir Francesca Archibugi
Laterna Magica Prize
BLACK CAT WHITE CAT (Germany/France/Yugoslavia/
Austria/Greece)
Dir Emir Kusturica
Anicaflash Prize
TRAIN DE VIE (France/Belgium)
Dir Radu Mihaileanu
Elvira Notari Prize
PASTI, PASTI, PASTICKY (Czech Republic)
Dir Vera Chytilová
Elvira Notari Prize (Special Mention)
NEW ROSE HOTEL (US)
Dir Abel Ferrara
FEDIC Award
DEL PERDUTO AMORE (Italy)
Dir Michele Placido
FEDIC Award (Special Mention)
OSPITI (Italy)
Dir Matteo Garrone and STO LAVORANDO (Italy) Dir
Daniele Segre
Max Factor Award
Jenny Shircore for ELIZABETH (UK)
Dir Shekhar Kapur
FIPRESCI Award (Best First Work)
TRAIN DE VIE (France/Belgium)
Dir Radu Mihaileanu
FIPRESCI Award (Best Film)
BURE BARUTA
(France/Greece/Turkey/Serbia/Macedonia)
Dir Goran Paskaljevic
Filmcritica Prize
NEW ROSE HOTEL (US)
Dir Abel Ferrara
Pasinetti Award (Best Actress)
Giovanna Mezzogiorno
Sergio Trasatti Award
I GIARDINI DELLÔEDEN (Italy)
Dir Alessandro DÔAlatri

Sergio Trasatti Award (Special Mention)
CONTE DÔAUTOMNE (France)
Dir Eric Rohmer
COSÌ RIDEVANO (Italy)
Dir Gianni Amelio
Le SILENCE (France/Iran)
Dir Mohsen Makhmalbaf
UNESCO Award
COLONEL BUNKER (Albania/Poland/France/Germany)
Dir Kujtim Çashku
UNESCO Award (Special Mention)
La NUBE (Argentina/France/Germany/Italy)
Dir Fernando E. Solanas
Isvema Award
ORPHANS (UK)
Dir Peter Mullan
'Cult Network Italia' Prize
ORPHANS (UK)
Dir Peter Mullan
Kodak Award
ORPHANS (UK)
Dir Peter Mullan
Prix Pierrot
ORPHANS (UK)
Dir Peter Mullan
'CinemAvvenire' Award (Man, Nature)
Le SILENCE (France/Iran)
Dir Mohsen Makhmalbaf
'CinemAvvenire' Award (Best Film in Competition)
La NUBE (Argentina/France/Germany/Italy)
Dir Fernando E. Solanas
'CinemAvvenire' Award (Best First Work)
VIVRE AU PARADIS (Belgium/Norway/France)
Dir Bourdem Guerdjou
UNICEF Award (Special Mention)
LÔALBERO DELLE PERE (Italy)
Dir Francesca Archibugi

Awards 1999 – January to June

BAFTA FILM AWARDS
11th April 1999, London
195 Piccadilly
London W1V OLN
Tel: 020 7734 0022
Website: www.bafta.org

The Academy Fellowship
Elizabeth Taylor
The Michael Balcon Award for Outstanding British Contribution to Cinema
Michael Kuhn
The Alexander Korda Award for the Outstanding British Film of the Year
ELIZABETH (UK)
Dir   Shekhar Kapur
Best Film
SHAKESPEARE IN LOVE (US)
Dir   John Madden
The David Lean Award for Best Achievement in Direction
Peter Weir for The TRUMAN SHOW (US)
Best Original Screenplay
Andrew Niccol for The TRUMAN SHOW (US)
Dir Peter Weir
Best Adapted Screenplay
Elaine May for PRIMARY COLORS (US)
Dir Mike Nichols
Best Actress
Cate Blanchett for ELIZABETH (UK)
Dir Shekhar Kapur
Best Actor
Roberto Benigni for La VITA È BELLA (Italy)
Dir Roberto Benigni
Best Supporting Actress
Judi Dench for SHAKESPEARE IN LOVE (US)
Dir John Madden
Best Supporting Actor
Geoffrey Rush for SHAKESPEARE IN LOVE (US)
Dir John Madden
Best Film not in the English Language
CENTRAL DO BRASIL (Brazil/France/Spain/Japan)
Dir Walter Salles
The Anthony Asquith Award for Achievement in Film Music
David Hirschfelder for ELIZABETH (UK)
Dir Shekhar Kapur
The Carl Foreman Award for Most Promising Newcomer in British Film
Richard Kwietniowski
Best Cinematography
Remi Adefarasin for ELIZABETH (UK)
Dir Shekhar Kapur
Best Production Design
Dennis Gassner for The TRUMAN SHOW (US)
Dir Peter Weir
Best Costume Design
Sandy Powell for VELVET GOLDMINE (UK/US)
Dir Todd Haynes
Best Editing
David Gamble for SHAKESPEARE IN LOVE (US)
Dir John Madden

Best Sound
Gary Rydstrom, Ronald Judkins, Gary Summers, Andy Nelson, Richard Hymns
for SAVING PRIVATE RYAN (US)
Dir Steven Spielberg
Best Special Visual Effects
Stefen Fangmeier, Roger Guyett, Neil Corbould for SAVING PRIVATE RYAN (US)
Dir Steven Spielberg
Best Make-Up/Hair
Jenny Shircore for ELIZABETH (UK)
Dir Shekhar Kapur
Best Short Animated Film
The CANTERBURY TALES (UK Wales)
Dir Dave Antrobus, Ashley Potter, Mic Graves, Joanna Quinn, Aida Zyablikova, Valeri Ugarov, Sergei Olifirenko, Damian Gascoigne
Best Short Film
HOME (UK) Prod
Hannah Lewis
Orange Audience Award
LOCK, STOCK AND TWO SMOKING BARRELS (UK)
Dir Guy Ritchie

BAFTA TELEVISION AWARDS
9th May 1999
195 Piccadilly
London W1V OLN
Tel: 020 7734 0022
Website: www.bafta.org

The Academy Fellowship
Eric Morecambe and Ernie Wise
The Alan Clarke Award for Outstanding Creative Contribution to Television
Jimmy Mulville, Denise O'Donoghue
The Richard Dimbleby Award for Outstanding Personal Contribution to Factual Television
Trevor McDonald
The Dennis Potter Award
David Renwick
The Special Award
Richard Curtis
The Lew Grade Award for the Most Popular Television Programme
GOODNIGHT MISTER TOM (Carlton Television for ITV)
Best Actress
Thora Hird for TALKING HEADS 2: WAITING FOR THE TELEGRAM (Slow Motion Limited for BBC2)
Best Actor
Tom Courtenay for A RATHER ENGLISH MARRIAGE (BBC/Wall to Wall Television for BBC2)
Best Light Entertainment Performance
Michael Parkinson for PARKINSON (BBC1)
Best Comedy Peformance
Dermot Morgan for FATHER TED
(Hat Trick Productions for C4)
Best Single Drama
A RATHER ENGLISH MARRIAGE
(BBC/Wall to Wall Television for BBC2)
Best Drama Series
The COPS (World Productions for BBC2)
Best Drama Serial
OUR MUTUAL FRIEND
(BBC/Canadian Broadcasting Company for BBC2)
Best Soap
EASTENDERS (BBC1)

Best Factual Series
The HUMAN BODY
(BBC Science/The Learning Channel for BBC1)
Best Light Entertainment Programme or Series
WHO WANTS TO BE A MILLIONAIRE?
(Celador Productions for ITV)
Best Comedy
FATHER TED (Hat Trick Productions for C4)
The Huw Wheldon Award for Best Arts Programme or Series
The BRIAN EPSTEIN STORY (ARENA) (BBC2)
The Flaherty Documentary Award
SURVIVING LOCKERBIE (Scottish Television Enterprises for ITV)
Live Outside Broadcast Coverage
C4 RACING – DERBY DAY (Highflyer Productions for C4)
News and Current Affairs Journalism
DISPATCHES – INSIDE THE ANIMAL LIBERATION FRONT (C4)
Best Features (Programme or Series)
BACK TO THE FLOOR (BBC2)
Originality
The HUMAN BODY (BBC Science/The Learning Channel for BBC1)
Best International Programme or Series
The LARRY SANDERS SHOW (Brillstein Grey/HBO)
Best Make-Up/Hair
Lisa Westcott for OUR MUTUAL FRIEND
(BBC/Canadian Broadcasting Company for BBC2)
Best Photography (Factual)
George Jesse Turner for 42 UP (Granada Television for BBC1)
Best Photography and Lighting (Fiction/Entertainment)
John Daly for FAR FROM THE MADDING CROWD
(Granada Television/WGBH (Boston) for ITV)
Best Costume Design
Frances Tempest for A RESPECTABLE TRADE
(BBC/Irish Screen Entertainment for BBC1)
Best Graphic Design
Tim Goodchild, David Haith for The HUMAN BODY
(BBC Science/The Learning Channel for BBC1)
Best Sound (Factual)
The LIFE OF BIRDS (BBC TV/Public Broadcasting Service for BBC1)
Best Sound (Fiction/Entertainment)
Paul Hamblin, Catherine Hodgson, Graham Headicar, Richard Manton for OUR MUTUAL FRIEND
(BBC/Canadian Broadcasting Company for BBC2)
Best Editing (Factual)
Brian Tagg for LOCKERBIE: A NIGHT REMEMBERED
(Castle Haven Digital for C4)
Best Editing (Fiction/Entertainment)
Dave King for A RATHER ENGLISH MARRIAGE
(BBC/Wall to Wall Television for BBC2)
Best Design
Malcolm Thornton for OUR MUTUAL FRIEND
(BBC/Canadian Broadcasting Company for BBC2)
Best Original Television Music
Jim Parker for A RATHER ENGLISH MARRIAGE
(BBC/Wall to Wall Television for BBC2)

49TH BERLIN INTERNATIONAL FILM FESTIVAL
10th-21st February 1999, Berlin
Internationale Filmfestspiele Berlin
Budapester Strasse 50
10787 Berlin
Tel: (49) 30 25 489-0
Website: www.berlinale.de

Golden Berlin Bear
The THIN RED LINE (US)
Dir Terrence Malick
Silver Berlin Bear (Jury Grand Prix)
MIFUNES SIDSTE SANG – DOGME 3
(Denmark/Sweden)
Dir Søren Kragh-Jacobsen
Silver Berlin Bear – Best Director
Stephen Frears for The HI-LO COUNTRY (US)
Silver Berlin Bear – Best Actress
Juliane Köhler and Maria Schrader for AIMÉE & JAGUAR (Germany)
Dir Max Färberböck
Silver Berlin Bear – Best Actor
Michael Gwisdek for NACHTGESTALTEN (Germany)
Dir Andreas Dresen
Silver Berlin Bear for Oustanding Single Achievement
Marc Norman and Tom Stoppard for their screenplay of SHAKESPEARE IN LOVE (US)
Dir John Madden
Silver Berlin Bear for Outstanding Artistic Achievement
David Cronenberg for EXISTENZ (Canada/UK)
Dir David Cronenberg
The Blue Angel
Yesim Ustaoglu for GÜNESE YOLCULUK
(Turkey/Netherlands/Germany)
Dir Yesim Ustaoglu
The Alfred Bauer Prize
KARNAVAL (Belgium/France/Germany/Switzerland)
Dir Thomas Vincent
A Special Mention for his outstanding work as Director of Photography
John Toll for The THIN RED LINE (US)
Dir Terrence Malick
A Special Mention for the young actress
Iben Hjejle for MIFUNES SIDSTE SANG – DOGME 3
(Denmark/Sweden)
Dir Søren Kragh-Jacobsen
A Special Mention for its subject matter
ÇA COMMENCE AUJOURD'HUI (France)
Dir Bertrand Tavernier
Gay Teddy Bear – Best Feature
FUCKING ÅMÅL (Sweden)
Dir Lukas Moodysson
Gay Teddy Bear – Best Documentary
The MAN WHO DROVE WITH MANDELA (UK)
Dir Greta Schiller
Gay Teddy Bear Jury Award – Wieland Speck
Prizes for Short Films
Golden Berlin Bear
FARAON (Russia)
Dir Sergej Ovtscharov and to MASKS (Germany/Poland)
Dir Piotr Karwas
Silver Berlin Bear
DESSERTS (UK)
Dir Jeff Stark
Gay Teddy Bear
LIU AWAITING SPRING (Australia)
Dir Andrew Soo

BROADCASTING PRESS GUILD TELEVISION AND RADIO AWARDS 1998
26th March 1999, London
c/o Richard Last
Tiverton, The Ridge
Woking
Surrey GU22 7EQ
Tel: 01483 764895

Best Single Documentary
42UP (Granada Television for BBC1)
Writer's Award
Caroline Aherne, Craig Cash and Henry Normal for The
ROYLE FAMILY (Granada Television
for BBC Manchester)
Best Documentary Series
The LIFE OF BIRDS (BBC TV/Public Broadcasting
Service for BBC1)
Best Drama Series/Serial
OUR MUTUAL FRIEND (BBC TV/Canadian
Broadcasting Corporation for BBC2)
Best Actress
Daniela Nardini for UNDERCOVER HEART (BBC1)
Best Actor
Timothy Spall for OUR MUTUAL FRIEND (BBC
TV/Canadian Broadcasting Corporation for BBC2)
Best Entertainment
COLD FEET (Granada Television for ITV) and
GOODNESS GRACIOUS ME (BBC2)
Best Single Drama
A RATHER ENGLISH MARRIAGE (Wall to Wall
Productions for BBC2)
Best Performer
Michael Parkinson

52nd CANNES FESTIVAL
12th-23rd May 1999, Cannes
99 Boulevard Malesherbes
75008 Paris
Tel: (33) 1 45 61 66 00
Web site: www.festival-cannes.org

Palme d'Or
ROSETTA (Belgium/France)
Dir Luc and Jean-Pierre Dardenne
Grand Jury Prize
L'HUMANITÉ (France)
Dir Bruno Dumont
Best Actress
Séverine Caneele for L'HUMANITÉ (France)
Dir Bruno Dumont, and Emilie Dequenne for
ROSETTA (Belgium/France)
Dir Luc and Jean-Pierre Dardenne
Best Actor
Emmanuel Schotté for L'HUMANITÉ (France)
Dir Bruno Dumont
Best Director
Pedro Almodovar for TODO SOBRE MI MADRE
(Spain/France)
Best Screenplay
Yuri Arabov and Marina Koreneva for MOLOCH
(Russia/Germany/France)
Dir Alexandre Sokourov
Jury Prize for Daring and Originality
A CARTA (Portugal/France/Spain)
Dir Manoel de Oliveira

Camera d'Or
MARANA SIMHASANAM (India/UK)
Dir Murali Nair
**Grand Prix Technique de la Commission Supèrieure
Technique de L'image et du Son**
JING KE CI QIN WANG
(Japan/China/France)
Dir Chen Kaige
Short Films
Palme d'Or
WHEN THE DAY BREAKS (Canada)
Dir Wendy Tilby and Amanda Forbis
Grand Jury Prize
STOP (France)
Dir Rodolphe Marconi, and SO-POONG (Republic of
Korea)
Dir Song Ilgon

24th CÉSARS
Awarded in Paris 6th March 1999

Best Film
La VIE RÊVÉE DES ANGES (France)
Dir Erick Zonca
Best Director
Patrice Chéreau for CEUX QUI M'AIMENT
PRENDRONT LE TRAIN (France)
Best Actress
Élodie Bouchez for La VIE RÊVÉE DES ANGES
(France)
Dir Erick Zonca
Best Actor
Jacques Villeret for Le DÎNER DE CONS (France)
Dir Francis Veber
Best Foreign Film
La VITA È BELLA (Italy)
Dir Roberto Benigni
Best First Film
DIEU SEUL ME VOIT (VERSAILLES-CHANTIERS)
(France)
Dir Bruno Podalydès
Best New Actress
Natacha Régnier for La VIE RÊVÉE DES ANGES
(France)
Dir Erick Zonca
Best New Actor
Bruno Putzulu for PETITIS DÉ SORDRES AMOUREUX
(France/Switzerland/Spain)
Dir Olivier Péray
Best Sound
Vincent Tulli and Vincent Arnardi for TAXI (France/Italy)
Dir Gérard Pirès
Best Sets
Jacques Rouxel for LAUTREC (France/Spain)
Dir Roger Planchon
Best Costume Design
Jean-Pierre Larroque for LAUTREC (France/Spain)
Dir Roger Planchon
Best Editing
Véronique Lange for TAXI (France/Italy)
Dir Gérard Pirès
Best Music
Tony Gatlif for GADJO DILO (France)
Dir Tony Gatlif
Best Short Film
L'INTERVIEW (France)
Dir Xavier Giannoli

Best Supporting Actress
Dominique Blanc for CEUX QUI M'AIMENT
PRENDRONT LE TRAIN (France)
Dir PatriceChéreau
Best Supporting Actor
Daniel Prévost for Le DÎNER DES CONS (France)
Dir Francis Veber
Best Screenplay
Francis Veber for Le DÎNER DES CONS (France)
Dir Francis Veber
Best Photography
Eric Gautier for CEUX QUI M'AIMENT PRENDRONT
LE TRAIN (France)
Dir Patrice Chéreau
Honorary Césars
Pedro Almodóvar
Jean Rochefort
Johnny Depp

EVENING STANDARD BRITISH FILM AWARDS 1998
Awarded in London 7th February 1999

Best Film
The GENERAL (Ireland/UK)
Dir John Boorman
Best Actress
Julie Christie for AFTERGLOW (US)
Dir Alan Rudolph
Best Actor
Derek Jacobi for LOVE IS THE DEVIL: STUDY FOR A
PORTRAIT OF FRANCIS BACON
(UK/France/Japan)
Dir John Maybury
Best Screenplay
Eileen Atkins for MRS DALLOWAY (UK)
Dir Marleen Gorris
Best Technical Achievement
Ashley Rowe for TWENTYFOURSEVEN (UK)
Dir Shane Meadows, The WOODLANDERS (UK)
Dir Phil Agland, STILL CRAZY (UK)
Dir Brian Gibson, The GOVERNESS (UK)
Dir Sandra Goldbacher
Most Promising Newcomer
Guy Ritchie for LOCK, STOCK AND TWO SMOKING
BARRELS (UK)
Dir Guy Ritchie
Peter Sellers Award for Comedy
Bill Nighy for STILL CRAZY (UK)
Dir Brian Gibson
Special Awards:
Ken Loach, Michael Caine

56th GOLDEN GLOBE AWARDS
24th January 1999, Los Angeles
292 South La Cienega Blvd
Suite 316, Beverly Hills
CA 9021-3055
Web site: www.hfpa.com

FILM
Best Motion Picture (Drama)
SAVING PRIVATE RYAN (US)
Dir Steven Spielberg
Best Actress (Drama)
Cate Blanchett for ELIZABETH (UK)
Dir Shekhar Kapur
Best Actor (Drama)
Jim Carrey for The TRUMAN SHOW (US)
Dir Peter Weir
Best Motion Picture (Comedy or Musical)
SHAKESPEARE IN LOVE (US)
Dir John Madden
Best Actress (Comedy or Musical)
Gwyneth Paltrow for SHAKESPEARE IN LOVE (US)
Dir John Madden
Best Actor (Comedy or Musical)
Michael Caine for LITTLE VOICE (UK/US)
Dir Mark Herman
Best Foreign Language Film
CENTRAL DO BRASIL (Brazil/France/Spain/Japan)
Dir Walter Salles
Best Supporting Actress
Lynn Redgrave for GODS AND MONSTERS (US/UK)
Dir Bill Condon
Best Supporting Actor
Ed Harris for The TRUMAN SHOW (US)
Dir Peter Weir
Best Director
Steven Spielberg for SAVING PRIVATE RYAN (US)
Best Screenplay
Marc Norman and Tom Stoppard for SHAKESPEARE IN
LOVE (US)
Dir John Madden
Best Original Score
Burkhard Dallwitz / additional music by Philip Glass for
The TRUMAN SHOW (US)
Dir Peter Weir
Best Original Song
David Foster and Carole Bayer Sager (Italian translation
Alberto Testa and Tony Renis) for "The Prayer",
QUEST FOR CAMELOT THE MAGIC SWORD (US)
Dir Frederick Du Chau
Cecil B. deMille Award
Jack Nicholson

TELEVISION
Best TV Series (Drama)
The PRACTICE (David E. Kelley/Twentieth Century-Fox
Film Corporation)
Best Actress (Drama Series)
Keri Russell for FELICITY (Imagine TV/Touchstone Television)
Best Actor (Drama Series)
Dylan McDermott for The PRACTICE (David E.
Kelley/Twentieth Century-Fox Film Corporation)
Best TV Series (Comedy or Musical)
ALLY McBEAL (David E. Kelley Productions/20th
Century Fox TV)
Best Actress (Musical or Comedy Series)
Jenna Elfman for DHARMA AND GREG
(Chuck Lorre/4 to 6 Productions/Fox Broadcasting Company)

Best Actor (Musical or Comedy Series)
Michael J. Fox for SPIN CITY (UBU Productions/Lottery Hill/Dreamworks SKG)
Best Mini-Series or TV Movie
FROM THE EARTH TO THE MOON (HBO/Clavius Base/Imagine Entertainment)
Best Actress (Mini-Series or TV Movie)
Angelina Jolie for GIA (Marvin Worth Productions/Citadel Entertainment/Kahn Power Pictures)
Best Actor (Mini-Series or TV Movie)
Stanley Tucci for WINCHELL (Fried Films/HBO Pictures)
Best Supporting Actress (Series, Mini-Series or TV Movie)
Camryn Manheim for The PRACTICE (David E. Kelley/Twentieth Century-Fox Film Corporation) and Faye Dunaway for GIA (Marvin Worth Productions/Citadel Entertainment/Kahn Power Pictures)
Best Supporting Actor (Series, Mini-Series or TV Movie)
Don Cheadle for The RAT PACK (HBO Pictures/Moritz Original) and Gregory Peck for MOBY DICK (Whale Productions/Southern Whale/Nine Network/UK-Australian Co-Productions/USA Pictures)

39th GOLDEN ROSE OF MONTREUX
22 April 1999, Montreux
Television Suisse Romande
Quai E Anserment 20
CP 234/1211 Geneva 8, Switzerland
Tel: (41) 22 708 85 99
Web site: www.rosedor.ch

Golden Rose
The LEAGUE OF GENTLEMEN (BBC2)
Silver Rose (Comedy)
FIKTIV (Prime Productions)
Bronze Rose (Comedy)
BIG TRAIN (Talkback for BBC2)
Comedy Special Mention
VENTIL (SF/DRS) (Switzerland) and SPANK! (Omer Productions) (Isr)
Silver Rose (Sitcom)
FATHER TED (Hat Trick Productions for Channel 4)
Bronze Rose (Sitcom)
THIRD ROCK FROM THE SUN (Carsey-Werner Productions) (US)
Sitcom Special Mention
KISS ME KATE (BBC1) and IN EXILE (Assembly Film & Television) (Isr)
Silver Rose (Music)
NOBODY DOES IT BETTER: THE MUSIC OF JAMES BOND (NVC Arts for Channel 4)
Silver Rose (Variety)
WHATEVER YOU WANT (Hat Trick Productions for BBC1)
Bronze Rose (Variety)
DIVA AND THE MAESTRO (The Multimedia Group of Canada) (CA)
Silver Rose (Game Shows)
WHO WANTS TO BE A MILLIONAIRE? (Celador Productions for ITV)
Bronze Rose (Game Shows)
BRING ME THE HEAD OF LIGHT ENTERTAINMENT (Anglia Television/United Film and Television Productions for Channel 5)
Special Prize of the City of Montreux
A HYMN FOR ALVIN ALLEY (Thirteen/WNET) (US)
Press Prize
DINNERLADIES (Good Fun/Pozzitive Television for BBC1)

GRIERSON AWARD 1998
25 March 1999, London
The Grierson Memorial Trust
37 Gower Street
London WC1E 6HH
Tel: 020 7580 1502

Best Documentary
INSIDE STORY: TONGUE TIED (BBC1 Dir Olivia Lichtenstein)
Jury Commendation
BORN IN THE USSR – 14UP (BBC1 Dir Sergei Miroshnichenko) and The NAZIS: A WARNING FROM HISTORY – THE ROAD TO TREBLINKA (BBC2 Dir Laurence Rees)
Special Award
Michael Apted

LONDON CRITICS' CIRCLE FILM AWARDS
Awarded at the Dorchester Hotel, London 1999

Director of the Year
Peter Weir for The TRUMAN SHOW (US)
Film of the Year
SAVING PRIVATE RYAN (US)
Dir Steven Spielberg
Foreign Language Fim of the Year
SHALL WE DANSU? (Japan)
Dir Masayuki Suo
Actress of the Year
Cate Blanchett for ELIZABETH (UK)
Dir Shekhar Kapur
Actor of the Year
Jack Nicholson for AS GOOD AS IT GETS (US)
Dir James L. Brooks
British Newcomer of the Year
Peter Mullan for MY NAME IS JOE (Germany/UK/France)
Dir Ken Loach
Screenwriter of the Year
Andrew Niccol for The TRUMAN SHOW (US)
Dir Peter Weir
British Film of the Year
LOCK, STOCK AND TWO SMOKING BARRELS (UK)
Dir Guy Ritchie
British Producer of the Year
Alison Owen, Tim Bevan and Eric Fellner for ELIZABETH (UK)
Dir Shekhar Kapur
British Screenwriter of the Year
Guy Ritchie for LOCK, STOCK AND TWO SMOKING BARRELS (UK)
Dir Guy Ritchie
British Actress of the Year
Helena Bonham Carter for WINGS OF THE DOVE (US/UK)
Dir Iain Softley
British Actor of the Year
Brendan Gleeson for The GENERAL (Ireland/UK)
Dir John Boorman
British Director of the Year
John Boorman for The GENERAL (Ireland/UK)
British Supporting Actress of the Year
Minnie Driver for GOOD WILL HUNTING (US)
Dir Gus Van Sant and Kate Beckinsale for The LAST DAYS OF DISCO (US)
Dir Whit Stillman

British Supporting Actor of the Year
Nigel Hawthorne for The OBJECT OF MY AFFECTION
(US)
Dir Nicholas Hytner
The Dilys Powell Award
Albert Finney and John Hurt
Lifetime Achievement Award
John Boorman and John Box

39th MONTE CARLO TELEVISION FESTIVAL

Held 18th-24th February 1999, Monte Carlo
4 Boulevard de Jardin Exotique
98000 Monte Carlo
Monaco
Tel: (37) 793 10 40 60
Website: www.tvfestival.com/

Special Prize of H.S.H. Prince Rainier III
OPERATION HVIDVASK (DR TV) (Denmark)
Prize of the Monaco Red Cross
L'ENFANT DES TERRES BLONDES (France 3)
(France)
AMADE & UNESCO Prize
L'ENFANT DES TERRES BLONDES (France 3) (France)
Prix Unda (Best Television Film)
Le BONHEUR D'AUTRUI (Télévision Polonaise)
(Poland)
European Producer Award
Telfrance (France) for its fiction productions over the last
2 years
FILMS FOR TV
Gold Nymph (Best Film)
L'ENFANT DES TERRES BLONDES (France 3) (France)
Silver Nymph (Best Script)
Shin-Ichi Ichikawa for YU-KON (Chubu-Nippon
Broadcasting Co) (Japan)
Silver Nymph (Best Direction)
Edouard Niermans for L'ENFANT DES TERRES
BLONDES (France 3) (France)
Silver Nymph (Best Actress)
Amanda Burton for The GIFT (Tetra Films for BBC1) (UK)
Silver Nymph (Best Actor)
Neil Dudgeon for The GIFT (Tetra Films for BBC1) (UK)
MINI-SERIES
Gold Nymph (Best Mini-Series)
OPERNBALL (Atlas International Film) (Germany)
Silver Nymph (Best Script)
Sandro Petraglia and Stefano Rulli for La VITA CHE
VERRA (Rai Due) (Italy)
Silver Nymph (Best Direction)
Urs Egger for OPERNBALL (Atlas International Film)
(Germany)
Silver Nymph (Best Actress)
Lena Mossegard for The WOMAN IN THE LOCKED
ROOM (Sveriges Television) (Sweden)
Silver Nymph (Best Actor)
Tony Doyle for AMONGST WOMEN (Parallel Film
Productions for BBC Northern Ireland) (UK)
Special Mention
VANITY FAIR (BBC1) (UK)
NEWS & CURRENT AFFAIRS PROGRAMMES
Gold Nymph
PROFESSION REPORTER: EMBARGO (TF1) (France)
Silver Nymph
Les HOMMES EN NOIR (Télévision Suisse Romande)
(Switzerland)

Silver Nymph
CORRESPONDENT SPECIAL: THE UNFINISHED
WAR (BBC2) (UK)
Silver Nymph
VILLAGE HEAD ELECTION (China Control TV)
(China)
Special Mention
Les CRAMPONS DE LA LIBERTE (Doc en Stock)
(France)

71st OSCARS – ACADEMY OF MOTION PICTURE ARTS AND SCIENCES

21st March 1999, Los Angeles
AMPAS
8949 Wilshire Blvd
Beverly Hills
California 90211
Tel: (1) 310 247 3000
Website: www.oscars.org/awards

Best Film
SHAKESPEARE IN LOVE (US)
Dir John Madden
Best Director
Steven Spielberg for SAVING PRIVATE RYAN (US)
Best Original Screenplay
Marc Norman and Tom Stoppard for
SHAKESPEARE IN LOVE (US)
Dir John Madden
Best Screenplay Adaptation
Bill Condon for GODS AND MONSTERS (US/UK)
Dir Bill Condon
Best Actress
Gwyneth Paltrow for SHAKESPEARE IN LOVE (US)
Dir John Madden
Best Actor
Roberto Benigni for La VITA È BELLA (Italy)
Dir Roberto Benigni
Best Supporting Actress
Judi Dench for SHAKESPEARE IN LOVE (US)
Dir John Madden
Best Supporting Actor
James Coburn for AFFLICTION (US)
Dir Paul Schrader
Best Cinematography
Janusz Kaminski for SAVING PRIVATE RYAN (US)
Dir Steven Spielberg
Best Original Song
Stephen Schwartz for "When You Believe"
The PRINCE OF EGYPT (US)
Dir Brenda Chapman
Best Costume Design
Sandy Powell for
SHAKESPEARE IN LOVE (US)
Dir John Madden
Best Make-Up
Jenny Shircore for ELIZABETH (UK)
Dir Shekhar Kapur
Best Art Direction
Martin Childs and Jill Quertier for
SHAKESPEARE IN LOVE (US)
Dir John Madden
Life Achievement Award
Elia Kazan
Best Documentary Feature
The LAST DAYS (US)
Dir Jim Moll

Best Documentary Short
The PERSONALS: IMPROVISATIONS ON ROMANCE
IN THE GOLDEN YEARS (US)
Dir Keiko Ibi
Best Visual Effects
Joel Hynek, Nicholas Brooks, Stuart Robertson and Kevin
Mack for WHAT DREAMS MAY COME (US/NZ)
Dir Vincent Ward
The Irving G. Thalberg Award
Norman Jewison
Best Editing
Michael Kahn for SAVING PRIVATE RYAN (US)
Dir Steven Spielberg
Best Original Dramatic Score
Nicola Piovani for La VITA È BELLA (Italy)
Dir Roberto Benigni
Best Original Musical or Comedy Score
Stephen Warbeck for SHAKESPEARE IN LOVE (US)
Dir John Madden
Best Foreign Language Film
La VITA È BELLA (Italy)
Dir Roberto Benigni
Best Sound
Gary Rydstrom, Gary Summers, Andy Nelson and Ronald
Judkins for SAVING PRIVATE RYAN (US)
Dir Steven Spielberg
Best Sound Effects Editing
Gary Rydstrom and Richard Hymns for SAVING
PRIVATE RYAN (US)
Dir Steven Spielberg
Best Short Film (Animated)
BUNNY (US)
Dir Chris Wedge
Best Short Film (Live Action)
ELECTION NIGHT (Denmark) Dir Anders Thomas Jensen

ROYAL TELEVISION SOCIETY AWARDS
100 Gray's Inn Road
London WC1X 8AL
Tel: 020 7430 1000
Website: www.rts.org.uk/

RTS PROGRAMME AWARDS
Awarded in London 29th March 1999

Single Drama
A RATHER ENGLISH MARRIAGE
(Wall to Wall Television for BBC2)
Drama Series
JONATHAN CREEK (BBC Production for BBC1)
Drama Serial
A YOUNG PERSON'S GUIDE TO BECOMING A
ROCK STAR (Company TV for Channel 4)
Team
GOODNESS GRACIOUS ME
(BBC Production for BBC2)
Network Newcomer (Behind the Screen)
Damien O'Donnell for THIRTY FIVE ASIDE
(Clingfilm Productions for BBC2)
Network Newcomer (On Screen)
Tony Maudsley for A LIFE FOR A LIFE
(Celtic/Picture Palace for ITV)
Best Actress
Thora Hird for TALKING HEADS: WAITING FOR THE
TELEGRAM (Slow Motion for BBC2)
Best Actor
Ray Winstone for OUR BOY (Wall to Wall Television for BBC1)

Regional Programme
A LIGHT IN THE VALLEY (BBC Wales)
Regional Documentary
PUT TO THE TEST
(Brian Waddell Productions for BBC Northern Ireland)
Regional Presenter
Noel Thompson (BBC Northern Ireland)
Presenter
David Attenborough for LIFE OF BIRDS
(BBC Production for BBC1)
Television Performance
Rory Bremner for RORY BREMNER WHO ELSE?
(Vera Productions for Channel 4)
Writer's Award
Peter Berry for A LIFE FOR A LIFE
(Celtic/Picture Palace for ITV)
Entertainment
WHO WANTS TO BE A MILLIONAIRE?
(Celador Productions for ITV)
Situation Comedy and Comedy Drama
COLD FEET (Granada Television)
Children's Drama
MICROSOAP
(BBC Production/Buena Vista Productions for BBC1)
Children's Entertainment
The FIRST SNOW OF WINTER
(Hibbert Ralph Entertainment for BBC1)
Children's Factual
The FAME GAME (BBC Scotland for BBC1)
Documentary Series
WINDRUSH (BBC Production for BBC2)
Documentary Strand
The NATURAL WORLD (BBC Production for BBC2)
Single Documentary
MODERN TIMES:
DRINKING FOR ENGLAND (Century Films for BBC2)
Features (Prime Time)
TIME TEAM (Videotext/Picture House for Channel 4)
Features (Daytime)
CITY HOSPITAL (Topical Television for BBC1)
Arts
CLOSE UP: THIS ENGLAND
(BBC Production for BBC2)
Special Award
FATHER TED (Hat Trick Productions for Channel 4)

RTS EDUCATIONAL AWARDS
Awarded in London on 15th April 1999

SCHOOLS TELEVISION
Pre-School & Infants
RAT-A-TAT-TAT – WINNIE THE WITCH
(Open Mind Productions for Channel 4)
Primary (Arts)
MUSIC MAKERS: PROFESSOR ALLEGRO – IN THE
FIELDS (BBC Education)
Primary (Humanities)
ALL ABOUT US – KARL'S STORY
(Television Junction for Channel 4)
Primary (Science)
STAGE TWO SCIENCE – ACTION FORCES –
PUSHING AND PULLING
(Scottish Television for Channel 4)
Secondary (Arts)
SPORTSBANK DANCE TV DANCE ATHLETES
(BBC Education)
Secondary (Humanities)
TURNING POINTS:

EMMA'S STORY (BBC Education)
Secondary (Science)
SHORT CIRCUIT:
BLOOD (BBC Education)
ADULT EDUCATIONAL TELEVISION
Education and Training
STUDENT CHOICE '98
(Wobbly Picture Productions for BBC Education)
Personal Education
SMASHED – ALCOHOL SEASON – LAST ORDERS
(Evans Woolfe for Channel 4)
General
The DROP DEAD SHOW
(Granada Production for Channel 4)
Campaigns and Seasons
COMPUTERS DON'T BITE (BBC Education)
RTS/NIACE
The DROP DEAD SHOW
(Granada Production for Channel 4)
Multimedia Award
Dynamo Website
(www.bbc.co.uk/education/parents/dynamo/) (BBC
Education)

RTS TELEVISION SPORTS AWARDS
Awarded in London 29th April 1999

Live Outside Broadcast Coverage of the Year
The FIRST DIVISION PLAY-OFF (Sky Sports)
Sports Documentary
The MAN WHO JUMPED TO EARTH
(BBC Wales for BBC1)
Sports News
NEWS AT TEN – WORLD CUP TROUBLE
(ITN News on ITV)
Sports Commentator
Clive Tyldesley (ITV Sport)
Sports Presenter
Desmond Lynam (BBC Sport)
Sports Pundit
Martin Brundle
Regional Sports Documentary
BRED FOR THE RED:
HOME TRUTHS (BBC Northern Ireland)
Regional Sports Programme (Actuality)
GOODWOOD HISTORIC RACING
(Meridian Broadcasting)
Regional Sports Programme (Entertainment)
EXTREME (Westcountry Television)
Regional Sports Presenter or Commentator
Hazel Irvine (BBC Scotland)
Regional Sports News
MERIDIAN TONIGHT (Meridian Broadcasting)
Newcomer
Guy Mowbray (Eurosport)
Sports Innovation
CHELTENHAM – WIRE CAM (Channel 4)
Sports Programme of the Year (Entertainment)
A QUESTION OF SPORT (BBC Production for BBC1)
Television Sports Award of the Year
Sky Sports Football Production Team
Judges Award
Jimmy Hill

RTS JOURNALISM AWARDS
Awarded in London 11th May 1999

News Award (International)
NINE O'CLOCK NEWS – The Massacre at Drenica
(BBC News)
News Award (Home)
GMTV – Drumcree
Portadown Divided (GMTV/Reuters for ITV)
Regional Daily News Magazine
LONDON TONIGHT (London News Network)
Television Technician of the Year
Nikki Millard (BBC News)
Interview of the Year
Dermot Murnaghan (interview of Peter Mandelson)
(ITN News on ITV)
Regional Current Affairs
The GHOST OF PIPER ALPHA (TV6 for BBC Scotland)
Current Affairs (International)
The SERBS LAST STAND (BBC2)
Current Affairs (Home)
DISPATCHES: INSIDE THE ALF
(David Monaghan Productions)
Television Journalist of the Year
David Loyn (BBC News)
Young Journalist of the Year
Peter Lane (5 News ITN)
Programme of the Year
NEWS AT TEN (ITN News on ITV)
Judges' Award
WORLD IN ACTION (Granada Television for ITV)

British Successes in the Academy Awards 1927–1998

The following list chronicles British successes in the Academy Awards. It includes individuals who were either born, and lived and worked, in Britain into their adult lives, or those who were not born here but took on citizenship.
Compiled by Erinna Mettler

1927/28 (1st) held in 1930

Charles Chaplin – Special Award (acting, producing, directing and writing):
THE CIRCUS

1928/29 (2nd) held in 1930

Frank Lloyd – Best Direction:
THE DIVINE LADY

1929/30 (3rd) held in 1930

George Arliss – Best Actor:
THE GREEN GODDESS

1932/33 (6th) held in 1934

William S. Darling – Best Art Direction:
CAVALCADE
Charles Laughton – Best Actor:
THE PRIVATE LIFE OF HENRY VIII
Frank Lloyd – Best Direction:
CAVALCADE

1935 (8th) held in 1936

Gaumont British Studios – Best Short Subject:
WINGS OVER MT. EVEREST
Victor Mclaglen – Best Actor:
THE INFORMER

1938 (11th) held in 1939

Ian Dalrymple, Cecil Lewis & W.P. Lipscomb – Best Screenplay:
PYGMALION

1939 (12th) held in 1940

Robert Donat – Best Actor:
GOODBYE MR. CHIPS
Vivien Leigh – Best Actress:
GONE WITH THE WIND

1940 (13th) held in 1941

Lawrence Butler & Jack Whitney – Special Visual Effects:
THE THIEF OF BAGDAD
Vincent Korda – Best Colour Set Design:
THE THIEF OF BAGDAD

1941 (14th) held in 1942

British Ministry of Information – Honorary Award:
TARGET FOR TONIGHT
Donald Crisp – Best Supporting Actor:
HOW GREEN WAS MY VALLEY
Joan Fontaine – Best Actress:
SUSPICION
Jack Whitney & The General Studios Sound Department – Best Sound:
THAT HAMILTON WOMAN

1942 (15th) held in 1943

Noel Coward – Special Award:
IN WHICH WE SERVE
Greer Garson – Best Actress:
MRS. MINIVER

1943 (16th) held in 1944

British Ministry of Information – Best Documentary:
DESERT VICTORY
William S. Darling – Best Art Direction:
THE SONG OF BERNADETTE

1945 (18th) held in 1946

The Governments of the United States & Great Britain – Best Documentary:
THE TRUE GLORY
Ray Milland – Best Actor:
THE LOST WEEKEND
Harry Stradling – Best Cinematography (b/w):
THE PICTURE OF DORIAN GRAY

1946 (19th) held in 1947

Muriel & Sydney Box – Best Original Screenplay:
THE SEVENTH VEIL
Clemence Dane – Best Original Story:
VACATION FROM MARRIAGE
Olivia de Havilland – Best Actress:
TO EACH HIS OWN
Laurence Olivier – Special Award:
HENRY V
Thomas Howard – Best Special Effects:
BLITHE SPIRIT
William S. Darling – Best Art Direction (b/w):
Anna And the King Of Siam

1947 (20th) held in 1948

John Bryan – Best Art Direction:
GREAT EXPECTATIONS
Jack Cardiff – Best Cinematography (col):
BLACK NARCISSUS
Ronald Colman – Best Actor:
A DOUBLE LIFE
Guy Green – Best Cinematography (b/w):
GREAT EXPECTATIONS
Edmund Gwen – Best Supporting Actor:
MIRACLE ON 34TH STREET

1948 (21st) held in 1949

Carmen Dillon & Roger Furse – Best Art Direction
(b/w):
HAMLET
Brian Easdale – Best Score:
THE RED SHOES
Roger Furse – Best Costume Design:
HAMLET
Laurence Olivier – Best Picture:
HAMLET
Laurence Olivier – Best Actor:
HAMLET

1949 (22nd) held in 1950

British Information Services – Best Documentary:
DAYBREAK IN UDI
Olivia de Havilland – Best Actress:
THE HEIRESS

1950 (23rd) held in 1951

George Sanders – Best Supporting Actor:
ALL ABOUT EVE

1951 (24th) held in 1952

James Bernard & Paul Dehn – Best Motion Picture Story:
SEVEN DAYS TO NOON
Vivien Leigh – Best Actress:
A STREETCAR NAMED DESIRE

1952 (25th) held in 1953

T.E.B. Clarke – Best Story & Screenplay:
THE LAVENDER HILL MOB
London Films Sound Dept. – Best Sound:
THE SOUND BARRIER

1954 (26th) held in 1954

British Information Services – Best Documentary
Short Subject:
THURSDAY'S CHILDREN
S. Tyne Jule – Best Song:
THREE COINS IN THE FOUNTAIN
Jon Whitely & Vincent Winter – Special Award (Best
Juvenile Performances):
THE KIDNAPPERS

1956 (29th) held in 1957

George K. Arthur – Best Short Subject:
THE BESPOKE OVERCOAT

1957 (30th) held in 1958

Malcolm Arnold – Best Musical Score:
THE BRIDGE ON THE RIVER KWAI
Alec Guinness – Best Actor:
THE BRIDGE ON THE RIVER KWAI
Jack Hildyard – Best Cinematography:
THE BRIDGE ON THE RIVER KWAI
David Lean – Best Director:
THE BRIDGE ON THE RIVER KWAI
Pete Taylor – Best Editing:
THE BRIDGE ON THE RIVER KWAI

1958 (31st) held in 1959

Cecil Beaton – Best Costumes:
GIGI
Wendy Hiller – Best Supporting Actress:
SEPARATE TABLES
Thomas Howard – Special Visual Effects:
TOM THUMB
David Niven – Best Actor:
SEPARATE TABLES

1959 (32nd) held in 1960

Hugh Griffith – Best Supporting Actor:
BEN HUR
Elizabeth Haffenden – Best Costume Design (col.):
BEN HUR

1960 (33rd) held in 1961

Freddie Francis – Best Cinematography (b/w):
SONS & LOVERS
James Hill – Best Documentary:
GIUSEPPINA
Hayley Mills – Special Award (Best Juvenile
Performance):
POLLYANNA
Peter Ustinov – Best Supporting Actor:
SPARTACUS

1961 (34th) held in 1962

Vivian C. Greenham – Best Visual Effects:
THE GUNS OF NAVARONE

1962 (35th) held in 1963

John Box & John Stoll – Best Art Direction:
LAWRENCE OF ARABIA
Anne V. Coates – Best Editing:
LAWRENCE OF ARABIA
Jack Howells (Janus Films) – Best Documentary:
DYLAN THOMAS
David Lean – Best Director:
LAWRENCE OF ARABIA

Shepperton Studios Sound Dept. (John Cox Sound Director) – Best Sound:
LAWRENCE OF ARABIA
Freddie Young – Best Cinematography:
LAWRENCE OF ARABIA

1963 (36th) held in 1964

John Addison – Best Score:
TOM JONES
John Osborne – Best Adapted Screenplay:
TOM JONES
Tony Richardson – Best Director:
TOM JONES
Tony Richardson (Woodfall Films) – Best Picture:
TOM JONES
Margaret Rutherford – Best Supporting Actress:
THE V.I.P.S

1964 (37th) held in 1965

Julie Andrews – Best Actress:
MARY POPPINS
Cecil Beaton – Best Art Direction (col):
MY FAIR LADY
Cecil Beaton – Best Costume Design (col):
MY FAIR LADY
Rex Harrison – Best Actor:
MY FAIR LADY
Walter Lassally – Best Cinematography (b/w):
ZORBA THE GREEK
Harry Stradling – Best Cinematography (col):
MY FAIR LADY
Peter Ustinov – Best Supporting Actor:
TOPKAPI
Norman Wanstall – Best Sound Effects:
GOLDFINGER

1965 (38th) held in 1966

Julie Christie – Best Actress
DARLING
Robert Bolt – Adapted Screenplay
DOCTOR ZHIVAGO
Frederic Raphael – Original Screenplay
DARLING
Freddie Young – Colour Cinematography
DOCTOR ZHIVAGO
John Box, Terence Marsh – Best Art Direction (colour)
DOCTOR ZHIVAGO
Julie Harris – Costume (b/w)
DARLING
Phyllis Dalton – Costume (col)
DOCTOR ZHIVAGO
John Stears – Special Visual Effects
THUNDERBALL

1966 (39th) held in 1967

John Barry – Best Original Score:
BORN FREE
John Barry & Don Black – Best Song:
BORN FREE
Robert Bolt – Best Adapted Screenplay:
A MAN FOR ALL SEASONS

Joan Bridge & Elizabeth Haffenden – Best Costume (col):
A MAN FOR ALL SEASONS
Gordon Daniel – Best Sound:
GRAND PRIX
Ted Moore – Best Cinematography (col):
A MAN FOR ALL SEASONS
Ken Thorne – Best Adapted Score:
A FUNNY THING HAPPENED ON THE WAY TO THE FORUM
Peter Watkins – Best Documentary Feature:
THE WAR GAME

1967 (40th) held in 1968

Leslie Bricusse – Best Song:
DOCTOR DOLITTLE (TALK TO THE ANIMALS)
Alfred Hitchcock – Irving Thalberg Memorial Award
John Poyner – Best Sound Effects:
THE DIRTY DOZEN

1968 (41st) held in 1969

John Barry – Best Original Score:
THE LION IN WINTER
Vernon Dixon & Ken Muggleston – Best Art Direction:
OLIVER!
Carol Reed – Best Director:
OLIVER!
Shepperton Sound Studio – Best Sound:
OLIVER!
Charles D. Staffell – Scientific, Class I Statuett –
for the development of a successful embodiement of the reflex background projection system for composite cinematography
John Woolf – Best Picture:
OLIVER!

1969 (42nd) held in 1970

Margaret Furfe – Best Costume:
ANNE OF THE THOUSAND DAYS
Cary Grant – Honorary Award
John Schlesinger – Best Director:
MIDNIGHT COWBOY
Maggie Smith – Best Actress:
THE PRIME OF MISS JEAN BRODIE

1970 (43rd) held in 1971

The Beatles – Best Original Score:
LET IT BE
Glenda Jackson – Best Actress:
WOMEN IN LOVE
John Mills – Best Supporting Actor:
RYAN'S DAUGHTER
Freddie Young – Best Cinematography:
RYAN'S DAUGHTER

1971 (44th) held in 1972

Robert Amram – Best Short:
SENTINELS OF SILENCE

Ernest Archer, John Box, Vernon Dixon & Jack
Maxsted – Best Art Direction:
NICHOLAS & ALEXANDRA
Charles Chaplin – Honorary Award
David Hildyard & Gordon K. McCallum – Best Sound:
FIDDLER ON THE ROOF
Oswald Morris – Best Cinematography:
FIDDLER ON THE ROOF

1972 (45th) held in 1973

Charles Chaplin – Best Original Score:
LIMELIGHT
David Hildyard – Best Sound:
CABARET
Anthony Powell – Best Costume Design:
TRAVELS WITH MY AUNT
Geoffrey Unsworth – Best Cinematography:
CABARET

1973 (46th) held in 1974

Glenda Jackson – Best Actress:
A TOUCH OF CLASS

1974 (47th) held in 1975

Albert Whitlock – Special Achievement In Visual
Effects:
EARTHQUAKE

1975 (48th) held in 1976

Ben Adam, Vernon Dixon & Roy Walker – Best Art
Direction:
BARRY LYNDON
John Alcott – Best Cinematography:
BARRY LYNDON
Bob Godfrey – Best Animated Short:
GREAT
Albert Whitlock – Special Achievement In Visual
Effects:
THE HINDENBERG

1976 (49th) held in 1977

Peter Finch – Best Actor:
NETWORK

1977 (50th) held in 1978

John Barry, Roger Christians & Leslie Dilley – Best
Art Direction:
STAR WARS
John Mollo – Best Costume Design:
STAR WARS
Vanessa Redgrave – Best Supporting Actress:
JULIA
John Stears – Best Visual Effects:
STAR WARS

1978 (51st) held in 1979

Les Bowie, Colin Chilvers, Denys Coop, Roy Field &
Derek Meddings – Special Achievement In Visual
Effects:
SUPERMAN
Michael Deeley, John Peverall & Barry Spikings – Best
Picture:
THE DEER HUNTER
Laurence Oilvier – Lifetime Achievement Award
Anthony Powell – Best Costume Design:
DEATH ON THE NILE
Maggie Smith – Best Supporting Actress:
CALIFORNIA SUITE

1979 (52nd) held in 1980

Nick Allder, Denis Ayling & Brian Johnson – Special
Achievement In Visual Effects:
ALIEN
Alec Guinness – Honorary Award
Tony Walton – Best Art Direction:
ALL THAT JAZZ

1980 (53rd) held in 1981

Brian Johnson – Special Achievement In Visual Effects:
THE EMPIRE STRIKES BACK
Lloyd Phillips – Best Live Action Short:
THE DOLLAR BOTTOM
Anthony Powell – Best Costume Design:
TESS
David W. Samuelson – Scientific and Engineering
Award –
for the engineering and development of the Louma
Camera Crane and remote control system for motion
picture production
Jack Stevens – Best Art Direction:
TESS
Geoffrey Unsworth – Best Cinematography:
TESS

1981 (54th) held in 1982

Leslie Dilley & Michael Ford – Best Art Direction:
RAIDERS OF THE LOST ARK
John Gielgud – Best Supporting Actor:
ARTHUR
Nigel Nobel – Best Documentary Short:
CLOSE HARMONY
David Puttnam – Best Picture:
CHARIOTS OF FIRE
Arnold Schwartzman – Best Documentary Feature:
CLOSE HARMONY
Colin Welland – Best Original Screenplay:
CHARIOTS OF FIRE
Kit West – Special Achievement In Visual Effects:
RAIDERS OF THE LOST ARK

1982 (55th) held in 1983

Richard Attenborough – Best Picture:
GANDHI
Richard Attenborough – Best Director:
GANDHI

John Briley – Best Original Screenplay:
GANDHI
Stuart Craig, Bob Laing & Michael Seirton – Best Art
Direction:
GANDHI
Ben Kingsley – Best Actor:
GANDHI
John Mollo – Best Costume Design:
GANDHI
Sarah Monzani – Best Achievement In Make Up:
QUEST FOR FIRE
Colin Mossman & Rank Laboratories – Scientific and
Engineering Award -
for the engineering and implementation of a 4,000
meter printing system for motion picture laboratories
Christine Oestreicher – Best Live Action Short:
A SHOCKING ACCIDENT
Ronnie Taylor & Billy Williams – Best Cinematography:
GANDHI

1983 (56th) held in 1984

Gerald L. Turpin (Lightflex International) – Scientific
And Engineering Award
- for the design, engineering and development of an on-
camera device providing contrast control, sourceless
fill light and special effects for motion picture
photography

1984 (57th) held in 1985

Peggy Ashcroft – Best Supporting Actress:
A PASSAGE TO INDIA
Jim Clark – Best Editing:
THE KILLING FIELDS
George Gibbs – Special Achievement In Visual Effects:
INDIANA JONES AND THE TEMPLE OF DOOM
Chris Menges – Best Cinematography:
THE KILLING FIELDS
Peter Shaffer – Best Adapted Screenplay:
AMADEUS

1985 (58th) held in 1986

John Barry – Best Original Score:
OUT OF AFRICA
Stephen Grimes – Best Art Direction:
OUT OF AFRICA
David Watkin – Best Cinematography:
OUT OF AFRICA

1986 (59th) held in 1987

Brian Ackland-Snow & Brian Saregar – Best Art
Direction:
A ROOM WITH A VIEW
Jenny Beavan & John Bright – Best Costume Design:
A ROOM WITH A VIEW
Michael Caine – Best Supporting Actor:
HANNAH & HER SISTERS
Simon Kaye – Best Sound:
PLATOON
Lee Electric Lighting Ltd. – Technical Achievement
Award
Chris Menges – Best Cinematography:

THE MISSION
Peter D. Parks – Technical Achievement Award
William B. Pollard & David W. Samuelson – Technical
Achievement Award
John Richardson – Special Achievement In Visual
Effects:
ALIENS
Claire Simpson – Best Editing:
PLATOON
Don Sharpe – Best Sound Effects Editing:
ALIENS
Vivienne Verdon-Roe – Best Documentary Short:
WOMEN – FOR AMERICA, FOR THE WORLD

1987 (60th) held in 1988

James Acheson – Best Costume Design:
THE LAST EMPEROR
Sean Connery – Best Supporting Actor:
THE UNTOUCHABLES
Mark Peploe – Best Adapted Screenplay:
THE LAST EMPEROR
Ivan Sharrock – Best Sound:
THE LAST EMPEROR
Jeremy Thomas – Best Picture:
THE LAST EMPEROR

1988 (61st) held in 1989

James Acheson – Best Costume Design:
DANGEROUS LIAISONS
George Gibbs – Special Achievement In Visual Effects:
WHO FRAMED ROGER RABBIT
Christopher Hampton – Best Adapted Screenplay:
DANGEROUS LIAISONS

1989 (62nd) held in 1990

Phyllis Dalton – Best Costume:
HENRY V
Daniel Day-Lewis – Best Actor:
MY LEFT FOOT
Freddie Francis – Best Cinematography:
GLORY
Brenda Fricker – Best Supporting Actress:
MY LEFT FOOT
Anton Furst – Best Art Direction:
BATMAN
Richard Hymns – Best Sound Effects Editing:
INDIANA JONES AND THE LAST CRUSADE
Jessica Tandy – Best Actress:
DRIVING MISS DAISY
James Hendrie – Best Live Action Short:
WORK EXPERIENCE

1990 (63rd) held in 1991

John Barry – Best Original Score:
DANCES WITH WOLVES
Jeremy Irons – Best Actor:
REVERSAL OF FORTUNE
Nick Park – Best Animated Short:
CREATURE COMFORTS

1991 (64th) held in 1992

Daniel Greaves – Best Animated Short:
MANIPULATION
Anthony Hopkins – Best Actor:
SILENCE OF THE LAMBS

1992 (65th) held in 1993

Simon Kaye – Best Sound:
THE LAST OF THE MOHICANS
Tim Rice – Best Original Song:
ALADDIN (A WHOLE NEW WORLD)
Emma Thompson – Best Actress:
HOWARDS END
Ian Whittaker – Best Art Direction:
HOWARDS END

1993 (66th) held in 1994

Richard Hymns – Best Sound Effects Editing:
JURASSIC PARK
Nick Park – Best Animated Short:
THE WRONG TROUSERS
Deborah Kerr – Career Achievement Honorary Award

1994 (67th) held in 1995

Ken Adam & Carolyn Scott – Best Art Direction:
THE MADNESS OF KING GEORGE
Peter Capaldi & Ruth Kenley-Letts – Best Live Action Short:
FRANZ KAFKA'S IT'S A WONDERFUL LIFE
Elton John & Tim Rice – Best Song:
THE LION KING (CAN YOU FEEL THE LOVE TONIGHT)
Alison Snowden & David Fine -Best Animated Short:
BOB'S BIRTHDAY

1995 (68th) held in 1996

James Acheson – Best Costume Design:
RESTORATION
Jon Blair – Best Documentary Feature:
ANNE FRANK REMEMBERED
Lois Burwell & Peter Frampton – Special Achievement In Make Up:
BRAVEHEART
Emma Thompson – Best Adapted Screenplay:
SENSE & SENSIBILITY
Nick Park – Best Animated Short:
A CLOSE SHAVE

1996 (69th) held in 1997

Anthony Minghella – Best Director:
THE ENGLISH PATIENT
Rachel Portman – Best Original Score Musical or Comedy:
EMMA
Tim Rice & Andrew Lloyd Webber – Best Original song:
EVITA (YOU MUST LOVE ME)
Stuart Craig & Stephanie McMillan – Best Art Direction:
THE ENGLISH PATIENT

1997 (70th) held in 1998

Peter Lamont and Michael Ford – Best Achievement In Art Direction:
TITANIC
Anne Dudley – Best Original Score Musical or Comedy:
THE FULL MONTY
Jan Pinkava – Best Animated Short:
GERI'S GAME

1998 (70th) held in 1999

David Parfitt – Best Film
SHAKESPEARE IN LOVE
Judi Dench – Best Actress in a Supporting Role
SHAKESPEARE IN LOVE
Tom Stoppard – Best Original Screenplay
SHAKESPEARE IN LOVE
Martin Childs and Jill Quertier Best Art Direction
SHAKESPEARE IN LOVE
Sandy Powell – Best Costume Design
SHAKESPEARE IN LOVE
Jenny Shircore – Best Make-up
ELIZABETH
Stephen Warbeck – Best Original Score Musical or Comedy
SHAKESPEARE IN LOVE
Andy Nelson – Best Sound
SAVING PRIVATE RYAN

BOOKS

Below is a selective list of books, in the English language, published in 1998 on the subject of film and television, all of which can be found at the BFI National Library. An ISBN has been provided where known. Compiled by Anastasia Kerameos

ADAMAH: A VANISHED FILM TRYSTER
Hillel (ed.)
Jerusalem: Steven Spielberg Jewish Film Archive.

ADVANCED STUDIES IN MEDIA
NICHOLAS
Joe; PRICE, John
Walton-on-Thames: Nelson.
ISBN 0174900473

ADVENTURES IN A TV NATION
MOORE
Michael; GLYNN, Kathleen
New York: Harper Perennial.
ISBN 0060988096

THE ADVENTURES OF ROBERTO ROSSELLINI
GALLAGHER
Tag
New York: Da Capo Press.
ISBN 0306808730

THE AESTHETICS AND PSYCHOLOGY OF THE CINEMA MITRY
Jean KING, Christopher (translator)
London: Athlone Press.
ISBN 0485300842

Series: French film directors
AGNÈS VARDA
SMITH, Alison
Manchester: Manchester University Press.
ISBN 0719050618

ALAN CLARKE
KELLY, Richard (ed.)
London: Faber and Faber.
ISBN 0571196098

Series: Contemporary film and television series
ALEXANDER KLUGE: THE LAST MODERNIST

LUTZE, Peter C.
Detroit, MI: Wayne State University Press.
ISBN 0814326560

Series: Bloomsbury movie guides; no. 4
THE ALIEN QUARTET: THE ULTIMATE A-Z
THOMSON, David
London: Bloomsbury.
ISBN 0747538034

Series: Bibliographies and indexes in the performing arts, no. 22
AMERICAN FILM CYCLES: THE SILENT ERA
LANGMAN, Larry
Westport, CT; London: Greenwood Press.
ISBN 0313306575

AMERICAN SCIENCE FICTION TELEVISION SERIES OF THE 1950S: EPISODE GUIDES AND CASTS AND CREDITS FOR TWENTY SHOWS
LUCANIO, Patrick; COLVILLE, Gary
Jefferson, NC; London: McFarland.
ISBN 0786404345

AMERICAN TELEVISION ABROAD: HOLLYWOOD'S ATTEMPT TO DOMINATE WORLD TELEVISION
SEGRAVE, Kerry
Jefferson, NC; London: McFarland & Company.
ISBN 0786405821

Series: Cinema & history
AMISTAD
GOLD, Claudia; WALL, Ian
London: Film Education.

ANALYSING MUSICAL MULTIMEDIA
COOK, Nicholas
Oxford: Clarendon Press.
ISBN 0198165897

ANATOMY OF FILM (3rd ed.)
DICK, Bernard F.
New York: St. Martin's Press.
ISBN 0312153996

AND THE MIRROR CRACKED: FEMINIST CINEMA AND FILM

THEORY
SMELIK, Anneke
London: Macmillan.
ISBN 0333693248

Series: Cinetek series
ANTÔNIO DAS MORTES
JOHNSON, Randal
Trowbridge, Wilts: Flicks Books.
ISBN 0948911107

Series: Faber classic screenplays
THE APARTMENT
WILDER, Billy; DIAMOND, I.A.L.
London: Faber and Faber.
ISBN 0571194095

Series: Bloomsbury movie guides, no. 1
APOCALYPSE NOW: THE ULTIMATE A-Z
FRENCH, Karl
London: Bloomsbury.
ISBN 0747538042

APPROACHES TO MEDIA DISCOURSE
BELL, Allan; GARRETT, Peter (eds.)
Oxford: Blackwell.
ISBN 0631198881

ARAB CINEMA: HISTORY AND CULTURAL IDENTITY
SHAFIK, Viola
Cairo: American University in Cairo Press.
ISBN 9774244753

ARE WE THERE YET?: THE SIMPSONS: GUIDE TO SPRINGFIELD
GIMPLE, Scott M.
MORRISON, Bill (ed.)
London: Boxtree.
ISBN 0752224034

ARE YOU BEING SERVED?: A CELEBRATION OF TWENTY-FIVE YEARS
WEBBER, Richard; CROFT, David; LLOYD, Jeremy
London: Orion.
ISBN 0752817957

ART DIRECTORS IN CINEMA: A WORLDWIDE BIOGRAPHICAL DICTIONARY
STEPHENS, Michael L.

Jefferson, NC; London: McFarland & Company.
ISBN 0786403128

ART IN MOTION: ANIMATION AESTHETICS
FURNISS, Maureen
Sydney: John Libbey & Co.
ISBN 1864620390

ARTIST UNKNOWN: AN ALTERNATIVE HISTORY OF THE ARTS COUNCIL
WITTS, Richard
London: Little, Brown.
ISBN 0316878200

THE ART OF MULAN
KURTTI, Jeff
New York: Hyperion.
ISBN 0786863889

THE ART OF THE STORYBOARD: STORYBOARDING FOR FILM, TV, AND ANIMATION
HART, John
Boston, MA: Focal Press.
ISBN 0240803299

THE ARTS COUNCIL OF ENGLAND NATIONAL LOTTERY FILM PROGRAMME: CONSULTATION PAPER ON CINEMA DISTRIBUTION
ARTS COUNCIL OF ENGLAND
London: Arts Council of England.

Series:　Critical perspectives on Asian Pacific Americans
ASIAN AMERICA THROUGH THE LENS
XING, Jun
London/ New Delhi: Sage Publications.
ISBN 076199176X

THE ASIAN FILM LIBRARY REFERENCE TO JAPANESE FILM 1998: VOLUME 1: FILMS
CREMIN, Stephen (Ed./Comp.)
London: Asian Film Library.

THE ASIAN FILM LIBRARY REFERENCE TO JAPANESE FILM 1998: VOLUME 2: CAST STAFF
CREMIN, Stephen (Ed./Comp.)
London: Asian Film Library.

AUDIO-VISUAL COMMUNICATIONS AND THE REGULATION OF BROADCASTING: MINUTES OF EVIDENCE, THURSDAY 29 JANUARY 1998
GREAT BRITAIN House of Commons

KAUFMAN, Gerald (chairman)
London: The Stationery Office, 29 January 1998.
[HC 520-i]
ISBN 010218898X

AUDIO-VISUAL COMMUNICATIONS AND THE REGULATION OF BROADCASTING: MINUTES OF EVIDENCE, THURSDAY 5 FEBRUARY 1998
GREAT BRITAIN House of Commons
KAUFMAN, Gerald (chairman)
London: The Stationery Office, 5 February 1998.
[HC 520-ii]
ISBN 0102190984

AUDIO-VISUAL COMMUNICATIONS AND THE REGULATION OF BROADCASTING: MINUTES OF EVIDENCE, THURSDAY 12 FEBRUARY 1998
GREAT BRITAIN House of Commons
KAUFMAN, Gerald (chairman)
London: The Stationery Office, 12 February 1998.
[HC 520-iii]
ISBN 0102227985

AUDIO-VISUAL COMMUNICATIONS AND THE REGULATION OF BROADCASTING: MINUTES OF EVIDENCE, THURSDAY 19 FEBRUARY 1998
GREAT BRITAIN House of Commons
KAUFMAN, Gerald (chairman)
London: The Stationery Office, 19 February 1998.
[HC 520-iv]
ISBN 0102237980

AUDIO-VISUAL COMMUNICATIONS AND THE REGULATION OF BROADCASTING: MINUTES OF EVIDENCE, THURSDAY 26 FEBRUARY 1998
GREAT BRITAIN House of Commons
KAUFMAN, Gerald (chairman)
London: The Stationery Office, 26 February 1998.
[HC 520-v]
ISBN 0102255989

AUDIO-VISUAL COMMUNICATIONS AND THE REGULATION OF BROADCASTING· MINUTES OF EVIDENCE, THURSDAY 5 MARCH 1998

GREAT BRITAIN House of Commons
KAUFMAN, Gerald (chairman)
London: The Stationery Office, 5 March 1998.
[HC 520-vi]
0102254982

AUDIO-VISUAL COMMUNICATIONS AND THE REGULATION OF BROADCASTING: MINUTES OF EVIDENCE, THURSDAY 19 MARCH 1998
GREAT BRITAIN House of Commons
KAUFMAN, Gerald (chairman)
London: The Stationery Office, 19 March 1998.
[HC 520-vii]
ISBN 0102282986

Series:　Statistics in focus: distributive trades, services and transport, 1998, no. 2
THE AUDIO-VISUAL SECTOR IN THE EUROPEAN ECONOMIC AREA IN THE 1990s
EUROSTAT; KOHVAKKA, Rauli
Luxembourg: Eurostat.

AUSTRALIAN FILM 1900 - 1977: A GUIDE TO FEATURE FILM PRODUCTION
PIKE, Andrew; COOPER, Ross
Melbourne: Oxford University Press.
ISBN 0195507843

Series:　National Film and Television Archive Filmographies Series, no. 8
AVANT GARDE: FILM AND TV HOLDINGS IN THE NFTVA
FINN, Eugene (compiler)
London: BFI, National Film and Television Archive.

AVATARS OF THE WORLD: FROM PAPYRUS TO CYBERSPACE
O'DONNELL, James J.
Cambridge, MA; London: Harvard University Press.
ISBN 0674055454

THE AVENGERS: ORIGINAL MOVIE SCREENPLAY
MACPHERSON, Don
London: Titan Books.
ISBN 1852869321

THE AVENGERS: THE MAKING OF THE MOVIE
ROGERS, Dave
London: Titan Books.
ISBN 185286933X

A-Z OF SILENT FILM COMEDY
MITCHELL, Glenn
London: B.T. Batsford.
ISBN 0713479396

BABYLON 5: SEASON BY SEASON: SIGNS AND PORTENTS
KILLICK, Jane
New York: Del Rey Book/Ballantine.
ISBN 0345424476

 BACK IN THE SADDLE AGAIN: NEW ESSAYS ON THE WESTERN
BUSCOMBE, Edward; PEARSON, Roberta E. (eds.)
London: British Film Institute.
ISBN 0851706614

BACK IN THE SADDLE: ESSAYS ON WESTERN FILM AND TELEVISION ACTORS
YOGGY, Gary A. (ed.)
Jefferson, NC; London: McFarland & Company.
ISBN 078640566X

THE BAD AND THE BEAUTIFUL: A SCREENPLAY
SCHNEE, Charles
BRUCCOLI, Matthew J. (ed.)
Carbondale, IL; Edwardsville, IL: Southern Illinois University Press.
ISBN 0809321823

BAD GIRLS AND SICK BOYS: FANTASIES IN CONTEMPORARY ART AND CULTURE
KAUFFMAN, Linda S.
Berkeley; Los Angeles; London: University of California Press.
ISBN 0520210328

BAD LANGUAGE: WHAT ARE THE LIMITS?
HARGRAVE, Andrea Millwood
London: Broadcasting Standards Commission.

BANNED IN THE MEDIA: A REFERENCE GUIDE TO CENSORSHIP IN THE PRESS, MOTION PICTURES, BROADCASTING, AND THE INTERNET
FOERSTEL, Herbert N.
Westport, CT; London: Greenwood Press.
ISBN 0313302456

"BANNED IN THE USA": BRITISH FILMS IN THE UNITED STATES AND THEIR CENSORSHIP, 1933-1960
SLIDE, Anthony
London; New York: I.B.Tauris.
ISBN 1860642543

Series: Media manuals
BASIC STUDIO DIRECTING
FAIRWEATHER, Rod
Oxford: Focal Press.
ISBN 0240515250

BATTLE ON!: AN UNAUTHORIZED, IRREVERENT LOOK AT XENA: WARRIOR PRINCESS
COX, Greg
New York: ROC.
ISBN 0451457315

THE BBC BEYOND 2000 BRITISH BROADCASTING CORPORATION
London: British Broadcasting Corporation.

BECAUSE I TELL A JOKE OR TWO: COMEDY, POLITICS AND SOCIAL DIFFERENCE
WAGG, Stephen (ed.)
London; New York: Routledge.
ISBN 0415129214

BEDSIDE MANNERS: GEORGE CLOONEY AND ER
KEENLEYSIDE, Sam
Toronto: ECW Press.
ISBN 1550223364

BEFORE THE EXORCIST: WILLIAM PETER BLATTY'S OWN STORY OF TAKING HIS NOVEL TO FILM
BLATTY, William Peter
Eye, Suffolk: ScreenPress Books.

THE BEGINNINGS OF THE CINEMA IN ENGLAND 1894-1901. VOLUME ONE: 1894-1896
BARNES, John
MALTBY, Richard (ed.)
Exeter: University of Exeter Press.
ISBN 0859895645

BEHIND THE SCENES AT TIME TEAM
TAYLOR, Tim
BENNETT, Chris (photographer)
London; Basingstoke: Channel Four.
ISBN 075221327X

Series: Contemporary film and television series
BERTOLUCCI'S THE LAST EMPEROR: MULTIPLE TAKES
SKLAREW, Bruce H.; KAUFMAN, Bonnie S.; SPITZ, Ellen Handler; BORDEN, Diane (eds.)
Wayne State University Press.
ISBN 0814327001

BETWEEN SILK AND CYANIDE: THE STORY OF SOE'S CODE WAR

MARKS, Leo
London: HarperCollins.
ISBN 0002559447

A BIGGER PICTURE: THE REPORT OF THE FILM POLICY REVIEW GROUP FILM POLICY REVIEW GROUP; DEPARTMENT FOR CULTURE, MEDIA AND SPORT
London: Department for Culture, Media and Sport.

THE BIG LEBOWSKI
COEN, Ethan; COEN, Joel
London: Faber and Faber.
ISBN 0571193358

 Series: BFI film classics
THE BIRDS
PAGLIA, Camille
London: British Film Institute.
ISBN 0851706517

BLACKADDER: THE WHOLE DAMN DYNASTY
CURTIS, Richard; ELTON, Ben; ATKINSON, Rowan
London: Michael Joseph.
ISBN 0718143728

THE BLACK FAMILY OF SUNDERLAND: THEIR CIRCUITS AND THEIR CINEMAS
MANDERS, Frank
Wakefield: Mercia Cinema Society.
ISBN 0946406472

BLACK IN THE BRITISH FRAME: BLACK PEOPLE IN BRITISH FILM AND TELEVISION 1896-1996
BOURNE, Stephen
London: Cassell.
ISBN 0304333743

Series: Bloomsbury movie guides, no. 3
BLUE VELVET: THE ULTIMATE A-Z
DRAZIN, Charles
London: Bloomsbury.
ISBN 0747538891

Series: Faber classic screenplays
BONNIE AND CLYDE
NEWMAN, David; BENTON, Robert
WAKE, Sandra; HAYDEN, Nicola (eds.)
London: Faber and Faber.
ISBN 0571194532

BOOGIE NIGHTS
ANDERSON, Paul Thomas
London: Faber and Faber.
ISBN 0571195393

THE BOOK OF MOVIE LISTS: AN OFFBEAT, PROVOCATIVE COLLECTION OF THE BEST AND WORST OF EVERYTHING IN MOVIES
MCBRIDE, Joseph
Chicago: Contemporary Books.
ISBN 0809228912

BOXED SETS: TELEVISION REPRESENTATIONS OF THEATRE
RIDGMAN, Jeremy (ed.)
Luton: John Libbey Media/Arts Council of England.
ISBN 1860205194

THE BOY AIN'T RIGHT
AIBEL
Jonathan
London: HarperCollins.
ISBN 0006531105

Series: Bloomsbury film classics: the original novel
THE BOYS FROM BRAZIL
LEVIN
Ira
London: Bloomsbury.
ISBN 0747542384

BRIAN FRIEL'S DANCING AT LUGHNASA
McGUINNESS, Frank
London: Faber and Faber.
ISBN 0571196063

THE BRITISH AT WAR: CINEMA, STATE AND PROPAGANDA 1939-1945
CHAPMAN, James
London: I.B.Tauris.
ISBN 186064158X

BROADCASTING: THE BROADCASTING (LOCAL DELIVERY SERVICES) ORDER 1998
GREAT BRITAIN, Statutory Instruments
London: The Stationery Office, 15th May 1998.
[S.I. 1998; no. 1240]
ISBN 0110790456

BROADCASTING: THE BROADCASTING ACT 1996 (COMMENCEMENT NO. 3) ORDER 1998
GREAT BRITAIN, Statutory Instruments
London: The Stationery Office, 28th January 1998.
[S.I. 1998; no. 188 (C.1)]
ISBN 0110654862

BROADCASTING: THE CHANNEL 4 (APPLICATION OF EXCESS REVENUES) ORDER 1998
GREAT BRITAIN, Statutory Instruments
London: The Stationery Office.
[S.I. 1998; no. 2915]
ISBN 0110798627

BROADCASTING: THE DISSOLUTION OF THE BROADCASTING COMPLAINTS COMMISSION AND THE BROADCASTING STANDARDS COUNCIL ORDER 1998
GREAT BRITAIN, Statutory Instruments
London: The Stationery Office.
[S.I. 1998; no. 2954]
ISBN 0110798821

BROADCASTING: THE FOREIGN SATELLITE SERVICE PROSCRIPTION (NO.2) ORDER 1998
GREAT BRITAIN, Statutory Instruments
London: The Stationery Office.
[S.I. 1998; no. 3083]
ISBN 0110799259

BROADCASTING: THE TELEVISION BROADCASTING REGULATIONS 1998
GREAT BRITAIN, Statutory Instruments
London: The Stationery Office.
[S.I. 1998; no. 1998]
ISBN 0110803280

BUFFY X-POSED: THE UNAUTHORIZED BIOGRAPHY OF SARAH MICHELLE GELLAR AND HER ON-SCREEN CHARACTER
EDWARDS, Ted
Rocklin, CA: Prima.
ISBN 076151368X

BUILDING A COMPANY: ROY O. DISNEY AND THE CREATION OF AN ENTERTAINMENT EMPIRE
THOMAS, Bob
New York: Hyperion.
ISBN 0786862009

THE BUREAU OF MOTION PICTURES AND ITS INFLUENCE ON FILM CONTENT DURING WORLD WAR II: THE REASONS FOR ITS FAILURE
MYERS, James M.
Lewiston, NY; Queenston, Ont; Lampeter: The Edwin Mellen Press.
ISBN 0773483047

CARTOON CRAZY?: CHILDREN'S PERCEPTIONS OF "ACTION" CARTOONS
CHAMBERS, Sue; KARET, Nicki; SAMSON, Neil
London: Independent Television Commission.
ISBN 0900485698

CARY GRANT: A LIFE IN PICTURES
CURTIS, Jenny
New York: MetroBooks.
ISBN 1567995659

THE CATHOLIC CRUSADE AGAINST THE MOVIES, 1940-1975
BLACK, Gregory D.
Cambridge: Cambridge University Press.
ISBN 0521594189

CELEBRATING 1895: THE CENTENARY OF CINEMA
FULLERTON, John (ed.)
Sydney: John Libbey & Co.
ISBN 1864620153

THE CELLULOID COUCH: AN ANNOTATED INTERNATIONAL FILMOGRAPHY OF THE MENTAL HEALTH PROFESSIONAL IN THE MOVIES AND TELEVISION, FROM THE BEGINNING TO 1990
RABKIN, Leslie
Lanham, MD: Scarecrow Press.
ISBN 0810834626

Series: Critical studies in communication and in the cultural industries
CELLULOID MUSHROOM CLOUDS: HOLLYWOOD AND THE ATOMIC BOMB
EVANS, Joyce A.
Boulder, CO; Oxford: Westview Press.
ISBN 0813326133

CHANGING CHANNELS: THE PROSPECTS FOR TELEVISION IN A DIGITAL WORLD
STEEMERS, Jeanette (ed.)
Luton, Bedfordshire: John Libbey Media/University of Luton Press.
ISBN 1860205445

CHANNEL 4 LICENSE
INDEPENDENT TELEVISION COMMISSION
London: Independent Television Commission.

CHANNELING VIOLENCE: THE ECONOMIC MARKET FOR VIOLENT TELEVISION

PROGRAMMING
HAMILTON, James T.
Princeton, NJ: Princeton University
Press.
ISBN 0691048487

Series: Creation Cinema
Collection, 10
CHARLIE'S FAMILY: AN
ILLUSTRATED SCREENPLAY
VAN BEBBER, Jim
London: Creation Books.
ISBN 1871592941

CHICK FLICKS
RICH, Ruby
Durham, NC: Duke University
Press.
ISBN 0822321211

CHILDREN AND MEDIA
VIOLENCE: YEARBOOK FROM
THE UNESCO
INTERNATIONAL
CLEARINGHOUSE ON
CHILDREN AND VIOLENCE ON
THE SCREEN 1998
CARLSSON, Ulla; FEILITZEN,
Cecilia von (eds.)
Gothenburg: UNESCO International
Clearinghouse on Children and
Violence on the Screen
ISBN 9163063581

CHINATOWN THE LAST
DETAIL
TOWNE, Robert
London: Faber and Faber.
ISBN 0571150853

CHOOSE LIFE: EWAN
MCGREGOR AND THE
BRITISH FILM REVIVAL
BROOKS, Xan
London: Chameleon Books.
ISBN 0233994106

THE CINE GOES TO TOWN:
FRENCH CINEMA, 1896-1914
ABEL, Richard
Berkeley; Los Angeles; London:
University of California Press.
ISBN 0520079361

Series: Film culture in
transition
CINEMA FUTURES: CAIN,
ABEL OR CABLE?: THE
SCREEN ARTS IN THE
DIGITAL AGE
ELSAESSER, Thomas; HOFFMAN,
Kay (eds.)
Amsterdam: Amsterdam University
Press.
ISBN 9053563121

CINEMAGOING ASIA
COULING, Katharine;

GRUMMITT, Karsten-Peter
Leicester: Dodona Research.
ISBN 1872025110

CINEMAGOING AUSTRALASIA
COULING, Katharine; GRUMMITT,
Karsten-Peter
Leicester: Dodona Research.
ISBN 1872025064

CINEMAGOING EUROPE:
FRANCE BENELEUX
COULING, Katharine; GRUMMITT,
Karsten-Peter
Leicester: Dodona Research.
ISBN 1872025951

CINEMAGOING EUROPE:
GERMANY EASTERN EUROPE
COULING, Katharine; GRUMMITT,
Karsten-Peter
Leicester: Dodona Research.
ISBN 1872025900

CINEMAGOING EUROPE:
SOUTHERN EUROPE
COULING, Katharine; GRUMMITT,
Karsten-Peter
Leicester: Dodona Research.
ISBN 1872025854

CINEMAGOING EUROPE:
SUMMARY
COULING, Katharine; GRUMMITT,
Karsten-Peter
Leicester: Dodona Research.
ISBN 1872025013

CINEMAGOING EUROPE:
UNITED KINGDOM IRELAND
COULING, Katharine; GRUMMITT,
Karsten-Peter
Leicester: Dodona Research.
ISBN 1872025803

CINEMAS OF ILFRACOMBE
VERNON, Chris; HORNSEY, Brian
Wakefield: Mercia Cinema Society.
ISBN 1901425479

CINEMAS OF TRAFFORD: A
SOUVENIR OF 100 YEARS OF
CINEMA
RENDELL, Douglas (compiler)
Altrincham: Douglas Rendell.
ISBN 0951256017

Series: Screencraft
CINEMATOGRAPHY
ETTEDGUI, Peter
RotoVision.
ISBN 2880463564

Series: The Brantwood Outline
History Series
CINEPLEX ODEON: AN
OUTLINE HISTORY
TURNER, Philip

Brantwood Books.
ISBN 0953102149

CLOSE UP 1927-1933: CINEMA
AND MODERNISM
DONALD, James; FRIEDBERG,
Anne; MARCUS, Laura (eds.)
New Jersey: Princeton University
Press.
ISBN 0691004633

CODES OF GUIDANCE
Broadcasting Standards Commission
London: Broadcasting Standards
Commission, June 1998
ISBN 1872521312

Series: French film directors
COLINE SERREAU
ROLLET, Brigitte
Manchester; New York: Manchester
University Press.
ISBN 071905088X

COME BY SUNDAY: THE
FABULOUS, RUINED LIFE OF
DIANA DORS
WISE, DAMON
Basingstoke; London: Sidgwick &
Jackson.
ISBN 028306305X

COMMUNICATION, CINEMA,
DEVELOPMENT: FROM
MOROSITY TO HOPE
ROBERGE, Gaston
New Delhi: Manohar.
ISBN 8173041490

COMMUNICATION FROM THE
COMMISSION TO THE
EUROPEAN PARLIAMENT AND
THE COUNCIL OF MINISTERS:
AUDIOVISUAL POLICY: NEXT
STEPS
Commission of the European
Communities
Luxembourg: Office for Official
Publications of the European
Commission.
COM(98) 446 final
ISBN 9278384194

Series: Media, culture & society
series
COMMUNISM, CAPITALISM
AND THE MASS MEDIA
SPARKS, Colin; READING, Anna
London; Thousand Oaks, CA; New
Delhi: SAGE Publications.
ISBN 0761950753

THE COMPLETE INDEX TO
WORLD FILM SINCE 1895
GOBLE, Alan
East Grinstead, West Sussex:
Bowker-Saur.
ISBN 1857392523

CONFESSIONS OF A LATE NIGHT TALK SHOW HOST: THE AUTOBIOGRAPHY OF LARRY SANDERS
SHANDLING, Garry; RENSIN, David
New York: Simon & Schuster.
ISBN 0684812045

CONTEMPORARY CINEMA
ORR, John
Edinburgh: Edinburgh University Press.
ISBN 0748608362

CONTEMPORARY SPANISH CINEMA
JORDAN, Barry; MORGAN-TAMOSUNAS, Rikki
Manchester: Manchester University Press.
ISBN 0719044138

CONTROVERSIES IN MEDIA ETHICS
GORDON, A. David; KITTROSS, John M.
New York: Longman.
ISBN 0801330254

COPPOLA
COWIE, Peter
London: Faber and Faber.
ISBN 0571196772

COPYCAT TELEVISION: GLOBALISATION, PROGRAM FORMATS AND CULTURAL IDENTITY
MORAN, Albert
Luton: University of Luton Press.
ISBN 1860205372

CORONATION STREET: AROUND THE HOUSES
LITTLE, Daran
London; Basingstoke: Boxtree.
ISBN 0752211749

CRACKS IN THE PEDESTAL: IDEOLOGY AND GENDER IN HOLLYWOOD
GREEN, Philip
Amherst, MA: University of Massachusetts Press.
ISBN 1558491201

CREATING 3-D ANIMATION: THE AARDMAN BOOK OF FILMMAKING
LORD, Peter; SIBLEY, Brian
New York: Abrams.
ISBN 0810919966

CREATIVE BRITAIN
SMITH, Chris
London: Faber and Faber.
ISBN 0571196659

A CRITICAL CINEMA 3: INTERVIEWS WITH INDEPENDENT FILMMAKERS
MACDONALD, Scott
Berkeley; Los Angeles; London: University of California Press.
ISBN 0520209435

A CRITICAL HISTORY OF TELEVISION'S THE TWILIGHT ZONE, 1959-1964
PRESNELL, Don; McGEE, Marty
Jefferson, NC; London: McFarland.
ISBN 0786404485

Series: The Television Series
CUE THE BUNNY ON THE RAINBOW: TALES FROM TV'S MOST PROLIFIC SITCOM DIRECTOR
RAFKIN, Alan
Syracuse, NY: Syracuse University Press.
ISBN 0815605420

CULT TV: THE COMEDIES: THE ULTIMATE CRITICAL GUIDE
LEWIS, Jon E.; STEMPEL, Penny
London: Pavilion.
ISBN 186205245X

Series: SUNY series, human communication processes
CULTURAL DIVERSITY AND THE U.S. MEDIA
KAMALIPOUR, Yahya R.; CARILLI, Theresa (eds.)
New York: State University of New York Press.
ISBN 0791439305

Series: House of Commons papers, session 1997-98; 1090
CULTURE, MEDIA AND SPORT COMMITTEE, EIGHTH REPORT: REPORT AND ACCOUNTS OF THE BBC FOR 1997-98: REPORT, TOGETHER WITH PROCEEDINGS OF THE COMMITTEE AND MINUTES OF EVIDENCE
GREAT BRITAIN House of Commons
KAUFMAN, Gerald (chairman)
London: The Stationery Office, 3 November 1998.
ISBN 0105550833

Series: House of Commons papers, session 1997-98; 1159
CULTURE, MEDIA AND SPORT COMMITTEE: MINUTES OF PROCEEDINGS
GREAT BRITAIN House of Commons
KAUFMAN, Gerald (chairman)
London: The Stationery Office, 18

November 1998.
ISBN 0105551163

Series: House of Commons papers, session 1997-98; 1110
CULTURE, MEDIA AND SPORT COMMITTEE, NINTH REPORT: THE FUTURE OF NEWS AT TEN: REPORT, TOGETHER WITH PROCEEDINGS OF THE COMMITTEE, MINUTES OF EVIDENCE AND APPENDICES
GREAT BRITAIN House of Commons
KAUFMAN, Gerald (chairman)
London: The Stationery Office, 3 November 1998.
ISBN 0105550868

CURRENT COPYRIGHT LAW
HENRY, Michael
London: Butterworths.

DAD'S ARMY: THE LOST EPISODES
PERRY, Jimmy; CROFT, David
London: Virgin.
ISBN 1852277572

DARK CITY: THE LOST WORLD OF FILM NOIR
MULLER, Eddie
London: Titan Books.
ISBN 1852869844

DAVID LLOYD GEORGE: THE MOVIE MYSTERY
BERRY, David; HORROCKS, Simon (eds.)
Cardiff: University of Wales Press.
ISBN 070831371X

Series: A Directors Guild of America oral history series, no. 16
THE DAYS OF LIVE: TELEVISION'S GOLDEN AGE AS SEEN BY 21 DIRECTORS GUILD OF AMERICA MEMBERS
SKUTCH, Ira (ed.)
Lanham, MD: Scarecrow Press.
ISBN 0810834928

DECIPHERING VIOLENCE: THE COGNITIVE STRUCTURE OF RIGHT AND WRONG
CERULO, Karen A.
New York; London: Routledge.
ISBN 0415917999

THE DECLINE AND FALL OF PUBLIC SERVICE BROADCASTING
TRACEY, Michael
Oxford: Oxford University Press.
ISBN 0198159242

DEJA VU: A SCREENPLAY
FOYT, Victoria; JAGLOM, Henry
Hollywood, CA: Rainbow
Filmbooks/Samuel French Trade.
ISBN 1878965050

Series: Bloomsbury film classics
DELIVERANCE
DICKEY, James
London: Bloomsbury.
ISBN 0747540888

**DENNIS POTTER: A
BIOGRAPHY**
CARPENTER, Humphrey
London: Faber and Faber.
ISBN 0571176852

**DENNIS POTTER: BETWEEN
TWO WORLDS: A CRITICAL
REASSESSMENT**
CREEBER, Glen
Basingstoke, Hampshire: Macmillan.
ISBN 0333713907

**Series: House of Commons
papers, session 1997-98; 984-i**
**THE DEVELOPMENT OF
PARLIAMENTARY
BROADCASTING: MINUTES OF
EVIDENCE, WEDNESDAY 15
JULY 1998**
GREAT BRITAIN House of
Commons
London: The Stationery Office, 15
July 1998.
ISBN 010555068X

**DEVILS AND ANGELS:
TELEVISION, IDEOLOGY AND
THE COVERAGE OF POVERTY**
DEVEREUX, Eoin
Luton, Bedfordshire: John Libbey
Media/University of Luton Press.
ISBN 1860205453

**THE DE-VOICING OF SOCIETY:
WHY WE DON'T TALK TO
EACH OTHER ANY MORE**
LOCKE, John L.
New York: Simon & Schuster.
ISBN 0684843331

**DICTIONARY OF TELEVISION
AND AUDIOVISUAL
TERMINOLOGY**
MOSHKOVITZ, Moshe
Jefferson, NC: McFarland.
ISBN 078640440X

**DIFFERENCES IN THE DARK:
AMERICAN MOVIES AND
ENGLISH THEATER**
GILMORE, Michael T.
New York: Columbia University
Press.
ISBN 0231112246

**Series: Media, education and
culture**
**DIGITAL DIVERSIONS: YOUTH
CULTURE IN THE AGE OF
MULTIMEDIA**
SEFTON-GREEN, Julian (ed.)
London: UCL Press.
ISBN 1857288572

**DIRECTING SINGLE CAMERA
DRAMA**
CRISP, Mike
Oxford: Focal Press.
ISBN 0240514785

**DIRECTING THE
DOCUMENTARY**
RABIGER, Michael
Boston; Oxford: Focal Press.
ISBN 0240802705

DIVORCING JACK
BATEMAN, Colin
London: HarperCollins.
ISBN 0006512747

**THE DOCUMENTARY FILM
MOVEMENT: AN ANTHOLOGY**
AITKEN, Ian (ed.)
Edinburgh: Edinburgh University
Press.
ISBN 0748609482

**DOCUMENTING OURSELVES:
FILM, VIDEO, AND CULTURE**
SHERMAN, Sharon R.
Lexington, KY: University Press of
Kentucky.
ISBN 0813109345

**Series: Contemporary film and
television series**
**DOCUMENTING THE
DOCUMENTARY: CLOSE
READINGS OF DOCUMENTARY
FILM AND VIDEO**
GRANT, Barry Keith;
SLONIOWSKI, Jeanette (eds.)
Detroit, MI: Wayne State University
Press.
ISBN 0814326390

**DON QUIXOTE'S ART
TELEVISION: SEEING THINGS
IN ART AND TELEVISION**
RUSHTON, Dave
Edinburgh: Institute of Local
Television.
ISBN 189940502X

**DOROTHY DANDRIDGE: A
BIOGRAPHY**
BOGLE, Donald
New York: Boulevard Books.
ISBN 1572972920

**Series: Contemporary French
film and society**

**DOUBLE TAKES: CULTURE
AND GENDER IN FRENCH
FILMS AND THEIR AMERICAN
REMAKES**
DURHAM, Carolyn A.
Hanover, N.H: University Press of
New England.
ISBN 0874518741

**THE DOUBLE VISION OF STAR
TREK: HALF-HUMANS, EVIL
TWINS, AND SCIENCE FICTION**
HERTENSTEIN, Mike
Chicago: Cornerstone Press Chicago.
ISBN 0940895420

**Series: Filmmakers series, no.
62**
**DOWN BUT NOT QUITE OUT IN
HOLLOW-WEIRD: A
DOCUMENTARY IN LETTERS
OF ERIC KNIGHT**
GEHMAN, Richard; GEHMAN,
Geoff
Lanham, MD; London: Scarecrow
Press.
ISBN 0810834464

**DOWN THE TUBE: AN INSIDE
ACCOUNT OF THE FAILURE
OF AMERICAN TELEVISION**
BAKER, William F.; DESSART,
George
New York: Basic Books.
ISBN 0465007228

**DRAMA QUEENS: WILD
WOMEN OF THE SILVER
SCREEN**
STEPHENS, Autumn
Berkeley, CA: Conari Press.
ISBN 1573241369

**DRUMS OF TERROR: VOODOO
IN THE CINEMA**
SENN, Bryan
Baltimore: Midnight Marquee Press.
ISBN 1887664181

DUE SOUTH
MOULAND, Michael
Toronto, Ontario: Key Porter Books.
ISBN 1550139665

**DUKE: THE LIFE AND IMAGE
OF JOHN WAYNE**
DAVIS, Ronald L.
Norman: University of Oklahoma
Press.
ISBN 0806130156

**EASY RIDERS, RAGING BULLS:
HOW THE SEX-DRUGS-AND-
ROCK'N'ROLL GENERATION
SAVED HOLLYWOOD**
BISKIND, Peter
New York: Simon & Schuster.
ISBN 0684809966

EDDIE IZZARD: DRESS TO KILL
IZZARD, Eddie; QUANTICK, David; DOUBLE, Steve
London: Virgin.
ISBN 1852277637

THE EISENSTEIN READER
EISENSTEIN, Sergei M.
TAYLOR, Richard (Ed./Translator); POWELL, William (Translator)
London: British Film Institute.
ISBN 0851706762

Series: Cinetek series
THE EMPEROR'S NAKED ARMY MARCHES ON = YUKIYUKITE SHINGUN
RUOFF, Jeffrey; RUOFF, Kenneth
Trowbridge, Wilts: Flicks Books.
ISBN 0948911050

EMPLOYMENT PATTERNS AND TRAINING NEEDS 1997/8: THE ANIMATION INDUSTRY
WOOLF, Myra; CHISNALL, Alan; HOLLY, Sara; Skillset
London: Skillset.

EMPTY MOMENTS: CINEMA, MODERNITY AND DRIFT
CHARNEY, Leo
Durham, NC; London: Duke University Press.
ISBN 0822320908

EMULATION, FEARS AND UNDERSTANDING: A REVIEW OF RECENT RESEARCH ON CHILDREN AND TELEVISION ADVERTISING
YOUNG, Brian
London: Independent Television Commission.
ISBN 0900485728

ENCYCLOPEDIA OF CHINESE FILM
ZHANG, Yingjin (au./ed.); XIAO, Zhiwei
London; New York: Routledge.
ISBN 0415151686

ENCYCLOPEDIA OF CONTEMPORARY FRENCH CULTURE
HUGHES, Alex; READER, Keith (ed.)
London; New York: Routledge.
ISBN 0415131863

THE ENCYCLOPEDIA OF NOVELS INTO FILMS
TIBBETTS, John C.; WELSH, James Michael
New York: Facts On File.
ISBN 081603317X

ENGLAND IS MINE: POP LIFE IN ALBION FROM WILDE TO GOLDIE
BRACEWELL, Michael
London: Flamingo.
ISBN 0006550150

ENTERTAINERS IN BRITISH FILMS: A CENTURY OF SHOWBIZ IN THE CINEMA
GIFFORD, Denis
Trowbridge, Wilts: Flicks Books.
ISBN 094891176X

 ENTERTAINING THE NATION: EDUCATION RESOURCE PACK
PEARCE, Hilary (ed.)
British Film Institute Museum of the Moving Image
London: British Film Institute Museum of the Moving Image.

 ENTERTAINING THE VICTORIANS: EDUCATION RESOURCE PACK
PEARCE, Hilary (ed.)
British Film Institute Museum of the Moving Image
London: British Film Institute Museum of the Moving Image.

Series: Creation Cinema Collection, 9
EROS IN HELL: SEX, BLOOD AND MADNESS IN JAPANESE CINEMA
HUNTER, Jack
London: Creation Books.
ISBN 1871592933

 ETHNIC NOTIONS: TOWARDS A CINEMA OF CULTURAL DIVERSITY
SULICK, Sarah (ed./compiler)
London: BFI Films.

EUROFICTION: TELEVISION FICTION IN EUROPE: SECOND REPORT, 1998
BUONANNO, Milly (ed.)
Strasbourg: European Audiovisual Observatory.

EWAN MCGREGOR
PENDREIGH, Brian
London: Orion.
ISBN 0752817876

EXILES IN HOLLYWOOD: MAJOR EUROPEAN FILM DIRECTORS IN AMERICA
PHILLIPS, Gene D.
London: Associated University Presses.
ISBN 0934223491

Series: BFI modern classics
THE EXORCIST
KERMODE, Mark
London: British Film Institute.
ISBN 0851706738

Series: Classic Screenplays
THE EXORCIST LEGION
BLATTY, William Peter
London: Faber and Faber.
ISBN 057120015X

FATAL ATTRACTIONS: RESCRIPTING ROMANCE IN CONTEMPORARY LITERATURE AND FILM
PEARCE, Lynne; WISKER, Gina (eds.)
London: Pluto Press.
ISBN 0745313817

FATHER TED: THE CRAGGY ISLAND PARISH MAGAZINES
MATHEWS, Arthur; LINEHAN, Graham
London: Boxtree.
ISBN 0752224727

Series: Communications and culture
FEMALE STORIES, FEMALES BODIES: NARRATIVE, IDENTITY AND REPRESENTATION
CURTI, Lidia
Basingstoke: Macmillan.
ISBN 0333471652

LA FEMME NIKITA X-POSED: THE UNAUTHORIZED BIOGRAPHY OF PETA WILSON AND HER ON-SCREEN CHARACTER
EDWARDS, Ted
Rocklin, CA: Prima.
ISBN 0761514546

FEMME NOIR: BAD GIRLS OF FILM
HANNSBERRY, Karen Burroughs
Jefferson, NC; London: McFarland.
ISBN 0786404299

FIFTY YEARS OF THE FUTURE: A CHRONICLE OF THE INSTITUTE OF CONTEMPORARY ARTS 1947-1997
Institute of Contemporary Arts (Corp Auth)
London: Institute of Contemporary Arts.

FILM AND LITERATURE: AN INTRODUCTION AND READER
CORRIGAN, Timothy
Upper Saddle River, NJ: Prentice

Hall.
ISBN 0135265428

Series: Garland studies in American popular history and culture
FILM AND THE NUCLEAR AGE: REPRESENTING CULTURAL ANXIETY
PERRINE, Toni
New York; London: Garland Publishing.
ISBN 0815329326

FILM CARTOONS: A GUIDE TO 20TH CENTURY AMERICAN ANIMATED FEATURES AND SHORTS
MCCALL, Douglas L.
Jefferson, NC; London: McFarland & Company.
ISBN 0786405848

THE FILM FESTIVAL GUIDE: FOR FILMMAKERS, FILM BUFFS, AND INDUSTRY PROFESSIONALS
LANGER, Adam
Chicago: Chicago Review Press.
ISBN 1556522851

FILMING ALL QUIET ON THE WESTERN FRONT: 'BRUTAL CUTTING, STUPID CENSORS, BIGOTED POLITICOS'
KELLY, Andrew
London: I.B.Tauris.
ISBN 1860643612

FILMING EMERGING AFRICA: A PIONEER CINEMATOGRAPHER'S SCRAPBOOK FROM THE 1940S TO THE 1960S
MANGIN, Geoffrey
Cape Town: Geoffrey Mangin.
ISBN 062022021X

FILMING ROBERT FLAHERTY'S THE LOUISIANA STORY: THE HELEN VAN DONGEN DIARY
ORBANZ, Eva (ed.)
New York: Museum of Modern Art, New York.
ISBN 0870700812

THE FILM 100
SMITH, Scott
Secaucus, NJ: Carol.
ISBN 0806519401

FILM POSTERS OF THE 70S: THE ESSENTIAL MOVIES OF THE DECADE, FROM THE REEL POSTER GALLERY COLLECTION
NOURMAND, Tony; MARSH,

Graham (eds.)
London: Aurum.
ISBN 185410585X

FILM PROPAGANDA: SOVIET RUSSIA AND NAZI GERMANY
TAYLOR, Richard
London; New York: I.B.Tauris.
ISBN 1860641679

THE FILMS OF FRANKENHEIMER: FORTY YEARS IN FILM
PRATLEY, Gerald
Cranbury, NJ: Lehigh University Press.
ISBN 1900541408

THE FILMS OF LON CHANEY
BLAKE, Michael F.
Lanham, MD; London: Vestal Press.
ISBN 1879511266

THE FILMS OF MACK SENNETT: CREDIT DOCUMENTATION FROM THE MACK SENNETT COLLECTION AT THE MARGARET HERRICK LIBRARY
SHERK, Warren (ed.)
Lanham, MD: Scarecrow Press.
ISBN 081083443X

Series: Cambridge film classics
THE FILMS OF MICHELANGELO ANTONIONI
BRUNETTE, Peter
Cambridge: Cambridge University Press.
ISBN 0521380855

THE FILMS OF PETER WEIR
RAYNER, Jonathan
London; New York: Cassell.
ISBN 0304701238

THE FILMS OF ROGER CORMAN: "SHOOTING MY WAY OUT OF TROUBLE"
FRANK, Alan
London: Batsford.
ISBN 0713482729

Series: Teach yourself books
FILM STUDIES
BUCKLAND, Warren
London: Hodder and Stoughton.
ISBN 0340697687

FILM VERSUS DRAMA: RELATIVE ACCEPTABILITY OF THE TWO GENRES ON TELEVISION
Counterpoint Research; HANLEY, Pam
London: Independent Television Commission.
ISBN 0900485779

THE FINEST YEARS: BRITISH CINEMA OF THE 1940S
DRAZIN, Charles
London: Andre Deutsch.
ISBN 0233989854

FIVE ROUNDS RAPID!: THE AUTOBIOGRAPHY OF NICHOLAS COURTNEY, DOCTOR WHO'S BRIGADIER
COURTNEY, Nicholas
NATHAN-TURNER, John (ed.)
London: Virgin.
ISBN 1852277823

FLESH & BLOOD: BOOK ONE
FENTON, Harvey (ed.)
Guildford, Surrey: FAB Press.
ISBN 0952926032

Series: SUNY series, cultural studies in cinema/video
THE FOLKLORE OF CONSENSUS: THEATRICALITY IN THE ITALIAN CINEMA, 1930-1943
LANDY, Marcia
Albany, NY: State University of New York Press.
ISBN 079143804X

FOR THE LOVE OF PLEASURE: WOMEN, MOVIES AND CULTURE IN TURN-OF-THE-CENTURY CHICAGO
RABINOVITZ, Lauren
London: Rutgers University Press.
ISBN 0813525330

FOR THE TIME BEING: COLLECTED JOURNALISM
BOGARDE, Dirk
London: Viking.
ISBN 0670880051

43 WAYS TO FINANCE YOUR FEATURE FILM: A COMPREHENSIVE ANALYSIS OF FILM FINANCE
CONES, John W.
Carbondale, IL; Edwardsville, IL: Southern Illinois University Press.
ISBN 0809322021

FRANCIS X. BUSHMAN: A BIOGRAPHY AND FILMOGRAPHY
MATURI, Richard J.; MATURI, Mary Buckingham
Jefferson, NC; London: McFarland & Company.
ISBN 078640485X

Series: Culture and the moving image
FRANK CAPRA: AUTHORSHIP AND THE STUDIO SYSTEM
SKLAR, Robert; ZAGARRIO, Vito

(eds.)
Philadelphia: Temple University
Press.
ISBN 1566396085

**FRANK SINATRA AND
POPULAR CULTURE: ESSAYS
ON AN AMERICAN ICON**
MUSTAZZA, Leonard (ed.)
Westport, CT; London: Praeger.
ISBN 0275964957

**Series: French film directors
FRANÇOIS TRUFFAUT**
HOLMES, Diane; INGRAM, Robert
Manchester: Manchester University
Press.
ISBN 0719045533

**FREAKS TALK BACK:
TABLOID TALK SHOWS AND
SEXUAL NONCONFORMITY**
GAMSON, Joshua
Chicago; London: University of
Chicago Press.
ISBN 0226280640

**FRENCHY'S GREASE
SCRAPBOOK**
CONN, Didi
London: Chameleon Books.
ISBN 0233994637

**FROM BARBIE TO MORTAL
KOMBAT**
CASSELL, Justine and JENKINS,
Henry (ed.)
Cambridge, MA; London: MIT Press.
ISBN 0262032589

**Series: Routledge research in
media and cultural studies
FROM SATELLITE TO SINGLE
MARKET: NEW
COMMUNICATION
TECHNOLOGY AND
EUROPEAN PUBLIC SERVICE
TELEVISION**
COLLINS, Richard
London; New York: Routledge.
ISBN 041517970X

**FULL-FRONTAL: MALE
NUDITY VIDEO GUIDE**
STEWART, Steve (ed./compiler)
California: Companion Press.
ISBN 1889138118

**FUNDING INFORMATION AND
COMMUNICATIONS
TECHNOLOGY IN THE
HERITAGE SECTOR: POLICY
RECOMMENDATIONS TO THE
HERITAGE LOTTERY FUND
JANUARY 1998**
HUMANITIES ADVANCED
TECHNOLOGY & INFORMATION
INSTITUTE

Glasgow: University of Glasgow.

**Series: Cinetek series
A FUNNY DIRTY LITTLE WAR =
NO HABRÁ MÁS PENAS NI
OLVIDO**
FOSTER, David William
Trowbridge, Wilts: Flicks Books.
ISBN 0948911069

**Series: The Aurum film
encyclopedia
GANGSTERS**
HARDY, Phil (ed.)
London: Aurum.
ISBN 1854105655

**GARY COOPER: AMERICAN
HERO**
MEYERS, Jeffrey
New York: William Morrow.
ISBN 0688154948

GATES OF EDEN: STORIES
COEN, Ethan
London: Doubleday.
ISBN 0385410379

**Series: Berg French Studies
GAY SIGNATURES: GAY AND
LESBIAN THEORY, FICTION
AND FILM IN FRANCE, 1945-
1995**
HEATHCOTE, Owen; WILLIAMS,
James S.; HUGHES, Alex (eds.)
Oxford; New York, NY: Berg.
ISBN 1859739873

THE GENERAL
BOORMAN, John
London: Faber and Faber.
ISBN 0571196462

**LES GENS DU CINEMA = THE
PEOPLE OF THE MOVIE
WORLD**
SISCOT, Andre
Bruxelles: Memor.
ISBN 2930133317

**GET A LIFE!: THE LITTLE RED
BOOK OF THE WHITE DOT
ANTI-TELEVISION CAMPAIGN**
BURKE, David; LOTUS, Jean
London: Bloomsbury.
ISBN 0747536899

**GET BACK: THE BEATLES'
LET IT BE DISASTER**
SULPY, Doug; SCHWEIGHARDT,
Ray
London: Helter Skelter Publishing.
ISBN 0900924129

**GET ME A MURDER A DAY!: A
HISTORY OF MASS
COMMUNICATION IN BRITAIN**
WILLIAMS, Kevin

London: Arnold.
ISBN 0340614668

**GIRL REPORTER: GENDER,
JOURNALISM, AND THE
MOVIES**
GOOD, Howard
Lanham, MD; London: Scarecrow
Press.
ISBN 0810833980

**Series: Contemporary film and
television series
GIVING UP THE GHOST:
SPIRITS, GHOSTS, AND
ANGELS IN MAINSTREAM
COMEDY FILMS**
FOWKES, Katherine A.
Detroit, MI: Wayne State University
Press.
ISBN 0814327214

**Series: Bloomsbury movie
guides, no. 2
GOLDFINGER: THE ULTIMATE
A-Z**
TURNER, Adrian
London: Bloomsbury.
ISBN 0747538883

GOOD WILL HUNTING
DAMON, Matt; AFFLECK, Ben
London: Faber and Faber.
ISBN 057119611X

**GOODNIGHT, SEATTLE: THE
UNAUTHORISED GUIDE TO
THE WORLD OF FRASIER**
BAILEY, David; MARTYN, Warren
London: Virgin.
ISBN 0753502860

**GOOD SCRIPTS, BAD SCRIPTS:
LEARNING THE CRAFT OF
SCREENWRITING THROUGH
25 OF THE BEST AND WORST
FILMS IN HISTORY**
POPE, Thomas
New York, USA: Three Rivers Press.
ISBN 0609801198

**THE GOOD VIBRATIONS
GUIDE: ADULT VIDEOS**
WINKS, Cathy
San Francisco: Down There Press.
ISBN 0940208229

**Series: Studies in
communication, media, and public
opinion
GOVERNING WITH THE
NEWS: THE NEWS MEDIA AS A
POLITICAL INSTITUTION**
COOK, Timothy E.
Chicago; London: University of
Chicago Press.
ISBN 0226115003

GRAMOPHONE FILM MUSIC GOOD CD GUIDE
WALKER, Mark (ed.)
Harrow: Gramophone Publications Limited.
ISBN 0902470973

GRAMOPHONE MUSICALS GOOD CD GUIDE
WALKER, Mark (ed.)
Harrow: Gramophone Publications Limited.
ISBN 0902470981

THE GRANADA THEATRES
EYLES, Allen
London: Cinema Theatre Association/British Film Institute.
ISBN 0851706800

Series: Reference guides to the world's cinema
GUIDE TO AFRICAN CINEMA
RUSSELL, Sharon A.
Westport, CT: Greenwood Press.
ISBN 0313296219

Series: Reference guides to the world's cinema
GUIDE TO AMERICAN CINEMA, 1965-1995
CURRAN, Daniel
Westport, CT: Greenwood Press.
ISBN 0313296669

THE GUINNESS BOOK OF FILM: THE ULTIMATE GUIDE TO THE BEST FILMS EVER
GUINNESS
London: Guinness.
ISBN 0851120733

HANIF KUREISHI: POST-COLONIAL STORYTELLER
KALETA, Kenneth C.
Austin, TX: University of Texas Press.
ISBN 0292743335

HANS RICHTER: ACTIVISM, MODERNISM AND THE AVANT-GARDE
FOSTER, Stephen C. (ed.)
Cambridge, MA; London: MIT Press.
ISBN 0262061961

HAPPINESS
SOLONDZ, Todd
London: Faber and Faber.
ISBN 0571197922

HENRY FOOL
HARTLEY, Hal
London: Faber and Faber.
ISBN 0571195199

HERCULES AND XENA: THE UNOFFICIAL COMPANION
VAN HISE, James
Los Angeles: Renaissance Books.
ISBN 1580630014

HIGH CONCEPT: DON SIMPSON AND THE HOLLYWOOD CULTURE OF SUCCESS
FLEMING, Charles
New York: Doubleday.
ISBN 0385486944

HIGH-DEFINITION TELEVISION: A GLOBAL PERSPECTIVE
DUPAGNE, Michel; SEEL, Peter
Iowa: Iowa State University Press.
ISBN 0813829259

Series: SUNY series in psychoanalysis and culture
HITCHCOCK'S BI-TEXTUALITY: LACAN, FEMINISMS, AND QUEER THEORY
SAMUELS, Robert
Albany, NY: State University of New York Press.
ISBN 0791436101

bfi **HOLLYWOOD AND EUROPE: ECONOMICS, CULTURE, NATIONAL IDENTITY 1945-95**
NOWELL-SMITH, Geoffrey; RICCI, Steven (eds.)
London: British Film Institute.
ISBN 0851705979

HOLLYWOOD DIVA: A BIOGRAPHY OF JEANETTE MACDONALD
TURK, Edward Baron
Berkeley; Los Angeles; London: University of California Press.
ISBN 0520212029

HOLLYWOOD DRESSED UNDRESSED: A CENTURY OF CINEMA STYLE
SCHRIER, Sandy
New York: Rizzoli.
ISBN 0847821102

Series: Creation Cinema Collection
HOLLYWOOD HEX: DEATH AND DESTINY IN THE DREAM FACTORY
BROTTMAN, Mikita
London: Creation Books.
ISBN 1871592852

HOLLYWOOD HOOPLA: CREATING AND SELLING STARS IN THE GOLDEN AGE OF HOLLYWOOD
SENNETT, Robert S.

New York: Billboard Books.
ISBN 0823083314

HOLLYWOOD ON LAKE MICHIGAN: 100 YEARS OF CHICAGO AND THE MOVIES
BERNSTEIN, Arnie
Chicago: Lake Claremont Press.
ISBN 0964242621

HOLLYWOOD RENAISSANCE: THE CINEMA OF DEMOCRACY IN THE ERA OF FORD, CAPRA, AND KAZAN
GIRGUS, Sam B.
Cambridge: Cambridge University Press.
ISBN 0521625521

HOLLYWOOD'S INDIAN: THE PORTRAYAL OF THE NATIVE AMERICAN IN FILM
ROLLINS, Peter C.; O'CONNOR, John E. (eds.)
Lexington, KY: University Press of Kentucky.
ISBN 0813120446

HOLLYWOOD'S LATIN LOVERS: LATINO, ITALIAN AND FRENCH MEN WHO MAKE THE SCREEN SMOLDER
THOMAS, Victoria
Santa Monica, CA: Angel City Press.
ISBN 1883318416

HOLLYWOOD STUNT PERFORMERS: A DICTIONARY AND FILMOGRAPHY OF OVER 600 MEN AND WOMEN, 1922-1996
FREESE, Gene Scott
Jefferson, NC; London: McFarland & Company.
ISBN 0786405112

HOMICIDE: LIFE ON THE SCREEN
HOFFMAN, Tod
Toronto: ECW Press, 1998.
ISBN 1550223585

THE HORSE WHISPERER: AN ILLUSTRATED COMPANION TO THE MAJOR MOTION PICTURE
EHRLICH, Gretel
London: Bantam.
ISBN 0593044711

Series: Bloomsbury film classics
THE HUSTLER
TEVIS, Walter
London: Bloomsbury.
ISBN 0747539723

Series: Social futures
HYPERREALITY AND GLOBAL

CULTURE
PERRY, Nick
London; New York: Routledge.
ISBN 0415105153

IDEOLOGY OF THE HINDI FILM: A HISTORICAL CONSTRUCTION
MADHAVA PRASAD, M.
Oxford: Oxford University Press.
ISBN 019564218X

IMAGE AND REPRESENTATION: KEY CONCEPTS IN MEDIA STUDIES
LACEY, Nick
London: Macmillan.
ISBN 0333644360

IMAGES IN THE DARK: AN ENCYCLOPEDIA OF GAY AND LESBIAN FILM AND VIDEO
MURRAY, Raymond
London: Titan.
ISBN 1840230339

IMAGES OF THE PASSION: THE SACRAMENTAL MODE IN FILM
FRASER, Peter
Trowbridge, Wilts: Flicks Books.
ISBN 0948911786

IMAGINENATIVE: ABORIGINALLY PRODUCED FILM VIDEO
ABORIGINAL FILM & VIDEO ART ALLIANCE; V/ TAPE
Toronto: V/Tape.

IMPS OF THE PERVERSE: GAY MONSTERS IN FILM
SAUNDERS, Michael William
Westport, CT; London: Praeger.
ISBN 0275957616

THE INCOMPARABLE REX: A MEMOIR OF REX HARRISON IN THE 1980S
GARLAND, Patrick
London; Basingstoke: Macmillan.
ISBN 0333717961

INCUBI NOTTURNI: IL BUIO OLTRE LO SCHERMO: UN FILO ROSSO SANGUE TRA CINEMA E MUSICA = DEAD OF NIGHT: DARKNESS BEYOND THE SCREEN: A BLOOD RED LINE THROUGH CINEMA AND MUSIC
PINTABONA, Giuseppe (ed.)
Genova: Erga Edizioni.
ISBN 8881631164

bfi Series: BFI modern classics
INDEPENDENCE DAY, OR HOW

I LEARNED TO STOP WORRYING AND LOVE THE ENOLA GAY
ROGIN, Michael
London: British Film Institute.
ISBN 0851706622

INDEPENDENT TELEVISION IN BRITAIN: VOLUME 5: ITV AND THE IBA: THE OLD RELATIONSHIP CHANGES
BONNER, Paul; ASTON, Lesley
Basingstoke; London: Macmillan.
ISBN 0333647734

INDIAN POPULAR CINEMA: A NARRATIVE OF CULTURAL CHANGE
GOKULSING, K. Moti; DISSANAYAKE, Wimal
Stoke-on-Trent: Trentham Books.
ISBN 1858560969

IN SEARCH OF DONNA REED
FULTZ, Jay
Iowa City: University of Iowa Press.
ISBN 0877456259

INSIDE HOLLYWOOD: A WRITER'S GUIDE TO RESEARCHING THE WORLD OF MOVIES AND TV
WILSON, John Morgan
Cincinnati, Ohio: Writer's Digest Books.
ISBN 0898798329

Series: The society for cinema studies tranlsation series
INSIDE THE GAZE: THE FICTION FILM AND ITS SPECTATOR
CASETTI, Francesco
ANDREW, Nell; O'BRIEN, Charles (translators)
Bloomington, IN; Indianapolis, IN: Indiana University Press.
ISBN 0253212324

INSIDE THE PRISONER: RADICAL TELEVISION AND FILM IN THE 1960S
RAKOFF, Ian
London: B.T. Batsford.
ISBN 0713484136

INTELLECTUAL IMPOSTURES: POSTMODERN PHILOSOPHERS' ABUSE OF SCIENCE
SOKAL, Alan; BRICMONT, Jean
London: Profile Books.
ISBN 1861970749

Series: Critical media studies
INTERACTIONS: CRITICAL STUDIES IN COMMUNICATION, MEDIA

AND JOURNALISM
HARDT, Hanno
Lanham, MD: Rowman and Littlefield.
ISBN 0847688887

INTERNATIONAL RELATIONS ON FILM
GREGG, Robert W.
Boulder, CO: Lynne Reinner Publishers.
ISBN 1555876757

Series: Cambridge studies in film
INTERPRETING THE MOVING IMAGE
CARROLL, Noel
Cambridge: Cambridge University Press.
ISBN 0521589703

IN THE COMPANY OF WOMEN: CONTEMPORARY FEMALE FRIENDSHIP FILMS
HOLLINGER, Karen
Minneapolis: University of Minnesota Press.
ISBN 0816631786

IN THE PUBLIC GOOD?: CENSORSHIP IN NEW ZEALAND
WATSON, Chris; SHUKER, Roy
Palmerston North, N.Z: Dunmore Press.
ISBN 0864693052

bfi Series: National Film and Television Archive Filmographies Series; 7
IRISH HISTORY AND THE TROUBLES: FICTION FILM AND TV HOLDINGS IN THE NFTVA
FINN, Eugene (compiler)
London: British Film Institute.

ITALIAN HORROR FILMS OF THE 1960S: A CRITICAL CATALOG OF 62 CHILLERS
McCALLUM, Lawrence
Jefferson, NC: McFarland.
ISBN 0786404353

THE ITC CODE OF ADVERTISING STANDARDS AND PRACTICE, AUTUMN 1998
INDEPENDENT TELEVISION COMMISSION
London: Independent Television Commission.

ITC RULES ON THE AMOUNT AND SCHEDULING OF ADVERTISING, AUTUMN 1998
INDEPENDENT TELEVISION COMMISSION

London: Independent Television Commission.

JACK SMITH: FLAMING CREATURE: HIS AMAZING LIFE AND TIMES
LEFFINGWELL, Edward; HEIFERMAN, Marvin; KISMARIC, Carole (eds.)
London: Serpent's Tail.
ISBN 185242429X

JACKIE BROWN
TARANTINO, Quentin
London: Faber and Faber.
ISBN 0571194753

JACK LONDON'S THE SEA WOLF: A SCREENPLAY
ROSSEN, Robert
FUMENTO, Rocco; WILLIAMS, Tony (eds.)
Carbondale, IL; Edwardsville, IL: Southern Illinois University Press.
ISBN 0809321793

JACQUES TOURNEUR: THE CINEMA OF NIGHTFALL
FUJIWARA, Chris
Jefferson, NC; London: McFarland.
ISBN 0786404914

JAMES WHALE: A NEW WORLD OF GODS AND MONSTERS
CURTIS, James
London: Faber and Faber.
ISBN 0571192858

JAMES WILLIAMSON: STUDIES AND DOCUMENTS OF A PIONEER OF THE FILM NARRATIVE
SOPOCY, Martin
Cranbury, NJ; London: Associated University Presses.
ISBN 0838637167

JANE AUSTEN IN HOLLYWOOD
TROOST, Linda; GREENFIELD, Sayre (eds.)
Lexington, KY: University Press of Kentucky.
ISBN 0813120845

JAPANESE CINEMA: THE ESSENTIAL HANDBOOK
WEISSER, Thomas; MIHARA WEISSER, Yuko
Miami, FL: Vital Books Inc./Asian Cult Cinema Publications.
ISBN 1889288500

JEAN COCTEAU
MAURIÈS, Patrick
London: Thames and Hudson.
ISBN 0500237603

Series: **Conversations with filmmakers series**
JEAN-LUC GODARD: INTERVIEWS
STERRITT, David (ed.)
Jackson, MS: University Press of Mississippi.
ISBN 1578060818

JEAN VIGO
SALLES GOMES, P.E.
London: Faber and Faber.
ISBN 0571196101

JERRY MAGUIRE A JERRY MAGUIRE JOURNAL
CROWE, Cameron
London: Faber and Faber.
ISBN 0571196721

JOHN BARRY: A SIXTIES THEME: FROM JAMES BOND TO MIDNIGHT COWBOY
FIEGEL, Eddi
London: Constable.
ISBN 0094785309

Series: **Bio-bibliographies in the performing arts, no. 78**
JOHN FORD: A BIO-BIBLIOGRAPHY
LEVY, Bill
Westport, CT; London: Greenwood Press.
ISBN 0313275149

JOHN SAYLES, FILMMAKER: A CRITICAL STUDY OF THE INDEPENDENT WRITER-DIRECTOR; WITH A FILMOGRAPHY AND A BIBLIOGRAPHY
RYAN, Jack
Jefferson, NC: McFarland.
ISBN 0786405295

Series: **Filmmakers series, no. 59**
JOSEPH H. LEWIS: OVERVIEW, INTERVIEW, AND FILMOGRAPHY
NEVINS, Francis M.
Lanham, MD; London: Scarecrow Press.
ISBN 0810834073

Series: **The Princess Grace Irish Library lectures, no.5**
JOYCE, HUSTON, AND THE MAKING OF THE DEAD
HART, Clive
Gerrards Cross: Colin Smythe.

JUNGIAN REFLECTIONS WITHIN THE CINEMA: A PSYCHOLOGICAL ANALYSIS OF SCI-FI AND FANTASY ARCHETYPES

IACCINO, James F.
Westport, CT; London: Praeger.
ISBN 0275950484

Series: **A life in pictures**
KATHARINE HEPBURN: A LIFE IN PICTURES
HARVEY, Diana Karanikas; HARVEY, Jackson
New York: MetroBooks.
ISBN 1567995667

KEEPING SCORE: FILM AND TELEVISION MUSIC, 1988-1997
MARILL, Alvin H.
Lanham, MD: Scarecrow Press.
ISBN 0810834162

KING PULP: THE WILD WORLD OF QUENTIN TARANTINO
WOODS, Paul A.
London: Plexus.
ISBN 085965270X

Series: **Cinema & history**
THE LAND GIRLS
GOLD, Claudia; WALL, Ian
London: Film Education.

THE LANGUAGE OF CINEMA
JACKSON, Kevin
Manchester: Carcanet.
ISBN 1857542320

THE LAST DAYS OF MARILYN MONROE
WOLFE, Donald H.
New York: William Morrow.
ISBN 0688162886

THE LAST DINOSAUR BOOK: THE LIFE AND TIMES OF A CULTURAL ICON
MITCHELL, W.J. Thomas
Chicago; London: University of Chicago Press.
ISBN 0226532046

THE LAST MOGUL: LEW WASSERMAN, MCA, AND THE HIDDEN HISTORY OF HOLLYWOOD
MCDOUGAL, Dennis
New York: Crown Publishers.
ISBN 0517704641

bfi Series: **BFI modern classics**
LAST TANGO IN PARIS
THOMPSON, David
London: British Film Institute.
ISBN 0851705456

LENYA THE LEGEND: A PICTORIAL AUTOBIOGRAPHY
FARNETH, David (ed.)
LENYA, Lotte

London: Thames and Hudson.
ISBN 050001888X

LEONARDO DICAPRIO: ROMANTIC HERO
BEGO, Mark
London: Ebury Press.
ISBN 0091865670

LEONARDO: UP CLOSE AND PERSONAL
LOOSELEAF, Victoria
New York: Ballantine.
ISBN 0345432223

LIGHT AND ILLUSION: THE HOLLYWOOD PORTRAITS OF RAY JONES
ZIMMERMAN, Tom
JONES, John (ed.)
Glendale, Ca: Balcony Press.
ISBN 1890449008

LIFE THE MOVIE: HOW ENTERTAINMENT CONQUERED REALITY
GABLER, Neal
New York: Alfred A. Knopf.
ISBN 0679417524

LINDSAY ANDERSON: MAVERICK FILM-MAKER
HEDLING, Erik
London: Cassell.
ISBN 030433605X

LIVING COLOR: RACE AND TELEVISION IN THE UNITED STATES
TORRES, Sacha (ed.)
Durham, NC; London: Duke University Press.
ISBN 0822321785

LIVING PICTURES: THE ORIGINS OF THE MOVIES
ROSSELL, Deac
Albany, NY: State University of New York Press.
ISBN 079143768X

Series: Faber film
LOACH ON LOACH
FULLER, Graham (ed.)
London: Faber and Faber.
ISBN 0571179185

LOCK, STOCK & TWO SMOKING BARRELS
RITCHIE, Guy
London: Headline.
ISBN 0747262055

LOST IN SPACE: THE TRUE STORY
SHIFRES, Edward B.
Salt Lake City, Utah: Windsor House Publishing Group.

ISBN 1881636178

Series: French film directors
LUC BESSON
HAYWARD, Susan
Manchester: Manchester University Press.
ISBN 0719050758

LUCY LAWLESS AND RENEÉ O'CONNOR: WARRIOR STARS OF XENA
STAFFORD, Nikki
Toronto: ECW Press.
ISBN 155022347X

LULU ON THE BRIDGE
AUSTER, Paul
London: Faber and Faber.
ISBN 0571195865

Series: Feminist cultural studies, the media, and political culture
MADCAPS, SCREWBALLS, AND CON WOMEN: THE FEMALE TRICKSTER IN AMERICAN CULTURE
LANDAY, Lori
Philadelphia: University of Pennsylvania Press.
ISBN 0812216512

MAKING MISCHIEF: THE CULT FILMS OF PETE WALKER
CHIBNALL, Steve
Surrey: FAB Press.
ISBN 0952926016

MAKING MOVIES ON YOUR OWN: PRACTICAL TALK FROM INDEPENDENT FILMMAKERS
LINDENMUTH, Kevin J.
Jefferson, NC; London: McFarland & Company.
ISBN 0786405171

(bfi)   MAKING MOVIES: CARTOONS BY ALAN PARKER
PARKER, Alan (au./illustator)
London: British Film Institute.
ISBN 0851706797

THE MAKING OF GODZILLA
ABERLY, Rachel
London: Titan Books.
ISBN 1852869054

THE MAKING OF HORNBLOWER: THE OFFICIAL COMPANION TO THE ITV SERIES
MCGREGOR, Tom
London; Basingstoke: Boxtree.
ISBN 0752211897

THE MAKING OF LOST IN SPACE
CADIGAN, Pat
London: Titan Books.
ISBN 1852869062

THE MAKING OF THE SCARLET PIMPERNEL: THE OFFICIAL COMPANION TO THE BBC SERIES
TIBBALLS, Geoff
London; Basingstoke: Boxtree.
ISBN 0752213016

Series: International series in social psychology
MAKING SENSE OF TELEVISION: THE PSYCHOLOGY OF AUDIENCE INTERPRETATION
LIVINGSTONE, Sonia
London; New York: Routledge.
ISBN 041518536X

Series: Cinema & history,no. 4
THE MAN IN THE IRON MASK: STUDY GUIDE
WALL, Ian; Film Education
London: Film Education.

Series: Cinetek series
THE MANCHURIAN CANDIDATE
BADSEY, Stephen
Trowbridge, Wilts: Flicks Books.
ISBN 094891162X

Series: Bloomsbury film classics: the original novel
MARATHON MAN
GOLDMAN, William
London: Bloomsbury.
ISBN 0747539731

MARIHUANA, MOTHERHOOD AND MADNESS: THREE SCREENPLAYS FROM THE EXPLOITATION CINEMA OF DWAIN ESPER
ESPER, Dwain
WOOD, Bret; SLIDE, Anthony (eds.)
Lanham, MD: Scarecrow Press.
ISBN 0810833751

MARILYN MONROE
LEAMING, Barbara
London: Weidenfeld & Nicolson.
ISBN 0297816721

MARILYN, HITLER AND ME: THE MEMOIRS OF MILTON SHULMAN
SHULMAN, Milton
London: Andre Deutsch.
ISBN 0233994084

Series: Close up
MARTIN SCORSESE

DOUGAN, Andy
New York: Thunder's Mouth Press.
ISBN 1560251611

**THE MATERIAL GHOST:
FILMS AND THEIR MEDIUM**
PEREZ, Gilberto
Baltimore; London: Johns Hopkins
University Press.
ISBN 0801856736

**MAYHEM: VIOLENCE AS
PUBLIC ENTERTAINMENT**
BOK, Sissela
Reading, Massachusetts: Addison-
Wesley.
ISBN 0201489791

**MEAT IS MURDER: AN
ILLUSTRATED GUIDE TO
CANNIBAL CULTURE**
BROTTMAN, Mikita
London: Creation Books.
ISBN 1871592909

**THE MEDIA: AN
INTRODUCTION**
BRIGGS, Adam; COBLEY, Paul
(eds.)
Harlow: Longman.
ISBN 0582277981

**MEDIA, CULTURE, AND THE
RELIGIOUS RIGHT**
KINTZ, Linda; LESAGE, Julia (eds.)
Minneapolis: Minnesota University
Press.
ISBN 0816630852

**THE MEDIA IN AMERICAN
POLITICS: CONTENTS AND
CONSEQUENCES**
PALETZ, David L.
New York: Longman.
ISBN 0321029917

**MEDIA INDUSTRY
DOCUMENTATION**
HENRY, Michael
London; Edinburgh; Dublin:
Butterworths.
ISBN 0406905126

**MEDIA INDUSTRY
TRANSACTIONS**
HENRY, Michael
London; Edinburgh; Dublin:
Butterworths.
ISBN 0406049777

**THE MEDIA IN QUESTION:
POPULAR CULTURES AND
PUBLIC INTERESTS**
BRANTS, Kees; HERMES, Joke;
ZOONEN, Liesbet van (eds.)
London; Thousand Oaks, CA; New
Delhi: Sage.
ISBN 0761957235

**MEDIA POLICY:
CONVERGENCE,
CONCENTRATION AND
COMMERCE**
MCQUAIL, Denis; SIUNE, Karen
(eds.)
Euromedia Research Group
(Commissioner)
London; Thousand Oaks; New Delhi:
Sage Publications.
ISBN 0761959408

Series: Communication and
society
**MEDIA, RITUAL AND
IDENTITY**
LIEBES, Tamar; CURRAN, James
(eds.)
London; New York: Routledge.
ISBN 041515992X

bfi Series: BFI Education
research report
**MEDIA STUDIES: WHAT
STUDENTS THINK**
BARRATT, A.J.B.; BRITISH FILM
INSTITUTE. EDUCATION
London: British Film Institute.

**MEGAMEDIA: HOW GIANT
CORPORATIONS DOMINATE
MASS MEDIA, DISTORT
COMPETITION, AND
ENDANGER DEMOCRACY**
ALGER, Dean
Lanham, MD: Rowman and
Littlefield.

**MEMORIES OF TYNE TEES
TELEVISION**
PHILLIPS, Geoff
Durham: G. P. Electronic Services.
ISBN 0952248069

**THE MEMORY OF TIRESIAS:
INTERTEXTUALITY AND FILM**
IAMPOLSKI, Mikhail
RAM, Harsha (Translator)
Berkeley; Los Angeles; London:
University of California Press.
ISBN 0520085302

MEN WITH GUNS LONE STAR
SAYLES, John
London: Faber and Faber.
ISBN 057119527X

Series: Cinetek series
MESSIDOR
LEACH, Jim
Trowbridge, Wilts: Flicks Books.
ISBN 0948911018

**METHODOLOGY, CULTURE,
AUDIOVISUALITY**
WILK, Eugeniusz (ed.)
Katowice: Slask.
ISBN 8371640994

MICHAEL HANEKE
HORWATH, Alexander;
SPAGNOLETTI, Giovanni (eds.)
Turin: Lindau.
ISBN 8871802527

Series: Hispanic Issues, vol.16
**MODES OF REPRESENTATION
IN SPANISH CINEMA**
TALENS, Jenaro; ZUNZUNEGUI,
Santos (eds.)
Minneapolis: Minnesota University
Press.
ISBN 0816629757

**MOJO A FILM-MAKER'S
DIARY**
BUTTERWORTH, Jez
London: Faber and Faber.
ISBN 0571192181

**MONSTERS ARE ATTACKING
TOKYO!: THE INCREDIBLE
WORLD OF JAPANESE
FANTASY FILMS**
GALBRAITH IV, Stuart
Venice, CA: Feral House.
ISBN 0922915474

**MORE THAN NIGHT: FILM
NOIR IN ITS CONTEXTS**
NAREMORE, James
Berkeley; Los Angeles; London:
University of California Press.
ISBN 0520212932

MORECAMBE & WISE
MCCANN, Graham
London: Fourth Estate.
ISBN 1857027353

Series: Allyn and Bacon series
in mass communication
**THE MOTION PICTURE MEGA-
INDUSTRY**
LITMAN, Barry Russell
Needham Heights, Mass: Allyn &
Bacon.
ISBN 0205200265

**MURDER: A TALE OF MODERN
AMERICAN LIFE**
KNOX, Sara L.
Durham, NC: Duke University Press.
ISBN 0822320665

MY AUTOBIOGRAPHY
BRIGGS, Johnny; CODD, Pat
London: Blake.
ISBN 1857822064

**NATIONAL
DECONSTRUCTION:
VIOLENCE, IDENTITY, AND
JUSTICE IN BOSNIA**
CAMPBELL, David
Minneapolis: University of
Minnesota Press.

ISBN 0816629374

NECRONOMICON: BOOK TWO
BLACK, Andy (ed.)
London: Creation Books.
ISBN 1871592380

NEGATIVE SPACE: MANNY FARBER ON THE MOVIES
FARBER, Manny
London: Da Capo.
ISBN 0306808293

THE NEW AMERICAN CINEMA
LEWIS, Jon (ed.)
Durham, NC; London: Duke University Press.
ISBN 0822321157

Series: Images of Asia
NEW CHINESE CINEMA
TAM, Kwok-kan; DISSANAYAKE, Wimal
Oxford; New York, NY: Oxford University Press.
ISBN 0195906071

THE NEW HISTORICAL DICTIONARY OF THE AMERICAN FILM INDUSTRY
SLIDE, Anthony
Chicago; London: Fitzroy Dearborn Publishers.
ISBN 1579580564

NEW LINKS FOR THE LOTTERY: PROPOSALS FOR THE NEW OPPORTUNITIES FUND, PRESENTED TO PARLIAMENT BY THE SECRETARY OF STATE FOR CULTURE, MEDIA AND SPORT BY COMMAND OF HER MAJESTY, NOVEMBER 1998
GREAT BRITAIN Department for Culture, Media and Sport
London: The Stationery Office.
[Cm 4166]
ISBN 0101416628

NEW MEDIA AND AMERICAN POLITICS
DAVIS, Richard; OWEN, Diana
New York: Oxford University Press.
ISBN 0195120612

NINETY YEARS OF CINEMA IN MONTROSE, PORTOBELLO AND KELSO
HORNSEY, Brian
[s.l.]: [s.n.].
ISBN 1901425509

NINETY YEARS OF CINEMA IN PETERBOROUGH
HORNSEY, Brian
[s.l.]: [s.n.].
ISBN 1873969279

9TH EUROPEAN TELEVISION AND FILM FORUM 6-8, NOVEMBER 1997, LISBON: NEW MEDIA STRATEGIES: CONVERGENCE OR COMPETITION?
CONTAMINE, Claude; WHITTLE, Stephen; DELEVILLE-McGUIRE, Sophie (eds.)
Dusseldorf: European Institute for the Media.
ISBN 3929673258

NO GO THE BOGEYMAN: SCARING, LULLING AND MAKING MOCK
WARNER, Marina
London: Chatto & Windus.
ISBN 0701165936

NO OTHER WAY TO TELL IT: DRAMADOC/DOCUDRAMA ON TELEVISION
PAGET, Derek
Manchester: Manchester University Press.
ISBN 0719045339

NORDIC NATIONAL CINEMAS
SOILA, Tytti; SODERBERGH WIDDING, Astrid; IVERSEN, Gunnar
London: Routledge.
ISBN 0415081955

NOW THAT'S FUNNY!: WRITERS ON WRITING COMEDY
BRADBURY, David; McGRATH, Joe
London: Methuen.
ISBN 0413725200

Series: BFI film classics

LA NUIT AMÉRICAINE
CRITTENDEN, Roger
London: British Film Institute.
ISBN 085170672X

Series: Cinetek series
OCCUPATION IN 26 PICTURES: OKUPACIJA U 26 SLIKA
GOULDING, Daniel J.
Trowbridge, Wilts: Flicks Books.
ISBN 0948911646

THE OFFICIAL THREE STOOGES ENCYCLOPEDIA: THE ULTIMATE KNUCKLEHEAD'S GUIDE TO STOOGEDOM - FROM AMALGAMATED ASSOCIATION OF MORONS TO ZILLER, ZELLER, AND ZOLLER
KURSN, Robert
Chicago: Contemporary Books.
ISBN 0809229307

OL' BLUE EYES: A FRANK SINATRA ENCYCLOPEDIA
MUSTAZZA, Leonard
Westport, CT; London: Greenwood.
ISBN 0313304866

Series: Cinetek series
OMAR GATLATO
ARMES, Roy
Trowbridge, Wilts: Flicks Books.
ISBN 0948911182

Series: Filmmakers series, no. 63
ON ACTORS AND ACTING: ESSAYS BY ALEXANDER KNOX
KNOX, Alexander
SLIDE, Anthony (ed.)
Lanham, MD; London: Scarecrow Press.
ISBN 081083499

ON SUNSET BOULEVARD: THE LIFE AND TIMES OF BILLY WILDER
SIKOV, Ed
New York: Hyperion.
ISBN 0786861940

ON TELEVISION AND JOURNALISM
BOURDIEU, Pierre
FERGUSON, Patricia Parkhurst (Translator)
London: Pluto Press.
ISBN 0745313337

Series: BFI modern classics
ONCE UPON A TIME IN AMERICA
MARTIN, Adrian
London: British Film Institute.
ISBN 0851705448

THE ONLY FOOLS AND HORSES STORY
CLARK, Steve
London: BBC.
ISBN 056338445X

OONA: LIVING IN THE SHADOWS: A BIOGRAPHY OF OONA O'NEILL CHAPLIN
SCOVELL, Jane
New York: Warner Books.
ISBN 0446517305

OPEN SECRET: GAY HOLLYWOOD, 1928-1998
EHRENSTEIN, David
New York: William Morrow.
ISBN 0688153178

THE ORAL HISTORY READER
PERKS, Robert; THOMSON, Alistair (eds.)
London; New York: Routledge.
ISBN 0415133521

OSCAR AND LUCINDA
JONES, Laura
London: Faber and Faber.
ISBN 0571194702

OUR FATHER: A TRIBUTE TO DERMOT MORGAN
MORGAN, Don; MORGAN, Robert;
MORGAN, Ben
Dublin: New Island.
ISBN 1874597960

OUT OF TUNE: DAVID HELFGOTT AND THE MYTH OF SHINE
GROSS, Tom
New York: Warner Books.
ISBN 0446523836

OVER THE LIMIT: MY SECRET DIARIES 1993–8
MONKHOUSE, Bob
London: Century.
ISBN 0712677070

THE OXFORD GUIDE TO FILM STUDIES
HILL, John; GIBSON, Pamela
Church (eds.)
Oxford: Oxford University Press.
ISBN 0198711158

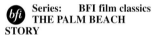
Series: BFI film classics
THE PALM BEACH STORY
PYM, John
London: British Film Institute.
ISBN 0851706711

Series: Faber classic screenplays
PEEPING TOM
MARKS, Leo
London: Faber and Faber.
ISBN 0571194036

THE PENGUIN BOOK OF HOLLYWOOD
SILVESTER, Christopher (ed.)
London: Viking.
ISBN 0670880655

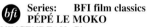
Series: BFI film classics
PÉPÉ LE MOKO
VINCENDEAU, Ginette
London: British Film Institute.
ISBN 0851706746

Series: BFI film classics
PERFORMANCE
MACCABE, Colin
London: British Film Institute.
ISBN 0851706703

Series: Media monographs, no. 24
PERSPECTIVES OF PUBLIC SERVICE TELEVISION IN EUROPE

WOLDT, Runar; DRIES, Josephine;
GERBER, Arnaud; KONERT,
Bertram
Dusseldorf: European Institute for the Media.
ISBN 3929673320

PETULA CLARK FILM COMPANION
WARNER, Steven
London: Meeting Point Publications.

Series: SUNY series, cultural studies in cinema/video
THE PHANTOM OF THE CINEMA: CHARACTER IN MODERN FILM
MICHAELS, Lloyd
Albany, NY: State University of New York Press.
ISBN 0791435687

A PHILOSOPHY OF MASS ART
CARROLL, Noel
Oxford: Clarendon Press.
ISBN 0198742371

PI
ARONOFSKY, Darren
London: Faber and Faber.
ISBN 0571200427

PLAGUE YEARS: A LIFE IN UNDERGROUND MOVIES
HOOLBOOM, Mike
REINKE, Steve (ed.)
Ontario, Canada: YYZ Books.
ISBN 0920397212

PLANET OF THE APES AS AMERICAN MYTH: RACE, POLITICS AND POPULAR CULTURE
GREENE, Eric
Hanover, N.H: University Press of New England.
ISBN 0819563293

PLAY IT AGAIN, SAM: RETAKES ON REMAKES
HORTON, Andrew; MCDOUGAL,
Stuart Y.; HORTON, Andrew;
MCDOUGAL, Stuart Y. (eds.)
Berkeley; Los Angeles; London:
University of California Press.
ISBN 0520205928

PLAYING FOR SUCCESS: A WHITE PAPER ON THE UK LEISURE SOFTWARE INDUSTRY
ELSPA
Offenham: ELSPA.

PLAYING TO THE CAMERA: FILM ACTORS DISCUSS THEIR CRAFT
CARDULLO, Bert (ed.)

New Haven, CT; London: Yale University Press.
ISBN 0300069839

Series: Cinetek series
POISON
WYATT, Justin
Trowbridge, Wilts: Flicks Books.
ISBN 0948911212

THE POLITICAL FILM: AN INTRODUCTION
GENOVESE, Michael A.
Needham Heights, Mass: Simon & Schuster.
ISBN 0536012504

Series: Praeger series in political communication
POLITICS AND POLITICIANS IN AMERICAN FILM
GIANOS, Phillip L.
Westport, CT; London: Praeger.
ISBN 0275960714

POLITICS AND THE MEDIA: HARLOTS AND PREROGATIVES AT THE TURN OF THE MILLENNIUM
SEATON, Jean (ed.)
Oxford: Blackwell.
ISBN 0631209417

POP OFF: THE REGULAR 8 FACTION
KOVACOVA, Milada (Curator)
PORTER, John; STEELE, Lisa (Contributors)
Toronto: XYZ Artists' Outlet.
ISBN 0920397190

PORNOCOPIA: PORN, SEX, TECHNOLOGY AND DESIRE
O'TOOLE, Laurence
London: Serpent's Tail.
ISBN 1852423951

POSTMODERNISM IN THE CINEMA
DEGLI-ESPOSITO, Cristina (ed.)
New York; Oxford: Berghahn Books.
ISBN 1571811052

POST-TRAUMATIC CULTURE: INJURY AND INTERPRETATION IN THE NINETIES
FARRELL, Kirby
Baltimore; London: Johns Hopkins University Press.
ISBN 0801857872

A PRICE ABOVE RUBIES
YAKIN, Boaz
London: Faber and Faber.
ISBN 0571196446

THE PRINCE OF EGYPT: A NEW VISION IN ANIMATION
SOLOMON, Charles
MAGEE, Rhion (Designer)
London: Thames and Hudson.
ISBN 0500019134

PRODUCING PUBLIC TELEVISION, PRODUCING PUBLIC CULTURE
DORNFELD, Barry
Princeton, NJ: Princeton University Press.
ISBN 0691044678

PRODUCTION RESEARCH: AN INTRODUCTION
CHATER, Kathy
Oxford: Focal Press.
ISBN 0240514661

PROJECTIONS 8: FILM-MAKERS ON FILM-MAKING
BOORMAN, John; DONOHUE, Walter (eds.)
London: Faber and Faber.
ISBN 0571193552

Series: Twayne's Filmmakers Series
PUMP 'EM FULL OF LEAD: A LOOK AT GANGSTERS ON FILM
YAQUINTO, Marilyn
New York: Twayne Publishers.
ISBN 0805738924

PUPPETS, PLAYBOYS PRISONERS: YOUR GUIDE TO THE VERY BEST ITC SERIES
ROGERS, Dave; GILLIS, S.J.
London: Cult TV.

PURE DRIVEL
MARTIN, Steve
Harmondsworth, Middlesex: Viking.
ISBN 0670885215

QUENTIN TARANTINO: INTERVIEWS
PEARY, Gerald (ed.)
Jackson, MS: University Press of Mississippi.
ISBN 1578060516

RADIO TIMES GUIDE TO TV COMEDY
LEWISOHN, Mark
London: British Broadcasting Corporation.
ISBN 0563369779

RAISING CAIN: BLACKFACE PERFORMANCE FROM JIM CROW TO HIP HOP
LHAMON, W.T. Jnr
Cambridge, MA; London: Harvard University Press.
ISBN 0674747119

RAT PACK CONFIDENTIAL: FRANK, DEAN, SAMMY, PETER, JOEY THE LAST GREAT SHOWBIZ PARTY
LEVY, Shawn
London: Fourth Estate.
ISBN 1841150002

READING THE RABBIT: EXPLORATIONS IN WARNER BROS. ANIMATION
SANDLER, Kevin S. (ed.)
New Brunswick, NJ: Rutgers University Press.
ISBN 0813525381

REALITY TRANSFORMED: FILM AS MEANING AND TECHNIQUE
SINGER, Irving
Cambridge, MA; London: MIT Press.
ISBN 0262194031

RECONSTRUCTING WOODY: ART, LOVE, LIFE IN THE FILMS OF WOODY ALLEN
NICHOLS, Mary P.
Lanham, MD: Rowman and Littlefield.
ISBN 0847689891

Series: Cinetek series
RED PSALM = MÉG KÉR A NÉP
PETRIE, Graham
Trowbridge, Wilts: Flicks Books.
ISBN 0948911115

Series: Praeger series in political communication
REELPOLITIK: POLITICAL IDEOLOGIES IN '30S AND '40S FILMS
KELLEY, Beverly Merrill
Westport, CT: Praeger.
ISBN 0275960196

REEVES MORTIMER
DESSAU, Bruce
London: Orion.
ISBN 0752817817

REFIGURING AMERICAN FILM GENRES: HISTORY AND GENRE
BROWNE, Nick (ed.)
Berkeley; Los Angeles; London: University of California Press.
ISBN 0520207319

REGULATING COMMUNICATIONS: APPROACHING CONVERGENCE IN THE INFORMATION AGE
GREAT BRITAIN Department of Trade; GREAT BRITAIN Department for Culture, Media and Sport

London: The Stationery Office, July 1998.
[Cm 4022]
ISBN 0101402228

REGULATING THE MEDIA
GIBBONS, Thomas
London: Sweet and Maxwell.
ISBN 0421606606

RENEGADE SISTERS: GIRL GANGS ON FILM
ZALCOCK, Beverley
London; San Francisco: Creation Books.
ISBN 1871592925

REPRESENTING "RACE": IDEOLOGY, IDENTITY AND THE MEDIA
FERGUSON, Robert
London: Arnold.
ISBN 0340692391

THE REPUBLIC PICTURES CHECKLIST: FEATURES, SERIALS, CARTOONS, SHORT SUBJECTS AND TRAINING FILMS OF REPUBLIC PICTURES CORPORATION, 1935-1959
MARTIN, Len D.
Jefferson, NC; London: McFarland & Company.
ISBN 0786404388

RETURN OF THE JEDI: THE ILLUSTRATED SCREENPLAY
KASDAN, Lawrence; LUCAS, George
New York: Del Rey Book/Ballantine.
ISBN 0345420799

Series: Princeton series in opera
RICHARD WAGNER, FRITZ LANG AND THE NIBELUNGEN: THE DRAMATURGY OF DISAVOWAL
LEVIN, David J.
Princeton, NJ: Princeton University Press.
ISBN 0691026211

RINGMASTER!
SPRINGER, Jerry; MORTON, Laura
New York: St. Martin's Press.
ISBN 0312201885

ROADRACERS
RODRIGUEZ, Robert
London: Faber and Faber.
ISBN 0571194265

ROBERT BOLT: SCENES FROM TWO LIVES
TURNER, Adrian
London: Hutchinson.
ISBN 0091801761

ROBERT SIODMAK: A BIOGRAPHY, WITH CRITICAL ANALYSES OF HIS FILMS NOIRS AND A FILMOGRAPHY OF ALL HIS WORKS
ALPI, Deborah Lazaroff
Jefferson, NC; London: McFarland & Company.
ISBN 0786404892

THE ROGERS GILLIS GUIDE TO THE AVENGERS
ROGERS, Dave; GILLIS, S.J.
SJG Communications Services.
ISBN 0952844141

RONNIE BARKER: THE AUTHORISED BIOGRAPHY
McCABE, Bob
London: Chameleon Books.
ISBN 0233993827

ROUNDERS: A SCREENPLAY
LEVIEN, David; KOPPELMAN, Brian
New York: Hyperion; Miramax Books.
ISBN 0786884223

RUBY KEELER: A PHOTOGRAPHIC BIOGRAPHY
MARLOW-TRUMP, Nancy
Jefferson, NC: McFarland & Company.
ISBN 0786405244

SAEED: AN ACTOR'S JOURNEY
JAFFREY, Saeed
London: Constable.
ISBN 009476770X

Series: Console-ing passions
SATURDAY MORNING CENSORS: TELEVISION REGULATION BEFORE THE V-CHIP
HENDERSHOT, Heather
Durham, NC; London: Duke University Press.
ISBN 0822322404

SATYAJIT RAY: AN INTIMATE MASTER
DAS, Santi (ed.)
Calcutta: Allied Publishers.
ISBN 8170237483

SAUCER MOVIES: A UFOLOGICAL HISTORY OF THE CIMEMA
MEEHAN, Paul
Lanham, MD: Scarecrow Press.
ISBN 0810835738

SAVING PRIVATE RYAN: A FILM BY STEVEN SPIELBERG
JAMES, David (Photographer)
SUNSHINE, Linda (ed.)

London; Basingstoke: Boxtree.
ISBN 0752213482

SCIENCE FICTION AND FANTASY FILM FLASHBACKS: CONVERSATIONS WITH 24 ACTORS, WRITERS, PRODUCERS AND DIRECTORS FROM THE GOLDEN AGE
WEAVER, Tom
Jefferson, NC; London: McFarland.
ISBN 0786405643

Series: ARENA working papers, no. 3
SCOTLAND'S PARLIAMENT: DEVOLUTION, THE MEDIA AND POLITICAL CULTURE
SCHLESINGER, Philip
Oslo: ARENA.

SCREAMS NIGHTMARES: THE FILMS OF WES CRAVEN
ROBB, Brian J.
London: Titan Books.
ISBN 1852869453

SCREAMS OF REASON: MAD SCIENCE AND MODERN CULTURE
SKAL, David J
New York; London: W.W. Norton.
ISBN 039304582X

SCREEN HISTORIES: A SCREEN READER
KUHN, Annette; STACEY, Jackie (eds.)
SCREEN
Oxford: Oxford University Press.
ISBN 0198159498

SCREENING THE PAST: FILM AND THE REPRESENTATION OF HISTORY
BARTA, Tony (ed.)
Westport, CT; London: Praeger.
ISBN 0275954021

THE SCRIPT OF ELIZABETH
HIRST, Michael
London; Basingstoke: Boxtree.
ISBN 0752224549

THE SEARCH FOR A METHOD: FOCUS GROUPS AND THE DEVELOPMENT OF MASS COMMUNICATION RESEARCH
MORRISON, David E.
Luton: University of Luton Press.
ISBN 1860205402

SEATS IN ALL PARTS...: MANSFIELD'S STAGE AND SCREEN HISTORY
ORTON, Leslie; BRADBURY, David J.; Old Mansfield Society
Nottinghamshire: Old Mansfield

Society.
ISBN 0951794833

bfi **THE SECOND WORLD SUMMIT ON TELEVISION FOR CHILDREN: SUMMIT LIBRARY CATALOGUE**
BROWN, Lucy (Compiler)
London: British Film Institute.

THE SECRET ART OF ANTONIN ARTAUD
DERRIDA, Jacques; THÉVENIN, Paule
CAWS, Mary Ann (Translator)
Cambridge, MA; London: MIT Press.
ISBN 0262041650

THE SECRET POLITICS OF OUR DESIRES: INNOCENCE, CULPABILITY AND INDIAN POPULAR CINEMA
NANDY, Ashis (ed.)
London; New York: Zed Books.
ISBN 1856495159

SEDUCING AMERICA: HOW TELEVISION CHARMS THE MODERN VOTER
HART, Roderick P.
Thousand Oaks, CA; London; New Delhi: SAGE Publications.
ISBN 0761916237

SEEKING THE CENTRE: THE AUSTRALIAN DESERT IN LITERATURE, ART AND FILM
HAYNES, Roslynn
Cambridge: Cambridge University Press.
ISBN 0521571111

THE SEINFELD UNIVERSE: THE ENTIRE DOMAIN
GATTUSO, Greg
London: BBC.
ISBN 0563384336

Series: Filmmakers series, no. 60
SEPTEMBER SONG: AN INTIMATE BIOGRAPHY OF WALTER HUSTON
WELD, John
Lanham, MD; London: Scarecrow Press.
ISBN 0810834081

SEX MURDER ART: THE FILMS OF JÖRG BUTTGEREIT
KEREKES, David
Manchester: Headpress.
ISBN 0952328844

Series: Film and culture
SEXUAL POLITICS AND NARRATIVE FILM:

HOLLYWOOD AND BEYOND
WOOD, Robin
New York; Chichester, West Sussex:
Columbia University Press.
ISBN 0231076053

Series: New casebooks
SHAKESPEARE ON FILM
SHAUGHNESSY, Robert (ed.)
Basingstoke; London: Macmillan.
ISBN 0333720164

Series: Popular culture bio-
bibliographies
**SHIRLEY TEMPLE BLACK: A
BIO-BIBLIOGRAPHY**
HAMMONTREE, Patsy Guy
Westport, CT; London: Greenwood
Press.
ISBN 0313258481

SHOOTING FROM THE LIP
PUCKRIK, Katie
London: Headline.
ISBN 0747260168

SHOOTING THE PAST
POLIAKOFF, Stephen
London: Methuen.
ISBN 0413731405

**SHOOTING TO KILL:
FILMMAKING AND THE
"TROUBLES" IN NORTHERN
IRELAND**
McILROY, Brian
Trowbridge, Wilts: Flicks Books.
ISBN 0948911530

**SHOOTING TO KILL: HOW AN
INDEPENDENT PRODUCER
BLASTS THROUGH THE
BARRIERS TO MAKE MOVIES
THAT MATTER**
VACHON, Christine; EDELSTEIN,
David
New York: Avon Books.
ISBN 0380798549

**SID AND MARTY KROFFT: A
CRITICAL STUDY OF
SATURDAY MORNING
CHILDREN'S TELEVISION,
1969-1993**
ERICKSON, Hal
Jefferson, NC: McFarland.
ISBN 078640518X

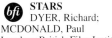 **SIGNS AND MEANINGS IN
THE CINEMA**
WOLLEN, Peter
London: British Film Institute.
ISBN 0851706479

Series: Film/fiction, v. 3
**SISTERHOODS: ACROSS THE
LITERATURE/MEDIA DIVIDE**
CARTMELL, Deborah; HUNTER,

I.Q.; KAYE, Heidi; WHELEHAN,
Imelda (eds.)
London: Pluto Press.
ISBN 0745312187

SLAM
STRATTON, Richard;
WOZENCRAFT, Kim (ed.)
New York: Grove Press.
ISBN 0802135757

**SLEEPING WHERE I FALL: A
CHRONICLE**
COYOTE, Peter
Washington, D.C: Counterpoint.
ISBN 1887178678

Series: Filmmakers series;
No.58
**SMILE WHEN THE RAINDROPS
FALL: THE STORY OF
CHARLEY CHASE**
ANTHONY, Brian; EDMONDS,
Andy
Lanham, MD: Scarecrow Press.
ISBN 0810833778

**SO CLOSE TO THE STATE/S:
THE EMERGENCE OF
CANADIAN FEATURE FILM
POLICY**
DORLAND, Michael
Toronto: University of Toronto Press.
ISBN 080208043X

**THE SOCIOLOGY OF
JOURNALISM**
MCNAIR, Brian
London: Arnold.
ISBN 0340706155

SOPHIA LOREN: A BIOGRAPHY
HARRIS, Warren G.
New York: Simon & Schuster.
ISBN 0684802732

**THE SOUND OF SILENCE:
CONVERSATIONS WITH 16
FILM AND STAGE
PERSONALITIES WHO
BRIDGED THE GAP BETWEEN
SILENTS AND THE TALKIES**
ANKERICH, Michael G.
Jefferson, NC; London: McFarland.
ISBN 078640504X

**SOUNDTRACKS: AN
INTERNATIONAL DICTIONARY
OF COMPOSERS FOR FILM**
CRAGGS, Stewart R.
Aldershot: Ashgate.
ISBN 1859281893

Series: Film and culture
**THE SOUNDS OF COMMERCE:
MARKETING POPULAR FILM
MUSIC**
SMITH, Jeff

New York; Chichester, West Sussex:
Columbia University Press.
ISBN 023110863X

SPEAKING ABOUT GODARD
SILVERMAN, Kaja; FAROCKI,
Harun
New York; London: New York
University Press.
ISBN 0814780660

Series: The SUNY series in
postmodern culture
**SPEEDING TO THE
MILLENIUM: FILM AND
CULTURE 1993-1995**
NATOLI, Joseph
Albany, NY: State University of New
York Press.
ISBN 0791437280

Series: Cinetek series
**THE SPIRIT OF THE BEEHIVE
= EL ESPÍRITU DE LA
COLMENA**
HIGGINBOTHAM, Virginia
Trowbridge, Wilts: Flicks Books.
ISBN 0948911123

STAR WARS ENCYCLOPEDIA
SANSWEET, Stephen J.
London: Virgin.
ISBN 185227736X

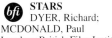 **STARS**
DYER, Richard;
MCDONALD, Paul
London: British Film Institute.
ISBN 0851706436

STEPHEN SONDHEIM: A LIFE
SECREST, Meryle
London: Bloomsbury.
ISBN 0747535353

STILL CRAZY
CLEMENT, Dick; LA FRENAIS, Ian
Eye, Suffolk: ScreenPress Books.
ISBN 1901680215

STILL ME
REEVE, Christopher
London: Century.
ISBN 0712678646

**"THE STORY OF THE
CENTURY!: AN
INTERNATIONAL NEWSFILM
CONFERENCE: PAPERS,
PRESENTATIONS AND
PROCEEDINGS**
JEAVONS, Clyde; MERCER, Jane;
KIRCHNER, Daniela (eds.)
London: British Universities Film &
Video Council.
ISBN 0901299693

STORY: SUBSTANCE,

STRUCTURE, STYLE AND THE PRINCIPLES OF SCREENWRITING
McKEE, Robert
London: Methuen.
ISBN 0413715507

STRANGER THAN PARADISE: MAVERICK FILM-MAKERS IN RECENT AMERICAN CINEMA
ANDREW, Geoff
London: Prion.
ISBN 1853752746

STUDYING THE MEDIA: AN INTRODUCTION
O'SULLIVAN, Tim; DUTTON, Brian; RAYNER, Philip
London: Arnold.
ISBN 034067685X

SUBJECT: CINEMA, OBJECT: WOMAN: A STUDY OF THE PORTRAYAL OF WOMEN IN INDIAN CINEMA
CHATTERJI, Shoma A.
Calcutta: Parumita Publications.

Series: BFI film classics
 SUNRISE: A SONG OF TWO HUMANS
FISCHER, Lucy
London: British Film Institute.
ISBN 0851706681

Series: Faber classic screenplays
SWEET SMELL OF SUCCESS
ODETS, Clifford; LEHMAN, Ernest
London: Faber and Faber.
ISBN 0571194109

SYDNEY POLLACK: A CRITICAL FILMOGRAPHY
MEYER, Janet
Jefferson, NC: McFarland.
ISBN 0786404868

TABLOID TELEVISION: POPULAR JOURNALISM AND THE "OTHER NEWS"
LANGER, John
London; New York: Routledge.
ISBN 0415066360

TAKARAZUKA: SEXUAL POLITICS AND POPULAR CULTURE IN MODERN JAPAN
ROBERTSON, Jennifer
Berkeley; Los Angeles; London: University of California Press.
ISBN 0520211510

TALK OF DRAMA: VIEWS OF THE TELEVISION DRAMATIST NOW AND THEN
DAY-LEWIS, Sean
Luton: John Libbey Media/University of Luton Press.
ISBN 1860205127

TALKIN' WITH YOUR MOUTH FULL: CONVERSATIONS WITH THE VIDEOS OF STEVE FAGIN
FAGIN, Steve (ed.)
Durham, NC; London: Duke University Press.
ISBN 082232069X

TALKING HEADS 2
BENNETT, Alan
London: BBC Worldwide.
ISBN 0563384603

TALL IN THE SADDLE: GREAT LINES FROM CLASSIC WESTERNS
THOMPSON, Peggy; USUKAWA, Saeko
San Francisco: Chronicle Books.
ISBN 081181730X

TEACHING AFRICAN CINEMA
ASHBURY, Roy; HELSBY, Wendy; O'BRIEN, Maureen
London: British Film Institute.
ISBN 085170560X

TEACHING POPULAR CULTURE: BEYOND RADICAL PEDAGOGY
BUCKINGHAM, David (ed.)
London: UCL Press.
ISBN 1857287932

Series: LEA's communication series
TEACHING THE MEDIA: INTERNATIONAL PERSPECTIVES
HART, Andrew (ed.)
Mahwah, NJ: Lawrence Erlbaum.
ISBN 0805824766

Series: Library of contemporary thought
TEAM RODENT: HOW DISNEY DEVOURS THE WORLD
HIAASEN, Carl
New York: Ballantine.
ISBN 0345422805

TECHGNOSIS: MYTH, MAGIC AND MYSTICISM IN THE AGE OF INFORMATION
DAVIS, Erik
New York: Harmony.
ISBN 0517704153

TEENAGE CONFIDENTIAL: AN ILLUSTRATED HISTORY OF THE AMERICAN TEEN
BARSON, Michael; HELLER, Steven
San Francisco: Chronicle Books.
ISBN 0811815846

Series: Media, education and

culture
TEEN SPIRITS: MUSIC AND IDENTITY IN MEDIA EDUCATION
RICHARDS, Chris
London: UCL Press.
ISBN 1857288599

TELEGRAPHS: THE WIRELESS TELEGRAPHY (TELEVISION LICENCE FEES) AMENDMENT) REGULATIONS 1998
GREAT BRITAIN, Statutory Instruments
London: The Stationery Office.
[S.I. 1998; no. 558]

TELEVISION ACROSS THE YEARS: THE BRITISH PUBLIC'S VIEW
SVENNEVIG, Michael
Luton: University of Luton Press.
ISBN 0900485787

TELEVISION: A MEDIA STUDENT'S GUIDE
MCQUEEN, David
London: Arnold.
ISBN 034070604X

Series: Documents in contemporary history
TELEVISION AND THE PRESS SINCE 1945
NEGRINE, Ralph (ed.)
Manchester; New York: Manchester University Press.
ISBN 0719049210

TELEVISION: AN INTERNATIONAL HISTORY
SMITH, Anthony (ed.); with PATERSON, Richard
Oxford: Oxford University Press.
ISBN 0198742495

Series: IEE history of technology series; vol 22
TELEVISION: AN INTERNATIONAL HISTORY OF THE FORMATIVE YEARS
BURNS, R.W.
Stevenage: Institution of Electrical Engineers.
ISBN 0852969147

TELEVISION NEWS AND THE SUPREME COURT: ALL THE NEWS THAT'S FIT TO AIR?
SLOTNICK, Elliot E.; SEGAL, Jennifer A.
Cambridge: Cambridge University Press.
ISBN 0521576164

THE TELEVISION STUDIES

BOOK
GERAGHTY, Christine; LUSTED,
David (ed.)
London: Arnold.
ISBN 0340662328

TELEVISION UNDER THE
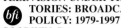 **TORIES: BROADCASTING**
POLICY: 1979-1997
GOODWIN, Peter
London: British Film Institute.
ISBN 0851706142

TELEVISION VIOLENCE AND
PUBLIC POLICY
HAMILTON, James T. (ed.)
USA: University of Michigan Press.
ISBN 0472109030

TERMS OF ENDEARMENT:
HOLLYWOOD ROMANTIC
COMEDY OF THE 1980S AND
1990S
EVANS, Peter William; DELEYTO,
Celestino (eds.)
Edinburgh: Edinburgh University
Press.
ISBN 0748608850

THIRD COMMUNICATION
FROM THE COMMISSION TO
THE COUNCIL AND THE
EUROPEAN PARLIAMENT ON
THE APPLICATION OF
ARTICLES 4 AND 5 OF
DIRECTIVE 89/552/EEC
"TELEVISION WITHOUT
FRONTIERS" FOR THE
PERIOD 1995-96...
COMMISSION OF THE
EUROPEAN COMMUNITIES
Luxembourg: Office for Official
Publications of the European
Community.
COM(1998) 199 final
ISBN 9278329193

THREADING THE NEEDLE:
THE PAX NET STORY
PAXSON, Lowell; TEMPLETON,
Gary
New York: HarperBusiness.
ISBN 0887309488

THREADS OF TIME: A
MEMOIR
BROOK, Peter
London: Methuen.
ISBN 0413696200

Series: BFI modern
 classics
THE "THREE COLOURS"
TRILOGY
ANDREW, Geoff
London: British Film Institute.
ISBN 0851705693
THREE COLOURS TRILOGY:

BLUE, WHITE, RED
KIESLOWSKI, Krzysztof;
PIESIEWICZ, Krzysztof
STOK, Danusia (translator)
London: Faber and Faber.
ISBN 0571178928

THREE MORE SCREENPLAYS
BY PRESTON STURGES
HORTON, Andrew (ed.)
Berkeley; Los Angeles; London:
University of California Press.
ISBN 0520210042

A TIME OF CHANGE
WOODWARD, John; British
Film Institute
London: BFI Directorate.

TIME OUT: INTERVIEWS, 1968-
1998
BROUGHTON, Frank (ed.)
Harmondsworth, Middlesex:
Penguin.

TITANIC AND THE MAKING OF
JAMES CAMERON: THE
INSIDE STORY OF THE THREE-
YEAR ADVENTURE THAT
REWROTE MOTION PICTURE
HISTORY
PARISI, Paula
London: Orion Media.
ISBN 0752817981

TITANIC: JAMES CAMERON'S
ILLUSTRATED SCREENPLAY
CAMERON, James
London; Basingstoke: Boxtree.
ISBN 0752213202

Series: Cinema & history, 1
TITANIC: STUDY GUIDE
WALL, Ian; Film Education
London: Film Education.

TITANIC TOWN
DEVLIN, Anne
London: Faber and Faber.
ISBN 0571196756

TOMMY COOPER: JUST LIKE
THAT
NOVICK, Jeremy
London: Chameleon Books.
ISBN 0233994114

TOTALLY, TENDERLY,
TRAGICALLY: ESSAYS AND
CRITICISM FROM A LIFELONG
LOVE AFFAIR WITH THE
MOVIES
LOPATE, Phillip
New York: Anchor Press/Doubleday.
ISBN 0385492502

Series: Contemporary film and

television series
TRACKING KING KONG: A
HOLLYWOOD ICON IN WORLD
CULTURE
ERB, Cynthia
Detroit, MI: Wayne State University Press.
ISBN 0814326862

Series: The SUNY series in
postmodern culture
THE TRANSPARENCY OF
SPECTACLE: MEDITATIONS
ON THE MOVING IMAGE
DIXON, Wheeler Winston
Albany, NY: State University of New
York Press.
ISBN 0791437825

TRAVOLTA: THE LIFE
ANDREWS, Nigel
London: Bloomsbury.
ISBN 0747531749

Series: SUNY series in feminist
criticism and theory
TRIANGULATED VISIONS:
WOMEN IN RECENT GERMAN
CINEMA
MAJER O'SICKEY, Ingeborg;
ZADOW, Ingeborg von (eds.)
Albany, NY: State University of New
York Press.
ISBN 0791437183

TRUMAN CAPOTE: IN WHICH
VARIOUS FRIENDS, ENEMIES,
ACQUAINTANCES AND
DETRACTORS RECALL HIS
TURBULENT CAREER
PLIMPTON, George
London: Picador.
ISBN 0330368710

Series: NHB shooting script
series
THE TRUMAN SHOW
NICCOL, Andrew
London: Nick Hern Books.
ISBN 1854594176

TV MANIA: A TIMELINE OF
TELEVISION
PAVESE, Edith; HENRY, Judith
New York: Abrams.
ISBN 0810938928

TV OR NOT TV: TELEVISION,
JUSTICE AND THE COURTS
GOLDFARB, Ronald L.
New York; London: New York
University Press.
ISBN 0814731120

UNDERSTANDING ANIMATION
WELLS, Paul
London: Routledge.
ISBN 0415115973
UNDERSTANDING GLOBAL

NEWS: A CRITICAL INTRODUCTION
VAN GINNEKEN, Jaap
London: SAGE Publications.
ISBN 0761957081

UNDERSTANDING SOCIETY, CULTURE AND TELEVISION
MONACO, Paul
Westport, CT; London: Praeger.
ISBN 0275960579

UNFINISHED BUSINESS: SCREENPLAYS, SCENARIOS AND IDEAS
ANTONIONI, Michelangelo
DI CARLO, Carlo; TINAZZI, Giorgio (eds.)
New York: Marsilio.
ISBN 156886051X

THE UNKNOWN THIRTIES: AN ALTERNATIVE HISTORY OF THE BRITISH CINEMA 1929-39
RICHARDS, Jeffrey (ed.)
London: I.B.Tauris.
ISBN 1860643035

UNSPEAKABLE SHAXXXSPEARES: QUEER THEORY AND AMERICAN KIDDIE CULTURE
BURT, Richard
Basingstoke; London: Macmillan.
ISBN 0333753275

THE UNTOUCHABLES
VAHIMAGI, Tise
London: British Film Institute.
ISBN 0851705634

Series: LEA's communication series
THE V-CHIP DEBATE: CONTENT FILTERING FROM TELEVISION TO THE INTERNET
PRICE, Monroe E. (ed.)
Mahwah, NJ: Lawrence Erlbaum.
ISBN 0805830626

VALENTINO: A DREAM OF DESIRE
BRET, David
London: Robson Books.
ISBN 1861051239

VERTIGO: THE MAKING OF A HITCHCOCK CLASSIC
AUILER, Dan
New York: St. Martin's Press.
ISBN 0312169159

VIDEOJOURNALISM: THE DEFINITIVE GUIDE TO MULTI-SKILLED TELEVISION PRODUCTION
GRIFFITHS, Richard

Oxford: Focal Press.
ISBN 0240515080

Series: Theories of Contemporary Culture, 21
VIRTUALITIES: TELEVISION, MEDIA ART, AND CYBERCULTURE
MORSE, Margaret
Bloomington, IN; Indianapolis, IN: Indiana University Press.
ISBN 0253211778

VISCONTI: EXPLORATIONS OF BEAUTY AND DECAY
BACON, Henry
Cambridge: Cambridge University Press.
ISBN 0521599601

THE VISIBLE WALL: JEWS AND OTHER ETHNIC OUTSIDERS IN SWEDISH FILM
WRIGHT, Rochelle
Carbondale, IL; Edwardsville, IL: Southern Illinois University Press.
ISBN 0809321645

VISIONS OF ARMAGEDDON
VAZ, Mark Cotta
New York: Hyperion.
ISBN 0786883472

VISIONS OF MODERNITY: REPRESENTATIONS, MEMORY, TIME AND SPACE IN THE AGE OF THE CAMERA
MCQUIRE, Scott
London; Thousand Oaks, CA; New Delhi: Sage.
ISBN 0761953000

WAR AND THE MEDIA: PROPAGANDA AND PERSUASION IN THE GULF WAR
TAYLOR, Philip M.
Manchester: Manchester University Press.
ISBN 0719055504

WATCHING M*A*S*H, WATCHING AMERICA: A SOCIAL HISTORY OF THE 1972-1983 TELEVISION SERIES
WITTEBOLS, James H.
Jefferson, NC; London: McFarland & Company.
ISBN 0786404574

THE WEREWOLF COMPLEX: AMERICA'S FASCINATION WITH VIOLENCE
DUCLOS, Denis
PINGREE, Amanda (translator)
Oxford; New York, NY: Berg.
ISBN 1859731465
WESTERN GUNSLINGERS IN

FACT AND ON FILM: HOLLYWOOD'S FAMOUS LAWMEN AND OUTLAWS
RAINEY, Buck
Jefferson, NC: McFarland.
ISBN 0786403969

THE WESTERN READER
KITSES, Jim; RICKMAN, Gregg (ed.)
New York: Limelight Editions.
ISBN 0879102683

WHAT IT IS... WHAT IT WAS!: THE BLACK FILM EXPLOSION OF THE '70S IN WORDS AND PICTURES
MARTINEZ, Gerald; MARTINEZ, Diana; CHAVEZ, Andres
New York: Miramax Books/Hyperion.
ISBN 0786883774

WHEN THE SNOW MELTS: THE AUTOBIOGRAPHY OF CUBBY BROCCOLI
BROCCOLI, Albert R.; ZEC, Donald
London; Basingstoke: Boxtree.
ISBN 0752211625

WHITEWASH: RACIALIZED POLITICS AND THE MEDIA
GABRIEL, John
London: Routledge.
ISBN 0415149703

WHY WE WATCH: THE ATTRACTIONS OF VIOLENT ENTERTAINMENT
GOLDSTEIN, Jeffrey (ed.)
Oxford; New York, NY: Oxford University Press.
ISBN 0195118219

Series: Filmmakers series
WIFE OF THE LIFE OF THE PARTY
CHAPLIN, Lita Grey; VANCE, Jeffrey
Lanham, MD; London: Scarecrow Press.
ISBN 0810834324

WINONA RYDER: THE BIOGRAPHY
GOODALL, Nigel
London: Blake.
ISBN 1857822145

THE WINTER GUEST
MACDONALD, Sharman; RICKMAN, Alan
London: Faber and Faber.
ISBN 0571194796

Series: Media, education and

culture
**WIRED-UP: YOUNG PEOPLE
AMD THE ELECTRONIC
MEDIA**
HOWARD, Sue (ed.)
London: UCL Press.
ISBN 1857288041

**WISECRACKER: THE LIFE
AND TIMES OF WILLIAM
HAINES, HOLLYWOOD'S FIRST
OPENLY GAY STAR**
MANN, William J.
New York: Viking Penguin.
ISBN 0670871559

**WITNESS: THE MAKING OF
SCHINDLER'S LIST**
PALOWSKI, Franciszek
WARE, Anna; WARE, Robert G.
(translators)
London: Orion.
ISBN 0752817906

**WOMEN FILMMAKERS THEIR
FILMS**
UNTERBURGER, Amy L. (ed.)
Detroit, MI: St. James Press.
ISBN 1558623574

WOMEN IN FILM NOIR
KAPLAN, E. Ann (ed.)
London: British Film Institute.
ISBN 0851706665

**WOMEN IN HOLLYWOOD:
FROM VAMP TO STUDIO HEAD**
SOVA, Dawn B.
New York: Fromm International
Publishing Corporation.
ISBN 0880642327

**WOODY ALLEN: A
BIOGRAPHY**
BAXTER, John
London: HarperCollins.
ISBN 0002557754

**WORKING GIRLS: GENDER
AND SEXUALITY IN POPULAR
CINEMA**
TASKER, Yvonne
London: Routledge.
ISBN 0415140056

**WORKING-CLASS
HOLLYWOOD: SILENT FILM
AND THE SHAPING OF CLASS
IN AMERICA**
ROSS, Steven J.
Princeton, NJ: Princeton University
Press.
ISBN 0691032343

Series: Contemporary Japanese
society
**THE WORLDS OF JAPANESE
POPULAR CULTURE: GENDER,**

**SHIFTING BOUNDARIES AND
GLOBAL CULTURES**
MARTINEZ, D.P. (ed.)
Cambridge: Cambridge University
Press.
ISBN 0521637295

**WRITER'S GUIDE TO
HOLLYWOOD PRODUCERS,
DIRECTORS, AND
SCREENWRITER'S AGENTS
1999-2000**
PRESS, Skip
Rocklin, CA: Prima.
ISBN 0761514848

**WRITING DIALOGUE FOR
SCRIPTS**
DAVIS, Rib
London: A & C Black.
ISBN 0713648023

**"YOU AIN'T HEARD NOTHIN'
YET": THE AMERICAN
TALKING FILM, HISTORY AND
MEMORY, 1927-1949**
SARRIS, Andrew
New York: Oxford University Press.
ISBN 0195038835

BOOKSELLERS

Stock

A   **Books**
B   **Magazines**
C   **Posters**
D   **Memorabilia eg Stills**
E   **Cassettes, CDs,**
      Records and Videos
F   **Postcards and**
      Greetings Cards

Arnolfini Bookshop
16 Narrow Quay
Bristol BS1 4QA
Tel: 0117 9299191
Fax: 0117 9253876
Peter Begen, Bookshop Manager
Open: 10.00-7.00 Mon-Sat,
12.00-6.30 Sun
Stock: A, B, F
Based in the Arnolfini Gallery,
concentrating on the visual arts. No
catalogues issued. Send requests for
specific material with SAE

At the Movies
9 Cecil Court
London WC2N 4EZ
Tel: 020 7240 7221
Stock includes books, stills and
memorabilia. No catalogue
Open: 11.00-6.00 Mon-Fri
11.30-6.00 Sat

Blackwell's
48-51 Broad Street
Oxford OX1 3BQ
Tel: 01865 792792
Fax: 01865 794143
email: blackwells.extra@blackwell.
co.uk
Website: www.blackwell.
co.uk/bookshops/
Open: 9.00-6.00 Mon, Wed-Sat, 9.30-
6.00 Tue, 11.00-5.00 Sun
Stock: A
Literature department has sections on
cinemas and performing arts,
sociology department has a Media
Studies section `and performing arts.
International charge and send service
available

Blackwell's Art & Poster Shop
27 Broad Street
Oxford OX1 2AS
Tel: 01865 792792
Open: 9.00-6.00 Mon, Wed-Sat, 9.30-
6.00 Tues, 11.00-5.00 Sun
Stock: A, B, C, F
A wide selection of books, posters,
cards, calendars and gift items, all
available by mail order

Brockwell Books
5 Old School House Court
High Street
Honiton
Devon EX14 8NZ
Tel: 01404 42826
Stock: A, B, C, D
Film books offered by mail order
only. Mainly deal in out of print
books but also some new titles.
Catalogue 'Serious about Cinema'
produced three times a year

Cinegrafix Gallery
4 Copper Row
Shad Thames
Tower Bridge Piazza
London SE1 2LH
Tel: 020 7234 0566
Fax: 020 7234 0577
Gallery open Tues-Sat 11.00-7.00
Stock: A, B, C, D, F
Specialist in rare film posters. Poster
catalogues available at £5. Fully
illustrated Portrait catalogue available
at £4

The Cinema Bookshop
13-14 Great Russell Street
London WC1B 3NH
Tel: 020 7637 0206
Fax: 020 7436 9979
Open: 10.30-5.30 Mon-Sat
Stock: A, B, C, D
Comprehensive stock of new, out-of-
print and rare books. Posters,
Pressbooks and stills etc. No
catalogues are issued. Send requests
for specific material with SAE

The Cinema Store
Unit 4B, Orion House
Upper Saint Martin's Lane
London WC2H 9EJ
Tel: 020 7379 7838 (general
enquiries)
Fax: 020 7240 7689
email: cinemastor@aol.com
Website: www. atlasdigital.com/
cinemastore
Tel: 020 7379 7865
(laserdiscs, mail order books, cd's)
Tel: 020 7379 7895
(trading cards, VHS)
Open: 10.00-6.00 Mon-Wed, Sat,
10.00-7.00 Thu-Fri
12-6 Sun
Stock: A, B, C, D, E, F
Mail order available worldwide.
Latest and vintage posters/stills,
magazines, models and laser discs,
new/rare VHS, soundtracks and
trading cards

Cornerhouse Books
70 Oxford Street

Manchester M1 5NH
Tel: 0161 228 7621
Fax: 0161 236 7323
Stock: A, B, F
Open: 12.00-8.30 daily
No catalogues issued. Send requests
for specific material with SAE

Culture Vultures Books
329 St Leonard's Road
Windsor SL4 3DS
Tel: 01753 851 693
Fax: 01923 224714
Stock: A
Mail order only. Periodic catalogues
issued (separate catalogues for
cinema, theatre, music). SAE
appreciated. Comprehensive stock of
out-of-print titles

Ray Dasilva Puppet Books
63 Kennedy Road
Bicester
Oxfordshire OX6 8BE
Tel: 01869 245793
Mail order (visitors by appointment).
New and secondhand books on
puppetry and animation including
film and television. Catalogue
available

David Drummond at Pleasures of Past Times
11 Cecil Court
Charing Cross Road
London WC2H 0AA
Tel: 020 7836 1142
Open: 11.00-2.30, 3.30-5.45 Mon-
Fri. First Sat in month 11.00-2.30
Stock: A, D, F
Extended hours and other times by
arrangement. No catalogue

Decorum Books
24 Cloudsley Square
London N1 0HN
Tel: 020 7278 1838
Fax: 020 7837 6424
Mail order only. Secondhand books
on film and theatre; music and art.
Also secondhand scores and sheet
music

Dress Circle
57-59 Monmouth Street
Upper St Martin's Lane
London WC2H 9DG
Tel: 020 7240 2227
Fax: 020 7379 8540
Open: 10.00-7.00 Mon-Sat
Stock: A, B, C, D, E, F
Specialists in stage music and
musicals. Catalogue of the entire
stock issued annually with updates
twice yearly. Send SAE for details

Anne FitzSimons
62 Scotby Road
Scotby

Carlisle CA4 8BD
Tel: 01228 513815
Stock: A, B, C, D, F
Mail order only. Antiquarian and out-
of-print titles on cinema,
broadcasting and performing arts. A
catalogue is issued twice a year. Send
three first-class postage stamps for
current issue

Flashbacks
6 Silver Place
Beak Street
London W1R 3LJ
Tel: 020 7437 8562
Fax: 020 7437 8562
email: Flashbacks@freeserve.co.uk
Website: www.dacre.simpleton.com/
Stock: C, D
Shop and mail order service. Send
SAE and 'wanted' list for stock details

Forbidden Planet
71-75 New Oxford Street
London WC1A 1DG
Tel: 020 7836 4179
Fax: 020 7240 7118
Open: 10.00-6.00 Mon-Wed, Sat,
10.00-7.00 Thur, Fri
Stock: A, B, C, D, E, F
Science fiction, horror, fantasy and
comics specialists. Mail order service
available on 020 7497 2150

Grant and Cutler
Language Booksellers
55-57 Great Marlborough Street
London W1V 2AY
Tel: 020 7734 2012
Fax: 020 7734 9272
email: postmaster@grant-c.demon.
co.uk
Website: www.grant-c.demon.co.uk
Stock A,E
Foreign language book specialist.
World cinema books and screenplays
Open 9:00 to 17:30   Monday to
Saturday
Thursdays, 9:00 to 19:00

Hay Cinema Bookshop (including Francis Edwards)
The Old Cinema
Castle Street
Hay-on-Wye
via Hereford HR3 5DF
Tel: 01497 820071
Large secondhand stock. Open 9.00-
7.00 Mon-Sat,
11.30-5.30 Sun

Heffers Booksellers
20 Trinity Street
Cambridge CB2 3NG
Tel: 01223 568568
Fax: 01223 568591
Open: 9.00-5.30 Mon-Sat
11.00-5.00 Sun
Stock: A, E

Catalogues of videocassettes and
spoken word recordings issued.
Copies are available on request.

David Henry
PO Box 9146
London W3 8WZ
Tel: 020 8993 2859
email: Filmbooks@Compuserve.com
Stock: A, B
Mail order only. A catalogue of out-
of-print and second-hand books is
issued two or three times a year and
available on request. Search service
for titles not in stock. New books can
be obtained to order, including those
published in USA

LV Kelly Books
6 Redlands
Blundell's Road
Tiverton
Devon EX16 4DH
Tel: 01884 256170
Fax: 01884 242550
email: lenkelly@eclipse.co.uk
Website:www.lvkellybooks.webjump.
com
Stock: A, B, E
Principally mail order but visitors
welcome by appointment. Catalogue
issued regularly on broadcasting and
mass communications. Occasional
lists on cinema, music, journalism

Ed Mason
Room 301
Third Floor
River Bank House Business Centre
1, Putney Bridge Approach
London SW6 3JD
Tel: 020 7736 8511
Stock: A, B, C, D
Specialist in original film
memorabilia from the earliest
onwards. Also organises the
Collectors' Film Convention six
times a year
Office only – all memorabilia stock
is re-located to Rare Discs (see entry)

National Museum of Photography, Film & Television
Pictureville
Bradford BD1 1NQ
Tel: 01274 202030
Fax: 01274 723155
Website: www.nmsi.ac.uk/nmpft
Bookshop run by A Zwemmer
Open: 10.00-6.00 Tue-Sun
Closed Mondays (except Bank
Holidays and School Holidays)
Stock: A, C, D, F
Mail order available. Send SAE with
requests for information

Offstage Theatre & Film Bookshop
37 Chalk Farm Road
London NW1 8AJ
Tel: 020 7485 4996
Fax: 020 7916 8046
Free cinema and media catalogues available. Send SAE. Open 7 days a week

C D Paramor
25 St Mary's Square
Newmarket
Suffolk CB8 0HZ
Tel: 01638 664416
Fax: 01638 664416
Stock: A, B, C, F, E
Mail order only. Visitors welcome strictly by appointment. Catalogues and most of the performing arts issued regularly free of charge

Pullman Everyman Cinema
Holly Bush Vale
Hampstead
London NW3 6TX
Tel: 0207 431 4828
Fax: 0207 435 2292
email: filmbooks@pullmancinemas.com
Tomislav Terek
Stock: A, B, C, D, E, F
Based at the Pullman Everyman Cinema, offers wide range of materials for scholars and enthusiasts alike

Rare Discs
18 Bloomsbury Street
London WC1B3 QA
Tel: 020 7580 3516
Open: 10.00-6.30 Mon-Sat
Stock: E
Retail shop with recorded mail order service. Over 7,000 titles including soundtracks, original cast shows, musicals and nostalgia. Telephone for information

Spread Eagle Bookshop (Incorporates Greenwich Gallery)
9 Nevada Street
London SE10 9JL
Tel: 020 8305 1666
Fax: 020 8305 1666
Open: 10.00-5.30 daily
Stock: A, B, C, D
All second-hand stock. Memorabilia, ephemera. Large stock of books on cinema, theatre, posters and photos

Stable Books
Holm Farm
Coldridge
Crediton
Devon EX17 6BR
Tel: 01363 83227

Mail order (visitors by appointment only). secondhand stock concerning theatre, cinema and puppetry

Stage Door Prints
9 Cecil Court
London WC2N 4EZ
Tel: 020 7240 1683
General stock of performing arts titles including antiquarian prints, ephemera and movie memorobilia. Open 11.00-6.00 Mon-Fri, 11.30-6.00 Sat

Treasure Chest
61 Cobbold Street
Felixstowe
Suffolk 1P11 7BH
Tel: 01394 270717
secondhand stock specialising in cinema and literature. Open 9.30-5.30 Mon-Sat

Vintage Magazine Co
39-43 Brewer Street
London W1R 3FD
Tel: 020 7439 8525
Open: 10.00-8.00 Mon-Sat, 12.00-7.00 Sun
Stock: B, C, D, F
247 Camden High Street
London NW1
Tel: 020 7482 0587
Open: 10.00-6.00
Mon-Fri, 10.00-7.00 Sat, Sun
Stock: B,C,D,F

Peter Wood
20 Stonehill Road
Great Shelford
Cambridge CB2 5JL
Tel: 01223 842419
Stock: A, D, F
Mail order. Visitors are welcome by appointment. A free catalogue is available of all books in stock

A Zwemmer
80 Charing Cross Road
London WC2H 0BB
Tel: 020 7240 4157
Open: 9.30-6.00 Mon-Fri, 10.00-6.00 Sat
Stock: A, B
A catalogue of new and in-print titles on every aspect of cinema is available on request. Mail order service for all books available through Mail Order Department

CABLE, SATELLITE AND DIGITAL

Information in this section is provided by David Fisher, Editor of Screen Digest whose continuing support we gratefully acknowledge

As the number of channels and digital services expands, the number of companies involved in delivering multichannel television to UK homes is rapidly diminishing. In the satellite orbit there has been one dominant operator – British Sky Broadcasting (BSkyB) – for some years. The cable business is moving towards a comparable position now that the third largest operator, NTL, has taken over the domestic cable television operations of the biggest, Cable & Wireless Communications, leaving only two major multiple system operators (MSOs). The second largest MSO, Telewest, is widely expected to become part of one major cable company in due course through a merger with NTL. The cost to NTL of the CWC acquisition is £8.2 billion, whilst Cable & Wireless is paying £6.5 billion to take full ownership of CWC's business operations. These figures indicate the massive financial scale of cable investment and costs.

This process of merger and takeover has radically altered the structure of the UK's broadband cable industry as envisaged when the first franchises were awarded in November 1983. With 12.5m homes already passed by cable systems that are continuing to build—and only 4m homes outside franchise areas—a new phase is beginning as the exclusivity that operators enjoyed as part of their franchises is abandoned. Competition between cable companies is thus possible, although the prospect of operators spending huge sums of money on building competitive cable networks in the foreseeable future is remote.

MULTIPLE SYSTEM OPERATORS

Almost all franchises are held as part of groups of holdings. Such groups are called multiple system operators (MSOs). Extensive consolidation has taken place since 1995 and especially during the first half of 1998, which resulted in the emergence of three dominant groups: Cable & Wireless Communications, NTL and Telewest. However, in mid 1999 NTL agreed to acquire the cable operations of Cable & Wireless

AT&T
US telecom operator, which acquired Tele-Communications Inc (TCI), the largest US cable operator, holder of 50% share in TW Holdings, which owns 53% of Telewest [qv]

Atlantic Telecom Group
303 King Street
Aberdeen AB2 3AP
Tel: 01224 646644
Fax: 01224 644601
Website: http://www.atlantic-telecom.co.uk
Areas: Aberdeen

British Telecommunications (BT)
87-89 Baker Street
London W1M 2LP
Tel: 020 7 487 1254
Fax: 020 7 487 1259
Areas:
as BT New Towns Cable TV Services: Milton Keynes
as Westminster Cable Company: Westminster LB.
Also upgrade systems at Barbican (London), Brackla, Martlesham, Walderslade, Washington
Note: BT is to sell its Milton Keynes and Westminster cable systems. It has also been authorised to deliver cable television services to the 17 per cent of UK homes outside franchised areas. From 1 January 2001 BT will be allowed to compete in delivery of television-related services with existing cable networks.

Cable & Telecoms (UK)
PO Box 319
Whipsnade
Dunstable
Bedfordshire LU6 2LT
Tel: 01582 873006
Fax: 01582 873003
Ownership: US Cable Corporation, McNicholas Construction, Morgan Cable
as Ayrshire Cable & Telecoms: Ayr
as Cumbria Cable & Telecoms: Carlisle; Cumbria, Central
as Northumberland Cable & Telecoms: Northumberland
as South Cumbria Cable & Telecoms: Cumbria, South

Cable & Wireless Communications
26 Red Lion Square
London WC1R 4HQ
Tel: 020 7 528 2000
Website: http://www.cwcom.co.uk
Formed 1997 by merger of cable operators Bell Cablemedia (inc Videotron), Nynex Cablecomms and telecom operator Mercury
Ownership: Cable & Wireless 52.6%, Nynex 18.5%, Bell Canada International (BCI) 14.2%, others 14.7%
Areas:
Aylesbury/Amersham/Chesham, Bolton, Bournemouth/Poole/Christchurch, Brighton/Hove/Worthing, Bromley, Bury/Rochdale, Cheshire North, Chichester/Bognor, Dartford/Swanley, Derby/Spondon, Durham South /North Yorkshire, Ealing, Eastbourne/Hastings, Epping Forest/Chigwell/Loughton/Ongar, Fenland, Great Yarmouth/Lowestoft/Caister, Greater London East, Greenwich/Lewisham, Harrogate/Knaresborough, Harrow, Havering, Hertfordshire South, Kensington/Chelsea, Kent South East, Lambeth/Southwark, Lancashire East, Leeds, London North West, Macclesfield/Wilmslow, Manchester/Salford, Newham/Tower Hamlets, Norwich, Oldham/Tameside, Peterborough, Portsmouth/Fareham/Gosport/Havant, Southampton/Eastleigh, Stockport, Stoke-on-Trent/Newcastle, Surrey North, Surrey North East,

Thamesmead, Totton/Hythe, Waltham Forest, Wandsworth, Wearside, Whittlesey/March/Wisbech, Winchester, The Wirral, York
CWC is being acquired by NTL [qv].

Convergence Group
Premiere House
3 Betts Way
Crawley, West Sussex RH10 2GB
Tel: 01293 540444
Fax: 01293 540900
Areas: East Grinstead, Haywards Heath
50% in Taunton/Bridgewater, Yeovil (with Orbis Trust (Guernsey))
Cox Communications
US cable operator
10% stake in Telewest (23% of preference shares) [qv]

Eurobell (Holdings)
Multi-Media House
Lloyds Court, Manor Royal
Crawley, West Sussex RH10 2PT
Tel: 01293 400444
Fax: 01293 400440
Ownership: Detecon (Deutsche Telepost Consulting)
Areas: Crawley/Horley/Gatwick, Devon South, Kent West
General Cable
Acquired by Telewest June 1998
Metro Cable
Areas: Irvine
Shareholder in Ayrshire Cable & Telecoms

NTL
Bristol House
1 Lakeside Road
Farnborough
Hampshire GU14 6XP
Tel 01252 402662
Fax 01252 402665
Website: http://www.cabletel.co.uk
HQ:
110 East 59th Street, New York, NY 10022 USA
Tel +1/212 906 8440
Fax +1/212 752 1157
Formerly: International CableTel
Ownership: Rockefeller family, Capital Cities Broadcasting Company (subsidiary of Walt Disney Company), Microsoft, France Télécom (eventually will be largest shareholder with 25%)
NTL is acquiring Cable & Wireless Communications cable franchises.
Areas:
former CableTel franchises
as CableTel Bedfordshire: Bedford
as CableTel Glasgow: Bearsden/Milngavie, Glasgow Greater, Glasgow North West/Clydebank, Invercylde, Paisley/Renfrew

as CableTel Herts & Bedfordshire: Luton/South Bedfordshire
as CableTel Hertfordshire: Hertfordshire Central, Hertfordshire East,
as CableTel Kirklees: Huddersfield/Dewsbury
as CableTel Northern Ireland: Northern Ireland
as CableTel South Wales: Cardiff/Penarth, Glamorgan West, Glamorgan/Gwent, Newport/Cwmbran/Pontypool
as CableTel Surrey: Guildford/West Surrey
former Comcast UK franchises:
as Anglia Cable: Harlow/Bishops Stortford/Stansted Airport
as Cambridge Cable: Cambridge/Ely/Newmarket,
as Comcast Teesside: Darlington, Teesside
as East Coast Cable: Colchester/Ipswich/etc,
as Southern East Anglia Cable: East Anglia South,
Sold its 50% stake in Cable London to Telewest (qv) August 1999.
former ComTel franchises:
Andover/Salisbury/Romsey, Daventry, Corby/Kettering/Wellingborough, Hertfordshire West, Litchfield/Burntwood/Rugeley, Northampton, Nuneaton/Bedworth/Rugby, Oxford/Abingdon, Stafford/Stone, Swindon, Tamworth/North Warwickshire/Meriden, Thames Valley, Warwick/Stratford-upon-Avon/Kenilworth/Leamington Spa
former Diamond Cable franchises:
Bassetlaw, Burton-on-Trent, Coventry, East Derbyshire, Grantham, Grimsby/Immingham/Cleethorpes, Hinckley/Bosworth, Huddersfield/Dewsbury, Leicester, Lincoln, Lincolnshire/South Humberside, Loughborough/Shepshed, Mansfield/Sutton/Kirkby-in-Ashfield, Melton Mowbray, Newark-on-Trent, Northern Ireland, Nottingham, Ravenshead, Vale of Belvoir
SBC International
Ownership: Southwestern Bell Telecom [US telecom operator]
10% stake in Telewest (23% of preference shares) [qv]
Telecential Communications
Acquired by NTL June 1998

Telewest Communications
Unit 1, Genesis Business Park
Albert Drive
Woking, Surrey GU21 5RW
Tel: 01483 750900

Fax 01483 750901
Website: http://www.telewest.co.uk
Ownership: TW Holdings (= Tele-Communications International (TINTA) 50% and US West International 50%) 53%, Microsoft 29.9%, Liberty Media (=AT&T), Cox Communications 10%, SBC International (= Southwestern Bell Telecom) 10%
Acquired NTL's (formerly Comcast UK's) half-share in Cable London in August 1999.
Areas:
as Birmingham Cable: Birmingham/Solihull, Wythall
as Cable Corporation: Hillingdon/Hounslow, Windsor
as Cable London: Camden, Enfield, Hackney & Islington, Haringey
as Telewest London & the South East): Croydon, Kingston/Richmond, Merton/Sutton, Thames Estuary North, Thames Estuary South
as Telewest Midlands & the South West: Avon, Black Country, Cheltenham/Gloucester, Taunton/Bridgewater, Telford, Worcester
as Telewest North West): Blackpool/Fylde, Lancashire Central, Liverpool North/Bootle/Crosby, Liverpool South, St Helens/Knowsley, Southport, Wigan
as Telewest Scotland & North East: Cumbernauld, Dumbarton, Dundee, Edinburgh, Falkirk/West Lothian, Fife, Glenrothes/Kirkaldy/Leven, Motherwell/East Kilbride/Hamilton/Wishaw/Lanark, Perth/Scone, Tyneside
as Yorkshire Cable Communications: Barnsley, Bradford, Calderdale, Doncaster/Rotherham, Sheffield, Wakefield/Pontefract/Castleford
US West International
50% share in TW Holdings, which owns 53% of Telewest [qv]

CABLE FRANCHISES

All broadband cable franchises to date were granted by the Cable Authority (apart from 11 previously granted by the Department of Trade and Industry), the role of which was taken over by the Independent Television Commission (ITC) in January 1991, under the Broadcasting Act 1990.

The Act empowered the ITC to grant fifteen-year 'local delivery licences', which can include use of microwave distribution. Licences must be awarded to the highest bidder on the basis of an annual cash bid in addition to forecasts of the sums that will be paid to the Exchequer as a percentage of revenue earned in the second and third five-year periods of the licence.

The franchises are arranged in alphabetical order of area. Where appropriate the principal towns in the area are identified under the area name; cross references are provided for these and other principal towns at the appropriate alphabetical point. 'Homes in area' is the number of homes in the franchise area at the time of the last census before award of the franchise. 'Build completed' is indicated where all homes nominally in the area are passed by cable. 'Homes passed' is the number of homes to which a cable service is available and marketed. 'Subscribers' (abbreviated to 'Subs') are those taking at least the basic service, with the percentage this represents of homes passed. Unless stated, services have not yet begun.

Extensive consolidation of ownership has occurred since the last edition of the Handbook. To reflect this, the name of the parent franchise or local delivery licence holder is given, with a cross-reference to the listing under the Group Ownership heading, where any significant local trading names are given. However, for marketing reasons such local variations are expected to disappear in time.

In some towns an older cable system still exists. These are not franchised but are licensed by the ITC to provide limited services. They are gradually being superseded by new broadband networks

Aberdeen
Franchise holder: Aberdeen Cable Services = Atlantic Telecom Group (see MSOs)
Homes in area: 91,000 (build complete)
Awarded: 29 Nov 83
Service start: 1 May 85
Homes passed: 97,628
Subs: 16,875 = 17.3% (1 Apr 99)

Abingdon
see Oxford

Accrington
see Lancashire, East

Airdrie
see Cumbernauld

Alconbury
Narrowband upgrade system operated by Cablecom Investments (see MSOs)

Aldershot
see Guildford

Amersham
see Aylesbury

Andover/Salisbury/Romsey
Franchise holder: NTL (see MSOs)
Homes in area: 84,500
Awarded: Andover Apr 89, Salisbury/Romsey 6 Apr 90
Service start: Andover Mar 90, Salisbury/Romsey Jun 95
Homes passed: 53,648 (1 Apr 99)
Subs: 10,757 = 20.1% (1 Apr 99)
Franchises awarded separately but amalgamated

Ashford
see Kent, South-east

Avon
Bristol, Bath, Weston-super-Mare, Frome, Melksham etc
Franchise holder: Telewest (see MSOs)
Homes in area: 300,000 (build complete)
Awarded: 16 Nov 88
Service start: 14 Sept 90
Homes passed: 306,366 (1 Apr 99)
Subs: 80,010 = 26.1% (1 Apr 99)

Aylesbury/Amersham/Chesham/Wendover
Franchise holder: Cable & Wireless Communications (see MSOs)
Homes in area: 89,000
Awarded: 31 May 90; acquired Jul 94
Service start: Apr 96
Homes passed: 37,707 (1 Apr 99)
Subs: 4,896 = 13.0% (1 Apr 99)

Ayr
Local delivery franchise holder:
Cable & Telecoms (see MSOs)
Homes in area: 155,000
Awarded: July 1997
Area includes narrowband system in Irvine.

Baldock
see Hertfordshire, Central

Banstead
see East Grinstead

Barking/Dagenham, London Borough of
see Greater London East

Barnet, London Borough of
see London, North West

Barnsley
Franchise holder: Telewest (see MSOs)
Homes in area: 82,000
Awarded: 14 Jun 90; acquired Apr 93
Homes passed: 36,463 (1 Apr 99)
Subs: 5,276 = 14.5% (1 Apr 99)

Barrow in Furness
see Cumbria, South

Basildon
see Thames Estuary North

Basingstoke
see Thames Valley

Bassetlaw
Local delivery licence holder: NTL (see MSOs)
Homes in area: 32,800
Date awarded: 13 Jul 95
Bath see Avon
Bearsden/Milngavie
Franchise holder: CableTel Glasgow (see MSOs)
Homes in area: 16,000
Awarded: 7 Jun 90
Homes passed: 13,168 (1 Apr 99)
Subs: 4,928 = 37.4% (1 Apr 99)

Bedford
Franchise holder: CableTel Bedfordshire (see MSOs)
Homes in area: 55,000 (build complete)
Awarded: 14 Jun 90
Service start: Nov 1994
Homes passed: 56,304 (1 Apr 99)
Subs: 19,128 = 34.0% (1 Apr 99)

Bedworth
see Nuneaton

Beith
Narrowband upgrade system operated by A Thomson (Relay)

Belfast
Franchise revoked from Ulster Cablevision
Homes in area: 136,000

Awarded: 29 Nov 83
see Northern Ireland

Belper
see Derbyshire, East

Berkhamsted
see Hertfordshire, West

Bexley, London Borough of
see Greater London East
Birmingham/Solihull
Franchise holder: Birmingham Cable
(see MSOs)
Homes in area: 465,000
Awarded: 19 Oct 88
Service start: Dec 89
Homes passed: 415,959 (1 Apr 99)
Subs: 117,713 = 28.3% (1 Apr 99)

Bishops Stortford
see Harlow

Black Country
Dudley, Sandwell, Walsall,
Wolverhampton, urban parts of
Bromsgrove, Cannock,
Kidderminster
Franchise holder: Telewest (see
MSOs)
Homes in area: 470,000
Awarded: 14 Jul 89
Service start: Sept 91
Homes passed: 384,800 (1 Apr 99)
Subs: 93,060 = 24.2% (1 Apr 99)

Blackburn
see Lancashire, East

Blackpool and Fylde
Local delivery franchise holder:
Telewest (see MSOs)
Homes in area: 101,000
Date awarded: Sept 94
Homes passed: 38,875 (1 Apr 99)
Subs: 7,985 = 20.5% (1 Apr 99)

Blaenau Ffestiniog
Narrowband upgrade system operated
by John Sulwyn Evans

Bognor
see Chichester

Bolsover
see Derbyshire, East

Bolton
Franchise holder: Cable & Wireless
Communications (see MSOs)
Homes in area: 135,000
Awarded: 13 Aug 85; acquired 22
Mar 93
Service start: Jul 90
Homes passed: 127,195 (1 Apr 99)
Subs: 25,358 = 19.9% (1 Apr 99)

Bootle
see Liverpool, North

Borehamwood
see Hertfordshire, South

Bosworth
see Hinkley

**Bournemouth/Poole/Christc
hurch**
Franchise holder: Cable & Wireless
Communications (see MSOs)
Homes in area: 143,000
Awarded: 6 Apr 90
Service start: mid 94
Home passed: 119,119 (1 Apr 99)
Subs: 29,718 = 24.9% (1 Apr 99)

Bracknell
see Thames Valley

Bradford
Franchise holder: Telewest (see
MSOs)
Homes in area: 175,000
Awarded: 14 Jun 90
Service start: Jul 92
Homes passed: 143,551 (1 Apr 99)
Subs: 25,251 = 17.6% (1 Apr 99)

Braintree
see East Anglia, South
Brecon
Narrowband upgrade system operated
by Metro Cable

Brent, London Borough of
see London, North West

Brentwood
see Thames Estuary North

Brighouse
see Calderdale

Brighton/Hove/Worthing
Franchise holder: Cable & Wireless
Communications (see MSOs)
Homes in area: 160,000 (build
complete)
Awarded: 20 Oct 89; acquired 22
Mar 93
Service start: Apr 1992
Homes passed: 157,817 (1 Apr 99)
Subs: 37,914 = 23.7% (1 Apr 99)
Separate upgrade system in Brighton
operated by CDA Communications

Bristol
see Avon

Broadstairs
see Thanet, Isle of

**Bromley, London Borough
of**
Franchise holder: Cable & Wireless
Communications (see MSOs)
Homes in area: 117,000 (build
complete)
Awarded: 16 Mar 90
Service start: Jan 93

Homes passed: 116,565 (1 Apr 99)
Subs: 27,610 = 23.7% (1 Apr 99)

Burgess Hill
see Haywards Heath

Burnley
see Lancashire, East

Burntwood
see Stafford

Bury St Edmunds
see East Anglia, South

**Burton-on-Trent/
Swadlincote/Ashby-de-la-
Zouch/Coalville/Uttoxeter**
Local delivery franchise holder: NTL
(see MSOs)
Homes in area: 77,675
Awarded: Jun 95
Original franchise revoked from N-
Com Cablevision

Bury/Rochdale
Franchise holder: Cable & Wireless
Communications (see MSOs)
Homes in area: 143,000
Awarded: 17 May 90; acquired 4
May 93
Homes passed: 72,652 (1 Apr 99)
Subs: 16,732 = 22.9% (1 Apr 99)
Separate upgrade system in Rochdale
operated by CDA Communications

Bushey
see Hertfordshire, South

Calderdale
Halifax, Brighouse
Franchise holder: Telewest (see
MSOs)
Homes in area: 75,000
Awarded: 14 Jun 90
Homes passed: 30,704 (1 Apr 99)
Subs: 4,262 = 13.9% (1 Apr 99)

Camberley
see Guildford

Cambridge and district
Cambridge, Newmarket, Ely, Saffron
Walden, Huntingdon, St Ives, St
Neots, Royston, etc
Franchise holder: Cambridge Cable =
Comcast Europe (see MSOs)
Homes in area: 132,000
Awarded: 4 Jun 89
Service start: Jul 91
Homes passed: 126,860 (1 Apr 99)
Subs: 29,111 = 22.9% (1 Apr 99)

**Camden, London Borough
of**
Franchise holder: Telewest (see
MSOs)
Homes in area: 70,000 (build
complete)
Awarded: 1 Feb 86

Service start: Dec 89
Homes passed: 83,071 (1 Apr 99)
Subs: 20,146 = 22.9% (1 Apr 99)
Canterbury/Thanet
No applicants for local delivery
franchise (January 1997)
Upgrade systems in Canterbury and
Isle of Thanet operated by CDA
Communications

Cardiff/Penarth
Franchise holder: CableTel South
Wales (see MSOs)
Homes in area: 103,000
Awarded: 5 Feb 86
Service start: Sept 94
Homes passed: 93,269 (1 Apr 99)
Subs: 38,588 = 41.4% (1 Apr 99)
Carlisle
Local delivery licence holder: Cable
& Telecoms (UK) (see MSOs)
Homes in area: 35,000
Awarded: Nov 95
Original franchise surrendered by
Carlisle Cablevision (awarded: 21
Jun 90)

Carmarthen
Narrowband upgrade system operated
by Metro Cable

Castleford
see Wakefield

Chatham
see Thames Estuary South

Chelmsford
see Thames Estuary North

Cheltenham/Gloucester
Franchise holder: Telewest (see
MSOs)
Homes in area: 90,000
Awarded: 13 Aug 85
Service start: Aug 94
Homes passed: 55,802 (1 Apr 99)
Subs: 13,206 = 23.7% (1 Apr 99)

Cheshire, North
Chester, Ellesmere Port, Warrington,
Widnes, Runcorn
Franchise holder: Cable & Wireless
Communications (see MSOs)
Homes in area: 175,000
Awarded: 12 Jan 90; acquired 21 Apr
93
Homes passed: 114,216 (1 Apr 99)
Subs: 27,179 = 23.8% (1 Apr 99)

Chesham
see Aylesbury

Cheshunt
see Hertfordshire, East

Chesterfield
see Derbyshire, East

Chichester/Bognor

Local delivery franchise holder:
Cable & Wireless Communications
(see MSOs)
Homes in area: 67,100
Awarded: Nov 95

Chigwell
see Epping Forest

Chorley
see Southport

Chorleywood
see Hertfordshire, South

Christchurch
see Bournemouth

Clacton on Sea
see East Anglia, South

Cleethorpes
see Grimsby

Clydebank
see Glasgow, North West

Coalville
see Burton-on-Trent
Coatbridge see Cumbernauld

Colchester/Ipswich/Felixstowe /Harwich/Woodbridge
Franchise holder: East Coast Cable =
Comcast Europe (see MSOs)
Homes in area: 126,000
Awarded: 21 Jul 89
Service start: late 94
Homes passed: 84,506 (1 Apr 99)
Subs: 16,220 = 19.2% (1 Apr 99)

Colne
see Lancashire, East
Consett/Stanley (Derwentside)
Local delivery franchise holder:
Telewest (see MSOs)
Homes in area: 37,000
Awarded: 27 Jul 98

Corby
see Northampton, North-east

Coventry
Franchise holder: Coventry Cable =
NTL (see MSOs)
Homes in area: 119,000 (build
complete)
Awarded: 29 Nov 83
Service start: 1 Sept 85
Homes passed: 117,000
Subs: 20,522 = 17.5% (1 Apr 99)

Crawley/Horley/Gatwick
Franchise holder: Eurobell (see
MSOs)
Homes in area: 44,000 (build
complete)
Awarded: 27 Apr 89
Service start: Jun 93
Homes passed: 43,315 (1 Apr 99)
Subs: 9,929 = 22.9% (1 Apr 99)

Crosby
see Liverpool, North

Croydon, London Borough of
Franchise holder: Telewest (see
MSOs)
Homes in area: 115,000 (build
complete)
Awarded: 1 Nov 83
Service start: 1 Sept 85
Homes passed: 124,534 (1 Apr 99)
Subs: 29,564 = 23.7% (1 Apr 99)

Cumbernauld/Kilsyth/ Airdrie/Coatbridge
Franchise holder: Telewest (see MSOs)
Homes in area: 55,000
Awarded: 27 Apr 89
Service start: May 95

Cumbria, Central
Local delivery franchise holder:
Cable & Telecoms (UK) (see MSOs)
Homes in area: 84,000
Awarded: Oct 96

Cumbria, South
Barrow-in-Furness, South Lakeland
District
Local delivery franchise holder:
South Cumbria Cable & Telecoms =
Cable & Telecoms (UK) (see MSOs)
Homes in area: 61,500
Awarded: May 97

Cwmbran
see Newport

Dagenham
see Greater London East

Darlington
Franchise holder: Comcast Teesside
(see MSOs)
Homes in area: 34,000
Awarded: 21 Jun 90
Service start: Jun 95
Homes passed: 34,485 (1 Apr 99)
Subs: 9,420 = 27.3% (1 Apr 99)

Dartford/Swanley
Franchise holder: Cable & Wireless
Communications (see MSOs)
Homes in area: 35,000
Awarded: 16 Mar 90
Service start: Dec 94
Homes passed: 23,732 (1 Apr 99)
Subs: 4,376 = 18.4% (1 Apr 99)

Daventry
Local delivery franchise holder: NTL
(see MSOs)
Homes in area: 8,710
Awarded: Nov 96
Homes passed: 19,262 (1 Apr 99)
Subs: 4,355 = 22.6% (1 Apr 99)

Deal
see Kent, South East

Derby/Spondon
Franchise holder: Cable & Wireless
Communications (see MSOs)
Homes in area: 83,000 (build
complete)
Awarded: 16 Feb 90; acquired 22 Mar 93
Service start: Oct 91
Homes passed: 93,344 (1 Apr 99)
Subs: 18,393 = 19.7% (1 Apr 99)

Derbyshire, East
Chesterfield, Bolsover, Matlock,
Belper
Local delivery franchise holder: NTL
(see MSOs)
Homes in area: 89,000
Awarded: Jun 96

Devon, South
Exeter, Plymouth, Torbay, Totnes,
Newton Abbot
Franchise holder: Eurobell (see
MSOs)
Homes in area: 236,000
Awarded: 15 Dec 89
Service start: May 1996
Homes passed: 99,170 (1 Apr 99)
Subs: 14,679 = 14.8% (1 Apr 99)

Dewsbury
see Kirklees

Diss
see East Anglia, South

Doncaster/Rotherham
Franchise holder: Telewest (see
MSOs)
Homes in area: 192,000
Awarded: 10 May 90
Homes passed: 69,284 (1 Apr 99)
Subs: 9,580 = 13.8% (1 Apr 99)
Dorset, West

**Dorchester, Weymouth,
Portland**
Homes in area: 35,000
Awarded: 10 Feb 90
Franchise revoked from Coastal
Cablevision = Leonard
Communication (US)

Dover
see Kent, South East

Droitwich
see Worcester

Dudley
see Black Country

Dumbarton/Vale of Leven
Franchise holder: Telewest (see
MSOs)
Homes in area: 17,000 (build
complete)
Awarded: 27 Apr 89
Service start: Nov 96
Homes passed: 19,898 (1 Apr 99)
Subs: 9,387 = 47.2% (1 Apr 99)

Dumfries and Galloway
Local delivery franchise holder:
Dumfries and Galloway Cable &
Telecoms
Ownership: US Cable Group,
McNicholas Construction, Morgan
Cable
PO Box 319
Whipsnade
Bedfordshire LU6 2LT
Tel: 01582 873006
Fax: 01582 873003
Homes in area: 155,000
Awarded: Dec 97

**Dundee/Broughty
Ferry/Monifieth/Carnoustie**
Franchise holder: Telewest (see
MSOs)
Homes in area: 95,000
Awarded: 19 Jan 90
Service start: Jan 91
Homes passed: 66,295 (1 Apr 99)
Subs: 11,903 = 18.0% (1 Apr 99)
Dunstable see Luton
Durham, South/North Yorkshire
Local delivery franchise holder:
Cable & Wireless Communications
(see MSOs)
Homes in area: 155,000
Awarded: Apr 96

Durham
see Wearside

Ealing, London Borough of
Franchise holder: Cable & Wireless
Communications (see MSOs)
Homes in area: 105,000
Awarded: 8 Nov 83
Service start: 1 Nov 86
Homes passed: 81,088 (1 Apr 99)
Subs: 20,165 = 24.9% (1 Apr 99)

East Anglia, South
Bury St Edmunds, Sudbury,
Braintree, Clacton on Sea,
Stowmarket, Thetford, Diss
Local delivery licence holder:
Southern East Anglia Cable =
Comcast Europe (see MSOs)
Homes in area: 205,000
Date awarded: Jan 95

East Grinstead
East Grinstead, Crowborough, parts
of Banstead and Reigate
Local delivery licence holder:
Convergence (East Grinstead) (see
MSOs)
Homes in area: 30,300
Date awarded: 11 Jul 96

East Kilbride
see Motherwell

Eastbourne/Hastings
Local delivery franchise holder:
Cable & Wireless Communications

(see MSOs)
Homes in area: 150,000
Awarded: Feb 96
Separate upgrade systems in
Eastbourne and Hastings operated by
CDA Communications

Eastleigh
see Southampton

East Lothian
see Lothian

Edinburgh
Franchise holder: Telewest (see
MSOs)
Homes in area: 183,000 (build
complete)
Awarded: 5 Feb 86
Service start: May 92
Homes passed: 243,865 (1 Apr 99)
Subs: 65,036 = 26.7% (1 Apr 99)
see also Lothian

Ellesmere Port
see Cheshire, North

Elmbridge
see Surrey, North

Elstree
see Hertfordshire, South

Enfield
Franchise holder: Telewest (see
MSOs)
Homes in area: 105,000 (build
complete)
Awarded: 31 May 90
Service start: Oct 91
Homes passed: 107,931 (1 Apr 99)
Subs: 30,171 = 28.0% (1 Apr 99)

**Epping
Forest/Chigwell/Loughton/
Ongar**
Franchise holder: Cable & Wireless
Communications (see MSOs)
Homes in area: 45,000
Awarded: 3 May 90
Service start: Dec 94
Homes passed: 34,048 (1 Apr 99)
Subs: 4,979 = 14.6% (1 Apr 99)

Epsom
see Surrey, North East

Exeter
see Devon, South

Falkirk/West Lothian
Franchise holder: Telewest (see
MSOs)
Homes in area: 30,000
Awarded: 21 Jun 90
Service start: Oct 94

Fareham
see Portsmouth

Farnborough
see Guildford

Faversham
Narrowband upgrade system operated by CDA Communications (see MSOs)

Felixstowe
see Colchester

Fenland
Wisbech, March, Whittlesey
Franchise holder: Cable & Wireless Communications (see MSOs)
Homes in area: 21,000
Awarded: 5 Jul 90
Service start: Apr 97
Homes passed: 12,036 (1 Apr 99)
Subs: 2,755 = 22.9% (1 Apr 99)

Fife
Kingdom of Fife excluding Glenrothes and Kirkcaldy
Local delivery franchise holder: Telewest (see MSOs)
Homes in area: 35,000
Awarded: Jul 97

Folkestone
see Kent, South East

Gateshead
see Tyneside

Gatwick
see Crawley

Gillingham
see Thames Estuary South

Glamorgan, West
Swansea, Neath, Port Talbot
Franchise holder: CableTel South Wales (see MSOs)
Homes in area: 110,000
Awarded: 16 Nov 89
Service start: Dec 90
Homes passed: 107,012 (1 Apr 99)
Subs: 49,595 = 46.3% (1 Apr 99)
Separate narrowband upgrade systems operated in parts of the area by Metro Cable

Glamorgan/Gwent
Franchise holder: CableTel South Wales (see MSOs)
Homes in area: 230,000
Awarded: Oct 95
Service start: Apr 97 on existing network
Homes passed: 19,641 (1 Apr 99)
Subs: 8,919 = 45.4% (1 Apr 99)
Separate narrowband upgrade systems operated in parts of the area by Metro Cable

Glasgow, Greater
Franchise holder: CableTel Glasgow (see MSOs)

Homes in area: 274,000
Awarded: 7 Jun 90
Homes passed: 89,288 (1 Apr 99)
Subs: 33,172 = 37.2% (1 Apr 99)

Glasgow, North West/Clydebank
Franchise holder: CableTel Glasgow (see MSOs)
Homes in area: 112,000; 16,000 business premises
Awarded: 29 Nov 83
Service start: 1 Oct 85
Homes passed: 114,407 (1 Apr 99)
Subs: 29,071 = 25.4% (1 Apr 99)

Glenrothes/Kirkcaldy/Leven /Buckhaven/Methil
Franchise holder: Telewest (see MSOs)
Homes in area: 60,000
Awarded: 21 Jun 90
Service start: Oct 91
Homes passed: 51,461 (1 Apr 99)
Subs: 14,886 = 28.9% (1 Apr 99)

Gloucester
see Cheltenham

Godalming
see Guildford

Gosport
see Portsmouth

Gourock
see Inverclyde

Grantham
Franchise holder: NTL (see MSOs)
Homes in area: 30,000
Awarded: 26 Apr 90
Service start: Oct 95
Homes passed: 13,945 (1 Apr 99)
Subs: 3,194 = 22.9% (1 Apr 99)

Gravesend
see Thames Estuary South

Great Yarmouth/ Lowestoft/Caister
Franchise holder: Cable & Wireless Communications (see MSOs)
Homes in area: 64,000
Awarded: 5 Jul 90
Service start: Jun 96
Homes passed: 20,220 (1 Apr 99)
Subs: 4,447 = 22.0% (1 Apr 99)

Greater London East
Boroughs of Barking/Dagenham, Bexley, Redbridge
Franchise holder: Cable & Wireless Communications (see MSOs)
Homes in area: 229,000
Awarded: 15 Dec 88
Service start: Dec 90
Homes passed: 200,539 (1 Apr 99)
Subs: 44,431 = 22.2% (1 Apr 99)

Greenock
see Inverclyde

Greenwich/Lewisham, London Boroughs of
Franchise holder: Cable & Wireless Communications (see MSOs)
Homes in area: 175,000
Awarded: 7 Apr 89
Service start: Jan 91
Homes passed: 141,578 (1 Apr 99)
Subs: 31,043 = 21.9% (1 Apr 99)

Grimsby/Immingham/ Cleethorpes
Franchise holder: NTL (see MSOs)
Homes in area: 63,000
Awarded: 5 Jul 90
Service start: Jun 95
Homes passed: 62,734 (1 Apr 99)
Subs: 13,814 = 22.0% (1 Apr 99)

Guildford/West Surrey/ East Hampshire
Guildford, Aldershot, Farnborough, Camberley, Woking, Godalming
Franchise holder: CableTel UK (see MSOs)
Flagship House
Reading Road North
Surrey GU13 8XR
Tel: 01252 652000
Fax: 01252 652100
Homes in area: 22,000 + 115,000
Awarded: 29 Nov 83 + Aug 85
Service start: 1 Jul 87
Homes passed: 132,901 (1 Apr 99)
Subs: 51,5223 = 38.8% (1 Apr 99)

Gwent
see Glamorgan/Gwent

Hackney/Islington, London Boroughs of
Franchise holder: Telewest (see MSOs)
Homes in area: 150,000
Awarded: 13 Apr 90
Service start: Apr 95
Homes passed: 116,015 (1 Apr 99)
Subs: 26,788 = 23.1% (1 Apr 99)

Halifax
see Calderdale

Hamilton
see Motherwell

Hammersmith and Fulham, London Borough of
see London, North West

Haringey, London Borough of
Franchise holder: Telewest (see MSOs)
Homes in area: 85,000
Awarded: Sept 89
Homes passed: 74,816 (1 Apr 99)
Subs: 19,490 = 26.1% (1 Apr 99)

Harlow/Bishops Stortford/Stansted Airport
Franchise holder: Anglia Cable =
Comcast Europe (see MSOs)
Homes in area: 43,000 (build
complete)
Date awarded: 23 Mar 90
Service start: Jun 93
Homes passed: 46,738 (1 Apr 99)
Subs: 13,938 = 29.8% (1 Apr 99)

Harpenden
see Hertfordshire, West

Harrogate/Knaresborough
Franchise holder: Cable & Wireless
Communications (see MSOs)
Homes in area: 78,000
Awarded: 30 Mar 90, acquired Apr
94
Service start: Sep 95
Homes passed: 32,368 (1 Apr 99)
Subs: 4,425 = 13.7% (1 Apr 99)
Harrow
Franchise holder: Cable & Wireless
Communications (see MSOs)
Homes in area: 79,000
Awarded: 24 May 90
Service start: Dec 91
Homes passed: 68,103 (1 Apr 99)
Subs: 16,780 = 24.6% (1 Apr 99)

Hartlepool
see Teesside

Harwich
see Colchester

Hastings
see Eastbourne

Hatfield
see Hertfordshire, Central

Havant
see Portsmouth

Haverfordwest
Narrowband upgrade system operated
by Metro Cable

Havering, London Borough of
Franchise holder: Cable & Wireless
Communications (see MSOs)
Homes in area: 90,000
Awarded: 6 Apr 90
Service start: Sept 93
Homes passed: 82,654 (1 Apr 99)
Subs: 8,719 = 10.5% (1 Apr 99)

Haywards Heath
Local delivery franchise holder:
Convergence Group (see MSOs)
Homes in area: 31,150
Original franchise revoked from N-
Comm Cablevision

Heathrow
see Windsor

Hemel Hempstead
see Hertfordshire, West

Henley-on-Thames
see Thames Valley

Herne Bay
Narrowband upgrade system operated
by CDA Communications (see
MSOs)

Hertford
see Hertfordshire, East

Hertfordshire, Central
Stevenage, Welwyn, Hatfield,
Hitchin, Baldock, Letchworth
Franchise holder: CableTel
Hertfordshire (see MSOs)
Homes in area: 100,000
Awarded: 3 Nov 89
Homes passed: 89,302 (1 Apr 99)
Subs: 49,970 = 56.0% (1 Apr 99)
Separate upgrade system operated in
Hatfield by Metro Cable

Hertfordshire, East
Hertford, Cheshunt, Ware, Lea
Valley, Hoddesdon
Franchise holder: CableTel
Bedfordshire (see MSOs)
Homes in area: 60,000
Awarded: 31 May 90
Homes passed: 48,595 (1 Apr 99)
Subs: 17,881 = 36.8% (1 Apr 99)

Hertfordshire, South
Watford, Chorleywood,
Rickmansworth, Bushey, Radlett,
Elstree, Borehamwood, Potters Bar
Franchise holder: Cable & Wireless
Communications (see MSOs)
Homes in area: 95,000
Awarded: 3 Nov 89
Service start: Apr 92
Homes passed: 87,304 (1 Apr 99)
Subs: 23,216 = 26.6% (1 Apr 99)

Hertfordshire, West
Harpenden, Hemel Hempstead, St
Albans, Berkhamsted, Tring,
Redbourne
Franchise holder: NTL (see MSOs)
Homes in area: 100,000
Awarded: 3 Nov 89
Service start: Mar 91
Homes passed: 98,945 (1 Apr 99)
Subs: 19,477 = 19.9% (1 Apr 99)

High Wycombe
see Thames Valley

Hillingdon
see Middlesex

Hinckley/Bosworth
Local delivery franchise holder: NTL
(see MSOs)
Homes in area: 31,200
Awarded: Jun 95

Original franchise revoked from N-
Comm Cablevision

Hitchin
see Hertfordshire, Central

Hoddesdon
see Hertfordshire, East

Horley
see Crawley

Hounslow
see Middlesex

Hove
see Brighton

Huddersfield
see Kirklees

Hull
see Kingston upon Hull

Immingham
see Grimsby

Inverclyde
Greenock, Port Glasgow, Gourock,
Kilmacolm
Franchise holder: CableTel Glasgow
(see MSOs)
Homes in area: 32,000
Awarded: 5 Jul 90
Service start: 1995
Homes passed: 22,260 (1 Apr 99)
Subs: 10,397 = 46.7% (1 Apr 99)

Ipswich
see Colchester

Isle of Thanet see Thanet, Isle of
Isle of Wight
Local delivery franchise holder: Isle
of Wight Cable and Telephone
Company
Elm Farm
Elm Lane
Calbourne
Isle of Wight PO30 4JY
Ownership: Utility Cable, Fortuna
Advanced Communications
Networks
Homes on area: 43,000
Awarded: May 1997

Islington
see Hackney

Jersey
Franchise holder: Jersey Cable (not
ITC licensed)
3 Colomberie
St Helier, Jersey
Channel Islands JE4 9SY
Tel: 01534 66477
Fax: 01534 66681
Ownership: Carveth 50.4%, Mattbrel
30%, others 19.6%

Homes in area: 28,000
Service start: 1987
Franchise renewed: Jan 94
Homes passed: 3,500 cable, 4,600 SMATV

Kenilworth
see Warwick

Kensington/Chelsea, London Borough of
Franchise holder: Cable & Wireless Communications (see MSOs)
Homes in area: 82,000
Awarded: 4 Feb 88
Service start: Sep 89
Homes passed: 70,590 (1 Apr 99)
Subs: 14,958 = 21.2% (1 Apr 99)

Kent, South East
Ashford, Deal, Dover, Folkestone
Local delivery franchise holder:
Cable & Wireless Communications (see MSOs)
Homes in area: 116,300
Awarded: May 90
Service start: Sep 96
Homes passed: 41,705 (1 Apr 99)
Subs: 4,673 = 11.2% (1 Apr 99)
Separate upgrade system in Ashford operated by CDA Communications

Kent, West
Tunbridge Wells, Tonbridge, Sevenoaks
Local delivery franchise holder:
Eurobell (see MSOs)
Homes in area: 90,600
Awarded: May 94

Kettering
see Northampton, North-east

Kidderminster
see Black Country

Kilbirnie
Narrowband upgrade system operated by A Thomson (Relay)

Kilsyth
see Cumbernauld

Kingston and Richmond, London Boroughs of
Franchise holder: Telewest (see MSOs)
Homes in areas: 124,000
Awarded: 6 May 89
Service start: Jan 91
Homes passed: 106,219 (1 Apr 99)
Subs: 24,729 = 23.3% (1 Apr 99)

Kingston upon Hull
Narrowband upgrade system operated by Hull Cablevision = Atlantic Telecom Group (see MSOs)

Kirkcaldy
see Glenrothes

Kirkby-in-Ashfield
see Mansfield

Kirklees
Huddersfield, Dewsbury
Franchise holder: CableTel Kirklees (see MSOs)
Homes in area: 148,000
Awarded: 14 Jun 90
Service start: Jun 95
Homes passed: 88,691 (1 Apr 99)
Subs: 35,610 = 40.2% (1 Apr 99)

Knaresborough
see York

Knowsley
see St Helens

Lakenheath
Narrowband upgrade system operated by Cablecom Investments (see MSOs)

Lambeth/Southwark, London Boroughs of
Franchise holder: Cable & Wireless Communications (see MSOs)
Homes in area: 191,000
Awarded: 6 Jul 89
Service start: Jul 91
Homes passed: 141,756 (1 Apr 99)
Subs: 30,234 = 21.3% (1 Apr 99)

Lanark
see Motherwell

Lancashire, Central
Preston, Leyland
Franchise holder: Telewest (see MSOs)
Homes in area: 114,000
Awarded: 5 Feb 86
Build start: Jun 90
Homes passed: 96,372 (1 Apr 99)
Subs: 18,934 = 19.6% (1 Apr 99)

Lancashire, East
Blackburn, Burnley, Accrington, Nelson, Colne, Rossendale Valley
Franchise holder: Cable & Wireless Communications (see MSOs)
Homes in area: 168,000
Awarded: 9 May 88; acquired 21 Apr 93
Service start: 30 Nov 89
Homes passed: 116,696 (1 Apr 99)
Subs: 23,187 = 19.9% (1 Apr 99)
Narrowband upgrade system in Burnley operated by Cablecom Investments (see MSOs)

Lancaster/Morecambe
No applications
Homes in area: 40,000

Lancashire West
see Southport
Largs
Narrowband upgrade system operated

by Harris of Saltcoats (see MSOs)

Lea Valley
see Hertfordshire, East

Leamington Spa
see Warwick

Leeds
Franchise holder: Cable & Wireless Communications (see MSOs)
Homes in area: 289,000
Awarded: Mar 90
Service Start: Jun 94
Homes passed: 211,789 (1 Apr 99)
Subs: 40,844 = 19.3% (1 Apr 99)

Leicester/ Loughborough/Shepshed
Franchise holder: NTL (see MSOs)
Homes in area: Leicester 170,670 + Loughborough 30,000
Awarded: Leicester 22 Sept 89, Loughborough 9 March 90
Service start: 1 Mar 91
Homes passed: 131,919 (1 Apr 99)
Subs: 29,307 = 22.2% (1 Apr 99)
Separate upgrade system in Leicester operated by CDA Communications

Leighton Buzzard
see Luton

Letchworth
see Hertfordshire, Central

Lewes
Narrowband upgrade system operated by CDA Communications (see MSOs)

Leyland
see Lancashire, Central

Lichfield
see Stafford

Lincoln
Franchise holder: NTL (see MSOs)
Homes in area: 42,000
Awarded: 5 Jul 90
Service start: Jul 95
Homes passed: 46,754 (1 Apr 99)
Subs: 9,506 = 20.3% (1 Apr 99)

Lincolnshire/South Humberside
Local delivery franchise holder: NTL (see MSOs)
Homes in area: 144,000
Awarded: Jan 96

Liverpool, North/Bootle/Crosby
Franchise holder: Telewest (see MSOs)
Homes in area: 119,000 (build complete)
Awarded: 5 Jul 90
Homes passed: 121,695 (1 Apr 99)
Subs: 34,148 = 28.1% (1 Apr 99)

Liverpool, South (Merseyside)
Franchise holder: Telewest (see MSOs)
Homes in area: 125,000
Awarded: 29 Nov 83
Service start: Oct 90
Homes passed: 117,182 (1 Apr 99)
Subs: 30,502 = 26.0% (1 Apr 99)

Llandeilo
Narrowband system operated by John Jones

London
see also Greater London East and individual boroughs
London, North West
Boroughs of Barnet, Brent, Hammersmith and Fulham
Franchise holder: Cable & Wireless Communications (see MSOs)
Homes in area: 280,000
Awarded: 19 Jan 89
Service start: Jul 91
Homes passed: 142,114 (1 Apr 99)
Subs: 25,410 = 17.9% (1 Apr 99)
Separate upgrade system operated in Brent by Sapphire

Lothian
East Lothian, Midlothian, parts of City of Edinburgh
Local delivery franchise applicant: Telewest (see MSOs)
Homes in area: 30,000

Loughborough
see Leicester

Loughton
see Epping Forest

Lowestoft
see Great Yarmouth

Luton/Dunstable/Leighton Buzzard
Franchise holder: CableTel Bedfordshire (see MSOs)
Homes in area: 97,000
Awarded: Jul 86
Service start: Nov 86 on upgrade system, Mar 90 on new build network
Homes passed: 96,725 (1 Apr 99)
Subs: 34,322 = 35.5% (1 Apr 99)

Macclesfield/Wilmslow
Franchise holder: Cable & Wireless Communications (see MSOs)
Homes in area: 45,000
Awarded: 11 Jul 90; acquired 4 May 93
Homes passed: 40,454 (1 Apr 99)
Subs: 8,085 = 20.0% (1 Apr 99)

Maidenhead
see Windsor

Maidstone
see Thames Estuary South

Manchester/Salford/ Trafford
Franchise holder: Cable & Wireless Communications (see MSOs)
Homes in area: 363,000
Awarded: 17 May 90; acquired 22 Mar 93
Service start: Oct 94
Homes passed: 214,391 (1 Apr 99)
Subs: 46,310 = 21.6% (1 Apr 99)
Separate upgrade system in Salford operated by CDA Communications

Mansfield/Sutton/ Kirkby-in-Ashfield
Franchise holder: NTL (see MSOs)
Homes in area: 58,000 (build complete)
Awarded: 3 Mar 90
Homes passed: 78,218 (1 Apr 99)
Subs: 19,946 = 25.5% (1 Apr 99)

March
see Fenland

Margate
see Thanet, Isle of

Market Harborough
see Northampton, North-east

Marlow
see Thames Valley

Matlock
see Derbyshire, East

Melton Mowbray
Franchise holder: NTL (see MSOs)
Homes in area: 30,000
Awarded: 26 Apr 90
Service start: Oct 95

Meriden
see Stafford

Merton and Sutton, London Boroughs of
Franchise holder: Telewest (see MSOs)
Homes in area: 135,000 (build complete)
Awarded: 6 May 89
Service start: Mar 90
Homes passed: 135,522 (1 Apr 99)
Subs: 31,876 = 23.5% (1 Apr 99)

Middlesbrough
see Teesside

Middlesex
Hillingdon, Hounslow (franchises awarded separately but since combined)
Franchise holder: Telewest (see MSOs)
Homes in area: 186,886

Awarded: 24 May 90
Service start: Nov 91
Homes passed: 169,119 (1 Apr 99)
Subs: 26,854 = 15.9% (1 Apr 99)

Midlothian
see Lothian

Mildenhall
Narrowband upgrade system operated by Cablecom Investments (see MSOs)

Milford Haven
Narrowband upgrade system operated by Metro Cable

Milton Keynes
Local delivery franchise holder: BT New Towns Cable TV (see MSOs)
51 Alston Drive
Bradwell Abbey
Milton Keynes MK13 9HB
Tel: 01908 322522
Fax: 01908 319802
Homes in area: 114,000
Awarded: 29 May 1997
Homes passed: 51,965 (1 Apr 99)
Subs: 42,144 = 81.1% (1 Apr 99)

Mole Valley
see Surrey, North East

Monifieth
see Dundee

Morecambe
see Lancaster

Motherwell/East Kilbride/Hamilton/Wishaw/ Lanark
Franchise holder: Telewest (see MSOs)
Homes in area: 125,000 (build complete)
Awarded: 27 Apr 89
Service start: Mar 92
Homes passed: 159,689 (1 Apr 99)
Subs: 45,364 = 28.4% (1 Apr 99)

Neath
see Glamorgan, West

Nelson
see Lancashire, East

Newark on Trent
Franchise holder: NTL (see MSOs)
Homes in area: 35,000
Awarded: 26 Apr 90
Service start: Sep 95
Homes passed: 17,771 (1 Apr 99)
Subs: 3,852 = 21.7% (1 Apr 99)

Newbury
see Thames Valley

Newcastle-under-Lyne
see Stoke-on-Trent

Newcastle-upon-Tyne
see Tyneside

Newham and Tower Hamlets, London Boroughs of
Franchise holder: Cable & Wireless
Communications (see MSOs)
Homes in area: 127,000
Awarded: 13 Aug 85
Service start: May 87
Homes passed: 114,058 (1 Apr 99)
Subs: 19,144 = 16.8% (1 Apr 99)

Newport/Cwmbran/ Pontypool
Franchise holder: CableTel South
Wales (see MSOs)
Homes in area: 85,000
Awarded: 11 Jul 90
Homes passed: 48,983 (1 Apr 99)
Subs: 23,204 = 47.4% (1 Apr 99)

Newton Abbot
see Devon, South

Neyland
Narrowband upgrade system operated
by Metro Cable

Northampton
Franchise holder: NTL (see MSOs)
Homes in area: 72,000
Awarded: 19 Jan 89
Service start: 1988 on 13-channel
upgrade network (classified as
broadband), Mar 91 on new-build
network
Homes passed: 57,786 (1 Apr 99)
Subs: 13,064 = 22.6% (1 Apr 99)
Separate upgrade system operated by
CDA Communications

Northamptonshire, North-east
Corby, Kettering, Wellingborough,
Market Harborough
Franchise holder: NTL (see MSOs)
Homes in area: 90,000
Awarded: 21 Jun 90
Service start: Dec 94
Homes passed: 97,200 (1 Apr 99)
Subs: 16,104 = 16.6% (1 Apr 99)

Northern Ireland
Franchise holder: CableTel Northern
Ireland (see MSOs)
Homes in area: 428,000
Date awarded: May 95
Homes passed: 156,553 (1 Apr 99)
Subs: 61,157 = 39.1% (1 Apr 99)

Northumberland
Local delivery franchise holder:
Cable & Telecoms
Homes in area: 125,000

Awarded: Oct 97
Norwich
Franchise holder: Cable & Wireless
Communications (see MSOs)
Homes in area: 83,000
Awarded: 21 Jul 89, acquired Jul 94
Service start: Jun 90
Homes passed: 69,074 (1 Apr 99)
Subs: 12,553 = 18.2% (1 Apr 99)

Nottingham
Franchise holder: NTL (see MSOs)
Homes in area: 160,000
Awarded: 22 Sept 89
Service start: 10 Sept 90
Homes passed: 208,586 (1 Apr 99)
Subs: 43,204 = 20.7% (1 Apr 99)

Nuneaton/Bedworth/Rugby
Franchise holder: Telecential
Communications (see MSOs)
Homes in area: Nuneaton 44,000 +
Rugby 23,000 (awarded as two
separate franchises)
Awarded: 6 Apr 90
Service start: Feb 96

Oldham/Tameside
Franchise holder: Cable & Wireless
Communications (see MSOs)
Homes in area: 172,000
Awarded: 17 May 90; acquired 4
May 93
Service start: Oct 94
Homes passed: 100,839 (1 Apr 99)
Subs: 23,188 = 23.0% (1 Apr 99)

Ongar
see Epping Forest

Oxford/Abingdon
Franchise holder: NTL (see MSOs)
Homes in area: 72,000 (build
complete)
Awarded: 14 Jun 90
Service start: Sept 95
Homes passed: 128,328 (1 Apr 99)
Subs: 15,787 = 12.3% (1 Apr 99)

Paisley/Renfrew
Franchise holder: CableTel Glasgow
(see MSOs)
Homes in area: 67,000
Awarded: 7 Jun 90
Service start: Aug 94
Homes passed: 61,732 (1 Apr 99)
Subs: 27,661 = 44.8% (1 Apr 99)

Pembroke Dock
Narrowband upgrade system operated
by Metro Cable

Penarth
see Cardiff

Perth/Scone
Franchise holder: Telewest (see
MSOs)
Homes in area: 18,000
Awarded: 19 Jan 90

Service start: 1997
Homes passed: 19,422 (1 Apr 99)
Subs: 4,612 = 23.7% (1 Apr 99)
Separate upgrade system operated in
Perth by Perth Cable TV

Peterborough
Franchise holder: Cable & Wireless
Communications (see MSOs)
Homes in area: 58,000
Awarded: 21 Jul 89
Service start: May 90
Homes passed: 55,014 (1 Apr 99)
Subs: 13,537 = 24.6% (1 Apr 99)

Plymouth
see Devon, South

Pontefract
see Wakefield

Pontypool
see Newport

Poole
see Bournemouth

Port Glasgow
see Inverclyde

Port Talbot
see Glamorgan, West

Portsmouth/Fareham/ Gosport/Havant/East Hampshire
Franchise holder: Cable & Wireless
Communications (see MSOs)
Homes in area: 213,000
Awarded: 2 Feb 90
Service start: Sept 91
Homes passed: 210,019 (1 Apr 99)
Subs: 60,603 = 28.9% (1 Apr 99)

Potters Bar
see Hertfordshire, South

Preston
see Lancashire, Central

Radlett
see Hertfordshire, South

Ramsgate see Thanet, Isle of

Ravenshead
Local delivery licence holder: NTL
(see MSOs)
Homes in area: 2,500
Date awarded: 13 July 95

Reading
see Thames Valley

Redbourne
see Hertfordshire, West

Redbridge, London Borough of
see Greater London East

Reddish
see Worcester

Redhill
see Surrey, North East

Reigate
see Surrey, North East and East
Grinstead

Renfrew
see Paisley

**Richmond, London Borough
of**
see Kingston

Rickmansworth
see Hertfordshire, South

Rochdale
see Bury

Rochester
see Thames Estuary South

Romsey
see Andover

Rossendale Valley
see Lancashire, East

Rotherham
see Doncaster

Rugby
see Nuneaton

Rugeley
see Stafford

Runcorn
see Cheshire, North

Runnymede
see Surrey, North

St Albans
see Hertfordshire, West

St Helens/Knowsley
Franchise holder: Telewest (see
MSOs)
Homes in area: 121,000
Awarded: 5 Jul 90
Service start: Jun 92
Homes passed: 106,544 (1 Apr 99)
Subs: 28,580 = 26.8% (1 Apr 99)

Salford
see Manchester

Salisbury
see Andover

Saltcoats
Narrowband upgrade system operated
by Harris of Saltcoats (see MSOs)

Sandwell
see Black Country

Sefton
see Southport

Scone
see Dundee

Sheffield
Franchise holder: Telewest (see
MSOs)
Homes in area: 210,000
Awarded: 31 May 90
Service start: Apr 94
Homes passed: 89,206 (1 Apr 99)
Subs: 15,187 = 17.0% (1 Apr 99)

Shepshed
see Leicester

Shrewsbury
Local delivery licence holder: Cable
& Telecoms (see MSOs)
Homes in area: 90,000
Awarded: Jan 96
Licence revoked Dec 97

Sittingbourne
see Thames Estuary South
Skelmersdale
Narrowband upgrade system operated
by Tawd Valley Cable

Slough
see Windsor

Solihull
see Birmingham

South Ribble
see Southport

Southampton/Eastleigh
Franchise holder: Cable & Wireless
Communications (see MSOs)
Homes in area: 119,371
Awarded: 12 Sept 86
Service start: 1 Dec 90
Homes passed: 106,720 (1 Apr 99)
includes Winchester
Subs: 25,897 = 24.3% (1 Apr 99)
includes Winchester

**Southport/Sefton/West
Lancashire/South
Ribble/Chorley**
Local delivery licence holder:
Telewest
Homes in area: 90,000
Awarded: Jan 96
Service start: Jun 97

Southend
see Thames Estuary North

**Southwark, London
Borough of**
see Lambeth

Stafford/Stone
Franchise holder: NTL (see MSOs)
Homes in area: 30,600

Awarded: 1 Dec 89
Service start: Sept 95
merged with Local delivery licences
for
Lichfield/Burntwood/Rugeley
(Homes in area: 39,290)
Tamworth/North
Warwickshire/Meriden (Homes in
area: 43,315)
Awarded: Jun 95
Service start: Mar 97
Homes passed: 92,094 (1 Apr 99)
Subs: 14,694 = 16.0% (1 Apr 99)

Staines
see Windsor

Stanley
see Consett

Stanwell
see Windsor

Stevenage
see Hertfordshire, Central

Stockport
Franchise holder: Cable & Wireless
Communications (see MSOs)
Homes in area: 113,000
Awarded: 17 May 90; acquired 4
May 93
Service start: Oct 94
Homes passed: 103,577 (1 Apr 99)
Subs: 23,478 = 22.7% (1 Apr 99)

Stockton
see Teesside

**Stoke-on-Trent/Newcastle-
under-Lyne**
Franchise holder: Cable & Wireless
Communications (see MSOs)
Homes in area: 156,000
Awarded: 1 Dec 89; acquired 21 Apr
93
Homes passed: 123,855 (1 Apr 99)
Subs: 21,425 = 17.3% (1 Apr 99)

Stone
see Stafford

Stowmarket
see East Anglia, South

Stratford-upon-Avon
see Warwick

Sudbury
see East Anglia, South

Sunderland
see Wearside

Surrey, North/North East
Banstead, Caterham, Chertsey,
Cobham, Dorking, Elmbridge,
Epsom, Ewell, Leatherhead, Reigate,
Redhill, Sunbury, Weybridge etc
Franchise holder: Cable & Wireless

Communications (see MSOs)
Homes in area: 71,000 + 98,000
(awarded as two franchises)
Awarded: 21 Jun 90
Service start: Apr 93
Homes passed: 152,486 (1 Apr 99)
Subs: 30,521 = 20.0% (1 Apr 99)

Sutton
see Mansfield

Sutton, London Borough of
see Merton

Swansea
see Glamorgan, West

Swindon
Franchise holder: Swindon Cable =
NTL (see MSOs)
Homes in area: 65,000 (build
complete)
Service start: 1 Sep 84
Homes passed: 68,000 (1 Apr 99)
Subs: 23,875 = 35.1% (1 Apr 99)

Tameside
see Oldham

Tamworth
see Stafford

Taunton/Bridgwater
Local delivery licence holder:
Telewest
Homes in area: 71,300
Awarded: Feb 97

Teesside
Middlesbrough, Stockton, Hartlepool
Franchise holder: Comcast Teesside
(see MSOs)
Homes in area: 195,000
Awarded: 5 Jul 90
Service start: Jun 95
Homes passed: 181,048 (1 Apr 99)
Subs: 55,366 = 30.6% (1 Apr 99)

Telford
Franchise holder: Telewest (see
MSOs)
Homes in area: 55,000
Awarded: 26 Apr 90
Service start: May 92
Homes passed: 53,213 (1 Apr 99)
Subs: 15,152 = 28.5% (1 Apr 99)

Thames Estuary North
Southend, Basildon, Billericay,
Brentwood, Chelmsford etc
Franchise holder: Telewest (see
MSOs)
Homes in area: 300,000
Awarded: 16 Nov 88
Service start: Jun 94
Homes passed: 190,661 (1 Apr 99)
Subs: 54,853 = 28.8% (1 Apr 99)
Separate upgrade system in Basildon
operated by CDA Communications

Thames Estuary South
Gravesend, Chatham, Rochester,
Gillingham, Maidstone, Sittingbourne
Franchise holder: Telewest (see
MSOs)
Homes in area: 145,000
Awarded: 16 Nov 88
Homes passed: 102,664 (1 Apr 99)
Subs: 29,402 = 28.6% (1 Apr 99)
Separate upgrade systems in
Chatham and Sittingbourne operated
by CDA Communications

Thames Valley
Reading, Twyford, Henley-on-
Thames, Wokingham, High
Wycombe, Marlow, Bracknell,
Basingstoke, Ascot, Newbury,
Thatcham
Franchise holder: NTL (see MSOs)
Homes in area: 215,000
Awarded: 2 Dec 88
Service start: Dec 91
Homes passed: 195,367 (1 Apr 99)
Subs: 38,334 = 19.6% (1 Apr 99)

Thamesmead
Franchise holder: Cable & Wireless
Communications (see MSOs)
Homes in area: 11,000
Awarded: 31 May 90
Service start: Jul 91
Homes passed: 8,544 (1 Jul 98)
Subs: 2,577 = 30.2% (1 Jul 98)

Thanet, Isle of
Margate, Ramsgate, Broadstairs
Franchise revoked from Coastal
Cablevision = Leonard
Communications
Homes in area: 51,000
Awarded: 16 Feb 90
Separate narrowband upgrade system
operated CDA Communications (see
MSOs)

Thetford
see East Anglia, South

Torbay
see Devon, South

Totnes
see Devon, South

Totton/Hythe
Local delivery franchise holder:
Cable & Wireless Communications
(see MSOs)
Homes in area: 25,200
Awarded: Sep 95
Service start: Apr 97

Tower Hamlets, London Borough of
see Newham

Tring
see Hertfordshire, West

Twyford
see Thames Valley

Tyneside
Newcastle-upon-Tyne, Gateshead,
North and South Tyneside
Franchise holder: Telewest (see
MSOs)
Homes in area: 325,000
Awarded: 14 Dec 89
Service start: Sept 90
Homes passed: 229,462 (1 Apr 99)
Subs: 65,563 = 28.6% (1 Apr 99)

Upper Heyford
Narrowband upgrade system operated
by Cablecom Investments (see
MSOs)

Uttoxeter
see Burton-on-Trent

Vale of Belvoir
Local delivery franchise holder: NTL
(see MSOs)
Homes in area: 4,545
Awarded: Jul 96

Wakefield/Pontefract/ Castleford
Franchise holder: Telewest (see
MSOs)
Homes in area: 94,000
Awarded: 2 Mar 90; acquired Apr 93
Homes passed: 45,158 (1 Apr 99)
Subs: 5,643 = 12.5% (1 Apr 99)

Walsall
see Black Country

Waltham Forest, London Borough of
Franchise holder: Cable & Wireless
Communications (see MSOs)
Homes in area: 83,000
Awarded: 28 Sept 89
Service start: Feb 94
Homes passed: 81,205 (1 Apr 99)
Subs: 16,895 = 20.8% (1 Apr 99)

Wandsworth, London Borough of
Franchise holder: Cable & Wireless
Communications (see MSOs)
Homes in area: 100,000
Awarded: 13 Aug 85
Service start: Aug 93
Homes passed: 65,060 (1 Apr 99)
Subs: 12,203 = 18.8% (1 Apr 99)

Ware
see Hertfordshire, East

Warrington
see Cheshire, North

Warwick/Stratford-upon-Avon/Kenilworth/ Leamington Spa

Franchise holder: NTL (see MSOs)
Homes in area: 50,000 (build complete)
Awarded: 30 Mar 90
Homes passed: 119,043 (1 Apr 99)
Subs: 16,134 = 13.6% (1 Apr 99)

Watford
see Hertfordshire, South

Wearside
Sunderland, Durham, Washington
Franchise holder: Cable & Wireless Communications (see MSOs)
Homes in area: 200,000
Awarded: 14 Jun 90
Service start: Aug 96
Homes passed: 61,576 (1 Apr 99)
Subs: 10,148 = 16.5% (1 Apr 99)

Wellingborough
see Northampton, North-east

Welwyn
see Hertfordshire, Central

Wendover
see Aylesbury

West Lothian
see Falkirk

Westminster, London Borough of
Franchise holder: Westminster Cable Company = British Telecom (see MSOs)
87-89 Baker Street
London W1M 1AG
Tel: 020 7 935 6699
Fax: 020 7 486 9447
Homes in area: 120,000
Awarded: 29 Nov 83
Service start: Sept 85
Homes passed: 101,024 (1 Apr 99)
Subs: 22,680 = 22.5% (1 Apr 99)

Weymouth
see Dorset, West

Whittlesey
see Fenland

Widnes
see Cheshire, North

Wigan
Franchise holder: Telewest (see MSOs)
Homes in area: 110,000
Awarded: 17 May 90
Service start: Jun 92
Homes passed: 108,810 (1 Apr 99)
Subs: 27,403 = 25.3% (1 Apr 99)

Wilmslow
see Macclesfield

Winchester
Franchise holder: Cable & Wireless

Communications (see MSOs)
Homes in area: 19,000
Awarded: 6 Apr 90
Service start: 1995
Homes passed and subs included with Southampton/Eastleigh

Windsor/Slough/ Maidenhead/Ashford/ Staines/Stanwell/Heathrow/ Iver
Franchise holder: Telewest (see MSOs)
Homes in area: 110,000 (build complete)
Awarded: 1 Nov 83; Iver added subsequently to create contiguity with Middlesex
Service start: 1 Dec 85
Homes passed: 108,618 (1 Apr 99)
Subs: 16,213 = 14.9% (1 Apr 99)

Wirral, The
Franchise holder: Cable & Wireless Communications (see MSOs)
Homes in area: 120,000
Awarded: 11 Jul 90
Homes passed: 77,337 (1 Apr 99)
Subs: 16,650 = 21.5% (1 Apr 99)
Separate upgrade system operated by CDA Communications

Wisbech
see Fenland

Wishaw
see Motherwell

Woking
see Guildford

Wokingham
see Thames Valley

Wolverhampton
see Black Country

Worcester/Redditch/ Droitwich
Franchise holder: Telewest (see MSOs)
Homes in area: 70,000
Awarded: 14 Jun 90
Service start: 1997
Homes passed: 27,396 (1 Apr 99)
Subs: 7,806 = 28.5% (1 Apr 99)

Worthing
see Brighton

Wythall
Local delivery franchise holder: Birmingham Cable (see MSOs)
Homes in area: 4,000
Awarded: Sep 95
Service start: Apr 97

Yeovil
Local delivery licence holder: Convergence Group

Ownership: Convergence Group (see MSOs), Orbis Trust (Guernsey)
Homes in area: 62,300
Awarded: Jul 96

York
Franchise holder: Cable & Wireless Communications (see MSOs)
Homes in area: 78,000
Homes passed: 3,925 (upgrade system)
Awarded: 30 Mar 90, acquired Apr 94
Service start: Sep 95
Homes passed: 29,710 (1 Apr 99)
Subs: 4,450 = 15.0% (1 Apr 99)

Yorkshire, North
see Durham, South

SATELLITE AND CABLE TELEVISION CHANNELS

All channels transmitting via cable or satellite within or to the UK, wholly or partly in the English language or intended for viewing by other linguistic groups within the UK. Services are licensed and monitored by the Independent Television Commission (ITC). Channels not intended for reception in the UK are excluded, as are those that are licensed but not actively broadcasting (many licensed channels never materialise).

The television standard and encrypting system used are indicated after the name of the satellite. Services for which a separate charge is made are marked 'premium' after the programming type.

The advent of digital television from the fourth quarter 1998 has already created several new channels, although initially most digital channels are conversions of services already available in analogue form.

MULTIPLE SERVICE PROVIDERS (MSP)

BBC Digital Programme Services
Broadcasting House
Portland Place
London W1A 1AA
Tel: 020 8 752 5045
Services: BBC Knowledge
BBC Worldwide
Woodlands
80 Wood Lane
London W12 0TT
Tel: 020 8 576 2000
Services: Animal Planet 50%, BBC News 24, UK Arena 50%, UK Gold 50%, UK Horizons 50%, UK Style 50%

British Sky Broadcasting (BSkyB)
6 Centaurs Business Park
Grant Way, Syon Lane
Isleworth
Middlesex TW7 5QD
Tel: 020 8 782 3000
Fax: 020 8 782 3030
Website: www.sky.co.uk
Ownership: News International Television 39.88 %, BSB Holdings (= Pathé 30.27%, Granada 36.22%, Pearson 4.29%) 12.82 %, Pathé 12.71 %, Granada Group 6.48 %
Services: The Computer Channel, The History Channel 50%, National Geographic Channel 50%, Nickelodeon 50%, QVC 20%, Sky Box Office, Sky Cinema, Sky MovieMax, Sky News, Sky One, Sky Premier, Sky Soap, Sky Sports1 , Sky Sports 2, Sky Sports 3, Sky Sports Extra, Sky Travel
40% stake in Granada Sky Broadcasting

Carlton Communications
45 Fouberts Street
London W1V 2DN
Tel: 020 7 432 9000
Fax: 020 7 432 3151
Services: Carlton Food Network, Carlton Select

Discovery Communications
160 Great Portland Street
London W1N 5TB
Tel: 020 7 462 3600
Fax: 020 7 462 3700
Services: Animal Planet, Discovery Channel Europe, TLC Europe
Flextech Television

160 Great Portland Street
London W1N 5TB
Tel: 020 7 299 5000
Fax: 020 7 299 5400
Ownership: Tele-Communications International (TINTA)
Services: Bravo, Challenge TV, Living, Trouble, UK Arena 50%, UK Gold 50%, UK Horizons 50%, UK Style 50%
Service management: Discovery, Discovery Home & Leisure, Playboy TV, Screenshop, TV Travel Shop

Granada Sky Broadcasting
Franciscan Court
16 Hatfields
London SE1 8DJ
Tel: 020 7 578 4040
Fax: 020 7 578 4176
Ownership: Granada Group 60%, British Sky Broadcasting 40%
Services: Granada Breeze, Granada Plus, Granada Men & Motors

Home Video Channel
Aquis House, Station Road
Hayes
Middlesex UB3 4DX
Tel: 020 8 581 7000
Fax: 020 8 581 7007
Ownership: Spice Entertainment Companies
Services: The Adult Channel, HVC

Landmark Communications
64-66 Newman Street
London W1P 3PG
Tel: 020 7 665 0600
Fax: 020 7 665 0601
Ownership: Landmark Communications Inc
Services: Travel Channel

Portland Enterprises
Portland House, Portland Place
London E14 9TT
Tel: 020 7 308 5095
Services: Gay TV, Television X The Fantasy Channel

Turner Broadcasting System (TBS)
CNN House
19-22 Rathbone Place
London W1P 1DF
Tel: 020 7 637 6700
Fax: 020 7 637 6768
Ownership: Time Warner
Services: Cartoon Network, CNN International, Turner Network Television

UK Channel Management
160 Great Portland Street
London W1N 5TB
Tel: 020 7 765 1959
Ownership: BBC Worldwide, Flextech [qqv]

CHANNELS

The Adult Channel
Ownership: Home Video Channel
[see MSP above]
Service start: Feb 1992
Satellite: Astra 1B (PAL/Videocrypt)
Programming: 'adult' entertainment
(premium)
email: adultch@spicecos.com
Website: www.cyberspice.com

Animal Planet
Ownership: BBC Worldwide,
Discovery Communications [see
MSP above]
Service start: Sep 98
Satellite: Astra 1E, Hot Bird 1
(PAL/encrypted)
Programming: natural history
documentaries
Website: www.animal.discovery.com

Asianet
Unit 1, Endsleigh Industrial Estate
Endsleigh Road
Uxbridge
Middlesex UB2 5QR
Tel: 020 8 930 0930
Fax: 020 8 930 0546
Cable only from videotape
Programming: movies and
entertainment in Hindi, Punjabi and
other languages

BBC Choice
Ownership: BBC Worldwide [See
MSP above]
Programming: general entertainment
Digital

BBC Knowledge
Ownership: BBC Digital Programme
Services [See MSP above]
Programming: educational
Digital

BBC News 24
Ownership: BBC Worldwide [See
MSP above]
Programming: news

Bloomberg Television
City Gate House
39-45 Finsbury Square
London EC2A 1PQ
Tel: 020 7 330 7500
Fax: 020 7 256 5326
Service start: 1 Nov 1995
Satellite: Astra 1E, Eutelsat II-F1
Programming: business and finance
Website: www.bloomberg.co.uk
The Box
Imperial House
11-13 Young Street
London W8 5EH
Tel: 020 7 376 2000

Fax: 020 7 376 1313
Ownership: Emap
Service start: 2 Mar 1992
Satellite: Astra 1A (PAL/Videocrypt;
cable only)
Programming: interactive pop music
Website: www.thebox.com

Bravo
Ownership: Flextech Television [see
MSP above]
Service start: Sept 1985
Satellite: Astra 1C (PAL/Videocrypt)
Programming: old movies and
television programmes
Website: www.bravo.co.uk

British Eurosport
55 Drury Lane
London WC2B 5SQ
Tel: 020 7 468 7777
Fax: 020 7 468 0024
Ownership: ESO Ltd = TF1 34%,
Canal Plus 33%, ESPN 33%
Service start: Feb 89
Satellite: Astra 1A, Hot Bird 1
(PAL/clear)
Programming: sport
Website: www.eurosport-tv.com
Also digital

Carlton Cinema
Ownership: Carlton Communications
[see MSP above]
Service start: 2 Sep 1996
Website: www.carltoncinema.co.uk
Digital, included in ONdigital
Carlton Food Network
Ownership: Carlton Communications
[see MSP above]
Service start: 2 Sep 1996
Satellite: Intelsat 601 (MPEG2
encrypted)
Programming: Food
Website: www.cfn,co.uk
Also digital

Carlton Kids
Ownership: Carlton Entertainment
[see MSP above]
Programming: children's
Digital, included in ONdigital

Carlton Select
Ownership: Carlton Communications
[see MSP above]
Service start: 1 Jun 1995
Satellite: Intelsat 601 (MPEG2
encrypted); cable exclusive
Programming: entertainment; classic
TV shows
Website: www.carltonselect.co.uk
Also digital

Carlton World
Ownership: Carlton Entertainment
[see MSP above]
Programming: documentary
Digital, included in ONdigital

Cartoon Network
1 Soho Square
London W1V 5FD
Tel: 020 7 478 1000
Ownership: Turner Broadcasting [see
MSP above]
Service start: Sept 93
Satellite: Astra 1C, Astra 1F
(PAL/clear)
Programming: children's animation
Website: www.cartoonnetwork.co.uk
Also digital

Challenge TV
Ownership: Flextech [see MSP
above]
Service start: 3 Feb 1997
Satellite: Astra 1C (PAL/Videocrypt)
Programming: general entertainment,
game shows
Website: www.challengetv.co.uk

The Channel Guide
1a French's Yard
Amwell End
Ware, Herts SG12 9HP
Tel: 01920 469238
Fax: 01920 468372
Ownership: Picture Applications
Service start: May 1990
Cable only (text)
Programming: programme listings

Channel One
PO Box 336
Old Hall Street
Liverpool L69 3TE
Tel: 0151 4722700
Ownership: Daily Mail & General
Trust
Service start: 30 Nov 94 (in London)
Cable only on Liverpool/Merseyside
cable systems
Programming: news and general
features in rolling format

Chinese News and Entertainment (CNE)
Marvic House
Bishops Road, Fulham
London SW6 7AD
Tel: 020 7 610 3880
Fax: 020 7 610 3118
email: chinesemarkets@
cnetv.demon.co.uk
Ownership: The CNT Group
Service start: Nov 92
Satellite: Astra 1C (PAL/Clear)
Programming: news, current affairs,
films, dramas, lifestyle

Christian Channel Europe
Christian Channel Studios
Stonehills, Shields Road
Gateshead NE10 0HW
Tel: 0191 4952244
email: info@godnetwork.com
Service start: 1 Oct 1995
Satellite: Astra 1B

Programming: Christian
Website: www.indigo.ie/
spugradio/cce.html

CNBC Europe
10 Fleet Place
London EC4M 7QS
Tel: 020 8 653 9300
email: talkback@nbc.com
Website: www.cnbceurope.com
Ownership: NBC and Dow Jones
Service start: 11 Mar 1996
Satellite: Astra 1E
Programming: business news

CNN International
Ownership: Turner Broadcasting [see MSP above]
Service start: Oct 1985
Satellite: Astra 1B, Intelsat 605 (PAL/clear)
Programming: news
Website: www.europe.cnn.com

The Computer Channel
Ownership: British Sky Broadcasting (see MSP)
Satellite: Astra 1D
Programming: computer topics and programs

The Discovery Channel Europe
Ownership: Discovery Communications [see MSP above]
Service start: Apr 89
Satellite: Astra 1C, Hot Bird 1 (PAL/encrypted)
Programming: documentaries
Website: www.discovery.com/digitnets/international/europe/europe.html

Discovery Home & Leisure
Ownership: Discovery Communications [see MSP above]
Service start: Mar 1992
Satellite: Astra 1C, Hot Bird 1 (PAL/encrypted)
Programming: lifestyle
Website: www.discovery.com/digitnets/learning/learning.html

The Disney Channel UK
Beaumont House
Kensington Village
Avonmore Road
London W14 8TS
Tel: 020 8 222 1000
Ownership: Walt Disney Company
Satellite: Astra 1B (PAL/Videocrypt)
Programming: children's (supplied as bonus with Sky Premier and Moviemax)
Website: www.disneychannel.co.uk

EBN: European Business News
10 Fleet Place

London EC4M 7RB
Tel: 020 7 653 9300
Fax: 020 7 653 9333
Website: www.ebn.co.uk
Ownership: Dow Jones & Co 70%, Flextech 30%
Service start: 27 Feb 95
Satellite: Eutelsat II F6 (PAL/clear)
Programming: financial and business news

EDTV (Emirates Dubai TV)
c/o Teleview Productions
7a Grafton Street
London W1X 3LA
Tel: 020 7 493 2496
Fax: 020 7 629 6207
Ownership: Dubai government
Service start: Dec 93
Satellite: Arabsat 2A, Intelsat K
Programming: news (from ITN), entertainment, film, sports, children's in Arabic and English
Website: www.edtv.com

Euronews
60 Chemin des Mouilles
69130 Ecully
France
Tel: (33) 4 72 18 80 00
Fax: (33) 4 73 18 93 71
Ownership: 18 European Broadcasting Union members 51%, Générale Occidentale 49%
Service start: 1 Jan 1993
Satellite: Hot Bird 3, Eutelsat II-F1 (PAL/clear)
Programming: news in English, French, Spanish, German and Italian

Film Four
124 Horseferry Road
London SW1P 2TX
Tel: 020 7 396 4444
Ownership: Channel Four Television
Programming: feature and short films [premium]
Website: www.channel4.com
Digital

Fox Kids Network
Ownership: Fox Television (managed by BSkyB, see MSP above)
Satellite: Astra 1A (PAL/Videocrypt)
Programming: children's
Website: www.foxkids.co.uk

Front Row
Front Row Television
19 Newman Street
London W1P 3HB
Tel: 020 7 307 2222
Ownership: NTL, Telewest
Programming: movies [pay-per-view]
Gay TV
Ownership: Portland Enterprises [see MSP above]
Satellite: Astra 1C (PAL/encrypted)
Programming: erotic

GMTV2
The London Television Centre
Upper Ground
London SE1 9TT
Tel: 020 7 827 7000
Programming: morning general interest
Digital

Granada Breeze
Ownership: Granada Sky Broadcasting [see MSP above]
Satellite: Astra 1E (PAL/encrypted)
Programming: lifestyle
Website: www.gsb.co.uk/breeze/home.html
Also digital

Granada Men & Motors
Ownership: Granada Sky Broadcasting [see MSP above]
Satellite: Astra 1A (PAL/Videocrypt)
Programming: male-oriented, motoring
Website: www.gsb.co.uk/men/home.html
Also digital

Granada Plus
Ownership: Granada Sky Broadcasting [see MSP above]
Satellite: Astra 1A (PAL/Videocrypt)
Programming: classic TV programmes
Website: www.gsb.co.uk/plus/home.html
Also digital

The History Channel
Ownership: BSkyB 50%, A&E Television Networks 50%
Service start: 1 Nov 1995
Satellite: Astra 1B (PAL/Videocrypt)
Programming: history
Website: www.thehistorychannel.co.uk
Also digital
HVC: Home Video Channel
Ownership: Home Video Channel [see MSP above]
Service start: Sept 1985
Satellite: Astra 1D (cable exclusive)
Programming: movies (premium)
Website: www.cyberspice.com

ITV2
200 Gray''s Inn Road
London WC1X 8HF
Tel: 020 7 843 8000
Ownership: ITV companies
Website: www.itv.co.uk
Digital; also on analogue cable
Japan Satellite TV (JSTV)

The Landscape Channel
Landscape Studios
Hye House
Crowhurst, East Sussex TN33 9BX
Tel: 01424 83688

Fax: 01424 83680
email: info@landscapetv.com
Service start: Nov 1988 (on
videotape); Apr 1993 (on satellite)
Satellite: Orion, Hispasat (PAL/clear)
Programming: music and visual
wallpaper
Website: www.landscapetv.com

Live TV
24th floor
1 Canada Square
Canary Wharf
London E14 5AP
Tel: 020 7 293 3900
Fax: 020 7 293 3820
email: cable@livetv.co.uk
Ownership: Mirror Group
Newspapers
Service start: 12 June 95
Programming: general entertainment
Website: www.livetv.co.uk

Living
Ownership: Flextech [see MSP
above]
Service start: Sept 93
Satellite: Astra 1C (PAL/Videocrypt)
Programming: daytime lifestyle,
evening general entertainment
Website: www.livingtv.co.uk

MBC: Middle East Broadcasting Centre
80 Silverthorne Road
Battersea
London SW8 3XA
Tel: 020 7 501 1111
Fax: 020 7 501 1110
Service start: Sept 91
Programming: general and news in
Arabic

MTV UK
180 Oxford Street
London W1N 0DS
Tel: 020 7 478 6000
Ownership: Viacom
Service start: Aug 87
Satellite: Astra 1A (PAL/Videocrypt)
Programming: pop music
Website: www.mtv.co.uk
Also digital

Muslim TV Ahmadiyyah
16 Gressenhall Road
London SW18 5QL
Tel: 020 8 870 8517
Fax: 020 8 870 0684
email: mta/mtl@dial.pipex.com
Ownership: Al-Shirkatul Islamiyyah
Service start: Jan 94
Satellite: Intelsat 601
Programming: spiritual, educational,
training
Website: www.alislam.org/mta

MUTV
Manchester United Television

274 Deansgate
Manchester M3 4SB
Tel: 0161 834 1111
Ownership: Manchester United FC,
BSkyB, Granada
Programming: Manchester United FC
Web Site: www.manutd.com

Namaste Television
7 Trafalgar Business Centre
77-87 River Road
Barking
Essex IG11 0EZ
Tel: 020 8 507 8292
Fax: 020 8 507 8292
Service start: Sept 92
Satellite: Intelsat 601
Programming: Asian entertainment
Website: www.namastev.co.uk
National Geographic Channel
Ownership: British Sky Broadcasting
(see MSP), National Geographic
Telephone: 020 8 847 4319
Service start: 1997
Satellite: Astra 1A (PAL/Videocrypt)
Programming: natural history
documentaries
Website: www.nationalgeographic.
com

Nickelodeon
15-18 Rathbone Place
London W1P 1DF
Tel: 020 7 462 1000
Fax: 020 7 462 1030
Ownership: British Sky Broadcasting
50% [see MSP above], MTV
Networks 50%
Service start: 1 Sept 93
Satellite: Astra 1C (PAL/Videocrypt)
Programming: children's
Website: www.nick.uk.com

The Paramount Comedy Channel
15-18 Rathbone Place
London W1P 1DF
Tel: 020 7 462 1200
Fax: 020 7 462 1030
Ownership: British Sky Broadcasting
[see MSP above], Viacom
Service start: 1 Nov 1995
Satellite: Astra 1C (PAL/Videocrypt)
Programming: comedy
Website: www.paramountcomedy.
com

The Parliamentary Channel
160 Great Portland Street
London W1N 5TB
Tel: 020 7 299 5000
Fax: 020 7 299 6000
Ownership: consortium of cable
operators
Service start: Jan 92
Satellite: Intelsat 601 (PAL/clear)
Programming: coverage of British
parliamentary debates
Website: www.parlchan.co.uk

Performance: The Arts Channel
60 Charlotte Street
London W1P 2AX
Tel: 020 7 927 8808
Ownership: Arts & Entertainment
Service start: Oct 92
Cable only from videotape
Programming: opera, jazz and
classical concerts, drama

Playboy TV
Ownership: Flextech 51% [see MSP
above], BSkyB, Playboy
Service start: 1 Nov 1995
Satellite: Astra 1B (PAL/Videocrypt)
Programming: erotic (premium)
Website: www.playboytv.co.uk

Quick House
65 Clifton Street
London EC2A 4JE
Tel: 020 7 426 7330
Fax: 020 7 426 7333
Ownership: NHK, private Japanese
investors
Satellite: Astra 1E (PAL/Videocrypt)
Programming: Japanese news, drama,
documentary, entertainment, sport
Website: www.jstv.co.uk

QVC: The Shopping Channel
Marcopolo House, Chelsea Bridge
Queenstown Road
London SW8 4NQ
Tel: 020 7 705 5600
Fax: 020 7 705 5602
Ownership: QVC (= Comcast, TCI)
80%, BSkyB 20%
Satellite: Astra 1C (soft scrambled)
Service start: Oct 93
Programming: home shopping
Website: www.qvc.com

The Racing Channel
17 Corsham Street
London N1 6DR
Tel: 020 7 253 2232
Fax: 020 7 696 8681
email: info@satelliteinfo.co.uk
Service start: Nov 1995
Satellite: Astra 1D
Programming: horse racing

The Sci-Fi Channel Europe
77 Charlotte Street
London W1P 2DD
Tel: 020 7 805 6100
Fax: 020 7 805 6150
Service start: 1 Nov 1995
Satellites: Astra 1B, Hot Bird 1
(PAL/encrypted)
Programming: science fiction
Website: www.scifi.com/
sfeurope/index.html

S4C2
Sianel Pedwar Cymru

Parc Ty-Glas
Llanisien
Cardiff CF4 5DU
Wales
Tel: 029 20747 444
Fax: 029 20754 444
Programming: Coverage of the Welsh
Assembly in session initially, news
and general entertainment in Welsh
and English
Digital

Shop! The Home Shopping Channel
Sir John Moores Building
100 Old Hall Street
Liverpool
Merseyside L70 1AB
Tel: 0151 235 2055
Ownership: The Home Shopping
Channel Ltd
Digital

Sky Box Office
Ownership: British Sky Broadcasting
[see MSP above]
Service start: 1 Dec 97
Satellite: Astra 1E (PAL/Videocrypt)
Programming: movies, concerts,
events (pay-per-view)
Also digital

Sky Cinema
Ownership: British Sky Broadcasting
[see MSP above]
Service start: Oct 92
Satellite: Astra 1C (PAL/Videocrypt)
Programming: movies (premium)

Sky MovieMax
Ownership: British Sky Broadcasting
[see MSP above]
Service start: Feb 89
Satellite: Astra 1A (PAL/Videocrypt)
Programming: movies (premium)
Also digital

Sky News
Ownership: British Sky Broadcasting
[see MSP above]
Service start: Feb 89
Satellite: Astra 1A (PAL/Videocrypt)
Programming: news

Sky One
Ownership: British Sky Broadcasting
[see MSP above]
Service start: Feb 89
Satellite: Astra 1A (PAL/Videocrypt)
Programming: entertainment
Also digital

Sky Premier
Ownership: British Sky Broadcasting
[see MSP above]
Service start: Apr 91
Satellite: Astra 1B (PAL/Videocrypt)
Programming: movies (premium)
Also digital

Sky Soap
Ownership: British Sky Broadcasting
[see MSP above]
Satellite: Astra 1B (PAL/Videocrypt)
Programming: entertainment

Sky Sports 1
Ownership: British Sky Broadcasting
[see MSP above]
Service start: Apr 91
Satellite: Astra 1B (PAL/Videocrypt)
Programming: sport (premium)
Also digital

Sky Sports 2
Ownership: British Sky Broadcasting
[see MSP above]
Service start: Aug 94
Satellite: Astra 1C (PAL/Videocrypt)
Programming: sport (premium)
Also digital

Sky Sports 3
Ownership: British Sky Broadcasting
[see MSP above]
Service start: Aug 94
Satellite: Astra 1B (PAL/Videocrypt)
Programming: sport (premium)
Also digital

Sky Sports Extra
Ownership: British Sky Broadcasting
[see MSP above]
Service start: Aug 99
Satellite: Astra 1B (PAL/Videocrypt)
Programming: sport (bonus with
premium channels)
Digital

Sky Travel
Ownership: British Sky Broadcasting
[see MSP above]
Satellite: Astra 1C (PAL/Videocrypt)
Programming: travel documentaries

STEP-UP
University of Plymouth
Notte Street
Plymouth PL1 2AR
Tel: 01752 233635
Programming: educational and business

Tara Television
The Forum
74-80 Camden Street
London NW1 0EG
Tel: 020 7 383 3330
Fax: 020 7 383 3450
Service start: 15 Nov 1996
Satellite: Intelsat 601 (MPEG-2
encrypted)
Programming: Irish entertainment
Website: http://www.tara-tv.co.uk
TCC
Ownership: Flextech [see MSP above]
Service start: Sept 1984
Satellite: Astra 1C (PAL/Videocrypt)
Programming: children's
Website: www.tcc.flextech.co.uk/

Television X: The Fantasy Channel
Portland House
Portland Place
Millharbour
London E14 9TT
Tel: 020 7 987 5095
Service start: 2 Jun 1995
Satellite: Astra 1C (PAL/Videocrypt)
Programming: erotic (premium)
Website:www.televisionx.co.uk

TNT Classic Movies
1 Soho Square
London W1V 5FD
Tel: 020 7 478 1000
Ownership: Turner Broadcasting [see
MSP above]
Service start: Sept 93
Satellite: Astra 1C, Astra 1F
(PAL/clear)
Programming: movies, entertainment

Travel Channel
66 Newman Street
London W1P 3LA
Tel: 020 7 636 5401
Fax: 020 7 636 6424
Ownership: Landmark
Communications [see MSP above]
Service start: 1 Feb 94
Satellite: Astra 1E
Programming: travel
Website: www.travelchannel.co.uk

Trouble
Ownership: Flextech Television [see
MSP above]
Service start: Sept 1985
Satellite: Astra 1C (PAL/Videocrypt)
Programming: teenagers
email: webmaster@trouble.co.uk
Website: www.trouble.co.uk

[.tv]
96-97 Wilton Road
London SW1V 1DW
Tel: 020 7 599 8938
Satellite: Astra 1E
Programming: computer-related
topics
Website: www.tvchannel.co.uk/dottv/

TV Travel Shop
Satellite: Astra 1C
Website: www.tvtravelshop.co.uk

TVBS Europe
30-31 Newman Street
London W1P 3PE
Tel: 020 7 636 8888
Satellite: Astra 1E (digital)
Programming: Chinese-language
Website: www.chinese-channel.co.uk

UK Arena
Ownership: UKTV – BBC
Worldwide, Flextech [see MSP
above]

Satellite: Astra 1E
Programming: arts
Also digital

UK Gold

Ownership: UKTV = BBC
Worldwide, Flextech [see MSP
above]
Service start: Nov 92
Satellite: Astra 1B (PAL/Videocrypt)
Programming: entertainment
Also digital

UK Horizons

Ownership: UKTV = BBC
Worldwide, Flextech [see MSP
above]
Satellite: Astra 1E
Programming: documentaries
Also digital

UK Play

Ownership: UKTV = BBC
Worldwide, Flextech [see MSP
above]
Programming: popular music,
comedy
Digital

UK Style

Ownership: UKTV = BBC
Worldwide, Flextech [see MSP
above]
Satellite: Astra 1E
Programming: lifestyle
Also digital

VH-1

180 Oxford Street
London W1N 0DS
Tel: 020 7 284 7777
Fax: 020 7 284 7788
Ownership: MTV Networks =
Viacom (100%)
Satellite: Astra 1B (PAL/encrypted)
Programming: pop music
Website: www.vh1.com
Also digital

Zee TV Europe

Unit 7
Belvue Business Centre
Belvue Road
Northolt
Middlesex UB5 5QQ
Tel: 020 8 839 4000
Fax: 020 8 842 3223
Ownership: Asia TV Ltd
Service start: Mar 1995
Satellite: Astra 1E (PAL/Videocrypt)
Programming: films, discussions,
news, game shows in Hindi, Punjabi,
Urdu, Bengali, Tamil, English, etc
Website:www.zeetelevision.com/

DIGITAL TELEVISION

ONdigital

346 Queenstown Road
London SW8 4NE
Tel: 020 7819 8000
Fax: 020 819 8100
Website: www.ondigital.co.uk

Sky Digital

6 Centaurs Business Park
Grant Way
Syon Lane
Isleworth
Middlesex TW7 5QD
Tel: 020 8 782 3000
Fax: 020 8 782 3030
Website: www.skydigital.co.uk

CAREERS AND TRAINING

CAREERS

No one organisation gives individually-tailored advice about careers in the media industries, but it is an area much written about, and we have included in this section details of some books and other sources or contacts that may help. Compiled by David Sharp.

There is no doubt that the media industries are perceived as being "glamourous" and young people are attracted to them. Opportunities in television appear to be increasing as the number of companies and organisations continues to grow, boosted by the growth of digital delivery and the new technologies. The film sector too, continues to appear reasonably healthy. Anyone wanting to work in these industries should expect to be open to the idea of working with new technologies and should anticipate the need to update their skills regularly. Offering a range of skills, rather than just one can be to an applicant's benefit.

Finally, it is important to recognise that this area of training and learning, like many others, has been undergoing shifts of emphasis that provide vocational alternatives to more traditional ways of obtaining qualifications and experience. Health warning! it is still the case that formal qualifications are only part of the picture. If you do get a foot in the door and show initiative and skill you can still get on.

For these reasons it is important that anyone considering a career in the industry takes care to investigate what courses are available that will help prepare the way, and if possible, although this is rarely easy, talks to someone already doing a job similar to the one they are interested in.

The Jobs

The media industry contains a wide range of jobs, some of which, usually of a support or administrative nature (eg librarian; accountant) have equivalents in many other areas, and some of which are quite specialised and have unique, though possibly misleading titles (eg best boy; gaffer).

The bibliography, below, will help guide you.

Bibliography

Below is a selected list, based on holdings at the BFI National Library. These will give you some guidance as to the range of jobs available, the structure of the industry, and they will offer some general guidance on preparing a CV. There are publications (and short courses) devoted to creating and presenting CVs, and you should check with your nearest library about these.

GETTING INTO FILMS & TELEVISION
Angell, Robert
How To Books, 5th ed., 1999
ISBN 1-85703-413-9

HOW TO GET INTO THE FILM & TV BUSINESS
Gates, Tudor
Alma House, 1995
ISBN 0-415-15112-0

Inside Broadcasting
Newby, Julian
Routledge, 1997
ISBN 0-415-15112-0

bfi **LIGHTS, CAMERA, ACTION! CAREERS IN FILM, TELEVISION, VIDEO**
Langham, Josephine
BFI, 2nd ed., 1996
ISBN 0-85170-573-1

MAKING ACTING WORK
Salt, Chrys
Bloomsbury, 1997
ISBN 0-74753-595-7

A WOMAN'S GUIDE TO JOBS IN FILM AND TELEVISION
Muir, Anne Ross
Pandora Press, 1987
ISBN 0-86358-061-0

WORKING IN TELEVISION, FILM & RADIO
Foster, Val et al
DfEE, 1997
ISBN 0-86111-0696-2

Courses
The following titles are recommended for information on courses. You will need to consider what balance between theory, practice and academic study you wish to undertake, and plan accordingly. Decide what qualifications and skills you want to acquire, check who validates the course, and for practical courses, what equipment is available to learn with.

bfi **MEDIA COURSES UK**
Orton, Lavinia
BFI, Annual.

bfi **MEDIA AND MULTIMEDIA SHORT COURSES**
Orton, Lavinia
BFI/Skillset (3 issues per year)
This is also available on the BFI website; and at some Regional Arts Boards

FLOODLIGHT
(covers the Greater London region) and other local guides to courses may be worth checking at your local library

Courses Abroad
COMPLETE GUIDE TO AMERICAN FILM SCHOOLS AND CINEMA AND TELEVISION COURSES
PINTOFF, Ernest
Penguin, 1994
ISBN 0-1401-7226-2

COMPLETE GUIDE TO ANIMATION AND COMPUTER GRAPHICS SCHOOLS
Pintoff, Ernest
Watson-Guptill, 1995
ISBN 0-8230-2177-7
Restricted to American courses only

VARIETY INTERNATIONAL FILM GUIDE
COWIE, Peter, ed.
This annual guide includes an international film schools section.

WHERE TO GET MULTIMEDIA TRAINING IN EUROPE
Institut National de L' Audiovisuel
1997
ISBN 2-86938-136-0

There are two other contacts for courses abroad:

CILECT (CENTRE INTERNATIONAL DE LIAISON ECOLES DE CINEMA ET DE TÉLÉVISION)
8 rue Theresienne
1000 Bruxelles
Belgique
Tel: 00 32 2 511 98 39
Fax: 00 32 2 511 00 35
Contact: Executive Secretary, Henry Verhasselt. email:
hverh.cilect@skynet.be

Training Organisations

All Regional Arts Boards and Media Development Agencies are involved with or have information on training. These are listed in the Funding section of the Handbook.

Broadcast Training Wales

Cyfle
BTW and Cyfle are part of the same grouping, with BTW focusing on English speakers and Cyfle on Welsh speakers and reasonably advanced learners of Welsh. They support the training needs of the Welsh film and television industry
3rd Floor/3ydd Llawr
Crichton House/Ty Crichton
11-12 Mount Stuart Square/Sgwar Mount Stuart
Cardiff/Cardydd CF1 6EE
Tel: 029 20 465533
Fax: 029 20 463344
also at:
Gronant, Penrallt Isaf
Caernarfon, Gwynedd
LL55 1NS
Tel: 01286 671000
Fax: 01286 678831
email: cyfle@cyfle-cyf.demon.co.uk
Website: http://www.cyfle-cyf.demon.co.uk

Film Education
Alhambra House
27-31 Charing Cross Road
London WC2H 0AU
Tel: 020 7976 2291
Fax: 020 7839 5052
Website: http://www.filmeducation.org
Fact sheets about how to get ahead in film, describing some of the key jobs are located on their website. Film Education also produce packs for teachers on recently released films, which give some background on the production process

ft2 – Film & Television Freelance Training
4th Floor Warwick House
9 Warwick Street
London W1 R 5RA
Tel: 020 7734 5141
Fax: 020 7287 9899
Website: www.ft2.org.uk
FT2 is the only UK-wide provider of new entrant training for young people wishing to enter the freelance sector of the industry in the junior construction, production and technical grades. Funded by Skillset,

Freelance Training Fund, European Social Fund, the AFVPA and Channel 4, ft2 is the largest industry training managed training provider in its field and has a 100% record of people graduating from the scheme and entering the industry

4FIT
Managed by ft2 (see above) this is Channel 4's training programme for people from ethnic minority backgrounds wishing to train as new entrants to junior production grades

Gaelic Television Training Trust
c/o Sabhal Mór Ostaig College
An Teanga
Isle of Skye, IV44 8RQ
Tel: 01471 844373
Fax: 01471 844383
Website: http://www.smo.uhi.ac.uk

Mediaskill
Broadcasting Centre
Barrack Road
Newcastle upon Tyne
NE99 2NE
Tel: 0191 232 5484
Fax: 0191 232 8871

Midlands Media Training Consortium
Birmingham office:
The Big Peg
120 Vyse Street
Birmingham B18 6NF
Tel: 0121 248 1515
Fax: 0121 248 1616
email: training@mmtc.co.uk

Nottingham office:
Nottingham Fashion Centre
Huntingdon Street
Nottingham NG1 3LH
Tel/Fax: 0115 993 0151
email: training@mmtc.co.uk
Midlands Media Training Consortium provides substantial funding to Midlands professional freelancers and broadcast staff to help them keep up with new technology, new working practices and new markets

National Film & Television School
National Short Course Training Programme
Beaconsfield Film Studios
Station Road
Beaconsfield
Bucks HP9 1LG
Tel:01494 677903
Fax: 01494 678708
Short course training for those already working in the industry

Northern Ireland Film Commission
21 Ormeau Avenue
Belfast BT2 8HD
Tel: 028 9023244
Fax: 028 90239918
email: info@nifc.co.uk
Website: http://www.nifc.co.uk

North West Media Training Consortium
c/o Mersey Television
Campus Manor
Childwall Abbey Road
Liverpool L16 0JP
Tel: 0151 722 9122
Fax: 0151 722 6839
Regional Training body with a brief to develop a training strategy for those who already have industry experience

Scottish Screen Training
249 West George Street
Glasgow G2 4RB
Tel: 0141 302 1700
Fax: 0141 302 1711

Skillnet South West
Regional Training Consortium for the South West
59 Prince Street
Bristol BS1 4QH
Tel: 0117 925 4011
Fax: 0117 925 3511
email: skillnetsw@bfv.co.uk

Skillset
2nd Floor
91-101 Oxford Street
London W1R 1RA
Tel: 020 7534 5300
Fax: 020 7534 5333
email: info@skillset.org
Website: http://www.skillset.org
Skillset is the National Training Organisation for broadcast, film, video and multimedia. It takes an overview but does not carry out training itself. It produces a careers handbook (send SAE with £1 stamp), also available on the website . A separate publication on TV for 14-17-year olds is available (send A4 sae with 66p 1st class postage)

Yorkshire Media Training Consortium
30-38 Dock Street
Leeds LS10 1JF
Tel: 0113 294 4410
Fax: 0113 294 4989
email: info@ymtc.co.uk
A regional agency, YMTC is concerned to develop a strategy to identify, develop and provide training for those who are already working within the industry in the region

Paying Your Way

It is important to be clear on the cost of any course you embark on and sources of grants or other funding. Generally speaking short courses do not attract grants, but your local authority or local careers office may be able to advise on this, or your nearest Training and Enterprise Council. Find out where they are, and check directories of sources for grants at your local library

CD ROMS

The following list comprises of CD ROM titles currently held in the BFI National Library's Reading Room, with a brief description of contents. Compiled by Sean Delaney

Academy Players
AMPAS, Beverly Hills, CA.
CD ROM version of the long-running directory. Contains stills and contact for American actors. User is also able to search by physical type for casting purposes.

Complete Index to World Film since 1895
(by Alan Goble)
Bowker-Saur, London
Revamped and re-titled, the complete index contains details for over 300,000 film titles including animations, documentaries, shorts and TV movies. Although user can search by title, keyword, production company, director, actor, and other major credits, keyword, records offer little more than basic credits.

FIAF International Index to Film Periodicals
Film International des Archives du Film, Brussels
Very important periodical index covering film and television journals since 1972. Contains the usual title/director/actor/keyword search options. Although character based, this CD ROM also contains listings of major articles by journal title and, almost uniquely, a most useful author search capability. There is an emphasis upon French language

bfi Film Index International
BFI/Chadwyck-Healey, London/Oxford
Based on the BFI National Library's SIFT database, this is probably one of the most useful CD ROM's for film research. It contains over 1 million cast and credit references for over 100,000 films and over 40,000 personalities up to 1997.

Attached to these are over 400,000 articles based on records collected since the 1930s. As well as the basic searches by title and personality, there are also searches by country of production, year of production and by synopsis, which can be combined and refined to help user find out how many types of film were made in a particular country in a particular year.

The Knowledge
Miller Freeman, Tonbridge, Kent
Easy to use CD ROM based on the standard reference work for UK film and television production. User is able to call up either specific contact information for companies and personnel or display listings of relevant companies.

Motion Picture Guide
Cinebooks, USA
Based on the well established hard copy version, this CD ROM covers films dating back to 1925. Users can search by title, personality, year of release and keyword. Searches can be combined e.g. number of films about space produced in 1956. Entries offer more than its Complete Index rival offering credits and critical synopsis.

Players Guide
The Spotlight, London
American version of the Spotlight directories (see below)

Spotlight Actors/Actresses/ Walk-on & Supporting Artists
The Spotlight, London
CD ROM versions of the famous long running directory. Supplies contact information and stills for UK based actors and actresses. It contains searches that allow casting searches by physical type that are easier to use than the Academy Players equivalent.

TBI Yearbook
FT Media & Telecoms, London.
Containing listings for over 200

countries for terrestrial, cable and satellite television. Entries by country contain contact points for all major governmental and trade organisations as well as the major companies. The country entries also cover recent developments and issues in handy and informative summaries. Companies can be searched for directly in A-Z index. The world television industry is discussed in a useful Top 100 analysis that is accompanied by a Top 100 table.

Also available

Annuaire du Cinema, Television & Video
(France – production directory)

Audio Visual Materials for Higher Education
[featuring the Avance database] (UK, produced by the British Universities Film & Video Council)

Australian Feature Films
(Australia, filmographic)

British-Humanities Index
(UK, general periodical index)

Corel All-Movie Database
(US, general filmographic)

Cremer Filmdatenbank
(Germany, production directory)

Cultural Connections
(Australia, based on the Australian National Film & Sound Archive collections)

Cannes Film Festival
(France, 1995 promo that also contains data on previous festivals)

Kays Production Database
(UK, based on the venerable hard copy directory)

Kinopalatsi
(Finland, filmographic)

Lexikon des Internationalen Films
(Germany, filmographic)

Quigley's Entertainment Industry Reference
(US, contact information)

Scotland on Location
(UK, production)

Schweizer Filme/Films Suisses/Swiss Films
(Switzerland, filmographic)

Svenska Langfilmen
(Sweden, filmographic)

Truffaut
(France, biographical)

Tuttofellini
(Italy, biographical)

Rudolfo Valentino
(Spain, biographical)

Variety Compact
(US, contacts and statistical information)

Wilson Art Index
(US, periodical index)

ZDF Jahrbuch auf CD ROM
(Germany, television directory)

CINEMAS

Listed below are the companies who control the major cinema chains and multiplexes in the UK, followed by the cinemas themselves listed by county and town, and including seating capacities. The listing also includes disabled access information, where available. Compiled by Allen Eyles

KEY TO SYMBOLS

 bfi supported – either financial and/or programming assistance

P/T Part-time screenings
S/O Seasonal openings

DISABILITY CODES

West End/Outer London

E Hearing aid system installed. Always check with venue whether in operation
W Venue with unstepped access (via main or side door), wheelchair space and adapted lavatory
X Venue with flat or one step access to auditorium
A Venue with 2-5 steps to auditorium
G Provision for Guide Dogs

England/Channel Islands/Scotland/Wales/Northern Ireland

X Accessible to people with disabilities (advance arrangements sometimes necessary – please phone cinemas to check)
E Hearing aid system installed. Always check with venue whether in operation

The help of Artsline, London's Information and Advice Service for Disabled People on Arts & Entertainment, in producing this section, including the use of their coding system for venues in the Greater London area, is gratefully acknowledged. Any further information on disability access would be welcome.

CINEMA CIRCUITS

ABC Cinemas
80 Great Portland Street
London W1N 5PA
Tel: 020 7291 9000
Fax: 020 7580 1080
Operates 62 sites including 4 multiplexes in mid-1999

Apollo Leisure Group
7 Palatine Suite
Coppull Enterprises Centre
Mill Lane, Coppull
Lancs PR7 5AN
Tel: 01257 471012
Fax: 01257 794109
Operates 14 cinemas with 61 screens in the North West of England, Wales, Yorkshire and the Midlands and is opening a 9 screen multiplex at Paignton, Devon

Artificial Eye Film Company
14 King Street
London WC2E 8HN
Tel: 020 7240 5353
Fax: 020 7240 5242
Film distributors operating the Chelsea Cinema and Renoir in London's West End

Caledonian Cinemas
1st Floor, Highland Rail House
Station Square
Inverness IV1 1LE
Tel: 01463 718888
Fax: 01463 718180
Operates 15 screens on 5 sites, all in Scotland

Cine-UK Ltd
Chapter House
22 Chapter Street
London SW1P 4NP
Tel: 020 7932 2200
Fax: 020 7932 2222
Operates 11 multiplexes (128 screens) in summer 1999 with others under construction at Runcorn, Weymouth, Wood Green, Milton Keynes and more planned for Huntingdon, Isle of Wight, Bury St. Edmunds, Llandudno Junction, Bishop's Stortford, Burton upon Trent and Jersey

City Screen
86 Dean Street
London W1V 5AA
Tel: 020 7734 4342
Fax: 020 7734 4027
Operates the Picture House cinemas in Clapham, Brighton, Oxford, Exeter, Stratford upon Avon, Stratford East, London, East Grinstead, York and Cambridge. The company also operates Maltings Cinema Ely and programmes or manages the Curzon group of cinemas in London's West End and others

Film Network
23 West Smithfield
London EC1A 9HY
Tel: 020 7489 0531
Fax: 020 7248 5781
Operates nine screens on two sites at Greenwich and Peckham in South East London

Mainline Pictures
37 Museum Street
London WC1A 1LP
Tel: 020 7242 5523
Fax: 020 7430 0170
Website: www.screencinemas.co.uk
Operates Screen cinemas at Baker Street, Haverstock Hill, Islington Green, Reigate, Walton-on-Thames and Winchester with a total of 10 screens

National Amusements (UK)
Showcase Cinema
Redfield Way
Lenton
Nottingham NG27 2UW
Tel: 0115 986 2508
Owners and operators of 15 Showcase cinemas with 199 screens in Nottingham, Derby, Peterborough, Leeds, Liverpool, Walsall, Birmingham, Coventry, Manchester, Stockton, Bristol, Wokingham (Reading), Newham (London) and two in the Glasgow area near Coatbridge and Linwood with others announced for Birmingham, Cardiff, Dudley and Pontypridd

Oasis Cinemas
20 Rushcroft Road
Brixton
London SW2 1LA

Tel: 020 7733 8989
Fax: 020 7733 8790
Owns the Gate Notting Hill and
Cameo Edinburgh, and the Ritzy
Brixton which is a five-screen
multiplex

Odeon Cinemas
Rank Leisure Division
Stafferton Way
Maidenhead
Bucks SL6 1AY
Tel: 01628 504000
Fax: 01628 504383
The Odeon chain totalled 451 screens
on 80 sites in May 1999, with new
multiplexes opening at Coventry,
Dunfermline and Epsom and others
under development at Bradford,
Uxbridge, Wimbledon and elsewhere

Picturedrome Theatres
1 Duchess Street
London W1N 3DE
Tel: 01372 460 108
Independent chain o f8 cinemas at
Bognor, Bristol, Cannock,
Chippenham, Newport & Ryde (Isle
of Wight), Sittingbourne and
Weymouth

Robins Cinemas
Studio 3B
Highgate Business Centre
33 Greenwood Place
London NW5 1DH
Tel: 020 7482 3842
Fax: 020 7482 4141
Operates 8 buildings with 21screens
in mid-1999

Scott Cinemas
Alexandra
Newton Abbot
Devon
Tel: 01626 65368
West Country circuit with cinemas at
Bridgwater, Exmouth, Lyme Regis,
Newton Abbot, Sidmouth and
Teignmouth

UCI (UK) Ltd
7th Floor, Lee House
90 Great Bridgewater Street
Manchester M1 5JW
Tel: 0161 455 4000
Fax: 0161 455 4076
Website: www.uci-cinemas.co.uk
Operators of 26 purpose-built
multiplexes with 235 screens in the
UK plus the Empire and Plaza in
London's West End with more
multiplexes scheduled for
Manchester (Printworks) and
Maidenhead

Virgin Cinemas
6th Floor, Adelaide House
626 High Road
Chiswick
London W4 5RY
Tel: 020 8987 5000
Fax: 020 8742 7984
Operates 29 multiplexes in UK and 4
traditional cinemas in mid-1999. Has
further multiplexes opening at
Dundee, Edinburgh and Cardiff with
others announced for Glasgow, West
India Quay (London), Enfield,
Oldham, Birmingham V Ways, Hull,
Middlesborough and Parrs Wood
(Manchester)

Ward-Anderson Cinema Group
Film House
35 Upper Abbey Street
Dublin 1
Ireland
Tel: (353) 1 872 3422/3922
Fax: (353) 1 872 3687
Leading cinema operator in Northern
and Southern Ireland. Sites include
Ballymena, Belfast, Londonderry,
Lisburn and Newry

Warner Village Cinemas
79 Wells Street
London W1P 3RD
Tel: 020 7465 4090
Fax: 020 7465 4919
Currently operating 24 multiplex
cinemas in the UK with 222 screens,
including the 9-screen Warner Village
West End in London's Leicester
Square. A further 30 multiplexes will
be launched into the new
Millennium, the majority of which
are currently under construction at
locations throughout the UK

LONDON WEST END – PREMIERE RUN

BAKER STREET
Screen on Baker Street
Baker Street, NW1
Tel: 020 7935 2772
Seats: 1:95, 2:100

BAYSWATER
UCI Whiteleys, Queensway, W2
WG
Tel: 0870 603 4567
Seats: 1:333, 2:281, 3:196, 4:178,
5:154, 6:138, 7:147, 8:125

BLOOMSBURY
Renoir
Brunswick Square, WC1
Tel: 020 7837 8402
Seats: 1:251, 2:251

CHELSEA
Chelsea Cinema
Kings Road, SW3
Tel: 020 7351 3742
Seats: 713

Virgin Cinemas
Kings Road, SW3
Tel: 0870 907 0710
Seats: 1:220, 2:238, 3:122, 4:111

CITY OF LONDON
Barbican
Silk Street, EC2
WE
Tel: 020 7638 8891/638 4141
Seats: 1:288, 2:255

FULHAM ROAD
Virgin Cinemas
Fulham Road, SW10
Tel: 0870 907 0711
Seats: 1:348 X, 2:329 X, 3:173 X,
4:203 X, 5:218, 6:154,

HAVERSTOCK HILL
Screen on the Hill
Haverstock Hill, NW3
A
Tel: 020 7435 3366/9787
Seats: 339

HAYMARKET
Virgin Cinemas
Haymarket, SW1
Tel: 0870 907 0718
Seats: 1:448, 2:200, 3:201

Odeon
Haymarket SW1

A
Tel: 020 8315 4212
Seats: 566

ISLINGTON
 The Lux Cinema
2-4 Hoxton Square, N1
Tel: 020 7684 0200/0201
Seats: 120

Screen on the Green
Upper Street, Islington, N1
A
Tel: 020 7226 3520
Seats: 280

KENSINGTON
Odeon
Kensington High Street, W8
Tel: 020 8315 4214
Seats: 1:520, 2:66, 3:91, 4:265 X,
5:171 X, 6:204 X

KILBURN
Tricycle Cinema
269 Kilburn High Road, NW6
EWG
Tel: 020 7 328 1000/1900
Seats: 289

KNIGHTSBRIDGE
Curzon Minema
45 Knightsbridge, SW1X 7NL
Tel: 020 7369 1723
Seats: 68

LEICESTER SQUARE
ABC Panton St
Panton Street, SW1
Tel: 020 7930 0631/2
Seats: 1:127 X, 2:144 X, 3:138, 4:136

ABC Swiss Centre
Swiss Centre, W1
Tel: 020 7439 4470/437 2096
Seats: 1:97, 2:101, 3:93, 4:108

Empire
Leicester Square, WC2
Tel: 0870 603 4567
Seats: 1:1,330 X, 2:353, 3:77

Odeon Leicester Square
Leicester Square, WC2
Tel: 020 8315 4215
Seats: 1,943 EX; Mezzanine: 1:60 W,
2:50, 3:60, 4:60, 5:60

Odeon West End
Leicester Square, WC2
E
Tel: 020 8315 4221
Seats: 1:503, 2:838

Prince Charles
Leicester Place, WC2

X
Tel: 020 7437 8181
Seats: 488

Warner Village West End
Leicester Square, WC2
Tel: 020 7437 4347/3484
Seats: 1:178, 2:126, 3:300, 4:298,
5:414, 6:264, 7:410, 8:180, 9:303

THE MALL
 ICA Cinema
The Mall, SW1
AG
Tel: 020 7930 3647
Seats: 185, C'thèque: 45

MARBLE ARCH
Odeon
Edgware Road, W1
E
Tel: 020 8315 4216
Seats: 1:254, 2:126, 3:174, 4:229, 5:239

MAYFAIR
Curzon Mayfair
Curzon Street, W1
Tel: 020 7369 1720
Seats: 542

NOTTING HILL GATE
Coronet
Notting Hill Gate, W11
A
Tel: 020 7727 6705
Seats:396

Gate
Notting Hill Gate, W11
X
Tel: 020 7727 4043
Seats: 240

PICCADILLY CIRCUS
ABC
Piccadilly, W1
Tel: 020 7437 3561
Seats: 1:124, 2:118

IMAX Trocadero Centre
Piccadilly Circus, W1
Seats: 300

Metro
Rupert Street, W1
W
Tel: 020 7437 0757
Seats: 1:195, 2:84

Plaza
Lower Regent Street, W1
Tel: 020 7437 0757/734 1506
Seats: 1:752, 2:370 X, 3:161, 4:187

Virgin Cinemas
Trocadero Centre

Piccadilly Circus, W1
XE
Tel: 020 7434 0032
Seats: 1:548, 2:240, 3:146, 4:154,
5:122, 6:94, 7:89

PORTOBELLO ROAD
Electric
Portobello Road, W11
X
Seats: 400
(Temporarily closed)

SHAFTESBURY AVENUE
ABC
Shaftesbury Avenue, WC2
Tel: 020 7836 6279/8606
Seats: 1:616, 2:581

Curzon Soho
Shaftesbury Avenue, W1
Tel: 020 7734 2255
Seats: 1:249, 2:110, 3:130

SOUTH KENSINGTON
Ciné Lumière
French Institute
Queensberry Place, SW7
Tel: 020 7838 2144/2146
Seats: 350

Goethe Institute
50 Princes Gate,
Exhibition Rd, SW7
Tel: 020 7596 4000
Seats: 170

TOTTENHAM COURT ROAD
ABC
Tottenham Court Road, W1
Tel: 020 7636 6148/6749
Seats: 1:328, 2:145, 3:137

WATERLOO
 **bfi London IMAX**
Charlie Chaplin Walk, SE 1
Tel: 020 7902 1234
Seats: 482

National Film Theatre
South Bank, Waterloo, SE1
WE
Tel: 020 7928 3232
Seats: 1:450, 2:160, 3:135

Queen Elizabeth Hall
South Bank, Waterloo, SE1
X
Tel: 020 7928 3002
Seats: 906

Royal Festival Hall
South Bank, Waterloo, SE1
X
Tel: 020 7928 3002
Seats: 2,419

OUTER LONDON

ACTON
Warner Village
Royale Leisure Park, Park Royal
Tel: 020 8896 0099
Seats: 1:424, 2:155, 3:201, 4:272,
5:312, 6:272, 7:201, 8:155, 9:424

BARNET
Odeon
Great North Road
Tel: 020 8315 4210
Seats: 1:522 E, 2:178, 3:78, 4:190 W,
5:158

BECKENHAM
ABC
High Street
Tel: 020 8650 1171/658 7114
Seats: 1:478, 2:228 A, 3:127 A

Studio
Beckenham Road
Tel: 020 8663 0103
Seats: 84

BEXLEYHEATH
Cineworld The Movies
The Broadway
Tel: 020 8303 0015
Seats: 1:157, 2:128, 3:280, 4:244,
5:88, 6:84, 7:111, 8:168, 9:221

BOREHAMWOOD
Cinema
Leisure Centre
Shenley Road
WG
Tel: 020 8207 2028
Seats: 1:180, 2:144, 3:111, 4:108

BRENTFORD
Watermans Arts Centre
High Street
WEG
Tel: 020 8568 1176
Seats: 240

BRIXTON
Ritzy
Brixton Oval
Coldharbour Lane SW2
Tel: 020 7737 2121
Seats: 1:353, 2:179, 3:125, 4:108,
5:84

BROMLEY
Odeon
High Street
Tel: 020 8315 4211
Seats: 1:392, 2:129 X, 3:105 X,
4:273

CAMDEN TOWN
Odeon
Parkway
Tel: 020 8315 4229
Seats: 1:403, 2:92, 3:238, 4:90, 5:99

CATFORD
ABC
Central Parade SE6 2TF
Tel: 020 8698 3306/697 6579
Seats: 1:519 X, 2:259

CLAPHAM
Picture House
Venn Street, SW4
Tel: 020 7498 3323
Seats: 1:212, 2:153 X, 3:135 X,
4:110

CROYDON
Safari
London Road
Tel: 020 8688 3422
Seats: 1:650, 2:399 X, 3:187 X

David Lean Cinema
Clock Tower
Katherine St
X
Tel: 020 8253 1030
Seats: 68

Fairfield Halls/Ashcroft Theatre
Park Lane
Tel: 020 8688 9291
Seats: Fairfield: 1,552 WEG
Ashcroft: 750

Warner Village
Purley Way
Tel: 020 8680 6881
Seats: 1:253, 2:205, 3:178, 4:396,
5:396, 6:178, 7:205, 8:253

DAGENHAM
Warner Village
Dagenham Leisure Park,
off Cook Road
Tel: 020 8592 2211
Seats: 1:402, 2:144, 3:187, 4:250,
5:297, 6:250, 7:187, 8:144, 9:402

DALSTON
Rio
Kingsland High Street, E8
WEG
Tel: 020 7254 6677/249 2722
Seats: 405

EALING
Gorsai
Northfield Avenue, W13
Tel: 020 8567 1075
Seats: 1:155, 2:149

Virgin Cinemas,
Uxbridge Road, W5
Tel: 0870 907 0719
Seats: 1:576, 2:371, 3:193

EAST FINCHLEY
Phoenix
High Road, N2
XG
Tel: 020 8444 6789
Seats: 308

EAST HAM
Boleyn
Barking Road
Tel: 020 8471 4884
Seats: 1:800, 2:250, 3:250

EDGWARE
Belle-Vue
Station Road
Tel: 020 8381 2556
Seats: 1:700, 2:200, 3:158

ELEPHANT & CASTLE
Coronet Film Centre
New Kent Road, SE1
Tel: 020 7703 4968/708 0066
Seats: 1:546, 2:271 X, 3:211X

FELTHAM
Cineworld The Movies
Leisure West Browells Lane
Tel: 020 8867 0888
Seats: 1:104, 2:116, 3:132, 4:205,
5:253, 6:351, 7:302, 8:350, 9:265,
10:90, 11:112, 12: 137, 13:124, 14:99

FINCHLEY ROAD
Warner Village Cinemas
02 Centre
Tel: 020 7604 3066
Seats: 1:359, 2:324, 3:159, 4:261,
5:376, 6:258, 7:134, 8:86

GOLDERS GREEN
ABC
Finchley Road, NW11
Tel: 020 8455 1724/4134
Seats: 524

GREENWICH
Greenwich Cinema
High Road, SE10
WEG
Tel: 020 8293 0101
Seats: 1:350, 2:288, 3:144

HAMMERSMITH
Virgin Cinemas
King Street, W6
Tel: 0870 907 0718
Seats: 1:322, 2:322, 3:268 A,
4:268 A

Riverside Studios
Crisp Road, W6
E
Tel: 020 7420 0100
Seats: 200

HAMPSTEAD
ABC
Pond Street, NW3
Tel: 020 7794 4000/6603
Seats: 1:476, 2:198 X, 3:193 X

Pullman Everyman
Holly Bush Vale, NW3
X
Tel: 0845 606 2345
Seats: 184

HARRINGEY
New Curzon
Frobisher Road
Tel: 020 8347 6664
Seats: 498

HARROW
Safari
Station Road
Tel: 020 8426 0303
Seats: 1:612, 2:133

Warner Village
St George's Centre, St. Ann's Road
Tel: 020 8427 9900/9009
Seats: 1:347, 2:288, 3:424, 4:296,
5:121, 6:109, 7:110, 8:87, 9:96

HAYES
Beck Theatre
Grange Road
XE
Tel: 020 8561 8371
Seats: 518

HOLLOWAY
Odeon
Holloway Road, N7
Tel: 020 8315 4213
Seats: 1:243, 2:192, 3:223, 4:328,
5:301,6:78, 7:112, 8:124

ILFORD
Cinema
High Road
Seats: 600

Odeon
Gants Hill
Tel: 020 8315 4223
Seats: 1:768, 2:255 X, 3:290 X,
4:190, 5:62

KILBURN
Tricycle Cinemas
High Road
Tel: 020 7328 1000
Seats: 280

KINGSTON
ABC Options
Richmond Road
Tel: 020 8546 0404/547 2860
Seats: 1:287 X, 2:273 X, 3:200

LAMBETH
Imperial War Museum
Lambeth Road, SE1
X
Tel: 020 7735 8922
Seats: 216

LEE VALLEY
UCI
Picketts Lock Lane
Meridian Way,
Edmonton
X
Tel: 0870 603 4567
Seats: 164 (6 screens), 206
(4 screens), 426 (2 screens)

MILE END
Genesis
Mile End Road
Tel: 020 7780 2000
Seats: 1:575, 2:159, 3:159, 4:101,
5:95

MUSWELL HILL
Odeon
Fortis Green Road, N10
Tel: 020 8315 4216
Seats: 1:568, 2:173 X, 3:169 X

NEWHAM
Showcase Cinemas
Jenkins Lane, off A13
X
Tel: 020 8477 4520
Seats: 3,664 (14 screens)

NORTH FINCHLEY
Warner Village
Great North Leisure Park, North
Circular Road, Chaplin Square,
N12
Tel: 020 8446 9977/9344
Seats: 1:367, 2:164, 3:219, 4:333,
5:333, 6:219, 7:164, 8:367

PECKHAM
Premier
Rye Lane
X
Tel: 020 7732 1010
Seats: 1:397, 2:255, 3:275, 4:197,
5:218, 6:112

PUTNEY
ABC
High Street, SW15
AWG
Tel: 020 8788 3003/785 3493
Seats: 1:433, 2:313, 3:147

RICHMOND
Filmhouse
Water Lane
WG
Tel: 020 8332 0030
Seats: 150

Odeon
Hill Street
Tel: 020 8315 4218
Seats: 1:412, 2:179 X, 3:179 X

Odeon Studio
Red Lion Street
Tel: 020 8315 4218
Seats: 1:81, 2:78, 3:78, 4:92

ROMFORD
ABC
South Street
Tel: 01708 743848/747671
Seats: 1:652, 2:494 A, 3:246 X

Odeon Liberty 2
Mercury Gardens
Tel: 01708 729040
Seats: 1:412 W, 2:255, 3:150, 4:181,
5:181, 6:150, 7:331, 8:254

SIDCUP
ABC
High Street
Tel: 020 8300 2539/300 3603
Seats: 1:503 A, 2:309

STAPLES CORNER
Virgin Cinemas
Geron Way
WE
Tel: 0870 907 0717
Seats: 1:455, 2:362, 3:214, 4:210,
5:166, 6:166

STRATFORD
Picture House
Gerry Raffles Square
Salway Road E15
Tel: 020 8555 3311/66
Seats: 1:212, 2:236, 3:256, 4:157

STREATHAM
ABC
High Road, SW16
Tel: 020 8769 1928/6262
Seats: 1:630, 2:427 X, 3:227 X

Odeon
High Road, SW16
Tel: 020 8315 4219
Seats: 1:1,092, 2:231 X, 3:201 X,
4:253, 5:198

SURREY QUAYS
UCI Cinemas
Redriff Road, SE16
Tel: 0870 603 4567

Seats: 1:411, 2:401, 3:328, 4:200, 5:198, 6:198, 7:164, 8:164, 9:164

SUTTON
Secombe Centre
Cheam Road
XE
Tel: 020 8661 0416
Seats: 330

UCI
St Nicholas Centre
St Nicholas Way
X
Tel: 0870 603 4567
Seats: 1:305, 2:297, 3:234, 4:327, 5:261, 6:327

SWISS COTTAGE
Odeon
Finchley Road, NW3
Tel: 020 8315 4220
Seats: 1:715, 2:111, 3:220, 4:120, 5:154, 6:156

WALTHAMSTOW
ABC
Hoe Street, E17
Tel: 020 8520 7092
Seats: 1:592, 2:183 A, 3:174 A

WELL HALL
Coronet
Well Hall Road, SE9
Tel: 020 8850 3351
Seats: 1:450, 2:131 XG

WILLESDEN
Belle Vue
Willesden Green Library Centre, NW10
Tel: 020 8830 0822
Seats: 204

WIMBLEDON
Odeon
The Broadway, SW19
Tel: 020 8315 4222
Seats: 1:662, 2:90, 3:190 X, 4:175, 5:226 X

WOODFORD
ABC
High Road, E18
Tel: 020 8989 3463/4066
Seats: 1:561, 2:199 X, 3:131 X

WOOD GREEN
Cineworld the Movies
Shopping City
High Road
Seats: 2,200 (12 screens)
(Scheduled to open March 2000)

Hoyts
Spouters Corner
Seats: 1,600 (6 screens)
(Scheduled to open Spring 2000)

ENGLAND

AVON

Bath
ABC, Beau Nash, Westgate Street
X
Tel: 01225 461730/462959
Seats: 727

Little Theatre, St Michael's Place
Tel: 01225 466822
Seats: 1:192, 2:74

Robins, St John's Place
Tel: 01225 461506
Seats: 1:151, 2:126 X, 3:49

Bristol Avon
Arnolfini, Narrow Quay
XE
Tel: 0117 929 9191
Seats: 176

Cube
King Square
X
Tel: 0117 907 4190/4191
Seats: 124

Cineworld The Movies
Hengrove Leisure Park,
Hengrove Way
Tel: 01275 831099
Seats: 1:97, 2:123, 3:133, 4:211, 5:264, 6:343, 7:312, 8:344, 9:262, 10:88, 11:113, 12:152, 13:123, 14:98

Orpheus, Northumbria Drive, Henleaze
Tel: 0117 962 1644
Seats: 1:186, 2:129, 3:125

ABC, Whiteladies Road, Clifton
Tel: 0117 973 0679/973 3640
Seats: 1:372, 2:252 X, 3:135 X

Odeon, Union Street
Tel: 0117 929 0884
Seats: 1:399, 2:244, 3:215

Showcase Cinemas, Avon Meads off Albert Road, St Phillips Causeway
Tel: 0117 972 3800
Seats: 3,408 (14 screens)

bfi Watershed, 1 Canon's Road, BS1 5TX
XE
Tel: 0117 927 6444/925 3845
Seats: 1:200, 2:50

Warner Village Cinemas
The Venue, Cribbs Causeway
Leisure Complex
Tel: 0117 950 0222
Seats: 1:385, 2:124, 3:124, 4:166,

5:239, 6:273, 7:273, 8:239, 9:166, 10:124, 11:124, 12:385

Warner Village Cinemas,
Aspects Leisure Park, Kingswood
Tel: 0117 960 0185
Seats: 1:385, 2:167, 3:125, 4:125, 5:167, 6:293, 7:337, 8:293, 9:167, 10:125, 11:125, 12:167, 13:385
(Scheduled to open November 1999)

Clevedon
Curzon, Old Church Road
Tel: 01275 871000
Seats: 392

Nailsea
Cinema, Scotch Horn Leisure Centre, Brockway (P/T)
Tel: 01275 856965
Seats: 250

Weston-Super-Mare
Odeon, The Centre
Tel: 01934 641251
Seats: 1:586, 2:109, 3:126, 4:268

Playhouse, High Street (P/T)
Tel: 01934 23521/31701
Seats: 658

BEDFORDSHIRE

Bedford
Civic Theatre, Horne Lane (P/T)
Tel: 01234 44813
Seats: 266

Virgin Cinemas, Aspect Leisure Park, Newnham Avenue
XE
Tel: 0541 555 130
Seats: 1:340, 2:300, 3:300, 4:300, 5:200, 6:200

Leighton Buzzard
Theatre, Lake Street (P/T)
Tel: 01525 378310
Seats: 170

Luton
ABC, George Street
Tel: 01582 727311
Seats: 1:562, 2:436, 3:272

Cineworld The Movies
The Galaxy, Bridge Street
Tel: 01582 401092/400705
Seats: 1:114, 2:75, 3:112, 4:284, 5:419, 6:212, 7:123, 8:217, 9:137, 10:213, 11:240

Artezium, Arts and Media Centre
Tel: 01582 707100
Seats: 96

St George's Theatre
Central Library (P/T)

Tel: 01582 547440
Seats: 238

BERKSHIRE

Bracknell
South Hill Park Arts Centre
X
Tel: 01344 427272/484123
Seats: 1:60, 2:200 m

UCI, The Point
Skimpedhill Lane
X
Tel: 0870 603 4567
Seats: 1:177, 2:205, 3:205, 4:177,
5:316, 6:316, 7:177, 8:205, 9:205,
10:177

Newbury
Corn Exchange,
Market Place (P/T)
X
Tel: 01635 522733
Seats: 370

Reading
Film Theatre, Whiteknights (P/T)
Tel: 01734 868497/875123
Seats: 409

Odeon, Cheapside
Tel: 01734 576803
Seats: 1:410, 2:221, 3:221

Warner Village Cinemas,
Oracle Centre
Tel: 0118 956 0043
Seats: 1:134, 2:147, 3:251, 4:372,
5:191, 6:232, 7:232, 8:148, 9:118,
10:88
(Scheduled to open November 1999)

Slough
Virgin Cinemas,
Queensmere Centre
Tel: 0870 603 4567
Seats: 1,821 (10 screens)

Sunninghill
Novello Theatre, High Street (P/T)
Tel: 01990 20881
Seats: 160

Windsor
Arts Centre, St Leonards Road (P/T)
Tel: 01753 8593336
Seats: 108

Wokingham
Showcase Cinemas, Loddon
Bridge, Reading Road,
Winnersh
X
Tel: 01189 306922
Seats: 2,980 (12 screens)

BUCKINGHAMSHIRE

Aylesbury
ABC
Seats: 1: 396, 2:283, 3:266, 4:230,
5:133, 6:205

Odeon, Cambridge Street
Tel: 01296 339588
Seats: 1:450, 2:108, 3:113

Chesham
Elgiva Theatre, Elgiva Lane (P/T)
XE
Tel: 01494 774759
Seats: 328

Gerrards Cross
ABC, Ethorpe Crescent
Tel: 01753 882516/883024
Seats: 1:350, 2:212

Halton
Astra, RAF Halton (P/T)
Tel: 01296 623535
Seats: 570

High Wycombe
UCI Wycombe 6,
Crest Road, Cressex
X
Tel: 0870 603 4567
Seats: 1:388, 2:388, 3:284, 4: 284,
5:202, 6:202

Milton Keynes
Cineworld The Movies
Xscape Sno Dome Complex,
Avebury Road
Seats: 3,450 (16 screens)
(Scheduled to open May 2000)

UCI The Point 10
Midsummer Boulevard
Tel: 0870 603 4567
Seats: 1:156, 2:169, 3:250, 4:222,
5:222, 6:222, 7:222, 8:250

CAMBRIDGESHIRE

Cambridge
Arts Picture House
St Andrews Street
Tel: 01223 504444/572929
Seats: 1: 250, 2:150, 3:108

Warner Village,
Grafton Centre, East Road
XE
Tel: 01223 460442/460225
Seats: 1:163, 2:180, 3:194, 4:205,
5:175, 6:177, 7:335, 8:442

Ely
The Maltings, Broad Street (P/T)
Tel: 01353 666388
Seats: 200

Huntingdon
Cromwell Centre, Princes Street
Tel: 01480 433499
Seats: 264

Peterborough
Showcase Cinemas
Mallory Road, Boon Gate
X
Tel: 01733 555636
Seats: 3,365 (13 screens)

Ramsey
Grand, Great Whyte (P/T)
Tel: 01487 710221
Seats: 173

CHANNEL ISLANDS

Forest Guernsey
Mallard Cinema, Mallard Hotel
La Villiaze
Tel: 01481 64164
Seats: 1:154, 2:54, 3:75, 4:75

St Helier Jersey
Odeon, Bath Street
Tel: 01534 22888
Seats: 1:409, 2:244, 3:213, 4:171

St Peter Port Guernsey
Beau Sejour Centre
Tel: 01481 26964
Seats: 250

St Saviour Jersey
Cine Centre, St Saviour's Road
Tel: 01534 871611
Seats: 1:400, 2:291, 3:85

CHESHIRE

Cheshire Oaks
Warner Village Cinemas,
The Coliseum, Coliseum Way,
Ellesmere Port
Tel: 0151 356 2265
Seats: 3,600 (15 screens) + 300
(Iwerks Extreme Screen)
(Scheduled to open December
1999/January 2000)

Chester
Virgin Cinemas,
Chaser Court
Greyhound Park,
Sealand Road
XE
Tel: 01244 380459/380301/380155
Seats: 1:366, 2:366, 3:265, 4:232,
5:211, 6:211

Odeon, Northgate Street
Tel: 01244 343216
Seats: 1:408, 2:148, 3:148, 4:122,
5:122

Crewe
Apollo, High Street
Tel: 01270 255708
Seats: 1:107, 2:110, 3:91

Lyceum Theatre, Heath Street (P/T)
Tel: 01270 215523
Seats: 750

Victoria Film Theatre,
West Street l
Tel: 01270 211422
Seats: 180

Ellesmere Port
Epic Cinema,
Epic Leisure Centre (P/T)
X
Tel: 0151 355 3665
Seats: 163

Knutsford
Studio, Toft Road
X
Tel: 01565 633005
Seats: 400

Nantwich
Civic Hall, Market Street (P/T)
Tel: 01270 628633
Seats: 300

Northwich
Regal, London Road
Tel: 01606 43130
Seats: 1:797, 2:200

Runcorn
Cineworld The Movies,
Trident Retail Park
Seats: 1,600 (9 screens)
(Scheduled to open December 1999)

Warrington
UCI 10, Westbrook Centre,
Cromwell Avenue
X
Tel: 0990 888990
Seats: 1:186, 2:180, 3:180, 4:186,
5:276, 6:276, 7:186, 8:180, 9:180,
10:186

Wilmslow
Rex, Alderley Road (P/T)
Tel: 01625 522266
Seats: 838

CLEVELAND
Billingham
Forum Theatre,
Town Centre (P/T)
Tel: 01642 552663
Seats: 494

Hartlepool
Warner Village Cinemas
The Lanyard, Marina Way
Tel: 01429 261 177/263 263
Seats: 1:303, 2:345, 3:160, 4:204,
5:431, 6:204, 7:160

Middlesbrough
Odeon, Corporation Road
Tel: 01426 981167
Seats: 1:611, 2:129, 3:148, 4:254

Redcar
Regent
Tel: 01642 482094
Seats: 350

Stockton
Dovecot Arts Centre
Dovecot Street
Tel: 01642 611625/611659
Seats: 100

Showcase Cinemas, Aintree Oval
Teeside Leisure Park
Tel: 01642 633111
Seats: 3,400 (14 screens)

CO DURHAM
Consett
Empire, Front Street
XE
Tel: 01207 506751
Seats: 535

Darlington
Arts Centre, Vane Terrace (P/T)
XE
Tel: 01325 483168/483271
Seats: 100

ABC, Northgate
Tel: 01325 462745/484994
Seats: 1:578, 2:201, 3:139

Durham
Robins, North Road
Tel: 0191 384 3434
Seats: 1:312 X, 2:98, 3:96, 4:74

Hordern
WMR Film Centre,
Sunderland Road
Tel: 01783 864344
Seats: 1:156, 2:96

Stanley
Civic Hall (P/T)
Tel: 01207 32164
Seats: 632

CORNWALL
Bude
Rebel, off A39, Rainbow
Trefknic Cross

Tel: 01288 361442
Seats: 120

Falmouth
Arts, Church Street
Tel: 01326 212300
Seats: 199

Looe East
Cinema, Higher Market Street
Tel: 015036 2709
Seats: 95

Padstow
Cinedrome, Lanadwell Street
Tel: 01841 532344
Seats: 183

Penzance
Savoy, Causeway Head
Tel: 01736 363330
Seats: 1:200, 2:50, 3:50

Redruth
Regal Film Centre, Fore Street
Tel: 01209 216278
Seats: 1:171, 2:121, 3:600, 4:95

St Austell
Film Centre, Chandos Place
Tel: 01726 73750
Seats: 1:274, 2:134, 3:133, 4:70, 5:70

St Ives
Royal, Royal Square
Tel: 01736 796843
Seats: 1:350, 2:150, 3:63

Truro
Plaza, Lemon Street
Tel: 01872 272 894
Seats: 1:300, 2:198, 3:135, 4:70

Wadebridge
Regal, The Platt
Tel: 01208 812791
Seats: 1:224, 2:98

CUMBRIA
Ambleside
Zeffirelli's, Compston Road
X
Tel: 01539 431771
Seats: 1:205, 2:63

Barrow
Apollo, Abbey Road
Tel: 01229 832772
Seats: 1:531, 2:260, 3:230, 4:115

Apollo, Hollywood Park,
Hindpool Road
Tel: 01229 825354
Seats: 1:118, 2:103, 3:258, 4:258,
5:118, 6:118

Bowness-on-Windermere
Royalty, Lake Road
X
Tel: 01539 443364
Seats: 1:400, 2:100, 3:65

Carlisle
Lonsdale, Warwick Road
Tel: 01228 514654
Seats: 1:375, 2:216, 3:54

City Cinemas 4 & 5, Mary Street
X
Tel: 01228 514654
Seats: 4:122, 5:112

Warner Village Cinemas
Botchergate
Seats: (7 screens)
(Scheduled to open May 2000)

Kendal
Brewery Arts Centre
Highgate, LA9 4HE (S/O)
XE
Tel: 01539 725133
Seats: 246

Keswick
Alhambra
St John Street (S/O)
Tel: 017687 72195
Seats: 313

Millom
Palladium, Horn Hill (S/O)
Tel: 01657 2441
Seats: 400

Penrith
Alhambra, Middlegate
Tel: 01768 62400
Seats: 1:170, 2:90

Ulverston
Laurel & Hardy Museum
Upper Brook Street (P/T) (S/O)
Tel: 01229 52292/86614
Seats: 50

Roxy, Brogden Street
Tel: 01229 53797/56211
Seats: 310

Whitehaven
Gaiety
Tangier Street
Tel: 01946 693012
Seats: 330

Workington
Rendezvous,
Murray Road
Tel: 01900 602505
Two screens

DERBYSHIRE
Chesterfield
Cineworld The Movies
Derby Road, Alma Leisure Park
Tel: 0246 229172/278000
SeatsL 1:245, 2:128, 3:107, 4:150,
5:291, 6:291, 7:150, 8: 107, 9:128,
10:237

Derby
(bfi) Metro Cinema
      Green Lane, DE1 1SA
XE
Tel: 01332 340170/347765
Seats: 128

Ilkeston
Scala, Market Place
Tel: 0115 932 4612
Seats: 500

Matlock
Ritz, Causeway Lane
Tel: 01629 580 607
Seats: 1:176, 2:97

DEVON
Barnstaple
Astor, Boutport Street
Tel: 01271 42550
Seats: 360

Dartington
(bfi) Barn Theatre
      Arts Society
The Gallery, TQ9 6EJ (P/T)
X
Tel: 01803 865864/863073
Seats: 208

Exeter
Northcott Theatre,
Stocker Road (P/T)
Tel: 01392 54853
Seats: 433

Odeon, Sidwell Street
Tel: 01392 217175
Seats: 1:740, 2:121, 3:106, 4:344

Picture House
51 Bartholomew Street West
Tel: 01392 251341
Seats: 1:220, 2:160

Exmouth
Savoy, Rolle Street
Tel: 01395 268220
Seats: 1:204, 2:100, 3:70

Ilfracombe
Pendle Stairway, High Street
X
Tel: 01271 863260
Seats: 460

Newton Abbot
Alexandra, Market Street
X
Tel: 01626 65368
Seats: 1:206, 2:127

Okehampton
Carlton, St James Street
Tel: 01837 52167
Seats: 380

Paignton
Apollo Cinemas, Esplanade
Tel: 01803 558822
Seats: 1:360, 2:184, 3: 184, 4:219,
5:360, 6:77, 7:86, 8:33, 9:97

Torbay, Torbay Road
Tel: 01803 559544
Seats: 484

Plymouth
Arts Centre, Looe Street
X
Tel: 01752 660060
Seats: 73

Odeon, Derry's Cross
Tel: 01752 668825
Seats: 1:422, 2:164, 3:164, 4:218,
5:133

ABC, Derry's Cross
Tel: 01752 663300/225553
Seats: 1:582, 2:380, 3:115

Warner Village Cinemas
Barbican Leisure Park
Shapters Road, Coxside
Tel: 01752 223435
Seats: 1:175, 2:189, 3:153, 4:196,
5:188, 6:133, 7:292, 8:454, 9:498,
10:257, 11:215, 12:133, 133:127,
14:190, 15:187

Sidmouth
Radway, Radway Place
Tel: 01395 513085
Seats: 400

Tavistock
The Wharf, Canal Street (P/T)
Tel: 01822 613928
Seats: 212

Teignmouth
Riviera, Den Crescent
Tel: 01626 774624
Seats: 417

Tiverton
Tivoli, Fore Street
Tel: 01884 252157
Seats: 364

Torquay
Odeon, Abbey Road
Tel: 01803 295805
Seats: 1:304, 2:333

Torrington
Plough, Fore Street
Tel: 01805 622552/3
Seats: 108

DORSET

Bournemouth
ABC, Westover Road
Tel: 01202 292612
Seats: 1:652, 2:585, 3:223

Odeon, Westover Road
Tel: 01202 293554
Seats: 1:757, 2:359, 3:266, 4:120,
5:121, 6:146

Bridport
Palace, South Street
(temporarily closed)
Seats: 420

Christchurch
Regent Centre, High Street (P/T)
Tel: 01202 479819
Seats: 485

Dorchester
Plaza, Trinity Street
Tel: 01305 262488
Seats: 1:100, 2:320

Lyme Regis
Regent, Broad Street
X
Tel: 01297 442053
Seats: 400

Poole
Arts Centre, Kingsland Road (P/T)
X
Tel: 01202 685222
Seats: 143

UCI Tower Park,
Mannings Heath
Tel: 0870 603 4567
Seats: 1:194, 2:188, 3:188, 4:194,
5:276, 6:276, 7:194, 8:188, 9:188,
10:194

Shaftesbury
Arts Centre, Bell Street (P/T)
Tel: 01747 854321
Seats: 160

Swanage
Mowlem, Shore Road
Tel: 01929 422239
Seats: 411

Wareham
Rex, West Street
Tel: 01929 552778
Seats: 151

Weymouth
Cineworld The Movies
New Bond Street
Seats: 1,500 (9 screens)
(Scheduled to open December 1999)

Picturedrome
Gloucester Street
Tel: 01305 785847
Seats: 418

Rosehill Theatre, Moresby (P/T)
X
Tel: 01946 694039/692422
Seats: 208

Wimborne
Tivoli, West Borough (P/T)
Tel: 01202 848014
Seats: 500

EAST SUSSEX

Bexhill
Curzon, Western Road
Tel: 01424 210078
Seats: 175

Brighton
ABC, East Street
Tel: 01273 327010/202095
Seats: 1:345, 2:271, 3:194

Cinematheque, Media Centre,
Middle Street
Tel: 01273 384 300

Duke of York's Premier Picture
House, Preston Circus
Tel: 01273 626 261
Seats: 359

Gardner Arts Centre,
University of Sussex, Falmer (P/T)
Tel: 01273 685861
Seats: 354

Virgin Cinemas, Brighton Marina
Tel: 0541 555 145
Seats: 1:351, 2:351, 3:251, 4:251,
5:223, 6:223, 7:202, 8:203

Odeon Kingswest, West Street
Tel: 01273 207977
Seats: 1:388, 2:883, 3:504, 4:273,
5:242, 6:103

Chichester
Minerva Studio Cinema
Chichester Festival Theatre
Oaklands Park (S/O)
X

Tel: 01243 781312
Seats: 212

New Park Film Centre
New Park Road
X
Tel: 01243 786650
Seats: 120

Eastbourne
Curzon, Langney Road
Tel: 01323 731441
Seats: 1:530, 2:236, 3:236

Virgin Cinemas, Crumbles
Harbour Village
Pevensey Bay Road
XE
Tel: 01323 470070
Seats: 1:322, 2:312, 3:271, 4:254,
5:221, 6:221

Hastings
ABC, Queens Road
Tel: 01424 420517/431180
Seats: 1:387, 2:176, 3:129

St Mary-in-the-Castle Arts Centre,
Pelham Crescent
Tel: 01424 781624
Seats: 590

Uckfield
Picture House, High Street
Tel: 01825 763822/764909
Seats: 1:150, 2:100

EAST YORKSHIRE

Beverley
Playhouse, Market Place
Tel: 01482 881315
Seats: 310

ESSEX

Basildon
Robins, Great Oaks
Tel: 01268 527421/527431
Seats: 1:644, 2:435, 3:90

Towngate (P/T)
Tel: 01268 532632
Seats: 552, (Mirren Studio) 158

UCI
Festival Leisure Park
Pipps Hill
Tel: 0870 603 4567
Seats: 2,909 (12 screens)

Brentwood
ABC, Chapel High
Tel: 01277 212931/227574
Seats: 1:300, 2:196

Burnham-on-Crouch
Rio, Station Road

Tel: 01621 782027
Seats: 1:220, 2:60

Canvey Island
Movie Starr Cineplex
Eastern Esplandade
Tel: 01268 695000
Seats: 1:134, 2:122, 3:104, 4:73

Chelmsford
Central Theatre
High Street (P/T)
Tel: 01634 403868

Odeon, Kings Head Walk
EX
Tel: 01245 495068
Seats: 1:338, 2:110, 3:160, 4:236,
5:174, 6:152, 7:131, 8:141

Clacton
Flicks, Pier Avenue
Tel: 01255 429627
Seats: 1:625, 2:135

Colchester
Odeon, Crouch Street
Tel: 01206 760707
Seats: 1:480, 2:237, 3:118, 4:133,
5:126, 6:177

Grays
Thameside, Orsett Road (P/T)
Tel: 01375 382555
Seats: 303

Halstead
Empire, Butler Road
Tel: 01787 477001
Seats: 320

Harlow
Virgin Cinemas, Queensgate
Centre, Edinburgh Way
XE
Tel: 0870 907 0713
Seats: 1:356, 2:260, 3:240, 4:234,
5:233, 6:230

Odeon, The High
Tel: 01279 635067
Seats: 1:450, 2:239, 3:200

Playhouse, The High (P/T)
XE
Tel: 01279 431945
Seats: 330

Harwich
Electric Palace,
King's Quay Street (P/T)
Tel: 01255 553333
Seats: 204

South Woodham Ferrers
Flix, Market Street

Tel: 01245 329777
Seats: 1:249, 2:101

Southend
Odeon, Victoria Circus
XE
Tel: 01702 393544
Seats: 1:200, 2:264, 3:148, 4:224,
5:394, 6:264, 7:264, 8:200

West Thurrock
UCI Lakeside 10
Lakeside Retail Park
X
Tel: 0870 6034567
Seats: 276 (2 screens), 194
(4 screens), 188 (4 screens)

Warner, Lakeside Shopping Centre
X
Tel: 01708 891010/890567/890600
Seats: 1:382, 2:184, 3:177, 4:237,
5:498, 6:338, 7:208

GLOUCESTERSHIRE
Cheltenham
Odeon, Winchcombe Street
Tel: 01242 514421
Seats: 1:252, 2:184, 3:184, 4:90,
5:129, 6:104, 7:177

Wotton Under Edge
Town Cinema
Tel: 01453 521666
Seats: 200

Cirencester
Regal, Lewis Lane
Tel: 01285 658755
Seats: 1:100, 2:100

Coleford
Studio, High Street
Tel: 01594 833331
Seats: 1:200, 2:80

Gloucester
Guildhall Arts Centre,
Eastgate Street (P/T)
X
Tel: 01452 505086/9
Seats: 1:120, 2: 150

Virgin Cinemas,
Peel Centre,
St. Ann Way, Bristol Road
XE
Tel: 0541 555 174
Seats: 1:354, 2:354, 3:238, 4:238,
5:219, 6:219

Tewkesbury
Roses Theatre (P/T)
Tel: 01684 295074
Seats: 375

GREATER MANCHESTER
Ardwick
Apollo, Ardwick Green (P/T)
X
Tel: 0161 273 6921
Seats: 2,641

Ashton-under-Lyne
Metro, Old Street
Tel: 0161 330 1993
Seats: 987

Bolton
Warner Village
Middlebrook Leisure Park
Tel: 01204 66968
Seats: 1:368, 2:124, 3:124, 4:166,
5:244, 6:269, 7:269, 8:244, 9:166,
10:124, 11:124, 12:368

Virgin Cinemas
Eagley Brook Way
Tel: 01204 366200
Seats: 1: 143, 2:144, 3:118, 4:155,
5:230, 6:467, 7:635, 8:522, 9:233,
10:156, 11:156, 12:193, 13:193,
14:72, 15:72

Bury
Warner Village, Pilsworth
Industrial Estate, Pilsworth Road
X
Tel: 0161 766 2440/1121
Seats: 1:559, 2:322, 3:278, 4:434,
5:208, 6:166, 7:166, 8:208, 9:434,
10:278, 11:322, 12:573

Gatley
Tatton, Gatley Road
Tel: 0161 491 0711
Seats: 1:648, 2:247, 3:111

Heaton Moor
Savoy, Heaton Manor Road
Tel: 0161 432 2114
Seats: 476

Hollinwood
Roxy, Hollins Road
Tel: 0161 681 1441
Seats: 1:470, 2:130, 3:260, 4:260,
5:320, 6:96, 7:140

Manchester
Arena 7, Nynex Arena Complex
X
Tel: 0161 839 0700
Seats: 1:138, 2:143, 3:287, 4:257,
5:221, 6:370, 7:156

Cine City, Wilmslow Road,
Withington
Tel: 0161 445 9888
Seats: 1:150, 2:130, 3:130

 Cornerhouse
70 Oxford Street

M1 5NH
XE
Tel: 0161 228 2467/7621
Seats: 1:300, 2:170, 3:60

Odeon, Oxford Street
Tel: 0161 236 0537
Seats: 1:629 E, 2:346 E, 3:144 X,
4:97, 5:203 E, 6:143 X, 7:86

Showcase Cinemas
Hyde Road, Belle Vue
Tel: 0161 220 8505
Seats: 3,191 (14 screens)

UCI, Trafford Centre
Barton Dock Road
Tel: 0870 603 4567
Seats: 1:427, 2:427, 3:371, 4:301,
5:243, 6:243, 7:181, 8:181, 9:181,
10:181, 11:181, 12:181, 13:152,
14:152, 15:140, 16:140, 17:112,
18:112, 19:112, 20:112

UCI, Printworks
(Scheduled to open during 2000)

Marple
Regent, Stockport Road
X
Tel: 0161 427 5951
Seats: 285

Monton
Princess, Monton Road
Tel: 0161 789 3426
Seats: 580

Rochdale
ABC Sandbrook Way
Sandbrook Park
Tel: 01706 719 955
Seats: 1:474, 2:311, 3:311, 4:236,
4:236, 5:236, 6:208, 7:208, 8:165,
9:165

Stalybridge
New Palace, Market Street
Tel: 0161 338 2156
Seats: 414

Stockport
**Virgin Cinemas, Grand Central
Square, Wellington Road South**
XE
Tel: 0161 476 5996
Seats: 1: 303, 2:255, 3:243, 4:243,
5:122, 6:116, 7:96, 8:120, 9:84, 10:90

Urmston
Curzon, Princess Road
Tel: 0161 748 2929
Seats: 1:400, 2:134

Walkden
**Apollo, Ellesmere Centre,
Bolton Road**

Tel: 0161 790 9432
Seats: 1:118, 2:108, 3:86, 4:94

Wigan
**Virgin Cinemas,
Robin Park Road, Newtown**
X
Tel: 01942 218005
Seats: 1:554, 2:290, 3:290, 4:207,
5:207, 6:163, 7:163, 8:163, 9:163,
10:207, 11:129

HANTS
Aldershot
ABC, High Street
Tel: 01252 317223/20355
Seats: 1:313, 2:187, 3:150

West End Centre, Queens Road
X
Tel: 01252 330040
Seats: 98

Alton
Palace, Normandy Street
Tel: 01420 82303
Seats: 111

Andover
Savoy, London Street
Tel: 01264 352624
Seats: 250

Basingstoke
Anvil, Churchill Way (P/T)
X
Tel: 01256 844244
Seats: 70

**Warner Village, Basingstoke,
Leisure Park, Churchill Way West**
XE
Tel: 01256 818739/818448
Seats: 1:427, 2:238, 3:223, 4:154,
5:157, 6:157, 7:154, 8:223, 9:238,
10:427

Cosham
ABC, High Street
Tel: 023 92376635
Seats: 1:441, 2:118, 3:107

Crookham
Globe, Queen Elizabeth Barracks
Tel: 01252 876769
Seats: 340

Eastleigh
**Point Dance and Arts Centre
Town Hall Centre, Leigh Road
(P/T)**
Seats: 264

Fawley
Waterside, Long Lane

Tel: 023 80891335
Seats: 355

Gosport
**St Vincent's College Leisure
Centre, Mill Lane (P/T)**
Tel: 023 92523451
Seats: 150

Ritz, Walpole Road
Tel: 023 92501231
Seats: 1,136

Havant
Arts Centre, East Street (P/T)
X
Tel: 023 92472700
Seats: 130

Hayling Island
Hiads Theatre, Station Road
Tel: 023 92462573
Seats: 150

Lymington
Community Centre, New Street (P/T)
Tel: 015907 2337
Seats: 110

Portsmouth
ABC, Commercial Road
Tel: 023 92823538/839719
Seats: 1:542, 2:255, 3:203

Odeon, London Road, North End
Tel: 023 92651434
Seats: 1:631, 2:225, 3:173, 4:259

**Rendezvous
Lion Gate Building
University of Portsmouth (S/O)**
Tel: 023 92833854
Seats: 90

UCI Port Way, Port Solent, Cosham
X
Tel: 0870 603 4567
Seats: 1:214, 2:264, 3:318, 4:264,
5:257, 6:190

Southampton
 **The Gantry, Off Blechynden
Terrace, SO1 0GW**
X
Tel: 01703 229319/330729
Seats: 198

 **Harbour Lights
Ocean Village SO14 3TL**
Seats: 1:350, 2:150
(Scheduled to re-open October 1999)

**Mountbatten Theatre
East Park Terrace (P/T)**
Tel: 023 80221991
Seats: 515

Northguild Lecture Theatre
Guildhall (P/T)
XE
Tel: 023 80632601
Seats: 118

Odeon, Leisure World
West Quay Road
Tel: 023 80333515
Seats: 1:540, 2:495, 3:169, 4:111,
5:112, 6:139, 7:270, 8:318, 9:331,
10:288, 11:502, 12:102, 13:138

Virgin Cinemas, Ocean Way
Ocean Village
Tel: 0541 555132
Seats: 1:421, 2:346, 3:346, 4:258,
5:258

Tadley
Cinema Royal, Boundary Road (P/T)
Tel: 01734 814617

Winchester
The Screen at Winchester,
Southgate Street
X
Tel: 01962 877007
Seats: 1:214, 2:170

Theatre Royal, Jewry Street (P/T)
Tel: 01962 842122
Seats: 405

HEREFORD & WORCS

Evesham
Regal, Port Street
Tel: 01386 446002
Seats: 540

Hereford
ABC, Commercial Road
Tel: 01432 272554
Seats: 378

The Courtyard Theatre and Arts
Centre, Edgar Street (P/T)
X
Tel: 01432 359252
Seats: 1:364, (Studio) 124

Malvern
Cinema, Winter Gardens Complex
Grange Road
Tel: 01684 892277/892710
Seats: 407

Rubery
Virgin Cinemas, Great Park
Tel: 0121 453 0465
Seats: 1:165, 2:187, 3:165, 4:149,
5:288, 6:194, 7:523, 8:247, 9:400
10:149 11:187 12:165, 13:82

Worcester
Odeon, Foregate Street

Tel: 01905 24006
Seats: 1:306, 2:201, 3:125, 4:99,
5:68, 6:306, 7:131

Warner Village Cinemas
Friar Street
Seats: 1,800 (6 screens)
(Scheduled to open March 2000)

HERTS

Hatfield
UCI, The Galleria
Comet Way
Tel: 01707 264662/270222/272734
Seats: 1:172, 2:235, 3:263, 4:167,
5:183, 6:183, 7:260, 8:378, 9:172

Hemel Hempstead
Odeon, Leisure World,
Jarmans Park
XE
Tel: 01442 232224
Seats: 1:136, 2:187, 3:187, 4:320,
5:260, 6:435, 7:168, 8:168

Hoddesdon
Broxbourne Civic Hall
High Street (P/T)
Tel: 01992 441946/31
Seats: 564

Letchworth
Broadway, Eastcheap
Tel: 01462 681 223
Seats: 1:488, 2:176 X, 3:174 X

Potters Bar
Wyllyotts Centre,
Darkes Lane (P/T)
X
Tel: 01707 645005
Seats: 345

Rickmansworth
Watersmeet Theatre
High Street (P/T)
Tel: 01923 771542
Seats: 390

Royston
Priory, Priory Lane
Tel: 01763 243133/248527
Seats: 305

St Albans
Alban Arena, Civic Centre (P/T)
XE
Tel: 01727 844488
Seats: 800

Stevenage
Gordon Craig Theatre
Lytton Way (P/T)
Tel: 01438 766 866
Seats: 507

Cineworld The Movies,
Stevenage Leisure Park
Six Hills Way
Tel: 01438 740944/740310
Seats: 1:357, 2:289, 3:175, 4:148,
5:88, 6:99, 7:137, 8:112, 9:168,
10:135, 11:173, 12:286

Stourport
Civic Centre, Civic Hall,
New Street
Tel: 01562 820 505
Seats: 399

Tenbury Wells
Regal, Teme Street
Tel: 01584 810971
Seats: 260

Watford
Warner Village,
Woodside Leisure Park
Garston
Tel: 01923 682222
Seats: 1:251, 2:233, 3:264, 4:330,
5:221, 6:198, 7:215, 8:301

Welwyn Garden City
Campus West,
The Campus, AL8 6BX (P/T)
Tel: 01707 332880/357197
Seats: 300

Worksop
Regal, Carlton Road
Tel: 01909 482896
Seats: 1:326 (P/T) , 2:154

HUMBERSIDE

Bridlington
Forum, The Promenade
Tel: 01262 676767
Seats: 1:202, 2:103, 3:57

Hull
Odeon, Kingston Street
X
Tel: 0148 258 6420
Seats: 1:172, 2:172, 3:152, 4:174,
5:168, 6:275, 7:134, 8:152, 9:110,
10:91

 Screen, Central Library
Albion Street HU1 3TF
XE
Tel: 01482 226655
Seats: 247

UCI St Andrew's Quay
Clive Sullivan Way
X
Tel: 0870 6034567
Seats: 1:166, 2:152, 3:236, 4:292,
5:292, 6:236, 7:152, 8:166

Goole
The Gate, Dunhill Road
Tel: 01405 720219
Seats: 90

Grimsby
ABC, Freeman Street
Tel: 01472 342878/349368
Seats: 1:393, 2:236, 3:126
Screen, Crosland Road, Willows
DN37 9EH (P/T)
X
Tel: 01472 240410
Seats: 206

Scunthorpe
Majestic, Oswald Road
Tel: 01724 842352
Seats: 1:176, 2:155 X, 3:76 X,
4:55 X, 5:38

Screen, Central Library
Carlton Street, DN15 6TX (P/T)
X
Tel: 01724 860190/860161
Seats: 253

ISLE OF MAN

Douglas
Palace Cinema
Tel: 01624 76814
Seats: 1:319, 2:120

Summerland Cinema
Tel: 01624 25511
Seats: 200

ISLE OF WIGHT

Lake
Screen De Luxe, Sandown Road
Tel: 01983 404050
Seats: 150

Newport
Picturedrome, High Street
Tel: 01983 527169
Seats: 1:380, 2:277

Medina Theatre, Mountbatten
Centre, Fairlee Road (P/T)
XE
Tel: 01983 527020
Seats: 419

Ryde
Commodore, Star Street
Tel: 01983 564064
Seats: 1:186, 2:184, 3:180

KENT

Ashford
Cineworld The Movies
Eureka Leisure Park

Trinity Road
Tel: 01233 620568/622226
Seats: 1:344, 2:75, 3:63, 4:89, 5:156,
6:254, 7:254, 8:156, 9:89, 10:63,
11:215, 12:345

Bluewater
Hoyts
Tel: 0870 242 7070
Seats: 1:129, 2:197, 3:361, 4:464,
5:245, 6:176, 7:80, 8:139, 9:298,
10:379, 11:193, 12:132, Studio:86

Broadstairs
Windsor, Harbour Street
Tel: 01843 865726
Seats: 120

Canterbury
 Cinema 3, Cornwallis South,
University of Kent CT2 7NX
Tel: 01227 769075/764000 x4017
Seats: 300

ABC, St Georges Place
Tel: 01227 462022/453577
Seats: 1:536, 2:404

Chatham
ABC, High Street
Tel: 01634 846756/842522
Seats: 1:520, 2:360, 3:170

Dartford
Orchard Theatre
Home Gardens (P/T)
XE
Tel: 01322 343333
Seats: 930

Deal Kent
Flicks, Queen Street
Tel: 01304 361165
Seats: 1:162, 2:99

Showcase Cinemas,
Foresters Park Osmaston Park
Road at Sinfin Lane
X
Tel: 01332 270300
Seats: 2,557 (11 screens)

UCI Meteor Centre 10,
Mansfield Road
X
Tel: 0870 603 4567
Seats: 1:191, 2:188, 3:188, 4:191,
5:276, 6:276, 7:191, 8:188, 9:188,
10:191

Dover
Silver Screen, White Cliffs
Experience, Gaol Lane
Tel: 01304 228000
Seats: 110

Faversham
New Royal, Market Place
Tel: 01795 591211
Seats: 448

Folkestone
Silver Screen, Guildhall Street
Tel: 01303 221230
Seats: 1:435, 2:106

Gravesend
ABC, King Street
Tel: 01474 356947/352470
Seats: 1:571, 2:296, 3:109

Herne Bay
Kavanagh, William Street
X
Tel: 01227 365676
Seats: 1:137, 2:95

Maidenhead
UCI Cinemas
Seats: 2,000 (8 screens)
(Scheduled to open during 2000)

Maidstone
Odeon, Lockmeadow
Tel: 01622 755 741
Seats: 1:86, 2:89, 3:127, 4:111,
5:240, 6:240, 7:398, 8:347

Odeon, Knights Park
Seats: 1:1,646 (8 screens)

Margate
Dreamland, Marine Parade
Tel: 01843 227822
Seats: 1:378, 2:376

Ramsgate
Granville Premier, Victoria Parade
(P/T)
Tel: 01843 591750
Seats: 1:300, 2:240

Rochester
Virgin Cinemas
Chariot Way, Strood
Tel: 0541 560 568
Seats: 1:485, 2:310, 3:310, 4:217,
5:220, 6:199, 7:199, 8:92, 9:142

Sandwich
Empire, Delf Street
Tel: 01304 620480
Seats: 136

Sevenoaks
Stag Theatre and Majestic 1 & 2,
London Road
Tel: 01732 450175/451548
Seats: 1:470 m, 2:140, 3:111

Sittingbourne
Picturedrome, High Street

Tel: 01795 423984/426018
Seats: 1:300, 2:110

Tonbridge
Angel Centre, Angel Lane (P/T)
Tel: 01732 359588
Seats: 306

Tunbridge Wells
ABC, Mount Pleasant
Tel: 01892 541141/523135
Seats: 1:450 X, 2:402, 3:130

Odeon, Knights Way
Tel: 01892 616 662
Seats: 1:439, 2:272, 3;258, 4:221,
5:139, 6:272, 7:258, 8:221, 9:139

Westgate-on-Sea
Carlton, St Mildreds Road
Tel: 01843 832019
Seats: Premiere: 297, Century: 56,
Bijou: 32

Whitstable
Imperial Oyster
Tel: 01227 770829
Seats: 144

LANCASHIRE
Blackburn
Apollo Five, King William Street
Tel: 01254 695979
Seats: 1:295, 2:205, 3:115, 4:100,
5:95

Blackpool
ABC, Church Street
Tel: 01253 27207/24233
Seats: 1:714, 2:324, 3:225

Odeon, Rigby Road
Tel: 01253 297 906
Seats: 1:422, 2:139, 3:346, 4:153,
5:200, 6:397, 7:159, 8:351, 9:381,
10:201

Blyth Northumberland
Wallaw, Union Street
Tel: 01670 352504
Seats: 1:850, 2:150, 3:80

Burnley
Apollo, Hollywood Park
Centenary Way, Manchester Road
Tel: 01282 456222/456333
Seats: 1:61, 2:238, 3:93, 4:339, 5:93,
6:339, 7:93, 8:238, 9:93

Clitheroe
Civic Hall, York Street
Tel: 01200 423278
Seats: 400

Horwich
Leisure Centre, Victoria Road

(P/T)
Tel: 01204 692211
Seats: 400

Lancaster
ABC, King Street
Tel: 01524 64141/841149
Seats: 1:250, 2:244

 The Dukes Playhouse,
Moor Lane, LA1 1QE (P/T)
XE
Tel: 01524 66645/67461
Seats: 307

Leamington Spa Warwicks
Apollo, Portland Place
Tel: 01926 426106/427448
Seats: 1:309 X, 2:199 X, 3:138, 4: 112 X

Royal, Spa Centre,
Newbold Terrace
Tel: 01926 887726/888997
Seats: 208

Longridge
Palace, Market Place
Tel: 01772 785600
Seats: 200

Lytham St. Annes
Pleasure Island Cinemas,
South Promenade
Tel: 01253 780085
Four screens

Oldham
Roxy, Hollins Road
Tel: 0161 683 4759
Seats: 1:400, 2:300, 3:130

Morecambe
Apollo, Central Drive
Tel: 01524 426642
Seats: 1:207, 2:207, 3:106, 4:106

Preston
Guild Hall, Lancaster Road (P/T)
X
Tel: 01772 258858

UCI Riversway
Ashton-on-Ribble
X
Tel: 0870 603 4567
Seats: 1:194, 2:188, 3:188, 4:194,
5:276, 6:276, 7:194, 8:188, 9:188,
10:194

Warner, The Capitol Centre,
London Way, Walton-le-dale
X
Tel: 01772 881100
Seats: 1:180, 2:180, 3:412, 4:236,
5:236, 6:412, 7:192

Salford Quays
Virgin Cinemas
Clippers Quay
Tel: 0161 873 7279
Seats: 1:287, 2:265, 3:249, 4:249,
5:213, 6:213, 7:177, 8:177

Skelmersdale
Premiere Film Centre
Tel: 01695 25041
Seats: 1:230, 2:248

LEICESTERSHIRE
Leicester
Belle Vue, Abbey Street
Tel: 0116 262 0005
Seats: 1:250, 2:180

Bollywood, Melton Road
Tel: 0116 268 1422
Seats: 1:450, 2:150

Odeon, Aylestone Road,
Freemans Park
XE
Tel: 0116 255 7069
Seats: 1:128, 2:164, 3:154, 4;239,
5:210, 6:632, 7:332, 8:212, 9:329,
10:154, 11:164, 12:126

 Phoenix Arts
16 Upper Brown Street
LE1 5TA (P/T)
XE
Tel: 0116 255 4854/255 5627
Seats: 274

Warner Village,
Meridian Leisure Park
Brownstone
Tel: 0116 282 7733
Seats: 1:423, 2:158, 3:202, 4:266,
5:306, 6:266, 7:202, 8:158, 9:423

Loughborough
Curzon, Cattle Market
Tel: 01509 212261
Seats: 1:420, 2:303, 3:199, 4:186,
5:140, 6:80

Stanford Hall Cinema at the
Co-operative College (P/T)
Tel: 01509 852333
Seats: 352

Melton Mowbray
Regal, King Street
Tel:0116 267 3127
Seats: 226

LINCOLNSHIRE
Boston
Blackfriars Arts Centre,
Spain Lane (P/T)
Tel: 01205 363108
Seats: 237

Regal, West Street
Tel: 01205 350553
Seats: 182

Gainsborough
Trinity Arts Centre
Trinity Street (P/T)
X
Tel: 01427 810710
Seats: 210

Grantham
Paragon, St Catherine's Road
X
Tel: 01476 570046
Seats: 1:270, 2:160

Lincoln
Odeon, Tritton Trading Estate,
Valentine Road
Tel: 01522 512747
Seats: 1:279, 2:164, 3:181, 4:138,
5:134, 6:138

Louth
Playhouse, Cannon Street
Tel: 01507 603333
Seats: 1:215, 2:158 X, 3:78 X

Mablethorpe
Loewen, Quebec Road
Tel: 0150 747 7040
Seats: 1:203, 2:80

Skegness
Odeon, Butlins Family
Entertainment Resort
Roman Bank
Tel: 01754 762311
Seats: 1:120, 2:120

Tower, Lumley Road
Tel: 01754 3938
Seats: 401

Sleaford
Picture Drome, Southgate
Tel: 01529 303187
Seats: 60

Spilsby
Phoenix, Reynard Street
Tel: 01790 753 675
Seats: 264

Stamford
Arts Centre, St. Mary's Street
Tel: 01780 763203
Seats: 166

Woodhall Spa
Kinema in the Woods
Coronation Road
Tel. 01526 352166
Seats: 1:290, 2:90

MERSEYSIDE
Birkenhead
Warner Village Cinemas
Conway Park, Europa Boulevard
Tel: 0151 649 8811
Seats: 1:298, 2:359, 3:164, 4:206,
5:433, 6:206, 7:164

Bromborough
Odeon,
Wirral Leisure Retail Park
Welton Road
X
Tel: 0151 334 0777
Seats: 1:465, 2:356, 3:248, 4:203,
5:338, 6:168, 7:168, 8:86, 9:135,
10:71, 11:122

Crosby
Plaza, Crosby Road North, Waterloo
Tel: 0151 474 4076
Seats: 1:600, 2:92, 3:74

Liverpool
ABC, Allerton Road
Tel: 0151 724 3550/5095
Seats: 472

Odeon, London Road
Tel: 01426 950072
Seats: 1:482, 2:157, 3:152, 4:149,
5:195, 6:132, 7:130

Philharmonic Hall, Hope Street (P/T)
X
Tel: 0151 709 2895/3789
Seats: 1,627

Showcase Cinemas, East
Lancashire Road, Norris Green
X
Tel: 0151 549 2021
Seats: 3,415 (12 screens)

Virgin Cinemas, Edge Lane Retail
Park, Binns Road
XE
Tel: 0151 252 0544
Seats: 1:356, 2:354, 3:264, 4:264,
5:220, 6:220, 7:198, 8:200

Woolton, Mason Street
X
Tel: 0151 428 1919
Seats: 256

Southport
Arts Centre, Lord Street (P/T)
X
Tel: 01704 540004/540011
Seats: 400

ABC, Lord Street
X
Tel: 01704 530627
Seats: 1:504, 2:385

Switch Island
Odeon, Dunnings Bridge Road,
Netherton
Tel: 0151 524 0340
Seats: 1:373, 2: 230, 3:132, 4:161,
5:245, 6:615, 7:343, 8:230, 9:132,
10:151, 11:245, 12:158

Wallasey
Apollo 6, King Street
Tel: 0151 639 0828
Seats: 1:181, 2:111, 3:161, 4:90,
5:89, 6:89

MIDDLESEX
Staines
ABC, Clarence Street
Tel: 01784 453316/459140
Seats: 1:586, 2:363 X, 3:174 X

Uxbridge
Odeon, High Street
Tel: 01895 813139
Seats: 1:236, 2:445

NORFOLK
Cromer
Regal, Hans Place
Tel: 01263 513311
Seats: 1:129, 2:136, 3:66, 4:55

Dereham
Hollywood, Dereham,
Entertainment Centre,
Market Place
Tel: 01362 693261
Seats: 1:160, 2:90, 3:108

Great Yarmouth
Hollywood, Marine Parade
Tel: 01493 842043
Seats: 1:500, 2:296, 3:250, 4:250

Hunstanton
Princess Theatre, The Green (P/T)
Tel: 01485 532252
Seats: 467

King's Lynn
Arts Centre, King Street
Tel: 01553 774725/773578
Seats: 359

Majestic, Tower Street
Tel: 01553 772603
Seats: 1:450, 2:123, 3:400

Norwich
ABC, Prince of Wales Road
Tel: 01603 624677/623312
Seats: 1:523, 2:343, 3:186, 4:105

 Cinema City,
St Andrew's Street NR2 4AD
X

Tel: 01603 625145/622047
Seats: 230

Odeon, Anglia Square
E
Tel: 01603 621903
Seats: 1:442, 2:197, 3:195 X

Star Century, Castle Mall
Seats: 1,850 (screens)
(Scheduled to open April 2000)

UCI Cinemas
Tel: 0870 6034567
Seats: 1:171, 2:372, 3:126, 4:171,
5:160, 6:290, 7:471, 8:286, 9:160,
10:141, 11:141, 12:160, 13:288,
14:212
(Scheduled to open November 1999)

Sheringham
Little Theatre
Station Road (S/O)
Tel: 01263 822347
Seats: 198

Thetford
Diamond Screen
Tel: 01842 750075
Seats: 1:230, 2:115

Toftwood
CBA, Shipham Road
Tel: 01362 693261
Seats: 30

NORTHUMBERLAND
Alnwick
Playhouse, Bondgate Without
(P/T)
Tel: 01665 510785
Seats: 272

Berwick
Maltings Art Centre, Eastern Lane
(P/T)
Seats: 100

Playhouse, Sandgate
Tel: 01289 307769
Seats: 650

Hexham Northumberland
Forum, Market Place
(Temporarily closed)

Morpeth
Coliseum, New Market
Tel: 01670 516834
Seats: 1:132, 2:132

NORTH YORKSHIRE
Elland
Rex, Coronation Street
X

Tel: 01422 372140
Seats: 294

Holmfirth
Picturedome, Market Walk
Tel: 01484 689759
Seats: 200

Harrogate
Odeon, East Parade
Tel: 0142 352 0412
Seats: 1:532, 2:105 X, 3:78 X, 4:339

Leyburn
Elite, Railway Street (P/T)
Tel: 01969 624488
Seats: 173

Pickering
Castle, Burgate
Tel: 01751 472622
Seats: 250

Scarborough
Futurist, Forshaw Road (P/T)
X
Tel: 01723 370742
Seats: 2,155

Hollywood Plaza
North Marine Road
Tel: 01723 365119
Seats: 275

Stephen Joseph Theatre,
Westborough (P/T)
XE
Tel: 01723 370541
Seats: 165 (McCarthy Auditorium)

YMCA Theatre, St Thomas Street
(P/T)
Tel: 01723 506750
Seats: 290

Skipton
Plaza, Sackville Street
X
Tel: 01756 793417
Seats: 320

Thirsk
Ritz
Tel: 01845 523484
Seats: 238

York
City Screen Picture House
Coney Street
Seats: 1:240, 2:140, 3:140
(Scheduled to open November 1999)

 Film Theatre, City Screen,
Yorkshire Museum, Museum
Gardens, YO1 2DR (P/T)
X

Tel: 01904 612940
Seats: City Screen 300,
Film Theatre 720

Odeon, Blossom Street
Tel: 0190 462 3040
Seats: 1:832, 2:115 X, 3:115 X

Warner Village, Clifton Moor
Centre, Stirling Road
X
Tel: 01904 691199/691094
Seats: 1:128, 2:212, 3:316, 4:441,
5:185, 6:251, 7:251, 8:185, 9:441,
10:316, 11:212, 12:128

NORTHANTS
Kettering
Odeon, Pegasus Court,
Wellingborough Road
Tel: 01536 485 522
Seats: 1:174, 2:125, 3:232, 4:349,
5:105, 6:83, 7:105, 8:310

Northampton
Virgin Cinemas
Sixfields Leisure
Weeden Road, Upton
Tel: 0541 560564
Seats: 1:452, 2:287, 3:287, 4:207,
5:207, 6:147, 7:147, 8:147, 9:147

 Forum Cinema, Lings
Forum, Weston Favell
Centre, NN3 4JR (P/T)
Tel: 01604 401006/ 402 833
Seats: 270

Rushden
Ritz, College Street
Tel: 01933 312468
Seats: 822

Wellingborough
Castle,
Castle Way
Off Commercial Way
Tel: 01933 270007
Seats: 500

NOTTS
Hucknall
Byron, High Street
Tel: 0115 963 6377
Seats: 430

Kirkby-in-Ashfield
Regent
Tel: 01623 753866
Seats: 180

Mansfield
ABC, Mansfield Leisure Park
Park Lane

Tel: 01623 422 462
Seats: 1:390, 2:390, 3:246, 4:246,
5:221, 6:221, 7:193, 8:193

Newark
Palace Theatre,
Appleton Gate (P/T)
Tel: 01636 671156
Seats: 351

Nottingham
 Broadway,
Nottingham Media Centre
14 Broad Street, NG1 3AL
Tel: 0115 952 6600/952 6611
Seats: 1:379 E, 2:155 XE

Odeon, Angel Row
Tel: 0142 695 7022
Seats: 1:903, 2:557, 3:150, 4:150,
5:113, 6:100

Royal Centre, Theatre Square (P/T)
Tel: 0115 989 5555
Seats: 1,000

Savoy, Derby Road
Tel: 0115 947 2580/941 9123
Seats: 1:386, 2:128, 3:168

Showcase Cinemas
Redfield Way, Lenton
Tel: 0115 986 6766
Seats: 3,307 (13 screens)

OXFORDSHIRE
Banbury
ABC, Horsefair
Tel: 01295 262071
Seats: 1:431, 2:225

Chipping Norton
The Theatre, Spring Street (P/T)
Tel: 01608 642349/642350
Seats: 195

Henley-on-Thames
Kenton Theatre, New Street (P/T)
X
Tel: 01491 575698
Seats: 240

Regal, Broma Way, off Bell Street
Tel: 01491 414160
Seats: 1:152, 2:101, 3:85

Oxford
ABC, George Street
Tel: 01865 244607/723911
Seats: 1:626, 2:327, 3:140

ABC, Magdalen Street
Tel: 01865 243067
Seats: 864

Phoenix Picture House,

57 Walton Street
X
Tel: 01865 554909
Seats: 1:206, 2:100

Ultimate Picture Palace, Jeune Street
X
Tel: 01865 245288
Seats: 185

Wallingford
Corn Exchange (P/T)
Tel: 01491 825000
Seats: 187

Wantage
Regent, Newbury Street
Tel: 01235 771 155
Seats: 1:110, 2:87

Witney
Corn Exchange, Market Square
(P/T)
Tel: 01993 703646
Seats: 207

SHROPSHIRE
Bridgnorth
Majestic, Whitburn Street
Tel: 01746 761815/761866
Seats: 1:500, 2:86, 3:86

Ludlow
Assembly Rooms
Mill Street (P/T)
X
Tel: 01584 878141
Seats: 320

Market Drayton
Royal Festival Centre (P/T)
Seats: 165

Shrewsbury
Cineworld The Movies
Old Potts Way
Tel: 01743 340726/240350
Seats: 1: 224, 2:157, 3:226, 4:280,
5:135, 6:100, 7:80, 8:222

The Film Theatre,
The Music Hall,
The Square, SY1 1LH
Tel: 01743 350763/352019
Seats: 100

Telford
UCI Telford Centre 10,
Forgegate
X
Tel: 0870 603 4567
Seats: 1:194, 2:188, 3:188, 4:194,
5:276, 6:276, 7:194, 8:188, 9:188,
10:194

SOMERSET
Bridgwater
Film Centre, Penel Orlieu
Tel: 01278 422383
Seats: 1:223, 2:232

Burnham-on-Sea
Ritz, Victoria Street
Tel: 01278 782871
Seats: 204

Frome
Westway, Cork Street
Tel: 01373 465685
Seats: 304

Minehead
Odeon, Butlin's Summerwest World
X
Tel: 01643 703331
Seats: 218

Shepton Mallet
Amusement Centre, Market Place
(P/T)
Tel: 01749 3444688
Seats: 270

Street
Strode Theatre, Strode College,
Church Road, BA16 0AB (P/T)
XE
Tel: 01458 442846/46529
Seats: 400

Taunton
Odeon, Heron Gate, Riverside
X
Tel: 01823 443237
Seats: 1:125, 2:126, 3:372, 4:258,
5:304

Wellington
Wellesley, Mantle Street
Tel: 01823 666668/666880
Seats: 432

Wells
Film Centre, Princes Road
Tel: 01749 672036/672195
Seats: 1:150, 2:60

Wincanton
Plaza, South Street
Seats: 380

Yeovil
ABC, Court Ash Terrace
Tel: 01935 413333/413413
Seats: 1:602, 2:248, 3:246

SOUTH YORKSHIRE
Barnsley
Odeon, Eldon Street

Tel: 0122 620 5494
Seats: 1:416, 2:619X

Doncaster
Civic Theatre, Waterdale (P/T)
Tel: 01302 62349
Seats: 547

Odeon, Hallgate
X
Tel: 0130 234 2523
Seats: 1:1,003, 2:155, 3:158

Warner Village, Doncaster Leisure
Park, Bawtry Road
Tel: 01302 371313
Seats: 1:224, 2:212, 3:252, 4:386,
5:252, 6:212, 7:224

Penistone
Metro, Town Hall
Tel: 01226 762004
Seats: 348

Sheffield
 The Showroom
Media and Exhibition Centre
Paternoster Row, S1 2BX
X
Tel: 0114 275 7727
Seats: 1:83, 2:110, 3:178, 4:282

Odeon, Arundel Gate
Tel: 0114 272 3981
Seats: 1:253 XE, 2:231 X,
3:250 XE, 4:117 XE, 5:115 XE,
6:131, 7:170, 8:160, 9:161, 10:123

UCI Crystal Peaks 10
Eckington Way, Sothall
X
Tel: 0870 603 4567
Seats: 1:202: 2:202, 3:230, 4:226,
5:316, 6:316, 7:226, 8:230, 9:202,
10:202

Virgin Cinemas, Broughton Lane
Tel: 0114 242 1237
Seats: 1:143, 2:141, 3:164, 4:262,
5:262, 6:551, 7:691, 8:551, 9:262,
9:262, 10:262, 11:173, 12:193,
13:115, 14:197, 15:197, 16:197,
17:197, 18:93, 19:82, 20:82

Warner Village
Meadowhall Shopping Centre
X
Tel: 0114 256 9444
Seats: 1:199, 2:198, 3:98, 4:233,
5:198, 6:362, 7:192, 8:192, 9:80,
10:190, 11:329

STAFFORDSHIRE
Burton-on-Trent
Robins, Guild Street
Tel: 01283 563200
Seats: 1:502, 2:110, 3:110

Cannock
Picturedrome, Walsall Road
Tel: 01543 502226
Seats: 1:368, 2:185

Lichfield
Civic Hall, Castle Dyke
Tel: 01543 254021
Seats: 278

Hanley
ABC, Broad Street
Tel: 01782 212320/268970
Seats: 1:572, 2:248, 3:171

Forum Theatre,
Stoke-on-Trent City Museum,
Bethesda Street (P/T)
Tel: 01782 232799
Seats: 300

Stafford
Apollo, New Port Road
Tel: 01785 251277
Seats: 1:305, 2:170, 3:164

Stoke-on-Trent
 Film Theatre,
College Road, ST4 2DE
Tel: 01782 411188/413622
Seats: 212

Odeon, Etruria Road
X
Tel: 0178 221 5805
Seats: 1:201, 2:216, 3:368, 4:162,
5:169, 6:185, 7:564, 8:162, 9:104,
10:75

Tamworth
Palace, Lower Gungate (P/T)
Tel: 01827 57100
Seats: 325

UCI, Bolebridge Street
X
Tel: 0870 603 4567
Seats: 203 (8 screens),
327 (2 screens)

SUFFOLK
Aldeburgh
Aldeburgh Cinema
High Street
X
Tel: 01728 452996
Seats: 286

Bury St Edmunds
ABC, Hatter Street
Tel: 01284 754477
Seats: 1:196, 2:117

Felixstowe
Palace, Crescent Road

Tel: 01394 282787
Seats: 1:150, 2:90

Haverhill
Arts Centre, High Street (P/T)
Tel: 01440 714140
Seats: 200

Ipswich
 Film Theatre, Corn Exchange,
King Street, IP1 1DH
XE
Tel: 01473 255851/215544
Seats: 1:220, 2:40

Odeon, St Margaret's Street
Tel: 01473 287717
Seats: 1:509, 2:320, 3:292, 4:220,
5:220

Virgin Cinemas, Cardinal Park,
Greyfriars Road
Tel: 0870 907 0748
Seats: 1:168, 2:186, 3:168, 4:270,
5:179, 6:510, 7:238, 8:398, 9:186,
10:168, 11:83

Leiston
Film Theatre, High Street
Tel: 01728 830549
Seats: 288

Lowestoft
Hollywood, London Road South
Tel: 01502 564567
Seats: 1:200, 2:175, 3:65, 4:40

Marina Theatre, The Marina
(P/T)
Tel: 01502 573318
Seats: 751

Stowmarket
Regal, Ipswich Street (P/T)
Tel: 01449 612825
Seats: 234

Sudbury
Quay Theatre, Quay Lane
Tel: 01787 374745
Seats: 129

Woodbridge
Riverside Theatre, Quay Street
Tel: 01394 382174/380571
Seats: 280

SURREY
Camberley
ArtsLink, Knoll Road (P/T)
Tel: 01276 707600
Seats: 338

Robins, London Road
Tel: 01276 63909/26768
Seats: 1:420, 2:114, 3:94

Globe, Hawley (P/T)
Tel: 01252 876769
Seats: 200

Cranleigh
Regal, High Street
Tel: 01483 272373
Seats: 268

Dorking
Premier, Dorking Halls
Tel: 01306 881717
Seats: 198

UCI Merry Hill
Shopping Centre 10
X
Tel: 0870 603 4567
Seats: 1:350, 2:350, 3:274, 4:274,
5:224, 6:224, 7:254, 8:254, 9:178,
10:178

Epsom
Odeon, Upper High Street
Seats: 2,000 (8 screens)
(Scheduled to open early 2000)

Playhouse, Ashley Avenue (P/T)
XE
Tel: 01372 742555/6
Seats: 300

Esher
ABC, High Street
Tel: 01372 465639/463362
Seats: 1:918 A, 2:117

Farnham
Redgrave Theatre, Brightwells
X
Tel: 01252 727 720
Seats: 362

Godalming
Borough Hall (P/T)
Tel: 01483 861111
Seats: 250

Guildford
Odeon, Bedford Road
Tel: 01483 578017
Seats: 1:430, 2:361, 3:343, 4:273,
5:297, 6:148, 7:112, 8:130, 9:130

Haslemere
Haslemere Hall, Bridge Road (P/T)
Tel: 01428 2161
Seats: 350

Oxted
Plaza, Station Road West
X
Tel: 01883 712567
Seats: 442

Reigate
Screen, Bancroft Road
Tel: 01737 223200
Seats: 1:139, 2:142

Redhill
The Harlequin
Warwick Quadrant (P/T)
X
Tel: 01737 765547
Seats: 494

Walton on Thames
Screen, High Street
Tel: 01932 252825
Seats: 1:200, 2:140

Woking
Ambassador Cinemas
Peacock Centre off Victoria Way
X
Tel: 01483 761144
Seats: 1:434, 2:447, 3:190, 4:236,
5:268, 6:89

TYNE AND WEAR

Boldon
Virgin Cinemas, Boldon Leisure
Park, Boldon Colliery
Tel: 0541 550512
Seats: 1:284, 2:197, 3:80, 4:119,
5:263, 6:529, 7:263, 8:136, 9:119,
10:197, 11:284

Gateshead
UCI Metro 11, Metro Centre
Tel: 0191 493 2022/3
Seats: 1:200, 2:200, 3:228, 4:256,
5: 370, 6:370, 7:256, 8:228, 9:200,
10:200, 11:520

Newcastle-upon-Tyne
Odeon, Pilgrim Street
Tel: 01426 950527
Seats: 1:1,1171, 2:155, 3:250, 4:361

Tyneside,
10-12 Pilgrim Street, NE1 6QG
XE
Tel: 0191 232 8289
Seats: 1:383, 2:155

 UCI Cinemas, Silverlink
Tel: 0870 6034567
Seats: 1:326, 2:156, 3:185, 4:198,
5:410, 6:198, 7:185, 8:156, 9:326

Warner Village
New Bridge Street
Tel: 0191 221 0202/0545
Seats: 1:404, 2:398, 3:236, 4:244,
5:290, 6:657, 7:509, 8:398, 9:248

South Shields
Customs House, Mill Dam

Tel: 0191 455 6655
Seats: 1:400, 2:160

Washington
Fairworld, Victoria Road
Tel: 0191 416 2711
Seats: 1:227, 2:177

Whitley Bay
Playhouse, Marine Avenue
Tel: 0191 252 3505
Seats: 746

WARWICKS

Nuneaton
ABC, Bermuda Park
Tel: 024 76 388588
Seats: 1:475, 2:390, 3:318, 4:318,
5:257, 6:257, 7:212, 8:212

Stratford-on-Avon
Picture House, Windsor Street
X
Tel: 01789 415511
Seats: 1:208, 2:104

WEST MIDLANDS

Birmingham
Electric, Station Street
X
Tel: 0121 643 7277
Seats: 1:200, 2:100

Virgin Cinemas,
Arcadian Centre, Hurst Street
XE
Tel: 0121 622 3323
Seats: 1:419, 2:299, 3:275, 4:240,
5:192, 6:222, 7:210, 8:196, 9:168

MAC
Cannon Hill Park
Tel: 0121 440 3838
Seats: 1:202, 2:144

Odeon, New Street
Tel: 0121 643 6103
Seats: 1:231, 2:390, 3:298, 4:229,
5:194, 6:180, 7:130, 8:80

Piccadilly, Stratford Road
Sparkbrook
Tel: 0121 773 1658

Showcase Cinemas,
Kingsbury Road
Erdington
Tel: 0121 382 9779
Seats: 3,599 (12 screens)

Warner Village Cinemas
Star City
Seats: 6,100 (30 screens)
(Scheduled to open June 2000)

Coventry

Odeon
Seats: 1,934 (9 screens)
(Scheduled to open October 1999)

Showcase Cinemas, Cross Point, Hinckley Road
Tel: 024 76 602111
Seats: 4,413 (14 screens)

Warwick Arts Centre, University of Warwick, CV4 7AL
X
Tel: 024 76 524524/523060
Seats: 240

Dudley

Limelight Cinema, Black Country Living Museum
Tel: 0121 557 9643
Seats: 100

Quinton

ABC, Hagley Road West
Tel: 0121 422 2562/2252
Seats: 1:300, 2:236, 3:232, 4:121

Smethwick

Princes, High Street
Tel: 0121 565 5202
Seats: 600

Solihull

UCI 8, Highlands Road, Shirley
X
Tel: 0870 603 4567
Seats: 286 (2 screens), 250 (2 screens), 214 (2 screens), 178 (2 screens)

Sutton Coldfield

Odeon, Birmingham Road
Tel: 0121 354 2714
Seats: 1:590, 2:128 X, 3:110 X, 4:330 X

Walsall

Showcase Cinemas, Bentley Mill Way, Darlaston
X
Tel: 01922 22123
Seats: 2,870 (12 screens)

West Bromwich

Kings, Paradise Street
X
Tel: 0121 553 0192
Seats: 1:326, 2:287, 3:462

Wolverhampton

Cineworld The Movies, Wednesfield Way Wednesfield
Tel: 01902 305418
Seats: 1:103, 2:113, 3:151, 4:205, 5:192, 6:343, 7:379, 8:343, 9:184, 10:89, 11:105, 12:162, 13:143, 14:98

Light House, Chubb Buildings, Fryer Street
XE
Tel: 01902 716055
Seats: 1:242, 2:80

WEST SUSSEX

Bognor Regis

Picturedrome, Canada Grove
Tel: 01243 823138
Seats: 1:399, 2:100

Odeon, Butlin's Southcoast World
Tel: 01243 819916
Seats: 1:240, 2:240

Burgess Hill

Orion, Cyprus Road
Tel: 01444 232137/243300
Seats: 1:150, 2:121

Crawley

ABC, High Street
Tel: 01293 527497/541296
Seats: 1:294, 2:212, 3:110

Virgin Cinemas, Crawley Leisure Park London Road
Tel: 01293 537415
Seats: 1:236, 2:421, 3:186, 4:551, 5:186, 6:129, 7:129, 8:318, 9:173, 10:231, 11:184, 12:156, 13:173, 14:173, 15:70
Seats: 3,158 (15 screens)
(Scheduled to open December 1998)

East Grinstead

King Street Picture House Atrium Building, King Street
Tel: 01342 322 238
Seats: 1:240, 2:240

Haywards Heath

Clair Hall, Perrymount Road (P/T)
Tel: 01444 455440/454394
Seats: 350

Horsham

Arts Centre (Ritz Cinema and Capitol Theatre), North Street (P/T)
Tel: 01403 268689
Seats: 1:126, 2:450

Littlehampton

Windmill Theatre, Church Street (P/T)
Tel: 01903 724929
Seats: 252

Worthing

Connaught Theatre, Union Place (P/T)
Tel: 01903 231799/235333
Seats: 1:514, 2 (Ritz): 220

Dome, Marine Parade
Tel: 01903 200461
Seats: 600

WEST YORKSHIRE

Bradford

National Museum of Photography, Film and Television, Prince's View (P/T)
Tel: 01274 732277/727488
Seats: 340 (IMAX)

Odeon, Prince's Way
Tel: 0142 691 5550
Seats: 1:466, 2:1,117, 3:244

Odeon, Phoenix Park
Seats: 3,000 (13 screens)
(under construction)

 Pictureville Cinema, NMPFTV, Pictureville, BD1 1NQ
X
Tel: 01274 732277
Seats: 306

Priestley Centre for the Arts Chapel Street Little Germany BD1 5DL
XE
Tel: 01274 820666
Seats: 290

Halifax

ABC, Ward's End
Tel: 01422 352000/346429
Seats: 1:670, 2:199, 3:172

Hebden Bridge

Picture House, New Road
XE
Tel: 01422 842807
Seats: 498

Huddersfield

Tudor, Queensgate, Zetland Street
Tel: 01484 530874
Two screens

UCI, McAlpine Stadium Bradley Mills Road
Tel: 0870 6034567
Seats: 1:375, 2:296, 3:296, 4:268, 5:268, 6:176, 7:176, 8:148, 9:148

Keighley

Picture House
Tel: 01535 602561
Seats: 1:364, 2:95

Leeds

Cottage Road Cinema Headingley
Tel: 0113 230 2562
Seats: 468

Hyde Park Cinema
Brudenell Road
Tel: 0113 275 2045
Seats: 360

Lounge, North Lane, Headingley
Tel: 0113 275 1061/258932
Seats: 691

ABC, Vicar Lane
Tel: 0113 245 1013/245 2665
Seats: 1:670, 2:483, 3:228

Odeon, The Headrow
Tel: 0142 697 7333
Seats: 1:975, 2:385 X, 3:198 X,
4:172, 5:110

Showcase Cinemas
Gelderd Road, Birstall
X
Tel: 01924 420622
Seats: 4,250 (16 screens)

Warner Village Cinemas
Cardigan Fields
Kirkstall Road
Tel: 0113 279 9855
Seats: 1: 345, 2: 124, 3:166, 4: 245,
5: 252, 6: 245, 7:166, 8:124, 9:345

Pontefract
Crescent, Ropergate
Tel: 01977 703788
Seats: 412

Shipley
Flicks, Bradford Road
Tel: 01274 583429
Seats: 1:89, 2:72, 3:121, 4:94

Wakefield
Cineworld The Movies,
Westgate Leisure Centre
X
Tel: 01924 332114
Seats: 1:323, 2:215, 3:84, 4:114,
5:183, 6:255, 7:255, 8:183, 9:114,
10:84, 11:215, 12:323

Wetherby
Film Theater, Crossley Street
Tel: 01937 580544
Seats: 156

WILTSHIRE
Chippenham
Astoria, Marshfield Road
Tel: 01249 652498
Seats: 1:215, 2:215

Devizes
Palace, Market Place
Tel: 01380 722971
Seats: 253

Salisbury
Odeon, New Canal
Tel: 01722 335924
Seats: 1:471, 2:281 X, 3:128 X, 4:111
X, 5:70

Swindon
Arts Centre, Devizes Road,
Old Town (P/T)
E
Tel: 01793 614 837
Seats: 228

Cineworld The Movies,
Greenbridge Retail & Leisure
Park, Drakes Way
Tel: 01793 484322/420710
Seats: 1:327, 2:282, 3:170, 4:154,
5:94, 6:102, 7:134, 8:105, 9:139,
10:129, 11:137, 12:263

Virgin Cinemas, Shaw Ridge
Leisure Park, Whitehill Way
XE
Tel: 0541 555134
Seats: 1:349, 2:349, 3:297, 4:297,
5:272, 6:166, 7:144

Wyvern, Theatre Square (P/T)
Tel: 01793 524481
Seats: 617

SCOTLAND

A number of BFI-supported
cinemas in Scotland also
receive substantial central
funding and programming/
management support via
Scottish Screen

BORDERS
Galashiels
Pavilion, Market Street
Tel: 01896 752767
Seats: 1:335, 2:172, 3:147, 4:56

Kelso
Roxy, Horse Market
Tel: 01573 224609
Seats: 260

CENTRAL
Falkirk
ABC, Princess Street
Tel: 01324 631713/623805
Seats: 1:690, 2:140 X, 3:137

FTH Arts Centre, Town Hall,
West Bridge Street
Tel: 01324 506850

Stirling
Allanpark Cinema, Allanpark
Tel: 01786 474137
Seats: 1:399, 2:289

  MacRobert Arts Centre,
University of Stirling,
FK9 4LA (P/T)
XE
Tel: 01786 461081
Seats: 495

DUMFRIES & GALL
Annan
Ladystreet, Moat Road (S/O)
Tel: 01461 202796
Seats: 1:110, 2:60

Castle Douglas
Palace, St Andrews Street (S/O)
Tel: 01556 2141
Seats: 400

Dumfries
ABC, Shakespeare Street
Tel: 01387 253578
Seats: 526

Lockerbie
Rex, Bridge Street (S/O)
Tel: 01576 202547
Seats: 195

Newton Stewart
Cinema, Victoria Street
Tel: 01671 403 333

FIFE

Dunfermline
Odeon, Harbeath Leisure Park
Seats: 2,000 (10 screens)
(Scheduled to open during 2000)

Robins, East Port
Tel: 01383 623535
Seats: 1:209, 2:156, 3:78

Glenrothes
Kingsway, Church Street
Tel: 01592 750980
Seats: 1:294, 2:223

Kirkcaldy
 Adam Smith Theatre
Bennochy Road, KY1 1ET (P/T)
XE
Tel: 01592 412929
Seats: 475

ABC, High Street
Tel: 01592 260143/201520
Seats: 1:546, 2:285 X, 3:235 X

St Andrews
New Picture House, North Street
Tel: 01334 473509
Seats: 1:739, 2:94

GRAMPIAN

Aberdeen
Odeon, Justice Mill Lane
Tel: 01244 587160
Seats: 1:415, 2:123, 3:123, 4:225, 5:225

Virgin Cinemas, Queens Link, Leisure Park, Links Road
Tel: 01224 572228
Seats: 1:160, 2:86, 3:208, 4:290, 5:560, 6:280, 7:208, 8:160, 9:160

Peterhead
Playhouse, Queen Street
Tel: 01779 471052
Seats: 731

Elgin
Moray Playhouse, High Street
Tel: 01343 542680
Seats: 1:300, 2:250

HIGHLANDS

Aviemore
Speyside, Aviemore Centre
X
Tel: 01479 810624/810627
Seats: 721

Fort William
Studios 1 and 2, Cameron Square
Tel: 01397 705095
Seats: 1:126, 2:76

Inverness
Eden Court Theatre
Bishops Road
Tel: 01463 234234
Seats: 84

La Scala, Strothers Lane
Tel: 01463 233302
Seats: 1:429, 2:250

Warner Village Cinemas
Inverness Retail and Business Park, Eastfield Way
Tel: 01463 711 175/147
Seats: 1:314, 2:352, 3:160, 4:203, 5:430, 6:203, 7:160

ISLE OF BUTE

Rothesay
MBC Cinema, Winter Gardens, Promenade, Victoria Street
Tel: 01700 505462
Seats: 98

LANARKSHIRE

Motherwell
Civic Theatre, Civic Centre (P/T)
Tel: 01698 66166
Seats: 395

LOTHIAN

Edinburgh
Cameo, Home Street, Tollcross
X
Tel: 0131 228 4141
Seats: 1:253, 2:75, 3:66

Dominion, Newbattle Terrace
Tel: 0131 447 2660/4771
Seats: 1:586, 2:317, 322:47, 4:67

 Filmhouse, 88 Lothian Road
EH3 9BZ
XE
Tel: 0131 228 2688/6382
Seats: 1:280, 2:97, 3:73

ABC, Lothian Road
Tel: 0131 228 1638/229 3030
Seats: 1:868, 2:730 X, 3:318 X

ABC, Westside Plaza, Wester Hailes Road
Tel: 0131 442 2200
Seats: 1:416, 2:332, 3:332, 4:244, 5:228, 6:213, 7:192, 8:171

The Lumière, Royal Museum
Lothian Street,
Edinburgh EH1 1JF

Tel: 0131 247 4219
Seats: 280

Odeon, Clerk Street
Tel: 0131 667 7331
Seats: 1:675, 2:301 X, 3:203 X, 4:262, 5:173

UCI Kinnaird Park,
Newcraighall Road
Tel: 0870 603 4567
Seats: 170 (6 screens), 208 (4 screens), 312 (2 screens)

Virgin Cinemas
Seats: 2,900 (13 screens)
(Scheduled to open November 1999)

ORKNEY

Kirkwall
Cinema, Pickaquoy Centre
Seats: 240

STRATHCLYDE

Ayr
Odeon, Burns Statue Square
Tel: 01426 979722
Seats: 1:388, 2:168, 3:135, 4:371

Brodick, Arran
Brodick, Hall Cinema
Tel: 01770 302065/302375
Seats:250

Campbeltown
Picture House, Hall Street (P/T)
Tel: 01825 553899
Seats: 265

Clydebank
UCI Clydebank 10, Clyde Regional
Centre, Britannia Way
Tel: 0870 603 4567
Seats: 1:202, 2:202, 3:230, 4:253, 5:390, 6:390, 7:253, 8:230, 9:202, 10:202

Coatbridge
Showcase Cinemas
Langmuir Road, Bargeddie, Bailleston
X
Tel: 01236 434 434
Seats: 3,664 (14 screens)

Robert Burns Centre Film Theatre, Mill Road (P/T)
Tel: 01387 264808
Seats: 67

Dunoon
Studio, John Street
Tel: 01369 4545
Seats: 1:188, 2:70

East Kilbride

Arts Centre, Old Coach Road (P/T)
Tel: 01355 261000

UCI, Olympia Shopping Centre
Rothesay Street, Town Centre
Tel: 01355 249699
Seats: 1:319, 2:206, 3:219, 4:207,
5:207, 6:219, 7:206, 8:206, 9:219

Girvan

Vogue, Dalrymple Street (S/O)
Tel: 01465 2101
Seats: 500

Glasgow

ABC, Clarkston Road, Muirend
X
Tel: 0141 637 2641
Seats: 1:482, 2:208, 3:90

ABC, Sauchiehall Street
Tel: 0141 332 9513/0490
Seats: 1:970, 2:872 E (rear), 3:384,
4:206 E, 5:194 E

Bombay Cinema, Lorne Road
Ibrox
Tel: 0141 419 0722

 Glasgow Film Theatre,
12 Rose Street, G3 6RB
XE
Tel: 0141 332 6535/8128
Seats: 1:404, 2:144

Grosvenor, Ashton Lane,
Hillhead
Tel: 0141 339 4298
Seats: 1:274, 2:252

Odeon, Springfield Quay,
Paisley Road
Tel: 0141 418 0345 X
Seats: 1:428, 2:128, 3:89, 4:201,
5:200, 6:277, 7:321, 8:128, 9:89,
10:194, 11:242, 12:256

Odeon, Renfield Street
X
Tel: 0141 333 9551
Seats: 1:555, 2:152, 3:113, 4:173,
5:196, 6:239, 7:247, 8:257, 9:222

Virgin Cinemas, The Forge
Parkhead
XE
Tel: 0141 556 4282
Seats: 1:434, 2:434, 3:322, 4:262,
5:208, 6:144, 7:132

Greenock

Waterfront
off Container Way
Tel: 01475 732201
Seats: 1:258, 2:148, 3:106, 4:84

Hamilton

Odeon, Townhead Street
Tel: 01698 283802/422384
Seats: 1:466, 2:226, 3:310

Irvine

Magnum, Harbour Street
X
Tel: 01294 278381
Seats: 323

WMR Film Centre, Bank Street
X
Tel: 01294 279900/276817
Seats: 252

Kilmarnock

Odeon, Queens Drive
Tel: 01563 572 421
Seats: 1:308, 2:308, 3: 145, 4:145,
5:185, 6:185, 7:437, 8:201

Largs

Barrfield Cinema, Greenock Road
Tel: 01475 689777
Seats: 470

Millport

The Cinema (Town Hall)
Clifton Street (S/O)
Tel: 01475 530741
Seats: 250

Oban

Highland Theatre, George Street
(P/T)
Tel: 01631 563794
Seats: 1:277, 2:25

Paisley

Showcase Cinemas,
Phoenix Business Park,
Linwood
Tel: 0141 887 0011
Seats: 3,784 (14 screens)

Wishaw

Arrow Cinema
Wishaw Retail Park
Tel: 01698 371 000
Seats: 1:242, 2:82, 3:188, 4:80

TAYSIDE

Dundee

Odeon, The Stack Leisure Park
Harefield Road
X
Tel: 01382 400855
Seats: 1:574, 2:210, 3:216, 4:233,
5:192, 6:221

Dundee Contemporary Arts
Nethergate
Tel: 01382 432000

 Steps Theatre
Central Library,
The Wellgate
Dundee DD1 1DB
Tel: 01382 432082
Seats: 250

Virgin Cinemas,
Camperdown
Seats: 2,888 (11 screens)
(Scheduled to open October 1999)

Perth

Playhouse, Murray Street
Tel: 01738 623126
Seats: 1:606, 2:56, 3:156, 4:144,
5:131, 6:113, 7:110

Pitlochry

Regal, Athal Road (S/O)
Tel: 01796 2560
Seats: 400

WESTERN ISLES

Stornoway

Twilights, Seaforth Hotel
James Street (P/T)
Tel: 01851 702740
Seats: 60

WALES

CLWYD

Mold
Theatr Clwyd, County Civic
Centre, CH7 1YA
X
Tel: 01352 756331/755114
Seats: 1:530, 2:129

Prestatyn
Scala, High Street
Tel: 01745 854365
Seats: 314

Rhyl
Apollo, Children's Village
West Promenade
Tel: 01745 353856
Seats: 1:206, 2:206, 3:117, 4:107,
5:107

Wrexham
Odeon Plas Coch Retail Park
Plas Coch Road
Tel: 01978 310656
Seats: 1:354, 2:191, 3:148, 4:254,
5:112, 6:112, 7:112

DYFED

Aberystwyth
Arts Centre, Penglais, Campus,
University of Wales (P/T)
Tel: 01970 623232
Seats:125

Commodore, Bath Street
Tel: 01970 612421
Seats: 410

Brynamman
Public Hall, Station Road
Tel: 01269 823232
Seats: 838

Fishguard
Theatr Gwaun, West Street
Tel: 01348 873421/874051
Seats: 252

Cardigan
Theatr Mwldan,
Bath House Road (P/T)
X
Tel: 01239 621200
Seats: 210

Carmarthen
Lyric
King's Street (P/T)
Tel: 01267 232632
Seats: 740

Cross Hands
Public Hall
Tel: 01269 844441
Seats: 300

Haverefordwest
Palace, Upper Market Street
Tel: 01437 767675
Seats: 500

Llanelli
Entertainment Centre, Station Rd
Tel: 01554 774057/752659
Seats: 1:516, 2:310, 3:122

Tenby
Royal Playhouse
White Lion Street
Tel: 01834 844809
Seats: 479

Milford Haven
Torch Theatre, St Peters Road
Tel: 01646 695267
Seats: 297

GWENT

Brynmawr
Market Hall, Market Square
Tel: 01495 310576
Seats: 320

Blackwood
Miners' Institute, High Street (P/T)
X
Tel: 01495 227206
Seats: 409

Cwmbran
Scene, The Mall
Tel: 016338 66621
Seats: 1:115, 2:78, 3:130

Monmouth
Savoy, Church Street
Tel: 01600 772467
Seats: 450

Newport
Virgin Cinemas,
Retail Park
Seven Styles Avenue
Tel: 0541 550516
Seats: 1:199, 2:178, 3:123, 4:187,
5:267, 6:405, 7:458, 8:287, 9:180,
10:123, 11:211, 12:156, 13:77

Pontypool
Scala, Osborne Road
Tel: 0149 575 6038
Seats: 197

GWYNEDD

Bala
Neuadd Buddig (P/T)

Tel: 01678 520 800
Seats: 372

Bangor
Plaza, High Street
X
Tel: 01248 371080
Seats: 1:310, 2:178

Theatr Gwynedd, Deiniol Road
X
Tel: 01248 351707/351708
Seats: 343

Bethesda
Ogwen, High Street (P/T)
Tel: 01286 676335
Seats: 315

Harlech
Theatr Ardudwy Coleg Harlech
(P/T)
Tel: 01766 780667
Seats: 266

Holyhead
Empire
Stanley Street
Tel: 01407 761458
Seats: 160

Llandudno
Palladium, Gloddaeth Street
Tel: 01492 876244
Seats: 334

Portmadoc
Coliseum, Avenue Road
Tel: 01766 512108
Seats: 582

Tywyn
The Cinema, Corbett Square
X
Tel: 01654 710260
Seats: 368

Pwllheli
Odeon, Butlin's Starcoast World
Tel: 01758 612112
Seats: 200

Town Hall Cinema (P/T)
Tel: 01758 613371
Seats: 450

MID GLAMORGAN

Aberaman
Grand Theatre, Cardiff Road (P/T)
Tel: 01685 872310
Seats: 950

Abercwmboi
Capitol Screen
Tel: 01443 475766
Seats: 280

Aberdare
Coliseum, Mount Pleasant Street
(P/T)
X
Tel: 01685 882380
Seats: 621

Blaengarw
Workmen's Hall, Blaengarw Rd (P/T)
X
Tel: 01656 871142
Seats: 250

Bridgend
Odeon, McArthur Glen Designer
Outlet
Tel: 01656 647 476
Seats: 1:433, 2:329, 3:255, 4:248,
5:222, 6:179, 7:157, 8:165, 9:112

Cwmaman
Public Hall, Alice Place (P/T)
Tel: 01685 876003
Seats: 344

Ferndale
Cinema, Hall, High Street (P/T)
Seats: 190

Llantwit Major
St Donat's Arts Centre
St Donat's Castle
Tel: 01446 799099
Seats: 220

Maesteg
Town Hall Cinema, Talbot Street
Tel: 01656 733269
Seats: 170

Merthyr Tydfil
Castle
Tel: 01685 386669
Seats: 1:98, 2:198

Pontypridd
Muni Screen, Gelliwastad Rd (P/T)
XE
Tel: 01443 485934
Seats: 400

Porthcawl
Grand Pavilion (S/O) (P/T)
Tel: 01656 786996
Seats: 500

Treorchy
Parc and Dare Theatre
Station Road
Tel: 01443 773112
Seats: 794

Welshpool
Pola, Berriew Street
Tel: 01938 555715
Seats: 1:150, 2:40

Ystradgynlais
Miners' Welfare and Community
Hall, Brecon Road (P/T)
X
Tel: 01639 843163
Seats: 345

POWYS

Brecon
Coliseum Film Centre
Wheat Street
Tel: 01874 622501
Seats: 1:164, 2:164

Builth Wells
Wyeside Arts Centre, Castle Street
Tel: 01982 552555
Seats: 210

Newtown
Regent, Broad Street
Tel: 01686 625917
Seats: 210

SOUTH GLAMORGAN

Barry
Theatre Royal, Broad Street
Tel: 01446 735019
Seats: 496

Cardiff
 Chapter, Market Road
Canton, CF5 1QE
X
Tel: 029 20304 400
Seats: 1:194, 2:68

Chapter Globe, Albany Road
Tel: 029 20304 400
Seats: 200

Monico, Pantbach Road, Rhiwbina
Tel: 029 20693426
Seats: 1:500, 2:156

Odeon, Queen Street
Tel: 029 20237846
Seats: 1:424, 2:635

Odeon, Capitol Shopping Centre
Station Terrace
Tel: 029 20377410
Seats: 1:433, 2:257, 3:220, 4:183,
5:158

St David's Hall, The Hayes (P/T)
Tel: 029 20371236/42611
Seats: 1,600

UCI, Hemingway Road
Atlantic Wharf, Cardiff Bay
Tel: 0870 603 4567
Seats: 1:520, 2:353, 3:351, 4:313,
5:267, 6:267, 7:200, 8:200, 9:153,
10:153, 11:147, 12:147

WEST GLAMORGAN

Pontardawe
Arts Centre, Herbert Street
Tel: 01792 863722
Seats: 450

Port Talbot
Apollo, Hollywood Park
Aberavon Sea Front
Princess Margaret Way
Tel: 01639 895552
Seats: 1:118, 2:103, 3:258, 4:258,
5:118, 6:118

Swansea
Taliesin Arts Centre, University
College, Singleton Park, SA2 8PZ
XE
Tel: 01792 296883/295491
Seats: 328

UCI, Quay Parade, Parc Tawe
Tel: 01792 645005
Seats: 1:180, 2:188, 3:188, 4:194,
5:276, 6:276, 7:194, 8:188, 9:188,
10:180

NORTHERN IRELAND

ANTRIM

Antrim
Cineplex, Fountain Hill
Tel: 028 94 461 111
Seats: 1:312, 2:232, 3:132, 4:112

Ballymena
IMC, Larne Link Road
Tel: 028 25 631111
Seats: 1:342, 2:261, 3:160, 4:160,
5:109, 6:112, 7:109

Belfast
Cineworld, Kennedy Centre
Falls Road
E
Tel: 028 90 600988
Seats: 1:296, 2:190, 3:178, 4:178,
5:165

Movie House,
Yorkgate Shopping Centre
X
Tel: 028 90 755000
Seats: 1:314, 2:264, 3:248, 4:181,
5:172, 6:97, 7:97, 8:332, 9:72, 10:67,
11:67, 12:83, 13:83, 14:475

 Queen's Film Theatre,
25 College Gardens, BT9 6BS
X
Tel: 028 90 244857/667687
Seats: 1:250, 2:150

Virgin Cinemas, Dublin Road
Tel: 028 90 245700
Seats: 1:436, 2:354, 3:262 X, 4:264
X, 5:252, 6:272, 7:187 X, 8:187 X,
9:169, 10:118 X

The Strand, Hollywood Road
Tel: 028 90 673500
Seats: 1:250, 2:193, 3:84, 4:98

Glengormley
Movie House, Glenville Road
Tel: 028 90 833424
Seats: 1:309, 2:243, 3:117, 4:110,
5:76, 6:51

Lisburn
Omniplex, Governors Road
Tel: 028 92 663664
Seats: 1:487, 2:180, 3:132, 4:164,
5:259, 6:220, 7:66, 8:66, 9:66, 10:66,
11:42, 12:66

Larne
Regal, Curran Road
Tel: 028 28 277711
Seats: 1:300, 2:220, 3:120, 4:120

Portrush
Playhouse, Mainstreet
Tel: 01265 823917
Seats: 1:299, 2:65

ARMAGH

Armagh
City Film House
Tel: 028 37 511033
Four screens

Lurgan
Centre Point Cinemas
Portadown Road
Tel: 01762 324667
Seats: 1:281, 2:182, 3:142, 4:90

DOWN

Banbridge
Iveagh, Hanratty Road
Tel: 01820 662423
Seats: 863

Bangor
Cineplex, Valentine's Road
Castlepark
Tel: 028 91454729
Seats: 1:287, 2:196, 3:164, 4:112

Kilkeel
Vogue
Seats: 295

Newry
Savoy 2, Merchant's Quay
Tel: 028 028 30260000
Seats: 1:197, 2:58

Omniplex, Quays Shopping Centre,
Albert Basin
Tel: 028 30256098
Seats: 2,100 (9 screens)

FERMANAGH

Enniskillen
Ardhowen Theatre,
Dublin Road (P/T)
Tel: 028 66325440
Seats: 295

Cineworld, Raceview
Factory Road
Tel: 028 66324172
Seats: 1:302, 2:193, 3:130

LONDONDERRY

Coleraine
Jet Centre, Riverside Park
Tel: 01265 58011
Seats: 1:273, 2:193, 3:152, 4:104

Dungiven
St Canice's Hall, Main Street
Seats: 300

Londonderry
Orchard, Orchard Street
Tel: 028 71 267789
Seats: 132, 700 m

Strand, Quayside Centre, Strand
Road
Tel: 028 71373939
Seats: 1:317, 2:256, 3:227, 4:227,
5:134, 6:124, 7:90

Maghera
Movie House, St Lurach's Road
Tel: 028 796 43872/42936
Seats: 1:221, 2:117, 3:95

Magherafelt
Queen Street
Tel: 028 796 33172
Seats: 1:230, 2:75

TYRONE

Cookstown
Ritz, Burn Road
Tel: 016487 65182
Seats: 1:208, 2:126

Omagh
Studios 1-4, Quin Road
Seats: 1:800, 2:144, 3:300, 4:119

COURSES

Listed here is a selection of educational establishments which offer courses in film and television. (P) indicates where a course is mainly practical. Emphasis on the remaining courses is usually on theoretical study; some of these courses include minor practical components.

A wider range of courses and more detailed information can be found in two indispensable BFI publications, *Media Courses UK 2000* and *Media & Multimedia Short Courses*, both edited by Lavinia Orton.

It is also worth checking individual college websites for fuller course details.

AFECT (Advancement of Film Education Charitable Trust)
4 Stanley Buildings
Pancras Road
London NW1 2TD
Tel: 020 7 837 5473
Patron: Mike Leigh
Makes professional-level, practical film education available on a part-time basis to those who may have neither the means nor the time to attend a full-time film course
(P) Practical Part-time 16mm Film-making Course
Two year course integrating learning with production. Bias is traditional narrative; despite limitations of scale, students are enabled to realise personal, artistic, social and cultural expression in this medium. Term 1: Shoot 35mm stills storyboard. Instruction/practicals camera. Interior lit sequence. Editing. Term 2: Script/shoot/edit group mute film with individual sequences, rotating crewing jobs. Term 3: Individual shot-mute three minute films. Term 4: Obtaining and adding sound. Dubbing. Sync-sound intro. Term 5: Individual six minute sync-sound

film each. Term 6: Completing these. Year 3: Advanced projects; semi-independent productions

AIU – London
(American InterContinental University—formerly the American College in London)
Department of Media Production
110 Marylebone High Street
London W1M 3DB
Tel: 0171-467-5600
Fax: 0171935-8144
WebSite:www.aiulondon.ac.uk/
(P) BA in Media Production
The Bachelor of Fine Arts is a three-to four-year full time degree program. Students can select classes from the areas of Videography, Audio and Electronic Music, Scriptwriting and Journalism, Photography, Multimedia, Production Management, Animation and Computer Graphics, and Post-production. The curriculum is a balance of theoretical and practical courses and focuses on preparing students for employment within the media industry. There are general education requirements for the degree. Equipment is digitally based utilising DVC-Pro, Sony Mini DV, Final cut Pro, and Avid. Class sizes are kept small and practical work is group based. Courses are designed as a modular format delivered over three to five academic terms per year. Students are expected to produce a major thesis project for public exhibition at the end of their academic career.
(P) AA in Media Production
Associate of Arts degree in Media Production is a two-year full time course in which students take foundation knowledge classes. The curriculum is a balance of theoretical and practical courses and focuses on preparing students for employment within the media industry. Equipment is digitally based utilising DVC-Pro, Sony Mini DV, Final cut Pro, and Avid. Courses are delivered in a modular format over three to five academic terms per year.

Barking College
Dagenham Road
Romford RM7 0XU
Tel: 01708 766841

Fax: 01708 731067
(P) B/TEC National Diploma Media
This two year broad-based media course covers video, radio and sound recording, print and journalism. Facilities include: television studio; portable video; video editing suites; sound recording studio and DTP equipment. There is a practical and vocational emphasis and students are prepared for either a career in the media industries, or for entry to higher education. Applications from mature students are welcome
RSA – Lens Based Media (Video and Photography)
This one year course provides an introduction to media work and has a 50 per cent practical 'hands on' approach to video production and photography. It is equivalent to a GNVQ Intermediate qualification – but has a more specialist emphasis. BTEC National Diploma courses in either Media or Photography would be a suitable progression
Access to Media
This ne year evening class – two evenings a week – prepares students for Higher Education in Media Studies/Production and includes some practical work

University of Bath
School of Modern Languages and International Studies
Claverton Down
Bath BA2 7AY
Tel: 01225 826482
Fax: 01225 826099
Website: www.bath.ac.uk
BA (Hons) European Studies and modern Languages
First year: Introduction to language, history, and theory of film. Second year: Options on French, German, Italian, and Russian Film. Final year: options include French New Wave; surrealist film; Russian and East European film; German and Italian film. Also an option in European Film
From September 2000
MA in European Cinema

Birkbeck College University of London
Department of Media Studies
Centre for Extra-Mural Studies

26 Russell Square
London WC1B 5DQ
Tel: 020 7 631 6667/6639
Fax: 020 7 631 6683
Website: www.birkbeck.ac.uk/
Extra-Mural Certificate and Diploma in Media Studies
Part-time courses in film, television, journalism and in areas of media practice such as screenwriting, freelance journalism, video, radio, leading to the Certificate/Diploma in Media Studies or in Media Practice.
Contact: Manize Talukdar
BA Humanities
Four year part-time interdisciplinary course, including 4-6 media modules.
Contact: Cathy Moore

University of Birmingham
Cultural Studies Department
Faculty of Commerce and Social Science
PO Box 363
Birmingham B15 2TT
Tel: 0121 414 6060
Website: www.birmingham.ac.uk
Ann Gray
BA Media, Culture and Society
Full degree or combined half degree, looking at a range of contemporary social and cultural issues, in a cross-disciplinary way.

Bournemouth University
School of Media Arts and Communication, Poole House
Talbot Campus, Fern Barrow
Poole
Dorset BH12 5BB
Tel: 01202 595553
email: srose@bournemouth.ac.uk
Website: www.bournemouth.ac.uk
(P) BA (Hons) Media Production
A three year course covering the academic, practical, aesthetic, technical and professional aspects of work in the media. The course is divided equally between practical and theoretical studies. Students work in audio, video and interactive multimedia leading to a major project in Year 3 produced as an interactive CD Rom. In addition, students complete a piece of individual written research.
(P) BA (Hons) Scriptwriting for Film and Television
A comprehensive three year programme, taught by practising scriptwriters, comprising theoretical and practical work specifically designed to meet the needs of new writers in the industry. All graduates will have a thorough knowledge of the industry and a portfolio of work developed to a very high standard. Applications from mature students

are encouraged.
(P) BA (Hons) Television and Video Production
A three year degree course which enables students to work with broadcast-quality equipment to produce video and television programmes. There are supporting courses dealing with media, communication and film theories, professional studies, and the history of cinema and broadcasting.
(P) PGDip/MA in Television and Video Production
A one year full-time course for graduates or proven practitioners who seek ultimately to become directors or producers. Using Betacam SP, the course centres on practical productions on location and in the studio, supported by theoretical and professional studies.The MA element is a continuation period of 3-6 months part time study and includes a dissertation on a selected research topic.
(P) MA in Music Design for Film and Television
This course centres on composing for film and television. It offers tuition in and experience of the practical and theoretical aspects of combining music with moving pictures. The syllabus includes: Composition; Film Music Analysis; Film Theory; Production Theory; Law of Contract & Copyright; and Technology. Each composer spends the entire year based at his/her dedicated workstation which is designed to produce music at the highest broadcast standard

The Arts Institute at Bournemouth School of Media
Wallisdown
Poole,
Dorset BH12 5HH
Tel: 01202 363281
Fax: 01202 537729
(P) B/TEC National Diploma Audio Visual Design
Contact: Jon Towlson
Tel: 01202 363289
Fax: 01202 537729
Two-year vocational course centred around the disciplines of video and audio production. These practical studies are supported by elements of design studies, drama, music, scriptwriting, animation, Contextual Studies, Business and Professional Studies. The course is recognised by BKSTS
(P) BA Hons Film and Animation Production
Contact: Nik Stratton

Tel: 01202 363269
Fax: 01202 537729
The course offers experience of film and video production for either live action or animation and, within this, the opportunity to specialise in either camera editing, producing or directing etc. It also encourages engagement with the history of the moving image of the relationship between contemporary media theory and practice. In 1998 the Arts Institute was awarded the Queen's Anniversary Prize for Higher Education in recognition of its achievements in education for the film and animation industries

University of Bradford
Department of Electronic Imaging and Media Communications
Richmond Road
Bradford BD7 1DP
Tel: 01274 234011
Fax: 01274 233727
email: P.E.Dale@bradford.ac.uk
Website: www.bradford.ac.uk
(P) BSc Electronic Imaging and Media Communications
A three year, full-time course, developed by a group of staff with various specialities – electronics, art and design, digital music, sociology, photography and television. The breadth of the course is unusual and offers real advantages in preparing students for a career in the media. A Foundation Year is available
(P) BSc Media Technology and Production
In this course high calibre candidates will be able to develop full media products in realistic environments

Brighton Film School
Admin Office
13 Tudor Close
Dean Court Road
Rottingdean, East Sussex BN2 7DF
Tel: 01273 302166
Fax: 01273 302163
Website: www. tbfs.8m.com
Director and Senior Lecturer: Frank Tuscanny
Director of Admissions: Meryl von Habsburg
Foundation Course in Cinematography
This module is offered as a short part-time course (usually 10 weeks) designed for those who want to explore their own skills and interests in filmmaking. Theoretical tuition by a variety of lecturers in all disciplines of film production is combined with film company visits, providing a route which may also be available as an Access Course to other

establishments offering full-time degree courses

Diploma Course in Cinematography

A one year part-time course spanning three years over an academic year, the third being for a practical assignment. All these courses are designed to meet industry needs and include coursework to test competence. Committed to gaining academic recognition and, inter alia, accreditation by the BKSTS, to which our students are encouraged to belong

University of Bristol
Department of Drama
Cantocks Close
Woodland Road
Bristol BS8 1UP
Tel: 0117 928 9000
Fax: 0117 928 7832
email: mark.sinfield@bristol.ac.uk
Website: www.bristol.ac.uk
Mark Sinfield
(P) BA Drama

Three year course with theatre, film and TV options. Alongside theatre-based Units, critical and theoretical approaches to film and TV are part of the core syllabus in year 1. Additional critical and practical options are offered in years 2 and 3. Practical work is group-based, extends and enriches critical study in a range of forms in fiction and non-fiction, and results in the production of original work. Theoretical work may be developed through individual dissertations as well as a range of seminar courses

(P) MA in Film and Television Production

This one-year course was the first of its kind in a British university and has produced numerous distinguished practitioners working internationally. It offers a broad grounding in practical skills in film and television production, regular consultation with professional practitioners, and a collective forum for the development of critical thinking and creative practice. Based around a core of group-based practical work, the course offers modular options in a range of practical and critical disciplines, leading to group-based production for public festival entry and/or broadcast, and individual analysis. Production platforms include broadcast-standard video and 16mm film, as well as digital media. The course enjoys widespread support from film and television organisations and leading practitioners

Brunel University
Department of Human Sciences
Uxbridge, Middx UB8 3PH
Tel: 01895 274000
Fax: 01895 232806
Website: www.brunel.ac.uk
Ian Hurchby
BSc Media and Communications Studies

Four year interdisciplinary course which aims to give an understanding of the social, intellectual and practical dimensions of the communications media, with particular reference to the new information technologies

MA Communications and Technology

This course offers detailed study of the new communications and information technologies

Canterbury Christ Church College
Dept of Radio, Film and Television
North Holmes Road
Canterbury CT1 1QU
Tel: 01227 767700
Fax: 01227 470442
Website: www.cant.ac.uk
email: P.Simpson@cant.ac.uk
(P) BA or BSc (Hons) Radio, Film & Television with one other subject
Contact: Philip Simpson

RFTV is one half of a three year joint honours degree and may be combined with Art, American Studies, English, Geography, History, Mathematics, Sport Science, Music, Religious Studies and Science. The course introduces students to an understanding and appreciation of radio, film and television as media of communication and creative expression, stressing their relevance to the individual and to society. It also offers an opportunity to develop and practice production skills in each of the three media

(P) MA Media Production
Contact: Dickon Reed

A one year taught MA which concentrates on production in radio, film and television. Part I of the course introduces relevant production skills; in Part II members will fulfil a measurable major role in a production project. Course members with practical experience can update their skills and concentrate on one medium in Part I. All course members attend theory seminars through the course. Assessment will be based on the major piece of practical work and an extended essay

The City College Manchester
School of Art and Design,
Manchester M23 0DD
Tel: 0161 957 1749
Fax: 0161 949 3854
(P) B/TEC National Diploma Audio-Visual Design

Multi-disciplinary course working between video, film animation, photography, graphics, sound and Digital Imaging. Assessment is continuous, based on practical projects linked to theoretical studies

Coventry University
Coventry School of Art and Design
Priory Street
Coventry CV1 5FB
Tel: 024 76838690
Fax: 024 76838667
Website: www.alvis.coventry.ac.uk
BA (Hons) Communication Studies

Three year course which includes specialities in Cultural and Media Studies, and in Communication Management, built around a core of studies in communication, culture and media, with a range of other options from which students select. European exchange and work placement programmes are included; also options in journalism, photography and video. Projects enable students to combine theoretical and practical work according to their particular interests

Postgraduate Programme Communication, Culture and Media: MA or PgC/PgD

One full-time, two year part-time. The programme is a modular scheme with core theory and research elements, specialist options, and a selection of electives which include film theory and psychoanalysis, journalism, media policy, television culture and politics. Students may specialise in applied communications, or cultural policy, or media and culture for the MA qualification

De Montfort University Bedford
Polhill Avenue
Bedford MK41 9EA
Tel: 01234 351967
Fax: 01234 217738
Website: www.dmu.ac.uk/Bedford
BA (Hons) Dance and Drama with another subject
Modular BA/BSc Programme (Arts Pathway) Film Studies

First, Second and Third level modules studying film as a cultural product and a social practice through lectures, screenings, seminars. Level

1: Intro to Film Studies; Level 2: double module – early to contemporary mainstream cinema; Level 3: single module – Art Cinema plus optional research module
Television and Drama
Two third level modules. 1: forms of television drama and study of key practitioners; 2: television as a cultural practice

De Montfort University Leicester
School of Arts
The Gateway
Leicester LE1 9BH
Tel: 0116 255 1551 or 0116 257 8391
Fax: 0116 257 7199
Website: www.dmu.ac.uk/Leicester
Dr Paul Wells/Tim O'Sullivan
BA (Hons) Media Studies (Single, Joint or Combined Honours Degrees)
As a Single Honours degree, Media Studies offers a range of courses which focus specifically on Film, Television/Video, Photography and Media institutions. It offers courses in both theoretical and practical work which provide students with the opportunity to develop their skills and learning through detailed analysis of media texts, through understanding the social and political processes of media industries and institutions and through practical work in video, photography, radio and journalism. With Joint Honours, it is possible to take Media Studies in conjunction with one other arts discipline; for Combined Honours, with two other disciplines

University of Derby
School of Art and Design,
Green Lane,
Derby DE1 1RX
Tel: 01332 622282
Fax: 01332 622296
Website: www.derby.ac.uk
BA Film and Television Studies
Specialist critical and theoretical course with no practical component

Dewsbury College
Batley School of Art & Design
Wheelwright Campus
Birkdale Road
Dewsbury, West Yorks WF13 4HQ
Tel: 01924 451649
Fax: 01924 469491
(P) BA (Hons) Moving Image Design
This course provides an opportunity to study one of the most rapidly developing areas of design. Using computer technology, the course combines live action video techniques

with 3D animation to produce time-based imagery for the broadcast media, advertising and publicity. The course demands an imaginative approach with an understanding of both 2D and 3D design
B/TEC National Diploma Design (Audio-Visual)
Two year full-time course developing creative and technical skills in audio-visual and video production, sound recording, photography and AV graphics. Supporting studies include film and business studies

University of East Anglia
School of English and American Studies,
Norwich NR4 7TJ
Tel: 01603 456161
Website: www.uea.ac.uk
BA (Hons) Film and English Studies
A Joint Major programme which integrates Film and Television history and theory with work on English literature, history and cultural studies; the film work deals mainly with Hollywood, but also with British cinema. Course includes instruction in film and video production, and the option of submitting a practical project. All students submit an independent dissertation on a film or television topic.
BA (Hons) Film and American Studies
A four year Joint Major programme which integrates Film and Television history and theory with work on American literature, history, cultural studies and politics. Course includes instruction in film and video production, and the option of submitting a practical project. All students spend a year at a University in the USA, and submit an independent dissertation on a film or television topic.
BA (Hons) Modular System
Students admitted to the University to major in other subjects including Literature, Drama, American Studies etc have the option of taking one or more units in film and television study: together, these may comprise up to one third of the degree work. No practical element.
MA Film Studies
One year full-time taught programme. MA is awarded 50 per cent on coursework and 50 per cent on dissertation. Within the School's modular system, it is possible to replace one or two of the four film seminars with others chosen from a range of topics in literary theory,

creative writing, American studies and cultural studies. The film seminars deal with early cinema, British film history, film and narrative theory, screen costume and theories of the image, and research resources and methodology. Dissertation topics are freely chosen and may deal with television as well as cinema.
MA Film Studies: Film Archive option
One year full-time taught programme, run in conjunction with the East Anglian Film Archive (located in the University). Students take two of the MA film seminars, plus two more that deal with the practical and administrative aspects of film archive work. Course includes visits to other archives, and a one-month placement at a chosen archive in Britain or overseas. Assessment is based on two essays, a video production, a placement report, and an independent dissertation (counting 50 per cent)
MPhil and PhD
Students are accepted for research degrees. Areas of special expertise include early cinema, British film history, television history, gender and cinema, classical and contemporary Hollywood, and screen costume

University of East London
Faculty of Design Built Environment
Greengate Street
London E14 0BG
Tel: 0181 590 7722
Fax: 0181 849 3694
Website: www.uel.ac.uk
(P) BA (Hons) Fine Art, Time Based Art
During the first year students can experiment with each of the disciplines that are available but can also specialise in film, video and video animation throughout the three years
BA Visual Theories: Film Studies
A specialist pathway within the university's modular structure and the range of options is generally extensive with theoretical work on the history of cinema and avant-garde film

Department of Cultural Studies
Longbridge Road, Dagenham
Essex RM8 2AS
Tel: 0181 590 7722 x 2741
Fax: 0181 849 3598
BA (Hons) in Media Studies
Media Studies is offered as a single honours degree or as a major, minor or joint degree in combination with

other subjects (eg Cultural Studies; History; Literature and Women's Studies)

Department of Innovation Studies
Maryland House, Manbey Park
Road
London E15 1EY
Tel: 0181 590 7722 x 4216
Fax: 0181 849 3677
BSc (Hons) New Technology:
Media & Communication
This degree examines the media industries in the context of a study of technological change in society. Covers the social relations of technology, the film, recording, newspaper, television, cable and satellite industries
BA (Hons) Moving Image Design
Using computer technology, the course combines live action video techniques with 3D animation to produce time-based imagery for the broadcast media, advertising and publicity

Edinburgh College of Art
School of Visual Communication
Lauriston Place
Edinburgh EH3 9DF
Tel: 0131 221 6138
Fax: 0131 221 6100
These courses are strongly based on practical production work and run for three years.
(P) BA (Hons) Visual
Communications (Film and
Television)
The course runs for three years and most applicants have done either a foundation course in art and design, or a further education course in video/audio-visual. Film/television students will generally combine individual projects with participation in group projects. All kinds of work can be tackled – drama, documentary and experimental. The course includes possibilities of cross-disciplinary projects with other departments in the school – animation, illustration, photography, and graphic design. All students are also encouraged to use the school's computer workshop
(P) Masters Degree
A small number of postgraduates can be accepted, studying either for a diploma (three terms) or a masters degree (four terms). In both cases there is no formal taught course – the programme is tailored to the practical production proposals of the individual student. Postgraduates must already have appropriate skills and experience to use the resources available. The masters degree is

awarded on the strength of the practical work produced

University of Exeter
School of English,
Queen's Building,
The Queen's Drive
Exeter EX4 4QH
Tel: 01392 264263
Fax: 01392 264361
Website: www.ex.ac.uk
BA (Hons) English Studies
Students can take up to half of their degree in Film Studies, including courses on British Cinema, Hollywood and Europe and an introduction to Key Issues in Film Studies. No practical component
(P) MA Programme in the History
of Cinema and Popular Culture
The core modules in this programme concentrate on key moments in cinema history and the relationship between cinema and 19th Century optical media and popular entertainment. Optical modules cover a variety of theoretical and historical topics including Cult Movies and Postcolonial Cinema.
Mphil and PhD
Applications for postgraduate study in British Cinema, Early and Pre Cinema History, and Cinema and Cultural Theory will be particularly welcome
School of Modern Languages
The Queen's Building
Queen's Drive
Exeter EX4 4QH
Tel: 01392 264231
Fax: 01392 264377
BA (Single, Combined Hons and
Modular) Italian
Italian cinema option for second/third- and final-year students. In general, Neo-realism to the present day. Films are studied for their intrinsic merit, as commercial products, and as part of Twentieth-century Italian culture.
BA (Single and Combined Hons)
Spanish
Option in Spanish cinema. Spanish films 1963 to 1990. Selection covering social, literary and war themes, film censorship and its circumvention

Farnborough College of Technology
Media and Visual Arts
Boundary Road, Farnborough
Hants GU14 6SB
Tel: 01252 407270
Fax: 01252 407271
email: A.Harding@Farnet ac uk
Website: www.farnct.ac.uk
(P) HND Media Technology and

Business
Two year full-time course to study media production techniques with business studies. Course includes television and video production, video and audio systems, radio, journalism and finance in the media
(P) HND Design Technology
(Multimedia, Video Graphics &
Animation)
Provides training in television and video production, animation and computerised video graphics. In the first and second years, all students undertake the following modules: visual studies, television and video production, animation and graphics, historical and contextual studies and business management. In the second year, students select three options from the following: video systems, documentary and drama production, advertising copywriting, photography, marketing and the media, journalism, desktop publishing and radio production
(P) BSc (Hons) Media (Production)
Technology
This popular degree adopts a bi-media approach studying both Television and Radio. Students will be expected to develop and demonstrate technical skills, as well as an understanding of the appropriate theories and concepts. This will be achieved by practical units in television/video and radio, as well as theoretical ones such as audio-visual systems, television and film, radio in society etc. Optional units enable the students to create a vocational or academic pathway of their choice
(P) Higher National Diploma in
Media Technology (Broadcast
Engineering)
This new programme has been created at the specific request of the broadcast industries. As a result of he digital revolution there is a dramatic increase in the number of broadcasters of both television and radio. Through this programme of study students learn to become broadcast engineers using and maintaining a range of equipment necessary to provide television and radio broadcasts

University of Glasgow
Department of Theatre,
Film and Television Studies
University of Glasgow
Glasgow G12 8QQ
Tel: 0141 330 5162
Fax: 0141 330 4142
email: tfts.office@arts.gla.ac.uk
Website: www.arts.gla.ac.uk/tfts/

Ian P. Craven
MA Joint Honours Film and Television Studies
Four year undergraduate course. Film/Television Studies represents 50 per cent of an Honours degree or 30 per cent of a non-Honours degree. Year 1 is concerned with Film and TV as 'languages', and with the institutional, industrial and technological contexts of cinema and television. Year 2 is structured under two headings; Film and Television: Theories and Methods and Film and Television: National and Cultural Identities. Years 3 and 4 consist of a range of Honours optional courses, seven to be taken over two years in addition to a dissertation. There is also a compulsory practical course, involving either the production of a video, a contractual work placement or an applied research project
MPhil Screen Studies
One-year postgraduate course. Consisting of a core course on research methods, a range of specialist options and a supervised dissertation component, the M.Phil. in Screen Studies aims to offer an opportunity for advanced level study of cinema and television. It is geared towards the needs of well-qualified students contemplating a career in media research, criticism or administration, and also seeks to provide a preparation for applicants whose intention is to pursue research in Film and Television Studies at Doctoral level. Options within the course vary from year to year, according to the research priorities of academic staff. Please contact the department at the addresses above for further details

Department of French
Glasgow G12 8QQ
Tel: 0141 339 8855
Contact: Jim Steel, Ramona Fotiade
MA (Hons) French
Study of French cinema is a one year special subject comprising one two-hour seminar per fortnight and weekly screenings

Glasgow Caledonian University
Department of Language & Media
Cowcaddens Road
Glasgow G4 0BA
Tel: 0141 331 3259
Fax: 0141 331 3264
email: dhu@gcal.ac.uk
Website: www.gcal.ac.uk
BA Communication and Mass Media
Four year course (unclassified and

Honours) examining the place of mass communication in contemporary society. Includes practical studies in television, advertising and public relations

Goldsmiths College
University of London
Lewisham Way
London SE14 6NW
Tel: 020 7 919 7171
Fax: 020 7 919 7509
email: admissions@gold.ac.uk
Website: www.goldsmiths.ac.uk
(P) BA Media and Communications
This course brings together theoretical analyses in social sciences and cultural studies with practical work in creative writing (fiction), electronic graphics and animation, photography, print journalism, radio, script writing or television (video and film) production. The practical element constitutes 50 per cent of the total degree course. The theoretical element includes media history and sociology, textual and cultural studies, anthropology and psychology and media management
BA Anthropology and Communication Studies
Half of this course constitutes Communication Studies. The course is mainly theoretical but does include two short practical courses of ten weeks in length in two of the practice areas. These include television, videographics and animation, radio, print journalism, photography, creative writing and script writing. The theory component is concerned with media history, sociology, psychology, textual and cultural studies
BA Communication Studies/Sociology
Communication Studies constitutes half this course and is split into theoretical studies and two ten-week practical courses. Practical options include television, videographics and animation, radio, print journalism, photography, creative writing and script writing. The theory component is concerned with psychology, media sociology, cultural studies, semiotics and media history
MA Image and Communication (Photography or Electronic Graphics)
One year full-time course combines theory and practice, specialising in either photography or electronic graphics. Practical workshops cover medium and large format cameras, flash, colour printing, lighting,

computer and video graphics, design, desktop publishing, animation, animatics, two and three dimensional computer animation. Assessment by coursework, practical production and viva voce
MA Television (TV Drama or Documentary)
One year full-time course specialising in either documentary or drama modes, taught by practical and theoretical sessions. Course covers script writing, programme planning, camera work, studio and location work, interviewing, sound and post production. Assessment is by coursework, practical production and viva voce
MA Media and Communication Studies
This course offers an inter-disciplinary approach as well as the opportunity to specialise in media and communications. The course is based around a series of compulsory courses and options drawing on theoretical frameworks from cultural studies, political economy, sociology, anthropology, and psychology to develop a critical understanding of the role of the media and communications industries in contemporary culture. Assessment is by coursework, written examinations and dissertation

University of Hertfordshire
Watford Campus, Wall Hall,
Aldenham, Watford,
Herts WD2 8AT
Tel: 01707 285643
BA (Hons) Humanities
Full- or part-time degree. Within the Historical Studies major/minor and single honours there is a second year option, Film and History, which examines the inter-war period through film and focuses on the historian's use of film

The Hull School of Art and Design
University of Lincolnshire & Humberside
Queens Gardens
Kingston-upon-Hull HU1 3DQ
Tel: 01482 440550
Fax: 01482 462101
All courses in The Hull School of Art & Design are 80 per cent practice and 20 per cent theory and are provided with extensive facilities including: SVHS, DV, DAT, Digital, Analogue, 16mm; production and post production including non linear editing; and current professional programmes for Macs and PCs.

Kent Institute of Art and Design

School of Visual Communication
Maidstone College
Oakwood Park
Maidstone, Kent ME16 8AG
Tel: 01622 757286
Fax: 01622 692003
email: kiadmarketing@kiad.ac.uk
Website: www.kiad.ac.uk
(P) BA (Hons) Visual Communication – Time Based Media
Explores all aspects of the moving image, including video, film, sound and animation. The emphasis is on personal authored work, mainly in video, but traditional production roles and values are also taught. The pathway encourages creative and investigative video production, and is a pioneer of the 'multi-skilled' approach used today in all aspects of professional and independent TV and Video production
Master of Arts in Visual Communication
This Master of Arts Programme has been developed for designers, illustrators, photographers, film/video makers, and theorists who wish to develop their practices either as a single discipline or combination of disciplines within an ethos of interdisciplinarity. Each application to the programme is determined by an individually proposed MA Project defined within the speculative framework of the programme. All graduates in Visual Communication are part of one programme but develop their Master of Arts projects within a negotiated study plan drawn from the School's principal study areas.
Time Based Media with Electronic Imaging
Time Based Media with Electronic Imaging (TBN) includes video/film production, conventional and digital animation, multi-media and sound.
Visual Theory
This aspect of the programme provides an introduction to a range of theoretical frameworks for understanding the role of visual media in contemporary society. For further information contact the Register on: 01622 757286 or Fax 01622 692003
MPhil and PHd Study
Applicants for MPhil/PhD must demonstrate an understanding of research methodologies. These are taught as part of MPhil study. Students wishing to register for PhD will normally be required to register for MPhil in the first instance.

Conversion to PhD is dependent upon completion of MPhil requirements (two years) and evidence of sufficient aptitude and ability to sustain the research project through to the Doctoral award. The areas of expertise that the Institute is initially providing for research degree activity includes Electronic and Time-Based Media. For further information contact the Registrar on: 01622 757286 or Fax: 01622 692003

University of Kent

Rutherford College
Canterbury
Kent CT2 7NX
Tel: 01227 764000
Fax: 01227 827846
Website: www.ukc.ac.uk
BA Combined Hons
A Part 1 course on Narrative Cinema is available to all Humanities students in Year 1. The Part 2 component in Film Studies in Years 2 and 3 can vary from 25 per cent to 75 per cent of a student's programme. Courses include film theory, British cinema, non-narrative cinema, comedy, and sexual difference and cinema. The rest of a student's programme consists of courses from any other humanities subject. No practical component
BA Single Hons
This includes a practical film production option
MA, MPhil and PhD
An MA in Film is also available, which combines courses in film history and archiving, with courses in film criticism and film theory. An MA combining Film and Art History is also available. Students are also accepted for MA, MPhil and PhD by thesis

King Alfred's College Winchester (Affiliated to Southampton University)

School of Community and Performing Arts
Sparkford Road
Winchester SO22 4NR
Tel: 01962 841515
Fax: 01962 842280
Website: www.wkac.ac.uk
BA (Hons) Drama, Theatre and Television Studies
Three year course relating theories of contemporary television and drama to practical work in both media. The course looks at both the institutions and the practices of the two media from the perspectives of the ideology and aesthetic contexts in which work is produced together with critical ideologies of the Twentieth Century.

It includes television projects in which students work in groups to produce documentaries or drama documentaries. These projects are community based
Media and Film Studies
Further details available from Dr Maggie Andrews: Head of Media Film School of Cultural Studies

Kingston University

School of Three Dimensional Design, Knights Park
Kingston-Upon-Thames
Surrey KT1 2QJ
Tel: 0181 547 2000 ext 4165
Website: www.kingston.ac.uk
MA Design for Film and Television
One year MA Course in scenic design tailored to the needs of those who wish to enter the industry with the eventual aim of becoming production designers or art directors. The course is constructed as a series of design projects to cover different types of film and television production

School of Art and Design History
Tel: 0181 547 7112
BA/BA (Hons) Combined Studies: History of Art, Architecture and Design
Five to six year part-time or three year full-time. Optional film strand: three Film Studies modules, each representing one sixth of a full-time student's yearly programme, one third of a part-time student's. Foundation level: concepts of 'Art' cinema. Intermediate level: photographic issues. Advanced level: the study of a selected artist.

School of Languages
Penrhyn Road
Kingston-Upon-Thames
Surrey KT1 2EE
Tel: 0181 547 2000
Fax: 0181 547 7392
BA (Hons) French Full and Half-field, Full and Part-time
Introduction to French Cinema. Year two on French Cinema. Year four special subject on New Wave Cinema

University of Leicester

Centre for Mass Communication Research
104 Regent Road
Leicester LE1 7LT
Tel: 0116 252 3863
Fax: 0116 252 3874
Website: www.le.ac.uk
BSc Communications and Society
A three-year social science based undergraduate course. The modules taught cover a wide range of areas

including media institutions, research methods in mass communications, film and TV forms abd television production. Students are assessed by a combination of continuous assessment and examination

MA Mass Communications
One year taught course studying the organisation and impact of the mass media both nationally and internationally and providing practical training in research methods

MA Mass Communications (by Distance Learning)
Two year part-time course by distance learning. Organized in 10 modules plus dissertation. Course materials include 60 course units, readers, set books, AV materials. Contributions from a team of international experts. The course covers media theories, history, regulation, media in global context, methodology, media industries, professional practices, audiences, texts and issues of representation. Options include media education, film. Day and weekend schools are voluntary but highly recommended

University of Liverpool
School of Politics and Communication Studies
Roxby Building
PO Box 147
Liverpool L69 3BX
Tel: 0151 794 2890
Fax: 0151 794 3948
Website: www.liv.ac.uk

BA Combined Hons (Social and Environmental Studies)
BA Joint Hons (English and Communication Studies)
BA Joint Hons (Politics and Communication Studies)
In all these programmes, students combine work in the Communication Studies Department with largely non media-related work in other Departments; Communication Studies forms up to 50 per cent of their programme. Year 1: Communication: a programme of introductory work on communication and cultural analysis. Year 2: courses on Broadcasting, Film Studies and Drama. Year 3: courses available include Documentary, exploring a range of work in literature, photography, film and television. No practical component

MA Cultural Research and Analysis
The purpose of this degree is to introduce students to current work in the area of research on popular cultural institutions, forms and behaviours. Core courses look at the

mass media and culture, at culture and national identity, and at city culture and urban life. There is a particular emphasis on research of a broadly ethnographic character, involving students in the field work within the Merseyside area

Liverpool John Moores University
School of Media, Critical and Creative Arts
Dean Walters Building
St James Road
Liverpool L1 7BR
Tel: 0151 231 5052
Website: www.livjm.ac.uk

(P) BA (Hons) Media and Cultural Studies
Three year, full-time or four-year, part-time course.

BA (Hons) Screen Studies
Course spans history of film and television

BA (Hons) Media Professional Studies
Brings together theoretical and vocational approaches to the study of television and related media.

London College of Printing & Distributive Trades
Media School, Back Hill
Clerkenwell Road
London EC1R 5EN
Tel: 020 7514 6500

MA Screenwriting, MA Documentary Research, MA Independent Film & Video
These are part-time (1 day a week), two years. Enquiries to the course leaders: Screenwriting – Phil Parker; Documentary Research – Michael Chanan; Independent Film & Video – Liz Wells

London Guildhall University
Sir John Cass Department of Art
133 Whitechapel High Street
London E1 7QA
Tel: 020 7 320 3455/3456
Fax: 020 7 320 3462
Website: www.lgu.ac.uk

BA (Hons) Communication and Audio-Visual Production Studies (Early Specialisation)
This degree includes both practical and theoretical studies. Practical units include film television and video production, photo-journalism, radio journalism and writing for the media. Theoretical units include cultural history and cultural studies. The degree may be studied full-time or part-time. Communication Studies may also be studied as half of a joint degree or as a minor component of a degree.

London International Film School
Department F17
24 Shelton Street
London WC2H 9HP
Tel: 020 7 836 9642
Fax: 020 7 497 3718
Website: www.lifs.org.uk

(P) Diploma in Film Making
A two year full-time practical course teaching skills to professional levels. All students work on one or more films each term and are encouraged to interchange unit roles termly to experience different skill areas. Approximately half each term is spent in film making, half in practical instruction, seminars, workshops, tutorials, and script writing. Established for over 40 years, the school is constituted as an independent, non profit-making, educational charity and is a member of NAHEFV and CILECT – respectively the national and international federations of film schools. Graduates include Bill Douglas, Danny Huston, John Irwin, Mike Leigh, Michael Mann and Franc Roddam. The course is accredited by BECTU and widely recognised by local education authorities for grants. New courses commence each January, April and September

London School of Economics and Political Science
Department of Social Psychology
Media and Communications
Houghton Street
London WC2A 2AE
Tel: 020 7 955 7710/7714
Fax: 020 7 955 7565
Website: www.lse.ac.uk

MSc Media and Communications
One year MSc programme (two years part-time) provides an advanced understanding of the development and forms of media systems (eg text, audience, organisation, effects) in Britain and elsewhere. Students take two core courses, one inter-disciplinary theoretical approaches to media and communications, and one research methodology in media and communications. Additionally, students choose from a range of optional courses reflecting social science approaches to media and communications, and complete an original, supervised, research report on a subject of their choice

The Lux Centre
2-4 Hoxton Square
London N1 6NU

The London
International
Film School

- Training film makers for 40 years •
- Graduates now working worldwide •
- Located in Covent Garden in the heart of London •
- 16mm documentary & 35mm studio filming •
- Two year Diploma course in film making •
- Commences three times a year: January, May, September •

London International Film School,
Department F23. 24 Shelton Street, London WC2H 9HP
Tel: 0171 836 9642/0171 240 0168 Fax: 0171 497 3718
Email: lifs@dial.pipex.com Web Page: http://www.tecc.co.uk/lifs/index.html

Tel: 020 7684 2787
Fax: 020 7684 222
email: lux@lux.org.uk
The training and educatin programme
at the lux Centre aims to broaden
practical and theoretical
understanding of film, video and
digital art. From talks and events in
the Lux Gallergy to monthly open
submissions screenings in the Lux
Cinema, participation in the lux's
exhibition programme is encouraged.
Lux Education also offers an
extensive short course programme,
approaching training both from a
creative and technical angle. Courses
cover everything from 16mm Film
Production (from script to post-
production) to multimedia authoring,
and a host of specialised areas such
as Super 8 editing, AVID editing,
optical printing, rostrum animation
and studies in film history and theory
organised with Birkbeck college

University of Manchester
Department of Drama
Oxford Road, Manchester M13
9PL
Tel: 0161 275 3347
Fax: 0161 275 3349
Website: www.man.ac.uk
BA Single and Joint Honours

**Drama and BA in Drama and
Screen Studies**
Two films studies courses on
Hollywood and European cinema
compulsory in Year 1 and 2, with
additional film studies and video
production courses optional in Years
2 and 3.
MPhil/PhD
Opportunity for research theses on
aspects of film and television and
documentary
MA module course in Screen Studies

Manchester Metropolitan University
Department of Communication
Media, Chatham Building
Cavendish Street
Manchester M15 6BR
Tel: 0161 247 1284
Fax: 0161 247 6393
**(P) BA (Hons) Television
Production**
A three year, full-time course based
around practical projects. Typically,
these include dramas, documentaries,
corporate productions and magazine
programmes. Students work mainly
in groups and are encouraged to
experience different production roles.
Emphasis is placed on development
of original programme material

through individually based research
and scripting. Equipment includes a
four-camera TV studio and non-linear
editing. Complimentary studies
include media history, narrative
studies and semiology. Subject to
validation

**Department of English
Geoffrey Manton Building
Rosamond Street West
Manchester M15 6LL**
Tel: 0161 247 1731/2
Fax: 0161 247 6345
**BA English Studies/BA Humanities
& Social Studies**
The Theory and Practice of
Television. Second Year optional
Course. Film & Film Theory;
Modern War Literature & Cinema;
American Cinema. Three Third Year
optional courses

Middlesex University
Faculty of Art, Design &
Performing Arts
Cat Hill, Barnet
Herts EN4 8HT
Tel: 0181 362 5000
Fax: 0181 440 9541
email: admissions@mdx.ac.uk
Website: www.mdx.ac.uk
BA (Hons) Visual Culture

Modular system degree. Film studies develops from a first level in Art and Design History. Critical and theoretical approaches to film are covered, including production, distribution and reception. The set allows detailed studies of different genres and modes of production in filmmaking, and raises issues of gender, nationality, representation and narrative

(P) MA Video

A one year full-time course (45 wks) emphasising the creative aspects of professional video production in the independent sector. Intended for graduate students with considerable lo-band video experience. The course covers all aspects of the production cycle, with an emphasis on scriptwriting. 50 per cent practical; 50 per cent theoretical

BA Honours Film Studies (combined with another subject-modular)

Modular system degree. Students combine Film Studies and another subject chosen from some 80 different subjects available

Napier University

Department of Photography, Film and Television
61 Marchmont Road
Edinburgh EH9 1HU
Tel: 0131 466 7321
Website: www.napier.ac.uk
(P) BA (Hons) Photography, Film and Television
With option of specialising in Film and Television production from the start of the 3rd year. At the end of the 2nd year students take either the still image stream or the moving image stream in this four year course
MPhil/PhD
A 2/3 year research programme with tutorial support facilitating opportunities for advanced study in creative practice in the moving image, including production of a major film or multimedia project

National Film and Television School

Beaconsfield Studios
Station Road, Beaconsfield
Bucks HP9 1LG
Tel: 01494 671234
Fax: 01494 674042
email: cad@nftsfilm-tv.ac.uk
Website: www.nftsfilm-tv.ac.uk
(P) A full-time professional training leading to an NFTS Associateship in specialisation producing, fiction direction, documentary direction, screenwriting, cinematography, editing, animation direction, screen

design, screen sound, screen music and television. The School now offers a 2-year Diploma course and a 1-year, project-based, Advanced Programme for those who already have substantial experience, either in the media or a related field. Shortlisted applicants are offered short courses prior to final selection. Assistant level training is also available and the NSCTP offers a wide range of short courses for industry professionals. The School is funded by a partnership of Government and industry (film, television and video). Its graduates occupy leading roles in all aspects of film and television production

University of Newcastle upon Tyne

Centre for Research into Film
Newcastle upon Tyne NE1 7RU
Tel: 0191 222 7492
Fax: 0191 222 5442
email: p.p.powrie@ncl.ac.uk
Website: www.ncl.ac.uk/ncrif
Diploma/MA in Film Studies
One year full-time; two year part-time course. Obligatory research training and introduction to the study of film, followed by 4 from 19 day-time and evening options, although not all are taught in every year: 6 on Hollywood cinema (the Biblical Epic; Lubitsch; romantic comedy; film noir; the Western; gender in the action film); 3 on British Cinema (pre-50s; post-60s; class and sex); on French cinema (New Wave; cinema and conflict since 1968; the contemporary nostalgia film & postmodern cinema (1960-1979; 1980-present) 2 on Spanish Cinema (60s-70s; 80s-90s); 4 on Media and Industry (Broadcasting in France; TV Comedy; Programming and Marketing; Financial Structures). Dissertation required for the MA
MLitt in Film Studies
Research-based course tailor-made for individual students. Three/four essays followed by a dissertation on negotiated topic in British, French, Hollywood, or Spanish cinemas
PhD in Film Studies
Supervision offered in British, French, Hollywood, and Spanish cinemas. for current and suggested postgraduate projects
Department of French Studies
Newcastle upon Tyne NE1 7RU
Tel: 0191 222 7441
Fax: 0191 222 5442
BA (Hons) French, French/Spanish, French/German
Optional modules in film studies. Stage 1: introduction to the study of

film. Stage 2: introduction to film theory; Classic French cinema. Stage 3: French cinema in the 1980s; cinema and conflict post-1968

Newham College of Further Education

East Ham Campus
High Street South
London E6 4ER
Tel: 0181 257 4000
Fax: Fax; 0181 257 4307
Offers part-time study up to level 4. Video Production, Photography and Digital Imaging

University of North London

School of Literary and Media Studies
116-220 Holloway Road
London N7 8DB
Tel: 020 7 753 5111
BA (Hons) Humanities
Film Studies may be taken as a major, joint or minor with one of 13 other subjects within BA (Hons) Humanities

Northern School of Film and Television

Leeds Metropolitan University
2 Queen Square
Leeds LS2 8AF
Tel: 0113 283 1900
Fax: 0113 283 1901
email: nsftv@lmu.ac.uk
Website: www.lmu.ac.uk/
This is run by Leeds Metropolitan University, with the support of Yorkshire Television, providing postgraduate level professional training in practical film production
(P) MA/PgD Scriptwriting for Film and TV (Fiction)
An intensive practical course running from February, one year full-time, and one year part-time (off site). Staffed largely by working professional writers, it covers the various forms of fiction scriptwriting for film and television – short film, feature film, television drama, soap opera, series etc. The course has a strong emphasis on professional presentation, and aims to help graduates to set up a credible freelance practice. Work consists of a short film script, a 30 minute script, a 60 minute script proposal and a full length feature script or television equivalent.
(P) PgD Film Production (Fiction)
An intensive one year practical course running from October to October. Students are admitted into specialist areas: Direction (six students per year), Production (six), Camera (three), Art-Direction (six),

Editing (three) and Sound (three). Students work in teams to produce six short films, in two batches of three. The resulting films may be broadcast on Yorkshire Television, which provide the base production funding and some facilities. Scripts are normally drawn from the product of the Scriptwriting Course and the emphasis is on team working and joint creativity under pressure. It is not a course for 'auteur' film makers. There is also a theoretical studies component

MA Film Production (Fiction)
Part-time course. Normally taken up by students who have completed the Postgraduate Diploma (see above), the MA is available via several options: 1) a 10,000 word dissertation; 2) 2 x 5,000 word extended essays; 3) exchange placement with one of NSFTV's exchange partners (Poland, Germany, Holland) and report

University of Northumbria at Newcastle
Faculty of Art & Design
Squires Building
Sandyford Road
Newcastle upon Tyne NE1 8ST
Tel: 0191 227 4935
Fax: 0191 227 3632
Website: www.unn.ac.uk
(P) BA (Hons) Media Production
Practical three year course with fully integrated theoretical and critical components in which students are offered the opportunity to specialise in individual programmes of work.
BA (Hons) History of Modern Art, Design and Film
Offered as a three year full-time course. Film Studies is given equal weighting with painting and design in the first year. In the second year up to 60 per cent of a student's time can be devoted to Film Studies, with this rising to nearly 100 per cent in the third year
MPhil
There are possibilities for research degrees in either film theory or practice

Nova Camcorder School
11a Winholme
Armthorpe
Doncaster DN3 3AF
Tel: 01302 833422
Fax: 01302 833422
email: NCS@novaonline.co.uk
Website: www.novaonline.co.uk
(P) Practical evening course for camcorder beginners
A 10-week course, one night a week, for people who want to learn how to use their camcorders properly. The course explains all the features and functions of a camcorder before moving onto basic film-making techniques and home editing and titling. The course is specifically designed for beginners, and participants receive a worksheet every week which summarises the topics covered

Plymouth College of Art and Design
School of Media and Photography
Tavistock Place
Plymouth
Devon PL4 8AT
Tel: 01752 203434
Fax: 01752 203444
(P) B/TEC HND Media Production
(in partnership with the University of Plymouth). A two year modular course with pathways in film, video, animation and electronic imaging. All areas of film, video and television production are covered and the course is well supported by visiting lecturers and workshops. Strong links with the industry have been developed and work based experience forms an important part of the course. The course has BKSTS accreditation. Opportunities exist through the ERASMUS programme to undertake a programme of exchange with European universities or polytechnics during the course. In addition suitably qualified students can progress to third level modules for the award of a BA (Hons) in PhotoMedia
Advanced Diploma Photography, Film and Television leading to the BIPP Professional Qualifying Exam
A one year course post HND and postgraduate. The photography, film and television option allows students to plan their own line of study, including practical work, dissertation and an extended period of work based experience. Students from both courses have had considerable success in film and video scholarships and competitions. Students on both courses have the opportunity for three month work placements in the media industry in Europe
NCFE Foundation in Lens Based Media
A one year full time foundation course for those wishing to progress to Higher Education in one of the many exciting areas of lens based media. This practical course covers: photography, video, electronic imaging, multi-imaging and contextual studies. The course aims to help the student develop a portfolio which shows how the student has integrated technical skills with creative concepts and critical analysis. (This course may also be studied part time over two academic years)
National Diploma Programmes
ND Photography; ND MultiMedia, ND Media Studies

University of Portsmouth
Department of Design
Lion Gate Building, Lion Terrace
Portsmouth PO1 3HF
Tel: 01705 843805
Fax: 01705 843808
email: lingardm@env2.enf.port.ac.uk
Website: www.port.ac.uk
BA (Hons) Art, Design and Media
Three year unitised programme has six specialist pathways. All are structured around historical, cultural and theoretical analysis which form an important part of the degree. Student placements in Europe and the UK and outside projects maintain the degree's links with industry and art practice.
Media Arts – Moving Image Strand
In the first and second years, students undertake briefs around personal and cultural identity, gender, media arts practice, documentary as intervention etc. Students work in video, sound, multimedia and photography. In the third year students work on self-directed projects
Media Arts – Photography Strand
Encourages collaborative work with moving image and sound artists
Communication Design
Design for television, video graphics and multimedia are central areas of concern
History and Cultural Theory
Aim to produce graduates with particular skills in research and communication

School of Social and Historical Studies, Milldam
Burnaby Road
Portsmouth PO1 3AS
Tel: 01705 876543
Fax: 01705 842174
BA (Hons) Cultural Studies
Year 3: options on British Cinema 1933-70, British Television Drama, Avant-Garde Films and Feminism

Ravensbourne College of Design & Communication
School of Television
Walden Road, Chislehurst
Kent BR7 5SN
Tel: 0181 289 4900

Fax: 0181 325 8320
(P) B/TEC HND Professional Broadcasting (Engineering Pathway)
Two year full-time vocational course designed in consultation with the broadcasting industry leading to employment opportunities as technician engineers. Students develop skills in installing, aligning and maintaining a wide range of professional broadcast equipment using analogue and digital technologies
B/TEC HND Professional Broadcasting (Technical Operations pathway)
Two year full-time vocational course designed in consultation with the TV broadcasting industry leading to employment opportunities in television and video production as members of programme making presentation and transmission teams. Students develop skills in budgeting, production management and lighting, camera operation, sound, video recording and editing, vision-mixing,

Telecine, and audio-recording
BA (Hons) in Professional Broadcasting
90 week full-time vocational course designed in consultation with the broadcasting industry leading to employment opportunities for creative, team-centred individuals possessing a fundamental competence for working in the production process, business practice and technology of a changing and highly competitive industry
BSc (Hons) Communication and Technology
A two-year course which explores the use of communication technology in both broadcast and non-broadcast environments. In doing so, it provides students with 3 main tool kits: technology (broadcast video and computer technology), design (especially for screen) and management (marketing, finance and project management).
(P) BEng Broadcast Engineering
This three year programme is offered in conjunction with the University of

Sussex, Ravensbourne's partner institution. Exploring the application of electronic engineering and computing principles to television and broadcast technology, this course maximises the potential for employment

University of Reading
Department of Film and Drama
Bulmershe Court
Woodlands Ave
Reading RG6 IHY
Tel: 0118 931 8878
Fax: 0118 931 8873
Website: www.reading.ac.uk
BA Film and Drama (Single Subject)
After the first two terms in which three subjects are studied (two being in film and drama), students work wholly in film and drama. The course is critical but with significant practical elements which are designed to extend critical understanding. It does not provide professional training
BA Film and Drama with English, German, Italian
Students in general share the same teaching as Single Subject students
MA Film and Drama
One year taught course, incorporating study of both film and drama, practical assignments and research methodologies
MPhil and PhD
Research applications for MPhil and PhD degrees are also invited in areas of cinema, television and twentieth century theatre

Department of English
Whiteknights
Reading RG6 6AA
Tel: 0118 931 8361
Fax: 0118 931 6561
BA (Hons) English
Second year optional course on film, television and literature. Third year optional course in media semiotics
PhD
Research can be supervised on the history of the BBC and other mass media topics

Department of French Studies
Whiteknights
Reading RG6 6AA
Fax: 0118 931 8122
BA (Hons) French
First year introductory course: detailed study of one film (one half-term). Final year: Two-term option: French cinema, with special emphasis on the 30s, 40s and the Nouvelle Vague. Includes introductory work on the principle of

film study. Available also to students combining French with certain other subjects.

Department of Italian Studies
Whiteknights
Reading RG6 2AA
BA (Hons) Italian/French and Italian with Film Studies
First year introductory course: Post-War Italian Cinema (one half-term). Second year course: Italian Cinema (three terms). Final year course: Italian Cinema in its European and American context (two terms). Dissertation on an aspect of Italian cinema. These courses available to students reading other subjects in the Faculty.
MA Italian Cinema
One year full-time or two year part-time course on Italian cinema: compulsory theory course, options on film and literature, Bertolucci, Italian industry and genre – the Spaghetti Western.
MPhil and PhD
Research can be supervised on Italian cinema for degree by thesis

Department of German Studies, University of Reading
Whiteknights
Reading RG6 6AA
Tel: 0118 931 8332
Fax: 01118 931 8333
email: j.e.sandford@reading.ac.uk
BA (Hons) German
Two-term Finals option: The German Cinema. Course covers German cinema from the 1920s to the present, with special emphasis on the Weimar Republic, the Third Reich, and the 'New German Cinema'.

College of Ripon and York St John
Faculty of Creative and Performing Arts
Lord Mayor's Walk
York 7EX
Tel: 01904 616672
Fax: 01904 616931
Website: www.ucrysj.ac.uk
Bill Pinner
(P) BA (Hons) Theatre, Film and Television
This degree programme embraces theoretical and practical aspects of theatre, film and television. 'Core' theories and concepts are taught alongside practical, production modules and all activity is focused on the development of both intellectual and practical skills. Emphasis is placed upon the interrelationship of the three areas alongside theories and skills specific to each. Workshops

and specialist modules allow a focus of interests and skills, but students are expected to engage with all three areas of the degree. There are opportunities to study abroad in Europe or North America, and to undertake work placements and internships. There are excellent facilities for performance activity and video production

Roehampton Institute, London
Faculty of Arts and Humanities
Digby Stuart College
Roehampton Lane
London SW15 5PU
Tel: 0181 392 3230
Fax: 0181 392 3289
email: j.ridgman@roehampton.ac.uk
Website: www.roehampton.ac.uk
BA Film and Television Studies
A three-year modular degree programme, which may be combined with a variety of other subjects. Several core courses are available (Film Narrative, British Television Drama, Cultural Theory and Media, Representing Women etc) to which may be added selected topic modules. The course includes up to 40 per cent practical work in television and video, moving from principles of single camera production in year one to sustained, independent project work in the final year

Royal College of Art
Department of Film and Television
School of the Moving Image
Kensington Gore
London SW7 2EU
Tel: 020 7 584 5020
Fax: 020 7 589 0178
email: j.smith@rca.ac.uk
Website: www.rca.ac.uk/Design
(P) Cinematography
The aim of the Cinematography Specialism is to create opportunities for students to increase their practical knowledge and creative experience
(P) Design for Film and Television
The Design Specialism aims to cover all aspects of production design in film and television through theoretical and practical teaching
(P) Direction – Film and TV Drama
A high-level of professional skill combined with original talent is expected of all students and the syllabus is designed to develop the practice of their creative and technical abilities
(P) Documentary – Film and TV
This is a new specialism on the course and is open to a few,

dedicated documentary students.
(P) Editing
This course offers editors the opportunity to develop technical and creative excellence and to further their skills by interweaving the study of film with maximum practical experience
(P) Production
The aim of the Production Specialism is to develop the skills of creative producers and to give them the practical opportunity to take total responsibility for film and television productions from initial concept through to marketing the finished product
Sound Design
The Sound Specialism aims to develop a full understanding of the technique and role of sound in film and video and to increase the students skill in sound recording, sound editing, post-sync recording

St Helens College
School of Arts, Media and Design
Brook Street
St Helens
Merseyside WA10 1PZ
Tel: 01744 623322
BA (Hons) Media Production
Modular course in television, video, film and radio production skills
BA Media and Cultural Studies

University of Salford
School of Media, Music and Performance
Adelphi, Peru Street
Salford, Manchester M3 6EQ
Tel: 0161 295 6026
Fax: 0161 295 6023
Website: www.salford.ac.uk
International Media Centre
Director and Head of School: Ron Cook
Adelphi House, The Crescent
Salford, Manchester M3 6EN
BA (Hons) Television and Radio
BA (Hons) Media and Performance
BA (Hons) Media, Language and Business
BSc (Hons) Media Technology
B/TEC HND Media Production
B/TEC HND Media Performance
MA Television Feature and Documentary Production
MA Scriptwriting for Television and Radio (part-time)
Plus – degree courses in Band Musicianship; Popular Music & Recording; Music, Acoustics & Recording; Composition; Performance
Visiting Professor: David Plowright. Fellows: Richard Ellis, Ray Fitzwalter. Professional Patrons: Ken

Russell, Ben Kingsley, Liz Forgan, Robert Powell, Gareth Morgan, Sir George Martin CBE, Jack Rosenthal CBE, Stuart Prebble, Leslie Woodhead OBE, Gillian Lynne. All courses are 50 per cent practical production/performance based. The Granada Education Awards are available to ethnic students. MA Documentary is supported by Channel 4, Avid Technology and Granada TV

University of Sheffield
Department of English Literature
Shearwood Mount
Shearwood Road
Sheffield S10 2TD
Tel: 0114 222 8480
Fax: 0114 282 8481
Website: www.shef.ac.uk
BA (Hons) English Literature
Students may study one or two Special Subjects in Film in their second or third years

Sheffield Hallam University
Communications Subject Group
School of Cultural Studies
36 Collegiate Crescent
Sheffield S10 2BP
Tel: 0114 255 5555
Fax: 0114 253 2344
Website: www.shu.ac.uk
BA (Hons) Communication Studies
Course covers all aspects of human communication, one area being Mass Communication. Option course in Television Fiction in Year 3. Some practical work
MA/PgD/Certificate Communication Studies
Part-time course to gain certificate in three terms, Diploma in six terms, MA in 8 terms. Aims to develop theoretical understandings and analytical skills in relation to the processes and practices of communication in modern society. Students attend for two sessions of 2+ hours each week. Full-time/route 12 months. 8 hours per week

School of Cultural Studies
Psalter Lane
Sheffield S11 8UZ
Tel: 0114 253 2601 /272 0911
Film and Media Studies Programme
BA (Hons) Film Studies
BA (Hons) Media Studies
The Film and Media Studies Programme consists of two degree routes. The courses provide opportunities for the study of film and a range of media (including television, radio and journalism) from a variety of perspectives including historical development,

social, political and economic contexts, and the artistic and aesthetic dimensions of film and media. The courses also provide a grounding in basic media production skills with units in film, video etc and scriptwriting
(P) BA (Hons) History of Art, Design and Film
Film studies is a major component of this course. Year 1: introduction to film analysis and history. Year 2: special study on Hollywood. Year 3: critical and theoretical studies in Art, Design and Film and Contemporary Film Theory and Practice.
MA Film Studies
Two year part-time course; two evenings per week, plus dissertation to be written over two terms in a third year. Main areas of study: Problems of Method; The Classical Narrative Tradition; British Cinema 1927-45; Hollywood and Popular culture
BA (Hons) Fine Art (Combined and Media Arts)
After initial work with a range of media, students can specialise in film and/or video. Film productions range from short 8mm films to 16mm documentaries or widescreen features, to small 35mm productions

Northern Media School
The Workstation
15 Paternoster Row
Sheffield S1 2BX
Tel: 0114 272 0994
Fax: 0114 275 6816
(P) PgDip Broadcast Journalism
Main focus is on practical work. Much of the teaching is conducted through workshops and practical exercises supplemented by seminars and lectures
(P) PgDip and MA in Screenwriting (Fiction)
Intensive practical course covering fiction scriptwriting for film and television

South Bank University
Education, Politics and Social Science
103 Borough Road
London SE1 1AA
Tel: 020 7 928 8989
Fax: 020 7 815 8273
email: registry@sbu.ac.uk
Website: www.sbu.ac.uk
(P) BSc (Hons) Media and Society
Three year full time course. Two thirds critical studies, one third practical work. This course combines units assessing the social and political significance of the mass media, together with units

introducing practical production skills. Critically, the course grows from studies of the media in the Britain during year one, to studies of European and global media in years tow and three. Other units also address the understanding of media audiences, news forms and media law. Individual research leads to the completion of a dissertation thesis in year three. Practically, the course develops skills in audio, radio, video and multimedia production. These skills are then employed by students in the creation of their own final year projects

South Kent College
DASH
Maison Dieu Road
Dover CT16 1DH
Tel: 01304 204573
Fax: 01304 204573
B/TEC National Diploma Media Studies
Two year full-time course covering video, film, print/DTP, photography and radio. Students complete advertising, drama, news and documentary projects closely linked to community groups. The course is modular and work experience is offered

South Thames College
Department of Design and Media
Wandsworth High Street
London SW18 2PP
Tel: 020 8 918 7043
Bsc (Hons) Media and Society
Course run in conjunction with South Bank University. Practical areas include: television, radio, audio, photography, and computer-aided design

The University of Southampton
Research and Graduate School of Education
Faculty of Educational Studies
Southampton
Hants SO9 5NH
Tel: 01703 593387
Fax: 01703 593556
Website: www.soton.ac.uk
Certificate and Diploma Advanced Educational Studies – Media Education
Certificate is one year course involving 60 hours of contact time; the Diploma is taken over two years, with 120 hours of contact time. Both include a range of media courses. The Certificate is also available as a distance learning package, involving 240 hours of independent study
MA (Ed)
The MA in Education is run on a

modular basis as a full- or part-time taught course. The course as a whole requires the completion of 12x15-hour units and a supervised dissertation. Included are Television, Media Education, Training

MPhil and PhD
Research degrees in any area of Media Education, Media Studies, Educational Broadcasting and Educational Technology are available

Southampton University
New College
School of Culture and Language
The Avenue
Southampton SO17 1BG
Tel: 01703 597317
Fax: 01703 230944
BA (Hons) Humanities, Humanities (English Studies); Humanities (English Studies and Historical Studies)
These degree courses offer a number of optional film modules eg American cinema, European Cinema, Film and History, Film and Political Metaphor

School of Research & Graduate Studies, Highfield
Southampton
Hants SO17 1BJ
Tel: 01703 593406/592248
Fax: 01703 593288/595437
email: fnl@soton.ac.uk
MA Film Studies
The course aims to equip students with the capacity to engage intellectually with significant developments in film theory and history, together with the skills required to undertake contextual and textual analysis of films and critical writing. The weight given to European cinemas, including British cinema, and to transnational perspectives, is a unique feature, and Hollywood and American independent cinema represent core elements. Tutors include Tim Bergfelder, Caroline Blinder, Pam Cook, Deniz Göktürk, Sylvie Lindeperg, Bill Marshall, Lucy Mazdon, David Vilaseca and Linda Ruth Williams

Staffordshire University
School of Humanities & Social Sciences
Field of Media and Cultural Studies
PO Box 661, College Road
Stoke on Trent ST4 2XW
Tel: 01782 294413
Fax: 01782 294760
Website: www.staffs.ac.uk
BA (Hons) Film, Television and Radio Studies

This single Honours degree provides a broad study of the media, with an emphasis on film, television and radio, but offering opportunities to consider new technologies, journalism and advertising, together with a strand of practical work in scriptwriting and production which runs throughout the degree.
After a foundation year in which students are introduced to key problems and issues of media study, there is a wide choice of options which enables students to construct a programme to suit their own interests. Students can, for instance, choosed to focus more strongly on one of the media offered – film, television or radio – or they might decide to spread their study evenly across the diversity of the media. By the final year it is possible to spend up to half their time on independent projects such as researching and writing a dissertation, producing a script, radio or video production, or developing and costing a project proposal for a media organisation or funding body
BA (Joint/Combined Hons) in Film Studies
In the half degree in Film Studies students are introduced to the diversity of practices involved in the cinema, including film-making, film-going, and film funding. A series of options enable contemporary and historical, American and British, European and non-European. Students also have the opportunity to explore some of the problems and issues involved in understanding cinema through practical work such as scriptwriting or video production.
BA (Joint/Combined Hons) in Media Studies
The half degree in Media Studies begins with an introduction to ways of studying the media, with core modules on the British Press and Broadcasting History. It then goes on to explore the operation of the mass media in society through a focus on the broadcast media, together with consideration of the press, advertising and new technologies. Within this focus students are introduced to different theories and methodologies for analysing the relation between the media and society, including such issues as: the development of new technologies, their national and global implications, changing media audiences and patterns of consumption, and public debates about media policies and practices. As well as studying media problems

and issues, a series of options offers modules in broadcasting history and different radio, television or journalistic forms. Students also have the opportunity to engage with media practices, formats and problems through practical work such as scriptwriting or audio/video production

University of Stirling
Film and Media Studies
Stirling FK9 4LA
Tel: 01786 467520
Fax: 01786 466855
Website: www.stir.ac.uk
BA (Hons) Film and Media Studies (Single and Joint Hons)
Four year degree in the theory and analysis of all the principal media. All students take courses in the theories of mass communication and in cultural theories, as well as problems of textual analysis and then select from a range of options, including practical courses in the problems of news reporting in radio and television and in television documentary. As a joint honours degree Film and Media Studies can be combined with a variety of other subjects
BA General Degree
Students can build a component of their degree in film and media studies ranging from as much as eight units (approximately 50 per cent of their degree) if they take a major in the subject, down to as little as three if they wish merely to complete a Part 1 major. For the most part students follow the same units as do Film and Media Studies Honours students
MSc/Diploma Media Management
One year full-time programme consisting of two taught terms (Sept-May) followed by a dissertation (May-Aug). Internationally oriented and comparative in approach, the course offers media practitioners a wider analytical perspective on the key issues affecting their work and offers graduates a rigorous foundation for a career in the media industry. Areas covered include media policy and regulation, media economics, management and marketing, analytical methods and case studies and advanced media theory
MLitt and PhD
The specialist fields of the Stirling Media Research Institute: Media and National/Cultural identity; Political Communication and the Sociology of Journalism; Screen Interpretation; Media Management and Media

policy; public relations. Further details of the Institute's work are obtainable on request

Msc/Diploma Public Relations
Available in full time (12 months) and distance learning (30 months) formats. The degree develops the key analytical and practical skills for a career in Public Relations. Areas covered include; Public Relations; management and organisational studies; research and evaluation; media and communication studies; marketing and political communication

The University of Sunderland
School of Arts, Design & Communications, Forster Building
Chester Road
Sunderland SR1 3RL
Tel: 0191 515 2125
Fax: 0191 515 2178
Website: www.sunderland.ac.uk
BA (Hons) Photography, Video and Digital Imaging
Amalgamates three areas within a creative and fine art context
BA (Hons) Communication and Cultural Studies
Options include study of film, broadcasting and popular culture at each level. Up to 20 per cent practical study of the media is possible, including video, radio, photography, and broadcast and print journalism
(P) BA (Hons) Media and Cultural Studies
Comprises study of social, historical and artistic aspects of the mass media and popular culture together with development of practical skills in media arts
MA Cultural and Textual Studies
One year full-time or two year part-time MA. Postgraduate courses are constructed from a wide range of modules. The compulsory module provides students with a flexible theoretical foundation, and a multi-media and comparative study of verbal and visual forms of cultural communication, representing both 'high' and 'popular' culture. Students are then asked to choose three other modules, and to write a dissertation which allows them to specialise in film studies if they wish
MA Woman, Culture and Identity
One year full-time or two year part-time MA. The compulsory module introduces students to feminist theory and criticism in the areas of film and media studies, cultural studies, literary studies and philosophy. Students are then asked to choose

three other specialist modules, and to write a dissertation, which allows them to specialise in feminist film and/or media studies if they wish

Surrey Institute of Art and Design
Faculty of Arts and Media
Falkner Road, The Hart
Farnham, Surrey GU9 7DS
Tel: 01252 722441
Fax: 01252 732213
BA (Hons) Photography
BA (Hons) Film and Video
BA (Hons) Animation
The approach in each course is essentially practical, structured to encourage a direct and fundamental appraisal of photography, film, video and animation through practice and by theoretical study. 70 per cent practical, 30 per cent theoretical. Courses are BECTU accredited
BA (Hons) Media Studies
A range of theoretical approaches to the mass media are examined. Emphasis is placed on the critical application of such theories to the actual production and consumption of media, primarily visual, culture. Units on professional practice, the European context of media production, and the learning of a modern European language prepare students for a career in the media industry

University of Sussex
School of Cultural and Community Studies
Media Studies Co-Ordinator
Essex House, Falmer
Brighton BN1 9RQ
Tel: 01273 678019
Fax: 01273 678644
email: a.m.oxley@sussex.ac.uk
Website: www.sussex.ac.uk
BA Media Studies
The degree course in Media Studies enables students to develop a critical understanding of the press, cinema, radio, television, new information technologies and of the particular character of media communications. The Major in Media Studies is taught in two Schools of Studies – Cultural and Community Studies (CCS) and European Studies (EURO): different School Courses accompany it according to the School. The course in EURO also involves study of a modern European language and an additional year abroad in Europe
BA English and Media Studies
BA Music and Media Studies
A three year full-time degree course which includes analysis of television, film and other media, together with

some opportunity to be involved in practical television, video and radio production
MA in Media Studies
The MA comprises a two-term core course in media theory and research which students study the conceptual, methodological and policy related issues emerging from the study of the media. In addition, students choose, in each of the first two terms, an optional course from: European Media in Transition; Media Technology and Everyday Life; Media Audiences; The Political Economy of the New Communications Media; Promotional Culture; Queering Popular Culture; Sexual Difference; Theories of Representation; Memories of the Holocaust
(P) MA in Media Studies (Multimedia)
The course shares a core course, Media Theory and Research, with the MA in Media Studies. In addition, students take two dedicated courses: The Political Economy of the New Communications Media, and Theory and Practice of Interactive Multimedia. After two terms students either complete an academic dissertation, or undertake an industry placement and a multimedia project

Thames Valley University, London
London College of Music and Media
St Mary's Road
Ealing
London W5 5RF
Tel: 020 8 231 2304
Fax: 020 8 231 2656
Website: www.tvu.ac.uk
BA (Hons) Design & Media Management
Multi-disciplinary course. Students take design and management studies which are compulsory, and media production units including photography, sound, computer videographics, video production and multi-image
MA Cultural Studies
Part-time taught evening course of six units plus dissertation. Topics include film and television, popular culture

Trinity and All Saints College
(A College of the University of Leeds)
Brownberrie Lane, Horsforth
Leeds LS18 5HD
Tel: 0113 283 7100
Fax: 0113 283 7200

email: J.Foale@tasc.ac.uk
Website: www.tasc.ac.uk
Diploma/MA in BiMedia or Print Journalism
The course takes the form of a Postgraduate Diploma which, for suitable candidates, can be enhanced to Master's level. The Diploma consists of three taught modules: Basic Journalism, Journalism Skills (Bimedia or Print and Essential Knowledge. The Diploma courses run full-time for 39 weeks and include a minimum attachment at a news organisation

University of Ulster at Belfast
School of Design & Communication
Faculty of Art and Design
York Street
Belfast BT15 1ED
Tel: 01232 328515
Fax: 01232 321048
(P) DipHE/BA (Hons) Visual Communication
Practical and theoretical film/video/media studies available to all students plus a specialist pathway,

Screen Based Imaging (SBI) which includes Video production, Animation and Multimedia Design
(P) DipHE/BA (Hons) Combined Studies
Students choose from modules across all courses and many specialise in a combination of Visual/Communication SBI and Fine Art Video plus media studies theory modules
School of Fine and Applied Arts
DIPHE/BA Hons Fine and Applied Arts
Students specialising in the Fine Art pathway may specialise in video from year two

University of Ulster at Coleraine
School of Media and Performing Arts, Coleraine
Co Londonderry
Northern Ireland BT52 1SA
Tel: 01265 324196
Fax: 01265 324964
(P) BA (Hons) Media Studies
Three year course integrating theoretical, critical and practical approaches to film, television,

photography, radio and the press. Important practical component
MA Media Studies
A two year part-time course combining advanced study of the mass media with media practice. There are also specialist options dealing with media education and cultural identity. MA is awarded 40 per cent on coursework, 60 per cent on dissertation (which may incorporate production element)
MPhil and DPhil
Students are accepted for MPhil and DPhil by thesis. Particular expertise is offered in the area of the media and Ireland, although supervision is provided in most areas of Media Studies
MA International Media Studies
A one year full-time course in association with Aichi Shukutoku University, Nagoya, Japan. The course is concerned with the mass media in an international context and students spend one semester at ASU, in Japan and one semester at UUC, in Northern Ireland

University of Wales, College of Cardiff

PO Box 908
French Section/German Section, EUROS
Cardiff CF1 3YQ
Tel: 029 20874000
Fax: 029 20874946
BA French
Study of Francophone African cinema included as part of optional courses. Small practical component
BA German
Study of contemporary German cinema forms part of optional courses

University of Wales College, Newport

University Information Centre
Caerleon Campus
PO Box 101
Newport NP6 1YH
Tel: 01633 432432
Fax: 01633 432850
email: uic@newport.ac.uk
Website: www.newport.ac.uk
BA (Hons) Film and Video
The course is intended for students wishing to explore the moving image in the broadest possible sense as an expressive and dynamic medium. It provides them with a programme of work designed to support and stimulate their personal development as creative and aware practitioners of film, regardless of their ultimate ambition. The practice of film is studied in a wider culture and intellectual context and students are encouraged to be analytical and critical. Their study acknowledges existing conventions in dominant cinema but seeks to extend them through experimentation and exploration
(P) BA (Hons) Animation
Intended for students wishing to use animation as part of a wider personal practice, as well as becoming professional animators working in independent production, advertising and design. The course is designed to develop students imaginations and ideas to explore and extend their animation technique. Therefore it is presented in a cultural context which promotes critical debate and rigorous analysis in terms of representation and expression. In Year 3 students develop their own programme for the production of major pieces of animation on high quality production equipment to broadcast standards
BA (Hons) Media and Visual Culture
At a time when our culture seems dominated as never before by the presence of media systems and images, this stimulating programme critically examines issues relating to media and visual culture. Specialist courses in the theory and history of film, photography design and contemporary art complement the central study of media culture. Practical options in subjects such as film, photography and new media can be selected, leading to major work involving practice in the final year
(P) MA Film
This practical MA programme will offer an opportunity to: complete a short broadcast standard film explore and challenge the notions of the cinematic subject and language explore developing forms and changing technologies
The course will include:
teaching through group and individual tutorials
close links with the film and television industry and media agencies in Wales
visiting masterclasses and facilities made available in professional production houses. The discursive and practical work on a short film wil be in one of the following areas; Fiction, Faction, Animation, Non-genre/experimental. Acceptance of the course will be based on interview including: the submission of a treatment of a proposed film to be made during the course, the screening of a previous film, some fees/production bursaries could be available

University College Warrington

University College (A college of the University of Manchester)
Media and Performing Arts
Padgate Campus
Crab Lane WA2 0DB
Tel: 01925 494494
Fax: 01925 816077
email: Media@Warr.ac.uk
Website: www.warr.ac.uk
(P) BA Hons Media and Cultural Studies
Students on this single Honours programme undertake wide-ranging academic study in media and cultural studies, extensive production work chosen from television, radio, commercial music production or multimedia journalism, and a lengthy period of work placement in the media industry. They are eligible to apply for the Granada TV internship scheme.
(P) BA Hons Media (Television Production)
(P) BA Hons Media (Radio Production)
(P) BA Hons Media (Commercial Music Production)
(P) BA Hons Media (Multimedia Journalism)
These degrees are available as single and joint Honours programmes. Students who take media as single honours, or as a major or minor subject within a joint honours programme undertake academic analysis of the media through core modules in media forms, issues in media representation, media institutions and audiences, and media professional issues, as well as modules from a broad range of optional units. Single honours and major subject students undertake extensive specialist production work chosen from television, radio or commercial music production and multimedia journalism, and have an extensive period of work experience in the media industry. These students are also eligible to apply for the interneeship scheme run in association with Granada TV. Production modules are not available to students who take media as a minor subject. Students on joint honours programmes can combine media with other subjects such as leisure management, performing arts, business and sports studies
MA/PGDip Screen Studies
Offered on a one year full-time or two year part-time basis. Students take the same 3 core units as in the MA Media and Cultural Studies, but then choose 3 optional units specifically related to aspects of screen culture, including new media technologies. To gain the award of MA, students complete a 20,000 word dissertation
(P) MA/PGDip Television Production (in association with Granada TV)
Run in association with Granada TV, this is a one year full-time fast track vocational course for those with serious aspirations to work in television production. Following intensive skills workshops, students are expected to produce largely, though not exclusively, factual-based programming to professional standards on Beta, using programme budgets supplied by Granada TV. The course includes 3-4 weeks work experience at Granada or BBC North. In addition to extensive production work, students develop an understanding of the contemporary broadcasting, independent and corporate sectors, and engage with aspects of television theory. To gain

the award of MA, students complete a written project, which can be a conventional academic study, an industrial study or an original script. Granada TV bursaries are available for successful applicants

University of Warwick
Department of Film and Television Studies, Faculty of Arts
Coventry CV4 7AL
Tel: 024 76523523
Fax: 024 76524757
Website: www.warwick.ac.uk
BA Joint Degree Film and Literature
Four courses offered each year, two in film and two in literature. Mainly film studies but some television included
BA in Film with Television Studies
Four courses offered each year, three of which on film and, from year two, television. Further options available in film and/or television in year three
BA French or Italian with Film Studies
This degree puts a particular emphasis on film within and alongside its studies of French or Italian language, literature and society
Various Degrees
Options in film studies can be taken as part of undergraduate degrees in other departments
MA Film and Television Studies
Taught courses on Textual Analysis, Methods in Film History, Modernity and Innovation, and Issues of Representation, Introduction to Film and Television Studies for Graduates
MA for Research in Film and Television Studies
Combination of taught course and tailor-made programme of viewing and reading for students with substantial knowledge of film and television studies at BA level. For students wishing to proceed to PhD research
MA, MPhil and PhD
Students are accepted for research degrees

University of Westminster
School of Communication, Design and Media
Harrow Campus
Northwick Park HA1 3TP
Tel: 020 7 911 5903
Fax: 020 7 911 5955
email: hw06@wmin.ac.uk
Website: www.wmin.ac.uk
BA (Hons) Film and Television
A modular degree course for young and mature students interested in film-making (fiction, documentary

and experimental), television drama and documentary, screenwriting and film and television theory and criticism. The course emphasises creative collaboration and encourages some specialisation. It aims to equip students with understanding and competence in relevant critical ideas and the ability to work confidently and professionally in film and allied media using traditional and new technologies
BA (Hons) Media Studies
This degree studies the social context in which the institutions of mass communications operate, including film and television, and teaches the practice of print and broadcasting journalism and video production. On levels 2 and 3 students choose one of the following pathways: radio, journalism or video production. The course gives equal emphasis to theory/criticism and practice. The video pathway is accredited by BECTU
MA PgD Film and Television Studies
Advanced level part-time course taught in Central London (evenings and study weekends) concerned with theoretical aspects of film and television. Modular credit and accumulation scheme, with exemption for work previously done. The MA is normally awarded after three years' study (120 credits). A Postgraduate Certificate can be awarded after one year (45 credits) or a Diploma after two years (75 credits)
(P) BA (Hons) Contemporary Media Practice
A modular three year full-time course offering an integrated approach to photography, film, video and digital-imaging. Students are encouraged to use a range of photographic and electronic media and theoretical studies are considered crucial to the development of ideas. In Years 1 and 2, the taught programme covers basic and applied skills on a project basis; these are complemented by a range of options. In Year 3 students are given the opportunity to develop their own programme of study, resulting in the production of major projects in practice and dissertations

Weymouth College
Creative & Performing Arts
Cranford Avenue
Weymouth
Dorset DT4 7LQ
Tel: 01305 208856
Fax: 01305 208892
(P) GNVQ Intermediate and

Advanced Levels Media Communication and Production BTEC)
Intermediate level: one year course designed to give a foundation in media theory and production across audio, video and print media
BTEC National Diploma in Media
The two year, full-time programme offers a broad foundation in media production skills, working practices and contextual knowledge. Core components include: video and audio production techniques; desktop publishing; photography; writing for the media; and research presentation skills. The second year allows for more specialisation in video or audio production but in a multi-skilled context. The programme is sponsored by Total Video Ltd, providing work experience and professional support for students

Wimbledon School of Art
Merton Hall Road
London SW19 3QA
Tel: 020 8 540 0231
Fax: 020 8 543 1750
(P) BA (Hons) Technical Arts: Design
Training of set designers for theatre, film and television

University of Wolverhampton
School of Humanities and Social Sciences, Castle View, Dudley
West Midlands DY1 3HR
Tel: 01902 323400
Fax: 01902 323379
Website: www.wolverhampton.ac.uk
BA (Hons) Media and Cultural Studies
This is a modular programme which may be studied as a Specialist or Combined Award. Students follow a core programme covering key theoretical, historical and critical debates in both Media and Cultural Studies. A level 2 module in Research Methods prepares students for a final year project. Alongside the core students choose option modules drawn from the following themes: Film Studies; Video and Professional Communications (including Print and Broadcast Journalism, European Broadcasting and Organisational Communication); Gender and Representation (including Fashion, Style and Consumption). All students have the option of a Student Link, in which they undertake a small-scale research project in an organisation or company. This is not principally a practical programme but students taking the Video and Professional

Communications Theme will undertake a range of practical work for assessment. This programme includes the option of studying a foreign language.

BA (Hons) Applied Communications

This modular programme may be studied as a Specialist or Combined Award and is concerned with issues and problems of human communication in their professional or industrial context. It draws upon media studies and planned communication, including marketing, journalism, public relations, corporate communication and interactive multimedia. The programme offers a balance between the theory and practice of different forms of planned communications. Specialists take a professional placement within an appropriate sector of the communication industry as part of their final year. This programme combines theory and practice and on completion students will have acquired a range communications skills in marketing, journalism, design for interactive multimedia and public relations. This programme includes the options of studying a foreign language

BA (Hons) Film Studies

This modular programme is available as a joint degree, which can be studied in combination with another subject. Students take a general foundation in Media Studies and then follow modules which introduce approaches to the analysis of films, studies of different genres (musicals, melodrama, film noir), theories of authorship, and the Hollywood studio system. The study of national cinemas includes options on British, French and Spanish cinema and special study of contemporary America. Film modules are taught at Wolverhampton's award-winning Light House Media Centre, which offers two purpose-built and fully equipped cinemas, library and exhibition facilities. The majority of films studied are screened in full cinema format. Additional library resources are housed on the Dudley and Wolverhampton campuses

DISTRIBUTORS (NON-THEATRICAL)

Companies here control UK rights for non-theatrical distribution (for domestic and group viewing in schools, hospitals, airlines and so on).

For an extensive list of titles available non -theatrically with relevant distributors' addresses, see the *British National Film & Video Catalogue*, available for reference from the BFI National Library and major public libraries. Other sources of film and video are listed under Archives and Film Libraries, and Workshops

Amber Films
5 Side
Newcastle upon Tyne NE1 3JE
Tel: 0191 232 2000
Fax: 0191 230 3217
email: amberside@btinternet.com

Arts Council Film and Video Library
Concord Video and Film Council
201 Felixstowe Road
Ipswich 1P3 9BJ
Tel: 01473 726012
Fax: 01473 274531

BBC for Business
Woodlands
80 Wood Lane
London W12 0TT
Tel: 020 8576 2088
Fax: 020 8576 2867

Big Bear Records
PO Box 944
Birmingham B16 8UT
Tel: 0121 454 7020/8100
Fax: 0121 454 9996
email:
bigbearmusic@compuserve.com

Boulton-Hawker Films
Hadleigh
near Ipswich
Suffolk IP7 5BG
Tel: 01473 822235
Fax: 01473 824519
Educational films and videos: health education, social welfare, home

economics, P.S.E., P.E., Maths, biology, physics, chemistry, geography

British Film Institute
21 Stephen Street
London W1P 2LN
Tel: 020 7 957 8909
Fax: 020 7580 5830
email: bookings@bfi.org.uk
Handles non-theatrical 16mm, 35mm and video. Subject catalogues available

BUFVC (British Universities Film & Video Council)
77 Wells Street
London W1P 3RE
Tel: 020 7393 1500
Fax: 020 7393 1555
Video cassettes and videodiscs for sale direct from above address. Also off-air recording back-up service for education. Hire via Concord Video and Film Council

Carlton UK Television
Video Resource Unit
Lenton Lane
Nottingham NG7 2NA
Tel: 0115 986 3322
Fax: 0115 964 5202

Central Office of Information (COI)
Films and Video
Hercules Road
London SE1 7DU
Tel: 020 7261 8594
Fax: 020 7261 8874
Website: www.coi.gov.uk/
via CFL Vision

CFL Vision
PO Box 35
Wetherby
Yorks LS23 7EX
Tel: 01937 541010
Fax: 01937 541083
email: euroview@compuserve.com
Website: www.euroview.co.uk

Chain Production
2 Clanricarde Gardens
London W2 4NA
Tel: 020 7219 4277
Fax: 020 7229 0861
Specialist in European films and world cinema, cult classics, handling European Film Libraries with all

rights to over 1,000 films - also clip rights and clip search

Cinenova (Women's Film and Video Distribution)
113 Roman Road
London E2 0QN
Tel: 020 8981 6828
Fax: 020 8983 4441
email: admin@cinenova.demon.co.uk
Website: www.luton.ac.uk/cinenova/
Promotion and distribution of films and videos by women spanning 90 years of film-making from around the world

Concord Video and Film Council
201 Felixstowe Road
Ipswich, Suffolk IP3 9BJ
Tel: 01473 726012
Fax: 01473 274531
email: ericwalker@gn.apc.org
Lydia Vulliamy
Videos and films for hire/sale on domestic and international social issues - counselling, development, education, the arts, race and gender issues, disabilities, etc - for training and discussion. Also incorporates Graves Medical Audio Visual Library

CTVC Video
Hillside Studio, Merry Hill Road
Bushey
Watford WD2 1DR
Tel: 020 8950 4426
Fax: 020 8950 1437
Website: www.ourworld.compuserve.com/homepage/ctvc/
Christian, moral and social programmes

Derann Film Services
99 High Street
Dudley
West Mids DY1 1QP
Tel: 01384 233191/257077
Fax: 01384 456488
Website: www.danilo.demon.co.uk/
D Simmonds, S Simmonds
8mm package movie distributors; video production; bulk video duplication; laser disc stockist

Education Distribution Service
Education House
Castle Road
Sittingbourne

Kent ME10 3RL
Tel: 01795 427614
Fax: 01795 474871
email: eds@edist.co.uk
Distribution library for many clients
including film and video releases.
Extensive catalogue available

Educational and Television Films
247 Upper Street
London N1 1RU
Tel: 020 7226 2298
Fax: 020 7226 8016
Website: www.etvltd.demon.co.uk/
Documentary films from Eastern
Europe. Archive film library

Educational Media, Film & Video
235 Imperial Drive
Rayners Lane
Harrow HA2 7HE
Tel: 020 8868 1908/1915
Fax: 020 8868 1991
Lynda Morrell
Distributors of British and overseas
educational, health, training/safety
video games as well as new CD-
ROM titles. Act as agent for the
promotion of British productions
overseas. Free catalogue

Electricity Association Video Library
30 Millbank
London SW1P 4RD
Tel: 020 7963 5827
Fax: 020 7963 5800

Film Quest Ltd
71 (b) Maple Road
Surbiton
Surrey KT6 4AG
Tel: 020 8390 3677
Fax: 020 8390 1281
Booking agents for university, school
and private film societies

Filmbank Distributors
Grayton House
498-504 Fulham Road
London SW6 5NH
Tel: 020 7386 9909/5411
Fax: 020 7381 2405
Bookings Department
Filmbank represents all of the major
film studios for the non-theatrical
market (group screenings) and
distributes titles on either 16mm film
or video

First Take Ltd
19 Liddell Road
London NW6 2EW
Tel: 020 7328 4676

Golds
The Independent Home

Entertainment Wholesaler
Gold House
69 Flempton Street
Leyton
London E10 7NL
Tel: 020 8539 3600
Fax: 020 8539 2176
Contact: Garry Elwood, Sales &
Marketing Director
Gold product range ever increasing
multi-format selection including:
Audio cassettes, CDs, T-Shirts, DVD,
Spoken Word Cassettes and CDs,
Video, CD Rom, CDi, Video CD,
Laserdisc, computer games and
accessories to all formats. 42 years of
service and expertise 32 years spent
in home entertainment market

IAC (Institute of Amateur Cinematographers)
24c West Street, Epsom
Surrey KT18 7RJ
Tel: 01372 739672

Imperial War Museum
Film and Video Archive (Loans)
Lambeth Road
London SE1 6HZ
Tel: 020 7416 5000
Fax: 020 7416 5379
Brad King/Toby Haggith
Documentaries, newsreels and
propaganda films from the Museum's
film archive on 16mm, 35mm and
video

IUN Entertainment
Centre 500
500 Chiswick High Road
London W4 5RG
Tel: 020 8956 2454
Fax: 020 8956 2339

Leeds Animation Workshop (A Women's Collective)
45 Bayswater Row
Leeds LS8 5LF
Tel: 0113 248 4997
Fax: 0113 248 4997
Milena Dragic
Producers and distributors of
animated films on social issues

The Lux Centre
2-4 Hoxton Square
London N1 6NU
Tel: 020 7684 2782
Fax: 020 7684 1111
email: dist@lux.org.uk
Website: www.lea.org.uk
The Lux Centre house the
distribution collections of the former
London Film Makers' Co-op and
London Electronic Arts, with over
3,500 artists' films, videos and works
in new media, ranging from 1920s
animations by Len Lye through
classic avant garde films by Maya

Deren, Stan Brakhage and others, to
the latest work by international artists
such as Sadie Benning and John
Maybury

Melrose Film Productions
Dumbarton House
68 Oxford Street
London WIN OLH
Tel: 020 7627 8404
Fax: 020 7622 0421

National Educational Video Library
Arfon House
Bontnewydd
Caernarfon
Bangor
Gwynedd LL57 7NN
Tel: 01286 676001
Fax: 01286 676001
Supply of educational videotapes and
loan of sponsored videotapes and
film

National Film and Television School
Beaconsfield Studios
Station Road, Beaconsfield
Bucks HP9 1LG
Tel: 01494 671234
Fax: 01494 674042
Karin Farnworth

Open University Worldwide
The Berrill Building
Walton Hall
Milton Keynes MK7 6AA
Tel: 01908 858785
Fax: 01908 858787
email: D.M.Ruault@open.ac.uk

Post Office Video and Film Library
PO Box 145
Sittingbourne
Kent ME10 1NH
Tel: 01795 426465
Fax: 01795 474871
email: poful@edist.co.uk
Includes many video programmes
and supporting educational material
including curriculum guidelines. Also
a comprehensive range of extension
and other curriculum linked material.
TV rights available

Royal Danish Embassy
55 Sloane Street
London SW1X 9SR
Tel: 020 7333 0200
Fax: 020 7333 0270

RSPCA
Causeway
Horsham
West Sussex RH12 1HG
Tel: 01403 264181
Fax: 01403 241048

Sheila Graber Animation Limited
50 Meldon Avenue
South Shields
Tyne and Wear NE34 0EL
Tel: 0191 455 4985
Fax: 0191 455 3600
email: sheila@graber.demon.co.uk
Over 70 animated shorts available -
16mm, video and computer
interactive featuring a range of 'fun'
educational shorts on art, life, the
universe and everything. Producers
of interactive CD-Roms

The Short Film Bureau
68 Middle Street
Brighton BN1 1AL
Tel: 01273 235524/5
Fax: 01273 235528
email: Matt@shortfilmbureau.com
Specialising in the promotion and
distribution of short films for
theatrical and non-theatrical release
world wide

South West Arts
Bradninch Place
Gandy Street
Exeter EX4 3LS
Tel: 01392 218188
Fax: 01392 413554
Vikki Scott, Kirsty Hayes

Team Video Productions
Canalot
222 Kensal Road
London W10 5BN
Tel: 020 8960 5536
Fax: 020 8960 9784
Chris Thomas, Billy Ridgers
Producer and distributor of
educational video resources

THE (Total Home Entertainment)
National Distribution Centre
Rosevale Business Park
Newcastle-under-Lyme
Staffs ST5 7QT
Tel: 01782 566566
Fax: 01782 565400
Jed Taylor
Exclusive distribution for Quantum
Leap, ILC, Mollin Video, IMS,
Mistique Productions, Primetime
Promotions and distribution of over
6,000 other titles (see also Video
Labels)

Training Services
Brooklands House
29 Hythegate
Werrington
Peterborough PE4 7ZP
Tel: 01733 327337
Fax: 01733 575537
email: tipton@training

services.demon.co.uk
Distribute programmes from the
following producers:
3E's Training
Aegis Healthcare
Angel Productions
Barclays Bank Film Library
CCD Product & Design
Flex Training
Grosvenor Career Services
Hebden Lindsay Ltd
Kirby Marketing Associates
McPherson Marketing
Promotions Sound & Vision
Schwops Productions
Touchline Training Group
Video Communicators Pty
John Burder Films
Easy-i Ltd

TV Choice
22 Charing Cross Road
London WC2H 0HR
Tel: 020 7379 0873
Fax: 020 7379 0263

Vera Media
30-38 Dock Street
Leeds LS10 1JF
Tel: 0113 242 8646
Fax: 0113 242 8739
email: vera@vera-media.demon.co.uk
Website: www.vera.media.co.uk

Video Arts
Dumbarton House
68 Oxford Street
London W1N 0LH
Tel: 020 7637 7288
Fax: 020 7580 8103
Video Arts produces and exclusively
distributes the John Cleese training
films; Video Arts also distributes a
selection of meeting breaks from
Muppet Meeting Films TM as well as
Tom Peters programmes (produced
by Video Publishing House Inc) and
In Search of Excellence and other
films from the Nathan/Tyler Business
Video Library

Viewtech Film and Video
7-8 Falcons Gate
Northavon Business Centre
Dean Road Yate
Bristol BS37 5NH
Tel: 01454 858055
Fax: 01454 858056
email: info@viewtech.co.uk
Website: www.viewtech.co.uk
Safety films

Westbourne Film Distribution
1st Floor
17 Westbourne Park Road
London W2 5PX
Tel: 020 7221 1998
Fax: 020 7221 1998

Agents for broadcasting/video sales
for independent animators from
outside the UK, particularly Central
Eastern Europe. Classic children's
film *The Singing Ringing Tree*

The University of Westminster
School of Communications, Design
and Media
Harrow Campus
Northwick Park HA1 3TP
Tel: 020 7911 5003
Fax: 020 7911 5955
email: hwo6@wmin.ac
Applications: com.3@wmin.ac.uk

WFA
9 Lucy Street
Manchester M15 4BX
Tel: 0161 848 9782/5
Fax: 0161 848 9783
email:wfa@timewarp.com.uk

Yorkshire International Thomson Multimedia
Television Centre
Leeds LS3 1JS
Tel: 0113 222 8369
Fax: 0113 243 4884
email: yitminfo@yitm.co.uk
Distributor for many ITV companies,
including Yorkshire-Tyne Tees,
Thames, and Channel 4. Has an
educational catalogue, containing
videos and CD-Rom's, and further
industry catalogue, providing training
packages for companies

DISTRIBUTORS (THEATRICAL)

Alibi Communications
12 Maiden Lane
London WCZE 7NA
Tel: 020 7845 0430
Gareth Jones, Hilary Davis, Juliette Gill

Alliance Releasing
2nd Foor
184-192 Drummond Street
London NW1 3HP
Tel: 020 7391 6900
Fax: 020 7383 0404
Film distribution:
1998
Eve's Bayou
The Hanging Garden
Kitchen
The Governess
Hana Bi
Gadjo Dilo
Kiss or Kill
1999
eXistenZ
Cookie's Fortune
The Taste of Sunshine
The Room for Romeo Brass
Titanic Town
Bedrooms & Hallways
Seul Contre Tous
Besieged
Mifune
Sitcom
Following
Beautiful People

Apollo Film Distributors
14 Ensbury Park Road
Bournemouth BH9 2SJ
Tel: 01202 520962
Fax: 01202 539969

Arrow Film Distributors
18 Watford Road
Radlett
Herts WD7 8LE
Tel: 01923 858 306
Fax: 01923 859673
Website: www.arrowfilms.co.uk/

Artificial Eye Film Company
14 King Street
London WC2E 8HN
Tel: 020 7240 5353
Fax: 020 7240 5242
Robert Beeson, Sam Shinton
1998
The End of Violence
Clubbed to Death

La Maman et La Putain
Mrs Dalloway
Happy Together
Western
Taste of Cherry
Journey to the Beginning of the World
The Thief
Dance of the Wind
Psycho
Secret Defense
Love Is the Devil
Rien ne va Plus
The Eel
Year of the Horse
The Apple
1999
Affliction
Painted Angels
An Autumn Tale
Black Cat White Cat
Eternity and a Day
Touch of Evil
The Polish Bride
A la place du coeur
The Sacrifice
Late August, Early September
L'Argent
Place Vendôme
The Big Sleep
Pola X
The Scar
Alice et Martin

bfi Films
21 Stephen Street
London W1P 2LN
Tel: 020 7957 8905
Fax: 020 7580 5830
email: bookings@bfi.org.uk
Website: www.bfi.org.uk
Heather Stewart
Ultimate Hitchcock season at the NFT: opening fim *The Ring*, closing film *The Lodger*
First run: *The Man Who Knew Too Much*
Robert Bresson season includes: *Mouchette; Au Hasard Balthazar*
Akira Kurosawa season includes: *Yojimbo; Seven Samurai; Throne of Blood; The Hidden Fortress; Ikiru*
Releases 1999
To Have and Have Not
The Night of the Hunter
Get Carter
Croupier
Nights of Cabiria
Kes
Cat People/Curse of the Cat People

Releases 2000
A Matter of Life and Death

Blue Dolphin Film & Video
40 Langham Street
London W1N 5RG
Tel: 020 7255 2494
Fax: 020 7580 7670
Joseph D'Morais

Blue Light
231 Portobello Road
London W11 1LT
Tel: 020 79791
Fax: 020 79871
(See Made in Hong Kong)

Brian Jackson Films Ltd
39/41 Hanover Steps
St George's Fields
Albion Street
London W2 2YG
Tel: 020 7402 7543
Fax: 020 7262 5736

Buena Vista International (UK)
3 Queen Caroline Street
Hammersmith
London W6 9PE
Tel: 020 8222 1000
Fax: 020 8222 2795
Daniel Battsek

John Burder Films
7 Saltcoats Road
London W4 1AR
Tel: 020 8995 0547
Fax: 020 8995 3376
email: jburder@aol.com
Website: www.johnburder.co.uk
Broadcast TV programmes

Carlton Film Distributors
127 Wardour Street
London W1V 4AD
Tel: 020 7224 3339
Fax: 020 7434 3689
(Formerly Rank Film Distributors)

Cavalcade Films
Regent House
235-241 Regent Street
London W1R 8JU
Tel: 020 7734 3147
Fax: 020 7734 2403

Chain Production
2 Clanricarde Gardens
London W2 4NA
Tel: 020 7229 4277

Fax: 020 7229 0861
Specialist in European films and world cinema, cult classics, handling European Film Libraries with all rights to over 1,000 films - also clip rights and clip search

Children's Film Unit
Unit 8 Princeton Court
55 Felsham Road
London SW15
Tel: 020 8785 0350
Fax: 020 8785 0351
email: cfilmunit@aol.com

Cinenova
113 Roman Road
London E2 0QN
Tel: 020 8981 6828
Fax: 020 8983 4441
email: admin@cinenova.demon.co.uk
Website: www.luton.ac.uk/cinenova/
Promotion and distribution of women's film and video
B/Side
Deviant Beauty
Dialogues with Madwomen
Jodie: An Icon
A Life in a Day with Helena Goldwater
Mad, Bad and Barking
Sluts and Goddesses Video Workshop
True Blue Camper

City Screen
86 Dean Street
London W1V 5AA
Tel: 020 7734 4342
Fax: 020 7734 4027

Columbia TriStar Films (UK)
Europe House
25 Golden Square
London W1R 6LU
Tel: 020 7533 1111
Fax: 020 7533 1105
Feature releases from Columbia, TriStar, and Orion Pictures

Contemporary Films
24 Southwood Lawn Road
Highgate
London N6 5SF
Tel: 020 8340 5715
Fax: 020 8348 1238
Strangers on a Train
Battleship Potemkin

David Lamping Co
13 Berners Street
London W1P 3DE
Tel: 020 7580 0088
Fax: 020 7580 3468
David Lamping

Documedia International Films Ltd
Programme Sales/Acquistitions

19 Widegate Street
London E1 7HP
Tel: 020 7625 6200
Fax: 020 7625 7887
Disbributors of award winning drama specials, drama shorts and feature films for theatrical release, also video sales/Internet and video on demand.

Double: Take
21 St Mary's Grove
London SW13 0JA
Tel: 020 8788 5743
Fax: 020 8785 3050
Maya Kemp
Distributors and producers of children's TV and video
The Clangers
Crystal Tipps and Alistair
Fred Basset
Ivor the Engine
Willo the Wisp

Downtown Pictures Ltd
4th Floor, Suite 2
St Georges House
14-17 Wells Street
London W1P 3FP
Tel: 020 7323 6604
Fax: 020 7636 8090
Martin McCabe, Alan McQueen, Alan Latham, Anne Rigby

Electric Triangle
191 Portobello Road
London W11 2ED
Tel: 020 7792 2020
Fax: 020 7792 2617
Brian Bonaparte

Entertainment Film Distributors
27 Soho Square
London W1V 6HU
Tel: 020 7439 1606
Fax: 020 7734 2483

Eros International
Bollywood EROS network limited
Unit 26
Park Royal Metro Centre
Britannia Way
Coronation Road
London NW10 7PA
Tel: 020 8963 8778
Fax: 020 8963 8779
email:b4u@b4utv.com
Website:www.b4utv.com

Feature Film Company
68-70 Wardour Street
London W1V 3HP
Tel: 020 7734 2266
Fax: 020 7494 0309
Ulee's Gold
My Son the Fanatic
The Blackout
It's a Wonderful Life
Quadrophenia

Das Boot; the Director's Cut
Wild Man Blues
Gang Related

Film and Video Umbrella
2 Rugby Street
London WC1N 3QZ
Tel: 020 7831 7753
Fax: 020 7831 7746
email: fvu@fvu.co.uk
Promoting innovation with film and the electronic image

Film Four Distributors
76-78 Charlotte Street
London W1P 1LX
Tel: 020 7868 7700
Fax: 020 7868 7767
Website: www.filmfour.com

Gala
26 Danbury Street
Islington
London N1 8JU
Tel: 020 7226 5085
Fax: 020 7226 5897

GVI Distributors
2 King Street
Southall
 Middlesex UB2 4DA
Tel: 020 8813 8059
Fax: 020 8813 8062

Hemdale Communications
10 Avenue Studios, Sydney Close,
Chelsea
London SW3 6HW
Tel: 020 7581 9734
Fax: 020 7581 9735
The Legend of Wolf Mountain
Little Nemo - Adventures in Slumberland
The Magic Voyage
The Mighty Kong
Quest of the Delta Knights
Savage Land

ICA Projects
12 Carlton House Terrace
London SW1Y 5AH
Tel: 020 7873 0056
Fax: 020 7930 9686
email: projects@ica.org.uk
La vie de Jesus
Moment of Innocence
Hamam - The Turkish Bath
Afterlife
The Buttoners
Made in Hong Kong

Indy UK
Independent Feature Film Distributors
13 Mountview
Northwood
Middlesex HA6 3NZ
Tel: 07000 Indyuk (463985)
Fax: 0870 161 7339

email: indyuk@realit.demo.co.uk
The Scarlet Tunic
The Usual Children

Kino Kino!
76 Cheeseman's Terrace
London W14 9XG
Tel: 020 8 881 9463
Fax: 020 8 881 9463
email: vitaly@kinokino.u-net.com
Hands (dir Artur Aristakisyan)
released in 1998. *Brother* (dir Alexei
Balabaov)

Made in Hong Kong/Blue Light
231 Portobello Road
London W11 1LT
Tel: 020 7792 9791
Fax: 020 7792 9871
Made in Hong Kong releases the
finest in Hong Kong cinema
Bullet in the Head
Chinese Ghost Story
City on Fire
Days of Being Wild
Full Contact
Heroic Trio
The Killer
Saviour of the Soul
Blue Light distributes European and
other titles

Mainline Pictures
37 Museum Street
London WC1A 1LP
Tel: 020 7242 5523
Fax: 020 7430 0170

Manga Entertainment Ltd
40 St Peter's Road
London W6 9BD
Tel: 020 8748 9000
Fax: 020 8748 0841
Ghost in the Shell
Dancehall Queen
Razor Blade Smile
Gravesend
Perfect Blue

Mayfair Entertainment UK Ltd
110 St Martins Lane
London WC2N 4AD
Tel: 020 7304 7922
Fax: 020 7867 1121

Medusa Communications & Marketing Ltd
Regal Chambers, 51 Bancroft
Hitchin
Herts SG5 1LL
Tel: 01462 421818
Fax: 01462 420393

Metro Tartan Distribution Ltd
79 Wardour Street
London W1V 3TH

Tel: 020 7734 8508/9
Fax: 020 7287 2112
Drifting Clouds
Tierra
Deep Crimson
Kissed
Prisoner of the Mountain
Un air de famille
Les Voleurs
JunkMail
Ponette
Dobermann
Funny Games
To Have and to Hold

Metrodome Distribution
3rd Floor
25 Maddox Street
London W1R 9LE
Tel: 020 7408 2121
Fax: 020 7409 1935
Metrodome Distribution is part of the
Metrodome Group. The distribution
arm was set up in order to distribute
films that Metrodome Films
produces, as well as to actively
acquire and release another 8-10
films per year.
Buffalo '66
The Real Blonde
The Day Trippers
Human Traffic
The Bride of Chucky
Tango

Millivres Multimedia
Ground Floor
Worldwide House
116-134 Bayham St
London NW1 0BA
Tel. 020 7482 2576

Miracle Communications
38 Broadhurst Avenue
Edgware
Middx HA8 8TS
Tel: 020 8958 8512
Fax: 020 8958 5112
Martin Myers
Handles all First Independent titles

New Line International
25-28 Old Burlington Street
London W1X 1LB
Tel: 020 7440 1040
Fax: 020 7439 6118
Please see Entertainment Film
Distributors

Oasis Cinemas and Film Distribution
20 Rushcroft Road
Brixton
London SW2 1LA
Tel: 020 7733 8989
Fax: 020 7733 8790
email: oasiscinemas@compuserve
.co.uk
Laws of Gravity

The Lunatic
The Secret Rapture
Dance Hall Queen
Gravesend

Optimum Releasing
1st Floor
143 Charing Cross Road
London WC2M OEE
Tel: 020 7478 4466
Fax: 020 7734 3044

Pathé Distribution
Kent House
14-17 Market Place
Great Titchfield Street
London W1N 8AR
Tel: 020 7323 51 51
Fax: 020 7631 3568
Website: www.pathe.co.uk/

PD&B Films
68 Middle Street
Brighton
East Sussex BN1 1AL
Tel: 01273 235525
Fax: 01273 235528
email: info@pdbfilms.com
Website: www.pdbfilms.com

Pilgrim Entertainment
1 Richmond Mews
London W1
Tel: 020 7287 6314
Fax: 020 8961 6454
White Angel

Portman Entertainment
167 Wardour Street
London W1V 3TA
Tel: 020 7468 3400
Fax: 020 7468 3499
China Dream (TVM), *Crossmaheart*
(TVM), *Lucia* (feature), *Mayday*
(TVM), *Midnight Flight* (TVM),
Paranoia (feature), *Saving Grace*
(feature), *The Trench* (feature)

Poseidon Film Distributors
Hammer House
117 Wardour Street
London W1V 3TD
Tel: 020 7734 4441
Fax: 020 7437 0638
Autism
Dyslexia
Russian Composers - Writers
The Steal
Animation series The Bears
"The Odyssey"
The Night Witches

Redbus Film Distributors
53 Frith Street
London W1V 5TE
Tel: 020 7734 0890
Fax. 020 7734 0899
Website: www.films.redbus.co.uk

The Samuel Goldwyn Company
St George's House
14-17 Wells Street
London W1P 3FP
Tel: 020 7436 5105
Fax: 020 7580 6520
Angels and Insects
I Shot Andy Warhol
Reckless

Smoking Dogs Films
21b Brooksby Street
Islington
London N1 1EX
Tel: 020 7697 0747
Fax: 020 7697 0757
John AkomFrah, Lina Gopaul, David Lawson
Independent films
The Call of Mist (BBC Arts)
Goldie - When Saturn Returns (C4)
The Wonderful World of Louis Armstrong (BBC Omnibus)

Squirrel Films Distribution
119 Rotherhithe Street
London SE16 4NF
Tel: 020 7231 2209
Fax: 020 7231 2119
Slate of 6 feature films for children in preparation - release due November 1999

Supreme Film Distributors
3 Ferndown
Emerson Park
Hornchurch
Essex RM11 3JL
Tel: 01708 450352
Fax: 01708 470282

TKO Communications
PO Box 130
Hove, East Sussex BN3 6QU
Tel: 01273 550088
Fax: 01273 540969
email: jkruger02@aik,com
Gallavants (Gallavants)
3 Musketeers (Animated)
In Concert with Marvin Gaye
Jerry Lee Lewis - live in concert

Twentieth Century Fox Film Co
20th Century House
31-32 Soho Square
London W1V 6AP
Tel: 020 7437 7766
Fax: 020 7734 3187
Website: www.fox.co.uk/

UIP (United International Pictures (UK))
12 Golden Square
London W1A 2JL
Tel: 020 7534 5200
Fax: 020 7636 4118
Website: www.uip.com/

Releases product from Paramount, Universal, MGM/UA and SKG DreamWorks

United Media
68 Berwick Street
London W1V 3PE
Contact: Dena Blakeman
Tel: 020 7287 2396
Fax: 020 7287 2398

Universal Pictures International (UPI)
1 Sussex Place
Hammersmith
London W6 9QB
Tel: 020 8910 5000
Fax: 020 8910 5121

Warner Bros Distributors
98 Theobald's Road
London WC1X 8WB
Tel: 020 7984 5400
Website: www.warnerbros.com/
Nigel Sharrocks

Westbourne Film Distribution
1st Floor,
17 Westbourne Park Road
London W2 5PX
Tel: 020 7221 1998
Fax: 020 7221 1998
Agents for broadcasting/video sales for independent animators from outside the UK, particularly Central Eastern Europe. Classic children's film *The Singing Ringing Tree*

Winstone Film Distributors
18 Craignish Avenue
Norbury
London SW16 4RN
Tel: 020 8765 0240
Fax: 020 8765 0564
Mike.G.Ewin
Sub-distribution for Canal + Image UK Ltd)- Library only
1998
Girls Night
Kurt and Courtney
Mojo
Eskiya
Rothschild's Violin
Marquise
East Side Story
Left Luggage
Marie Baie des anges
Monk Dawson
1999
Insomnia
Classe de neige
The 39 Steps
Festen
High Art
Brylcreem Boys
Crush Proof
Via Satellite
Respect

Yashraj Films
3rd Floor Wembley Point
1 Harrow Road
Middlesex HA9 6DE
Tel: 0870 7397345
Fax: 0870 7397346
email:ukoffice@yashrajfilms.com
Website: www.yashraj.com

FACILITIES

Abbey Road Studios
3 Abbey Road
London NW8 9AY
Tel: 020 7 266 7000
Fax: 020 7 266 7250
Website: www.abbeyroad.co.uk/
Four studios; music to picture; 35mm
projection; film sound transfer
facilities; audio post-production.
Sonic Solutions computer sound
enhancement system; residential
accommodation, restaurant and bar.
Multimedia design and authoring,
dvd authoring

AFM Lighting Ltd
Waxlow Road
London NW10 7NU
Tel: 020 8233 7000
Fax: 020 8233 7001
Gary Wallace
Lighting equipment and crew hire;
generator hire

After Image Facilities
32 Acre Lane
London SW2 5SG
Tel: 020 7737 7300
Fax: 020 7326 1850
email: Jane@arc.co.uk
Jane Thorburn
Full broadcast sound stage - Studio A
(1,680 sq ft, black, chromakey, blue,
white cyc) and insert studio (730 sq
ft hard cyc). Multiformat broadcast
on-line post production. Special
effects - Ultimatte/blue screen

Air Studios
Lyndhurst Hall, Lyndhurst Road
Hampstead
London NW3 5NG
Tel: 020 7794 0660
Fax: 020 7794 8518
Alison Burton
Lyndhurst Hall: capacity - 500 sq m
by 18m high with daylight; 100 plus
musicians; four separation booths.
Full motion picture scoring facilities.
Neve VRP Legend 72ch console,
flying fader automation. LCRS
monitoring. Studio 1: capacity - 60
sq m with daylight. 40 plus
musicians. Neve/Focusrite 72ch
console; GML automation; LCRS
monitoring. Studio 2: Mixing Room;
SSL8000G plus series console with
Ultimation; ASM system. Film and
TV dubbing facilities; two suites
equipped with AMS Logic II

consoles; 16 output; AudioFile
spectra plus; LCRS monitoring.
Exabyte back-up. One suite equipped
with an AMS Logic III console.
Every tape machine format available

Alphabet Communications
Parkgate Industrial Estate
Knutsford
Cheshire WA16 8DX
Tel: 01565 755678
Fax: 01565 634164
email: info@alphabet.co.uk
Digital Beta on line digital edit
suites,
Charisma DVE
Aston Motif caption generator
Sony 6000 vision switcher
Sony 9100 edit controller
Beta SP component edit suite
Avid 800 offline 18Gbyte memory
2D Computer graphic Pixell Collage
3D Computer graphics Softimage 3D
Extreme Mental Ray render
Standards conversion
All tape formats available
Commentary recording and rostrum
camera
1800sq ft drive in studio
Crews
Digital Beta DVW700P 16: 9 & 4:3
camera
Beta SP
VHS Duplication
Authoring of Interactive CD ROM
packages
Website building
CD ROM duplication services

Angel Recording Studios
311 Upper Street
London N1 2TU
Tel: 020 7354 2525
Fax: 020 7226 9624
Gloria Luck
Two large orchestral studios with
Neve desks, and one small studio. All
with facilities for recording to picture

Anvil Post Production Ltd
Denham Studios
North Orbital Road, Denham
Uxbridge
Middx UB9 5HL
Tel: 01895 833522
Fax: 01895 835006
email: *@anvil.nildram.co.uk
Sound completion service; re-
recording, ADR, post-sync, Fx
recording, transfers, foreign version

dubbing; non-linear and film editing
rooms, neg cutting, off-line editing,
production offices

ARRI Lighting Rental
20a The Airlinks,
Spitfire Way,
Heston,
Middx TW5 9NR
Tel: 020 8561 6700
Fax: 020 8569 2539
Tim Ross
Lighting equipment hire

Jim Bambrick and Associates
William Blake House
8 Marshall Street
London W1V 2AJ
Tel: 020 7434 2351
Fax: 020 7734 6362
6 x Avid Editing Suite with versions
6.5 software, 35mm Steinbeck

Barcud
Cibyn
Caernarfon
Gwynedd LL55 2BD
Tel: 01286 671671
Fax: 01286 671679
Video formats: 1"C, Beta SP, D2 OB
Unit 1: up to 7 cameras 4VTR OB
Unit 2: up to 10 cameras 6VTR,
DVE, Graphics Betacam units.
Studio 1: 6,500 sq ft studio with
audience seating and comprehensive
lighting rig. Studio 2: 1,500 sq ft
studio with vision/lighting control
gallery and sound gallery. Three edit
suites; two graphics suites, one with
Harriet. DVE: three channels
Charisma, two channels Cleo. Two
Sound post-production suites with
AudioFile and Screen Sound; BT
lines. Wales' leading broadcast
facility company can supply OB
units, studios, Betamac Kits (all fully
crewed if required) and full post
production both on and off-line

Bell Digital Facilities
Lamb House
Church Street
Chiswick Mall
London W4 2PD
Tel: 020 8996 9960
Fax: 020 8996 9966
email: sales@bel-media.co
ProTools IV sound dubbing studio
with non-linear picture. VocAlign &

other ADR and outboard tools. Voice booth accessible from all suites. Extensive 3D animation & 2D graphics studio. Sound proofed, air-conditioned. 600 sq ft video studio available as 4-waller or with cameras. Avid off and on-line and After Effects

Blue Post Production
58 Old Compton Street
London W1V 5PA
Tel: 020 7437 2626
Fax: 020 7439 2477
Contact: Catherine Spruce, Director of Marketing
Digital Online Editing with Axial edit controllers, GVG 4000 digital vision mixers, Kaleidoscope DVEs, disc recorders, Abekas A72, digital audio an R-Dat
Quantel Edit Box 4000 with 2 hours non-compressed storage
Sound Studio with Avid Audio Vision, 32 input MTA fully automated desk
Offline Editing on Avid Media Composer 800
Telecine Ursa Diamond System, incorporating Pogle Platinium DCP with ESR & TWiGi

BUFVC
77 Wells Street
London W1P 3RE
Tel: 020 7393 1500
Fax: 020 7393 1555
email: bufvc@open.ac.uk
16mm video steenbeck plus 35mm and 16mm viewing facilities.
Betacam 2 machine edit facility for low-cost assembly off-line work

Canalot Production Studios
222 Kensal Road
London W10 5BN
Tel: 020 8960 8580
Fax: 020 8960 8907
Nieves Heathcote
Media business complex housing over 80 companies, involved in TV, film, video and music production, with boardroom to hire for meetings, conferences and costings

Capital FX
21A Kingly Court
London W1R 5LE
Tel: 020 7439 1982
Fax: 020 7734 0950
Graphic design and production, laser subtitling, opticals effects and editing

Capital Studios
Wandsworth Plain
London SW18 1ET
Tel: 020 8877 1234
Fax: 020 8877 0234
Central London: 3,000 and 2,000 sq

ft fully equipped broadcast standard television studios. 16x9/4x3 switchable, two on-line edit suites (D3, D2, D5, Digital Betacam & Beta SP). Avid on/off line editing. Multi track and digital sound dubbing facilities with commentary booth. 'Harriet' graphics suite. BT lines. All support facilities. Car park. Expert team, comfortable surroundings

Chromacolour International Ltd
11-16 Grange Mills
Weir Road
London SW12 0NE
Tel: 020 8675 8422
Fax: 020 8675 8499
Animation supplies/equipment

Cinebuild
Studio House
Rita Road
Vauxhall
London SW8 1JU
Tel: 020 7582 8750
Fax: 020 7793 0467
Special effects: rain, snow, fog, mist, smoke, fire, explosions; lighting and equipment hire. Studio: 200 sq m

Cinecontact
27 Newman Street
London W1P 4AR

Tel: 020 7323 0618
Fax: 020 7323 1215
Contact: Jacqui Timberlake
Documentary film-makers. Avid post
production facilities

Cinesite (Europe) Ltd
9 Carlisle Street
London W1V 5RG
Tel: 020 7973 4000
Fax: 020 7973 4040
Website: www.cinesite.com
Utilising state-of-the art technology,
Cinesite provides expertise in every
area of resolution-free digital
imaging and digital special effects for
feature films. Our creative and
production teams offer a full
spectrum of services from the
storyboard to the final composite,
including digital effects, and shoot
supervision. Credits include: *Devil's
Advocate, Air Force One, Event
Horizon, Tommorrow Never Dies,
Batman and Robin, Jerry Maguire,
Space Jam, Smilla's Sense of Snow*

Colour Film Services Group
10 Wadsworth Road
Perivale
Middx UB6 7JX
Tel: 020 8998 2731
Fax: 020 8997 8738

Communicopia Ltd
The Old Town Hall
Albion Street
Southwick
West Sussex BN42 4AX
Tel: 01273 278575
Fax: 01273 416082
email: info@communicopia.co.uk
Website: www.communicopia.co.uk
Post production facility. Includes:
Fast 601 non-linear video post
production suite. Broadcast quality
MPEG2 601. GEM WK4 music
workstation. Voice-over sound suite.
Digital sound mixer. Track laying
and audio mixing to picture.
Broadcast standard, non-linear
editing. 3D effect/DVE. Unlimited
layering , all with colour correction,
keying and DVE. High-speed
background rendering . 36 Gigabytes
of media storage. Huge picture
library. Lightwave 5 graphics system.
3D full-featured animation system.
CD ROM, CD Burner and CD
Players. DAT player/recorder. VHS
and S-VHS recorders. Music and
sound effects library. Zip dives. ISDN

Complete
Slingsby Place
Off Long Acre
London WC2E 9AB
Tel: 020 7379 7739
Fax: 020 7497 9305

email: info@complete.co.uk
Richard Ireland,
Richard Ireland, Lucy Pye, Sarah
Morgan, Lisa Sweet and Holly Ryan
Henry, Flame, Harriet. Digital
editing. C-reality-Hires-Telecine. 3D
Animation with Alias wave front and
soft/maxDigital Ursa Diamond
Telecine with Russell Square DI tape
grading. Digital playouts and ISDN
links

Connections Communications Centre
Palingswick House
241 King Street
Hammersmith
London W6 9LP
Tel: 020 8741 1766
Fax: 020 8593 9134
email: Info@cccmedia.demon.co.uk
Website: www.cccmedia.demon.
co.uk
Production Equipment
BETA SP, DV, DVCPRO, SVHS
cameras. Wide range of lighting and
sound including SQN stereo mixer
and portable D.A.T.
Post Production Equipment
Avid Xpress Deluxe Non-Linear Edit
system. BETA SP 3 machine suite
with computerised edit controller
SVHS on-line and off-line editing

Corinthian Television Facilities (CTV)
87 St John's Wood Terrace
London NW8 6PY
Tel: 020 7483 6000
Fax: 020 7483 4264
Website: www.ctv.co.uk
OBs: Multi-camera and multi-VTR
vehicles. Post Production: 3 suites, 1
SP component, 2 multi-format with
1", D2, D3, Abekas A64, A72, Aston
and colour caption camera. Studios: 2
fully equipped television studios (1 in
St John's Wood, 1, in Piccadilly
Circus), 1-5 camera, multi-format
VTRs, BT lines, audience seating.
Audio: SSL Scrrensound digital
audio editing and mixing system

Dateline Productions
79 Dean Street
London W1V 5HA
Tel: 020 7437 4510
Fax: 020 7287 1072
Avid non-linear editing

De Lane Lea Sound Centre
75 Dean Street
London W1V 5HA
Tel: 020 7439 1721
Fax: 020 7437 0913
2 high speed 16/35mm Dolby stereo
dubbing theatres with Dolby SR;
high speed ADR and FX theatre

(16/35mm and NTSC/PAL video);
Synclavier digital FX suite; digital
dubbing theatre with Logic 2
console; 3 x AudioFile preparation
rooms; sound rushes and transfers;
video transfers to VHS and U-Matic;
Beta rushes syncing. 24 cutting
rooms/offices. See also under studios

Denman Productions
60 Mallard Place
Strawberry Vale
Twickenham TW1 4SR
Tel: 020 8891 3461
Fax: 020 8891 6413
Video and film production, including
3D computer animation and web
design

Diverse Production
6 Gorleston Street
London W14 8XS
Tel: 020 7603 4567
Fax: 020 7603 2148
Ray Nunney
TV post-production. Digital on-line
editing; off-line editing;
comprehensive graphic design
service; titles sequences, programme
graphics, generic packaging, sets and
printwork

Dolby Laboratories
Wootton Bassett
Wilts SN4 8QJ
Tel: 01793 842100
Fax: 01793 842101
Cinema processors for replay of
Dolby Digital, and Dolby SR
(analogue) film soundtracks; audio
noise reduction equipment. Sound
consultancy relating to Dolby film
productions and Dolby Surround
productions for television

Dubbs
25-26 Poland Street
London W1V 3DB
Tel: 020 7629 0055
Fax: 020 7287 8796
email: customer_services@dubbs.
co.uk
Website: www.dubbs.co.uk
Videotape duplication: All digital
formats; BeatSP 1", BVU SP, SVHS,
VHS, U-matic, Hi-8 and Video 8.
Standards Conversion: Alchemist Ph
C, Adac, Tetra. Audio: Tascam
DA88, DAT, Audio cassette. Full
labelling, packing and despatch
service available

Edinburgh Film and Video Productions
Edinburgh Film and TV Studios
Nine Mile Burn
By Penlculk
Midlothian EH26 9LT
Tel: 01968 672131

Fax: 01968 672685
Stage: 50 sq m; 16/Super 16/35mm
cutting rooms; preview theatre; edge
numbering; lighting grip equipment
hire; scenery workshops

Edinburgh Film Workshop Trust
29 Albany Street
Edinburgh EH1 3QN
Tel: 0131 557 5242
Fax: 0131 557 3852
email: post@efwt.demon.co.uk
Website: www.efwt.demon.co.uk
Production and post-production on
tape and film. Umbrella production
for new producers and consultancy to
individuals and organisations

Edric Audio-visual Hire
34-36 Oak End Way
Gerrards Cross
Bucks SL9 8BR
Tel: 01753 884646
Fax: 01753 887163
Audiovisual and video production
facilities

Elstree Light and Power
Millennium Studios
Elstree Way
Borehamwood
Herts WD6 1SF
Tel: 020 8236 1300

Fax: 020 8236 1333
Tony Slee
TV silent generators; Twin Sets HMI,
MSR and Tungsten Heads.
Distribution to BS 5550.Rigging
Specialists

Faction Films
28-29 Great Sutton Street
London EC1V 0DU
Tel: 020 7608 0654/3
Fax: 020 7608 2157
Avid MC1000 composer; Montage
22 suite; 6 plate 16mm Steenbeck
edit suite; Low-band U-matic suite;
Sony VX1000 digi-cam; Sony Hi-8;
HHB Portadat; Nagra 4.2; Production
office space; Experienced Editors and
Sound recordist available

The Film Centre
Leathermarket
Weston Street
London SE1
Tel: 020 7261 1115 or 0700
FILMCENTRE (345623)
Fax: 0118 961 7392
email: info@filmcentre.co.uk
35/16mm Camera Equipment hire,
primarily to the independent sector.
Also film editing and off-line hire,
rostrum, lighting truck, audio
equipment, film/video projectors,
multimedia authoring. Production

office and crewing facilities.
Film Centre Shop: one stop for stock
and consumables

The Film Factory at VTR
64 Dean Street
London W1V 5HG
Tel: 020 7437 0026
Fax: 020 7494 0059
email: info@vtr.co.uk
Website: www.filmfactory.com
The Film Factory at VTR is one of
London's major feature film post
production facilities specialising in
high-resolution digital special effects.
Creative teams cover all aspects of
feature visual post production work
including special effects filming,
extensive CGI work, and high
resoultion compositing. The Domino
system is an inegral part of The Film
Factory. Already proven for its
extensive US work on Independence
Day, the Domino is an ideal and
versatile medium for 35mm high
resolution compositing at 3,000 lines.
Experienced producer teams, one of
the largest CGI feature film units in
the UK and highly-experienced
Domino high-resolution compositing
teams, make the Film Factory one of
the most exciting feature film post
production facilities in London

Film Work Group
Top Floor, Chelsea Reach
79-89 Lots Road
London SW10 0RN
Tel: 020 7352 0538
Fax: 020 7351 6479
Loren Squires, Nigel Perkins
Video and Film post-production
facilities. AVID on-line (2:1) and off-
line editing. 36 gigs storage, Digital
Animation Workstations (draw, paint,
image, modification, edit). 3 machine
Hi-Band SP and mixed Beta SP/Hi-
Band with DVE. 2 machine Lo-Band
off-line with sound mixing. 6 plate
Steenbeck. Special rates for grant
aided, self-funded and non-profit
projects

FinePoint Broadcast
Furze Hill
Kingswood
Surrey KT20 6EZ
Tel: 01737 370033
Fax: 01737 370088
email: hire@finepoint.co.uk
Website: www.finepoint.co.uk
Broadcast equipment hire. Cameras,
lenses, control units, cables, VTRs,
edit controllers, digital video effects,
vision mixers, monitors, sound kit,
full outside broadcast unit

Fisher Productions Europe Ltd
Studio House
Rita Road
Vauxhall
London SW8 1JU
Tel: 020 7582 8750
Fax: 020 7793 0467
(See Cinebuild)

FrameStore
9 Noel Street
London W1V 4AL
Tel: 020 7208 2600
Fax: 020 7208 2626
email:mandy.wells@framestore.co.uk
Website: www.framestore.co.uk
Digital effects for film and video.
The latest technology, including Ursa
Diamond Telecine, 2x inferno/flame,
4x Henry, Digital Edit Suite, 3D
Computer Animation, Avid Editing
for commercials, broadcast and
graphic design projects. Plus digital
film opticals for feature effects,
repairs, pick-ups, restoration, titles
and tape to film transfers. Call
bookings or post-producers: Fiona,
Lottie, AJ and Drew for advice on
projects

Mike Fraser
Unit 6
Silver Road
White City Industrial Park
London W12 7SG

Tel: 020 8749 6911
Fax: 020 8743 3144
Mike Fraser
Mike Fraser, Rod Wheeler
Telecine transfer 35mm, 16mm and
S16; rushes syncing; non-linear edit
suites; film video list management,
post-production through OSC/R to
negative cutting. Storage

Frontline Television Services
44 Earlham Street
Covent Garden
London WC2H 9LA
Tel: 020 7836 0411
Fax: 020 7379 5210
Charlie Sayle
Extensive edit, duplication, computer
animation and multimedia facilities -
5 Avid Media Composers, Avid
Symphony, DS, Linear Digital
Betacam Suite. Low volume, low
cost, quick turnaround duplication.
2D and 3D animation and graphics.
Multimedia facilities including
encoding

FX Projects
Studio House
Rita Road
Vauxhall
London SW8 1JU
Tel: 020 7582 8750
Fax: 020 7793 0467
(See Cinebuild)

General Screen Enterprises
Highbridge Estate
Oxford Road
Uxbridge
Middx UB8 1LX
Tel: 01895 231931
Fax: 01895 235335
Pinewood Studios
Iver Heath
Bucks SL0 0NH
Tel: 01753 650260
Fax: 01753 650259
Studio: 100 sq m. 16mm, 35mm
opticals including matting, aerial
image work, titling, editing, trailers,
promos, special effects, graphics.
Cineon Digital Fx Unit, Film
Opticals, Motion Control Stage,
VistaVision; computerised rostrum
animation motion control; video
suite; preview theatre

Goldcrest Post Production
Facilities Ltd
Entrance 1 Lexington Street
36/44 Brewer Street
London W1R 3HP
Tel: 020 7439 4177 or 020 7437
7972
Fax: 020 7437 5402
email:mailbox@goldcrest-post.co.uk
John Spirit
John Spirit, Louise Seymour

Theatre One with SSL5000 console,
Dolby SRD, film + video projection;
Theatre Two with Harrison Series 12
Console & Synclavier 9600 16 track
direct to disk; Dolby SRD ADR +
effects recording, built-in Foley
surfaces and extensive props; AMS
AUDIOFILE suite with Yamaha
digital desk; SOUND TRANSFER
BAYS all film and video formats
with Dolby SRD; Rank Cintel
MKIIC TELECINE enhanced 4:2:2,
Pogle and secondary colour
correction. Keycode + Aaton code
readers, Electronic Wetgate; Video
transfers to 1", Beta SP, U-Matics,
VHS and D2, ADAC standards
conversion. Non Linear editing Avid
or Lightworks available. 40 Cutting
Rooms; Production offices; Duplex
apartments available

Headline Video Facilities
3 Nimrod Way
Elgar Road
Reading
Berks RG2 0EB
Tel: 0118 975 1555
Fax: 0118 986 1482
email: post@headlinevideo.demon.
co.uk
Tom Street
Talented and experienced designers
and editors who create and produce
quality Broadcast graphics and
editing. Quantel Hal Express, Harriet
and 3D Studio Max with fully
integrated Highly Specified Digital
Betacam and Beta SP editing suites.
Avid and VHS offline, duplication
and standards conversion

Hillside Studios
Merry Hill Road
Bushey
Herts WD2 1DR
Tel: 020 8950 7919
Fax: 020 8421 8085
email: hillside@ctvc.co.uk
Website: www.ctvc.co.uk
Production and Post-Production
facilities to Broadcast standards.
1500 sq ft studio with 16 x 9
switchable cameras and Digital
Mixer. Smaller studio and single
camera location units available.
Sounds Studios and Dubbing Suites,
Non-Linear and Digital Editing.
Graphics, Set Design and
Construction. Offices, restaurant and
parking

Holloway Film & TV
68-70 Wardour Street
London W1V 3HP
Tel. 020 7494 0777
Fax: 020 7494 0309
Matt Stoddart

D5, D3, D2, Digital Betacam, 3 m/c
Digital Betacam suite, AVID
(AVRTT) on-line/Offline. Betacam
SP, 1"C, BVU, Lo-Band Hi-8,
Video-8, S-VHS, VHS, Standards
Conversion, Audio Laybacks/Layoffs

Hull Time Based Arts
8 Posterngate
Hull HU1 2JN
Tel: 01482 586340
Fax: 01482 589952
email: lab@htba.demon.co.uk
Website: www.htba.demon.co.uk
Avid Media Composer 8000 on line
digital non linear video editing suite.
Avid Media Composer 400 off line
digital non linear video editing suites.
DVC Pro and DV video cameras.
DAT recorders, Video/Data projectors
and all anciliary video equipment
available. Special rates for non
commercial projects

Humphries Video Services
Unit 2, The Willow Business
Centre
17 Willow Lane
Mitcham
Surrey CR4 4NX
Tel: 020 8648 6111/020 7636 3636
Fax: 020 8648 5261
email: sales@hvs.bdx.co.uk
Website: www.hvs.co.uk

David Brown, Emma Lincoln
Video cassette duplication: all
formats, any standard. Standards
convertors. Macrovision anti-copy
process, labelling, shrink wrapping,
packaging and mail out services, free
collections and deliveries in central
London. Committed to industrial and
broadcast work

ITN
200 Gray's Inn Road
London WC1X 8XZ
Tel: 020 7430 4134
Fax: 020 7430 4655
Martin Swain
Martin Swain, Jenny Mazzey
2400 sq ft studio; live or recorded
work; comprehensive outside source
ability; audience 65; crews; video
transfer; Westminster studio; graphics
design service using Flash Harry,
Paintbox etc; Training offered; Sound
and dubbing; tape recycling;
experienced staff

Terry Jones PostProductions Ltd
The Hat Factory
16-18 Hollen Street
London W1V 3AD
Tel: 020 7434 1173
Fax: 020 7494 1893
Terry Jones

Paul Jones or Matt Nutley
Lightworks V.I.P. online and
Heavyworks editing suites. Plus
computerised Beta offline and 35mm
film editing facilities. Experiencd and
creative, award winning editors
handling commercials,
documentaries, features and
corporate work

Lee Lighting
Wycombe Road
Wembley
Middlesex HAO 1QD
Tel: 020 8900 2900
Fax: 020 8902 5500
Website: www.lee.co.uk
Film/TV lighting equipment hire

Light House Media Centre
The Chubb Buildings
Fryer Street
Wolverhampton WV1 1HT
Tel: 01902 716044
Fax: 01902 717143
Contact: Technical department
Three machine U-Matic edit suite
(hi-band - BVE 900, lo-band BVE
600) VHS/U-Matic/Betacam/ENG
kits, also animation and chroma
keying

Lighthouse
Brighton Media Centre

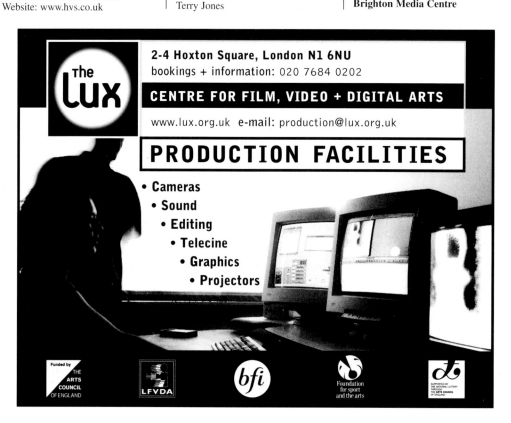

9-12 Middle Street
Brighton BN1 1AL
Tel: 01273 384222 Facilities: 01273
384255
Fax: 01273 384233
email: info@lighthouse.org.uk
Jane Finnis
Jane Finnis, Caroline Freeman
A training and production centre,
providing courses, facilities and
production advice. Avid off- and
online edit suites. Apple Mac
graphics and animation workstations.
Digital video capture &
manipulation. Output to/from
Betacam SP. SVHS offline edit suite.
Post Production and Digital Artists
equipment bursaries offered three
times a year

The Lux Centre
Lux Production Facilities
f2-4 Hoxton Square
London N1 6NU
Tel: 020 7684 0101
Fax: 020 7684 1111
email: facilities@lux.org.uk
Subsidised facilities for film, video
and digital media production. 8mm &
16mm film cameras, digital video
cameras, film and multi-format video
editing, online and offline. Avids,
Telecine and video transter, digital
audio editing, multimedia and
Internet workstations, graphics,
animation and much more. LCD
video projectors, monitors and
playback equipment for exhibition
and events. Optical Printer for gauge
transfers, colouring and all kinds of
optical manipulation of film: Macs
with Adobe Premiere for editing and
Macromedia Director for interactive
multimedia authoring: state of the art
Avid editing suite: 16mm black and
white film processing: Super 8,
16mm and Super 16 camera kits;
Lighting including standard blonde
and redhead kits and the latest
Dedolight and Kino Flo Kits;
Analogue editing suites with
Steenbecks, plus a rare Super 8
Steenbeck; sound transfer room;
Rostrum Camera for animation, titles
and effects; broadcast quality
Telecine

MAC Sound Hire
1-2 Attenburys Park
Park Road
Altrincham
Cheshire WA14 5QE
Tel: 0161 969 8311
Fax: 0161 962 9423
Professional sound equipment hire

The Machine Room
54-58 Wardour Street
London W1V 3HN

Tel: 020 7734 3433
Fax: 020 7287 3773
David Atkinson
2 wet/dry gate digital Telecine suites
with DVNR. VT viewing and sound
layback suite. Most digital and
analogue video tape formats in both
PAL and NTSC. Standards
conversion with Alchemist Phc and
Vector Motion Compensation
(VMC). Programme dubbing. VHS
duplication. Macrovision anti-piracy
system, 2 edit suites. FACT
accredited. Special rates for archive
film transferFull range of film
treatment services. See also Film
Treatment Centre under Laboratories.
Nitrate handling and nitrate storage
vaults. DVD Authoring and encoding

Metro Broadcast
6-7 Great Chapel Street
London W1V 3AG
Tel: 020 7439 3494
Fax: 020 7437 3782
Mark Cox
Nayle Kemah
Broadcast Hire: Avid: MCO, Film
compsers, 9000,
Camera formats - Digital Beta, Beta
SX, Beta SP, DVC Pro, DV Cam,
Mini DV. VTRs, D2, D3, D5, DVW
A500 Broadcast crews available.
Duplication: Alchemist standards
conversion from/to all formats.
Technical assessment. Format
include: D1, D2, D3, Digital Beta,
Beta SX, DVC Pro DV Cam mini
DV. CD ROM, DVD

The Mill/Mill Film
40/41 Great Marlborough Street
London W1V 1DA
Tel: 020 7287 4041
Fax: 020 7287 8393
Dan Macey
Post Production for commercials and
feature films using Spirit, Ursa,
Inferno, Flame, Cineon, Henry, Harry
and digital editing

Millennium Studios
Elstree Way
Borehamwood
Herts WD6 1SF
Tel: 020 8236 1400
Fax: 020 8236 1444
Kate Tufano
Sound stage 80'x44'x24' with
6'x44'x11' balcony flying and cyc
grid. In house suppliers of: lighting;
generators; rigging; photography;
crew catering and fully licensed bar

Mister Lighting Studios Ltd
2 Dukes Road
Western Avenue
London W3 0SL

Tel: 020 8956 5600
Fax: 020 8956 5604
Steve Smith
Lighting equipment/studio hire

Molinare
34 Fouberts Place
London W1V 2BH
Tel: 020 7439 2244
Fax: 020 7734 6813
Video formats: Digital Betacam, D1,
D2, D3, 1", Beta SP, BVU, U-Matic,
VHS. NTSC: 1", Beta SP, U-Matic &
VHS. Editing: Editbox, three D1
serial digital suite; two component
multi-format; one composite multi-
format. DVEs: two A57, four A53,
DME, four ADO, Encore. Storage:
two A66, A64. Caption Generators:
Aston Motif, A72, Aston Caption,
Aston 3. Graphics: Harry with V7
Paintbox, Encore and D1. Harriet
with V7 Paintbox, D1 and Beta SP.
3D graphics with Silicon Graphics
and Softimage. Telecine: Ursa Gold
with Pogle + DCP, A57, Rank Cintel
111 with 4.2.2 digital links, wetgate,
Pogle and DCP controller and
secondary colour grading, 35mm,
16mm, S16mm/S8. Audio: two
digital studios, two 24 track and
AudioFile studios, track-laying studio
with DAWN, voice record studios,
transfer room, sound Fx libraries.
Duplication, standards conversion,
Matrix camera, BT landlines, satellite
downlink

The Moving Picture Company
127 Wardour Street
London W1V 4AD
Tel: 020 7434 3100
Fax: 020 7437 3951/287 5187
Video formats: D1, D2, Digital
Betacam, Betacam SP, 1" C format,
hi-/lo-band.
Editing: 3xD1/Disk based edit suites,
Sony 9100 and Abekas A84 (8
layers) A57 DVE, A64, A60 and A66
Disks; A72 and Aston Motif caption
generator. Video Rostrum and Colour
Caption Camera
Non Linear Offline Editing: 1 x Avid
4000 with Betacam SP. 35/16mm
cutting room
Telecine: 2 URSA Gold 4 x 4 with
Pogle DCP/Russell Square Colour
Correction Jump Free, Low
Speed/Silk Scan Options, Matchbox
Stills Store, Key Code, noise
reduction
SFX: Discreet Logic 2 x Flame, 1 x
Flint and Quantel 2 x Henry
3D: Hardware: 7 x SGI systems (3 x
High Impacts and 4 x Indigo 2
Extremes). Software: Alias
Poweranimator, Custom

Programming and Procedural Effects, Matador, 3D Studio Paint, Elastic Reality and Pandemonium. Rendering: SGI Challenge and Onyx (x2). Digital Film: High resolution 35mm digital film post production, comprising 7 x Kodak Cineon, 1 x Discreet Logic Inferno and Matador. Filmtel TM video tape to 35mm transfer. Mac: Disk or ISDN input of artwork. File transfer, Photoshop and Illustrator and stills output to 35mm or high resolution 5 x 4 transparencies
Studio: 47' x 30' with L cyc

Northern Light
35/41 Assembly Street
Leith
Edinburgh EH6 7RG
Tel: 0131 553 2383
Fax: 0131 553 3296
Gordon Blackburn
Stage lighting equipment hire. Mains distribution, staging, PA equipment hire. Sale of colour correction pyrotechnics etc

Oasis Television
6-7 Great Pulteney Street
London W1V 3LF
Tel: 020 7434 4133
Fax: 020 7494 2843
Helen Leicester
14 online suites (including digital linear, analogue linear, Jaleo Digital, Non-linear, Avid Online). 2 fully digital audiodubbing suites. 11 Avid and Lightworkds offline services. 5 graphics suites C2D and 3D, including illusion), standards conversion. Full duplication facilities multimedia

Ocean Post
5 Upper James Street
London W1R 3HF
Tel: 020 7287 2297
Fax: 020 7287 0296
email: bookings@oceanpost.co.uk
Editbox suite, Avid online suites, Avid offline suites

Omnititles
28 Manor Way
London SE3 9EF
Tel: 020 8297 7877
Fax: 020 8297 7877
email: Omnititles@compuserve.com
Spotting and subtitling services for film, TV, video, satellite and cable. Subtitling in most world languages

Oxford Film and Video Makers
The Stables
North Place
Headington
Oxford OX3 7RF

Tel: 01865 741682 or 01865 60074 (course enquiries)
Fax: 01865 742901
email: ofvm@ox39hy.demon.co.uk
Film and video equipment hire - including Beta SP and non-linear editing facility (FAST). Wide range of evening and weekend courses

Panavision Grips
5-11 Taunton Road
Metropolitan Centre
Greenford
Middx UB6 8UQ
Tel: 020 8578 2382
Fax: 020 8578 1536
email: pangrip.co.uk
Grip equipment and studio hire
The Greenford Studios
5-11 Taunton road
Metropolitan Centre
Greenford Middx UB6 8UQ
Tel: 020 8575 7300
Fax: 020 8839 1640

The Pierce Rooms
Pierce House
Hammersmith Apollo
Queen Caroline Street
London W6 9QH
Tel: 020 8563 1234
Fax: 020 8563 1337
Complete surround sound facilities: surround sound to picture recording. Foley and mixing. Large and accurate main control room - Neve VR 72-60 console with flying fader automation, recall and digital surround automation. Dynaudio M4-surround sound monitoring. Separate digital preproduction room. Permanent tie lines to Apollo theatre for studio quality live recordings. In house team of engineers and programmers; 24 hour maintenance; private parking

Pinewood Studios
Sound Dept
Pinewood Road
Iver Heath, Bucks SL0 0NH
Tel: 01753 656301
Fax: 01753 656014
email: graham_hartstone@rank.com
Graham Hartstone
Two large stereo dubbing theatres with automated consoles, all digital release formats. 35mm and Digital dubbing, Akai DD8 dubbers & recorders, ADR & Foley recording. Large ADR/Fx recording theatre, 35mm or AVID AUDIOVISION, removable drives, ISDN Dolbyfax with timecode in aux data. Digital dubbing theatres with AMS/NEVE Logic 2 and AudioFile Spectra 16. Preview theatre 115 seats. Formats 35/70mm Dolby SR.D, DTS and SDDS. Comprehensive transfer bay.

Stereo Optical Negative transfer including Dolby SR.D, SDDS and DTS. Cutting rooms

PMPP Facilities
69 Dean Street
London W1V 5HB
Tel: 020 7437 0979
Fax: 020 7434 0386
Website: www.pmpp.dircon.co.uk
Off-line editing: BVW SP, lo-band and VHS. Non-linear editing: 5 custom built Avid suites either self drive or with editor. On-line editing: Digital Betacam, D3, D2, Beta SP, 1", BVU SP and Hi-8 formats. Three suites with Charisma effects Aston or A72 cap gen and GVG mixers. Graphics: Matisse Painting, Softimage 3D, Acrobat 3D, animation and T-Morph morphing on Silicon Graphics workstations. Sound dubbing on Avid Audiovision or AudioFile. Voiceover studio/A-DAT digital multi-track recording. Full transfer, duplication and standards conversion service. Pack shot studio

Post Box
8 Lower James Street
London W1R 3PL
Tel: 020 7439 0600
Fax: 020 7439 0700
Jo Smith
Jo Beddington, Jason Elliott, Alice Valdes-Scott
UK and international post production. Offline, online, editbox, Magnum and more - offering the whole package for broadcasters

Red Post Production
Hammersley House
Hammersley House
London W1R 6JD
Tel: 020 7439 1449
Fax: 020 7439 1339
email: Red-Post@Demon.co.uk
email: Redfx@Demon.co.uk
Post production company specialising in design and technical special effects for commercials, video promos, broadcast titles and idents, feature film projects, broadcast projects utilising computer animation techniques. Motion capture, Flame, Henry, Flash Harry. Full technical supervision

Redapple
214 Epsom Road
Merrow
Guildford
Surrey GU1 2RA
Tel: 01483 455044
Fax: 01483 455022
Video formats: Beta SP, Beta Sx, NTSC/PAL. Cameras: Sony DNW 90WSP 4:3016:9, IKEGAMI, V-55

Camcorders; Transport; VW
Caravelle and Volvo Camera Cars

Redwood Studios Recording & Film Post Production
1-6 Falconberg Court
London W1V 5FG
Andre Jacquemin - Managing
Director - Sound Designer
Post production for features including
large f/x library and digital audio
post work

Richmond Film Services
The Old School
Park Lane
Richmond
Surrey TW9 2RA
Tel: 020 8940 6077
Fax: 020 8948 8326
Sound equipment available for hire,
sales of tape and batteries, and UK
agent for Ursta recordists' trolleys
and Denecke timecode equipment

Salon Post-Productions
10 Livonia Street
London W1V 3PH
Tel: 020 7437 0516
Fax: 020 7437 6197
Website: www.salon.ndirect.co.uk
Editing Equipment rental -
non linear systems including Avid
Film Composer & Lightworks, hard
disk storage, BetaSP and DAT etc
Film equipment - including 35mm
and 16mm Steenbecks and all editing
accessories and supplies. Edit suites
in Soho or delivered to any location.
Digital sound editing systems include
Audiovision, AKAI, Protools

Michael Samuelson VFG Lighting
Pinewood Studios
Iver Heath
Bucks SL0 0NH
Tel: 01753 631133
Fax: 01753 630485
Unit 9 Maybrook Industrial Park
Armley Road
Leeds LS12 2EL
Tel: 0113 242 8232
Fax: 0113 245 4149
Unit K, Llantrisant Business Park
Llantrisant,
Mid Glamorgan CF7 8LF
Tel: 01443 227777
Fax: 01443 223656
Units 7/8, Piccadilly Trading
Estate, Great Ancoats Street
Manchester M1 2NP
Tel: 0161 272 8462
Fax: 0161 273 8729
Meridian Studios, Television
Centre, Northam
Southampton SO2 0TA
Tel: 023 80 222555

Fax: 01703 335050
Hire of film and television lighting
equipment and generators. Six UK
depots. Largest range of MSR
discharge equipment in Europe
including the powerful SUNPAR
range from France

Sheffield Independent Film
5 Brown Street
Sheffield S1 2BS
Tel: 0114 272 0304
Fax: 0114 279 5225
Colin Pons, Gloria Ward,
Alan Robinson
Aaton XTR + (S16/St 16). Vision 12
tripod S16/St 16. 6-plate Steenbeck,
Picsync. Nagra IS. SQN 45 mixer.
Microphones: 416, 816, ECM 55s.
SVHS edit suite. Avid MSP edit suite
Sony DXC537. UVW100
Betakit/Betacam (PVE 2800)/Hi-
band SP (BVU 950)/Hi-8, 2 and 3
machine edit suite. Three Chip
cameras. Lighting equipment. 1,200
ft studio. Sony DVC Digital
Camcorder

Shepperton Sound
Shepperton Studios
Studios Road, Shepperton
Middx TW17 0QD
Tel: 01932 572676
Fax: 01932 572396
three Dubbing Theatres (16mm,
35mm, video) Post-sync, and
footsteps; effects, theatre, in-house
sound transfers

Shepperton Studios
Studios Road
Shepperton
Middx TW17 0QD
Tel: 01932 562611
Fax: 01932 568989
email: sheppertonstudios@dial.pipex.
com
Cutting rooms; 16mm, 35mm
viewing theatres

Studio Pur
c/o Gargoyle Graphics
16 Chart St
London N1 6UG
Tel: 020 7490 5177
Fax: 020 7490 5177
email: sbayly@ich.ucl.ac.uk
Website: www.ace.mdx.ac.uk
/hyperhomes/houses/pur/index.htm
Simon Bayly, Lucy Thane
Media 100 & After Effects, Pro
Tools, Sony DSR-200 DVCAM
camcorder & tripod, Tascam portable
DAT, audio effects processing, 500
lumens video projector, multimedia
workstation, mics, lights & PA
equipment

SVC Television
142 Wardour Street
London W1V 3AU
Tel: 020 7734 1600
Fax: 020 7437 1854
Tracey Whitaker
Video Post Production including the
following: Diamond Telecini, Flame,
3 Henrys, Computer Animation & 2
Motion Control Studios

Tele-Cine
Video House
48 Charlotte Street
London W1P 1LX
Tel: 020 7208 2000
Fax: 020 7208 2250/1
Website: www.telecine.co.uk
Siân Morgan
Component digital editing; composite
editing graphics 13D; Avid non-linear
editing telecine; audio post-
production laser disc preparation
multi-media applications; copy and
duplication commercials playouts; 2"
quad/archive retrieval; standards
conversion: telecom lines; satellite
downlink

Tiny Epic Video Co
37 Dean Street
London W1V 5AP
Tel: 020 7437 2854
Fax: 020 7434 0211
Non-linear offlining on Avid, and
D/Vision. Tape offlining on Umatic
& VHS with and without shotlister.
Rushes dubbing. Tape transfers -
most formats including Hi-8 and
DAT. EDL Generation and
Translation

TVi
Film House
142 Wardour Street
London W1V 3AU
Tel: 020 7878 0000
Fax: 020 7878 7800
Website: www.tvi.co.uk
Mark Ottley
Mark Ottley, Joy Hancock
Post production; Telecine; sound
dubbing; copying and conversion.
Extensive integrated services
especially for film originated
programmes. Full digital compo-nent
environment. Wetgate digital
Telecine with Aaton and ARRI and
full range of gates including Super
16mm and 35mm wide aperture
wetgate transfers. Full film rushes
transfer service. Free film preparation
service. Wide range of VTRs
including Digital Betacam

TVMS, TV Media
420 Sauchiehall Street
Glasgow G2 3JD
Tel: 0141 331 1993

Fax: 0141 332 9040
Peter McNeill, Chas Chalmers
Media 100 off-line and on-line with
Beta SP and Digital facilities for
Broadcast, Commercials, and
Corporate Productions

TVP Videodubbing Ltd
2 Golden Square
London W1R 3AD
Tel: 020 7439 7138
Fax: 020 7434 1907
Jaqui Winston
Telecine transfer from 35mm, Super
16mm, 16mm and Super 8mm to all
video formats with full grading,
blemish concealment and image
restoration service. Video mastering,
reformatting and duplication to and
from any format; standards
conversion service including motion
compensation via the Alchemist Ph.
C. digital converter. Also landlines
for feeds to the BT Tower and
commercials playouts. Laserdisc pre-
mastering and full quality
assessment. Packaging

Twickenham Film Studios
St Margaret's
Twickenham
Middx TW1 2AW
Tel: 020 8607 8888
Fax: 020 8607 8889
Gerry Humphreys,
ISDN: 020 8744 1415
Gerry Humphreys, Caroline Tipple
Two dubbing theatres; ADR/Foley
theatre; 40 cutting rooms;
Lightworks, Avid, 16/35mm

Vector Television
Battersea Road, Heaton Mersey
Stockport, Cheshire SK4 3EA
Tel: 0161 432 9000
Fax: 0161 443 1325
Martin Tetlow
Vector Graphics; Vector Digital
Audio; Vector Digital editing; Vector
Studios; 2D/3D design and
visualisation consultancy

Video Film & Grip Company
23 Alliance Court
Alliance Road
London W3 0RB
Tel: 020 8993 8555
Fax: 020 8896 3941
Contact: G.Stubbings
Unit 9, Orchard Street Industrial
Estate, Salford
Manchester M6 6FL
Tel: 0161 745 8146
Fax: 0161 745 8161
Cardiff Studios, Culverhouse
Cross, Cardiff CF5 6XT
Tel: 029 20599777
Fax: 029 20597957

Suppliers of 35mm camera equipment.
16mm camera equipment for
documentaries, Digital SP and Beta SP
video equipment for broadcast, and
extensive range of cranes, dollies and
ancillary grip equipment

The Video Lab
Back West Crescent
St Annes on Sea
Lancs FY8 1SU
Tel: 01253 725499/712011
Fax: 01253 713094
Cintel Telecine 9.5/8/Super
8/16/35mm, slides and stills. Video
formats: 2", 1"C, BVU, U-Matic,
Beta SP. Cameras: Sony. Duplication,
standards conversion. Specialists in
transfer from discontinued videotape
formats. Library of holiday videos
(Travelogue), corporate and TV
production, TV and cinema
commercial production

Videola (UK)
162-170 Wardour Street
London W1V 3TA
Tel: 020 7437 5413
Fax: 020 7734 5295
Video formats: 1", U-Matic, Beta SP.
Camera: JVC KY35. Editing: three
machine Beta SP. Computer rostrum
camera. Lightworks offline

Videolondon Sound
16-18 Ramillies Street
London W1V 1DL
Tel: 020 7734 4811
Fax: 020 7494 2553
email: info@videolon.ftech.co.uk
Website: www.ftech.net/~videolon
Five sophisticated sound recording
studios with overhead TV projection
systems. 16mm, 35mm and video
post-sync recording and mixing. Two
Synclavier digital audio suites with
four further Synclaviers, five
AvidAudiovision, two StudioFrame
and one AudioFile assignable to any
of the studios. All sound facilities for
film or video post-production
including D3, DigiBetacam, Betacam
SP, 1" PAL and Dolby Surround for
TV with three Lightworks non-linear
editing systems

Videosonics Cinema Sound
68a Delancey Street
London NW1 7RY
Tel: 020 7209 0209
Fax: 020 7419 4470
2 x All Digital THX Film Dubbing
Theatres. Dolby Digital and SR 35
mm, 16mm and Super 16mm. All
aspect ratios, all speeds. Video
Projection if required Theatre I:
AMS-Neve Logic II console (112
channels) with 24track Audiofile.
Theatre II (Big Blue): AMS-Neve

DFC console (224 channels) with 2 x
24 track Audio files. 3 x additional
television Sound Dubbing Suites, 2
with AMS-Neve digital consoles, 1 x
SSL console. 6 x Digital Audio
Editing rooms, 35mm film editing,
Facilities for Lightworks and Avid 2
x Foley and ADR Studios. A total of
14 AMS Audiofiles. Parking by
arrangement. Wheelchair Access

VTR Ltd
64 Dean Street
London W1V 5HG
Tel: 020 7437 0026
Fax: 020 7439 9427
email: info@vtr.co.uk
Website: www.vtr.co.uk
Anthony Frend
VTR is one of London's major digital
non-linear post production facilities
specialising in commercials,
corporates and promos. Facilities
include: 2 x Spirit DataCines the
world's first real-time high resolution
film scanner for 35mm, 16mm and
super 16mm; Ursa Gold telecines
with Pogle Platinum and full range of
Ursa optical effects incl.
Kaleidoscope; Inferno and Flame for
resolution independent special effects
for TV and cinema. 3x Henry Infinity
for non-linear digital editing and
effects. 3D Computer Graphics and
Animation with Maya Software; Flint
RT, 3 x Macs; dubbing, ISDN and
playout facilities. Domino (digital
film effects) see under 'The Film
Factory at VTR.'

Windmill Lane Pictures
4 Windmill Lane, Dublin 2
Ireland
Tel: (353) 1 6713444
Fax: (353) 1 6718413
Liz Murphy
Telecine, digital on-line, AVID off-
line, Henry, Flame, Flint, EFP Crews
and number 4 Audio Studio

Worldwide Television News (WTN Facilities)
The Interchange, Oval Road
Camden Lock
London NW1
Tel: 020 7410 5410
Fax: 020 7410 5335
Anne Marie Phelan
2 TV studios (full cyc and
component key); Digital Betacam
and Beta SP editing (PAL and
NTSC), Quantel Newsbox Non-linear
online editing; Vistek VMC Digital
standards conversion; Soundstation
Digital Audio dubbing; UK and
international satellite delivery and
crews

FESTIVALS

Listed below by country of origin are a selection of international film, television and video festivals with contact addresses and brief synopses

Australia

Melbourne International Film Festival
– July/August
PO Box 2206, Fitzroy Mail Centre
Fitzroy 3065
Victoria
Tel: (61) 3 417 2011
Fax: (61) 3 417 3804
Non-competitive showcase for Australian and International features, documentaries, animation together with an international short film competition

Sydney Film Festival
– June
PO Box 950
Glebe NSW 2037
Tel: (61) 2 9660 3844
Fax: (61) 2 9692 8793
email: sydfilm@ozonline.com.au
Website: www.sydfilm-fest.com.au/
A broad-based non-competitive Festival screening around 200 films not previously shown in Australia: features, documentaries, shorts, animation, video and experimental work. Competitive section for Australian short films only. Audience votes for best documentary, short and feature

Austria

Viennale – Vienna International Film Festival
– 15-27 October 1999
Stiftgasse 6
A-1070
Vienna
Tel: (43) 1 526 5947
Fax: (43) 1 523 4172
email: office@viennale.or.at
Website: www.viennale.or.at
Non-competitive for features and documentaries. Additional categories: Twilight Zone; Tributes; Historical Retrospective

Belgium

Brussels International Festival of Fantasy, Thriller and Science Fiction Films
– 11 March 2000
144 avenue de la Reine
1030 Brussels
Tel: (32) 2 201 17 13
Fax: (32) 2 201 14 69
Website: www.bifff.org/
Competitive for features and shorts (less than 20 mins)

Brussels International Film Festival
– 20-31 January 1999
Chaussée de Louvain 30
B–1210 Brussels
Tel: (32) 2 227 39 80
Fax: (32) 2 218 18 60
email: infoffb@netcity.be
Website: www.ffb.cinebel.com
This is a competitive festival for European general interest films, annually showing about 100 features and 120 shorts. European features and shorts eligible to compete for Crystal Star Award. Belgian shorts eligible to compete for Golden Iris Award. Sections include European Competition, Kaleidoscope of the World Cinema, Belgian Focus with a National Competition, Special Events and Tributes. Feature entries should be over 60 minutes and shorts should be under 30 minutes. Formats accepted: 35 mm, 16mm. Deadline: 31st October. No entry fee

Flanders International Film Festival – Ghent
– 5-16 October 1999
1104 Kortrijksesteenweg
B-9051 Ghent
Tel: (32) 9 221 89 46
Fax: (32) 9 221 90 74
email: filmfestival@glo.be
Website: www.filmfestival.be
Contact: Jacques Dubrulle, Secretary-general, Walter Provo, Programme Executive
Marian Ponnet, Guest Officer.
Belgium's most prominent yearly film event. Competitive, showing 150 feature films and 80 shorts from around the world. Best film award $35,000. Deadline for entry forms mid August

Brazil

Gramado International Film Festival – Latin and Brazilian Cinema
– August
Avenida das Hortensias 2029
Grande 95670-000
Gramado – Rio do Sul
Tel: (55) 54 286 2335
Fax: (55) 54 286 2397
email: festival@via-rs.com.br
Website: www.viadigital.com.br/gramado
For exhibition of audiovisual products from Latin language speaking countries

Mostra Rio – Rio de Janeiro Film Festivals
– September
Rua Voluntários dá Pátria 97
CEP 22270-010
Rio de Janeiro RJ
Tel: (55) 21 539 1505
Fax: (55) 21 539 1247
Website: www.estacao.ignet.com.br/mostra/
Non-competitive, promoting films that would not otherwise get to Brazilian screens

São Paulo International Film Festival
– 15-29 October 1999
Alameda 937, Cj 303
São Paulo SP 01424-001
Tel: (55) 11 883 5137/3064-5819
Fax: (55) 11 853 7936
email: info@mostra.org
Website: www.mostra.org
Two sections, international selection (for features, shorts, documentary, animation.) and a competitive section for films of new directors (first, second or third feature), produced during two years preceding the festival

Burkina Faso

Panafrican Film and TV Festival of Ouagadougou
February/March odd years
Secrétariat Général Permanent du FESPACO
01 BP 2505
Ouagadougou 01
Tel: (226) 30 75 38

Fax: (226) 31 25 09
Competitive, featuring African diaspora and African film-makers, whose work has been produced during the three years preceding the Festival, and not shown before at FESPACO

Canada

Banff Television Festival
– June
1516 Railway Avenue
Canmore, Alberta, T1W 1P6
Tel: (1) 403 678 9260
Fax: (1) 403 678 9269
email: banff@banfftvfest.com
Website: www.banfftvfest.com
Competitive for programmes made for television, including short and long drama, limited and continuing series, arts and social and political documentaries, children's programmes, comedy, performance specials, information and animation programmes broadcast for the first time in the previous year and popular science programmes

Festival International du Film Sur L'Art (International Festival of Films on Art)
– 9-14 March 1999
640 rue St Paul Ouest
Bureau 406
Montreal, Quebec H3C 1L9
Tel: (1) 514 874 1637
Fax: (1) 514 874 9929
email: Fifa@maniacom.com
Website: www.maniacom.com /fifa.html
The Festival encompasses all the arts, of any period or style. Films and videos must preferably be in French, otherwise in English, in their original, subtitled or dubbed version

Montreal International Festival of New Cinema and New Media
– 14-24 October 1999 (28th edition)
Boulevard Saint-Laurent 3536
Montreal
Quebec H2X 2V1
Tel: (1) 514 847 9272
Fax: (1) 514 847 0732
email: montrealfest@fcmm.com
Website: www.fcmm.com
Claude Chamberlan
Discovery and promotion of outstanding international films, video and new media creations produced during previous two years, which have not been previously screened in Canada. Non-competitive (although some prizes in cash are awarded)

Montreal World Film Festival (+ Market)
– August/September
1432 de Bleury St
Montreal
Quebec H3A 2JI
Tel: (1) 514 848 3883
Fax: (1) 514 848 3886
Competitive festival recognized by the International Federation of Film Producers Associations. Categories: Official Competition; World Greats; World Cinema: Reflections of Our Time; Cinema of Tomorrow: New Trends; Latin American Cinema; Focus on Irish Cinema; Panorama Canada; Films for Television (documentaries and fiction films); Tributes

Ottawa International Animation Festival
– September/October even years
2 Daly Avenue
Ottawa
Ontario K1N 6E2
Tel: (1) 613 232 6727
Fax: (1) 613 232 6315
Website: www.awn.com.ottawa/
Competitive

The Atlantic Film Festival (Halifax)
– 17-25 September 1999
PO Box 36139
Halifax
Nova Scotia B3J 3S9
Tel: (1) 902 422 3456
Fax: (1) 902 422 4006
email: festival@atlanticfilm.com
Website: www.atlanticfilm.com
Gordon Whittaker – Executive Director, Lia Rinaldo – Program Director
Entry Deadline: 11 June 1999
A nine-day celebration of film which is known for its warm and festive atmosphere. The Festival showcases the finest film and videomaking from Atlantic Canada and the rest of the world

Toronto International Film Festival
– September
Suite 1600 2 Carlton Street
Toronto
Ontario M5B 1J3
Tel: (1) 416 967 7371
Fax: (1) 416 967 9477
Non-competitive for feature films and shorts not previously shown in Canada. Also includes some American premieres, retrospectives and national cinema programmes. Films must have been completed within the year prior to the Festival to be eligible

Vancouver International Film Festival
Suite 410, 1008 Homer Street
Vancouver
British Columbia V6B 2X1
Tel: (1) 604 685 0260
Fax: (1) 604 688 8221
email: viff@viff.org
Website: Webstite: http://www.viff.org
Third largest festival in North America, with special emphasis on East Asian, Canadian and documentary films. Also British and European cinema and 'The Screenwriter's Art'. Submission deadline mid-July – only feature film entries accepted from outside of Canada

Croatia

World Festival of Animated Films – Zagreb
– June even years
Koncertna direkcija Zagreb
Kneza Mislava 18
10000 Zagreb
Tel: (385 - 1) 46 11 808/46 11 709/46 11 598
Fax: (385 - 1) 46 11 807/46 11 808
email: kdz@zg.tel.hr
Website: www.animafest.hr/
Competitive for animated films (up to 30 mins). Categories: a) films from 30 secs-6 mins, b) films from 6-15 mins, c) 15 min-30mins. Awards: Grand Prix, First Prize in each category (ABC), Best First Production (Film Debut) Best Student Film, Five Special Distinctions. Films must have been completed in two years prior to the Festival and not have been awarded prizes

Cuba

International Festival of New Latin American Cinema
– December
Calle 23
1155 Vedado
Havana 4
Tel: (53) 7 552841 552849
Fax: (53) 7 33 30 78 /33 4273
Competitive for films and videos

Czech Republic

'Golden Prague' International TV Festival
– May
Czech Television
Kavci Hory
140 70 Prague 4

Tel: (42) 2 6113 4405/4028
Fax: (42) 2 6121 2891
Competitive for television music
programmes and other types of
serious music, dance, jazz and world
music.music programmes. Entry
forms must be submitted by 31st
January and videos by 15th February

Karlovy Vary International Film Festival
– 2-10 July
Film Servis Festival Karlovy Vary
Panská 1
110 00 Prague 1
Tel: (420) – 2 2423 5412
Fax: (420) – 2 2423 3408
Website: www.iffkv.cz/
Feature film competition, information
sections, Eastern Europe, Asia and
Czech panorama, retrospectives

Denmark

Balticum Film and TV Festival
– 5-11 June
Skippergade 8
3740 Svaneke
Tel: (45) 7023 0024
Fax: (45) 7023 0025
Website: www.dk-web.com/bbf/
Competitive for documentaries from
the countries around the Baltic Sea.
Three categories: Best Film less than
35 minutes; Best film more than 35
minutes. Three prizes in each
category in the Balticum competition:
a special press juries prize. The Film
School Competition: Only European
Film Schools can enter new projects.
2 Prizes: Best film school
documentary and best film school
fiction

Copenhagen Film Festival
– September
FSI
Vesterbrogade 35
1620 Copenhagen V
Tel: (45) 33 25 25 01
Fax: (45) 33 25 57 56
email: fside@datashopper.dk
Festival for the public. Previews of
American, European and Danish
films, both by established filmmakers
and those less well known. Around
120 films, plus seminars and
exhibition

International Odense Film Festival
– 16-21 August 1999
Vindegade 18
5100 Odense C
Tel: (45) 6613 1372 x4044
Fax: (45) 6591 4318
email: filmfestival@post.odkomm.dk

Website: www.filmfestival.dk/
Competitive for fairy-tale and
experimental-imaginative films.
Deadline for entries 1 April

Egypt

Cairo International Film Festival
November/December
17 Kasr El Nil Street
Cairo
Tel: (20) 2 392 3562/3962/393 3832
Fax: (20) 2 393 8979
Competitive for feature films, plus a
film, television and video market

Cairo International Film Festival for Children
September
17 Kasr el El Nil Street
Cairo
Tel: (20) 2 392 3562/3962/393 3832
Fax: (20) 2 393 8979
Competitive for children's films:
features, shorts, documentaries,
educative, cartoons, television films
and programmes for children up to
14 years

Finland

Midnight Sun Film Festival
Jäämerentie 9
99600 Sodankylä
June
Tel: (358) (0)16 614 524/614 522
Fax: (358) (0)16 618 646
Non-competitive for feature films,
held in Finnish Lapland

Tampere 30th International Short Film Festival
– 8-12 March 2000
PO Box 305
33101 Tampere
Tel: (358) 3 2130034
Fax: (358) 3 2230121
email: film.festival@tt.tampere.fi
Competitive for short films, max. 30
mins. Categories for animated, fiction
and documentary short films,
completed on or after 1 January
1998. Videos (VHS) accepted for
selection only 16mm and 35mm
screening prints. 10-15 large
retrospectives and tributes of short
films from all over the world.
Competition deadline December
1999

France

19th Amiens International Film Festival
– November
MCA – 2 place Léon Gontier
F-8000 Amiens

Tel: (33) 322 713570
Fax: (33) 322 92 53 04
Films completed after 15 September
1997, and which make a contribution
to the identity of people or an ethnic
minority, are eligible for entry. They
may be either full-length or short,
fiction or documentary films

Annecy International Festival of Animation (+ Market)
– May
JICA/MIFA
BP 399
74013 Annecy Cédex
Tel: (33) 04 50 10 09 00
Fax: (33) 04 50 10 09 70
Competitive for animated short films,
feature-length films, TV films,
commercials, produced in the
previous 26 months

Cannes International Film Festival
– 18 May 2000
99 Boulevard Maiesherbes
75008 Paris
Tel: (33) 1 45 61 66 00
Fax: (33) 1 45 61 97 60
email: festival@cannes.bull.net
Website: www.festival-cannes.fr/
Competitive section for feature films
and shorts (up to 15 mins) produced
in the previous year, which have not
been screened outside country of
origin nor been entered in other
competitive festivals, plus non-
competitive section: Un Certain
Regard. Other non-competitive
events: Directors Fortnight
(Quinzaine des Réalisateurs) and
Programme of French Cinema
(Cinémas en France)
215 rue du Faubourg St Honoré
75008 Paris
Tel: (33) 1 45 61 01 66
Fax: (33) 1 40 74 07 96
Critic's Week (Semaine de la
Critique)
73 rue de Lourmel
75015 Paris
Tel: (33) 1 45 75 68 27
Fax: (33) 1 40 59 03 99

Cinéma du Réel, (International Festival of Visual Anthropology)
March
Bibliothèque Publique d'Information
19 rue Beaubourg
75197 Paris Cedex 04
Tel: (33) 1 44 78 44 21/45 16
Fax: (33) 1 44 78 12 24
Documentaries only (film or video).
Competitive – must not have been
released commercially or been
awarded a prize at an international

festival in France. Must have been made in the year prior to the Festival

Cognac International Thriller Film Festival

April
Le Public Systeme
36 rue Pierret
92200 Neuilly-sur-Seine
Tel: (33) 1 46 40 55 00
Fax: (33) 1 46 40 55 39
email: cognac@pobox.com
Competitive for thriller films, which have not been commercially shown in France or participated in festivals in Europe (police movies, thrillers, 'film noirs', court movies, investigations etc)

Deauville Festival of American Film

September
36 rue Pierret
92200 Neuilly-sur-Seine
Tel: (33) 1 46 40 55 00
Fax: (33) 1 46 40 55 39
email: deauville@pobox.com
Studio previews (non competitive)
Independent Films Competition and panorama. US productions only

Festival Cinématographique d'Automne de Gardanne

– 22 October/2 November 1999
Cinéma 3 Casino
11 cours Forbin
13120 Gardanne
Tel: (33) (0)442 51 44 93
Fax: (33) (0) 442 58 17 86
Includes European Competition of Shorts. Aims to discover high quality European cinema. Also junior section and retrospectives. All films for competition to be submitted on VHS, and to have been produced in the year prior to the Festival

Festival des Trois Continents

– November
BP 43302
44033 Nantes Cedex 1
Tel: (33) 2 40 69 74 14
Fax: (33) 2 4073 55 22
Feature-length fiction films from Africa, Asia, Latin and Black America. Competitive section, tributes to directors and actors, panoramas

Festival du Film Britannique de Dinard

– September
47 boulevard Féart
35800 Dinard
Tel: (33) 99 88 19 04
Fax: (33) 99 46 67 15
Competitive, plus retrospective and

exhibition; tribute meeting between French and English producers

Festival International de Films de Femmes

– 24 April 2000
Maison des Arts
Place Salvador Allende
94000 Créteil
Tel: (33) 1 49 80 38 98
Fax: (33) 1 43 99 04 10
email: filmsfemme@wanadoo.fr
Website: www.gdebussac.fr/filmfem
Jacki Buet
Competitive for feature films, documentaries, shorts, retrospectives directed by women and produced in the previous 23 months and not previously shown in France

FIFREC (International Film and Student Directors Festival)

16 chemin de Pommier
69330 Jons/Lyon
June
Tel: (33) 72 02 48 64
Fax: (33) 72 02 20 36
Official film school selections (three per school) and open selection for directors from film schools, either students or recent graduates. Categories include fiction, documentaries and animation. Also best film school award. Films to be under 40 mins

French-American Film Workshop

– June
10 Montée de la Tour
30400 Villeneuve-les-Avignon
Tel: (04) 90 25 93 23
Fax: (04) 90 25 93 24
198 Avenue of the Americas
New York, NY 10013
USA
Tel: (212) 343 2675
Fax: (212) 343 1849
email: JHR2001@AOL
Contact: Jerome Henry Rudes, General Director
The Workshop brings together independent filmmakers from the United States and France at the Avignon/New York Film Festival and Rencontres Cinématographiques Franco-Américaines d'Avignon (see below). French and American independent film is celebrated with new films, retrospectives, round-tables on pertinent issues and daily receptions
Avignon/New York Film Festival
(April)
Alliance Française/French Institute, 22 East 60th Street, New York, NY –

with 'the 21st Century Filmmaker Awards'
Rencontres Cinématographiques Franco-Américaines d'Avignon
(June)
Cinéma Vox, Place de l'Horloge, Avignon, France – with 'The Tournage Awards'

Gérardmer-Fantastic Arts International Fantasy Film Festival

– January
36 rue Pierret
92200 Neuilly-sur-Seine
Tel: (33) 1 46 40 55 00
Fax: (33) 1 46 40 55 39
email: fantasticarts@pdox.com
Competitive for international fantasy feature films (science-fiction, horror, supernatural etc)

International Festival of European Cinema La Boule

– October
97 Rue Raumur
75002 Paris
Tel: (33) 1 4041 0454
Fax: (33) 1 4026 5478
Categories for European feature, short film, animation and documentary. Prizes for best director, actor and actress

MIP-TV

– April
Reed MIDEM Organisation
179 avenue Victor Hugo
75116 Paris
Tel: (33) 1 44 34 44 44
Fax: (33) 1 44 34 44 00
International television programme market, held in Cannes

MIPCOM

– October
Reed MIDEM Organisation
179 avenue Victor Hugo
75116 Paris
Tel: (33) 1 44 34 44 44
Fax: (33) 1 44 34 44 00
International film and programme market for television, video, cable and satellite, held in Cannes

Germany

Berlin International Film Festival

– 10-21 February 1999
Internationale Filmfestspiele Berlin
Budapester Strasse 50
10787 Berlin
Tel: (49) 30 254 890
Fax: (49) 30 254 89249
Website: www.berlinale.de/
Competitive for feature films and shorts (up to 10 mins), plus a

separate competition for children's films – feature length and shorts – produced in the previous year and not entered for other festivals. Also has non-competitive programme consisting of forum of young cinema, panorama, film market and New German films

Feminale, 9th International Women's Film Festival
– *30 June*
Feminale
Maybachstr, 111
50670 Cologne
Tel: (49) 221 130029/1300 225
Fax: (49) 221 1300281
email: Feminale@t-online.de
Website: www.dom.de./filmworks/Feminale
Non-competitive for films by women directors only made in last two years, all genres, formats, lengths. Retrospectives, special programmes

Femme Totale – International Frauen Film Festival
– *10-14 March 1999*
c/o Kulturbüro der Stadt Dortmund
Kleppingstr 21-23
44122 Dortmund
Tel: (49) 231 50 25 162
Fax: (49) 231 50 22 497
email: femmetotale@compuserve.com
Website: www.femmetotale.de
Silke Johanna Räbiger
Held every two years. Women Film-makers' Festival screens features, short films, documentaries and videos. Workshops and seminars.

Filmfest Hamburg
– *September*
Friedensallee 1
22765 Hamburg
Tel: (49) 40 398 26 210
Fax: (49) 40 398 26 211
Non-competitive, international features and shorts for cinema release (fiction, documentaries), presentation of one film country/continent, premieres of Hamburg-funded films, and other activities

International Festival of Animated Film Stuttgart
– *April*
Festivalbüro
Teckstrasse 56 (Kulturpark Berg)
70190 Stuttgart
Tel: (49) 711/925460
Fax: (49) 711/9254615
Competitive for animated short films of an artistic and experimental nature, which have been produced in

the previous two years and not exceeding 35 mins. Animation, exhibitions and workshops. DM 139.000 worth of prizes

International Film Festival Mannheim – Heidelberg
– *October*
Collini-Center, Galerie
68161 Mannheim
Tel: (49) 621 10 29 43
Fax: (49) 621 29 15 64
email: ifmh@mannheim-filmfestival.com
Additional parts of the annual event are the 'Co-Production Meetings' for producers seeking co-production partners and the 'Independent Market Service' for buyers. Deadline for entry: 25 July, 1999

International FilmFest Emden
– *May*
An der Berufsschule 3
26721 Emden
Tel: (49) 49 21 91 55 35
Fax: (49) 49 21 91 55 91
A festival for European feature films and shorts. Competitive section for feature films and a short and animation films (not more than 20 minutes in length) (35mm and 16mm) from northwestern Europe and German speaking countries (Audience Awards 15 000 DM 6000 DM) Regular Sections: New British and New German Films. Retrospectives, tributes to directors, children's films, midnight talks

Internationales Filmwochenende Würzburg
– *January*
Gosbertsteige 2
97082 Würzburg
Tel: (49) 931 414 098
Fax: (49) 931 416 279
Competitive section for recent European and international productions, plus non-competitive section including tributes to directors as well as panoramas. Videos accepted for selection only

Internationales Leipziger Festival für Dokumentar und Animationsfilm
– *October/November*
Box 940
04009 Leipzig
Tel: (49) 341 9 80 39 21
Fax: (49) 341 9 80 48 28
Competition, special programmes, retrospectives, international juries and awards

Munich Film Festival
– *April/May*
Internationale Münchner Filmwochen
Kaiserstrasse 39
80801 Munich
Tel: (49) 89 38 19 04 0
Fax: (49) 89 38 19 04 26
Non-competitive for feature films, shorts and documentaries which have not previously been shown in Germany

Munich International Documentary Festival
– *April/May*
Troger Strasse 46
Munich D-81675
Tel: (49) 89 470 3237
Fax: (49) 89 470 6611

Nordic Film Days Lübeck
– *4-7 November 1999*
23539 Lübeck
Tel: (49) 451 122 41 05
Fax: (49) 451 122 41 06
email: filmtage@luebeck.de
Website: www.filmtage.luebeck.de
Festival of Scandinavian and Baltic films. Competitive for feature, children's, documentary, and Nordic countries' films

Oberhausen International Short Film Festival
– *22-27 April 1999*
Grillostrasse 34
46045 Oberhausen
Tel: (49) 208 825 2652
Fax: (49) 208 825 5413
email: info@kurzfilmtage.de
Website: www.shortfilm.de
Competitive for documentaries, animation, experimental, short features and videos (up to 35 mins), produced in the previous 28 months; international competition and German competition; international symposia

Prix Europa
– *September/October*
Sender Freies Berlin
Masurenallee 8-14
14046 Berlin
Tel: (49) 30 3031 1610
Fax: (49) 30 3031 1619
Competitive for fiction, non-fiction, series/serials in television. Open to all television stations and television producers in Europe. Eight awards of 6,150 ECU

Prix Futura Berlin
– *May/April odd years*
International Radio and TV Contest
Sender Freies Berlin
14046 Berlin

Tel: (49) 30 3031 1610
Fax: (49) 30 3031 1619
Competitive, one entry per category
(documentary and drama). Open to
all broadcasting organisations; radio
evening competition for newcomers
in drama and features; three
television competitions for films
from Asia, Africa and Latin America
in evenings

Prix Jeunesse International
– *June*
Bayerischer Rundfunk
80300 Munich
Tel: (49) 89 5900 2058
Fax: (49) 89 5900 3053
email: ubz@prixjeunesse.de
Website: www.prixjeunesse.de
Competitive for children's and youth
television programmes (age groups
up to 7, 7-12 and 12-17), in fiction
and non-fiction, produced in the
previous two years. (In odd years:
seminars in children's and youth
television)

Greece

International Thessaloniki Film Festival
– *November*
36 Sina Street
10672 Athens
Tel: (30) 1 3610418/3620907/
3620962
Fax: (30) 1 362 1023
Dedicated to the promotion of
independent cinema from all over the
world. International Competition for
first or second features (Golden
Alexander worth approx. $43,000,
Silver Alexander $27,000). Official
non competitive section for Greek
films produced in 1999, informative
section with the best independent
films of the year, retrospectives (last
year's retrospective dedicated to
Claude Chabrol and Arturo Ripstein),
exhibitions, special events etc

Hong Kong

Hong Kong International Film Festival
– *April*
Level 7, Admin Building, Hong
Kong Cultural Centre
10 Salisbury Road, Tsimshatsui
Kowloon
Tel: (852) 2734 2892
Fax: (852) 2366 5206
Non-competitive for feature films,
documentaries and invited short
films, which have been produced in
the previous two years, also a local
short film competition

Hungary

Hungarian Film Week
– *February*
Magyar Filmunio
Varosligeti fasor 38
H – 1068 Budapest
Tel: (361) 351 7760
Fax: (361) 351 7766
Competitive festival for Hungarian
features, shorts and documentaries

India

Bombay International Film Festival for Documentary, Short and Animation Films
Feb even years)
Films Division, Ministry of
Information and Broadcasting
Government of India
24-Dr G Deshmukh Marg
Bombay 400 026
Tel: (91) 22
3864633/3873655/3861421/3861461
Fax: (91) 22 3860308
Competitive for fiction, non-fiction
and animation films, plus
Golden/Silver Conch and cash
awards and Information Section.

Mumbai International Film Festival
March
24– Dr Gopalrao Deshmukh Marg
Mumbai
400 026
Tel: (91) (22) 386 46 33
Fax: (91) (22) 380 00 308
email: films@giasbm01.Vsnl.net.in

International Film Festival of India (IFFI)
– *January*
Directorate of Film Festivals
Fourth Floor, Lok Nayak Bhavan
Khan Market,
New Delhi 110 003
Tel: (91) 11 4615953/4697167
Fax: (91) 11 4623430
Malti Sahai (Director)
Organised from January 10-20, each
year and recognised by FIAPF. It is
held in different Indian Film Cities
by rotation including New Delhi,
Bangalore, Bombay, Calcutta,
Hyderbad and Trivandrum. IFFI'98
was organised in New Delhi and
featured a specialised competition
section for Asian film makers

International Film Festival of Kerala
– *April*
Kerala State Chalachitra Academy
Elankom Gardens
Vellyambalam

Trivandrum 695 010
Kerala
Tel: 91 471 310323
Fax: 91 471 310322
email: chitram@md3.vsn.net.in
Asian Cinema. Retrospectives of
European, African and Japanese
Cinema. International advertising films

Iran

Tehran International Market (TIM)
c/o CMI
53 Koohyari Street
Fereshteh Avenue, Tehran 19658
Tel: (98) 21 254 8032
Fax: (98) 21 255 1914
The fourth Tehran International
Market is designed to provide major
producers from the West a
personalised arena to target regional
program buyers and theatrical
distributors in the lucrative Middle
East market and surrounding areas.
Buyers will also represent the Persian
Gulf States, Asia and the Indian
subcontinent, Central and Eastern
Europe. More than 1,500 hours of
programming was brought by Iranian
TV alone during TIM'96

Ireland

Cork International Film Festival
– *October*
Hatfield House, Tobin Street
Cork
Tel: (353) 21 271711
Fax: (353) 21 275945
email: ciff@indigo.ie
Non-competitive, screening a broad
range of features, shorts and
documentaries from over 40
countries. Films of every category
welcomed for submission.
Competitive: short films

Dublin Film Festival
– *March*
1 Suffolk Street
Dublin 2
Tel: (353) 1 679 2937
Fax: (353) 1 679 2939

Israel

Haifa International Film Festival
– *25-30 September*
142 Hanassi Avenue
Haifa 34633
Tel: (972) 4 8353530/8353521
Fax: (972) 4 8384327
The biggest annual meeting of
professionals associated with the film
industry in Israel. Competitions: 1.

'Golden Anchor' award $25,000 for mediterranean cinema. 2. Israeli Film Competition award $30,000

Jerusalem Film Festival
– July
PO Box 8561, Wolfson Gardens
Hebron Road
91083 Jerusalem
Tel: (972) 2 672 4131
Fax: (972) 2 673 3076
Finest in recent international cinema, documentaries, animation, avant garde, retrospectives, special tributes and homages, Mediterranean and Israeli cinema, retrospectives, restored class Best Israeli Screenplay. Three international awards: Wim van Leer In Spirit of Freedom focus on human rights; Mediterranian Cinema; Jewish Theme Awards

Italy

Cinema Giovani – Torino Film Festival
– 19-27 November
Via Monte di Pietá 1
10121 Torino
Tel: (39) 11 5623309
Fax: (39) 11 5629796
email: cinemagiovani@torinofilmfest.org
Website: www.torinofilmfest.org
Competitive sections for feature and short films. Italian Space section (videos and films) open solely to Italian work. All works must be completed during 13 previous months, with no prior release in Italy

Da Sodoma a Hollywood
– April
Turin Lesbian and Gay Film Festival, Associazione Culturale L'Altra Communicazione
Piazza San Carlo 161
10123 Turin
Tel: (39) 11 534 888
Fax: (39) 11 534 796
email: glfilmfest@assioma.com
Specialist lesbian/gay themed festival. Competitive for features, shorts and documentaries. Also retrospectives and special showcases for both cinema and television work

Europa Cinema & TV Viareggio, Italy
– September
Via XX Settembre Mo 3
Tel: (39) 6 42011184 (39) 6 42000211
Fax: (39) 6 42010599
An international competition of European Films; a section of films regarding food; a retrospective

section of films about 'The European Roots of American Cinema'; a retrospective of Radford's films; a section of Arte's (a European Cultural conference organised by ACE (Atelier du Cinéma Européen); a RAI première (opening day); screening of Ballando, Ballando by E.Scola (closing day)

Festival dei Popoli – International Review of Social Documentary Films
– November
Borgo Pinti 82r
50121 Firenze
Tel: (39) 55 244 778
Fax: (39) 55 241364
email: fespopol@dadait
Mario Simondi (Secretary General)
Patricia Baroni (Assistant)
Franco Lucchesi (President)
Competitive and non-competitive sections for documentaries on sociological, historical, political, anthropological subjects, as well as music, art and cinema, produced during the year preceding the festival. The films for the competitive section should not have been screened in Italy before

Giffoni Film Festival
– July/August
Piazza Umberto I
84095 Giffoni Valle Piana
Tel: (39) 89 868 544
Fax: (39) 89 866 111
Competitive for full-length fiction for children 12-14 and 12-18 years. Entries must have been produced within two years preceding the festival

MIFED
– November
Largo Domodossola 1
20145 Milan
Tel: (39) 2 480 12912 -48012920
Fax: (39) 2 499 77020
International market for companies working in the film and television industries

Mystery & Noir Film Festival
– December
Via Tirso 90
00198 Rome
Tel: 39 6 8848030 – 8844672
Fax: 39 6 8840450
Giorgio Gosetti
Competitive for thrillers between 30-180 mins length, which have been produced in the previous year and not released in Italy. Festival now takes place at Courmayeur (at the foot of Mount Blanc)

Pesaro Film Festival (Mostra Internazionale del Nuovo Cinema)
– June & October
Via Villafranca 20
00185 Rome
Tel: (39) 6 4456643/491156
Fax: (39) 6 491163
email: pesarofilmfest@mclink.it
Non-competitive. Particularly concerned with the work of new directors and emergent cinemas, with innovation at every level. In recent seasons the festival has been devoted to a specific country or culture

Pordenone Film Fair
– October
c/o Le Giornate del Cinema Muto
c/o La Cineteca del Frioli
Via G.Biui, Polozzo Guiisotti
33013 Gemona (UD)
Tel: 39 434 520446
Fax: 39 434 520584
email: gcm@proxima.conecto.it
Website: www.cinetec@del.frivli.org/gcm
An exhibition of books and journals, collectibles and ephemera presented by the Giornate del Cinema Muto. The Film Fair is held near the Verdi Theatre which will host the film screenings. Authors attending the festival are invited to discuss their latest works. An auction sale of cinema memorabilia is part of the program

Pordenone Silent Film Festival (La Giornate del Cinema Muto)
– 9-16 October 1999
c/o La Cineteca del Friuli
Via G.Bini, Polozzo Gurisotti
33013 Gemona (UD)
Tel: (39) 432 98 04 58
Fax: (39) 432 97 05 42
email: gcm@proxima.conecto.it
Website: www.cinetecadelfriuli.org.gcm/inglese/
David Robinson, Director
Non-competitive silent film festival. Annual award for restoration and preservation of the silent film heritage

Prix Italia
– September
RAI Radiotelevisione Italiana
Borgo Sant Angelo, 23
00193 Rome
Tel: (39) 06 68889016-7
Fax: (39) 06 68889172-3
Competitive for television and radio productions from national broadcasting organisations. Radio categories: music, fiction (single plays and serials), documentary

(factual and cultural). A maximum of four programmes can be submitted to the Radio competition. TV categories: performing arts, fiction (single plays and serials), documentary (factual and cultural). Only one programme can be submitted to each category

Salerno International Film Festival
– October
PO Box 137
84100 Salerno
Tel: (39) 89 223 632
Fax: (39) 89 223 632
All films – feature, documentaries, experimental and animated films – which are entered in the competitive section are eligible for the "Gran Premio Golta di Salerno"

Taormina International Film Festival
– July
Palazzo Firenze
Via Pirandello 31
98039 Taormina
Sicily
Tel: (39) 942 21142
Fax: (39) 942 23348
Competitive for features. Recognised by FIAPF, category B. Emphasis on new directors and cinema from developing countries

Venice Film Festival
– September
Mostra Internazionale d'Arte Cinematografica
La Biennale di Venezia
Ca' Giustinian
San Marco, 30124 Venice
Tel: (39) 41 5218711
Fax: (39) 41 5227539
Website: www.labiennale.it
Competitive for feature films competitive for shorts (up to 30 mins); has competitive sections, perspectives, night and stars, Italian section; retrospective. Non-participation at other international festivals and/or screenings outside country of origin. Submission by 30 June

Japan

International Animation Festival Hiroshima
– 24-28 August 2000
4-17 Kako-machi
Naka-ku
Hiroshima 730-0812
Tel: (81) 82 245 0245
Fax: (81) 82 245 0246
email: hiroanim@urban.ne.jp
Website: www.urban.ne.jp/home/

hiroanim/
Competitive biennial festival. Also retrospective, symposium, exhibition etc. For competition, animated works under 30 mins, and completed during preceding two years are eligible on either 16mm, 35mm, 3/4" videotape (NTSC, PAL, SECAM) or Betacam (only NTSC)

Tokyo International Film Festival
– October
Organising Committee
4F, Landic Ginza Bldg II
1-6-5 Ginza, Chuo-Ku
Tokyo 104-0061
Tel: (81) 3 3563 6305
Fax: (81) 3 3563 6310
Competitive for International Films and Young Cinema sections. Also special screenings, cinema prism, Nippon cinema classics, symposium, no film market

Tokyo Video Festival
– January
c/o Victor Co of Japan Ltd
1-7-1 Shinbashi
Victor Bldg, Minato-ku
Tokyo 105
Tel: (81) 3 3289 2815
Fax: (81) 3 3289 2819
Competitive for videos; compositions on any theme and in any style accepted, whether previously screened or not, but maximum tape playback time must not exceed 20 minutes

Malta

Golden Knight International Amateur Film & Video Festival
– November
PO Box 450
Valletta CMR,01
Tel: (356) 222345/236173
Fax: (356) 225047
Three classes: amateur, student, professional – maximum 30 mins

Martinique

Festival du Film Caribéen Cinéma, Vidéo: Images Caraïbes
– June even years
77 route de la Folie
97200 Fort-de-France
Tel: (596) 69 10 12/70 23 81
Fax: (596) 69 21 58/62 23 93
Competitive for all film and video makers native to the Caribbean Islands – features, shorts and documentary

Monaco

Monte Carlo Television Festival and Market
– February
4, boulevard du Jardin Exotique
Monte-Carlo 98000 Monaco
Tel: 337 93 10 40 60
Fax: 337 93 50 70 14
Contact: David Tomatis
Annual festival and market, includes awards for television films, mini-series and news categories. In 1996 joined with Imagina conference

The Netherlands

Cinekid
– 25 October 1999
Weteringschans 249
1017 Xy
Amsterdam
Tel: (31) 2 624 7110
Fax: (31) 2 620 9965
email: engel2x2xsyall.nl
Website: www.cinekid.nl
International children's film and television festival. Winning film is guaranteed distribution in the Netherlands

Dutch Film Festival
– 22 September – 1 October
Stichting Nederlands Film Festival
PO Box 1581
3500 BN Utrecht
Tel: (31) 30 2322684
Fax: (31) 30 2313200
email: ned.filmfest@inter.nl.net
Website: www.nethlandfilm.nl/
Annual screening of a selection of new Dutch features, shorts, documentaries, animation and television drama. Retrospectives, seminars, talkshows, Cinema Militans Lecture, Holland Film Meeting, outdoor programme. Presentation of the Grand Prix of Dutch Film: the Golden Calf Awards

International Documentary Filmfestival Amsterdam
– 24 November/2 December
Kleine-Gartmanplantsoen 10
1017 RR Amsterdam
Tel: (31) 20 6273329
Fax: (31) 20 6385388
Website: www.idfa.nl/
Competition programme: compet-itive for documentaries of any length, 35mm or 16mm, produced in 15 months prior to the festival; retrospectives; Joris Ivens award; Top 10 selected by well-known filmmaker; competitive video-programme; forum for international co-financing of European documentaries. Workshop, seminar and debates

International Film Festival Rotterdam

– 26 January/6 February
PO Box 21696
3001 AR Rotterdam
Tel: (31) 10 411 8080
Fax: (31) 10 413 5132
Website: www.lffrotterdam.nl/
Comprising 200 features, documentaries, shorts. Main programme presents international premiers, and a selection of the last year's festivals. Several sidebars and retrospectives. Cinemart: co-production market for films in progress. Deadline for entries 1 November. Tiger Award competition: three premiums, each US$10,000 for promising new film-makers

Le Nombre d'Or, International Widescreen Festival, Amsterdam

– 8-12 September 2000
IBC Office
Savoy Place
London WC2R OBL
Tel: 020 7240 3839
Fax: 020 7240 8830
email: show@ibc.org.uk
Website: www.ibc.org.uk/ibc
Jarlath O'Connel, Festival Co-ordinator
Competitive television Festival celebrating widescreen production in all genres and held as part of IBC in Amsterdam. Programmes must have been broadcast or have a broadcast date scheduled. The focus is on mainstream programming with documentaries, dramas and musci programmes making up the bulk of the entries. Programmes must have been shot on widescreen video (including HD) or in Super 16 or 35mm film as long as they have been electronically edited. Around 30 programmes are screened before an International Jury over three days of screenings and winning programmes are then re-screened on the final days. IBC also includes Masterclasses, Panel Discussions and Workshops aimed at the production community. The recent Festival attracted 105 entries from 18 countries. Deadline for entries is early June each year

New Zealand

Auckland International Film Festival

– July
PO Box 9544
Te Aro
Wellington 6035

Tel: (64) 4 385 0162
Fax: (64) 4 801 7304
Festival includes feature films, short films, documentaries, video and animation

Wellington Film Festival

– July
C/o New Zealand Film Festival
PO Box 9544
Te Aro
Wellington
Tel: (64) 4 385 0162
Fax: (64) 4 801 7304
email: enzedff@actrix.gen.nz
Festival includes feature films, short films, documentaries, video and animation

Norway

Norwegian International Film Festival

August
PO Box 145
5501 Haugesund
Tel: (47) 52 73 44 30
Fax: (47) 52 73 44 20
Non-competitive film festival, highlighting a selection of films for the coming theatrical season. New Nordic films – a market presenting Nordic films with a potential outside the Nordic Countries

Poland

International Short Film Festival in Kraków

– May/June
c/o PIF 'Apollo Film'
ul. Pychowicka 7
30-364 Kraków
Tel: (48) 12 67 23 40/67 13 56
Fax: (48) 12 67 15 52
Festival Director: Wit Dudek
Competitive for short films (up to 35 mins), including documentaries, fiction, animation, popular science and experimental subjects, produced in the previous 15 months

Portugal

Cinanima (International Animated Film Festival)

– November
Apartado 743
4501 Espinho Codex
Tel: (351) 2 734 4611/734 1621
Fax: (351) 2 734 6015
Competitive for animation short films, features, advertising and institutional, didactic and information, first film, title sequences and series. Entries must have been completed from January 1999 onwards

Encontros Internacionais de Cinema Documental

– November
Centro Cultural Malaposta
Rua Angola, Olival Basto
2675 Odivelas
Tel: (351) 9388570/407
Fax: (351) 9389347
email: amascultura@mail.telepac.pt
Director: Manuel Costa e Silva
Two categories: film and video (competition). Only event dedicated to documentary in Portugal, to increase awareness of the form and show work from other countries

Fantasporto '2000 – 20th Oporto International Film Festival

– 25 February/4 March 2000
Cinema Novo – Multimedia Centre
Rua da Constituição 311
4200 Porto
Tel: (351) 2 5073880
Fax: (351) 2 5508210
email: fantas@caleida.pt
Website: www.caleida.pt.fantasporto
Mario Dorminsky
Competitive section for feature films and shorts, particularly fantasy and science fiction films. Includes 10th New Directors week with an official competition, a Fantasia sectin dedicated to Eastern films and a Retrospective section. The Festival runs now in 8 theatres (2,700 seats altogether) and screens nearly 300 feature films each year. Also includes, in conjunction with the Portugese Film Institute, a programme of Potuguese film

Festival Internacional de Cinema da Figueira da Foz

– August/September
Apartado de Correios 5407
1709 Lisbon Codex
Tel: (351) 1 812 62 31
Fax: (351) 1 812 62 28
email: jose.marques@ficff.pt
Website: www.ficff.pt
Competitive for fiction and documentary films, films for children, shorts and video. Some cash prizes. Special programmes on different directors and countries. Also retrospective of Portuguese cinema. Entries must have been produced during 20 months preceding Festival

Festival Internacional de Cinema de Troia

– June
International Film Festival
Forum Luisa Todi
Avenida Luisa Todi, 61-65
2900 Setúbal
Tel: (351) 65 52 59 08 – 53 40 59

Fax: (351) 65 52 56 81
Three categories: Official Section,
First Films, Man and His
Environment, also information
section. The Official Section is
devoted to films coming from those
countries which have a limited
production (less than 21 features per
year). Films must not have been
screened previously in Portugal and
must have been produced during 12
months preceding the Festival. Also
film market, retrospectives in the
information section, Gay and Lesbian
section, Jury selection

Puerto Rico

Puerto Rico International Film Festival
– November
70 Mayagüez Street, Suite B1
Hato Rey PR 00918
Tel: (1) 809 764 7044
Fax: (1) 809 753 5367
Non-competitive international, full-length feature event with emphasis
on Latin American, Spanish and
women directors. FIPRESCI jury for
the Latin American selection

Russia

International Film Festival of Festivals
– June
10 Kamennoostrovsky Avenue
St Petersburg 197101
Tel: (7) 812 237 0304
Fax: (7) 812 233 2174
Non-competitive, aimed at promoting
films from all over the world that meet
the highest artistic criteria, and the
distribution of non-commercial cinema

Moscow International Film Festival
– July
Interfest, General Management of
International Film Festivals
10 Khokholski Per
Moscow 109028
Tel: (7) 95 917 9154
Fax: (7) 95 916 0107

Serbia

Belgrade International Film Festival
– January/February
Sava Centar
Milentija Popovica 9
11070 Novi Beograd
Tel: (38) 11 222 49 61
Fax: (38) 11 222 11 56
Non-competitive for features
refl-ecting high aesthetic and artistic
values and contemporary trends

Singapore

Singapore International Film Festival – April
29A Keong Saik Road
Singapore 089136
Tel: (65) 738 7567
Fax: (65) 738 7578
email: filmfest@pacific.net.sg
Specialised competitive festival for
Best Asian Film. Non-competitive
includes panorama of international
film. 8mm, 16mm, 35mm and video
are accepted. Films must not have
been shown commercially in
Singapore

Slovakia

Forum – Festival of First Feature Films
– October
Brectanova
833 14 Bratislava 1
Tel: (42) 7 378 8290
Fax: (42) 7 378 8290
International competition for first
feature films at least 50 minutes long,
and made or first shown in the 16
months preceding the Festival

South Africa

Cape Town International Film Festival
– April/May
University of Cape Town
Private Bag
Rondebosch 7700
Tel: (27) 21 23 8257/8
Fax: (27) 21 24 2355
Annual festival which runs over a three
week period during April/May.
Screenings are in 35mm, 16mm as well
as video with an emphasis on
contemporary, international feature films

Durban International Film Festival
University of Natal
Centre for Creative Arts
4014 Durban
Tel: (27) 31 260 2506
Fax: (27) 31 260 3074
The Festival aims to showcase films
of quality to local audiences,
including screenings in peri-urban
areas of the city

Spain

Bilbao International Festival of Documentary & Short Films
– November/December
Colón de Larreátegui 37, 4o drcha
48009 Bilbao

Tel: (34) 4 248698/247860
Fax: (34) 4 245624
Competitive for animation, fiction
and documentary

International Film Festival For Young People of Gijón
– November/December
Maternidad 2-20
33207 Gijón
Tel: (34) 8 5343739
Fax: (34) 8 5354152
Competitive for features and shorts.
Must have been produced during 18
months preceding the festival and not
awarded a prize at any other major
international film festival

International Short Film Contest 'Ciudad de Huesca'
– June
C/Del Parque 1,2
(Circulo Oscense)
Huesca 22002
Tel: (34) 974 212582
Fax: (34) 974 210065
email: huescafest@tsai.es
Website: www.huescafilmfestival.
com
Competitive for short films (up to 30
mins) on any theme except tourism
and promotion

L'Alternativa, International Independent Film Festival of Barcelona
November
Centre de Cultura Contemporànea
de Barcelona
C/Montalegre 5
08001 Barcelona
Tel: (34) 93 306 41 00
Fax: (34) 93 306 41 04
email: alternativa@cccb.org
Contact: Tessa Renaudd
L'Alternativa is dedicated to
screening creative and innovative
cinema from around the world.
Composed of three official sections
(short, feature and documentary) all
films compete in front of an
international jury. A film market,
retrospective screenings and seminars
run parallel to the official sections

Mostra de Valencia/Cinema del Mediterrani
– October
Pza del Arzobispo 2 bajo
46003 Valencia
Tel: (34) 6 392 1506
Fax: (34) 6 391 5156
Competitive official section.
Informative section, special events
section, 'mostra' for children, and
International Congress of Film Music

Ourense Film Festival

– *26 September/2 October*
C/Cardenal Quiroga 15, 3o Of. 25
32003 Ourense
Tel: (34) 88 215885
Fax: (34) 88 215885
Festival Internacional de Cine
Independiente de Ourense – Second
international festival for independent
cinema. Competitive sections for
every independent short or long
length film

San Sebastian International Film Festival

Plaza OQuendo S/N
20004 San Sebastian
Tel: (34) 943 48 12 12
Fax: (34) 943 48 12 18
email: ssiff@mail.ddnet.es
Website: www.sabsebastianfestival.
com
Diego Galan
Competitive for feature films
produced in the previous year and not
released in Spain or shown in any
other festivals. Non-competitive for
Zabaltegi/Open Zone. Also
retrospective sections. New
Director's Prize to the best first or
second film. 150,000 ECUS given to
the producer and director of the
winning film as co-production for
their next film

Sitges International Film Festival of Catalonia

– *October*
Av Josep Tarradellas
135 ESC A, 3r. 2a.
08029 Barcelona
Tel: (34) 3 93 419 3635
Fax: (34) 3 93 439 7380
email:cinsit@sitgesfur.com
Website: www.sitges.com/cinema
Two official sections. One for fantasy
films and others for non-genre files.
Also shorts, retrospective and
animation sections

Valladolid International Film Festival

– *October*
PO Box 646
47080 Valladolid
Tel: (34 83) 30 57 00/77/88
Fax: (34 83) 30 98 35
email: festval.ladolid@seminci.com
Website: www.seminic.com
Director: Fernando Lara
Competitive for 35mm features and
shorts, plus documentaries, entries
not to have been shown previously in
Spain. Also film school tributes,
retrospectives and selection of new
Spanish productions

Sweden

Gotebörg Film Festival

– *28 January/6 February 2000*
Box 7079
402 32 Gothenburg
Tel: (46) 31 41 05 46
Fax: (46) 31 41 00 63
email:goteborg@filmfestivl.org
Website: www.goteborg.filmfestival.
org
Non-competitive for features,
documentaries and shorts not
released in Sweden

Stockholm International Film Festival

– *November*
PO Box 7673
103 95 Stockholm
Tel: (46) 8 67 75 000
Fax: (46) 8 20 05 90
Competitive for innovative current
feature films, focus on American
Independents, a retrospective,
summary of Swedish films released
during the year, survey of world
cinema. Around 100 films have their
Swedish premiere during the festival.
FIPRESCI jury, FIAPF accredited.
'Northern Lights' – Critics Week

Umea International Film Festival

– *September*
PO Box 43
S 901 02
Umea
Tel: (46) 90 13 33 88
Fax: (46) 90 77 79 61
email: film.festival@ff.umea.se
Non-competitive festival with focus
mainly on features but does except
shorts and documentaries. About 150
films are screened in several sections.
The festival also organises seminars

Uppsala International Short Film Festival

– *18-24 October*
Box 1746
S-751 47 Uppsala
Tel: (46) 18 12 00 25
Fax: (46) 18 12 13 50
email: uppsala@shortfilmfestival.
com
Website: www.shortfilmfestival.com
Competitive for shorts (up to 60
mins), including fiction, animation,
experimental films, documentaries,
children's and young people's films.
16 and 35mm only

Switzerland

19th Vevey International Comedy Film Festival

– *22 September/8 October 2000*
CP 421
1800 Vevey
Tel: (41) 21 925 80 31
Fax: (41) 21 925 80 35
Competitive for medium and short
films, hommage and retrospective

Festival International de Films de Fribourg

– *12-19 March 2000*
Rue de Locarno 8
CH -1700 Fribourg
Tel: (41) (26) 322 22 32
Fax: (41) (26) 322 79 50
email: info@fiff.ch
Website: www.fiff.ch
Martial Knoebel
Competitive for films from Africa,
Asia and Latin America (16/35mm,
video). Films (16/35mm) may be
circulated throughout Switzerland
after the Festival

Golden Rose of Montreux TV Festival

– *April*
Télévision Suisse Romande
PO Box 234
1211 Geneva 8
Tel: (41) 22 708 8599
Fax: (41) 22 781 5249
email: gabrielle.bucher@tsr.ch
Competitive for television
productions (24-60 mins) of light
entertainment, music and variety, first
broadcast in the previous 14 months

International Film – Video – Multimedia Festival Lucerne

– *VIPER 27-31 October 1999*
PO Box 4929
6002 Lucerne
Tel: (41) 41 362 17 17
Fax: (41) 41 362 17 18
email: info@viper.ch
Website: www.viper.ch
The festival presents new
international innovative,
experimental and artistic media
productions: Film, Video, CD-ROM,
internet-projects. Two competitions:
International competition for Film
and Video (award sum SFR 10.000)
and national competition for Film
and Video (award sum SFR 5.000
plus material assets). VIPER also
includes the "Videogallery", an
outstanding selection of film and
video work which is run by co-
operating European festivals

Locarno International Film Festival

Via della Posta 6
CP 844
6601 Locarno

Tel: (41) 91 751 02 32
Fax: (41) 91 751 74 65
email: info@pardo.ch
Website: www.pardo.ch
Programme includes: a) Competition reserved for fiction features representative of Young Cinema (first or second features) and New Cinema (films by more established filmmakers who are innovating in film style and content and works by directors from emerging film industries). b) A (non-competitive) selection of films with innovative potential in style and content. c) A retrospective designed to enlarge perspectives on film history

Nyon International Documentary Film Festival – Visions du Réel
– 1-7 May 2000
PO Box 593
CH-1260 Nyon
Tel: (41) 22 361 60 60
Fax: (41) 22 361 70 71
International competition

Semaine Internationale du Vidéo/International Video Week
– November odd years
Saint Gervais Gèneve, Centre pour l'image contemporaire
5 rue du Temple
1201 Geneva
Tel: (41) 22 908 20 60
Fax: (41) 22 908 20 01
Competition with international entries; seminars and conferences; retrospectives; special programmes; installations; Swiss art school programme

Tunisia

Carthage Film Festival
– October/November
The JCC Managing Committee
5 Avenue Ali Belahouane
2070 La Marsa
Tel: (216) 1 745 355
Fax: (216) 1 745 564
Official competition open to Arab and African short and feature films. Entries must have been made within two years prior to the festival, and not have been awarded first prize at any previous international festival in an African or Arab country. Also has an information section, an international film market (MIPAC) and a workshop

Turkey

International Istanbul Film Festival
– April

Istanbul Foundation for Culture and Arts
Istiklal Cad Luvr
Apt No: 146
80070 Beyoglu
Istanbul
Tel: (90) 1 212 293 3133
Fax: (90) 1 212 249 7771
Two competitive sections, international and national. The International Competition for feature films on art (literature, theatre, cinema, music, dance and plastic arts) is judged by an international jury and the 'Golden Tulip Award' is presented as the Grand Prix. Entry by invitation

United Kingdom

Bath Film Festival
– October 13-5 November 2000
7 Terrace Walk
Bath BA1 1LN
Tel: 01225 401149
Fax: 01225 401149
Chris Baker, co-ordinator
Non-competitive, screening c30, preview, current, recent and classic features. 'Events Programme' of workshops, seminars, courses, film with other art forms especially music, screenings of the work of emergent filmmakers, and one or two 'keystone' events each year aimed at attracting national interest

BBC British Short Film Festival
Room A214
BBC Centre House
56 Wood Lane
London W12 7SB
Tel: 020 8743 8000 ext 62222/62052
Fax: 020 8740 8540
Competitive for short film in all categories (up to 40 mins). Thematic and specialised programmes and special events. Prizes awarded include Best British and International Productions. Closing date for entries is early June

Birmingham International Film and TV Festival
9 Margaret Street
Birmingham, B3 3BS
Tel: 0121 212 0777
Fax: 0121 212 0666
email: info@film-tv-festival.org.uk
Non-competitive for features and shorts, plus retrospective and tribute programmes. The Festival hosts conferences debating topical issues in film and television production

Bite the Mango
– September
National Museum of Photography,

Film & Television
Pictureville, Bradford BD1 1NQ
Tel: 01274 203320/203300
Fax: 01274 770217
Europe's only annual festival for South Asian and Black film and television. Entries accepted from South Asian and Black film and video-makers

Black Sunday – The British Genre Film Festival
51 Thatch Leach Lane
Whitefield
Manchester M25 6EN
Tel: 0161 766 2566
Fax: 0161 766 2566
Non-competitive for horror, thriller, fantasy, science-fiction and film noir genres produced in the previous year. First choice festival for UK premieres of many of the above genre films. Special guests and retrospective programmes

Blackpool Film Festival
– June/July
20 Glen Eldon Road
St Anne's-on-Sea
Lancashire FY8 2AU
Tel: 0253 721800
Fax: 0253 721800
Peter Stamford

Bradford Animation Festival
– March
National Museum of Photography
Film and Television
Pictureville
Bradford BD1 1NQ
Tel: 01274 203320/203300
Competitive festival for animated shorts in four categories: under 16s, non-professional, professional, experimental. Features closing awards night, interviews with animators, and international animation

Bradford Film Festival
– September
National Museum of Photography, Film & Television
Pictureville
Bradford BD1 1NQ
Tel: 01274 770000/ 01274 732277/203320
Fax: 01274 770217
Non-competitive for feature films. Strands include widescreen with world's only Cinerama Screen and IMAX. Focus on national cinema of selected European countries

Brief Encounters – Bristol Short Film Festivals
PO Box 576
Bristol BS99 2BD
Tel: 0117 9224628
Fax: 0117 9222906

THE NATIONAL MUSEUM OF PHOTOGRAPHY, FILM & TELEVISION

 6th Bradford Film Festival   3 – 18 March 2000

 Bradford Animation Festival   June 2000

 Bite the Mango   22 - 30 September 2000

Europe's Premier
Black and Asian Film Festival

- Film and Television Galleries
- Cubby Broccoli and
  Pictureville Cinemas
- 2D and 3D IMAX®
  Cinema Experience
- Double band
  35/16mm Preview Facilities

**NATIONAL
MUSEUM**

**PHOTOGRAPHY
FILM & TELEVISION**

National Museum of Photography,
Film & Television, Bradford BD1 1NQ

(01274) 20 20 30

Fax (01274) 72 31 55   www.nmpft.org.uk
talk.nmpft@nmsi.ac.uk

email: brief.encounters@dial.pipex.com

Competitive for short film in all categories (up to 30 mins). Thematic and specialised programmes and special events. Audience award. Closing date for entries end of July

Cambridge Film Festival
– July
Arts Cinema
8 Market Passage
Cambridge CB2 3PF
Tel: 01223 504444
Fax: 01223 578956
email: festival@cambarts.co.uk
Non-competitive; new world cinema selected from international festivals. Also featuring director retrospectives, short film programmes, thematic seasons and revived classics. Conference for independent exhibitors and distributors. Public debates and post-screening discussions

Chichester Film Festival
– 19 August/5 September
New Park Film Centre
New Park Road, Chichester
West Sussex PO19 1XN
Tel: 01243 784881/01243
Fax: 01243 539853
Contact: Roger Gibson
This is a non-competitive festival that focuses on previews, retrospectives of British film makers, with a special emphasis on UK and other European productions

Cinemagic – International Film Festival for Young People
– December
4th floor, 38 Dublin Road
Belfast BT2 7HN
Tel: 01232 311900
Fax: 01232 319709
Contact: Frances Cassidy
Competitive for international short and feature films aimed at 4-18 year-olds. The next festival will include the usual charity premieres, educational workpacks, practical workshops, directors talks and masterclasses with industry professionals. The Belfast event is to be held at Virgin Cinemas, Dublin Road

CineWomen
Cinema City
St.Andrew's Street
Norwich NR2 4AD
Tel: 01603 632366
Fax: 01603 7678238
email: j.h.morgan@uea.ac.uk
Jayne Hathor Morgan, Festival Director

Edinburgh Fringe Film and Video Festival
– February
29 Albany Street
Edinburgh EH1 3QN
Tel: 0131 556 2044
Fax: 0131 557 4400
Competitive for low-budget/independent/innovative works from Britain and abroad. All submissions welcome

Edinburgh International Film Festival
– 15– 29 August 1999
Filmhouse
88 Lothian Road
Edinburgh EH3 9BZ
Tel: 0131 228 4051
Fax: 0131 229 5501
email: info@edfilmfest.org.uk
Website: www.edfilmfest.org.uk
Patron: Sean Connery
Chairman: John McCormick
Director: Lizzie Francke
Producer: Ginnie Atkinson
Oldest continually running film festival in the world. Patron: Sean Connery. Programme sections: Gala (World, European or British premieres); Rosebud; Focus on British Section; Scene by Scene (illustrated lectures by film-makers); Retrospectives (film-makers and themes); Documentary; Mirrorball (music videos and music related projects); NBX (market place for UK productions); Also animation, out-door cinema events and short films. Prizes for Best British Feature, Best Animation, Best New Film etc. Submissions must be received by April

Edinburgh International Television Festival
– August
2nd Floor
24 Neal Street
London WC2H 9PS
Tel: 020 7370 4519
Fax: 020 7836 0702
email: EITF@festival.demon.co.uk
A unique forum for discussion between programme makers and broadcasters, comprising around 30 workshops, lectures and debates

European Short Film Festival
– annually 2nd weekend in November
11 Holbein House
Holbein Place
London SW1 8NH
Tel: 020 7460 3901
Fax: 020 7259 9278
email: pearl@bogo.co.uk
Website: www.bogo.co.uk/kohle/film
Fritz Kohle, Festival Director
Drama, documentaries, film/video up to 20 minutes in length. Technical

requirements: VHS preview tape. 35mm, 16mm, Beta SP or VHS screening copy. Films must have been made during the last three years. Awards include Audience Award, Best Director, Best Producer, Best Cast, Best Drama, Best Documentary, Best Experimental Deadline 30 September.

Festival of Fantastic Films
– September
33 Barrington Road
Altrincham
Cheshire WA14 1H2
Tel: 0161 929 1423
Fax: 0161 929 1067
email: 101341.3352@compuserve.com
Festival celebrates science fiction and fantasy film. Features guests of honour, interviews, signing panels, dealers, talks and over 30 film screenings

Foyle Film Festival
– November
The Nerve Centre
2nd Floor, Northern Counties Building, 8 Custom House Street
Derry BT48 6AE
Tel: 01504 267432
Fax: 01504 371738
email: S.Kelpie@nerve-centre.org.uk
Shauna Kelpie (Festival Director)
Northern Ireland's major annual film event celebrated its 10th year in 1996. The central venue is the Orchard cinema in the heart of Derry city centre

French Film Festival
– November
13 Randolph Crescent
Edinburgh EH3 7TX
Tel: 0131 225 5366
Fax: 0131 220 0648
The UK's only festival devoted solely to French cinema including feature films and shorts. Section on first or second films qualifies for the Hennessy Audience Award. Retrospectives, panorama of new productions, and debates. Based at venues in three cities: Filmhouse, Edinburgh, Glasgow Film Theatre and Aberdeen Belmont Centre

Green Screen (London's International Environmental Film Festival)
– November
45 Shelton Street
London WC2H 9JH
Tel: 020 7379 7390
Fax: 020 7379 7197
Non-competitive selection of international environmental films, question and answer sessions

following every film showing with well known environmentalists, film-makers, media personalities and celebrities with environmental clout

International Animation Festival, Cardiff
– June
18 Broadwick Street
London W1V 1FG
Tel: 020 7494 0506
Fax: 020 7494 0807

International Celtic Film and Television Festival
– March
The Library, Farraline Park
Inverness IV1 1LS
Tel: 01463 226 189
Fax: 01463 716 368
Competition for films whose subject matter has particular relevance to the Celtic nations

Italian Film Festival
– April
82 Nicolson Street
Edinburgh EH8 9EW
Tel: 0131 668 2232
Fax: 0131 668 2777
A unique UK event throwing an exclusive spotlight on il cinema italiano over ten days in Edinburgh (Filmhouse) Glasgow (Film Theatre); and London (Riverside). Visiting guests and directors, debates, first and second films, plus a broad range of current releases and special focuses on particular actors or directors

IVCA Awards
– October
IVCA
Bolsover House
5-6 Clipstone Street
London W1P 8LD
Tel: 020 7580 0962
Fax: 020 7436 2606
email: info@ivca.org
Website: www.ivca.org
Competitive for non-broadcast industrial/training films and videos, covering all aspects of the manufacturing and commercial world, plus categories for educational, business, leisure and communications subjects. Programme, Special and Production (Craft) Awards, and industry award for effective communication. Closing date for entries December

Kino Festival of New Irish Cinema
– March
48 Princess Street
Manchester M1 6HR
Tel: 0161 288 2494
Fax: 0161 281 1374

email: John.kino@good.co.uk
Website: www.kinofilm.org.uk
John Wojowski
Irish Film Festival devoted solely to new work. The festival features both short films and features. Low budget, innovative features especially welcome. Short films of all categories (inc student work) can be submitted. Special categories of new work by expatriate Irish Film makers. Work can be submitted any time before the deadline date. Deadline for submissions 25 January (late submissions only by arrangement). Work must have been completed within the last 18 months. Six awards (funding permitting). Application forms can be obtained by tel/fax/email

KinoFilm
– October/November
Manchester International Short Film and Video Festival
48 Princess Street
Manchester M1 6HR
Tel: 0161 288 2494
Fax: 0161 281 1374
email: John.kino@good.co.uk
Website: www.kinofilm.org.uk
John Wojowski
Kinofilm is dedicated to short films and videos from every corner of the world. Emphasis is placed on short innovative, unusual and off-beat productions. Films on any subject or theme can be submitted providing they are no longer than 30 minutes and were produced within the last two years and have not been previously submitted. All sections of film/video making community are eligible. Particularly welcome are applications from young film-makers and all members of the community who have never had work shown at festivals. Special categories include: Gay and Lesbian, Black Cinema, New Irish Cinema, New American Underground, Eastern European Work, Super 8 Film. Closing date for submissions for 2000 is August 2000 Please telephone or fax for an application form. Entry fee £2.50 National, £5.00 International. Application forms can be downloaded from the Kino website. Competive strand was introduced for 1999

Leeds International Film Festival
– October
Town Hall
The Headrow
Leeds LS1 3AD
Tel: 0113 247 8389
Fax: 0113 247 8397
Non-competitive for feature films,

documentaries and shorts, plus thematic retrospective programme. Lectures, seminars and exhibitions

London Film Festival
– November
National Film Theatre
South Bank
London SE1 8XT
Tel: 020 7815 1322/1323
Fax: 020 7633 0786
Non-competitive for feature films, shorts and video, by invitation only, which have not previously been screened in Great Britain. Some entries travel to regional film theatres as part of a national tour from November to December

London Jewish Film Festival
– June
National Film Theatre
South Bank
London SE1 8XT
Tel: 020 7815 1323/1324
Fax: 020 7633 0786
Non-competitive for film and video made by Jewish directors and/or concerned with issues relating to Jewish identity and other issues. Some entries travel to regional film theatres as part of a national tour

London Latin American Film Festival – September
Metro Pictures
79 Wardour Street
London W1V 3TH
Tel: 020 7434 3357
Fax: 020 7287 2112
Non-competitive, bringing to London a line up of contemporary films from Latin America and surveying current trends

London Lesbian and Gay Film Festival
– 30 March – 13 April 2000
Festivals Office National Film Theatre, South Bank
London SE1 8XT
Tel: 020 7815 1323/1324
Fax: 020 7633 0786
Non-competitive for film and videos of special interest to lesbian and gay audiences. Some entries travel to regional film theatres as part of a national tour from April to June

Raindance Film Showcase
81 Berwick Street
London W1V 3PF
Tel: 020 7287 3833
Fax: 020 7439 2243
Britain's only film market for independently produced features, shorts and documentaries. Deadline 1 September

Sheffield International Documentary Festival

– *October*
The Workstation
15 Paternoster Row
Sheffield S1 2BX
Tel: 0114 276 5141
Fax: 0114 272 1849
email: shefdoc@info.sidf.co.uk
Website: www.sidf.co.uk
The only UK festival dedicated to excellence in documentary film and television. The week long event is both a public film festival and an industry gathering with sessions, screenings and discussions on all the new developments in documentary. The festival is non-competitive

Shots in the Dark– Crime, Mystery and Thriller Festival

– *June*
Broadway
14-18 Broad Street
Nottingham NG1 3AL
Tel: 0115 952 6600/6611
Fax: 0115 952 6622
Non-competitive for all types of mysteries and thrillers. Includes previews of new movies, retrospectives, television events, special guests. Honorary Patron: Quentin Tarantino

Television and Young People (TVYP)

– *August*
24 Neal Street
London WC2H 9PS
Tel: 020 7379 4519
Fax: 020 7836 0702
email: TVYP@festival.demon.co.uk
Website: www.typ.org
Varsha Patel
Television and Young People is the educational arm of the Guardian Edinburgh International Television Festival and the UK's leading forum for young people aspiring to work in television. TVYP is a five day festival of events giving new entrants an insight into every aspect of the television industry through a programme of masterclasses, workshops, screenings, can career surgeries, and the opportunity to meet, work with, and learn from some of the leading creative talent in the industry. TVYP offers 150 places to young people aged 18-21 from the UK. Other than their travel to Edinburgh, all expenses are covered by TVYP

Video Positive

– *March/April 2000*
International Biennale of Video and Electronic Media Art

Foundation for Art and Creative Technology (FACT)
Bluecoat Chambers
School Lane
Liverpool L1 3BX
Tel: 0151 709 2663
Fax: 0151 707 2150
Non-competitive for video and electronic media art produced worldwide in the two years preceding the festival. Includes community and education programmes, screenings, workshops and seminars. Some commissions available

Welsh International Film Festival, Aberystwyth

– *November*
c/o Premiere Cymru Wales Cyf
Unit 6G, Cefn Llan
Aberystwyth
Dyfed SY23 3AH
Tel: 01970 617995
Fax: 01970 617942
email: wff995@aber.ac.uk
Non-competitive for international feature films and shorts, together with films from Wales in Welsh and English. Also short retrospectives, workshops and seminars. D M Davies Award (£25,000) presented to the best short film submitted by a young film maker from Wales

Wildscreen

– *7-13 October 2000*
PO Box 366, Deanery Road
College Green
Bristol BS99 2HD
Tel: 0117 909 6300
Fax: 0117 909 5000
email: info@widscreen.org.uk
International festival of moving images from the natural world. Competitive: Panda Awards include Conservation, Revelation, Newcomer, Children's, Outstanding Achievement, Craft and multimedia. Eligible productions completed after 1 January 1998 and not entered in Wildscreen 98. Week long festival includes screenings, discussions, video kiosks, masterclasses and workshops

Uruguay

International Children's Film Festival

– *March/April*
Cinemateca Uruguaya
Carnelli 1311,
Casilla de Correo 1170
11200 Montevideo
Tel: (598) 2 408 24 60
Fax: (598) 2 409 45 72
Competitive for fiction international films, documentaries and animation for children

International Film Festival of Uruguay

– *April*
Cinemateca Uruguaya
Carnelli 1311,
Casilla de Correo 1170
11200 Montevideo
Tel: (598) 2 48 24 60
Fax: (598) 2 49 45 72
Competitive for fiction and Latin American videos

USA

AFI Los Angeles International Film Festival

– *October*
2021 N Western Avenue
Los Angeles
CA 90027
Tel: (1) 213 856 7707
Fax: (1) 213 462 4049
email: afifest@afionline.org
Competitive, FIAPF accredited. Features, documentaries, shorts by invitation

AFI National Video Festival

– *October*
2021 N Western Avenue
Los Angeles
CA 90027
Tel: (1) 213 856 7707
Fax: (1) 213 462 4049
Non-competitive. Screenings in Los Angeles, Washington. Accepts: 1" U-Matic, NTSC/PAL/SECAM (No Beta, no 1"

AFM (American Film Market)

9th Floor, 10850 Wiltshire Blvd,
Los Angeles
CA 90024
Tel: (1) 310 446 1000
Fax: (1) 310 446 1600
Annual market for film, television and video

Asian American International Film Festival

– *July*
c/o Asian CineVision
32 East Broadway, 4th Floor
New York, NY 10002
Tel: (1) 212 925 8685
Fax: (1) 212 925 8157
Non-competitive, all categories and lengths. No video-to-film transfers accepted as entries. Films must be produced, directed and/or written by artists of Asian heritage

Chicago International Children's Film Festival

– *October*
Facets Multimedia
1517 West Fullerton Avenue

Chicago IL 60614
Tel: (1) 773 281 9075
Fax: (1) 773 929 5437 or 773 929 0266
email: kidsfest@facets.org
Competitive for entertainment films, videotapes and television programmes for children. Deadline for entries 28 May 1999

35th Chicago International Film Festival
– 6-21 October 1999
32 West Randolph Street
Suite: 600
Chicago
Illinois 60601 USA
Tel: (1) 312 425 9400
Fax: (1) 312 425 0944
email: filmfest@wwa.com
Website: www.chicago.ddbn.com/filmfest/
Contact: Michael Kutza
Founder & Artistic director
Competitive for feature films, documentaries, shorts, animation, student and First and Second Features

Cleveland International Film Festival
1621 Euclid Avenue, Suite 428
Cleveland
OH 44115
Tel: (1) 216 623 0400
Fax: (1) 216 623 0103
Non-competitive for feature, narrative, documentary, animation and experimental films. Competitive for shorts, with $2,500 prize money

Columbus International Film and Video Festival (a.k.a. The Chris Awards)
20-22 October 1999
5701 High Street
Suite 200
Worthington
Ohio 43085
Fax: (1) 614 841 1666
email: chrisawd@infinet.com
Website: www.infinet.com/~chrisawd
The Chris Awards is one of the longest-running competitions of its kind in North America, specialising in honouring documentary, education, business and information films and videos, as well as categories for the arts and entertainment. Entrants compete within categories for the first place Chris statuette, second place Bronze plaque and third place Certificate of Honorable Mention Expanded public screenings. Entry deadline 1 July

Denver International Film Festival
– October

1430 Larimer Square
Suite 201
Denver
CO 80202
Tel: (1) 303 595 3456
Fax: (1) 303 595 0956
email: dfs@denverfilm.org
Non-competitive. New international features, tributes to film artists, independent features, documentaries, shorts, animation, experimental works, videos and children's films

Flagstaff International Film Festival – Worldfest Flagstaff
PO Box 56566
Houston, Texas
77256
Tel: (1) 713 965 9955
Fax: (1) 713 965 9960
email: worldfest@aol.com
Website: www.worldfest.org
Competitive for features and shorts. Production seminar and workshop series of three seminars. Cash awards, plus Worldfest Discovery programme. Winners introduced to organisers of top 200 international festivals. Screenplay category: winning screenplays submitted to top 100 US creative agencies

Florida Film Festival
1300 South Orlando Avenue
Maitland
FL 32751
Tel: (1) 407 629 1088
Fax: (1) 407 629 6870
A 10 day event involving over 100 films, several seminars and social events. It includes an American Independent Film Competition with three categories: dramatic, documentary and short films

Fort Lauderdale International Film Festival
– October/November
1402 East Lasolas Blvd 007
Fort Lauderdale
FL 33301
Tel: (1) 954 760 9898
Fax: (1) 954 760 9099
The festival typically features 40 – 50 full length features, plus documentaries, an art on film series, short subjects, as well as animation. Awards are presented for Best Film, Best Foreign Language Film, Documentary, Short, Director, Actor, Actress and an Audience Award. The Festival also features an international student film competition with cash prizes totalling over $5,000 with an additional $5,000 in product grants from Kodak

Hawaii International Film Festival
– 5-21 November 1999
1001 Bishop Street, Paacific Tower
Suite 745
Honolulu HI 96813
Tel: (1) 808 528 3456
Fax: (1) 808 528 1410
email: hiffinfo@hiff.org
Website: www.hiff.org
Entries must be produced in Asia, North America or the Pacific, or concern those areas and relate to the Festival's cross-cultural emphasis. Any genres welcomed. Awards given include best feature film promoting cultural understanding and best documentary film and audience award. Deadline 12 July 1999

Houston International Film and Video Festival – Worldfest Houston (+ Market)
April
PO Box 56566
Houston
TX 77256-6566
Tel: (1) 713 965 9955
Fax: (1) 713 965 9960
email: worldfest@aol.com
Website: www.worldfest.org
Competitive for features, shorts, documentary, television production and television commercials. Independent and major studios, experimental and video. Worldfest Discovery Programme where winners are introduced to organisers of top 200 international festivals. Screenplay category. Winning screenplays submitted to top 100 US creative agencies

Independent Feature Film Market
– September
12th Floor, 104 West 29th Street
New York
NY 1001-5310
Tel: (1) 212 465 8200
Fax: (1) 212 465 8525
email: IFPNY@ifp.org
Website: Web site: www.ifp.org
The Independent Feature Film Market is the largest running market devoted to new, emerging American independent film talent seeking domestic and foreign distribution. It is the market for discovering projects in development, outstanding documentaries, and startling works of fiction. Domestic and foreign filmmakers, distributors, and feature films. Sales agents, producers, festival representatives and casting directors attend to acquire and

evaluate both completed films and projects in development

Miami Film Festival
– January/February
Film Society of Miami
444 Brickell Avenue, Suite 229
Miami FL 33131
Tel: (1) 305 377 3456
Fax: (1) 303 577 9768
Non-competitive; screenings of 25-30 international films; all cate-gories considered, 35mm film only. Entry deadline 1 November

Mobius Advertising Awards Competition – February
841 North Addison Avenue
Elmhurst, IL 60126-1291
Tel: (1) 630 834 7773
Fax: (1) 630 834 5565
email:mobiusinfo@mobiusawards.com
Website: www.mobiusawards.com
International awards competition for television and radio commercials produced or released in the 12 months preceding the annual 1 October entry deadline. Founded in 1971

National Educational Media Network (formerly National Educational Film & Video Festival)
– November
655 Thirteenth Street
Oakland
CA 94612
Tel: (1) 510 465 6885
Fax: (1) 510 465 2835
email: nemn@nemn.org
Website: www.nemn.org
National Educational Media Network is the only US media organisation dedicated to recognising and supporting excellence in educational media, ranging from documentaries to moving image media designed especially for classroom and training programs. NEMN's internationally acclaimed annual Apple Awards competition is the largest in the US, with over 1,000 entrants yearly. The competition recognises excellence and innovation in educational film, video, television and multimedia works intended for national and international distribution. Awards are given to media programs demonstrating technical and artistic skill that educate, inform and empower the end-user.

New York Film Festival
Film Society of Lincoln Center
70 Lincoln Center Plaza, 4th Floor
New York NY 10023
Tel: (1) 212 875 5610
Fax: (1) 212 875 5636
Website: www.filmlinc.com
Non-competitive for feature films, shorts, including drama, documentary, animation and experimental films. Films must have been produced one year prior to the Festival and must be New York premieres

Nortel Palm Springs International Film Festival
– August
PO Box 2230
Palm Springs
California
CA 92263
Tel: (1) 760 322 2930
Fax: (1) 760 322 4087
At each festival world premieres mix with social functions, cultural events, industry seminars, student activities and directors workshops

Portland International Film Festival
– 11-28 February 2000
Northwest Film Center
1219 SW Park Avenue
Portland, OR 97205
Tel: (503) 221 1156
Fax: (503) 294 0874
email: info@nwfilm.org
Website: www.nwfilm.org
Invitational survey of New World cinema. Includes over 100 features, documentary and short films from more than two dozen countries. Numerous visiting artists. Attendance for the 23rd Festival is expected to be 35,000, drawn from throughout the North West of America

San Francisco International Film Festival
– April/May
1521 Eddy Street
San Francisco
CA 94115-4102
Tel: (1) 415 929 5014
Fax: (1) 415 921 5032
Feature films, by invitation, shown non-competitively. Shorts, documentaries, animation, experimental works and television productions eligible for Golden Gate Awards competition section.
Deadline for Golden Gate Awards entries early December

San Francisco International Lesbian & Gay Film Festival
– June
Frameline
346 Ninth Street
San Francisco CA 94103
Tel: (1) 415 703 8650
Fax: (1) 415 861 1404
Largest lesbian/gay film festival in the world. Features, documentary, experimental, short film and video.
Deadline for entries 15 February

Seattle International Film Festival
– May/June
911 Pine St 86th Fl.
Seattle
WA 98101
Tel: (1) 206 464 5830
Fax: (1) 206 264 7919
email: mail@seattle.com
Website: www.seattlefilm.com
Jury prize for new director and American independent award. Other audience-voted awards. Submissions accepted 1 Jan to 15 March

Sundance Film Festival
– 20-30 January 2000
PO Box 16450
Salt Lake City
UT 84116
Tel: (1) 801 328 3456
Fax: (1) 801 575 5175
Competitive for American independent dramatic and documentary feature films. Also presents a number of international and American premieres and short films, as well as sidebars, special retrospectives and seminars

Telluride Film Festival
– September
PO Box B-1156
53 South Main Street, Suite 212
Hanover NH 03755
Tel: (1) 603 643 1255
Fax: (1) 603 643 5938
email: tellufilm@aol.com
Website: www.elluridemm.com/filmfest.htm
Non-competitive. World premieres, archival films and tributes. Entry deadline 31 July

US International Film & Video Festival
– June
841 North Addison Avenue
Elmhurst
IL 60126-1291
Tel: (1) 630 834 7773
Fax: (1) 630 834 5565
email:filmfestinfo@filmfestawards.com
Website: www.filmfestawards.com
International awards competition for business, television, industrial and informational productions, produced or released in the 18 months preceding the annual 1 March entry deadline. Formerly the US Industrial Film and Video Festival, founded 1968

FILM SOCIETIES

Listed below are UK film societies which are open to the public (marked OP after the society name), those based in educational establishments (ST), private companies and organisations (CL), and some corporate societies (CP). Societies providing disabled access to their venues are marked (DA) – always contact the organiser beforehand to confirm details. Secretaries' addresses are grouped in broad geographical areas, along with the BFFS regional officers who can offer specific local information. Compiled by Tom Brownlie

British Federation of Film Societies (BFFS) Constituent Groups

British Federation of Film Societies (BFFS)
The Secretary
BFFS
PO BOX 1DR
London W1A 1DR
Tel: 020 7734 9300
Fax: 020 7734 9093

Eastern
Bedfordshire, Cambridgeshire, Essex, Hertfordshire, Lincolnshire, Norfolk, Suffolk

London
32 London Boroughs and the City of London

Midlands
Derbyshire (excluding High Peak District), Leicestershire, Northamptonshire, Nottinghamshire, Hereford and Worcester, Shropshire, Staffordshire, Warwickshire, Metropolitan districts of

Birmingham, Coventry, Dudley, Sandwell, Solihull, Walsall, Wolverhampton

North West
Cheshire, High Peak district of Derbyshire, Lancashire, Metropolitan districts of Bolton, Bury, Knowsley, City of Liverpool, Manchester, Oldham, Rochdale, St Helens, Salford, Sefton, Stockport, Tameside, Trafford, Wigan, Wirral, Northern Ireland

Northern
Cleveland, Cumbria, Durham, Northumberland, Metropolitan districts of Gateshead, Newcastle, North Tyneside, South Tyneside, Sunderland

Scotland
Aberdeen, Angus, Ayrshire, Dumfries, Edinburgh, Faroe Islands, Fife, Glasgow, Isle of Lewis, Isle of Skye, Livingston, Perth, Shetland, Stirling, Strathblane, West Lothian

South East
Kent, Surrey, East Sussex, West Sussex

South West
Avon, Channel Islands, Cornwall, Devon, Dorset (except districts of Bournemouth, Christchurch and Poole), Gloucestershire, Somerset

Southern
Berkshire, Buckinghamshire, Hampshire, Isle of Wight, Oxfordshire, Wiltshire, Districts of Bournemouth, Christchurch, Poole

Wales
Dyfed, Cardiff, Cardigan, Gwent, Merthyr Tydfil, Mid-Glamorgan, Powys, Swansea

Yorkshire
Humberside, North Yorkshire, Metropolitan districts of Barnsley, Bradford, Calderdale, Doncaster, Kirklees, Leeds, Rotherham, Sheffield, Wakefield

Eastern

Eastern Group BFFS
Gerry Dobson,
Kennel Cottage
Burton, Nr Lincoln,
Lincs LN1 2RD

Bedford Film Society OP
PJ Clark
33 The Ridgeway
Bedford MK41 8ES

Berkhamsted Film Society OP DA
Jenny Walsh
8 Cherry Gardens
Tring
Herts HP23 4EA

Bury St Edmunds Film Society OP DA
Don Smith
Rectory Cottage, Drinkstone
Bury St Edmunds
Suffolk IP30 9SP

Chelmsford Film Club OP DA
Coline Hewitt
Sixth Ave
Chelmsford, Essex CM1 4ED

Epping Film Society OP DA
Mrs A Berry
10 Bury Road
Epping, Essex CM16 5EU

Great Yarmouth Film Society OP
E C Hunt
21 Park Lane
Norwich, Norfolk NR2 3EE

Ipswich Film Society
Terry Cloke
4 Burlington Road
Ipswich
Suffolk IP1 2EU

Letchworth Film Society OP DA
Peter Griffiths
35 Broadwater Dale
Letchworth, Herts SG6 3HQ

Lincoln Film Society OP
Gerry Dobson
Kennel Cottage

Burton by Lincoln
Lincoln, Lincs LN1 2RD

Peterborough Film Society OP

Allan Bunch
196 Lincoln Road
Peterborough,
Cambs PE1 2NQ

Screen in the Barn

Brian Guthrie
Field House
Thrandeston, Diss
Norfolk 1P21 4BU

Trinity Arts Centre

Catherine Harrison
Trinity Street,
Gainsborough DN21 2AL

UEASU Film Society ST DA

Di Anderson
Students Union, UEA
Norwich
Norfolk NR4 7TJ

University of Essex Film Society ST

Matt McDonnell
Students' Union Building
Wivenhoe Park
Colchester, Essex CO4 3SQ

LONDON

British Federation of Film Societies (BFFS)

The Secretary
PO BOX 1DR
London W1A 1DR
Tel: 020 7734 9300
Fax: 020 7734 9093

Avant-Garde Film Society OP DA

Chris White
9 Elmbridge Drive
Ruislip, Middx HA4 7XD

Balham Film Festival

Peter Milton
22 Childebert Road
London SW17 8EX

Barclays Bank Film Society CL DA

Liza Castellino
c/o IUKRB HR, 5th Floor
St Swithin's House
11-12 St Swithin's Lane
London EC4P 8AS

BBC Film Club

61 Northdene
Chigwell
Essex 1GF 5JS

Chairman: Nigel Messenger
Membership: David Charlton

Brunel Film Society ST DA

The President
Brunel University
Uxbridge
Middx UB8 3PH

Chertsey Film Society

A Proctor
28 Wheatash Road
Addlestone
Surrey KT15 2ER

Imperial College Union Film Society ST DA

Ian Nicol
5 Sterling Place
South Ealing
London W5 4RA

Institut Francais Film Society OP

The Secretary
(Cinema Dept)
17 Queensberry Place
London SW7 2DT

John Lewis Partnership Film Society CL DA

Peter Allen
Business Information Department
John Lewis plc
171 Victoria Street
London SW1E 5NN

London Socialist Film Co-op

Nicola Seyd
13 Foundling Road
Brunswick Centre
London WC1N 1QE

National Physical Laboratory (NPL) Film Society CL

Roger Townsend
National Physical Laboratory
Queens Road
Teddington, Middx TW11 0LW

POSK Film Society

Zofia Binder, Membership Secretary
5 Rowan Road
London W6 7DT

Richmond Film Society

John Smith
16 Brackley Road
Chiswick
London W4 2HN

South London Film Society OP

Dr M Essex-Lopresti
14 Oakwood Park Road
Southgate
London N14 6QG

UCL Film Society ST

Simon Mesterten
University College London
25 Gordon Street
London WC1A 0AH

UCLU Film Society

Andrew Blackwell
25 Gordon Street
London WC1H OAH

University of Greenwich Film Society ST

William Clarke
University of Greenwich
Student's Union
Thomas Street, Woolwich
London SE18 6HU

Midlands

Midlands Group BFFS

Robert Johnson
The Villas, 86 School Lane,
Cookshill, Caverwall,
Stoke-on-Trent ST11 9EN

Derby University

The Secretary
Derby University FS
UDSU
Kedleston Road

Flicks in the Sticks

Ian Kerry
Further Up, Long Row
Lower Down
Lydbury North
Shrops SH7 8BB

Kinver Film Society OP DA

P M Hassall
13 Bredon Avenue
Stourbridge
West Midlands DY9 7NR

Loughborough Students Union Film Society ST

The Secretary
Student Union Building
Ashby Road
Loughborough, Leics LE11 3TT

Malvern Film Society OP

Sylvia Finnemore
Ledbury Terr, 17 Wyche Road,
Malvern Worcs

Nottingham Trent University Film Society

Laura Rowan
Byron House, Shakespeare Street
Nottingham

Octagon Film Club

Mike Lee
The Community Office

Welland Park Community College
Welland Park Road
Market Harborough, Leics, LE16

Open Film Society
David Reed
Faculty of Technology
The Open University, Walton Hall
Milton Keynes MK7 6AA

Rewind
Ian Killick
11 Framlington Grove
Kenilworth
Warwickshire CV8 2PS

Solihull Film Society OP DA
Steve Wharam
2 Coppice Road
Solihull, West Midlands B2 9JY

Stafford Film Society OP DA
Gerry McPherson
Orchard View, Mill Lane
Acton Gate
Stafford ST14 ORA

Three Rivers Film Society
Jon Taylor
222b New Road, Croxley Green
Rickmansworth, Herts, WD3 3HH

UCESU Film Society ST/OP
Jonathan King
University of Central England
Students Union
Perry Barr
Birmingham B3 3HQ

University of Keele Film Society ST
Nova Dudley
c/o Media & Communications
Keele University,
Staffs ST5 5BG

University of Warwick Film Society ST DA
The Secretary
Students Union
University of Warwick
Coventry CV4 7AL

North West

North West Group BFFS
Chris Coffey
BFFS North West Group
64 Dale Crescent,
St Helens,
Merseyside WA9 4YE

Aldham Roberts Learning Resources Centre
Liverpool John Moores University
Mount Pleasant, Liverpool L3 5UZ

Birkenhead Library Film Society
Susan Boote
Central Library, Borough Road
Birkenhead
Wirral L41 2XB

Bolton Institute Film Society
Laurette Evans
Arts Office
Chadwick Campus
Bolton BL2 1JW

Bolton School Arts and Conferences
Duncan Kyle
Chorley New Road
Bolton BL1 4PA

Chester Film Society OP
Tony Slater
2 Avon Close
Neston
S Wirral L64 OTH

Chorley Film Society OP
Chris Collinson
47 Bolton Road
Chorley, Lancs PR7 3AU

Cineast
Jonathan Redman
220 Manchester Road
Burnley, Lancashire BB11 4HG

Deeside Film Society OP DA
Peter Saunders
13 Manor Road, Hoylake, Wirral
Merseyside

Frodsham Film Society
Michael Donovan
58 The Willows
Frodsham
Cheshire WA6 7QS

Heswall Film Society OP DA
Alvin Sant
18 Fairlawn Court, Bidston Road
Birkenhead, L43 6UX

Hulme Hall Film Society
David Butler
Houldsworth 51
Hulme Hall, Oxford Place
Manchester M14 5RR

Kino Film Club CL
John Wojonski
13 Mersey Crescent
West Didsbury
Manchester M20 2ZJ

Lancaster University Film Society
Nicola Langham
Lonsdale College

University of Lancashire
Lancs LA1 4GT

Lytham St Annes Film Society OP DA
Alan Payne
18 Cecil Street
Lytham St Annes
Lancs FY8 5NN

Manchester and Salford Film Society OP DA
Tom Ainsworth
64 Egerton Road, Fallowfield
Manchester M14 6RA

Manchester University Film Society ST DA
The Secretary
Union Building
Oxford Road
Manchester M13 9PL

Peak Film Society
Adrian Smith
30 Green Lane
Simmondley
Glossop SK13 6XY

Preston Film Society OP DA
Michael Lockwood
14 Croftgate
Highgate Park, Fulwood
Preston
Lancs PR2 8LS

Saddleworth Film Society
Philip Adams
11 Huddersfield
Delph, Oldham

St Helen's Film Society CP
Chris Coffey
64 Dale Crescent
St Helens
Merseyside WA9 4YE

Society of Fantastic Films
Harry Nadler
5 South Mesnefield Road
Salford M7 0QP

Southport Film Guild OP
Irene Gunn
5 Chandley Close, Ainsdale
Southport
Merseyside PR8 2SJ

Northern

Northern Group BFFS
c/o Scottish Group
28 Thornyflat Road,
Ayr KA8 0LX

Bede Film Society
Christian Errington
College of St Hild & St Bede

University of Durham
Durham DH1 1SZ

Darlington Arts Centre
Stef Hynd
Vane Terrace
Darlington
Co Durham DL3 7AX

Durham University Film Unit ST DA
Heidi Moore
Durham Student's Union
Dunelm House
New Elvet
Durham, DH1 3AN

Film Club at the Roxy OP
Phil Evans
55 Hibbert Road
Barrow-in-Furness
Cumbria LA14 5AF

Kenswick Film Club
Paul Buttle
18 Brewery Lane
Keswick, Cumbria

Sunderland University Film and Video Society
John Davison
The Gallery
Ashburne House
Ryhope Road
Tyne & Wear S22 7EF

Scotland

Scottish Group BFFS
Ronald Currie
28 Thornyflat Road,
Ayr KA8 0LX

Aberdeen University Cinema Society
Garath Took
50/52 College Bounds
Old Aberdeen AB2 3DS

Ayr & Craigie Film Society OP DA
Ronald Currie
28 Thornyflat Road
Ayr
Ayrshire

Barony Film Society
Maureen Maciver
1 Lower Granton Road
Edinburgh EH5 2RX

Bathgate Regal
Margaret Hardy
Regal Community Theatre
24-34 North Bridge Street
Bathgate
West Lothian EH48 4PS

Callander Film Society OP
David Hinton
25 Bridgend
Callander, Perthshire FK17 8AG

Cove & Kilgreggan Film Society
Sally Garwood
Upper Flat, Cragowlet West,
Shore Road, Cove G84 OLS

Crieff Film Society OP
Charles Lacaille
5 Gilfillan Court
Commercial Lane
Comrie
Perthshire PH6 2DP

Dundee University FS
Paul McQuade
c/o DUSA
Airlie Place
Dundee DD1

Edinburgh University Film Society ST DA
Societies' Centre
60 The Pleasance
Edinburgh EH8 9TJ

Electric Shadows – Glasgow University Film Club
Leah Panos
Flat 1/3, 61 Cecil Street
Glasgow G12 8RW

Linlithgow Film Society OP
Jenny Gilford
81 Belsyde Court
Linlithgow
West Lothian EH49 7RL

The Park Film Society
Mrs J Marchant
15 Kennedy Court
Braidnom Cres
Glasgow, Strathclyde

Portree Film Society
James Cryer
1 Camastianavaig
Braes by Portree
Isle of Skye IV51 9LQ

Queen Margaret College Film Society OP DA
Andrew Meneghini
Queen Margaret College
Grainger Stewart A6
Clerwood Terrace
Edinburgh EH12 8TS

RGU Film Society
Alec Grant
Faculty of Management
Robert Gordon University
Garthdee Road
Aberdeen AB10 7QE

St Brides Film Society
George Williamson
St Brides, 10 Orwell Terrace,
Edinburgh EH11 2DY

Shetland Film Club
Stuart Hubbard
Nethaburn
Wester Quarff
Shetland ZE2 9EZ

Stirling Film Society
Alan McMaster
10a Wallace St
Stirling FK8 1NP

Stirling University Film Club
The President
SUSA, Stirling University
Stirling FK9 4LA

Ten Day Weekend
Shelagh Stewart
Unit 14, Firhill Business Centre
76 Firhill Road
Glasgow G20 7BA

Tweedale Film Club OP DA
Jeanette Carlyle
Top Floor, 23 Marchmont Road
Edinburgh EH9 1HY

Uist Art Association
Helen McDonald
Liniclate School
Benbecula
Western Isles HS7 SPT

South East

South East Group
c/o Southern Group, 1 Vanstone
Cottages, Bagshot Road, Englefield
Green, Egham,
Surrey TW20 ORS

Buckingham and Winslow Film Society
J Childs
22a Aylesbury Road, Wing
Leighton Buzzard

Dover Film Society OP
D Pratt
19 Bramley Avenue
Canterbury
Kent CT1 3XW

Eastbourne Film Society
Barbara Wilson
2 Chalk Farm Close
Willingdon
Eastbourne
East Sussex BN20 9HY

Lewes Film Guild OP DA
Mary Burke

6 Friars Walk
Lewes, East Sussex BN7 2LE

Maidstone Film Society
Moira Hancock
2 Brockenhurst Avenue,
Maidstone, Kent ME15 7ED

Steyning Film Society
J Rampton
Woodbine Cottage, 124 High Street
Steyning , W Sussex BN44 3RD

Studio Film Society
Chris Archer
28 Beckenham Road
Beckenham BR3 4LS

Walton & Weybridge Film Society
Joan Westbrook
28 Eastwick Road
Walton on Thames
Surrey KT12 5AD

South West

South West Group BFFS
Brian Clay
The Garden Flat,
71 Springfield Road, Cotham
Bristol BS6 5SW

Bradford on Avon Film Society
Chris Jenkinson
16 Trowbridge Road
Bradford on Avon
Wiltshire BA15 1AG

Bath Film Festival
Chris Baker
7 Terrace Walk
Bath, NE Somerset BA1 1LN

Bath Film Society
Andree Peacock
Lower Byway, Chapel Lane
Box, Corsham, Wilts SN13 8NU

Bath University Film Society
The Secretary
c/o BUSU
University of Bath, Bath BA2 7AY

Blandford Forum Film Society OP DA
B Winkle
6A Bayfran Way
Blandford Forum
Dorset DT11 7RZ

Bournemouth and Poole Film Society OP
Peter Coles
2 Lytchett Drive, Broadstone
Dorset BH18 9LB

Bridport Film Society
Mary Wood
9 Bowhayes
Greenways
Bridport, Dorset DT6 4EB

Cheltenham Film Society OP DA
Geoff Luck
8 Edgeworth, Miserden Road
Cheltenham, Glos GL51 6BW

Cinema at the Warehouse OP
Jo Canning
High Wells, West Street, Hnton St
George, Somerset TA17 8SA

Cinematheque Yeovil OP DA
G Rixon
The Old Police House
Church Street, Ilchester,
Somerset BA22 8LL

City of Bath College
James Trice
Student's Union
Aron Street, Bath BA1 1UP

Dartmouth Film Society
Karen Wale
146 Bayards Castle Steps
South Town
Dartmouth, Devon TQ6

Dorchester Film Society OP DA
Ann Evans
62 Casterbridge Road
Dorchester, Dorset DT1 2AG

Exeter University Film Society
Debra Pascoe
c/o Guild of Students
Devonshire House
University of Exeter, Stocker Road
Exeter EX4 4PZ

Falmouth Film Society OP DA
Kate Rogers
Falmouth Arts Centre
Church Street, Falmouth
Cornwall TR11 3EG

The Film Club at the Odeon
8 The Old Mill
Culmstock, Cullompton
Devon EX15 3JL

Gloucester Film Society OP DA
C Toomey
8 Garden Way
Longlevens
Gloucester GL2 9UL

Holsworthy Film Society
Tony Langham
The Old Rectory
Pyworthy, Holsworthy
Devon EX22 6LA

Jersey Film Society OP DA
Paula Thelwell
Boulivot de Bas
Le Boulivot, Grouville, Jersey
Channel Islands JE3 9UH

Lyme Regis Film Society OP DA
M Rose
Frathings, Colway Lane, Lyme
Regis, Dorset DT7 3AR

The Octagon Film Society OP
Clifford Edwards
Okehampton College
Mill Road
Okehampton, Devon EX20 1PW

Penwith Film Society
Martin Hunt
19 Morrab Place
Penzance, Cornwall TR18 4DQ

Regal Film Society
Victoria Thomas
Wagside Cottage, Cutcombe
Wheddon Cross
Somerset TA24 7AP

Shaftesbury Arts Centre Film Society OP DA
Paul Schilling
5 Well Lane
Enmore Green
Shaftesbury, Dorset SP7 8LP

South Molton Film Society
Phillip Norman
20 Brook Meadow
South Molton
Devon

Stroud and District Film Society OP DA
Tim Mugford
Manor Farm, Besbury Common
Minchinhampton
Stroud
Glos GL6 9ES

Weston-Super-Mare Film Society
Richard Morgan
23 Ashcombe Gardens
Western-Super-Mare
Somerset

Southern

Southern Group BFFS
Dudley Smithers

1 Vanstone Cottages, Bagshot
Road, Englefield Green, Egham,
Surrey TW20 ORS

**Abingdon College &
District Film Society ST DA**
Mike Bloom
Abingdon College of FE
Northcourt Road
Abingdon, Oxon 0X14 1NN

**Ashcroft Arts Centre Film
Society OP DA**
Steve Rowley
Osborn Road
Fareham, Hants PO16 7DX

Bracknell Film Society
Ian Neall
Creedy Cottage, 30 Addiscombe
Road, Crowthorn,
Berks RG45 7JX

Chiltern Film Club
Derek Goddard
9 Hospital Hill
Chesham
Bucks

Cranbrook Film Society
Vanessa Nicholson
Horserace House, Sissinghurst
Kent TN17 2AT

**Eton College Film Society
ST**
G.J.Savage
Eton College
Windsor, Berks SL4 6DW

Farnham Film Society
Pamela Woodroffe
c/o The Maltings, Bridge Square
Farnham
Surrey GU9 7QR

Forest Arts
Nadine Fry
Old Milton Road
New Milton, BH25 6DS

Harwell Film Society CL DA
Lorraine Watling
Building 156
Harwell Laboratory
Didcot, Oxon OX11 0RA

Havant Film Society OP DA
M Short
14 South Street, Havant
Hampshire PO9 1DA

**Henley-on-Thames Film
Society**
M Whittaker
10 St Andrews Rd
Henley-on-Thames
Oxon RG9 IHP

Hook Norton Film Society
Dr ME White
Wisteria House, High Street
Hook Norton
Oxon OX15 5NF

Horsham Film Society
Norman Chapman
Farthings
King James Lane
Henfield
Sussex BN5 9ER

HIADS Ltd
Helena Dyer
Station Theatre, Station Road
Hayling Island
Hants PO11 OEH

**Intimate Cinema Film
Society**
A Henk
10 Aston Way
Espom
Surrey KT18 5LZ

**Marlborough College Senior
Film Society ST DA**
Ross Birkbeck
Marlborough College
Marlborough, Wilts SN8 1PA

**Newbury Film Society OP
DA**
Chris Martin
Swandene, The Mount, Highclere
Newbury RG20 9QZ

Oscar Film Unit
The Secretary
University of Surrey
Guildford, Surrey GU2 5XH

**Oxford University Film
Foundation**
Joe Perkins
Balliol College
Oxford, OX1 3BJ

Rye Film Club
The Old Grammar School
High Street, Rye,
East Sussex TN31 7JF

**Slough Co-Operative Film
Society**
Jo Hughes
58 St Judes Road
Englefield Green, Egham
Surrey TW20 0BT

**Southampton Film Theatre
– The Phoenix OP DA**
Staff Club Office
University of Southampton
University Road
Southampton SO17 1BJ

Southampton University
The Secretary Union Films
Student's Union
Highfield
Southampton SO17 1BJ

Surbiton Film Club
Hugh Peacock
9 Bockhampton Road,
Kingston Upon Thames
Surrey KT2 5JU

Swindon Film Society OP
Julia Edwards
9 Westlecot Road
Old Town, Swindon
Wilts SN1 4EZ

**University of Sussex Film
Society**
Film Society Pigeon Hole
Students Union, Falmer House
Sussex University
Falmer, Brighton BN1 9QF

**Winchester College Film
Society ST**
Dr J Webster
Winchester College
Winchester
Hants SO23 9NA

Winchester Film Society OP DA
Judith Altshul
17 Bramshaw Close
Winchester
Hants SO22 6LT

Woking's New Cinema Club
Barbara Millington
184 Alexandra Gardens
Knaphill, Woking
Surrey GU21 2DW

Wales

Welsh Group BFFS
Rupert Clarke
Felin Llwyngwair, Newport, Pembs
SA42 OLX

**Abergavenny Film Society
OP DA**
Carol Phillips
Tybryn, Tal-y-coed
Monmouth
Gwent NP5 4HP

Brecon Film Society OP DA
Becky Morton
6 Mount Streetm Brecon,
Powys LD3 7LU

Cambria Cinema Club
M Wilson
Dewina, Llanddewi-Brefi
Tregaron
Ceredigion

Fishguard Film Society OP
Frances Chivers
Iscoed-Pont Cilrhedyn
Abergwaun
Pembs SA65 9SB

Haverfordwest Film Society OP DA
Kay Green
Summerhill
16A Haverfordwest Road
Letterston
Dyfed SA62 5UA

Llanidloes Film Society
Dr A Scrase
Prospect Farm, Newchapel
Llanidloes, Powys SY18 6JY

North East Wales Film Society
G. Jones
11 Cedar Gardens, Deeside,
Flintshire, Clwyd CH5 1XJ

Narbeth Film Society
John Baum
Llalihaden,
S Pembrokeshire SA67 8HL

Phoenix Film Club OP DA
Neil Hammond
c/o Phoenix Centre, Church Road,
Ton Pentre, Rhondda, CF41 7EH

Presteigne Film Society OP DA
Patricia Wilson
Penkevel, School Lane
Norton, Presteigne LD8 2EL

Swansea Film Society OP
David Phillips
13 Oaklands Terr, Mount Pleasant
Swansea SA1 6JJ

Theatr Mwldan Film Society OP DA
Mary Champion
Pengarn Fawr, Cippyn
Cardigan, Dyfed SA43 3LT

UWCC Film Society
Steven Griffiths
220 Corporation Road
Grangetown
Cardiff

The Valleys Film Society
Geoffrey Nicholson
Aber Rhaedr Farmhouse
Llanrhaedr-Yu-Mochnant, Powys
SY10 OAX

The Windswept Film Society
Bel Crewe
Tan-y-Cefn, Nantmel, Nr
Rhayader,
Powys LD6 5PD

Yorkshire

Yorkshire Group BFFS
Richard Fort
8 Bradley Grove
Silsden
Keighley
West Yorks BD20 9LX

Bradford Student Cinema
Tim Anglish
Students Union
University of Bradford
Richmond Road
Bradford BD7 1DP

Halifax Playhouse Film Club OP DA
Sylvia Drake
7 North Road
Barkisland
Halifax HX4 0AH

Harrogate Film Society OP
James Lamb
19A Lynton Gardens
Harrogate
North Yorks

Hebden Bridge Film Society OP
Diane Stead
Mytholm House, Mytholm
Hebden Bridge
West Yorks HX7 6DS

Ilkley Film Society OP DA
Richard Fort
8 Bradley Grove
Silsden
Keighley
West Yorks BD20 9LX

Leeds Film Society
N Smith
14 Lindsey Road, Leeds LS9 7LT

Otley Film Society
J Bennett
24 Grange View, Otley LS21 2SE

Ryedale Film Society
Karin Doose
25 West End
Kirkby Moorside YO6 6AD

Scarborough Film Society OP
Tony Davison
29 Peasholm Drive, Scarborough
North Yorks YO12 7NA

Sheffield University SU Film Unit ST DA
The Secretary
Student's Union
Sheffield University
Western Bank
Sheffield S10 2TG

University of Huddersfield Student Union Film Society ST
Karen McDonald
Student Union
Queensgate
Huddersfield, W Yorks HD1 3DH

Whitby Film Society
James Liddle
Lisvane, Grosment, Nr Whitby
N Yorks YO22 5PE

York Student Cinema ST DA
Nadine Bullock
Student Union Corridor
Goodriche College
University of York
Heslington
York YO1 5DD

Overseas

British Council Film Club & Video Angelica Oserwalder
Rothenbaumchausse 34
2000 Hamburg 13
Germany

British Embassy Cinema Club
E Miskey, PO Box 393
Jeddah
Saudia Arabia

Cine Club of Calcutta
Sudhin Banerjee
2 Jawaharlal, Nehru Road
Calcutta 700 013
India

Irish Federation of Film Societies
Brenda Gannon
The Irish Film Centre
6 Eustace Street
Dublin 2

W Australian Federation of Film Societies
Barry King
P O Box 90, Subiaco 600B
Western Australia,
Australia

FUNDING

In April 2000 the Film Council will start its role as the government funded body responsible for encouraging commercial and cultural activity across the film production, exhibition and distribution industries. The Film Council will also be distributor of Lottery funds for film production in England. At the time of writing the Film Council is expected to incorporate staff and activities of the British Film Commission, *bfi* Production and the Arts Council of England Lottery Film Department.

In some cases list of schemes in this years section is likely to reflect the intermediate period up to the Film Council establishing itself. They mainly cover production but some include development, distribution, exhibition etc. The funds fall into three main categories; direct grants, production finance and reimbursable loans. In almost all cases these schemes are not open to students.

For a more comprehensive look at UK funding *Lowdown The Low Budget Funding Guide 1999/2000* published by the *bfi* is thoroughly recommended.

ADAPT (Access for Disabled People to Arts Premises Today)
The ADAPT Trust
8 Hampton Terrace
Edinburgh EH12 5JD
Tel: 0131 346 1999
Fax: 0131 346 1991
Development Manager: Stewart Coulter
Charitable trust providing advice and challenge funding to arts venues - cinemas, concert halls, libraries, heritage and historic houses, theatres, museums and galleries - throughout Great Britain. ADAPT also provides a consultancy service and undertakes access audits and assessments. Grants and Awards for 1999 advertised as available

ADAPT (Northern Ireland)
185 Stranmillis Road
Belfast
BT9 5DU
Tel: 01232 683463
Fax: 01232 661715

Arts Council of England
14 Great Peter Street
London SW1P 3NQ
Tel: 020 7333 0100
Fax: 020 7973 6581
email: enquires@artscouncil.org.uk
Website: www.artscouncil.org.uk
The Arts Council of England and Lottery Funding For Film
In the course of the next 12 months, the Arts Council will hand over responsibility for National Lottery film funding to the Film Council. In the meantime, the Arts Council will continue to administer its Lottery Film Programme, including the supervision of the film franchises. Approximately £9 million will be available for individual films up to April 2000. The Arts Council will not introduce any new schemes during the period and it is expected that the Arts Council Lottery Film Department will transfer to the Film Council in the autumn of 1999.
Arts Council of England Lottery Film Department
14 Great Peter Street
London SW1P 3NQ
Tel: 020 7312 0123
Fax: 020 7973 6571
Website: www.artscouncil.org.uk

Director of Lottery Film: Carolyn Lambert
The Visual Arts Department
The Visual Arts Department will continue to work with national agencies for artists' film and video and there may be opportunities for commissioning
Artists' Film and Video Production Awards
Offers support of up to £15,000 to individual artists for production.
Animate!
Animate!, is a co-commissioning scheme with Channel 4 for experimental animation, for publications and for multimedia projects

Arts Council of Northern Ireland
Lottery Department
MacNeice House
Belfast BT9 6AQ
Tel: 01232 667000
Fax: 01232 664766
Lottery Director: Tanya Greenfield

Arts Council of Wales
Lottery Unit
Holst House
9 Museum Place
Cardiff CF1 3NX
Tel: 029 20 376500
Fax: 029 20 395284
email: information@ccc-acw.org.uk
Website: www.ccc.acw.org.uk
Lottery Director: Robert Edge

BBC 10x10
Bristol Television Features
Whiteladies Road
Bristol BS8 2LR
Tel: 0117 974 6746
Fax: 0117 974 7452
email: 10x10@BBC.co.uk
Series Producer: Jeremy Howe
Produces 10 ten-minute films per series, documentary or fiction films for broadcast on BBC2. It is an initiative to encourage and develop new and innovative filmmaking talent in all genres, through the provision of modest production finance combined with practical guidance. The scheme is open to any director with no commissioned broadcast UK Network directing credit. All applications must include a showreel with their proposals -

which should be treatments for
documentary, scripts for drama

bfi Production
21 Stephen Street
London W1P 2LN
Tel: 020 7255 1444
Fax: 020 7580 9456
Website: www.bfi.org.uk
Head of Production: Roger Shannon
BFI Production will be incorporated
in to the Film Council (which should
be set up by April 2000). In the
ensuing period BFI Production
intends to complete the 1999 New
Directors slate of short films and
aspires to launch a limited number of
script development schemes with
national and regional partners

British Council
11 Portland Place
London W1N 4EJ
Tel: 020 7930 8466
Fax: 020 7389 3199
Website: www.britcoun.org/
Assists in the co-ordination and
shipping of films to festivals, and in
some cases can provide funds for the
film-maker to attend when invited. A
limited amount of fundraising is
available for UK filmmakers to
attend European seminars/workshops
such as Arista, Eave, Sources etc

British Screen Finance Limited
14-17 Wells Mews
London W1P 3FL
Tel: 020 7323 9080
Fax: 020 7323 0092
email: BS@cd-online.co.uk
Invests in British feature films
including, through the European Co-
production Fund Limited, films made
under co-production treaties with
other countries. Scripts should be
submitted with full background
information. All scripts are read.
Scripts submitted by producers with a
fully developed production package
are given priority, and projects must
have commercial potential in the
theatrical market. British Screen's
contribution is capped at £500,000,
and is never more than 30 per cent of
a film's budget

Channel 4/MOMI Animators
Professional Residencies
Museum of the Moving Image
South Bank
London SE1 8XT
Tel: 020 7815 1376
Four professional residencies are
awarded to young or first time
animators who receive a fee of

£2,910 plus a budget of up to £1,612
towards materials. At the end of the
residencies projects will be
considered for commission by
Channel 4

The Glasgow Film Fund
249 West George Street
Glasgow G2 4RB
Tel: 0141 302 1757
Fax: 0141 302 1714
Contact: Judy Anderson
The Glasgow Film Fund (GFF)
provides production funding for
companies shooting films in the
Glasgow area or produced by
Glasgow-based production
companies. Applications are accepted
for films intended for theatrical
release and with a budget of at least
£500,000. The maximum investment
made by the GFF in any one project
is normally £150,000, however,
where there is an exceptionally high
level of economic benefit the GFF
may consider raising its maximum
investment to £250,000. GFF
application forms, meeting dates,
submission deadlines and further
information are available from the
GFF office. Production credits
include, *Shallow Grave, Small Faces,
Carla's Song, Regeneration,
Orphans, My Name Is Joe, The Acid
House* and *The Debt Collector*

Kraszna-Krausz Foundation
122 Fawnbrake Avenue
London SE24 0BZ
Tel: 020 7738 6701
Fax: 020 7738 6701
email: K-K@dial.pipex.com
Andrea Livingstone
Annual awards, with prizes for books
on the moving image (film,
television, video and related media),
alternating with those for books on
still photography. Books, to have
been published in previous two years,
can be submitted from publishers in
any language. Prize money around
£10,000, with awards in two
categories. The 1999 awards are for
books on the moving image

National Disability and Video Project (NDVP)
**West Midlands Disability Arts
Forum**
**Unit 007, The Custard Factory,
Gibb Street**
Digbeth
Birmingham B9 4AA
Tel: 0121 242 2248
Fax: 0121 242 2268
Funded by the Arts Council of
England, the NDFVP supports the
production of film, video and digital

media projects by disabled
people.Awards are available for
research and development (up to
£2,000) and production (up to
£19,000). Two production awards are
available for projects of up to 10
minutes with budgets of up to
£25,000, the balance of funding to be
obtained from other sources

Nicholl Fellowships in Screenwriting
**Academy of Motion Picture Arts
and Sciences**
8949 Wilshire Boulevard
Beverly Hills, CA 90211
USA
Tel: (1) 310 247 3059
Website: www.oscars.org/nicholl
**Annual Screenwriting Fellowship
Awards**
Up to five fellowships of US$25,000
each to new screenwriters. Eligible are
writers in English who have not earned
money writing for commercial film or
television. Collaborations and
adaptations are not eligible. A
completed entry includes a feature film
screenplay approx 100-130 pages long,
an application form and a US$30 entry
fee. Send self-addressed envelope for
rules and application form

Northern Ireland Film Commission
21 Ormeau Avenue
Belfast BT2 8HD
Tel: 01232 232444
Fax: 01232 239918
email: info@nifc.co.uk
Website: www.nifc.co.uk
The Northern Ireland Film
Development Fund offers loans to
production companies for the
development of feature films or
television drama series or serials that
are intended to be produced primarily
in Northern Ireland. NIFDF offers
interest-free loans of up to 50 per
cent of the cost of developing
projects. Loans are unlikely to
exceed £40,000 for a television
drama series or serial or £15,000 for
a single feature film.

The Prince's Trust
18 Park Square East
London NW1 4LH
Tel: 0800 842842
Fax: 020 7543 1200
The Prince's Trust aims to help
young people to succeed by
providing opportunities which they
would otherwise not have. This is
achieved through a nationwide
network which delivers training,
personal development, support for
business start ups, development

awards and educational support.
Richard Mills Travel Fellowship
In association with the Gulbenkian
Foundation and the Peter S Cadbury
Trust, offers three grants of £1,000
for people working in community
arts, in the areas of housing, minority
arts, special needs, or arts for young
people, especially the unemployed.
The Fellowships are applicable to
people under 35

Scottish Arts Council
Lottery Department
12 Manor Place
Edinburgh EH3 7DD
Tel: 0131 226 6051
Fax: 0131 477 7240
Website: www.sac.org.uk
Lottery Director: David Bonnar

Scottish Screen
249 West George Street
Glasgow G2 4RB
Tel: 0141 302 1700
Fax: 0141 302 1711
email: info@scottishscreen.com
Website: www.scottishscreen.com
Chief Executive: John Archer
Scottish Screen is responsible to the
Scottish Parliament for developing all
aspects of screen industry and culture
in Scotland through script and
company development, short film
production, distribution of National
Lottery film production finance,
training, education, exhibition
funding, the film Commission
locations support and the Scottish
Film and Television Archive
Film Schemes
Cineworks (Production Awards up to
£10,000 and £15,000 and completion
funding up to £5,000)
Tartan Shorts (£60,000)
New Found Land (£45,000)
New Gaelic-language short film
scheme to be supported by the
Comataidh Craolaidh Gaidhlig is
currently being finalised
Development
Advice and Finance for the
development of feature films
(Development Awards of up to
£20,000, Interim Awards of up to
£5,000, Writers' Awards of up to
£5,000)
MEDIA
At Scottish Screen MEDIA Atenna
Scotland can help you access
MEDIA II and other European
support programmes

Sgrîn, Media Agency for Wales
The Bank, 10 Mount Stuart Square
Cardiff Bay
Cardiff CF1 6EE

Tel: 029 20 333300
Fax: 029 20 333320
email: sgrin@sgrinwales.demon.
co.uk
Website: www.sgrinwales.demon.co
Production coordinator. Gaynor
Messer Price
Sgrîn, Media Agency for Wales, is
the primary organisation for film,
television and new media in Wales.
Sgrîn operates an independent filmmakers' fund, offering grants for
development, production and
completion of short films. It also
provides funding support for cinema
venues, both public and private,
cultural and interpretive printed and
audiovisual material which
complements and promotes
exhibition programmes, and events.
Guidelines and deadlines are
available on request

Regional Arts Boards and Regional schemes

Croydon Film & Video Awards
Croydon Clocktower
Katharine Street
Croydon CR9 1ET
Tel: 020 8760 5400 ext 1048
Co-ordinator: Mark Wilcox
The Croydon Film & Video Awards
are an ongoing production initiative
co-funded by the LFVDA and the
London Borough of Croydon. The
£10,000 scheme was established in
1997 to support local film and video
makers to make fictional,
documentary or experimental shorts.
In February 2000 three new shorts
will be premiered at the Croydon
Cuts short film festival in the David
Lean Cinema.

East Midlands Arts Board
Mountfields House
Epinal Way
Loughborough
Leics LE11 0QE
Tel: 01509 218292
Fax: 01509 262214
email: carol.clarke@em-arts.co.uk
Film, Video and Broadcasting
Assistant Officer: Carol Clarke
A limited number of small-scale, low
budget Script Development Awards;
Completion Grants; Materials
Awards. A limited number of awards
for short films, including First Cut
and Co-Production challenge
schemes up to £10,000

Eastern Arts Board
Cherry Hinton Hall
Cherry Hinton Road
Cambridge CB1 8DW
Tel: 01223 215355
Fax: 01223 248075
email: cinema@eastern-arts.co.uk
Website: www.arts.org.uk/
Cinema and Broadcasting Officer:
Martin Ayres
Media Assistant: Helen Dixon
Eastern Arts Board is the regional
arts development and funding agency
for the counties of Bedfordshire,
Cambridgeshire, Essex,
Hertfordshire, Norfolk and Suffolk,
and the unitary authorities of Luton,
Peterborough, Rochford and
Thurrock. The new East of England
Regional Arts Lottery Programme
and Small Scale Capital Scheme
includes priority support for film,
video, cinema and multimedia

activity. EAB Open Access schemes will offer support for individuals. EAB assists a network of agencies and venues, including first take (see entry for first take) with Anglia Television. Policy, information, development services and funding for Cinema & Broadcasting covers five interlocking areas: Collections, Education & Training, Exhibition, Production, and Artists Film & Video & Multimedia. From Autumn 1999 EAB specialist film and video production, scriptwriting, co-commissioning funding and development services will be delivered through first take (see entry for first take).

East of England Regional Production Fund
Launched in Autumn 1999, this fund seeks to assist innovative practice and creative experimentation in a range of genres, styles and formats. It offers seed funding for the realisation, development and production of one-off moving image projects

first take films
Anglia Television
Anglia House
Norwich
Norfolk NR1 3JG
Tel: 01603 615151
Fax: 01603 764665
email: cnorbury@angliatv.co.uk
Executive Producer: Caroline Norbury
Administrator: Annette Culverhouse
Marketing & Distribution: Kate Gerova
first take films is a joint initiative set up by Eastern Arts Board and Anglia Television. It is a regional cultural production agency whose principal function is to facilitate, encourage and promote the creative arts of film, video and moving image in the East of England. The first take series is Anglia TV's annual showcase for up and coming new directors, and submissions are usually accepted in February

Light House Media Centre
9-12 Middle Street
Brighton BN1 1AL
Tel: 01273 384222

London Arts Board
Elme House
133 Long Acre
Covent Garden
London WC2E 9AF
Tel: 020 7240 1313
Fax: 020 7240 4578
Chairman: Trevor Phillips
Chief Executive: Sue Robertson

London Film and Video Development Agency_
114 Whitfield Street
London W1P 5RW
Tel: 020 7383 7755
Fax: 020 7383 7745
Chief Executive: Gill Henderson
Projects Officer: Andrea Corbett
Provides revenue funding to a range of production, training facilities and exhibition organisations, including the London Production Fund (q.v.).
Also:
Project Funding
Support for training courses, film and video exhibition and festivals in London
The LFVDA is the assessing body for London film and video applications to the National Lottery. The LFVDA runs the London Production Fund

London Production Fund
114 Whitfield Street
London W1
Tel: 020 7383 7766
Fax: 020 7383 7745
Production Advisor: Maggie Ellis
The London Production Fund aims to support and develop film, video and television projects by independent film-makers living/working in the London region. It is run by the London Film and Video Development Agency and receives financial support from Carlton Television, Channel 4 and the LFVDA. It has an annual budget of approximately £200,000
Development Awards
Support of up to £3,000 each to assist in the development of scripts, storyboards, project packages, pilots
Production and Completion Awards
Offers support of up to £15,000 each for production or part-production costs. Awards will be made on the basis of written proposals and applicants' previous work. The Fund is interested in supporting as diverse a range of films and videos as possible

North West Arts Board
Manchester House
22 Bridge Street
Manchester M3 3AB
Tel: 0161 834 6644
Fax: 0161 834 6969
Website: www.arts.org.uk/
Director, Visual & Media Arts: Howard Rifkin
NWAB offers a range of funding schemes covering Production, Exhibition, Training and Media Education for those resident in the NWAB region

Northern Arts Board
9-10 Osborne Terrace
Jesmond
Newcastle upon Tyne NE2 1NZ
Tel: 0191 281 6334
Fax: 0191 281 3276
email: jcl@norab.demon.co.uk
Website: www.arts.org.uk
Head of Film Media and Literature: Janice Campbell
Northern Production Fund (NPF)
The aim of NPF is to support the production of short and long form drama, for film, television and radio, animation, creative documentaries, and all forms of experimental film-making, including work for gallery exhibition. The foremost concern of NPF is for the quality of the production. NPF to support productions which are imaginative, innovative, thoughtful, courageous and powerful. NPF normally holds three meetings per year to consider applications under the small scale production, development and feature film development headings.
Production
Support of up to £30,000 for production or part-production costs or completion costs.
Development
Support of up to £5,000 to assist in the development of scripts, storyboards, full treatments, pilot production, etc. This includes research and development for feature films, short drama for film or radio, animation, documentary projects and innovative television drama.
Feature Film Developments
A maximum of £10,000 awards for feature film development will be available for projects each year. These awards will normally be made to production companies, working with a Northern-based writer, who are able to demonstrate their ability to match the Northern Arts contribution. Matching funding may include the cost of feature film development expertise and/or the contribution of another funding partner.
Company Support
Support for companies is available to assist in the development of a programme of work. Company support will normally be awarded to support several projects rather than production costs.
Broadcaster Partnership Schemes
The Northern Production Fund also works in partnership with broadcasters to offer production schemes for short drama and documentary production

South East Arts

Union House
Eridge Road
Tunbridge Wells
Kent TN4 8HF
Tel. 01892 515210
Fax: 01892 549383
email: info.sea@artsfb.org.uk
Website: www.arts.org.uk
Production Development Manager:
Croline Freeman
Production Grants
Offers grants of up to £10,000 for
full or part-funding of films or videos
for more experienced filmmakers.
Grants of up to £1,000 are available
to newcomers or those with little
production experience

South West Arts

Bradninch Place
Gandy Street
Exeter EX4 3LS
Tel: 01392 218188
Fax: 01392 413554
John Prescott Thomas
Chief Executive: Nick Capaldi

South West Media Development Agency

59 Prince Street
Bristol BS1 4QH
Tel: 0117 927 3226
Fax: 0117 927 6216
Website: www.swmediadevagency.
co.uk
Director: Judith Higginbottom
The South West Media Development
Agency is the funding and
development body for film, video
and television in the south west. It
provides advice and financial support
for: low budget and independent
production, animation, script
development, artists' film and video
commissioning, exhibition of
independent art-house, historic and
experimental cinema. Applicants for
financial support must be resident in
the South West Media Development
region. For details of available
funding, please contact Sarah-Jane
Meredith

Southern Arts Board

13 St Clement Street
Winchester
Hants SO23 9DQ
Tel: 01962 855099
Fax: 01962 861186
Film and Video production grants
available in two categories:
production (up to £5,000) and
completion (up to £3,000). Co-
production funding is strongly
encouraged. First Cut (with Central)
and Taped Up (with Meridian) are
both broadcast schemes to support

filmmakers new to television to make
short films for broadcast. The David
Alsthul Award is a competitive award
for creative achievement in film and
video production available to those
who live or work in the Southern
region including students. Annual
prize money of £1,000. Exhibition
Development Fund supports
programming, marketing, training
and research and includes support for
artists working with digital
technology and installation work.
Media Education Development Fund
supports strategic development of
regional media education. Full details
on all the above on application

West Midlands Arts Board

82 Granville Street
Birmingham B1 2HJ
Tel: 0121 631 3121
Fax: 0121 643 7239
email: info@west-midlands-
arts.co.uk
**"First Cut" Film and Video
Production Scheme.**
A broadcast initiative supported by
West Midlands Arts, Birmingham
City Council, the Media
Development Agency for the West
Midlands (MDAWM), Central
Broadcasting, BBC Resources
Midlands and East, and the Midland
Media Training Consortium. The aim
is to produce a range of diverse
programmes for regional television.
Recipients of the award work with a
Production Co-ordinator based at
(MDAWM) to develop a project
through training, production support
and access to the broadcast industry.
A minimum of five awards are made
with budgets of up to £7,500. The
scheme results in the Central
Television 'First Cut' programme
which will be broadcast in the
Autumn of 2000. Application
deadline January 2000.
New Work and Commissions
Offer artist film and video makers an
opportunity to produce new work in
film, video and new technology. The
scheme seeks proposals which
demonstrate innovation and
experimentation. Awards are made for
pieces up to ten minutes with a
maximum budget of £5,000. The
scheme favours work for screening in
conventional, sites specific and other
contexts. Application deadlines
February/September. Research and
Development Awards
Enables makers to develop their
proposals for future productions.
Research and Development Awards
are expected to range between £200 to
£1,000. Deadline February/September

Yorkshire Arts

21 Bond Street
Dewsbury
West Yorks WF13 1AX
Tel: 01924 455555
Fax: 01924 466522
email: tony.dixon.yha@artsfb.org.uk
**Short Film and Video Production
Awards 2000**
More information will be available
later in the year regarding the
deadline and details for the Short
Film & Video Production Fund,
following implementation of the
restructure of Yorkshire Arts, and in
the light of major changes in the
national structure for funding moving
image work. The deadline is unlikely
to be before the end of March 2000.
Contact: Yorkshire Arts directly for
details
Development Awards 1999
Awards of £500 are available for
projects to be developed to a stage
where applications can be made to
YHA for short film production
funding. An award can be used in
any way which advances the project.
For example: scriptwriting, research,
fees. Applications will be accepted
from writers, producers, directors etc.
Deadline 12 noon 29 October 1999

European and Pan-European Sources

Eurimages
Council of Europe
Palais de l'Europe
67075 Strasbourg Cédex
France
Tel: (33) 3 88 41 26 40
Fax: (33) 3 88 41 27 60
Website: www.culture.coe.fr/
eurimages
Provides financial support for feature-length fiction films, documentaries, distribution and exhibition. Applications from the UK can only be accepted if a UK producer is a fourth co-producer in a tripartite co-production or the third in a bipartite, provided his/her share does not exceed 30 per cent of the co-production

European Co-production Association
c/o France 2
22 Avenue Montaigne
75387 Paris
Cédex 08
France
Tel: (33) 1 4421 4126
Fax: (49) 1 4421 5179
Secretariat: Claire Heinrich
A consortium of European public service TV networks for the co-production of TV fiction series. Can offer complete finance. Development funding is also possible. Proposals should consist of full treatment, financial plan and details of proposed co-production partners. Projects are proposed directly to Secretariat or to member national broadcasters (Channel 4 in UK)

European Co-production Fund
c/o British Screen Finance
14-17 Wells Mews
London W1P 3FL
Tel: 020 7323 9080
Fax: 020 7323 0092
email: info@britishscreen.co.uk
The Fund's aim is to enable UK producers to collaborate in the making of films which the European market demonstrably wishes to see made but which could not be made without the Fund's involvement. The ECF offers commercial loans, up to 30 per cent of the total budget capped at £500,000, for full length feature films intended for theatrical release. The film must be a co-production involving at least two production companies, with no link of common ownership established in separate EU states

FilmFörderung Hamburg
Friedensallee 14-16
22765 Hamburg
Germany
Tel: (49) 40 398 370
Fax: (49) 40 398 3710
email: filmfoerderung-hamburg@ffhh.de
Eva Hubert
Producers of cinema films can apply for a subsidy amounting to at most 50 per cent of the overall production costs of the finished film. Foreign producers can also apply for this support. We recommend to co-produce with a German partner. It is necessary to spend at least 150 per cent of the subsidy in Hamburg. Part of the film should be shot in Hamburg. Financial support provided by the FilmFörderung Hamburg can be used in combination with other private or public funding, including that of TV networks

MEDIA II Programme

MEDIA II is a programme of the European Union, managed by the European Commission in Brussels. MEDIA II, which follows on from MEDIA I, started in 1996 and will conclude in the year 2000

European Commission
Directorate General X:
Information, Communication, Culture, Audio-visual
200, rue de la Loi
1040 Brussels, Belgium
Tel: (32) 2 299 11 11
Fax: (32) 2 299 92 14
Website: www.europa.eu.int/comm
Head of MEDIA Unit: Jacques Delmoly
Who is eligible?
All member states of the European Unin and countries belonging to the European Economic Area are eligible for MEDIA II. The Programme is also open to Cyprus, Malta, Central and Eastern European countries subject to special agreements with the Commission
Objectives
The Commission publishes in the Official Journal of the European Commission calls for projects and deadlines for submission for the following areas of support: Training, Development and Distribution/ Promotion
Media Contacts
As part of a network of 29 Desks and Antennae throughout Europe, the members of the UK MEDIA team listed below should be the first point of contact for UK companies seeking information and advice of the MEDIA Programme. Guidelines and application forms for al the MEDIA II schemes are available from them. They produce regular newsletters and other printed information detailing upcoming deadlines, training courses and markets

MEDIA Services England
249 West George Street
Glasgow G2 4QE
Tel: 0870 0100 791
Fax: 0141 302 1778
email: media.england@
scottishscreen.com

MEDIA Antenna Scotland
c/o Scottish Screen
249 West George Street
Glasgow G2 4RB
Tel: 0141 302 1776/7
Fax: 0141 302 1778

email: louise.scott@dial.pipex.com
Website: www.scottishscreen.com
Contact: Louise Scott

MEDIA Antenna Wales
c/o Sgrîn: The Media Agency for Wales
The Bank, 10 Mount Stuart Square
Llantrisant Road
Cardiff CF10 5EE
Tel: 029 20 333 304
Fax: 029 20 333 320
email: antenna@
scrwales.demon.co.uk
Website: www.sgrin.wales.demon
.co.uk
Contact: Gwarr Hughes

MEDIA Northern Ireland
MEDIA Services Northern Ireland
c/o Northrn Ireland Film
Commission
21 Ormeau Avenue
Belfast BT2 8HD
Tel: 01232 232 444
Fax: 01232 239 918
email: media@nifc.com
Heike Meyer -Döring

Training Support
Support is available for training
institutions or bodies which provide
initial and continuous vocational
training courses in: Screenplay
techniques, economic and
commercial management, new
technologies
Development Support
MEDIA Development offers support
in the form of interest free loans in
two main areas: Project development:
fiction and creative documentary,
animation, multimedia projects, state
funding. Company development:
business plans, company
development
**Distribution and Promotional
Support**
The MEDIA Distribution scheme
aims at improving the transnational
distribution of European audio-visual
works. The areas of support are:
Cinema distribution, Video and
multimedia publishing, TV
distribution, Marketing of licensing
rights. Support is also given to
organisations which: facilitate access
by independent producers and
distributors of European markets
Organise thematic markets or
specialist events
Film Festival Support
Networking and exchange of ideas,
experience, good practice and
product is encouraged between
festivals and events. Support is given
for: activities organised by networks
of audio-visual events, audio-visual

festivals carried out in partnership
MEDIA also support two specialist
sectors: animation and exhibition

CARTOON (European Association of Animation Film)
418 Boulevard Lambermont
B-1030 Brussels
Belgium
Tel: (32) 2 245 12 00
Fax: (32) 2 245 46 89
email: cartoon@skynet.be
Website: www.cartoon-media.be
Contact: Corinne Jenart, Marc
Vandeweyer
CARTOON, based in Brussels, is a
European animation network which
organises the annual CARTOON
FORUM, co-ordinates the grouping
of European animation studios and
runs specialist training courses in
animation

Europa Cinemas
54, rue Beaubourg
F-75 003 Paris, France
Tel: (33) 1 42 71 53 70
Fax: (33) 1 42 71 47 55
email: europacinema@magic.fr
Website: www.europa-cinemas.org
Contact: Claude-Eric Poiroux, Fatima
Djoumer
This project encourages screenings
and promotion of European films in a
network of cinemas in European
cities. It offers a financial support for
screening European films, for
promotional activities and for special
events

MEDIA Salles
Via Soperga, 2
1-20 127 Milan, Italy
Tel: (39) 02 66 98 4405
Fax: (39) 02 669 1574
Website: www.mediasalles.it/
Contact: Elisabetta Brunella
MEDIA Salles with Euro Kids
Network is an initiative aimed at
consolidating the availability of
'cinema at the cinema' for children
and young people in Europe, and at
raising the visibility of European film
to a younger audience

INTERNATIONAL SALES

Below is a selection of companies which acquire rights to audiovisual products for sale to foreign distributors in all media – see also Distributors (Non-Theatrical) and (Theatrical)

Action Time
Wrendal House
2 Whitworth Street West
Manchester M1 5WX
Tel: 0161 236 8999
Fax: 0161 236 8845
Specialises in international format sales of game shows and light entertainment.

All American Fremantle International
57 Jamestown Road
London NW1 7DB
Tel: 020 7284 0880
Fax: 020 7916 5511
London arm of NY-based Fremantle Int. Produces and distributes game shows and light entertainment programmes

Jane Balfour Films
Burghley House
35 Fortress Road
London NW5 1AQ
Tel: 020 7267 5392
Fax: 020 7267 4241
email: Jbf@janebalfourfilms.co.uk
Jane Balfour, Mary Barlow, Sarah Banbery, Méabh O'Donovan
International sales agent for independent producers and some of Channel 4, output handling drama, documentaries, and specialised feature films

BBC Worldwide
Woodlands
80 Wood Lane
London W12 0TT
Tel: 020 8576 2000
Fax: 020 8749 0538
Website: www.bbc.worldwide.com
Programme, Sales and Marketing – the sales and licensing of BBC programmes and international broadcasters, and the generation of co-production business; Channel Marketing – the development of new cable and satellite delivered television channels around the world

Beyond Films
3rd Floor
22 Newman Street
London W1V 3HB
Tel: 020 7636 9613
Fax: 020 7636 9614
Dee Emerson
Films: *Strictly Ballroom, Love & Other Catastrophes, Love Serenade, Kiss or Kill, Heaven's Burning, SLC Punk, Orphans, Two Hands, Paperback Hero, Kick, Fresh Air, In a Savage Land*

bfi
21 Stephen Street
London W1P 2LN
Tel: 020 7957 8927
Fax: 020 7580 5830
email: films@bfi.org.uk
John Flahive, Film Sales Manager
Sales of BFI Production and BFI TV features, shorts and documentaries, archival and acquired titles including: *Love is the Devil, Under the Skin, Speak Like a Child,* early Peter Greenaway and Derek Jarman features and shorts, *Lee Marvin a Personal Portrait* by John Boorman, *South* and Silent Shakespeare

bfi Archival Footage Sales Unit
21 Stephen Street
London W1P 2LN
Tel: 020 7957 8934
Fax: 020 7580 5830
email: footage.films@bfi.org.uk
Website: www.bfi.org.uk
Jan Faull or Simon Brown
Material from the largest collection of film footage in Britain – the National Film and Television Archive. Television, films, documentaries, newsreels and animation are all covered with over 350,000 titles to choose from, including material dating back to 1895. First stop for serious research on subjects that have shaped the 20th century. Research facilities available.

BRITE (British Independent Television Enterprises)
The London Television Centre
Upper Ground
London SE1 9LT
Tel: 020 7737 8603
Fax: 020 7737 8320
Website: www.brite.tv.co.uk

Nadine Nohr
International programme sales and distribution for Granada Television, London Weekend Television and Yorkshire-Tyne Tees Television. Leading titles include *Cracker, Prime Suspect*

British Home Entertainment
5 Broadwater Road
Walton-on-Thames
Surrey KT12 5DB
Tel: 01932 228832
Fax: 01932 247759
email: clive@bhe.prestel.co.uk
Clive Williamson
Video distribution/TV marketing. An *Evening with the Royal Ballet, Othello, The Mikado, The Soldier's Tale, Uncle Vanya, King and Country, The Hollow Crown*

Capitol Films
23 Queensdae Place
London W11 4SQ
Tel: 020 7471 6000
Fax: 020 7471 6012
email: films@capitolfilms.com
Valencia Haynes
Recent productions include: *Dancing at Lughnasa, Mad Cows, Among Giants, Wilde* and *A Soldier's Daughter Never Cries*

Carlton International
35-38 Portman Square
London W1H 0NU
Tel: 020 7224 3339
Fax: 020 7486 1707
Director of Sales: Louise Sexton
International TV programme and film sales agent, now representing Carlton Television, Central Television, HTV, ITN Productions and Meridian Broadcasting as well as a growing number of independent production companies.
The ITC Collection
The ITC Library was acquired in 1999 by Carlton International.. The library includes such celebrated films as *The Eagle has Landed,The Big Easy,The Boys from Brazil, On Golden Pond, Farewell My Lovely, Sophie's Choice and The Last Seduction.* It also features a huge array of classic series including *The Saint, The Prisoner, Randall and Hopkirk (Deceased)* and *Space 1999* and some of the most popular

children's programmes including
*Gerry Anderson's Thunderbirds, Joe
90* and *Captain Scarlet*

Castle Target International
A 29 Barwell Business Park
Leatherhead Road
Chessington
Surrey KT9 2NY
Tel: 020 8974 1021
Fax: 020 8974 3707
Brian Leafe
*Buddy's Song, The Monk, That
Summer of White Roses, Conspiracy*

CBC International Sales
43-51 Great Titchfield Street
London W1P 8DD
Tel: 020 7412 9200
Fax: 020 7323 5658
Susan Hewitt, Michelle Payne, Janice
Russell
The programme sales division of
Canadian Broadcasting Corporation
and Société Radio-Canada

Chatsworth Television Distributors
97-99 Dean Street
London W1V 5RA
Tel: 020 7734 4302
Fax: 020 7437 3301

CiBy Sales
10 Stephen Mews
London W1P 1PP
Tel: 020 7333 8877
Fax: 020 7333 8878
Wendy Palmer
Established in 1992, CiBy Sales is
responsible for the international
multi-media exploitation of films
produced by French production
company Ciby 2000 and other
independent producers. Titles
include: *Muriel's Wedding, The
Piano, Secrets and Lies*

Cine Electra
National House
60-66 Wardour Street
London W1V 3HP
Tel: 020 7287 1123
Fax: 020 7722 4251
Julia Kennedy
Established in 1991, Cine Electra has
continued to diversify its activities
within international sales and
production. From its acquisition, the
company now represents a library of
150 titles including such directors as
Peter Greenaway, Andrzej Wajda,
Jacques Rivette and Idrissa
Ouedraogo

Circle Communications PLC
45-49 Mortimer Street
London W1N 7TD
Tel: 020 7636 9421

Fax: 020 7436 7426
Circle is an international television
rights group. Based in the UK, and
trading in all the major territories of
the world, Circle provides a range of
services for producers and
broadcasters. Circle comprises
distinct businesses principally
engaged in the creation, acquisition,
marketing and licensing of visual
entertainment rights. The companies
within Circle Communications are:
Carnival (Films & Theatre)
Pavilion International
Delta Ventures
Production Finance &
Management
Independent Wildlife
Harlequin Films & Television
Oxford Scientific Films
La Plante International

Columbia TriStar International Television
Sony Pictures, Europe House
25 Golden Square
London W1R 6LU
Tel: 020 7533 1000
Fax: 020 7533 1246
European TV production and
network operations and international
distribution of Columbia TriStar's
feature films and TV product

CTVC
Hillside Studios
Merry Hill Road
Bushey
Watford WD2 1DR
Tel: 020 8950 4426
Fax: 020 8950 6694
Website: www.ctvc.co.uk
Ann Harvey
International programme sales and
co-productions in documentary,
music, children's, drama and arts
programmes

DLT Entertainment UK Ltd
10 Bedford Square
London WC1B 3RA
Tel: 020 7631 1184
Fax: 020 7636 4571
John Reynolds; Martin Booth
Specialising in entertainment
programming. Recent titles include:
As Time Goes By, series seven for
BBC Television; *Bloomin'
Marvellous,* eight-part comedy series
for BBC Television

Documedia International Films Ltd
19 Widegate Street
London E1 7HP
Tel: 020 7625 6200
Fax: 020 7625 7887
Distributors of innovative and award

winning drama specials, drama
shorts, serials, tele-movies and
feature films; documentary specials
and series; for worldwide sales and
co-production

EVA Entertainment
Studio 8
125 Moore Park Road
London SW6 4PS
Tel: 020 7384 1002

FilmFour International
76-78 Charlotte Street
London W1P 2TX
Tel: 020 7868 7700
Fax: 020 7868 7766
Website: www.filmfour.com
Head of International Marketing:
Bridget Pedgrift
Director of Worldwide Sales and
Marketing: Susan Bruce Smith
Film Sales Manager: Andrea Klein
International sales arm of FilmFour
Ltd, UK-based film production arm
of Channel 4. Recent titles include
*East is East, Hotel Splendide, Sugar
Town, The War Zone, The Debt
Collector*

Goldcrest Films and Television
65/66 Dean Street
London W1V 5HD
Tel: 020 7437 8696
Fax: 020 7437 4448
Thierry Wase-Bailey
Major feature film production, sales
and finance company

Grampian Television
Queen's Cross
Aberdeen AB15 4XJ
Tel: 01224 846846
Fax: 01224 846800
Alistair Gracie (Controller) Hilary I.
Buchan (Head of Public Relations)
North Scotland ITV station
producing a wide range of
programming including
documentaries, sport, children's,
religion and extensive daily news and
current affairs to serve ITV's largest
region

Hollywood Classics
8 Cleveland Gardens
London W2 6HA
Tel: 020 7262 4646
Fax: 020 7262 3242
email: HollywoodClassicsUK
@compuserve.com
Melanie Tebb
Hollywood Classics has offices in
London and Los Angeles and sells
back catalogue titles from major
Hollywood studios for theatrical
release in all territories outside North
America. Also represents an

increasing library of European and independent American titles and has all rights to catalogues from various independent producers

Icon Entertainment International
The Quadrangle , 4th Floor
18 Wardour Street
London W1V 3AA
Tel: 020 7494 8100
Fax: 020 7494 8101
Ralph Kamp: Chief Executive
Jamie Carmichael: Head of Sales
Michaela Piper: Marketing Manager

ITC Library
Tel: 020 7836 7701
(See Carlton International)

J & M Entertainment
2 Dorset Square
London NW1 6PX
Tel: 020 7723 6544
Fax: 020 7724 7541
Julia Palau, Michael Ryan,
Specialise in sales of all media, distribution and marketing of independent feature films

Kushner-Locke International
83 Marylebone High Street
London W1M 3DE
Tel: 020 7935 9498
Fax: 020 7935 9486
Website: www.kushner-locke.com
Company led by Donald Kushner and Peter Locke has expanded its existing successful television production and distribution activities into international theatrical feature films, taking on Gregory Cascante and Eleanor Powell, partners of August Entertainment

Link Entertainment
7 Baron's Gate
33-35 Rothschild Road
Chiswick
London W4 5HT
Tel: 020 8996 4800
Fax: 020 8747 9452
email: info@linklic.demon.co.uk
Claire Derry, David Hamilton, Jo Kavanagh-Payne
Specialists in children's programmes for worldwide distribution and character licensing

London Films
35 Davies Street
London W1Y 1FN
Tel: 020 7499 7800
Fax: 020 7499 7994
Andrew Luff
Founded in 1932 by Alexander Korda, London Films is renowned for the production of classics. Co-productions with the BBC include

Poldark and *I Claudius*. More recent series include *Lady Chatterley* directed by Ken Russell and *The Scarlet Pimpernell* starring Richard E.Grant

London Television Service
21-25 St Anne's Court
London W1V 3AW
Tel: 020 7434 1121
Fax: 020 7734 0619
email: lts@londontv.com
Website: www.londontv.com
LTS is a specialist production and distribution organisation that handles the promotion and marketing of British documentary and magazine programmes worldwide to television, cable, satellite and non-broadcast outlets. The flagship science and technology series Perspective has sold to television in over 100 countries

MCA TV
1 Hamilton Mews
London W1V 9FF
Tel: 020 7491 4666
Fax: 020 7493 4702
Website: www.mca.com/tv/
Roger Cordjohn, Penny Craig
UK operation for the major US corporation which owns Universal Pictures

National Film Board of Canada
Canada House
Trafalgar Square
London SW1Y 5BJ
Tel: 020 7258 6480
Fax: 020 7258 6532
Jane Taylor
European sales office for documentary, drama and animation productions from Canada's National Film Board

NBD Television
Unit 2, Royalty Studios
105 Lancaster Road
London W11 1QF
Tel: 020 7243 3646
Fax: 020 7243 3656
Nicky Davies Williams, Charlotte Felia, Carolyne Waters
Company specialising in music and light entertainment

Orbit Media Ltd
7-11 Kensington High Street
London W8 5NP
Tel: 020 7221 5548
Fax: 020 7727 0515
Chris Ranger, Jordan Reynolds
Specialises in vintage product from the first decade of American TV: The Golden Years of Television and 65 x 30 mins Series NoireTV series

Paramount Television
49 Charles Street
London W1X 8LU
Tel: 020 7318 6400
Fax: 020 7491 2086
Stephen Tague

PD&B Films
68 Middle Street
Brighton
East Sussex BN1 1AL
Tel: 01273 235525
Fax: 01273 235528
email: info@pdbfilms.com
Website: www.pdbfilms.com
PD&B Films is an international sales agent for short films

Pearson Television International
1 Stephen Street
London W1P 1PJ
Tel: 020 7691 6000
Fax: 020 691 6060
Website: www.pearsontv.com
Managing Director: Brian Harris
Executive Vice President: Joe Abrams
Represents worldwide sales efforts for the companies under the Pearson Television International marque, including, ACI, All American, Alomo, Grundy and Thames Television as well as programming from independent producers. Catalogue includes: 10 volumes of ACI television movies – most recently *Behind the Mask* starring Donald Sutherland, *Deep in My Heart* with Anne Bancroft; comedy from *Benny Hill* and *Mr Bean*; sitcoms including *Men Behaving Badly, Goodnight Sweetheart, Birds of a Feather*; long running series *Neighbours, Shortland Street, Family Affairs, Homicide: Life on the Street* and *The Bill*; and Francis Ford Coppola's sci-fi series First Wave

Photoplay Productions
21 Princess Road
London NW1 8JR
Tel: 020 7722 2500
Fax: 020 7722 6662
Kevin Brownlow, David Gill, Patrick Stanbury
European dealer for the Blackhawk 16mm library of silent and early sound films

Portman Entertainment Ltd
167 Wardour Street
London W1V 3TA
Tel: 020 7468 3443
Fax: 020 7468 3469
Xavier Marchand, Gary Mitchell, Jane Baker
International feature film sales

division of the Portman Entertainment Group. Handles all media sales of both Portman's own productions as well as pre-financing and acquiring feature films and television programming from independent producers for worldwide sales. Recent titles include *The Clandestine Marriage, The Trench, Savage Honeymoon, Scarfies, Nancherrow* (TV miniseries)

Primetime Television Associates
Seymour Mews House
Seymour Mews, Wigmore Street
London W1H 9PE
Tel: 020 7935 9000
Fax: 020 7935 1992
Simon Willock, Richard Leworthy
Production and distribution.
Production includes: *Nicholas Nickleby, Porgy and Bess, Great Expectations, Othello*. Distribution includes: *Home and Away,* 99-1, *In the Wild, Finney, Our Friends in the North*

Reuters Television
85 Fleet Street
London EC4P 4AJ
Tel: 020 7250 1122
Fax: 020 7542 4995
Distribution of international TV news and sports material to broadcasters around the world

RM Associates
46 Great Marlborough Street
London W1V 1DB
Tel: 020 7439 2637
Fax: 020 7439 2316
Sally Fairhead
In addition to handling the exclusive distribution of programmes produced/co-produced by RM Arts, RM Associates works closely with numerous broadcasters and independent producers to bring together a comprehensive catalogue of music and arts programming

S4C International
Parc Ty Glas
Llanishen
Cardiff CF4 5DU
Tel: 029 20747444
Fax: 029 20754444
Rhianydd Darwin/Teleri Roberts/Helen Howells
Distribute programmes plus co-productions commissioned by S4C from independent producers – animation, drama, documentaries

Safir Films Ltd
49 Littleton Rd
Harrow
Middx HA1 3SY

Tel: 020 8423 0763
Fax: 020 8423 7963
email: Safir@ibm.net
Lawrence Safir
Hold rights to numerous Australian, US and UK pictures, including Sam Spiegel's Betrayal

The Sales Company
62 Shaftesbury Avenue
London W1V 7DE
Tel: 020 7434 9061
Fax: 020 7494 3293
Alison Thompson, Rebecca Kearey and Joy Wong. The Sales Company is owned by British Screen, BBC Worldwide, Zenith Productions and The Film Consortium handles international sales for their films, for all rights. Recent films include: *The Snapper, Priest, Butterfly Kiss, Antonia's Line, Stonewall, Land and Freedom,The Van, I Went Down, My Name is Joe* and *Hideous Kinky*. Also occasionally handles product from the international arena including *Safe, La Seconda Volta, Jerusalem* and *Private Confessions*

The Samuel Goldwyn Company
St George's House
14-17 Wells Street
London W1P 3FP
Tel: 020 7436 5105
Fax: 020 7580 6520
Betsy Spanbock, Katerina Mattingley
Acquisition, development, sales, distribution and marketing of films and television product worldwide. Recent film titles include *The Perez Family, The Madness of King George, Napoleon, Go Fish, Suture, Oleanna, Angels and Insects*. Television product includes: *Flipper, Camp Gladiators*

Scottish Television International
Cowcaddens
Glasgow G2 3PR
Tel: 0141 300 3000
Fax: 0141 300 3256
Ian Jones, Director
Anita Cox, Teleri Roberts
Sales and Marketing of STV, Grampian and Third Party Programming Worldwide, including: *McCallum, Taggart, Blobs, Hot Rod Dogs*. In the Field of Drama, Children's and Factual Programming

Screen Ventures
49 Goodge Street
London W1P 1FB
Tel: 020 7580 7448
Fax: 020 7631 1265
email: screenventures@easynet.

co.uk
Christopher Mould, Mike Evans
Worldwide television sales agents for international record companies and independent producers. Screen Ventures is also an independent producer of television documentaries and music programming

Smart Egg Pictures
11&12 Barnard Mews
Barnard Road
London SW11 1QU
Tel: 020 7924 6284
Fax: 020 7924 5650
Tom Sjoberg, Judy Phang
Independent foreign sales company. Titles include *Spaced Invaders, Dinosaurs, Montenegro, The Coca-Cola Kid, Rave Dancing to a Different Beat, Phoenix* and the *Magic Carpet* and *Evil Ed*

Stranger Than Fiction Film Sales Ltd
23 West Smithfield
London EC1A 9HY
Tel: 020 7248 9999
Fax: 020 7329 3333
email:cinechix@aol.com
Grace Carley
Boutique-style sales agency dealing primarily in arthouse features from the UK, US and Ireland. Recent titles include: Final Cut from Fugitive Films, Urban Ghost Story, from Living Spirit Productions and the award-winning documentary feature Southpaw

TCB Releasing
Stone House
Rudge, Frome
Somerset BA11 2QQ
Tel: 01373 830769
Fax: 01373 831028
Angus Trowbridge
Sales of jazz and blues music programmes to broadcast television and the home-video media (extracts, single programmes, series): Jazz Legends series (26 x 1 hr episodes), Mingus Sextet in Oslo concert, Monk in Oslo concert, Bill Evans in Oslo concert, BBC Jazz 625 series (20 x half-hour episodes), Blues Legends (8 x 1hr episodes), Individual Voices (11 x 1 hour episodes), *Live at the Village Vanguard* (6x 1 hr episodes), Stars of Jazz series, *The Soundies*

Trans World International
TWI House
23 Eyot Gardens
London W6 9TR
Tel: 020 8233 5000
Fax: 020 8233 5401
Eric Drossart, Bill Sinrich, Buzz Hornett

The world's largest independent producer and distributor of sports programmes, TWI is owned by Mark McCormack's IMG Group and specialises in sports and arts programming. Titles include: *Trans World Sport, Futbol Mundial, PGA European Tour productions, ATP Tour highlights, West Indies Test Cricket, Oddballs, A-Z of Sport, Goal!, The Olympic Series, Century and The Whitbread Round The World Race*

Turner International Television Licensing
CNN House
19 Rathbone Place
London W1P 1DF
Tel: 020 7637 6900
Fax: 020 7637 6925
Ross Portugeis
US production and distribution company of films and programmes from Hanna-Barbera (animation), Castle Rock, New Line, Turner Pictures Worldwide, World Championship Wrestling, Turner Original Productions (non-fiction), plus a library of over 2,500 films, 1,500 hours of television programmes and 1,000 cartoons from the MGM (pre-1986) and Warner Bros (pre-1950) studios

Twentieth Century Fox Television
31-32 Soho Square
London W1V 6AP
Tel: 020 7437 7766
Fax: 020 7439 1806
Website: www.fox.co.uk/
Stephen Cornish, Vice President
Randall Broman, Director of Sales
TV sales and distribution. A News Corporation company

Universal Pictures International
Oxford House
76 Oxford Street
London W1N 0H9
Tel: 020 7307 1300
Fax: 020 7307 1301

VCI Programme Sales
VCI
76 Dean Street
London W1V 5HA
Tel: 020 7396 8888
Fax: 020 7396 8890
Paul Hembury
A wholly owned subsidiary of VCI PLC, responsible for all overseas activities. Distributes a wide variety of product including music, sport, children's, fitness, documentary, educational, special interest and features

Victor Film Company Ltd
2b Chandos Street
London W1M 9DG
Tel: 020 7636 6620
Fax: 020 7636 6511
Alasdair Waddell, Vic Bateman, Carol Philbin, Alexandra Roper, Eliana Celiberti
International sales agent for independent producers of commercial films

Vine International Pictures
Astoria House
62 Shaftesbury Avenue
London W1V 7DE
Tel: 020 7437 1181
Fax: 020 7494 0634
Website: www.vineinternational. co.uk
Marie Vine, Barry Gill
Sale of feature films such as *Rainbow, The Pillow Book, The Ox and the Eye, Younger and Younger, The Prince of Jutland, Erik the Viking, Let Him Have It, Trouble in Mind*

Walt Disney Television International The
3 Queen Caroline Street
Hammersmith
London W6 9PA
Tel: 020 8222 1000
Fax: 020 8222 2795
MD: Etienne de Villiers
VP, Sales & Marketing: Keith Legoy
International television arm of a major US production company

Warner Bros International Television
98 Theobald's Road
London WC1X 8WB
Tel: 020 7984 5400
Richard Milnes, Donna Brett, Tim Horan, Ian Giles
TV sales, marketing and distribution. A division of Warner Bros Distributors Ltd, A Time Warner Entertainment Company, LP

Worldwide Television News Corporation (WTN)
The Interchange
Oval Road, Camden Lock
London NW1 7EP
Tel: 020 7410 5200
Fax: 020 7413 8327 (Library)
Gerry O'Reilly, David Simmons
International TV news, features, sport, entertainment, documentary programmes and archive resources. Camera crews in major global locations, plus in-house broadcasting and production facilities

Yorkshire-Tyne Tees Enterprises
15 Bloomsbury Square
London WC1A 2LJ
Tel: 020 7312 3700
Fax: 020 7312 3777
Sarah Doole, Susan Crawley, Ann Gillham
International sales division of Yorkshire-Tyne Tees TV

LABORATORIES

Bucks Laboratories Ltd
714 Banbury Avenue
Slough
Berks SL1 4LR
Tel: 01753 501500
Fax: 01753 691762
Website: www.bucks.co.uk
Darren Fagg
Comprehensive lab services in Super
35mm and 35mm, Super 16mm and
16mm, starting Sunday night. West
End rushes pick up unit 10.30 pm.
Also day bath. Chromakopy: 35mm
low-cost overnight colour reversal
dubbing prints. Photogard: European
coating centre for negative and print
treatment. Chromascan: 35mm and
16mm video to film transfer

Colour Film Services Group
10 Wadsworth Road
Perivale
Middx UB6 7JX
Tel: 020 8998 2731
Fax: 020 8997 8738
Steve Kyte
Film Laboratory: full 16mm and
35mm colour processing laboratory,
with Super 16mm to 35mm blow up
a speciality. Video Facility:
broadcastt standard wet gate telecines
and full digital edit suite. Video
duplication, CD mastering and
archiving to various formats.
Superscan: unique tape to film
transfer system in both Standard
Resolution and High Resolution.
Sounds Studios: analogue and digital
dubbing, track laying, synching,
voice overs and optical transfer bay

Colour-Technique
Cinematograph Film Laboratories
Finch Cottage, Finch Lane
Knotty Green
Beaconsfield HP9 2TL
Tel: 01494 672757
Specialists in 8mm, Super 8mm and
9.5mm blown up to 16mm with wet
gate printing. Stretch printing 16 and
18 Fps to 24, 32 and 48 Fps. 16mm
to 16mm optical copies with wet gate
and stretch printing. World leader for
archival film copying for 8mm,
Super 8mm, 9.5mm and 16mm with
wet gate printing from old shrunk
films, B/w dupe negs and colour
internegs. Also Super 8mm blown up
to Super 16mm wet gate printing and
stretch printing. 16mm to Super

16mm wet gate and stretch printing.
Colour internegs and B&W dupe
negatives. Super 8mm blown to 35 mm

Deluxe Laboratories Limited
North Orbital Road
Denham, Uxbridge
Middlesex UB9 5HQ
Tel: 01895 832323
Fax: 01895 832446
David Dowler
Deluxe London, together with sister
laboratories Deluxe Hollywood and
Deluxe Toronto, is a subsidiary of
Deluxe Entertainment Services. The
laboratories offer comprehensive
worldwide services to the Motion
Picture, Commercials and Television
industries. Deluxe London and
Toronto also include video transfer
suites. Deluxe Toronto includes
complete sound mixing and dubbing
suites. The well-known special
effects and optical house, General
Screen Enterprises, is also part of the
London operation

East Anglian Film Archive
University of East Anglia
Norwich NR4 7TJ
Tel: 01603 592664
Fax: 01603 458553
Specialises in blow-up printing of Std
8mm, Super 8mm, 9.5 mm, and
17.5mm b/w or colour, onto 16mm film

Film and Photo Ltd
13 Colville Road
South Acton Industrial Estate
London W3 8BL
Tel: 020 8992 0037
Fax: 020 8993 2409
email: film-photo@demon.co.uk
Website: www.film-
photo.demon.co.uk
Managing Director: Tony Scott
Post production motion picture
laboratory. 35/16mm Colour & B/W
reversal dupes. Tape to film transfers
– Optical effects. Nitrate
restoration/preservation

Film Lab North Ltd
Croydon House
Croydon Street
Leeds LS11 9RT
Tel: 0113 243 4842
Fax: 0113 2434323
email: fin@globalnet.co.uk
Mike Varley, Peter Wright

Full service in 16mm colour
Negative Processing, 16mm colour
printing, 35mm colour printing video
transfer. Super 16mm a speciality –
Plus 35mm colour grading and
printing

Hendersons Film Laboratories
18-20 St Dunstan's Road
South Norwood
London SW25 6EU
Tel: 020 8653 2255
Brian Pritchard
Preserves nitrate film footage. A total
black and white Laboratory Service
in 35mm and 16mm . Printing and
processing all black and white stocks
including 16mm reversal, plus
developing super 8mm reversal

The Lux Centre
2-4 Hoxton Square
London N1 6NU
Tel: 020 7684 0202
Fax: 020 7684 2222
Paul Murray
16mm b/w printing and processing

Metrocolor London
91-95 Gillespie Road
Highbury
London N5 1LS
Tel: 020 7226 4422
Fax: 020 7359 2353
Len Brown, Dave Kelly
Terry Lansbury, Alan Douglas
Offers complete service for features,
commercials, television productions
and pop promos for 16mm, Super
16mm, 35mm and Super 35mm. Day
and night processing and printing
colour, b/w and vnf. Overnight
rushes and sound transfer. Overnight
'best-light' and 'gamma' Telecine
rushes transfer and sync sound.
Computerised logging and negative
matching. Sound transfer to optical
negative – Dolby stereo, Dolby SRD
Digital stereo and DTS Timecode.
Specialist Super 16mm services
include: 35mm fully graded blow-up
prints; 35mm fully graded blow-up
immediates; fully graded prints re-
formatted to standard 16mm retaining
1.66:1 aspect ratio

Soho Images
8-14 Meard Street
London W1V 3HR

Tel: 020 7437 0831
Fax: 020 7734 9471
Soho Laboratories offer day and
night printing and processing of
16mm (including Super 16mm) and
35mm colour or b/w film

Technicolor Film Services
Technicolor Ltd
Bath Road
West Drayton
Middx UB7 0DB
Tel: 020 8759 5432
Fax: 020 8759 6270
West End pick-up and delivery point:
Goldcrest Ltd
1 Lexington Street
London W1R 3HP
Tel: 020 7439 4177
A 'Technicolor' logo in the end
credits has always been synonymous
with high quality film processing.
For almost 60 years Technicolor has
been at the forefront of film handling
technology. A 24 hours-a-day service
in all film formats; Europe's leading
65/70m laboratory facility (with
specialist support for large 'space
theatre' formats) and a comprehensive
sound transfer service, are highlights
of Technicolor's broad based
package. The laboratory is fully
equipped to make SRD, SDDS and
DTS prints too

Todd-AO UK
13 Hawley Crescent
London NW11 8NP
Tel: 020 7284 7929
Fax: 020 7284 7908
Roger Harlow
Complete 35mm, Super 16 and
16mm film processing laboratory and
sound transfer service with full video
post-production facility including
Digital Wet Gate Telecines, D3,
Digital Betacam, Betacam SP and
other video formats. On-line editing,
duplication and standards conversion.
Sync sound and A+B roll negative to
tape transfer, neg cutting service

LEGISLATION

This section of the Handbook has a twofold purpose, first to provide a brief history of the legislation relating to the film and television in the United Kingdom, and second to provide a short summary of the current principal instruments of legislation relating to film, television and video industries in the United Kingdom and in the European Community. Current legislation is separated into four categories: cinema and broadcasting; finance; copyright and European Union legislation. This section was compiled by Michael Henry of solicitors Henry Hepworth whose continued support we gratefully acknowledge

Legislative History

Cinema

Legislation for the cinema industry in the United Kingdom goes back to 1909, when the Cinematograph Act was passed providing for the licensing of exhibition premises, and safety of audiences. The emphasis on safety has been maintained through the years in other enactments such as the Celluloid and Cinematograph Film Act 1922, Cinematograph Act 1952 and the Fire Precautions Act 1971, the two latter having been consolidated in the Cinemas Act 1985.

The Cinematograph Films (Animals Act) 1937 was passed to prevent the exhibition and distribution of films in which suffering may have been caused to animals. The Cinematograph (Amendment) Act 1982 applied certain licensing requirements to pornographic cinema clubs. Excluded from licensing were the activities of bona fide film societies and 'demonstrations' such as those used in shops, as well as exhi-

bitions intended to provide information, education or instruction. Requirements for licensing were consolidated in the Cinemas Act 1985.

The Sunday Entertainments Act 1932 as amended by the Sunday Cinema Act 1972 and the Cinemas Act 1985 regulated the opening and use of cinema premises on Sundays.

The Sunday Entertainments Act 1932 also established a Sunday Cinematograph Fund for 'encouraging the use and development of cinematograph as a means of entertainment and instruction'. This was how the British Film Institute was originally funded.

Statutory controls were imposed by the Cinematograph Films Act 1927 in other areas of the film industry, such as the booking of films, quotas for the distribution and renting of British films and the registration of films exhibited to the public. This Act was modified by the Cinematograph Films Acts of 1938 and 1948 and the Film Acts 1960, 1966, 1970 and 1980 which were repealed by the Films Act 1985.

The financing of the British film industry has long been the subject of specific legislation. The National Film Finance Corporation was established by the Cinematograph Film Production (Special Loans) Act 1949. The Cinematograph Film Production (Special Loans) Act 1952 gave the National Film Finance Corporation the power to borrow from sources other than the Board of Trade. Other legislation dealing with film finance were the Cinematograph Film Production (Special Loans) Act 1954 and the Films Acts 1970 and 1980. The Cinematograph Films Council was established by the Cinematograph Films Act 1948, but like the National Film Finance Corporation, the Council was abolished by the Films Act 1985.

The Cinematograph Films Act 1957 established the British Film Fund Agency and put on a statutory foot-

ing the formerly voluntary levy on exhibitors known as the 'Eady levy'. Eady money was to be paid to the British Film Fund Agency, which in turn was responsible for making payments to British film-makers, the Children's Film Foundation, the National Film Finance Corporation, the British Film Institute and towards training film-makers. The Film Levy Finance Act 1981 consolidated the provisions relating to the Agency and the exhibitors' levy. The Agency was wound up in 1988 pursuant to a statutory order made under the Films Act 1985.

The British Film Institute used to obtain its funding from grants made by the Privy Council out of the Cinematograph Fund established under the Sunday Entertainments Act 1932 and also from the proceeds of subscriptions, sales and rentals of films. The British Film Institute Act 1949 allows for grants of money from Parliament to be made to the British Film Institute as the Lord President of the Privy Council thinks fit.

Broadcasting

The BBC first started as the British Broadcasting Company (representing the interests of some radio manufacturers) and was licensed in 1923 by the Postmaster General under the Wireless Telegraphy Act 1904 before being established by Royal Charter. The company was involved in television development from 1929 and in 1935 was licensed to provide a public television service.

The Independent Television Authority was established under the Television Act 1954 to provide additional television broadcasting services. Its existence was continued under the Television Act 1964 and under the Independent Broadcasting Act 1973, although its name had been changed to the Independent Broadcasting Authority by the Sound Broadcasting Act 1972 (which also permitted it to provide local sound broadcasting services).

The Broadcasting Act 1981 amended and consolidated certain provisions contained in previous legislation including the removal of the prohibition on certain specified people from broadcasting opinions expressed in proceedings of Parliament or local authorities, the extension of the IBA's functions to the provision of programmes for Channel 4 and the establishment of the Broadcasting Complaints Commission.

Cable programme services and satellite broadcasts were the subject of the Cable and Broadcasting Act 1984. This Act and the Broadcasting Act 1981 were repealed and consolidated by the Broadcasting Act 1990 which implemented proposals in the Government's White Paper Broadcasting in the 1990's: Competition Choice and Quality (Cm 517, November 1988). Earlier recommendations on the reform of the broadcasting industry had been made in the Report of the Committee on Financing the BBC (the Peacock Report) (Cmnd 9824, July 1986) and the Third Report of the Home Affairs Committee's inquiry into the Future of Broadcasting (HC Paper 262, Session 1987-88, June 1988).

Current UK/EU Legislation

BROADCASTING AND CINEMAS

Broadcasting Act 1996

The Broadcasting Act 1996 makes provision for digital terrestrial television broadcasting and contains provisions relating to the award of multiplex licences. It also provides for the introduction of radio multiplex services and regulates digital terrestrial sound broadcasting. In addition, the Act amends a number of provisions contained in the Broadcasting Act 1990 relating to the funding of Channel Four Television Corporation, the funding of Sianel Pedwar Cymru, and the operation of the Comataidh Craolidgh Gaialig (the Gaelic Broadcasting Committee). The Act also dissolves the Broadcasting Complaints Commission and Broadcasting Standards Council and replaces these with the Broadcasting Standards Commission. The Act also contains other provisions relating to the transmission network of the BBC and television coverage of listed events.

Broadcasting Act 1990

The Broadcasting Act 1990 established a new framework for the regulation of independent television and radio services, and for satellite television and cable television. Under the Act, the Independent Broadcasting Authority (IBA) and the Cable Authority were dissolved and replaced by the Independent Television Commission. The Radio Authority was established in respect of independent radio services. The Broadcasting Standards Council was made a statutory body and the Act also contains provisions relating to the Broadcasting Complaints Commission. Besides reorganising independent broadcasting, the Act provided for the formation of a separate company with responsibility for effecting the technical arrangements relating to independent television broadcasting – National Transcommunications Limited – as a first step towards the privatisation of the former IBA's transmission functions.

The Broadcasting Act 1990 repealed the Broadcasting Act 1981 and the Cable and Broadcasting Act 1984, amended the Wireless Telegraphy Act 1949, the Wireless Telegraphy Act 1967, the Marine [&c] Broadcasting (Offences) Act 1967, and the Copyright, Designs and Patents Act 1988, and also implements legislative provisions required pursuant to Directive 89/552 – see below.

The Broadcasting Act 1990 requires the British Broadcasting Corporation, all Channel 3 Licensees, the Channel Four Television Corporation, S4C (the Welsh Fourth Channel Authority) and the future Channel 5 Licensee to procure that not less than 25 per cent of the total amount of time allocated by those services to broadcasting "qualifying programming" is allocated to the broadcasting of a range and diversity of "independent productions". The expressions "qualifying programming" and "independent productions" are defined in the Broadcasting (Independent Productions) Order 1991.

Cinemas Act 1985

The Cinemas Act 1985 consolidated the Cinematographic Acts 1909 to 1952, the Cinematographic (Amendment) Act 1982 and related enactments. The Act deals with the exhibition of films and contains provisions for the grant, renewal and transfer of licences for film exhibition. There are special provisions for Greater London.

The Cinemas Act specifies the conditions of Sunday opening, and provides for exempted exhibition in private dwelling houses, and for non-commercial shows in premises used only occasionally.

Video Recordings Act 1984

The Video Recordings Act 1984 controls the distribution of video recordings with the aim of restricting the depiction or simulation of human sexual activity, gross violence, human genital organs or urinary or excretory functions. A system of classification and labelling is prescribed. The supply of recordings without a classification certificate, or the supply of classified recordings to persons under a certain age or in certain premises or in breach of labelling regulations, is prohibited subject to certain exemptions.

Classification certificates are issued by the British Board of Film

Classification. It is an offence to supply or offer to supply, or to have in possession for the purposes of supplying, an unclassified video recording. Supplying recordings in breach of classification, supplying certain classified recordings otherwise than in licensed sex shops, supplying recordings in breach of labelling requirements and supplying recordings with false indications as to classification, are all offences under the Act. The Video Recordings Act provides for powers of entry, search and seizure and for the forfeiture of video recordings by the court.

Telecommunications Act 1984

The Telecommunications Act 1984 prohibits the running of a telecommunications system within the United Kingdom subject to certain exceptions which include the running of a telecommunication system in certain circumstances by a broadcasting authority. A broadcasting authority means a person who is licensed under the Wireless Telegraphy Act 1949 (see below) to broadcast programmes for general reception. Telecommunications systems include, among other things, any system for the conveyance of speech, music, other sounds and visual images by electric, magnetic, electro-magnetic, electro-chemical or electro-mechanical energy.

Wireless Telegraphy Acts 1967 and 1949

The 1967 Act provides for the Secretary of State to obtain information as to the sale and hire of television receiving sets. The Act allows the Secretary of State to prohibit the manufacture or importation of certain wireless telegraphy apparatus and to control the installation of such apparatus in vehicles.

The 1949 Act provides for the licensing of wireless telegraphy and defines "wireless telegraphy" as the sending of electro-magnetic energy over paths not provided by a material substance constructed or arranged for that purpose. The requirements to hold a licence under the Wireless Telegraphy Act 1949 or the Telecommunications Act 1984 are separate from the television and radio

broadcast licensing provisions and cable programme source licensing provisions contained in the Broadcasting Act 1990.

Marine [&c] Broadcasting (Offences) Act 1967

The making of broadcasts by wireless telegraphy (as defined in the Wireless Telegraphy Act 1949) intended for general reception from ships, aircraft and certain marine structures is prohibited under this Act.

The Cinematograph Films (Animals) Act 1937

The Cinematograph Films (Animals) Act 1937 provides for the prevention of exhibiting or distributing films in which suffering may have been caused to animals.

Celluloid and Cinematograph Film Act 1922

This Act contains provisions which are aimed at the prevention of fire in premises where raw celluloid or cinematograph film is stored or used. Silver nitrate film which was in universal use until the 1950s and was still used in some parts of the world (notably the former USSR) until the 1970s, is highly inflammable and becomes unstable with age. The purpose of the legislation was to protect members of the public from fire risks.

FINANCE

Finance (No 2) Act 1997

Section 48 Finance (No 2) Act 1997 introduced new rules for writing-off production and acquisition expenditure of British qualifying films costing £15 million or less to make. The relief applies to expenditure incurred between 2 July 1997 and 1 July 2000. Section 48 allows 100 per cent write-off for production or acquisition costs when the film is completed.

A British qualifying film is one certified as such by the Department of Culture Media and Sport under the Films Act 1985. In order to be certified a number of criteria must be met. These include the requirement for the maker of the film to be a UK/European Economic Area ("EEA") company and the requirement for a certain percentage of labour costs to be spent on UK/EEA nationals. The prohibition on using a

foreign studio was relaxed in 1999.

The Inland Revenue made an announcement on 25 March 1998 that the Government intends to extend the time limit for relief under section 48 from 3 years to 5 years in a future Finance Bill. The relief will then apply to expenditure incurred between 2 July 1997 and 1 July 2002. The Film Review Group issued a report on 25 March 1998 which sets out an action plan for delivery by April 1999.

The Finance Act 1990, Capital Allowances Act 1990 and Finance (No 2) Act 1992

Section 80 and Schedule 12 to the Finance Act 1990 deals with the tax issues relating to the reorganisation of independent broadcasting provided for in the Broadcasting Act 1990.

Section 68 of the Capital Allowances Act 1990 replaces Section 72 of the Finance Act 1982 providing for certain expenditure in the production of a film, tape or disc to be treated as expenditure of a revenue nature.

Sections 41-43 of the Finance (No 2) Act 1992 amend the tax regime to provide accelerated relief for pre-production costs incurred after 10 March 1992 and production expenditure on films completed after that date. Section 69 of the Act makes certain consequential amendments to Section 68 of the Capital Allowances Act 1990.

Films Act 1985

The Films Act 1985 dissolved the British Film Fund Agency, ending the Eady levy system established in 1951. The Act also abolished the Cinematograph Film Council and dissolved the National Film Finance Corporation, transferring its assets to British Screen Finance Limited. The Act repealed the Films Acts 1960 – 1980 and also repealed certain provisions of the Finance Acts 1982 and 1984 and substituted new provisions for determining whether or not a film was 'British' film eligible for allowances. Under the Finance Acts 1997 (No 2), 1992 (No2) and 1990. These provisions have been further amended to relax the prohibition on using a foreign studio

National Film Finance Corporation Act 1981

The National Film Finance Corporation Act 1981 repealed the Cinematograph Film Production (Special Loans) Acts of 1949 and 1954 and made provisions in relation to the National Film Finance Corporation which has since been dissolved by the Films Act 1985. The National Film Finance Corporation Act 1981 is, however, still on the statute book.

Film Levy Finance Act 1981

Although the British Film Fund Agency was dissolved by the British Film Fund Agency (Dissolution) Order 1988, SI 1988/37, the Film Levy Act itself is still in place.

COPYRIGHT

Copyright, Designs and Patents Act 1988

This Act is the primary piece of legislation relating to copyright in the United Kingdom. The Act provides copyright protection for original literary, dramatic, musical and artistic works, for films, sound recordings, broadcasts and cable programmes, and for typographical arrangements of published editions.

The Act repeals the Copyright Act 1956 which in turn repealed the Copyright Act 1911, but the transitional provisions of the Copyright, Designs and Patents Act 1988 apply certain provisions of the earlier legislation for the purpose of determining ownership of copyright, type of protection and certain other matters. Because the term of copyright for original literary, dramatic and/or musical works is the life of the author plus 50 years, the earlier legislation will continue to be relevant until well into the next century. The provisions of the Act have been amended by EU harmonisation provisions contained in Directive 93/98 extending the term of copyright protection in relation to literary, dramatic, musical and artistic works originating in countries within the European Economic Area or written by nationals of countries in the EEA, to the duration of the life of the author or last surviving co-author plus, 70 years calculated from 31 December in the relevant year of decrease.

The Act provides a period of copyright protection for films and sound recordings which expires 50 years from the end of the calendar year in which the film or sound recording is made, or if it is shown or played in public or broadcast or included in a cable programme service, 50 years from the end of the calendar year in which this occurred.

The provisions of the Act have been amended by EU harmonisation provisions contained in Directive 93/98 extending the term of copyright protection for films, to a period equal to the duration to the lifetime of the last to die of the persons responsible for the making of the film, plus 70 years calculated from 31 December in the relevant year of decrease.

The Act introduced three new moral rights into United Kingdom legislation. In addition to the right not to have a work falsely attributed to him or her, an author (of a literary dramatic musical or artistic work) or director (of a film) has the right to be identified in relation to their work, and the right not to permit their work to suffer derogatory treatment. A derogatory treatment is any addition, deletion, alteration or adaptation of a work which amounts to a distortion or mutilation of the work, or is otherwise prejudicial to the honour or reputation of the author or director. A person who commissions films or photographs for private and domestic purposes enjoys a new right of privacy established by the Act.

Another new development is the creation of a statutory civil right for performers, giving them the right not to have recordings of their performances used without their consent. United Kingdom copyright legislation was amended following a decision in Rickless -v- United Artists Corporation – a case which was brought by the estate of Peter Sellars and involved The Trail of the Pink Panther. The legislation is retrospective and protects performances given 50 years ago, not just in the United Kingdom, but in any country if the performers were "qualifying persons" within the meaning of the relevant Act. The performances which are covered include not only dramatic and musical performances, but readings of literary works, variety programmes and even mime.

Numerous other provisions are contained in the Copyright, Designs and Patents Act including sections which deal with the fraudulent reception of programmes, the manufacture and sale of devices designed to circumvent copy-protection, and patent and design law.

EUROPEAN COMMUNITY LEGISLATION

Directive 89/552 – on television without frontiers

The objective of the Directive is to eliminate the barriers which divide Europe with a view to permitting and assuring the transition from national programme markets to a common programme production and distribution market. It also aims to establish conditions of fair competition without prejudice to the public interest role which falls to be discharged by television broadcasting services in the EC.

The laws of all Member States relating to television broadcasting and cable operations contain disparities which may impede the free movement of broadcasts within the EC and may distort competition. All such restrictions are required to be abolished.

Member States are free to specify detailed criteria relating to language etc. Additionally, Member States are permitted to lay down different conditions relating to the insertion of advertising in programmes within the limits set out in the Directive. Member States are required to provide where practicable that broadcasters reserve a proportion of their transmission time to European works created by independent producers. The amount of advertising is not to exceed 15 per cent of daily transmission time and the support advertising within a given one hour period shall not exceed 20 per cent.

Directive 92/100 – on rental rights

Authors or performers have, pursuant to the Directive, an unwaiveable right to receive equitable remuneration. Member States are required to provide a right for performers in relation to the fixation of their performances, a right for phonogram and film producers in relation to their phonograms and first fixations of their films and a right for broadcasters in relation to the fixation of broadcasts and their broadcast and cable transmissions. Member States must also provide a 'reproduction right' giving performers, phonogram producers, film producers and broadcasting organisations the right to authorise or prohibit the direct or indirect reproduction of their copyright works. The Directive also requires Member States to provide for performers, film producers, phonogram producers and broadcasting organisations to have exclusive rights to make available their work by sale or otherwise – known as the 'distribution right'.

Directive 93/83 on Satellite Transmission and Cable Retransmission

This Directive is aimed at eliminating uncertainty and differences in national legislation governing when the act of communication of a programme takes place. It avoids the cumulative application of several national laws to one single act of broadcasting.

The Directive provides that communication by satellite occurs in the member state where the programming signals are introduced under the control of a broadcaster into an uninterrupted chain of communication, leading to the satellite and down towards earth. The Directive also examines protection for authors, performers and producers of phonograms and broadcasting organisations, and requires that copyright owners may grant or refuse authorisation for cable retransmissions of a broadcast only through a collecting society.

Directive 98/98 on harmonising the term of protection of copyright and certain related rights

This Directive is aimed at harmonising the periods of copyright throughout the European Union where different states provide different periods of protection. Although the minimum term established by the Berne Convention on Copyright is 50 years post mortem auctoris, a number of states have chosen to provide for longer periods. In Germany the peri-

od of literary dramatic musical and artistic works is 70 years pma, in Spain 60 years (or 80 years for copyrights protected under the Spanish law of 1879 until its reform in 1987). In France the period is 60 years pma or 70 years for musical compositions.

In addition to the differences in the term of rights post mortem auctoris, further discrepancies arise in protection accorded by different member states through wartime extensions. Belgium has provided a wartime extension of 10 years, Italy 12 years, France six and eight years respectively in relation to the First and Second World Wars. In France, a further period of 30 years is provided in the case of copyright works whose authors were killed in action – such as Antoine de Saint-ExupÈry.

The Directive also provides that rights of performers shall run from 50 years from the date of performance or if later, from the point at which the fixation of the performance is lawfully made available to the public for the first time, or if this has not occurred from the first assimilation of the performance. The rights of producers of phonograms run 50 years from first publication of the phonogram, but expire 50 years after the fixation was made if the phonogram, but expire 50 years after the fixation was made if the phonogram has not been published during that time. A similar provision applies to the rights of producers of the first fixations of cinematographic works and sequences of moving images, whether accompanied or not by sound. Rights of broadcasting organisations run from 50 years from the first transmission of the broadcast.

The Directive provides that the person who makes available to the public a previously unpublished work which is in the public domain, shall have the same rights of exploitation in relation to the work as would have fallen to the author for a term of 25 years from the time the work was first made available to the public. The Directive applies to all works which are protected by at least one member state on 1 July 1995 when the Directive came into effect. As a result of the differing terms in European states, many works which were treated as being in the 'public

domain' in the United Kingdom will have their copyright revived. Works by Beatrix Potter, James Joyce and Rudyard Kipling are all works which will benefit from a revival of copyright. The provisions relating to the term of protection of cinematographic films are not required to be applied to films created before 1 July 1994. Each member state of the European Union's required to implement the Directive. The precise manner of implementation and the choice of transitional provisions, are matters which each state is free to determine.

Directive 93/98 was implemented in the United Kingdom by the Rights in Performances Regulations 1995/3297 which took effect from 1 January 1996. The term of copyright protection for literary dramatic musical or artistic works expires at the end of the period of 70 years from the last day of the calendar year in which the author dies. Copyright in a film expires 70 years from the end of the calendar year in which the death occurs of the last to die of the principal director, the author of the screenplay, the author of the dialogue or the composer of the music specially created for and used for the film. The period of copyright previously applying to films under the Copyright, Designs and Patents Act 1988 ended 50 years from the first showing or playing in public of a film, and the effect of the implementation of Directive 93/98 is to create a significant extension of the period in which a film copyright owner has the exclusive economic right to exploit a film. If, as anticipated, the United States of America also extends the duration of the copyright period applying to films, the value of intellectual property rights in audiovisual productions may increase significantly.

LIBRARIES

This section provides a directory of libraries and archives which have collections of books, periodicals and papers covering film and television. It includes the libraries of colleges and universities with graduate and post-graduate degree courses in the media. Most of these collections are intended for student and teaching staff use: permission for access should always be sought from the Librarian in charge. Where possible a breakdown of types of resources available is provided

bfi National Library
21 Stephen Street
London W1P 2LN
Tel: 020 7 255 1444
      020 7436 0165 (Information)
Fax: 020 7436 2338

The *bfi's* own library is extensive and hold's the world's largest collection of documentation on film and television. It includes both published and unpublished material ranging from books and periodicals to news cuttings, press releases, scripts, theses, and files of festival material
Reading Room opening hours:
Mon, Fri   10.30am – 5.30pm
Tues Thurs   10.30am – 8.00pm
Wed   01.00pm – 8.00pm
Library library pass: £33.00
NFT Members pass: £25.00
Discount passes (£20.00) are available to Senior Citizens, Registered Disabled and Unemployed upon proof of eligibility. Students may also apply for a discounted library pass. Day passes are available (£6.00) to anyone and space may be reserved by giving 48 hours notice.

Enquiry Lines:
The Enquiry Line is available for short enquiries. Frequent callers subscribe to an information service. The line is open from 10.00am to 5.00pm Monday to Friday via the BFI switchboard (020 7255 1444)

Research Services:
For more detailed enquiries, users should contact the Information Service by fax or mail.

RESOURCES

A   Specialist sections
B   Film/TV journals
C   Film/TV/CD Roms
D   Video loan service
E   Internet access
F   Special collections

Aberdeen

Aberdeen University Library
Queen Mother Library, Meston Walk, Aberdeen
Grampian AB24 3UE
Tel: 01224 272579
Fax: 01224 487048
email: library@abdn.ac.uk
Website: www.abdn.ac.uk/library/
Contact: University Librarian

Bangor

Normal College
Education Library, Bangor
Gwynedd LL57 2P
Tel: 01248 370171
Fax: 01248 370461
Contact: Librarian

Barnet

Middlesex University Cat Hill Library
Cat Hill, Barnet
Herts EN4 8HT
Tel: 020 8362 5042
Fax: 020 8440 9541
Contact: Art and Design Librarian

Bath

Bath University Library
Claverton Down
Bath BA2 7AY
Tel: 01225 826084
Fax: 01225 826229
Contact: University Librarian

Belfast

Belfast Central Library
Royal Avenue
Belfast
Co. Antrim BT1 1EA
Tel. 01232 332819
Fax: 01232 312886
Contact: Chief Librarian

Northern Ireland Film Commission
21 Ormeau Avenue
Belfast BT2 8HD
Tel: 01232 232 444
Fax: 01232 239 918
email: Contact: Information Officer
Resources: B, D

Queen's Film Theatre
25 College Gardens
Belfast BT9 6BS
Tel: 01232 667687 ext. 33
Fax: 01232 663733
email:mofen@qub.ac.uk
Website: www.qub.uk/
Contact: Administrator/Programmer
Resources: B, C, E, F

Birmingham

BBC Pebble Mill
Information Research Library
Pebble Mill Road
Birmingham B5 7QQ
Tel: 0121 414 8922
Contact: Information Research Librarian
Resources: B, C, E

Birmingham University Library
Edgbaston
Birmingham B15 2TT
Tel: 0121 414 5817
Fax: 0121 414 5815
Contact: Librarian, Arts and Humanities

Central Broadcasting Ltd
Broad Street
Birmingham B1 2JP
Tel: 0121 643 9898
Contact: Reference Librarian

Information Services
Franchise Street
Perry Barr
Birmingham B42 2SU
Tel: 0121 331 5300
Fax: 0121 331 6543
Contact: Dean of Information Services

University of Central England
Birmingham Institute of Art & Design
Gosta Green
Birmingham B4 7DX

Tel: 0121 331 5860
Contact: Library staff

Vivid – Birmingham's Centre for Media Arts
Unit 311 The Big Peg
120 Vyse Street
Birmingham B18 6ND
Tel: 0121 233 4061
Fax: 0121 212 1784
email:vivid@waveriden.co.uk
Website: www.wavespace.waverider
.co.uk
Contact: Head of Service: Yasmeen Baig
Resources: A, B, D, E,

Brighton

University of Brighton Faculty of Art, Design and Humanities
St Peter's House Library
16-18 Richmond Place
Brighton BN2 2NA
Tel: 01273 643221
Contact: Librarian

University of Sussex Library
Falmer
Brighton
East Sussex BN1 9QL
Tel: 01273 678163
Fax: 01273 678441
Contact: Enquiries and Information Services

Bristol

Bristol City Council
Leisure Services
Central Library, Reference Library, College Green
Bristol BS1 5TL
Tel: 0117 927 6121
Fax: 0117 922 6775
Contact: Head of Reference & Information Services

University of Bristol
University Library
Tyndall Avenue
Bristol BS8 1TJ
Tel: 0117 928 9017
Fax: 0117 925 5334
Website: www.bris.ac.uk/Depts
/Library
Contact: Librarian
Resources: A,B, C, E

University of Bristol Theatre Collection
Department of Drama
Cantocks Close
Bristol BS8 1UP
Tel: 0117 928 7836
Fax: 0117 928 7832
email: theatre.collection@bris.ac.uk
Website: www.bris.ac.uk/depts/drama

West of England University at Bristol
Library, Faculty of Art, Media & Design
Bower Ashton Campus
Clanage Road
Bristol BS3 2JU
Tel: 0117 966 0222 x4750
Fax: 0117 976 3946
Contact: Steve Morgan, Campus/Subject Librarian, Art, Media and Design

Canterbury

Canterbury College Library
Kent Institute of Art & Design
New Dover Road, Canterbury
Kent CT1 3AN
Tel: 01227 769371
Fax: 01227 451320

Christ Church College Library
North Holmes Road
Canterbury
Kent CT1 1QU
Tel: 01227 767700
Fax: 01227 767530
Website: www.cant.ac.uk./
depts/services/library/library1.html
Contact: Director of Library Services
Resources: A, B, C, D, E

Kent Institute of Art & Design at Canterbury
New Dover Road
Canterbury
Kent CT1 3AN
Tel: 01227 769371
Fax: 01227 451320
Contact: Learning Resources Manager

Templeman Library
University of Kent at Canterbury
Canterbury
Kent CT2 7NU
Tel: 01227 764000
Fax: 01227 459025
Contact: Librarian

Cardiff

Coleg Glan Hafren
Trowbridge Road
Rumney
Cardiff CF3 8XZ
Tel: 029 20250250
Fax: 029 20250339
Contact: Learning Resources Development Manager

University of Wales College
Cardiff, Bute, Library
PO Box 430
Cardiff CF1 3XT

Tel: 029 20874000
Fax: 029 20874192
Website: www.cardiff.ac.uk
Contact: Librarian

Carlisle

Cumbria College of Art and Design Library
Brampton Road
Carlisle
Cumbria CA3 9AY
Tel: 01228 25333 x206
Contact: Librarian

Chislehurst

Ravensbourne College of Design and Communication Library
Walden Road, Chislehurst
Kent BR7 5SN
Tel: 020 8289 4900
Fax: 020 8325 8320
email: library@rave.ac.uk
Contact: Librarian

Colchester

University of Essex
The Albert Sloman Library
Wivenhoe Park
Colchester CO4 3SQ
Tel: 01206 873333
Contact: Librarian

Coleraine

University of Ulster
Library
Coleraine
Northern Ireland BT52 1SA
Tel: 01265 32 4345
Fax: 01265 32 4928
Contact: Pro-Librarian
Resources: A, B, C, D

Coventry

Coventry City Library
Smithford Way
Coventry CV1 1FY
Tel: 024 76832314
Fax: 024 76832440
email: covinfo@discover.co.uk
Contact: Librarian – Karen Berry

Coventry University, Art & Design Library
Priory Street
Coventry CV1 5FB
Tel: 024 76838546
Fax: 024 76838686
Website: www.coventry.ac.uk./irary/
Contact: Sub-Librarian, Art & Design

Warwick University Library
Gibbet Hill Road

Coventry CV4 7AL
Tel: 024 76524103
Fax: 024 76524211
Contact: Librarian
Resources: A, B, C, D, E, F*
* Collection of German film
programme from the 1930s

Derby

Derby University Library
Kedleston Rd
Derby DE3 1GB
Tel: 01332 622222 x 4061
Fax: 01332 622222 x 4059
Contact: Librarian

University of Derby
Library and Learning Resources
Derby DE1 !RX
Tel: 01332 622222 Ext 3001
Website: www.derby.ac.uk/library
/homelib.html
Contact: Subject Adviser, Art &
Design
Resources: A, B, C, D, E

Dorking

Surrey Performing Arts
Library
Vaughan Williams House
West Street
Dorking, Surrey RH4 1BY
Tel: 01306 887509
Fax: 01306 875074
email: p.arts@dial.pipex.com
Website: www.surreycc.gov.uk/
libraries/direct/perfarts.html
Senior Librarian: G.Muncy
Contact: Librarian
Resources: A, B, C, D, E, F*
*Scripts

Douglas

Douglas Corporation
Douglas Public Library
Ridgeway Street
Douglas
Isle of Man
Tel: 01624 623021
Fax: 01624 662792
Contact: Borough Librarian

Dundee

Library Duncan of
Jordanstone College
University of Dundee
13 Perth Road
Dundee DD1 4HT
Tel: 01382 345255
Fax: 01382 229283
Contact: College Librarian
Resources: A, B, C, D, E, F*
* Few scripts

Egham

Royal Holloway University
of London Library
Egham Hill
Egham
Surrey TW20 OEX
Tel: 01784 443330
Fax: 01784 437520
Website: www.rhbnc.ac.uk
Contact: Librarian
Resources: A, B, C, D, E

Exeter

Exeter University Library
Stocker Road
Exeter
Devon EX4 4PT
Tel: 01392 263869
Fax: 01392 263871
Website: www.exe.ac.uk/@
JACrawle/lib.film.html
Contact: Librarian
Resources: A, B, C, D, E, F*
*The Bill Douglas Centre for the
History of Cinema and Popular
Culture

Farnham

Surrey Institute of Art &
Design, University College
Falkner Road, The Hart
Farnham
Surrey GU9 7DS
Tel: 01252 722441
Fax: 01252 892616
Contact: Institue Librarian
Resources: A, B, C, D*, E*
*Registered users only

Gateshead

Gateshead Libraries and
Arts Department
Central Library
Prince Consort Road
Gateshead
Tyne and Wear NE8 4LN
Tel: 0191 477 3478
Fax: 0191 477 7454
Contact: The Librarian

Glasgow

Glasgow Caledonian
University Library
Cowcaddens Road
Glasgow G4 0BA
Tel: 0141 331 3858
Fax: 0141 331 3005
Website: /www.gcal.ac.uk/library/
index.html
Contact: Assistant Academic Liaison
Librarian for Language and Media
Resources: A, B, C, D, E

Glasgow City Libraries
Mitchell Library
North Street
Glasgow G3 7DN
Tel: 0141 287 2933
Fax: 0141 287 2815
Contact: Departmental Librarian, Art
Department

Glasgow School of Art
Library
167 Renfrew Street
Glasgow G3 6RQ
Tel: 0141 353 4551
Fax: 0141 332 3506
Contact: Principal Librarian

Scottish Council for
Educational Technology
Dowanhill
74 Victoria Crescent Road
Glasgow G12 9JN
Tel: 0141 337 5000
Fax: 0141 337 5050
Website: www.sect.com
Contact: Librarian
Resources: D

Scottish Screen
249 West George Street
Glasgow G2 4RB
Tel: 0141 302 1700
Fax: 0141 302 1711
email: info@scottishscreen.com
Website: www.scottishscreen.com
Chief Executive: John Archer
Resources: D, F*
* Access to the Shiach Script library
with over 100 feature and short film
scripts, Video, publications resource.
Internet site, National Archive
collection of factual documentary
material reflecting Scotland's social
and cultural histor. Available to
braodcasters, programme makers,
educational history. Available to
broadcasters, programme makers,
educational users and researchers.
Distribution of Scottish shorts with
back catalogue

University of Glasgow
The Library
Hillhead Street
Glasgow G12 8QQ
Tel: 0141 330 6704/5
Fax: 0141 330 4952
Contact: Librarian

Gravesend

VLV – Voice of the
Listener and Viewer
101 King's Drive
Gravesend
Kent DA12 5BQ
Tel: 01474 352835
Fax: 01474 351112

Contact: Information Officer
In addition to its own VLV holds archives of the former independent Broadcasting Research Unit (1980-1991) and the former British Action for Children's Television (BACTV) (1988-1994) and makes these available for a small fee together with its own archives and library. VLV represents the citizen and consumer interest in broadcasting
Resources: A, E, F

Huddersfield

Kirklees Cultural Services
Central Library
Princess Alexandra Walk
Huddersfield HD1 2SU
Tel: 01484 221967
Fax: 01484 221974
Contact: Reference Librarian
Resources: C, D, E

Hull

Hull University Brynmor Jones Library
Cottingham Road
Hull
North Humberside HU6 7RX
Tel: 01482 465440
Fax: 01482 466205
Contact: Librarian

Humberside

Humberside University
School of Art, Architecture and Design Learning Support Centre
Guildhall Road
Hull HU1 1HJ
Tel: 01482 440550
Fax: 01482 449627
Contact: Centre Manager

Keele

Keele Information Services
Keele University
Keele
Staffs ST5 5BG
Tel: 01782 583239
Fax: 01782 711553
Contact: Visual Arts Department
Resources: B, C, D, E

Kingston upon Thames

Kingston Museum & Heritage Service
North Kingston Centre
Richmond Road
Kingston upon Thames
Surrey KT2 5PE
Tel: 020 8547 6738 or 6755

Website: http://www.kingston.ac.uk/muytexto.htm
Contact: T. Everson, Local History Officer
Resources: E, F*
*Eadweard Maybridge Collection

Kingston University Library Services
Art and Design Library
Knights Park
Kingston Upon Thames
Surrey KT1 2QJ
Tel: 020 8547 2000 x 4031
Fax: 020 8547 7011
Contact: Senior Faculty Librarian (Design)

Kingston University Library Services
Library & Media Services
Penrhyn Road
Kingston Upon Thames
Surrey KT1 2EE
Tel: 020 8547 2000
Contact: Head of Media Services

Leeds

Leeds City Libraries
Central Library
Municipal Buildings
Calverley Street
Leeds, West Yorkshire LS1 3AB
Tel: 0113 247 8265
Fax: 0113 247 8268
Contact: Director of Library Services

Leeds Metropolitan University
City Campus Library
Calverley Street
Leeds, West Yorkshire LS1 3HE
Tel: 0113 283 2600 x3836
Fax: 0113 242 5733
Contact: Tutor Librarian, Art & Design

Trinity and All Saints College Library
Brownberrie Lane, Horsforth
Leeds, West Yorkshire LS18 5HD
Tel: 0113 283 7100
Fax: 0113 283 7200
Website: www.tasc.ac.uk
Contact: Librarian
Resources: A, B, D, E

Leicester

Centre For Mass Communication Research
104 Regent Road
Leicester LE1 7LT
Tel: 0116 2523863
Fax: 0116 2523874
Contact: Director

De Montfort University Library
Kimberlin Library
The Gateway
Leicester LE1 9BH
Tel: 0116 255 1551
Fax: 0116 255 0307
Contact: Senior Assistant Librarian (Art and Design)

Leicester Central Lending Library
54 Belvoir Street
Leicester LE1 6QL
Tel: 0116 255 6699
Contact: Area Librarian
Resources: D, E,

Leicester University Library
PO Box 248
University Road
Leicester LE1 9QD
Tel: 0116 252 2042
Fax: 0116 252 2066
Website: www.le.ac.uk
Contact: Librarian
Resources: A, B, E

Liverpool

Aldham Robarts Learning Resource Centre
Liverpool John Moores University
Mount Pleasant
Liverpool L3 5UZ
Tel: 0151 231 3104
Contact: Senior Information Officer (Media, Critical and Creative Arts)

Liverpool City Libraries
William Brown Street
Liverpool L3 8EW
Tel: 0151 225 5429
Fax: 0151 207 1342
Contact: Librarian

Liverpool Hope University College
Hope Park
Liverpool L16 9LB
Tel: 0151 291 2000
Fax: 0151 291 2037
Website: www.livhope.ac.uk
Contact: Director of Learning Resources
Resources: A, B, C, D, E

London

Barbican Library
Barbican Centre
London EC2Y 8DS
Tel: 020 7638 0569
Fax: 020 7638 2249
Contact: Librarian

BKSTS – The Moving Image Society
63-71 Victoria House

Vernon Place
London WC1B 4DA
Tel: 020 7242 8400
Fax: 020 7405 3560
email:
movimage@bksts.demon.co.uk
Contact: John Graham

British Universities Film & Video Council Library
77 Wells Street
London W1P 3RE
Tel: 020 7393 1508
Fax: 020 7393 1555
Website: www.bufvc.ac.uk
Contact: Head of Information
Resources: B, C, D*, E, F**
* Film loans
** British Universities Newsreel Project database

Brunel University
Twickenham Campus
300 St Margarets Road
Twickenham TW1 1PT
Tel: 020 8891 0121
Fax: 020 8891 0240
Contact: Director of Library Services
Resources: A, B, C, E

Camberwell College of Arts Library
London Institute
Peckham Road
London SE5 8UF
Tel: 020 7514 6349
Fax: 020 7514 6324
Contact: College Librarian
Resources: A, B, E

Camden Public Libraries
Swiss Cottage Library
88 Avenue Road
London NW3 3HA
Tel: 020 7413 6527
Website: swisslib@camden.gov.uk
Contact: Librarian
Resources: A, B, D, E

Carlton Screen Advertising Ltd
127 Wardour Street
London W1V 4NL
Tel: 020 7439 9531
Fax: 020 7439 2395
Contact: Secretary

The College of North East London Learning Resource Centre
High Road, Tottenham
London N15 4RU
Tel: 020 8442 3013
Fax: 020 8442 3091
Contact: Head of Learning Resources

Guildhall University Library Services
Calcutta House

Old Castle Street
London E1 7NT
Tel: 020 7320 1000
Fax: 020 7320 1177
Contact: Head of Library Services

Independent Television Commission Library
33 Foley Street
London W1P 7LB
Tel: 020 7306 7763
Fax: 020 7306 7750
Contact: Librarian
Resources: A, B, C, E, F*
* Press cuttings

Institute of Education Library (London)
20 Bedford Way
London WC1H OAL
Tel: 020 7612 6080
Fax: 020 7612 6093
email: lib.enquiries@ioe.ac.uk
Contact: Librarian

International Institute of Communications
Library and Information Service
Tavistock House South
Tavistock Square
London WC1H 9LF
Tel: 020 7388 0671
Fax: 020 7380 0623
Contact: Information & Library Manager

London Borough of Barnet Libraries
Hendon Library
The Burroughs
Hendon
London NW4 4BQ
Tel: 020 8359 2628
Fax: 020 8359 2885
Contact: Librarian

London College of Printing & Distributive Trades
Media School
Backhill
Clerkenwell EC1R 5EN
Tel: 020 7514 6500
Fax: 020 7514 6848
Contact: Head of Learning Resources

Middlesex University Library
Bounds Green Road
London N11 2NQ
Tel: 020 8362 5240
Contact: University Librarian

Roehampton Institute
Information Services
Roehampton Institute London
Learning Resources Centre
Digby Stuart College
Roehampton Lane
London SW15 5SZ

Tel: 020 8392 3251
Contact: Information Adviser
(Performing Arts)
Resources: B, C, E

Royal College of Art
Kensington Gore
London SW7 2EU
Tel: 020 7590 4224 – Library Desk
Tel: 020 7590 4444 – College
Fax: 020 7590 4500
Contact: Library Manager

Royal Television Society, Library & Archive
Holborn Hall
100 Grays Inn Road
London WC1X 8AL
Tel: 020 7430 1000
Fax: 020 7430 0924
Contact: Archivist

Slade/Duveen Art Library
University College London
Gower Street
London WC1E 6BT
Tel: 020 7504 2594
Fax: 020 7380 7373
email: r.dar@ucl.ac.uk
Contact: Art Librarian: Ruth Dar
Resources: A, B, C, E*
* For UCL staff and students

Thames Valley University Library
Learning Resources Centre
18-22 Bond Street W5 5AA
Tel: 020 8231 2248
Fax: 020 8231 2631
Contact: Humanities Librarian

University of East London
Greengate House Library
School of Art & Design
89 Greengate Street
London E13 0BG
Tel: 020 8590 7000 x 3434
Contact: Site Librarian

University of London: Goldsmiths' College Library
Lewisham Way
London SE14 6NW
Tel: 020 7919 7168
Fax: 020 7919 7165
email: lbslpm@gold.ac.uk
Website: www.gold.ac.uk
Contact: Subject Librarian: Media & Communications
Resources: A, B, C, D

University of North London
The Learning Centre
236-250 Holloway Road
London N7 6PP
Tel: 020 7607 2789 x 2720
Fax: 020 7753 5079
Contact: Film Studies Librarian
Resources: B, C, D, E

University of Westminster
Harrow Learning Resources
Centre, Watford Road
Northwick Park
Harrow HA1 3TP
Tel: 020 7911 5000
Website: http://www.wmin.ac.uk
Contact: Design, Media &
Communications Co-ordinator
Resources: A, B, C, D, E

Westminster Reference Library
35 St Martins Street
London WC2H 7HP
Tel: 020 7641 4636
Fax: 020 7641 4640
Contact: Margaret Girvan, Arts
Librarian
Resources: A, B, C, E

Loughborough

Loughborough University Pilkington Library
Loughborough University
Loughborough LE11 3TU
Tel: 01509 222360
Fax: 01509 234806
Contact: Assistant Librarian

Luton

University of Luton Library
Park Square
Luton LU1 3JU
Tel: 01582 734111
Contact: Faculty Information Officer

Maidstone

Kent Institute of Art & Design at Maidstone
Oakwood Park, Maidstone
Kent ME16 8AG
Tel: 01622 757286
Fax: 01622 692003
Contact: College Librarian

Manchester

John Rylands University Library
Oxford Road
Manchester M13 9PP
Tel: 0161 275 3751/3738
Fax: 0161 273 7488
Contact: Lending Services Librarian

Manchester Arts Library
Central Library
St Peters Square
Manchester M2 5PD
Tel: 0161 234 1974
Fax: 0161 234 1963
Contact: Arts Librarian
Resources: A, B, D, E

Manchester Metropolitan University Library
All Saints Building
Grosvenor Square
Oxford Road
Manchester M15 6BH
Tel: 0161 247 6104
Fax: 0161 247 6349
Contact: Senior Subject Librarian

North West Film Archive
Manchester Metropolitan
University
Minshull House
47-49 Chorlton Street
Manchester M1 3EU
Tel: 0161 247 3097
Fax: 0161 247 3098
email: n.w.filmarchive@mmu.ac.uk
Website: www.mmu.ac.uk/services
/library/wst.htm
Director: Maryann Gomes
Enquiries: Liza Warren/Anoush
Simon
Resources: D, E, F*
* Ephemera

Newcastle upon Tyne

Newcastle Upon Tyne University Robinson Library
Robinson Library
Newcastle Upon Tyne NE2 4HQ
Tel: 0191 222 7713
Fax: 0191 222 6235
Website: www.ncl.ac.uk/library
Contact: The Librarian
Resources: A, B, C, D, E

University of Northumbria at Newcastle Library Building
Ellison Place
Newcastle Upon Tyne NE1 8ST
Tel: 0191 227 4132
Fax: 0191 227 4563
Website: www.unn.ac.uk
Contact: Jane Shaw, Senior Officer,
Information Services Department

Newport

University of Wales College Newport
Caerleon
Newport NP6 1XJ
Tel: 01633 430088
Fax: 01633 432108
Contact: Art and Design Librarian

Northumberland

Northumberland Central Library
The Willows, Morpeth

Northumberland NE61 1TA
Tel: 01670 511156
Fax: 01670 518012
Website: www.amenities@
northumberland.gov.uk
Contact: The Librarian
Resources: A, B, C, D, E

Norwich

East Anglian Film Archive
Centre for East Anglian Studies
University of East Anglia
Norwich NR4 7TJ
Tel: 01603 592664
Fax: 01603 458553
Contact: Assistant Archivist

University of East Anglia
University Library
Norwich NR4 7TJ
Tel: 01603 456161
Fax: 01603 259490
Contact: Film Studies Librarian

Nottingham

Nottingham Central Library
Angel Row
Nottingham NG1 6HP
Tel: 0115 941 2121
Fax: 0115 953 7001
Contact: Librarian

Nottingham Trent University Library
The Boots Library
Goldsmith Street
Nottingham NG1 5LS
Tel: 0115 848 2110
Fax: 0115 848 2286
Website: www.ntu.ac.uk
Contact: Faculty Liaison Officer (Art
& Design)
Resources: A, B, C, D, E

University of Nottingham Library
Hallward Library
University Park
Nottingham NG7 2RD
Tel: 0115 951 4584
Fax: 0115 951 4558
Website: www.nottingham.ac
.uk/library
Contact: Humanities Librarian
Recources: A, B, C, E

Plymouth

College of St Mark and St John Library
Derriford Road, Plymouth
Devon PL6 8BH
Tel: 01752 636700
Fax: 01752 636712
Contact: Resources Librarian
Resources: B, C, E

**Plymouth College of Art &
Design Library**
Tavistock Place
Plymouth
Devon PL4 8AT
Tel: 01752 203412
Fax: 01752 203444
Contact: Librarian
Resources: A, B, C, D, E

Pontypridd

University of Glamorgan
Learning Resources Centre
Pontypridd
Mid Glamorgan CF37 1DL
Tel: 01443 482625
Fax: 01443 482629
Contact: Head of Learning Resource

Poole

**Bournemouth & Poole
College of Art & Design**
Fern Barrow,
off Wallisdown Road, Poole
Dorset BH12 5HH
Tel: 01202 533011
Fax: 01202 537729
Contact: University Librarian

**Bournemouth University
Library**
Talbot Campus, Fern Barrow,
off Wallisdown Road
Poole
Dorset BH12 5BB
Tel: 01202 595011
Contact: Librarian

Portsmouth

Highbury College Library
Cosham
Portsmouth
Hants PO6 2SA
Tel: 023 92 283213
Fax: 023 92 325551
Contact: College Librarian

**Portsmouth University
Library**
Frewen Library, Cambridge Road
Portsmouth, Hampshire PO1 2ST
Tel: 023 92 843222
Fax: 023 92 843233
Website: www.libr.port.ac.uk
Contact: University Librarian
Resources: A, B, C, D, E

Preston

**University of Central
Lancashire Library**
St Peter's Square
Preston
Lancashire PR1 2HE

Tel: 01772 201201 x 2266
Fax: 01772 892937
Contact: Senior Subject Librarian

Reading

**Reading University
Bulmershe Library**
Woodlands Avenue
Reading RG6 1HY
Tel: 0118 987 5123 ext 4824
Fax: 0118 931 8651
Contact: Faculty Team Manager
(Education & Community Studies)

Rochdale

**Rochdale Metropolitan
Borough Libraries**
Wheatsheaf Library, Wheatsheaf
Centre, Baillie Street, Rochdale
Lancashire OL16 1AQ
Tel: 01706 864914
Fax: 01706 864992
Contact: Librarian

Salford

**University of Salford,
Academic Information
Services (Library)**
Adelphi Campus
Peru Street
Salford
Greater Manchester M3 6EQ
Tel: 0161 295 6183/6185
Fax: 0161 295 6103
Website: www.salford.ac.
uk/ais/homepage.html
Contact: Sue Slade (Faculty co-
ordinator)
Contact: Andy Callen (Information
Officer, Music & Media Productions)
Resources: A, B, C, D, E, F*
* Scripts

Sheffield

**Sheffield Hallam University
Library**
Psalter Lane Site, Sheffield
South Yorkshire S11 8UZ
Tel: 0114 590 4444
Fax: 0114 225 2717
Website: www.shu.ac.uk/services/ic/
Contact: Librarian, School of
Cultural Studies
Resources: A, B, C, D, E

**Sheffield Libraries &
Information Services**
Arts and Social Sciences Section
Central Library
Surrey Street
Tel: 0114 273 4747/8
Fax: 0114 273 5009
Contact: Librarian

Sheffield University Library
Main Library
University of Sheffield
Western Bank,
Sheffield
South Yorkshire S10 2TN
Tel: 0114 222 7200/1
Fax: 0114 273 9826
Contact: Head of Reader Services

Solihul

Solihull College
Chelmsley Campus, Partridge
Close, Chelmsley Wood
Solihull B37 6UG
Tel: 0121 770 5651
Contact: Librarian

Southampton

**Periodical Office, Hartley
Library**
University of Southampton
University Road, Highfield
Southampton
Hants SO17 1BJ
Tel: 023 80 593521
Fax: 023 80 593007
Contact: Assistant Librarian, Arts
Resources: B, D, E, F*
* Personal papers, pressbooks

**Southampton Institute,
Mountbatten Library**
East Park Terrace, Southampton
Hampshire SO17 1BJ
Tel: 023 80 319000
Fax: 023 80 3576161
Website: www.solent.ac.uk/library/
Contact: Information Librarian
(Communications)
Resources: D*, E*
* For existing Institute staff and students

**University of Southampton
New College**
The Avenue
Southampton SO17 1BG
Tel: 023 80 216220
Fax: 023 80 230944
Contact: Librarian

Stirling

**University of Stirling
Library**
Stirling FK9 4LA
Tel: 01786 467 235
Fax: 01786 51335
Contact: Librarian

Stoke on Trent

**Staffordshire University
Library and Information
Service**

College Road, Stoke-On-Trent
Staffordshire ST4 2DE
Tel: 01782 294770/294809
Fax: 01782 744035
Contact: Art & Design Librarian

Sunderland

City Library and Art Centre
Fawcett Street
Sunderland SR1 1RE
Tel: 0191-514 1235
Fax: 0191-514 8444
Contact: Librarian

Sunderland University Library
Langham Tower
Ryhope Road
Sunderland SR2 7EE
Tel: 0191 515 2900
Fax: 0191 515 2423
Contact: Librarian

Sutton

Sutton Central Library
Music and Arts Department
St Nicholas Way
Sutton
Surrey SM1 1EA
Tel: 020 8770 4764/5
Fax: 020 8770 4777
Contact: Arts Librarian

Swansea

Swansea Institute of Higher Education Library
Townhill Road
Swansea, SA2 0UT
Tel: 01792 481000
Fax: 01792 298017
Contact: Librarian
Resources: B, C, E

Teddington

Cinema Theatre Association
44 Harrowdene Gardens
Teddington, Middlesex TW11 0DJ
Tel: 020 8977 2608
Contact: Secretary

Uxbridge

Brunel University Library
Uxbridge
Middlesex UB8 3PH
Tel: 01895 274000
Fax: 01895 232806
Contact: Librarian

Warrington

Warrington Collegiate Institute
University College Library

Padgate Campus
Crab Lane
Warrington WA2 0DB
Tel: 01925 494284
Website: www.narr.ac.uk
Contact: College Librarian

Wellingborough

Tresham Institute of Further and Higher Education Library
Church Street
Wellingborough
Northamptonshire NN8 4PD
Tel: 01933 224165
Fax: 01933 441832
Contact: Librarian

King Alfred's College Library
Sparkford Road, Winchester
Hampshire SO22 4NR
Tel: 01962 827306
Fax: 01962 827443
Website: www.kc.wkac.ac.uk
Contact: Librarian

Winchester School of Art
Park Avenue, Winchester
Hampshire SO23 8DL
Tel: 01962 842500
Fax: 01962 842496
Website: www.soton.ac.uk/
Contact: Head of Learning Resources
Resources: B, E

Wolverhampton

Light House
Media Reference Library
The Chubb Buildings
Fryer Street
Wolverhampton WV1 1HT
Tel: 01902 716055
Fax: 01902 717143
email: lighthse@waverider.co.uk
Contact Library: Librarian
Exhibitions/Cultural Events: Evelyn Wilson
Chief Executive: Frank Challenger
Resources: A, B, E, F*
* Scripts, pressbooks

Wolverhampton Libraries and Information Services
Central Library
Snow Hill
Wolverhampton WV1 3AX
Tel: 01902 312 025
Fax: 01902 714 579
Contact: Librarian
Resources: B, D

Wolverhampton University
Dudley Learning Centre
University of Wolverhampton
Castle View

Dudley
West Midlands DY1 3BQ
Tel: 01902 323 560
Fax: 01902 323 354
Website: www.wlv.ac.uk.llb
Learning Centre Manager
Resources: A, B, C, D, E

Wolverhampton University
Art and Law Library
54 Stafford Street
Wolverhampton WV1 3AX
Tel: 01902 321597
Fax: 01902 322668
Contact: Art and Design Librarian

York

University College of Ripon and York St John Library
Lord Mayors Walk
York YO3 7EX
Tel: 01904 616700
Fax: 01904 612512
Website:
www.ucrysj.ac.uk/services/library/index.htm
Contact: Librarian
Resources: B, C, D, E, F*
* Ripon campus of college houses – Yorkshire Film Archive

ORGANISATIONS

Listed below are the main trade/government organisations and bodies relevant to the film and television industries in the UK. This is followed by a separate list of Regional Film Commissions. Finally, a small selection of organisations from the US concludes this section

ABC (Association of Business Communicators)
1 West Ruislip Station
Ruislip
Middx HA4 7DW
Tel: 01895 622 401
Fax: 01895 631 219
Roger Saunders
Trade association of professionals providing the highest standards of audiovisual/video equipment/services for use in corporate communication

ACCS (Association for Cultural and Communication Studies)
Dept of Literature & Languages
Nottingham Trent University
Clifton Site
Nottingham NG11 8NS
Tel: 0115 941 8418 x3289
Fax: 0115 948 6632
Georgia Stone
Provides a professional forum for teachers and researchers in Media, Film, Television and Cultural Studies in both further and higher education. Its Executive Committee is drawn from the college and university sectors. Organises an Annual Conference, seeks to facilitate the exchange of information among members and liaises with various national bodies including 'sister' organisations: AME, NAHEFV and BUFVC

Advertising Association
Abford House
15 Wilton Road
London SW1V 1NJ
Tel: 020 7828 2771/828 4831
Fax: 020 7931 0376
email: aa@adassoc.org.uk
Website: www.adassoc.org.uk
Andrew Brown
A federation of 27 trade associations and professional bodies representing advertisers, agencies, the advertising media and support services. It is the central organisation for the UK advertising business, on British and European legislative proposals and other issues of common concern, both at national and international levels, and as such campaigns actively to maintain the freedom to advertise and to improve public attitudes to advertising. It publishes UK and European statistics on advertising expenditure, instigates research on advertising issues and organises seminars and courses for people in the communications business. Its Information Centre is one of the country's leading sources for advertising and associated subjects

Advertising Film and Videotape Producers' Association (AFVPA)
26 Noel Street
London W1V 3RD
Tel: 020 7434 2651
Fax: 020 7434 9002
email: afvpa@easynet.co.uk
Website: www.afvpa@easynet.co.uk
Cecilia Garnett
Represents most producers of TV commercials. It negotiates with recognised trade unions, with the advertisers and agencies and also supplies a range of member services

Advertising Standards Authority (ASA)
Brook House
2 Torrington Place
London WC1E 7HW
Tel: 020 7580 5555
Fax: 020 7631 3051
Website: www.asa.org.uk

AFMA Europe
49 Littleton Road
Harrow
Middx HA1 3SY
Tel: 020 8423 0763
Fax: Tel: 020 8423 7963
Chairman: Lawrence Safir
Hold rights to numerous Australian, US and UK pictures, including Sam Spiegel's Betrayal

AIM (All Industry Marketing for Cinema)
22 Golden Square
London W1R 3PA
Tel: 020 7437 4383
Fax: 020 7734 0912
John Mahony
Unites distribution, exhibition and cinema advertising in promoting cinema and cinema-going. Funds film education, holds Cinema Days for regional journalists, markets cinema for sponsorship and promotional ventures and is a forum for cinema marketing ideas

Amalgamated Engineering and Electrical Union (AEEU)
Hayes Court,
West Common Road,
Bromley,
Kent BR2 7AU
Tel: 020 8462 7755
Fax: 020 8462 4959
Website: www.aeeu.org.uk
Trade union representing – among others -people employed in film and TV lighting/electrical/electronic work

AMPS (Association of Motion Picture Sound)
28 Knox Street
London W1H 1FS
Tel: 020 7402 5429
Fax: 020 7402 5429
Brian Hickin
Promotes and encourages science, technology and creative application of all aspects of motion picture sound recording and reproduction, and seeks to promote and enhance the status of those therein engaged

APRS – The Professional Recording Association
2 Windsor Square
Silver Street
Reading RG1 2TH
Tel: 01803 868600
Fax: 01803 868444
Mark Broad – Chief Executive
Represents the interests of the professional sound recording industry, including radio, TV and audio studios and companies providing equipment and services in the field. The Recording Technology exhibition is running at the Business Design Centre in June

Arts Council of England
Visual Arts Department
14 Great Peter Street

London SW1P 3NQ
Tel: 020 7973 6443
Fax: 020 7973 6410
Website: www.artscouncil.org.uk
David Curtis, Gary Thomas
The Visual Arts Department works
with national agencies for artists' film
and video and supports the production
of film and video work by artists, and
related activities, including festivals
and publications, through the Artists'
Film and Video National Funds:
Production, Exhibition

Arts Council of Wales
9 Museum Place
Cardiff CF1 3NX
Tel: 029 20376500
Fax: 029 20395284
Website: www.ccc.acw.org.uk
Chief Executive: Emyr Jenkins

ASIFA
International Animated Film
Association
94 Norton Gardens
London SW16 4TA
Tel: 020 8681 8988
Fax: 020 8688 1441
Pat Raine Webb
A worldwide association of individuals
who work in, or make a contribution
to, the animation industry, including
students. Activities include
involvement in UK and international
events and festivals, an Employment
Databank, Animation Archive,
children's workshops. The UK group
provides an information service to
members and a news magazine

Audio Visual Association
Herkomer House
156 High Street
Bushey
Herts WD2 3DD
Tel: 020 8950 5959
Fax: 020 8950 7560
email: multimedia@visual-
arena.co.uk
Website: www.visual-arena.co.uk
Mike Simpson FBIPP
The Audio Visual Association is a
Special Interest Group within the
British Institute of Professional
Photography. With the Institute's
current thinking of lateral
representation within all categories of
imaging and imaging technology, the
AVA represents those individuals
involved in the various disciplines of
audiovisual

Authors' Licensing &
Collecting Society
Marlborough Court
14-18 Holborn
London EC1 N 2LE
Tel: 020 7395 0600

Fax: 020 7395 0660
email: alcs@alcs.co.uk
Website: www.alcs.co.uk
The ALCS is the British collecting
society for all writers. Its principal
purpose is to ensure that hard-to-
collect revenues due to authors are
efficently collected and speedily
distributed. These include the
simultaneous cable retransmission of
the UK's terrestrial and various
international channels, educational
off-air recording, BBC World Service
and BBC Prime television. Contact
the ALCS office for more
information

BAFTA (British Academy of
Film and Television Arts)
195 Piccadilly
London W1V OLN
Tel: 020 7734 0022
Fax: 020 7734 1792
Website: www.bafta.org/
Ron Allison
BAFTA was formed in 1946 by
Britain's most eminent filmmakers as
a non-profit making company. It aims
to advance the art and technique of
film and television and encourage
experiment and research.
Membership is available to those
who have worked, or have been
working actively within the film
and/or television industries for not
less than three years. BAFTA has
facilities for screenings, conferences,
seminoars and discussion meetings
and makes representations to
parliamentary committees when
appropriate. Its Awards for Film and
Television are annual televised
events. There are also Awards for
Children's films and programmes and
for Interactive Entertainment. The
Academy has branches in Liverpool,
Manchester, Glasgow, Cardiff, Los
Angeles and New York. See also
under Awards and Preview Theatres

BARB (Broadcasters'
Audience Research Board)
5th Floor, North Wing
Glenthorne House
Hammersmith Grove
London W6 0ND
Tel: 020 8741 9110
Fax: 020 8741 1943
Succeeding the Joint Industries'
Committee on Television Audience
Research (JICTAR), BARB
commissions audience research on
behalf of the BBC and ITV

BECTU (Broadcasting
Entertainment Cinematograph
and Theatre Union)
111 Wardour Street

London W1V 4AY
Tel: 020 7437 8506
Fax: 020 7437 8268
Website: www.bectu.org.uk
General Secretary: Roger Bolton
Press Officer: Janice Turner
BECTU is the UK trade union for
workers in film, broadcasting and the
arts. Formed in 1991 by the merger
of the ACTT and BETA, the union is
30,000 strong and repre-sents
permanently employed and freelance
staff in television, radio, film,
cinema, theatre and entertainment.
BECTU provides a comprehensive
industrial relations service based on
agreements with the BBC, ITV
companies, Channel 4, PACT,
AFVPA and MFVPA, Odeon, MGM,
Apollo, Society of Film Distributors,
National Screen Services,
independent exhibitors and the BFI
itself. Outside film and television, the
union has agreements with the
national producing theatres and with
the Theatrical Management
Association, the Society of London
Theatres and others

BECTU History Project
111 Wardour Street
London W1V 4AY
Fax: 0207 437 8506
email: histproj@bectu.org.uk
The Project seeks to record and
preserve the history of film and
television in the UK, and the
influence of personnel from the UK
working abroad, by interviewing
those who have been involved

BKSTS – The Moving Image
Society
63-71 Victoria House
Vernon Place
London WC1B 4DF
Tel: 020 7242 8400
Fax: 020 7405 3560
email:movimage@bksts.
demon.co.uk
Website: www.bksts.com
Executive Director: Anne Fenton
Formed in 1931, the BKSTS is the
technical society for film, television
and associated industries. A wide
range of training courses and
seminars are organised with special
rates for members. The society
produces many publications
including a monthly journal Image
Technology and a quarterly Cinema
Technology both free to members.
Corporate members must have
sufficient qualifications and
experience, however student and
associate grades are also available.
Biennial conference has become a
platform for new products and

developments from all over the world. The BKSTs also has a college accreditation scheme and currently accredits 9 courses within the HE + FE sector

BREMA (British Radio & Electronic Equipment Manufacturers' Association)
Landseer House
19 Charing Cross Road
London WC2H 0ES
Tel: 020 7930 3206
Fax: 020 7839 4613
Trade association for British consumer electronics industry

British Academy of Songwriters, Composers and Songwriters
The Penthouse
4 Brook Street
Mayfair
London W1Y 1AA
Tel: 020 7629 0992
Fax: 020 7629 0993
email: info@britishacademy.com
Website: www.britishacademy.com
Rosemary Dixson
(Formerly the Association of Professional Composers (APC), the Composers' Guild of Great Britain, and the British Academy of Songwriters, Composers and Authors (BASCA)). The Academy represents the interests of composers and songwriters across all genres, providing advice on professional and artistic matters. The Academy publishes a quarterly magazine and administers a number of major awards and events including the Ivor Novello Awards

British Actors Equity Association
Guild House
Upper St Martin's Lane
London WC2H 9EG
Tel: 020 7379 6000
Fax: 020 7379 7001
email: info@equity.org.uk
Website: www.equity.org.uk
General Secretary: Ian McGarry
Equity was formed in 1930 by professional performers to achieve solutions to problems of casual employment and short-term engagements. Equity has 40,000 members, and represents performers (other than musicians), stage managers, stage directors, stage designers and choreographers in all spheres of work in the entertainment industry. It negotiates agreements on behalf of its members with producers' associations and other employers. In some fields of work

only artists with previous professional experience are normally eligible for work. Membership of Equity is treated as evidence of professional experience under these agreements. It publishes Equity Journal four times a year

British Amateur Television Club (BATC)
Grenehurst
Pinewood Road
High Wycombe
Bucks HP12 4DD
Tel: 01494 528899
email: memsec@batc.org.uk
Website: www.batc.org.uk
Non-profit making organisation run entirely by volunteers. BATC publish a quarterly technical publication CQ-TV which is available via subscription

British Board of Film Classification (BBFC)
3 Soho Square
London W1V 6HD
Tel: 020 7439 7961
Fax: 020 7287 0141
Website: www.bbfc.co.uk
The 1909 Cinematograph Films Act required public cinemas to be licensed by their local authority. Originally this was a safety precaution against fire risk but was soon interpreted by the local authorities as a way of censoring cinema owners' choice of films. In 1912, the British Board of Film Classification was established by the film industry to seek to impose a conformity of view-point: films cannot be shown in public in Britain unless they have the BBFC's certificate or the relevant local authorisation. The Board finances itself by charging a fee for the films it views. When viewing a film, the Board attempts to judge whether a film is liable to break the law, for example by depraving and corrupting a significant proportion of its likely audience. It then assesses whether there is material greatly and gratuitously offensive to a large number of people. The Board seeks to reflect contemporary public attitudes. There are no written rules but films are considered in the light of the above criteria, previous decisions and the examiners' personal judgement. It is the policy of the Board not to censor anything on political grounds. Five film categories came into effect in 1982, with the introduction of a '12' category in August 1989:
In questions of classification, the

Board is primarily concerned with the protection of children, and the category system was changed in 1982 so as to provide clear and concise information to parents and the public generally. Only if a film fails to fall naturally into one of the following categories will cuts be considered.
  U – UNIVERSAL. Suitable for all.
PG – PARENTAL GUIDANCE. Some scenes may be unsuitable for young children.
12 – Suitable only for persons of twelve years and over (introduced on video 1st July 1994)
15 – Suitable only for persons of fifteen years and over
18 – Suitable only for persons of eighteen years and over.
R18 – FOR RESTRICTED DISTRIBUTION ONLY, through specially licensed cinemas or sex shops to which no one under eighteen is admitted. The '12', '15' and '18' categories are subject to age bars at the cinema box office and at the counters of video shops. The video industry has asked for an additional category, to be used for works to be stocked on the children's shelves of video shops:
Uc – UNIVERSAL. Particularly suitable for young children.
The final decision, however, still lies with the local authority. In 1986 the GLC ceased to be the licensing authority for London cinemas, and these powers devolved to the Borough Councils. Sometimes films are passed by the BBFC and then banned by local authorities (*Straw Dogs, Caligula, Crash*). Others may have their categories altered (*Monty Python's Life of Brian, Mrs Doubtfire*). Current newsreels are exempt from censorship

British Broadcasting Corporation (BBC)
Television Centre
Wood Lane
London W12 7RJ
Tel: 020 8743 8000
Website: www.bbc.co.uk
The BBC provides two national television networks, five national radio networks, as well as local radio and regional radio and television services. They are funded through the Licence Fee. The BBC is a public corporation, set up in 1927 by Royal Charter. Government proposals for the future of the BBC were published in a White Paper in July 1994. The BBC also broadcasts overseas through World Service Radio and Worldwide Television, but these are not funded through the Licence Fee

British Copyright Council

29-33 Berners Street
London W1P 4AA
Tel: 01986 788 122
Provides liaison between societies
which represent the interest of those
who own copyright in literature,
music, drama and works of art,
making representation to Government
on behalf of its member societies

The British Council

Films and Television Department
11 Portland Place
London W1N 4EJ
Tel: 020 7389 3065
Fax: 020 7389 3041
Website: www.britcoun.org/
The British Council is Britain's
international network for education,
culture and technology. It is an
independent, non-political
organisation with offices in over 100
countries. Films and Television
Department acts as a clearing house
for international festival·screenings
of British short films and videos,
including animation and experimental
work. Using its extensive 16mm
library, and 35mm prints borrowed
from industry sources, it also ensures
British participation in a range of
international feature film events. The
department arranges seminars
overseas on themes such as
broadcasting freedom and the future
of public service television. It
publishes the International Directory
of Film and Video Festivals
(biennial) and the annual British
Films Catalogue. a 15-seat Preview
Theatre (16mm, 35mm, video) is
available for daytime use by UK
filmmakers

British Design & Art Direction

9 Graphite Square
Vauxhall Walk
London SE11 5EE
Tel: 020 7840 1111
Fax: 020 7840 0840
Marketing Manager: Marcelle
Johnson
A professional association, registered
as a charity, which publishes an
annual of the best of British and
international design, advertising,
television commercials and videos,
and organises travelling exhibitions.
Professional awards, student awards,
education programme, lectures.
Membership details are available on
request

British Federation of Film Societies (BFFS)

BFFS

PO BOX 1DR
London W1A IDR
Tel: 020 7734 9300
Fax: 020 7734 9093
The BFFS exists to promote the work
of some 300 film societies in the UK

British Film Commission

70 Baker Street
London W1M 1DJ
Tel: 020 7224 5000
Fax: 020 7224 1013
email: info@britfilmcom.co.uk
Website: www.britfilmcom.co.uk
The British Film Commission is
funded by central Government to
promote the UK as an international
production centre and to encourage
the use of British locations, services,
facilities and personnel. It provides
information services at no charge to
enquirers and on all matters relevant
to overseas producers contemplating
production in the UK. For more
details on area and city film
commissions in the UK, see end of
section

British Film Designers Guild

24 St Anslem's Place
London W1Y 1FG
Tel: 020 7499 4336
Fax: 020 7499 4336
Promotes and encourages activities of
all members of the art department.
Full availability and information
service open to all producers

(bfi) British Film Institute

21 Stephen Street
London W1P 2LN
Tel: 020 7255 1444
Fax: 020 7436 7950
Website: www.bfi.org.uk
Founded in 1933, the BFI was
incorporated by Royal Charter in
1983; it is the UK national agency
with responsibility for encouraging
the arts of film and television and
conserving them in the national
interest. Approximately half the
BFI's funding comes from the
Department for Culture, Media and
Sport. The rest is raised from the
subscriptions of its members,
provision of services, sponsorship
and donations

British Institute of Professional Photography

Fox Talbot House
Amwell End, Ware
Herts SG12 9HN
Tel: 01920 464011
Fax: 01920 487056
Website: www.bipp.com
Company Secretary: Alex Mair
The qualifying body for professional
photography and photographic

processing. Members represent
specialisations in the fields of
photography, both stills and moving
images

British Interactive Multimedia Association Ltd

5/6 Clipstone Street
London W1P 7EB
Tel: 020 7436 8250
Fax: 020 7436 8251
email: enquiries@bima.co.uk
Website: www.bima.co.uk
Norma Hughes, General Secretary

British Phonographic Industry Ltd (BPI)

25 Savile Row
London W1X 1AA
Tel: 020 7287 4422
Fax: 020 7287 2252
email: general@bpi.co.uk
Website: www.bpi.co.uk
John Deacon, Director General
BPI is the industry association for
record companies in the UK. It
provides professional negotiating
skills, legal advice, information and
other services for its 200 members. It
protects rights, fights piracy and
promotes export opportunities.
Organises the BRIT Awards.
Information service available

British Screen Advisory Council (BSAC)

19 Cavendish Square
London W1M 9AB
Tel: 020 7499 4177
Fax: 020 7306 0329
email:bsac@bsacouncil.co.uk
Director: Fiona Clarke-Hackston,
Chairman: David Elstein
Events & Communications Officer:
Anna Pottle
BSAC is an independent, advisory
body to government and policy makers
at national and European level. It is a
source of information and research for
the screen media industries. BSAC
provides a unique forum for the audio
visual industry to discuss major issues
which effect the industry. Its
membership embraces senior
management from all aspects of
television, film, and video. BSAC
regularly commissions and oversees
research on the audio visual industry
and uses this research to underpin its
policy documents. In addition to regular
monthly meetings, BSAC organises
conferences, seminars, industry
briefings and an annual reception in
Brussels. BSAC is industry funded

British Screen Development (BSD)

14-17 Wells Mews

London W1P 3FL
Tel: 020 7323 9080
Fax: 020 7323 0092
Head of Development: Emma
Berkofsky
BSD makes loans for the
development of British and European
cinema feature films. Films such as
Photographing Fairies; Wilde; Before
the Rain; Antonia's Line; Land and
Freedom; Rob Roy; House of
America; The Tango Lesson; Jilting
Joe. It has a two-tier loan system:
screenplay loans for new writers;
development loans for production
companies to pay writers, and
ancillary costs. BSD also part-
finances, administers and oversees
the production of a variety of short
films around the country. In 1999
some 15 short films will be
commissioned with budgets of
around £25,000. In Europe, BSD
supports and sponsors candidates
through the SOURCES, ACE and
ARISTA programmes

British Screen Finance
14-17 Wells Mews
London W1P 3FL
Tel: 020 7323 9080
Fax: 020 7323 0092
email: BS@cd-online.co.uk
Since January 1986, British Screen, a
private company aided by
Government grant, has taken over the
role and the business of the National
Film Finance Corporation which was
dissolved following the Films Act
1985. British Screen exists primarily
to support new talent in
commercially viable productions for
the cinema which might find
difficulty in attracting mainstream
commercial funding. Between 1986
and 1998 it invested in more than
140 productions, and hopes to
support a further 12-15 in 1999.
Recent successful films include *The
Crying Game, Orlando, Naked, Land
and Freedom , Sliding Doors* and
Hiliary and Jackie. Through British
Screen Development it also runs
programmes of short films made in
Northern Ireland and English regions

British Society of Cinematographers (BSC)
11 Croft Road
Chalfont St Peter
Gerrards Cross
Bucks SL9 9AE
Tel: 01753 888052
Fax: 01753 891486
email: BritCinematographers
@compuserve.com
Frances Russell
Promotes and encourages the pursuit

of the highest standards in the craft
of motion picture photography.
Publishes a Newsletter and the BSC
Directory

British Tape Industry Association
Ambassador House
Brigstock Road
Thornton Heath CR7 7JG
Tel: 020 8665 5395
Fax: 020 8665 6447
email: bbia@admin.co.uk
Trade association for the
manufacturers of blank audio and
videotape

Broadcasting Press Guild
Tiverton
The Ridge
Woking
Surrey GU22 7EQ
Tel: 01483 764895
Fax: 01483 765882
Secretary: Richard Last
An association of journalists who
specialise in writing about the media
in the national, regional and trade
press. Membership by invitation.
Monthly lunches with leading
industry figures as guests. Annual
Television and Radio Awards voted
for by members

Broadcasting Research Unit
VLV Librarian
101 King's Drive
Gravesend
Kent DA12 5BQ
Tel: 01474 352835
Fax: 01474 351112
The Broadcasting Research Unit was
an independent Trust researching all
aspects of broadcasting, development
and technologies, which operated
from 1980-1991. Its publications and
research are now available from the
above address

Broadcasting Standards Commission
7 The Sanctuary
London SW1P 3JS
Tel: 020 7233 0544
Fax: 020 7233 0397
Deputy Chairs: Jane Leighton and
Lord Warner
Director: Stephen Whittle
The Broadcasting Standards
Commission is the statutory body for
both standards and fairness in
broadcasting. It is the only
organisation within the regulatory
framework of UK broadcasting to
cover all television and radio. This
includes BBC and commercial
broadcasters as well as text, cable,
satellite and digital services. As an

independent organisation
representing the interests of the
consumer, the Broadcasting
Standards Commission considers the
portrayal of violence, sexual conduct
and matters of taste and decency. As
an alternative to a court of law, it
provides redress for people who
believe they have been unfairly
treated or subjected to unwarranted
infringement of privacy. The
Commission has three main tasks
which are set out in the 1996
Broadcasting Act: – produces codes
of practice relating to standards and
fairness; considers and adjudicates on
complaints; monitors, researches and
reports on standards and fairness in
broadcasting. The Commission does
not have the power to preview or to
censor broadcasting

BUFVC (British Universities Film and Video Council)
77 Wells Street
London W1P 3RE
Tel: 020 7393 1500
Fax: 020 7393 1555
email: bufvc@open.ac.uk
Website: www.bufvc.ac.uk
Murray Weston
An organisation, funded via the Open
University, with members in many
institutions of higher education. It
provides a number of services to
support the production and use of
film, television and other audiovisual
materials for teaching and research. It
operates a comprehensive
Information Service, produces a
regular magazine Viewfinder,
catalogues and other publications
such as the Researchers' Guide to
British Film and Television
Collections and the BUFVC
Handbook for Film and Television in
Education, organises conferences and
seminars and distributes specialised
film and video material. It runs a
preview and editing facility for film
(16mm) and video (Betacam and
other formats). Researchers in history
and film and programme researchers
come to the Council's offices to use
the Slade Film History Register, with
its information on British newsreels.
BUFVC's off-air recording back-up
service records the fiveUK terrestrial
channels between 10.00am and
2.10am each day. The recordings are
held indefinitely allowing educational
establishments to request copies if
they have failed to record the
material locally under ERA licence

BVA (British Video Association)
167 Great Portland Street

London W1 5FD
Tel: 020 7436 0041
Fax: 020 7436 0043
Website: www.bva.org.uk/
Represents, promotes and protects the collective rights of its members who produce and/or distribute video cassettes for rental and sale to the public

Cable Communications Association
5th Floor
Artillery House
Artillery Row
London SW1P 1RT
Tel: 020 7222 2900
Fax: 020 7799 1471
Chief Executive: Bob Frost
Represents the interests of cable operators, installers, programme providers and equipment suppliers. For further information on cable, see under Cable and Satellite

Campaign for Press and Broadcasting Freedom
8 Cynthia Street
London N1 9JF
Tel: 020 7278 4430
Fax: 020 7837 8868
email: cpbf@arcitechs.com
Website: www.architechs.com/cpbf
A broad-based membership organisation campaigning for more diverse, accessible and accountable media in Britain, backed by the trade union movement. The CPBF was established in 1979. The mail order catalogue is regularly updated and includes books on all aspects of the media from broadcasting policy to sexism; its bi-monthly journal Free Press examines current ethical, industrial and political developments in media policy and practice. CPBF acts as a parliamentary lobby group on censorship and media reform.

Celtic Film and Television Festival Company
1 Bowmont Gardens
Glasgow G12 9LR
Tel: 0141 342 4947
Fax: 0141 342 4948
email: mail@celticfilm.co.uk
Frances Hendron
Organises an annual competitive festival/conference, itinerant Scotland, Ireland, Cornwall, Wales and Brittany in March/April. Supports the development of television and film in Celtic nations and indigenous languages

Central Office of Information (COI)
Films and Video

Hercules Road
London SE1 7DU
Tel: 020 7261 8495
Fax: 020 7261 8877
Ian Hamilton
COI Films and Video is responsible for government filmmaking on informational themes. The COI organises the production of a wide range of TV commercials and trailers, documentary films, video programmes and CD ROMs. It uses staff producers, and draws on the film and video industry for production facilities

CFL Vision
PO Box 35
Wetherby
Yorks LS23 7EX
Tel: 01937 541010
Fax: 01937 541083
email: euroview@compuserve.com
Website: www.euroview.co.uk
CFL Vision is one of the oldest established video library operations in the UK. It is part of the Central Office of Information and distributes their video and CD ROM productios, as well as programmes acquired from both public and private sectors. Over 200 titles are available for loan or purchase by small businesses, industry, local authorities and schools

Chart Information Network
No8, Montague Close
London Bridge
London SE1 9UR
Tel: 020 7334 7333
Fax: 020 7921 5942
Supplies BVA members with detailed sales information on the sell-through video market. Markets and licenses the Official Retail Video Charts for broadcasting and publishing around the world

Children's Film and Television Foundation (CFTF)
Elstree Film Studios
Borehamwood
Herts WD6 1JG
Tel: 020 8953 0844
Fax: 020 8207 0860
In 1944 Lord Rank founded the Children's Entertainment Film Division to make films specifically for children. In 1951 this resulted in the setting up of the Children's Film Foundation (now CFTF), a non-profit making organisation which, up to 1981, was funded by an annual grant from the BFFA (Eady money). The CFTF no longer makes films from its own resources but, for suitable children's/family cinema/television

projects, is prepared to consider financing script development for eventual production by commercial companies. Films from the Foundation's library are available for hiring at nominal charge in 35mm, 16mm and video format

Church of England Communications Unit
Church House
Great Smith Street
London SW1P 3NZ
Tel: 020 7222 9011 x356/7
Fax: 020 7222 6672
Rev Jonathan Jennings
(Out of office hours: 020 7222 9233)
Responsible for liaison between the Church of England and the broadcasting and film industries. Advises the C of E on all matters relating to broadcasting

Cinema Advertising Association (CAA)
12 Golden Square
London W13 3AF
Tel: 020 7534 6363
Fax: 020 7534 6464
Website: www.adassoc.org.uk
Bruce Koster
The CAA is a trade association of cinema advertising contractors operating in the UK and Eire. First established as a separate organisation in 1953 as the Screen Advertising Association, its main purpose is to promote, monitor and maintain standards of cinema advertising exhibition including the pre-vetting of commercials. It also commissions and conducts research into cinema as an advertising medium, and is a prime sponsor of the CAVIAR annual surveys

Cinema & Television Benevolent Fund (CTBF)
22 Golden Square
London W1R 4AD
Tel: 020 7437 6567
Fax: 020 7437 7186
The CTBF is the trade fund operating in the UK for retired and serving employees (actors have their separate funds) who have worked for two or more years in any capacity, in the cinema, film or independent television industries'. The CTBF offers caring help, support and financial assistance, irrespective of age, and the Fund's home in Wokingham, Berkshire offers full residential and convalescent facilities

Cinema and Television Veterans
Elanda House

9 The Weald
Ashford
Kent TN24 8RA
Tel: 01233 639967
An association open to all persons
employed in the United Kingdom or
by United Kingdom companies in the
cinema and/or broadcast television
industries in any capacity other than
as an artiste, for a total of at least
thirty years

Cinema Exhibitors' Association (CEA)

22 Golden Square
London W1R 3PA
Tel: 020 7734 9551
Fax: 020 7734 6147
The first branch of the CEA in the
industry was formed in 1912 and
consisted of cinema owners.
Following a merger with the
Association of Independent Cinemas
(AIC) it became the only association
representing cinema exhibition. CEA
members account for the vast
majority of UK commercial cinemas,
including independents, Regional
Film Theatres and cinemas in local
authority ownership. The CEA
represents members' interests –
within the industry and to local,
national and European Government.
It is closely involved with legislation
(current and proposed) emanating
from the UK Government and the
European Commission which affects
exhibition

Cinema Theatre Association

44 Harrowdene Gardens
Teddington
Middx TW11 0DJ
Tel: 020 8977 2608
Adam Unger
The Cinema Theatre Association was
formed in 1967 to promote interest in
Britain's cinema building legacy, in
particular the magnificent movie
palaces of the 1920s and 1930s. It is
the only major organisation
committed to cinema preservation in
the UK. It campaigns for the
protection of architecturally
important cinemas and runs a
comprehensive archive. The CTA
publishes a bi-monthly bulletin and
the magazine *Picture House*

Cinergy

Minema Cinema
45 Knightsbridge
London SW1X 7NL
Tel: 020 7235 4226
Fax: 020 7235 3426
Creative Director: Nick Walker
Co-ordinatior: Damian Spandley
Multimeidator: Nick Perry

Cinergy is a multimedia cabaret club
with a special emphasis on short
films. It is open to the public and
welcomes submissions from
filmmakers on all formats and with
high, low or no budgets.

Comataidh Craolaidh Gaidhlig (Gaelic Broadcasting Committee)

4 Harbour View, Cromwell Street
Stornoway
Isle of Lewis HSI 2DF
Tel: 01851 705550
Fax: 01851 706432
The Gaelic Television Fund and
Comataidh Telebhisein Gaidhlig was
set up under the provisions of the
Broadcasting Act 1990. Funds made
available by the Government were to
be paid to the ITC for the credit of
the fund to be known as the Gaelic
Television Fund. The Fund was to be
managed by the body known as the
Gaelic Television Committee. Under
the Broadcasting Act 1996 the Gaelic
Television Fund was redesignated as
the Gaelic Broadcasting Fund and the
Gaelic Television Committee became
the Gaelic Broadcasting Committee

Commonwealth Broadcasting Association

17 Fleet Street
London ECHY 1AA
Tel: 020 7583 5550
Fax: 020 7583 5549
email: cba@cba.org.uk
Website: www.oneworld.org/cba
An association of 90 public service
broadcasting organisations in 54
Commonwealth countries

Critics' Circle

Critics' Circle
4 Alwyne Villas
London N1 2HQ
Tel: 020 7226 2726
Fax: 020 7354 2574
Chairman: Christopher Tookey
Vice-Chairman: John Marriott
Hon. Secretary: Tom Hutchinson
Hon. Treasurer: Peter Cargin
The film section of the Critics' Circle
brings together leading national
critics for meetings, functions and the
presentation of annual awards

Deaf Broadcasting Council

70 Blacketts Wood Drive
Chorleywood, Rickmansworth
Herts WD3 5QQ
Tel: 01923 283127
Fax: 01923 283127
email: dmyers@cix.co.uk
An umbrella consumer group
working as a link between hearing
impaired people and TV broadcasters

– aiming for increased high quality
access to television and video

Defence Press and Broadcasting Advisory Committee

Room 2235
Ministry of Defence
Main Building
Whitehall
London SW1A 2HB
Tel: 020 7218 2206
Fax: 020 7218 5857
Secretary: Rear Admiral David
Pulvertaft
The Committee is made up of senior
officials from the Ministry of
Defence, the Home Office and the
Foreign & Commonwealth Office
and representatives of the media. It
issues guidance, in the form of DA
Notices, on the publication of
information which it regards as
sensitive for reasons of national
security

Department for Culture, Media and Sport – Media Division (Films)

2-4 Cockspur Street
London SW1Y 5DH
Tel: 020 7211 6000
Fax: 020 7211 6249
Website: www.culture.gov.uk
Contacts:
For BFI, British Screen Finance
(BSF), European Co-production fund
(ECPF): Aidan McDowell
Tel: 020 7211 6429
For Enquiries concerning film which
might be made under UK Co-
production Agreements: Diana Brown
Tel: 020 7211 6433
For MEDIA Programme, British Film
Commission (BFC), National Film
and Television School (NFTS) and
Audiovisual Eureka (AVE): Peter
Wright
Tel: 020 7211 6435
The Department for Culture Media
and Sport is responsible for
Government policy on film, relations
with the film industry and
Government funding for: the British
Film Institute, British Screen
Finance, the European Co-Production
Fund (administered by British Screen
Finance), the British Film
Commission and the National Film
and Television School. It is also
responsible for Government policy
on and contribution to, the EC Media
Programme and Audiovisual Eureka.
It also acts as the UK competent
authority for administering the UK's
seven bilateral co-production
agreements and the European Co-
production Convention

Department for Education and Employment (DFEE)
Sanctuary Buildings
Great Smith Street
London SW1P 3BT
Tel: 020 7925 5000
Fax: 020 7925 6000
email: info@dfee.gov.uk
Website: www.dfee.gov.uk
Public enquiries: 020 7925 5555
The DFE is responsible for policies for education in England and the Government's relations with universities in England, Scotland and Wales

Directors' and Producers' Rights Society, The
15-19 Great Titchfield Street
London W1P 7FB
Tel: 020 7631 1077
Fax: 020 7631 1019
email: dprs@dial.pipex.com
Suzan Dormer
The Directors' and Producers' Rights Society is a collecting society which administers authorials rights payments on behalf of British film and television Directors

Directors' Guild of Great Britain
15-19 Great Titchfield Street
London W1P 7FB
Tel: 020 7436 8626
Fax: 020 7436 8646
email: guild@dggb.co.uk
Website: www.dggb.co.uk
Sarah Wain
Represents interests and concerns of directors in all media. Publishes regular magazine *DIRECT*

Educational Policy Services, BBC
BBC White City
201 Wood Lane
London W12 7TS
Tel: 020 8752 4204
Fax: 020 8752 4441
email: Lucia.jones@bbc.co.uk
EPS supports the work of BBC Education radio and television production departments. It services the Educational Broadcasting Council representing professional users

Educational Television & Media Association (ETMA)
37 Monkgate
York YO31 7A3
Tel: 01904 639212
Fax: 01904 639212
email: josie.key@etma.u-net.com
Website: www.etma.org.uk
A dynamic association comprising a wide variety of users of television and other electronic media in education. International competition for educational videos (including Broadcast, a student category and multi-media packages) – deadline November. Journal of Educational Media , Annual Conference and Exhibition in the Spring. Regional meetings/workshops/training programmes. Patrons: BBC Education, Canford Audio, Channel 4, JVC Professional, MarCom Systems, Panasonic Broadcast, Sony Broadcast, Strand Lighting. New members welcome – contact Administrator

Federation Against Copyright Theft (FACT)
7 Victory Business Centre
Worton Road
Isleworth
Middx TW7 6DB
Tel: 020 8568 6646
Fax: 020 8560 6364
R Dixon, Director General
DNL Lowe, Company Secretary
FACT, Federation Against Copyright Theft, is an investigative organisation funded by its members to combat counterfeiting, piracy and misuse of their products. The members of FACT are major companies in the British and American film, video and television industries. FACT is a non-profit making company limited by guarantee. FACT assists all statutory law enforcement authorities and will undertake private criminal prosecutions wherever possible

Federation of Entertainment Unions (FEU)
1 Highfield
Twyford
Nr Winchester
Hants SO21 1QR
Tel: 01962 713134
Fax: 01962 713288
email: harris@interalpha.co.uk
The FEU is a lobbying and campaigning group and meets regularly with statutory bodies and pressure groups ranging from the BBC and ITC and the British Film Commission through to the Parliamentary All Party Media Committee and the Voice of the Listener and Viewer. The Federation comprises British Actors' Equity Association, Broadcasting Entertainment Cinematograph and Theatre Union, Musicians' Union, National Union of Journalists, Writers' Guild of Great Britain and Amalgamated Engineering & Electrical Union (Electricians Section). It has three standing committees covering Film and Electronic Media, European Affairs and Training

The Feminist Library
5a Westminster Bridge Road
London SE1 7XW
Tel: 020 7928 7789
The Feminist Library provides information about women's studies, courses, and current events. It has a large collection of fiction and non-fiction books, pamphlets, papers etc. It holds a wide selection of journals and newsletters from all over the world and produces its own quarterly newsletter. Social events are held and discussion groups meet every other Tuesday. The library is run entirely by volunteers. Membership library. Open Tuesday (11.00am-8.00pm) Wednesday (3.00pm -5.00pm) and Saturday (2.00-5.00pm)

Film Artistes' Association (FAA)
111 Wardour Street
London W1V 4AY
Tel: 020 7437 8506
Fax: 020 7437 8268
Spencer MacDonald
The FAA represents extras, doubles, stand-ins. Under an agreement with PACT, it supplies all background artistes in the major film studios and within a 40 mile radius of Charing Cross on all locations

Film Complaints Panel
22 Golden Square
London W1R 3PA
Chief Administrator: Annette Bradford

Film Education
Alhambra House
27-31 Charing Cross Road
London WC2H 0AU
Tel: 020 7976 2291
Fax: 020 7839 5052
email: post@film-ed.u-net.com
Website: www.filmeducation.org
Ian Wall
Film Education is a registered charity supported by the UK film industry. For over a decade it has been at the forefront of the development of Film and Media Studies in schools and colleges and now has more than 20,000 named primary and secondary teacher contacts on its unique database.
The main aims of Film Education are to develop the use of film in the school curriculum and to facilitate the use of cinemas by schools. To this end it publishes a variety of free teaching materials, produces BBC Learning Zone programmes, organises Inset and runs a range of workshops and school screenings. All Film Education resources are

carefully researched and written by teachers for teachers

Film & Television Commission

North West England
Pioneer Buildings
65-67 Dale Street
Liverpool L2 2NS
Tel: 0151 330 6666
Fax: 0151 330 6611
FTC north west is the official film commission for the north west of England, working in partnership with the film offices of Liverpool, Manchester, Lancashire, Isle of Man and Cheshire

Film Unit Drivers Guild

22 Ferraro Close
Heston
Middlesex
Tel: 020 8569 5001
Fax: 020 8569 5002
B. Newell
FUDG represents its freelance members in the Film and Television industry when they are not on a production. It supplies them with work, such as pick ups and drops to any destination the client wishes to travel. Guild members are made up of professional film unit drivers and will look after all transportation needs

First Film Foundation

9 Bourlet Close
London W1P 7PJ
Tel: 020 7580 2111
Fax: 020 7580 2116
Provides training, guidance, and promotional schemes for new British and Irish producers, writers and directors in feature film production and development

FOCAL International Ltd (Federation of Commercial Audio-Visual Libraries)

Pentax House
South Hill Avenue
Northolt Road
South Harrow
Middx HA2 0DU
Tel: 020 8423 5853
Fax: 020 8933 4826
email: anne@focalltd.demon.co.uk
Website: www. focalltd.demon.co.uk
Administrator: Anne Johnson
An international, non-profit making professional trade association representing commercial film/audiovisual libraries and interested individuals. Among other activities, it organises regular meetings, maximises copyright information, and produces a directory of libraries and quarterly journal

German Federal Film Board and German Film Export Union

4 Lowndes Court
Carnaby Street
London W1V 1PP
Tel: 020 7437 2047
Fax: 020 7439 2947
Iris Kehr
UK representative of the German Federal Film Board (Filmförderungsanstalt), the government industry organisation, and the German Film Export Union (Export Union des Deutschen Films), the official trade association for the promotion of German films abroad. For full details see entries under Organisations (Europe)

Glasgow Film Fund

249 West George Street
Glasgow G2 4RB
Tel: 0141 302 1757
Fax: 0141 302 1714
Judy Anderson
The Glasgow Film Fund provides production funding for companies making feature films in the Glasgow area or produced by Glasgow-based production companies. Applications are accepted for films intended for theatrical release, with a budget of at £500,000. The maximum investment made by the Glasgow Film Fund in any one project will be £150,000, however, where there is an exceptionally high level of local economic benefit the GFF may consider raising its maximum investment to £250,000. Glasgow Film Fund application forms, meeting dates, submission deadlines and further details are available from the GFF office. Production credits include: *Shallow Grave*, *The Near Room*, *Small Faces*, *Carla's Song*, *The Slab Boys*, *Regeneration*, *The Life of Stuff*, *Orphans*, *My Name is Joe*, *The Acid House* and *The Debt Collector*

Grierson Memorial Trust

c/o Ivan Sopher & co
5 Elstree Gate
Elstree Way
Borehamwood
Herts WD6 1JD
Tel: 020 8207 0602
Fax: 020 8207 6758
email: accountants@ivansopher.co.uk
Website: www.editor.net/griersontrust
John Chittock, Chairman

Guild of British Animation

26 Noel Street
London W1V 3RD
Tel: 020 7434 2651

Fax: 020 7434 9002
Cecilia Garnett
Represents interests of producers of animated films. AFVPA acts as secretariat for this association

Guild of British Camera Technicians

5-11 Taunton Road
Metropolitan Centre
Greenford
Middx UB6 8UQ
Tel: 020 8578 9243
Fax: 020 8575 5972
Office manager: Maureen O'Grady
Magazine Editors, Eyepiece: Charles Hewitt and Kerry-Anne Burrows
The Guild exists to further the professional interests of technicians working with film or video motion picture cameras. Membership is restricted to those whose work brings them into direct contact with these cameras and who can demonstrate competence in their particular field of work. By setting certain minimum standards of skill for membership, the Guild seeks to encourage its members, especially newer entrants, to strive to improve their art.
Through its publication, Eyepiece: disseminates information about both creative and technical developments, past and present, in the film and television industry

Guild of British Film Editors

Travair, Spurlands End Road
Great Kingshill , High Wycombe
Bucks HP15 6HY
Tel: 0149 712313
Fax: 0149 712313
email: cox.gbfe@btinternet.com
To ensure that the true value of film and sound editing is recognised as an important part of the creative and artistic aspects of film production

Guild of Film Production Accountants and Financial Administrators

Pinewood Studios
Pinewood Road
Iver Heath
Bucks SL0 0NH
Tel: 01753 651767
Fax: 01753 652803
email: secretary@gfpa.org.uk
Website: www.gfpa.org.uk
John Sargent – Honorary Administrator
To update members with information on methods, practice and legislation affecting the film industry. To promote and maintain a high standard of film production accounting, cost and financial administration

Guild of Film Production Executives
Pinewood Studios
Iver Heath
Bucks SL0 0NH
Tel: 01753 656850
Fax: 01753 656850
email: sales@sargent-disc.com
Contact: Angela Pyle
The Guild has sought to achieve the highest standards of its membership and includes a broad spectrum of experienced Producers, Associate and Line Producers, Production Supervisors and Managers, 1st Assistant Directors and Location Managers, capable of handling feature and television productions of all sorts and sizes

Guild of Regional Film Writers
9 Heather Close
Southampton
Hants SO40 4LE
Chairman: Darren Vaughan
The Guild of Regional Film Writers was formed in 1987 and now has over 90 members on its list. The organisation exists to support, encourage and promote the work of regional film journalists, in an industry that is seen to centre its' attention around the nation's capital. Through a self-funding organisation, the Guild works closely with AIM, who provide support for Cinema Days. These four day events take place three times a year at regional cinemas where members take-in up to 15 movies, accompanied by relevant press conferences

Guild of Stunt and Action Co-ordinators
72 Pembroke Road
London W8 6NX
Tel: 020 7602 8319
Sally Fisher
To promote the highest standards of safety and professionalism in film and television stunt work

Guild of Television Cameramen
1 Churchill Road
Whitchurch, Tavistock
Devon PL19 9BU
Tel: 01822 614405
Fax: 01822 615785
Sheila Lewis
The Guild was formed in 1972 'to ensure and preserve the professional status of the television cameramen and to establish, uphold and advance the standards of qualification and competence of cameramen'. The Guild is not a union and seeks to avoid political involvement

Guild of Vision Mixers
147 Ship Lane
Farnborough
Hants GU14 8BJ
Tel: 01252 514953
Fax: 01252 656756
Peter Turl
The Guild aims to represent the interests of vision mixers throughout the UK and Ireland, and seeks to maintain the highest professional standards in vision-mixing

IAC (Institute of Amateur Cinematographers)
24c West Street
Epsom
Surrey KT18 7RJ
Tel: 01372 739672
Encouraging amateurs interested in the art of making moving pictures and supporting them with a variety of services

Imperial War Museum Film and Video Archive
Lambeth Road
London SE1 6HZ
Tel: 020 7416 5000
Fax: 020 7416 5379
See entry under Archives and Film Libraries

Incorporated Society of British Advertisers (ISBA)
44 Hertford Street
London W1Y 8AE
Tel: 020 7499 7502
Fax: 020 7629 5255
Website: www.isba.org.uk
Deborah Morris
The ISBA was founded in 1900 as an association for advertisers, both regional and national. Subscriptions are based on advertisers' expenditure and the main objective is the protection and advancement of the advertising interests of member firms. This involves organised representation, co-operation, action and exchange of information and experience, together with conferences, workshops and publications. ISBA offer a communications consultancy service for members on questions as varied as assessment of TV commercial production quotes to formulation of advertising agency agreements

Incorporated Society of Musicians (ISM)
10 Stratford Place
London W1N 9AE
Tel: 020 7629 4413
Fax: 020 7408 1538
email: membership@ism.org
Website: www.ism.org

Chief Executive: Neil Hoyle
Professional association for all musicians: teachers, performers and composers. The ISM produces various publications, including the monthly Music Journal, and gives advice to members on all professional issues

Independent Film Distributors' Association (IFDA)
10a Stephen Mews
London W1P 0AX
Tel: 020 7957 8957
Fax: 020 7957 8968
IFDA was formed in 1973, and its members are mainly specialised film distributors who deal in both 16mm and 35mm and every type of film from classic features to 'popular music.' Supply many users including universities, schools, hospitals, prisons, independent cinemas, hotels, film societies, ships etc

Independent Television Commission (ITC)
33 Foley Street
London W1P 7LB
Tel: 020 7255 3000
Fax: 020 7306 7800
email: Publicaffairs@itc.org.uk
The ITC is the public body responsible for licensing and regulating commercially funded television services. These include Channel 3 (ITV), Channel 4, Channel 5, public teletext and a range of cable, local delivery and satellite services and digital television services

Institute of Practitioners in Advertising (IPA)
44 Belgrave Square
London SW1X 8QS
Tel: 020 7235 7020
Fax: 020 7245 9904
The representative body for UK advertising agencies. Represents the collective views of its member agencies in negotiations with Government departments, the media and industry and consumer organisations

International Arts Bureau
4 Baden Place
Crosby Row
London SE1 1YW
Tel: 020 7403 7001
Fax: 020 7403 2009
Director: Rod Fisher
The International Arts Bureau specialises in providing information and advice on a range of international arts issues, including cultural policies, networks and funding programmes from around the world. They offer a free enquiry service for

clients of the Arts Council of England and Regional Arts Boards; monthly one-to-one funding advice 'surgeries'; a range of publications including a bi monthly journal called International Arts Navigator; they run training seminars on European policies, structures and funding opportunities, and undertake research and consultancy for national, regional and local cultural agencies

International Association of Broadcasting Manufacturers (IABM)
Broad Oaks
Parish Lane
Farnham Common
Slough SL2 3JW
Tel: 01753 645682
Fax: 01753 645682
email: info@iabm.org.uk
Website: www.iabm.org.uk
Secretariat: Brenda White
IABM aims to foster the interests of manufacturers of broadcast equipment from all countries. Areas of membership include liaison with broadcasters, standardisation, other technical information, an annual product Award for design and innovation and exhibitions. All companies active in the field of broadcast equipment manufacturing are encouraged to join

International Federation of the Phonographic Industry (IFPI)
IFPI Secretariat
54 Regent Street
London W1R 5PJ
Tel: 020 7878 7900
Fax: 020 7878 7950
Director General: Nicholas Garnett
An international association of 1,300 members in 71 countries, representing the copyright interests of the sound recording and music video industries

International Institute of Communications
Tavistock House South
Tavistock Square
London WC1H 9LF
Tel: 020 7388 0671
Fax: 020 7380 0623
The IIC promotes the open debate of issues in the communications field worldwide. Its current interests cover legal and policy, economic and public interest issues. It does this via its: bi-monthly journal Intermedia; through its international communications library; annual conference; sponsored seminars and research forums

International Teleproduction Society
c/o PACT
45 Mortimer Street
London W1N 7TD
Tel: 020 7331 6000
Fax: 020 7331 6700
The ITS UK Chapter (International Teleproduction Society) is the trade association serving the professional community of businesses that provide creative and technical services in pictures and sound

ITV Network Ltd
200 Gray's Inn Road
London WC1X 8HF
Tel: 020 7843 8000
Fax: 020 7843 8158
Chief Executive: Richard Eyre
Director of Programmes: David Liddiment
A body wholly owned by the ITV companies which independently undertakes the commissioning and scheduling of those television programmes which are shown across the ITV Network. It also provides a range of services to the ITV companies where a common approach is required

IVCA (International Visual Communication Association)
Bolsover House
5-6 Clipstone Street
London W1P 8LD
Tel: 020 7580 0962
Fax: 020 7436 2606
email: info@ivca.org
Chief Executive: Wayne Drew
The IVCA is the largest European Association of its kind, representing a wide range of organisations and individuals working in the established and developing technologies of visual communication. With roots in video, film and business events industries, the Association has also developed significant representation of the new and fast growing technologies, notably business television, multimedia, interactive software and the internet. It provides business services for its members: legal help, internet service, insurance, arbitration etc. and holds events/seminars for training, networking and for all industry related topics

Kraszna-Krausz Foundation
122 Fawnbrake Avenue
London SE24 0BZ
Tel: 020 7738 6701
Fax: 020 7738 6701

email: k-k@dial.pipex.com
Administrator: Andrea Livingstone
The Foundation offers small grants to assist in the development of new or unfinished projects, work or literature where the subject specifically relates to the art, history, practice or technology of photography or the moving image (defiended as film, television, video and related screen media)

London Screenwriters' Workshop
114 Whitfield Street
London W1P 5RW
Sandland St
London WC1R 4PZ
Tel: 020 7387 5511
Promotes contact between screenwriters and producers, agents, development executives and other film and TV professionals through a wide range of seminars. Practical workshops provide training in all aspects of the screenwriting process. Membership is open to anyone interested in writing for film and TV, and to anyone in these and related media

Mechanical-Copyright Protection Society (MCPS)
29/33 Berner Street
London W1P 4AA
Tel: 020 8664 4400
Fax: 020 8769 8792
email: info@mcps.co.uk
Website: www.mcps.co.uk
Contact: Non-retail Licensing Department
MCPS is an organisation of music publishers and composers, which issues licences for the recording of its members' copyright musical works in all areas of television, film and video production. Free advice and further information is available on request

Media, Communication and Cultural Studies Association (MeCCSA)
The Surrey Institute of Art and Design University College
Falkner Road
Farnham
Surrey GU9 7DS
Tel: 01252 892806
email: hdavis@surrart.ac.uk
Website: www.surrat.ac.uk/media/meccsa
Dr Helen Davis
MeCCSA is the leading subject association for the field of Media, Communication and Cultural Studies in UK higher education. It represents the interests of individual academics and HEIs across the field

Mental Health Media Council

The Resource Centre
356 Holloway Road
London N7 6PA
Tel: 020 7700 0100
Fax: 020 7700 0099
An independent charity founded in
1965, MHMC provides information,
advice and consultancy on film/video
use and production relevant to health,
mental health, physical disability,
learning difficulties and most aspects
of social welfare. Resource lists on
audiovisual material, quarterly
newsletter Mediawise. Producers of
video and broadcast programmes

Metier

Glyde House
Glydegate
Bradford BD5 0BQ
Tel: 01274 738 800
Fax: 01274 391 566
Chief Exec: Duncan Sones
A National Training Organisation,
developing National and Scottish
Vocational Qualifications for
occupations in performing and visual
arts, arts administration, front-of-
house, arts development &
interpretation and technical support
functions in the arts and
entertainment sector. It is responsible
for strategic action to improve the
quality, availability and effectiveness
of vocational training within its
industrial sector

Music Film and Video Producers' Association (MFVPA)

26 Noel Street
London W1V 3RD
Tel: 020 7434 2651
Fax: 020 7434 9002
The MFVPA was formed in 1985 to
represent the interests of pop/music
promo production companies. It
negotiates agreements with bodies
such as the BPI and BECTU on
behalf of its members. Secretariat
support is run through AFVPA

Music Publishers Association Ltd

3rd Floor, Strandgate
18/20 York Buildings
London WC2N 6JU
Tel: 020 7839 7779
Fax: 020 7839 7776
The only trade association repre-
senting UK music publishers. List of
members available at £10.00

Musicians' Union (MU)

60-62 Clapham Road
London SW9 0JJ

Tel: 020 7582 5566
Fax: 020 7793 9185
email: info@musiciansunion.org.uk
Media Department Contacts: Howard
Evans, Marilyn Stoddart
Represents the interests of virtually
all professional musicians in the UK.
The media department deals with all
music related issues involving film
and TV: day to day working and
interpretation of the MU/PACT
agreement, synchronisation of audio
recordings and advertisements and
film and rights clearances. Queries
regarding video, DVD, promotional
filming, EPK's, contractors,
musicians, composers and arrangers

National Association for Higher Education in Film and Video (NAHEFV)

c/o London International Film
School
24 Shelton Street
London WC2H 9HP
Tel: 020 7836 9642/240 0168
Fax: 020 7497 3718
The Association's main aims are to
act as a forum for debate on all
aspects of film, video and TV
education and to foster links with
industry, the professions and
Government bodies. It was
established in 1983 to represent all
courses in the UK which offer a
major practical study in film, video
or television at the higher educational
level

National Campaign for the Arts

Francis House
Francis Street
London SW1P 1DE
Tel: 020 7828 4448
Fax: 020 7931 9959/020 7233 6564
email: nca@ecna.org
Website: www.ecna.org./nca/
Director: Jennifer Edwards
The NCA specialises in lobbying,
campaigning research and
information. It provides facts and
figures for politicians, journalists and
any other interested parties. It is
independent and funded by its
members – individuals and
organisations

National Council for Educational Technology (NCET)

Milburn Hill Road
Science Park
University of Warwick
Coventry CV4 7JJ
Tel: 024 76116994
Fax: 024 76411418
Formerly the National Council for

Educational Technology (NCET), the
new remit will be to ensure that
technology supports the DfEE's
objectives to drive up standards, in
particular to provide the professional
expertise the DfEE needs to support
the future development of the
National Grid for Learning. BECTA
will also have a role in the further
education sector's developing use of
ICT, in the identification of ICT
opportunities for special educational
needs, and in the evaluttion of new
technologies as they come on stream

National Film and Television School

Beaconsfield Studios
Station Road
Beaconsfield
Bucks HP9 1LG
Tel: 01494 671234
Fax: 01494 674042
email: cad@nftsfilm-tv.ac.uk
Website: www.nftsfilm-tv.ac.uk
Director: Stephen Bayly
The National Film and Television
School provides advanced training
and retraining in all major disciplines
to professional standards. Graduates
are entitled to BECTU membership
on gaining employment. It is an
autonomous non-profit making
organisation funded by the
Department for Culture, Media and
Sport and the film and television
industries. See also under Courses

National Film Trustee Company (NFTC)

14-17 Wells Mews
London W1P 3FL
Tel: 020 7580 6799
Fax: 020 7636 6711
An independent revenue collection
and disbursement service for
producers and financiers. The NFTC
has been in business since 1971. It is
a subsidiary of British Screen Finance

National Museum of Photography Film & Television

Pictureville
Bradford BD1 1NQ
Tel: 01274 202030
Fax: 01274 723155
Website: www.nmsi.ac.uk/nmpft
Bill Lawrence, Head of Cinema
The world's only museum devoted to
still and moving pictures, their
technology and history. Features
Britain's first giant IMAX film
system; the world's only public
Cinerama; interactive galleries and
'TV Heaven', reference library of
programmes and commercials

National Screen Service
15 Wadsworth Road
Greenford
Middx UB6 7JN
Tel: 020 8998 2851
Fax: 020 8997 0840
2 Wedgwood Mews
12-13 Greek Street
London W1V 6BH
Tel: 020 7437 4851
Fax: 020 7287 0328
John Mahony, Brian McIlmail,
Norman Darkins
Formed in 1926 as a subsidiary of a
US corporation and purchased by its
present British owner/directors in
1986. It distributes trailers, posters
and other publicity material to UK
cinemas and carries out related
printing activity

National Union of Journalists
314 Gray's Inn Road
London WC1X 8DP
Tel: 020 7278 7916
Fax: 020 7837 8143
Deputy General Secretary: John Fray
Direct line to Broadcasting Office:
020 7843 3726
Represents nearly 5,000 journalists
working in broadcasting in the areas

of news, sport, current affairs and
features. It has agreements with all
the major broadcasting companies
and the BBC. It also has agreements
with the main broadcasting agencies,
WTN, Reuters Television and PACT

National Viewers' & Listeners' Association (NVALA)
All Saints House, High Street
Colchester
Essex CO1 1UG
Tel: 01206 561155
Fax: 01206 766175
email: info@nvala.org
Director: John C Beyer
Founder & President Emeritus: Mary
Whitehouse CBE
President: Rev Graham Stevens
Concerned with moral standards in
the media

Network of Workshops (NoW)
c/o Video in Pilton
30 Ferry Road Avenue
West Pilton
Edinburgh EH4 4BA
Tel: 0131 343 1151
Fax: 0131 343 2820
A membership organisation which is
open to all independent collective

film and video groups who are
committed to the cultural aims stated
in the BECTU workshop declaration

Networking
c/o Vera Media
30-38 Dock Street
Leeds LS10 1JF
Tel: 0113 2428646
Fax: 0113 2451238
email: networking@vera-
media.demon.co.uk
Membership organisation for women
working, seeking work or
interested/involved in film, video or
television, colleges, libraries, careers
depts., production companies
welcome to join. Members receive
quarterly 20-page newsletter with
events, production info., letters,
reports, news and views; entry in
NETWORKING index; individual
advice and help; campaigning voice.
£15 pa (UK), £18 (abroad)

New Producers Alliance (NPA)
9 Bourlet Close
London W1P 7PJ
Tel: 020 7580 2480
Fax: 020 7580 2484
email: administrator@npa.org.uk
Established in 1993 by a group of

young producers building upon their shared desire to make commercial films for an international audience, NPA has now grown to a membership of more than 1,300. NPA is an independent networking organisation providing members with access to contacts, information, free legal advice and general help regarding film production. NPA publishes a monthly newsletter and organises meetings, workshops and seminars. Membership is available to producers, directors and writers affiliates (individuals other than the above) and corporate bodies

Northern Ireland Film Commission
21 Ormeau Avenue
Belfast BT2 8HD
Tel: 01232 232 444
Fax: 01232 239 918
The Northern Ireland Film Commission promotes the growth of film and television culture and the industry in Northern Ireland

Office for National Statistics
1 Drummond Gate
London SW1V 2QQ
Tel: 020 7533 5725

Office of Fair Trading
Field House
15-25 Bream's Buildings
London EC4A 1PR
Tel: 020 7242 2858
Fax: 020 7269 8800
The Director General of Fair Trading has an interest in the supply of films for exhibition in cinemas. Following a report by the Monopolies and Mergers Commission (MMC) in 1994, the Director General has taken action to ensure that the adverse public interest findings of the MMC are remedied. Under the Broadcasting Act 1990, he also has two specific roles in relation to the television industry. In his report published in December 1992 he assessed the Channel 3 networking arrangement and from 1 January 1993 he had to monitor the BBC's progress towards a statutory requirement to source 25 per cent of its qualifying programming from independent producers

PACT (Producers Alliance for Cinema and Television)
45 Mortimer Street
London W1N 7TD
Tel: 020 7331 6000
Fax: 020 7331 6700
email: enquiries@pact.co.uk

Website: www.pact.co.uk
Chief Executive: Shaun Williams
Membership Officer: David Alan Mills
PACT exists to serve the feature film and independent television production sector. Currently representing 1,400 companies, PACT is the UK contact point for co-production, co-finance partners and distributors. Membership services include a dedicated industrial relations unit, legal documentation and back-up, a varied calendar of events, courses and business advice, representation at international film and television markets, a comprehensive research programme, publication of a monthly magazine, an annual members' directory, a number of specialist guidebooks, affiliation with European and international producers' organisations, plus extensive information and production advice. PACT works for participants in the industry at every level and operates a members' regional network throughout the UK with a divisional office in Scotland. PACT lobbies actively with broadcasters, financiers and governments to ensure that the producer's voice is heard and understood in Britain and Europe

Performing Right Society (PRS)
29-33 Berners Street
London W1P 4AA
Tel: 020 7580 5544
Fax: 020 7306 4050
Website: www.prs.co.uk
PRS is a non-profit making association of composers, authors and publishers of musical works. It collects and distributes royalties for the use, in public performances, broadcasts and cable programmes, of its members' copyright music and has links with other performing right societies throughout the world

Phonographic Performance (PPL)
1 Upper James Street
London W1R 3HG
Tel: 020 7534 1000
Fax: 020 7534 1111
Head of External Affairs:
Colleen Hue
Controls public performance and broadcasting rights in sound recordings on behalf of approximately 2,000 record companies in the UK. The users of sound recordings licensed by PPL range from BBC and independent TV and Radio, pan-European satellite

services, night clubs and juke boxes, to pubs, shops, hotels etc

Production Managers Association (PMA)
Ealing Studios
Ealing Green
Ealing
London W5 5EP
Tel: 020 8758 8699
Fax: 020 8758 8658
Represents over 140 broadcast production managers who all have at least three years experience and six broadcast credits. Provides a network of like-minded individuals

Radio, Electrical and Television Retailers' Association (RETRA)
Retra House
St John's Terrace
1 Ampthill Street
Bedford MK42 9EY
Tel: 01234 269110
Fax: 01234 269609
Fred Round
Founded in 1942, RETRA represents the interests of electrical retailers to all those who make decisions likely to affect the selling and servicing of electrical and electronic products

Reel Women
57 Holmewood Gardens
London SW2 3NB
Tel: 020 8678 7404
A networking organisation for all women in film, video and television. It places particular emphasis on the creative interaction between women from the broadcast, non-broadcast and independent sectors and higher education, aiming to provide a forum for debate around issues affecting women in all areas of production and training, as well as around broader concerns about the representation and position of women in the industry and on screen. Seminars, screenings and workshops are held as well as regular 'nights out'

The Royal Photographic Society
Milsom Street
Bath, Avon BA1 1DN
Tel: 01225 462841
Fax: 01225 448688
email: rps@rps.org
Website: www.rps.org
A learned society founded for the promotion and enjoyment of all aspects of photography. Contains a specialist Film and Video Group, secretary John Tarby, FRPS, with a regular journal, meetings and the

opportunity to submit productions for the George Sewell Trophy and the Hugh Baddeley Trophy; and an Audiovisual group, secretary Brian Jenkins, LRPS, offering an extensive programme of events, seminars and demonstrations, and the bi-monthly magazine AV News. Membership open to both amateur and professional photographers

Royal Television Society
Holborn Hall
100 Grays Inn Road
London WC1X 8AL
Tel: 020 7430 1000
Fax: 020 7430 0924
Exec. Director: Michael Bunce
Dep. Exec. Director: Claire Price
The RTS, founded in 1927, has over 4,000 members in the UK and overseas, which are serviced by the Society's 17 regional centres. The Society aims to bring together all the disciplines of television by providing a forum for debate on the technical, cultural and social implications of the medium. This is achieved through the many lectures, conferences, symposia and workshops and master classes organised each year. The RTS does not run formal training courses. The RTS publishes a journal eight times a year Television. The RTS Television Journalism and Sports Awards are presented every year in February and the Programme Awards in May. There are also Craft & Design, Educational Television Awards and student video awards

Scottish Arts Council
12 Manor Place
Edinburgh EH3 7DD
Tel: 0131 226 6051
Fax: 0131 225 9833
Director: Seona Reid
See entry for Scottish Screen, the lead body for film in Scotland

Scottish Screen
249 West George Street
Glasgow G2 4RB
Tel: 0141 302 1700
Fax: 0141 302 1711
email: info@scottishscreen.com
Website: www.scottishscreen.com
Chief Executive: John Archer
(See Regional Film Commission)
Scottish Screen is responsible to the Scottish Parliament for developing all aspects of screen industry and culture in Scotland through script and company development, short film production, distribution of National Lottery film production finance, training, education, exhibition funding, the film Commission

locations support and the Scottish Film and Television Archive

The Script Factory
Linton House
24 Wells Street
London W1P 3FG
Tel: 020 7323 1414
Fax: 020 7323 9464

Sgrîn (Media Agency for Wales)
The Bank, 10 Mount Stuart Square
Cardiff Bay
Cardiff CF1 6EE
Tel: 029 20333300
Fax: 029 20333320
email:
sgrin@sgrinwales.demon.co.uk
Website: www.screenwales.org.uk/
Chief Executive: J. Berwyn Rowlands
Incorporating the Wales Film and Television Archive, Media Antenna Wales and the Production Fund. Formed in 1997 by the merger of the Wales Film Council and Screen Wales. Sgrin offers a coordinated vision for all aspects, cultural and industrial, of film television and related media in Wales

The Shape Network
c/o Ithaca
Unit 1, St John Fisher School
Sandy Lane West
Blackbird Leys
Oxford OX4 5LD
Tel: 01865 714652
Fax: 01865 714822
Chair: Anna Thornhill
A federation of independent arts organisations working to increase access to the arts for many groups of people who are usually excluded. The role of the Network is to share information, advice and support and to lobby on arts and disability issues nationally

The Short Film Bureau
68 Middle Street
Brighton
East Sussex BN1 1AL
Tel: 01273 235524
Fax: 01273 23558
email: infro@shortfilmbureau.com
Website: www.shortfilmbureau.com
Patrons: Sir Sydney Samuelson OBE
Steve Woolley, Brian Cox
The Bureau has two goals: To help new filmmakers find audiences for their work an dto raise the profile and acceptance of short films in general. This is done by offering advice and support on funding, production, marketing and distribution. The website offers proffessional and practical advice on all aspects of

short film making. The Cinema Programme provides an opportunity for filmmakers to have their work assessed for potential theatrical release by UK distributors and exhibitiors.

SKILLSET
The National Training Organisation for Broadcast, Film, Video and Multimedia
91-101 Oxford Street
London W1R 1RA
Tel: 020 7534 5300
Fax: 020 7534 5333
email: info@skillset.org
Website: www.skillset.org
Chief Executive: Dinah Caine
Director of Standards and Qualifications: Kate O'Connor
Communications Manager: Flora Teh-Morris
Founded and managed by the key employers and unions within the industry, SKILLSET operates at a strategic level providing relevant labour market and training information, encouraging higher levels of investment in training and developing and implementing occupational standards and the National and Scottish Vocation Qualifications based upon them. It seeks to influence national and international education and training policies to the industry's best advantage, strives to create greater and equal access to training opportunities and career development and assists in developing a healthier and safer workforce. SKILLSET is a UK-wide organisation

Society for the Study of Popular British Cinema
Department of Media and Cultural Production
Faculty of Humanities and Social Science
Gateway House
De Montfort University
Leicester LE1 9BH
Fax: 0116 2577199
Contact: Alan Burton, Secretary
Society which produces a newsletter and encourages an interest in British films

Society of Authors' Broadcasting Group
84 Drayton Gardens
London SW10 9SB
Tel: 020 7373 6642
Fax: 020 7373 5768
email: authorsoc@writer.org.uk
Specialities: Radio, television and film scriptwriters

Society of Cable Telecommunication Engineers (SCTE)
Fulton House Business Centre
Fulton Road, Wembley Park
Middlesex HA9 0TF
Tel: 020 8902 8998
Fax: 020 8903 8719
Mrs Beverley K Allgood FSAE
Aims to raise the standard of cable telecommunication engineering to the highest technical level, and to elevate and improve the status and efficiency of those engaged in cable telecommunication engineering

Society of Film Distributors (SFD)
22 Golden Square
London W1R 3PA
Tel: 020 7437 4383
Fax: 020 7734 0912
General Secretary: D C Hunt
SFD was founded in 1915 and membership includes all the major distribution companies and several independent companies. It promotes and protects its members' interests and co-operates with all other film organisations and Government agencies where distribution interests are involved

Society of Television Lighting Directors
4 The Orchard
Aberthin
Cowbridge
South Glamorgan CF7 7HU
The Society provides a forum for the exchange of ideas in all aspects of the TV profession including techniques and equipment. Meetings are organised throughout the UK and abroad. Technical information and news of members' activities are published in the Society's magazine

Sovexportfilm
11b Paveley Drive
Morgans Walk
London SW11 3TP
Tel: 020 7358 1226
Fax: 020 7358 1226
Exports Russian films to different countries and imports films to Russia. Provides facilities to foreign companies wishing to film in Russia. Co-production information for producers

TAC (Welsh Independent Producers)
Gronant
Caernarfon
Gwynedd LL55 1NS
Tel: 01286 671123
Fax: 01286 678890

TAC is the trade association representing the 95 production companies working for Welsh broadcasters. It offers a full IR service and conducts negotiations on standard terms of trade with the broadcasters

Variety Club of Great Britain
Variety Club House
93 Bayham Street
London NW1 0AG
Tel: 020 7428 8100
Fax: 020 7428 8111
Charity dedicated to helping disabled and disadvantaged children throughout Great Britain

Videola (UK)
Paramount House
162/170 Wardour Street
London W1V 3AT
Tel: 020 7437 2136
Fax: 020 7437 5413

VLV – Voice of the Listener and Viewer
101 King's Drive
Gravesend
Kent DA12 5BQ
Tel: 01474 352835
Fax: 01474 351112
An independent non-profit making society which represents the citizen and consumer voice in broadcasting and which supports the principle of public service in broadcasting. Founded in 1983, by Jocelyn Hay, VLV is the only consumer body speaking for listeners and viewers on the full range of broadcasting issues. VLV has over 2,000 members, more than 20 corporate members (most of which are registered charities) and over 50 colleges and university departments in academic membership. VLV is funded by its members and free from any sectarian, commercial or political links. Holds public lectures, conferences and seminars and arranges exclusive visits for its members to broadcasting centres in different parts of the country. Publishes a quarterly newsletter and briefings on broadcasting developments. Has responded to all parliamentary and public inquiries on broadcasting since 1984 and to consultations by the ITC, Radio Authority, BBC and Broadcasting Standards Council since 1990. Is in frequent touch with MPs, civil servants, the BBC and independent broadcasters, regulators, academics and relevant consumer bodies at UK and European level. Holds the archive of the former

independent Broadcasting Research Unit and of the former British Action for Children's Television (BACTV) and makes these available for a small fee together with its own archives and library. Set up the VLV Forum for Children's Broadcasting in 1994

Women in Film and Television (UK)
Garden Studios
11-15 Betterton Street
London WC2H 9BP
Tel: 020 7379 0344
Fax: 020 7379 1625
Director: Kate Norrish
Administrator: Donna Coyle
A membership organisation for women working in the film and television industries. WFTV aims to provide information and career support through a monthly programme of events that are free to members. In addition WFTV safeguards the interests of the members through its lobbying and campaigning. Annual Awards Ceremony at the Dorchester remains the only industry event that solely celebrates the achievements of women. WFTV is part of an international network of organisations – currently 37 chapters world-wide

Writers' Guild of Great Britain
430 Edgware Road
London W2 1EH
Tel: 020 7723 8074
Fax: 020 7706 2413
email: postie@wggb.demon.co.uk
Website: www.writers.org.uk/guild
The Writers' Guild is the recognised TUC-affiliated trade union for writers working in film, television, radio, theatre and publishing

Regional Film Commissions and Film Offices

Bath Film Office
Abbey Chambers
Abbey Churchyard
Bath BA1 1LY
Tel: 01225 477711
Fax: 01225 477221
email: Richard_Angell@
Bathnes.gov.uk
Under the umbrella of the British Film
Commission, the Bath Film Office
offers a free service to the TV, film
and commercials industry. It maintains
a database of over 800 locations in
and around the city of Bath

Central England Screen Commission
Unit 5, Holliday Wharf
Holliday Street
Birmingham B1 1TJ
Tel: 0121 643 9309
Fax: 0121 643 9064

East Midlands Screen Commission
Broadway
14-18 Broad Street
Nottingham NG1 3AL
Tel: 0115 910 5564
Covers Nottinghamshire,
Northamptonshire, Derbyshire,
Leicestershire, Rutland

Eastern Screen
Anglia TV
Norwich NR1 3JG
Tel: 01603 767077
Fax: 01603 767191
The Film Commission for the East of
England offering free help and advice
on locations, facilities companies
local services and crew to anyone
intending to film within the region

Edinburgh and Lothian Screen Industries Office
Castlecliff
25 Johnston Terrace
Edinburgh EH1 2NH
Tel: 0131 622 7337
Fax: 0131 622 7338
George Carlaw, Ros Davis
The Film Commission for the City of
Edinburgh and the coastline,
countryside and counties of Lothian.
Advice on locations, crews and
facilities and local authority liaison.
A free service provided by the City
of Edinburgh and West, East, and
Midlothian Councils, to encourage
film, video and television production
in the area

Glasgow Film Office
City Chambers
Glasgow G2 YDU
Tel: 0141 302 1757
Гах. 0141 287 0311
Website: www.glasgowfilm.org.uk

Herts Film Link
South Way
Leavesden
Hertfordshire WD2 7LT
Tel: 01923 495 051
Fax: 01923 333007
email: hfl@herts-filmlink.co.uk
Website: www.hertsfilmlink.com
Roger Harrop

Isle of Man Film Commission
Illiam Dhone House
2 Circular Road
Douglas
Isle of Man 1M1 1PJ
Tel: 01624 685864
Fax: 01624 685454

Lancashire Film and Television Office
Enterprise plc
17 Ribblesdale Place
Preston PR1 3NA
Tel: 01772 203 020
Fax: 01772 252 640

Liverpool Film Office
Pioneer Buildings
67 Dale St
Liverpool L2 2NS
Tel: 0151 291 9191
Fax: 0151 291 9199
Film Commissioner: Brigid Marray
Locations Officer: Lynn Saunders
Provides a free film liaison service,
and assistance to all productions
intending to use locations, resources,
services and skills in the Merseyside
area. Undertakes research and
location scouting, liaises with local
agencies and the community. Offers
access to the best range of locations
in the UK through its extensive
locations library

London Film Commission
20 Euston Centre
Regent's Place
London NW1 3JH
Tel: 020 7387 8787
Fax: 020 7387 8788
email: lfc@london-film.co.uk
Dominic Reid, Film Commissioner
Julia Willis, Production Co-ordinator
The London Film Commission
encourages and assists film and
television production in London and
holds databases of locations,
personnel and facilities. Funded by
Government, the film industry and

other private sector sponsors, it
works to promote London as a first
choice destination for overseas filmmakers. It collaborates with the Local
Authorities, the police and other
services to create a film friendly
atmosphere in the capital

Media Development Agency for the West Midlands incorporating Central Screen Commission
Broad Street House
3rd Floor, 212 Broad Street
Birmingham B15 IAY
Tel: 0121 643 9309
Fax: 0121 643 9064
email: info@mda-wm.org.uk
Website: www.mda-wm.org.uk
Media Development Agency for the
West Midlands and Screen
Commission, Directory & Database
of local production facilities, crews
and talents; location finding and
liaison: low budget production
funding including 1st Academy;
information resources and
counselling service; legal surgeries;
seminars and masterclasses; media
business development support;
copyright registration scheme

Mid Wales Film Commission
6G Science Park Cefn Llan,
Aberystwyth
Ceredigion SY23 3AH
Tel: 01970 617995
Fax: 01970 617942
email: info@midwalesfilm.com
Website: www.midwalesfilm.com
Mid Wales Film Commission seeks
to promote the use of Mid Wales
facilities and locations for the
production of films, television
programmes and commercial

North Wales Film Commission The
Council Offices
Shire Hall Street
Caernarfen
Gwynedd LL55 1SH
Tel: 01286 679685
Fax: 01286 673324
email: fil@gwynedd.gov.uk
Hugh Edwin Jones, Peter Lowther
Area film liaison office for
information on filming in the county
of Gwynedd and Anglesey.
Information provided on locations,
facilities and crew

Northern Screen Commission (NSC)
Great North House
Sandyford Road
Newcastle Upon Tyne NE1 8ND
Tel: 0191 204 2311

Fax: 0191 204 2209
email:nsc@filmhelp.demon.co.uk
Paul Mingard
Seeking to attract film, video and
television production to the North of
England, NSC can provide a full
liaison service backed by a network
of local authority contacts and public
organisations. Available at no cost is
a locations library, a database on
local facilities and services as well as
a full list of local crew or talent

Scottish Highlands and Islands Film Commission
Comisean Fiolm na
Gaidhealtachd's nan Eilean Alba
Inverness Castle
Inverness 1V2 3EG
Tel: 01463 702000
Fax: 01463 710848
The Scottish Highlands and Islands
Film Commission provides a free,
comprehensive liaison service to the
film and television industry,
including information and advice on
locations, permissions, crew and
services etc. We cover Argyll and
Bute, Highland, Moray, Orkney,
Shetland and the Western Isles, and
have a network of local film liaison

officers able to provide quick and
expert local help, whatevern your
project

Scottish Screen
249 West George Street
Glasgow G2 4RB
Tel: 0141 302 1700
Fax: 0141 302 1711
email: info@scottishscreen.com
Website: www.scottishscreen.com
Chief Executive: John Archer
Scottish Screen promotes Scotland as
an international filming destination
and encourages incoming production
by co-ordinating locations enquiries.
Working in partnership with are
offices Scottish Screen provides
detailed support on locations,
crewing and facilities and has a
library of 35,000 stills covering 4,000
locations, all on database

South Wales Film Commission
The Media Centre
Culverhouse Cross
Cardiff Cf5 6XJ
Tel: (01222) 590240
Fax: (01222) 590511
email: 106276.223@compuserve.com

A member of the British Film
Commission and AFCI, providing
location, research and information on
facilities and services across South
Wales for film and television
production

South West Film Commission (South)
18 Belle Vue Road, Saltash,
Cornwall PL12 E5
Tel: 01752 841199
Fax: 01752 841254
email: infosouth@swfilm.co.uk
Film Commissioner: Sue Dalziel
Offers professional assistance to
productions shooting in Devon,
Cornwall, Somerset, Dorset, Bristol
City, Gloucestershire, Wiltshire
South West Film Commission (North)
59 Prince Street
Bristol B51 4QH
Tel: 0117 907 4315
Fax: 0117 907 4384
email: swfilminfonorth
@swfilm.co.uk

South West Scotland Screen Commission
Gracefield Arts Centre
28 Edinburgh Road

Dumfries DG1 1NW
Tel: 01387 263666
Fax: 01387 263666
An unrivalled variety and wealth of
locations to suit any style of shoot or
budget, plus a free location finding
and film liaison service for South
West Scotland

Southern Screen Commission
Brighton Media Centre
9-12 Middle Street
Brighton BN1 1AL
Tel: 01273 384211
Fax: 01273 384211
Website: www.adh.bton.ac.uk/
southernscreen/
Southern Screen promotes and
markets locations, personnel and
services in the South East to the film
and television industries

Yorkshire Screen Commission
The Workstation
15 Paternoster Row
Sheffield S1 2BX
Tel: 0114 2799115/2766511
Fax: 0114 2796522/2798593
Screen Commissioners: Sue Lathan,
Information Co-ordinator: Shuna
Frood, Crew Manager: Penny Finerty
Assists film & TV production
companies in finding locations,
facilities and crew in the Yorkshire
region

US Organisations

American Film Institute
P.O. Box 27999/ 2021
North Western Avenue
Los Angeles, CA 90027
Tel: (323) 856-7600
Fax (323) 467-4578
The John F. Kennedy Center for
the Performing Arts
Washington, D.C. 20566
Tel: (202) 828-4000
Fax (202) 659-1970
Website: www.afionline.org/
Organisation dedicated to preserving
the heritage of film and television

AMPAS (Academy of Motion Picture Arts & Sciences)
8949 Wilshire Boulevard
Beverly Hills
CA 90211
Tel: (1) 310 247 3000
Fax: (1) 310 859 9619
Organisation of producers, actors and
others which is responsible for
widely promoting and supporting the
film industry, as well as for awarding
the annual Oscars

Hollywood Foreign Press Association
292 S. La Cienega Blvd, #316
Beverly Hills
CA 90211
Tel: (1) 310 657 1731
Fax: (1) 310 657 5576
Journalists reporting on the
entertainment industry for non-US
media. Annual event: Golden Globe
Awards – awarding achievements in
motion pictures and television

Museum of Television and Radio
25 West 52 Street
New York, NY 10019
Tel: (1) 212 621 6600/6800
Fax: (1) 212 621 6715
The Museum (formerly The Museum
of Broadcasting) collects and
preserves television and radio
programmes and advertising
commercials, and makes them
available to the public. The
collection, which now includes
nearly 60,000 programmes, covers 70
years of news, public affairs
programmes, documentaries,
performing arts, children's
programming, sports, and comedy.
The Museum organises exhibitions,
and screening and listening series

ORGANISATIONS (EUROPE)

The following is a list of some of the main pan-European film and television organisations, entries for countries of the European Union and the various MEDIA II projects instigated by the European Commission

ACE (Ateliers du Cinéma Européen/European Film Studio)
rue de Rivoli 68
75004 Paris
France
Tel: (33) 1 44 61 88 30
Fax: (33) 1 44 61 88 40
email: ace@pelnet.com
Director: Claudie Cheval
ACE was established as a joint project of the Media Business School and the European Producers Club, to work with producers during the development stages of their projects, guiding them in a way that maximises their chances of reaching the largest possible target audience

AGICOA (Association de Gestion Internationale Collective des Oeuvres Audio-Visuelles)
rue de St-Jean 26
1203 Geneva
Switzerland
Tel: (41) 22 340 32 00
Fax: (41) 22 340 34 32
Rodolphe Egli, Luigi Cattaneo
AGICOA ensures the protection of the rights of producers worldwide when their works are retransmitted by cable. By entering their works in the AGICOA Registers, producers can claim royalties collected for them

Audio-Visual EUREKA
Permanent Secretariat
rue de la Bonté 5-7
1000 Brussels,
Belgium
Tel: (32) 2 543 76 60
Fax: (32) 2 538 04 39
email: secretariat@aveureka.be
Website: www.aveureka.be
Director: Sylivie Forbin
Audiovisual Eureka is a Pan-European Intergovernmental Organisation for the promotion of cooperation in the European Audiovisual Sector. Membership consists of the 35 members including the European Commission (member) and the Council of Europe (associate member). From 1996-1998 Audiovisual Eureka concentrated on Training (1996), Development (1997) and Distribution (1998). Currently Audiovisual Eureka is focussing on consolidation of the works undertaken so far and accomplishing an external evaluation of the actions and initiatives launched since 1996

Bureau de Liaison Européen du Cinéma
c/o Fédération Internationale des Associations de Distributeurs de Films (FIAD)
boulevard Malesherbes 43
75008 Paris, France
Tel: (33) 1 42 66 05 32
Fax: (33) 1 42 66 96 92
Gilbert Grégoire
Umbrella grouping of cinema trade organisations in order to promote the cinema industry, including CICCE, FEITIS, FIAD, FIAPF, FIPFI and UNIC

Centre for Cultural Research
Am Hofgarten 17
53113 Bonn
Germany
Tel: (49) 228 211058
Fax: (49) 228 217493
Scharfschwerdtstr. 10
16540 Hohen Neuendorf
c/o IKM, Karlsplatz 2
1010 Vienna, Austria
Prof Andreas Johannes Wiesand
Research, documentation, and advisory tasks in all fields of the arts and media, especially with 'European' perspectives. Participation in arts and media management courses at university level. Produces publications and is founding seat of the European Institute for Comparative Cultural Policy and the Arts (ERIC Arts) with members in 21 European countries

EURIMAGES
Council of Europe
Palais de l'Europe
avenue de l'Europe
67075 Strasbourg Cédex, France
Tel: (33) 88 41 26 40
Fax: (33) 88 41 27 60
Website:
www.culture.coe.fr/eurimages
Contact: Executive Secretary
Founded in 1988 by a group of Council of Europe member states. Its objective is to stimulate film and audio-visual production by partly financing the co-production, distribution and exhibition of European cinematographic and audio-visual works. Eurimages now includes 24 member states

Eurocréation Media
rue Debelleyme 3
75003 Paris, France
Tel: (33) 1 44 59 27 01
Fax: (33) 1 40 29 92 46
Jean-Pierre Niederhauser, Anne-Marie Autissier (Consultant)
Eurocréation Media develops consultation and expertise in the field of European audio-visual and cinema (research, support for the organisation and conception of European events, training activities)

European Academy for Film & Television
rue Verte 69
1210 Brussels, Belgium
Tel: (32) 2 218 66 07
Fax: (32) 2 217 55 72
Permanent Secretary: Dimitri Balachoff
The purpose of the Academy, a non-profit making association, is the research, development and disclosure of all matters relating to cinema and television chiefly in the European continent, and also in other continents, taking into account artistic, commercial, cultural, economic, financial, historical, institutional, pedagogical, trade union and technical aspects. Quarterly newsletter, ACANEWS. Other activities: Blue Angel Award, presented every year at the Berlin International Film Festival for the Best European Film in Competition

European Audio-visual Observatory
76 allée de la Robertsau
67000 Strasbourg, France
Tel: (33) 3 88 144400
Fax: (33) 3 88 144419
Website: www.obs.coe.int/
Executive Director: Nils Klevjer

AAS. A Pan-European institution
working in the legal framework of
the Council of Europe. The
Observatory is a public service centre
providing information on the
European television, film and video
industries, aimed at the audio-visual
industry, and available in English,
French and German. It provides
legal, economic and market, and film
and television funding related
information and counselling, and is
working with a network of partner
organisations on the developing
harmonisation of data covering the
whole of Europe. The Observatory
also publishes a monthly newsletter
(IRIS) on legal development in all of
its 33 member States, as well as an
annual Statistical Yearbook on Film,
Television, Video and New Media.
The Observatory provides
information through an individualised
document delivery service in the
legal information area

European Broadcasting Union (EBU)
Ancienne Route 17a
1218 Grand-Saconnex
Geneva, Switzerland
Tel: (41) 22 717 2111
Fax: (41) 22 717 2200
Website: www.ebu.ch/
Jean-Pierre Julien
The EBU is a professional
association of national broadcasters
with 117 members in 79 countries.
Principal activities: daily exchange
of news, sports and cultural
programmes for television
(Eurovision) and radio (Euroradio);
Tv coproductions; technical studies
and legal action in the international
broadcasting sphere

European Coordination of Film Festivals
64 rue Philippe le Bon
1000 Bruxelles
Tel: (32) 2 280 13 76
Fax: (32) 2 230 91 41
email: cefc@skypro.be
Website: www.eurofilmfest.org
Marie José Carta
A network of 150 audio-visual
festivals in Europe to promote the
diversity of the European moving
image through collaboration projects
such as touring programmes, staff
exchanges, reserach and conferences
on the socio-economic impact of film
festivals, electronic subtitling and
sponsorship, the quarterly newsletter
(EuroFilmFest). The Coordination is
funded by MEDIA

European Co-production Association
c/o France 2
22 avenue Montaigne
75387 Paris Cédex 08
France
Tel: (33) 1 4421 4126
Fax: (33) 1 4421 5179
A consortium of, at present, six
European public service television
networks for the co-production of
television programmes. Can offer
complete finance. Proposals should
consist of full treatment, financial
plan and details of proposed co-
production partners. Projects are
proposed to the ECA Secretariat or to
member national broadcasters

European Co-production Fund (ECF)
c/o British Screen Finance
14-17 Wells Mews
London W1P 3FL
Tel: 020 7323 9080
Fax: 020 7323 0092
email: info@britishscreen.co.uk
In November 1996, the Department
of National Heritage (DNH) (as it
was – now the DCMS) announced
that it would continue funding ECF
at the current level of £2 million per
year until March 2000. The Fund is
available for investment in feature
films made by European co-
producers and for investment in
European film development work.
The ECF administers the fund (it is a
wholly owned subsidy of BSF) for
disbursing the Fund to producers in
the form of loans on commercial
terms. The Fund aims to improve the
opportunity for UK producers to co-
produce with EC partners. Successful
recent films include: *Orlando, Before
the Rain, Antonia's Line*

European Film Academy (EFA)
Kurfurstendamm 225
D-10719 Berlin
Germany
Tel: (49) 30 88 71 67 - 0
Fax: (49) 30 88 71 67 77
Chairman: Nik Powell,
Director: Marion Döring
Promotes European cinema
worldwide to strengthen its
commercial and artistic position, to
improve the knowledge and
awareness of European cinema and to
pass on the substantial experience of
the Academy members to the
younger generation of film
professionals. The European Film
Academy presents the annual
European Film Awards

European Institute for the Media (EIM)
Kaistrasse 13
40221 Düsseldorf, Germany
Tel: (49) 211 90 10 40
Fax: (49) 211 90 10 456
Head of Research: Runar Woldt
Head of East-West: Dusoun Rejic
Acting Head of Library,
Documentation and Statistics Centre:
Helga Schmid
A forum for research and
documentation in the field of media
in Europe. Its activities include:
research into the media in Europe
with a political, economic and
juridicial orientation; the organisation
of conferences and seminars such as
the annual European Television and
Film Forum; East-West Co-operation
Programme; the development of an
advanced studies programme for
students and media managers.
Publication of the Bulletin in
English/French/German, quarterly on
European media development, and of
the Ukrainian and Russian Bulletin as
well as research reports. Officers in
Kiev and Moscow. Organises the
European Media Summer School, an
annual course on media development
for advanced students and
professionals, and facilitates an
information request service

EUTELSAT (European Telecommunications Satellite Organisation)
Tour Maine-Montparnasse
avenue du Maine 33
75755 Paris Cédex 15, France
Tel: (33) 1 45 38 47 47
Fax: (33) 1 45 38 37 00
Website: www.eutelsat.org/
Vanessa O'Connor
EUTELSAT operates a satellite
system for intra-European
communications of all kinds. Traffic
carried includes Television and Radio
channels, programme exchanges,
satellite newsgathering, telephony
and business communications

Fédération Européenne des Industries Techniques de l'Image et du Son (FEITIS)
avenue Marceau 50
75008 Paris
France
Tel: (33) 1 47 23 07 45
Fax: (33) 1 47 23 70 47
A federation of European
professional organisations
representing those working in film
and video services and facilities in all
audio-visual and cinematographic
markets

Federation Internationale de la Press et Cinématographique (International Federation of Film Critics) (FIPRESCI)
Schleissheimer Str 83
D-80797 Munich
Tel: (49) 89 18 23 03
Fax: (49) 89 18 47 66
Klaus Eder, General Secretary

Fédération Internationale des Producteurs de Films Indépendants (FIPFI)
avenue Marceau 50
75008 Paris,
France
Tel: (33) 1 47 23 70 30
Fax: (33) 1 47 20 78 17
Federation of independent film producers, currently with members in 21 countries. It is open to all independent producers, either individual or groups, provided they are legally registered as such. FIPFI aims to promote the distribution of independent films, to increase possibilities for co-production, to share information between member countries and seeks to defend freedom of expression

FIAD (Fédération Internationale des Associations de Distributeurs de Films)
boulevard Malesherbes 43
75008 Paris, France
Tel: (33) 1 42 66 05 32
Fax: (33) 1 42 66 96 92
Président: Gilbert Grégoire
Président d'honneur: Luc Hemelaer
Vice Président: Stephan Hutter
Secrétaire Général: Antoine Virenque
Represents the interests of film distributors

FIAPF (Fédération Internationale des Associations de Producteurs de Films)
avenue des Champs-Elysées 33
75008 Paris, France
Tel: (33) 1 42 25 62 14
Fax: (33) 1 42 56 16 52
An international level gathering of national associations of film producers (23 member countries). It represents the general interests of film producers in worldwide forums (WIPO, UNESCO, WCO, GATT) and with European authorities (EC, Council of Europe, Audio-visual EUREKA), it lobbies for better international legal protection for film and audio-visual producers

FIAT/IFTA (International Federation of Television Archives)
Tevearkivet
Sveriges Television AB RH-N2G
S-105 10 Stockholm
Sweden
Tel: (+468) 784 5740
Fax: (+468) 660 4000
FIAT membership is mainly made up of the archive services of broadcasting organisations. However it also encompasses national archives and other television-related bodies. It meets annually and publishes its proceedings and other recommendations concerning television archiving

IDATE (Institut de l'audio-visuel et de télécommunications en Europe)
BP 4167
34092 Montpelier Cédex 5
France

Institut de Formation et d'Enseignement pour les Métiers de l'Image et du Son (FEMIS)
rue Francoeur 6
75018 Paris
France
Tel: (33) 1 42 62 20 00
Fax: (33) 1 42 62 21 00
High level technical training in the audio-visual field for French applicants and those from outside France with a working knowledge of French. Organises regular student exchanges with other European film schools

Institut de Journalisme Robert Schuman – European Media Studies
rue de l'Association 32-34
1000 Brussels
Belgium
Tel: (32) 2 217 2355
Fax: (32) 2 219 5764
Anne de Boeck
Postgraduate training in journalism. Drawing students from all over Europe, it offers nine months intensive training in journalism for press, radio and television

International Cable Communications Council
boulevard Anspach 1, Box 34
1000 Brussels
Belgium
Tel: (32) 2 211 94 49
Fax: (32) 2 211 99 07
International body gathering European, Canadian, North American

and Latin American cable television organisations

International Federation of Actors (FIA)
Guild House
Upper St Martin's Lane
London WC2H 9EG
Tel: 020 7379 0900
Fax: 020 7379 8260
Trade union federation founded in 1952 and embracing 60 performers' trade unions in 44 countries. It organises solidarity action when member unions are in dispute, researches and analyses problems affecting the rights and working conditions of film, television and theatre actors as well as singers, dancers, variety and circus artistes. It represents members in the international arena on issues such as cultural policy and copyright and publishes twice yearly newsheet FOCUS

ISETU/FISTAV
(International Secretariat for Arts, Mass Media and Entertainment Trade Unions/International Federation of Audio-Visual Workers)
IPC, boulevard Charlemagne 1
PO Box 5
1040 Brussels, Belgium
Tel: (32) 2 238 09 51
Fax: (32) 2 230 00 76
General Secretary: Jim Wilson
Caters to the special concerns of unions and similar associations whose members are engaged in mass media, entertainment and the arts. It is a clearing house for information regarding multi-national productions or movement of employees across national borders, and acts to exchange information about collective agreements, legal standards and practices at an international level. It organises conferences, has opened a campaign in support of public service broadcasting, and has begun initiatives ranging from defending screen writers to focusing on the concerns of special groups

Prince's Trust Partners in Europe, The
8 Bedford Row
London WC1R 4BA
Tel: 020 7405 5799
Contact: Anne Engel
Offer 'Go and See' grants (max £500) towards partnership projects in Europe to people under 26 out of full time education

Telefilm Canada/Europe
5 rue de Constantine
Paris 75007
Director: Sheila de La Varende
Canadian government organisation
financing film and television
productions. European office
provides link between Canada, UK
and other European countries

UK EUREKA Unit
Department of Trade and Industry,
3rd Floor, Green Core
151 Buckingham Palace Road
London SW1W 9SS
Tel: 020 7215 1618
Fax: 020 7215 1700
For Advanced Broadcasting
Technology: Brian Aldous
Tel: 020 7215 1737
A pan-European initiative to
encourage industry-led, market-
driven collaborative projects aimed at
producing advanced technology
products, processes and services

**UNIC (Union
Internationale des Cinémas)**
15 Rue de Berri
75008 Paris
France
Tel: (33) 1 53 93 76 76
Fax: (33) 1 45 53 29 76
Defends the interests of cinema
exhibitors worldwide, particularly in
matters of law and economics. It
publishes UNIC News and a Bulletin.
Also provides statistical information
and special studies concerning the
exhibition sector, to members and
others

**URTI (Université
Radiophonique et
Télévisuelle Internationale)**
General Secretariat
116, avenue du Président Kennedy
75786 Paris Cedex 16
France
Tel: (33) 1 42 30 39 98
Fax: (33) 1 40 50 89 99
President: Roland Faure
A non-governmental organisation
recognised by UNESCO and founded
in 1949, URTI is an association of
professionals in the audio-visual field
from all over the world. Promotes
cultural programmes and organisation
of projects including the International
Grand Prix for Creative
Documentaries, the Young Television
Prize at the Monte Carlo
International Television Festival, the
Grand Prix for Radio (since 1989)

Austria

**Animation Studio for
Experimental Animated
Films**
University of Applied Arts
Vienna
A – 1010 Wien Salzgries 14
Tel: (43) 1 7120392/71133-521
Fax: (43) 1 7120392
Hubert Sielecki

**Association of Audio-visual
and Film Industry**
Wiedner Haupstrasse 63
1045 Wien
PO Box 327
Tel: (43) 1 50105/3010
Fax: (43) 1 50105/276
email: film@fafo.at
Dr Elmar Peterlunger

Austrian Film Commission
Stiftgasse 6
A-1070 Vienna
Tel: (43) 1 526 33 23/200
Fax: (43) 1 526 68 01
email: afilmco@magnet.at
Website: www.afc.at
The Austrian Film Commission is a
central information and promotion
agency. The organization, financed
by public funds, offers a wide variety
of services for Austrian producers
and creative artists, it acts as
consultant whenever its productions
are presented in international
festivals, and it provides members of
the profession in all sectors with
comprehensive information as to
current activity in the Austrian film
industry. It is the aim of all activities
to enhance the perception of Austrian
film-making both at home and
abroad. In addition to the major
festivals in Berlin, Cannes and
Venice, the Austrian Film
Commission currently provides
support for 70 international film
festivals and fairs. The catalogue
Austrian Films published annually,
offers an overview, divided in
sections, of current Austrian film-
making. The Austrian Film Guide
provides a concise source of
addresses for Austrian producers,
distributors, institutions associated
with film, funding organisations etc.
Also published is Austrian Film
News, written about and for the
Austrian film industry

Austrian Film Institute
Spittelberggasse 3
A-1070 Wien
Tel: (43) 1 526 97 30
Fax: (43) 1 526 97 30/440
email: oefi@filminstitut.or.at

Website: www.filminstitut.or.at
Film funding, Eurimages and
MEDIA II

Filmakademie Wien
National Film School
Vienna Hochschule für Musik und
darstellende Kunst
Metternichgasse 12
A-1030 Wien
Tel: (43) 1 713 52 12 0
Fax: (43) 1 713 52 12 23

**Wiener
Filmfinanzierungsfonds
(WFF)**
Stiftgasse 6 /2/3
1070 Vienna
Tel: (43) 1 526 50 88 – 0
Fax: (43) 1 526 50 88 – 20
The WFF concedes interest free loans
in order to support full-length feature
films and creative documentaries for
cinema and television. Besides
production, the WFF assists
scriptwriting, project development,
exploitation/distribution and the
improvement of Viennese film
industry infrastructure

Belgium

**Cinémathèque Royale de
Belgique/Royal Film
Archive**
Rue Ravenstein 23
1000 Brussels
Tel: (32) 2 507 83 70
Fax: (32) 2 513 12 72
Gabrielle Claes
Film preservation. The collection can
be consulted on the Archive's
premises for research purposes. Edits
the Belgian film annual

**Commission de Sélection de
Films**
Ministère de la Culture et des
Affaires Sociales
Direction de l'Audio-visuel
Boulevard Léopold II 40
1080 Brussels
Tel: (32) 2 413 22 39
Fax: (32) 2 413 22 42
Christiane Dano, Serge Meurant
Assistance given to the production of
short and long features, as well as
other audio-visual production by
independent producers

Commission du Film
Ministère de la Culture et des
Affaires Sociales
Direction de l'Audiovisuel
Boulevard Léopold II 44
1080 Brussels
Tel: (32) 2 413 22 21
Fax: (32) 2 413 20 68

Gives official recognition to Belgian films; decides whether a film has sufficient Belgian input to qualify as Belgian

Film Museum Jacques Ledoux
Rue Baron Horta 9
1000 Brussels
Tel: (32) 2 507 83 70
Fax: (32) 2 513 12 72
email: filmmuseum@ledoux.be
Gabrielle Claes
Permanent exhibition of the prehistory of cinema. Five screenings per day – three sound, two silent. Organises one double festival a year: L'Age d'Or Prize and prizes for the distribution of quality films in Belgium

IDEM
227 Chaussee D'ixelles
1050 Brussels
Tel: (32) 2 640 77 31
Fax: (32) 2 640 98 56
Trade association for television producers

Radio-Télévision Belge de la Communauté Française (RTBF)
Blvd Auguste Reyers 52
1044 Brussels
Tel: (32) 2 737 21 11
Fax: (32) 2 737 25 56
Administrateur Général: Jean-Louis Stalport
Public broadcaster responsible for French language services

VRT
Auguste Reyerslaan 52
1043 Brussels
Tel: (32) 2 741 3111
Fax: (32) 2 734 9351
Managing Director: Bert De Graeve
Television: Piet Van Roe
Radio: Chris Cleeren
Public television and radio station serving Dutch speaking Flemish community in Belgium

Denmark

Danish Film Institute/Archive and Cinemateque
Vognmagergade 10
DK – 1120 Copenhagen
Tel: (45) 3374 3400/3374 3575
Fax: (45) 3374 3599
The Archive and Cinematheque, founded in 1941, is one of the world's oldest film archives. It has a collection of 25,000 titles from almost every genre and country, and has daily screenings. There is also an extensive library of books and pamphlets, periodicals, clippings, posters and stills

DFI (Danish Film Institute)
Vognmagergade 10
DK – 1120 Copenhagen
Tel: (45) 33 74 34 30
Fax: (45) 33 74 34 01
An autonomous self-governing body under the auspices of the Ministry of Culture, financed through the state budget. Provides funding for the production of Danish feature films, shorts and documentaries, and also supports distribution and exhibition of feature films. Promotes Danish films abroad and finances two community access workshops. FurthermoreDFI purchases and rents out shorts and documentaries on 16mm and video to educational institutions/Libraries and private persons

Danmarks Radio (DR)
Morkhojvej 170
2860 Soborg
Tel: (45) 35 20 30 40
Fax: (45) 35 20 26 44
Public service television and radio network

Film-og TV
Arbejderforeningen
Danish Film and Television
Workers Union
Kongens Nytorv 21
Baghuset 3. sal
1050 Copenhagen K
Tel: (45) 33 14 33 55
Fax: (45) 33 14 33 03
Trade union which organises film, video and television workers, and maintains the professional, social, economic and artistic interests of its members. Negotiates collective agreements for feature films, documentaries, commercials, negotiating contracts, copyright and authors' rights. Also protection of Danish film production

Producenterne
Kronprinsensgade 9B
1114 Copenhagen K
Tel: (45) 33 14 03 11
Fax: (45) 33 14 03 65
The Danish Producers' Association of Film, Television, Video and AV

Finland

AVEK – The Promotion Centre for Audio-visual Culture in Finland
Hietaniemenkatu 2
FIN – 00100 Helsinki
Tel: (358) 9 43152350

Fax: (358) 9 43152388
email: avek@avek.kopiosto.fi
Website: www.kopiostofi/avek
AVEK was established in 1987 to promote cinemas, video and television culture. It is responsible for the management of funds arising from authors' copyright entitlements and is used for authors' common purposes (the blank tape levy). AVEK's support activities cover the entire field of audio-visual culture, emphasis being on the production support of short films, documentaries and media art. The other two activity sections are training of the professionals working in the audio-visual field and audiovisual culture in general

Finnish Film Archive/Suomen Elokuva-arkisto
Pursimiehenkatu 29-31 A
PO Box 177
FIN-00151
Helsinki
Tel: (358) 9 615 400
Fax: (358) 9 615 40 242
email: sea@sea.fi
Website: www.sea.fi
Matti Lukkarila
Stock: 10,000 feature film titles; 30,000 shorts and spots; 18,000 video cassettes; 20,000 books and scripts; 330,000 different stills, 110,000 posters; and 40,000 documentation files. The archive arranges regular screenings in Helsinki and other cities. Documentation, database, publications (Finnish national filmography). Publications

Finnish Film Foundation
Kanavakatu 12
Fin-Helsinki
Tel: (358) 0 6220 300
Fax: (358) 0 6220 3050
Film funding for script, development and production of feature film and documentaries. Audio post production and auditorio services. Distribution and screening support. International activities (cultural export and promotion of Finnish Film)

France

Les Archives du Film du Centre National de la Cinématographie
7 bis rue Alexandre Turpault
78390 Bois d'Arcy
Tel: (33) 1 30 14 80 00
Fax: (33) 1 34 60 52 25
Michelle Aubert
The film collection includes some 131,000 titles, mostly French

features, documentaries and shorts from 1895 to date through the new legal deposit for films which includes all categories of films shown in cinemas including foreign releases. Since 1991, a special pluriannual programme for copying early films, including nitrate film, has been set up. So far, some 8,000 titles have been restored including the whole of the Lumière brothers film production from 1895 to 1905 which covers 1,400 short titles. A detailed catalogue of the Lumiére production is available in print and CD-Rom. Enquiries and viewing facilities for film are available on demand

Bibliothèque du Film (BIFI)
100 rue du Faubourg Saint-Antoine
75012 Paris
Tel: (33-1) 53 02 22 30
Fax: (33-1) 53 02 22 39
Website: www.bifi.fr
Contact: Laurent Billia
Documentation
Contact: Marc Vernet
Head Manager

Centre National de la Cinématographie (CNC)
rue de Lübeck 12
75016 Paris
Tel: (33) 1 45 05 1440
Fax: (33) 1 47 55 04 91
Director-General: Dominique Wallon, Press, Public & Internal Relations: Patrick Ciercoles
A government institution, under the auspices of the Ministry of Culture. Its areas of concern are: the economics of cinema and the audio-visual industries; film regulation; the promotion of the cinema industries and the protection of cinema heritage. Offers financial assistance in all aspects of French cinema (production, exhibition, distribution etc). In 1986, the CNC was made responsible for the system of aid offered to the production of films made for television. These include fiction films, animated films and documentaries. The aim here corresponds to one of the principal objectives of public sector funding, where support is given to the French television industry while the development of a high standard of television is encouraged

Cinémathèque Française – Musée du Cinéma
4, rue de Longchamp
75016 Paris
Tel: (33) 1 53 65 74 57
Fax: (33) 1 53 65 74 97

Marianne de Fleury
Founded in 1936 by Henri Langlois, Georges Franju and Jean Mitry to save, conserve and show films. Now houses a cinema museum, screening theatres, library and stills and posters library

Fédération de la Production Cinématographique Française
rue du Cirque 5
75008 Paris
Tel: (33) 1 42 25 70 63
Fax: (33) 1 42 25 94 27
Alain Poiré, Pascal Rogard
National federation of French cinema production

Fédération Nationale des Distributeurs de Films
boulevard Malesherbes 43
75008 Paris
Tel: (33) 1 42 66 05 32
Fax: (33) 1 42 66 96 92
President: Fabienne Vonier, Délégué général: Antoine Virenque
National federation of film distributors

Fédération Nationale des Industries Techniques duCinéma et de l'Audio-visuel
(FITCA)
avenue Marceau 50
75008 Paris
Tel: (33) 1 47 23 75 76
Fax: (33) 1 47 23 70 47
A federation of technical trade associations which acts as intermediary between its members and their market. Maintains a database on all technical aspects of production, and helps French and European companies find suitable partners for research and development or commercial ventures

Forum des images (ex Vidéothèque de Paris)
Forum des Halles
2, Grande Galerie
Porte Saint-Eustache
75001 Paris
Tel: 01 44 76 62 00
Website: www.vdp.fr/

France 2
avenue Montaigne 22
75008 Paris
Tel: (33) 1 44 21 42 42
Fax: (33) 1 44 21 51 45
France's main public service terrestrial television channel

Institut National de l'Audiovisuel (INA)
4, avenue de l'Europe

94366 Bry-sur-Marne Cédex
Tel: (33) 1 49 83 20 00
Fax: (33) 1 49 83 25 80
Website: www.ina.fr/
Television and radio archive; research into new technology; research and publications about broadcasting; production of over 130 first works for television and 15 major series and collections. INA initiates major documentaries and cultural series involving partners from Europe and the rest of the world

TF1
1 Quai du Point du Jour
92656 Boulogne, Cédex
Tel: (33) 1 41 41 12 34
Fax: (33) 1 41 41 29 10
Privatised national television channel

Germany

ARD (Arbeitsgemeinschaft der öffentlich rechtlichen Rundfunkanstalten der Bundesrepublik Deutschland)
Programme Directorate of Deutsches Fernsehen
Arnulfstrasse 42
Postfach 20 06 22
80335 Munich
Tel: (49) 89 5900 01
Fax: (49) 89 5900 32 49
One of the two public service broadcasters in Germany, consisting of 10 independent broadcasting corporations

Beauftragtr der Bundersregierung für Anglelegesheiten der Kulter und de Mediar
Postfach 170290
53108 Bonn
Tel: (49) 228 681 5566
Fax: (49) 228 681 5504
Friedrich-Wilhelm Moog
Awards prizes, grants funds for the production and distribution of German feature films, short films, films for children and young people and documentaries. Promotes film institutes, festivals and specific events. Supervisory body of the Federal Archive for national film production

BVDFP (Bundesverband Deutscher Fernseh – produzenten)
Widenmayerstrasse 32
80538 Munich
Tel: (49) 89 21 21 47 10
Fax: (49) 89 228 55 62
Trade association for independent television producers

Deutsches Filminstitut-DIF
Schaumainkai 41
60596 Frankfurt/Main
Tel: (49) 69 9612200
Fax: (49) 69 620 060
The German Institute for Film
Studies is a non-profit making
organisation, and its remit includes
amassing culturally significant films
and publications and documents
about film; to catalogue them and
make them available for study and
research. It also supports and puts on
screenings of scientific, cultural and
art films

Deutsches Filmmuseum
Schaumainkai 41
60596 Frankfurt/Main
Tel: (49) 69 21 23 33 69
Fax: (49) 69 21 23 78 81
email:filmmuseum@stadt-
frankfurt.de
Permanent and temporary
exhibitions, incorporates the Cinema,
the municipally administered
cinémathéque. Film archive and
collections of equipment,
documentation, stills, posters and
designs, music and sound. Library
and videothéque

Export-Union des Deutschen Films (EXU)
Türkenstrasse 93
80799 München
Tel: (49) 89-390095
Fax: (49) 89-395223
Board of Directors: Jochem Strate,
Antonio Excoustos, Rolf Bahr,
Michel Weber
Managing Director: Christian Dorsch
PR Manager: Susanne Reinker
The Export-Union des Deutschen
Films (EXU) is the official trade
association for the promotion of the
export of German films, with
overseas offices located in London,
Paris, Rome, Madrid, Buenos Aires,
Tokyo, Hongkong, New York and
Los Angeles. The EXU maintains a
presence at all major film and TV
festivals (ie Berlin, Cannes,
Montreal, Toronto, Locarno, Venice,
MIP-TV, MIPCOM and MIFED). It
has a switchboard function for
German film companies working
abroad as well as for foreign
companies and buyers looking for
media outlets and coproduction
facilities in Germany

FFA (Filmförderungsanstalt)
Budapester Strasse 41
10787 Berlin
Tel: (49) 30 254090-0
Fax: (49) 30 254090-57

Rolf Bahr, Dr. Karl Guhlke –
Directors General
The German Federal Film Board
(FFA), incorporated under public law,
is the biggest film funding institution
in the country. Its mandate is the all-
round raising of standards of quality
in German film and cinema and the
improvement of the economic
structure of the film industry. The
annual budget of about 60 million
Deutschmarks is granted by a levy
raised from all major German
cinemas and video providers. The
administrative council of 29 members
is a reprsentative cross section of the
German film industry including
members of the government's upper
and lower house as well as public
and private TV stations. Funding is
offered in the following areas: full-
length features, shorts, screenplays,
marketing, exhibition, additional
prints and professional training. The
Export-Union des Deutschen Films
e.V. largely represents the FFA's
interests abroad

Film Förderung
Hamburg GmbH
Friedensalle14-16
22765 Hamburg
Tel: (49) 40 39837-0
Fax: (49) 40 39837-10
Managing director: Eva Hubert
Subsidies available for: script
development; pre-production; co-
production and distribution

FSK (Freiwillige Selbstkontrolle der Filmwirtschaft)
Kreuzberger Ring 56
65205 Wiesbaden
Tel: (49) 611 77 891 0
Fax: (49) 611 77 891 39
Film industry voluntary self-
regulatory body. Activities are: to
examine together with official
competent representatives which
films can be shown to minors under
18 year olds and under; to discuss the
examination of films with youth
groups; to organise seminars on the
study of film, videos and new media.
Adult films (age group from 18) are
approved only by delegates of films
and video industry

Kunsthochschule für Medien Köln (Academy of Media Arts)
Peter-Welter-Platz 2
50676
Cologne
Tel: (49) 221 201890
Fax: (49) 221 2018917
The first academy of Arts in

Germany to embrace all the audio-
visual media. It offers an Audio-
visual Media graduate programme
concentrating on the areas of
Television/Film, Media Art, Media
Design and Art and Media Science

Stiftung Deutsche Kinemathek
Heerstr 18-20
14052 Berlin
Tel: (49) 30 3009030
Fax: (49) 30 30090313
Hans Helmut Prinzler
German Film Archive with collection
of German and foreign films, cine-
historical documents and equipment
(approx. 10,000 films, over a million
photographs, around 20,000 posters,
15,000 set-design and costume
sketches, projectors, camera and
accessories from the early days of
cinema to the 80s). Member of FIAF

ZDF (Zweites Deutsches Fernsehen)
ZDF-Strasse
PO Box 4040
55100 Mainz
Tel: (49) 6131 702060
Fax: (49) 6131 702052
A major public service broadcaster in
Germany

Greece

ERT SA (Hellenic Broadcasting Corporation)
Messoghion 402
15342 Aghia Paraskevi
Athens
Tel: (30) 1 639 0772
Fax: (30) 1 639 0652
National public television and radio
broadcaster, for information,
education and entertainment

Greek Film Centre
10 Panepistimiou Avenue
10671 Athens
Tel: (30) 1 361 7633/363 4586
Fax: (30) 1 361 4336
Governmental organisation under the
auspices of the Ministry of Culture.
Grants subsidies for production,
promotion and distribution

Ministry of Culture
Cinema Department
Boulinas Street 20
10682 Athens
Tel: (30) 1 322 4737

Ireland

An Chomhairle Ealaíon/The Arts Council
70 Merrion Square

Dublin 2
Tel: (353) 1 6180200
Fax: (353) 1 6761302
The Arts Council/An Chomhairle Ealaion is the principal channel of Government funding for the arts in Ireland. In the area of film the Council focuses its support on the development of film as an art form and on the individual film-maker as artist. With a budget for film of £975,000 in 1998 the Council supports a national film centre and archive, four film festivals and a number of film resource organisations. It administers an awards scheme for the production of short dramas, experimental films and community video. It also co-operates with the Irish Film Board and RTE Television in Frameworks, an animation awards scheme

Bord Scannán na hÉireann/Irish Film Board
Rockfort House
St. Augustine Street
Galway
Tel: (353) 91 561398
Fax: (353) 91 561405
email: film@iol.ie
Website: www.iol.ie/filmboard
Chief Executive: Rod Stoneman
Business Manager: Leslie Kelly
Applications Officer: Paddy Hayes
Information Co-ordinator: Cynthis O'Murchu
Bord Scannán na hÉireann promotes the creative and commercial elements of Irish film-making and film culture for a home and international audience. Each year it supports a number of film projects by providing development and production loans. Normally three submission deadlines annually. Dates and application procedures available from the office

Film Censor's Office
16 Harcourt Terrace
Dublin 2
Tel: (353) 1 676 1985
Fax: (353) 1 676 1898
Sheamus Smith
The Official Film Censor is appointed by the Irish Government to consider and classify all feature films and videos distributed in Ireland

Film Institute of Ireland
Irish Film Centre
6 Eustace Street, Temple Bar
Dublin 2
Tel: (353) 1 679 5744/677 8788
Fax: (353) 1 677 8755
email: info@ifc.ie
The Film Institute promotes film culture through a wide range of

activities in film exhibition and distribution, film/media education, various training programmes and the Irish Film Archive. Its premises, the Irish Film Centre in Temple Bar, are also home to Film Base, MEDIA Desk, The Junior Dublin Film Festival, The Federation of Irish Film Societies, and Hubbard Casting. The Building has conference facilities, a bar cafe and a shop as well as 2 cinemas seating 260 and 115

RTE (Radio Telefis Eireann)
Donnybrook
Dublin 4
Tel: (353) 1 208 3111
Fax: (353) 1 208 3080
Public service national broadcaster

Italy

ANICA (Associazione Nazionale Industrie Cinematografiche e Audiovisive)
Viale Regina Margherita 286
00198 Rome
Tel: (39) 6 442 31 480
Fax: (39) 6 442 31 296/6 440 41 28
Gino de Dominicis
Trade association for television and movie producers and distributors, representing technical industries (post-production companies/dubbing/studios/labs); home video producers and distributors; television and radio broadcasters

Centro Sperimentale di Cinematografia Cineteca Nazionale
Via Tuscolana 1524
00173 Rome
Tel: (39) 6 722 941
Fax: (39) 6 721 1619

Fininvest Television
Viale Europa 48
20093 Cologno Monzese, Milan
Tel: (39) 2 251 41
Fax: (39) 2 251 47031
Adriano Galliani
Major competitor to RAI, running television channels Canale 5, Italia Uno and Rete Quattro

Fondazione Cineteca Italiana
Via Palestro 16
20121 Milan
Tel: (39) 2 76022847
Fax: (39) 2 798289
email: cinetecaitaliana@digibank.it
Film Museum
Palazzo Dugnani
Via D Manin 2/b

Milan
Tel: (39) 2 6554977
Gianni Comencini
Film archive, film museum. Set up to promote the preservation of film as art and historical document, and to promote the development of cinema art and culture

Istituto Luce S.p.A
Via Tuscolana 1055
00173 Rome
Tel: (39) 6 722931/729921
Fax: (39) 6 7222493/7221127
Presiolente e Administratore
Delegato: Angelo Guglieluni Diretore
Ufficio Stampa e Pubblicità: Patrizia de Cesari
Diretiore Commerciale: Leonardo Tiberi
Created to spread culture and education through cinema. It invests in film, distributes films of cultural interest and holds Italy's largest archive

Museo Nazionale del Cinema
Via Montebello 15
10124 Turin
Tel: (39) 11 8154230
Fax: (39) 11 8122503
Giuliano Soria, Paolo Bertetto, Sergio Toffetti, Donata Pesenti Campagnoni, Luciana Spina. The museum represents photography, pre-cinema and cinema history. Its collections include films, books and periodicals, posters, photographs and cinema ephemera

RAI (Radiotelevisione Italiana)
Viale Mazzini 14
00195 Rome
Tel: (39) 6 361 3608
Fax: (39) 6 323 1010
Italian state broadcaster

Luxembourg

Surproduction S.A.S
Via del Rosso Fiorentino 2/b
50142 Firenze
Tel: (39) 055 712127
Fax: (39) 055 712127
Nicola Melloni

Cinémathèque Municipale – Ville de Luxembourg
rue Eugène Ruppert 10
2453 Luxembourg
Tel: (352) 4796 2644
Fax: (352) 40 75 19
Official Luxembourg film archive, preserving international film heritage. Daily screenings every year 'Live Cinema' performances – silent films with music. Member of FIAF,

(13,000 prints/35mm, 16mm, 70mm)

CLT Multi Media
Blvd Pierre Frieden 45
1543 Luxembourg
Tel: (352) 42 1 42 2170
Fax: (352) 42 1 42 2756
Director of Corporate
Communications: Karin Schintgen
Radio, television; co production/
distribution; press; rights aquisitions

The Netherlands

Filmmuseum
PO Box 74782
1070 BT Amsterdam
Tel: (31) 20 589 1400
Fax: (31) 20 683 3401
email: filmmuseum@nfm.nl
Website: www.nfm.nl/filmmuseum
Film museum with three public
screenings each day, permanent and
temporary exhibitions, library, film
café and film distribution

Ministry of Education, Culture and Science (OCW)
Film Department
PO Box 25.000
2700LZ Zoetermeer
Tel: (31) 79-3234368
Fax: (31) 79-3234959
Rob Docter, Séamus Cassidy
The film department of the Ministry
is responsible for the development
and maintenance of Dutch film
policy. Various different
organisations for production,
distribution, promotion and
conservation of film are subsidised
by this department

Nederlandse Omroep Stichting (NOS)
Postbus 26444
1202 JJ Hilversum
Tel: (31) 35 779 222
Fax: (31) 35 773 586
Louis Heinsman
Public corporation co-ordinating
three-channel public television

Vereniging van Onafhankelijke Televisie Producenten (OTP)
Sumatralaan 45
PO Box 27900
1202 KV Hilversum
Tel: (31) 35 6231166
Fax: (31) 6280051
Director: Andries M. Overste
Trade association for independent
television producers (currently 14
members)

Portugal

Cinemateca Portuguesa - Museu do Cinema
Rua Barata Salgueiro 39
1200 Lisbon
Tel: (351) 1 54 62 79
Fax: (351) 1 352 31 80
President: João Bénard da Costa, vice
President: José Manuel Costa
National film museum and archive,
preserving, restoring and showing
films. Includes a public
documentation centre, a stills and
posters archive

Instituto Português da Arte Cinematográfica e Audiovisual (IPACA)
Rua S Pedro de Alcântara 45-1o
1250 Lisbon
Tel: (351) 1 346 66 34
Fax: (351) 1 347 27 77
President: Zita Seabra, Vice-
Presidents: Paulo Moreira, Salvato
Telles de Menezes
Assists with subsidies, improvement,
regulation and promotion of the
television and film industry

RTP (Radiotelevisão Portuguesa)
Avenida 5 de Outubro 197
1094 Lisbon Cedex
Tel: (351) 1 793 1774
Fax: (351) 1 793 1758
Maria Manuela Furtado
Public service television with two
channels: RTP1 – general, TV2 –
cultural and sports. One satellite
programme, RTP International,
covering Europe, USA, Africa, Macau

Spain

Academia de las Artes y de las Ciencias Cinematográficas de España
General Oraá 68
28006 Madrid
Tel: (34) 1 563 33 41
Fax: (34) 1 563 26 93

Filmoteca Española
Carretera de la Dehesa de la Villa
s/n, 28040 Madrid
Tel: (34) 1 549 00 11
Fax: (34) 1 549 73 48
Director: José Maria Prado; Deputy
Director: Catherine Gautier;
Documentation: Dolores Devesa
National Film Archive, member of
FIAF since 1958. Preserves 26,000
film titles including a large collection
of newsreels. Provides access to
researchers on its premises. The
library and stills departments are
open to the public. Publishes and co-
produces various books on film every
year. Five daily public screenings
with simultaneous translation or
electronic subtitles are held at the
restored Cine Doré, C/Santa Isabel 3,
in the city centre, where facilities
include a bookshop and cafeteria

ICAA (Instituto de la Cinematografia y de las Artes Audio-visuales)
Ministerio de Cultura
Plaza del Rey No1
28071 Madrid
Tel: (34) 1 532 74 39
Fax: (34) 1 531 92 12
Enrique Balmaseda Arias-Dávila
The promotion, protection and
diffusion of cinema and audiovisual
activities in production, distribution
and exhibition. Gives financial
support in these areas to Spanish
companies. Also involved in the
promotion of Spanish cinema and
audio-visual arts, and their influence
on the different communities within
Spain

RTVE (Radiotelevision Española)
Edificio Prado del Rey – 3a planta
Centro RTVE, Prado Del Rey,
22224 Madrid
Tel: (34) 1 5 81 70 00
Fax: (34) 1 5 81 77 57
Head of International Sales RTVE:
Teresa Moreno
National public service broadcaster,
film producer and distributor

Sweden

Oberoende Filmares Förbund (OFF)/Independent Film Producers Association
Box 27 121
102 52 Stockholm
Tel: (46) 8 665 12 21
Fax: (46) 8 663 66 55
email: off.se
OFF is a non-profit organisation,
founded 1984, with some 300
members. OFF promotes the special
interests of filmmakers and
independent Swedish producers of
documentaries, short and feature
films. Our purpose is twofold: to
raise the quality of Swedish
audiovisual production and to
increase the quantity of domestic
production. OFF works on many
levels. The organisation partakes in
public debate, organises seminars,
publishes a quarterly newsletter, does
lobby-work on a national level
besides nordic and international

networking. OFF aids its producers with legal counsel as well as copyright, economic and insurance policy advisement

Statens biografbyrå
Box 7728
103 95 Stockholm
Tel: (46) 8 24 34 25
Fax: (46) 8 21 01 78
email: registrator@statensbiografbyra.se
Website: www.statensbiografbyra.se
The Swedish National Board of Film Classification (Statens biografbyrå) was founded in 1911. Films and videos must be approved and classified by the Board prior to showing at a public gathering or entertainment. For videos intended for sale or hire, there is a voluntary system of advance examination

Svenska Filminstitutet (Swedish Film Institute)
Box 27 126
Filmhuset
Borgvägen 1-5
S-10252 Stockholm
Tel: (46) 8 665 11 00
Fax: (46) 8 661 18 20
email: janerik.billinger@sfi.se
Jan-Erik Billinger: Head of the Information Department
The Swedish Film Institute is the central organisation for Swedish cinema. Its activities are to: support the production of Swedish films of high merit; promote the distribution and exhibition of quality films; preserve films and materials of interest to cinematic and cultural history and promote Swedish cinematic culture internationally

Sveriges Biografägareförbund
Box 1147
S 171 23 Solna
Tel: (946) 8 735 97 80
Fax: (946) 8 730 25 60
The Swedish Exhibitors Association is a joint association for Swedish cinema owners

Sveriges Filmuthyrareförening upa
Box 23021
S-10435 Stockholm
Tel: (946) 8 441 55 70
Fax: (946) 8 34 38 10
Kay Wall
The Swedish Film Distributors Association is a joint association for film distributors

Swedish Women's Film Association
Po Box 27182

S-10251 Stockholm
Visitors address: Filmhuset, Borgvägen 5
Tel: (46) 8 665 1100/1293
Fax: (46) 8 666 3748
Anna Hallberg
Workshops, seminars, festivals and international exchange programme

The MEDIA II Programme

MEDIA II is a programme of the European Union, managed by the European Commission in Brussels. MEDIA II, which follows on from MEDIA I, started in 1996 and will conclude in the year 2000

European Commission
Directorate General X:
Information, Communication, Culture, Audio-visual
rue de la Loi, 200
1040 Brussels, Belgium
Tel: (32) 2 299 11 11
Fax: (32) 2 299 92 14
Head of Programme: Jacques Delmoly

MEDIA Contacts
As part of a network of 29 Desks and Antennae throughout Europe, the members of the UK MEDIA team listed below should be the first point of contact for UK companies seeking information and advice of the MEDIA Programme. Guidelines and application forms for al the MEDIA II schemes are available from them. They produce regular newsletters and other printed information detailing upcoming deadlines, training courses and markets

MEDIA Services England
249 West George Street
Glasgow G2 4QE
Tel: 0870 0100 791
Fax: 0141 302 1778
email: media.england@scottishscreen.com
Chris Miller

MEDIA Antenna Scotland
c/o Scottish Screen
249 West George Street
Glasgow G2 4RB
Tel: 0141 302 1776/7
Fax: 0141 302 1778
email: media.scotland@scottishscreen.com
Contact: Louise Scott or Pam Murray

MEDIA Antenna Cymru Wales
The Bank, 10 Mount Stuart Square
Cardiff CF10 5EE
Llantrisant Road
Cardiff CF5 2PU
Tel: 01222 333 304
Fax: 01222 333 320
email: antenna@sgrinwales.demon.co.uk
Website: www.screenwales.org.uk/
Contact: Gwarr Hughes

MEDIA Northern Ireland

MEDIA Services Northern Ireland
c/o Northrn Ireland Film
Commission
21 Ormeau Avenue
Belfast BT2 8HD
Tel: 01232 232 444
Fax: 01232 239 918
email: media@nifc.com
Heike Meyer -Döring

Intermediary Organisations

The MEDIA II Programme
contracted three companies to act as
Intermediary Organisations (IOs) for
the five year period of MEDIA II to
assist Brussels in administering and
processing applications in each of the
three areas of support (Training,
Development and Distribution) and
dealing with payments.

TRAINING

Media Research and Consultancy Spain

(MRC) Madrid
Claudio Coello 43 – 2OD
E-28001 Madrid, Spain
Tel: (34) 1 577 94 04
Fax: (34) 1 575 71 99
email: mrc@mad.servicom.es
Head of office: Fernando Labrada

DEVELOPMENT

European Media Development Agency

(EMDA) London
39c Highbury Place
London N5 1QP
Tel: (44) 171 226 9903
Fax: (44) 171 354 2706
Head of office: David Kavanagh

DISTRIBUTION

D&S Media Services

Brussels, Munich and Dublin
Rue Pere Deken 33
B – 1040 Brussels
Tel: (32) 2 743 22 44
Fax: (32) 2 743 22 45
Head of office: John Dick

CARTOON (European Association of Animation Film)

418 Boulevard Lambermont
1030 Brussels, Belgium
Tel: (32) 2 245 12 00
Fax: (32) 2 245 46 89
email: cartoon@skynet.be
Website: www.cartoon-media.be
Contact: Corinne Jenart, Marc
Vandeweyer
CARTOON, based in Brussels, is a
European animation network which
organises the annual CARTOON
FORUM, co-ordinates the grouping
of European animation studios and
runs specialist training courses in
animation

EXHIBITION NETWORKS

Europa Cinemas

54, rue Beaubourg
F-75 003 Paris, France
Tel: (33) 1 42 71 53 70
Fax: (33) 1 42 71 47 55
email: europacinema@magic.fr
Website: www.europa-cinemas.org
Claude-Eric Poiroux, Fatima
Djoumer
This project encourages screenings
and promotion of European films
through a network of cinemas in
European cities. It offers financial
support for screening European films,
for promotional activities and for
special events

MEDIA Salles

Via Soperga, 2
20127 Milan, Italy
Tel: (39) 02 66 98 44 05
Fax: (39) 02 669 15 74
email: infocinema@mediasalles.it
Website: www.mediasalles.it/
Elisabetta Brunella
MEDIA Salles with Euro Kids
Network is an initiative aimed at
consolidating the availability of
'cinema at the cinema' for children
and young people in Europe, and at
raising the visibility of European film
to a younger audience

PR COMPANIES

These are a selection of companies which handle aspects of publicity and promotion for film and video production companies and/or individual productions

The Associates
34 Clerkenwell Close
London EC1R OAU
Tel: 020 7608 2204
Fax: 020 7250 1756
Catherine Flynn, Alison Marsh

Avalon Publicity Limited
4a Exmoor Street
Lonodn W10 6BD
Tel: 020 7598 7222
Fax: 020 7598 7223
Zoe Godfrey
Specialist entertainment based pr agency providing services from pr and unit publicity to transmission publicity and media launches

Byron Advertising, Marketing and PR
Byron House
Wallingford Road
Uxbridge
Middx UB8 2RW
Tel: 01895 252131
Fax: 01895 252137
Les Barnes

Jacquie Capri Enterprises
3rd Floor
46/47 Chancery Lane
London WC21 1JB
Tel: 020 7831 4545
Fax: 020 7831 2557

Emma Chapman Publicity
25 Frith Street
London W1V 5TR
Tel: 020 7734 9619
Fax: 020 7494 3884
Contact: Emma Chapman

CJP Public Relations Ltd
29a Chippenham Mews
London W9 2AN
Tel: 020 7266 0167
Fax: 020 7266 0165
email: cjp@globalnet.co.uk
Carolyn Jardine

Max Clifford Associates
109 New Bond Street
London W1Y 9AA
Tel: 020 7408 2350
Fax: 020 7409 2294
Max Clifford

Corbett and Keene
122 Wardour Street
London W1V 3LA
Tel: 020 7494 3478
Fax: 020 7734 2024
Ginger Corbett, Sara Keene, Charlotte Tudor

Dennis Davidson Associates (DDA)
Royalty House
72-74 Dean Street
London W1V 5HB
Tel: 020 7439 6391
Fax: 020 7437 6358
email: info@ddapr.com
Dennis Davidson, Stacy Wood, Chris Paton

FEREF Associates
14-17 Wells Mews
London W1A 1ET
Tel: 020 7580 6546
Fax: 020 7631 3156
Peter Andrews, Ken Paul, Robin Behling, David Kemp, Brian Bysouth, Gareth Shepherd

Soren Fischer
67 Parkway Drive
Queens Park
Bournemouth BH8 9JS
Tel: 01202 393033
Fax: 01202 301516
email: Sorenfischer@Compuserve.com
Soren Fischer
PR co-ordinator and British representative, Berlin Film Festival

Lynne Franks PR
327-329 Harrow Road
London W9 3RB
Tel: 020 7724 6777
Fax: 020 7724 8484
Julian Henry

Sue Hyman Associates
70 Chalk Farm Road
London NW1 8AN
Tel: 020 7485 8489/5842
Fax: 020 7267 4715
email: sue.hyman.@btinternet.com
Sue Hyman

JAC Publicity
1st Floor, Playhouse Court
64 Southwark Bridge Road
London SE1 0AS
Tel: 020 7261 1211
Fax: 020 7261 1214
Claire Forbes

Richard Laver Publicity
3 Troy Court
Kensington High Street
London W8 7RA
Tel: 020 7937 7322
Fax: 020 7937 8670
email: Richard@Lavpub.u-net.com
Richard Laver

McDonald and Rutter
14-18 Ham Yard
Gt. Windmill Street
London W1P 7PD
Tel: 020 7734 9009
Fax: 020 7734 1151
email: mcdonaldrutter@btinternet.com
Charles McDonald, Jonathan Rutter

New Focus Communications Ltd
Thorpe House
44 Spittal Street
Marlow
Bucks, SL7 1DB
Tel: 01628 488533
Fax: 01628 488633
Ms Ray Hodges, MCam MiPR

Optimum Communications
34 Hanway Street
London W1P 9DE
Tel: 020 7580 5352
Fax: 020 7636 3945
Nigel Passingham

Porter Frith Publicity & Marketing
26 Danbury Street
London N1 8JU
Tel: 020 7359 3734
Fax: 020 7226 5897
Sue Porter, Liz Frith

S.S.A. Public Relations
Suite 323/324
The Linen Hall
162-168 Regent Street
London W1R 5TB
Tel: 020 7494 2755
Fax: 020 7494 2833
Céline Brook, Andrew O'Driscoll
S.S.A Public Relations is a full service public relations firm that

provides trade and consumer
publicity for a wide range of
corporate and entertainment clients.
The company specialises in key
areas, representing television and
theatrical film production and
distribution companies

Judy Tarlo Associates
85 Ashworth Mansions
Grantully Road
London W9 ILN
Tel: 020 7286 6025
Fax: 020 7289 8969
Judy Tarlo, Louise Hanson

Peter Thompson Associates
134 Great Portland Street
London W1N 5PH
Tel: 020 7436 5991/2
Fax: 020 7436 0509
Peter Thompson, Amanda Malpass

Town House Publicity
45 Islington Park Street
London N1 1QB
Tel: 020 7226 7450
Fax: 020 7359 6026
email: townhouse@lineone.net
Mary Fulton

UpFront Television Ltd
39-41 New Oxford Street
London WC1A 1BH
Tel: 020 7836 7701
Fax: 020 7836 7702
email: upfront@binternet.com

Warren Cowan/Phil Symes Associates
35 Soho Square
London W1V 6AX
Tel: 020 7439 3535
Fax: 020 7439 3737
Phil Symes, Warren Cowan

Stella Wilson Publicity
130 Calabria Road
London N5 1HT
Tel: 020 7354 5672
Fax: 020 7354 2242
email: stella@starmaker.demon.co.uk
Stella Wilson

PRESS CONTACTS

The following is a list of magazines and newspapers which cover film, television and video. Circulation figures may have altered since going to press. Also listed are the news and photo agencies which handle media news syndication, and television and radio programmes concerned with the visual media

6degrees.co.uk
220 Tower Bridge Road
London SE1 2UP
Tel: 020 7407 2728
Fax: 020 7357 7654
email: publisher@6degrees.co.uk
Website: www.6degrees.co.uk
Publisher: Justin Bowyer
Editor: Nick Walker
6degrees is the online UK independent film magazine, covering independ, art house and world cinema news, reviews and article – plus free weekly newsletter

19 (Monthly)
IPC Magazines
King's Reach Tower
Stamford Street
London SE1 9LS
Tel: 020 7261 6410
Fax: 020 7261 7634
Film: Corrine Barraclough
Magazine for young women
Lead time: 8 weeks
Circulation: 187,740

Arena (Bi-monthly)
Third Floor, Block A
Exmouth House
Pine Street
London EC1R 0JL
Tel: 020 7689 2266
Fax: 020 7689 0900
Magazine for men covering general interest, film, literature, music and fashion
Lead time: 6-8 weeks
Circulation: 100,000

Ariel (Weekly, Tues)
Room 123, Henry Wood House
3 and 6 Langham Place
London W1A 1AA
Tel: 020 7765 3623
Fax: 020 7765 3646

Editor: Robin Reynolds
BBC staff magazine
Lead time: Tuesday before publication
Circulation: 26,000

Art Monthly
Britannia Art Publications, Suite 17
26 Charing Cross Road
London WC2H 0DG
Tel: 020 7240 0389
Fax: 020 7497 0726
email: artmonthly@compuserve.com
Editor: Patricia Bickers
Aimed at artists, art dealers, teachers, students, collectors, arts administrators, and all those interested in contemporary visual art
Lead time: 4 weeks
Circulation: 4,000 plus

Asian Times (Weekly, Tues)
138-148 Cambridge Heath Road
London E1 5QJ
Tel: 020 7702 8012
Fax: 020 7702 7937
Editor: Sanjay Gohil
National, weekly newspaper for Britain's English-speaking, Asian community
Press day: Thurs
Circulation: 30,000

The Big Issue (Weekly, Mon)
236-240 Pentonville Road
Kings Cross
London N1 9JY
Tel: 020 7418 0418
Fax: 020 7418 0427
email: london@bigissue.com
Website: www.bigissue.com
Editor: Becky Gardiner
Arts: Tina Jackson
Film editor: Xan Brooks
General interest magazine, with emphasis on homelessness. Sold by the homeless
Lead time: Tues, 3 weeks before
Circulation: ABC figure 142,937

British Film and TV Facilities Journal
Gullimanor Ltd
12 Eton Street
Richmond upon Thames
Surrey TW9 1EE
Tel: 020 8332 1644
Fax: 020 8332 1755

email: editorial@cdial.pipex.com
Editor: Colin Lenthall
Journal for those working in British film, TV and video industry

British Film (Quarterly)
Arts and Entertainment Publishing Ltd
24 Sandyford Place
Glasgow G3 7NG
Tel: 0141 221 4241
Fax: 0141 221 4247
Editor: Robert McColl
British Film covers Film making and broadcasting within the UK. Primarily a trade magazine distributed to all production companies and facility houses within the UK
Circulation: 20,000

Broadcast (Weekly, Fri)
EMAP Media
33-39 Bowling Green Lane
London EC1R 0DA
Tel: 020 7505 8014
Fax: 020 7505 8050
Publisher/Editor: Jon Baker
Broadcasting industry news magazine with coverage of TV, radio, cable and satellite, corporate production and international programming and distribution Press day: Wed. Lead time: 2 weeks Circulation: 13,556

The Business of Film (Monthly)
Suite 3
2a New Cavendish Street
London W1M 7RP
Tel: 020 7486 1996
Fax: 020 7486 1969
Publisher/executive editor: Elspeth Tavares
Aimed at film industry professionals – producers, distributors, exhibitors, investors, financiers
Lead time: 2 weeks

Cable and Satellite Communications International (Monthly)
104 City View
463 Bethnal Green Road
London E2 9QY
Tel: 020 7613 5553
Fax: 020 7729 7723
email:de81@dial.pipex.com
Editor: Joss Armitage
Business magazine for professionals

in the cable and satellite television industry
Circulation: 4,029

Capital Gay (Weekly, Thur)
1 Tavistock Chambers
Bloomsbury Way
London WC1A 2SE
Tel: 020 7242 2750
Fax: 020 7242 3334
Film editor: Pas Paschal
TV editor: Michael Mason
Newspaper for lesbians and gay men in the South East combining news, features, arts and entertainment, what's on guide
Lead time: 1 week (Mon)
Circulation: 22,000

Caribbean Times
incorporating African Times (Weekly, Mon)
138-148 Cambridge Heath Road
London E1 5QJ
Tel: 020 7702 8012
Fax: 020 7702 7937
Editor: Clive Morgan
Tabloid dealing with issues pertinent to community it serves
Press day: Fri
Circulation: 25,000

City Life (Fortnightly)
164 Deansgate
Manchester M60 2RD
Tel: 0161 839 1416
Fax: 0161 839 1488
Website: www.poptel.org.uk/citylife/
Editor: Chris Sharratt
Film editor: Melanie Dakin
What's on in and around Greater Manchester
Circulation: 20,000

COIL (journal of the moving image)
PO Box 14649
London EC2A 3RD
Tel: 0411 069569
Fax: 020 7613 0378
email: probascis@easynet.co.uk
Website: www.easyweb.easynet.co.uk/~probascis
Frequency: two issues per year
Editor: Giles Lane
Project Manager: Joan Johnston

Company (Monthly)
National Magazine House
72 Broadwick Street
London W1V 2BP
Tel: 020 7439 5000
Fax: 020 7439 5117
Glossy magazine for women aged 18-30
Lead time: 10 weeks
Circulation: 272,160

Cosmopolitan (Monthly)
National Magazine House
72 Broadwick Street
London W1V 2BP
Tel: 020 7439 5000
Fax: 020 7439 5101
Editor: Mandi Norwood
Arts/General: Sarah Kennedy
For women aged 18-35
Lead time: 12 weeks
Circulation: 461,080

Creation (Monthly)
MDI Ltd
30/31 Islington Green
London N1 8DU
Tel: 020 7226 8585
Fax: 020 7226 8586
Editor: Clare Mount
Film, television, new media publication
Circulation: 8,000

Creative Review (Monthly)
St. Giles House
50 Poland Street
London W1V 4AX
Tel: 020 7439 4222
Fax: 020 7734 6748
Editor: Lewis Blackwell
Publisher: Morag Arman-Addey
Trade paper for creative people covering film, advertising and design. Film reviews, profiles and technical features
Lead time: 4 weeks
Circulation: 15,206

Daily Mail
Northcliffe House
2 Derry Street
London W8 5TT
Tel: 020 7938 6000
Fax: 020 7937 4463
Chief showbusiness writer: Baz Bamigboye
Film: Christopher Tookey
TV: Peter Paterson
National daily newspaper
Circulation: 2,163,676

Daily Star The
Ludgate House
245 Blackfriars Road
London SE1 9UX
Tel: 020 7928 8000
Fax: 020 7922 7962
Film: Sandro Monetti
TV: Pat Codd
Video: Sandro Monetti and Pat Codd
National daily newspaper
Circulation: 654,866

Daily Telegraph
1 Canada Square
Canary Wharf
London E14 5DT
Tel: 020 7538 5000
Fax: 020 7538 6242

Film critic: Quentin Curtis
Arts Editor: Sarah Crompton
TV: Marsha Dunstan
National daily newspaper
Lead time: 1 week
Circulation: 1,117,439

Diva (Monthly)
Ground Floor
Worldwide House
116-134 Bayham Street
London NW1 0BA
Tel: 020 7482 2576
Fax: 020 7284 0329
email: diva@gaytimes.co.uk
Website: www.gaytimes.co.uk
Editor: Gillian Rodgerson
Lesbian news and culture
Lead times: 4-6 weeks
Circulation: 35,000

Eclipse (Monthly)
Phoenix Magazines Limited
PO Box 33, Liskeard
Cornwall PL14 4YX
Tel: 01579 344313
Fax: (01579) 344313
email: phoenixmgs@aol.com
Editor: Simon Clarke
Magazine covering the entire spectrum of science fiction in books, cinema, television and comics, along with role playing and computer games. News, reviews, interviews, competitions, features, profiles, etc.
Lead time: six weeks
Circulation: 15,000

Economist The (Weekly)
25 St James's Street
London SW1A 1HG
Tel: 020 7830 7000
Fax: 020 7839 2968
Website: www.economist.com
Film/video/television (cultural): Tony Thomas;
(business): Frances Cairncross
International coverage of major political, social and business developments with arts section
Press day: Wed
Circulation: 327,689

Elle (Monthly)
Endeavour House
189 Shaftesbury Avenue
London WC2H 8JG
Tel: 020 7208 3458
Fax: 020 7208 3599
Editor: Fiona McIntosh
Arts Ed: Jenny Dyson
Glossy magazine aimed at 18-35 year old working women
Lead time: 3 months
Circulation: 205,623

Empire (Monthly)
Mappin House
4 Winsley Street

London W1N 4AR
Tel: 020 7436 1515
Fax: 020 7312 8249
email: empire@delphi.com
Website: www.empireonline.co.uk
Quality film monthly incorporating
features, interviews and movie news
as well as reviews of all new movies
and videos
Lead time: 3 weeks
Circulation: 161,503

The European (Weekly, Thurs)
200 Gray's Inn Road
London WC1X 8NE
Tel: 020 7418 7777
Fax: 020 7713 1840/1870
Arts Editor: Andrew Harvey
Editor in Chief: Andrew Neil
In-depth coverage of European news,
politics and culture
Press day: Thurs
Circulation: 160,511

Evening Standard (Mon-Fri)
Northcliffe House
2 Derry Street
London W8 5EE
Tel: 020 7938 2648
Fax: 020 7937 3193
Film: Alexander Walker, Neil
Norman
Media editor: Victor Sebestyen
London weekday evening paper
Circulation: 438,136

Everywoman (Monthly)
9 St Alban's Place
London N1 0NX
Tel: 020 7704 8440
Fax: 020 7226 9448
Arts editor: Nina Rapi
Feminist magazine covering
mainstream issues
Lead time: 6 weeks
Circulation: 15,000

The Express on Sunday
Ludgate House
245 Blackfriars Road
London SE1 9UX
Tel: 020 7928 8000
Fax: 020 7620 1656
Film: Chris Peachment
TV: Nigel Billen
National Sunday newspaper
Circulation: 1,159,759

The Express
Ludgate House
245 Blackfriars Road
London SE1 9UX
Tel: 020 7928 8000
Fax: 020 7620 1654
Showbusiness editor: Annie Leask
Film: Jason Solomons
TV/Theatre critic: Robert Goe-
Langton

Showbusiness Correspondent: David
Wigg
National daily newspaper
Circulation: 1,227,971

The Face (Monthly)
Second Floor, Block A
Exmouth House
Pine Street
London EC1R 0JL
Tel: 020 7689 9999
Fax: 020 7689 0300
Film: Charles Gant, Adam
Higginbotham
Visual-orientated youth culture
magazine: emphasis on music,
fashion and films
Lead time: 4 weeks
Circulation: 100,744

FHM (Monthly)
Mappin House
London W1N 7AR
Tel: 020 7436 1515
Fax: 020 7312 8191
Editor: Anthony Noguera
Deputy Editor: Gavin Newsham
Assistant Editor: Richard Galpin
Men's lifestyle magazine
Lead time: 6 weeks
Circulation: 755,000

Film Guide (Monthly – Free)
Film Guide Ltd
30 North End Road
London W14 0SH
Tel: 020 7602 9790
Fax: 020 7602 2063
Editor: Alan Jones
Film news, features and interviews
Circulation: 125,000

Film (Quarterly)
Suite 210
29 Great Pulteney Street
London W1R 3DD
Tel: 020 7734 9300
Fax: 020 7734 9093
Editor: Tom Brownlie
Thematically-based journal with
information for Film Societies and
other film exhibitors
Lead time: 2 weeks
Circulation: 2,000

Film Review
(Monthly + 4 specials)
Visual Imagination
9 Blades Court, Deodar Road
London SW15 2NU
Tel: 020 8875 1520
Fax: 020 8875 1588
Editor: Neil Corry
Reviews of films on cinema screen
and video; star interviews and
profiles; book and CD reviews
Lead time: 1 month
Circulation: 50,000

Financial Times
1 Southwark Bridge
London SE1 9HL
Tel: 020 7873 3000
Fax: 020 7873 3076
Website: www.ft.com
Arts: Annalena McAfee
Film: Nigel Andrews
TV: Christopher Dunkley
National daily newspaper
Circulation: 316,578

Flicks (Monthly)
25 The Coda Centre
189 Munster Road
London SW6 6AW
Tel: 020 7381 8811
Fax: 020 7381 1811
Editor: Nick Thomas
Managing Director: Val Lyon
Magazine of the film industry, for
sale in cinemas throughout the UK,
or by subscription
Lead time: 6 weeks
Circulation: 200,000

Gay Times (Monthly)
Ground Floor
Worldwide House
116-134 Bayham Street
London NW1 0BA
Tel: 020 7482 2576
Fax: 020 7284 0329
email: edit@gaytimes.co.uk
Arts editor: James Cary Parkes
Britain's leading lesbian and gay
magazine. Extensive film, television
and arts coverage. Round Britain
guide
Lead time: 6-8 weeks
Circulation: 65,000

The Guardian
119 Farringdon Road
London EC1R 3ER
Tel: 020 7278 2332
Fax: 020 7837 2114
Website: www.guardian.co.uk
Film: Derek Malcolm, Johnathan
Romney
TV critic: Nancy Banks-Smith
Media editor: John Mulholland
Arts editor: Claire Armitstead
Head of Press, PR & Corporate
Affairs: Camilla Nicholls
Weekend editor: Deborah Orr
National daily newspaper
Circulation: 407,870

Harpers & Queen (Monthly)
National Magazine House
72 Broadwick Street
London W1V 2BP
Tel: 020 7439 5000
Fax: 020 7439 5506
Arts & Films: Anthony Quinn
Glossy magazine for women

The hottest movie director in town

Whatever you need to know about movies, Film Unlimited is your indispensable internet guide. The website provides an essential online film resource, with detailed rundowns on actors, directors and producers, listings and information on every single cinema in the UK and a schedule for up-coming video releases. There are also updates on British film production and an exclusive insider's guide to all the latest industry gossip. So when you want to get into film, go straight to the biggest movie mogul in Europe.

www.**film**Unlimited.co.uk

Lead time: 12 weeks
Circulation: 93,186

Heat
4th Floor, Mappin House
4 Winsley Street
London W1N 7AR
Tel: 020 7436 1515
Fax: 020 7817 8847
email: heat@ecm.emap.com

The Herald
195 Albion Street
Glasgow G1 1QP
Grays Inn House
127 Clerkenwell Road
London EC1R 5DB
Tel: 020 7405 2121
Fax: 020 7405 1888
Film critic: William Russell (London address)
TV editor: Ken Wright
Scottish daily newspaper
Circulation: 107,527

The Hollywood Reporter (daily; weekly international, Tues)
23 Ridgmount Street
London W1CE 7AH
Tel: 020 7332 6686
Fax: 020 7323 5513
email: cdunkley@hollywoodreporter.com
European bureau chief: Ray Bennett
Deputy bureau chief/European News
Editor: Cathy Dunkley
Showbusiness trade paper
Circulation: 39,000

i-D Magazine (Monthly)
Universal House
251-255 Tottenham Court Road
London W1P 0AE
Tel: 020 7813 6170
Fax: 020 7813 6179
Film & TV: David Sandhu
Youth/fashion magazine with film features
Lead time: 8 weeks
Circulation: 45,000

Illustrated London News (2 pa)
20 Upper Ground
London SE1 9PF
Tel: 020 7805 5555
Fax: 020 7805 5911
Editor: Alison Booth
News, pictorial record and commentary, and a guide to coming events
Lead time: 8-10 weeks
Circulation: 30,000

In Camera (Quarterly)
Professional Motion Imaging
PO Box 66, Hemel Hempstead
Herts HP1 1JU

Tel: 01442 844875
Fax: 01442 844987
Editor: Josephine Ober
Business editor: Giosi Gallotli
Journal for motion picture industry, primarily for cinematographers, but also for other technicians and anyone in the industry
Lead time: 4 weeks
Circulation: 45,000

The Independent on Sunday
1 Canada Square
Canary Wharf
London E14 5DL
Tel: 020 7293 2000
Fax: 020 7293 2027
Film critic: Kevin Jackson
TV: Robin Boss
National Sunday newspaper
Lead time: 2 weeks
Circulation: 275,000

The Independent
1 Canada Square
Canary Wharf
London E14 5DL
Tel: 020 7293 2000
Fax: 020 7293 2047
Film: Sam Taylor
TV: Tom Sutcliffe, Gerard Gilbert
Media: Rob Brown
National daily newspaper
Circulation: 257,594

International Connection
1st Floor, 23 South Quay
Gt Yarmouth
Norfolk NR30 2RG
Tel: 07071 224091
Fax: 01493 330565
Film and TV industry business magazine

Interzone (Monthly)
217 Preston Drove
Brighton BN1 6FL
Tel: 01273 504710
Editor: David Pringle
Film: Nick Lowe
Science-fiction magazine
Lead time: 8 weeks
Circulation: 10,000

Jewish Chronicle (Weekly, Friday)
25 Furnival Street
London EC4A 1JT
Tel: 020 7405 9252
Editor: Edward J Temko
Film critic: Alan Montague
TV critic: Helen Jacobus
Lead time: 2 days
Press day: Wed
Circulation: 47,273

The List
(Fortnightly, Thur)
14 High Street

Edinburgh EH1 1TE
Tel: 0131 558 1191
Fax: 0131 557 8500
email: editor@List.co.uk
Editor: Alan Morrison
Film editor: Alan Morrison
TV: Brian Donaldson
Glasgow/Edinburgh events guide
Lead time: 1 week
Circulation: 15,000

Mail on Sunday
Northcliffe House
2 Derry Street
London W8 5TS
Tel: 020 7938 6000
Fax: 020 7937 3829
Film: Jane Preston
TV critic: Brian Viner
National Sunday newspaper
Press day: Fri/Sat
Circulation: 2,137,872

Marie Claire (Monthly)
2 Hatfields
London SE1 9PG
Tel: 020 7261 5240
Fax: 020 7261 5277
Film: Anthony Quinn
Arts: Louise Clark
Women's magazine
Lead time: 3 months
Circulation: 457,034

Media Week (Weekly, Thur)
Quantum House
19 Scarbrook Road
Croydon CR9 1LX
Tel: 020 8565 4317
Fax: 020 8565 4394
email: mweeked@media.emap.co.uk
Editor: Susannah Richmond
News magazine aimed at the advertising and media industries
Press day: Wed
Circulation: 13,209 ABC

Melody Maker (Weekly, Weds)
26th Floor
King's Reach Tower
Stamford Street
London SE1 9LS
Tel: 020 7261 6229
Fax: 020 7261 6706
Editor: Mark Sutherland
Film: Ben Knowles/Colin Kennedy
Pop/rock music newspaper
Press day: Fri
Circulation: 40,349

Midweek (Weekly, Thur/West End, Mon/City)
7-9 Rathbone Street
London W1P 1AF
Tel: 020 7636 6651
Fax: 020 7255 2352
Editor: Bill Williamson

Film editor: Derek Malcolm
General interest male/female London living and arts oriented.
18-35 target age readership
Lead time: 2 weeks
Circulation: 100,000

The Mirror
1 Canada Square
Canary Wharf
London E14 5DP
Tel: 020 7293 3000
Fax: 020 7293 3409
Film: Simon Rose
TV : Tony Purnell
National daily newspaper with daily/weekly film and television column
Circulation: 2,355,285
incorporating The Daily Record (Scottish daily newspaper)

Morning Star
1-3 Ardleigh Road
London N1 4HS
Tel: 020 7254 0033
Fax: 020 7254 5950
Film/TV: Mike Parker
The only national daily oned by its readers as a co-operative. Weekly film and TV reviews
Circulation: 9,000

Movie Plus (Monthly)
Inside Publications
16 Brand Street
Hitchin, Herts SG5 1JE
Tel: 01462 436785
Fax: 01462 436806
Editor: Carole Childs

Moving Pictures (Monthly)
151-153 Wardour Street
London W1V 3TB
Tel: 020 7287 0070
Fax: 020 7287 9637
Editor: Christian de Schutter
Worldwide coverage of television, film, video and new media
Circulation: 8,500

Ms London (Weekly, Mon)
7-9 Rathbone Street
London W1P 1AF
Tel: 020 7636 6651
Fax: 020 7255 2352
Films: Dee Pilgrim
Free magazine with drama, video, film and general arts section
Lead time: 2 weeks
Press day: Thurs
Circulation: 94,100

New Musical Express (Weekly, Wed)
25th Floor
King's Reach Tower
Stamford Street
London SE1 9LS

Tel: 020 7261 5723
Fax: 020 7261 5185
Website: www.nme.com
Film/TV editor: John Mulvey
Rock music newspaper
Lead time: Mon, 1 week before press day
Circulation: 121,001

New Scientist (Weekly, Sat avail Thur)
151 Wardour Street
London W1V 4BN
London SE1 9LS
Tel: 020 7331 2701
Fax: 020 7331 2772
email: news@newscientist.com
Website: www.newscientist.com
Editor: Alun Anderson
Contains articles and reports on the progress of science and technology in terms which the non-specialist can understand
Press day: Mon
Circulation: 120,744

New Statesman and Society (Weekly, Fri)
7th Floor,
Victoria Station House
191 Victoria Street
London SW1E 5NE
Tel: 020 7828 1232
Fax: 020 7828 1881
Editor: Peter Wilby
Arts films: Angus Mackinnon
Independent radical journal of political, social and cultural comment
Press day: Mon
Circulation: 26,000

News of the World
News International
1 Virginia Street
London E1 9XR
Tel: 020 7782 1000
Fax: 020 7583 9504
Editor: Phil Hall
Films: Johnathon Ross
TV critic: Charles Catchpole
National Sunday newspaper
Press day: Sat
Circulation: 4,434,856

Nine to Five (Weekly, Mon)
7-9 Rathbone Street
London W1P 1AF
Tel: 020 7636 6651
Fax: 020 7255 2352
Film: Bill Williamson
Free London magazine
Press day: Wed
Circulation: 160,000

Observer Life Magazine (Weekly, Sun)
119 Farringdon Road

London EC1R 3ER
Tel: 020 7278 2332
Fax: 020 7239 9837
Supplement to The Observer

The Observer (Weekly, Sun)
119 Farringdon Road
London EC1R 3ER
Tel: 020 7278 2332
Fax: 020 7713 4250
Arts editor: Jane Ferguson
Film critic: Philip French
TV: Mike Bradley
National Sunday newspaper
Lead time: 1 week
Press day: Fri
Circulation: 450,831

Options (Monthly)
King's Reach Tower
Stamford Street
London SE1 9LS
Tel: 020 7261 5000
Fax: 020 7261 7344
Film: Susy Feag
TV: Stuart Husband
Women's glossy magazine
Lead time: 3 months
Circulation: 146,692

The PACT Magazine
Producers Alliance for Cinema and Television
published by MDI Ltd
30/31 Islington Green
London N1 8DU
Tel: 020 7226 8585
Fax: 020 7226 8586
Editor: Clare Mount
PACT members' monthly
Circulation:2,000

The People (Weekly, Sun)
1 Canada Square
Canary Wharf
London E14 5AP
Tel: 020 7510 3000
Fax: 020 7293 3810
Films: Jane Simon
TV: Rachel Lloyd
National Sunday newspaper
Press day: Sat
Circulation: 1,932,237

Picture House (Annual)
Cinema Theatre Association
5 Coopers Close
Burgess Hill
West Sussex RH15 8AN
Tel: 01444 246893
Documents the past and present history of cinema buildings
Lead time: 8 weeks
Circulation: 2,000

The Pink Paper (Weekly, Thur)
Cedar House

72 Holloway Road
London N7 8NZ
Tel: 020 7296 6210
Fax: 020 7957 0046
Editor: Alistair Pegg
Film/TV: Neil Edwards
Britain's national lesbian and gay
newspaper
Lead time: 14 days
Circulation: 53,780

PIX
21 Stephen Street
London W1P 2LN
Tel: 020 7255 1444
Fax: 020 7436 7950
Ilona Halberstadt
A counterpoint of images and critical
texts, PIX brings together
experimental, independent and
commercial cinema from all over the
world and explores its relation to
other arts

Premiere (Monthly)
37-39 Millharbour
London E14 9TZ
Tel: 020 7972 6791
Fax: 020 7972 6791
Editor: Matt Mueller
A 16-page UK film supplement in
issues of American Premiere sold in
the UK, containing personality
profiles, on the set reports, news and
reviews
Lead time: 3 months
Circulation: 40,000

Press Gazette
19 Scarbrook Road
Croydon
Surrey CR9 1LX
Tel: 020 7565 4200
Fax:020 7565 4295
Editor: Adam Leyland
Weekly magazine covering all
aspects of the media industry:
journalism; advertising; broadcast;
freelance
Press day: Thurs
Circulation: 8,500

Q (Monthly)
1st Floor
Mappin House
4 Winsley Street
London W1N 7AR
Tel: 020 7436 1515
Fax: 020 7312 8247
Website: www.qonline.co.uk/
Editor: David Davies
Specialist music magazine for 18-45
year olds. Includes reviews of new
albums, films and books
Lead time: 14 days
Circulation: 212,607

Radio Times (Weekly, Tues)
Woodlands
80 Wood Lane
London W12 0TT
Tel: 020 8576 3999
Fax: 020 8576 3160
Website: www.rtguide.beeb.com
Editor: Sue Robinson
Films: Barry Norman
Features: Kim Newson
Listings: Caroline Meyer
Weekly guide to UK television, radio
and satellite programmes
Lead time: 14 days
Circulation: 1,406,152

Regional Film & Video (Monthly)
Flagship Publishing
164-165 North Street
Belfast BT1 IGF
Tel: 01232 319008
Fax: 01232 319101
Editor: Steve Preston
Film and Video Trade Newspaper
Circulation: 12,000

Satellite TV Europe
531-533 King's Road,
London SW10 0TZ
Tel: 020 7351 3612
Website: www.satellite-tv.co.uk/

Scotland on Sunday
20 North Bridge
Edinburgh EH1 1YT
Tel: 0131 225 2468
Fax: 0131 220 2443
email: spectrum_sos@scotsman.com
Film: Allan Hunter
Arts and Features: Adrian Turpin
TV: Stewart Hennessey
Scottish Sunday newspaper
Lead time: 10 days
Circulation: 110,000

The Scotsman
20 North Bridge
Edinburgh EH1 1YT
Tel: 0131 225 2468
Fax: 0131 243 3686
Arts Editor: Robert Dowden Scott
Film critic: Trevor Johnston
Scottish daily newspaper
Circulation: 77,057

Scottish Film (Quarterly)
Arts and Entertainment Publishing
Ltd
24 Sandyford Place
Glasgow G3 7NG
Tel: 0141 221 4241
Fax: 0141 221 4247
Editor: Robert McColl
Filmmaking and broadcasting within
Scotland. Scottish Film is distributed
throughout Scotland to all the

production companies, facility houses
and broadcasters
Circulation: 20,000

Screen Digest (Monthly)
Lyme House Studios
38 Georgiana Street
London NW1 0EB
Tel: 020 7482 5842
Fax: 020 7580 0060
email: screendigest@compuserve
.com
Managing director: Allan Hardy
Editor: David Fisher
Executive editor: Ben Keen
Deputy editor: Mark Smith
International industry news digest
and research report covering film,
television, cable, satellite, video and
other multimedia information. Has a
centre page reference system every
month on subjects like law, statistics
or sales. Now also available on a
computer data base via fax at 020
7580 0060 under the name Screenfax
(see entry under Screenfax)

Screen Finance (Fortnightly)
FT Newsletters
30-31 Great Sutton Street
London EC1V 0DX
Tel: 020 7454 1185
Fax: 020 7490 1686
email: x 25@compuserve.com
Editor: Neil McCartney
Detailed analysis and news coverage
of the film and television industries
in the UK and Europe
Lead time: 1-3 days

Screen International (Weekly, Thur)
EMAP Media
33-39 Bowling Green Lane
London EC1R 0DA
Tel: 020 7505 8056/8080
Fax: 020 7505 8117
Managing Editor: Denis Seguin
Features: Leo Barraclough
International trade magazine for the
film, television, video, cable and
satellite industries. Regular news,
features, production information from
around the world
Press day: Tue
Features lead time: 3 months
Circulation: 10,000

Screen (Quarterly)
The Gilmorehill Centre
University of Glasgow
Glasgow G12 8QQ
Tel: 0141 330 5035
Fax: 0141 330 3515
email: screen@arts.gla.ac.uk
Website: www.arts.gla.ac
.uk/tfs/screen.html

Journal of essays, reports, debates and reviews on film and television studies. Organises the annual Screen Studies Conference
Circulation: 1,400

Screenfax (Database)
Screen Digest
Lyme House Studios
38 Georgiana Street
London NW1 0EB
Fax: 020 7580 0060
Available on-line via Dialog, Profile, Data-Star, MAID and most other on-line databases, or by fax: 020 7580 0060. Provides customised print-outs on all screen media subjects with summaries of news developments, market research. See entry under Screen Digest

SFX
Future Publishing
30 Monouth Street
Bath BA1 2BW
Tel: 01225 442244
Fax: 01225 480696
email: sfx@futurenet.co.uk
Website: www.sfx.co.uk
Editor: Dave Golder

Shivers (Monthly)
Visual Imagination
9 Blades Court
Deodar Road
London SW15 2NU
Tel: 020 8875 1520
Fax: 020 8875 1588
Editor: David Miller
Horror film reviews and features
Lead time: 1 month
Circulation: 30,000

Sight and Sound (Monthly)
British Film Institute
21 Stephen Street
London W1P 2LN
Tel: 020 7255 1444
Fax: 020 7436 2327
Editor: Nick James
Incorporating 'Monthly Film Bulletin'. Includes regular columns, feature articles, a book review section and review/synopsis/credits of every feature film theatrically released, plus a brief listing of every video
Copy date: 4th of each month
Circulation: 26,000

South Wales Argus
Cardiff Road
Newport
Gwent NP9 1QW
Tel: 01633 810000
Fax: 01633 462202
Film & TV editor: Lesley Williams
Regional evening newspaper

Lead time: 2 weeks
Circulation: 32,569

The Spectator (Weekly, Thur)
56 Doughty Street
London WC1N 2LL
Tel: 020 7405 1706
Fax: 020 7242 0603
Arts editor: Elizabeth Anderson
Film: Mark Steyn
TV: James Delingpole and Simon Hoggart
Independent review of politics, current affairs, literature and the arts
Press day: Wed
Circulation: 56,313

Stage Screen & Radio (10 issues a year)
111 Wardour Street
London W1V 4AY
Tel: 020 7437 8506
Fax: 020 7437 8268
Editor: Janice Turner
Journal of the film, broadcasting, theatre and entertainment union BECTU. Reporting and analysis of these industries and the union's activities plus coverage of technological developments
Lead time: 4 weeks
Circulation: 34,600

Stage The (incorporating Television Today) (Weekly, Thurs)
Stage House
47 Bermondsey Street
London SE1 3XT
Tel: 020 7403 1818
Fax: 020 7357 9287
Website: www.thestage.co.uk
Editor: Brian Attwood
Weekly trade paper covering all aspects of entertainment
Circulation: 39,258

Starburst
(Monthly + 4 Specials + German language version)
Visual Imagination
9 Blades Court
Deodar Road
London SW15 2NU
Tel: 020 8875 1520
Fax: 020 8875 1588
email: Star@cix.compulink.co.uk
Website: www.wisimag.com
Editor: Stephen Payne
Science fiction, fantasy and horror films, television and video
Lead time: 1 month
Circulation: 45,000

Subway Magazine
The Attic
62 Kelvingrove Street

Glasgow G3 7SA
Tel: 0141 332 9088
Fax: 0141 331 1477
Editor: Gill Mill

The Sun
PO Box 481
1 Virginia Street
London E1 9XP
Tel: 020 7782 4000
Fax: 020 7488 3253
Films: Nick Fisher
Showbiz editor: Dominic Mohan
TV editor: Danny Buckland
TV News: Sarah Crosbie
National daily newspaper
Circulation: 3,875,329

Sunday Express Magazine
Ludgate House
245 Blackfriars Road
London SE1 9UX
Tel: 020 7922 7150
Fax: 020 7922 7599
Editor: Katy Bravery
Supplement to The Express on Sunday
Lead time: 6 weeks

Sunday Magazine
1 Virginia Street
London E1 9BD
Tel: 020 7782 7000
Fax: 020 7782 7474
Editor: Judy McGuire
Deputy Editor: Jonathan Worsnop
Supplement to News of the World
Lead time: 6 weeks
Circulation: 4,701,879

Sunday Mirror
1 Canada Square
Canary Wharf
London E14 5AP
Tel: 020 7293 3000
Fax: 020 7293 3939
Film critic: Quentin Falk
TV: David Rowe, Pam Francis
National Sunday newspaper
Circulation: 2,268,263

Sunday Telegraph
1 Canada Square
Canary Wharf
London E14 5DT
Tel: 020 7538 5000
Fax: 020 7513 2504
Arts: John Preston
Film: Anne Billson
TV: Judy Rumbold
National Sunday newspaper
Circulation: 886,377

Sunday Times
1 Virginia Street
London E1 9BD
Tel. 020 7782 5000
Fax: 020 7782 5731
Film: Tom Shone

TV reviews: A A Gill
Video: George Perry
National Sunday newspaper
Press day: Wed
Circulation: 1,314,576

Sunday Times Magazine
Admiral House
66-68 East Smithfield
London E11 9XW
Tel: 020 7782 7000
Fax: 020 7867 0410
Editor: Robin Morgan
Supplement to Sunday Times
Lead time: 4 weeks
Circulation: 1,314,576

Talking Pictures (Quarterly)
34 Darwin Crescent
Laira, Plymouth PL3 6DX
Tel: 01752 347200
Fax: 020 7737 4720
email: stntpublishingltd@
btinternet.com
Website: Weebsite:
www.filmcentre.co.uk
Editor: Nigel Watson
Devoted to a serious yet entertaining
look at film, computer entertainment,
television and video
Lead time: 2 months
Circulation: 500

Tatler (Monthly)
Vogue House, 1 Hanover Square
London W1R 0AD
Tel: 020 7499 9080
Fax: 020 7409 0451
Website: www.tatler.co.uk
Editor: Jane Procter
Arts: Celia Lyttleton
Smart society magazine favouring
profiles, fashion and the arts
Lead time: 3 months
Circulation: 88,235

The Teacher (8 p.a.)
National Union of Teachers
Hamilton House, Mabledon Place
London WC1H 9BD
Tel: 020 7380 4708
Fax: 020 7387 8458
Editor: Mitch Howard
Circulation: 250,000 mailed direct to
all NUT members and to educational
institutions

Telegraph Magazine
1 Canada Square
Canary Wharf
London E14 5AU
Tel: 020 7538 5000
Fax: 020 7513 2500
TV films: Jessamy Calkin
Supplement to Saturday edition of
the Daily Telegraph
Lead time: 6 weeks
Circulation: 1,300,000

Television (9 p.a.)
Royal Television Society
Holborn Hall
100 Gray's Inn Road
London WC1X 8AL
Tel: 020 7430 1000
Fax: 020 7430 0924
email: info@rts.org.uk
Website: www.rts.org.uk
Editor: Peter Fiddick
Television trade magazine
Lead time: 2 weeks
Circulation: 5,000

Televisual (Monthly)
St. Giles House, 50 Poland Street
London W1V 4AX
Tel: 020 7970 6666
Fax: 020 7970 6733
Editor: Mundy Ellis
Assistant Editor; Keely Winstone
Monthly business magazine for
production professionals in the
business of moving pictures
News lead time: 1 month
Features lead time: 2 months
Circulation: 8,040

Time Out (Weekly, Tues)
Universal House
251 Tottenham Court Road
London W1P 0AB
Tel: 020 7813 3000
Fax: 020 7813 6028
Website: www.timeout.co.uk
Film: Geoff Andrew, Tom Charity
Video: Derek Adams
TV: Alkarim Jivani
London listings magazine with
cinema and television sections
Listings lead time: 8 days
Features lead time: 1 week
Circulation: 100,000 plus

The Times Educational Supplement Scotland (Weekly, Fri)
Scott House, 10 South St Andrew
Street, Edinburgh EH2 2AZ
Tel: 0131 557 1133
Fax: 0131 558 1155
Editor: Willis Pickard
Press day: Wed
Circulation: 10,000

The Times Educational Supplement (Weekly, Fri)
Admiral House
66-68 East Smithfield
London E1 9XY
Tel: 020 7782 3000
Fax: 020 7782 3200
Editor: Caroline St John-Brooks
Film/TV editor: Janette Wolf
Press day: Tuesday
Lead time for reviews: copy 14-21
days
Circulation: 150,000

The Times Higher Educational Supplement (Weekly, Fri)
Admiral House
66-68 East Smithfield
London E1 9XY
Tel: 020 7782 3000
Fax: 020 7782 3300
Film/TV editor: Sean Coughlan
Press day: Wed
Lead time for reviews: copy 10 days
before publication
Circulation: 26,666

The Times Literary Supplement (Weekly, Fri)
Admiral House
66-68 East Smithfield
London E1 9XY
Tel: 020 7782 3000
Fax: 020 7782 3100
Arts editor: Will Eaves
Press day: Tues
Lead time: 2 weeks
Circulation: 34,044

The Times
1 Pennington Street
London E1 9XN
Tel: 020 7782 5000
Fax: 020 7488 3242
Website: www.the-times.co.uk
Film/video critic: Geoff Brown
Film writer: David Robinson
TV: Matthew Bond
National daily newspaper
Circulation: 747,054

Top Review
1st Floor, 23 South Quay
Gt Yarmouth
Norfolk NR30 2RG
Tel: 01493 331042
Fax: 01493 330565
Film, video, car, computer book,
travel and DIY reviews
Circulation: 60,000

Total Film
Future Publishing, 99 Baker Street
London W1M 1FB
Tel: 020 7317 2600
Fax: 020 7317 2644
email: totalfilm@futurenet.co.uk
Website: www.futurenet.co.uk
Editor: Emma Cochrane

Tribune (Weekly, Fri)
308 Gray's Inn Road
London WC1X 8DY
Tel: 020 7278 0911
Fax: 020 7833 0385
Review editor: Caroline Rees
Political and cultural weekly
Lead time: 14 days
Circulation: 10,000

TV Quick (Weekly, Mon)
25-27 Camden Road

London NW1 9LL
Tel: 020 7284 0909
Fax: 020 7284 0593
Editor: Jon Gower
Mass market television magazine
Lead time: 3 weeks
Circulation: 799,000

TV Times (Weekly, Tues)
10th Floor
King's Reach Tower
Stamford Street
London SE1 9LS
Tel: 020 7261 7000
Fax: 020 7261 7777
Editor: Liz Murphy
Film editor: David Quinlan
Weekly magazine of listings and
features serving viewers of
independent TV, BBC TV, satellite
and radio
Lead time: 6 weeks
Circulation: 981,311

TV Zone
(Monthly + 4 specials)
Visual Imagination Limited
9 Blades Court
Deodar Road
London SW15 2NU
Tel: 020 8875 1520
Fax: 020 8875 1588
email: star@cix.compulink.co.uk
Editor: Jan Vincent-Rudzki
Magazine of cult television, past,
present and future, with emphasis on
science fiction and fantasy
Lead time: 1 month
Circulation: 45,000

Uncut
IPC Magazines Ltd
King's Reach Tower
Stamford Street
London SE1 9LS
Tel: 020 7261 6992
Fax: 020 7261 5573
Website: www.uncut.net
Editor: Allan Jones

Variety (Weekly, Mon) and Daily (Mon-Fri)
6 Bell Yard
London WC2A 2JR
Tel: 020 7520 5222
Fax: 020 7520 5220
email: adam.dawtrey@rbi.co.uk
Website: www.variety.com
European editor: Adam Dawtrey
International showbusiness
newspaper
Press day: Thurs
Circulation: 36,000

Video Home Entertainment (Weekly, Fri)
Strandgate
18-20 York Buildings
London WC2 6JU

Tel: 020 7839 7774
Fax: 020 7839 4393
Editor: John Ferguson
Video trade publication for rental and
retail
Lead time: Monday before publication
Circulation: 7,613

View
Oakwood House
422 Hackney Road
London E2 7SY
Tel: 020 7729 6881
Fax: 020 7729 0988
Editor: Branwell Johnson
A weekly trade magazine for the
video industry covering news
relevant to the business from a retail
to distributor level. It carries a
complete listing of the month's rental
releases and a highlighted sell
through list. Regular features include
coverage from the US and interviews
with leading industry figures
Circulation: 8,000

Viewfinder (3 p.a.)
BUFVC
77 Wells Street
London W1P 3RE
Tel: 020 7393 1511
Fax: 020 7393 1555
Editor: Martyn Glanville
Periodical for people in higher
education and research, includes
articles on the production, study and
use of film, television and related
media. Deadlines: 10th Jan, 1st Apr,
1st Oct
Lead time: 6 weeks
Circulation: 5,000

Vogue (Monthly)
Vogue House
Hanover Square
London W1R 0AD
Tel: 020 7408 0559
Fax: 020 7493 1345
Website: www.vogue.co.uk
Editor: Alexandra Shulman
Films: Susie Forbes
Glossy magazine for women
Lead time: 12 weeks
Circulation: 201,187

The Voice (Weekly, Monday)
370 Coldharbour Lane
London SW9 8PL
Tel: 020 7737 7377
Fax: 020 7274 8994
Editor: Annie Stewart
Arts: Omega Douglas
Britain's leading black newspaper
with mainly 18-35 age group
readership. Regular film, television
and video coverage
Press day: Friday
Circulation: 52,000

The Web
Media House, Adlington Park
Macclesfield SK10 4NP
Tel: 01625 878888
Fax: 01625 879967
email: web@idg.co.uk
Editor: Mike Cowley
Focusing on lifestyle and culture on
the Net, film and television is
extensively covered with features,
leaders and listing
Lead time: 2 weeks

Western Mail
Thomson House
Cardiff CF1 1WR
Tel: 029 20 223333
Fax: 029 20 583652
Film: Carolyn Hitt
Daily newspaper
Circulation: 60,251

What DVD?
Future Publishing
Beauford Court
30 Monmouth Street
Bath BA1 2BW
Tel: 01225 442244
Fax: 01225 732282
Website: www.futurenet.com/

What's On In London (Weekly, Tues)
180 Pentonville Road
London N1 9LB
Tel: 020 7278 4393
Fax: 020 7837 5838
Editor: Michael Darvell
Films & Video: David Clark
London based weekly covering
cinema, theatre, music, arts, books,
entertainment and video
Press day: Mon
Lead time: 10 days
Circulation: 42,000

What's On TV (Weekly, Tues)
King's Reach Tower
London SE1 9LS
Tel: 020 7261 7769
Fax: 020 7261 7739
Editor: Mike Hollingsworth
TV listings magazine
Lead time: 3 weeks
Circulation: 1,676,000

Yorkshire Post
Wellington Street
Leeds
West Yorkshire LS1 1RF
Tel: 0113 238 8536
Fax: 0113 244 3430
TV editor: Angela Barnes
Regional daily morning newspaper
Deadline: 10.00 pm
Circulation: 100,126

BBC Radio

BBC
Broadcasting House
Portland Place
London W1A 1AA
Tel: 020 7580 4468
Fax: 020 7637 1630

**BBC CWR (Coventry &
Warwickshire)**
25 Warwick Road
Coventry CV1 2WR
Tel: 01203 559911
Fax: 01203 520080

BBC Essex
198 New London Road
Chelmsford
Essex CM2 9XB
Tel: 01245 262393
Fax: 01245 492983

BBC GMR Talk
PO Box 951
Oxford Road
Manchester M60 1SD
Tel: 0161 200 2000
Fax: 0161 228 6110

BBC Hereford & Worcester
Hylton Road
Worcester WR2 5WW
Tel: 01905 748485
Fax: 01905 748006

BBC Radio Bristol
Broadcasting House
Whiteladies Road
Bristol BS8 2LR
Tel: 0117 974 1111
Fax: 0117 923 8323

BBC Radio Cambridgeshire
Broadway Court
Broadway
Peterborough PE1 1RP
Tel: 01733 312832
Fax: 01733 343768

BBC Radio Cleveland
PO Box 95FM
Broadcasting House
Newport Road
Middlesbrough TS1 5DG
Tel: 01642 225211
Fax: 01642 211356

BBC Radio Cornwall
Phoenix Wharf
Truro TR1 1UA
Tel: 01872 275421
Fax: 01872 240679

BBC Radio Cumbria
Hartington Street
Barrow-in-Furness
Cumbria LA14 5SC

Tel: 01228 835252
Fax: 01228 870008

BBC Radio Derby
PO Box 269
Derby DE1 3HL
Tel: 01332 361111
Fax: 01332 290794

BBC Radio Devon
PO Box 5
Broadcasting House
Seymour Road
Mannamead
Plymouth PL3 5YQ
Tel: 01752 260323
Fax: 01752 234599

BBC Radio Foyle
8 Northland Road
Londonderry BT48 7JD
Tel: 01504 378 600
Fax: 01504 378666

BBC Radio Guernsey
Commerce House
Les Banques
St Peter Port
Guernsey GY1 2HS
Tel: 01481 728977
Fax: 01481 713557

BBC Radio Humberside
9 Chapel Street
Hull HU1 3NU
Tel: 01482 323232
Fax: 01482 226409

BBC Radio Jersey
18 Parade Road
St Helier
Jersey JE2 3PL
Tel: 01534 87000
Fax: 01534 32569

BBC Radio Lancashire
Darwen Street
Blackburn
Lancs BB2 2EA
Tel: 01254 262411
Fax: 01254 680821

BBC Radio Leeds
Broadcasting House
Woodhouse Lane
Leeds LS2 9PN
Tel: 0113 244 2131
Fax: 0113 242 0652

BBC Radio Leicester
Epic House
Charles Street
Leicester LE1 3SH
Tel: 0116 251 6688
Fax: 0116 251 1463

BBC Radio Lincolnshire
PO Box 219
Newport
Lincoln LN1 3XY

Tel: 01522 511411
Fax: 01522 511058

BBC Radio Merseyside
55 Paradise Street
Liverpool L1 3BP
Tel: 0151 708 5500
Fax: 0151 794 0909
Film and video reviewer: Ramsey
Campbell

BBC Radio Newcastle
Broadcasting Centre
Fenham
Newcastle Upon Tyne NE99 1RN
Tel: 0191 232 4141
Fax: 0191 232 5082

BBC Radio Norfolk
Norfolk Tower, Surrey Street
Norwich NR1 3PA
Tel: 01603 617411
Fax: 01603 633692

BBC Radio Northampton
Broadcasting House
Abington Street
Northampton NN1 2BH
Tel: 01604 239100
Fax: 01604 230709

BBC Radio Nottingham
PO York House
Mansfield Road
Nottingham NG1 3JB
Tel: 0115 955 0500
Fax: 0115 955 0501

BBC Radio Oxford
269 Banbury Road
Oxford OX2 7DW
Tel: 01865 311444
Fax: 01865 311996

BBC Radio Sheffield
Ashdell Grove
60 Westbourne Grove
Sheffield S10 2QU
Tel: 0114 268 6185
Fax: 0114 266 4375

BBC Radio Solent
PO Box 900
Dorchester DT1 1TP
Tel: 01305 269654
Fax: 01305 250910

BBC Radio Stoke
Cheapside
Hanley
Stoke-on-Trent ST1 1JJ
Tel: 01782 208080
Fax: 01782 289115

BBC Radio Sussex & Surrey
Broadcasting House
Guildford
Surrey GU2 5AP
Tel: 01483 306306
Fax: 01483 304952

BBC Radio WM
PO Box 206
Birmingham B5 7SD
Tel: 0121 414 8484
Fax: 0121 414 8817

BBC Somerset Sound
14-16 Paul Street
Taunton TA1 3PF
Somerset
Tel: 01823 251641
Fax: 01823 332539

BBC Southern Counties
Broadcasting Centre
Guildford GU2 5AP
Tel: 01483 306306
Fax: 01483 304952

BBC Three Counties Radio
PO Box 3CR , Hastings Street
Luton, Bedfordshire LU1 5XL
Tel: 01582 441000
Fax: 01582 401467

BBC Wiltshire Sound
Broadcasting House
Prospect Place, Swindon SN1 3RN
Tel: 01793 513626
Fax: 01793 513650

BBC World Service
Bush House, Strand
London WC2B 4PH
Tel: 020 7257 2171
Fax: 020 7240 3938

Independent Radio

GLR
35c Marylebone High Street
London W1A 4LG
Tel: 020 7224 2424
Fax: 020 7487 2908

Classic FM
Academic House
24-28 Oval Road
London NW1 7DQ
Tel: 020 7284 3000
Fax: 020 7713 2630

Longwave Radio
Atlantic 252
74 Newman Street
London W1P 3LA
Tel: 020 7637 5252
Fax: 020 7637 3925
Trim, Co Meath, Ireland
Tel/Fax: 00353 463655

Virgin 1215 AM
1 Golden Square
London W1R 4DJ
Tel: 020 7434 1215
Fax: 020 7434 1197

Television

Anglia Television
Anglia House
Norwich NR1 3JG
Tel: 01603 615151
Fax: 01603 615032
Website: www.anglia.tv.co.uk

BBC Television Centre
Wood Lane
London W12 7RJ
Tel: 020 8743 8000

Border Television
Television Centre
Carlisle CA1 3NT
Tel: 01228 25101
Fax: 01228 525101

Carlton Television
35-38 Portman Square
London W1H 0NU
Tel: 020 7486 6688
Fax: 020 7486 1132

Central Independent Television (East)
Carlton Studios
Lenton Lane
Nottingham NG7 2NA
Tel: 0115 986 3322
Fax: 0115 964 5018

Central Independent Television (South)
9 Windrush Court
Abingdon Business Park
Abingdon
Oxon OX14 1SA
Tel: 01235 554123
Fax: 01235 524024

Channel Five Broadcasting
22 Long Acre
London WC2E 9LY
Tel: 020 7550 5555
Fax: 020 7550 5554

Channel Four Television
124 Horseferry Road
London SW1P 2TX
Tel: 020 7396 4444
Fax: 020 7306 8353

Channel Television
Television House
Bulwer Avenue
St Sampsons
Guernsey GY2 4LA
Tel: 01481 41888
Fax: 01481 41889
The Television Centre
La Pouquelaye
St Helier
Jersey JE1 3ZD
Tel: 01534 816816
Fax: 01534 816689

GMTV
London Television Centre
Upper Ground
London SE1 9TT
Tel: 020 7827 7000
Fax: 020 7827 7249

Grampian Television
Queen's Cross
Aberdeen AB15 4XJ
Tel: 01224 846846
Fax: 01224 846802
North Tonight; Crossfire; Telefios;
Walking Back to Happiness; Top
Club; We the Jury; The Art Sutter
Show

Granada Television
Quay Street
Manchester M60 9EA
Tel: 0161 832 7211
Fax: 0161 827 2324
Albert Dock
Liverpool L3 4BA
Tel: 0151 709 9393
White Cross
Lancaster LA1 4XQ
Tel: 01524 606688
36 Golden Square
London W1R 4AH
Tel: 020 7734 8080
Bridgegate House
5 Bridge Place
Lower Bridge Street
Chester CH1 1SA
Tel: 01244 313966

HTV Wales
Television Centre
Culverhouse Cross
Cardiff CF5 6XJ
Tel: 029 20 590590
Fax: 029 20 590759

HTV West
Television Centre
Bath Road
Bristol BS4 3HG
Tel: 0117 9722722
Fax: 0117 972 3122
HTV News; The West This Week,
West Eye View

Independent Television News (ITN)
200 Gray's Inn Road
London WC1X 8XZ
Tel: 020 7833 3000

Meridian Broadcasting
TV Centre
Northam Road
Southampton SO14 0PZ
Tel: 023 80 222555
Fax: 023 80 335050
TV Weekly

S4C
Parc Ty Glas

Llanishen
Cardiff CF4 5DU
Tel: 029 20 747444
Fax: 029 20 754444
Head of Press and Public Relations:
David Meredith

Scottish Television
Cowcaddens
Glasgow G2 3PR
Tel: 0141 300 3000
Fax: 0141 332 9274

Tyne Tees Television
The Television Centre
City Road
Newcastle upon Tyne NE1 2AL
Tel: 0191 261 0181
Fax: 0191 232 7017

Ulster Television
Havelock House
Ormeau Road
Belfast BT7 1EB
Tel: 01232 328122
Fax: 01232 246695

Westcountry Television
Western Wood Way
Language Science Park
Plymouth PL7 5BQ
Tel: 01752 333333
Fax: 01752 333033

Yorkshire Television
The Television Centre
Kirkstall Road
Leeds LS3 1JS
Tel: 0113 243 8283
Fax: 0113 243 3655

News and photo agencies

Associated Press
12 Norwich Street
London EC4A 1BP
Tel: 020 7353 1515
Fax: 020 7583 0196

Bridge News
78 Fleet Street
London EC4Y 1HY
Tel: 020 7842 4000
Fax: 020 7583 5032
Business Information Service

Central Office of Information
Hercules Road
London SE1 7DU
Tel: 020 7928 2345
Fax: 020 7928 5037

Central Press Features
20 Spectrum House
32-34 Gordon House Road
London NW5 1LP
Tel: 020 7284 1433
Fax: 020 7284 4494
Film/TV: Chris King

Fleet Street News Agency
68 Exmouth Market
London EC1R 4RA
Tel: 020 7278 5661
Fax: 020 7278 8480

London News Service
68 Exmouth Market
London EC1R 4RA
Tel: 020 7278 5661
Fax: 020 7278 8480

Press Association
292 Vauxhall Bridge Road
London Sw1V 1AE
Tel: 0171-963 7000
Fax: 0171-963 7192
email: www@padd.press.net
Website: www.pa.press.net/

Reuters Ltd
85 Fleet Street
London EC4P 4AJ
Tel: 020 7250 1122
Fax: 020 7542 7921
Website: www.reuters.com
Media: Mary Ellen-Barker

United Press International
408 The Strand
London WC2R 0NE
Tel: 020 7333 0990
Fax: 020 7333 1690

PREVIEW THEATRES

BAFTA
195 Piccadilly
London W1V 0LN
Tel: 020 7465 0277
Fax: 020 7734 1009
Website: www.bafta.org
Formats: Twin 35mm all aspect
ratios. Dolby A, SR, SRD, DTS
sound. 35 Double head mono,
twin/triple track stereo plus Dolby
Matrix. Twin 16mm and super
16mm, 16 double head stereo plus
Dolby Matrix. BARCO 9200 Data
Video Projector VHS, Lo Band/Hi
Band U-matic, Beta, Beta SP, Digi
Beta. Interfaces for most PC outputs,
SVGA, MAC etc. 35mm slides
single, twin and disolve multi-wau
control, Audio, RGB Video Tie Lines
in Theatre. ISDN 2. Catering by
Roux Fine Dining. Seats: Princess
Anee Theatre, 213 Run Run Shaw
Theatre, 30 (not all formats
available), Function Room, up to 200

bfi British Film Institute
21 Stephen Street
London W1P 2LN
Tel: 020 7957 8976
Fax: 020 7580 5830
email: roger.young@bfi.org.uk
Website: www.bfi.org.uk
Formats: 35mm Dolby Opt/Mag
Stereo A/SR, Std 16mm Opt, Super
16 Mag Stereo A/SR, Large Screen
Video Projection PAL VHS, SVHS,
U-MATIC hi/lo band Triple Standard,
BETA SP, DVD (PAL/NTSC) Stereo
Large Screen Video Projection.
Disabled Access
Seats: 1: 36, 2: 36

BUFVC
77 Wells Street
London W1P 3RE
Tel: 020 7393 1500
Fax: 020 7393 1555
email: bufvc@open.ac.uk
Formats: Viewing rooms equipped
with 16mm double-head, Betacam,
SVHS, VHS, lo-band and hi-band U-
Matic, Betamax, Phillips 1500
Seats: 20-30 max

Carlton Preview Theatre
127 Wardour Street
London W1V 4AD
Tel: 020 7437 9020 x257
Fax: 020 7434 3689
Formats: U-Matic, 16mm, 35mm,

double-head, Dolby SR Stereo, VHS,
U-Matic, slides. Lift to theatre
Seats: 58

Century Preview Theatres
31-32 Soho Square
London W1V 6AP
Tel: 020 7437 7766
Fax: 020 7434 2170
Picture Formats: 1.1:33, 1.1:66,
1.1:85, Super 35, Scope
Sound Formats: (CP 500) Mono,
Dolby A, SR, SR-D+EX. DTS.
Double Head (Magnetic) 2000 ft.
Also: Spotlighting, microphones,
lecturns, for conventions. Video on
request
Seating Capacity: 73

Chapter Cinema
Market Road
Canton
Cardiff CF5 1QE
Tel: 01222 311050
Fax: 01222 313431
email: chaptercinema@easynet.co.uk
Formats: 35mm optical, 16mm
optical/sep mag, high quality video
projection, U-Matic/VHS – all
standards. Beta SP PAL2 Channel
infra-red audio
amplification/simultaneous
translation system in both screens.
Reception space, bars and restaurant
Seats: 1:194, 2:68

Columbia TriStar Films UK
Sony Pictures Europe House
25 Golden Square
London W1R 6LU
Tel: 020 7533 1095
Fax: 020 7533 1105
Formats: 35mm optical (SDDS,
Dolby "SR" + "A" type)/double
head, SVA Mag, 16mm optical
(Mono), Super 16 and Super 35.
BETA SP, BVU/U-Matic, VHS, High
Definition Video. Large reception
area. Seats: 80

Computer Film Company
19-23 Wells Street
London W1P 3FB
Picture Formats: 1.1:33, 1.1:66,
1.1:85, Super 35, Scope. Variable
speeds, reverse projection if required.
Sound Formats: Mono, Dolby A, SR,
SRD. Video on request. Bar area
Seating: 64

The Curzon Minema
45 Knightsbridge
London SW1X 7NL
Tel: 020 7235 4226
Fax: 020 7235 3426
email:info@minema.com
Website: www.minema.com
Formats: 35mm and 16mm, video
and AV presentations

Curzon Soho
93-107 Shaftesbury venue
London W1V 7AE
Tel: 020 7734 9209
Fax: 020 7724 1977
John Bateman
Picture Formats: 1.1:33, 1.1:66,
1.1:85, Scope. Kodak side projection,
video projection on request, PA on
request, all theatres to THX standard
Sound Formats: Mono, Dolby, A+SR,
SRD, Double headed (magnetic) 3
and 6 Track. Six channel A type and
SR Reduction
Seats: 1:249 2: 130 3: 110

De Lane Lea Sound Centre
75 Dean Street
London W1V 5HA
Tel: 020 7432 3800
Fax: 020 7437 0913
Picture Formats: 35mm. 1.1:33,
1.1:66, 1.1:85. Super 35, Scope
Sound Formats: Mono, Dolby, A +
SR with double-head capacity
(magnetic) 6,4,3 track stereo
Video: VHS, U-Matic, DVD, Beta
sp. Bar and catering available.
Seating Capacity: 37

Edinburgh Film & TV Studios
Nine Mile Burn
Penicuik EH26 9LT
Tel: 01968 672131
Fax: 01968 672685
Formats: 16mm and 35mm double-
head stereo, U-Matic, VHS
Seats: 100

Eon Theatre
Eon House
136 Piccadilly
London W1V 95H
Tel: 020 7 493 7953
Projection 35mm. Picture Formats:
1.1:33, 1.1:66, 1.1:85 Scope
Sound Formats: Mono, Dolby, A+SR
(Video Projection, Format VHS,
DVD, U-Matic. Boardroom and

hospitality suite
Seating: 22

Film Four Ltd
77-78 Charlotte Street
London W1P 1X
Tel: 020 7868 7700
Picture Formats: 35mm, 16mm, 16mm super. 1.1:33. 1.1:66, 1.1: 85, Scope
Sound Formats: Mono, Dolby, A+SR, SRD, Double headed (magnetic) (3 Track)
Seating Capacity: 30

ICA
12 Carlton House Terrace
London SW1Y 5AH
Tel: 020 7930 0493
Fax: 020 7873 0051
Formats:
Cinema 1: 185 seats 35mm com-opt, Dolby CP, 16mm com-opt, + Sep Mag; video projection Super 16mm
Cinema 2: 45 seats, 35mm com-opt, 16mm com-opt, Super 8, video projection all formats.
Both Cinmas available up to 4.30pm weekdays, 2pm at the weekend.
Two regency reception rooms also available, level access to cinemas.
Cafe bar available exclusively till noon

Imperial War Museum
(Corporate Hospitality)
Lambeth Road
London SE1 6HZ
Tel: 020 7416 5394
Fax: 020 7416 5392/020 7416 5374
Formats: 35mm and 16mm; Betacam, U-Matic, SVHS and VHS. Catering by arrangement. Large Exhibit Hall, capacity: 1,000 Disabled access
Seats: Cinema: 200

King's Lynn Arts Centre
27/29 King Street
King's Lynn
Norfolk PE30 1HA
Tel: 01553 765565
Fax: 01553 762141
Formats: 16mm, 35mm
Seats: 349

The Lux Cinema
2-4 Hoxton Square
London N1 6NU
Tel: 020 7684 2866
Fax: 020 7684 2222
email: lux@lux.org.uk
The Lux Cinema opens onto fashionable Hoxton Square with a distinctive lobby dominated by a back-projection wall and video floor, available for promotional use. The cinema has a polished, semi-sprung wooden floor with stylish, upholstered and fully removable

seating. It can be adapted from an auditorium to a 126 square meter shell for master-classes, live music, performance and studio production of film and video. All major projection formats are available, including data projection, with variable and fully programmable electronic screen, lighting and acoustic qualities. Full disabled access throughout, with lower level counter and induction loop
Seats 120

Mr Young's
14 D'Arblay Street
London W1V 3FP
Tel: 020 7437 1771
Fax: 020 7734 4520
Contact: Reuben/Andy/Derry
Formats: 16mm, Super 16mm, 35mm, Super 35mm, U-Matic, VHS, Betacam SP, Dolby stereo double-head optical and magnetic Dolby SR. Large screen video projection. Bar area, catering by request. Both theatres non-smoking
Seats: 1: 42, 2: 25, 3:45

Pinewood Studios
Pinewood Road
Iver Heath
Bucks SL0 0NH
Tel: 01753 656296
Fax: 01753 656014
email: helen_wells@rank.com
Contact: Helen Wells
Formats: 35mm, 70mm, Dolby SR, SR.D, DTS, SDDS. COMPOT, COMMAG, SEPMAG. Max screen width 31ft. Disabled access. Lounge available
Seats: 115 seats

Planet Hollywood
13 Coventry Street
London W1
Tel: 020 7437 7827
Fax: 020 7439 7827
Formats: 35mm, 70mm, SVHS/VHS, U-Matic, Laser Disc, Lucasfilm Ltd THX Sound Sytem, Dolby CP200 + SRD/DTS digital stereo. Super 35mm with separate magnetic tracks and remote volume control. Microphone facilities. Lifts for the disabled available
Seats: Cinema: 75, Dining area: 85, 120 (standing)

Prominent Facilities THX
68a Delancey Street
London NW1 7RY
Tel: 020 7284 1020
Fax: 020 7284 1202
Formats: 35mm Dolby optical and magnetic, 2,000' double-head, rock 'n' roll. All aspect ratios, and Super 35, 24-25 30fps, triple-track, interlock, Dolby A + SR stereo,

16mm double-head married. Fully air conditioned, kitchen and reception area. Wheelchair access. Seats: 26

RSA
8 John Adam Street
London WC2N 6EZ
Tel: 020 7839 5049
Fax: 020 7321 0271
email: Conference@rsa-uk.demon.co.uk
Website: www.rsa.org.uk
The Great Room
Video Formats: SVHS, Beta SP. Other formats by arrangement.
Barcographics 8100 Projector for Video and Data Projection. Loop system for hard of hearing, disabled access to all rooms. Full catering available: Seats: 202
Durham House Street Auditorium
Video Formats: SVHS, Low band U-matic. Other formats by arrangement.
Sony 1252 Projector for Video and Data Projection. Loop system for hard of hearing, disabled access to all rooms. Full catering available.
Seats: 60

Screen West
136-142 Bramley Road
London W10 6SR
Tel: 020 7437 6292
Carrie Snitcher
Enquiries: Sarah Alliston
Technical Enquiries: Peter Spence
State of the art preview theatre with luxury seating for 74 people.
Formats: 35mm, 16mm, Super 35mm, Double Head, Beta, VHS, PC. Surround Sound: Optical, Magnetic, Digital (SRD and DTS). and full catering facilities in the adjoining function room.

The Screening Room
Moving Picture Company
127-133 Wardour Street
London W1V
Tel: 020 7434 3100
Fax: 020 7287 9698
email: screening@moving-picture.co.uk
Website: www.moving-picture.co.uk
Picture Formats: 35mm Projection, 1.1:37, 1:1:66, 1.1:85, Super 35 Scope, Speeds, 0-50 FPS Forwards/Reverse, High speed shuttling @ 250 FPS, Xenon lamps with controlled colour temperature.
Sound Formats: Mono, Dolby, A+R, SRD. Magnetic 6 Track, 3 Track. 1 Track with/without SR, Noise reduction
Video: Digital projection, VHS/U-Matic, Digi-beta/DVD (All regions) 5.1, VGA, SVGA, & XGA.
Powerpoint

PA: CD/Cassette, stage and lecturn, autocue (by arrangement). Self-catering, bar facilities, foyer reception area up to 75 people. Air conditioned.
Seating capacity: 75

Shepperton Studios
Studios Road
Shepperton
Middx TW17 0QD
Tel: 01932 562611/572350
Fax: 01932 568989
email:
sheppertonstudios@dial.pipex.com
Formats: 35mm double-head and married, Dolby A + SR, Video U-Matic, NTSC, PAL, SECAM, VHS.
Seats: (35mm) 17

Total Film
99 Baker Street
London W1M 1FB
Tel: 020 7317 2600
Fax: 020 7486 5676
Graham Singleton
Fully air conditioned screening room facility with Crestron touch screen remote for computer generated presentations and adjacent boardroom facilities. Format: 35mm print, Betacam and VHS through an overhead CRT with line doubler. Ernemann 15-laser audio projector with both scope and flat lenses. Sony Betacam SP player and professional JVC HRH 507MS VCR with overhead CRT projector. Sound delivery by Sony Digital Camera System with Dolby SR set-up & installed by Dolby Laboratories
Seats: 24

Twentieth Century Fox
31-32 Soho Square
London W1V 6AP
Tel: 020 7735 7135
Fax: 020 7735 7138
Peter Holland

Twickenham Film Studios
St Margaret's
Twickenham
Middx TW1 2AW
Tel: 020 8607 8888
Fax: 020 8607 8889
Formats: 16mm, 35mm.
Seats: 31

UIP International Theatre
UIP House
45 Beardon Road
Hammersmith
London
Tel: 020 8741 9041
Picture Formats: 1.1:33, 1.1:66, 1.1:85, Scope
Sound Formats: Mono, Dolby, A+SR, SRD +EX, DTS, SDDS, Double head

(magnetic). Mono, SVA, 6 Track
Video: VHS, U-Matic, Beta SP
Seating capacity: 43

Warner Bros
98 Theobalds Road
London WC1X 8WB
Tel: 020 7984 5272

Watershed Media Centre
1 Canons Road
Bristol BS1 5TX
Tel: 0117 9276444
Fax: 0117 9213958
email:
watershed@online.redirect.co.uk
Formats: Super 8mm, 16mm double-head, 35mm, VHS U-Matic lo-band, Betacam SP, Dolby A + SR. Lift access, for wheelchair spaces each theatre (prior notification for C2 required)
Seats: 1: 200. 2: 55

PRODUCTION COMPANIES

Listed below is a selection of UK companies currently active in financing and/or making audio visual product for the UK and international media markets. Not generally listed are the numerous companies making television commercials, educational and other non-broadcast material.

Check Book 4 published by the British Film Commission is a useful guide to all aspects of film production in the UK. Two other reference works *PACT Directory of UK Movie Producers* and *British Films Catalogue 1999* both give useful contact information for both feature and short film production in the UK

LOTTERY FILM PRODUCTION FRANCHISES

On 15 May 1997 The Arts Council announced three National Lottery-funded commercial feature film production franchises. Each franchise will extend over a six year period. All franchise funds offered will serve as funding pre-allocations over that period and will be drawn down conditional upon Arts Council approval of individual film proposals.

Pathé Pictures
Kent House
Market Place
London W1N 8AR
Tel: 0171 323 5151
Fax: 0171 636 7594
Head of Production: Andrea Calderwood
Lottery award: £33 million
Number of films: 35
Pathé Productions is formed by six producers in association with Pathé Pictures. **Thin Man Films and Imagine Films; Allied Filmmakers and Allied Films Ltd; NFH;**
Pandora Productions; Sarah Radclyffe Productions;Fragile Films; MW Entertainment

The Film Consortium
6 Flitcroft Street
London WC2 8DJ
Tel: 0171 691 4440
Fax: 0171 691 4445
Head of Production and Development: Colin Vanes
Lottery award: £30.25 million
Number of films: 39
The Film Consortium is formed by four production companies **Greenpoint Films, Parallax Pictures, Scala Productions; Skreba** in association with Virgin Cinemas. It intends to make four to five features a year with budgets in the range of £1.5-£6 million. The Film Consortium (TFC) has a commitment to encourage the development of new writers, producers and directors

DNA Films
2-4 Noel Street
London W1 3RB
Tel: 0171 287 3209
Fax: 0171 287 3503
Lottery award: £29 million
Number of films: 16
Contact: Grace Hodge
Tel: 0171 485 4411
DNA Film Ltd is formed by **Toledo Pictures; Figment Films**. It intends to make three films per year. Each film's budget will be up to £4 million and will be fully funded by DNA Films

A19 Film and Video
21 Foyle Street
Sunderland SR1 1LE
Tel: 0191 565 5709
Fax: 0191 565 6288
Documentary programmes for television. Education/training material for distribution. Low budget fiction work. Production support offered to local and regionally based film-makers, schools, community groups etc

Aardman Animations
Gas Ferry Road
Bristol BS1 6UN
Tel: 0117 984 8485
Fax: 0117 984 8486
Website: www.aardman.com
Award winning character led model animation studio producing films, commercials and television series. Aardman's first theatrical feature film, Chicken Run, is currently in production

ABTV
Agran Barton Television
The Yacht Club
Chelsea Harbour
London SW10 0XA
Tel: 020 7351 7070
Fax: 020 7352 3528
Linda Agran, Nick Barton
Recent productions: Fusion (C4); Righteous Babes (C4); Previous productions: The Vanishing Man (ITV); Byzantium – The Lost Empire (TLC & C4)

Acacia Productions
80 Weston Park
London N8 9TB
Tel: 020 8341 9392
Fax: 020 8341 4879
email: acacia@dial.pipex.com
Website: www.greenindex.co.uk
Recent productions: Last Plant Standing , international series of programmes about the global conservation of plant genetic resources (4x50mins) Seeds of Hope for Rwanda (25 mins); A Future for Forests (25 mins); The Wokabout Somil (25 mins); Spirit of Trees (8 x 30 min, C4)

Action Time
Wrendal House
2 Whitworth Street

West Manchester M15WX
Tel: 0161 236 8999
Fax: 0161 236 8845
Entertainment programme devisors and producers in UK and Europe. Recent productions: *Mr & Mrs With Julian Clary* (ITV); *Catchphrase* (ITV)

Adventure Pictures
6 Blackbird Yard
Ravenscroft Street
London E2 7RP
Tel: 020 7613 2233
Fax: 020 7256 0842
Produced Sally Potter's *Orlando* and *The Tango Lesson* with other features in development. Television documentaries include: Death of a Runaway (RTS award nomination 1992); Child's Eye (RTS award nomination 1995); Looking for *Billy; Let Me See My Children; Our House; Searching for Susan; Child's Eye; Home Alone; Stepfamilies; The Test; Men Who Pay For Sex; Footballer's Wives; The End is Nigh*

After Image Ltd
32 Acre Lane
London SW2 5SG
Tel: 020 7737 7300
Fax: 020 7326 1850
email: jane@arc.co.uk
Currently developing dramas. Recent Productions include *Television Songs of Seduction*, a music drama; Pull, a sculptural dance. 2 documentaries shot in Africa. 2 television operas called *Camera* and *The Empress* (C4) plus *The Score* (BBC2) a classical music magazine series

Agenda Film
Castell Close
Enterprise Park
Swansea SA7 9FH
Tel: 01792 410510
Fax: 01792 775469
Wales' largest independent production company. Entertainment, drama, features for S4C, C4, BBC, corporate sector. Co-producer of Welsh-based feature films, like *TwinTown*

Alibi Communications
12 Maiden Lane
Covent Garden
London WCZE 7NA
Tel: 020 7845 0430
Gareth Jones
Hilary Davis, Juliette Gill, Nigel Thomas
Formed in 1999 consisting of Alibi Film International, Alibi Entertainment, and Alibi Pictures, with aim of producing quality theatrical feature films and TV drama and sitcom for international distribution

Alive Productions
37 Harwood Road
London SW6 4QP
Tel: 020 7384 2243
Fax: 020 7384 2026
TV programme production company including *Star Test* and *Star Chamber* (both for C4)

Allied Filmmakers
Kent House
Market Place
London W1N 8AR
Tel: 020 7323 5151
Fax: 020 7631 3568
(See Pathé Productions – Lottery Film Production Franchises)

Alomo Productions Ltd
45 Fouberts Place
London W1V 2DN
Tel: 020 7434 3060
Television comedy and drama: *Goodnight Sweetheart; Birds of a Feather; Love Hurts. A Pearson Company*

Amy International Productions
PO Box 17
Towcester
Northants NN12 8YJ
Tel: 01295 760256
Fax: 01295 760889
Such a Long Journey (in post production); *Dragon Under the Hill; The Liaison; Operation Farrier; Herculine Barbin*

Angelic Pictures
21 & 22 Colebrooke Row
Angel
Islington
London N1 8AP
Tel: 020 7359 9514
Fax: 020 7359 9153
email: rslw@hotmail.com
Website: www.angelicpictures.co.uk
Angelic Pictures supports a broad range of individual productions – both broadcast and non-broadcast, including the full production of corporate films, and multi-media packages for companies. Recently produced corporate films for DAE ltd. suppliers in petro chemicals to the oil and gas industry, and Metroski/Metroboard Ltd. technologically advanced ski-simulator and training equipment

Anglia Television Limited
Anglia House
Norwich NR1 3JG
Tel: 01603 615151
Fax: 01603 761245
Website: www.anglia.tv.co.uk

Anglo/Fortunato Films
170 Popes Lane
London W5 4NJ
Tel: 020 8932 7676
Fax: 020 8932 7491
Luciano Celentino
Feature film production company.
1994 Directed *Callan*; 1996 Produced, wrote directed *The Pinch*

The Animation Station
Leisure and Tourism Department
Cherwell District Council
Bodicote House
Bodicote, Banbury
Oxon OX15 4AA
Tel: 01295 252535
Fax: 01295 263155
Dex Mugan
A specialist arts education producer, distributor and trainer. Works in collaboration with innovative artists and performers from across the world, selecting and commissioning a broad range of high quality work

Animha Productions
121 Roman Road
Linthorpe
Middlesbrough TS5 5QB
Tel: 01642 813 137
Fax: 01642 813 137
email: animha@awn.com
Website: www.awn.com/animha

Animus Entertainments
67/71 Goswell Road
London EC1V 7EN
Tel: 020 7490 8234
Fax: 020 7490 8235
Ruth Beni

Antelope
29B Montague Street
London WC1B 5BH
Tel: 020 7209 0099
Fax: 020 7209 0098
email: antelope@antelope.co.uk
Mick Csaky, Krishan Aróra
Dramas and documentaries for broadcast TV in UK, USA, Europe and Japan. Recent productions: *444 Days, A Very British Psycho, Kung Fu Business, The Pier, Frostrup on Sunday, Himalaya*

Arcane Pictures
46 Wetherby Mansions
Earl Court Square
London SW5 9DI
Tel: 020 7244 6590
Fax: 565 4495
email: duffield@dircon.co.uk
Philippa Green. Producers: Meg Thomson, George Duffield
Recent productions: *Milk*

Arlington Productions Ltd
Pinewood Studios

Iver Heath
Bucks SLO ONH
Tel: 01723 651700
Fax: 01723 656050
TV filmmaker (previously through
Tyburn Film Productions Ltd): *The Masks of Death; Murder Elite; Peter Cushing: A One-Way Ticket to Hollywood*

Richard Attenborough Productions
Twickenham Studios
St Margaret's
Twickenham TW1 2AW
Tel: 020 8607 8873
Fax: 020 8744 2766
Recent productions: *Grey Owl; In Love and War*

Aurum Productions
PO Box 14703
London SE1 9WQ
Tel: 020 7401 2700
Fax: 020 7401 2702
Nicholas Burgess-Jones,
Director/Producer
Film and Video Production, Feature
Films-Pop Promos, documentaries

Avalon Television
4a Exmoor Street
London W10 6BD
Tel: 020 7598 7280
Fax: 020 7598 7281
The Frank Skinner Show (BBC1);
Harry Hill (Channel 4); *Quiz Ball*
(BBC1)

Bandung
Block H
Carkers Lane
53-79 Highgate Road
London NW5 1TL
Tel: 020 7482 5045
Fax: 020 7284 0930
email: bandung@gn.apc.org

Basilisk Communications
31 Percy Street
London W1P 9FG
Tel: 020 7580 7222
Fax: 020 7631 0572

Bazal
46-47 Bedford Square
London WC1B 3DP
Tel: 020 7462 9000
Fax: 020 7462 9998
Productions incldue: *Changing Rooms* (BBC1); *Food & Drink* (BBC2); *Ground Force* (BBC1)

BBC Films Ltd
Television Centre
302 Union House
London W12 7RJ
Tel: 020 7743 8000
Recent productions: *24 7; Mrs Brown; Face*

Beambright
Debnershe
The Street
Shalford
Surrey GU4 8BT
Tel: 01483 539343
Fax: 01483 539343

Beaver Films Ltd
Beaver Lodge
Richmond Green
Richmond-Upon-Thames
Surrey TW9 1NQ
Tel: 020 8940 7234
In production *Séance on a Wet Afternoon* (Remake)

Berwin and Dempsey Productions Ltd
37 Arteslan Road
London W2
Tel: 020 7792 5152
Dorothy Berwin, Ceci Dempsey
Recent production: *Bedrooms and Hallways*

BFI Production
21 Stephen Street
London W1P 2LN
Tel: 020 7636 5587
Fax: 020 7580 9456

The Big Group
22 Stephenson Way
London NW1 2HD
Tel: 020 7383 2335
Fax: 020 7383 0357
Producing for television and film

Black Coral Productions
Unit 130, Lea Valley
Technopark,
Ashley Road
London N17 9LN
Tel: 020 8281 0401
Fax: 020 8504 3338
Black Coral is actively involved in documentary and drama productions.

Blue Dolphin Film & Video
40 Langham Street
London W1N 5RG
Tel: 020 7255 2494
Fax: 020 7580 7670

Blue Heaven Productions Ltd
45 Leather Lane
London EC1N 7TJ
Tel: 020 7404 4222
Fax: 020 7404 4266
Producer of *The Ruth Rendell Mysteries* for Meridian/ITV Network

British Lion Film Corporation
Pinewood Studios
Iver Heath
Bucks SLO 0NH

Tel: 01753 651700
Fax: 01753 656391

Britt Allcroft Company PLC The
3 Grosvenor Square
Southampton SO15 2BE
Tel: 01703 331661
Fax: 01703 332206
Recent productions: *Thomas the Tank Engine and Friends*, 104 stories filmed in live-action animation

Bronco Films
Producer's Centre
61 Holland Street
Glasgow G2 4NJ
Tel: 0141 334 4971
Peter Broughan

Brook Lapping Productions
6 Anglers Lane
London NW5 3DG
Tel: 020 7482 3100
Fax: 020 7284 0626
Anne Lapping

Buena Vista Productions
Centre West
3 Queen Caroline Street
Hammersmith
London W4 9PE
Tel: 020 8222 1000
Fax: 020 8222 2795
International television production arm of The Walt Disney Studios

Burder Films John
7 Saltcoats Road
London W4 1AR
Tel: 020 8995 0547
Fax: 020 8995 3376
email: jburder@aol.com
Website: www.johnburder.co.uk
Corporate and broadcast worldwide, productions for many leading sponsors. Including The Common Sense Guides, and ABC of Guides

Buxton Raven Productions Ltd
159-173 St. John Street
London EC1V 4QJ
Tel: 020 7296 0012
Fax: 020 7296 0014
email: jb@buxtonraven.demon.co.uk
Contacts: Jette Bonnevie, Jens Ravn
Founded in 1988, Buxton Raven focuses on feature film development and production

Capitol Films
23 Queensdae Place
London W11 4SQ
Tel: 020 7471 6000
Fax: 020 7471 6012
email: films@capitolfilms.com
Valencia Haynes
Recent productions include: *Dancing*

at Lughnasa, Mad Cows, Among Giants, Wilde and A Soldier's Daughter Never Cries

Carlton Select
45 Fouberts Place
London W1V 2DN
Tel: 020 7434 3060
Fax: 020 7494 1421
Owned by Carlton Communications.
Includes: *Soldier Soldier; Peak Practice; Birds of a Feather, Goodnight Sweetheart*

Carnival (Films and Theatre) Ltd
12 Raddington Road
Ladbroke Grove
London W10 5TG
Tel: 020 8968 1818
Fax: 020 8968 0155
Recent productions: *Films – Firelight; Up on the Roof; The Mill on the Floss; Shadowlands; Under Suspicion; Television – The Tenth Kingdom; Agatha Christie's Poirot; Lucy Sullivan is Getting Married; Every Woman Knows A Secret; Oktober; BUGS; Crime Traveller; Jeeves & Wooster*

Cartwn Cymru
Screen Centre
Llantrisant Road
Cardiff CF5 2PU
Tel: 029 20 575999
Fax: 029 20 575919
Animation production. Recent productions: *Turandot: Operavox* (BBC2/S4C Animated Operas): *Testament: The Bible in Animation*; (S4C/BBC2). *The Miracle Maker* (SAC/BBC/British Screen/Icon); 90 minute theatrical feature. In production: *The Mabinogi* (SAC/BBC); animated feature of medieval epic; *The Fairy Oad* (HIT Entertainment): 75 minute TV feature for Tx on CITV Christmas '99

Catalyst Television
Brook Green Studios
186 Shepherd's Bush Road
London W6 7LL
Tel: 020 7603 7030
Fax: 020 7603 9519
Gardeners World (BBC); *Absolute Beginners* (C5); *Gardening From Scratch* (BBC)

Celador Productions
39 Long Acre
London WC2E 9JT
Tel: 020 7240 8101
Fax: 020 7836 1117
Television: primarily entertainment programming for all broadcast channels. Includes game shows, variety, with selected situation comedy, drama and factual output

Celtic Films
1-2 Bromley Place
London W1P 5HB
Tel: 020 7637 7651
Fax: 020 7436 5387
Sharpe (Carlton UK Productions), *Red Fox* (LWT), *Riszko* (ITV)

Chain Production
2 Clanricarde Gardens
London W2 4NA
Tel: 020 7229 4277
Fax: 020 7229 0861
Garwin Davison, Roberta Licurgo
Development and Co-Production
Feature Films, Previous Production
with India, Italy, USA, Partners

Channel X
22 Stephenson Way
London NW1 2HD
Tel: 020 7387 3874
Fax: 020 7387 0738
email: mail@channelx.co.uk
XYZ; Jo Brand Through the Cakehole; The Smell of Reeves and Mortimer; The Unpleasant World of Penn and Teller; Funny Business, Phil Kay Feels..., Food Fight, Barking . Turning Tricks with Paul Zenon; Families at War, The Cooler, Bang, Bang It's Reeves and Mortimer, Leftfield, All Back to Mine

Chatsworth Television
97-99 Dean Street
London W1V 5RA
Tel: 020 7734 4302
Fax: 020 7437 3301
email: television@chatsworth-tv.co.uk
Sister company to Chatsworth distribution and merchandising companies. Producers of light entertainment and drama. Best known for the long running *Treasure Hunt and The Crystal Maze* (C4), *Mortimer's Law* (BBC)

Cheerleader Productions
43 Whitfield Street
London W1P 6TG
Tel: 020 7258 6800
Fax: 020 7258 6888
Specialists in live and post-produced sports programmes, documentaries, leisure, entertainment

The Children's Film Unit
Unit 8, Princeton Court
55 Felsham Road
London SW15 1AZ
Tel: 020 8785 0350
Fax: 020 8785 0351
email: cfilmunit@aol.com
A registered Educational Charity, the CFU makes low-budget films for television and PR on subjects of concern to children and young

people. Crews and actors are trained at regular weekly workshops in Putney. Work is in 16mm and video, and membership is open to children from 8-18. Latest films for C4: *The Gingerbread House; Awayday; Administrator: Carol Rennie*

Chrysalis Films International Ltd
The Chrysalis Building
13 Bramley Road
London W10 6SP
Tel: 020 7465 6259
Fax: 020 7465 6159
Michael Pilsworth
Motion pictures arm of Chrysalis Visual Entertainment (see below). Recent productions: *Stiff Upper Lips; Richard III* (with United Artists); *Shooting Fish; I Love You – I Love You Not*

Chrysalis Visual Entertainment
The Chrysalis Building
13 Bramley Road
London W10 6SP
Tel: 020 7221 2213
Fax: 020 7465 6159
The following are all part of Chrysalis Visual Entertainment: Assembly Film and Television; Bentley Productions; Cactus TV, Chrysalis Television (includes Chrysalis sport, Chrysalis Sport USA, Mach1, Chrysalis TV, Chrysalis Television North, Chrysalis Creative). Lucky Dog, Red Rooster Television, Tandem Television,. Watchmaker Productions, Chrysalis Television International, Chrysalis Distribution, IDTV (The Netherlands), South Pacific Pictures (New Zealand)

Cinema Verity Productions Ltd
11 Addison Avenue
London W11 4QS
Tel: 020 7460 2777
Fax: 020 7371 3329

Circus Films Ltd
Shepperton Studios
Shepperton
Middlesex TW17 0QD
Tel: 01932 572680/1
Fax: 01932 568989

Clark Television Production
Cavendish House
128-134 Cleveland Street
London W1P 5DN
Tel: 020 7388 7700
Fax: 020 7388 3366
Dispatches; The Black Bag; The Chrystal Rose Show; Class Action; Hard News; Chrystal's Style Guide; Frontline

Comedy House The
6 Bayley Street
London WC1B 3HB
Tel: 020 7304 0047
Fax: 020 7304 0048
Set up in 1990 to develop comedy
films with British talent

The Comic Strip Ltd
Dean House
102 Dean Street
London W1V 5RA
Tel: 020 7734 1166
Fax: 020 7734 1105
Recent productions: Four Men in a
Car – a one-off 30 minute comedy
for C4

Company Pictures
184-192 Drummond Street
London NW1 3HP
Tel: 020 7388 9277
Fax: 020 7388 8107
Produces and develops feature films
and drama for television. Recent
productions include: *Titanic Town*

Connections Communications Centre Ltd
Palingswick House
241 King Street
Hammersmith
London W6 9LP
Tel: 020 8741 1767
Fax: 020 8563 1934
email: @cccmedia.demon.co.uk
Jacqueline Davis
A registered charity producing
promotional and educational videos
for the voluntary sector

Contrast Films
311 Katherine Road
London E7 8PJ
Tel: 020 8472 5001
Fax: 020 8472 5001
Produce documentaries and feature
films.Productions include:
Bangladesh 25: New Eastenders(BBC
Pebble Mill); *Rhythms* (C4); *Flame in
my Heart* (C4)

Cosgrove Hall Films
8 Albany Road
Chorlton-cum-Hardy
Manchester M21 0AW
Tel: 0161 882 2500
Fax: 0161 882 2555
Award-winning animation company
Producer of drawn and model
animation. Creators of:
*Dangermouse; The Wind in the
Willows; Count Duckula; The B.F.G.;
Noddy; Discworld, Foxbusters*

Judy Couniham Films Ltd
12a Newburgh Street
London W1V 1LG
Tel: 020 7287 4329

Fax: 020 7287 2303
Previous productions include:
*Antonia's Line, Before The Rain,
Before the Rain, Time to Love, Janice
Beard 45 wpm.* In development: see
Dakota Films

Dakota Films
12a Newburgh Street
London W1V 1LG
Tel: 020 7287 4329
Fax: 020 7287 2303
Previous productions: *Let Him Have
It; Othello; Janice Beard 45wpm*
In development: *Fade to Black; Me
Without You; Mother of Pearl;
Garnethill*

Dan Films Ltd
32 Maple Street
London W1P 5GD
Tel: 020 7916 4771
Fax: 020 7916 4773
email: office@danfilms.com
Website: www.danfilms.com
Cilla Ware (Director)
Julie Baines (Producer); Sarah Daniel
(Producer); Sara Sutton (Producer's
Assistant); Jason Newmark (Head of
Development). Recent productions:
LA Without a Map (feature); *The Rise
& Fall of Studio 54* (documentary);
Hothouse (single drama tv); *Butterfly
Kiss* (feature); *Madagscar Skin*
(feature)

De Warrenne Pictures
121 Free Trade Wharf
340 The Highway
London E1 9EU
Tel: 020 7790 8068
Fax: 020 7790 6850
Tom Waller
Feature film production company.
Recent projects include *Monk
Dawson* based on award winning
novel by Piers Paul Read. In
Production: *Butterfly Man*, by
Kaprice Kea; In development:
Famine, historical drama set in
Ireland. *Sally*, based on the bestseller
by Freya North

Dennis Woolf Productions
169 Didsbury Road
Stockport
Cheshire SK4 2AE
Tel: 0161 422 8175
Fax: 0161 442 8175

Dirty Hands
c/o Propaganda
2nd Floor
6-10 Lexington Street
London W1R 3HS
Tel: 020 7478 3207
Fax: 020 7734 7131

Diverse Productions
Gorleston Street
London W14 8XS
Tel: 020 7603 4567
Fax: 020 7603 2148
Established in 1982, Diverse is one
of Britain's leading independent
factual programme makers, and has
recently expanded into Interactive
media

DLT Entertainment UK Ltd
10 Bedford Square
London WC1B 3RA
Tel: 020 7631 1184
Fax: 020 7636 4571
Specialising in entertainment
programming

DNA Films
(See DNA Film Ltd – Lottery Film
Production Franchises)

Documedia International Films Ltd
Production Office
19 Widegate Street
London E1 7HP
Tel: 020 7625 6200
Fax: 020 7625 7887
Producers and distributors of
documentary and drama
programming; corporate and Internet
adaptations

Dogstar UK Ltd
5 Sherwood Street
London W1V 7RA
Tel: 020 7287 5944
Fax: 020 7287 1786
email: email@dogstar.co.uk
Liz Barron, Irena Brignull, Rose
Cottam, Alan Greenspan, Mike
Newell, David Parfitt

Domino Films
7 King Harry Lane
St Albans AL3 4S
Tel: 01727 750153
Fax: 01727 750153
email: Jo@dominofilms.co.uk
Well-established company producing
wide range of factual programmes
which include: the award-winning
*Selling Murder; Secret World of Sex;
Lost Children of the Empire; Heil
Herbie.* Other productions include:
*Eve Strikes Back; Breadline Britain
1990s; Soviet Citizens; Take Three
Girls; Windows on the World; What's
the Evidence*

Double Exposure
Unit 22-23
63 Clerkenwell Road
London EC1M 5PS
Tel: 020 7490 2499
Fax: 020 7490 2556
Production and distribution of

broadcast and educational
documentaries in the UK and abroad

Downtown Pictures Ltd
4th Floor, Suite 2
St Georges House
14-17 Wells Street
London W1P 3FP
Tel: 020 7323 6604
Fax: 020 7636 8090
Martin McCabe, Alan McQueen,
Alan Latham, Anne Rigby

Drama House The
20 Chalcot Square
London NW1 8YA
Tel: 020 7586 1000
Fax: 020 7586 1345

Dramatis Personae
19 Regency Street
London SW1P 4BY
Tel: 020 7834 9300

Ecosse Films
12 Quayside Lodge
Watermeadow Lane
London SW6 2UZ
Tel: 020 7371 0290
Fax: 020 7736 3436
Douglas Rae, Emma Crawford,
Robert Bernstein *Mrs. Brown, The
Ambassador, Unsuitable Job for a
Woman*

Edinburgh Film & Video Productions
Edinburgh Film and TV Studios
Nine Mile Burn by Penicuik
Midlothian EH26 9LT
Tel: 01968 672131
Fax: 01968 672685
Major Scottish production company
established in 1961

Elmgate Productions
Shepperton Studios,
Studios Road
Shepperton
Middx TW17 0QD
Tel: 01932 562611
Fax: 01932 569918
Feature films, television films and
series

Endboard Productions
114a Poplar Road
Bearwood
Birmingham B66 4AP
Tel: 0121 429 9779
Fax: 0121 429 9008
Producers of television programmes

Eon Productions
138 Piccadilly
London W1Z 9FH
Tel: 020 7493 7953
Fax: 020 7408 1236
Producers of James Bond films

Equilibrium Films
28 Sheen Common Drive
Richmond TW10 5BN
Tel: 020 8898 0150/ 876 3637
Fax: 020 8898 0150/ 876 3637
Titles include: *The Tribe That Time
Forgot* – an Equilibrium Film
production in association withWGBH
Boston/Nova for PBS;
*Jaguar People;Yemen's Cultural
Drug: Dream or Nightmare;Yemen's
Jambiya Cult;Sudan's Slave Trade;
First Contact – Last Rites* – a Bare
Faced Production for BBC; *Egypt
Powerplays, Burma's Final Solution,
Conquering The Mountain of Fire,
Barefoot Among The Tame Tigers,
Dispatches* C4

Festival Film and Television Ltd
Festival House
Tranquil Passage
Blackheath Village
London SE3 OBJ
Tel: 020 8297 9999
Fax: 020 8297 1155
The company concentrates mainly on
popular television drama and
continues production of its Catherine
Cookson mini-series for ITV. Recent
completed productions include: *The
Round Tower, Colour Blind* and *Tilly
Trotter*. Future projects include *The
Harrogate Secret* (3 part mini-series
for ITV). Series in development
include *Decline and Fall* by Evelyn
Wugh, *Mrs Pargeter*, based on the
books by Simon Brett, and *Lily
Josephine* based on the best selling
novel by Kate Saunders

Figment Films Ltd
2 Noel Street
London W1
Tel: 020 7287 3209
Fax: 020 7287 3503
Productions include: *Shallow Grave;
Trainspotting, Twin Town, A Life Less
Ordinary*
(See DNA Film – Lottery Film
Production Franchises)

Film and General Productions
10 Pembridge Place
London W2 4XB
Tel: 020 7221 1141
Fax: 020 7792 1167

The Film Consortium
9 Flitcroft Street
London WC28H 8DJ
Tel: 020 7691 4440
Fax: 020 7691 4445
Contact: Linda Gamble
Consists of: Greenpoint Films,
Parallax Pictures, Scala and Skreba

(See The Film Consortium – Lottery
Film Production Franchises)

Film Form Productions
64 Fitzjohn's Avenue
London NW3 5LT
Tel: 020 7794 6967
Fax: 020 7794 6967
Film/video production, drama and
documentary for television and video
distribution. Full crewing, writers,
producers and directors

FilmFair Animation
Unit 20 Mitre Bridge Industrial
Estate
Mitre Way
London W10 6AU
Tel: 020 8960 0735
Fax: 020 8964 1277
email: info@film.co.uk
Producers of model animation series,
special effects and commercials.
Productions include: *The Wombles;
Paddington Bear; Huxley Pig;
Gingerbread Man; Astro Farm ; The
Dreamstone; Brown Bear's Wedding;
White Bear's Secret; The Legend of
Treasure Island*

FilmFour Productions
76-78 Charlotte Street
London W1P 1LX
Tel: 020 7868 7700
Fax: 020 7868 7766
Website: www.filmfour.com
International film sales and
distribution arm of C4, often credited
as a co-production partner for UK
and international productions.
Decisions on programming and
finance relating to these productions
are initiated by Channel Four Films,
the film programming strand of C4's
drama department. Recent
productions: *Trainspotting; Brassed
Off; Fever Pitch; Welcome to
Sarajevo; Vigo – Passion For Life,
Martha – Meet Frank, Daniel &
Laurence; The Acid House;
Babymother*

Filmworks
65 Brackenbury Road
Hammersmith
London W6 0BG
Tel: 020 8741 5631
Fax: 020 8748 3198

Fine Line Features
25-28 Old Burlington Street
London W1X 1LB
Tel: 020 7440 1000
Fax: 020 7439 6105
European film production
*Shine,Sweet Hereafter
Deconstructing Harry*

The First Film Company
38 Great Windmill Street
London W1V 7PA
Tel: 020 7439 1640
Fax: 020 7437 2062
Feature film and television
production. *Dance with a Stranger*;
*Soursweet; The Commitments; The
Railway Station Man; A Kind of
Hush*. Among projects in
development: *Flying Hero Class*,
based on the novel by Thomas
Keneally; *Django Reinhardt*, an
original screenplay by Shelagh
Delaney; *No Man's Land*, an original
screenplay by John Forte. *The
Bombard Story* based on the novel by
Alain Bombard

Flashback Productions
22 Kildare Terrace
London W2 5LX
Tel: Tel/Fax: 020 7727 9904
Fax: Tel/Fax: 020 7727 9904

Flashback Television Ltd
11 Bowling Green Lane
London EC1R OBD
Tel: 020 7490 8996
Fax: 020 7490 5610
Award-winning producers of a wide
range of factual programming
including lifestyle, history, natural
history and sport documentaries

Flashlight Films
10 Golden Square
London W1R 3AF
Tel: 020 7287 4252
Fax: 020 7287 4232
email: flashlightfilms@
compuserve.com
Frank Mannion, Aaron Simpson

Focus Films
Rotunda Studios
Rear of 116-118 Finchley Road
London NW3 5HT
Tel: 020 7435 9004
Fax: 020 7431 3562
email: focus@pupix.demon.co.uk
David Pupkewitz, Marsha Levin,
Lisa Nicholson, Malcolm Kohll
Film and television production. Past
productions: Janet Suzman's
critically acclaimed *Othello; Gad
Hollander's Diary of a Sane Man,
Crimetime*, psychological drama,
starring Stephen Baldwin and Pete
Postlethwaite. Slate: *Secret Society;
The 51st State; The Sandmother; Cut
and Paste; On the Frontline; The
Favourite Game*

Mark Forstater Productions
27 Lonsdale Road
London NW6 6RA
Tel: 020 7624 1123
Fax: 020 7624 1124

Recent productions: Paper Marriage;
*The Touch; La Cuisine Polonaise;
Grushko*, BBC drama series; *Between
the Devil and the Deep Blue Sea; The
Last Resort; The Glitterball*

Fox Searchlight Pictures
(see Twentieth Century-Fox
Productions Ltd)
**Twentieth Century-Fox Film Co
Ltd**
Twentieth Century House
31-32 Soho Square
London W1V 6AP
Tel: 020 7437 7766
Fax: 020 7734 3187
Website: www.fox.co.uk/
Recent productions: *Smilla's Feeling
for Snow; Cousin Bette; Oscar and
Lucinda*

Fragile Films
95-97 Dean Street
London W1N 3XX
Tel: 020 7287 6200
Fax: 020 7287 0069
email: fragile@fragilefilms.com
(See Pathé Productions – Lottery
Film Production Franchises)
An Ideal Husband

Freedom Pictures
10 Rylett Crescent
Shepherds Bush
London W12 9RL
Tel: 020 8743 5330
Fax: 0468 855746

Front Page Films
23 West Smithfield
London EC1A 9HY
Tel: 020 7329 6866
Fax: 020 7329 6844
Owners of the Richmond Film-house.
Past productions: The Mini Sagas,
six theatrical shorts which were
released by UIP alongside *A Fish
Called Wanda, Parenthood and The
Naked Gun; Get Back*, a feature with
Paul McCartney directed by Richard
Lester. In development: a number of
feature films

Fugitive Films
21-22 Gate Street
London WC2A 3HP
Tel: 020 7242 6969
Fax: 020 7242 6970

Fulcrum Productions Ltd
254 Goswell Road
London EC1V 7RE
Tel: 020 7253 0353
Fax: 020 7490 0206
email: Sandra@FulcrumTV.com
Website: www.FulcrumTV.com
Sandra Leeming
Fulcrum Productions has made a
wide range of documentaries, current

affairs and arts programmes for
television. 1998 work: Feature Film:
Like it Is; BBC: *Crossing The Lines*;
ITV: *Diana – Secrets Behind the
Crash*; C4: *Foot & Hardy; NHS
Direct – The Fine Art of
Crime; Altered Minds – A Citizen's
Commission on Drugs; The Power
List; Dispatches – Nice Work If You
Can Get It; Witness – Jonestown;
Fusion – Looking For Dad;
Dispatches – Kicking the Habit;
Pulp; Dispatches – The No Car
Challenge*. C5: *First on Five*.
Discovery Channel: *Amazing Earth*

Gainsborough (Film & TV) Productions
The Groom Cottage
Pinewood Studios
Pinewood Lane
Iver Heath
Iver Bucks SLO ONH
Tel: 020 7409 1925
Fax: 020 7408 2042
In development: *Dangerous Love;
Bewitched; A Heart in the Highlands*

General Entertainment Investments
Bray Film Studios
Down Place, Windsor Road
Windsor
Berkshire SL4 5UG
Tel: 01628 22111
Fax: 01628 770381
Feature film producers/financiers

Global Vision Network
Elstree Film Studios
Borehamwood
Hertfordshire WD6 1JG
Tel: 020 8324 2333
Fax: 020 8324 2700
email: info@gvn.co.uk
Website: www.gvn.co.uk

Bob Godfrey Films
199 Kings Cross Road
London WC1X 9DB
Tel: 020 7278 5711
Fax: 020 7278 6809
Prominent studio, with recent
productions: *Small Talk,*
entertainment short, Oscar
nomination 1993; Children's TV
series: *Kevin Saves the World.
Entertainments The Many Deaths of
Norman Spittal*. Steve Bell: *The
Thatcher Legacy*

Goldcrest Films International
65-66 Dean Street
London W1V 6PL
Tel: 020 7437 8696
Fax: 020 7437 4448
Major feature film production, sales
and finance company. Recent

productions: *No Way Home; Bring Me The Head of Mavis Davis; Clockwatchers; Annabelle's Wish*

Goldwyn Films
10 Stephen Mews
London W1P 1PP
Tel: 020 7333 8877
Fax: 020 8333 8878

Granada Film
The London Television Centre
Upper Ground
London SE1 9LT
Tel: 020 7737 8681
Fax: 020 7737 8682
Head of Film: Pippa Cross
Established in 1989 – a subsidiary of the Granada Media Group. Feature films: *The Heart; Up On the Roof; Some Kind of Life; August; Jack & Sarah; The Field; My Left Foot; The Fruit Machine*

Greenpoint Films
5a Noel Street
London W1V 3RB
Tel: 020 7437 6492
Fax: 020 7437 0644
A loose association of ten filmmakers: Simon Relph, Christopher Morahan, Ann Scott, Richard Eyre, Stephen Frears, Patrick Cassavetti, John Mackenzie, Mike Newell, David Hare and Christopher Hampton
(See The Film Consortium – Lottery Film Production Franchises)

Griffin Productions
Global House
96-108 Great Suffolk Street
London WC1
Tel: 020 7620 1620
Fax: 020 7578 4390
Current productions: *Human Bomb* (Showtime), *Place of Lions* (Universal), *Pimpernel* (Showtime), *Prince of Mars* (Universal), *Week to Remember* (BBC), *Quintessial Verse* (BBC)

Gruber Films
1st Floor
74 Margaret Street
London W1N 7HA
Tel: 020 7436 3413
Fax: 020 7436 3402
Richard Holmes, Neil Peplow
Recent productions: *Walking Ned, Shooting Fish*
In development: *Raving Beauties, Snookered, Trilogy*

guerilla films
35 Thornbury Road
Iselworth
Middlesex TW7 4LQ
Tel: 020 8758 1716

Fax: 020 8758 9364
email: david@guerilla.u-net.com
Website: www.guerilla.u-net.com
David Nicholas Wilkinson
Productions include: *Dylan Thomas: Return Journey; James Herriot's Yorkshire; A Very English Madam*

HAL Films Ltd
45a Brewer Street
London W1R 3FD
Tel: 020 7434 4408
Recently founded British subsidiary of Miramax Films UK. In preparation: *Mansfield Park*

Halas & Batchelor
The Halas & Barchelor Collection Ltd
35a Pond Street
London NW3 2PN
Tel: 020 7435 8674
Fax: 020 7431 6835
Animation films from 1940

Hammer Film Productions
Millennium Studios, 5 Elstree Way
Borehamwood
Herts WD6 1SF
Tel: 020 8324 2284
Fax: 020 8905 1127
Graham Skeggs
The company responsible for many classic British horror films. In development: eight features for theatrical release; three projects for television production

Harcourt Films
58 Camden Square
London NW1 9XE
Tel: 020 7267 0882
Fax: 020 7267 1064
Producer of documentaries and arts programmes. Recent productions: 90 minute TV special *The Capeman* for HBO, One hour music docs

Hartswood Films
Twickenham Studios
The Barons
St Margarets
Twickenham
Middx TW1 2AW
Tel: 020 8607 8736
Fax: 020 8607 8744
Wonderful You (7X60min drama); *Men Behaving Badly* (6 series and 4 Christmas Specials, sitcom); *Is it Legal?* (3 series, sitcom); *In Love With Elizabeth* (1x60min, documentary); *Officers and Gentlemen* (1x60min, documentary); *The Red Baron* (1x60min, documentary); *Going to Chelsea* (1x60min, documentary); *My Good Friend* (2 series, comedy drama); *The English Wife* (drama); *A Woman's Guide to Adultery* (drama); *Code Name Kyril* (drama)

Hat Trick Productions
10 Livonia Street
London W1V 3PH
Tel: 020 7434 2451
Fax: 020 7287 9791
Denise O'Donoghue
Jimmy Mulville, Mary Bell, Hilary Strong
Specialising in comedy, light entertainment and drama.
Productions include: *Father Ted; Drop the Dead Donkey; Have I Got News For You; Confessions; Whatever You Want; Game On; The Peter Principle; If I Ruled the World; Clive Anderson All Talk; Room 101 and Whose Line is it Anyway?* The company's drama output includes: *A Very Open Prison; Boyz Unlimited; Eleven Men Against Eleven; Lord of Misrule; Crossing the Floor; Gobble* and *Underworld*

Hellion Pictures
1st Floor, 47 Dean Street
Soho
London W1V 5HL
Tel: 020 7924 0663
Fax: 01489 894 768
Chris Barfoot

Jim Henson Productions
30 Oval Road, Camden
London NW1 7DE
Tel: 020 7428 4000
Fax: 020 7428 4001
Producers of high quality children's/family entertainment for television and feature films, usually with a puppetry or fantasy connection. Recent productions: *Muppet Treasure Island* – feature

Holmes Associates
38-42 Whitfield Street
London W1P 5RF
Tel: 020 7813 4333
Fax: 020 7637 9024
Long-established UK independent production company for broadcast television

Hourglass Productions Ltd
24 Redding House
King Henry's Wharf
London SE18 5SR
Tel: 020 8858 6870/854 5557
Fax: 020 8858 6870
Founded in 1993 by John Walsh, now Vice Chair of the Directors Guild of Great Britain. Hourglass has become synominous with quality documentaries and dramas.
Productions include: the Oscar winning Ray Harryhausen; HRH Elizabeth II; The Comedy Store; the smash hit 15 part documentary series *Boyz & Girlz* from Channel Five and the internationally acclaimed feature

film Monarch. For 1999/2000 Hourglass has a new series for Channel Five entitled *Cowboyz and Cowgirlz* and a major feature film project

Hurll Television Michael
5th Floor, Avon House
Kensington Village
Avonmore Road
London W14 8TS
Tel: 020 7371 5354
Fax: 020 7371 5355

Iambic Productions
89 Whiteladies Road
Bristol BS8 2NT
Tel: 0117 923 7 222
Fax: 0117 923 8343
All Iambic's documentaries from 1991 to 1998 have won or been nominated for major awards in the UK or US, including BAFTAs and an international Emmy

Icon Entertainment International Ltd
37 Soho Square
London W1V 5DG
Tel: 020 7543 4300
Fax: 020 7543 4301
Recent productions: *Hamlet; Immortal Beloved; Braveheart; Anna Karenina.* In development: *Farenheit 451*

Idealworld Productions Ltd
St George's Studios
93-97 St George's Road
Glasgow G3 6JA
Tel: 0141 353 3222
Fax: 0141 353 3221
Film and television production. 1998 Productions *Deals On Wheels* (C4); *Tool Stories* (C4); *Equinox – Ekranoplan* (C4); *Beg To Differ* (C4); *Italian Cookbook* (C4); *1998 Transmissions Island Harvest* (BBC Scotland)

Illuminations Films/Koninck Studios
19-20 Rheidol Mews
Rheidol Terrace
London N1 8NU
Tel: 020 7226 0266
Fax: 020 7359 1151
email: griff@illumin.co.uk
Producers of fiction films for television and theatric release. Latest productions: *The Institute Benjamenta* by The Brothers Quay; *Robinson in Space* by Patrick Keiller; *Conspirators of Pleasure* by Jan Svankmajer; *Dance of the Wind* by Rajan Khosa: *The Falconer's Tale* by Chris Petit & Iain Sinclair; *Deadpan* by Steve McQueen

Illuminations Interactive
19-20 Rheidol Mews
Rheidol Terrace
London N1 8NU
Tel: 020 7226 0266
Fax: 020 7359 1151
email: terry@illumin.co.uk
Website: www.illumin.co.uk
Contact: Terry Braun
Partnered with Illuminations Television and Illuminations Films. Company developing and producing Interactive multi-media projects about history, culture and the visual and performing arts. Past interactive multimedia clients include: The Arts Council of England, the Museum of London, the Museum of Scotland, The Tate Gallery, The Horniman Museum and the European Community through its IMPACT initiative. Current interactive multimedia and World Wide Web clients include: Sadler's Wells Theatre, the American Symphony Orchestra League, the Imperial War Museum, the Museum of the Moving Image, The Museum of London, The Royal Festival Hall, The Hayward Gallery, the BFI, Granada Television and Channel 4 Television. Current productions include CD-Roms for the British Museum, Channel 4 Television and a website for the Museums and Galleries Commission

Illuminations Television
19-20 Rheidol Mews
Rheidol Terrace
London N1 8NU
Tel: 020 7226 0266
Fax: 020 7359 1151
email: illuminations@illumin.co.uk
Website: www.illumin.co.uk
Producers of cultural programmes for C4, BBC and others. Recent productions: *Richard II*, Deborah Warner's acclaimed production starring Fiona Shaw for BBC2 Performance; Tx 3 (BBC2), arts series; *The Net 4* (BBC2), magazine series about computers and the digital world; The Turner Prize 1997 (C4); *Is Painting Dead?* arts discussion programme (C4); *Things to Come* (C4); and *Dope Sheet* (C4), series about animation

Illustra Television
13-14 Bateman Street
London W1V 6EB
Tel: 020 7437 9611
Fax: 020 7734 7143

imaginary films
19 Ainsley St
London E2 ODL
Tel: 020 7613 5882

Fax: 020 7729 9280
email: brady@imagfilm.demon.co.uk
Website: www.imagfilm.co.uk
Ray and Deba Brady
An independent feature film production company, films include *Boy Meets Girl* (94), *Little England* (96), and *Kiss, Kiss Bang Bang* (97-98) all directed by Ray Brady. In development with BBNW are the features *Day of the Sirens* and *Little Angels* to be shot in (99) co-producers Annabel Nice and Kevin Watts, and Fate a psychological horror film, to be produced by Robert Sidoway and Mike Ashwell

Imagine Films Ltd
53 Greek Street
London W1V 5LR
Tel: 020 7287 4667
Fax: 020 7287 4668
(See Pathé Productions – Lottery Film Production Franchises)
Producers: Simon Channing-Williams; Stephanie Faugher; Finance Director: Eddie Kane

Impact Pictures Ltd
10/12 Carlisle Street (3rd floor)
London W1V 5RF
Registered address:
99 Kenton Road
Harrow
Middx HA3 OAN
Tel: 020 7734 9650
Fax: 020 7734 9652
James Roeber
Jeremy Bolt, Ariane Severin, Paul Anderson
Productions include: *Shopping*, directed by Paul Anderson and Stiff *Upper Lips*, directed by Gary Sinyor. In development: *Soldier* to be directed by Paul Anderson, with Gerry Weintraub. *Vigo* to be directed by Julien Temple with Nitrate Film/Channel 4

Insight Productions/Insight Pictures
Gidleigh Studio
Gidleigh, Chagford
Newton Abbot
Devon TQ13 8HP
Tel: 01647 432686
Fax: 01647 433141
Established in 1982, nearly 50 broadcast film credits

Interactive TV Productions
Mezzanine Floor
Mappin House
4 Winsley Street
London W1N 7AR
Tel: 020 7333 0444
Fax: 020 7333 0777

International Broadcasting Trust (IBT)
2 Ferdinand Place
London NW1 8EE
Tel: 020 7482 2847
Fax: 020 7284 3374
An independent, non-profit television production company and educational charity, specialising in making programmes on development, environment and human rights issues for UK and international broadcast. Recent productions include: *Dance of the People* – four programmes by young directors on anti-racism and cultural diversity, for BBC2; *The Bank, The President and the Pearl of Africa* a two-part fly-on-the-wall documentary series inside the World Bank, for Channel 4; *Paradise Blues* – a 30 minute documentary for Channel 4 following a Voluntary Services Overseas (VSO) mental health worker to Zanzibar; and *The India File* – five programmes for primary school pupils on the diversity of life in India, for Channel 4 Schools

J&M Entertainment Ltd
2 Dorset Square
London NW1 6PX
Tel: 020 7723 6544
Fax: 020 7724 7541
email: sales@jment.com
Recent productions: *Forever Mine, The Guilty Complicity, A Texas Funeral, History is Made at Night, Bruno*

Kai Film & TV Productions
1 Ravenslea Road
London SW12 8SA
Tel: 020 8673 4550
Fax: 020 8675 4760
Recent productions: *The Unbearable Shiteness of Being; Leopoldville*

Kensington Films
60 Charlotte Street
London W1P 2AX
Tel: 020 7927 8458
Fax: 020 7927 8798

Bill Kenwright Films
55-59 Shaftesbury Avenue
London W1V 7AA
Tel: 020 7439 4466
Fax: 020 7437 8370
Bill Kenwright
Recent productions: *Us Begins With You; Don't Go Breaking My Heart*

Kinetic Pictures
Video and Broadcast Production
The Chubb Buildings
Fryer Street
Wolverhampton WV1 1HT
Tel: 01902 837777
Fax: 01902 717143
email: kinetic@waverider.co.uk
Contact: Gary J Crozier, Creative Director

King Rollo Films
Dolphin Court
High Street
Honiton
Devon EX14 8LS
Tel: 01404 45218
Fax: 01404 45328
Produce top quality animated entertainment for children. In autumn 1993 the company's highly acclaimed line of *Spot* films was launched under licence by Disney for the North American home video market and now world sales of these titles approach two million cassettes. Producers of the animated series: *Mr Benn; King Rollo; Victor and Maria; Towser; Watt the Devil; The Adventures of Spot; The Adventures of Ric; Anytime Tales; Art; Play It Again; It's Fun to Learn with Spot; Buddy and Pip, Spot's Magical Christmas, Little Mr Jakob; Philipp; Happy Birthday; Good Night, Sleep Tight; Spot and his Grandparents go to the Carnival, Maisy*

Landseer Film & Television Productions
140 Royal College Street
London NW1 0TA
Tel: 020 7485 7333
Fax: 020 7485 7573
Documentary, music arts, dance and children's programming. Recent prouductions: *Petula Clark – South Bank Show* (LWT), *Routes of Rock* (Carlton), *Death of a Legend – Frank Sinatra* (LWT), *The Judas Tree* (Channel Four), *Benjamin Zander – Living on One Buttock* (BBC), *Zeffirelli – South Bank Show* (LWT), *Gounods Faust* (Channel Four), *Hear My Chanson – South Bank Show* (LWT), *Swinger* (BBC2)

Langham Productions (A division of the Man Alive Group)
Westpoint
33-34 Warple Way
London W3 0RG
Tel: 020 8743 7431
Fax: 020 8740 7454
Michael Latham, Michael Johnstone

Large Door Productions
2 Tunstall Road
London SW9 8BN
Tel: 020 7978 9500
Fax: 020 7978 9578
Founded in 1982 to specialise in documentaries about cinema and popular culture with an international emphasis

Leda Serene
31 Holberton Gardens
London NW10 6AY
Tel: 020 8969 7094/020 8346 4482
Fax: 020 8964 3044
email: ls@ledaserene.demon.co.uk
Frances-Anne Solomon, Rene Mohandas

Little Bird Co
7 Lower James Street
London W1
Tel: 020 7434 1131
Fax: 020 7434 1803
James Mitchell, Jonathan Cavendish
Feature films: *Nothing Personal; December Bride; Into the West; All Our Fault; A Man of No Importance; My Mother's Courage*. TV: *The Hanging Gale; Divine Magic*

Little Dancer
Avonway
Naseby Road
London SE19 3JJ
Tel: 020 8653 9343
Fax: 020 8653 9343
Recent productions in development: *Adios* by Sue Townsend; *Wilderness Years* by Sue Townsend. *Summer 99* a teen series; *Biff on TV*; digital Drama

Living Tape Productions
84 Newman Street
London W1P 3LD
Tel: 020 7299 1800
Fax: 020 7299 1818
Producers of documentary and educational programmes for television and video distribution

London Films
35 Davies Street
London W1Y 1FN
Tel: 020 7499 7800
Fax: 020 7499 7994
Founded in 1932 by Alexander Korda. Many co-productions with the BBC, including *Scarlet Pimpernel* starring Richard E. Grant for BBC TV/A+E Network, *Lady Chatterley, Resort to Murder; I, Claudius, Poldark* and *Testament of Youth*. Produced *The Country Girls* for C4.

M W Entertainments Ltd
48 Dean Street
London W1V 5HL
Tel: 020 7734 7707
Fax: 020 7734 7727
Film and theatre producer

Malachite Productions
East Kirkby House
Spilsby

Lincolnshire PE23 4BX
Tel: 01790 763538
Fax: 01790 763409
email:malachite Ltd@csi.com
London Office: 020 7487 5451
Charles Mapleston, Nancy Thomas,
Nikki Crane
Producers of people-based
documentary programmes on music,
design, painting, photography, arts,
anthropology and environmental
issues for broadcast television. The
company also produces dramatised
documentary programmes, is
developing micro-budget fiction
films, and is experimenting with new
technologies to communicate in new
ways. Recent productions: *John
Clare's Journey; Clarke's Penny
Whistle; A Voyage with Nancy
Blackett; Small Silver Screens;
Sequins in my Dreams*

Malone Gill Productions Ltd
9-15 Neal Street
London WC2H 9PU
Tel: 020 7460 4683
Fax: 020 7460 4679
email: ikonic@compuserve.com
Recent productions: *The Face of
Russia* (PBS); *Vermeer* (ITV);
Highlanders (ITV); *Storm Chasers*
(C4/Arts and Entertainment
Network); *Nature Perfected*
(C4/NHK/ABC/Canal Plus/RTE);
The Feast of Christmas (C4/SBS);
Nomads (C4/ITEL)

Manuel Productions Ltd Jo
11 Keslake Road
London NW6 6DG
Tel: 020 8930 0777
Fax: 020 8933 5475
Recent productions: *The Boy From
Mercury* directed by Martin Duffy
with Hugh O'Conor, Rita
Tushingham and Tom Courtenay.
Widow's Peak (Rank, Fineline,
British Screen), directed by John
Irvin with Mia Farrow, Joan
Plowright, Natasha Richardson. In
pre-production: *Mattie* starring Mia
Farrow, *Beyond the Meadow* (to be
directed by Richard Spense)

Maya Vision
43 New Oxford Street
London WC1A 1BH
Tel: 020 7836 1113
Fax: 020 7836 5169
email: maya@mayavisn.demon.co.uk
John Cranmer

Media Legal (Originations)
Media Legal
83 Clarendon Road
Sevenoaks
Kent TN13 1ET

Tel: 01732 460592
Production arm of Media Legal
developing legal projects for film and
TV

The Media Trust
3-7 Euston Centre
Regent's Place
Off Euston Road
London NW1 3JG
Tel: 020 7874 7600
Fax: 020 7874 7644
email: mediatrust@theframe.com
The Media Trust helps other charities
and voluntary organisations to
understand and access the media

Meditel Productions
4a Hollybush Place
London E2 9QX
Tel: 020 7613 5266
Fax: 020 7613 5398
Provides medical, science-based and
factual documentaries for television.
Past productions: *AZT – Cause for
Concern; The AIDS Catch; AIDS and
Africa* (C4 Dispatches); *Impotence –
One in Ten Men* (C4); *HRT – Pause
for Thought* (Thames TV This Week)

Mentorn Barraclough Carey
43 Whitfield Street
London W1P 67G
Tel: 020 7258 6800
Fax: 020 7258 6888
Website: www.mentorn.co.uk
Entertainment, drama, entertainment
news, documentaries, news and
current affairs, children's and features

Merchant Ivory Productions
46 Lexington Street
London W1P 3LH
Tel: 020 7437 1200/439 4335
Fax: 020 7734 1579
Producer Ismail Merchant and
director James Ivory together have
made, among other films, for
theatrical and television release

The Mersey Television Company
Campus Manor
Childwall Abbey Road
Liverpool L16 0JP
Tel: 0151 722 9122
Fax: 0151 722 1969
Independent production company
responsible for C4 thrice-weekly
drama series, *Brookside*

Mersham Productions
Newhouse, Mersham
Ashford
Kent TN25 6NQ
Tel: 01233 503636
Fax: 01233 502244

Mike Mansfield TV
5th Floor
41-42 Berners Street
London W1P 3AA
Tel: 020 7580 2581
Fax: 020 7580 2582

Mirage Enterprises
5 Wardour Mews
London W1R
Tel: 020 7734 3627
Recent productions: *Sliding Doors;
Sense and Sensibility; Out of Africa*

Miramax International (London)/Miramax Films UK Ltd
45a Brewer Street
London W1R 3FD
Tel: 020 7434 4408
David Aukin
Major US independent. Recent
productions: *Shakespeare in Love;
Little Voice; Velvet Goldmine*

Momentum Productions
63 Park Road
Teddington TW11 0AV
Tel: 020 8977 7333
Fax: 020 8977 6999
Specialists in on-screen marketing
and promotion of feature films – film
trailers, promos and commercials.
Producers of corporate films

Morningside Productions Inc
8 Ilchester Place
London W14 8AA
Tel: 020 7602 2382
Fax: 020 7602 1047

Mosiac Films Limited
The Old Butchers Shop
St Briavels
Glos GL15 6TA
email: info@mosaicfilms.com
Website: www.mosaicfilms.com
Adam Alexander
2nd Floor
8-12 Broadwick Street
London W1V 1FH
Tel: 020 7437 6514
Fax 020 7494 0595
Contact: Colin Luke
Recent productions: *Return to
Wonderland* – a series for BBC2;
Think of England for BBC Modern
Times; *Unholy Land* – a series for
C4; *Vyvan's Hotel* – for BBC Picture
This; Patriarchs, Presidents and
Profits – BBC Correspondent Special

MW Entertainments
48 Dean Street
Soho
London W1V 5HL
Tel: 020 7734 7707
Fax: 020 7734 7727

(See Pathé Productions – Lottery Film Production Franchises)

New Century Films Ltd
19 Little Russel Street
Bloomsbury
London WC1A 2HN
Tel: 020 7916 9723

New Realm Entertainments Ltd
2nd Floor, 25 Margaret Street
London W1
Tel: 020 7436 7800
Fax: 020 7436 0690

Noel Gay Television
1 Albion Court
Gelene Road
Hammersmith
London W6 OQT
Tel: 020 8600 5200
Fax: 020 8600 5222
TV Drama and TV entertainment. Associate companies: Grant Naylor Production. Noel Gay Motion Picture Company, Noel Gay Scotland, Rose Bay Film Productions, Sunbeam Productions, Pepper Productions

North South Productions
Woburn Buildings
1 Woburn Walk
London WC1H 0JJ
Tel: 020 7388 0351
Fax: 020 7388 2398
Development, travel and other international themes

Nova Productions
11a Winholme
Armthorpe
Doncaster DN3 3AF
Tel: (01302) 833422
Fax: (01302) 833422
email: info@novaonline.co.uk
Website: www.novaonline.co.uk
Andrew White, Maurice White, Gareth Atherton
Film and television production company, specialising in documentary, entertainment, special event and music promo production. Producer of programmes released on sell-through video on its own label via subsidiary Nova Home Entertainment and on other labels. Game show format development including *Bet To Win, Alphabeties and The Right Order*. Also training, promotional and multi-camera OB production for broadcast and non-broadcast. Recent productions: *The Doncaster Mansion House, More Buses of the South Yorkshire PTE: 1974-1986, 50 Years of Sheffield's Transport* – documentaries; *Beat Box* – karaoke music quiz game show;

Remembrance Sunday 1997 – multi-camera OB

Nunhead Films plc
Pinewood Studios
Pinewood Road
Iver Heath
Bucks SL0 0NH
Tel: 01753 656 158
Fax: 01753 655 700
email: info@nunheadfilms.com
Carol Lemon, John Stewart, Harry F Rushton
Feature film and television production

Orbit Media Ltd
7/11 Kensington High Street
London W8 5NP
Tel: 020 7221 5548
Fax: 020 7727 0515
Jordan Reynolds
Currently producing Richard O'Brien's *Midnight Matinee, History of Television*

Orlando TV Productions
Up-the-Steps
Little Tew
Chipping Norton
Oxon OX7 4JB
Tel: 01608 683218
Fax: 01608 683364
email: orlando.tv@btinternet.com
Producers of TV documentaries: *Nova* (WGBH-Boston); *Horizon* (BBC); *QED* (BBC)

Oxford Film and Video Makers
The Stables
North Place, Headington
Oxford OX3 9HY
Tel: 01865 741682
Fax: 01865 742901
Oxford Film and Video Makers supports a broad range of individual productions – both broadcast and non-broadcast – giving a voice to people normally under-represented in the media. Promoting experimental film and video art through 'Arteaters'. Supporting productions with campaigning groups through the CCD group. Production company facility now also available

Oxford Film Company
Studio 5
10/11 Archer Street
London W1V 7HG
Tel: 020 7439 0540
Fax: 020 7437 1182
Released *Hilary and Jackie* starring Emily Watson, directed by Anand Tucker and *The Dance*, an Icelandic/British/Dnish/German co-production directed by Agust Gudmundsson

Oxford Scientific Films
Lower Road
Long Hanborough
Oxford OX8 8LL
Tel: 01993 881881
Fax: 01993 882808

Pacesetter Productions Ltd
The Gardner's Lodge
Cloisters Business Centre
8 Battersea Park Road
London SW8 4BH
Tel: 020 7720 4545
Fax: 020 7720 4949

Pagoda Film & Television Corporation Ltd
Twentieth Century House
31-32 Soho Square
London W!V 6AP
Tel: 020 7534 3500
Fax: 020 7534 3501
In development: *Mary Stuart, That Funny Old Thing, The Corsican Sisters*

Paladin Pictures
22 Ashchurch Grove
London W12 9B7
Tel: 020 8740 1811
Fax: 020 8740 7220
Quality documentary, drama, music and arts programming. Recent productions include: *Plague Wars* (BBC1 series/WGBH Frontline); *Purple Secret* (C4-Secret History); *The Last Flight of Zulu Delta 576* (C4-Cutting Edge); *A Death In Venice* (BBC2-The Works); *Brothers & Sisters* (C4 series); *The Shearing Touch* (ITV-South Bank Show). Current Productions: *Georgiana – Duchess of Devonshire* (C4 historical biography); *Blood Family – a history of the Spencers* (C4 series); *Travels With My Tutu*, with Deborah Bull (BBC2 series on ballet); *The Secret Life of Daphne du Maurier* (BBC); *The Assassin's Wife* (2hr Movie of the Week)

paradogs Ltd
206 Panther House
38 Mount Pleasant
London WC1X OAP
Tel: 020 7833 1009
Fax: 020 7833 1009
Steven Eastwood, Writer/Director
Duncan Western, Editor/Camera-Op
Experimental, narrative, documentary and pop promo

Parallax Pictures
7 Denmark Street
London WC2H 8LS
Tel: 020 7836 1478
Fax: 020 7497 8062
Recent productions: Ken Loach's *Ladybird, Ladybird, Land and*

Freedom; Carla's Song; Les Blair's Jump the Gun; Bad Behaviour, Bliss; Philip Davis's ID; Christopher Monger's The Englishman Who Went Up the Hill, But Came Down a Mountain, Hold Back the Night (See The Film Consortium – Lottery Film Production Franchises)

Paramount-British Pictures Ltd
Paramount House
162-170 Wardour Street
London W1V
Tel: 020 7287 6767
Fax: 020 7734 0387
Sliding Doors, Event Horizon, Titanic

Partridge Films
The Television Centre
Bath Road
Bristol BS4 3HG
Tel: 0117 972 3777
Fax: 0117 971 9340
email: wildlife@partridge.co.uk
Michael Rosenberg (Director of Programmes), Andrew Buchanan (Head of Development), Jayne Clark (Director of Operations), Kate Edmondson (Library)
Makers of wildlife documentaries and videos for television and educational distribution. Recent productions include: *The Secret of Sharks and the Otters of Yellowstone* (BBC The Natural World and PBS) *Deadly Crocodiles and The Ten Deadliest Snakes in the World* (ITV), *Forces of the Wild* (Canal+ and PBS), *The Human Sexes* (The Learning Channel), *Amazing Animals* (Disney Channel), *Animal Alphabet* (C4)

Pathé Pictures
Kent House
Market Place
London W1N 8AR
Tel: 020 7323 5151
Fax: 020 7636 7594
Contact: Peter Scott
Consists of: Thin Man Films and Imagine Films, Allied Filmmakers and Allied Films Ltd, NFH, Pandora Productions, Sarah Radclyffe Productions, Fragile Films and MW Entertainment
(See Pathé Productions – Lottery Film Production Franchises)

PD&B Films
68 Middle Street
Brighton
East Sussex BN1 1AL
Tel: 01273 235525
Fax: 01273 235528
email: info@pdbfilms.com
Website: www.pdbfilms.com
Feature projects: *Out of Season; Anderson 3*

TV projects: *Hallowed Ground*: 6x1 hour European co-production series Movie Asylum: 4x40 minute L/E documentaries

Pearl Productions Ltd
11 Holbein House
London SW1 W8NH
email: info@pearlproductions.co.uk
Website: www.pearlproductions.co.uk
Camilla Doege-Kohle
Film production company. Also involved in the European Short Film Festival

Penumbra Productions Ltd
80 Brondesbury Road
London NW6 6RX
Tel: 020 7328 4550
Fax: 020 7328 3844
Cinema and television productions, specialising in contemporary issues and in the relationship between 'North' and 'South'. Recent productions: *China Rocks; Repomen; Bombay and Jazz; Divided By Rape; Stories My Country Told Me*. In development: a cinema feature, Sold; several documentary series relating to history, the environment and the future

Persistent Vision Productions
299 Ivydale Road
London SE15 3DZ
Tel: 020 7639 5596
Carol Lemon, John Stewart
In distribution: *Crash; The Gaol; The Break-In*

Peter Batty Productions
Claremont House
Renfrew Road
Kingston
Surrey KT2 7NT
Tel: 020 8942 6304
Fax: 020 8336 1661
Recent C4 productions: Swastika Over British Soil; A Time for Remembrance; The Divided Union; Fonteyn and Nureyev; The Algerian War; Swindle; Il Poverello. Independent productions: The Story of Wine; Battle for Warsaw; Battle for Dien Bien Phu; Birth of the Bomb; Search for the Super; Battle for Cassino; Operation Barbarossa; Farouk: Last of the Pharaohs

Photoplay Productions
21 Princess Road
London NW1 8JR
Tel: 020 7722 2500
Fax: 020 7722 6662
Kevin Brownlow, David Gill, Patrick Stanbury
Producers of documentaries and television versions of silent feature films

Picture Palace Films Ltd
19 Edis Street
London NW1 8LE
Tel: 020 7586 8763
Fax: 020 7586 9048
email: 100444.2737@ compuserve.com
Website: www.picturepalace.com
Malcolm Craddock, Alex Usborne
Specialise in feature film and TV drama and documentary
Recent productions: *A Life for a Life – The True Story of Stefan Kiszko* starring Olympia Dukakis (1 x 2hr film, co-production with Celtic Films); Irvine Welsh's *The Acid House* (feature). *Sharpe* (5 series, 14 x 2 hrs, Carlton), set in the Peninsular War. *Little Napoleons* (4 x 1 hr, C4), *Tales From a Hard City* (90 mins, C4/Yorkshire TV/La Sept/ARTE) In development: *The Spire* (feature) by Roger Spottiswoode, *Rebellion* (4 x 1 hour TV drama BBC Northern Ireland, Irish Film Board, Irish Screen, Media II) *Kolymsky Heights* (feature) with Jon Amil and *Sharpe's Tiger* (feature) with Celtic Films and Carlton Films

Planet 24 Productions
The Planet Building, Thames Quay
195 Marsh Wall
London E14 9SG
Tel: 020 7345 2424/512 5000
Fax: 020 7345 9400
Recent productions: *The Big Breakfast* (C4); *Hotel Babylon* (ITV); *Gaytime TV* (BBC2); *Nothing But the Truth* (C4); *The Word* (C4); *Delicious* (ITV);*The Weekend Show* (BBC)

Portman Productions
167 Wardour Street
London W1V 3TA
Tel: 020 7468 3400
Fax: 020 7468 3499
Major producer in primetime drama and feature films worldwide. Recent productions include: *Nancherrow* (2x2), *Savage Honeymoon* (feature), *Scarfies* (feature), *Clandestine Marriage* (feture),*Wrestling with Alligators* (feature); *Coming Home* (2x2); *Spanish Fly* (feature); *Rebecca* (2x2); *September* (2x2); *An Awfully Big Adventure* (feature); *Famous Five*, series I & II; *Hostage* (feature); *Fall From Grace* (4 x1); *Friday on my Mind* (3x1); *Blackwater Trail* (feature); *Little White Lies* (feature); *Seventh Floor* (feature); *Crime Broker* (feature); *A Woman of Substance* (4x1); *Via Satellite* (feature)

Praxis Films
PO Box 290

Market Rasen
Lincs LN3 6BB
Tel: 01472 398547
Fax: 01472 398683
email: 100625.232@compuserve.com
Film and video production of
documentaries, current affairs and
educational programmes. Recent
productions: series for Yorkshire
Television; films for C4's Secret
History, Dispatches, Cutting Edge,
3D and Secret Lives. Extensive
archive of sea, fishing, rural and
regional material

Presence Films
66a Great Titchfield Street
London W1P 7AE
Tel: 020 7636 8477
Fax: 020 7636 8722
Alan Dewhurst
In production: *The Ship*, directed by
Lucy Lee, the first British animated
IMAX film (principal funder:
Channel 4). In development: Bertolt
Brecht's *War Primer* (television arts
feature), *Eternity In An Hour* (low-
budget feature)

Prominent Features
34 Tavistock Street
London WC2E 7PB
Tel: 020 7497 1100
Company formed by Steve Abbott,
John Cleese, Terry Gilliam, Eric Idle,
Anne James, Terry Jones and
Michael Palin to produce in-house
features

Prominent Television
34 Tavistock Street
London WC2E 7PB
Tel: 020 7497 1100
Company formed by Steve Abbott,
John Cleese, Terry Gilliam, Eric Idle,
Anne James, Terry Jones and
Michael Palin to produce in-house
television programmes. 10 part travel
documentary series *Full Circle* with
Michael Palin (1997) a journey
around the Pacific rim

Sarah Radclyffe Productions
5th Floor
83-84 Berwick Street
London W1V 3PJ
Tel: 020 7437 3128
Fax: 020 7437 3129
email: srpltd@globalnet.co.uk
Sarah Radclyffe, Bill Godfrey, Dixie
Linder, Alison Jackson
Sarah Radclyffe previously founded
and was co-owner of Working Title
Films and was responsible for,
amongst others, *My Beautiful
Laundrette, Wish You Were Here*, and
A World Apart. Sarah Radclyffe
Productions was formed in 1993 and
productions to date are: *Second Best*,

dir Chris Menges; *Sirens*, dir. John
Duigan; *Cousin Bette*, dir. Des
McAnuff; *Bent*, dir. Sean Mathias;
Les Misérables, dir Bille August; *The
War Zone*, dir Tim Roth
(See Pathé Productions – Lottery
Film Production Franchises)

Ragdoll Productions
Pinewood Studios
Pinewood Road
Iver Heath
Bucks SL0 0NH
Tel: 01753 631800
Fax: 01753 631831
Specialist children's television
producer of live action and
animation, currently producing long-
running series *Teletubbies, Tots TV,
Rosie and Jim* (for ITV); *Teletubbies;
Brum* and *Open A Door* (for BBC)

Raw Charm
Ty Cefn
Rectory Road
Cardiff CF1 1QL
Tel: 029 20 641511
Fax: 029 20 668220
Pamela Hunt, Kate Jones Davies
Drama, documentaries, music,
entertainment. Recent productions:
Traffic in Children (BBC); *Trading
Places* (HTV); *The Plain* (HTV)

Recorded Picture Co
24 Hanway Street
London W1P 9DD
Tel: 020 7636 2251
Fax: 020 7636 2261
Managing Director: Jeremy Thomas
Films produced include: Nagisa
Oshima's *Merry Christmas,
Mr.Lawrence*, Stephen Frears' *The Hit*,
Nicolas Roeg's *Insignificance*, *The Last
Emperor* and *The Sheltering Sky* Dir
Bernardo Bertolucci, and *The Naked
Lunch, Crash* Dir David Cronenberg.
Recent productions: *Stealing Beauty*,
Dir Bernardo Bertolucci

Red Rooster Film & Television Entertainment
29 Floral Street
London WC2E 9DP
Tel: 020 7379 7727
Fax: 020 7379 5756
Grainne Marmion, Sarah Williams,
Tim Vaughan, Julia Ouston
The Chrysalis Group has bought the
remaining 50 per cent holding in the
company, and continues to maintain a
£1m fund to develop television
programmes and feature films.
Recent productions: *Wilderness*
(ITV); *Beyond Fear* (Channel 5)

Redwave Films (UK) Ltd
31-32 Soho Square
London W1V 6AP

Tel: 020 7753 7200
Fax: 020 7753 7201
Uberto Pasolini, Polly Leys, Rachel
Bennette

The Reel Thing
Airport House
Purley Way
Croydon
Surrey CRO 0XZ
Tel: 020 8395 7665
Fax: 020 8688 2598
Film and television production
company providing broadcast and
non-broadcast production services
across all delivery media from
terrestrial, satellite and Cable TV, to
multimedia delivery systems

Reeltime Pictures
70-72 Union Street
London SE1 0NW
Tel: 020 7620 3102
Fax: 020 7620 3104
Formed in 1984, Reeltime specialises
in the production of drama and
documentaries connected with cult
film and television for theatrical and
non-theatrical release. The company
also purchases and distributes sell-
through video under its own label
and aims to promote independent
genre film and television production.
Titles include *Myth Makers, Doctor
Who's Return to Devils End* (doc);
Wartime, Downtime, PROBE and *The
Stranger* (drama)

Regent Productions
The Mews
6 Putney Common
Putney
London SW15 1HL
Tel: 020 8789 5350
Fax: 020 8789 5332
Current productions: three new series
of the C4 quiz series *Fifteen-to-One*
(188 programmes). In development:
quiz shows; a seven-part drama
series; a current affairs project

Renaissance Films
34-35 Berwick Street
London W1V 3RF
Tel: 020 7287 5190
Fax: 020 7287 5191
Film production company formed by
Kenneth Branagh. Recent
productions include: *Wings of the
Dove*

Renegade Films
3rd Floor, Bolsover House
5/6 Clipstone Street
London W1P 8LD
Tel: 020 7637 0957
Fax: 020 7637 0959
email: renprism@dircon.co.uk
Robert Buckler, Amanda Mackenzie

Stuart, Ildiko Kemeny
Productions include: *Brothers in Trouble, Pressure, The Last Place on Earth, Facts of Life, Midnight Expresso, The Star, The Sin Eater Hotel Splendide* and (as Prisma Communications) *The Financial Times Business Toolkit*. Development projects include: *The Go Kart, Room To Rent, Hotel Sordide, The Thought Gang*

Replay
36 Ritherdon Road
London SW17 8QF
Tel: 020 7287 5334
Production of broadcast and corporate documentaries and drama

Revolution Films
10 Little Turstile
London WC1V 7DX
Tel: 020 7242 0372
Fax: 020 7242 0407
Recent productions: *Old New Borrowed Blue*

Richmond Light Horse Productions Ltd
3 Esmond Court
Thackeray Street
London W8
Tel: 020 7937 9315
Fax: 020 7938 4024

Riverchild Films
2nd floor, 26 Goodge St
London W1P 1FG
Tel: 020 7636 1122
Fax: 020 7636 1133
email: riverchild.demon.co.uk
Features and television drama

Riverfront Pictures
Dock Cottages, Peartree Lane
Glamis Road
Wapping
London E1 9SR
Tel: 020 7481 2939
Fax: 020 7480 5520
Specialise in music, arts and drama-documentaries. Independent productions for television. Recent productions for C4 *Cutting Edge* and BBC Arts

RM Associates
46 Great Marlborough Street
London W1V 1DB
Tel: 020 7439 2637
Fax: 020 7439 2316
RM Associates produces a broad range of music and arts programming and co-produces on an international basis with major broadcasters including BBC, C4, ARD and ZDF in Germany, NOS-TV in Holland, Danmarks Radio, SVT in Sweden and Thirteen/WNET in America

Roadshow Productions
c/o 6 Basil Mansions
Basil Street
London SW3 1AP
Tel: 020 7584 0542
Fax: 020 7584 1549

Rocket Pictures
7 King Street Cloisters
Clifton Walk
London W6 oGY
Tel: 020 8741 9009
Fax: 020 8741 9097
Recent productions include: *Women Talking Dirty*

Rodney Read
45 Richmond Road
Twickenham
Middx TW1 3AW
Tel: 020 8891 2875
Fax: 020 8744 9603
email: Rodney_Read@Compuserve.com
Film and video production offering experience in factual and entertainment programming. Also provides a full range of back-up facilities for the feature and television industries, including 'making of' documentaries, promotional programme inserts, on air graphics and title sequences, sales promos, trailers and commercials. Active in production for UK cable and satellite

Rogue Films
177 Wardour Street
London W1V 3FB
Tel: 020 7434 2222
Fax: 020 7494 7808
Commercials and music video production – UK, Europe, USA

RSPB Film and Video Unit
The Lodge, Sandy
Beds SG19 2DL
Tel: 01767 680551
Fax: 01767 692365
Producers of Osprey, Kingfisher, *Where Eagles Fly, Barn Owl, The Year of the Stork and Flying for Gold*. Recent productions: *The Flamingo Triangle; Skydancer*. The unit also acts as an independent producer of environmental films and videos

Samuelson Productions
4th Floor, 9 Hanover Street
London W1P 7LJ
Tel: 020 7495 3414
Fax: 020 7495 3415
Arlington Road dir Mark Pellington, starring Tim Robbins, Jeff Bridges, Joan Cusack and Hope Davis; *Wilde* dir Brian Gilbert, starring Stephen Fry, Jude Law, Vanessa Redgrave and Jennifer Ehle; *The Commissioner*

starring John Hurt and Armin Mueller-Stahl; *Dog's Best Friend* starring Richard Milligan and Shirley Jones; Previously: *Tom and Viv; Playmaker;* and documentaries *Man, God and Africa; Vicars; The Babe Business, Ultimate Frisbee*

Sands Films
119 Rotherhithe Street
London SE16 4NF
Tel: 020 7231 2209
Fax: 020 7231 2119
Recent productions: *The Butterfly Effect; As You Like It. Amahl and the Night Visitors. The Nutcracker Story*. In preparation and development: *A Midsummer Night's Dream, Nursery Rhymes, Cathedrals, Colla-Verdi*

Scala Productions
15 Frith Street
London W1V 5TS
Tel: 020 7734 7060
Fax: 020 7437 3248
email: scalaprods@aol.com
Nik Powell, Stephen Woolley, Amanda Posey, Rachel Wood, Finola Dwyer, Lurie Borg, Jonathan Karlsen
Recent productions: Shane Meadows' *Twentyfourseven* starring Bob Hoskins. Mark Herman's *Little Voice* starring Michael Caine, Brenda Blethyn, Ewan McGregor, Jane Horrocks. Chris Menges' *The Lost Son* starring Daniel Auteuil and Nastassja Kinski. Kay Mellor's *Fanny & Elvis* starring Kerry Fox and Ray Winstone. Deborah Warner's *The Last September* starring Maggie Smith and Michael Gambon Julian Fariono's *The Last Yellow* starring Mark Addy; Charlie Creed-Miles and Samantha Morton
Projects in development
Thanks for the Memories to be directed by Declan Lowney
Ben Elton's *Gridlock* to be directed by Chris Menges*The Brian Jones Project* to be directed by Frank Budgen *Jonathan Wild* to be directed by Richard Loncraine

Scottish Television Enterprises
Cowcaddens
Glasgow G2 3PR
Tel: 0141 300 3000
Fax: 0141 300 3030
Darrel James, Managing Director
Producers of: *Taggart* (drama), *Inspector Rebus* (drama), *Sherlock Holmes in the 22nd Century* (animation), *How 2* (teenage/education), *Fun House* (children's game show), *Get Wet* (children's gameshow), *The Last Musketeer* (drama)

Screen Ventures
49 Goodge Street
London W1P 1FB
Tel: 020 7580 7448
Fax: 020 7631 1265
email: screenventures@easynet.co.uk
Christopher Mould, Jack Bond,
Caroline Furness
Production and television sales
company. Producing music, drama
and documentaries. Recent projects:
Dani Dares a five part documentary
series for C4, *Mojo Working*, a 13-
part music series for C4, *Genet*, a
South Bank Show for LWT; Vanessa
Redgrave, a South Bank Show for
LWT. In development: *Falling*, a 90
minute feature backed by the
European Script Fund

September Films Ltd
Silver House
35 Beak Street
London W1R 3LD
Tel: 020 7494 1884
Fax: 020 7439 1194
David Green, Elaine Day, Sally Miles
TV Includes: *The Final Day*;
*Desperately Seeking Stardom; Teen
Spirit; Planet Showbiz*
Feature films: *House of America;
Solomon and Gaenor*

Siren Film and Video Ltd
5 Charlotte Square
Newcastle-upon-Tyne NE1 4XF
Tel: 0191 232 7900
Fax: 0191 232 7900
email: sirenfilms@aol.com
Film and television production
company specialising in work for and
about children

Siriol Productions
Phoenix Buildings
3 Mount Stuart Square
Butetown
Cardiff CF1 6RW
Tel: 029 20 488400
Fax: 029 20 485962
email: siriol@baynet.co.uk
Formerly Siriol Animation. Producers
of high quality animation for
television and the cinema. Makers of:
*SuperTed; The Princess and the
Goblin; Under Milk Wood; Santa and
the Tooth Fairies; Santa's First
Christmas; Tales of the Tooth Fairies,
The Hurricanes; Billy the Cat; The
Blobs; Rowland the Reindeer*

Skreba
5a Noel Street
London W1V 3RB
Tel: 020 7437 6492
Fax: 020 7437 0644
Ann Skinner, Simon Relph
(See The Film Consortium – Lottery
Film Production Franchises)

Skyline Films
PO Box 821U
London W41 1WH
Tel: 0836 275584
Fax: 020 8354 2219
Steve Clark-Hall, Mairi Bett
Recent productions: *The Winter
Guest* (with Ed Pressmann), *Love
and Death on Long Island, Small
Faces, Margaret's Museum, Still
Crazy* (for Margot Tandy)

Soho Communications
2 Percy Street
London W1P 9FB
Tel: 020 7637 5825
Fax: 020 7436 9740

Sony Pictures Europe UK Ltd
Sony Pictures Europe House
25 Golden Square
London W1R 6LU
Tel: 020 7533 1111
Fax: 020 7533 1105
Recent productions: *Virtual Sexuality*

Southern Star Primetime Limited
Southern Star Sales (UK) Limited
45-49 Mortimer Street
London W1N 7TD
Tel: 020 7636 9431
Fax: 020 7436 7426
Simon Willock: General Manager,
Wild & Real
Victoria Ryan, Head of European
Sales, Southern Star Primetime
Catherine Neubauer: Head of
European Sales, Southern Star Kids
Production and Distribution
Productions includes: *Nicholas
Nickleby, Porgy & Bess, Great
Expectations, Othello, Neville's
Island*
Distribution includes: *Bugs, Every
Woman Knows a Secret, Imogen's
Face, Home and Away, 99-1, In the
Wild, Our Friends in the North,
Bodyguards, Oklahoma, Famous
Five, Eyes on the World*

Specific Films
25 Rathbone Street
London W1P 1AG
Tel: 020 7580 7476
Fax: 020 7494 2676
Michael Hamlyn, Christian Routh
Recent productions: *the Last
Seduction 2*, dir Terry Marcel; *PAWS*
(exec. prod) dir Carl Zwicky; *The
Adventures of Priscilla, Queen of the
Desert*, directed by Stephan Elliott;
Mr Reliable dir by Nadia Tass.
Developing a number of feature film
projects

Spice Factory
81 The Promenade
Peacehaven
Brighton
East Sussex BN10 8LS
Tel: 01273 585275
Fax: 01273 585304
email: sfactory@fastnet.co.uk
Films, Games & Television
Production Company. Productions:
Killer Tongue (1997), *Dying to Go
Home* (1997), *Ricky 6* (1998), *New
Blood* (1998). In production: *Pilgrim*
(1999), *Shiney's Head* (1999),
Sabotage (1999). In development:
*Fry; Crush Hour; The Void;
Breaking the Code; Our Game; Bat
Out of Hell*. Television project in
development: Kremlin Contact;
Paramount/BBC/Bavaria based on
best selling book by Donald James

Stagescreen Productions
12 Upper St Martin's Lane
London WC2H 9DL
Tel: 020 7497 2510
Fax: 020 7497 2208
email: stgescreen@aol.com
Film, television and theatre company
whose work includes: *A Handful of
Dust; Death of a Son* (BBC TV);
*Where Angels Fear to Tread; Foreign
Affairs* (TNT)

Stephens Kerr
8-12 Camden High Street
London NW1 0JH
Tel: 020 7916 2124
Fax: 020 7916 212

Talent Television
2nd Floor Regent House
235 Regent Street
London W1R 7AG
Tel: 020 7434 1677
Fax: 020 7434 1577
John Kaye Cooper, Managing
Director
Current productions: h&p@bbc –
6x40 mins comedy. BBC
Vivienne Westwood 1x30 mins
documentary. ITV
The Veins of Britain 1x30 mins
documentary
Spaceship Earth TV Asahi/TEL
Recent credits: *Bill Bailey Live* – C4;
In the Presence of Julian Clary –
Carlton; *Alan Davies Urban Trauma*
– Entertainment. BBC1. *The Making
of Doctor Doolittle* – BBC1

Talisman Films Limited
5 Addison Place
London W11 4RJ
Tel: 020 7603 7474
Fax: 020 7602 7422
email: email@talismanfilms.com
Richard Jackson
Neil Dunn, Caroline Oulton

Production of theatric features and the whole range of television drama. Recent productions: *Complicity* (feature) starring Jonny Lee Miller, Brian Cox and Keeley Hawes: *The Secret Adveutures of Jules Verne* (22 part tv series) starring Michael Praed and Francesca Hunt; *Remember Me?* (Imelda Staunton; *Rob Roy* (feature for United Artists) starring Liam Neeson, Jessica Lange, John Hurt, Tim Roth; *Just William* (series I & II, BBC): *The Rector's Wife* (4x60 mins, C4) drama serial starring Lindsay Duncan

TalkBack Productions
36 Percy Street
London W1P 0LN
Tel: 020 7323 9777
Fax: 020 7637 5105
Productions include: *Smith and Jones* (+ 5 previous series, BBC1); *They Think It's All Over* (+3 previous series, BBC1); *Never Mind The Buzzcocks* (+ 1 previous series, BBC2); *The Lying Game* (BBC1); *In Search of Happiness* (BBC1); *Brass Eye* (Channel 4); *Knowing Me Knowing You...* with Alan Partridge (BBC2); *The Day Today* (BBC2); *Murder Most Horrid* (+ 2 previous series, BBC2)

Tall Stories
Studio 40
Clink Street Studios
1 Clink Street
London SE1 9DG
Tel: 020 7357 8050
Fax: 020 7357 0889

Richard Taylor Cartoon Films
River View, Waterloo Drive
Clun, Craven Arms
Shropshire SY7 8JD
Tel: 01588 640 073
Fax: 01588 640 074
Production of all forms of drawn animation

Telescope Pictures Ltd
Twickenham Film Studios
Saint Margarets
Twickenham
Middlesex TW1 2AW
Tel: 020 8607 8888
Fax: 020 8607 8889
Recent productions: *Princess Caraboo*, dir Michael Austin. In development: *Slow Train To Milan; Dorking Cocks; By Grand Central Station I Sat Down and Wept;* In production: *The Revengers' Comedies*

Teliesyn
26 Mortimer Road
Pont Canna

Cardiff CF1 2EH
Tel: 029 20 300876
Fax: 029 20 300877
Involved in feature film, television drama and television documentary/feature. In production: *Reel Truth*, docu/drama for S4C and C4; *Cyber Wales* and *Answering Back* for BBC Wales; *Dragon's Song* for C4. In development: *Video Pirates* (6 x 30 min drama) Coron yr Wythnos plus a number of feature film and drama series

Tempest Films
33 Brookfield
Highgate West Hill
London N6 6AT
Tel: 020 8340 0877
Fax: 020 8340 9309
In development: *The York Mysteries* with YTV. *Stop Press* – 6 part TV series; *The Actresses* – 3 part mini-series; *Mallory Short and the Very Big Bass* – feature film

Testimony Films
12 Great George Street,
Bristol BS1 5RS
Tel: 0117 925 8589
Fax: 0117 925 7668
Steve Humphries
Specialists in social history documentaries. Recent productions: *Labour of Love: Bringing up Children in Britain 1900-1950* (6 x 40 min, BBC2); *Forbidden Britain: Our Secret Past* (6 x 40 min, BBC2); *A Man's World: The Experience of Masculinity* (6 x 40 minutes, BBC2); *The Call of the Sea: Memories of a Seafaring Nation* (6 x 40 minutes, BBC2); *The Roses of No Man's Land* (1 x 60 minutes C4); *Sex in a Cold Climate* (1 x 60 minutes C4); *Hooked: Britain in Pursuit of Pleasure* (6 x 30 minutes C4). *Veterans: The Last Survivors of the Trench War* (2x50 mins BBC1); *Far Out: The Dawning of New Age Britain* (3x60 minutes C4); *Green and Pleasant Land* (6x60 minutes C4)

Thin Man Films
9 Greek Street
London W1V 5LE
Tel: 020 7734 7372
Fax: 020 7287 5228
Simon Channing-Williams, Mike Leigh
Recent productions: Career Girls; Secrets & Lies
(See Pathé Productions – Lottery Film Production Franchises)

Tiger Aspect Productions
5 Soho Square
London W1V 5DE
Tel: 020 7434 0672
Fax: 020 7287 1448

Harry Enfield and Chums (2 series BBC); *The Vicar of Dibley* (BBC1) *The Thin Blue Line* (BBC1) *The Village* (7 series for Meridian) *Howard Goodall's Organ Works* (Ch4) *Hospital* (Ch5) *Deacon Brodie* (Screen One for BBC 1)

Tiny Epic Video Co
37 Dean Street
London W1V 5AP
Tel: 020 7437 2854
Fax: 020 7434 0211

TKO Communications
PO Box 130, Hove
East Sussex BN3 6QU
Tel: 01273 550088
Fax: 01273 540969
email: jskruger@tkogroup.com
A division of the Kruger Organisation, making music programmes for television, satellite and video release worldwide as well as co-producing various series and acquiring rights to full length feature films for distribution. Co-production with Tros TV Holland will result in a new release "Marvin Gaye Live in Concert". 39x30 minutes TV Specials called "Masters of the Martial Arts" starring John Saxon and featuring 4 world champions demonstrating all aspects of the martial arts. A 30 minute special on Jerry Lee Lewis. Launching a library archive footage of stars including Glen Campbell, Vic Damone, Frankie Laine, Johnny Cash, Kris Kristofferson, Daniel O'Donnell, Willie Nelson, Conway Twitty, Dionne Warwick, George Burns, Jerry Lewis, The Stylistics, Anne Murray and many more. Distiributing for TV and Satellite and Video release of two digitalised, animated full length movie features, "Gallavants" and "The Three Musketeers"

Toledo Pictures
30 Oval Road
Camden
London NW1 7DE
Tel: 020 7485 4411
Fax: 020 7485 4422
Duncan Kenworthy
(See DNA – Lottery Film Production Franchises)

Topaz Productions
Manchester House
46 Wormholt Road
London W12 0LS
Tel: 020 8749 2619
Fax: 020 8749 0358
In production: ongoing corporate productions

Trans World International
TWI House
23 Eyot Gardens
London W6 9TR
Tel: 020 8233 5400
Fax: 020 8233 5401
Television and video sports production and rights representation branch of Mark McCormack's International Management Group, TWI produces over 2,500 hours of broadcast programming and represents the rights to many leading sports events including Wimbledon, British Open, US Open, and World Matchplay golf. Productions include: *Trans World Sport; Futbol Mundial; PGA European Tour; ATP Tour Highlights; West Indies, Indian and Pakistan Test cricket; Oddballs; A-Z of Sport; High 5; The American Big Match and Blitz; The Olympic Collection and The Whitbread Round The World Race*

Transatlantic Films
Studio 1
3 Brackenbury Road
London W6 OBE
Tel: 020 8735 0505
Fax: 020 8735 0605
email: mail@transatlanticfilms.com

Revel Guest, Corisande Albert, Ruth Sessions, Fiona Caldwell, Rob Albert. Current Co-Productions: *Horse Tales* 26x30 mins stories about the special bond between people and horses, for Animal Planet; *Trailblazers* – 26x60 mins, travel and adventure series for Discovery Europe, Travel Channel. Recent Programming: *Amazing Animal Adaptors* – 1x60 mins special for Discovery Channel; *History's Turning Points* – 26x30 mins about decisive moments in history, for Discovery Europe; *Lost Treasures of the Yangtze Valley* 1x60 mins & *The Three Gorges* 1x60 mins, the building of the World's biggest dam in China, for Discovery Channel/TLC.

Tribune Productions Ltd
22 Bentley Way
Stanmore
Middlesex HA7 3RP
Tel: 020 8420 7230
Fax: 020 8207 0860

Trijbits Productions
5a Noel Street
London W1V 3RB
Tel: 020 7439 4343
Fax: 020 7434 4447

Julia Caithness
Paul Trijbits' previous producer and executive producer credits include *Hardware, Dust Devil, The Young Americans, Boston Kickout, Roseanna's Grave, Milk*. In production: *Paranoia*, written and directed by John Duigan. In development: *Unnatural Murder* developed with BBC Films, *Maybe the Moon* with Ruby Films, *Diamond Geezers & the Delay*

Try Again Limited
Leigh Grove Farmhouse
Leigh Grove
Bradford on Avon
Wilts BA15 2RF
Tel: 01225 862 705
Fax: 01225 862 205
Michael Darlow, Rod Taylor, Chris Frederick
Produces drama, music, arts, documentary programmes. Recent productions include: *War Cries – Angels of Mercy?* C4 1 x 30 mins. *Martin Parr and the Ladies of the Valley* BBC 2 x 40 mins; 1:4; *The Lost Child – The Works* BBC 2 x 30 mins. *Something of a Different Pace – The Works* BBC 2 x 30 mins;

*Under the Skin, Dennis Potter –
Close Up* BBC2. 1 hour

TV Cartoons
39 Grafton Way
London W1P 5LA
Tel: 020 7388 2222
Fax: 020 7383 4192
John Coates, Norman Kauffman
Productions include: *The Snowman*,
Academy Award nominated film and
the feature film When the Wind
Blows, both adaptations from books
by Raymond Briggs; *Granpa*, a half
hour television special for C4 and
TVS; half hour special of Raymond
Briggs' *Father Christmas* (C4); *The
World of Peter Rabbit & Friends* (9 x
30 min), based on the books by
Beatrix Potter, *The Wind in the
Willows*, a TVC production for
Carlton UK Television and *Willows
in Winter, Famous Fred* Academy
Award Nominated 1998 (C4&S4C).
Latest productions are *The Bear* and
Oi Get off Our Train which was the
first film by Varga tvc

TV Choice
22 Charing Cross Road
London WC2H OHR
Tel: 020 7379 0873
Fax: 020 7379 0263
Chris Barnard, Norman Thomas
Producer and distributor of dramas
and documentaries about business,
technology and finance. TV Choice
videos and learning packs are used in
education and training in the UK and
overseas. Co-producers of feature
film Conspiracy with new features in
development

Twentieth Century Vixen
13 Aubert Park
Highbury
London N5 1TL
Tel: 020 7359 7368
Fax: 020 7359 7368
Film/video production and
distribution, mainly feature
documentaries. Recent projects:
documentary for BBC2 on the 'New
Marilyn' women's nightclub in
Shinjuku, Tokyo, Shinjuku Boys. and
Law Stories film about Shani'a Law
Courts in Iran for C4

Twentieth Century-Fox Productions Ltd
20th Century House
31-31 Soho Square
London W1V 6AP
Tel: 020 7437 7766
Fax: 020 7734 3187
Recent productions: *The Full Monty,
Braveheart, Stealing Beauty; Titanic*

Twenty Twenty Television
Suite 2, Grand Union House
29 Kentish Town Road
London Nw1 9NX
Tel: 020 7284 2020
Fax: 020 7284 1810
The company continues to produce
programmes exclusively for
broadcast television, specialising in
worldwide investigative journalism,
documentaries, productions, factually
based drama, science and childrens
programmes. Recent productions
include: *The Big Story* (Carlton);
Secret Lives Walt Disney (C4); *Un
Blues* (C4) and *Cutting Edge* (C4)

Tyburn Film Productions Ltd
Pinewood Studios
Iver Heath
Bucks SL0 ONH
Tel: 01753 651700
Fax: 01753 656050
Filmmaker: *The Creeping Flesh;
Persecution; The Ghoul; Legend of
the Werewolf*

UBA (United British Artists)
21 Alderville Road
London SW6 3RL
Tel: 01984 623619
Fax: 01984 623733
Production company for cinema and
TV projects. Past productions
include: K*eep the Aspidistra Flying*
for OFE; *Sweeney Todd* for
Showtime/Hallmark; *Champions* for
Embassy; *Ghost Hunter* for Granada;
Wind-prints for MCEG *Virgin Vision*;
Taffin for MGM; *Castaway* for
Cannon; *The Lonely Passion of
Judith Hearne* for HandMade Films;
Turtle Diary for the Samuel Goldwyn
Company;

Uden Associates
Chelsea Wharf
Lots Road
London SW10 0QJ
Tel: 020 7351 1255
Fax: 020 7376 3937
Film and television production
company for broadcast through C4,
BBC and corporate clients. Recent
productions: *Classic Trucks*, 6 x 30
min for C4 and various projects for
Equinox, *Cutting Edge (Nurses, A is
for Accident)* and Short Stories,
Classic Ships, 6 x 30 min for C4,
Autoerotic II, 3 x 30 min for C4,
Secret Lives: The Young Freud

Unicorn Organisation
Pottery Lane Studios
34a Pottery Lane
Holland Park

London W11 4LZ
Tel: 020 7229 5131
Fax: 020 7229 4999

Union Pictures
36 Marshall Street
London W1V 1LL
Tel: 020 7287 5110
Fax: 020 7287 3770
Recent productions include: *The
Crow Road; Deadly Voyage;
Masterchef; Junior Masterchef; The
Roswell Incident*

United Artists Corporation, Ltd (MGM/United Artists)
Pinewood Studios
Iver Heath
Buckinghamshire SL0 ONH
Tel: 01723 651700
Fax: 01723 656844
Recent productions: *Tomorrow Never
Dies, Man in the Iron Mask*

Universal Pictures International
Oxford House
76 Oxford Street
London W1N 0HQ
Tel: 020 7747 4000
Fax: 020 7747 4499

Universal Pictures Ltd
1 Hamilton Mews
London W1V 9FF
Tel: 020 7491 4666
Fax: 020 7493 4702
Recent productions: *The Jackal,
DragonHeart, Fierce Creatures*

UpFront Television Ltd
39-41 New Oxford Street
London WC1A 1BH
Tel: 020 7836 7701
Fax: 020 7836 7702
email: upfront@binternet.com

Vera Productions Ltd
3rd Floor
66/68 Margaret Street
London W1N 7FL
Tel: 020 7436 6116
Fax: 020 7436 6117/6016
Contact: Elaine Morris

Victor Film Company Ltd
2b Chandos Street
London W1M 9DG
Tel: 020 7636 6620
Fax: 020 7636 6511
Alasdair Waddell, Vic Bateman,
Carol Philbin, Alexandra Roper,
Eliana Celiberti
International sales agent for
independent producers of commercial
films. Titles include *Clockwork Mice,
Killing Time, Darklands, Aberration,
Preaching to the Perverted*

Videotel Productions
84 Newman Street
London W1P 3LD
Tel: 020 7299 1800
Fax: 020 7299 1818
Producers of educational and training
packages for television and video
distribution

Vine International Pictures
21 Great Chapel Street
London W1V 3AQ
Tel: 020 7437 1181
Fax: 020 7494 0634
Marie Vine, Barry Gill
Sale of feature films such as *Rainbow,
The Pillow Book, The Ox and the
Eye, Younger and Younger, The
Prince of Jutland, Erik the Viking, Let
Him Have It, Trouble in Mind*

Viz
4 Bank Street
Inverkeithing
Fife KY11 1LR
Tel: 01383 412811
Fax: 01383 418103

Wall To Wall Television
8-9 Spring Place
Kentish Town
London NW5 3ER
Tel: 020 7485 7424
Fax: 020 7267 5292
Alex Graham, Jane Root
Producers of quality innovative
programming including, drama:
*Statement of Affairs; You Me and It;
Plotlands*. Natural history: *Baby It's
You*. Leisure: *Eat Your Greens; Sophie's
Meat Course; For Love or Money*.
Entertainment: *Big City; Heartland;
The Big Country*. Arts and culture:
Fantasy by Gaslight; Rwandan Stories

Warner Bros. Productions Ltd
98 Theobald's Road
London WC1X 8WB
Tel: 020 7984 5400
Recent productions: *Eyes Wide Shut,
The Avengers*

Warner Sisters Film & TV Ltd, Cine Sisters Ltd
The Cottage
Pall Mall Deposit
124 Barlby Road
London W10 6BL
Tel: 020 8960 3550
Fax: 020 8960 3880
Directors: Lavinia Warner, Jane
Wellesley, Anne-Marie Casey and
Dorothy Viljoen
Founded 1984. Drama, Comedy. TV
and Feature Films. Output includes *A
Village Affair; Dangerous Lady;
Dressing for Breakfast; The Spy Who*

*Caught a Cold; Capital Sins; The
Bite; The Jump* – and feature film
Jilting Joe. Developing a wide range
of TV and feature projects

David Wickes Productions
169 Queen's Gate
London SW7 5HE
Tel: 020 7225 1382
Fax: 020 7589 8847
David Wickes, Heide Wilsher

Winchester Entertainment plc
29/30 Kingly Street
London W1R 5LB
Tel: 020 7434 4374
Fax: 020 7287 4334
Chief Executive: Gary Smith
Recent productions: *Shooting Fish;
Stiff Upper Lips; Divorcing Jack*

Working Title Films
Oxford House
76 Oxford Street
London W1N 9FD
Tel: 020 7307 3000
Fax: 020 7307 3001/2/3
Tim Bevan, Eric Fellner
Recent film productions: *The
Hudsucker Proxy; Four Weddings
and a Funeral; French Kiss; Loch
Ness; Moonlight and Valentino;
Fargo; Dead Man Walking*

Working Title Television
Oxford House
76 Oxford Street
London W1N 9FD
Tel: 020 7307 3000
Fax: 020 7307 3001/2/3
Simon Wright, Tim Bevan
Recent productions: *Edward II;
Amnesty – The Big 30; Further Tales
of the Riverbank; TV Squash; The
Borrowers* (series 1 & 2); T*ales of
the City; The Baldy Man, Land and
Woodley*

The Worldmark Production Company Ltd
7 Cornwall Crescent
London W11 1PH
Tel: 020 7792 9800
Fax: 020 8792 9801
David Wooster
Current productions: *Swimming with
Sharks* 1x52min for MNET South
Africa; England 2006 – FIFA World
Cup Bid Film for the Football
Association. Recent productions: *La
Coupe de la Glorie – 1998 FIFA
World Cup Official Film; Gary
Lineker's Golden Boots* 8x30 min for
BBC; *Living with Lions* – 2x120 min
for Sky Sports

X-Dream International
Stones, Wickham St Pauls

Halstead
Essex CO9 2PS
Tel: 01787 269089
Fax: 01787 269029
Specialises in the production,
distribution and representation of
sports TV, children's TV and film

Zenith North
11th Floor
Cale Cross House
156 Pilgrim Street
Newcastle upon Tyne NE1 6SU
Tel: 0191 261 0077
Fax: 0191 222 0271
email: zenithnorth@dial.pipex.com
Ivan Rendall, Peter Mitchell
(Managing Director), John Coffey
Productions include: *Byker Grove*
(BBC1); *Blues and Twos*
(Carlton/ITV); *The Famous Five*
(ITV); *Animal Ark* (HTV); *Dear
Nobody* (BBC); *Pass the Buck* (BBC);
Network First (Carlton ITV); music
specials for S4C; variety of regional
productions for Tyne Tees TV

Zenith Productions
43-45 Dorset Street
London W1H 4AB
Tel: 020 7224 2440
Fax: 020 7224 3194
email: zenith@zenith.tv.co.uk
Film and television production
company. Recent feature films: Todd
Haynes' *Velvet Goldmine*; Nicole
Holofcener's *Walking and Talking*;
Hal Hartley's *Amateur*. Recent
television drama: *The Uninvited*
(ITV); *Bodyguards* (Carlton);
Hamish Macbeth (3 series, BBC
Scotland); *Rhodes* (BBC1)

Zephyr Films
24 Colville Road
London W11 2BS
Tel: 020 7221 8318
Fax: 020 7221 9289

Zooid Pictures Limited
66 Alexander Road
London N19 5PQ
Tel: 020 7281 2407
Fax: 020 7281 2404
email: postmaster@zooid.co.uk
Website: www.zooid.co.uk
Producers of experimental and
television documentaries, various
shorts; documentaries; Anglo-
Brazilian-German co-productions

PRODUCTION STARTS

These are feature-length films intended for theatrical release with a significant British involvement (whether creative, financial or UK-based) which went into production between January and December 1998. The production start date is given where known. Single television dramas in production for the same period are indicated with *
Compiled by Laura Pearson

1998 UK PRODUCTION STARTS

1998
The Alchemist
L'Assedio
*Big Cat
Make Believe
A Monkey's Tale
Three Businessmen
Trouble On Earth

JANUARY
- Byron
- The Jesus Story
- Palmer's Pick-Up
- 3 Dreaming Of Joseph Lees
- 5 A Simple Plan
- 7 Mickey Blue-Eyes
- 12 The Lost Son
- 26 Still Crazy
- 30 Human Traffic

FEBRUARY
- 2 Arlington Road
- 4 Swing
- 13 The Killing Zone
- 16 Anthrakitis
- 21 Everybody Loves Sunshine

MARCH
- 1 My Summer With Des
- 2 Shakespeare In Love
- 2 War Zone
- 3 *Kiszko
- 4 Small Time Obsession
- 7 Onegin
- 10 To Walk With Lions
- 15 The Winslow Boy
- 22 Solomon And Gaenor

- 25 Eye Of The Beholder

APRIL
- The Debt Collector
- 6 eXistenZ
- 6 *Touch And Go
- 14 Grey Owl
- 15 This Year's Love
- 20 Notting Hill

MAY
- 1 Ashes To Ashes
- 2 *The Cater Street Hangman
- 3 Virtual Sexuality
- 4 The Mummy
- 4 Simon Magus
- 10 Gregory's 2 Girls
- 11 An Ideal Husband
- 18 Anxiety
- 18 The Big Tease
- 24 Beautiful People
- 24 Mad About Mambo

JUNE
- 1 Un Tè Con Il Duce
- 2 The American
- 6 Alien Love Triangle
- 8 Up At The Villa
- 15 24 Hours In London
- 22 The Diary
- 22 An Ideal Husband
- 22 Old New Borrowed Blue
- 29 Entrapment
- 30 Being Considered

JULY
- The Protagonist
- 6 Topsy Turvy
- 13 The Match
- 13 The Weekend
- 14 You're Dead
- 19 The Last Yellow
- 20 Freak Out
- 27 The Darkest Light
- 27 Lighthouse

AUGUST
- 3 *Alice Through The Looking Glass
- 3 Ratcatcher
- 3 Summer Rain
- 4 Undertakers Paradies - Meine Erste Asche
- 19 Lalla
- 20 Mansfield Park
- 24 Weak At Denise
- 25 The Closer You Get
- 31 Hold Back The Night
- 31 The Last September

SEPTEMBER
- 1 Johnny Hit And Run Pauline
- 3 *Rosen Im Sturm
- 4 Greenwich Mean Time
- 6 Bill Hicks Is Dead
- 7 The Clandestine Marriage
- 7 Rudy Valentino, Il Ritorno Dello Sceicco
- 13 Elephant Juice
- 13 Mad Cows
- 13 *Shadow Falls
- 21 Angela's Ashes
- 21 Felicia's Journey
- 23 A Room For Romeo Brass
- 24 Straight Shooter
- 26 The Xango Of Baker Street
- 27 Fanny And Elvis
- 27 Janice Beard 45 Wpm
- 28 Wonderland
- 29 Ordinary Decent Criminal
- 30 Mystery Plan

OCTOBER
- It Is Not Recommended To Offend Women
- 5 East Is East
- 5 Titus
- 12 Milk
- 19 *The Man
- 26 Texas Funeral
- 27 Accelerator

NOVEMBER
- 2 History Is Made At Night
- 2 The Wedding Tackle
- 3 Out Of Depth
- 5 The Trench
- 9 I Could Read The Sky
- 16 Peu M'Importe Si Tu M'Aimes...
- 17 Rancid Aluminium
- 23 *Oklahoma!
- 30 *Best

DECEMBER
- 3 *Tube Tales
- 14 Cotton Mary

ACCELERATOR

27 October

Production Companies: Imagine Films, Two For The Road in conjunction with Bord Scannán na hÈireann

Locations/Studio: Dublin, Belfast

Exec Prod: David Forrest, Beau Rogers

Producers: Michael Garland

Director: Vinnie Murphy

Screenplay: Vinnie Murphy, Mark Stewart

Film Editor: Peter Boyle

Director of Photography: Seamus Deasy

Cast: Stuart Sinclair Blyth, Mark Dunne, Georgina McKevitt, Gavin Kelty, Mary Ellen McCartan

The ALCHEMIST

Production Companies: Red Rooster Film and Television, Channel 5, CLT-Ufa

Exec Prod: Corinne Hollingsworth, Mick Pilsworth

Producers: Jill Green

Director: Peter Smith

Cast: Grant Show, Ruth Gemmell, Edward Hardwicke

*ALICE THROUGH THE LOOKING GLASS

3 August

Production Companies: Projector, IAC Film & Television, Channel Four, The Baltic Media Group, The Isle of Man Film Commission

Locations/Studio: Isle of Man

Exec Prod: Guy Collins

Producers: Trevor Eve, Simon Johnson, Paul Frift

Director: John Henderson

Screenplay: Nick Vivian

Film Editor: David Yardley

Director of Photography: John Ignatius

Cast: Kate Beckinsale, Sîan Phillips, Penelope Wilton, Michael Medwin, Geoffrey Palmer

ALIEN LOVE TRIANGLE (PART 1)

6 June

Production Companies: Figment Films, Dimension Films

Locations/Studio: Scotland, Los Angeles

Exec Prod: Bob Weinstein, Harvey Weinstein

Producers: Andrew MacDonald, Danny Boyle, Daniel Lupi

Director: Danny Boyle, Bill Forsyth

Screenplay: John Hodge, Bill Forsyth, Mark Protosevich

Cast: Courteney Cox, Kenneth Branagh, Heather Graham, Madeleine Stowe, Tony Shalhoub

The AMERICAN

2 June

Production Companies: BBC Films, Irish Screen, WGBH

Locations/Studio: Dublin

Exec Prod: Nigel Warren-Green, Kevin Menton, Simon Curtis, Rebecca Eaton

Producers: Fiona Finlay

Director: Paul Unwin

Screenplay: Michael Hastings

Film Editor: Kate Evans

Director of Photography: Tony Miller

Cast: Matthew Modine, Diana Rigg, Brenda Fricker, Aisling O'Sullivan, Andrew Scott

ANGELA'S ASHES

21 September

Production Companies: Scott Rudin Productions, Paramount Pictures, PolyGram Filmed Entertainment

Locations/Studio: Ireland

Exec Prod: Adam Schroeder

Producers: Scott Rudin, David Brown, Alan Parker

Director: Alan Parker

Screenplay: Laura Jones, Frank McCourt

Director of Photography: Michael Seresin

Cast: Emily Watson, Robert Carlyle

ANTHRAKITIS

16 February

Production Companies: Tiger Lily Films for the British Film Institute, Channel Four in association with The Arts Council of Wales Lottery Fund

Exec Prod: Kate Ogborn, Angie Daniell

Producers: Natasha Dack

Director: Sara Sugarman

Screenplay: Sara Sugarman

Film Editor: Lucia Zucchetti

Director of Photography: Julian Court

Cast: Liz Smith, Wendy Phillips, Kevin Phillips

ANXIETY

18 May

Production Companies: Mortal Films

Locations/Studio: Gainsborough Studios

Director: Alasdair Ogilvie

Director of Photography: Steve Brook-Smith

Cast: Susannah Morley, Ian Swan, Adrian Ross-Magenty, Ian Good

ARLINGTON ROAD

2 February

Production Companies: Samuelson Productions, PolyGram Filmed Entertainment

Lakeshore Entertainment

Locations/Studio: Texas, Washington DC

Exec Prod: Tom Rosenberg, Sigurjon Sighvatsson

Producers: Peter Samuelson, Marc Samuelson, Tom Gorai

Director: Mark Pellington

Screenplay: Ehren Kruger

Film Editor: Conrad Buff

Director of Photography: Bobby Bukowaki

Cast: Jeff Bridges, Tim Robbins, Joan Cusack, Robert Gossett, Hope Davis

ASHES TO ASHES

1 May

Production Companies: Red Moon Productions

Locations/Studio: London

Producers: Sherrie Trotman, Wayne Trotman

Director: Wayne Trotman

Screenplay: Wayne Trotman

Cast: Wayne Trotman, Gary Cameron, Ninh Coa

L'ASSEDIO

Production Companies: Fiction Cinematografica, Navert Film in co-production with Mediaset and in association with BBC Films

Locations/Studio: Rome (Italy), Nairobi (Kenya)

Producers: Massimo Cortesi

Director: Bernardo Bertolucci

Screenplay: Clare Peploe, Bernardo Bertolucci

Film Editor: Jacopo Quadri

Director of Photography: Fabio Cianchetti

Cast: Thandie Newton, David Thewlis, Claudio Santamaria, John C. Ojwang, Massimo De Rossi

BEAUTIFUL PEOPLE

24 May

Production Companies: Tall Stories, presented by the British Film Institute and Channel Four

Locations/Studio: London, Liverpool

Exec Prod: Roger Shannon, Ben Gibson

Producers: Ben Woolford

Director: Jasmin Dizdar

Screenplay: Jasmin Dizdar

Film Editor: Justin Krish

Director of Photography: Barry Ackroyd

Cast: Nicholas Farrell, Charles Kay, Rosalind Ayres, Charlotte Coleman, Gilbert Martin

BEING CONSIDERED

30 June

Production Companies: Serendipity Productions, Cattleya, Business

Affair Productions,
Film & General Productions
Locations/Studio: London, Brighton
Director: Jonathan Newman
Screenplay: Jonathan Newman
Director of Photography: Dirk Nel
Cast: James Dreyfus, Tania Levie,
Adam Levy, Viva Duce, Tom
Farrelly, Saeed Jaffrey

*BEST
30 November
Production Companies: Best Films,
with support from The Isle Of Man
Commission,
Pembridge Productions
Locations/Studio: Merseyside, Isle
of Man
Exec Prod: Mary McGuckian, John
Lynch, Guy Collins
Producers: Mary McGuckian
Director: Mary McGuckian
Screenplay: Mary McGuckian, John
Lynch
Director of Photography: Witold
Stok
Cast: John Lynch, Linus Roache, Cal
Macaninch, Ian Bannen, Jerome
Flynn, Ian Hart, Patsy Kensit

*BIG CAT
Production Companies: BBC
Drama
Exec Prod: Geoffrey Paget, Ruth
Mayorcas
Producers: Ruth Caleb
Director: Richard Spence
Screenplay: Lucy Gannon
Film Editor: Don Fairservice
Director of Photography: Chris
Seager
Cast: Amanda Root, David Morissey,
Gillian Taylforth, Stephen Crane,
Tracey Wilkinson

The BIG TEASE
18 May
Production Companies: Crawford P.
Locations/Studio: Los Angeles,
Scotland
Exec Prod: Craig Ferguson, Sacha
Gervasi, Kevin Allen
Producers: Philip Rose
Director: Kevin Allen
Screenplay: Sacha Gervasi, Craig
Ferguson
Film Editor: Chris Peppe
Director of Photography: Seamus
McGarvey
Cast: Craig Ferguson, Frances
Fisher, David Rasche, Mary
McCormack, Chris Langham

BILL HICKS IS DEAD
6 September
Production Companies: St Moritz
Productions
Locations/Studio: Edinburgh
Producers: Rebecca Knapp

Director: Faye Jackson
Screenplay: Faye Jackson
Film Editor: Faye Jackson
Director of Photography: Philip
Robertson
Cast: Wendy Wason, Kerry
Godliman, Kevin Kelly, Gavin
Mitchell, Monica Gibb

BYRON
January
Production Companies: Charter
International Productions
Locations/Studio: England, Italy,
Greece
Exec Prod: Richard Mortner
Producers: Billy Clark
Director: Charles Jarrott
Screenplay: Charles Jarrott
Director of Photography: Vilmos
Zsigmond
Cast: Jude Law, Omar Sharif,
Christopher Plummer, Ian
Richardson, Sadie Frost

*The CATER STREET HANGMAN
2 May
Production Companies: Ardent
Productions, Yorkshire Television,
A&E Network Television
Locations/Studio: Manchester,
Liverpool
Exec Prod: Eben Foggit, Keith
Richardson
Producers: June Wyndham-Davies
Director: Sarah Hellings
Screenplay: T. R. Bowen
Film Editor: Terry Warwick
Director of Photography: Doug
Hallows
Cast: Keeley Hawes, Eoin
McCarthy, Peter Egan, Richard
Lintern, John Castle

The CLANDESTINE MARRIAGE
7 September
Production Companies: RGO
Productions
Locations/Studio: Gloucestershire
Exec Prod: Steve Clark-Hall
Producers: Tim Buxton, Rod
Gunner, Jonathan Stables
Director: Christopher Miles
Screenplay: Trevor Bentham
Film Editor: George Akers
Director of Photography: Dennis
Crossan
Cast: Nigel Hawthorne, Joan Collins,
Timothy Spall, Paul Nicholls, Tom
Hollander

The CLOSER YOU GET
25 August
Production Companies: Redwave
Films, Fox Searchlight Pictures
Locations/Studio: Ireland

Producers: Uberto Pasolini
Director: Aileen Ritchie
Screenplay: William Ivory
Film Editor: Sue Wyatt
Director of Photography: Robert
Alazraki
Cast: Ian Hart, Sean McGinley,
Niamh Cusack, Ruth McCabe, Ewan
Stewart

COTTON MARY
14 December
Production Companies: Merchant
Ivory Productions, Canal Plus,
Universal Pictures
Locations/Studio: Kochi and
Chennai (India), London
Producers: Nayeem Hafizka, Gil
Donaldson
Director: Ismail Merchant
Screenplay: Alexandra Vietz
Film Editor: Roberto Silvi, Suresh
Sawant
Director of Photography: Pierre
Lhomme
Cast: Madhur Jaffrey, Greta Scacchi,
James Wilby, Natasha Richardson,
Sakina Jaffrey

The DARKEST LIGHT
27 July
Production Companies: Footprint
Films, Pathè Pictures, BBC Films,
Becker Group
Locations/Studio: North Yorkshire
Producers: Mark Blaney
Director: Bille Eltringham, Simon
Beaufoy
Screenplay: Simon Beaufoy
Film Editor: Ewa J. Lind
Director of Photography: Mary
Farbrother
Cast: Kerry Fox, Stephen Dillane,
Keri Arnold

The DEBT COLLECTOR
April
Production Companies: Dragon
Pictures, presented by Film Four,
presented in association with
Glasgow Film Fund
Locations/Studio: Edinburgh,
Glasgow
Producers: Graham Broadbent,
Damian Jones
Director: Anthony Neilson
Screenplay: Anthony Neilson
Film Editor: John Wilson
Director of Photography: Dick
Pope
Cast: Billy Connolly, Ken Stott,
Francesca Annis, Iain Robertson,
Annette Crosbie

The DIARY
22 June
Production Companies: Cult
Productions, DPI, M6, NDF
Locations/Studio: London

Producers: David Cherrill
Director: Edward Webber
Director of Photography: Frederick Farre
Cast: Mia Bailey, Abigail Olek, Jason Davies, Kestrel Boyle, Kim Haslinguis

DREAMING OF JOSEPH LEES
3 January
Production Companies: Midsummer Films, Fox Searchlight
Locations/Studio: Isle of Man
Exec Prod: Christopher Milburn, Mark Thomas
Producers: Christopher Milburn
Director: Eric Styles
Screenplay: Catherine Linstrum
Film Editor: Caroline Limmer
Director of Photography: Jimmy Dibling
Cast: Samantha Morton, Lee Ross, Rupert Graves, Miriam Margolyes, Holly Aird

EAST IS EAST
5 October
Production Companies: Assassin Films presented by Film Four in association with BBC Films
Locations/Studio: Salford, Ealing Studios
Exec Prod: Alan J. Wands
Producers: Leslee Udwin
Director: Damien O'Donnell
Screenplay: Ayub Khan-Din
Film Editor: Michael Parker
Director of Photography: Brian Tufano
Cast: Om Puri, Linda Bassett, Jordan Routledge, Archie Panjabi, Eric Marwa

ELEPHANT JUICE
13 September
Production Companies: Hal Films
Locations/Studio: London, Shepperton Studios
Exec Prod: Trea Hoving, David Aukin, Colin Leventhal
Producers: Sam Miller, Amy Jenkins, Sheila Fraser Milne
Director: Sam Miller
Screenplay: Amy Jenkins
Film Editor: Elen Lewis
Director of Photography: Adrian Wild
Cast: Emmanuelle Bèart, Sean Gallagher, Daniel Lapaine, Daniela Nardini, Mark Strong, Kimberly Williams

ENTRAPMENT
29 June
Production Companies: Twentieth Century Fox and Regency Enterprises present a Fountainbridge Films and a Michael Hertzberg production in association with

Taurus Film
Locations/Studio: Malaysia, London, Pinewood Studios
Exec Prod: Iain Smith, Ron Bass, Arnon Milchan
Producers: Michael Hertzberg, Rhonda Tollefson, Sean Connery
Director: John Amiel
Screenplay: Ron Bass, William Broyles
Film Editor: Terry Rawlings
Director of Photography: Phil Meheux
Cast: Sean Connery, Catherine Zeta-Jones, Ving Rhames, Will Patton, Maury Chaykin

EVERYBODY LOVES SUNSHINE
21 February
Production Companies: Everybody, IAC Holdings, Isle of Man Film Commission
Locations/Studio: Liverpool, Isle of Man
Exec Prod: Guy Collins, Heather Playford-Denman, Bjorg Veland, Simon Johnson
Producers: Joanne Reay
Director: Andrew Goth
Screenplay: Andrew Goth
Director of Photography: Julian Morson
Cast: Goldie, Andrew Goth, David Bowie, Rachel Shelley, Clint Dyer

EXISTENZ
6 April
Production Companies: Alliance Atlantis, Serendipity Point Films, Dimension Films in association with Natural Nylon Entertainment
Locations/Studio: Toronto, Ontario
Producers: Robert Lantos, Andras Hamori, David Cronenberg
Director: David Cronenberg
Screenplay: David Cronenberg
Film Editor: Ronald Sanders
Director of Photography: Peter Suschitzky
Cast: Jennifer Jason Leigh, Jude Law, Ian Holm, Don McKellar, Callum Keith Rennie

EYE OF THE BEHOLDER
25 March
Production Companies: Filmline International, Hit and Run Productions (UK)
Locations/Studio: Montreal
Exec Prod: Hilary Shor, Mark Damon
Producers: Nicolas Clermont, Tony Smith
Director: Stephan Elliott
Screenplay: Stephan Elliott
Director of Photography: Guy

Dufaux
Cast: Ewan McGregor, Ashley Judd, k d lang, Jason Priestly, Genevieve Bujold

FANNY AND ELVIS
27 September
Production Companies: Scala Productions, The Film Consortium
Locations/Studio: Yorkshire, London, Twickenham Studios
Exec Prod: Nik Powell
Producers: Laurie Borg
Director: Kay Mellor
Screenplay: Kay Mellor
Film Editor: Chris Blunden
Director of Photography: John Daly
Cast: Ray Winstone, Kerry Fox, David Morrissey, Colin Salmon, Gaynor Faye, Ben Daniels, Jennifer Saunders

FELICIA'S JOURNEY
21 September
Production Companies: Marquis Films, Icon Productions, Alliance Atlantis, Artisan Entertainment
Locations/Studio: Ireland, England, Shepperton Studios
Exec Prod: Paul Tucker, Ralph Kamp
Producers: Bruce Davey
Director: Atom Egoyan
Screenplay: Atom Egoyan
Film Editor: Susan Shipton
Director of Photography: Paul Sarossy
Cast: Bob Hoskins, Elaine Cassidy, Peter McDonald, Arsinèe Khanjian, Gerard McSorley

FREAK OUT
20 July
Production Companies: Beyond Therapy Entertainment, British Telecom, Atlantic International
Locations/Studio: Dorset
Exec Prod: Desmond Cullen-Jones, Stuart Munro
Producers: Christian James, Dan Palmer, John Swindel
Director: Christian James
Screenplay: Dan Palmer, Christian James
Director of Photography: Paul McIntyre
Cast: James Hicks, Dan Palmer, Suzanne Britten, Jim Sparrow, Ben Catchpole

GREENWICH MEAN TIME
4 September
Production Companies: Anvil Films and Recording Group, Icon Entertainment International
Locations/Studio: London
Producers: Taylor Hackford
Director: John Strickland

Screenplay: Simon Mirren
Film Editor: Patrick Moore
Director of Photography: Alan Almond
Cast: Steve John Shepherd, Anjela Lauren Smith, Karl Collins, Benjamin Waters, Alicya Eyo

GREGORY'S TWO GIRLS
10 May
Production Companies: Young Lake, Film Four, The Scottish Arts Council
Producers: Christopher Young
Director: Bill Forsyth
Screenplay: Bill Forsyth
Film Editor: John Glow
Director of Photography: John de Borman
Cast: John Gordon Sinclair, Carly Mackinnon, Maria Doyle, Martin Schwab, Dougray Scott

GREY OWL
14 April
Production Companies: Beaver/Ajawaan Productions Inc, Largo Entertainment
Locations/Studio: Montreal, Quebec, Canada and Hastings, England
Exec Prod: Barr B. Potter
Producers: Jake Eberts, Richard Attenborough, Claude Lèger
Director: Richard Attenborough
Screenplay: William Nicholson
Film Editor: Lesley Walker
Director of Photography: Roger Pratt
Cast: Pierce Brosnan, Annie Galipeau, Nathaniel Arcand, Renèe Asherson, Stephanie Cole, Graham Greene

HISTORY IS MADE AT NIGHT
2 November
Production Companies: Scala Productions, J&M Entertainment
Locations/Studio: Helsinki, New York
Exec Prod: Nik Powell, Stephen Woolley
Producers: Jonathan Karlsson
Director: Ilkka Jarvilaturi
Screenplay: Patrick Amos, Jean-Pierre Gorin
Film Editor: Alan Strachan
Director of Photography: Michael Amathieu
Cast: Bill Pullman, Irene Jacob

HOLD BACK THE NIGHT
31 August
Production Companies: Parallax Pictures, Film Consortium, FilmFour in association with the Arts Council of England, BIM Distribuzione, WavePictures
Producers: Sally Hibbin

Director: Phil Davis
Screenplay: Steve Chambers
Film Editor: Adam Ross
Director of Photography: Cinders Forshaw
Cast: Christine Tremarco, Sheila Hancock, Stuart Sinclair-Blyth, Richard Platt, Julie Ann Watson

HUMAN TRAFFIC
30 January
Production Companies: Fruit Salad Films presented by Irish Screen
Locations/Studio: Cardiff (Wales)
Exec Prod: Renata S. Aly
Producers: Allan Niblo, Emer McCourt
Director: Justin Kerrigan
Screenplay: Justin Kerrigan
Film Editor: Patrick Moore
Director of Photography: David Bennett
Cast: John Simm, Lorraine Pilkington, Shaun Parkes, Nicola Reynolds, Danny Dyer

I COULD READ THE SKY
9 November
Production Companies: Hot Property Films in association with Spider Pictures and Liquid Films with support from the British Film Institute, the Arts Council of England, Bord Scannán na hÈireann and Channel Four
Locations/Studio: Ireland, UK
Producers: Janine Marmot, Melanie Gore Grimes, Christopher Collins
Director: Nichola Bruce
Screenplay: Nichola Bruce, Timothy O'Grady
Director of Photography: Owen McPolin, Seamus McGarvey
Cast: Stephen Rea, Dermot Healy, Maria Doyle Kennedy, Brendan Coyle, Michael Lally

An IDEAL HUSBAND
11 May
Production Companies: Wilde Films, Scorpio Film Productions
Locations/Studio: London
Exec Prod: George Marshall
Producers: Daniel Figuero, Zygi Kamasa
Director: Bill Cartlidge
Screenplay: Bill Cartlidge
Film Editor: Matthew Glen
Director of Photography: Jake Polansky
Cast: James Wilby, Sadie Frost, Jonathan Firth, Prunella Scales, Robert Hardy

An IDEAL HUSBAND
22 June
Production Companies: Fragile

Films, Ideal Film Company in association with Icon Productions and Miramax Films, presentation by Pathè Pictures in association with the Arts Council of England, supported by the National Lottery through the Arts Council of England
Locations/Studio: London, Leavesden Studios
Exec Prod: Susan Landau, Ralph Kamp, Andrea Calderwood
Producers: Barnaby Thompson, Uri Fruchtmann, Bruce Davey
Director: Oliver Parker
Screenplay: Oliver Parker
Film Editor: Guy Bensley
Director of Photography: David Johnson
Cast: Cate Blanchett, Minnie Driver, Rupert Everett, Julianne Moore, Jeremy Northam

IT IS NOT RECOMMENDED TO OFFEND WOMEN
October
Production Companies: NTV-Profit
Locations/Studio: Russia, London
Producers: Igor Tolstunov, Sergei Kozlov
Director: Valery Akhadov
Screenplay: Valentin Tchernikh
Director of Photography: Valentin Piganov
Cast: Vera Glagoleva, Maxim Sukhanov

JANICE BEARD 45 WPM
27 September
Production Companies: Dakota Films presented by The Film Consortium in association with WavePictures, the Arts Council of England, Film Four Limited
Locations/Studio: London
Exec Prod: Jonathan Olsberg
Producers: Judy Counihan
Director: Clare Kilner
Screenplay: Ben Hopkins, Clare Kilner
Film Editor: Mary Finlay
Director of Photography: Peter Thwaite, Richard Greatrex
Cast: Eileen Walsh, Rhys Ifans, Patsy Kensit, David O'Hara, Sandra Voe

The JESUS STORY
January
Production Companies: S4C Films, Christmas Films sponsored by British Screen, BBC
Locations/Studio: Moscow
Director: Derek Hayes
Voices of: Ralph Fiennes, Julie Christie, William Hurt, Miranda Richardson

JOHNNY HIT AND RUN PAULINE
1 September
Production Companies: Storm Entertainment, Big Table Productions
Locations/Studio: UK
Exec Prod: Emma Thompson, H. Michael Heuser
Producers: Jenny Frankfurt
Director: Fay Lellios
Screenplay: Fay Lellios
Director of Photography: Frank Byers
Cast: Sherilyn Fenn, Phyllida Law, Paul McGann, Miranda Richardson

The KILLING ZONE
13 February
Production Companies: Seventh Twelfth Collective
Producers: Julian Boote
Director: Ian David Diaz
Screenplay: Ian David Diaz
Film Editor: Piotr Szkopiak
Director of Photography: Alan Dunlop
Cast: Padraig Casey, Oliver Young, Julian Boote, Mark Bowden, Richard Banks

*KISZKO
3 March
Production Companies: Celtic Films, Picture Palace Productions
Exec Prod: Muir Sutherland
Producers: Malcolm Craddock
Director: Stephen Whittaker
Screenplay: Peter Berry
Film Editor: Max Lemon
Director of Photography: James Aspinall
Cast: Olympia Dukakis, Tony Maudsley, Simon Shepherd, Malcolm Tierney, Tom Chadbon

LALLA
19 August
Production Companies: Frankfurter Filmproduktion
Locations/Studio: UK
Exec Prod: Michael Smeaon
Producers: Heidi Ulmke
Director: Hans Juergen Toegel
Screenplay: Gabriele Kister
Film Editor: Gabi Doll
Director of Photography: Rolf Greim
Cast: Nina Basquasat, Olivia Shilhavy, Elmar Wepper, Bjorn Kegel-Casapietra, Albert Fortell

The LAST SEPTEMBER
31 August
Production Companies: Zagros, Matrix Films and Television, Scala Productions in association with Bord Scannán na hÈireann, Radio Telefís Èireann with

the participation of British Sky Broadcasting, British Screen in association with IMA Films, Canal Plus
Locations/Studio: Drogheda
Exec Prod: Neil Jordan, Nik Powell, Stephen Woolley, Peter Fudakowski
Producers: Yvonne Thunder
Director: Deborah Warner
Screenplay: John Banville
Film Editor: Kate Evans, Marie-Therese Bioche
Director of Photography: Slawomir Idziak
Cast: Maggie Smith, Jane Birkin, Michael Gambon, Fiona Shaw, David Tennant

The LAST YELLOW
19 July
Production Companies: Scala Productions, Jolyon Symonds Productions, Hollywood Partners, the Arts Council of England, BBC Films
Locations/Studio: London, Pinewood Studios
Exec Prod: Nik Powell
Producers: Jolyon Symonds
Director: Julian Farino
Screenplay: Paul Tucker
Film Editor: Pia DiCiaula
Director of Photography: David Odd
Cast: Mark Addy, Charlie Creed-Miles, Samantha Morton, Kenneth Cranham, James Hooton

LIGHTHOUSE
27 July
Production Companies: Lighthouse Entertainment, Tungsten Pictures, the Arts Council of England, British Screen
Locations/Studio: London, Three Mills Island Studios
Producers: Mark Leake, Tim Dennison
Director: Simon Hunter
Screenplay: Simon Hunter
Director of Photography: Tony Imi
Cast: Rachel Shelley, Don Warrington, Chris Adamson, Bob Goody, Norman Mitchell

The LOST SON
12 January
Production Companies: Scala (Lost Son), IMA Films, presentation Film Consortium, Studio Canal Plus in association with the Arts Council of England, FilmFour, Canal+, France 2 Cinèma, France 3 Cinèma, supported by the National Lottery through the Arts Council of England, developed with the support of MEDIA II
Locations/Studio: London,

Felixstowe, Los Angeles, Tucson
Exec Prod: Nik Powell, Stephen Woolley, Georges Benayoun, Sarah Radclyffe
Producers: Finola Dwyer
Director: Chris Menges
Screenplay: Eric Leclere, Margaret Leclere, Mark Mills
Film Editor: Pamela Power, Luc Barnier
Director of Photography: Barry Ackroyd
Cast: Daniel Auteuil, Nastassja Kinski, Katrin Cartlidge, Ciaran Hinds, Marianne Denicourt,

MAD ABOUT MAMBO
24 May
Production Companies: Plurabelle Films, First City Features, Phoenix Pictures
Locations/Studio: Dublin
Exec Prod: Martin Bruce-Clayton
Producers: David Kelly, Gabriel Byrne
Director: John Forte
Screenplay: John Forte
Film Editor: David Martin
Director of Photography: Ashley Rowe
Cast: William Ash, Keri Russell, Theo Fraser Steele, Paul McLean, Joe Rea

MAD COWS
13 September
Production Companies: Flashlight Films
Locations/Studio: London
Producers: Frank Mannion, Aaron Simpson
Director: Sara Sugarman
Screenplay: Sara Sugarman
Film Editor: John Jympson
Director of Photography: Pierre Aïm
Cast: Anna Friel, Joanna Lumley, Greg Wise, Anna Massey, Phyllida Law

MAKE BELIEVE
Production Companies: Make Believe Productions
Exec Prod: Sarah Zincke
Producers: Alex Shaida
Director: Alex Shaida
Director of Photography: Roger Edwards
Cast: John Finn, Miles Harrison, Sarah White

*The MAN
19 October
Production Companies: Crucial Films produced for BBC Films
Locations/Studio: Hertfordshire, Tenerife
Exec Prod: Polly McDonald, Jane

Tranter
Producers: Colin Ludlow
Director: Betsan Morris Evans
Screenplay: Jon Canter
Film Editor: Jeremy Gibbs
Director of Photography: Simon
Maggs
Cast: Lenny Henry, Marianne Jean-
Baptiste, Morwenna Banks, Adrian
Edmondson, Julian Wadham

MANSFIELD PARK
20 August
Production Companies: HAL Films,
Miramax Film, BBC Films
Locations/Studio:
Northamptonshire, Cornwall, Ealing
Studios
Exec Prod: David Aukin, Trea
Horing
Producers: Elinor Day, Sarah Curtis
Director: Patricia Rozema
Screenplay: Patricia Rozema,
Maggie Wadey
Film Editor: Martin Walsh
Director of Photography: Mick
Coulter
Cast: Alessandro Nivola, Jonny Lee
Miller, Harold Pinter, Frances
O'Connor,
Embeth Davidtz

The MATCH
13 July
Production Companies: Propaganda
Films, Rafford Films, Alan Scott
Productions in association with
Irish Dream Time presented by
PolyGram Filmed Entertainment
Locations/Studio: Scotland
Exec Prod: Steve Golin, Pierce
Brosnan, Beau St. Clair, Robert
Kosberg
Producers: Allan Scott, Guymon
Casady
Director: Mick Davis
Screenplay: Mick Davis
Film Editor: Kate Williams
Director of Photography: Witold
Stok
Cast: Max Beesley, Isla Blair, James
Cosmo, Laura Fraser, Richard E.
Grant

MICKEY BLUE EYES
7 January
Production Companies: Simian
Films, Castle Rock Entertainment
Locations/Studio: New York
Producers: Elizabeth Hurley,
Charles Mulvehill
Director: Kelly Makin
Screenplay: Mark Lawrence, Adam
Scheinman, Robert Kuhn
Director of Photography: Donald
Thorin
Cast: Hugh Grant, Jeanne
Tripplehorn, James Caan, James Fox,
Burt Young

MILK
12 October
Production Companies: Gumfluh
Films
Locations/Studio: Oare (Wiltshire)
Exec Prod: Paul Trijbits
Producers: George Duffield, Meg
Thomson, Galt Niederhoffer
Director: William Brookfield
Screenplay: William Brookfield
Film Editor: Peter Hollywood
Director of Photography: Peter
Hannan
Cast: James Fleet, Phyllida Law,
Dawn French, Francesca Annis, Joss
Ackland

A MONKEY'S TALE
Production Companies: Les Films
du Triangle, Cologne Cartoon,
Ventureworld Films, Fabrique,
Kecskemetfilm
Locations/Studio: UK, France,
Germany
Producers: Steve Walsh
Director: Jean-Francois Laguionie
Screenplay: Norman Hudis, Jean-
Francois Laguionie
Voices of: John Hurt, Michael
Gambon, Rik Mayall, Diana Quick,
Matt Hill, Sally-Ann Marsh,
Shirley-Anne Field

The MUMMY
4 May
Production Companies: Universal
Pictures, Alphaville Productions
Locations/Studio: Morocco, UK,
Shepperton Studios
Exec Prod: Kevin Jarre
Producers: James Jacks, Sean Daniel
Director: Stephen Sommers
Screenplay: Stephen Sommers
Film Editor: Bob Ducsay, Kelly
Matsumoto
Director of Photography: Adrian
Biddle
Cast: Brendan Fraser, Rachel Weisz,
John Hannah, Kevin J. O'Connor,
Arnold Vosloo

MYSTERY PLAN
30 September
Production Companies: 891
Filmhouse
Locations/Studio: Harrow, Central
London
Producers: Sean Martin
Director: Sean Martin
Screenplay: Sean Martin
Film Editor: Loren Squires
Director of Photography: John Hoare
Cast: Tess Tomlinson, Tom
Chadwick, Jon McFarlane, Vicki
Simon, Jamie Jarvis

MY SUMMER WITH DES
1 March
Production Companies: BBC Films

Locations/Studio: London, Paris
Exec Prod: Jane Tranter
Producers: Joy Spink
Director: Simon Curtis
Screenplay: Arthur Smith
Film Editor: Philip Kloss
Director of Photography: Graham
Frake
Cast: Neil Morrissey, Rachel Weisz,
John Gordon Sinclair, Arabella Weir,
Desmond Lynam, Ned Sherrin

NOTTING HILL
20 April
Production Companies: PolyGram
Filmed Entertainment presents in
association with Working
Title Films a Duncan Kenworthy
production from Notting Hill Pictures
Locations/Studio: Notting Hill
(London), Ealing, Kenwood House
(Hampstead)
Shepperton Studios
Exec Prod: Tim Bevan, Richard
Curtis, Eric Fellner
Producers: Duncan Kenworthy
Director: Roger Michell
Screenplay: Richard Curtis
Film Editor: Nick Moore
Director of Photography: Michael
Coulter
Cast: Julia Roberts, Hugh Grant,
Hugh Bonneville, Emma Chambers,
James Dreyfus

*OKLAHOMA!
23 November
Production Companies: Oklahoma!
Screen Productions, Sky Productions
Locations/Studio: Shepperton
Studios
Producers: Richard Price
Director: Trevor Nunn
Director of Photography: Paul Wheeler
Cast: Maureen Lipman, Hugh
Jackman, Joselina Gabrielle, Shuler
Hensley, Jimmy Johnston

OLD NEW BORROWED BLUE
22 June
Production Companies: Revolution
Films presented by Miramax Films
and FilmFour
Locations/Studio: London, Belfast
(Northern Ireland), Pinewood Studios
Producers: Andrew Eaton
Director: Michael Winterbottom
Screenplay: John Forte
Film Editor: Trevor Waite
Director of Photography: Benoît
Delhomme
Cast: Yvan Attal, Dervla Kirwan,
Christopher Eccleston, Julie Graham,
Alun Armstrong

ONEGIN
7 March
Production Companies: Rysher

Entertainment
Locations/Studio: St. Petersburg (Russia), UK, Shepperton Studios
Exec Prod: Ralph Fiennes
Producers: Ralph Fiennes, Ileen Maisel
Director: Martha Fiennes
Cast: Ralph Fiennes, Liv Tyler, Toby Stephens, Lena Headey, Martin Donovan

ORDINARY DECENT CRIMINAL
29 September
Production Companies: Little Bird, Trigger Street, TATfilm
Locations/Studio: Dublin
Exec Prod: James Mitchell
Producers: Jonathan Cavendish
Director: Thaddeus O'Sullivan
Screenplay: Gerard Stembridge
Film Editor: David Ray
Director of Photography: Andrew Dunn
Cast: Kevin Spacey, Linda Fiorentino, Peter Mullan, David Hayman, Stephen Dillane

OUT OF DEPTH
3 November
Production Companies: Redbus Films, Out of Depth
Locations/Studio: London
Exec Prod: Paul Woolf
Producers: Stephen Cranny
Director: Simon Marshall
Screenplay: Simon Marshall
Film Editor: St. John O'Rorke
Director of Photography: Adam Suschitzky
Cast: Sean Maguire, Rita Tushingham, Josephine Butler, Phil Cornwell, Danny Midwinter

PALMER'S PICK-UP
January
Production Companies: Winchester Films, Plaster City Productions, ACC Entertainment & Co, KG Film
Locations/Studio: US
Exec Prod: Christopher Coppola, Chris Craib
Producers: Alain Silver
Director: Christopher Coppola
Screenplay: Nick Johnson
Film Editor: Nick Johnson
Director of Photography: Mark Kohl
Cast: Robert Carradine, Richard Hillman, Patrick Kilpatrick, Morton Downey Jr., Alice Ghostley

PEU M'IMPORTE SI TU M'AIMES...
16 November
Production Companies: Renn Productions, Pathé
Locations/Studio: London

Exec Prod: Timothy Burrill
Producers: Claude Berri
Director: Michel Blanc
Screenplay: Michel Blanc
Film Editor: Marilyn Montieux
Director of Photography: Barry Ackroyd
Cast: Daniel Auteuil, Stuart Townsend, Liza Walker, Peter Mullan, Claire Skinner

The PROTAGONIST
July
Production Companies: Surf Film, Chain Film
Locations/Studio: London
Producers: Massimo Vigliar
Director: Luca Guardignino
Screenplay: Luca Guardignino
Cast: Tilda Swinton, Patrick O'Kean

RANCID ALUMINIUM
17 November
Production Companies: Fiction Factory Production with support from Entertainment Film Distributors
Locations/Studio: London, Wales, Poland
Exec Prod: Nigel Green
Producers: Mark Thomas, Mike Parker
Director: Edward Thomas
Screenplay: James Hawes
Film Editor: Chris Lawrence
Director of Photography: Tony Imi
Cast: Rhys Ifans, Joseph Fiennes, Tara Fitzgerald, Sadie Frost, Steven Berkoff

RATCATCHER
3 August
Production Companies: Holy Cow Films, BBC Scotland presented by Pathé,
BBC Films in association with the Arts Council of England, Productions Lazennec, Studio Canal Plus
Locations/Studio: Glasgow
Exec Prod: Andrea Calderwood, Barbara McKissack, Sarah Radclyffe
Producers: Gavin Emerson
Director: Lynne Ramsay
Screenplay: Lynne Ramsay
Film Editor: Lucia Zucchetti
Director of Photography: Alwin Küchler
Cast: William Eadie, Tommy Flanagan, Mandy Matthews, Michelle Stuart, Lynne Ramsay Jr.

A ROOM FOR ROMEO BRASS
21 September
Production Companies: Company Pictures, BBC Films, the Arts Council of England
Locations/Studio: Nottingham
Exec Prod: András Hámori

Producers: George Faber, Charlie Pattinson
Director: Shane Meadows
Screenplay: Shane Meadows
Film Editor: Paul Tothill
Director of Photography: Ashley Rowe
Cast: Bob Hoskins, Andrew Shim, Benjamin Marshall, Frank Harper

*ROSEN IM STURM
3 September
Production Companies: Ufa Fernsehproduktion, ZDF
Locations/Studio: south of England
Producers: Wolf Bauer
Director: Stefan Bartmann
Screenplay: H Kugler, T Maier
Director of Photography: Marc Prill
Cast: Simone Heher, Harry Blank, Peter Bongartz

RUDY VALENTINO, IL RITORNO DELLO SCEICCO
7 September
Production Companies: Mediterranea Film
Locations/Studio: London, Paris, Milan, Puglia
Director: Nico Cirasola
Cast: Claudia Cardinale, Antonella Ponziani

*SHADOW FALLS
13 September
Production Companies: Ty Cefn
Locations/Studio: Cardiff
Exec Prod: Peter Edwards
Producers: Clive Waldron
Director: Endaf Emlyn
Screenplay: David Joss Buckley
Director of Photography: Peter Thornton
Cast: Philip Madoc, Ffion Wilkins, Simon Kunz, Caroline Berry, Sharon Morgan

SHAKESPEARE IN LOVE
2 March
Production Companies: Universal Pictures presents a Bedford Falls production
Locations/Studio: Broughton Castle (Banbury), Great Hall, Middle Coll (Eton),
Marble Hill House (Norfolk), Shepperton Studios
Exec Prod: Bob Weinstein, Julie Goldstein
Producers: David Parfitt, Donna Gigliotti, Harvey Weinstein, Edward Zwick, Marc Norman
Director: John Madden
Screenplay: Marc Norman, Tom Stoppard
Film Editor: David Gamble
Director of Photography: Richard

Greatrex
Cast: Joseph Fiennes, Gwyneth Paltrow, Judi Dench, Ben Affleck, Colin Firth

SIMON MAGUS
4 May
Production Companies: Jonescompany, Film Four, Lucky Red, ARP, Hollywood Partners, Silesia Film in association with the Arts Council of England
Locations/Studio: Wales, Shepperton Studios
Producers: Robert Jones
Director: Ben Hopkins
Screenplay: Ben Hopkins
Film Editor: Alan Levy
Director of Photography: Nic Knowland
Cast: Noah Taylor, Embeth Davidtz, Stuart Townsend, Rutger Hauer, Ian Holm

A SIMPLE PLAN
5 January
Production Companies: Paramount Pictures Corporation, Mutual Film Company, BBC, Marubeni Corporation, Toho-Towa, Tele-Munchen, Union General Cinematographique in association with Savoy Pictures Entertainment
Locations/Studio: Minnesota
Exec Prod: Gary Levinsohn, Mark Gordon
Producers: James Jacks, Adam Schroeder
Director: Sam Raimi
Screenplay: Scott B. Smith
Film Editor: Arthur Coburn, Eric L. Beason
Director of Photography: Alar Kivilo
Cast: Bill Paxton, Billy Bob Thornton, Bridget Fonda, Gary Cole, Brent Briscoe

SMALL TIME OBSESSION
4 March
Production Companies: Solo Films
Producers: Piotr Szkopiak
Director: Piotr Szkopiak
Screenplay: Piotr Szkopiak
Film Editor: Piotr Szkopiak
Director of Photography: Niels Johansen
Cast: Alex King, Juliette Caton, Oliver Young, Richard Banks

SOLOMON AND GAENOR
22 March
Production Companies: APT Film and TV in association with September Films, S4C presented by Film Four, the Arts Council of England, the Arts Council of Wales

Locations/Studio: south Wales
Exec Prod: Andy Porter, David Green
Producers: Sheryl Crown
Director: Paul Morrison
Screenplay: Paul Morrison
Film Editor: Kant Pan
Director of Photography: Nina Kellgren
Cast: Ioan Gruffudd, Nia Roberts, Sue Jones Davies, William Thomas, Mark Lewis Jones

STILL CRAZY
26 January
Production Companies: Marmot Tandy Production, 4U2 Production Services (Spanish), Televisionstones BV (Holland) with the participation of Greenlight Fund, supported by the National Lottery through the Arts Council of England, presented by Columbia Pictures Corporation
Locations/Studio: London
Exec Prod: Dick Clement, Ian La Frenais
Producers: Amanda Marmot
Director: Brian Gibson
Screenplay: Dick Clement, Ian La Frenais
Film Editor: Peter Boyle
Director of Photography: Ashley Rowe
Cast: Stephen Rea, Billy Connolly, Jimmy Nail, Timothy Spall, Bill Nighy

STRAIGHT SHOOTER
24 September
Production Companies: Perathon Film, Senator Film with backing from Filmfernseh Fonds Bayern, Filmstiftung Nordrhein-Westfalen, Filmförderungsanstalt
Locations/Studio: Cologne, Duisburg, Duesseldorf, London
Producers: Joseph Vilsmaier, Hanno Huth
Director: Thomas Bohn
Screenplay: Thomas Bohn
Film Editor: Norbert Herzner, Peter Adam
Director of Photography: Egon Werdin
Cast: Dennis Hopper, Heino Ferch, Katja Flint, Hannelore Hoger, Ulrich Muehe

SUMMER RAIN
3 August
Production Companies: Enterprise Films, Summer Rain Films
Locations/Studio: Brighton
Producers: Jonathan Glendening
Director: Jonathan Glendening
Screenplay: Chris Riley
Film Editor: Colin Chapman

Director of Photography: Peter Wignall
Cast: Clea Smith, Lara Clancy, Catherine Sampson, Paul Vaughan Evans, Andrew Crabb

SWING
4 February
Production Companies: Last Time Production, presented by Tapestry Films, Kushner-Locke Co
Locations/Studio: London, Liverpool
Exec Prod: Donald Kushner, Peter Locke, Robert L. Levy, Peter Abrams, J. P. Guerin
Producers: Louise Rosner, Su Lim
Director: Nick Mead
Screenplay: Nick Mead
Film Editor: Norman Buckley
Director of Photography: Ian Wilson
Cast: Hugo Speer, Lisa Stansfield, Tom Bell, Rita Tushingham, Alexei Sayle

Un TÈ CON IL DUCE/TEA WITH MUSSOLINI
1 June
Production Companies: Cattleya Films, Medusa, Cineritmo, Business Affair Productions, Film & General Productions
Locations/Studio: Florence, San Gimignano
Exec Prod: Marco Chimenz
Producers: Riccardo Tozzi, Giovannella Zannoni, Clive Parsons
Director: Franco Zeffirelli
Screenplay: John Mortimer, Franco Zeffirelli
Film Editor: Tariq Anwar
Director of Photography: David Watkin
Cast: Cher, Judi Dench, Joan Plowright, Maggie Smith, Lily Tomlin

TEXAS FUNERAL
26 October
Production Companies: Dragon Pictures, Jem Entertainment
Locations/Studio: Texas
Producers: Damian Jones, Graham Broadbent
Director: Blake Herron
Screenplay: Blake Herron
Cast: Robert Patrick, Joanna Whalley-Kilmer, Tony Goldwyn, Olivia D'Abo, Jane Adams

THIS YEAR'S LOVE
15 April
Production Companies: Kismet Film Company, Entertainment Film Distributors, The Scottish Arts Council Lottery Fund
Locations/Studio: Camden

(London), Three Mills Island Studio
Exec Prod: Nigel Green
Producers: Michele Camarda
Director: David Kane
Screenplay: David Kane
Film Editor: Sean Barton
Director of Photography: Robert
Alazraki
Cast: Kathy Burke, Jennifer Ehle,
Ian Hart, Douglas Henshall,
Catherine McCormack

THREE BUSINESSMEN
Production Companies:
Exterminating Angel Productions
VPRO TV, Film Funds Rotterdam
Locations/Studio: The Netherlands,
Liverpool, Hong Kong, Tokyo,
Mexico
Producers: Tod Davies
Director: Alex Cox
Screenplay: Tod Davies
Film Editor: Bob Robertson, Carlos
Puente
Director of Photography: Robert
Tregenza
Cast: Miguel Sandoval, Bob
Wisdom, Isabel Ampudia, Alex Cox

TITUS
5 October
Production Companies: Clear Blue
Sky Productions, Overseas Film
Group, NDF International
Locations/Studio: Rome, Croatia
Exec Prod: Jody Patton, Michiyo
Yoshizaki
Producers: Ellen Di Dionisio,
Robbie Little
Director: Julie Taymor
Screenplay: Julie Taymor
Film Editor: Francoise Bonnot
Director of Photography: Nicola
Pecorini
Cast: Anthony Hopkins, Jessica
Lange, Alan Cumming, Jonathan
Rhys Meyers, James Frain

TOPSY TURVY
6 July
Production Companies: Thin Man
Productions
Locations/Studio: London
Producers: Simon Channing-
Williams
Director: Mike Leigh
Screenplay: Mike Leigh
Film Editor: Robin Sales
Director of Photography: Dick
Pope
Cast: Jim Broadbent, Dexter
Fletcher, Allan Corduner, Timothy
Spall, Alison Steadman

*TOUCH AND GO
6 April
Production Companies: BBC Films
Locations/Studio: London, Leeds
Producers: Alan Wright

Director: Tim Fywell
Screenplay: Martin Allen
Film Editor: Roy Sharman
Director of Photography: Sean Van
Halles
Cast: Martin Clunes, Zara Turner,
Teresa Banham, Ewan Stewart, Ian
McElhinney

TO WALK WITH LIONS
10 March
Production Companies:
Kingsborough Greenlight Pictures,
Studio Eight Film Productions
Locations/Studio: Kenya
Exec Prod: John Buchanan
Producers: Pieter Kroonenburg,
Julie Allan
Director: Carl Schultz
Screenplay: Keith Ross Leckie
Film Editor: Angelo Corrao
Director of Photography: Jean
Lèpine
Cast: Richard Harris, John Michie,
Ian Bannen, Kerry Fox, Hugh
Quarshie

The TRENCH
5 November
Production Companies: Portman
Entertainment, Skyline Film &
Television Productions,
Blue PM, Galatèe Films with
participation of British Screen in
association with
the Arts Council of England,
Bonaparte Films with support of
Canal Plus
Locations/Studio: Bray Studios
Exec Prod: Xavier Marchand
Producers: Steve Clark-Hall
Director: William Boyd
Screenplay: William Boyd
Film Editor: Jim Clark, Laurence
Mèry-Clark
Director of Photography: Tony
Pierce-Roberts
Cast: Paul Nicholls, Daniel Craig,
Julian Rhind-Tutt, Danny Dyer,
James D`arcy,
Tam Williams, Antony Strachan

TROUBLE ON EARTH
Production Companies:
Rollercoaster Films
Producers: Alex Kaufman
Director: Alex Kaufman
Film Editor: Jami Maartin
Director of Photography: Michael
Carney
Cast: Andrew Jenner, Richard
Reeves, Roger Moss, Hermione
Gulliford

*TUBE TALES
3 December
Production Companies:
Horsepower Films
Locations/Studio: London

Underground
Exec Prod: Richard Jobson
Producers: Tony Thompson
Director: Stephen Hopkins, Bill
MacKinnon, Ewan McGregor, Jude
Law, Armando
Iannucci, Amy Jenkins, Charles
McDougal
Screenplay: Bob Hoskins, Amy
Jenkins, Armando Iannucci
Director of Photography: Brian
Tufano, Sue Gibson
Cast: Denise Van Outen, Rachel Weisz

24 HOURS IN LONDON
15 June
Production Companies: One World
Films
Locations/Studio: London, Bow
Studios
Exec Prod: Peter Jaques
Producers: Fergal McGrath
Director: Alexander Finbow
Screenplay: Alexander Finbow
Director of Photography: Chris
Plevin
Cast: Gary Olsen, Anjela Lauren
Smith, Amita Dhiri, James Olivier

UNDERTAKERS PARADIES
– MEINE ERSTE ASCHE
4 August
Production Companies: Claussen &
Wöbke Filmproduktion with funding
from MEDIA II,
Filmfernseh Fonds Bayern,
Bundesministerium des Innern
Locations/Studio: Aberystwyth
(Wales)
Producers: Jakob Claussen, Thomas
Woebke
Director: Matthias Oberg
Screenplay: Matthias Oberg, Tim
Dabringhaus
Film Editor: Barbara Giess
Director of Photography: Martin
Kukula
Cast: Thomas Schmauser, Ben
Gazzara, Emma Catherwood, Edward
Jewesbury,
Craig Kelly

UP AT THE VILLA
8 June
Production Companies: Up At The
Villa Productions, InterMedia Film
Equities, Mirage Enterprises,
Buckeye
Locations/Studio: Florence, Siena
Exec Prod: Guy East, Nigel Sinclair
Producers: Sydney Pollack, Stanley
F. Buchthal
Director: Philip Haas
Screenplay: Belinda Haas, Philip
Haas
Film Editor: Susan E. Morse
Director of Photography: Maurizio
Calvesi

Cast: Kristin Scott Thomas, Sean Penn, Anne Bancroft, James Fox, Jeremy Davies, Derek Jacobi, Massimo Glini

VIRTUAL SEXUALITY
3 May
Production Companies: Noel Gay Motion Picture Company, The Bridge
Locations/Studio: Swiss Cottage (London), Elstree Film Studios
Exec Prod: Jonathan Darby, Kevin Loader, Charles Armitage
Producers: Christopher Figg
Director: Nick Hurran
Screenplay: Nick Fisher
Film Editor: John Richards
Director of Photography: Brian Tufano
Cast: Laura Fraser, Rupert Penry-Jones, Luke De Lacey, Kieran O'Brien, Marcelle Duprey

WAR ZONE
2 March
Production Companies: FilmFour, Sarah Radclyffe Productions, Portobello Pictures
Exec Prod: Eric Abraham
Producers: Sarah Radclyffe, Dixie Linder
Director: Tim Roth
Screenplay: Alexander Stuart
Film Editor: Trevor Waite
Director of Photography: Seamus McGarvey
Cast: Ray Winstone, Tilda Swinton, Lara Belmont, Freddie Cunliffe, Kate Ashfield

WEAK AT DENISE
24 August
Production Companies: Peninsula Films
Locations/Studio: London
Producers: Julian Nott, Clare Erasmus
Director: Julian Nott
Screenplay: Julian Nott
Director of Photography: Marco Windham
Cast: Bill Thomas, Chrissie Cotterill, Craig Fairbrass, Edna Dore, Tilly Blackwood

The WEDDING TACKLE
2 November
Production Companies: Viking Films
Locations/Studio: London
Exec Prod: Donald Horne
Producers: Nigel Horne
Director: Rami Devir
Director of Photography: Shelley Hirst
Cast: James Purefoy, Leslie Grantham, Adrian Dunbar, Susan Vidler, Tony Slattery, Amanda Redman

The WEEKEND
13 July
Production Companies: Granada Film, Lunatics & Lovers, Yellow Room Productions
Locations/Studio: New York
Exec Prod: Pippa Cross, Janette Day
Producers: Ian Benson
Director: Brian Skeet
Screenplay: Brian Skeet
Director of Photography: Ron Fortunato
Cast: Gena Rowlands, Deborah Unger, Brooke Shields, David Conrad, James Duval

The WINSLOW BOY
15 March
Production Companies: Sony Pictures Classics
Locations/Studio: Clapham Common (London)
Producers: Sarah Green
Director: David Mamet
Screenplay: David Mamet
Film Editor: Barbara Tulliver
Director of Photography: Benoît Delhomme
Cast: Nigel Hawthorne, Jeremy Northam, Rebecca Pidgeon, Gemma Jones, Guy Edwards

WONDERLAND
28 September
Production Companies: Kismet Film Company, Revolution Films, PolyGram Filmed Entertainment, BBC Films
Locations/Studio: London
Exec Prod: Stewart Till, David M. Thompson
Producers: Andrew Eaton, Michele Camarda
Director: Michael Winterbottom
Screenplay: Laurence Coriat
Film Editor: Trevor Waite
Director of Photography: Sean Bobbitt
Cast: Shirley Henderson, Gina McKee, Molly Parker, Jack Shepherd, Ian Hart

The XANGO OF BAKER STREET
26 September
Production Companies: Skylight Cinema Foto Art
Locations/Studio: Porto (Portugal), Rio de Janeiro, London
Director: Miguel Faria Jr.

YOU'RE DEAD
14 July
Production Companies: Streamline Film Productions
Locations/Studio: London, Germany, MMC Studios (Cologne)
Exec Prod: Marco Weber

Producers: Marco Weber
Director: Andy Hurst
Screenplay: Andy Hurst
Film Editor: Andy Starke
Director of Photography: Wedigo von Schultzendorff
Cast: John Hurt, Claire Skinner, Rhys Ifans, Barbara Flynn, John Benfield

RELEASES

Listed here are feature-length films, both British and foreign, which had a theatrical release in the UK between January and December 1998. Entries quote the title, distributor, UK release date, certificate, country of origin, director/s, leading players, production company/ies, duration, gauge (other than 35mm), the Sight and Sound (S&S) reference. UK films or films with some UK involvement are followed by a Film Category reference. Re-releases are indicated by an asterisk and a Monthly Film Bulletin (MFB) reference. Compiled by Laura Pearson

1998 UK FILM RELEASES

UK Films (including co-productions and minority co-productions) in bold.
* Indicates re-release

The Disappearance of Finbar
Lost in Space
La Violon de Rothschild

JANUARY
2 Starship Troopers
2 The Wings of the Dove
2 Written on the Wind *
9 The End of Violence
9 The Jackal
9 Kissed
9 Picture Perfect
9 The Winter Guest
16 Boogie Nights
16 Bring Me the Head of Mavis Davis
16 Battleship Potemkin*
16 The Devil's Advocate
16 Devil's Island
16 Pretty Village Pretty Flame
23 Das Boot*
23 Breaking Up
23 Lewis & Clark & George
23 Lucie Aubrac
23 Titanic
23 Toute Vitesse
23 Up 'n' Under
23 The Winner
26 I Went Down
30 The Delta
30 Eskiya
30 In the Company of Men
30 Resurrection Man
30 Stella Does Tricks
30 Traveller

FEBRUARY
6 Clubbed to Death
6 Flubber
6 The Ice Storm
6 Ugetsu Monogatari*
6 The Woodlanders
13 The Blackout
13 Downtime
13 Fairytale A True Story
13 Good Burger
13 In & Out
13 Mortal Kombat 2 Annihilation
13 Paws
13 The Secret Agent
13 Sick The Life & Death of Bob

Flanagan Supermasochist
13 This is the Sea
20 The Boxer
20 The Butcher Boy
20 Kavkazskii Plennik
20 The Postman
20 Shin Heike Monogatari *
27 Breakdown
27 Desperate Measures
27 The Edge
27 La Maman et La Putain *
27 The Ugly

MARCH
6 Un Air de Famille
6 Bent
6 Bride of War
6 Good Will Hunting
6 Kiss the Girls
6 Middleton's Changeling
6 Mrs Dalloway
6 Retroactive
7 Frozen
13 As Good As It Gets
13 Fallen
13 Road to Nhill
13 Wag the Dog
20 Gattaca
20 The River
20 Jackie Brown
20 Love etc
20 Man in the Iron Mask
27 Anastasia
27 Best Men
27 Double Team
27 Mat i Syn
27 Twentyfourseven
27 Les Voleurs

APRIL
3 Kundun
3 La Lengua Asesina
3 Most Wanted
3 Mousehunt
3 Oscar and Lucinda
3 Out of the Past *
3 Sphere
3 Telling Lies in America
3 Ulee's Gold
10 Budbringeren
10 Different For Girls
10 The Twilight of the Ice Nymphs
17 Deconstructing Harry
17 Great Expectations
17 Gummo
17 Hard Rain
17 Like it Is
17 Midnight in the Garden of Good and Evil
24 The Big Lebowski

24 Body Count
24 Money Talks
24 The Rainmaker
24 US Marshalls
24 U Turn

MAY

1 My Son the Fanatic
1 Scream 2
1 Sliding Doors
8 Amy Foster
8 Designated Mourner
8 The Hanging Garden
8 Lolita
8 Martha – Meet Frank, Daniel and Laurence
8 Shall We Dansu?
8 Something to Believe in
8 Western
8 Wild Man Blues
15 Carne Trémula/Live Flesh/En Chair et en Os
15 Deep Impact
15 Gravesend
15 Liar
15 The Man Who Knew Too Little
15 Riget II
15 Wild Things
22 Blues Brothers 2000
22 "Chubby" Down Under and Other Sticky Regions
22 Guy
22 Mr. Magoo
22 The Real Blonde
22 Salut Cousin!
22 Star Kid
22 Der Unfisch
26 Viagen ao Principio do Mundo
29 Afterglow
29 Dark City
29 The General
29 Fists in the Pocket *
29 The James Gang
29 Once Upon a Time When We Were Colored
29 Un(c)ut
29 Washington Square
29 Wishmaster

JUNE

5 Dad Savage
5 Hurricane Street
5 Nowhere
5 Red Corner
5 The Replacement Killers
5 Ta'Ame-Gilas
5 The Wedding Singer
12 The Apostle
12 The Big Swap
12 The Girl With Brains in Her Feet
12 The Grass Harp
12 Hotel de Love
12 The Scarlet Tunic
12 Soul Food
12 Stiff Upper Lips
12 A Thousand Acres
19 City of Angels
19 Dream With the Fishes

19 The Full Monty
19 The Last Time I Committed Suicide
19 Point Blank *
19 Savior
26 Girl's Night
26 Going All the Way
26 Mimic
26 The Object of My Affection
26 Ponette
26 Palmetto
26 The War at Home

JULY

3 Grease *
3 Kurt & Courtney
3 Love and Death On Long Island
3 Six Days Seven Nights
10 Guru in Seven
10 Kiss or Kill
10 Mad City
10 Mojo
10 Sling Blade
10 Touch
17 Barnery's Great Adventure
17 Godzilla
17 Das Leben ist eine Baustelle
17 The Little Mermaid *
17 Sreda
17 Vor
24 Dance of the Wind
24 The Daytrippers
24 The Gingerbread Man
24 La Grande Illusion *
24 Hana-bi
24 The Magic Sword Quest for Camelot
24 Paulie
31 Dr. Dolittle
31 Lost in Space
31 Monk Dawson
31 Psycho *

AUGUST

7 Adventures of Robin Hood *
7 Armageddon
7 To Have and to Hold
7 Zero Effect
14 The Assignment
14 The Avengers
14 Dandy Dust
14 Eve's Bayou
14 Firelight
14 Gang Related
14 The Quiet Room
21 Le Bossu/On Guard!
21 The Day the Earth Stood Still *
21 The Life of Stuff
21 Gadjo Dilo
21 Metroland
21 The X Files
28 Basketball
28 The Horse Whisperer
28 Lock, Stock and Two Smoking Barrels
28 The Proposition
28 The Real Howard Spitz
28 Respect

28 Shigatsu Monogatari
28 The Spanish Prisoner
28 Yige Hao Ren

SEPTEMBER

4 Carícies
4 He Got Game
4 Ladoni
4 The Land Girls
4 The Last Days of Disco
4 Species II
4 Way Out West *
11 Babymother
11 Cousin Bette
11 Saving Private Ryan
11 La Vie de Jesus
18 The Doom Generation
18 Karakter
18 Kissing a Fool
18 Lethal Weapon 4
18 Love is the Devil
18 Men With Guns
18 Pépé le Moko *
25 Deep Rising
25 Secret Défense
25 There's Something About Mary
25 Thursday
25 Woo

OCTOBER

2 Buffalo '66
2 Divorcing Jack
2 Elizabeth
2 Mercury Rising
2 Moeder Dao de Schildpadgelijkende
2 Noon Va Goldoon
2 Sixth Happiness
9 Ever After
9 Marquise
9 A Soldier's Daughter Never Cries
9 Topless Women Talk About Their Lives
9 The Truman Show
16 Déjà Vu
16 Hamam
16 Kuch Kuch Hota Hai
16 Kuhle Wampe Oder Wem Gehört Die Welt?
16 Mulan
16 A Perfect Murder
16 Rien Ne Va Plus
16 Safe Men
16 La Vie Rêvée des Anges
23 Air Bud
23 The Disapperance of Finbar
23 For Richer or Poorer
23 The Governess
23 Halloween 20 Years Later
23 Small Soldiers
23 Velvet Goldmine
30 East Side Story
30 The Exorcist *
30 Funny Games
30 I Want You
30 Primary Colours
30 Razor Blade Smile
30 Still Crazy

NOVEMBER

6 Antz
6 Girls Town
6 My Name is Joe
6 The Players Club
6 Snake Eyes
10 The Nephew
13 Blade
13 Fear and Loathing in Las Vegas
13 Fire
13 Henry Fool
13 Hope Floats
13 Insomnia
13 Left Luggage
13 Al Massir
13 The Odd Couple II
13 Storefront Hitchcock
13 Das Wissen Vom Heilen
14 All the Little Animals
20 Dead Man's Curve
20 The Fountainhead *
20 Marie Baie Des Anges
20 Ronin
20 Rounders
20 Unagi
27 Lluvia en Los Zapatos
27 The Negotiator
27 Out of Sight
27 The Philadelphia Story *
27 Slums of Beverly Hills
27 T-Rex: Back to the Cretaceous
27 Victory
27 The Wisdom of Crocodiles

DECEMBER

4 Babe Pig in the City
4 Dancing at Lughnasa
4 It's a Wonderful Life *
4 On Connaît La Chanson
4 Rush Hour
4 Twilight
4 Underground
4 Year of the Horse Neil Young and
  Crazy Horse Live
11 The Boys
11 The Mask of Zorro
11 The Parent Trap
11 Playing God
11 Texas Chain Saw Massacre *
18 The Prince of Egypt
26 Enemy of the State
26 The Mighty
26 Practical Magic
26 What Dreams May Come
27 Sib

À TOUTE VITESSE/FULL SPEED

Dangerous to Know – 23 January
(not submitted) France, Dir Gaël Morel
with Élodie Bouchez, Pascal Cervo, Stéphane Rideau, Meziane Bardadi, Romain Auger, Salim Kechiouche
© **Magouric Productions/ Téléma/Rhône-Alpes Cinéma/France 2 Cinéma**
Magouric presents a Magouric Productions/Téléma/France 2 Cinéma/Rhône-Alpes Cinéma production with the participation of Cofimage 7/ Canal+/Region Rhône-Alpes/Centre National de la Cinématographie
With the support of the Fondation GAN pour le Cinéma/Procirep
85 minutes
S&S February 1998 p38

* The ADVENTURES OF ROBIN HOOD

BFI Films – 7 August
(U) USA, Dir Michael Curtiz
with Errol Flynn, Olivia de Havilland, Basil Rathbone, Claude Rains, Patric Knowles
Warner Bros.
101 minutes 45 seconds
MFB June 1938 p156

AFTERGLOW

Columbia TriStar Films (UK) – 29 May
(15) USA, Dir Alan Rudolph
with Nick Nolte, Julie Christie, Lara Flynn Boyle, Jonny Lee Miller, Jay Underwood
© **Afterglow, Inc**
Moonstone Entertainment presents a Sandcastle 5 and Elysian Dreams production
113 minutes 57 seconds
S&S June 1998 p38

AIR BUD

Warner Bros Distributors (UK) – 23 October
(U) USA/Luxembourg/Canada, Dir Charles Martin Smith
with Michael Jeter, Kevin Zegers, Wendy Makkena, Eric Christmas, Bill Cobbs
© **Buddy Films Inc.**
Walt Disney Pictures presents in association with Keystone Pictures, produced in association with CLT-UFA with the assistance of the Government of Canada – Canadian Film Production Tax Credit Program
97 minutes 48 seconds
S&S November 1998 p40

Un AIR DE FAMILLE

Metro/Tartan – 6 March
(15) France, Dir Cédric Klapisch
with Jean-Pierre Bacri, Jean-Pierre Darroussin, Catherine Frot, Agnès Jaoui, Claire Maurier
© **Téléma/Le Studio Canal+/France 2 Cinéma**
Charles Grassot presents a Téléma/Le Studio Canal+/France 2 Cinéma co-production with the participation of Canal+ /Cofimage 7
109 minutes 54 seconds (subtitles)
S&S March 1998 p36

ALL THE LITTLE ANIMALS

Entertainment Film Distribution Ltd – 14 November
(15) UK, Dir Jeremy Thomas
with John Hurt, Christian Bale, Daniel Benzali, James Faulkner, John O'Toole
© **RPC Animals Limited**
Recorded Picture Company presents in association with British Screen/J&M Entertainment/Isle of Man Film Commission/BBC Films/Entertainment Film Distributors, developed with the support of the European Script Fund and the assistance of Indigo
112 minutes 15 seconds
S&S September 1998 p36

AMISTAD

UIP – 27 February
(15) USA, Dir Steven Spielberg
with Morgan Freeman, Nigel Hawthorne, Anthony Hopkins, Djimon Hounsou, Matthew McConaughey
© **Dreamworks L.L.C.**
Dreamworks Pictures presents in association with HBO Pictures a Steven Spielberg film
154 minutes 49 seconds
S&S March 1998 p36

AMY FOSTER

Columbia TriStar – 8 May
(12) UK/USA/France, Dir Beeban Kidron with Vincent Perez, Rachel Weisz, Ian McKellen, Joss Ackland, Kathy Bates
© **Tapson Steel Films Limited**
Phoenix Pictures presents with the participation of The Greenlight Fund a Tapson Steel Films production supported by the National Lottery through the Arts Council of England in association with Canal+ Droits Audiovisuels, developed with the assistance of British Screen Finance Limited
112 minutes 54 seconds
S&S May 1998 p40
Alternative title:
SWEPT FROM THE SEA – THE STORY OF AMY FOSTER

ANASTASIA
20th Century Fox – 27 March
(U) USA, Dir Don Bluth, Gary
Goldman
with character voices by Meg Ryan,
John Cusack, Kelsey Grammer,
Christopher Lloyd, Hank Azaria
© Twentieth Century Fox Film
Corporation
Fox Family Films presents a Don
Bluth/Gary Goldman film
94 minutes 1 second
CinemaScope
S&S May 1998 p41

ANTZ
United International Pictures (UK)
Ltd – 6 November
(PG) USA, Dir Eric Darnell, Tim
Johnson
with character voices by Woody
Allen, Dan Aykroyd, Anne Bancroft,
Jane Curtin, Danny Glover
© Dream Works LLC
A Dream Works Pictures and PDI
presentation
83 minutes 7 seconds
S&S December 1998 p41

The APOSTLE
United International Pictures (UK)
Ltd – 12 June
(12) USA, Dir Robert Duvall
with Robert Duvall, Farrah Fawcett,
Todd Allen, John Beasley, June
Carter Cash
© Butchers Run Films
October Films presents a Butchers
Run production
133 minutes 33 seconds
S&S June 1998 p38

ARMAGEDDON
Buena Vista International (UK) –
7 August
(12) USA, Dir Michael Bay
with Bruce Willis, Billy Bob Thornton,
Liv Tyler, Ben Affleck, Will Patton
© Touchstone Pictures and Jerry
Bruckheimer, Inc
Touchstone Pictures presents a Jerry
Bruckheimer production in
association with Valhalla Motion
Pictures
150 minutes 20 seconds
S&S September 1998 p36

AS GOOD AS IT GETS
Columbia TriStar – 13 March
(15) USA, Dir James L. Brooks
with Jack Nicholson, Helen Hunt,
Greg Kinnear, Cuba Gooding Jr.,
Skeet Ulrich
© TriStar Pictures, Inc
TriStar Pictures presents a Gracie
Films production, a film by James
L. Brooks
138 minutes 27 seconds
S&S March 1998 p38

The ASSIGNMENT
Columbia TriStar Films (UK) –
14 August
(18) Canada/USA, Dir Christian
Duguay
with Aidan Quinn, Donald
Sutherland, Ben Kingsley, Liliana
Komorowska, Céline Bonnier
Allegro Film Productions V Inc.
Triumph Films presents an Allegro
Films production, produced with the
participation of Gouvernement du
Québec (Programme de Crédits
d'Impôt)/The Government of
Canada – Canadian Film or Video
Production Tax Credit Program/The
Movie Network/Super Écran
119 minutes 7 seconds
S&S November 1998 p40

The AVENGERS
Warner Bros Distributors (UK) –
14 August
(12) USA, Dir Jeremiah Chechik
with Ralph Fiennes, Uma Thurman,
Sean Connery, Jim Broadbent, Fiona
Shaw
© Warner Bros.
Warner Bros. presents a Jerry
Weintraub production
89 minutes 13 seconds
S&S October 1998 p38

BABE PIG IN THE CITY
United International Pictures (UK)
Ltd – 4 December
(U) USA/Australia, Dir George
Miller
with Magda Szubanski, James
Cromwell, Mickey Rooney, Mary
Stein, Paul Livingston
© Universal City Studios Inc
Universal Pictures presents a
Kennedy Miller film
95 minutes 37 seconds
S&S February 1999 p38

BABYMOTHER
Film Four Distributors Ltd -
11 September
(15) UK, Dir Julian Henriques
with Anjela Lauren Smith, Caroline
Chikezie, Jocelyn Esien, Wil
Johnson, Don Warrington
© Good Egg Productions, Inc
PolyGram Filmed Entertainment
presents in association with Lyrick
Studios
76 minutes 35 seconds
S&S September 1998 p38

BARNEY'S GREAT ADVENTURE
PolyGram Filmed Entertainment –
17 July
(U) USA, Dir Steve Gomer
with George Hearn, Shirley Douglas,
Trevor Morgan, Kyla Pratt, Diana Rice
© Good Egg Productions, Inc

PolyGram Filmed Entertainment
presents in association with Lyrick
Studios
76 minutes 35 seconds
S&S July 1998 p36

BASEKETBALL
United International Pictures (UK)
– 28 August
(15) US, Dir David Zucker with
Trey Parker, Matt Stone, Robert
Vaughn, Dian Bachar, Yasmine Bleeth
Universal Pictures
103 minutes 20 seconds
No S&S reference

BENT
Film Four Distributors – 6 March
(18) UK/USA/Japan, Dir Sean
Mathias
with Lothair Bluteau, Clive Owen,
Brian Webber, Ian McKellen, Mick
Jagger
© Channel Four Television
Corporation and Nippon Film
Development and Finance Inc
Channel Four Films presents in
association with NDF Inc/Ask
Kodansha Co Ltd and the Arts
Council of England supported by
the National Lottery through the
Arts Council of England a Bent
Production for Nippon Film
Development and Finance Inc. and
Channel 4
116 minutes 21 seconds
S&S March 1998 p39

BEST MEN
Film Four Distributors – 27 March
(15) USA/UK, Dir Tamra Davis
with Dean Cain, Andy Dick, Sean
Patrick Flanery, Mitchell Whitfield,
Luke Wilson
© Orion Pictures Corporation
Orion Pictures presents in
association with Rank Film
Distributors a Brad Krevoy/
Steve Stabler production
89 minutes 27 seconds
S&S April 1998 p36

The BIG LEBOWSKI
PolyGram Distribution – 24 April
(18) USA/UK, Dir Joel Coen
with Jeff Bridges, John Goodman,
Julianne Moore, Steve Buscemi,
David Huddleston
© PolyGram Filmed
Entertainment Inc
PolyGram Filmed Entertainment
presents a Working Title
production
116 minutes 53 seconds
S&S May 1998 p42

The BIG SWAP
Film Four Distributors Ltd –
12 June

(18) UK, Dir Niall Johnson
with Antony Edridge, Sorcha Brooks,
Richard Cherry, Julie-Ann Gillitt,
Kevin Howarth
© **Moonlit Pictures Limited**
Film Four Distributors presents a
Mayfair Entertainment
International presentation of a
Moonlit Pictures/Magic Box
production
121 minutes 31 seconds
S&S June 1998 p39

The BLACKOUT
Feature Film Company – 13
February
(18) USA/France, Dir Abel Ferrara
with Matthew Modine, Claudia
Schiffer, Béatrice Dalle, Sarah
Lassez, Dennis Hopper
© **Backlash Films, Inc**
Les Films Number One and CIPA
present in association with MDP
Worldwide an Edward R.
Pressman production
98 minutes 26 seconds
S&S March 1998 p40

BLADE
Entertainment Film Distributors
Ltd – 13 November
(18) USA, Dir Stephen Norrington
with Wesley Snipes, Stephen Dorff,
Kris Kristofferson, N'Bushe Wright,
Donal Logue
© **New Line Productions, Inc**
New Line Cinema presents an
Amen Ra Films production in
association with Imaginary Forces
120 minutes 9 seconds
S&S November 1998 p42

BLUES BROTHERS 2000
United International Pictures (UK)
Ltd – 22 May
(PG) USA, Dir John Landis
with Dan Aykroyd, John Goodman,
Joe Morton, J. Evan Bonifant, Aretha
Franklin
© **Universal City Studios, Inc**
Universal Pictures presents a
Landis/Belzberg production
123 minutes 28 seconds
S&S July 1998 p36

BODY COUNT
PolyGram Filmed Entertainment –
24 April
(18) USA/UK, Dir Robert Patton-
Spruill
with David Caruso, Linda Fiorentino,
John Leguizamo, Ving Rhames,
Donnie Wahlberg
© **Island Pictures Corp**
PolyGram Filmed Entertainment
presents an Island Pictures
production in association with
Jackson/McHenry Films and Main
Line Pictures

84 minutes 6 seconds
S&S June 1998 p40

BOOGIE NIGHTS
Entertainment – 16 January
(18) USA, Dir Paul Thomas Anderson
with Don Cheadle, Heather Graham,
Luis Guzman, Philip Baker Hall,
Philip Seymour Hoffman, Thomas
Jane
© **New Line Productions, Inc**
A New Line Cinema presentation
in association with Ghoulardi Film
Company
155 minutes 34 seconds
S&S January 1998 p36

* Das BOOT
Feature Film Company –
23 January
(15) Germany, Dir Wolfgang Petersen
with Jurgen Prochnow, Herbert
Gronemeyer, Klaus Wennemann,
Hubertus Bengsch, Martin
Semmelrogge
Bavaria Atelier GmbH/Radiant Film
207 minutes 53 seconds
No S&S reference
Expanded director's cut

Le BOSSU/ON GUARD!
Pathé Distribution Ltd – 21 August
(15) France/Italy/Germany, Dir
Philippe de Broca
with Daniel Auteuil, Fabrice Luchini,
Vincent Perez, Marie Gillain, Yann
Collette
© **Alicéleo/TFI Films**
Production/DA Films/Prima/Cecchi
Gori Group Tiger Cin.ca/Gemini
Film.
Patrick Godeau presents an
Alicéleo/TFI Films Production/D.A.
Films/Prima/Gemini
Filmproduktion/Cecchi Gori
Group Tiger Cinematografica co-
production, funded by
Eurimages, La Procirep and The
European Script Fund in
association with Cofimage 8 & 9,
with the participation of The
Centre National de la
Cinématographie and of Canal+
128 minutes 31 seconds (subtitles)
S&S September 1998 p39

The BOXER
UIP – 20 February
(15) Ireland/UK/USA, Dir Jim Sheridan
with Daniel Day-Lewis, Emily
Watson, Brian Cox, Ken Stott,
Gerard McSorley
© **Universal City Studios, Inc**
Universal Pictures presents a Hell's
Kitchen production, produced with
the support of investment
incentives for the Irish film
industry, produced with the
assistance of Bord Scannán na

hÉireann
113 minutes 32 seconds
S&S March 1998 p41

The BOYS
Film Four Distributors Ltd –
11 December
(18) Australia/UK, Dir Rowan Woods
with David Wenham, Toni Collette,
Lynette Curran, John Polson, Jeanette
Cronin
© **Arenafilm Pty Ltd/Australian**
Film Commission/Premium Movie
Partnership/SBS
Independent
An Arenafilm production in
Association with Axiom Films/The
Australian Film Commission/SBS
Independent/Premium Movie
Partnership, produced and
developed with the assistance of
Standard Asset Management
(Brian Price)
85 minutes 12 seconds
S&S November 1998 p43

BREAKDOWN
20th Century Fox – 27 February
(15) USA, Dir Jonathan Mostow
with Kurt Russell, J. T. Walsh,
Kathleen Quinlan, M. C. Gainey,
Jack Noseworthy
© **US/Canada: Paramount Pictures**
Corporation, all other territories:
Spelling Films Inc
Paramount Pictures presents in
association with Dino De
Laurentiis and Spelling Films
93 minutes 16 seconds
Super 35
S&S March 1998 p42

BREAKING UP
Warner Bros – 23 January
(15) USA, Dir Robert Greenwald
with Russell Crowe, Salma Hayek,
Abraham Alvarez
© **Monarchy Enterprises B.V. and**
Regency Entertainment (USA) Inc
Regency Enterprises presents a
Robert Greenwald film
89 minutes 8 seconds
S&S March 1998 p43

BRIDE OF WAR
Sgrin – Media Agency for Wales –
6 March
(12) UK/Poland, Dir Peter Edwards
with Huw Garmon, Anna Wojciewicz
Lluniau Lliw Cyf/Sianel Pedwar
Cymru/Telewizja Polska
115 minutes 36 seconds
No S&S reference

BRING ME THE HEAD OF MAVIS DAVIS
Feature Film Company –
16 January
(15) UK, Dir John Henderson

with Rik Mayall, Jane Horrocks,
Danny Aiello, Ronald Pickup,
Philip Martin-Brown, Ross Boatman
© **Goldcrest Films International**
BBC Films and Goldcrest Films
International present
a Mission film
99 minutes 23 seconds
S&S February 1998 p38

* BRONENOSETS POTEMKIN/BATTLESHIP POTEMKIN

Contemporary – 16 January
(PG) USSR, Dir Sergei M. Eisenstein
with Aleksandr Antonov, Vladimir
Barksy, Grigori V. Aleksandrov,
Mikhail S. Gomorov, Aleksandr I.
Levchin
First Studio Goskino
73 minutes 56 seconds
MFB March 1954 p35

BUDBRINGEREN/JUNK MAIL/POSTBUDET DER VIDSTE FOR MEGET

Metro/Tartan – 10 April
(15) Norway/Denmark, Dir Pål
Sletaune
with Robert Skjærstad, Andrine
Sæther, Per Egil Aske, Eli Anne
Linnestad, Trond Høvik
© **MovieMakers**
Moviemakers AS presents in
collaboration with Filmselskabet
Atlas A/S and Norsk Film A/S
supported by Norsk Filminstitutt
(Gunnar Svensrud)/Nordisk Film
& TV Fond/Norsk Film AS/
Atlas Film, Movieinvest/Det
Danske Filminstitutt/TV2
80 minutes 57 seconds (subtitles)
S&S April 1998 p40

BUFFALO '66

Metrodome Distribution Ltd –
2 October
(15) Canada/USA, Dir Vincent Gallo
with Vincent Gallo, Christina Ricci,
Ben Gazzara, Mickey Rourke,
Rosanna Arquette
© **Cinepix Film Properties, Inc**
Cinepix Film Properties presents a
Muse production
109 minutes 56 seconds
S&S October 1998 p39

The BUTCHER BOY

Warner Bros – 20 February
(15) USA, Dir Neil Jordan
with Stephen Rea, Fiona Shaw,
Eamonn Owens, Alan Boyle, Niall
Buggy
© **Geffen Pictures**
Geffen Pictures presents a Neil
Jordan film produced with the
support and investment incentives
for the Irish film industry

110 minutes 4 seconds
S&S March 1998 p44

CARÍCIES/CARESSES

Dangerous to Know – 4 September
(not submitted) Spain, Dir Ventura
Pons
with David Selvas, Laura Conejero,
Julieta Serrano, Montserrat Salvador,
Agustin González
© **Els Films de la Rambla, S.A.**
Barcelona
An Els Film de la Rambla, S.A.
production with the participation
of TVE – Televisió Espanyola, S.A./
TV3 – Televisió de Catalunyá, S.A.,
with the collaboration of
Departament de Cultura
Generalitat de Catalunyá
94 minutes 14 seconds (subtitles)
S&S October 1998 p40

CARNE TRÉMULA/LIVE FLESH/EN CHAIR ET EN OS

Pathé Distribution Ltd – 15 May
(18) Spain/France, Dir Pedro
Almodóvar
with Francesca Neri, Javier Bardem,
José Sancho, Angela Molina, Liberto
Rabal
© **El Deseo, S.A./CiBy 2000/**
France 3
El Deseo, S.A. presents an El
Deseo, S.A./CiBy 2000/France 3
co-production
developed with the support of the
European Script Fund
100 minutes 44 seconds
S&S May 1998 p50-51

The CASTLE

United International Pictures
(UK) Ltd
(15) Australia, Dir Bob Stich
with Michael Caton, Anne Tenney,
Stephen Curry, Anthony Simcoe,
Sophie Lee
© **Frontline Television Productions**
Pty Ltd/Village Roadshow Pictures
Pty Ltd
A Village Roadshow
Pictures/Working Dog presentation
85 minutes 31 seconds
S&S August 1998 p34

"CHUBBY" DOWN UNDER AND OTHER STICKY REGIONS

PolyGram Filmed Entertainment –
22 May
(18) UK, Dir Tom Poole
with Roy "Chubby" Brown
© **PolyGram Filmed**
Entertainment (UK) Ltd
A George Forster presentation
85 minutes 48 seconds
S&S August 1998 p35

CHUNGUANG ZHAXIE/HAPPY TOGETHER

Artificial Eye -24 April
(15) Hong Kong, Dir Wong Kar-Wai
with Leslie Cheung Kwok-Wing,
Tony Leung Chiu-Wai, Chang Chen
Block 2 Pictures Inc in association
with Prenom H Co. Ltd/Seawoo
Film Co. Ltd.
presents a Jet Tone Production
97 minutes 3 seconds (subtitles)
S&S May 1998 p49

CITY OF ANGELS

Warner Bros Distributors (UK) –
19 June
(12) USA/Germany, Dir Brad Silberling
with Nicolas Cage, Meg Ryan,
Dennis Franz, André Braugher, Colm
Feore
© **Warner Bros. Productions**
Limited/Monarchy Enterprises
B.V./Regency
Entertainment (USA), Inc
Warner Bros presents in
association with Regency Pictures
an Atlas Entertainment production
in association with Taurus Films
114 minutes 3 seconds
S&S July 1998 p37

CLUBBED TO DEATH

Artificial Eye – 6 February
(18) France/Portugal/Netherlands,
Dir Yolande Zauberman
with Élodie Bouchez, Roschdy Zem,
Béatrice Dalle, Richard Courcet,
Alex Descas, Gérald Thomassin
© **Madar/La Sept Cinéma/Grupo**
de Estudos e Realizacoes/
Meteor Film Productions
Madar presents a Franco Lusitano
Neerlandaise co-production
Produced by Madar/La Sept
Cinéma/Grupo de Estudos e
Realizacoe/Meteor Film
Productions with the participation
of Canal+
Supported by Eurimages with the
participation of Centre National
de la Cinématographie
88 minutes 12 seconds
S&S February 1998 p39

COUSIN BETTE

20th Century Fox (UK) –
11 September
(15) USA/UK, Dir Des McAnuff
with Geraldine Chaplin, John
Benfield, Hugh Laurie, Jessica
Lange, Paul Bandey
© **Twentieth Century Fox Film**
Corporation
Twentieth Century Fox presents a
Sarah Radclyffe production
108 minutes 27 seconds
S&S September 1998 p41

CUBE

First Independent Films Ltd –
25 September
(15) Canada, Dir Vincenzo Natali
with Nicole deBoer, Nicky Guadagni,
David Hewlett, Andrew Miller, Julian
Richings
© The Feature Film Project
The Feature Film Project presents
a Cube Libre production, produced
with the participation of Telefilm
Canada, Ontario Film
Development Corporation/The
Harold Greenberg Fund/Viacom
Canada
90 minutes 18 seconds
S&S November 1998 p44

DAD SAVAGE

PolyGram Filmed Entertainment –
5 June
(18) UK, Dir Betsan Morris Evans
with Patrick Stewart, Kevin McKidd,
Helen McCrory, Joe McFadden,
Marc Warren, Jake Wood
© PolyGram Films (UK) Ltd
PolyGram Filmed Entertainment
presents a Sweet Child film, Dad
Savage Ltd
104 minutes 16 seconds
S&S July 1998 p38

DANCE OF THE WIND/WARA MANDEL

Artificial Eye Film Company Ltd –
24 July
(U) Germany/UK/France/
Netherlands/India/Switzerland, Dir
Rajan Khosa
with Kitu Gidwani, Bhaveen
Gossain, B. C. Sanyal, Roshan Bano,
Kapila Vatsyayan
© Pandora Film Frankfurt and
Illumination Films London
Pandora Film and Elephant Eye
present in co-production with
Illuminations Films
(UK)/BA Production (France)/The
Filmcompany Amsterdam
(Netherlands)/NFDC
(India), produced with the
participation of The European Co-
production Fund (UK)/
Filmstiftung NRW/Hessischer
Rundfunk Filmförderung and in
association with ARTE
and WDR (Germany)/National
Film Development Corporation
(India)/The French Ministry
of Culture/The French Ministry of
Foreign Affairs
(France)/Fondazione
Montecinemaveritá
(Switzerland)/National Committee
for International Co-operation and
Sustainable Development/
Hubert Bals Fund/The
International Festival Rotterdam

(The Netherlands)
85 minutes 41 seconds (subtitles)
S&S August 1998 p36

DANCING AT LUGHNASA

Film Four Distributors Ltd –
4 December
(PG) Ireland/UK/USA, Dir Pat
O'Connor
with Meryl Streep, Michael Gambon,
Catherine McCormack, Kathy Burke,
Brid Brennan
© Ferndale Films Ltd
Ferndale Films/Capitol Films/Sony
Pictures Classics/Channel Four
Films in association with
Bord Scannán na hÉireann/The
Irish Film Board/Radio Telefís
Éireann presents
a Noel Pearson production
produced by Lenrey Ltd and
Ferndale Films Ltd
Produced with the support of
investment incentives for the Irish
Film Industry
Originally developed by Ferndale
Films for the screen in conjunction
with Radio Telefís Éireann
94 minutes 42 seconds
S&S December 1998 p42

DANDY DUST

Millivres Multimedia – 14 August
(18) UK/Austria, Dir Hans Scheirl
with Suzie Krueger, Leonora Rogers-
Wright, Tre Temperilli, Hans Scheirl,
Svar Simpson
Hans Scheirl/New Boys
Productions/DV8-Film,
Vienna/Hackneyed Productions
97 minutes
No S&S reference

DARK CITY

PolyGram Filmed Entertainment –
29 May
(15) USA/Australia, Dir Alex Proyas
with Rufus Sewell, Kiefer
Sutherland, Jennifer Connelly,
Richard O'Brien, Ian Richardson
© New Line Productions, Inc
New Line presents a Mystery
Clock production
100 minutes 19 seconds
S&S June 1998 p43

*The DAY THE EARTH STOOD STILL

[screened for 2 weeks at the
Barbican cinema] – 21 August
(not submitted) US, Dir Robert Wise
with Michael Rennie, Patricia Neal,
Hugh Marlowe, Sam Jaffe, Billy
Gray
Twentieth Century-Fox Film
Corporation
91 minutes 30 seconds
MFB November 1951 p355

The DAYTRIPPERS

Metrodome Distribution Ltd –
24 July
(15) USA, Dir Greg Mottola
with Hope Davis, Pat McNamara,
Anne Meara, Parker Posey, Liev
Schreiber
© Fiasco Photoplays & Trick
Films, Inc
86 minutes 56 seconds
S&S August 1998 p36

DEAD MAN'S CURVE

Metro Tartan Distributors –
20 November
(15) USA, Dir Dan Rosen
with Matthew Lillard, Michael
Vartan, Randall Batinkoff, Keri
Russell, Tamara Craig Thomas
© Mount Royal Entertainment
Alain Siritzky and Hope Street
Entertainment present in
association with Pierre
Kalfon/Michel Chambat/Ian Jessel
a Mount Royal Entertainment
production
90 minutes 33 seconds
S&S December 1998 p43

DECONSTRUCTING HARRY

Buena Vista International –
17 April
(18) USA, Dir Woody Allen
with Caroline Aaron, Woody Allen,
Kirstie Alley, Bob Balaban, Richard
Benjamin
© Magnolia Productions Inc and
Sweetland Films BV
A Jean Doumanian production
95 minutes 41 seconds
S&S May 1998 p42

DEEP IMPACT

United International Pictures (UK)
Ltd – 15 May
(12) USA, Dir Mimi Leder
with Robert Duvall, Téa Leoni,
Elijah Wood, Vanessa Redgrave,
Maximilian Schell
© Dream Works L.L.C./Paramount
Pictures/Amblin Entertainment
Dream Works Pictures and
Paramount Pictures present a
Zanuck/Brown production
120 minutes 45 seconds
S&S July 1998 p39

DEEP RISING

Entertainment Film Distributors
Ltd – 25 September
(15) USA, Dir Stephen Sommers
with Treat Williams, Famke Janssen,
Anthony Heald, Kevin J. O'Connor,
Wes Studi
© Hollywood Pictures Company
Hollywood Pictures presents a
Laurence Mark production

106 minutes 8 seconds
S&S November 1998 p45

DÉJÀ VU
United International Pictures (UK)
Ltd – 16 October
(15) USA/UK, Dir Henry Jaglom
with Stephen Dillane, Victoria Foyt,
Vanessa Redgrave, Glynis Barber,
Michael Brandon
© Jagtoria Film Company, Inc.
A Jagtoria film from Revere
Entertainment and The Rainbow
Film Company
117 minutes
S&S October 1998 p41

The DELTA
ICA – 30 January
(not submitted) US, Dir Ira Sachs
with Shayne Gray, Thang Chan,
Rachel Zan Huss, Colonius Davis
Charlie Guidance Productions
85 minutes
No S&S reference

The DESIGNATED MOURNER
[Short season at the NFT courtesy
of The Sales Co./BBC] – 8 May
(not submitted) UK, Dir David Hare
with Mike Nichols, Miranda
Richardson, David De Keyser
Presented by BBC Films/
Greenpoint Films
94 minutes
No S&S reference

DESPERATE MEASURES
Entertainment – 27 February
(15) USA, Dir Barbet Schroeder
with Michael Keaton, Andy Garcia,
Brian Cox, Marcia Gay Harden, Erik
King
© Mandalay Entertainment
Mandalay Entertainment presents
an Eaglepoint/Schroeder/Hoffman
production
100 minutes 24 seconds
S&S April 1998 p36

The DEVIL'S ADVOCATE
Warner Bros – 16 January
(18) USA, Dir Taylor Hackford
with Keanu Reeves, Al Pacino,
Charlize Theron, Jeffrey Jones,
Judith Ivey, Craig T. Nelson
© Warner Bros. Productions
Limited/Monarchy Enterprises B.V.
Warner Bros. presents in
association with
Regency Enterprises a Kopelson
Entertainment production
143 minutes 44 seconds
S&S January 1998 p38

DIFFERENT FOR GIRLS
Blue Dolphin – 10 April
(15) UK, Dir Richard Spence

with Steven MacKintosh, Rupert
Graves, Miriam Margolyes, Saskia
Reeves, Charlotte Coleman, Neil
Dudgeon
©1996. NFTC
BBC Films in association with
Maurice Marciano/Great Guns
present an X Pictures film

The DISAPPEARANCE OF FINBAR
Ian Rattray – 23 October
(15) Ireland/Sweden/France/UK Dir
Sue Clayton
with Luke Griffin, Jonathan Rhys
Myers (ie Meyers), Sean Lawlor
© 1996. First City Features
Ltd./Samson Films Ltd./Victoria
Film AB
a Film Four International
presentation
Channel Four Films and Pandora
Cinema present
a First City Features/Samson
Films/Victoria Film production,
produced with the
assistance of Bord Scannán na
hÉireann-The Irish Film
Board/Svenska Filminstitutet/
The Swedish Film Institute,
produced in association with
Midnight Sun Film & Cultural
Productions AB, this film was
supported by Eurimages Fund of
the Council of Europe, developed
with the European Script Fund
104 minutes 40 seconds
S&S November 1998 p46

DIVORCING JACK
Mosaic Movies – 2 October
(15) UK/France, Dir David Caffrey
with David Thewlis, Rachel Griffiths,
Jason Isaacs, Laura Fraser, Richard
Gant
© Scala (Divorcing Jack)
Limited/IMA Films/Le Studio
Canal+
BBC Films/Winchester Films/Scala
present in association with the Arts
Council of England and the Arts
Council of Northern Ireland a
Scala production in association
with IMA Films/Le Studio Canal+,
project developed and supported
by BBC Northern
Ireland, production partly funded
by Foundry Film Partners,
produced with the
assistance of The Northern Ireland
Film Commission with the
participation of Canal+
109 minutes 55 seconds
S&S October 1998 p41

DJÖFLAEYJAN/DEVIL'S ISLAND
Theatrical Experience – 16 January

(15) Iceland/Norway/Germany/
Denmark, Dir Fridrik Thor
Fridriksson
with Baltasar Kormákur, Gísli
Halldórsson, Sigurveig Jónsdóttir,
Halldóra Geirhardsdóttir, Sveinn
Geirsson, Gudmundur ólafsson
© íslenska
Kvikmyndasamsteypan/Filmhuset/
Peter Rommel Filmproduction
Icelandic Film Corporation
Production in association with
Zentropa Entertainments and in
co-production with
Peter Rommel Filmproduction
(Berlin)/Filmhuset (Oslo)
Supported by Eurimages, Film
Fund Baden-Wurttemberg,
Icelandic Film Fund/Nordic Film
& TV-Fund, ZDF-Arte
Developed with support of
European Script Fund
103 minutes 1 second
S&S January 1998 p39

The DOOM GENERATION
Metro Tartan Pictures –
18 September
(18) USA/France, Dir Gregg Araki
with James Duval, Rose McGowan,
Johnathon Schaech, Cress Williams,
Dustin Nguyen
Teen Angst Movie Company/Union
Générale
Cinématographique/Desperate
Pictures/Blurco/
Why Not Productions (France)
83 minutes 20 seconds
S&S June 1996 p37

DOUBLE TEAM
Columbia TriStar – 27 March
(18) USA, Dir Tsui Hark
with Jean-Claude Van Damme,
Dennis Rodman, Paul Freeman,
Mickey Rourke, Natacha Lindinger
© Mandalay Entertainment
Columbia Pictures and Mandalay
Entertainment present a Moshe
Diamant/One
Story Pictures production
93 minutes
S&S May 1998 p44

DOWNTIME
Film Four Distributors –
13 February
(15) UK/France, Dir Bharat Nalluri
with Paul McGann, Susan Lynch,
Tom Georgeson, David Roper,
Denise Bryson, Adam Johnston
© [UK]Channel Four Television
Corporation
[rest of world]Scala (Downtime)
Ltd/Ima Films SA
A Scala presentation in association
with Channel Four Films/
Arts Council of England/Moving

Image Development Agency and
Pandora Cinema A Scala/Pilgrim
production in association with IMA
Films with the participation of
Canal+ Produced in association with
Merseyside Film
Production Fund/sofica Sofinergie 4
Supported by the National Lottery
through the Arts Council of England
Developed with the support of the
European Script Fund
90 minutes 38 seconds
S&S February p40

DR. DOLITTLE
20th Century Fox (UK) – 31 July
(PG) USA, Dir Betty Thomas
with Eddie Murphy, Ossie Davis,
Oliver Platt, Peter Boyle, Richard
Schiff
© Twentieth Century Fox Film
Corporation
Twentieth Century Fox presents a
Davis Entertainment
Company/Joseph M. Singer
Entertainment production
85 minutes 18 seconds
S&S August 1998 p37

DREAM WITH THE FISHES
Columbia TriStar Films (UK) –
19 June
(18) USA, Dir Finn Taylor
with David Arquette, Brad Hunt,
Kathryn Erbe, Cathy Moriarty, J. E.
Freeman
© Dream With The Fishes
Productions, L.L.C.
3 Ring Circus Films presentation
96 minutes 52 seconds
S&S July 1998 p40

EAST SIDE STORY
Downtown Pictures – 30 October
(U) Germany/USA/France, Dir Dana
Ranga
with Erich Gusko, Karin Schröder,
Brigitte Ulbrich, Helmut Hanke,
Hans-Joachim Wallstein
© ANDA Films
An Anda Films presentation
produced in association with WDR,
with the participation of
DocStar/Canal+, produced with the
financial assistance of Filmstiftung
Nordrhein-Westfalen/
Kuratorium junger deutscher Film
Research funded by MAP-TV,
Filmboard Berlin-Brandenburg
80 minutes 11 seconds (subtitles,
English narration)
S&S October 1998 p42

The EDGE
20th Century Fox – 27 February
(15) USA, Dir Lee Tamahori
with Anthony Hopkins, Alec
Baldwin, Elle Macpherson, Harold
Perrineau,

L.Q.Jones, Kathleen Wilhoite
© Twentieth Century Fox Film
Corporation
Twentieth Century Fox presents an
Art Linson production
117 minutes 27 seconds
S&S February 1998 p41

ELIZABETH
PolyGram Filmed Entertainment –
2 October
(15) UK, Dir Shekhar Kapur
with Cate Blanchett, Geoffrey Rush,
Christopher Eccleston, Joseph
Fiennes, Richard Attenborough
© PolyGram Filmed
Entertainment, Inc
PolyGram Filmed Entertainment
presents in association with
Channel Four Films a
Working Title production
developed with the support of the
Media Programme of
the European Union
123 minutes 7 seconds
S&S November 1998 p47

The END OF VIOLENCE
Artificial Eye – 9 January
(15) USA/Germany/France, Dir Wim
Wenders
with Bill Pullman, Andie
MacDowell, Gabriel Byrne, Loren
Dean,
Traci Lind, Daniel Benzali
© CiBy Pictures, Inc. & Road
Movies Filmproduktion GmbH
CiBy 2000 presents a CiBy
Pictures/Road Movies/Kintop
Pictures
co-production
122 minutes 1 second
S&S January 1998 p40

ENEMY OF THE STATE
Buena Vista International (UK) –
26 December
(15) USA, Dir Tony Scott
with Will Smith, Gene Hackman, Jon
Voight, Regina King, Loren Dean
© Touchstone Pictures and Jerry
Bruckheimer, Inc
Touchstone Pictures presents a Don
Simpson/Jerry Bruckheimer
production in
association with Scott Free Productions
132 minutes
S&S January 1999 p45

ESKIYA
Rio Cinema – 30 January
(15) Turkey/France/Bulgaria, Dir
Yavuz Turgul with
Sener Sen, Ugur Yucel, Sermin Sen,
Yesim Salkim, Kamuran Usluer
Filma-Cass/ArtCam
International/Geopoly
127 minutes 36 seconds
No S&S reference

EVER AFTER
20th Century Fox – 9 October
(PG) USA, Dir Andy Tennant
with Drew Barrymore, Anjelica
Huston, Dougray Scott, Patrick
Godfrey, Megan Dodds
© Twentieth Century Fox Film
Corporation
Twentieth Century Fox presents a
Mireille Soria production
120 minutes 56 seconds
S&S October 1998 p43

EVE'S BAYOU
Alliance Releasing (UK) –
14 August
(15) USA, Dir Kasi Lemmons
with Samuel L. Jackson, Lynn
Whitfield, Debbi Morgan, Vondie
Curtis Hall, Branford Marsalis
© Trimark Pictures, Inc
Trimark Pictures presents a
Chubbco/Addis-Wechsler
production
108 minutes 18 seconds
S&S August 1998 p38

*The EXORCIST
Warner Bros Distributors (UK) –
30 October
(18) USA, Dir William Friedkin
with Ellen Burstyn, Max von Sydow,
Lee J. Cobb, Kitty Winn, Jack
MacGowran
Warner Bros/Hoya Productions
121 minutes 39 seconds
MFB April 1974 p71

FAIRYTALE A TRUE STORY
Warner Bros – 13 February
(U) USA, Dir Charles Sturridge
with Florence Hoath, Elizabeth Earl,
Paul McGann, Phoebe Nicholls, Bill
Nighy
© Anna K. Production C.V.
An Icon Entertainment
International presentation, an Icon
Productions/Wendy
Finerman production, production
financing provided by Newmarket
Capital Group, L.P.
97 minutes 47 seconds
S&S March 1998 p45

FALLEN
Warner Bros – 13 March
(15) USA, Dir Gregory Hoblit
with Denzel Washington, John
Goodman, Donald Sutherland,
Embeth Davidtz,
James Gandolfini
© Turner Pictures Worldwide, Inc
Turner Pictures presents an Atlas
Entertainment production
126 minutes 45 seconds
S&S March 1998 p46

FEAR AND LOATHING IN LAS VEGAS
United International Pictures (UK) Ltd – 13 November
(18) USA, Dir Terry Gilliam
with Johnny Depp, Benicio Del Toro, Tobey Maguire, Michael Lee Gogin, Larry Cedar
© Universal City Studios Productions Inc
Summit Entertainment and Universal Pictures present a Rhino Films/Laila Nabulsi production
118 minutes 8 seconds
Super 35
S&S November 1998 p48

FIRE
Guild Film Distribution – 13 November
(15) Canada, Dir Deepa Mehta
with Shabana Azmi, Nandita Das, Kulbushan Kharbanda, Jaaved Jaaferi, Ranjit Chowdhry
© Trial by Fire Films Inc
A Trial by Fire Films presentation
107 minutes 58 seconds
S&S January 1999 p46

FIRELIGHT
Buena Vista International (UK) – 14 August
(15) USA/UK, Dir William Nicholson
with Sophie Marceau, Stephen Dillane, Kevin Anderson, Lia Williams, Dominique Belcourt
©Hollywood Pictures
Hollywood Pictures presents a Wind Dancer/Carnival Films production
103 minutes 30 seconds
S&S August 1998 p39

FLUBBER
Buena Vista – 6 February
(U) US, Dir Les Mayfield
with Robin Williams, Marcia Gay Harden, Christopher McDonald, Raymond J. Barry, Clancy Brown
© Disney Enterprises, Inc
Walt Disney Pictures presents a Great Oaks production
93 minutes 49 seconds
S&S March 1998 p47-48

FOR RICHER OR POORER
United International Pictures (UK) Ltd – 23 October
(12) USA, Dir Bryan Spicer
with Tim Allen, Kirstie Alley, Jay O. Sanders, Michael Lerner, Wayne Knight
© Universal City Studios Inc. and The Bubble Factory LLC
A Universal Pictures release of a Universal/Bubble Factory presentation in association

with Yorktown Productions of a Sheinberg production
115 minutes 40 seconds
S&S November 1998 p49

* The FOUNTAINHEAD
BFI Films – 20 November
(PG) USA, Dir King Vidor
with Gary Cooper, Raymond Massey, Patricia Neal, Kent Smith, Robert Douglas
Warner Bros.
112 minutes 48 seconds
MFB September 1949 p.156

The FULL MONTY
20th Century Fox Film Co. – 19 June
(15) US/UK, Dir Peter Cattaneo
with Robert Carlyle, Tom Wilkinson, Mark Addy, Lesley Sharp, Emily Woof
Twentieth Century Fox Film Corporation/Redwave Films/Bodger Films
91 minutes
S&S September 1997 p43

FUNNY GAMES
Metro Tartan Distributors – 30 October
(18) Austria, Dir Michael Haneke
with Susanne Lothar, Ulrich M̯he, Arno Frisch, Frank Giering, Stefan Clapczynski
© Wega-Film, Wien
Supported by österreichisches Filminstitut/ORF/Wiener Filmfinanzierungsfond/Land österreich/
the 16:9 action plan of the European Union
108 minutes 59 seconds (subtitles)
S&S December 1998 p44

GADJO DILO
Alliance Releasing (UK) – 21 August
(15) France, Dir Tony Gatlif
with Romain Duris, Rona Hartner, Izidor Serban, Ovidiu Balan, Angela Serban
© Princes Films
Princes Films presents with the participation of Canal+/Centre National de la Cinématographie/Ministère de la Culture/SACEM
101 minutes 17 seconds (subtitles)
S&S August 1998 p40

GANG RELATED
The Feature Film Company – 14 August
(15) USA, Dir Jim Kouf
with James Belushi, Tupac Shakur, Lela Rochon, Dennis Quaid, James Earl Jones
© Orion Pictures Corporation
Orion Pictures presents a Brad

Krevoy/Steve Stabler production
111 minutes 10 seconds
S&S August 1998 p41

GATTACA
Columbia TriStar – 20 March
(15) USA, Dir Andrew Niccol
with Ethan Hawke, Uma Thurman, Alan Arkin, Jude Law, Loren Dean
© Columbia Pictures Industries, Inc
Columbia Pictures presents a Jersey Films production
106 minutes 18 seconds
Super 35
S&S March 1998 p48

The GENERAL
Warner Bros Distributors – 29 May
(15) Ireland/United Kingdom, Dir John Boorman
with Brendan Gleeson, Adrian Dunbar, Sean McGinley, Maria Doyle Kennedy, Angeline Ball
© Nattore Limited
A Merlin Films in association with J&M Entertainment production
123 minutes 51 seconds
S&S June 1998 p44

The GINGERBREAD MAN
PolyGram Filmed Entertainment – 24 July
(15) USA, Dir Robert Altman
with Kenneth Branagh, Embeth Davidtz, Robert Downey Jr., Daryl Hannah, Robert Duvall
© Island Pictures Corp.
PolyGram Filmed Entertainment presents an Island Pictures/Enchanter Entertainment production
113 minutes 59 seconds
S&S August 1998 p41

GIRLS' NIGHT
Granada Film – 26 June
(15) UK/USA, Dir Nick Hurran
with Brenda Blethyn, Julie Walters, Kris Kristofferson, George Costigan, James Gaddas
© Granada Film
Granada Film in association with Showtime Networks, Inc. presents a Granada Film production
102 minutes 24 seconds
S&S July 1998 p41

GIRLS TOWN
Metrodome Distribution Ltd – 6 November
(15) USA, Dir Jim McKay
with Lili Taylor, Bruklin Harris, Anna Grace, Aunjanue Ellis, Ramya Pratt
© Dolly Bell Pictures Inc
A C-Hundred Film Corp/Boomer Pictures film
88 minutes 56 seconds
S&S November 1998 p50

The GIRL WITH BRAINS IN HER FEET
Alliance Releasing – 12 June
(15) UK, Dir Roberto Bangura
with Amanda Mealing, Joanna Ward,
Jamie McIntosh, Jodie Smith,
Richard Claxton
© Lexington Films Limited
LFL – a Lexington Films
production
98 minutes 3 seconds
S&S June 1998 p45

GODZILLA
Columbia Tristar Films (UK) –
17 July
(PG) USA, Dir Roland Emmerich
with Matthew Broderick, Jean Réno,
Maria Pitillo, Hank Azaria, Kevin
Dunn
© TriStar Pictures, Inc
TriStar Pictures presents a
Centropolis Entertainment
production, a Fried Films and
Independent Pictures production
138 minutes 36 seconds
S&S August 1998 p42

GOING ALL THE WAY
PolyGram Filmed Entertainment –
26 June
(15) USA, Dir Mark Pellington
with Jeremy Davies, Ben Affleck,
Amy Locane, Rose McGowan,
Rachel Weisz
© Lakeshore Entertainment Corp
Lakeshore Entertainment presents
a Tom Gorai production, a
Gramercy Pictures release
103 minutes 2 seconds
S&S August 1998 p44

GOOD BURGER
UIP – 13 February
(PG) USA, Dir Brian Robbins
with Kenan Thompson, Kel Mitchell,
Abe Vigoda, Sinbad, Shar Jackson
© Paramount Pictures
Paramount Pictures present in
association with Nickelodeon
Movies a Tollin/ Robbins
production
95 minutes 9 seconds
S&S March 1998 p49

GOOD WILL HUNTING
Buena Vista – 6 March
(15) USA, Dir Gus Van Sant
with Robin Williams, Matt Damon,
Ben Affleck, Stellan Skarsgård,
Minnie Driver
© Miramax Film Corp
Miramax Films presents a
Lawrence Bender production
126 minutes 25 seconds
S&S March 1998 p50

The GOVERNESS
Alliance Releasing (UK) –
23 October
(15) UK/France, Dir Sandra
Goldbacher
with Minnie Driver, Tom Wilkinson,
Harriet Walter, Florence Hoath,
Bruce Myers
© Parallax (The Governess) Ltd
Pandora Cinema presents with the
participation of British Screen and
the Arts Council
of England in association with BBC
Films a Parallax picture developed
with the
support of British Screen Finance
Limited/Miramax Films supported
by the National Lottery through
the Arts Council of England
114 minutes 30 seconds
Super 35
S&S November 1998 p51

*La GRANDE ILLUSION
BFI – 24 July
(U) France, Dir Jean Renoir
with Jean Gabin, Dita Parlo, Pierre
Fresnay, Eric von Stroheim, Julien
Carette
Réalisations d'Art
Cinématographique
113 minutes
MFB January 1938 p21

The GRASS HARP
Pathé Distribution – 12 June
(PG) US, Dir Charles Matthau with
Piper Laurie, Sissy Spacek, Walter
Matthau, Edward Furlong, Nell Carter
© Grass Harp Productions, Inc
A Fine Line Features presentation
107 minutes
S&S December 1997 p43

GRAVESEND
Manga Entertainment – 15 May
(18) USA, Dir Salvatore Stabile
with Thomas Brandise, Tom Malloy,
Michael Parducci, Tony Tucci, Sean
Quinn
© Gravesend Productions
Island Digital Media, Oliver Stone
presents in association with
Brooklynwood Productions
84 minutes 51 seconds
S&S June 1998 p45

*GREASE
United International Pictures –
3 July
(PG) US, Dir Randal Kleiser
with John Travolta, Olivia Newton-
John, Stockard Channing, Jeff
Conaway, Barry Pearl
Paramount Pictures Corporation
110 minutes
MFB September 1978 p175

GREAT EXPECTATIONS
20th Century Fox – 17 April
(15) USA, Dir Alfonso Cuarón
with Ethan Hawke, Gwyneth Paltrow,
Hank Azaria, Chris Cooper, Anne
Bancroft
© Twentieth Century Fox Film
Corporation
Twentieth Century Fox presents an
Art Linson production
111 minutes 10 seconds
S&S May p45

GUMMO
Entertainment – 17 April
(18) USA, Dir Harmony Korine
with Jacob Sewell, Nick Sutton, Lara
Tosh, Jacob Reynolds, Darby
Dougherty
© New Line Productions Inc
A Fine Line Features presents an
Independent Pictures release
88 minutes 59 seconds
S&S April 1998 p38

GURU IN SEVEN
Ratpack Films Limited – 10 July
(18) UK, Dir Shani Grewal
with Saeed Jaffrey, Jacqueline
Pearce, Nitin Chandra Ganatra, Lea
Rochelle, Lynne Michelle
© Balhar Film Productions
Limited
Ratpack Films Limited and Balhar
Film Productions present
107 minutes 4 seconds
S&S July 1998 p42

GUY
PolyGram Filmed Entertainment –
22 May
(18) UK/Germany, Dir Michael
Lindsay-Hogg
with Vincent D'Onofrio, Hope Davis,
Kimber Riddle, Diane Salinger,
Richard Portnow
© PolyGram Films (UK) Limited
A PolyGram Filmed Entertainment
presentation in association with
Pandora Film
(Frankfurt) with the support of
Filmstiftung Nordrhein-Westfalen,
A Renée Missel-Tulchin/
Ades production
94 minutes 16 seconds
S&S July 1998 p43

HALLOWEEN H20 20 YEARS LATER
Buena Vista International (UK) –
23 October
(18) USA, Dir Steve Miner
with Jamie Lee Curtis, Adam Arkin,
Michelle Williams, Adam Hann-
Byrd, Jodi Lyn O'Keefe
© Miramax Film Corp
A Dimension Films release
Moustapha Akkad presents a
Nightfall production
85 minutes 52 seconds
S&S November 1998 p51

HAMAM IL BAGNO TURCO/HAMAM
ICA Projects – 16 October
(not submitted) Italy/Turkey/Spain,
Dir Ferzan Özpetek
with Alessandro Gassman, Francesca
D'Aloja, Halil Ergün, Serif Sezer,
Mehmet Günsür
© Sorpasso Film Srl
Marco Risi and Maurizio Tedesco
present a Sorpasso Film
(Rome)/Promete Film (Istanbul)/
Asbrell Productions (Madrid) co-
production with thanks to:
Telepiù/Eurimages/Tobav (Ankara)
94 minutes (subtitles)
S&S November 1998 p52

HANA-BI
Alliance Releasing (UK) – 24 July
(18) Japan, Dir Takeshi Kitano
with Beat Takeshi, Kayoko
Kishimoto, Ren Osugi, Susumu
Terajima, Tetsu Watanabe
© Bandai Visual/Television
Tokyo/Tokyo FM/Office Kitano
A Bandai Visual (Tokyo)/Tokyo
FM/Office Kitano presentation
103 minutes 5 seconds (subtitles)
S&S August 1998 p45

The HANGING GARDEN
Alliance Releasing – 8 May
(15) Canada/UK, Dir Thom
Fitzgerald
with Chris Leavins, Troy Veinotte,
Kerry Fox, Sarah Polley, Seana
McKenna
© 1195991 Ontario Ltd/9034-7287
Quebec Inc/3000788 Nova Scotia Ltd
Channel 4 and Alliance
Communications present a
Triptych Media/Galafilms/
Emotion Pictures production,
produced with the participation of
Telefilm Canada/
The Harold Greenberg
Fund/Channel 4/Nova Scotia Film
Development Corporation/
Nova Scotia Film Industry Tax
Credit/Gouvernement du Québec
(Programme de crédits
d'impô t) and Canadian Film and
Video Production Tax Credit/Nova
Scotia Department
of Education/Canada-Nova Scotia
Cooperation Agreement on
Cultural Development
91 minutes 8 seconds
S&S May 1998 p46

HARD RAIN
PolyGram Filmed Entertainment –
17 April
(15) USA/UK/Japan/
Germany/Denmark, Dir Mikael
Salomon
with Morgan Freeman, Christian
Slater, Randy Quaid, Minnie Driver,
Edward Asner
© Mutual Film Company,
LLC/PolyGram Films (U.K.)
Limited/Toho-Towa Company
Ltd/Tele-München Fernseh GmbH
& Co
Produktionsgesellschaft/British
Broadcasting
Corporation/UGC PH/Nordisk
Film Acquisition A/S
Mutual Film Company and
PolyGram Filmed
Entertainment/Marubeni/Toho-
Towa/Tele-München/BBC/UGC
PH/Nordisk Film present a Mark
Gordon/Gary Levinsohn
production,
production financing provided by
Newmarket Capital Group L.P.
and City National Bank
96 minutes 31 seconds
S&S May 1998 p49

HE GOT GAME
Buena Vista International -
4 September
(15) USA, Dir Spike Lee
with Denzel Washington, Ray Allen,
Milla Jovovich, Rosario Dawson,
Hill Harper
© Touchstone Pictures
Touchstone Pictures presents a 40
Acres and a Mule Filmworks
production
136 minutes 25 seconds
S&S October 1998 p44

HELIU/The RIVER
BFI – 20 March
(not submitted) Taiwan, Dir Tsai
Ming-Liang
with Miao Tian, Li Kangsheng, Lu
Xiaolin, Ann Hui, Chen Xiangqi
© Central Motion Pictures
Corporation
115 minutes (subtitles)
S&S April 1998 p51

HENRY FOOL
Columbia TriStar Films (UK) –
13 November
(18) USA, Dir Hal Hartley
with Thomas Jay Ryan, James
Urbaniak, Parker Posey, Kevin
Corrigan, Veanne Cox
© True Fiction Pictures & The
Shooting Gallery
A True Fiction and The Shooting
Gallery presentation, screenplay
developed in
association with Zenith
Productions
137 minutes 13 seconds
S&S November 1998 p53

HOPE FLOATS
20th Century Fox (UK) –
13 November
(PG) USA, Dir Forest Whitaker
with Sandra Bullock, Harry Connick
Jr., Gena Rowlands, Mae Whitman,
Michael Paré
© Twentieth Century Fox Film
Corporation
Twentieth Century Fox presents a
Lynda Obst production in
association with Fortis Films
114 minutes 20 seconds
S&S November 1998 p54

The HORSE WHISPERER
Buena Vista International (UK) –
28 August
(PG) USA, Dir Robert Redford
with Robert Redford, Kristin Scott
Thomas, Sam Neill, Dianne Wiest,
Scarlett Johansson
© Touchstone Pictures
Touchstone Pictures presents a
Wildwood Enterprises production
169 minutes 10 seconds
S&S September 1998 p43

HOTEL DE LOVE
Warner Bros Distributors (UK) –
12 June
(15) Australia/USA, Dir Craig
Rosenberg
with Aden Young, Saffron Burrows,
Simon Bossell, Pippa Grandison, Ray
Barrett
© Village Roadshow Pictures Pty
Ltd/Village Roadshow Film
Operator Pty Ltd
LIVE Entertainment presents a
Village Roadshow Pictures/Pratt
Films production
96 minutes 19 seconds
S&S August 1998 p45

HURRICANE
First Independent Films Ltd –
5 June
(15) USA, Dir Morgan J. Freeman
with Brendan Sexton III, Shawn
Elliott, José Zuñiga, David Roland
Frank, Carlo Alban
© [US/Canada] United Artists
Pictures Inc, [all other territories]
Hurricane LLC
Mayfair Entertainment
International, a (giv'en) production
88 minutes 42 seconds
S&S June 1998 p46

The ICE STORM
Buena Vista – 6 February
(15) USA, Dir Ang Lee
with Kevin Kline, Joan Allen, Henry
Czerny, Adam Hann-Byrd,
David Krumholtz, Tobey Maguire
© Twentieth Century Fox Film
CorporationFox Searchlight presents
a Good Machine production
112 minutes
S&S February p42

IN & OUT
UIP – 13 February
(12) USA, Dir Frank Oz
with Kevin Kline, Joan Cusack, Matt
Dillon, Debbie Reynolds,
Wilford Brimley, Bob Newhart
© Paramount Pictures
Paramount Pictures present in
association with Spelling Films
a Scott Rudin production
90 minutes 32 seconds
S&S February p43

INSOMNIA
United Media – 13 November
(15) Norway, Dir Erik Skjoldbjærg
with Stellan Skarsgård, Sverre Anker
Ousdal, Bjørn Floberg, Gisken
Armand, Maria Bonnevie
© Norsk Film AS/Nordic Screen
Production AS
Norsk Film AS in co-production
with Nordic Screen Production AS
with the support
of Norsk Filminstitutt presents a
film by Erik Skjoldbjærg
95 minutes 54 seconds (subtitles)
S&S December 1998 p46

IN THE COMPANY OF MEN
Alliance – 30 January
(18) USA, Dir Neil LaBute
with Aaron Eckhart, Stacy Edwards,
Matt Malloy, Emily Cline,
Jason Dixie, Chris Hayes
© Company One Productions
A Stephen Pevner/Atlantic
Entertainment production in
association with Fair and Square
Productions
97 minutes 12 seconds
S&S February p44

 *I PUGNI IN TASCA/ FISTS IN THE POCKET
BFI – 29 May
(not submitted) Italy, Dir Marco
Bellocchio with
Lou Castel, Paola Pitagora, Marino
Mase, Liliana Gerace, Pierluigi
Troglio
Doria Film
110 minutes 43 seconds
MFB June 1966 p91

*IT'S A WONDERFUL LIFE
Feature Film – 4 December
(U) USA/Dir Frank Capra with
James Stewart, Donna Reed, Lionel
Barrymore, Thomas Mitchell, Henry
Travers
Liberty Films
129 minutes
MFB April 1947 p50

I WANT YOU
PolyGram Filmed Entertainment –
30 October

(18) UK, Dir Michael Winterbottom
with Rachel Weisz, Alessandro
Nivola, Labina Mitevska, Luka
Petrusic, Graham Crowden
© PolyGram Films (UK) Limited
PolyGram Filmed Entertainment
presents a Revolution Films
production
87 minutes 19 seconds
S&S November 1998 p55

I WENT DOWN
Buena Vista – 26 January
(15) Ireland/Spain/UK, Dir Paddy
Breathnach
with Brendan Gleeson, Peter
McDonald, Peter Caffrey, Tony
Doyle, Antoine Byrne, David Wilmot
© Treasure Films Ireland Ltd
BBC Films and Bord Scannán na
hÉireann/Irish Film Board
present in association with Radio
Telefís Éireann and Euskal Media
a Treasure Films production
Produced with the support of
investment incentives for the Irish
Film Industry provided by the
Government of Ireland Developed
and produced with the assistance
of Bord Scannán na hÉireann
107 minutes 9 seconds
S&S February 1998 p44

The JACKAL
UIP – 9 January
(18) USA, Dir Michael Caton-Jones
with Bruce Willis, Richard Gere,
Sidney Poitier,
Diane Venora, Mathilda May,
J.K.Simmons
© Universal City Studios
Productions, Inc
Mutual Film Company and
Universal Pictures present an
Alphaville production
124 minutes 17 seconds
S&S February 1998 p45

JACKIE BROWN
Buena Vista – 20 March
(15) USA, Dir Quentin Tarantino
with Pam Grier, Samuel L. Jackson,
Robert Forster, Bridget Fonda,
Michael Keaton
© Mighty Mighty Afrodite
Productions, Inc
Miramax Films presents
A Band Apart
154 minutes 9 seconds
S&S April 1998 p39

The JAMES GANG
PolyGram Filmed Entertainment
Ltd – 29 May
(15) UK/Canada, Dir Mike Barker
with John Hannah, Helen McCrory,
Jason Flemyng, Toni Collette, Darren
Brownlie
© HandMade Films/BBC

Scotland/Revolution Films
BBC Films/Paragon Entertainment
Corporation/HandMade Films
present a Revolution
Films production
94 minutes 31 seconds
S&S June 1998 p47

JIDU HANLENG/FROZEN
Fortissimo – 7 March
(not submitted) Hong
Kong/Netherlands/China, Dir Wang
Xiaoshuai with
Jia Hongsheng, Ma Xiaoqing
Shu Kei's Creative
Workshop/Another Film Company
97 minutes
No S&S reference

KARAKTER/CHARACTER
Gala Film Distributors –
18 September
(15) Netherlands, Dir Mike van Diem
with Jan Decleir, Fedja van Huît,
Betty Schuurman, Tamar van den
Dop, Victor Löw
© Almerica Film B.V.
Laurens Geels & Dick Maas
present an Almerica Film B.V.
production in co-production
with NPS, made with the support
of Nederlandse Programma
Stichting/Stichting Nederlands
Fonds voor de Film/Stichting Co-
productiefonds Binnenlandse
Omroep/Stimuleringsfonds voor
Nederlandse Culturele
Omroepproducties/Fonds Film in
Vlaanderen/Stichting Film Fonds
Rotterdam/Gemeente
Rotterdam/Filmnet Benelux
B.V./ABN-AMBRO BANK N.V.
124 minutes 30 seconds (subtitles)
S&S September 1998 p40

KAVKAZSKII PLENNIK/PRISONER OF THE MOUNTAINS
Metro/Tartan – 20 February
(15) Russia/Kazakhstan, Dir Sergei
Bodrov
with Oleg Men'shikov, Sergei
Bodrov Jr., Susanna Mekhralieva,
Dzhemal Sikharulidze,
Aleksandr Bureev
© Karavan Joint Stock
Company/BG Productions
Karavan Joint Stock Company, BG
Productions, Cinema Committee of
the Russian Federation
98 minutes 45 seconds
S&S March 1998 p34,55

KISSED
Metro/Tartan – 9 January
(18) Canada, Dir Lynne Stopkewich
with Molly Parker, Peter
Outerbridge, Jay Brazeau, Natasha
Morley,

Jessie Winter Mudie, James Timmons
© Boneyard Film Company Inc
A Boneyard Film Company
production produced in association
with British Columbia Film
Produced with the assistance of
The Canada Council
(Media Arts Section)/National Film
Board of Canada (George
Johnson)/
UBC Department of Theatre &
Film (John Wright, Richard
Payment, Craig Volker)
and with the participation of
Telefilm Canada
78 minutes 24 seconds
S&S January 1998 p47

KISSING A FOOL

United International Pictures (UK)
Ltd – 18 September
(15) USA, Dir Doug Ellin
with David Schwimmer, Jason Lee,
Mili Avital, Bonnie Hunt, Vanessa
Angel
A Universal release presented in
association with R.L.
Entertainment and Largo
Entertainment of A Tag
Mendillo/Andrew Form production
93 minutes 31 seconds
S&S October 1998 p45

KISS OR KILL

Alliance Releasing (UK) – 10 July
(18) Australia, Dir Bill Bennett
with Frances O'Connor, Matt Day,
Chris Haywood, Barry Otto, Andrew
S. Gilbert
© Australian Film Finance
Corporation Limited/Australian
Asset Management Limited/
South Australian Film
Corporation/Movie Vision Pty
Limited/Bill Bennett Productions
Pty Limited
An Australian Film Finance
Corporation and Bill Bennett
presentation financed by the
Australian Film Finance
Corporation, produced with the
assistance of Movie Network/
South Australian Film
Corporation, script developed with
the assistance of the Australian
Film Commission
96 minutes 13 seconds
S&S July 1998 p44

KISS THE GIRLS

UIP – 6 March
(18) USA, Dir Gary Fleder
with Morgan Freeman, Ashley Judd,
Cary Elwes, Tony Goldwyn, Jay O.
Sanders
© Paramount Pictures
Paramount Pictures present in
association with Rysher
Entertainment a David Brown/

Joe Wizan production
115 minutes 29 seconds
S&S March 1998 p51

KUCH KUCH HOTA HAI/SOMETHING HAPPENED IN MY HEART

Yash Raj Films International –
16 October
(U) India, Dir Karan Johar with
Shah Rukh Khan, Kajol, Rani
Mukherjee, Farida Jalal, Archana
Puransingh
Dharma Productions
184 minutes 50 seconds
No S&S reference

*KUHLE WAMPE ODER WEM GEHÖRT DIE WELT?

BFI Films – 16 October
(not submitted) Germany, Dir Slatan
Dudow
with Hertha Thiele, Ernst Busch,
Martha Wolter, Lili Schönborn, Adolf
Fischer
Prometheus-Filmverleih und
Vertrieb/Praesens-Film AG
73 minutes 23 seconds (subtitled)
MFB July 1978 p146

KUNDUN

Buena Vista – 3 April
(12) USA, Dir Martin Scorsese
with Tenzin Thuthob Tsarong,
Gyurme Tethong, Tulku Jamyang
Kunga Tenzin,
Tenzin Yeshi Paichang, Tencho
Gyalpo
© Touchstone Pictures
Touchstone Pictures, a Capra/De
Fina production
134 minutes 9 seconds
S&S April 1998 p41

KURT & COURTNEY

Downtown Pictures – 3 July
(15) UK, Dir Nick Broomfield
with Nick Broomfield, Mari Earle,
Tracy Marander, Alice Wheeler,
Hank Harrison
© Strength Ltd
94 minutes 55 seconds
S&S July 1998 p44

LADONI/HANDS

Kino Kino! – 4 September
(PG) Russia, Dir Artur Aristakisyan
narrated by Artur Aristakisyan
VGIK
129 minutes 1 second
S&S September 1998 p42

The LAND GIRLS

Film Four Distributors Ltd –
4 September
(12) UK/France, Dir David Leland
with Catherine McCormack, Rachel
Weisz, Anna Friel, Steven

Mackintosh, Tom Georgeson
© InterMedia Land Girls
Ltd/Camera One/Arena films
InterMedia Films presents with the
participation of The Greenlight
Fund and Channel Four
Films a Greenpoint Film in
association with West Eleven
Films, supported by the
National Lottery through the Arts
Council of England
110 minutes 58 seconds
S&S September 1998 p44

The LAST DAYS OF DISCO

Warner Bros Distributors (UK) – 4
September
(15) USA, Dir Whit Stillman
with Chloî Sevigny, Kate Beckinsale,
Chris Eigeman, Mackenzie Astin,
Matt Keeslar
© Westerly Disco, Inc
A Gramercy release of a Castle
Rock Entertainment/Westerly
Films presentation
113 minutes 33 seconds
S&S September 1998 p44

The LAST TIME I COMMITTED SUICIDE

The Feature Film Company – 19
June
(15) USA, Dir Stephen Kay
with Thomas Jane, Keanu Reeves,
Adrien Brody, John Doe, Claire
Forlani
© Alpine Releasing Corporation
and The Kushner-Locke Company
The Kushner-Locke Company and
Tapestry Films present a Bates
Entertainment production
93 minutes 4 seconds
S&S June 1998 p48

Das LEBEN IST EINE BAUSTELLE/LIFE IS ALL YOU GET

City Screen Ltd – 17 July
(18) Germany, Dir Wolfgang Becker
with Jürgen Vogel, Christiane Paul,
Ricky Tomlinson, Armin Rohde,
Martina Gedeck
© X Filme creative pool GmbH
An X Filme in collaboration with
Filmstiftung NRW/WDR/ARTE/
Filmboard Berlin-Brandenburg
presentation
115 minutes 44 seconds (subtitles)
S&S August 1998 p47

LEFT LUGGAGE

Downtown Pictures – 13 November
(PG) Netherlands/Belgium/USA, Dir
Jeroen Krabbé
with Isabella Rossellini, Maximilian
Schell, Laura Fraser, Jeroen Krabbé,
Marianne Saegebrecht
© Left Luggage B.V.

Shooting Star FilmCompany BV/Flying Dutchman Prod. Inc present in association with Favourite Films NV/Greystone Films with the financial support of Creative Investment BV/ Dutch Film Fund/Cobo Fund/Flemish Film Fund/Vara Television with additional support of Greystone Communications Group Inc/Shooting Star FilmCompany BV/Wildganz BV/ Flying Dutchman Prod Inc/De Vensche BV
100 minutes 18 seconds
S&S November 1998 p55

La LENGUA ASESINA/KILLER TONGUE
Entertainment Film Distributors Ltd – 3 April
(18) Spain/UK, Dir Alberto Sciamma with Melinda Clarke, Jason Durr, Mapi Galán, Mabel Karr, Robert Englund
A production of Lolafilms/Sogetel/The Spice Factory/The Noel Gay Motion Picture, produced with the participation of The European Co-production Fund (UK)/Canal+ (Spain) in association with Sogepaq, developed with the support of the European Script Fund
98 minutes 35 seconds
S&S June 1998 p48

LEPA SELA LEPO GORE/PRETTY VILLAGE PRETTY FLAME
Guild Pathé – 16 January
(18) Serbia, Dir Srdan Dragojevic with Dragan Bjelogrlic, Nikola Kojo, Dragan Maksimovic, Velimir Bata Zivojinovic,
Zoran Cvijanovic, Milorad Mandic
Cobra Film Department RTV Serbia/Ministry of Culture of the Republic of Serbia
128 minutes 53 seconds (subtitles)
S&S January 1998 p51

LETHAL WEAPON 4
Warner Bros Distributors (UK) – 18 September
(15) USA, Dir Richard Donner with Mel Gibson, Danny Glover, Joe Pesci, Rene Russo, Chris Rock
© Warner Bros
Warner Bros. presents a Silver Pictures production in association with Doshudo Productions
125 minutes 44 seconds
S&S September 1998 p46

LEWIS & CLARK & GEORGE
[Short season at the NFT courtesy

of High Flyers Video Distribution/MDP Worldwide] – 23 January
(18) US, Dir Rod McCall with Rose McGowan, Salvator Xuereb, Dan Gunther, Art La Fleur, Aki Aleong
Davis Entertainment Classics/Dark Matter Productions
84 minutes
No S&S reference

LIAR
First Independent Films – 15 May
(18) USA, Dir Jonas Pate, Josh Pate with Tim Roth, Chris Penn, Michael Rooker, Renee Zellweger, Ellen Burstyn
© MDP Worldwide
MDP Worldwide presents a Peter Glatzer production
101 minutes 53 seconds
S&S June 1998 p49
US release title: **DECEIVER**

The LIFE OF STUFF
[screened for short season at the NFT courtesy of The Sales Co/BBC] – 21 August
(18) UK, Dir Simon Donald with Mabel Aitken, Ewen Bremner, Liam Cunningham, Jason Flemyng, Ciaran Hinds
© Prairie Pictures
Prairie Pictures in association with the Glasgow Film Fund, presented by BBC Films and the Scottish Arts Council
90 minutes
No S&S reference

LIKE IT IS
Dangerous to Know – 17 April
(18) UK, Dir Paul Oremland with Roger Daltrey, Dani Behr, Ian Rose, Steve Bell, Tony Van Silva
Dangerous to Know/Fulcrum Productions/Channel Four
96 minutes 32 seconds
No S&S reference

*The LITTLE MERMAID
Buena Vista – 17 July
(U) US, Dir John Musker, Ron Clements
with character voices by Rene Auberjonois, Christopher Daniel Barnes, Jodi Benson, Pat Carroll, Paddi Edwards
Walt Disney Company/Walt Disney Pictures in association with Silver Screen Partners IV
83 minutes
MFB October 1990 p298

LLUVIA EN LOS ZAPATOS/IF ONLY
Pathé Distribution – 27 November
(15) Spain/France/Canada/UK/

Luxembourg Dir Maria Ripoll with Lena Headey, Douglas Henshall, Penelope Cruz, Gustavo Salmeron, Mark Strong
© Esicma/Mandarin (The world except Canada) © Paragon Entertainment Corporation (only Canada)
HandMade Films/Paragon Entertainment Corp present an Esicma production in association with CLT/UFA International/Mandarin Films/Wild Rose Productions Developed in association with Parallel Picture (UK), developed with support of the MEDIA programme
94 minutes 31 seconds
S&S December 1998 p45

LOCK, STOCK AND TWO SMOKING BARRELS
PolyGram Filmed Entertainment – 28 August
(18) UK, Dir Guy Ritchie with Jason Flemyng, Dexter Fletcher, Nick Moran, Jason Statham, Steven Mackintosh
© Ska Films
The Steve Tisch Company/Ska Films presents a Matthew Vaughn production
106 minutes 22 seconds
S&S September 1998 p46

LOLITA
Pathé Distribution Ltd – 8 May
(18) France/USA, Dir Adrian Lyne with Jeremy Irons, Melanie Griffith, Frank Langella, Dominique Swain, Suzanne Shepherd
© Alphatex, S.A.
Mario Kassar presents a Pathé production
137 minutes 27 seconds
Super 35
S&S May 1998 p51

LOST IN SPACE
Entertainment Film Distributors Ltd – 31 July
(PG) USA, Dir Stephen Hopkins with Gary Oldman, William Hurt, Matt LeBlanc, Mimi Rogers, Heather Graham
© New Line Productions, Inc
A Prelude Pictures production in association with Irwin Allen Productions
129 minutes 53 seconds
S&S August 1998 p48-50

LOVE AND DEATH ON LONG ISLAND
Guild Film Distribution – 3 July
(15) UK/Canada, Dir Richard Kwietniowski

with John Hurt, Jason Priestley, Fiona Loewi, Sheila Hancock, Harvey Atkin
© Skyline Love & Death Ltd/IMX Lovdth Inc
A Skyline/Imagex production with the participation of British Screen/Telefilm Canada/ Arts Council of England/Nova Scotia Film Development Corporation in association with BBC Films/Mikado/The Sales Company, developed in association with Alfalfa Entertainments, developed with the support of British Screen Finance Limited/BBC Films/The Nova Scotia Film Industry Tax Credit and the European Script Fund, supported by the National Lottery through the Arts Council of England
93 minutes 12 seconds
S&S July 1998 p45-46

LOVE ETC.

Pathé – 20 March
(15) France, Dir Marion Vernoux
with Charlotte Gainsbourg, Yvan Attal, Charles Berling, Thibault de Montalembert, Elodie Navarre
© Alicéleo/Lumière/France 3 Cinéma/Le Studio Canal+
Patrick Godeau presents a production of Alicéleo/France 3 Cinéma/Le Studio Canal+
in association with Cofimage 7/Studio Images 3, with the participation of Canal+, supported by Centre National de la Cinématographie/Procirep and European Script Fund
104 minutes 10 seconds
S&S April 1998 p42

ⓑⓕⓘ LOVE IS THE DEVIL STUDY FOR A PORTRAIT OF FRANCIS BACON/ AI NO AKUMA

Artificial Eye Film Company Ltd – 18 September
(18) UK/France/Japan, Dir John Maybury
with Derek Jacobi, Daniel Craig, Anne Lambton, Karl Johnson, Annabel Brooks
© BBC and BFI
BBC Films and The British Film Institute present in association with The Arts Council of England/Première Heure/Uplink, a British Film Institute production in association with Partners in Crime with the assistance of STATE Screenplay, developed by BFI Production and BBC Films with

the support of The European Script Fund, initial development by Partners in Crime supported by The National Lottery through the Arts Council of England
90 minutes 36 seconds
S&S September 1998 p47

LUCIE AUBRAC

Pathé Distribution – 23 January
(12) France, Dir Claude Berri
with Carole Bouquet, Daniel Auteuil, Patrice Chéreau, Eric Boucher, Jean-Roger Milo, Heino Ferch
© Renn Productions/T.F.I Films Production/Rhône-Alpes Cinéma/D.A.Films/Pricel co-production with the participation of Région Rhônes-Alpes/Centre National de la Cinématographie with the participation of Canal+
115 minutes 38 seconds (subtitles)
S&S February 1998 p46

MAD CITY

Warner Bros Distributors (UK) – 10 July
(15) USA, Dir Costa-Gavras
with Dustin Hoffman, John Travolta, Alan Alda, Mia Kirshner, Ted Levine
© Warner Bros.
Warner Bros. presents an Arnold Kopelson production in association with Punch Productions
114 minutes 39 seconds
Super 35
S&S July 1998 p46

The MAGIC SWORD QUEST FOR CAMELOT

Warner Bros Distributors (UK) – 24 July
(U) USA, Dir Frederick Du Chau
with character voices of Jessalyn Gilsig, Andrea Corr, Cary Elwes, Bryan White, Gary Oldman
© Warner Bros.
85 minutes 51 seconds
S&S August 1998 p50

*La MAMAN ET LA PUTAIN

Artificial Eye – 27 February
(18) France, Dir Jean Eustache with Jean-Pierre Leaud, Francoise Lebrun, Bernadette Lafont, Isabelle Weingarten, Jacques Rendard
Films du Losange (Paris)/Elite Films/Cine Qua Non/Simar Films/V.M. Productions
217 minutes 20 seconds
MFB December 1974 p278

MAN IN THE IRON MASK

UIP – 20 March
(12) USA, Dir Randall Wallace

with Leonardo DiCaprio, Jeremy Irons, John Malkovich, Gérard Depardieu, Gabriel Byrne
© United Artists Pictures Inc
United Artists presents a Randall Wallace film, a United Artists Corporation Ltd production
132 minutes 1 second
S&S April 1998 p43

The MAN WHO KNEW TOO LITTLE

Warner Bros Distributors – 15 May
(12) USA/Germany, Dir Jon Amiel
with Bill Murray, Peter Gallagher, Joanne Whalley, Alfred Molina, Richard Wilson
© Monarchy Enterprises B.V. and Regency Entertainment (USA), Inc
Regency Enterprises presents an Arnon Milchan/Polar production in association with Taurus Films
93 minutes 29 seconds
S&S June 1998 p50

MARIE BAIE DES ANGES/ANGEL SHARKS

Blue Light – 20 November
(15) France, Dir Manuel Pradal
with Nicolas Welbers, Amira Casar, Swan Carpio, Jamie Harris, Frédéric Malgras
Les Films de la Suane presents a Studio Image 2/La Sept Cinéma/Lelia Films (Lionel Closson)/Les Films des Tournelles co-production with the participation of Canal+/Centre National de la Cinématographie with help from Région Provence-Alpes-Côte d'Azur/Région Languedoc-Rousillon with the financial co-operation of Cofiloisirs and the support of Equinoxe
93 minutes 23 seconds (subtitles)
S&S December 1998 p40

MARQUISE

Downtown Pictures – 9 October
France/Italy/Switzerland/Spain, Dir Véra Belmont
with Sophie Marceau, Bernard Giraudeau, Lambert Wilson, Patrick Timsit, Thierry Lhermitte
© Stéphan Films/France 3 Cinéma/AMLF
Stéphan Films/France 3 Cinéma/AMLF (France)/3 Emme Srl (Italy)/Alhena Films (Switzerland)/ Multivideo (Spain) supported by Eurimages with the participation of Canal+/Cofimage 5 with the support of Procirep
116 minutes 37 seconds
S&S November 1998 p57

MARTHA – MEET FRANK, DANIEL AND LAURENCE

Film Four Distributors – 8 May
(15) UK, Dir Nick Hamm
with Monica Potter, Rufus Sewell,
Tom Hollander, Joseph Fiennes, Ray
Winstone
© Channel 4 Television
Corporation
Channel Four Films presents a
Banshee production
87 minutes 47 seconds
S&S May 1998 p52

The MASK OF ZORRO

Columbia TriStar Films (UK) –
11 December
(PG) USA, Dir Martin Campbell
with Antonio Banderas, Anthony
Hopkins, Catherine Zeta Jones, Stuart
Wilson, Matt Letscher
© Global Entertainment
Productions GmbH & Co. KG
TriStar Pictures presents an
Amblin Entertainment production
in association with Zorro
Productions
137 minutes 47 seconds
S&S December 1998 p48

AI MASSIR/DESTINY

Flach-Pyramide/ICA –
13 November
(not submitted) France/Egypt, Dir
Youssef Chahine
with El Nour Sherif, Laila Eloui,
Mahmoud Hemeida, Safia El Emary,
Khaled El Nabaoui
Ognon Pictures/France 2
Cinéma/Misr International Film
135 minutes
No S&S reference

MAT I SYN/MUTTER UND SOHN/MOTHER AND SON

Blue Light – 27 March
(U) Russia/Germany, Dir Aleksandr
Sokurov
with Gudrun Geyer, Aleksei
Ananishnov
Goskino Rossii/Severnyi Fond, St.
Petersburg/Lenfilm, St.
Petersburg/Zero Film, Berlin/ö
Film, Berlin with Filmförderung
Hamburg and Deutches
Bundesministerium des Innern
70 minutes 55 seconds (subtitles)
S&S April 1998 p46

MEN WITH GUNS

Columbia TriStar Films (UK) –
18 September
(15) USA, Dir John Sayles
with Federico José Luppi, Damián
Alcázar, Tania Cruz, Damián
Delgado, Dan Rivera González
© Perdido Inc.

Lexington Road Productions and
Clear Blue Sky Productions in
association with
The Independent Film Channel
and Anarchists' Convention
present
127 minutes 54 seconds (subtitles)
S&S September 1998 p48

MERCURY RISING

United International Pictures (UK)
Ltd – 2 October
(15) USA, Dir Harold Becker
with Bruce Willis, Alec Baldwin,
Miko Hughes, Chi McBride, Kim
Dickens
© Universal City Studios, Inc
Universal Pictures and Imagine
Entertainment present a Brian
Grazer production
111 minutes 33 seconds
October 1998 p46

METROLAND

Metrodome Distribution Ltd – 21
August
(18) UK/France/Spain, Dir Philip
Saville
with Christian Bale, Lee Ross, Elsa
Zylberstein, Emily Watson, John
Wood
© Blue Horizon (Metroland)
Limited/Mact Productions
S.A./Filmania S.L.
Blue Horizon/Mact/Filmania
present in association with
Pandora Cinema and
the Arts Council of England, with
the participation of BBC
Films/Canal+ and
The European Co-production Fund
UK, with the support of The
Eurimages
Fund of the Council of Europe &
the collaboration of Sogepaq SA,
developed
with the support of the European
Script Fund, supported through
the proceeds
of the National Lottery by the Arts
Council of England, produced in
association with BBC Films
101 minutes 1 second
S&S August 1998 p51

MIDDLETON'S CHANGELING

United Independent Pictures Ltd –
6 March
(18) UK, Dir Marcus Thompson
with Ian Dury, Amanda Ray-King,
Colm Ó Maonlaí, Billy Connolly,
Campbell Morrison
© High Time Pictures Limited
High Time Pictures presents a
Marcus Thompson film
95 minutes 51 seconds
S&S April 1998 p43

MIDNIGHT IN THE GARDEN OF GOOD AND EVIL

Warner Bros – 17 April
(15) USA, Dir Clint Eastwood
with Kevin Spacey, John Cusack,
Jack Thompson, Irma P. Hall, Jude
Law
© Warner Bros
Warner Bros presents a Malpaso
production in association with
Silver Pictures
154 minutes 57 seconds
S&S March 1998 p52

The MIGHTY

Buena Vista International (UK) –
26 December
(PG) USA, Dir Peter Chelsom
with Sharon Stone, Gena Rowlands,
Harry Dean Stanton, Gillian
Anderson, James Gandolfini
© Miramax Film Corp.
Miramax Films presents a
Scholastic Productions/Simon
Fields production
100 minutes 20 seconds
S&S January 1999 p50

MIMIC

Buena Vista International (UK) –
26 June
(15) USA, Dir Guillermo del Toro
with Mira Sorvino, Jeremy Northam,
Josh Brolin, Giancarlo Giannini,
Alexander Goodwin
© Miramax Film Corp
A Dimension Films presentation
105 minutes 47 seconds
S&S July 1998 p47

Les MISÉRABLES

Entertainment Film Distributors
Ltd – 20 November
(12) USA, Dir Bille August
with Liam Neeson, Geoffrey Rush,
Uma Thurman, Claire Danes, Hans
Matheson
© Mandalay Entertainment
Mandalay Entertainment presents
a Sarah Radclyffe production/a
James Gorman production
133 minutes 50 seconds
S&S December 1998 p49

MOEDER DAO DE SCHILDPADGELIJKENDE/ MOTHER DAO THE TURTLELIKE

[short season at the Lux Cinema] –
2 October
(not submitted) Netherlands, Dir
Vincent Monnikendam
NPS Dutch Program
Services/Zeitgeist Films
88 minutes (subtitles)
No S&S reference

MOJO
Portobello Pictures – 10 July
(15) UK, Dir Jez Butterworth
with Ian Hart, Ewen Bremner, Aidan
Gillen, Martin Gwynn Jones, Hans
Matheson
© Mojo Films/Portobello Pictures
A BBC Films presentation with the
participation of British Screen of a
Mojo Films/
Portobello Pictures production
92 minutes 41 seconds
S&S July 1998 p48

MONEY TALKS
Entertainment – 24 April
(15) USA, Dir Bret Ratner
with Chris Tucker, Charlie Sheen,
Heather Locklear, Gerard Ismaël,
Damian Chapa,
Elise Neal
© New Line Productions, Inc
New Line Cinema presents a New
Line Cinema release
95 minutes 35 seconds
S&S April 1998 p44

MONK DAWSON
De Warrenne Pictures – 31 July
(18) UK, Dir Tom Waller
with John Michie, Ben Taylor, Paula
Hamilton, Martin Kemp, Rupert
Vansittart
© De Warrenne Pictures Ltd
De Warrenne Pictures
107 minutes 23 seconds
S&S August 1998 p52

MORTAL KOMBAT 2 ANNIHILATION
Entertainment – 13 February
(15) USA, Dir John R. Leonetti
with Robin Shou, Talisa Soto, Brian
Thompson, Sandra Hess, Lynn Red
Williams
© New Line Productions, Inc
New Line Cinema presents a
Lawrence Kasanoff/Threshold
Entertainment production
94 minutes 32 seconds
S&S April 1998 p45

MOST WANTED
**Entertainment Film Distributors
Ltd – 3 April**
(15) USA, Dir David Glenn Hogan
with Keenen Ivory Wayans, Jon
Voight, Jill Hennessy, Paul Sorvino,
Robert Culp
© New Line Productions, Inc
New Line Cinema presents an
Ivory Way production
98 minutes 54 seconds
S&S June 1998 p51

MOUSEHUNT
UIP – 3 April
(PG) USA, Dir Gore Verbinski
with Nathan Lane, Lee Evans, Maury
Chaykin, Christopher Walken, Vicki
Lewis
© Dream Works LLC
Dream Works Pictures presents an
Alan Riche/Tony Ludwig production
97 minutes 41 seconds
S&S April 1998 p47

MR. MAGOO
**Buena Vista International (UK) –
22 May**
(PG) USA, Dir Stanley Tong
with Leslie Nielsen, Kelly Lynch,
Ernie Hudson, Stephen Tobolowsky,
Nick Chinlund
© Disney Enterprises, Inc
Walt Disney Pictures presents a
Ben Myron production
87 minutes 24 seconds
S&S July 1998 p49

MRS DALLOWAY
Artificial Eye – 6 March
(PG) USA/UK/Netherlands, Dir
Marleen Gorris
with Vanessa Redgrave, Natascha
McElhone, Michael Kitchen, Alan
Cox, Sarah Badel
© Overseas Film Group,
Inc/Newmarket Capital Group L.P.
[Benelux only] Bergen Film
First Look Pictures presents a
Bayly/Paré production in association
with Bergen Film,
a Newmarket Capital Group/BBC
Films presentation with the
participation of The European Co-
production Fund U.K./NPS-
Television/Dutch Co-production
Fund (CoBo)/ The Dutch Film Fund
97 minutes 19 seconds
S&S March 1998 p53

MULAN
**Buena Vista International (UK)
Ltd – 16 October**
(U) USA, Dir Barry Cook, Tony
Bancroft
with character voices of Ming-Na
Wen, Lea Salonga, Soon-Teck Oh, B.
D. Wong, Donny Osmond
© Disney Enterprises, Inc
A Walt Disney Pictures presentation
87 minutes 41 seconds
S&S October 1998 p47

MY NAME IS JOE
**Film Four Distribution Ltd –
6 November**
(15) UK/Germany/France/
Italy/Spain, Dir Ken Loach
with Peter Mullan, Louise Goodall,
David McKay, Annemarie Kennedy,
Gary Lewis
© Parallax (Joe) Ltd and Road
Movies Vierte Produktionen
GmbH
A Parallax Pictures/Road Movies
Vierte Production with support of
the Scottish Arts Council National
Lottery Fund/The Glasgow Film
Fund/Filmstiftung Nordrhein-
Westfalen
in collaboration with Channel Four
Films/WDR/ARTE/La Sept
Cinéma, ARD/Degeto Film
and BIM Distribuzione/Diaphana
Distribution/Tornasol/Alta Films
104 minutes 53 seconds
S&S November 1998 p58

MY SON THE FANATIC
Feature Film Company – 1 May
(15) UK, Dir Udayan Prasad
with Om Puri, Rachel Griffiths,
Stellan Skarsgård, Akbar Kurtha,
Gopi Desai
© Son of Zephyr Limited
BBC Films in association with
UGC DA International &
the Arts Council of England
present a Zephyr Films production,
developed with the sole support of
BBC Films
86 minutes 58 seconds
S&S May 1998 p53

The NEGOTIATOR
**Warner Bros Distributors (UK) –
27 November**
(15) USA/Germany, Dir F. Gary Gray
with Samuel Jackson, Kevin Spacey,
David Morse, Ron Rifkin, John Spencer
© Monarchy Enterprises B.V. and
Regency Entertainment (USA) Inc.
Regency Enterprises
presents a Mandeville Films/New
Regency production in
association with Taurus Films
139 minutes 25 seconds
S&S December 1998 p52

The NEPHEW
**United International Pictures (UK)
Ltd – 10 November**
(12) Ireland, Dir Eugene Brady
with Donal McCann, Pierce Brosnan,
Sinéad Cusack, Aislín McGuckin,
Niall Toibín
© World 2000 Entertainment
Limited
Produced in Ireland by Nephew
Productions for Irish Dream Time
Inc/ World 2000 Entertainment
Ltd, developed with the support of
the European Script Fund,
produced with the support of
investment incentives for
The Irish Film Industry
104 minutes 55 seconds
S&S September 1998 p50

NOON VA GOLDOON/A MOMENT OF INNOCENCE
ICA Projects – 2 October
(not submitted)

Iran/France/Switzerland, Dir Mohsen
Makhmalbaf
with Mirhadi Taiebi, Ali Bakhshi,
Ammar Tafti, Mariyam Mohammad-
Amini, Fariba Faghiri
**Shirkate Pakhshiran with the
support of the Fondation
Montecinemaverità (Locarno,
Switzerland)/Diréction du
Développement de la Coopération
(D.C.C.) and the Départment
Fédération des Affaires Etrangères**
78 minutes (subtitles)
S&S December 1998 p50

NOWHERE
Pathé Distribution Ltd – 5 June
(18) USA/France, Dir Gregg Araki
with James Duval, Rachel True,
Nathan Bexton, Chiara Mastroianni,
Debi Mazar
© Kill
**Kill presents in association with
Desperate Pictures/Blurco/Why
Not Productions (France)**
81 minutes 35 seconds
S&S June 1998 p52

The OBJECT OF MY AFFECTION
20th Century Fox (UK) – 26 June
(15) USA, Dir Nicholas Hytner
with Jennifer Aniston, Paul Rudd,
John Pankow, Alan Alda, Tim Daly
**© Twentieth Century Fox Film
Corporation**
**Twentieth Century Fox presents a
Laurence Mark production**
111 minutes 27 seconds
S&S July 1998 p50

The ODD COUPLE II
**United International Pictures (UK)
Ltd – 13 November**
(15) USA, Dir Howard Deutch
with Jack Lemmon, Walter Matthau,
Christine Baranski, Barnard Hughes,
Jonathan Silverman
© Paramount Pictures Corporation
**Paramount Pictures presents a
Cort/Madden production**
96 minutes 23 seconds
S&S December 1998 p53

ONCE UPON A TIME... WHEN WE WERE COLORED
Winstone – 29 May
(not submitted) US, Dir Tim Reid
with Al Freeman Jr., Phylicia Rashad,
Leon, Paula Kelly, Salli Richardson
© BET Pictures
**Presented by BET
Pictures/produced by United Image
Entertainment**
112 minutes
No S&S reference

ON CONNAÎT LA CHANSON/SAME OLD SONG
Pathé Distribution – 4 December
(PG) France/Switzerland/UK, Dir
Alain Resnais
with Pierre Arditi, Sabine Azéma,
Jean-Pierre Bacri, André Dussollier,
Agnès Jaoui
**© Arena Films/Caméra
One/France 2 Cinéma/Vega
Film/Greenpoint**
**Arena Films/Caméra One/France 2
Cinéma/Vega Film/Greenpoint with
the participation
of Canal+/Cofimage
9/Sofineurope/Alia Film
(Rome)/Télévision Suisse
Romande/The European Co-
production Fund (London) with
the support of Eurimages/Centre
National de la
Cinématographie/Procirep/Office
Fédéral de la Culture (Berne)**
122 minutes (subtitles)
S&S December 1998 p54

OSCAR AND LUCINDA
20th Century Fox – 3 April
(15) USA/Australia, Dir Gillian
Armstrong
with Ralph Fiennes, Cate Blanchett,
Ciaran Hinds, Tom Wilkinson,
Richard Roxburgh
**© Twentieth Century Fox Film
Corporation/Australian Film
Finance Corporation Limited/
New South Wales Film and
Television Office/Dalton Films Pty
Limited**
**Fox Searchlight Pictures presents
in association with the Australian
Film Finance Corporation
and the New South Wales Film and
Television Office a Dalton Films
production, produced
in association with Meridian Films**
131 minutes 51 seconds
S&S April 1998 p48

OUT OF SIGHT
**United International Pictures (UK)
Ltd – 27 November**
(15) USA, Dir Steven Soderbergh
with George Clooney, Jennifer
Lopez, Ving Rhames, Don Cheadle,
Dennis Farina
**© Universal City Studios
Productions Inc**
**Universal Pictures presents a
Jersey Films production**
122 minutes 45 seconds
S&S December 1998 p55

*OUT OF THE PAST
BFI Films – 3 April
(PG) US, Dir Jacques Tourneur

with Robert Mitchum, Jane Greer,
Kirk Douglas, Rhonda Fleming,
Richard Webb
RKO Radio Pictures
96 minutes 58 seconds
MFB December 1947 p172

PALMETTO
**Warner Bros Distributors (UK) –
26 June**
(15) USA/Germany, Dir Volker
Schlöndorff
with Woody Harrelson, Elisabeth
Shue, Gina Gershon, Rolf Hoppe,
Michael Rapaport
© Castle Rock Entertainment
**Castle Rock Entertainment
presents a Rialto Film production**
113 minutes 22 seconds
S&S August 1998 p53

The PARENT TRAP
**Buena Vista International (UK) –
11 December**
(PG) USA, Dir Nancy Meyers
with Dennis Quaid, Natasha
Richardson, Lisa Ann Walter, Elaine
Hendrix, Simon Kunz
© Disney Enterprises, Inc
**Walt Disney Pictures presents a
Nancy Meyers/Charles Shyer film
produced in association
with The Meyers/Shyer Company**
127 minutes 59 seconds
S&S December 1998 p56

PAULIE
**United International Pictures (UK)
Ltd – 24 July**
(U) USA, Dir John Roberts
with Gena Rowlands, Tony Shalhoub,
Cheech Marin, Bruce Davison, Jay Mohr
© Dream Works LLC
**Dream Works Pictures present a
Mutual Film Company production**
91 minutes 38 seconds
S&S September 1998 p51

PAWS
PolyGram – 13 February
(PG) UK/Australia, Dir Karl Zwicky
with Billy Connolly, Nathan
Cavaleri, Emilie Francois, Joe
Petruzzi, Caroline Gillmer
**© PolyGram Films (UK)
Limited/Australian Film Finance
Corporation Limited/Latent
Image Productions Pty
Limited/New South Wales Film
and Television Office**
**PolyGram Filmed Entertainment
and The Australian Film Finance
Corporation
present a Latent Image production,
produced with the assistance and
finance from New South Wales and
Television Office**
83 minutes 32 seconds
S&S March 1998 p54

*PÉPÉ LE MOKO
BFI Films – 18 September
(not submitted) France, Dir Julien
Duvivier
with Jean Gabin, Gabriel Gabrio,
Saturnin Fabre, Fernand Charpin,
Lucas Gridoux
Paris Film Production
93 minutes
MFB April 1937 p86

A PERFECT MURDER
**Warner Bros Distributors (UK) –
16 October**
(15) USA, Dir Andrew Davis
with Michael Douglas, Gwyneth
Paltrow, Viggo Mortensen, David
Suchet, Sarita Choudhury
© **Warner Bros.**
**Warner Bros. presents a Kopelson
Entertainment production**
107 minutes 20 seconds
S&S October 1998 p48

 ***The PHILADELPHIA
STORY**
BFI Films – 27 November
(U) USA, Dir George Cukor
with Cary Grant, Katharine Hepburn,
James Stewart, Ruth Hussey, John
Howard
**Loew's Incorporated/Metro-
Goldwyn-Mayer**
112 minutes 27 seconds
MFB March 1941 p34

PICTURE PERFECT
20th Century Fox – 9 January
(PG) USA, Dir Glenn Gordon Caron
with Jennifer Aniston, Jay Mohr,
Kevin Bacon, Olympia Dukakis,
Illeana Douglas
© **Twentieth Century Fox Film
Corporation**
A 3 Arts production
101 minutes 40 seconds
S&S December 1998 p51

The PLAYERS CLUB
**Entertainment Film Distributors
Ltd – 6 November**
(18) USA, Dir Ice Cube
with Bernie Mac, Monica Calhoun, A.
J. Johnson, Ice Cube, Alex Thomas
© **New Line Productions, Inc**
**New Line Cinema presents an Ice
Cube/Pat Charbonnet production,
Ghetto Bird Productions**
102 minutes 55 seconds
S&S October 1998 p49

PLAYING GOD
**Blue Dolphin Film & Video –
11 December**
(18) USA, Dir Andy Wilson
with David Duchovny, Timothy
Hutton, Angelina Jolie, Michael
Massee, Peter Stormare
© **Beacon Communications Corp**

Touchstone Pictures presents in
association with Beacon Pictures
93 minutes 58 seconds
S&S January 1999 p53

 *POINT BLANK
BFI – 19 June
(15) US, Dir John Boorman with
Lee Marvin, Angie Dickinson,
Keenan Wynn, Carroll O'Connor,
Lloyd Bochner
Metro-Goldwyn-Mayer
91 minutes 51 seconds
MFB February 1968 p22

PONETTE
**Metro Tartan Distribution –
26 June**
(PG) France, Dir Jacques Doillon
with Victoire Thivisol, Matiaz
Bureau Caton, Delphine Schiltz,
Léopoldine Serre, Luckie Royer
© **Les Films Alain Sarde/Rhône-
Alpes Cinéma/Chrysalide Films**
**Alain Sarde presents a co-
production: Les Films Alain
Sarde/Rhône-Alpes Cinéma with
the participation of la Région
Rhône-Alpes/Centre National de la
Cinématographie and with the
participation of Canal+**
97 minutes 26 seconds (subtitles)
S&S July 1998 p51

The POSTMAN
Warner Bros – 20 February
(15) USA, Dir Kevin Costner
with Kevin Costner, Will Patton,
Larenz Tate, Olivia Williams, James
Russo
© **Warner Bros**
**Warner Bros presents a Kevin
Costner film, a Tig production**
177 minutes 31 seconds
S&S April 1998 p49

PRACTICAL MAGIC
**Warner Bros Distributors (UK) –
26 December**
(12) USA, Dir Griffin Dunne
with Sandra Bullock, Nicole Kidman,
Dianne Wiest, Stockard Channing,
Aidan Quinn
© **Warner Bros.**
(US/Canada/Bahamas/Bermuda)
© **Village Roadshow Films (BVI)
Limited (all other territories)**
**Warner Bros. presents in
association with Village Roadshow
Pictures a Di Novi Pictures
production in association with
Fortis Films**
104 minutes 4 seconds
S&S January 1999 p53

PRIMARY COLOURS
**United International Pictures (UK)
Ltd – 30 October**
(15) USA, Dir Mike Nichols

with John Travolta, Emma
Thompson, Billy Bob Thornton,
Adrian Lester, Maura Tierney
© **Universal City Studios Inc**
**Universal Pictures and Mutual
Film Company present an Icarus
production**
143 minutes 15 seconds
S&S October 1998 p50

The PRINCE OF EGYPT
**United International Pictures (UK)
Ltd – 18 December**
(U) USA, Dir Brenda Chapman,
Steven Hickner, Simon Wells
with character voices by Val Kilmer,
Ralph Fiennes, Michelle Pfeiffer,
Sandra Bullock, Jeff Goldblum
© **Dream Works LLC**
Dream Works LLC
98 minutes 53 seconds
S&S January 1999 p54

The PROPOSITION
**PolyGram Filmed Entertainment –
28 August**
(12) USA, Dir Lesli Linka Glatter
with Kenneth Branagh, Madeleine
Stowe, William Hurt, Neil Patrick
Harris, Robert Loggia
© **Interscope Communications** ©
**PolyGram Filmed Entertainment
Inc**
**PolyGram Filmed Entertainment
presents an Interscope
Communications production**
111 minutes 29 seconds
S&S November 1998 p60

*PSYCHO
**Artificial Eye Film Company – 31
July**
(15) USA, Dir Alfred Hitchcock
with Anthony Perkins, Vera Miles,
John Gavin, Martin Balsam, John
McIntire
**Shamley Productions/Paramount
Pictures Corporation**
108 minutes 27 seconds
MFB September 1960 p126

The QUIET ROOM
ICA – 14 August
(not submitted) Australia/Italy,
Dir Rolf de Heer
with Chloe Ferguson, Phoebe
Ferguson, Paul Blackwell, Celine
O'Leary
**Fandango Produzione
Cinematografica/Vertigo
Productions/Smile
Productions/SBS Independent**
91 minutes
No S&S reference

The RAINMAKER
UIP – 24 April
(15) Germany/USA, Dir Francis Ford
Coppola

with Matt Damon, Claire Danes, Jon
Voight, Mary Kay Place, Mickey
Rourke, Danny DeVito
© USA/Canada: Mont Blanc
Entertainment GmbH, © all other
countries: Bernina Film AG
Constellation Films presents a
Douglas/Reuther production in
association with American Zoetrope
135 minutes 30 seconds
S&S April 1998 p50

RAZOR BLADE SMILE
Manga Entertainment – 30 October
(18) UK, Dir Jake West
with Eileen Daly, Christopher
Adamson, Jonathan Coote, Kevin
Howarth, David Warbeck
**Palm Pictures presents a Manga
Live/Eye Deal Image production in
association with Beatnik films**
102 minutes 6 seconds
S&S December 1998 p57

The REAL BLONDE
Metrodome Distribution – 22 May
(15) USA, Dir Tom DiCillo
with Matthew Modine, Catherine
Keener, Daryl Hannah, Maxwell
Caulfield, Elizabeth Berkley
© Lakeshore Entertainment Corp.
and Paramount Pictures
Corporation
**Paramount Pictures and Lakeshore
Entertainment present a Marcus
Viscidi production**
104 minutes 58 seconds
S&S June 1998 p52

The REAL HOWARD SPITZ
The Mob – 28 August
(PG) UK/Canada, Dir Vadim Jean
with Kelsey Grammer, Amanda
Donohoe, Joseph Rutten, Patrick
McKenna, Genevieve Tessier
© Writer's Block Ltd/IMX
**Writer's Block Inc
A Metrodome/Imagex production,
TMN – The Movie Network**
101 minutes 14 seconds
S&S October 1998 p52

RED CORNER
United International Pictures (UK)
Ltd – 5 June
(15) USA, Dir Jon Avnet
with Richard Gere, Bai Ling, Bradley
Whitford, Byron Mann, Peter Donat
© Metro-Goldwyn-Mayer Pictures
Inc
**Metro-Goldwyn-Mayer Pictures
presents an Avnet/Kerner production**
122 minutes 24 seconds
S&S June 1998 p53

The REPLACEMENT KILLERS
Columbia TriStar Films (UK) –
5 June

(18) USA, Dir Antoine Fuqua
with Chow Yun-Fat, Mira Sorvino,
Michael Rooker, Jürgen Prochnow,
Carlos Gomez
© Columbia Pictures Industries,
Inc
**Columbia Pictures presents a
Bernie Brillstein/Brad Grey/WCG
Entertainment production**
87 minutes 25 seconds
Super 35
S&S June 1998 p54

RESPECT
[screened for 2 weeks at the
Electric Cinema] – 28 August
(18) GB, Dir Oz Hutchins
with Ama Leu, Eon John, Stephanie
Strohmann, Marcus Peters, Gary
McDonald
2C Productions
90 minutes
No S&S reference

RESURRECTION MAN
PolyGram – 30 January
(18) UK, Dir Marc Evans
with Stuart Townsend, Geraldine
O'Rawe, James Nesbitt, John
Hannah, Brenda Fricker
© PolyGram Film UK Ltd
**PolyGram Filmed Entertainment
presents a Revolution Films
production**
101 minutes 54 seconds
S&S February 1998 p47

RETROACTIVE
[screened for short season at the
NFT courtesy of High Fliers/Orion
Pictures] – 6 March
(not submitted) US, Dir Louis
Morneau with
James Belushi, Kylie Travis,
Shannon Whirry
**Orion Pictures Corporation/
Cohiba Pictures/Retroactive
Productions/Motion Picture
Corporation of America**
90 minutes
No S&S reference

RIEN NE VA PLUS
Artificial Eye Film Company –
16 October
(15) France/Switzerland, Dir Claude
Chabrol
with Isabelle Huppert, Michel
Serrault, François Cluzet, Jean-
François Balmer, Jackie Berroyer
© MK2 Productions/TF1 Films
Production/CAB Productions
SA/MK2 Productions 2/CED
Productions/Les Productions
Traversière
**Marin Karmitz and Véronique
Cayla present a Franco-Swiss co-
production: MK2 Productions/
TF1 Films Production/CAB**

Productions/Télévision Suisse
Romande/Téléclub/Rhône-Alpes
Cinéma with the participation of
Canal+ and the support of
Procirep, Office Fédéral de la
Culture (DFI) Suisse with the
participation of Région Rhône-
Alpes/Centre National de la
Cinématographie
105 minutes 36 seconds (subtitles)
S&S November 1998 p60

RIGET II/The KINGDOM [SERIES II]
ICA Projects – 15 May
(18) Denmark/Italy/Sweden/
Norway/France, Dir Lars von Trier,
Morten Arnfred
with Ernst-Hugo Järegård, Kirsten
Rolffes, Holger Juul Hansen, Søren
Pilmark, Ghita Nørby
© DR TV, Danish Broadcasting
Corporation and Zentropa
Entertainments ApS
**A Lars von Trier presentation
produced by Zentropa
Entertainments AsP/DR TV,
Danish Broadcasting Corporation
in co-production with Liberator
Productions S.a.r.l. and in
association with RAI Cinema
Fiction/Sveriges Television
Malmö/Norsk Riksringkasting/La
Sept/ARTE Unité de Programmes
Fictions, distributed with the
support of the MEDIA
Programme of the European
Union, 35mm version supported by
the Danish Filminstitute**
286 minutes (subtitles)
S&S August 1998 p46

ROAD TO NHILL
[screened for short season at the
Barbican cinema] – 13 March
(15) Australia, Dir Sue Brooks
with Bill Hunter, Tony Barry, Monica
Maughan, Lois Ramsey, Lynette
Curran
**Gecko Films/Australian Film
Finance Corporation/Film Victoria**
95 minutes
No S&S reference

RONIN
United International Pictures (UK)
Ltd – 20 November
(15) USA, Dir John Frankenheimer
with Robert De Niro, Jean Réno,
Natascha McElhone, Stellan
Skarsgård, Sean Bean
© United Artists Pictures Inc.
**United Artists Pictures presents an
FGM Entertainment production, a
United Artists
Corporation Ltd. production**
121 minutes 23 seconds
S&S December 1998 p58

ROUNDERS
Buena Vista International (UK) –
20 November
(15) USA, Dir John Dahl
with Matt Damon, Edward Norton,
John Turturro, Gretchen Mol, Famke
Janssen
© Miramax Film Corp.
A Miramax Films presentation of a
Spanky Pictures production
121 minutes 2 seconds
S&S December 1998 p59

RUSH HOUR
Entertainment Film Distributors
Ltd – 4 December
(15) USA, Dir Brett Ratner
with Jackie Chan, Chris Tucker, Tom
Wilkinson, Philip Baker Hall, Mark
Rolston
© New Line Productions Inc
New Line Cinema presents an
Arthur Sarkissian and Roger
Birnbaum production
97 minutes 41 seconds
S&S December 1998 p60

SAFE MEN
United International Pictures (UK)
Ltd – 16 October
(15) USA, Dir John Hamburg
with Sam Rockwell, Steve Zahn,
Mark Ruffalo, Josh Pais, Paul
Giamatti
© Safe Men Co., LLC
An Andell Entertainment
production in association with Blue
Guitar Films
87 minutes 49 seconds
S&S October 1998 p53

SALUT COUSIN!/HEY COUSIN!
Porter Frith/Arrow Film
Distributors – 22 May
(15) France/Belgium/Algeria/
Luxemburg, Dir Merzak Allouache
with Gad Elmaleh, Mess Hattou,
Magaly Berdy, Ann-Gisel Glass, Jean
Benguigui
© JBA Production/La Sept
Cinéma/Artémis
Productions/R.T.B.F./Flash Back
Audiovisuel/Samsa Film/Cléa
Productions
Les Films du Roseau/Jacques
Bidou presentation, this film was
supported by
Eurimages (du Conseil de
l'Europe) with the participation of
Canal+/Centre National
de la Cinématographie/Centre du
Cinéma et de
l'Audiovisuel/Communauté
Française de Belgique/Fonds
D'Action Sociale/La
Procirep/Ministère de la
Culture/La Sacem,

script developed with the support
of the European Script
Fund/Fondation Beaumarchais
102 minutes 26 seconds (subtitles)
S&S May 1998 p54

SAVING PRIVATE RYAN
United International Pictures (UK)
Ltd – 11 September
(15) USA, Dir Steven Spielberg
with Tom Hanks, Tom Sizemore,
Edward Burns, Barry Pepper, Adam
Goldberg
© Dream Works LLC and
Paramount Pictures Corporation
and Amblin Entertainment, Inc.
Paramount Pictures and Dream
Works Pictures present an Amblin
Entertainment
production in association with
Mutual Film Company, produced
with the support of
investment incentives for the Irish
film industry
169 minutes 37 seconds
S&S September 1998 p52

SAVIOR
First Independent Films Ltd –
19 June
(18) USA, Dir Peter Antonijevic
with Dennis Quaid, Nastassja Kinski,
Stellan Skarsgård, Natasa Ninkovic,
Pascal Rollin
© Savior Productions, Inc
Initial Entertainment Group
presents an Oliver Stone production
103 minutes 25 seconds
S&S July 1998 p51

The SCARLET TUNIC
Indy UK – Independent Feature
Film Distributors – 12 June
(12) UK, Dir Stuart St. Paul
with Jean-Marc Barr, Emma
Fielding, Simon Callow, Jack
Shepherd, John Sessions
© Scarlet Films PLC
A Scarlet Films PLC & The Bigger
Picture Company Ltd in
association with Scorpio
Productions Ltd production
92 minutes 5 seconds
S&S July 1998 p52

SCREAM 2
Buena Vista International – 1 May
(18) USA, Dir Wes Craven
with David Arquette, Neve Campbell,
Courteney Cox, Sarah Michelle
Gellar, Jamie Kennedy
© Miramax Film Corp.
A Dimension Films presentation, a
Konrad Pictures production in
association with Craven/
Maddalena Pictures
120 minutes 21 seconds
S&S May 1998 p55

The SECRET AGENT
20th Century Fox – 13 February
(12) USA/UK, Dir Christopher
Hampton
with Bob Hoskins, Patricia Arquette,
Gérard Depardieu, Jim Broadbent,
Christian Bale
© (UK) Capitol Films Ltd, (US)
Twentieth Century Fox Film
Corporation Capitol Films/Fox
Searchlight Pictures presents a
Heyman/Hoskins production
94 minutes 43 seconds
S&S April 1998 p52

SECRET DÉFENSE
Artificial Eye Company –
25 September
(PG) France/Switzerland/Italy, Dir
Jacques Rivette
with Sandrine Bonnaire, Jerzy
Radziwilowicz, Laure Marsac,
Grégoire Colin, Bernadette Giraud
© Pierre Grise Productions/La
Sept Cinéma /T & C Film AG
Pierre Grise Productions/La Sept
Cinéma (France)/ T & C Film AG
(Switzerland) with the
participation of Canal+/Sofica
Sofinergie 4, with the support of la
Procirep/Eurimages/Centre
National de la
Cinématographie/Programme
Media de l'Union
Européene/l'Office Fédéral de la
Culture of Départment Fédéral de
l'Intérieur (Switzerland)
173 minutes 27 seconds (subtitles)
S&S October 1998 p53

SHALL WE DANSU?
Buena Vista International – 8 May
(PG) Japan, Dir Masayuki Suo
with Koji Yakusho, Tamiyo Kusakari,
Naoto Takenaka, Eriko Watanabe,
Akira Emoto
© Daiei/NTV
Network/Hakuhodo/Nippon Shuppan
Altamura Pictures
118 minutes 52 seconds (subtitles)
S&S May 1998 p56

SHIGATSU MONOGATARI/APRIL STORY
Asian Film Library – 28 August
(not submitted) Japan,
Dir Shunji Iwai
with Takako Matsu, Seiichi Tanabe,
Kahori Fujii, Rumi, Kazuhiko Katô
© Rockwell Eyes
66 minutes 46 seconds (subtitles)
S&S October 1998 p38

bfi *SHIN HEIKE MONOGATARI/ TALES OF THE TAIRA CLAN
BFI – 20 February

(not submitted) Japan, Dir Kenji
Mizoguchi
with Raizo Ichikawa, Yoshiko Kuga,
Narutoshi Hayashi, Michiyo Kogure,
Ichijiro Oya
Daiei
108 minutes
MFB August 1973 p175

SIB/La POMME/The APPLE
Artificial Eye Film Company –
27 December
(PG) Iran/France, Dir Samirah
Makhmalbaf
with Massoumeh Naderi, Zahra
Naderi, Ghorban Ali-Naderi, Azizeh
Mohamadi, Zahra Sagharisaz,
Amir Hossein Khosrojerdi
© **MK2 Productions &**
Makhmalbaf Productions
85 minutes 19 seconds
S&S January 1999 p41

SICK THE LIFE & DEATH OF BOB FLANAGAN, SUPERMASOCHIST

BFI – **13 February**
(not submitted) USA, Dir Kirby Dick
with Bob Flanagan, Sheree Rose,
Cathy Flanagan, Bob Flanagan Sr,
Tim Flanagan, Sarah Doucette
© **Kirby Dick**
Funded in part with grants from
The Peter Norton Family
Foundation, Art Matters, Inc
90 minutes
S&S February 1998 p48

SIX DAYS SEVEN NIGHTS
Buena Vista International (UK) –
3 July
(12) USA, Dir Ivan Reitman
with Harrison Ford, Anne Heche,
David Schwimmer, Jacqueline
Obradors, Temuera Morrison
© **Touchstone Pictures**
Touchstone Pictures presents in
association with Caravan Pictures
a Roger Birnbaum/Northern
Lights Entertainment production
101 minutes 50 seconds
S&S August 1998 p53

SIXTH HAPPINESS
BFI Films – **2 October**
(not submitted) UK, Dir Waris
Hussein
with Firdaus Kanga, Souad Faress,
Khodus Wadia, Ahsen Bhatti, Indira
Varma
© **BBC and BFI**
BBC Films and the British Film
Institute present in association with
the Arts Council of England
a Kennedy Mellor production
supported by National Lottery

through the Arts Council of
England, developed by the BBC,
the BFI and with the support of the
European Script Fund
98 minutes 20 seconds
S&S October 1998 p54

SLIDING DOORS
United International Pictures (UK)
Ltd – **1 May**
(15) USA/UK, Dir Peter Howitt
with Gwyneth Paltrow, John Hannah,
John Lynch, Jeanne Tripplehorn, Zara
Turner
© **Mirage Enterprises and**
Intermedia Film Equities, Ltd
Paramount Pictures and Miramax
Films present in association with
Intermedia Films a
Mirage production, made with the
participation of British Screen
98 minutes 48 seconds
S&S June 1998 p55

SLING BLADE
Buena Vista International (UK) –
10 July
(15) USA, Dir Billy Bob Thornton
with Billy Bob Thornton, Dwight
Yoakam, J. T. Walsh, John Ritter,
Lucas Black
© **Sling Blade LLC**
A The Shooting Gallery presentation
134 minutes 39 seconds
S&S July 1998 p53

SLUMS OF BEVERLY HILLS
20th Century Fox (UK) –
27 November
(15) USA, Dir Tamara Jenkins
with Alan Arkin, Natasha Lyonne,
Kevin Corrigan, Jessica Walter, Rita
Moreno
© **Twentieth Century Fox Film**
Corporation
Fox Searchlight presents a South
Fork Pictures production
developed with the assistance
of the Sundance Institute
91 minutes 1 second
S&S December 1998 p61

SMALL SOLDIERS
United International Pictures (UK)
Ltd – **23 October**
(PG) USA, Dir Joe Dante
with Kirsten Dunst, Gregory Smith,
Jay Mohr, Phil Hartman, Kevin Dunn
© **Dream Works LLC/Universal**
City Studios, Inc/Amblin
Entertainment, Inc
A Universal Pictures and Dream
Works Pictures presentation
110 minutes 18 seconds
S&S October 1998 p55

SNAKE EYES
Buena Vista International (UK) –

6 November
(15) USA, Dir Brian De Palma
with Nicolas Cage, Gary Sinise, John
Heard, Carla Gugino, Stan Shaw
© **Paramount Pictures**
Corporation/Touchstone Pictures
Touchstone Pictures and
Paramount Pictures present a
DeBart production
98 minutes 14 seconds
S&S November 1998 p61

A SOLDIER'S DAUGHTER NEVER CRIES
Capitol Films – **9 October**
(15) UK, Dir James Ivory with
Virginie Ledoyen, Marie Henriau,
Samuel Gruen, LeeLee Sobieski,
Jesse Bradford
© **Merchant Ivory Productions Ltd**
Merchant Ivory Productions
presents in association with Capitol
Films and British Screen
126 minutes 50 seconds
S&S October 1998 p56

SOMETHING TO BELIEVE IN
Warner Brothers Distributors –
8 May
(PG) UK/Germany, Dir John Hough
with William McNamara, Maria
Pitillo, Tom Conti, Maria Schneider,
Ian Bannen
© **The Grade Company**
Lord Grade presents a co-
production with The Kirch Group
113 minutes 5 seconds
S&S May 1998 p57

SOUL FOOD
20th Century Fox (UK) – **12 June**
(15) USA, Dir George Tillman Jr.
with Vanessa L. Williams, Vivica A.
Fox, Nia Long, Michael Beach,
Mekhi Phifer
© **Twentieth Century Fox Film**
Corporation
Fox 2000 Pictures presents an
Edmonds Entertainment production
114 minutes 38 seconds
S&S July 1998 p53

The SPANISH PRISONER
Pathé Distribution Ltd – **28 August**
(PG) USA, Dir David Mamet
with Ben Gazzara, Felicity Huffman,
Ricky Jay, Steve Martin, Rebecca
Pidgeon
© **Jasmine Production,**
Inc/Sweetland Film B.V.
Sweetland Films presents a Jean
Doumanian production
110 minutes
S&S September 1998 p53

SPECIES II
United International Pictures (UK)
Ltd – **4 September**

USA, Dir Peter Medak
with Michael Madsen, Natasha
Henstridge, Marg Helgenberger,
Mykelti Williamson,
George Dzundza
© Metro-Goldwyn-Mayer Pictures
Inc
Metro-Goldwyn-Mayer Pictures
presents an FGM production
93 minutes 8 seconds
S&S September 1998 p53

SPHERE
Warner Bros – 3 April
(12) USA, Dir Barry Levinson
with Dustin Hoffman, Sharon Stone,
Samuel L. Jackson, Peter Coyote,
Queen Latifa
© Warner Bros
Warner Bros. presents a Baltimore
Pictures/Constant c production in
association with Punch Productions
134 minutes 5 seconds
S&S April 1998 p53

SREDA/WEDNESDAY 19.7.1961
Jane Balfour Films – 17 July
(not submitted)
Russia/Germany/UK/Finland, Dir
Viktor Kossakovsky
Roskomkino/Docstudios/Viola
Stephan Filmprodukten/Zweites
Deutsches Fernsehen/
BBC/YLE/Jane Balfour Films
93 minutes
No S&S reference

STAR KID
Entertainment Film Distributors
Ltd – 22 May
(PG) USA, Dir Manny Coto
with Joseph Mazzello, Richard
Gilliland, Corinne Bohrer, Alex
Daniels, Joey Simmrin
© Trimark Pictures, Inc
Trimark Pictures presents a Jennie
Lew Tugend/Trimark Pictures
production
100 minutes 45 seconds
S&S June 1998 p56

STARSHIP TROOPERS
Buena Vista – 2 January
(15) USA, Dir Paul Verhoeven
with Casper Van Dien, Dina Meyer,
Denise Richards, Jake Busey,
Neil Patrick Harris, Clancy Brown
© TriStar Pictures, Inc and
Touchstone Pictures
TriStar Pictures and Touchstone
Pictures present a Jon Davison
production
129 minutes 23 seconds
S&S January 1998 p53

 STELLA DOES TRICKS
BFI – 30 January
(18) UK, Dir Coky Giedroyc

with Kelly Macdonald, James Bolan,
Hans Matheson, Ewan Stewart,
Lindsay Henderson
© British Film Institute and
Channel Four Television
The British Film Institute and
Channel Four in association with
The Scottish Arts Council
Lottery Fund and the Scottish Film
Production Fund present a
Compulsive Films/Sidewalk
production, script developed by
BFI production, made with the
assistance from the
European Union's 16:9 Action Plan
98 minutes 31 seconds
S&S February 1998 p50

STIFF UPPER LIPS
Metrodome Distribution – 12 June
(15) UK, Dir Gary Sinyor
with Peter Ustinov, Prunella Scales,
Georgina Cates, Samuel West, Sean
Pertwee
© Ivory Hall Limited
A Cavalier Features/Impact
Pictures production in association
with Chrysalis Films
(UK), Yorkshire Films
International and the Isle of Man
Government
95 minutes 2 seconds
S&S July 1998 p54

STILL CRAZY
Columbia TriStar Films (UK) –
30 October
(15) USA/UK, Dir Brian Gibson
with Stephen Rea, Billy Connolly,
Jimmy Nail, Timothy Spall, Bill
Nighy
© Columbia Pictures Industries Inc
Columbia Pictures presents with the
participation of The Greenlight
Fund a Marmot Tandy production
supported by the National Lottery
through the Arts Council of England
95 min 35 seconds
S&S November 1998 p62

STOREFRONT HITCHCOCK
United International Pictures (UK)
Ltd – 13 November
(12) USA, Dir Jonathan Demme
with Robyn Hitchcock, Deni Bonet,
Tim Keegan
© Orion Pictures Corporation
Orion Pictures presents a Clinica
Estetico production
77 minutes 8 seconds
S&S January 1999 p57

TA'AME-GILAS/A TASTE OF CHERRY
Artificial Eye Film Company Ltd –
5 June
(PG) Iran, Dir Abbas Kiarostami
with Homayoon Irshadi, Abdol

Hossain Bagheri, Afshin Khorsid
Bakhtari, Safar Ali Moradi,
Mir Hossain Nouri
Abbas Kiarostami
99 minutes 8 seconds (subtitles)
S&S June 1998 p57

TELLING LIES IN AMERICA
First Independent – 3 April
(15) USA, Dir Guy Ferland
with Kevin Bacon, Brad Renfro,
Maximilian Schell, Calista Flockhart,
Paul Dooley
© Relevart, Inc.
Joe Eszterhas presents a Banner
Entertainment production in
association with Kuzui
Enterprises and Ben Myron
Productions
101 minutes 25 seconds
S&S April 1998 p54

*TEXAS CHAIN SAW MASSACRE
Blue Dolphin Film & Video –
11 December
(18) USA, Dir Tobe Hooper
with Marilyn Burns, Allen Danziger,
Paul A. Partain, William Vail, Teri
McMinn
Vortex
83 minutes 18 seconds
MFB December 1976 p258

THERE'S SOMETHING ABOUT MARY
20th Century Fox (UK) –
25 September
(15) USA, Dir Peter Farelly, Bobby
Farelly
with Cameron Diaz, Matt Dillon, Ben
Stiller, Lee Evans, Chris Elliott
© Twentieth Century Fox Film
Corporation
Twentieth Century Fox presents a
Farrelly Brothers movie
118 minutes 56 seconds
S&S October 1998 p57

THIS IS THE SEA
PolyGram – 13 February
(15) Ireland/USA/UK, Dir Mary
McGuckian
with Richard Harris, Gabriel Byrne,
John Lynch, Dearbhla Molloy, Ian
McElhinney
© Pembridge Pictures Limited
A Pembridge production,
developed with the support of the
European Script Fund,
produced with the financial
participation of Overseas
Filmgroup/Bord Scannàn na
hÉireann, produced with the
support of investment incentives
for the Irish film industry,
produced with

the participation of the European
Co-production fund (UK) and
Electric Pictures/PolyGram
Filmed Entertainment, made by
This is the Sea Limited for and on
behalf of Pembridge
Productions Limited and Judy
Counihan Films Limited
103 minutes 45 seconds
S&S March 1998 p55

A THOUSAND ACRES
PolyGram Filmed Entertainment –
12 June
(15) USA, Dir Jocelyn Moorhouse
with Michelle Pfeiffer, Jessica Lange,
Jennifer Jason Leigh, Colin Firth,
Keith Carradine
© Beacon Communications
Corp/Polygram Filmed
Entertainment, Inc
Touchstone Pictures present in
association with Propaganda Films
and Beacon Pictures
a Via Rosa/Prairie Films
production
105 minutes 23 seconds
S&S July 1998 p55

THURSDAY
PolyGram Filmed Entertainment –
25 September
(18) USA, Dir Skip Woods
with Thomas Jane, Aaron Eckhart,
Paulina Porizkova, James Le Gros,
Paula Marshall
© PolyGram Filmed
Entertainment, Inc.
PolyGram Filmed Entertainment
presents an Alan Poul production
87 minutes 29 seconds
S&S December 1998 p62

TITANIC
20th Century Fox – 23 January
(12) USA, Dir James Cameron
with Leonardo DiCaprio, Kate
Winslet, Billy Zane, Kathy Bates,
Frances Fisher
© Twentieth Century Fox Film
Corporation and Paramount
Pictures Corporation
Twentieth Century Fox and
Paramount Pictures present a
Lightstorm Entertainment
Production
194 minutes 36 seconds
S&S February 1998 p50

TO HAVE & TO HOLD
Metro Tartan Distribution –
7 August
(18) Australia, Dir John Hillcoat
with Tcheky Karyo, Rachel Griffiths,
Steve Jacobs, Anni Finsterer, David
Field
© Australian Film Finance
Corporation Pty Limited/Film
Victoria and Small Man

Productions Pty Ltd
A Small Man Production in
association with Calypso Films and
the Australian Film Finance
Corporation presentation,
produced with the assistance of the
QueenslandGovernment/Pacific
Film & Television Commission,
developed and produced with
the assistance of Film Victoria
99 minutes 32 seconds
S&S August 1998 p55

TOPLESS WOMEN TALK ABOUT THEIR LIVES
[Short season at the NFT courtesy
of New Zealand Film Commission]
– 9 October
(not submitted) New Zealand, Dir
Harry Sinclair
with Willa O'Neill, Danielle
Cormack, Stephen Lovatt, Andrew
Binns, Lucy Tucker
John Swimmer/New Zealand Film
Commission/New Zealand On Air
87 minutes
No S&S reference

TOUCH
Pathé Distribution Ltd – 10 July
(15) USA/France, Dir Paul Schrader
with Bridget Fonda, Christopher
Walken, Skeet Ulrich, Tom Arnold,
Gina Gershon
© Initial Productions
Lumière International presents a
Lila Gazès production
96 minutes 51 seconds
S&S June 1998 p58

TRAVELLER
First Independent – 30 January
(18) USA, Dir Jack Green
with Bill Paxton, Mark Wahlberg,
Julianna Margulies, James Gammon,
Luke Askew
© Traveler Production Company
L.L.C.
MDP Worldwide/October Films
presents a Banner Entertainment
production
100 minutes 26 seconds
S&S February 1998 p53

T-REX: BACK TO THE CRETACEOUS
Imax Corporation – 27 November
(U) USA, Dir Brett Leonard
with Peter Horton, Liz Stauber, Kari
Coleman, Laurie Murdoch, Tuck
Milligan
Imax Systems Corporation
45 minutes 47 seconds
IMAX
No S&S reference

The TRUMAN SHOW
United International Pictures (UK)
Ltd – 9 October

(PG) USA, Dir Peter Weir
with Jim Carrey, Laura Linney, Noah
Emmerich, Natascha McElhone,
Holland Taylor
© Paramount Pictures
Corporation
Paramount Pictures presents a
Scott Rudin production
102 minutes 54 seconds
S&S October 1998 p58

24 7 TWENTYFOURSEVEN
Pathé – 27 March
(15) UK, Dir Shane Meadows
Bob Hoskins, Mat Hand, Sun Hand,
Sarah Thom, Sammy Pasha
© BBC
BBC Films and Scala present a
Scala production for BBC Films
96 minutes 15 seconds (black and
white)
S&S April 1998 p55

TWILIGHT
United International Pictures (UK)
Ltd – 4 December
(15) USA, Dir Robert Benton
with Paul Newman, Susan Sarandon,
Gene Hackman, Stockard Channing,
Reese Witherspoon
© Paramount Pictures Corporation
Paramount Pictures presents a
Cinehaus production
94 minutes 33 seconds
S&S December 1998 p63

The TWILIGHT OF THE ICE NYMPHS
Alliance – 10 April
(not submitted) Canada, Dir Guy
Maddin
with Pascale Bussières, Shelley
Duvall, Frank Gorshin, Alice Krige,
R. H. Thomson
© Twilight Pictures Inc
Alliance Communications presents
a Marble Island picture, produced
with the participation
of Téléfilm Canada/Manitoba Film
and Sound Development
Corporation/The Harold
Greenberg Fund/The Government of
Canada/Canadian Film and Video
Production Tax Credit Program
91 minutes
S&S May 1998 p58

*UGETSU MONOGATARI
BFI Films – 6 February
(not submitted) Japan, Dir Kenji
Mizoguchi
with Masayuki Mori, Kinuyo Tanaka,
Ichisaburo Sawamura, Sakae Ozawa,
Mitsuko Mito
Daiei
96 minutes
MFB May 1962 p64

The UGLY

Metrodome – 27 February
(18) New Zealand, Dir Scott
Reynolds
with Paolo Rotondo, Rebecca Hobbs,
Roy Ward, Vanessa Byrnes, Sam
Wallace
© Essential Productions Ltd
The New Zealand Film
Commission, an Essential
Productions presentation
93 minutes 30 seconds
S&S March 1998 p56

ULEE'S GOLD

Feature Film Company – 3 April
(15) USA, Dir Victor Nunez
with Peter Fonda, Patricia
Richardson, Jessica Biel, J. Kenneth
Campbell, Christine Dunford
© Orion Pictures Corporation
Jonathan Demme presents a
Nunez-Gowan/Clinica Estetico
production
112 minutes 51 seconds
S&S April 1998 p56

UNAGI/The EEL

Metro Tartan Distributors –
20 November
(18) Japan, Dir Shohei Imamura
with Koji Yakusho, Misa Shimizu,
Fujio Tsuneta, Mitsuko Baisho,
Makoto Sato
© Eisei Gekijo (Satellite Cinema)
Co Ltd/KSS Films
Hisa Iino presents KSS Films/Eisei
Gekijo (Satellite Cinema) Co
Ltd/Groove Corp. in
association with Imamura
Productions a Shochiku Cinema
Japanesque presentation
108 minutes 59 seconds (subtitles)
S&S December p38,44

UN(c)UT

Millivres Multimedia – 29 May
(18) Canada, Dir John Greyson
with Michael Achtman, Damon
D'Oliveira, Matthew Ferguson,
Maria Reidstra, Alexandra Webb
© A Grey Zone production
A Grey Zone production, funding
by The Canada Council/The
Ontario Arts Council/The Toronto
Arts Council/Locarno Film Festival
Award/Telefilm Canada Award
(Montreal Film Festival)/Wexner
Center Media Arts Program (The
Ohio State University)
92 minutes 47 seconds
S&S October 1998 p59

UNDERGROUND

Creative Film Services Ltd –
4 December
(18) UK, Dir Paul Spurrier
with Billy Smith, Zoe Smale, Ian
Dury, Chrissie Cotterill, Nick Sutton

Creative Film Services Ltd
97 minutes 40 seconds
S&S August 1999 p53

Der UNFISCH

ICA – 22 May
(not submitted) Austria, Dir Robert
Dornhelm
with Karl Merkatz, Maria Schrader,
George Tabori, Eva Herzig, Andreas
Lust
Terra Film
98 minutes
No S&S reference

UP 'N' UNDER

Entertainment – 23 January
(12) UK, Dir John Godber
with Gary Olsen, Richard Ridings,
Samantha Janus, Ralph Brown, Neil
Morrissey
© Touchdown Film
Entertainment Film Distributors
presents a Touchdown film in
association with
Lluniau Lliw
98 minutes 30 seconds
Super 35
S&S February 1998 p54

U.S. MARSHALS

Warner Bros Distributors –
24 April
(15) USA, Dir Stuart Baird
with Tommy Lee Jones, Wesley
Snipes, Robert Downey Jr., Joe
Pantoliano, Daniel Roebuck
© Warner Bros
Warner Bros presents a Kopelson
Entertainment/Keith Barish
production
131 minutes
S&S June 1998 p58

U TURN

Buena Vista – 24 April
(18) USA/France, Dir Oliver Stone
with Sean Penn, Jennifer Lopez, Nick
Nolte, Powers Boothe, Claire Danes
© Phoenix Pictures
Phoenix Pictures presents an
Illusion Entertainment Group
production in
association with Clyde Is Hungry
Films in association with Canal+
Droits Audiovisuel
124 minutes 40 seconds
S&S May 1998 p58

VELVET GOLDMINE

Film Four Distributors Ltd –
23 October
UK/USA, Dir Todd Haynes
with Ewan McGregor, Jonathan Rhys
Meyers, Toni Collette, Christian
Bale, Eddie Izzard
© [UK/Eire] Channel Four
Television Corporation © [rest of
world] Velvet Goldmine

Productions
Ltd/Newmarket Capital LLC
A Zenith Productions/Killer Films
production in association with
Single Cell Pictures for Newmarket
Capital Group/Goldwyn
Films/Channel 4
123 minutes 31 seconds
S&S November 1998 p63

VIAGEM AO PRINCIPIO DO MUNDO/VOYAGE AU DÉBUT DU MONDE/JOURNEY TO THE BEGINNING OF THE WORLD

Artificial Eye Film Company – 26
June
(U) Portugal/France, Dir Manoel de
Oliveira
with Marcello Mastroianni, Jean-
Yves Gautier, Leonor Silveira, Diogo
Dória, Isabel de Castro
© Madragoa Filmes/Gemini Filmes
Paulo Branco presents a co-
production by Madragoa Filmes
and Gemini Filmes with the
participation of Instituto
Portugu|s da Arte
Cinematográfica e Audiovisual,
Radiotelevisi,o
Portuguesa/Canal+
94 minutes 56 seconds (subtitles)
S&S July 1998 p43

VICTORY

The Feature Film Company –
27 November
(15) UK/France/Germany, Dir Mark
Peploe
with Willem Dafoe, Sam Neill, Irène
Jacob, Rufus Sewell, Jean Yanne
© The Recorded Picture Company
Limited/UGC Images S.A./Studio
Babelsberg GmbH
UGC and RPC present a Recorded
Picture Company (UK)/UGC
Images (France)/Studio
Babelsberg/Extrafilm (Germany)
co-production with the support of
the Eurimages Fund of
the Council of Europe/Filmboard
Berlin-Brandenburg and with the
participation of British
Screen and Canal+ a Telescope
Films production
98 minutes 45 seconds
S&S December 1998 p64

La VIE DE JÉSUS/The LIFE OF JESUS

ICA Projects – 11 September
(not submitted) France, Dir Bruno
Dumont
with David Douche, Marjorie
Cottreel, Kader Chaatouf, Sébastien
Delbaere, Samuel Boidin
© 3B Productions/Norfilms

A 3B Productions/Norfilms/CRRAV co-production with the participation of Centre National de la Cinématographie, Ministère de la Culture/Canal+, with the support of la Procirep/Fondation Gan pour le Cinéma with help from la Région Nord/Pas de Calais
96 minutes (subtitles)
S&S September 1998 p55

La VIE R VÉE DES ANGES/The DREAM LIFE OF ANGELS
Gala Film Distributors – 16 October
(18) France, Dir Erick Zonca with Élodie Bouchez, Natacha Regnier, Grégoire Colin, Patrick Mercado, Jo Prestia
© Les Productions Bagheera/France 3 Cinéma/Diaphana/le CRRAV
A Les Productions Bagheera/France 3/Diaphana presentation with the participation of Centre National de la Cinématographie/Canal+ and the support of Conseil Régional du Centre/Fondation GAN pour le cinéma/Procirep with the support of Région Nord/Pas-de-Calais/Atelier de Production Centre Val de Loire Associate producer: Le Centre Régional des Ressources Audiovisuelles du Nord-Pas de Calais
Script development supported by Conseil Régional du Centre
113 minutes 21 seconds (subtitles)
S&S November 1998 p64

Le VIOLON DE ROTHSCHILD/ ROTHSCHILD'S VIOLIN/ ROTHSCHILDIN VIULU
(U)France/Switzerland/Finland/Hungary, Dir Edgardo Cozarinsky with Sergei Makovetsky, Dainius Kazlauskas, Miklós B. Székely, Mari Törocsik, Sándor Zsótér
© Les Films d'Ici/Imalyre – VTCOM France Télécom/La Sept – ARTE/CAB Productions/ Hansa Media/Hunnia Film Studio
Les Films d'Ici in co-production with Imalyre – VTCOM France Télécom/La Sept – ARTE (Paris)/CAB Productions (Lausanne)/Hansa Media (Helsinki), Hunnia Film Studio (Budapest)
with the participation of Fonds Eurimages/Office Fédéral de la Culture (DFI, Berne)/Centre

National de la Cinématographie/Fonds d'Action Sacem/Ministére de la Culture – Direction de la Musique et de la Danse/DOCUMENTARY-MEDIA programme with the support of Fondation d'entreprise France Télécom/Procirep
101 minutes 13 seconds (subtitles)
S&S April 1998 p51

Les VOLEURS/THIEVES
Metro/Tartan – 27 March
(18) France, Dir André Téchiné with Catherine Deneuve, Daniel Auteuil, Laurence Côte, BenoÔt Magimel, Fabienne Babe
© Les Films Alain Sarde/TFI Films Production/Rhône-Alpes Cinéma/D.A. Films
A co-production of Les Films Alain Sarde/TFI Films Production/Rhône-Alpes Cinéma/ D.A. Films with the participation of Région Rhône-Alpes/Centre National de la Cinématographie/ Canal+/Studio Images
116 minutes (subtitles)
S&S April p57

VOR/The THIEF
Artificial Eye Film Company Ltd – 17 July
(15) Russia/France, Dir Pavel Chukhrai with Vladimir Mashkov, Ekaterina Rednikova, Misha Filipchuk, Dima Chigarev, Amaliia Mordvinova
NTV-Profit (Russia)/Productions Le Pont (France)/Roissy Films (France) in association with The State Committee for Cinematography of the Russian Federation/Le Centre National de la Cinématographie (France)/Canal+ (France)
97 minutes 39 seconds (subtitles)
S&S August 1998 p54

WAG THE DOG
Entertainment – 13 March
(15) USA, Dir Barry Levinson with Dustin Hoffman, Robert De Niro, Anne Heche, Denis Leary, Willie Nelson
© New Line Productions, Inc
New Line Cinema presents a Tribeca/Baltimore Pictures/Punch production
97 minutes 2 seconds
S&S March 1998 p57

The WAR AT HOME
Metrodome Distribution Ltd – 26 June
(15) USA, Dir Emilio Estevez with Kathy Bates, Martin Sheen, Kimberly Williams, Emilio Estevez, Carla Gugino

© Avatar Entertainment, Inc
Touchstone Pictures presents an Avatar Entertainment production in association with Motion Picture Corporation of America
123 minutes 30 seconds
S&S August 1998 p56

WASHINGTON SQUARE
Buena Vista International – 29 May
(PG) USA, Dir Agnieszka Holland with Jennifer Jason Leigh, Albert Finney, Ben Chaplin, Maggie Smith, Judith Ivey
© Hollywood Pictures Company
Hollywood Pictures presents in association with Caravan Pictures a Roger Birnbaum production in association with Ann Dubinet (Alchemy Filmworks)
115 minutes 42 seconds
S&S June 1998 p59

*WAY OUT WEST
Vision Video Limited – 4 September
(U) USA, Dir James W. Horne with Stan Laurel, Oliver Hardy, Sharon Lynne, James Finlayson, Rosina Lawrence
Metro-Goldwyn Mayer Distributing Company presented by Hal Roach Studios
65 minutes 4 seconds
MFB May 1937 p105

The WEDDING SINGER
Entertainment Film Distributors Ltd – 5 June
(12) USA, Dir Frank Coraci with Adam Sandler, Drew Barrymore, Christine Taylor, Allen Covert, Angela Featherstone
© New Line Productions, Inc
New Line Cinema presents a Robert Simonds/Brad Grey production
96 minutes 33 seconds
S&S July 1998 p56

WESTERN
Artificial Eye – 8 May
(15) France, Dir Manuel Poirier with Sergi Lopez, Sacha Bourdo, Elisabeth Vitali, Marie Matheron, Daphné Gaudefroy D
© Salomé-Diaphana
A co-production of Salomé-Diaphana with the participation of Canal+/Le Centre National de la Cinématographie/sofica Sofinergie 4 with the support of Procirep
133 minutes 57 seconds (subtitles)
S&S May 1998 p59

WHAT DREAMS MAY COME
PolyGram Filmed Entertainment –

26 December
(15) USA/New Zealand, Dir Vincent Ward
with Robin Williams, Cuba Gooding Jr., Annabella Sciorra, Max von Sydow , Jessica Brooks Grant
© PolyGram Filmed Entertainment, Inc
PolyGram Filmed Entertainment presents an Interscope Communications production in association
with Metafilmics
113 minutes 18 seconds
S&S January 1999 p60

WILD MAN BLUES
Film Four Distributors – 8 May
(12) USA, Dir Barbara Kopple
with Woody Allen, Soon-Yi Previn, Letty Aronson, Jean Doumanian, John Doumanian
© Magnolia Productions, Inc and Sweetland Films, B.V.
Cabin Creek Films, Inc
105 minutes 24 seconds
S&S May 1998 p60

WILD THINGS
Entertainment Film Distributors Ltd – 15 May
(18) USA, Dir John McNaughton
with Kevin Bacon, Matt Dillon, Neve Campbell, Theresa Russell, Denise Richards
© Mandalay Entertainment
A Mandalay Entertainment presentation
107 minutes 50 seconds
S&S July 1998 p57

The WINGS OF THE DOVE
Buena Vista – 2 January
(15) USA/UK, Dir Iain Softley
with Helena Bonham Carter, Linus Roache, Alison Elliott, Elizabeth McGovern,
Michael Gambon, Alex Jennings
© Miramax Films and Renaissance Dove Ltd
Miramax Films presents a Renaissance Films production
101 minutes 50 seconds
S&S January 1998 p55

The WINNER
Feature Film Company – 23 January
(15) USA/Australia, Dir Alex Cox
with Rebecca DeMornay, Vincent D'Onofrio, Richard Edson, Saverio Guerra, Delroy Lindo
© Winner Productions Inc
Mark Damon Productions presents in association with Village Roadshow-Clipsal Films Partnership a Ken Schwenker production
88 minutes 54 seconds
S&S February 1998 p55

The WINTER GUEST
Film Four Distributors – 9 January
(15) USA/UK, Dir Alan Rickman
with Phyllida Law, Emma Thompson, Sheila Reid, Sandra Voe, Arlene Cockburn,
Gary Hollywood
© Pressman Lipper Productions
Film Four Distribution presents in association with Fine Line Features/Capitol Films/
The Scottish Arts Council National Lottery Fund a Pressman Lipper production for
Capitol Films/Fine Line Features/Channel Four Films with the participation of The Scottish Film Production Fund
109 minutes 43 seconds
S&S January 1998 p56

The WISDOM OF CROCODILES
Entertainment Film Distributors Ltd – 27 November
(18) UK, Dir Po Chih Leong
with Jude Law, Elina Löwensohn, Timothy Spall, Kerry Fox, Jack Davenport
© Zenith Productions Limited
Goldwyn Films International/Film Foundry Partners/Entertainment Film Distributors/Zenith Productions in association with the Arts Council of England present a Zenith film developed in association with Robert Jones supported by the National Lottery through the Arts Council of England developed with the support of the European Script Fund
98 minutes 37 seconds
S&S January 1999 p61

WISHMASTER
First Independent Films Ltd – 29 May
(18) USA, Dir Robert Kurtzman
with Tammy Lauren, Andrew Divoff, Kane Hodder, Tony Todd, Robert Englund
© LIVE Film and Mediaworks Inc
Wes Craven presents a Pierre David production
89 minutes 53 seconds
S&S June 1998 p61

Das WISSEN VOM HEILEN/The KNOWLEDGE OF HEALING
Artificial Eye Film Company – 13 November
(PG) Switzerland, Dir Franz Reichle
with H. H. Tenzin Gyatso [XIV Dalai Lama of Tibet], Tenzin Choedrak, Chimit-Dorzhi Dugarov, Karl Lutz, Alfred Hässig
© T&C Film Aä

T&C Film AG presents a film by Franz Reichle in collaboration with Schweizer Fernsehen DRS/Kulturfond Suissimage/Teleclub with contributions from Bundesamt für Kultur des Eidg. Departementes des Innern/Stadt und Kanton Zürich/Studiengruppe für Tibetische Medizin/Fondation Paraggi/Migros Kulturprozent/Hans Eggenberger Stiftung/Deh, Direktion für Entwicklungszusammen arbeit und Humanitäre Hilfe (Berne)/Zuger Kulturstiftung Landis & Gyr/Volkart Stiftung/Alfred Richterich Stiftung/Gemeinde Küsnacht/Beat Curti/Fritz Steiner
93 minutes 11 seconds (subtitles)
S&S December 1998 p48

WOO
Entertainment Film Distributors Ltd – 25 September
(15) USA, Dir Daisy V. S. Mayer
with Jada Pinkett Smith, Tommy Davidson, Dave Chappelle, Paula Jai Parker, LL Cool J
© New Line Productions, Inc.
New Line Cinema presents a New Deal/Gotham Entertainment production
84 minutes 34 seconds
S&S October 1998 p60

The WOODLANDERS
Pathé Distribution Ltd (UK) – 6 February
(PG) UK, Dir Phil Agland
with Rufus Sewell, Polly Walker, Jodhi May, Tony Haygarth, Cal MacAninch
© Channel Four Television Corporation/Pathe Productions Limited
Channel Four Films and Pathe Productions Ltd present in association with the Arts Council of England a River Films production supported by the National Lottery through the Arts Council of England
97 minutes 37 seconds
S&S February 1998 p56

WRITTEN ON THE WIND
BFI – 2 January
(PG) USA, Dir Douglas Sirk
with Rock Hudson, Lauren Bacall, Robert Stack, Dorothy Malone, Robert Keith
© Universal Pictures Company, Inc
Universal-International presentation
99 minutes 43 seconds
MFB November 1956 p139

The X FILES
20th Century Fox (UK) – 21
August
(15) USA, Dir Rob Bowman
with David Duchovny, Gillian
Anderson, John Neville, William B.
Davis, Martin Landau
© Twentieth Century Fox Film
Corporation
Twentieth Century Fox presents a
Ten Thirteen production
121 minutes 35 seconds
S&S September 1998 p55

YEAR OF THE HORSE
NEIL YOUNG AND CRAZY
HORSE LIVE
Artificial Eye Film Company –
4 December
(15) USA, Dir Jim Jarmusch
with Ralph Molina, Frank 'Poncho'
Sampedro, Billy Talbot, Neil Young,
Elliot Roberts
© Shakey Pictures
A Shakey Pictures presentation
107 minutes 18 seconds
S&S December 1998 p65

YIGE HAO REN/MR. NICE
GUY
Entertainment Film Distributors
Ltd – 28 August
(15) Hong Kong, Dir Samo Hung
[Hung Kam-Bo]
with Jackie Chan [Sing Lung],
Richard Norton, Miki Lee [Lee Ting-
Yee], Karen McLymont,
Gabrielle Fitzpatrick
© 1996 Golden Harvest Pictures Ltd
A Golden Harvest presentation, a
Leonard Ho [Ho Koon-Cheung]
production
88 minutes 8 seconds
S&S September 1998 p49

ZERO EFFECT
Warner Bros Distributors (UK) –
7 August
(15) USA, Dir Jake Kasdan
with Bill Pullman, Ben Stiller, Ryan
O'Neal, Kim Dickens, Angela
Featherstone
A Columbia Pictures/Castle Rock
Entertainment production of a
Manifest Film
Company production
115 minutes 58 seconds
S&S September 1998 p57

SPECIALISED GOOD AND SERVICES

This section has been divided into four parts. The first part features services specialising in actors, audiences and casting. The second is lists costume, make-up and prop services. The third section is a general section of specialised goods and services for the film, television and video industries including such items as film stock suppliers, effects units and music services. The final section combines legal and business services for the industry

Actors, Audiences and Casting

Avalon Publicity Limited
4a Exmoor Street
Lonodn W10 6BD
Tel: 020 7598 7222
Fax: 020 7598 7223
Zoe Godfrey
Provides audiences for TV productions

Bromley Casting (Film & TV Extras Agency)
77 Widmore Road
Bromley BR1 3AA
Tel: 020 8 466 8239
Fax: 020 8 466 8239
Website: www.showcall.co.uk
Providing quality background artisits to the UK film and TV industry

Central Casting Inc
13-14 Dean Street
London W1
Tel: 020 7437 4211

Dolly Brook Casting Agency
52 Sandford Road
East Ham
London E6 3QS
Tel: 020 8472 2561/470 1287
Fax: 020 8552 0733
Russell Brook
Specialises in walk-ons, supporting artistes, extras and small parts for films, television, commercials, modelling, photographic, voice-overs, pop videos

Downes Agency
96 Broadway
Bexleyheath
Kent DA6 7DE
Tel: 020 8304 0541
Fax: 020 8301 5591
Agents representing presenters and actors experienced in the fields of presentations, documentaries, commentaries, narrations, television dramas, feature films, industrial videos, training films, voice-overs, conferences and commercials

Lip Service Casting
4 Kingly Street
London W1R 5LF
Tel: 020 7734 3393
Fax: 020 7734 3373
Susan Mactavish
Voiceover agency for actors, and voiceover casting agency

Stone Casting Marcus
Georgian House
5 The Pavilions
Brighton BN2 1RA
Tel: 01273 670053
Fax: 01273 670053
Supplies television, film extras. Up to 1,000 extras available for crowd scenes

Costumes, Make-up and Props

Angels – The Costumiers
40 Camden Street
London NW1 OEN
Tel: 020 7 387 0999
Fax: 020 7 383 5603
email: angelscos.co.uk
Chairman: Tim Angel OBE
Contact: Richard Green
Contact: Jonathan Lipman
World's largest Costume Hire Company. Extensive ranges covering every historical period, including contemporary clothing, civil and military uniforms. Full in-house ladies and men's making service, millinery department, jewellry, glasses and watch hire. Branches also in Shaftesbury Avenue and Paris. Additional services:- experinced personal costumiers, designers office space, reference library and shipping department

Angels Wigs
40 Camden Street
London NW1 0EN
Tel: 020 7 387 0999
Fax: 020 7 383 5603
email: wigs@angelsacos.co.uk
Ben Stanton
All types of styles of wigs and hairpieces in either human hair bespoke or synthetic ready-to-wear. Large stocks held, ready to dress, for hire including legal wigs. In house craftsmen to advise on style or period. Facial hair made to order for sale

Cabervans
Caberfeidh
Cloch Road
Gourock
Nr. Glasgow PA19 1BA
Tel: 01475 638775
Fax: 01475 638775
Make-up and wardrobe units, dining coaches, motorhomes 3 & 4 bay artistes caravans, generators, toilets. One stop transport source in Scotland

European Communications & Media Ltd
Glinton

Milton Avenue
Gerrards Cross
Bucks SL9 8QW
Tel: 01753 888 880
Fax: 01753 888 886
email: info@ecml.demon.co.uk
Website: www.ecml.demon.co.uk
Robin Jathan
Prop suppliers, product placement,
branding, action vehicles

Faunus The Florists
Interior and Exterior Floral Design
69 Walmgate
York YO1 2TZ
Tel: 01904 613044
Contact: Robert Hale
Suppliers and designers of interior
floral decoration

Hirearchy Classic and Contemporary Costume
45 Palmerston Road
Boscombe
Bournemouth
Dorset BH1 4HW
Tel: 01202 394465
Specialising in the hire of ladies and
gents costumes from medieval to
present day. Also accessories, make-
up, wigs, militaria jewellery, textiles
and luggage

Hothouse Models & Effects
Design House
252 Western Avenue
Acton
London W3 6XJ
Tel: 020 8896 9070
Fax: 020 8896 9060
email: jezclarke@hothousefx.co.uk
Website: www.hothousefx.co.uk
Jeremy Clarke
All models props and effects for film
and television

Kevin Jones, Freelance Costume Designer & Assistant
32 Austen Walk
West Bromwich
West Midlands B71 1RD
Tel: (021) 586 6801
Costume designers, wardrobe for
films, television, commercials and
pop videos

Ten Tenths
106 Gifford Street
London N1 0DF
Tel: 020 7607 4887
Fax: 020 7609 8124
Props service specialising in vehicles
(cars, bikes, boats and planes)
ranging from 1901 to present day –
veteran, vintage, classic, modern
with complementary wardrobe
facilities

Film Services

Agfa-Gevaert
Motion Picture Division
27 Great West Road
Brentford
Middx TW8 9AX
Tel: 020 8 231 4301
Fax: 020 8 231 4315
Major suppliers to the Motion Picture
and Television Industries of Polyester
based Colour Print Film and Optical
Sound Recording Film

Any Effects
64 Weir Road
London SW19 8UG
Tel: 020 8944 0099
Fax: 020 8944 6989
Contact: Julianne Pellicci
Managing Director: Tom Harris
Mechanical (front of camera) special
effects. Pyrotechnics: simulated
explosions, bullet hits. Fine models
for close up camera work. Weather:
rain, snow, fog, wind. Breakaways:
shatterglass, windows, bottles,
glasses, collapsing furniture, walls,
floors. Specialised engineering rigs
and propmaking service

Bennett Underwater Productions Charlie
114 Addison Gardens
West Kensington
London W14 0DS
Tel: 020 7371 1964
email: chazben@aol.com
Ifafa, Main Street
Ashby Parva
Leicestershire LE17 5HU
Tel: 01455 209 405
Mobile: 0402 263 952
Contact: Charlie Bennett
Underwater services to the film and
television industry, including
qualified diving personnel and
equipment; underwater video, stills
photography and scuba instruction.
Advice, logistics and support offered
on an international scale with fluency
in Spanish, Portuguese, and French.
Registered HSE Diving contractor

Bonded Services

Aerodrome Way
Cranford Lane
Hounslow
Middx TW5 9QB
Tel: 020 8897 7973
Fax: 020 8897 7979
Inventory management, worldwide
freight, courier services, technical
facilities including film checking and
tape duplication, storage and distribution

Boulton-Hawker Films

Hadleigh
Ipswich
Suffolk IP7 5BG
Tel: 01473 822235
Fax: 01473 824519
Time-lapse, cinemicrography and
other specialised scientific filming
techniques

Connections Communications Centre Ltd

Palingswick House
241 King Street
Hammersmith
London W6 9LP
Tel: 020 8741 1767
Fax: 020 8563 1934
email: @cccmedia.demon.co.uk
Jacqueline Davis

A registered charity producing
promotional and educational videos
for the voluntary sector. Currently in
production Travelling Forward a 25
minute documentary commissioned
by the Thalidomide Society

Cool Million

Mortimer House
46 Sheen Lane
London SW14 8LP
Tel: 020 8878 7887
Fax: 020 8878 8687
Dot O'Rourke
Promotional merchandising, launch
parties and roadshows

De Wolfe Music

Shropshire House
2nd Floor East
11/20 Capper Street
London WC13 6JA
Tel: 020 7631 3600
Fax: 020 7631 3700
email: dewolfe_Music@
Compuserve.com
Warren De Wolfe, Alan Howe
World's largest production music
library. Represents 25 composers for
commissions, television and film
scores. Offices worldwide, sound FX
department, 3 x 24-track recording

studies all with music to picture
facilities, also digital editing

Diverse Design

Gorleston Street
London W14 8XS
Tel: 020 7603 4567
Fax: 020 7603 2148
email: design@diverse.co.uk
Daniel Creasey (Senior Producer)
Graphic design for television
including titles, format and content
graphics. Recent work: *The Lakes,
Cold War, Bad Blood, Booked,
Dispatches (Strand Titles), Badger,
An Unsuitable Job for a Woman,*

EOS Electronics AV

EOS House
Weston Square
Barry
South Glamorgan CF63 2YF
Tel: 01446 741212
Fax: 01446 746120
Specialist manufacturers of video
animation, video time laspsing and
video archiving equipment. Products:
Supertoon Low Cost School
Animation System, AC 580 Lo-band
Controller, BAC900 Broadcast
Animation Controller, LCP3
Compact Disc, Listening Posts

ETH Screen Music
17 Pilrig Street
Edinburgh EH6 5AN
Tel: 0131 553 2721
Harald Tobermann
Producer and publisher of original
music for moving images. Complete
creative team – composers, arrangers,
musicians

Eureka Location Management
51 Tonsley Hill
London SW18 1BW
Tel: 020 8870 4569
Fax: 020 8871 2158
Suzannah Holt
Finds and manages locations for film
and television in Britain and abroad.
Offices in London and Toronto

The Film Stock Centre Blanx
70 Wardour Street
London W1V 3HP
Tel: 020 7494 2244
Fax: 020 7287 2040
D John Ward
ndependent distributor of major
manufacturers' motion picture film
stock, professional video tape,
Polaroid, audio tape, related
products. Impartial advice,
competitive prices, SOR, special
deals for low-budgets. Weekdays
9.00am to 6.30pm

Harkness Hall Ltd
The Gate Studios
Station Road
Borehamwood
Herts WD6 1DQ
Tel: 020 8953 3611
Fax: 020 8207 3657
email: sales@harknesshall.com
Ian Sim, Robert Pickett
Projection screens and complete screen
systems, fixed and portable, front or
rear, flat, curved, flying, roller etc.
Curtain tracks, festoons, cycloramas,
raise and lower equipment, stage
equipment, installation and maintenance

Kodak Limited
Professional Motion Imaging
PO Box 66
Hemel Hempstead
Herts HP1 1JU
Tel: 01442 61122
Fax: 01442 844458
A Kennedy
Suppliers of the full range of Kodak
colour negative and print films,
including the new family of Vision
colour negative films

MBS Underwater Video Specialists
1 Orchard Cottages
Coombe Barton
Shobrooke, Crediton
Devon
Tel: 01363 775 278
Fax: 01363 775 278
email: mbscm@mail.eclipse.co.uk
Website: www.eclipse.co.uk.mbs
Contact: Colin Munro
MBS provides underwater stills
photography and videography
services, specialising in underwater
wildlife shots. We can provide full
HSE registered dive teams for UK
based work, and cover all aspects of
diving safety and support, vessel
servicing and specialist underwater
equipment supply

Media Education Agency
5A Queens Parade
Brownlow Road
London N11 2DN
Tel: 020 8888 4620
David Lusted
Consultancy, lectures and teacher in-
service education (INSET) in film,
television and media studies.
Contacts include academics,
educationists, broadcasters, writers
and actors

Midland Fire Protection Services
256 Foleshill Road
Coventry CV6 5AB
Tel: 024 7668 5252 (mobile) 0836
651408
Fax: 024 7663 7575
Specialists in fire and rescue cover
for location, studio and stage work.
Special services, firefighters, action
vehicles, fully equipped fire and
rescue appliances, 5,000 gallons of
water storage systems available,
throughout the UK 24 hour service

Moving Image Touring Exhibition Service (MITES)

Foundation For Art & Creative Technology (FACT)
Bluecoat Chambers
Liverpool L1 3BX
Tel: 0151 707 2881
Fax: 0151 707 2150
email: mites@fact.co.uk
Website: www.mites.org.uk
Simon Bradshaw
Courses for artists, gallery curators, technicians and exhibitors concerned with the commissioning and presentation of moving image art works. Also development, advice, consultation services, an extensive exhibition equipment resource, DVD authority and production

Oxford Scientific Films (OSF)

Lower Road
Long Hanborough
Oxford OX8 8LL
Tel: 01993 881 881
Fax: 01993 882 808
email: osf_ltd@compuserve.com
45-49 Mortimer Street
London W1N 7TD
Tel: 020 7323 0061
Fax: 020 7323 0161
Independent production company specialising in blue-chip natural history documentaries for broadcast. 30 years of experience and innovation in specialist camera techniques

Pirate Motion Control

St Leonards Road
London NW10 6ST
Tel: 020 8930 5000
Fax: 020 8930 5001
email: help@pirate.co.uk
Web: http://www.pirate.co.uk
Michael Ganss
Pirate Motion Control have the largest, most versatile video motion control studio facility in the UK. Located near AFM

ProDigital Audio Services

3 George Street
West Bay
Dorset DT6 4EY
Tel: 01308 422 866
Sound equipment, service and maintenance. Specialises in location sound equipment for the film and television industry – particularly DAT recorders

Radcliffes Transport Services

3-9 Willow Lane
Willow Lane Industrial Estate
Mitcham
Surrey CR4 4NA

Tel: 020 8687 2344
Fax: 020 8687 0997
Ken Bull
Specialist transport specifically for the film and television industry, both nationally and internationally. Fleet ranges from transit vans to 40' air ride articulated vehicles with experienced staff

The Screen Company

182 High Street
Cottenham
Cambridge CB4 4RX
Tel: 01954 250139
Fax: 01954 252005
Manufacture, supply and installation of all types of front and rear projection screens for video, slide, film and OHP

Security Archives Ltd

1-8 Capitol Park
Capitol Way
London NW9 0EQ
Tel: 020 8205 5544
Fax: 020 8200 1130
Secure storage for film, video and audio tape in bomb-proof vaults with thermohydrographic controls and Halon fire suppression. 24hr collection and delivery, computerised, bar-coded management and tracking of clients' material

Snow-Bound

37 Oakwood Drive
Heaton
Bolton BL1 5EE
Tel: 01204 841285
Fax: 01204 841285
Suppliers of artificial snow and the machinery to apply it for the creation of snow/winter scenes. The product is life-like (not poly beads or cotton wool) adheres to any surface and is fire-retardant, non-toxic and safe in use, and eco-friendly

Stanley Productions

36 Newman Street
London W1P 3PD
Tel: 020 7636 5770
Fax: 020 7636 5660
Richard Hennessy
Europe's largest distributor of video tape and equipment. Full demonstration facilities with independent advice on suitable equipment always available

Wrap it up

116a Acton Lane,
Chiswick
London W4 5HH
Tel: 020 8995 3357 (Mobiles 0973 198154)
Fax: 020 82348 3030

Wrap it up provides production services which include transcription, post production scripts, voice scripts and logging of rushes for production companies. Recent work: September Films – Teenagers British lifestyles – Transcription and Post Production Scripts. Horizon BBC – Transcription. Dennis and Gnasher, Tony Collingwood Productions – Voice Scripts

Zooid Pictures Limited

66 Alexander Road
London N19 5PQ
Tel: 020 7281 2407
Fax: 020 7281 2404
email: pictures@zooid.co.uk
Website: www.zooid.co.uk
Richard Philpott
For over 20 years, Zooid has been a one-stop media resources supplier and researcher for all copyright materials including film/video, stills, illustration, animation and sound, from archives, libraries, agencies, private collections and museums worldwide, for use in film, television, book publishing, CD-Rom, multimedia, presentations and on-line services. Zooid manage all aspects from first briefing through to licensing Zooid use advanced digital technologists and license their management system, Picture Desk, to leading international publishers

Legal and Business Services

Ashurst Morris Crisp
Broadwalk House
5 Appold Street
London EC2A 2HA
Tel: 0207 638 1111
Fax: 0207 972 7990
email: film.tv@ashursts.com
Website: www.ashursts.com
Tony Ghee, Tasha Stanford, Andrea Fessler, Charlotte Douglas, Vanessa Bertelli
Leading City law firm with a young and progressive media and telecommunications team. Advice is provided on all aspects of the film and television industry, including corporate, employment, property and tax issues. Clients include leading national broadcasters, cable network operators and a number of small independents

Barclays Bank Media Banking Centre
27 Soho Square
London W1A 4WA
Tel: 020 7445 5773 or 020 7445 5777
Fax: 020 7445 5784
Geoff Salmon or Clare Gamble
Large business centre providing a comprehensive range of banking services to all aspects of the film and television industry

Calibre Films
187 Wardour Street
London W1V 3FA
Tel: 020 7437 1552
Fax: 020 7437 1558
email: info@hexgo.ftech.co.uk
Contacts: Adam Sutcliffe and Paul Grindey
Offers experience in all aspects of the negotiation and drafting of agreements, film production, film financing and international co-productions, with an emphasis on concise and effective documents, and a practical 'business affairs' approach to legal matters for all those involved in the film-making and distribution process

Deloitte & Touche
Hill House
1 Little New Street
London EC4A 3TR
Tel: 020 7936 3000
Fax: 020 7583 8517/1198
Gavin Hamilton-Deeley, Robert Reed
Advisors to film, television and broadcasting organisations. Business plans and financial models for companies, tax planning and business advice for individuals, and information on legal and regulatory developments affecting the sector

Film Finances
1-11 Hay Hill
Berkeley Square
London W1X 7LF
Tel: 020 7629 6557
Fax: 020 7491 7530
G J Easton, J Shirras, D Wilder, H Penallt Jones
Provide completion guarantees for the film and television industry

Henry Hepworth
Media Law Solicitors
5 John Street
London WC1N 2HH
Tel: 020 7242 7999
Fax: 020 7242 7988
Michael Henry
A new specialist media and intellectual property practice with a distinctive high quality client base which is active across the entire spectrum of the copyright and intellectual property industries

Nicholson Graham & Jones
110 Cannon Street
London EC4N 6AR
Tel: 020 7648 9000
Fax: 020 7648 9001
Annmarie Pryor, Marketing Manager
A City law firm and founder member of the international GlobaLex network in the UK, USA, Europe and the Far East. The Intellectual Property Group handles film and television production, financing and distribution, cable, satellite and telecommunications work, book and newspaper publishing, syndication, advertising, merchandising, sponsorship and sports law. Also advise on technology transfer, patent, trade mark, service mark, know-how arrangements and franchising as well as computer hardware and software agreements and all intellectual property copyright, moral and performers' right issues

Olswang
90 Long Acre
London WC2E 9TT
Tel: 020 7208 8888
Fax: 020 7208 8800
email: olsmail@olswang.co.uk
Website: www.olswang.co.uk
One of the UK's leading entertainment and media law firms. It provides specialist advice in all aspects of broadcasting, satellite, cable, multimedia, IT & telecommunications, media convergence and music law, to the European and US markets

Richards Butler
Beaufort House
15 St Botolph Street
London EC3A 7EE
Tel: 020 7247 6555
Fax: 020 7247 5091
email: law@richards-butler.com
Richard Philipps, Barry Smith, Stephen Edwards, Martin Boulton
Richards Butler is an international law firm which has been associated with the media and entertainment industry for over 60 years

STUDIOS

BBC Television Centre Studios
Wood Lane
London W12 7RJ
Tel: 020 8576 7666
Fax: 020 8576 8806
8 full-facility television studios
TC1   10,250 sq ft
TC3   8,000 sq ft
TC4 and TC8   8,000 sq ft (digital and widescreen capable)
TC6   8,000 sq ft (digital)
TC2, TC5 and TC7 3,500 sq ft

The Boilerhouse
8 Nursery Road
Brixton
London SW9 8BP
Tel: 020 7737 7777
Fax: 020 7737 5577
Clive Howard, Michael Giessler
100 sq metre studio, dry/wet stage, special effect facilities, variable tank systems, rain rigs. Productions: Adidas, Cadbury Chocolate ads

Bray Studios
Down Place
Water Oakley
Windsor Road
Windsor SL4 5UG
Tel: 01628 622111
Fax: 01628 770381
Studio manager: Beryl Earl
STAGES
1 (sound) 955 sq metres
2 (sound) 948 sq metres
3 (sound) 238 sq metres
4 (sound) 167 sq metres
Murder Most Horrid, Talkback; *Midsummer Nights Dream*, Edenwood Productions; *Emma*, Mai Productions; *Mojo*, Portobello Pictures; *Velvet Goldmine*, Velvet Goldmine Productions Ltd

Capital FX
21A Kingly Court
London W1R 5LE
Tel: 020 7439 1982
Fax: 020 7734 0950
email: enquiries@capital.fx.co.uk
Website:www.capital.fx.co.uk
Graphic design and production, optical effects, film and laser subtitling

De Lane Lea Dean Street Studio
75 Dean Street
London W1V 5HA

Tel: 020 7439 1721/ 020 7432 3877 (direct line 24 hours)
Fax: 020 7437 0913
Studio manager: Dick Slade
STAGE
1 86 sq metres
40x23x18 SYNC
lighting rig, film and TV make-up rooms, one wardrobe, one production office, full fitted kitchen

Ealing Studios
Ealing Studios
Ealing Green
London W5 5EP
Tel: 020 8567 6655
Fax: 020 8758 8658
email: info@ealing-studios.co.uk
Operations Department
STAGES
1 (silent) – bluescreen/motion control = area 232m2
2 (sound) – 864m2
3A (sound) 530m2
3B (sound) 530m2
3A/B 9combined) 1,080m2
4 (model stage silent) 390,2
5 (sound) 90m2
FILMS
Wisdom of Crocodiles
East is East
Titanic Town
Mansfield Town
TELEVISION
Vanity Fair (BBC), *Murder Most Horrid* (Talkback for BBC2), *Bramwell* (Whitby Davison for Carlton), *A Christmas Carol* (Hallmark for TNT)

Halliford Studios
Manygate Lane
Shepperton
Middx TW17 9EG
Tel: 01932 226341
Fax: 01932 246336
Charlotte Goddard
STAGES
A 334 sq metres
B 223 sq metres

Holborn Studios
49/50 Eagle Wharf Road
London N1 7ED
Tel: 020 7490 4099
Fax: 020 7253 8120
Studio manager: Ivan Merrell
STAGES
4 2,470 sq feet
6 2,940 sq feet

7 2,660 sq feet
18 roomsets 3,125 sq feet
Also eight fashion studios, set building, E6 lab, b/w labs, KJP in house, canal-side restaurant and bar. Productions; National Lottery Stills; Advertisements for Scratch cards; Saatchis – photographer Dave Stewart

Isleworth Studios
Studio Parade
484 London Road
Isleworth
Middx TW7 4DE
Tel: 020 8568 3511
Fax: 020 8568 4863
STAGES
A 292 sq metres
B 152 sq metres
C 152 sq metres
D 152 sq metres

Lamb Studio
Bell Media Group
Lamb House
Church Street
Chiswick Mall
London W4 2PD
Tel: 020 8996 9960
Fax: 020 8996 9966
email: paul@belmedia.demon.co.uk
Sound proofed, air-conditioned studio. Total floor area of 575 sq ft. Average ceiling height of 12ft. Free parking, production office, kitchen, make-up room. Easy, access from central London, M4, M3 and M25. Ideal for talking heads, interviews, small dramas, pack shots, motion control, training. Post-production facilities also available

Leavesden Studios
PO Box 3000
Leavesden
Herts WD2 7LT
Tel: 01923 685 060
Fax: 01923 685 061
Studio Manager: Daniel Dark
STAGES
A 32,076sq feet
B 28,116 sq feet
C 11,285 sq feet
D 11,808 sq feet
F 15,427 sq feet
G 14,036 sq feet
Flight Shed 1 35,776
Effects 15,367 sq feet
Back Lot   100 acres

180 degrees of clear and uninterrupted horizon
Further 200,000 sq.ft of covered space available

FILMS
GoldenEye, Mortal Kombat, Annihilation; Sleepy Hollow, Star Wars: Episode One – The Phantom Menance, An Ideal Husband

Millennium Studios
Elstree Way
Herts WD6 1SF
Tel: 020 8236 1400
Fax: 020 8236 1444
Contact: Ronan Willson
'X' Stage: 327 sq metres sound stage with flying grid and cyc. Camera room, construction workshop, wardrobe, dressing rooms, edit rooms, hospitality suite and production offices are also on site. Recent productions: Carnivl Films 'Bug' Series

Pinewood Studios
Pinewood Road
Iver
Bucks SL0 0NH
Tel: 01753 651700
Fax: 01753 656844
Managing Director: Steve Jaggs
STAGES
A 1,685 sq metres
(Tank: 12.2m x 9.2m x 2.5m)
B 827 sq metres
C 827 sq metres
D 1,685 sq metres
(Tank: 12.2m x 9.2m x 2.5m)
E 1,685 sq metres
(Tank: 12.2m x 9.2m x 2.5m)
F 698 sq metres
(Tank: 6.1m x 6.1m x 2.5m)
G 247 sq metres
H 300 sq metres
J 824 sq metres
K 824 sq metres
L 880 sq metres
M 880 sq metres
N/P 767 sq metres
South Dock (silent)
1,547 sq metres
007 (silent) 4,225 sq metres (Tank: 90.5m x 22.3m x 2.7m Reservoir: 15.3m x 28.7m x 2.7m) Largest purpose-built silent stage in the world
Large Process 454 sq metres
Small Process 164 sq metres
Exterior Lot 50 acres, comprising formal gardens and lake, woods, fields, concrete service roads and squares
Exterior Tank 67.4m narrowing to 32m wide, 60.4 long, 1.06m deep. Capacity 764,000 gallons. Inner Tank: 15.5m x 12.2m x 2.7m. Backing 73.2m x 18.3m
Western Europe's largest outdoor Tank

FILMS
Mission: Impossible, The Fifth Element, Event Horizon, Eyes Wide Shut, Tomorrow Never Dies, Entrapment, Still Crazy, Plunkett & MacLeane, The World is not Enough
TELEVISION
Jonathan Creek, Little White Lies, Hornblower, Last of the Summer Wine, The Dark Room, Great Expectations, Harbour Lights, French & Saunders, The Tenth Kingdom

Riverside Studios
Crisp Road
Hammersmith
London W6 9RL
Tel: 020 8237 1000
Fax: 020 8237 1011
Jon Fawcett
Studio One 529 sq metres
Studio Two 378 sq metres
Studio Three 112 sq metres
Plus preview cinema, various dressing rooms, offices
TELEVISION
T.F.I. Friday, *'Collins & McConies Movie Club'*, Channel 4 Sitcom Festival, *'This Morning with Richard Not Judy'*

Rotherhithe Studios
119 Rotherhithe Street
London SE16 4NF
Tel: 020 7231 2209
Fax: 020 7231 2119
O Stockman, C Goodwin
STAGES
1 Rotherhithe 180 sq metres
Pre-production, construction, post-production facilities, costume making, props
FILMS
The Nutcracker Story (IMAX 3D)

Shepperton Studios
Studio Road
Shepperton
Middx TW17 0QD
Tel: 01932 562 611
Fax: 01932 568 989
Paul Olliver
STAGES
A 1,668 sq metres
B 1,115 sq metres
C 1,668 sq metres
D 1,115 sq metres
E 294 sq metres
F 294 sq metres
G 629 sq metres
H 2,660 sq metres
I 657 sq metres
J 1,394 sq metres
K 1,114 sq metres
L 604 sq metres
M 259 sq metres
T 261 sq metres
R 948 sq metres
S 929 sq metres

FILMS
Shakespeare in Love; Elizabeth, Hilary & Jackie; Sliding Doors; Notting Hill; Love's Labour's Lost; End of the Affair

Stonehills Studios
Shields Road
Gateshead
Tyne and Wear NE10 0HW
Tel: 0191 495 2244
Fax: 0191 495 2266
Studio Manager: Nick Walker
STAGES
1 1,433 sq feet
2   750 sq feet
The North's largest independent television facility comprising of Digital Betacam Edit Suite with the BVE 9100 Edit Controller, and Abekas ASWR 8100 mixer, A57 DVE and four machine editing, including two DVW 500s. Also three Avid off-line suites, 2D Matador and 3D Alias graphics and a Sound Studio comprising a Soundtracs 6800 24-track 32 channel desk and Soundscape 8-track digital editing machine
TELEVISION
Germ Genie, BBC 2; *The Spark*, Border; *Come Snow Come Blow*, Granada

Teddington Studios
Broom Road
Teddington
Middlesex TW11 9NT
Tel: 020 8977 3252
Fax: 020 8943 4050
David Carr
STUDIOS
1 653 sq metres
2 372 sq metres
3 120 sq metres
4 74 sq metres
TELEVISION
Kilroy; This is Your Life; Men Behaving Badly; Goodnight Sweetheart, Des O'Connor Tonight; Harry Hill; Babes in the Wood, All Along the Watchtower

Theed Street Studios
12 Theed Street
London SE1 8ST
Tel: 020 7928 1953
Fax: 020 7928 1952
Bill Collom
STAGE
A 151 sq metres
TELEVISION
Metropolis for BBC Continuing Education; *Reality on the Rocks* for C4; *Lost Civilisations* for Time Life

Three Mills Island Studios
Three Mill Lane
London E3 3DU

Tel: 020 7363 0033
Fax: 020 7363 0034
email: thremillscompuserve.com
Website: www.threemills.com
Edwin Shirley
STAGES
  1 31'x 28'x 18'
  2 33'x 28'x 18'
  3 14'x 28'x 18'
  4 87'x 77'x 23'7"
  5 143'x 74' x 22'
  6 101'x 77' x 27'
  7 212' x 77'x 33'5"
  8 84' x 49' x 31'
  9 104' x 84' x 31'
10 121' x 46' x 23'
11 106' x 89' x 33'
12 157' x 50' x 33'

Twickenham Film Studios
St Margaret's
Twickenham
Middx TW1 2AW
Tel: 020 8607 8888
Fax: 020 8607 8889
Gerry Humphreys, Caroline Tipple
(Stages)
STAGES
1 702 sq metres
with tank 37 sq metres x 2.6m deep
2 186 sq metres
3 516 sq metres
2 x dubbing theatres; 1 x ADR/Foley

theatre; 40 x cutting rooms;
Lightworks, Avid 35/16mm

Wembley Studios
10 Northfield Industrial Estate
Beresford Avenue
Wembley
Middlesex HAO 1RT
Tel: 020 8903 4296
Fax: 020 8900 1353
STAGES
Studio 290 sq metres
Cyc 193 sq metres
Power: 900 amps 3 phase
Production offices, dressing rooms,
kitchen

Westway Studios
8 Olaf Street
London W11 4BE
Tel: 020 7221 9041
Fax: 020 7221 9399
Steve/Kathy
STAGES
1 502 sq metres (Sound Stage)
2 475 sq metres
3 169 sq metres
4 261 sq metres

TELEVISION COMPANIES

Below are listed all British terrestrial television companies, with a selection of their key personnel, and in some cases programmes. A more comprehensive listing of programmes, producers and cast members can be found via the Web pages of each company. For details of feature films made for television see Production Starts

BBC Television

British Broadcasting Corporation
Television Centre
Wood Lane
London W12 7RJ
Tel: 020 8743 8000
Website: www.bbc.co.uk
Chairman: Sir Christopher Bland
Director-General: Greg Dyke
Chief Executive BBC Broadcast: Will Wyatt
Chief Executive BBC Worldwide: Rupert Gavin
Chief Executive BBC Broadcast: Will Wyatt
Chief Executive BBC Production: Matthew Bannister
Chief Executive BBC News: Tony Hall.
Chief Executive BBC Resources: Margaret Salmon
Chief Executive BBC World Service: Mark Byford
Director of Finance: John Smith
Director of Policy and Planning: Patricia Hodgson CBE
Director of Corporate Affairs: Colin Browne
The Board of Management also includes:
Director of Education: Michael Stevenson
Director of National and Regional Broadcasting: Mark Thompson
Director of Radio: Jenny Abramsky
Director of Television: Alan Yentob
Director of Production: Jana Bennett
Director of Technology: Philip Langsdale
Director of BBC Online Nigel Chapman

Director New Services and Deputy Director BBC Television: David Docherty
Managing Director UK Regions and Deputy Chief Executive BBC Worldwide: Peter Teague

BBC Broadcast Programme Acquisition
Centre House
56 Wood Lane
London W12 7RJ
Tel: 020 8743 8000
Fax: 020 8749 0893
Controller, Programme Acquisition: Alan Howden
Head of Programme Acquisition: Sophie Turner Laing
Selects and presents BBC TV's output of feature films and series on both channels

BBC Scotland
Broadcasting House
Queen Margaret Drive
Glasgow G12 8DG
Tel: 0141 338 2000
Fax: 0141 338 2660
email: enquiries.scot@bbc.co.uk

BBC Wales
Broadcasting House
Llandaff
Cardiff CF5 2YQ
Tel: 01222 322000

BBC Northern Ireland
Broadcasting House
Ormeau Avenue
Belfast BT2 8HQ
Tel: 01232 338224
email: ni@bbc.co.uk

BBC North East & Cumbria
Broadcasting Centre
Barrack Rd
Newcastle upon Tyne NE99 2NE
Tel: 0191 232 1313
Head of Regional & Local Programmes: Olwyn Hocking

BBC North West
New Broadcasting House
Oxford Road
Manchester. M60 1SJ
Tel: 0161 200 2020
Head of Regional & Local Programmes: Martin Brooks

BBC North
BBC Broadcasting Centre

Woodhouse Lane
Leeds LS2 9PX
Tel: 0113 244 1188
Head of Regional & Local Programmes: Colin Philpott

BBC West Midlands
Pebble Mill
Birmingham B5 7QQ
Tel: 0121 414 8888
Head, Regional & Local Progs: Laura Dalgleis

BBC East Midlands
East Midlands Broadcasting Centre, London Road, Nottingham NG2 4UU
Tel: 0115 955 0500
Head of Regional & Local Progs: Liam McCarthy (Acting)

BBC West
Broadcasting House
Whiteladies Road
Bristol BS8 2LR
Tel: 0117 973 2211
Head, Regional & Local Programmes: Leo Devine

BBC London & South East
Elstree Centre
Clarendon Road
Borehamwood
Herts WD6 1JF
Tel: 020 8953 6100
Head of Regional & Local Programmes: Jane Mote

BBC East
St Catherine's Close
All Saint's Green
Norwich, Norfolk
Tel: 01603 619331
Head, Regional & Local Programmes: David Holdsworth

BBC South West
Broadcasting House
Seymor Road
Mannamead
Plymouth PL3 5BD
Tel: 01752 229201
Head, Regional & Local Programmes: Eve Turner

BBC South
Broadcasting House
Whiteladies Road
Bristol BS8 2LR
Tel: 0117 973 2211

Independent Television Companies

Anglia Television

Anglia House
Norwich NR1 3JG
Tel: 01603 615151
Fax: 01603 631032
Website: www.anglia.tv.co.uk
Chairman: David McCall
Managing Director: Graham Creelman
Controller of Programmes and Production: Malcom Allsop
Network programmes:
Sunday Morning
Trisha
Touching Evil
Where the Heart is
About Anglia
Away With Words
Cover Story
Craven's Collectables
Crime Night
First Take
Kick-Off
Go Fishing with John Wilson
Liza's County
Off the Beaten Track
Out to Lunch with Brian Turner
The Road Show
Round the Houses
The Seventies
Take it On

Border Television

The Television Centre
Carlisle CA1 3NT
Tel: 01228 525101
Fax: 01228 541384
email: ian@border.tv.com
Website: www.border-tv.com
Chairman: James Graham
Chief Executive: Paul Corley
Executive Director: Melvyn Bragg
Managing Director: Peter Brownlow
Head of Programme Acqusitions: Neil Robinson
Programmes include:
Innovators

Carlton Television

101 St Martin's Lane
London WC2N 4AZ
Tel: 020 7240 4000
Fax: 020 7240 4171
Website: www.carlton.com
Chairman: Nigel Walmsley
Chief Executive: Clive Jones
Managing Director, Carloton Productions: Waheed Alli
Director of Programmes: Steve Hewlett
Chief Executive, Carlton Sales:

Martin Bowley
Finance Director: Mike Green
Commercial Director: Tom Betts
Controller of Public Affairs: Hardeep Kalsi
PRODUCTIONS
35-38 Portman Square
London W1H ONU
Tel: 020 7486 6688
Fax: 020 7486 1132
East Midlands

Carlton Studios
Lenton Lane
Nottingham NG7 2NA
Tel: 0115 863322
Fax: 0115 645552
Westcountry

Westcountry Television
Western Wood Way,
Language Sciene Park
Plymouth PL7 5BQ
Tel: 01752 333333
Fax: 01752 333444
Managing Director: Waheed Alli
Director of Programmes: Steve Hewlett
Controller, Business Affairs: Martin Baker
Director of Drama & Co-production: Jonathan Powell
Executive Producer, Drama: Rob Pursey
Executive Producer, Drama: Sharon Bloom
Controller of Children's & Young People's Programmes: Michael Forte
Executive Producer, Children & Young People's Programmes: David Mercer
Development Producer, Children's & Young People's Programmes: Jo Killingley
Controller of Entertainment: Mark Wells
Controller of Comedy: Nick Symons
Head of Development, Entertainment: Graeme Smith
Controller, Factual Programmes: Polly Bide
Head of Current Affairs and Feautres: Mike Morley
Head of Regional Programmes, Carlton: Emma Barker
Head of Regional Programmes Central: Mike Blair
Director of Programmes, Westcountry: Jane McCloskey
Controller, Carlton Digital Programmes: Peter Lowe

BROADCASTING
Carlton Broadcasting
London
101 St Martin's Lane,
London WC2N 4AZ
Tel: 020 7240 4000
Fax: 020 7240 4171

London Television Centre
Upper Ground
London SE1 9LT
Tel: 020 7620 1620
Fax: 020 7827 7500
Central Broadcasting:
West Midlands
Central Court
Gas Street
Birmingham B1 2JP
Tel: 0121 643 9898
Fax: 0121 643 4897
East Midlands
Carlton Studios,
Lenton Lane
Nottingham NG7 2NA
Tel: 0115 986 3322
Fax: 0115 964 5552
South Midlands
Windrush Court
Abingdon Business Park
Abingdon OX1 1SA
Tel: 01235 554123
Fax: 01235 524024
Westcountry Television
Western Wood Way,
Language Science Park
Plymouth PL7 5BQ
Tel: 01752 333333
Fax: 01752 333444
Managing Director, Carlton Broadcasting: Colin Stanbridge
Managing Director, Central Broadcasting: Ian Squires
Managing Director, Westcountry Television: Mark Haskell
Controller, Broadcasting: Coleena Reid
Director of Finance: Ian Hughes
Head of Aquisitions: John Broadbent
Head of Presentation: Wendy Chapman
Head of Presentation & Programme Planning (Central): David Burge
Controller, News & Operations (Central): Laurie Upshon
Controller, Sports (Central): Gary Newbon
Editor, Central News West: John Boileau
Editor, Central News East: Dan Barton
Editor, Central News South: Phil Carrodus
FACILITIES AND STUDIOS
Outside Broadcasting:
CARLTON 021
12-13 Gravelly Hill Industrial Estate, Gravelly Hill
Birmingham B24 8HZ
Tel: 0121 327 2021
Fax: 0121 327 7021
Managing Director: Ed Everest
CARLTON SALES
London
101 St Martin's Lane
London WC2N 4AZ
Tel: 020 7240 4000

Fax: 020 7240 4171
Manchester
Elizabeth House, 3rd Floor
St Peter's Square
Manchester M2 3DF
Tel: 0161 237 1881
Fax: 0161 237 1970
Westcountry
Westcountry Television
Western Wood Way
Language Science Park
Plymouth PL7 5BQ
Tel: 01752 333311
Fax: 01752 333316
Birmingham
Central Court
Gas Street
Birmingham B1 2JT
Tel: 0121 643 9898
Fax: 0121 634 4414
Chief Executive: Martin Bowley
Managing Director: Steve Platt
Sales Director: Gary Digby
Deputy Sales Director: Chris Solden
Sales Administration Director: Ron
Coomber
Marketing Director: Fran Cassidy
Director of Sponsorship: David
Prosser
Client Sales Director: Caroline Hunt
CARLTON BROADCASTING
101 St Martin's Lane
London WC2N 4AZ
Tel: 020 7240 4000
Fax: 020 7240 4171
Chairman: Nigel Walmsley
Managing Director: Colin Stanbridge
CENTRAL BROADCASTING
Central Court
Gas Street
Birmingham B1 2JT
Tel: 0121 643 9898
Fax: 0121 616 1531
email: centadutyoffice
@centraltv.co.uk
Website: www.centraltv.co.uk
Owned by Carlton
Chairman: Nigel Walmsley
Managing Director: Ian Squires
Carlton Studios
Lenton Lane
Nottingham NG7 2NA
Tel: 0115 986 3322
Fax: 0115 964 5552
Unit 9, Windrush Court
Abingdon Business Park
Abingdon OX1 1SA
Tel: 01235 554123
Fax: 01235 524024
Chairman: Nigel Walmsley
Managing Director: Ian Squires
Controller of News & Operations:
Laurie Upshon
Controller of Sport: Gary Newbon
Editor: Central News West: John
Boileau
Editor: Central News East: Dan
Barton

Editor: Central News South: Phil
Carrodus
WESTCOUNTRY
Langage Science Park
Western Wood Way
Banham
Plymouth PL7 5BG
Tel: 01752 333333
Fax: 01752 333444
Chairman: Clive Jones
Managing Director: Mark Haskell
Director of Programmes: Jane
McClosky
Head of Presentation: Graham
Stevens
CARLTON STUDIOS
Lenton Lane
Nottingham NG7 2NA
Tel: 0115 9863322
Fax: 0115 9645552
Managing Director: Ian Squires
Director of Operations: Paul
Flanaghan
Production Controller: John Revill

Channel 5 Broadcasting
22 Long Acre
London WC2E
Tel: 020 7550 5555
Fax: 020 7550 5554
Website: www.channel5.co.uk
Britain's fifth terrestrial channel
launched at the end of March 1997
Chief Executive: David Elstein
Director of Programming: Dawn
Airey

Channel Four Television
124 Horseferry Road
London SW1P 2TX
Tel: 020 7396 4444
Fax: 020 7306 8353
Website:www.channel4.com
Executive members
Chief Executive: Michael Jackson
Commercial Director: Andy Barnes
Director of Programmes: Tim
Gardam
Managing Director: David Scott
Director of Business Affairs: Janet
Walker
Director of Strategy and
Development: David Brook
Director and General Manager: Frank
McGettigan
Director of Strategy and
Development: David Brook
Non-Executive Members
Chairman: Vanni Travers
Deputy Chairman: Barry Cox
Murray Grigor
Sarah Radclyffe
Usha Prashar, CBE
Andrew Graham
Robin Miller
Joe Sinyor

Channel Television
Television Centre, La Pouquelaye
St Helier
Jersey JE1 3ZD
Tel: 01534 816816
Fax: 01534 816817
Website: www.channeltv.co.uk
Television Centre, Bulwer Avenue
St Sampsons
Guernsey GY1 2BH
Tel: 01481 723451
Fax: 01481 710739
Chief Executive: John Henwood
Director of TV: Michael Lucas
Directior of Productions: Phillipe
Bassett
Head of Programmes: Karen
Rankine
Head of Resource and Transmission:
Tim Ringsdore

GMTV
London Television Centre
Upper Ground
London SE1 9TT
Tel: 020 7827 7000
Fax: 020 7827 7001
Chairman: Charles Allen
Managing Director: Christopher
Stoddart
Director of Programmes: Peter
McHugh
Managing Editor: John Scammell
Editor: Gerry Melling
Head of Press & PR: Sue Brealey
Presenters: Eamonn Holmes, Fiona
Phillips, Lorraine Kelly, Penny
Smith, Matthew Lorenzo
6am-9.25am 7 days a week

Grampian Television
Queen's Cross
Aberdeen AB15 4XJ
Tel: 01224 846846
Fax: 01224 846800
Website:
www.scottishmediagroup.com
Chairman: Dr Calum A MacLeod
CBE

Granada Television
Granada Television Centre
Quay Street
Manchester M60 9EA
Tel: 0161 832 7211
Website: www.granadatv.com
36 Golden Square
London W1R 4AH
Tel: 020 7734 8080
Granada News Centre
Albert Dock, Liverpool L3 4BA
Tel: 0151 709 9393
Fax: 0151 709 3389
Granada News Centre
Bridgegate House
5 Bridge Place
Lower Bridge Street
Chester CH1 1SA

**SUPPORTING THE MAKING OF
GREAT BRITISH FILMS**

Tel: 01244 313966
Fax: 01244 320599
Granada News Centre
White Cross, Lancaster LA1 4XQ
Tel: 01524 60688
Fax: 01524 67607
Granada News Centre
Daisyfield Business Centre
Appleby Street
Blackburn BB1 3BL
Tel: 01254 690099
Fax: 01254 699299
Chief Executive: Charles Allen
Joint Managing Directors:
Andrea Wonfor, Jules Burns
Commercial Director: Katherine
Stross
Director of Production and
Resources: Brenda Smith
Director of Broadcasting: Julia
Lamaison
Sales Director: Mick Desmond
Director of Production: Max Graesser
Director of Public Affairs: Chris
Hopson
Technical Director: Roger Pickles
Controller of Drama: Sally Head
Controller of Entertainment and
Comedy: Andy Harris
Controller of Factual Programmes:
Dianne Nelmes
Controller of Programme Services
and Personnel: David Fraser
Head of Film: Pippa Cross
Head of Technical Operations: Chris
Hearn
Head of Entertainment: Bill Hilary
Head of Features: James Hunt
Head of Factual Drama: Ian McBride
Head of Regional Affairs: Rob
McLoughlin
Head of Planning and Marketing:
Colin Marsden
Head of Production Services: Jim
Richardson
Head of Music: Iain Rousham
Head of Regional Programmes: Mike
Spencer
Head of Design and Post Production:
Mike Taylor
Head of Current Affairs and
Documentaries: Charles Tremayne
Head of Transmission Operations:
Peter Williams
Head of Comedy: Antony Wood

HTV Wales
The Television Centre
Culverhouse Cross
Cardiff CF5 6XJ
Tel: 01222 590590
Fax: 01222 597183
Chairman HTV Wales: Gerald Davies
Managing Director – HTV Wales:
Henna Richards
Controller, Programming – HTV
Wales: Elis Owen
Human Resources and Site Services

Manager – HTV Wales
HTV West
The Television Centre
Bath Road
Bristol BS4 3HG
Tel: 0117 977 8366
Fax: 0117 972 2400
Chairman – HTV West: Louis
Sherwood
Managing Director – HTV West:
Jeremy Payne

Independent Television News
200 Gray's Inn Road
London WC1X 8XZ
Tel: 020 7833 3000
Fax: 020 7430 4700
Website: www.itv.co.uk
ITN is the news provider nominated
by the Independent Television
Commission to supply news
programme for the ITV network.
Subject to review, this licence is for a
ten year period from 1993. ITN also
provides news for Channel 4,
Channel 5 and for the Independent
Radio News (IRN) network. ITN is
recognised as one of the world's
leading news organisation whose
programmes and reports are seen in
every corner of the globe. In addition
to its base in London, ITN has
permanent bureaux in Washington,
Moscow, South Africa, the Middle
East, Hong Kong, and Brussels as
well as at Westminster and eight
other locations around the UK.

ITV Network Centre
200 Gray's Inn Road
London WC1X 8HF
Tel: 020 7843 8000
Fax: 020 7843 8160
Website: www.itv.co.uk
ITV is a federation of regional
broadcasters. National coverage is
achieved by 15 licensees,
broadcasting in 14 regional areas :
Anglia, Border, Carlton, Central,
Channel, Grampian, Granada, HTV,
LWT , Meridian, STV, UTV,
Westcountry, Tyne Tees, Yorkshire
(London has two licencees, one for
the weekday – Carlton and one for
the weekend – LWT)

LWT (London Weekend Television)
The London Television Centre
Upper Ground
London SE1 9LT
Tel: 020 7620 1620
Fax: 020 7261 1290
Website: www.lwt.co.uk
Chairman: Charles Allen
Managing Director: Steve Morrison
Controller of Arts: Melvyn Bragg

Controller of Drama: Sally Head
Controller of Entertainment: John
Kaye Cooper
Controller of Factual and Regional
Programmes: Simon Shaps
London's Burning
The South Bank Show
Gladiators
Blind Date

Meridian Broadcasting
TV Centre
Northam Road
Southampton SO14 0PZ
Tel: 01703 222555
Fax: 01703 335050
Website: www.meridiantv.co.uk
48 Leicester Square
London WC2H 7LY
Tel: 020 7839 2255
Fax: 020 7925 0665
West Point
New Hythe
Kent ME20 6XX
Tel: 01622 882244
Fax: 01622 714000
1-3 Brookway
Hambridge Lane
Newbury, Berks RG14 5UZ
Tel: 01635 522322
Fax: 01635 522620
Chairman: Clive Hollick
Chief Executive: Roger Laughton
Director of Public Affairs: Simon
Albury

S4C
Parc Ty Glas
Llanishen
Cardiff CF4 5DU
Tel: 01222 747444
Fax: 01222 754444
Website: www.s4c.co.uk
Chairman: Elan Closs Stephens
Chief Executive: Huw Jones
Director of Productions: Huw Eirug
Director of S4C International: Wyn
Innes
Testament – The Bible in Animation
9x30'
Co-production between S4C, BBC
and Christmas Films. Produced by
Cartwn Cymru, Right Angle and
Christmas Films
Animated stories from the Bible
Saints and Sinners – The History of
the Popes 6x50'
Co-production with RTE and La5
Production company: Opus 30
An insight into the power of the
Papacy, of Popes past and present
Ancient Egypt 5x60'
Co-production with Discovery
Communications and La 5
Production company: John Gwyn
An indepth journey through a
dynasty that lasted 6,000 years
The Making of Maps 1x99'

Co-production with BBC + British Screen
Production company: Gaucho
Film set in Wales during the Cuban Missile Crisis of 1962 featuring the loss of childhood innocence
Famous Fred 1x30'
A co-production between S4C, Channel 4 and TVC
Production company -TVC
The fabulous furry adventures of Fred – the home-loving cat who turns into a rock star glamourpuss at night
Cameleon 1x120'
Production Company – Elidir Films
An idealistic, wayward young man joins the army in search of a more exciting life but goes absent without leave after it fails to meet his expectations
The Jesus Story 1 x 90' or 4x30'
Co-production with BBC + Christmas Films + British Screen
Animated full length feature film from the makers of 'Testament', *Shakespeare The Animated Tales and 'Operavox The Animated Operas'*
The Heather Mountain 1x80'
Production Compay – Llun y Felin Productions
A feature film version of a classic Welsh story follows the story of a young girl growing up in North Wales at the turn of the Century
Wild Islands 24x30' or 8x50' + 50'
Raptor special
Co-production with STE + RTE
Production Company – Performance Films, Telesgop and Éamon de Buitléar
A unique insight into the wildlife and natural habitat of the national regions which make up Britain and Ireland

Scottish Television
Cowcaddens
Glasgow G2 3PR
Tel: 0141 300 3000
Fax: 0141 300 3030
Website: www.scottishmediagroup.com
20 Lincoln's Inn Field
London WC2A 3ED
Tel: 020 7446 7000
Fax: 020 7446 7010
Chairman: Gus Macdonald
Managing Director: Andrew Flanagan
Chief Executive Scottish Television Enterprises: Alistair Moffat
Director of Broadcasting/Head of Regional Programmes: Blair Jenkins
Doctor Finlay
Executive Producer: Robert Love
Taggart
Executive Producer: Robert Love
Glasgow detective series
High Road

Producer: John Temple
Drama serial set on Loch Lomond
Wheel of Fortune
Executive Producer: Sandy Ross
Popular network game show
Other programmes include:
Chart Bite
The Home Show
Kirsty
NB
Scotland Today
Scotsport
Scottish Passport
Scottish Women
Win, Lose or Draw

Tyne Tees Television
The Television Centre
City Road
Newcastle Upon Tyne NE1 2AL
Tel: 0191 261 0181
Fax: 0191 261 2302
Chairman: Sir Ralph Carr-Ellison TD
Deputy Chairman: R H Dickinson
Managing Director: John Calvert
Director of Broadcasting: Peter Moth
Group Head of Engineering: John Nichol
Controller of News: Graeme Thompson
Controller of Programme Administration and Planning: Peter MacArthur
Controller of Operations: Margaret Fay
Head of Current Affairs: Sheila Browne
Head of Light Entertainment: Christine Williams
Head of Young Peoples Programmes: Lesley Oakden
Head of Sports: Roger Tames
Chain Letters
Production Company: Tyne Tees Television
Producer: Christine Williams
Director: Ian Bolt
Presenter: Ted Robbins

Ulster Television
Havelock House
Ormeau Road
Belfast BT7 1EB
Tel: 01232 328122
Fax: 01232 246695
Chairman: J B McGuckian
Managing Director: J D Smyth
General Manager: J McCann
Controller of Programming: A Bremner
Head of Public Affairs: M McCann
UTV Live at Six
Five days a week hour-long news and features programme. Includes a wide range of strands – environment, health, home, entertainments, local communities, consumer affairs and sport

Westcountry Television
Western Wood Way
Langage Science Park
Plymouth PL7 5BG
Tel: 01752 333333
Fax: 01752 333444
Website: www.westcountry.co.uk
Westcountry Television is owned by Carlton
Managing Director: Mark Haskell
Director of Programmes: Jane McCloskey
Controller of News and Current Affairs: Brad Higgins
Controller of Features and Programme Development: Caroline Righton
Head of Broadcasting: Phil Barnes
Controller – Operations and Engineering : Mark Chaplin
Controller – Public Affairs: Mark Clare
Controller – Business Affairs: Peter Gregory

Yorkshire Television
The Television Centre
Leeds LS3 1JS
Tel: 0113 2 438283
Fax: 0113 2 445107
Global House
96-108 Great Suffolk Street
London SE1 OBE
Tel: 020 7578 4304
Fax: 020 7578 4320
Charter Square
Sheffield S1 3EJ
Tel: 0114 2 723262
Fax: 0114 275 4134
23 Brook Street
The Prospect Centre
Hull HU2 8PN
Tel: 01482 24488
Fax: 01482 586028
88 Bailgate
Lincoln LN1 3AR
Tel: 01522 530738
Fax: 01522 514162
Alexandra Dock Business Centre
Fisherman's Wharf
Alexandra Dock
Grimsby NE Lincs
DN21 1UL
Tel: 01472 357026
Fax: 01472 341967
8 Coppergate
York YO1 1NR
Tel: 01904 610066
Fax: 01904 610067
Director of Broadcasting: Mike Best
Controller, Features: Bridget Boseley
Controller of Factual Programmes: Chris Bryer
Controller of Commercial Affairs: Filip Cieslik
Head of International Facutal: Pauline Duffy
Head of Site Services: Peter Fox

Director of Production: David Fraser
Development Co-ordinator: Rachel Gilks
Executive Producer, Features and Factuals: Peter A. Gordon
Managing Director, Broadcasting: Richard Gregory
Group Head of Risk Management: John Hastings
PR & Regional Affairs Manager: Christine Hirst
Deputy Financial Controller – North East: Nick Holmes
Executive Producer, Schools Programmes: Chris Jelley
Head of News and Current Affairs: Clare Morrow
Controller of Drama, YTV: Carolyn Reynolds
Controller of Comedy Drama and Drama Features: David Reynolds
Controller of Drama: Keith Richardson
Head of Media Relations North: Sallie Ryle
Head of Engineering: John Nichol
Controller, Production Finance: Ian Roe
General Manager: Peter Rogers
Managing Editor of Factual Programmes: Helen Scott
Training and Development Manager: Sue Seager
Head of Personnel: Sue Slee
Controller of Comedy and Entertainment: Paul Spencer
Head of Sales and Planning: John Surtees
Deputy Controller of Children's, Granada Media Group
Director of Programmes: John Whinston
Programmes include:
Emmerdale
Heartbeat
A Touch of Frost
Bruce's Price is Right

VIDEO LABELS

These companies acquire the UK rights to all forms of audio-visual product and arrange for its distribution on videodisc, cassette or DVD at a retail level. Listed is a selection of titles released on each label. *Videolog* contains listings and crossreferences on currently available video titles and the companies distributing them

20:20 Vision Video UK
Horatio House
77-85 Fulham Palace Road
London W6 8JA
Tel: 020 8748 4034
Fax: 020 8748 4546
Little Women
Street Fighter
The Quick and the Dead

Arrow Film Distributors
18 Watford Road
Radlett
Herts WD7 8LE
Tel: 01923 858306
Fax: 01923 869673
Neil Agran
La Bonne Annee
Les Diaboliques
Europa Europa
Ginger and Fred
Montenegro
La Retour de Martin Guerre
Wages of Fear
Gulliver's Travels
Frank Sinatra: They Were Very Good Years
Leonardo DiCaprio: In His Own Words

Art House Productions
39-41 North Road
Islington
London N7 9DP
Tel: 020 7700 0068
Fax: 020 7609 2249
Richard Larcombe
Les Biches
Bicycle Thieves
Buffet Froid
Django
La Grande Bouffe
La Grande Illusion
The Harder They Come
Mephisto
Miranda
The Navigator
The Spirit of the Beehive
The Turning
Ultra

Artificial Eye Video
14 King Street
London WC2E 8HN
Tel: 020 7240 5353
Fax: 020 7240 5242
Robert Beeson, Roz Arratoon
Rien ne va Plus
The Eel
The Apple
The Stranger
An Autumn Tale
Black Cat White Cat
Eternity and a Day

BBC Video
Woodlands
80 Wood Lane
London W12 0TT
Tel: 020 8576 2236
Fax: 020 8743 0393
Blackadder
Dr Who
Match of the Day series
One Foot in the Grave
Pingu
Pole to Pole
Red Dwarf
Steptoe and Son

bfi Video
10a Stephen Mews
London W1P 0AX
Tel: 020 7957 8957
Fax: 020 7957 8968
bfi Video, incorporating Connoisseur and Academy, distributes over 250 titles (including DVDs) covering every decade of cinema, from the 1890s to the present. Recent Connoisseur releases:
Seven Samurai (VHS and DVD)
The Lodger
The Ring
South
British Transport Films
Nights of Cabiria
The Bat Whispers
Stella Does Tricks
Majorettes in Space
Frank Lloyd Wright
The New Deal Documentaries
Silent Shakespeare
Tales of the Taira Clan

Blue Dolphin Film & Video
40 Langham Street
London W1N 5RG
Tel: 020 7255 2494
Fax: 020 7580 7670
Joseph D'Morais
Video releases to date:
A Great Day in Harlem
A Fistful of Fingers
Invaders from Mars
Destination Moon
Flight to Mars
Mister Frost
The Square Circle
Loaded

Buena Vista Home Video
3 Queen Caroline Street
London W6 9PE
Tel: 020 8222 1000
Fax: 020 8222 2795
Distribute and market Walt Disney, Touchstone, Hollywood Pictures and Henson product on video

Carlton Video Limited
The Waterfront
Elstree Road
Elstree
Herts WD6 3BS
Tel: 020 8207 6207
Fax: 020 8207 5789
Carlton Video releases sections from Rank and Korda Collections. Also featuresThe Rohauer Collection, Godzila – Japanese Originals
Up on the Roof
Made in Britain
Meantime
Prick Up Your Ears
Children's Programmes including:
Tots TV, Bananas in Pyjamas, The World of Peter Rabbit and Friends, Old Bear and Friends, Rudolph the Red-Nosed Reindeer, annabelle's Wish, Dream Street, Big Garage, Jellikins, Kingdom of Rhymes, The Fairies, Extreme Dinosaurs, Timbuctoo, Potamus Park
TV Programmes: *Inspector Morse, Soldier Soldier, The Vice, Sharpe, Cadfael, Goodnight Mister Tom, The Scarlet Pimpernel, Kavanagh QC, Frenchman's Creek, Cider With Rosie, A Rather English Marriage, The Jump*

CIC UK
Glenthorne House

5-17 Hammersmith Grove
London W6 0ND
Tel: 020 8563 3500
Fax: 020 8563 3501
A Universal/Paramount Company
Clear and Present Danger
The Flintstones
Forrest Gump
Jurassic Park
The Paper
River Wild
Schindler's List
The Shadow
True Lies

Columbia TriStar Home Video

Sony Pictures Europe House
25 Golden Square
London W1R 6LU
Tel: 020 7533 1200
Fax: 020 7533 1172
Devil in a Blue Dress
First Knight
Higher Learning
It Could Happen to You
Legends of the Fall
Little Women
Mary Shelley's Frankenstein
Only You
The Quick and the Dead
Street Fighter

Curzon Video

13 Soho Square
London W1V 5FB
Tel: 020 7437 2552
Fax: 020 7437 2992
Belle Epoque
Daens
Deadly Advice
Decadence
L'Enfer
Fausto
The Hour of the Pig
How to be a Woman and Not Die in the Attempt
In Custody
Mina

Electric Pictures Video (Alliance Releasing)

184-192 Drummond Street
London NW1 3HP
Tel: 020 7580 3380
Fax: 020 7636 1675
Angel Baby
Arizona Dream
The Baby of Macon
Before the Rain
Belle de Jour
Blood Simple
Butterfly Kiss
The Celluloid Closet
Cold Fever
The Cook, The Thief, His Wife and Her Lover

Death and the Maiden
Delicatessen
La Dolce Vita
Drowning by Numbers
The Eighth Day
The Flower of my Secret
I Shot Andy Warhol
Kansas City
Kika
Ladybird, Ladybird
Love and Human Remains
Orlando
Priest
Prospero's Books
Raise the Red Lantern
Red Firecracker, Green Firecracker
Ridicule
The Runner
Shanghai Triad
The Story of Qiu Ju
Trees Lounge
The White Balloon
The Young Poisoner's Handbook
Walking and Talking

Entertainment in Video

27 Soho Square
London W1V 5FL
Tel: 020 7439 1979
Fax: 020 7734 2483
Kingpin
Last Man Standing
Leaving Las Vegas
Living in Oblivion
Nixon
Seven
Twelfth Night
Up Close and Personal

First Independent Films

99 Baker Street
London W1M 1FB
Tel: 020 7317 2500
Fax: 020 7317 2502/2503
Above the Rim
Automatic
Dumb and Dumber
The Lawnmower Man II
Little Odessa
Mortal Kombat
Nostradamus
Rainbow
Sleep With Me

FoxGuild Home Entertainment

Twentieth Century House
31-32 Soho Square
London W1V 6AP
Tel: 020 7753 0015
Fax: 020 7434 1435
Website: www.fox.co.uk/
Airheads
Braveheart
Johnny Mnemonic
Judge Dredd
The Scout
The Shawshank Redemption

Stargate
Trapped in Paradise
Wes Craven's New Nightmare

Granada LWT International

London Television Centre
Upper Ground
London SE1 9LT
Tel: 020 7620 1620
Fax: 020 7928 8476
Brideshead Revisited
Cracker – series 1 & 2
Gladiators
Hale & Pace – Greatest Hits
Jeeves & Wooster – series 1 & 2
Jewell in the Crown
London's Burning – series 1 & 6
Nicholas and Alexandra
Rik Mayhall Presents... – series 1 & 2

guerilla films

35 Thornbury Road
Iselworth
Middlesex TW7 4LQ
Tel: 020 8758 1716
Fax: 020 8758 9364
email: david@guerilla.u-net.com
Website: www.guerilla.u-net.com
David Nicholas Wilkinson
Includes films by Eric Rohmer,
*Barbet Shroeder, Jacques Rivette,
Jean-Claude*

Imperial Entertainment (UK)

Main Drive, GEC Estate
East Lane
Wembley
Middx HA9 7FF
Tel: 020 8904 0921
Fax: 020 8904 4306/908 6785
UK distributor of feature films
including Danielle Steele video titles

Jubilee Film and Video

Egret Mill
162 Old Street
Ashton-Under-Lyne
Manchester OL6 7ST
Tel: 0161 330 9555

Le Channel Ltd

10 Frederick Place
Weymouth
Dorset DT4 8HT
Tel: 01305 780446
Fax: 01305 780446
Art videos about famous paintings of the Western World. Palettes is a collection of very high standard videos about famous paintings of the Western World. Adapted from the French, the films have been researched by leading art historians and curators. Each Palette narrates the creation of a painting, the story of a painter, the progression of a Palette: Claude; Leonardo; Monet Poussin, Seurat, Vermeer

Lighthouse

Lumiere Video
167-169 Wardour Street
London W1V 3TA
Tel: **020 7413 0838**
Fax: 020 7734 1509
A catalogue of French, Spanish and
Italian titles from the Initial Groupe,
as well as the entire Weintraub
library
Fort Saganne
La Marge
Plein Soleil

Lumiere Classics

167-169 Wardour Street
London W1V 3TA
Tel: 020 7413 0838
Fax: 020 7413 0838
Eating Roual
Eva

Lumiere Home Video

167-169 Wardour Street
London W1V 3TA
Tel: 020 7413 0838
Fax: 020 7734 1509
The Avengers
12 titles from Hammer
Hue and Cry
Laughter in Paradise
Bruce Lee
Mighty Max
Moby Dick
Mona Lisa (widescreen)

Mainline Pictures

37 Museum Street
London WC1A 1LP
Tel: 020 7242 5523
Fax: 020 7430 0170
Bandit Queen
The Diary of Lady M
A Flame in my Heart
Go Fish
Let's Get Lost
Luck, Trust & Ketchup
The Premonition
Ruby in Paradise
The Wedding Banquet
Lovers
Crazy Love
Metropolitan
Chain of Desire

Media Releasing Distributors

27 Soho Square
London W1V 5FL
Tel: 020 7437 2341
Fax: 020 7734 2483
Day of the Dead
Eddie and the Cruisers
Kentucky Fried Movie
Return of Captain Invincible
Distributed through Entertainment In
Video (qv)

Medusa Communications & Marketing Ltd

Medusa Pictures Video Division
Regal Chambers, 51 Bancroft
Hitchin
Herts SG5 1LL
Tel: 01462 421818
Fax: 01462 420393
American Yakuza 2
The Babysitters
Crash
Evolver
The Final Cut
Freefall
F.T.W.
If These Walls Could Talk
Rent a Kid
When the Bough Breaks
A Woman Scorned 2

MGM Home Entertainment (Europe) Ltd

Glenthorne House
Hammersmith Grove
Tel: 020 8563 8383
Fax: 020 8563 2896

Nova Home Entertainment

11a Winholme
Armthorpe
Doncaster DN3 3AF
Tel: (01302) 833422
Fax: (01302) 833422
email: Library@novaonline.co.uk
Website: www.novaonline.co.uk
Contact: Andrew White, Maurice
White, Gareth Atherton
Sell-through video distributor, a
subsidiary of Nova Productions, with
a catalogue based specialist & local
interest documentaries and nostalgia
programming

Odyssey Video

15 Dufours Place
London W1V 1FE
Tel: 020 7437 8251
Fax: 020 7734 6941
Ambush in Waco
Beyond Control
Burden of Proof
Honour Thy Father & Mother
Lady Boss
Lucky/Chances
Out of Darkness
A Place for Annie
Remember
War & Remembrance

Orbit Media Ltd

7/11 Kensington High Street
London W8 5NP
Tel: 020 7221 5548
Fax: 020 7727 0515
Website: www.btinternet.com/orbitmedia
Chris Ranger, Jordan Reynolds
Screen classics label, feature films
and documentaries

Out on a Limb

Battersea Studios
Television Centre
Thackeray Road
London SW8 3TW
Tel: 020 7498 9643
Fax: 020 7498 1494
Being at Home with Claude
Forbidden Love
My Father is Coming
No Skin Off My Ass
Seduction: The Cruel Woman
Virgin Machine

Picture Music International

20 Manchester Square
London W1A 1ES
Tel: 020 7486 4488
Fax: 020 7465 0748
Blur: Showtime
Cliff Richard: The Hit List
David Bowie: The Video Collection
Iron Maiden: The First Ten Years
Kate Bush: The Line, The Cross and
The Curve
Peter Gabriel: Secret World Live
Pet Shop Boys: Videography
Pink Floyd: Pulse
Queen; Box of Flix
Tina Turner: Simply the Best

Quadrant Video

37a High Street
Carshalton
Surrey SM5 3BB
Tel: 020 8669 1114
Fax: 020 8669 8831
Sports video cassettes

Screen Edge

28-30 The Square
St Annes-on-Sea
Lancashire FY8 1RF
Tel: 01253 712453
Fax: 01253 712362
email: king@visicom.demon.co.uk
Website: www.visionary.co.uk
Rhythm Thief
Der Todesking
Pervirella

SIG Video Gems Ltd

The Coach House
The Old Vicarage
10 Church Street
Rickmansworth
Herts WD3 1BS
Tel: 01923 710599
Fax: 01923 710549
Black Beauty (TV series)
The Great Steam Trains
Minder
Moonlighting
Professionals
Return of the Incredible Hulk
Rumpole of the Bailey
Ruth Rendell
Sweeney

UK Gold Comdey Compilation
UK Gold Action/Drama Compilation

Tartan Video
Metro Tartan House
79 Wardour Street
London W1V 3TH
Tel: 020 7494 1400
Fax: 020 7439 1922
Cinema Paradiso
Man Bites Dog
Seventh Seal
The Umbrellas of Cherbourg
La Haine
The Dream Life of Angels
Kissed

Telstar Video Entertainment
The Studio
5 King Edward Mews
Byfeld Gardens
London SW13 9HP
Tel: 020 8846 9946
Fax: 020 8741 5584
A sell-through video distributor of
music, sport, special interest,
comedy, children and film
programmes
The Best Kept Secret in Golf
Foster & Allen: By Request
Harry Secombe Sings
Hollywood Women
John Denver: A Portrait
Michael Crawford: A Touch of
Music in the Night

Thames Video Home Entertainment
Pearson Television International
1 Stephen Street
London W1P 1PJ
Tel: 020 7691 6000
Fax: 020 7691 6079
Mr Bean; Tommy Cooper;
Wind in the Willows; World at War;
Men Behaving Badly; The Bill; The
Sweeney

THE (Total Home Entertainment)
National Distribution Centre
Rosevale Business Park
Newcastle under Lyme
Staffs ST5 7QT
Tel: 01782 566566
Fax: 01782 565400
Exclusive distributors for Paradox,
Pride, Kiseki, International Licencing &
Copyright Ltd, Grosvenor, Empire and
distributors of over 3,000 other titles –
Quantum Leap, Green Umbrella

Trumedia Ltd
PO Box 374
Headington
Oxford OX3 7NT
Tel: 01865 763097
Fax: 01865 763097
Literary video and audio resources

Universal Visual Programming
Oxford House
76 Oxford Street
London W1N 0HQ
Tel: 020 7307 7600
Fax: 020 7307 7639
Carey Weich
A subsidiary of Universal Pictures
International and acquiring
programmes for worldwide video
distribution across all genres: Popular
culture, comedy, music, and general
interest
Cats, Feet of Flames, Lord of the
Dance, Maisy, Barney, Mr Bean

Visionary Communications
28-30 The Square
St Annes-on-Sea
Lancashire FY8 1RF
Tel: 01253 712453
Fax: 01253 712362
email: king@visicom.demon.co.uk
Website: www.visionary.co.uk
Scorpio Rising
The Pope of Utah
Three Films' Burroughs'/Gysin
Destroy All Rational Thought
Cyberpunk
Angelic Conversation
In the Shadow of the Sun
The Gun is Loaded
Alice
Freaks
Island of Lost Souls
Mystery of the Wax Museum

WEBSITES

This section contains a small selection of useful websites based on the information in this book

ARCHIVE AND FILM LIBRARIES

FIAF
http://www.cinema.ucla.edu /FIAF

France – La Vidéoteque de paris
http://www.vdp.fr

National Film and Television Archive
http://www.bfi.org.uk

Scottish Film and Television Archive
http://www.scottishscreen.com

East Anglian Film Archive
http://www.uea.ac.uk/eafa

North West Film Archive
http://www.nwfa.mmu.ac.uk

National Museum of Photography Film & Television
http://www.nmsi.ac.uk/nmpft

AWARDS

BAFTA
http://www.bafta.org

Berlin
http://www.berlinale.de

Cannes
http://www.festival-cannes-fr

Edinburgh International Film Festival
http://www.edfilmfest.org.uk

Emmys
http://www.emmys.org

Emmys International
http://www.intlemmyawards.com

European Film Awards
http://www.europeanfilmacademy.org

Golden Globes
http://www.hfpa.com

Golden Rose of Montreux
http://www.rosedor.ch

Karlovy Vary
http://www.iffkv.cz

Locarno
http://www.pardo.ch

Oscars
http:// www.oscars.org/awards

Monte Carlo TV Festival
http://www.tvfestival.com

Royal Television Society Awards
http://www.rts.org.uk

BOOKS

BFI Publishing
http://www.bfi.org.uk

Oxford University Press
http://www.oup.co.uk

Routledge
http://www.routledge.com

BOOKSELLERS

Blackwell's
http://www.blackwell.co.uk/bookshops

Cinema Store
http://www.atlasdigital.com/cinema store

Waterstones
http://www.waterstones.co.uk

CABLE, SATELLITE AND DIGITAL

Cable/Satellite Guide
http://www.sceneone.co.uk/s1/TV

BSkyB
http://www.sky.co.uk

NTL
http://www.ntl.co.uk

ONDigital
http://www.ondigital.co.uk

SkyDigital
http://www.skydigital.co.uk

Telewest Communications
http://www.telewest.co.uk

CAREERS AND TRAINING

Film Education
http://www.filmeducation .org

National Film and Television School
http://www.nftsfilm-tv.ac.uk

Skillset
http://www.skillset.org

CD ROMS

International Film Index
http://www.bowker-saur.com/service

The Knowledge
http://www.mfplc.com

CINEMAS

Cinemas in the UK
http://www.aber.ac.uk/~jwp/cinemas

Apollo Cinemas
http://www.apollocinemas.co.uk

ABC Cinemas
http://www.abccinemas.co.uk

Caledonian Cinemas
http://www.caledoniancinemas.co.uk

Cineworld
http://www.cineworld.co.uk

Mainline
http://www.screencinemas.co.uk

Odeon
http://www.odeon.co.uk

Picturehouse
http://www.picturehouse-cinemas.co.uk

Showcase Cinemas
http://showcasecinemas.co.uk

UCI (UK) Ltd
http://www.uci-cinemas.co.uk

Warner Village
http://warnervillage.co.uk

COURSES

The American Intercontinental University
http://www.aiulondon.ac.uk

University of Bath
http://www.bath.ac.uk

Birkbeck College University of London
http://www.birkbeck.ac.uk

University of Birmingham
http://www.birmingham.ac.uk

Bournemouth University
http://www.bournemouth.ac.uk

University of Bradford
http://www.bradford.ac.uk

University of Bristol
http://www.bristol.ac.uk

Brunel University
http://www.brunel.ac.uk

Canterbury Christ Church College
http://www.cant.ac.uk

Coventry University
http://www.alvis.coventry.ac.uk

De Montfort University Bedford
http://www.dmu.ac.uk/Bedford

De Montfort University Leicester
http://www.dmu.ac.uk/Leicester

University of Derby
http://www.derby.ac.uk

University of East Anglia
http://www.uea.ac.uk

University of East London
http://www.bradford.ac.uk

University of Exeter
http://www.ex.ac.uk

University of Glasgow
http:// www.arts.gla.ac.uk/tfts

Glasgow Caledonian University
http://www.gcal.ac.uk

Goldsmiths College
http://www.goldsmiths.ac.uk

Kent Institute of Art and Design
http://www.kiad.ac.uk

University of Kent
http://www.ukc.ac.uk

King Alfred's College Winchester
http://www.wkac.ac.uk

Kingston University
http://www.kingston.ac.uk

University of Leicester
http://www.le.ac.uk

University of Liverpool
http://www.liv.ac.uk

Liverpool John Moores University
http://www.livjm.ac.uk

London Guildhall University
http://www.lgu.ac.uk

London International Film School
http://www.lifs..org.uk

London School of Economics and
Political Science
http://www.lse.ac.uk

University of Manchester
http://www.man.ac.uk

Middlesex University
http://www.mddx.ac.uk

Napier University
http://www.napier.ac.uk

National Film and Television School
http://www.nftsfilm-tv.ac.uk

University of Newcastle upon Tyne
http://www.ncl.ac.uk/ncrif

Northern School of Film and
Television
http:// www.lmu.ac.uk

University of Northumbria at
Newcastle
http://www.unn.ac.uk

Nova Camcorder School
http:// www.novaonline.co.uk

University of Portsmouth
http://www.port.ac.uk

University of Reading
http://www.reading.ac.uk

College of Ripon and York St John
http://www.ucrysj.ac.uk

Roehampton Institute
http://www.roehampton.ac.uk

Royal College of Art
http://www.rca.ac.uk/Design

University of Salford
http://www.salford.ac.uk

University of Sheffield
http://www.sheffield.ac.uk

Sheffield Hallam University
http://www.shef.ac.uk

South Bank University
http://www.sbu.ac.uk

Staffordshire University
http://www.staffs.ac.uk

University of Stirling
http://www.stir.ac.uk

The University of Sunderland
http://www.sunderland.ac.uk

University of Sussex
http://www.sussex.ac.uk

Thames Valley University
http://www.tvu.ac.uk

Trinity and All Saints College
http:// www.tasc.ac.uk

University of Wales College,
Newport
http://www.newport.ac.uk

University College Warrington
http://www.warr.ac.uk

University of Warwick
http://www.warwick.ac.uk

University of Westminster
http://www.wmin.ac.uk

University of Wolverhampton
http://www.wolverhampton.ac.uk

DISTRIBUTORS (NON-THEATRICAL)

Central Office of Information
http:// www.coi.gov.uk/

CFL Vision
http://www.euroview.co.uk

Educational and Television Films
http://: www.etvltd.demon.co.uk

Vera Media
http://www.vera.media.co.uk

DISTRIBUTORS (THEATRICAL)

Alliance Releasing
http://www.alliance.

bfi
http://www.bfi.org.uk

Buena Vista
http://www.bvimovies.com

FilmFour
http://www.filmfour.com

Pathe Distribution´
http://www.pathe.co.uk

Twentieth Century Fox
http://www.fox.co.uk

UIP (United International Pictures)
http://www.uip.com

Warner Bros
http://www.warnerbros.com

FACILITIES

Abbey Road Studios
http://www.abbeyroad.co.uk/

Cinesite (Europe) Ltd
http://www.cinesite.com

Communicopia Ltd
http://www.communicopia.co.uk

Connections Communications Centre
http://www.cccmedia.demon.co.uk

Dubbs
http://www.dubbs.co.uk

Edinburgh Film Workshop Trust
http://www.efwt.demon.co.uk

The Film Factory at VTR
http://www.filmfactory.com

FrameStore
http://www.framestore.co.uk

Hillside Studios
http://www.ctvc.co.uk

Hull Time Based Arts
http://www.htba.demon.co.uk

Lee Lighting
http://www.lee.co.uk

PMPP Facilities
http://www.pmpp.dircon.co.uk

Salon Post-Productions
http://www.salon.ndirect.co.uk

Tele-Cine
http://www.telecine.co.uk

VTR Ltd
http://www.vtr.co.uk

FESTIVALS

Film Festivals Servers
http://www.filmfestivals.com

Berlin
http://www.berlinale.de

Cannes
http://www.festival-cannes-fr

London Film Festival
http://www.lff.org.uk

FILM SOCIETIES

British Federation of Film Societies
http://www.shef.ac.uk/uni/union/
susoc/fu/sg/bffs

FUNDING

Arts Council
http://www.artscouncil.org.uk

bfi
http://www.bfi.org.uk

British Council
http://www.britcoun.org/

Scottish Screen
http://www.scottishscreen.com

Sgrin, Media Agency for Wales
http://www.sgrinwales.demon.co.uk

INTERNATIONAL SALES

BBC Worldwide
http://www.bbc.worldwide.com

BRITE (British Independent
Television Enterprises)
http://www.brite.tv.co.uk

FilmFour International
http://www.filmfour.com

London Television Service
http://www.londontv.com

Pearson Television International
http://www.pearsontv.com

Twentieth Century Fox Television
http://www.fox.co.uk

Vine International Pictures
http://www.vineinternational.co.uk

LIBRARIES

bfi National Library
http://www.bfi.org.uk

Library Association
http://www.la-hq.org.uk

ORGANISATIONS

American Film Institute
http://www.afionline.org/

Arts Council of England
http://www.artscouncil.org.uk

BBC
http://www.bbc.co.uk

British Council – British films
http://www.britfilms.com

British Film Commission
http://www.britfilmcom.co.uk

British Film Institute
http://www.bfi.org.uk

BKSTS – The Moving Image Society
http://www.bksts.demon.co.uk

BUFVC(British Universities Film
and Video Council
http://www.bufvc.ac.uk

Department for Culture, Media and
Sport (DCMS)
http://www.culture.gov.uk/

Directors' Guild of Great Britain
http://www.dggb.co.uk

EDI
http://www.entdata.com

National Museum of Photography,
Film and Television
http://www.nmsi.ac.uk/nmpft/

New Producer's Alliance
http://www.npa.org.uk

PACT – Producers Alliance for
Cinema and Television
http://www.pact.co.uk

Scottish Screen
http://www.scottishscreen.com

Skillset
http://www.skillset.org

ORGANISATIONS (EUROPE)

European Audio-visual Observatory
http:// www.obs.coe.int

EURIMAGES
http://www.culture.coe.fr/eurimages

European Broadcasting Union (EBU)
http:// www.ebu.ch/

EUTELSAT (European
Telecommunications Satellite
Organisation)
http://www.eutelsat.org

Belgium – The Flemish Film Institute
http://www.vfi-filminsituutbe

Denmark – Danish Film Institute
http://www.dfi.dk

Finland – AVEK – The Promotion
Centre for Audio-visual Culture in
Finland
http://www.kopiostofi/avek

Finnish Film Archive
http://www.sea.fi

The Finnish Film Foundation
http://www.ses.fi/ses

France – BibliothÈque du Film (BIFI)
http://www.bifi.fr

TV France International
http://www.tvfi.com

Germany – Filmf˜rderungsanstalt
http://www.ffa.de

Iceland – Icelandic Film Fund
http://www.centrum.is/filmfund

Ireland – Bord Scann·n na
hÉ.ireann/Irish Film Board
http://www.iol.ie/filmboard

Film Institute of Ireland
http://www.iftn.ie/ifc

Poland – Polish Cinema Database
http://info.fuw.edu.pl/Filmy

Portugal – Portuguese Film and
Audiovisual Institute
http://www.nfi.no/nfi.htm

Scottish Screen
http://www.scottishscreen.com

PRESS CONTACTS

6degrees.co.uk
http://www.6degrees.co.uk

Empire
http://www.empireonline.co.uk

Flicks
http://www.flicks.co.uk

Guardian online
http://www.guardian.co.uk/guardian

Premiere
http://www.premieremag.com

Radio Times
http://www.radiotimes.beeb.com

Screen
http://www.arts.gla.ac

Sunday Times
http://www.sunday-times.co.uk

Talking Pictures
http://www.filmcentre.co.uk

Television
http://www.rts.org.uk

Time Out
http://www.timeout.co.uk/

Total Film
http://www.futurenet.co.uk

Uncut
http:// www.uncut.net

Variety
http://www.variety.com

PREVIEW THEATRES

BAFTA
http://www.bafta.org

The Curzon Minema
http://www.minema.com

RSA
http://www.rsa.org.uk

The Screening Room
http://www.moving-picture.co.uk

PRODUCTION COMPANIES

Aardman Animations
http://www.aardman.com

British Film Commission
http://www.britfilmcom.co.uk

British Films Catalogue
http://www.britfilms.com/

FilmFour Productions
http://www.filmfour.com

Fox Searchlight Pictures
http://www.fox.co.uk

guerilla films
http://www.guerilla.u-net.com

imaginary films
http://www.imagfilm.co.uk

Mosiac Films Limited
http://www.mosaicfilms.com

New Producers Alliance
http://www.npa.org.uk

PACT
http://www.pact.co.uk

Zooid Pictures Limited
http://www.zooid.co.uk

SPECIALISED GOODS AND SERVICES

Ashurst Morris Crisp
http://www.ashursts.com

Bromley Casting (Film & TV Extras Agency)
http://www.showcall.co.uk

Hothouse Models & Effects
http://www.hothousefx.co.uk

MBS Underwater Video Specialists
http://www.eclipse.co.uk.mbs

Moving Image Touring Exhibition Service (MITES)
http://www.mites.org.uk

Olswang
http://www.olswang.co.uk

STUDIOS

Capital FX
http://www.capital.fx.co.uk

Elstree Film Studios
http://www.elstreefilmstudios.co.uk

Hillside Studios
http://www.ctvc.co.uk

Millennium Studios
http://www.elstree-online.co.uk

TELEVISION COMPANIES

TV Guides
http://www.link-it.com/TV
http://www.sceneone.co.uk/s1/TV

Anglia Television
http://www.anglia.tv.co.uk

BBC
http://www.bbc.co.uk

Border Television
http://www.border-tv.com

Carlton Television
http://www.carltontv.co.uk

Channel Television
http://www.channeltv.co.uk

Channel 4
http://www.channel4.co.uk

Granada Television
http://www.granada.co.uk

HTV
http://www.htv.co.uk

London Weekend Television (LWT)
http://www.lwt.co.uk

Meridian Broadcasting Ltd
http://www.meridan.tv.co.uk

S4C
http://www.s4c.co.uk/

Scottish Television
http://www.stv.co.uk

Ulster Television
http://www.utvlive.com

VIDEO LABELS

British Videogram Association
http://www.bva.org.uk

Blockbuster Entertainment
http://www.blockbuster.com

WEBSITES

Animation World Network
http://www.awn.com

Baseline
http://www.pkbaseline.com

Cyber Film School
http://www.cyberfilmschool.com

Hollywood Online
http://www.hollywood.com

Internet Movie Database
http://www.uk.imdb.com

Popcorn
http://www.popcorn.co.uk

WORKSHOPS

City Eye
http://www.city-eye.co.uk

Edinburgh Film Workshop Trust
www.efwt.demon.co.uk

Hull Time Based Arts
http://www.htba.demon.co.uk

The Lux Centre
http://www.lux.org.uk

Pilton Video
http://www.piltonvideo.co.uk

The Place in the Park Studios
http://www.screenhero.demon.co.uk

Real Time Video
http://www.rtvideo.demon.co.uk

Vera Media
http://www.vera-media.co.uk

Vivid
http://www.wavespace.waverider.co.uk/~vivid

WORKSHOPS

The selection of workshops listed below are generally non-profit distributing and subsidised organisations. Some workshops are also active in making audio-visual products for UK and international media markets. Those workshops with an asterisk after their name are BECTU-franchised

Amber Side Workshop*
5 Side, Newcastle upon Tyne NE1 3JE
Tel: 0191 232 2000
Fax: 0191 230 3217
Murray Martin
Film/video production, distribution and exhibition. Most recent productions include: Letters to Katiya, 1 hour documentary; Eden Valley 90 minute feature film; The Scar 115 minute feature film. The Workshops National Archive is based at Amber. Large selection of workshop production on VHS, a substantial amount of written material and a database. Access by appointment

Belfast Film Workshop
37 Queen Street
Belfast BT1 6EA
Tel: 01232 648387
Fax: 01232 246657
Alastair Hrron, Kate McManus
Film co-operative offering film/video/animation production and exhibition. Offers both these facilities to others. Made Acceptable Levels (with Frontroom); Thunder Without Rain: Available Light; a series on six Northern Irish photographers, various youth animation pieces and a series of videos on traditional music

Black Coral Training
130 Lea Valley Techno Park
Ashley Road
London N17 9LN
Tel: 020 8880 4861
Fax: 020 8880 4113
Black Coral Training is a non-profit making organisation specialising in 1-4 day foundation and intermediate level courses in: Production Management; Producing for low

budget features; business skills for freelancers; digtal sound editing; movie magic. Multi-skilling for broadcast television; composing music for film & television; research for documentary; presenting and directing. Screenwriting courses include: Live script readings; script reading skills; TV script editing; developing comedy skills; writing a first short film; adapting a story into a short screenplay. All courses taught by industry professionals. Supported by Skillset, LFVDA and Middlesex University

Black Media Training Trust (BMTT)
Workstation
15 Paternoster Row
Sheffield S12 BX
Tel: 01142 492207
Fax: 01142 492207
Contact: Carl Baker
Film and video training. Commercial media productions facility and training resource within and for all Asian, African and African Caribbean communities for community development purposes. Also various commercial media consultancy and project services and facilities hire. Funded by National Lottery Single Regeneration Budget and church urban fund

Caravel Media Centre
The Great Barn Studios
Cippenham Lane
Slough SL1 5AU
Tel: 01753 534828
Fax: 01753 571383
Denis Statham
Training, video production, distribution, exhibition and media education. Offers all these facilities to others. Runs national video courses for independent video-makers

Children's Film Unit The
Unit 8, Princeton Court
55 Felsham Road
London SW15 1AZ
Tel: 020 8785 0350
Fax: 020 8785 0351
email: cfilmunit@aol.com
Carol Rennie, Adminstrator
A registered educational charity, the CFU makes low-budget films for

television and PR on subjects of concern to children and young people. Crews and actors are trained at regular weekly workshops in Putney. Work is in 16mm and video and membership is open to children from 10 – 18. Latest films for Channel 4: Emily's Ghost; The Higher Mortals; Willies War; Nightshade; The Gingerbread House; Awayday. For the Samaritans: Time to Talk. For the Children's Film and Television Foundation: How's Business

City Eye
1st Floor, Northam Centre
Kent Street
Northam
Southampton SO14 5SP
Tel: 01703 634177
Fax: 01703 575717
email: info@city-eye.co.uk
Website: www.city-eye.co.uk
Richard McLaughlin
Film and video equipment hire. Educational projects. Production and post-production and multimedia services. Screenings. Community arts media development. Training courses all year in varied aspects of video, film, photography and radio. Committed to providing opportunities for the disadvantaged/under-represented groups. 50 per cent discount on all non-profit/educational work

Connections Communications Centre
Palingswick House
241 King Street
London W6 9LP
Tel: 020 8741 1766
Fax: 020 8563 9134
email: connections@cccmedia.demon.co.uk
Training in technical operations, video editing, production management and video technology. Betacam SP and SVHS editing facilities and production equipment available for hire

Cultural Partnerships
90 De Beauvoir Road
London N1 4EN
Tel: 020 7 254 8217
Fax: 020 7254 7541
Heather McAdam, Lol Gellor, Inge

Blackman
Arts, media and communications company. Offers various courses in digital sound training. Makes non-broadcast films, videos and radio programmes. Production-based training forms a vital part of the work. Studio facilities for dry/wet hire: fully air-conditioned and purpose built, 8000 sq ft multi-purpose studio. Analogue and Digital audio studios. Live audio studio

Depot Studios
Bond Street
Coventry CV1 4AH
Tel: 01203 525074
Fax: 01203 634373
email: info@covdepot.demon.co.uk
Contact: Deborah Martin-Williams, Audrey Droisen, Mike Roberts
A video and sound recording facility providing training, equipment hire, support and information. An expanding range of digital video and sound recording facilities available for hire. Projects and commissions also undertaken

Direct Films*
21b Brooksby Street
Islington
London
Tel: 020 7607 6161
Fax: 020 7607 7171
Avril Johnson, Lina Gopaul
Film and video production and consultancy. Committed to the development of black independent cinema and television. Productions include: Black Cab; Beaton But Unbowed; Handsworth Song; Twilight City; Testament; Mysteries of July; A Touch of the Tar Brush; Who Needs a Heart; Seven Songs for Malcolm X; The Darker Side of Black. Three Songs on Pain, Light and Time, The Last Angel of History, Mothership Connection, Memory Room 451, Martin Luther King – Days of Hope, Gangsta, Gangsta, The Tragedy of Tupac Shaku

Edinburgh Film Workshop Trust*
29 Albany Street
Edinburgh EH1 3QN
Tel: 0131 557 5242
Fax: 0131 557 3852
email: post@efwt.demon.co.uk
Website: www.efwt.demon.co.uk
David Halliday, Cassandra McGrogan, Robin MacPherson, Edward O'Donnelly
Scotland's only franchised workshop. Broadcast, non-broadcast and community integrated production. Facilities include Betacam

production; lo-band and hi-band U-Matic production; VHS, lo-band and hi-band edit suites; Nelson Hordell 16mm Rostrum camera; 8mm and 16mm cameras; film cutting room. Women's unit. Projects 1996 include: The Butterfly Man (C4), Short Stories: Huskies (C4)

Education on Screen Productions
64 All Saints Road
Kings Heath
Birmingham
Tel: 0121 444 3147
Fax: 0121 434 5154
Mike Kalemkerian, Neil Gammie
Independent company with extensive experience of drama/workshop based projects offering unique video production service to organisations in the West Midlands. Workshop-based approach encourages, where required, close and active client involvement particularly in pre-shoot stages. Also offers training projects to schools, colleges and businesses in the West Midlands

Exeter Phoenix
Media Centre
Bradninch Place
Gandy Street
Exeter
Devon EX4 3LS
Tel: 01392 667066
Fax: 01392 667596
email: media@exeterphoenix.org.uk
Video and multimedia training, access and activities. Media – 100, Betacam – SP, Digital – S (D9), Macintosh workstations, cinema, theatre and cafe

Film Fever Video Makers
13 All Saints Road
Ipswich
Suffolk IP1 4DG
Tel: 01473 250685
Small production Workshop offering occasional course in basic VHS and S-VHS production

Film House/Ty Ffilm
Chapter Arts Centre
Market Road
Canton
Cardiff CF5 1QE
Tel: 01222 409990

Film Work Group
Top Floor
Chelsea Reach
79-89 Lots Road
London SW10 0RN
Tel: 020 7352 0538
Fax: 020 7351 6479
Loren Squires, Nigel Perkins
Video and film post-production

facilities. Special rates for grant-aided, self-funded and non-profit projects.
Avid 'on line' (2:1) and 'off line' editing. 36 gigs storage. Digital Animation Workstations (draw, paint, image modification, edit).
3 machine Hi-Band SP and mixed Beta SP/Hi-Band with DVE
2 machine Lo-Band 'off line' with sound mixing.
6 plate Steenbeck.

First Take
Merseyside Innovation Centre
131 Mount Pleasant
Liverpool L3 5TF
Tel: 0151 708 5767
Fax: 0151 707 0230
email: firsttake@gn.apc.org
Mark Bareham, Lynne Harwood
First Take is an independent production and training organisation. It is the foremost provider of video training and production services to the voluntary, community, arts, education and local authority sectors across the North West. Professional video training by BBC Assessors and broadcast quality productions

Four Corners Film Workshop
113 Roman Road
Bethnal Green
London E2 0QN
Tel: 020 8981 6111
Fax: 020 8983 4441
Holds film production courses in S8mm and 16mm and film theory classes. A full programme runs all year round. Provides subsidised film and video equipment for low budget independent film-makers. Has a 40 seat cinema, S8mm, 16mm, Hi8 and U-Matic production and post-production facilities

Fradharc Ur
11 Scotland Street
Stornoway
Isle of Lewis PA87
Tel: 01851 703255
The first Gaelic film and video workshop, offering VHS and hi-band editing and shooting facilities. Production and training in Gaelic for community groups. Productions include: Under the Surface, Na Deilbh Bheo; The Weaver; A Wedding to Remember; As an Fhearran

Glasgow Film and Video Workshop
3rd Floor
34 Albion Street
Glasgow G1 1LH

Tel: 0141 553 2620
Fax: 0141 553 2660
Ian Reid, Paul Cameron, Aimara Recques
GFVW is an open access training/access resource for film and video makers. Offers equipment hire and training courses at subsidised rates. Facilities include; BetaSP, MiniDV, DVCPro, S-VHS and VHS, cameras and edit suites (including 2 AVIDs). Super 8 and 16mm production and support. Runs production and community based projects, distributes and promotes the exhibition of films and videos made through the workshop

Hull Time Based Arts
8 Posterngate
Hull HU1 2JN
Tel: 01482 216446
Fax: 01482 589952
email: Ron@htba.demon.co.uk
Website: www.htba.demon.co.uk
Film/video production, exhibition and education. Also promotes, produces and commissions experimental film, video, performance and music. Equipment for hire includes video projectors, Avid non-linear editing suites [Media Composer 8000 and 400] with output to Betacam SP and DVC Pro, with full training provided. DVC Pro cameras and production facilities are also available

Intermedia Film and Video
19 Heathcoat Street
Nottingham NG1 3AF
Tel: 0115 950 5434
Fax: 0115 955 9956
Malcolm Leick, Graham Forde
Offers facilities and training in 16mm production, Betacam SP, Lightworks non-linear editing. Has new three camera component studio. Provides production support for programme makers new to broadcast. Plus advice, information and customised training

Jubilee Arts Co Ltd
84 High Street
West Bromwich
West Midlands B70 6JW
Tel: 0121 553 6862
Fax: 0121 525 0640
email: @jubart.demon.co.uk
Jubilee Arts is a unique multi-media community arts team, formed in 1974. Skills include photography, video, drama, audio visual, music/sound, computers, training and graphic design We work with communities, using the arts as a tool to create opportunities for positive

ways for people to express themselves. Jubilee Arts works in partnership with a wide range of groups, agencies and voluntary and statutory bodies

Leeds Animation Workshop (A Women's Collective)*
45 Bayswater Row
Leeds LS8 5LF
Tel: 0113 248 4997
Fax: 0113 248 4997
Jane Bradshaw, Terry Wragg, Stephanie Munro, Janis Goodman, Milena Dragic
Production company making films on social issues. Distributing over 20 short films including – A World of Difference, Did You Say Hairdressing? Waste Watchers, No Offence, Through the Glass Ceiling, Out to Lunch, Give us a Smile, All Stressed Up. They also offer short training courses

Lighthouse
Brighton Media Centre
9-12 Middle Street
Brighton BN1 1AL
Tel: 01273 384222
Fax: 01273 384233
email: info@lighthouse.org.uk
Jane Finnis, Caroline Freeman
A training and production centre, providing courses, facilities and production advice for video and digital media. Avid off- and online edit suites. Apple Mac graphics and animation workstations. Digital video capture and manipulation. Output to/from Betacam SP. SVHS offline edit suite. Post Production and Digital Artists equipment bursaries offered three times a year

London Deaf Access Project
1-3 Worship Street
London EC2A 2AB
Tel: 020 7588 3522 (voice) Tel: 020 7588 3528 (text)
Fax: 020 7588 3526
email: Ldap@ndirect.co.uk
Translates information from English into British Sign Language (BSL) for Britain's deaf community, encourages others to do likewise and provides a consultancy/monitoring service for this purpose. Promotes the use of video amongst deaf people as an ideal medium for passing on information. Runs workshops and courses for deaf people in video production, taught by deaf people using BSL. Works with local authorities and government departments ensuring that public information is made accessible to sign language users. Titles include:

School Leavers, Access to Women's Services, Health issues

London Screenwriters' Workshop
114 Whitfield Street
London W1P 5RW
Sandland Street
London WC1R 4PZ
Tel: 020 7387 5511
Alan Denman, Paul Gallagher
The LSW is an educational charity whose purpose is to help new and developing writers learn the craft of screenwriting for film and television. It offers writing workshops, industry seminars, a newsletter and a script reading service. It is open at very reasonable cost to everyone.
Membership £30.00 p.a

Lux
Lux Building, 2-4 Hoxton Square
London N1 6NU
Tel: 020 7684 0101
Fax: 020 7684 111
email: info@lea.org.uk
Website: www.lux.org.uk
Lux (a merger of London Electronic Arts and London Film Makers' Co-op) is Britain's national centre for video and new media art. Offers a complete range of services including production based training, facility hire (production and post-production), distribution and exhibition of video and new media art and film

Media Arts
Town Hall Studios
Regent Circus
Swindon SN1 1QF
Tel: 01793 463224
Fax: 01793 463223
Ann Cullis, Shahina Johnson
Film & video production and training centre. Offers short courses and longer term media projects. First stop scheme offers funding for first time film/video makers. Also offers media education services, equipment hire, screenwriting advice and undertakes production commissions. Organises screenings and discussions

The Media Workshop
Peterborough Arts Centre
Media Department
Orton Goldhay
Peterborough PE2 0JQ
Tel: 01733 237073
Fax: 01733 235462
email: postmaster@p-arts.demon.co.uk
Video, multimedia and photography production, workshops and exhibitions. Offering DVCPRO, SVHS production/edit facilities and

Media 100 non-linear editing. Also full multimedia authoring and design

Mersey Film and Video
13-15 Hope Street
Liverpool L1 9BQ
Tel: 0151 708 5259
Fax: 0151 707 8595
email: mfv@hopestreet.u-net.com
Production facilities for: BETA SP, DVC PRO, MINI DV, multi-media stations, photoshop, Dolly and track, Jibarm, Lights, Mica, DAT etc. Post Production Avid, MC1000, SVHS, BBC FX & music library. Guidance and help for production, scripting, funding, budgets,

Migrant Media
90 De Beauvoir Road
London N1 4EN
Tel: 020 7254 9701
Fax: 020 7241 2387
Ken Fero, Ivan Ali Fawzi, Soulyman Garcia
Media production training and campaigning for migrants and refugees

Moving Image Touring Exhibition Services (MITES)
Moviola, Bluecoat Chambers
Liverpool L1 3BX
Tel: 0151 707 2881
Fax: 0151 707 2150
Courses for artists, gallery curators, technicians and exhibitors

Nerve Centre
2nd Floor
Northern Counties Building
8 Customs House Street
Derry BT48 6AE
Tel: 01504 260562

The Old Dairy Studios
156b Haxby Road
York YO3 7JN
Tel: 01904 641394
Fax: 01904 692052
Digital video production facilities inc. Fast video system, 32 Track digital recording studio, audio visual facilities with Adobe Photoshop, Radio Production and Midi Composition Studios are available. Courses in video production and editing, sound engineering, radio production, midi composition and digital imaging. Working with people with disabilities, unemployed people, people aged between 12 and 25 as well as with members of the community in general

Oxford Film and Video Makers
The Stables
North Place
Headington

Oxford OX3 7RF
Tel: 01865 741682 (01865 60074 course enquiries)
Fax: 01865 742901
email: ofvm@ox39hy.demon.co.uk
Accredited training in video, experimental film and 16mm film. Also offering courses in scriptwriting, directing and digital editing. Subsidised training for the unemployed and community groups. Production support through the OFVM millennium video project and regular screenings organised at local cinemas and the major summer music festivals. Fast professional digital editing facility available for hire with or without editor

Passing Light Syndicate
Beam Ends
Tincleton,
nr Dorchester DT2 8QP
Tel: 01305 849019
Lee Berry, John Rampley
Independent broad based film, video, mixed media creative outfit of varying members, assistance with fundraising, grants, advice. Broad-based creative collaboration re-film and video production, installation, performance, Internet and othe site specific spectatctulars etc. Always open to new people, ideas and projects.
Independent productions include: Polsow Hudol; Owth Ober Yn

Picture This: Moving Image Resource Centre
Kingsland House
Gas Lane
St Philips
Bristol BS2 0QL
Tel: 0117 972 1002
Fax: 0117 972 1750
email: info@picturethis.demon.co.uk
Josephine Lanyon, Director
Picture This provides:
Training – a range of courses from beginner level to longer term training for under-represented groups. Short courses available in video, film and animation production and post production.
Awards and bursaries – opportunities for new work, with cash grants, advice and access to resources
Production and distribution – facilitate and commission productions for galleries, film festivals broadcasting agencies and cinemas
Membership scheme – support, information, and advice for individuals and groups
Facilities – access to film and video production and post production facilities ranging from 16mm film up

to broadcast standard cameras and avid editing

Pilton Video*
30 Ferry Road Avenue
Edinburgh EH4 4BA
Tel: 0131 343 1151
Fax: 0131 343 2820
email: office@ piltonvido.freeserve.com
Website: www.piltonvideo.co.uk
Hugh Farrell, Joel Venet, Eleanor Hill, Graham Fitzpatrick
Training and production facilities in the local community; documentary and fiction for broadcast. 4 non-linear edit suites

The Place in the Park Studios
BellVue Road
Wrexham LL13 7NH
Tel: 01978 358522
email: knew@screenhero.demon.co.uk
Website: www.screenhero.demon.co.uk
Video/Film production access centre, offering subsidised facilities hire. Equipment includes Beta SP, Digital, 16mm and SVHS shooting and editing kit. The Place in The Park acts as a focal point/contact centre for independent film and video makers in the North Wales region and beyond

Platform Films and Video
3 Tankerton House
Tankerton Street
London WC1H 8HP
Tel: 020 7278 8394 Mobile: 0973 278 956
Fax: 020 7278 8394
Chris Reeves
Film/video production and distribution. Also equipment hire including complete Sony BVW400P shooting kit, Panasonic Hi-Fi sound VHS edit suite, Avid Media Composer 400, 9Gb, 20" monitors, Pro-Tools, title tool, Previs 2 fx, Sanyo 220 video projector. Titles include: Green Party General and Local election broadcasts 1998; From The Edge inserts for BBC2's Disability Programme Unit's magazine programme 1995-97; Proud Arabs and Texan Oilmen for C4's Criticial Eye 1993; The People's Flag series for C4 1987-88; The Miners' Campaign Tapes 1984-85; The Cause Of Ireland for C4 1983

Real Time Video
The Arts and Media Centre
21 South Street
Reading RG1 4QU
Tel: 0118 901 5205

Fax: 0118 901 5206
email: info@rtvideo.demon.co.uk
Website: www.rtvideo.demon.co.uk
Clive Robertson
Community access video workshop,
video production, training, exhibition
and consultancy. Runs workshops
and projects using video as
development and self advocacy tool.
Organises screenings and offers
training in production, post-
production, computer graphics and
community video practice. SVHS
edit suite with video and audio-
processing, and graphics available for
hire (reduced rates for non-profit
work)

Sankofa Film and Video*

Spectrum House
Unit K
32-34 Gordon House Road
London NW5 1LP
Tel: 020 7692 0393
Fax: 020 7485 2869
Maureen Blackwood, Johann
Insanally,
Film production and 16mm editing
facilities, training in film production
and scriptwriting, screenings.
Productions include: The Passion of
Remembrance; Perfect Image;
Dreaming Rivers; Looking for
Langston; Young Soul Rebels; In
between; A Family Called Abrew;
Des'ree EPK; Home Away From
Home; Father Sons; Unholy Ghosts;
Is it the design on the Wrapper? +
Vacuum

Sheffield Independent Film

5 Brown Street
Sheffield S1 2BS
Tel: 0114 272 0304
Fax: 0114 279 5225
Colin Pons
A resource base for independent film
and video-makers in the Sheffield
region. Regular training workshops;
access to a range of film and video
equipment; technical and
administrative backup; office space
and rent-a-desk; regular screenings of
independent film and video. Regular
producers sessions to help producers
keep abreast of developments in the
industry. Sister company Yorkshire
Media Production Agency. A grant
giving up to £200,000 or 25 per cent
of a film's budget

Signals Media Arts

Victoria Chambers
St Runwald Street
Colchester CO1 1HF
Tel: 01206 560255
Fax: 01206 369086
email: admin@signals.org.uk

Audrey Droisen
Film video and multimedia
production centre and facility.
Services in training, production,
media education and equipment hire.
Productions include: Three Hours in
High Heels is Heaven (C4), Coloured
(Anglia TV), Cutting Up (C4);
Garden of Eve (Anglia TV) and Fork
in the Road

Swingbridge Video

Norden House
41 Stowell Street
Newcastle upon Tyne NE1 4YB
Tel/Fax: 0191 232 3762
email: Swingvid@aol.com
Contact: Hugh Kelly
A producer of both broadcast and
non-broadcast programmes, including
drama and documentary formats and
specialising in socially purposeful
and educational subjects. Offers
training and consultancy services to
public sector, community and
voluntary organisations. Also
provides a tape distribution service.
Productions include: White Lies; An
English Estate; Happy Hour; Where
Shall We Go?; Sparks; Set You Free;
Mean Streets and many more

Trilith

Corner Cottage, Brickyard Lane
Bourton, Gillingham
Dorset SP8 5PJ
Tel: 01747 840750/840727
Trevor Bailey, John Holman
Specialises in rural television and
video on community action, rural
issues and the outlook and
experiences of country born people.
Also works with organisations
concerned with physical and mental
disability and with youth issues.
Produces own series of tapes,
undertakes broadcast and tape
commissions and gathers archive film
in order to make it publicly available
on video. Distributes own work
nationally. Recent work includes
broadcast feature and work with
farmers and others whose lives
revolve around a threatened livestock
market, and a production scripted and
acted by people with disabilities.
Another project enables young
people to make programmes for local
radio

Valley and Vale Community Arts Ltd

The Valley and Vale Media Centre,
Heol Dew, Sant
Betws
Mid Glamorgan CF32 8SU
Tel: 01656 729246/871911
Fax: 01656 729185/870507

Video production, training,
distribution and exhibition. Open
access workshop offering training to
community groups in
production/post-production, Hi8,
digital, Betacam SP and VHS
formats, with linear and non-linear
(media 100) editing facilities

Vera Media

30-38 Dock Street
Leeds LS10 1JF
Tel: 0113 2428646
Fax: 0113 242 8739
email: vera@vera-media.co.uk
Website: www.vera-media.co.uk
Alison Garthwaite, Catherine
Mitchell
Video production – documentary,
education, arts equality, public sector,
health. Training (ESF/other) for
women/mixed. Screenings.
Participatory productions.
Information resource. Runs
membership organisation
(NETWORKING) for women in
film, video and television

Video Access Centre

25a SW Thistle Street Lane
Edinburgh EH2 1EW
Tel: 0131 220 0220
Fax: 0131 220 0017
Lara Celini
A membership-based association
which provides resources and
training for individuals and
community groups to work with film
and video. Courses are short and at
basic or specialist level. Has VHS &
SVHS, Super 8 and 16mm
production facilities, runs bi-monthly
newsletter and information service

Vivid

Birmingham's Centre for Media
Arts
Unit 311
The Big Peg
120 Vyse Street
Birmingham B18 9ND
Tel: 0121 233 4061
Fax: 0121 212 1784
email: vivid@waverider.co.uk
Website:
www.wavespace.waverider.co.uk/~vi
vid/
Yasmeen BuigMarian Hall, Andrew
Robinson
Training, resources and support for
artists and media practitioners at all
levels. Facilities include 16mm film
production, Beta SX, DV Cam, Hi8
video production equipment, Avid,
Video Machine and linear video
editing, EOS animation, 5x4 medium
format and 35mm photographic
equipment and darkrooms, Power

Macs and PCs running Photoshop, premiere, director etc

Welfare State International (WSI)

The Ellers
Ulverston
Cumbria LA12 0AA
Tel: 01229 581127
Fax: 01229 581232
A consortium of artists, musicians, engineers and performers. Film/video production, hire and exhibition. Output includes community feature films King Real and the Hoodlums (script Adrian Mitchell) and work for television. Titles include: Piranha Pond (Border TV), RTS Special Creativity Award; Ulverston Town Map, community video; Community Celebration, Multinational Course leading to Lantern Procession (video) and Rites of Passage publications include: The Dead Good Funerals Book available from WSI. Recent Northern Arts Fellowships and exhibitions include Nick May, artist and filmmaker

West Yorkshire Media Services

Leeds Metropolitan University
Brunswick Terrace
Leeds LS2 813U
Tel: Te: 0113 283 1906
Fax: 0113 283 1906
email: m.spadafora@lmu.ac.uk
18 month Certificate in Film and Video Production courses accredited by Leeds Metropolitan University. A free course that welcomes applications from women and people people from minorities. Other courses and projects as per programme offers a thourough grounding in all aspects of film and video production.

WFA

Media and Cultural Centre
9 Lucy Street
Manchester M15 4BX
Tel: 0161 848 9785
Fax: 0161 848 9783
Main areas of work include media access and training, including City and Guilds 770 National Certificate, with a full range of production, post-production and exhibition equipment and facilities for community, semi-professional and professional standards. Video production unit (BECTU). Distribution and sale of 16mm films and videos, booking and advice service, video access library. Cultural work, mixed media events. Bookshop/outreach work

ABBREVIATIONS

ABC
Association of Business Communicators

ABSA
Association of Business Sponsorship of the Arts

ACCS
Association for Cultural and Communication Studies

ACE
Arts Council of England/Ateliers du Cinéma Européen

ADAPT
Access for Disabled People to Arts Premises today

AEEU
Amalgamated Engineering and Electrical Union

AETC
Arts and Entertainment Training Council

AFC
Australian Film Commission

AFCI
Association of Film Commissioners International

AFECT
Advancement of Film Education Charitable Trust

AFI
American Film Institute/Australian Film Institute

AFM
American Film Market

AFVPA
Advertising Film and Videotape Producers' Association

AGICOA
Association de Gestion Internationale Collective des Oeuvres Audiovisuelles

AIM
All Industry Marketing for Cinema

AMCCS
Association for Media, Cultural and Communications Studies

AME
Association for Media Education

AMFIT
Association for Media Film and Television Studies In Higher and Further Education

AMPAS
Adcademy of Motion Picture Arts and Sciences (USA)

AMPS
Association of Motion Picture Sound

APC
Association of Professional Composers

APRS
The Professional Recording Association

AVEK
The Promotion Centre for Audio Visual Culture in Finland

BAFTA
British Academy of Film and Television Arts

BARB
Broadcasters' Audience Research Board

BASCA
British Academy of Songwriters, Composers and Authors

BATC
British Amateur Television Club

BBC
British Broadcasting Corporation

BBFC
British Board of Film Classification

BCS
British Cable Services

BECTU
Broadcasting Entertainment Cinematograph and Theatre Union

BFB
Black Film Bulletin

BFC
British Film Commission

BFFS
British Federation of Film Societies

BFI
British Film Institute

BIEM
Bureau Internationale des Sociétés gérant les Droits d'Enregistrement

BIPP
British Institute of Professional Photography

BKSTS
British Kinematograph Sound and Television Society

BNFVC
British National Film and Video Catalogue

BPI
British Phonographic Industry

BREMA
British Radio and Electronic Equipment Manufacturers' Association

BSAC
British Screen Advisory Council

BSC
British Society of Cinematiographers

Broadcasting Standards Commission

BSD
British Screen Development

BSkyB
British Sky Broadcasting

BSS
Broadcasting Support Services

BTDA
British Television Distributors Association

BUFVC
British Universities Film and Video Council

BVA
British Video Association

CAA
Cinema Advertising Association

CARTOON
European Association of Animation Film

CAVIAR
Cinema and Video Industry Audience Research

CD
Compact Disc

CDI
Compact Disc Interactive

CD ROM
Compact Disc

Read Only Memory

CEA
Cinematograph Exhibitors' Association

CEPI
Co-ordination Européne des Producteurs Indépendantes

CFTF
Children's Film and Television
Foundation

CFU
Children's Film Unit

C4
Channel 4

CICCE
Comitédes Industries
Cinématographiques et
Audiovisuelles des Communautés
Européenes et de l'Europe
Extracommunautaire

CILECT
Centre Internationale de Liaison des
Ecoles de Cinéma et de Télévision

CNN
Cable News Network

COI
Central Office of Information

CPBF
Campaign for Press and Broadcasting
Freedom

CTA
Cable Television Association/

Cinema Theatre Association

CTBF
Cinema and Television Benevolent
Fund

DAT
Digital Audio Tape

DBC
Deaf Broadcasting Council

DCMS
Department for Culture Media and
Sport

DBS
Direct Broadcasting by Satellite

DFE
Department for Education

DFI
Danish Film Institute

DGGB
Directors' Guild of Great Britain

DTI
Department of Trade and Industry

DVI
Digital Video Interactive

DVD
Digital Versatile Disc

EAVE
European Audiovisual Entrepreneurs

EBU
European Broadcasting Union

ECF
European Co-Production Fund

EDI
Euopaaisches Dokumentarfilm
Institut/Entertainment Data
International

EFA
European Film Academy

EFCOM
European Film Commissioners

EFDO
European Film Distribution Office

EGAKU
European Committee of Trade
Unions in Arts, Mass Media and
Entertainment

EIM
European Institute for the Media

EITF
Edinburgh International Television
Festival

EMG
Euro Media Garanties

ENG
Electronic News Gathering

EU
European Union

EUTELSAT
European Telecommunications
Satellite Organisation

FAA
Film Artistes' Association

FACT
Federation Against Copyright Theft

FAME
Film Archive Management and
Entertainment

FBU
Federation of Broadcasting Unions

FEITIS
Fédération Européene des Industries
Techniques de l'Image et du Son

FEMIS
Institut de Formation et
d'Enseignement pour les Métiers de
l'Unage et du Son

FEPACI
Fédération Pan-Africain des
Cinéastes

FESPACO
Festivale Pan-Africain des Cinémas
de Ougadougou

FEU
Federation of Entertainment Unions

FIA
International Federation of Actors

FIAD
Fédération Internationale des
Associations de Distributeurs de Films

FIAF
Fédération Internaionale des Archives
du Film

FIAPF
International Federation of Film
Producers Associations

FIAT
Fédération Internationale des
Archives de Télévision

FICC
Fédération Internationale des Ciné-
Clubs

FIFREC
International Film and Student
Directors Festival

FIPFI
Fédération Internationale des
Producteurs de Films Indépendants

FIPRESCI
Fédération Internationale de la Presse
Cinématographique

FOCAL
Federation of Commercial Audio
Visual Libraries

FTVLCA
Film and Television Lighting
Contractors Association

FX
Effects/special effects

HBO
Home Box Office

HDTV
High Definition Television

HTV
Harlech Television

HVC
Home Video Channel

IABM
International Association of
Broadcasting Manufacturers

IAC
Institute of Amateur
Cinematographers

ICA
Institue of Contemporary Arts

IDATE
Insitut de l'Audiovisuel et des
Télécommunications en Europe

IFDA
Independent Film Distributors'
Association

IFFS
International Federation of Film
Societies (aka FICC)

IFPI
International Federation of the
Phonographic Industry

IFTA
International Federation of Television Archives (aka FIAT)

IIC
International Institute of Communications

ILR
Independent Local Radio

INR
Independent National Radio

IPA
Institute of Practitioners in Advertising

ISBA
Incorporated Society of British Advertising

ISETV
International Secretariat for Arts, Mass Media and Entertainment Trade Unions

ISM
Incorporated Society of Musicians

ITC
Independent Television Commission

ITN
Independent Television News

ITV
Independent Television

ITVA
Independent Television Association

IVCA
International Vsual Communications Association

IVLA
International Visual Literacy Association

JICTAR
Joint Industries' Committee for Television Audience Research

LAB
London Arts Board

LFF
London Film Festival

LFVDA
London Film and Video Development Agency

LSW
London Screenwriters' Workshop

LVA
London Video Access

LWT
London Weekend Television

MBS
Media Business School

MCPS
Mechanical Copyright Protection Society

MEDIA
Mesures pour Encourager le Développement de l'Industrie Audiovisuelle

MENU
Media Education News Update

MFVPA
Music, Film and Video Producers' Association

MGM
Metro Goldwyn Mayer

MHMC
Mental Health Media Council

MIDEM
MarchéInternational du Disque et de l'Edition Musicale

MIFED
 Mercato Internazionale del TV, film e del Documentario

MIPCOM
MarchéInternaional des Films et des Programmes pour la TV, la Vidéo, le C,ble et le Satellite

MIP-TV
MarchéInternational de Programmes de Télévision

MOMI
Museum of the Moving Image

MPA
Motion Picture Association of America

MPEAA
Motion Picture Export Association of American

MU
Musicians' Union

NAHEFV
National Association for Higher Education in Film and Video

NAVAL
National Audio Visual Aids Library

NCA
National Campaign for the Arts

NCC
National Cinema Centre

NCET
National Council for Educational Technology

NCVQ
National Council for Vocational Qualifications

NFDF
National Film Development Fund

NFT
National Film Theatre

NFTC
National Film Trustee Company

NFTS
National Film and Television School

NFTVA
National Film and Television Archive

NHMF
National Heritage Memorial Fund

NIFC
Northern Ireland Film Council

NMPFT
National Museum of Photography, Film and Television

NoW
Network of Workshops

NPA
New Producers Alliance

NSC
Northern Screen Commission

NTSC
National Television Standards Committee

NUJ
National Union of Journalists

NUT
National Union of Teachers

NVALA
National Viewers' and Listeners'Association

PACT
Producers Alliance for Cinema and Television

PAL
Programme Array Logic/

Phase Alternation Line

PPL
Phonographic Performance

PRS
Performing Right Society

RAB
Regional Arts Board

RETRA
Radio, Electrical and Television Retailers' Association

RFT
Regional Film Theatre

RTBF
Radio Television Belge de la CommunantéFranÁaise

RTS
Royal Television Society

S4C
Siandel Pedwar Cymru

S&S
Sight and Sound

SAC
Scottish Arts Council

SBFT
Scottish Broadcast & Film Training

SCALE
Small Countries Improve their
Audio-visual Level in Europe

SCTE
Society of Cable Television
Engineers

SECAM
Séquentiel couleur , mémoire

SFA
Short Film Agency

SFC
Scottish Film Council

SFD
Society of Film Distributors

SFPF
Scottish Film Production Fund

SFX
Special Effects

SIFT
Summary of Information on Film and
Television

SMATV
Satellite Mater Antenna Television

SOURCES
Stimulating Outstanding Resources
for Creative European Scriptwriting

TVRO
Television receive-only

UA
United Artists

UCI
United Cinemas International

UIP
United International Pictures

UNESCO
United Nations Educational,
Scientific and Cultural Organisation

UNIC
Union International des Cinémas

URTI
Université Radiophonique et
Télévisuelle Internationale

VCPS
Video Copyright Protection Society

VCR
Video Cassette Recorder

VHS
Video Home System

VLV
Voice of the Listener and Viewer

WGGB
Writers' Guild of Great Britain

WTN
Worldwide Television News

WTVA
Wider Television Access

YTV
Yorkshire Television

INDEX

N

O

U

Index of Advertisers